EPIDEMIOLOGY C
CHRONIC DISEASE
GLOBAL PERSPECTIVES

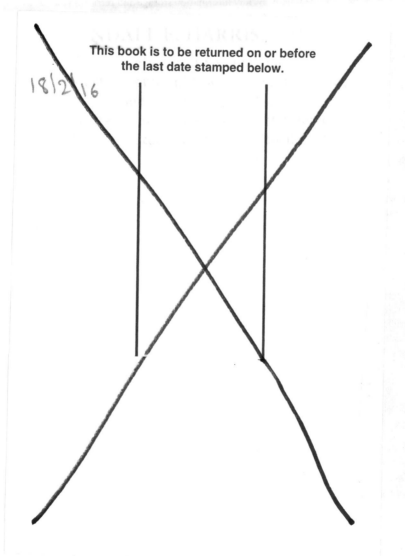

JONES & BARTLETT
LEARNING

World Headquarters
Jones & Bartlett Learning
5 Wall Street
Burlington, MA 01803
978-443-5000
info@jblearning.com
www.jblearning.com

Jones & Bartlett Learning books and products are available through most bookstores and online booksellers. To contact Jones & Bartlett Learning directly, call 800-832-0034, fax 978-443-8000, or visit our website, www.jblearning.com.

Epidemiology of Chronic Disease: Global Perspectives is an independent publication and has not been authorized, sponsored, or otherwise approved by the owners of the trademarks or service marks referenced in this product.

Some images in this book feature models. These models do not necessarily endorse, represent, or participate in the activities represented in the images.

This publication is designed to provide accurate and authoritative information in regard to the Subject Matter covered. It is sold with the understanding that the publisher is not engaged in rendering legal, accounting, or other professional service. If legal advice or other expert assistance is required, the service of a competent professional person should be sought.

Production Credits
Publisher: Michael Brown
Editorial Assistant: Chloe Falivene
Production Manager: Tracey McCrea
Senior Marketing Manager: Sophie Fleck Teague
Manufacturing and Inventory Control Supervisor: Amy Bacus
Composition: Cenveo Publisher Services
Cover Design: Kristin E. Parker
Rights & Photo Researcher: Sarah Cebulski
Rights & Photo Research Associate: Amy Rathburn
Cover Image: © Knorre/ShutterStock, Inc.
Printing and Binding: Edwards Brothers Malloy
Cover Printing: Edwards Brothers Malloy

To order this product, use ISBN: 978-1-4496-5328-6

Library of Congress Cataloging-in-Publication Data
Harris, Randall E.
  Epidemiology of chronic disease : global perspectives / Randall Harris.
     p. ; cm.
  Includes bibliographical references and index.
  ISBN 978-0-7637-8047-0 (pbk.)
  I. Title.
  [DNLM: 1. Chronic Disease—epidemiology. 2. World Health—statistics & numerical data.
3. Epidemiologic Methods—Statistics. WA 900.1]
  614.4'273—dc23

                                                    2011052773

6048
Printed in the United States of America
16 15 14 13 12   10 9 8 7 6 5 4 3 2 1

Contents

Chapter 3   Epidemiology of Ischemic (Coronary) Heart Disease   35

Chapter 4   Epidemiology of Myocardial Infarction   57

Chapter 5   Epidemiology of Stroke (Cerebral Infarction)   77

Chapter 15   Epidemiology of Stomach Cancer   163

Chapter 16   Epidemiology of Colorectal Cancer   169

Chapter 17   Epidemiology of Pancreatic Cancer   181

Chapter 33   Epidemiology of Obesity   417
Susanne K. Scott & Randall E. Harris

Preface

Epidemiology of Chronic Disease: Global Perspectives is a book written for all students and teachers of the health sciences, particularly those in epidemiology, public health, and medicine. Its main purpose is to present current and comprehensive information on the epidemiology, etiology, pathogenesis, risk factors, and preventive factors of common chronic diseases. In writing the book, I have made liberal use of the internet and drawn upon worldwide information to address the global landscape of chronic diseases.

Specific chapters are devoted to the epidemiology of each of forty major chronic diseases and conditions. The book is organized into eight distinct sections beginning with an introductory chapter on *"the epidemiologic transition"* whereby chronic diseases have replaced acute infectious conditions concurrent with improved health care and increasing longevity in many populations of the world. Subsequent sections cover cardiovascular and cerebrovascular diseases (coronary heart disease, myocardial infarction, stroke, hypertension), major forms of cancer (lung cancer, head and neck cancer, esophageal cancer, stomach cancer, colon cancer, pancreatic cancer, liver cancer, breast cancer, ovarian cancer, cervical cancer, prostate cancer, bladder cancer, kidney cancer, sarcoma, malignant melanoma, lymphoma, leukemia and brain tumors), diseases of the respiratory tract (chronic obstructive pulmonary disease, asthma), metabolic and digestive diseases (diabetes mellitus, obesity, thyroid disease, kidney disease, liver disease), musculoskeletal diseases (osteoporosis, arthritis), neurodegenerative diseases (Alzheimer's disease, Parkinson's disease, schizophrenia, epilepsy, multiple sclerosis), and finally, three infectious diseases (tuberculosis, malaria, and HIV disease) that often manifest as chronic conditions.

All chapters follow a similar format with subsections describing diagnostic criteria, historical perspectives, the global burden of disease, population differences and time trends in incidence, prevalence, disability and mortality, mechanisms of pathogenesis, risk factors, preventive factors and opportunities for disease prevention and control. Key epidemiologic studies and findings are presented in chronological order with supporting evidence and references selected to guide readers to further study. It is assumed that students and readers are building on a knowledge base of basic epidemiology and human biology. The text blends the traditional elements of epidemiology with human anatomy, physiology, and molecular biology.

It is my hope that the text will provide a forum for examining current hypotheses regarding chronic disease epidemiology. Subsections of each chapter focus upon controversial topics in the epidemiology of each disease. This format facilitates active student discussion of molecular mechanisms of disease pathogenesis and the relevant epidemiologic issues pertaining to the prevention and control of chronic diseases.

In essence, this book is an amalgamation of a longstanding continuum of the exchange of ideas and information with many colleagues in the fields of medicine, public health, epidemiology, biostatistics, genetics, pathology and molecular biology. I am therefore deeply indebted to mentors, colleagues, and particularly, students who have contributed to my education, research and teaching over the past four decades. I also gratefully acknowledge my coauthors, Susanne K. Scott, who wrote early drafts of the chapters on diabetes and obesity, and Zachary M. Harris, who contributed to the chapter on multiple sclerosis. The book clearly reflects the professional detail of the editorial and production staff of Jones & Bartlett Learning, and any errors and omissions in content as well as opinions on controversial issues are my responsibility. Finally, I am most grateful to my family for their support and understanding during the writing of this book.

Randall E. Harris

Contributors

Susanne K. Scott, PhD, MPH

Belgium, Wisconsin

Zachary M. Harris, MD (2014)

Tulane University School of Medicine

New Orleans, Louisiana

1

Global Epidemiology of Chronic Diseases: The Epidemiologic Transition

GLOBAL PANDEMIC OF CHRONIC DISEASES

A silent pandemic of chronic diseases is gradually enveloping the world population, spreading to all corners of the globe. This distinct spectrum of human afflictions is systemically replacing infectious and parasitic diseases as the leading cause of morbidity and mortality worldwide, thereby producing one of the greatest public health challenges of all time. According to global mortality data reported by the World Health Organization (WHO), chronic disorders such as coronary heart disease, stroke, cancer, chronic obstructive pulmonary disease, diabetes mellitus type 2, neurodegenerative disease, and renal failure caused 38 million deaths in 2009, more than 62% of all deaths worldwide (WHO, 2009a). The following excerpts from the 2008 WHO global report entitled *Preventing Chronic Diseases: A Vital Investment* captures the essence of the global pandemic of chronic diseases (WHO, 2008a).

> "Chronic diseases are the leading causes of death and disability worldwide. Disease rates from these conditions are accelerating globally, advancing across every region and pervading all socioeconomic classes. The World Health Report 2002 "Reducing Risks, Promoting Healthy Life" indicates that the mortality, morbidity and disability attributed to the major chronic diseases currently account for almost 60% of all deaths and 43% of the global burden of disease. By 2020 their contribution is expected to rise to 73% of all deaths and 60% of the global burden of disease. Moreover, 79% of the deaths attributed to these diseases occur in the developing countries. Four of the most prominent chronic diseases, cardiovascular diseases (CVD), cancer, chronic obstructive pulmonary disease (COPD), and type 2 diabetes, are linked by common and preventable biological risk factors, notably high blood pressure, high blood cholesterol and overweight, and by related major behavioral risk factors: unhealthy diet, physical inactivity, and tobacco use. Action to prevent these major chronic diseases should focus on controlling these and other key risk factors in a well-integrated manner."

The global pandemic of chronic diseases has emerged in concert with the changing demography of the world population. Overall, the world birth rate exceeds the death rate and the number of living individuals on the planet continues to increase. At the same time, more and more people are living to older ages thereby creating the phenomenon of "global aging." Aging populations are particularly evident in the industrialized and developed nations of the world, such as Japan, Italy, and Germany, where the proportion of elderly people (over 65 years of age) has increased from approximately 10% to 20% in the past half century (Hayutin, 2007). In large developing nations such as China and India, the proportion of elderly people is also expected to increase from current levels of about 5% to nearly 10% in the next few decades. In smaller underdeveloped nations where less than 5% of the people currently live beyond 65 years of age, population aging is also progressing, but at a slower pace. As a general consequence of the aging world population, long-term mechanisms of pathogenesis are more likely to cause disease late in life, thus resulting in vastly increased rates of chronic diseases, particularly among the elderly.

INCREASE IN WORLD POPULATION

As of December 31, 2009, The United States Census Bureau estimated that the world population consisted of 6.82 billion living human beings (United States Census Bureau, 2009). In that year, approximately 61 million people died and 139 million new babies were born, a net gain of 78 million people. Based upon projections of death rates and birth rates, the world population is expected to increase to nearly nine billion people by the year 2040 (**Figure 1.1**).

AGING OF THE WORLD POPULATION

The world population is not only increasing in number, but it is also growing older. Two demographic parameters are driving these phenomena: *longevity is increasing and the fertility rate is decreasing*. Studies at the World Health Organization (WHO, 2009a) and the Stanford Center of Longevity (Hayutin, 2007) clearly show that people around the world are living longer and women are having fewer children.

INCREASING LONGEVITY (LIFE EXPECTANCY)

The average life expectancy (also called longevity) for members of the world population born during 2005–2010 is 67 years (65 years for men and 70 years for women) (CIA World Fact Book, 2009). In the past half century, life expectancy has increased

dramatically throughout the world, particularly in populations of developing nations. Since 1950, life expectancy in highly populated nations such as China and India has increased from approximately 40 years to nearly 70 years (**Figure 1.2**).

In lesser developed nations, particularly those of central Africa where acute infectious and parasitic diseases prevail and greatly reduce the survival of children and young adults, life expectancy is much less, currently only about 50 years. In highly developed nations such as Japan, the United States, and European countries, longevity now approaches or surpasses 80 years and deaths are more likely due to chronic diseases of old age. The Japanese people currently enjoy the greatest longevity, about 82 years. Longevity in the United States currently stands at 78 years, only slightly higher than the average of more developed nations (**Figure 1.3**).

Life expectancy is the average number of years that a newborn could expect to live if he or she were to pass through life *subject to the age-specific death rates of the population of interest for the past year*. Derivation of life expectancy is usually presented as a "*two step*" process. For large populations, life expectancy is calculated by *first constructing a life table and recording the numbers of deaths and survivors that occur in a given year for successive intervals of the life span*. The numbers of deaths and survivors and corresponding age-specific death rates are usually tabulated for ages 0 to 1 years, 1 to 5 years, and successive 5-year age groups for ages 5 and above. From these data, a second life table is then constructed to represent the entire mortality

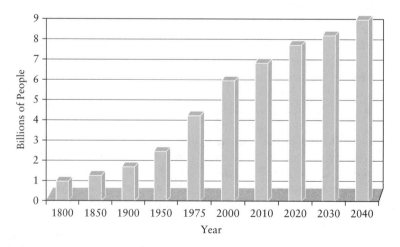

Figure 1.1 World Population.

Source: Data from the United States Census Bureau, International Data Base, 2009 (estimates for 2020–2040 are based on curvilinear regression).

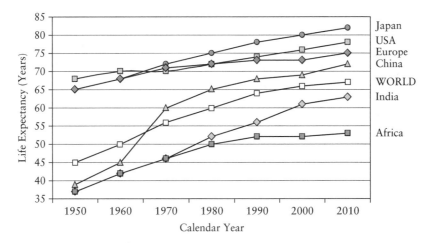

Figure 1.2 Longevity Trends in Selected Populations.

Source: Data from Population Division of the Department of Economic and Social Affairs of the United Nations Secretariat (2007). World Population Prospects: The 2006 Revision, Highlights. New York: United Nations. National Center for Health Statistics, 2009, USA.

experience from birth to death for a hypothetical cohort of 100,000 infants born alive and subject to the age-specific death rates that prevail in the population of interest for a particular year in time. Using the data from this second life table for 100,000 hypothetical individuals, life expectancy is simply calculated as the average years of life for all members since birth, e.g.,

life expectancy = total years of life for all members of the life table divided by the total number of persons at birth, *Life Expectancy* = Σ *years of life/100,000*. Life expectancy (longevity) at birth is therefore the mean years of life for individuals based entirely on the age-specific death rates for the population and year of interest (Colton, 1974).

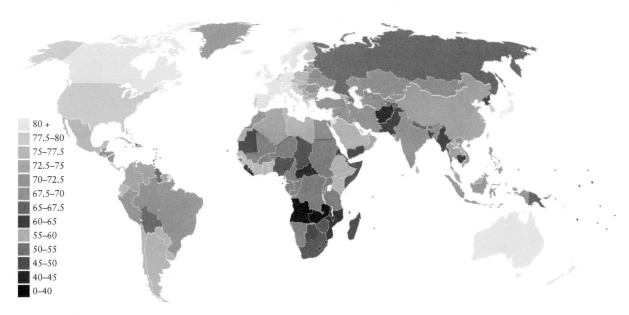

Figure 1.3 Global Longevity, 2011.

Source: CIA World Factbook, 2011 Estimates of Life Expectancy at Birth (Years).

GENDER DIFFERENCES IN LONGEVITY

Throughout the world, life expectancy (longevity) for women is 5–10 years greater than for men. With some exceptions in nations where high maternal death rates prevail due to lack of prenatal care, women have lower death rates and better survival at every age. In the industrialized world, improvements in prenatal care have reduced maternal mortality during the childbearing years thereby widening the gender gap in longevity during much of the 20th century. For example, the gender divergence in longevity in the US population gradually increased from about 2 years in 1900 to approximately 8 years in 1970, after which the difference shrank back to about 6 years, currently 81 years for women versus 75 years for men (**Figure 1.4**). The slight shrinkage of the US gender gap during the past 40 years is believed to reflect equalizing smoking rates among men and women (Pampel, 2002).

The survival differential favoring females actually begins at conception. Only about 90% of male fetuses survive to birth compared to nearly 100% of female fetuses. While precise causative factors for this disparity remain unclear, the relatively high rates of spontaneous abortions, miscarriages, and stillbirths among male fetuses could be due to hormonal incompatibilities of the male genotype in a milieu of female hormones such as estrogen and progesterone throughout gestation (Austad, 2006). At the other end of the life span, approximately 70% of individuals over 90 years of age are female, and remarkably, about 90% of centenarians (individuals over 100 years of age) are female (Perls, Hutter Silver, and Lauerman, 1999).

While no single factor can satisfactorily explain the clear survival advantage of women throughout life, certain environmental and biological differences are worth pointing out. The longer life span of women compared to men is undoubtedly related to gender differences in lifestyle. Despite the fact that men are, on average, bigger, stronger, faster, and more economically self-sufficient, their lifestyle choices and risky health behaviors obviously confer a clear survival advantage to women. In general, men have greater exposure to classical risk factors of disease such as tobacco and alcohol and, as a consequence, are more likely to die earlier from associated chronic conditions such as cardiovascular disease, lung cancer, chronic obstructive pulmonary disease, and cirrhosis of the liver. Men are also more likely to die from injuries, whether unintentional (motor vehicle or occupational accidents) or intentional (suicide, homicide, war). Reciprocally, women have traditionally been the "*sentinels of health*" for their families and communities at large. Due to their instinctive "*nurturing maternal instinct,*" women tend to take better care of themselves and make healthier lifestyle choices than men, thus contributing to their longer life span.

Hormonal differences between men and women may also influence their differences in lifestyle and longevity. Men are greater risk takers than women, particularly during the years of young adulthood when circulating levels of testosterone are highest. The biological effects of androgens and estrogens differ dramatically. Androgens have vasoconstrictive and inflammatory effects in blood vessels consistent with higher rates of cardiovascular disease in men whereas estrogens exert opposite effects and are thus cardioprotective in women, particularly during their reproductive years (Blackman et al., 2002; Parker et al., 2009). Moreover, gender differences in the balance of estrogens and androgens appear to confer heightened immunity and more resistance to

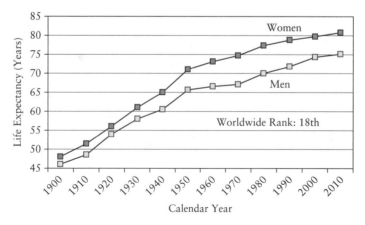

Figure 1.4 Life Expectancy, USA, Women and Men.

Source: Data from Population Division of the Department of Economic and Social Affairs of the United Nations Secretariat (2007). World Population Prospects: The 2006 Revision, Highlights. New York: United Nations. National Center for Health Statistics, 2009, USA.

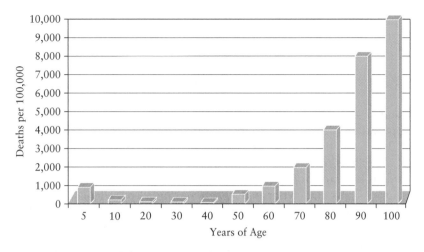

Figure 1.5 Characteristic Death Curve Modeled on the US Population 2002.

Source: Data from Aris, E. (2004). United States Life Tables, 2002. *National Vital Statistics Reports 53*(6):1–40.

infectious and degenerative diseases in women throughout life (Austad, 2006).

AGING AND DISEASE

Aging is a complex process involving a decline in physiological processes that are essential for life. As humans age, there is heightened susceptibility to life-threatening acute and chronic diseases. A characteristic "death curve" is depicted in **Figure 1.5**. The data points represent approximate all-cause annual mortality rates estimated for successive 10 year age brackets for the US population of 2002 (National Vital Statistics System, 2002). Note that the risk of death is elevated in the early years up to 5 years of age, after which there is a relatively long subtle increase in the risk of death until approximately

40 years of age, after which all-cause mortality exponentially rises for all successive age brackets.

Aging can thus be viewed as the general deterioration in human health over the life span generally associated with development of debilitating and life-threatening disease processes. Indeed, aging has been defined as the spectrum of changes that render human beings progressively more likely to die (Medawar, 1952). As shown in **Figure 1.6**, the prevalence of major chronic diseases (arthritis, heart disease, cancer, diabetes mellitus type 2, and chronic obstructive pulmonary disease) rises exponentially with age. It is obvious that the phenotype of human aging is one in which practically any system, tissue, or organ can fail, resulting in debilitation and death (Austad, 1997; Strehler, 1999). Nevertheless, it is important to stress that aging is not merely a collection of diseases. Rather, certain pathologic conditions progress

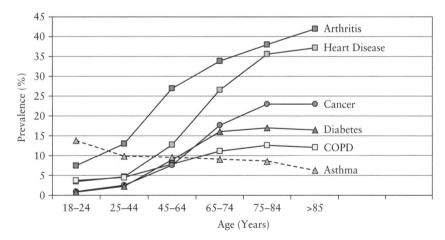

Figure 1.6 Prevalence of Selected Chronic Conditions Expressed as Percentages, as a Function of Age for the USA Population (2002–2003 Dataset).

Source: Data from National Center for Health Statistics, Data Warehouse on Trends in Health and Aging, 2003.

in parallel with the aging process while others, such as asthma, remain constant or even decline late in life.

AGING OF HUMAN CELL POPULATIONS

Aging is a complex and controversial subject. The aging phenomenon appears to be driven by deterioration in cellular health. It is estimated that the human body consists of tens of trillions of cells. This huge population of cells is divisible into subpopulations, each consisting of billions of cells that comprise certain anatomic structures, organs, and tissues. These component cell populations exist in a state of relative homeostasis performing the essential functions of life.

Studies of aging suggest that different cellular populations comprising the human body of a single individual do not all age at the same rate. Acceleration of the aging phenomenon in even one critical cell population may create a "weak link" for the entire system resulting in debilitation and death. However, as pointed out by Hayflick, the aging process does not share its elemental features with any particular disease (Hayflick, 2007). This observation led him to state that, *the fundamental aging process is not a disease but it increases vulnerability to disease.* To paraphrase, aging may be the cause but not necessarily the effect of a disease process.

The preservation of homeostasis among populations of normally functioning cells in the human body depends primarily upon the balance of cell death and cell replacement. If cells die faster than they are replaced, then the progressively greater demands placed upon those cells that remain may eventually lead to pathologic changes and rapid deterioration in cellular health. Any one of multiple intrinsic and extrinsic factors capable of upsetting the balance of cell death and cell replacement may therefore have considerable impact on the aging phenomenon, particularly for those cell populations that do not normally undergo cell division, e.g., neurons and mature muscle cells.

Programmed cell death (called apoptosis) and cell division are tightly regulated by genetic factors; nevertheless, both processes are also subject to modulation by extracellular as well as intracellular molecular factors. Aging may thus result from extrinsic or intrinsic factors that cause an accumulation of cellular and tissue damage; or alternatively, changes in gene expression related to DNA damage and somatic mutations, epigenetic factors such as methylation or acetylation of DNA, or structural modification of DNA by the intrinsic biological clock that regulates the number of cell divisions, e.g., telomere shortening in chromosomes (Campisi et al., 2000). The etiology of the aging phenomenon therefore appears similar to most complex human traits. Aging is influenced by genetic and environmental factors that interact to produce significant phenotypic variability. Two key theories of aging are briefly discussed in the following sections: one involves the energy rich microenvironment of the cell and the other the genetically controlled biological clock of cell division.

FREE RADICAL THEORY OF AGING

More than half a century ago, Denham Harman developed the free radical theory of aging (Harman, 1956). His theory states that aging is a consequence of accumulating oxidative damage to cells and cellular components over time (reviewed in Beckman and Ames, 1998). Harman later extended his theory to include mitochondrial production of free radicals during normal cellular respiration (Harman, 1972).

Free radicals and oxidants, commonly called reactive oxygen species (ROS), are highly unstable reactive molecules that can damage many vital cellular components (**Figure 1.7**). Rebecca Gerschman and colleagues discovered that ROS can originate from exogenous sources such as ultraviolet and ionizing radiation and first suggested that free radicals are toxic agents (Gerschman et al., 1954).

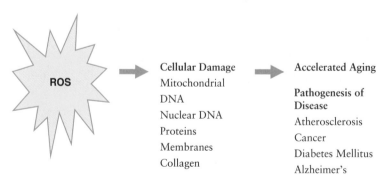

Figure 1.7 Free Radical Theory of Cell Damage, Aging, and Chronic Disease.

Reactive oxygen species (ROS) can be formed by exogenous processes such as irradiation and inflammation as well as normal cell metabolism. These short lived molecules include superoxide, peroxide, hydroxyl radicals, and reactive nitrogen species such as peroxynitrite, all of which are unstable and readily react with DNA to cause a variety of structural genetic alterations including base pair mutations, rearrangements, deletions, insertions, and DNA sequence amplification. While DNA mutations, alterations, and chromosomal abnormalities increase with age in mice and other laboratory animals, damage to nuclear diploid DNA by ROS remains an unproven cause of aging (Ames et al., 1993).

Oxidative phosphorylation is responsible for energy production within the mitochondria of virtually all cells. Since this process continually produces ROS such as superoxide and hydrogen peroxide, and since mitochondria possess haploid DNA unprotected by histones, many advocates of the free radical theory of aging consider that oxidative damage to mitochondria and the mitochondrial DNA has a primary role in the aging process (Harman, 1972; Linnane et al., 1989; de Grey, 1997; Barja, 2000).

Certain nutraceutical agents have gained favor as free radical scavengers that offer some protection against oxidation and the formation of ROS. These include ascorbic acid (vitamin C), tocopherol (vitamin E), carotenes, melatonin, and antioxidant enzymes such as superoxide dismutase (SOD), catalase, and glutathione peroxidase that are capable of degrading ROS into inert compounds (Ames et al., 1981).

TELOMERE SHORTENING AND AGING

Cell division is an extraordinarily precise process that gives rise to daughter cells that have *almost* exactly the same genetic constitution as their progenitors. However, with every cell division, there is incomplete duplication of the chromosomal tips (called telomeres). Successive cell divisions therefore result in shortening of chromosomes until a point is reached where the daughter cells are no longer capable of dividing (called the "*Hayflick Limit*" after its discoverer). Since cells that reach their Hayflick Limit cannot replicate, the balance of cell replication and cell death is interrupted and cellular health may deteriorate. This is the basis of the *Telomere Theory of Aging*; namely, as an ever-increasing percentage of cells reach their Hayflick Limit and are unable to reproduce, then defense, maintenance, and repair of the body becomes increasingly impaired. Thus, telomere attrition due to the Hayflick Limit could account for most of the decline in functional efficiency of cell populations and increases in vulnerability to chronic diseases that characterize the aging phenomenon (Hayflick, 1985, 2007; de Magalhaes and Faragher, 2008).

DECLINING FERTILITY IN WOMEN

Over the past half century, the worldwide fertility rate (*the average number of births per woman during the childbearing years*) has been cut in half, from 5.0 in the 1950s to 2.5 in the 21st century (**Figure 1.8**).

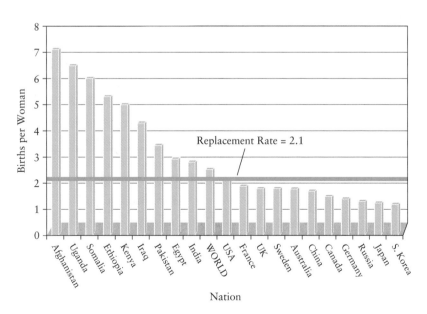

Figure 1.8 Selected Fertility Rates, 2006.

Source: Data from United Nations Department of Economic and Social Affairs, Population Division (2007). "United Nations World Population Prospects: 2006 revision, Table A.15." New York: UN; United Nations World Population Prospects 2006, CIA World Fact Book, 2009.

The decline in fertility rates has been sharpest in the most populous nations such as China, India, and Russia. For example, the fertility rate in China, which has the world's largest population (1.34 billion), decreased from more than 6 in 1970 to 1.6 births per woman in 2006, well below the worldwide replacement rate of 2.1. There are areas of Africa and the Middle East where fertility rates have remained high with populations consisting of predominately children and young adults. In industrialized nations such as Canada, Germany, Great Britain, and Japan, fertility rates are now well below the replacement rate. In the United States, the fertility rate has decreased from 3.5 in the 1960s to 2.0 currently, only slightly below the replacement rate. Worldwide birth control has likely contributed to the general decline in the global fertility rate (Hayutin, 2007).

A woman's potential for childbearing begins to gradually decline between 20 and 30 years of age and then exponentially decreases until the end of the reproductive years at menopause (Menken, Trussell, and Larsen, 1986; Rowe, 2006) (**Figure 1.9**). Widespread use of effective contraceptives, the accessibility of medical abortion, and the shifting paradigm for women to pursue professional careers rather than start families have combined to delay their having children. As a consequence of these factors, the reproductive window of childbearing years has been pushed back and dramatically reduced in women around the world. Furthermore, certain family planning incentives and policies such as China's "*one child policy*" in 1979 have further contributed to the steep decline in fertility in large populations of the world. These factors have all contributed to the global decline in fertility rates, particularly in the industrialized world (Hayutin, 2007).

CHROMOSOMAL ANEUPLOIDY AND OVARIAN RESERVE

Biological factors that reduce fertility in the aging female include increased chromosomal aneuploidy and diminished ovarian reserve with each successive menstrual cycle. As a woman ages, an ever-increasing proportion of the eggs she releases during each successive menstrual cycle are aneuploid (contain an abnormal number of chromosomes) and thus highly prone to spontaneous miscarriage.

The ovarian reserve (the remaining viable eggs in the ovaries) of each woman generally begins to decline about 15 years prior to menopause. Depletion of the ovarian reserve of eggs with aging is also an exponentially expanding phenomenon resulting in the markedly decreased fertility of women in their fifth decade of life. Notably, cigarette smoking is one of the most common and important factors that has been found to decrease ovarian reserve (Parker et al., 2009).

EPIDEMIOLOGIC TRANSITION

It is obvious that many developing and developed nations throughout the world are experiencing marked increases in life expectancy and decreases in fertility. This "*demographic transition*" has produced populations with a relative abundance of geriatric individuals compared to younger people and it is occurring in concert with a closely related phenomenon called the "*epidemiologic transition*."

In general, all nations of the world are in various stages of "*epidemiologic transition*," defined as the transition from acute infectious, parasitic, and

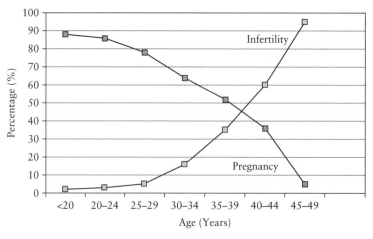

Figure 1.9 Pregnancy and Infertility Rates, Women, USA.

Source: Data from Menken et al. (1986). Age and infertility. *Science 233*:1389–1394; Rowe T (2006). Fertility and a woman's age. *J Reproductive Med 51*(3):157–163.

nutritional deficiency diseases as the predominant causes of morbidity and mortality to a predominance of noninfectious chronic diseases (Omran, 1971). This worldwide epidemiologic transition is undoubtedly a consequence of the improving economic standards of many nations, which has translated into better health and greater longevity for their native populations. Important contributing factors include adequate caloric intake throughout life, improved sanitation, vaccination against common infectious microbes, effective antibiotics to combat bacterial and parasitic diseases, effective drugs to reduce hypertension and other physiological disturbances, better health education for promotion of healthier lifestyles, advances in medical education, progress in medical technology, and overall improvements in healthcare systems.

From a historical perspective, until the beginning of the 20th century, epidemics of communicable (infectious) and parasitic diseases such as typhoid, cholera, smallpox, diphtheria, tuberculosis, bubonic plague, yellow fever, malaria, and influenza were the main causes of morbidity and mortality in all countries of the world. Although certain infectious and parasitic diseases such as tuberculosis and malaria remain epidemic in Third World countries, industrialization and progressive modernization of many nations have resulted in major improvements in housing, sanitation, water supply, nutrition, and health care. The discovery and availability of antibiotics and vaccines have radically changed the profile of diseases, initially in developed countries and later in many developing countries. Consequently, these improvements in medicine and public health have led to dramatic reductions in mortality from infectious and parasitic diseases.

Paradoxically, concurrent with decreases in morbidity and mortality from infectious and parasitic conditions, there has been a remarkable increase in the prevalence of chronic noncommunicable diseases such as cardiovascular disease, hypertension, stroke, chronic obstructive pulmonary disease, type 2 diabetes, and neurodegenerative pathologies such as Alzheimer's disease.

While good health coupled with increasing longevity is generally viewed as beneficial, it is also clear that the epidemiologic transition has produced a concomitant rise in chronic pathogenic processes typically manifested later in life. Cellular damage to vital tissues, organs, and systems of the human body by ROS, atherosclerosis, carcinogenesis, chronic inflammation, allergic reactions, insulin insensitivity, autoimmune reactions, and immunosuppression have produced a world pandemic of chronic diseases and conditions. Furthermore, the escalating spectrum of heart disease, cancer, hypertension, stroke, emphysema, chronic bronchitis, obesity, diabetes mellitus (type 2), cirrhosis of the liver, arthritis, autoimmune disease, kidney disease, and neurodegenerative disorders such as Alzheimer's disease is threatening to overwhelm the healthcare systems of many nations. As pointed out by Ernst L. Wynder, such chronic disease processes appear to be spurred by *metabolic overload* due to intake of high calorie diets with excessive fats and carbohydrates coupled with insufficient exercise and addictive use of tobacco and alcohol (Wynder, 1994). Fortunately, such metabolic insults are fundamentally preventable or correctable since they are largely controlled by personal behavior and lifestyle (please see discussion in the section on prevention).

It has become apparent that epidemiologic transitions are not necessarily unidirectional and should best be viewed as continuous transformation processes wherein some diseases may disappear while others may reappear. A case in point is the reemergence of infectious diseases in high income nations due to antibiotic or drug resistance of pathogenic bacteria, viruses, and other microbes. Epidemiologic transitions therefore reflect complex and dynamic patterns of health and disease due to demographic, socioeconomic, technological, cultural, environmental, and biological changes.

It is also important to realize that the populations of many lesser developed nations continue to manifest relatively short average life spans due to the impact of failing healthcare systems coupled with unstable governance, war, and pestilence. For example, life expectancy in sub-Saharan Africa is only about 45 years, largely due to infectious and parasitic diseases such as HIV/AIDS, tuberculosis, and malaria that produce life-threatening acute conditions such as diarrhea, pneumonia, and anemia. The following sections discuss the diseases and conditions that cause death in the world population and address the disparate profiles of disease among nations according to their economic status.

GLOBAL DEATH RATES

Crude annual death rates for the nations of the world are shown in **Figure 1.10**. The figure is derived from crude rates published by the World Health Organization in 2009 based upon data collected during 2002–2007 (WHO, 2009a; CIA World Factbook, 2009). It is stressed that crude rates are not adjusted for differences in the age distributions of the different populations. Hence, some populations with relatively

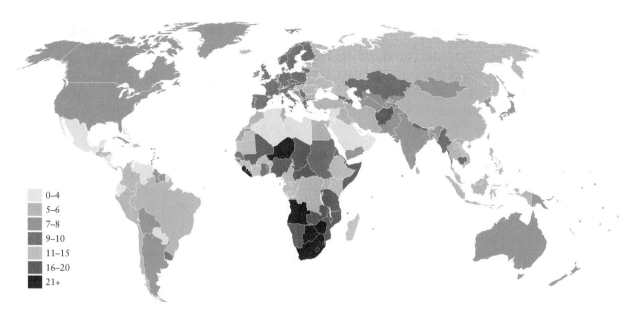

Figure 1.10 Global Death Rates, 2006.

Source: Data from CIA World Factbook, 2006 Estimates of Crude Death Rates per 1,000. Reprinted with permission: World Health Organization, 2009a: Annual Death Rates per 1,000.

more young people may have lower death rates than populations with more old people. Nevertheless, certain conclusions can be drawn by comparing the crude death rates among nations.

What is painfully obvious is that among the relatively young populations of central and southern Africa (sub-Saharan Africa), the death rates are the highest in the world. Compared to developed nations such as the United States, Canada, Japan, Great Britain, Australia, and many European nations, whose populations have far more older people, individuals in African nations such as Swaziland, Botswana, Angola, Niger, Chad, Mozambique, and Zimbabwe have a three to four times higher risk of dying. Even greater disparities in the crude death rates are apparent in the populations of sub-Saharan Africa (more than 20 deaths per 1,000) compared to those of the Mediterranean populations of northern Africa (less than 4 deaths per 1,000).

In sub-Saharan Africa, conditions of hunger and malnutrition cause life-threatening diarrhea in infants and children, killing 5 million every year before they reach the age of 5 years. Parasitic diseases such as malaria are left untreated, killing 1 million more children annually before they reach the age of 15 years. Infectious diseases such as HIV, hepatitis, and tuberculosis ravage the health of young adults, killing nearly 3 million young adults each year before

they reach the age of 45 years. Wars and strife due to political unrest kill 100,000 more young adults every year. And if an individual manages to live through these early afflictions, chronic conditions such as cardiovascular disease, stroke, diabetes, chronic obstructive pulmonary disease, and others manifest early and kill 3 million more adults before they reach the age of 65 years. Indeed, of the 60 million deaths that occur every year in the world population of approximately 6.8 billion, nearly 20%, about 12 million, occur in the central/southern African population of 0.8 billion people. Hence, just a single stratification of the world data divides individuals into two camps of death risk: populations residing in sub-Saharan Africa with crude average death rates exceeding 20 per 1,000 per year, and the rest of the world with an average rate less than 10 per 1,000 per year (Adetunji and Bos, 2006; Baingana and Bos, 2006; Bradshaw and Timaeus, 2006; Hill and Amouzou, 2006; Rao, Lopez, and Herned, 2006).

Other nations with high death rates include Afghanistan and member nations of the Russian Federation. The crude annual death rate in Afghanistan (nearly 20 per 1,000) reflects a war-torn impoverished population with little access to health care. The Afghanistan population has high rates of infant and maternal mortality, childhood mortality from malnutrition, and mortality in young adults from violence and diseases caused by addiction to tobacco, alcohol, and illicit drugs such as cocaine and opium (Duckett, 2005; WHO, 2009a).

In Russia, overall mortality has increased sharply since the disbanding of the Soviet Union during 1985–1991. Crude death rates for the Russian population during the 1980s were on par with other industrialized nations (about 8 per 1,000) but have since increased reaching a peak of nearly 15 per 1,000 in 2010. Recent studies have found a link between excessive alcohol consumption and mortality, particularly among men of working age. For example, Leon and colleagues reviewed the drinking habits of 2,835 men from the industrial city of Izhevsk who died at ages 25–54 years during 2003–2005 compared to 3,078 age-matched living controls. Results revealed that 51% of the men who died consumed *nonbeverage alcohol* (e.g., aftershave) or were problem drinkers compared to 13% of controls. Alcohol-related deaths included cirrhosis of the liver, hepatitis, certain malignancies (hepatocellular cancer, pancreatic cancer, and esophageal cancer), cardiovascular disease, accidents, and violence (homicide and suicide). The investigators estimated that 43% of deaths in men aged 25–54 years in Izhevsk were attributable to hazardous drinking (Leon et al., 2007).

In a recent study, a team of international investigators examined the drinking and smoking habits of 48,557 decedents from 3 Russian industrial cities (Tomsk, Barnaul, and Biysk) who died at ages 15–74 years during 1990–2001. Alcohol-related deaths included accidents, violence, heart disease, aerodigestive tract cancer, liver cancer, tuberculosis, pneumonia, hepatitis, liver cirrhosis, and pancreatic disease. Excess alcohol consumption accounted for 52% of all deaths at ages 15–54 years and 18% of deaths at later ages. The investigators concluded that alcohol and tobacco account for the large difference in adult mortality between Russia and other industrialized nations (Zaridze et al., 2009).

GLOBAL EPIDEMIOLOGY OF DISEASE

Figure 1.11 shows the number of deaths due to specific diseases based upon estimated mortality rates published by the World Health Organization (WHO) for the world population of 2009. Conditions of the heart (ischemic heart disease, congestive heart failure, valvular disease, cardiomyopathy) cause nearly 20% of deaths and various infectious/parasitic diseases (pneumonia, diarrhea, HIV, tuberculosis, malaria) rank a close second causing 19% of deaths. Cancer (12.5%), stroke (10%), and chronic obstructive pulmonary disease (7%) also rank high in relative mortality.

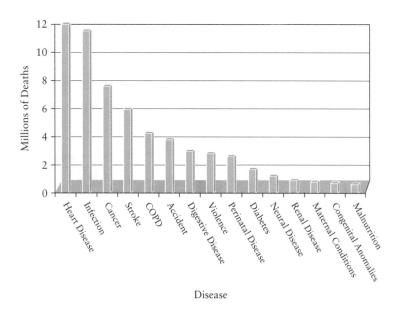

Figure 1.11 Worldwide Deaths from Disease, 2009.

Source: Data from WHO (2009a). World Health Statistics, 2009. World Health Organization, Geneva, Switzerland.

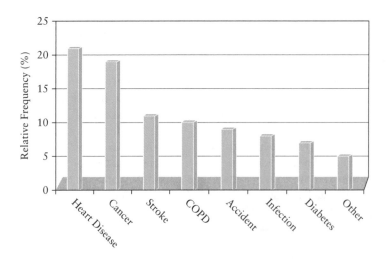

Figure 1.12 Relative Mortality for High Income Nations.

Source: Data from WHO (2009a). World Health Statistics, 2009. World Health Organization, Geneva, Switzerland.

Chronic noncommunicable diseases (heart disease, stroke, cancer, COPD; noninfectious digestive disease such as liver cirrhosis, diabetes, neurological disorders such as Alzheimer's disease, and chronic renal failure) caused approximately 60% (36 million) of all deaths whereas relatively acute conditions (infectious and parasitic diseases, accidents, violence, perinatal disease [low birth weight and failure to thrive], maternal conditions, congenital anomalies, and malnutrition) accounted for the remaining 40% (24 million) of deaths worldwide.

Diseases and conditions afflicting the human race show profound disparities arising from the prevailing environmental conditions and population susceptibilities. A crude but effective discriminant of the disease profile of a population is its economic status. Estimates of relative mortality for specific diseases in high income nations versus low income nations derived from WHO data are given in **Figures 1.12** and **1.13**.

In high income nations such as the United States, Japan, Canada, Australia, Great Britain, France, Germany, Italy, Finland, and Sweden (Figure 1.9), approximately 75% of deaths are due to noncommunicable chronic diseases such as heart disease (21%), cancer (19%), stroke (10%), chronic obstructive pulmonary disease (10%), diabetes mellitus (6%), and other chronic conditions (9%). The remaining 25%

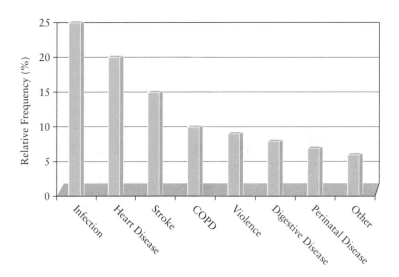

Figure 1.13 Relative Mortality for Low Income Nations.

Source: Data from WHO (2009a). World Health Statistics, 2009. World Health Organization, Geneva, Switzerland.

of deaths in these populations are attributable to relatively acute conditions such as pneumonia, influenza or other infections (16%), accidents (8%), suicide or homicide (2%).

The profile of life-threatening diseases for low income nations differs markedly from that of high income nations (Figures 1.12 and 1.13). In nations such as Afghanistan, Bangladesh, Cambodia, Central African Republic Chad, Democratic Government of Congo, Laos, Ethiopia, Guinea, Haiti, Laos, Liberia, Madagascar, Mali, Mozambique, Nepal, Niger, Rwanda, Somalia, Sudan, Tanzania, Uganda, Tanzania, Yemen, and Zambia, approximately 60% of deaths are attributable to relatively acute conditions such as infectious and parasitic diseases (24%), perinatal disease (16%), violence (10%), malnutrition (5%), and maternal or other acute conditions (5%). Remaining deaths are attributable to conditions associated with chronic disease processes such as heart disease (15%), cancer (12%), stroke (8%), and COPD (5%).

Remarkably, more than 5 billion people (about 75% of the world population) reside in the low income nations represented in Figure 1.13 (United Nations Department of Economic and Social Affairs, Population Division, [2007]). These populations exist on less than US$3 per person per day and have *little or no access* to clean water, proper sanitation and sewer systems, adequate nutrition, and health care.

In Figure 1.14, deaths from acute disease, chronic disease, and injury are further stratified according to the 2008 Gross National Income (GNI) per capita. The GNI groupings were calculated using the World Bank Atlas method for nations with populations exceeding 30,000 people (World Bank, 1993). Based on its 2008 GNI per capita, every economy was classified as low income, middle income (subdivided into lower middle income and upper middle income), or high income. The GNI groups translated into US dollars are as follows: low income, $975 or less; lower middle income, $976–$3,855; upper middle income, $3,856–$11,905; and high income, $11,906 or more.

Enormous differences are evident in the profiles of death-causing diseases according to economic level (**Figure 1.14**). Poverty with its attendant poor hygiene, malnutrition, inferior education, heavy use of tobacco and alcohol, and lack of access to effective health care is associated with acute diseases that tend to impact younger generations. Reciprocally, greater prosperity is associated with chronic diseases more likely to impact older individuals through improved public health practices, e.g., vaccination against infectious agents, adequate nutrition, higher education, avoidance of tobacco and alcohol, and more effective health care. Unfortunately, the latter scenario has created in many populations "*metabolic overload of caloric intake*" leading to an epidemic of obesity and related chronic diseases of adults and the elderly.

It is noteworthy that in lower middle income nations with large populations, such as India and China, deaths from chronic diseases now outnumber deaths from acute conditions by more than fivefold, and even in low income nations, the number of deaths from chronic diseases is approaching that of acute conditions. In higher middle income nations such as Poland, Russia, Mexico, and Argentina, mortality from chronic disease far outstrips that from acute disease. Their profile is similar to the mortality pattern of high income nations such as Sweden, the United States, the United Kingdom, Germany, and Japan.

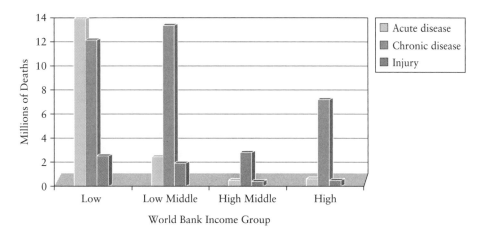

Figure 1.14 Worldwide Deaths by Major Cause and National Income, 2008.

Source: Data from WHO (2008a). Chronic Diseases: A Vital Investment. WHO Geneva, Switzerland.

These trends reflect the tremendous worldwide impact of the *epidemiologic transition*.

A disturbing trend in more prosperous nations is the heavy and indiscriminate use of antibiotics in the treatment of bacterial infections. Selection forces in these populations therefore favor the accumulation of resistant bacterial genes and plasmids resulting in the reemergence of certain infectious agents due to their evolving antibiotic resistance, e.g., *methicillin-resistant staphylococcus aureus (MRSA)*.

Risk Factors and Mortality

Worldwide mortality rates can also be examined according to major risk factors that are known to cause disease. Two major risk factors, tobacco and obesity, rival one another as perhaps the greatest public health menaces of all time. Another devastating menace to the status of public health is the problem of undernutrition which currently impacts millions of children, particularly in the underdeveloped nations of the world.

Global Tobacco Pandemic

Several comprehensive reports have addressed the global pandemic of disease resulting from tobacco addiction (Peto et al., 1996; Guindon and Boisclair, 2003; Doll et al., 2004; Jha et al., 2006; WHO, 2009b). According to estimates from these sources, 100 million people died from tobacco addiction (primarily cigarette smoking) during the 20th century, and if current smoking rates and trends prevail, one billion people will die from tobacco addiction in

the 21st century. Male smokers outnumber female smokers by more than fivefold in the populations of Africa, the Middle East, Asia, and the Western Pacific whereas female smoking rates are trending higher and may eventually approach male rates in the Americas and Europe (**Figure 1.15**). Worldwide, approximately 42% of men and 10% of women smoke, accounting for approximately 5.4 million deaths annually (**Figure 1.16**).

Prevention and Control of Tobacco Use

Recently, an international program of tobacco control titled the *Tobacco Free Initiative (TFI)* was ratified and implemented through the auspices of the World Health Organization to curb the epidemic of tobacco-related diseases throughout the world (WHO, 2009b). In addition to careful monitoring of tobacco use and prevention policies and their effectiveness in reducing tobacco-related morbidity and mortality, the *WHO TFI* advocates specific guidelines for the prevention of tobacco use and control of tobacco products. These are (1) primary prevention of initiating the smoking habit by early health education programs, (2) warning about the dangers of tobacco through hard-hitting antitobacco ads and graphic warnings on tobacco packaging, (3) protecting people from tobacco smoke by advocating smoke-free environments, (4) offering effective help to quit tobacco use through counseling and medications, (5) enforcing bans on tobacco advertising, promotion, and sponsorship, and, finally, (6) raising taxes on tobacco to generate revenues to support the program.

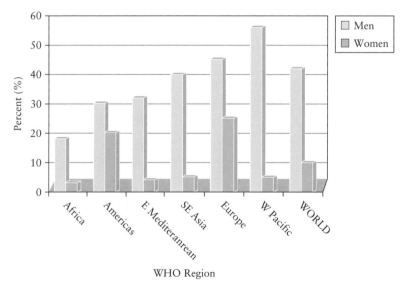

Figure 1.15 Worldwide Smoking Prevalence: 2005.

Source: Data from WHO (2009b). Report on the Global Tobacco Epidemic, 2009.

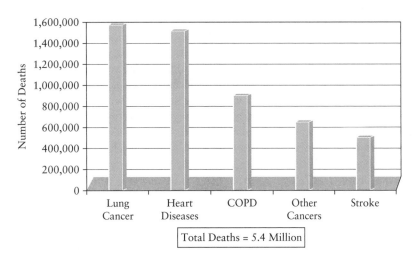

Figure 1.16 Worldwide Deaths Attributable to Cigarette Smoking, 2009.

Source: Data from WHO (2009b). Report on the Global Tobacco Epidemic, 2009.

Global Obesity Pandemic

The phenotype of an obese individual is characterized by an unnatural excess of body fat. This condition is commonly assessed by the body mass index (BMI) also known as the "*Quetelet Index*" calculated as weight in kilograms divided by the square of height in meters (kg/m^2). In adults, a BMI of 30 or more is defined as obese. In children, obesity is defined as weight above the 95th percentile for age-gender-specific growth charts.

As shown in **Figure 1.17**, approximately 10% of men and 12% of women are obese in the world population reflecting the global pandemic of overnutrition and metabolic overload (WHO, 2008a). The condition is particularly prominent in the developed nations of the Americas and Europe where over 20% of men and nearly 25% of women are in the obese category. According to surveys conducted by the WHO in 2009, there are more than 400 million clinically obese adults in the world population. Furthermore, the obesity pandemic is not restricted only to adults as the world population now contains approximately 22 million children under the age of 5 years that are either overweight or obese (International Obesity Task Force, 2009).

Obesity with its associated lipid engorgement of the fat cell (adipocyte) population often produces

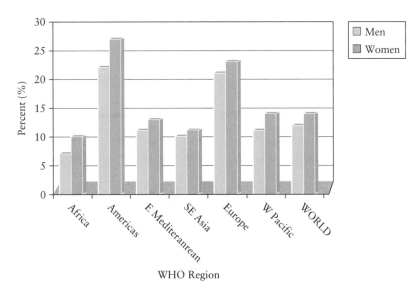

Figure 1.17 Worldwide Obesity Prevalence: 2009.

Source: Data from WHO (2009c). Obesity and Overweight. World Health Organization, Geneva, Switzerland.

adverse metabolic effects on blood pressure, cholesterol, triglycerides, and insulin resistance. Based on the results of recent epidemiologic investigations of diverse populations (Calle, 2007; Interheart, NCI bulletin), it is evident that as the BMI climbs above 30, there are corresponding risk increases in several chronic diseases including cardiovascular disease (hypertension, myocardial infarction, and stroke), chronic arthritis, type 2 diabetes, gallbladder disease, gastroesophageal reflux disease, and several cancers (Leach, Baumgard, and Broom, 1973; de Courten et al., 1997; Zimmet and Alberti, 2006; Caballero, 2007; Calle, 2007; Fisichella and Patti, 2009) (**Figure 1.18**). Gravid obesity (BMI > 40) has been found to be associated with greater than a twofold increase in the risk of all-cause mortality in both men and women (Calle, 2007).

Life-threatening conditions associated with obesity include hypertension, atherosclerosis, and hypercholesterolemia leading to catastrophic cardiovascular and cerebrovascular events such as myocardial infarction and stroke; insulin resistance resulting in type 2 diabetes; heightened carcinogenesis and development of certain types of malignant tumors, especially the hormonally related and large-bowel cancers. Nonfatal but debilitating health conditions associated with obesity include gastroesophageal reflux disease (GERD), cholelithiasis (genesis of gallstones), urolithiasis (genesis of kidney stones), and degenerative osteoarthritis.

The fundamental cause of obesity is an imbalance of energy input versus energy output. It should be realized that the development of obesity is *usually* not an acute process, but rather one that requires years or even decades of energy imbalance involving a sustained excess of calories consumed versus calories expended. Two primary risk factors are evident: (1) increased consumption of high calorie foods, particularly simple carbohydrates and other foods high in saturated fats and sugars, and (2) lack of sufficient physical activity. The inevitable consequence of calories taken in exceeding calories burned is obesity.

Societal changes and related behaviors are driving the obesity epidemic. With the globalization of food markets and continuing urbanization of the world population, low calorie diets with abundant complex carbohydrates are rapidly being replaced by high calorie diets with a high proportion of fats and sugars. At the same time, sedentary lifestyles characterized by little or no physical activity have become commonplace in the populations of modernized nations.

The International Obesity Task Force (IOTF) was established in 1996 to raise awareness and develop approaches to combat the emerging global pandemic of obesity. The IOTF membership consists of experts in the field of obesity research and represents 43 national organizations. The IOTF collaborates closely with the World Health Organization and other international health organizations concerned about the obesity problem.

The IOTF initiative on the prevention and management of obesity has four main goals: (1) to increase the awareness among governments, healthcare professionals, and the community that obesity is a serious medical condition and a major health problem with substantial economic costs; (2) to provide evidence and guidance for the development of better

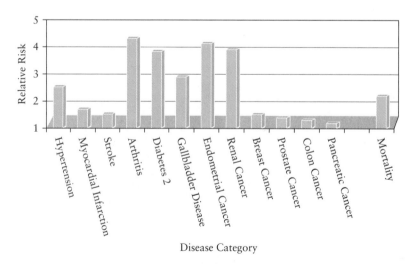

Figure 1.18 Obesity and Risk of Disease.

Source: Data from WHO (2008a). Chronic Diseases: A Vital Investment. WHO Geneva, Switzerland. Caballero B (2007). The Global Epidemic of Obesity: An Overview. *Epidemiologic Reviews* 29:1–5. Calle EE (2007). Obesity and cancer. *BMJ* 335(7630):1107–1108.

prevention and management strategies; (3) to secure the commitment of policy makers to action; and (4) to foster the development of national, regional, and international structures that will enable and support the implementation of action on the overweight and obesity.

The IOTF recommends several long-term strategies for the prevention and treatment of obesity and obesity-related diseases. Treatment centers incorporating effective weight loss programs should be developed with well-trained staff to ensure effective support to help individuals safely lose weight and maintain their optimum weight. Existing healthcare facilities should strive to develop and maintain an integrated team of physicians, dieticians, physical therapists, and other healthcare professionals, plus the necessary resources for the accurate diagnosis and effective treatment and management of obesity and obesity-related diseases.

A key element for success is primary prevention through promotion of healthy diets and regular physical activity beginning with health education programs initiated early in life. The following consensus statement from the British Medical Association is timely:

> "Such interventions at the family or school level will need to be matched by changes in the social and cultural context so that the benefits can be sustained and enhanced. Such prevention strategies will require a coordinated effort between the medical community, health administrators, teachers, parents, food producers and processors, retailers and caterers, advertisers and the media, recreation and sport planners, urban architects, city planners, politicians, and legislators. Environments that encourage healthy eating and active living are vitally important. The focus of such strategies should be to make it easier for the public to make healthy choices. Such strategies require funding for implementation, but should ultimately lead to a reduction in the costs from obesity related ill health."

Global Undernutrition and Malnutrition

Global estimates of relative mortality rates are shown for children under the age of 5 years in **Figure 1.19** (WHO, 2008b). It is evident that underweight children suffer from malnutrition and near starvation and are highly predisposed to infectious and parasitic diseases leading to diarrhea, dehydration, energy depletion, immunosuppression, and death. Such conditions currently exist in epidemic proportion in low income nations, particularly in sub-Saharan Africa.

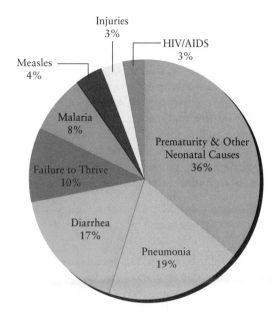

Figure 1.19 Relative Mortality Associated With Malnutrition and Underweight in Children Less Than Five Years of Age.

Source: Data from WHO (2008b). Global tuberculosis control 2008 report; WHO, UNAIDS, UNICEF (2008). Towards universal access: scaling up priority interventions in the health sector: progress report 2008.

Among the *10 million* children who die annually, WHO estimates that *6 million (60%)* succumb to conditions attributable to malnutrition and starvation (Caulfield et al., 2004).

Overall, the proportion of children under 5 years of age suffering from undernutrition (according to the WHO Child Growth Standards) declined from 27% in 1990 to 20% in 2005. However, progress has been uneven and an estimated 112 million children are underweight. Furthermore, every year some 536,000 women die of complications during pregnancy or childbirth, 99% of them in developing countries primarily in the populations of sub-Saharan Africa.

Reducing child mortality increasingly depends on approaches to improve neonatal survival. Globally, an estimated 37% of deaths among children under 5 years of age occur in the first month of life, most in the first week. Countries making the least progress are generally those affected by high prevalence rates of malnutrition and low birth weight, HIV/AIDS, indigenous infectious and parasitic diseases such as tuberculosis and malaria, economic hardship, and conflict. Much of the progress in reducing child mortality can be attributed to improved nutrition particularly during gestation and the neonatal period, increased immunization coverage against common infectious diseases such as measles, antiretroviral therapy for HIV/AIDS, use of oral rehydration therapies during episodes of diarrhea, use of insecticide-treated mosquito nets and access to combination therapies to combat malaria, efforts to eliminate disease due to *Haemophilus influenzae* type B infection, and ready access to clean water and sanitation facilities. However, because the availability and use of proven interventions at the community level remain low, pneumonia and diarrhea still kill 3.8 million children less than 5 years of age annually.

BODY MASS AND ALL-CAUSE MORTALITY

While no single biological factor can satisfactorily explain the disparate profiles of disease-specific mortality for different nations, there is one factor that does provide a crude but effective discriminant of all-cause mortality. Perhaps surprisingly, that factor is the body mass index (or Quetelet index) defined as weight in kilograms divided by height^2 in meters; $BMI = kg\ wt/(m\ ht)^2$. Its potential value as a measure of disease versus health is that BMI is a continuous variable that is easily calculated for every individual. The expectation is that low values are associated with nutritional deficiencies and high values with nutritional excesses.

Figure 1.20 shows all-cause mortality rates for adult men and women by eight categories of BMI ranging from extremely underweight (<14) to morbidly obese (>35) based upon a review of epidemiologic studies of 34 different populations from around the world. These data clearly reflect a U-curve for both genders where the optimum value corresponding to the lowest all-cause mortality is a BMI range of 21–25. As with most physiological factors, BMI shows a window of homeostasis wherein the potential

for good health is optimized and individuals with a BMI that is either too low or too high significantly increase their risk of dying. In particular, high BMI carries a fivefold increase of dying from obesity-linked conditions such as cardiovascular disease, stroke, diabetes, pulmonary disease, renal disease, and selected cancers such as breast cancer, colorectal cancer, and prostate cancer.

DISABILITY-ADJUSTED LIFE YEARS (DALY)

The *Disability-Adjusted Life Years (DALY)* is a measure of overall disease burden, expressed as the *number of years lost due to ill-health, disability, or early death*. The measure was originally developed by Christopher Murray and Alan López at Harvard University in order to characterize the overall burden of disease in populations (Murray and López, 1990, 1994). The World Health Organization subsequently adopted the measure in its *Global Burden of Disease Studies*.

The DALY is now widely used in the field of public health to assess the impact of death and disability in populations. This parameter is designed to extend the concept of potential years of life lost due to premature death to include equivalent years of "healthy" life lost due to states of poor health or disability. One DALY represents *one lost year of healthy life* and the sum of DALYs for all individuals of a population therefore quantifies the "gap" between current health status and ideal health where the entire population lives to an advanced age, free of disease and disability. The DALY therefore attempts to quantify mortality and morbidity in a single, common metric.

Traditionally, health liabilities were expressed as the expected or average number of *Years of Life*

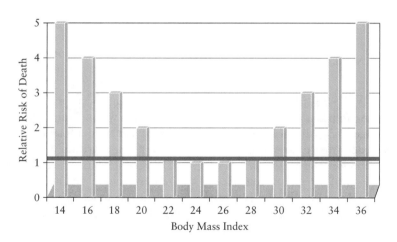

Figure 1.20 Body Mass Index & Mortality Window of Homeostasis.

Lost (YLL). This measure does not take into account the impact of disability or the number of years an individual lives with a severe disability. The population DALY for a disease or health condition is thus calculated as the sum of the years of life lost due to premature mortality in the population and the *Years Lost Due to Disability* (YLD) for incident cases of the specific health condition:

$$DALY = YLL + YLD$$

The YLL in a population for a particular disease is the product of the average life expectancy at average age of death for all individuals who died from that disease during a certain period of time (e.g., one year). The basic formula for YLL for a given cause, age, and gender is thus

$$YLL = N \times L_1$$

where N is the number of individuals who died from the disease in the population during the time period (year) of interest and L_1 is their standard life expectancy in years. Standard life expectancies for different ages are currently based upon life tables for the Japanese population, which has the highest biological life expectancy (80 years for men and 82.5 years for women).

To estimate YLD in a population for a particular disease in a particular time period, the average duration of disease (L_2) in years is weighted by a factor (DW) that reflects the severity of the disease on a scale from 0 (perfect health) to 1 (dead). The basic formula for YLD is thus

$$YLD = I \times DW \times L_2$$

where I denotes the number of new cases of disease, DW is the disability weight, and L_2 is the average duration of disease.

In calculating DALYs, the years of future life lost are weighted according to the formula

$$f(y) = 0.16243 \, y \, e^{-0.04y}$$

where y = the age at death or diagnosis of disease. This technique gives less weight to years of future life lost during periods of lesser productivity in the life span (childhood and late in life) and greater weight to years of future life lost during periods of higher productivity (late adolescence and adulthood). Furthermore, since a year of present life is considered more important than a year of future life, years of future life lost are discounted (reduced) at a standard rate of 3% per annum. Population estimates of DALYs for specific diseases are usually presented for a particular year per either 1,000 or 100,000 inhabitants (Murray and López, 1990, 1994, 1997).

Global Disability-Adjusted Life Year (DALY): All Causes

In 1997, Murray and López reported results of the first Global Burden of Disease Study using a standardized approach to epidemiologic assessment based upon estimates of DALY for various regions of the world. Estimates were calculated by age and gender for 107 disorders based upon cause-specific mortality and incidence rates, average age at onset, duration of disease, and severity of disability. Of the total DALY, 44% were due to communicable, maternal, perinatal, and nutritional disorders, 41% were due to noncommunicable diseases, and 15% were due to injuries. Among noncommunicable diseases, neurologic disease accounted for 10.5%; cardiovascular disease, 9.7%; and cancer, 5.1% of the total DALY. Communicable, maternal, perinatal, and nutritional disorders accounted for two-thirds of the disease burden in sub-Saharan Africa while noncommunicable diseases accounted for 80% of the burden in established market economies. The highest disease burdens were in sub-Saharan Africa and India (21.4% and 20.9% of the global DALY total, respectively). The authors noted that "*developing countries carried almost 90% of the global disease burden yet were recipients of only 10% of global health care funding*" (Murray and López, 1997).

Figure 1.21 depicts the worldwide pattern of DALY in 2004. The average DALY across all regions was 237 per 1,000 persons of which about 60% was due to years of life lost from premature death and 40% due to years of healthy life lost due to disability from nonfatal diseases (WHO, 2009c).

In the nations of sub-Saharan Africa, the DALY are more than twofold higher than the rest of the world, largely due to high mortality rates from both acute and chronic conditions as discussed earlier in this chapter. Higher than average DALY are also evident in the war torn nations of Afghanistan and Iraq.

The DALY and contributions of years of life lost due to premature death (YLL) and years of healthy life lost due to disability (YLD) are contrasted for various regions of the world in **Figure 1.22**. In regions with the highest DALY (Africa, East Mediterranean, and Southeast Asia), premature deaths account for more than two-thirds of the DALY whereas in Europe, America, and the Western Pacific, premature deaths and disability each account for roughly half of the disease burden. This pattern clearly reflects the impact of the *epidemiologic transition*, vis-à-vis the greater disease burden of communicable diseases and maternal, perinatal, and nutritional conditions in developing nations compared to the noncommunicable diseases that are more prominent in developed nations.

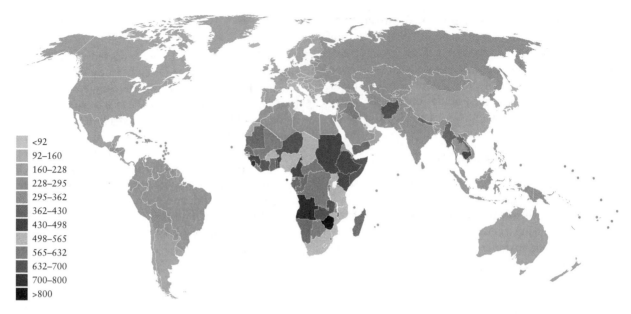

<92
92–160
160–228
228–295
295–362
362–430
430–498
498–565
565–632
632–700
700–800
>800

Figure 1.21 Disability Adjusted Life Years, 2004.

Source: Data from World Health Organization. The global burden of disease: 2004 update. Geneva, WHO, 2008. Available at www.who.int/evidence/bod

GLOBAL PREVENTION OF CHRONIC DISEASES

Four major groups of chronic diseases: cardiovascular diseases, cancers, chronic respiratory diseases, and diabetes represent the greatest burden to human health. These four diseases are the world's biggest killers, causing an estimated 36 million deaths each year and approximately 60% of all deaths globally.

Fortunately, these diseases are largely preventable. Up to 80% of heart disease, stroke, and type 2 diabetes, and over 30% of cancers can be prevented by eliminating shared risk factors, mainly tobacco addiction, unhealthy diet and obesity, sedentary lifestyle, and the harmful use of alcohol.

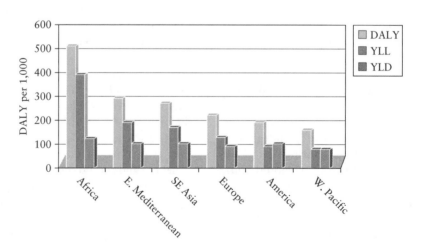

Figure 1.22 DALY, YLL, YLD by Region.

Source: Data from World Health Organization (2009). Death and DALY estimates for 2004 by cause for WHO Member States: Persons, all ages.

However, unless appropriately addressed with well-designed and effective disease prevention and health promotion programs, the mortality and disease burden from these health problems will continue to increase. WHO projects that, globally, deaths from these conditions will increase by 10–20% over the next 10 years. Due to high rates of smoking and alcohol abuse, increasing intake of diets ladened with salt, fat, and sugar, and a deficit in the access to health care, the populations of developing nations in Africa, Asia, and the Middle East are particularly susceptible.

Though proven cost-effective strategies currently exist to prevent and control the growing health burden of chronic diseases, high-level commitment, and concrete action are often missing or underfunded at the national level. On a global basis, it will be necessary to raise the priority accorded to chronic diseases and develop and implement effective disease prevention and health promotion strategies and policies for the populations at risk. There is an immediate call for the international public health communities to lobby and mobilize politicians, other international and regional agencies such as the United Nations Development Programme (UNDP), the United Nations Children's Fund (UNICEF), WHO, and the World Bank, and other international nongovernmental agencies to address the socioeconomic, behavioral, nutritional, and public health issues that have led to the current chronic disease epidemic. A multidisciplinary approach by governments that involves multiple ministries such as health, finance, education, sports, and agriculture can all contribute to a reversal of the underlying socioeconomic causes of the problem (Simpson et al., 1997; WHO, 1999; Zimmet, 1999, 2000; Zimmet, Alberti, and Shaw, 2001; Zimmet, Shaw, and Alberti, 2003; Alberti et al., 2004; WHO, UNAIDS, UNICEF, 2008).

Effective interventions should obviously target tobacco use, unhealthy diets, physical inactivity, and excessive alcohol consumption. Programs must also be implemented to promote research and develop international partnerships for the prevention and control of chronic diseases. To this end, improved registration systems of vital statistics are needed in order to monitor the incidence, prevalence, and mortality of chronic diseases, as well as their determinants, and to evaluate progress at the national, regional, and global levels (WHO, 1999; WHO, 2008a).

The World Health Organization working closely with its 193 Member States, has developed an Action Plan to prevent chronic diseases from occurring and to help the millions who are already affected to cope with these lifelong illnesses. This Action Plan, endorsed at the 61st World Health Assembly in May 2008, builds on the report of the Global Strategy for the Prevention and Control of Noncommunicable Diseases, 53rd World Health Assembly, May 2000. Key components of the plan are addressed in the following statement by Dr. Ala Alwan, Assistant Director-General, Noncommunicable Diseases and Mental Health, World Health Organization (Alwan, 2008).

"The action plan builds on the WHO Framework Convention on Tobacco Control and the WHO Global Strategy on Diet, Physical Activity, and Health. The Action Plan provides Member States, WHO, and the international community with a roadmap to establish and strengthen initiatives for the surveillance, prevention, and management of noncommunicable diseases. Furthermore, the Action Plan highlights the pressing need to invest in noncommunicable disease prevention as an integral part of sustainable socioeconomic development. NCD prevention is an all-government responsibility. Considerably more gains can be achieved by influencing policies of nonhealth sectors than by health policies alone. All stakeholders will need to intensify and harmonize their efforts to avert these preventable conditions and to save millions from suffering needlessly and dying prematurely."

For every individual, effective prevention of chronic disease is contingent upon the total avoidance of major known risk factors. Many of these risk factors are well established and primary prevention is straightforward; avoidance of cigarette smoking (and other forms of tobacco addiction), avoidance of excessive alcohol consumption, control of blood pressure by avoidance of high-salt fat-laden diets, control of blood glucose by avoidance of high carbohydrate (sugar-based) diets and foods with high glycemic indices, maintenance of body weight within normal limits, intake of calories matched to energy expenditure, daily intake of antioxidant and anti-inflammatory nutraceutical agents (fresh fruits and vegetables), daily aerobic exercising, daily stress release, and maintenance of a positive attitude in meeting life's challenges.

• • • REFERENCES

Adetunji, J., & Bos, E.R. (2006). Levels and trends in mortality in sub-Saharan Africa: An overview. In: Jamison, E.D., Feachem, R.G., Makgoba, M.W., et al. (Eds.). *Disease and Mortality in Sub-Saharan Africa* (2nd Edition, pp. 11–14). Washington, DC: The World Bank.

Alberti, G., Zimmet, P., Shaw, J., et al. (2004). Consensus Workshop Group: Type 2 diabetes in the young: The evolving epidemic: The International Diabetes Federation consensus workshop. *Diabetes Care, 27*, 1798–1811.

Alwan, A. (2008). 2008–2013 Action Plan for the Global Strategy for the Prevention and Control of Noncommunicable Diseases. Geneva, Switzerland: World Health Organization.

Ames, B., Cathcart, R., Schwiers, E., & Hochstein, P. (1981). Uric acid provides an antioxidant defense in humans against oxidant- and radical-caused aging and cancer: A hypothesis. *Proc Natl Acad Sci USA, 78*(11), 6858–6862.

Ames, B.N., Shigenaga, M.K., & Hagen, T.M. (1993). Oxidants, antioxidants, and the degenerative diseases of aging. *Proc Natl Acad Sci USA, 90*(17), 7915–7922.

Aris, E. (2004). United States Life Tables, 2002. *National Vital Statistics Reports, 53*(6), 1–40.

Austad, S.N. (1997). *Why We Age: What Science Is Discovering about the Body's Journey through Life.* New York: John Wiley & Sons.

Austad, S.N. (2006). Why women live longer than men: Sex differences in longevity. *Gend Med, 3*(2), 79–92.

Baingana, F.K., & Bos, E.R. (2006). Changing patterns of disease and mortality in Sub-Saharan Africa: An overview. In: Jamison, E.D., Feachem, R.G., Makgoba, M.W., et al. (Eds.). *Disease and Mortality in Sub-Saharan Africa* (2nd ed., pp. 1–10). Washington DC: The World Bank.

Barja, G., & Herrero, A. (2000). Oxidative damage to mitochondrial DNA is inversely related to maximum life span in the heart and brain of mammals. *Faseb J, 14*(2), 312–318.

Beckman, K.B., & Ames, B.N. (1998). The free radical theory of aging matures. *Physiol Rev, 78*, 547–581.

Blackman, M.R., Sorkin, J.D., Münzer, T., et al. (2002). Growth hormone and sex steroid administration in healthy aged women and men: A randomized controlled trial. *JAMA, 288*(18), 2282–2292.

Bradshaw, D., & Timaeus, I.M. (2006). Levels and trends of adult mortality. In: Jamison, E.D., Feachem, R.G., Makgoba, M.W., et al. (Eds.). *Disease and Mortality in Sub-Saharan Africa* (2nd ed., pp. 31–42). Washington, DC: The World Bank.

Caballero, B. (2007). The global epidemic of obesity: An overview. *Epidemiologic Reviews, 29*, 1–5.

Calle, E.E. (2007). Obesity and cancer. *BMJ, 335*(7630), 1107–1108.

Campisi, J., Kim, S.H., Lim, C.S., & Rubio, M. (2001). Cellular senescence, cancer and aging: The telomere connection. *Exp Gerontol, 36*(10), 1619–1637.

Caulfield, L.E., de Onis, M., Blössner, M., & Black, R.E. (2004). Undernutrition as an underlying cause of child deaths associated with diarrhea, pneumonia, malaria, and measles. *American Journal of Clinical Nutrition, 80*, 193–198.

CIA World Fact Book. (2009). *United Nations World Population Prospects 2006.*

Colton, T. (1974). *Statistics in Medicine.* Boston: Little, Brown and Company.

de Courten, M., Bennett, P., Tuomilehto, J., & Zimmet, P. (1997). Epidemiology of NIDDM in non-Europids. In: Alberti, K.G.M.M, DeFronzo, R.A., & Zimmet, P. (Eds.). *International Textbook of Diabetes Mellitus* (2nd ed., pp. 143–170). Chichester: Wiley.

de Magalhaes, J.P., & Faragher, R.G. (2008). Cell divisions and mammalian aging: Integrative biology insights from genes that regulate longevity. *Bioessays, 30*(6), 567–578.

Doll, R., Peto, R., Boreham, J., & Sutherland, I. (2004). Mortality in relation to smoking: 50 years' observations in male British doctors. *BMJ, 328*(7455), 1519.

Duckett, P. (2005). Globalized violence, community psychology and the bombing and occupation of Afghanistan and Iraq. *J Community Applied Social Psychology, 15*, 414–423.

Fisichella, P.M., & Patti, M.G. (2009). Gastro-esophageal reflux disease and morbid obesity: Is there a relation? *World J Surg, 33*, 2034–2038.

Gerschman, R., Gilbert, D.L., Nye, S.W., Dwyer, P., & Fenn, W.O. (1954). Oxygen poisoning and x-irradiation: A mechanism in common. *Science, 119*(3097), 623–626.

Guindon, G.E., & Boisclair, D. (2003). *Past, current and future trends in tobacco use.* Washington, DC: The International Bank for Reconstruction and Development, The World Bank, pp. 13–16.

Harman, D. (1956). Aging: A theory based on free radical and radiation chemistry. *J Gerontol, 11*(3), 298–300.

Harman, D. (1972). A biologic clock: The mitochondria? *Journal of the American Geriatrics Society, 20*(4), 145–147.

Hayflick, L. (1985). The cell biology of aging. *Clin Geriatr Med, 1*(1), 15–27.

Hayflick, L. (2007). Entropy explains aging, genetic determinism explains longevity, and undefined terminology explains misunderstanding both. *PLoS Genet, 3*(12), e220.

Hayutin, A. (2007). Global demographic shifts create challenges and opportunities. *PREA Quarterly*, (Fall), 46–53.

Hill, K., & Amouzou, A. (2006). Trends in child mortality. In: Jamison, E.D., Feachem, R.G., Makgoba, M.W., et al. (Eds.). *Disease and Mortality in Sub-Saharan Africa* (2nd ed., pp. 15–30). Washington, DC: The World Bank.

International Obesity Task Force. (2010). Obesity the Global Epidemic. London, United Kingdom.

Leach, R.E., Baumgard, S., & Broom, J. (1973). Obesity: Its relationship to osteoarthritis of the knee. *Clin Orthop, 1973*, 93271–93273.

Leon, D.A., Saburova, L., Tomkins, S., et al. (2007). Hazardous alcohol drinking and premature mortality in Russia: A population based case-control study. *Lancet, 369*(9578), 2001–2009.

Linnane, A.W., Marzuki, S., Ozawa, T., & Tanaka, M. (1989). Mitochondrial DNA mutations as an important contributor to aging and degenerative diseases. *Lancet, 1*(8639), 642–645.

Medawar, P.B. (1952). *An Unsolved Problem of Biology.* London: H. K. Lewis.

Menken, J., Trussell, J., & Larsen, U. (1986). Age and infertility. *Science, 233*, 1389–1394.

Murray, C.J.L., & López, A.D. (1990). Global and regional cause-of-death patterns in 1990. *Bulletin of the World Health Organization, 72*, 447–480.

Murray, C.J.L., & López, A.D. (1994). Quantifying disability: Data, methods and results. *Bulletin of the World Health Organization, 72*, 481–494.

Murray, C.J.L., & López, A.D. (1997). Global mortality, disability, and the contribution of risk factors: Global Burden of Disease Study. *Lancet, 349*(9063), 1436–1442.

Omran, A.R. (1971). The epidemiological transition: A theory of the epidemiology of population change. *Milbank Memorial Fund Quarterly, 49*, 509–538.

Pampel, F. (2002). Cigarette use and the narrowing sex differential in mortality. *Popul Dev Rev, 28*, 77–104.

Parker, W.H., Broder, M.S., Chang, E., et al. (2009). Ovarian conservation at the time of hysterectomy and long-term health outcomes in the Nurses' Health Study. *Obstet Gynecol, 113*, 1027–1037.

Perls, T.T., Hutter Silver, M., & Lauerman, J.F. (1999). *Living to 100: Lessons in Living to Your Maximum Potential at Any Age.* New York: Basic Books.

Peto, R., Lopez, A.D., Boreham, J., Thun, M., Heath, C., & Doll, R. (1996). Mortality from smoking worldwide. *British Medical Bulletin, 52*, 12–21.

Jha, P., Chaloupka, F.J., Corrao, M., & Jacob, B. (2006). Reducing the burden of smoking world-wide: Effectiveness of interventions and their coverage. *Drug and Alcohol Review, 25*(6), 597–609.

Rao, C., Lopez, A.D., & Herned, Y. (2006). Causes of death. In: *Disease and Mortality in Sub-Saharan Africa*, 2nd Edition, Editors (Jamison, E.D., Feachem, R.G., Makgoba, M.W., et al.), The World Bank, Washington DC, 2006, pp. 43–58.

Rowe, T. (2006). Fertility and a woman's age. *J Reproductive Med*, 51(3), 157–163.

Simpson, R.W., Tuomilehto, J., Lindstrom, J., Shaw, J.E., & Zimmet, P. (1997). Prevention of type 2 diabetes. In: DeFronzo, R.A., Ferranini, E., Keen, H., Zimmet, P., eds. *International Textbook of Diabetes Mellitus*. 3rd ed. John Wiley Chichefster, UK, 1997, pp. 1899–1913.

Strehler, B.L. (1999). *Time, Cells, and Aging*. 3rd ed. Larnaca: Demetriades Brothers.

United Nations Department of Economic and Social Affairs, Population Division. (2007). *United Nations World Population Prospects: 2006 revision*, Table A.15. New York: United Nations.

United States Census Bureau. (2009). International Data Base.

WHO. (1999). *The World Health Report 1999: Making a Difference*. Geneva, Switzerland.

WHO. (2008a). *Chronic Diseases: A Vital Investment*. Geneva, Switzerland.

WHO. (2008b). *Global tuberculosis control 2008 report*. Geneva, Switzerland.

WHO, UNAIDS, UNICEF. (2008). *Towards universal access: Scaling up priority interventions in the health sector; Progress report 2008*.

WHO. (2009a). *World Health Statistics, 2009*. Geneva, Switzerland.

WHO. (2009b). *Report on the Global Tobacco Epidemic, 2009*. Geneva, Switzerland.

WHO. (2009c). *Death and DALY estimates for 2004 by cause for WHO Member States: Persons, all ages*. Geneva, Switzerland.

World Bank. (1993). *World Development Report 1993: Investing in Health: World Development Indicators*. Oxford, UK: University Press Oxford.

Wynder, E.L. (1994). Principles of disease prevention from discovery to application. *International J Public Health*, 39(5), 167–172.

Zaridze, D., Brennan, P., Boreham, P., et al. (2009). Alcohol and cause-specific mortality in Russia: A retrospective case-control study of 48,557 adult deaths. *Lancet*, 373(9682), 2201–2214.

Zimmet, P. (1999). Diabetes epidemiology as a trigger to diabetes research. *Diabetologia*, 42, 499–518.

Zimmet, P. (2000). Globalization, coca-colonization and the chronic disease epidemic: Can the doomsday scenario be averted? *J Intern Med*, 247, 301–310.

Zimmet, P., Alberti, K.G., & Shaw, J. (2001). Global and societal implications of the diabetes epidemic. *Nature, 414*, 782–787.

Zimmet, P., Shaw, J., & Alberti, K.G. (2003). Preventing type 2 diabetes and the dysmetabolic syndrome in the real world: A realistic view. *Diabet Med, 20*, 693–702.

Zimmet, P.Z., & Alberti, G.M.M. (2006). Introduction: Globalization and the noncommunicable disease epidemic. *Obesity, 14*, 1–3.

2

Global Epidemiology of Cardiovascular Disease

GLOBAL EPIDEMIOLOGY OF CARDIOVASCULAR DISEASE

Cardiovascular disease (CVD) in its various forms is the leading cause of death worldwide, ranking first in both developing and developed nations. The total number of annual deaths due to CVD is more than 17 million, approximately 29% of all deaths. Furthermore, concurrent with increasing longevity throughout the world population, the burden of CVD no longer has its greater impact in the developed world. According to the most recent World Health Organizaiton (WHO) data, more than 80% of all CVD deaths occurred in developing (low and middle income) countries compared to developed (high income) countries (WHO 2009; WHO, 2010). **Figure 2.1** shows the marked excess of CVD deaths in low and middle income countries compared to high income countries (14 million versus 3 million).

Cardiovascular disease not only causes death but can also result in severe disability, particularly among those who survive a myocardial infarction or stroke. One measure of overall disease burden that is commonly used to measure the impact of *both* death and disability is *disability-adjusted life years* (DALY). The DALY extends the concept of *potential years of life lost due to premature death* (YLL) to include *years of healthy life lost due to disability* (YLD). In other words, the DALY combines mortality and morbidity into a single common measurement calculated as DALY = YLL + YLD.

Figure 2.2 depicts the burden of cardiovascular disease measured by DALY where one DALY is equivalent to the loss of one year of healthy life (WHO, 2009). Clearly, the CVD burden is higher in many of the developing nations of Asia, South America, and Africa (DALY > 5,100 per 100,000) than in the more advanced societies of North America, Europe, and Australia (DALY < 3,000 per 100,000). The composition of DALY also varies by economic region. Developing nations with high DALY rates suffer more lost years of healthy life due to premature death from CVD (60–70%) whereas developed nations lose more years of healthy life due to disability from CVD (50–60%).

SPECTRUM OF CARDIOVASCULAR DISEASE

Categorization of the pathologies underlying CVD is complex since the primary disease processes are often interdependent. Even so, more than 95% of all CVD can be categorized according to a few major pathologic conditions (Braunwald et al., 1997). Furthermore, more than 75% of deaths from CVD are attributable to either ischemic heart disease culminating in myocardial infarction or stroke culminating in cerebral infarction. These two conditions, ischemic heart disease and stroke, account for nearly one quarter of all deaths worldwide.

The approximate cause-specific global mortality rates due to the various forms of CVD are shown in **Table 2.1**. Of the 17.1 million deaths attributable to CVD every year, 7.2 million are due to ischemic (coronary) heart disease resulting in myocardial infarction (heart attack); 5.7 million are due to cerebrovascular disease (stroke), and an additional 2.2 million are due to hypertensive disease and/or congestive heart failure. The remaining deaths are due to rheumatic heart disease and inflammatory conditions (myocarditis, endocarditis, and pericarditis), aortic aneurysms, pulmonary emboli, and other cardiovascular conditions. Major diseases and conditions in

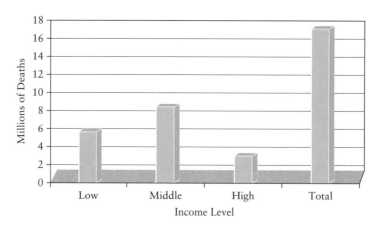

Figure 2.1 Global CVD Mortality, 2009.

Source: Data from WHO (2010). World Health Statistics 2010. World Health Organization Statistical Information System (WHOSIS), Geneva, Switzerland. Countries are grouped by national annual income per capita: Low: < $826, Middle: $826–$10,065, High: > $10,065.

the spectrum of CVD are briefly defined in the following paragraphs and separate chapters of this text are devoted to the epidemiology of these conditions.

Ischemic Heart Disease (Coronary Heart Disease) is caused by narrowing and obstruction of one or more blood vessels supplying the heart muscle itself (the myocardium). Ischemia means lack of oxygen (obviously due to the absence or lack of blood without which the heart muscle quickly dies). The catastrophic culminating event of obstructive coronary heart disease is a myocardial infarction (heart attack), which is frequently fatal. Coronary heart disease is almost always due to the presence of atherosclerotic plaque that impedes blood flow in one or more of the small caliber arteries of the heart. The development of atherosclerotic plaque (a process called atherogenesis) begins early in life and progresses over many years (usually decades) throughout the life span. Atherosclerotic

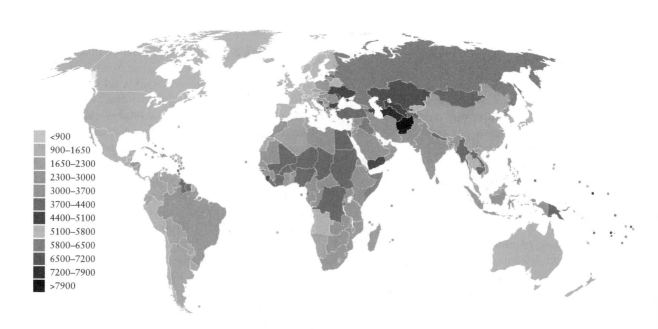

Figure 2.2 Cardiovascular Disease: Disability-Adjusted Life Years (DALY), 2004.

Source: Data from World Health Organization. The global burden of disease: 2004 update. Geneva, WHO, 2008. Available at www.who.int/evidence/bod. Age-standardized DALY from cardiovascular disease by country (per 100,000 inhabitants). Disability-adjusted life years (DALY) are rates per 100,000 people that combine Years of Life Lost (YLL) due to premature disease mortality in the population and the Years Lost due to Disability (YLD) for incident nonfatal cases of the disease (DALY = YLL + YLD). One DALY represents the loss of one year of healthy life.

Table 2.1	Relative Mortality Due to Cardiovascular Disease		
• Ischemic (Coronary) Heart Disease	7.2 Million	43%
• Cerebrovascular Disease (Stroke)	5.7 Million	33%
• Congestive Heart Failure	1.2 Million	7%
• Hypertensive Heart Disease	1.0 Million	6%
• Rheumatic Heart Disease	0.3 Million	2%
• Myocarditis/Endocarditis/Pericarditis	0.2 Million	1%
• Cardiomyopathy	0.2 Million	1%
• Congenital Heart Disease	0.1 Million	1%
• Peripheral Vascular/Aortal Disease	0.1 Million	1%
• Other Conditions	1.0 Million	6%
TOTAL	17.1 Million	

Mortality rates were estimated from worldwide data published by WHO, 2004. The relative mortality due to congestive heart failure is projected from data for the US population (National Center for Health Statistics, 2006: Heron et al., 2009).

plaque may develop over time in one or more coronary arteries eventually leading to stenosis and obstruction; or plaque may develop in a larger artery upstream, e.g., the aorta, that may rupture producing plaque remnants and thrombotic fragments (blood clots) that travel to smaller vessels such as the coronary arteries where they lodge and become obstructive. The process of atherogenesis is discussed in some detail in a following section of this chapter.

Myocardial Infarction (Heart Attack) is caused by acute obstruction of a coronary artery, usually one in which blood flow is already compromised by the presence of significant atherosclerotic plaque. Most infarcts of the myocardium arise due to ischemic heart disease as a consequence of long-standing atherosclerosis. There is controversy regarding the exact sequence of events leading to a myocardial infarction, and it is likely that there is considerable variability in the process from patient to patient. One proposed scenario involves rupture of an atherosclerotic plaque followed by platelet aggregation and possibly thrombotic occlusion in key coronary arteries, e.g., the right or left anterior descending or the left circumflex artery. Albeit, the end result of a myocardial infarction is significant necrosis of the myocardium which can quickly progress to arrhythmia and sudden cardiac death.

Cerebrovascular Disease (Stroke) is caused by acute disruption of the blood supply to the brain due to either blockage (ischemic stroke) or rupture of a blood vessel (hemorrhagic stroke). As with ischemic heart disease, strokes are usually caused by atherosclerotic plaque either developing in place or dislodged from a larger (upstream) artery. Plaque rupture, platelet aggregation, and thrombotic occlusion may all be involved.

Congestive Heart Failure is the seqeula of antecedent pathologies of the cardiovascular system, primarily (but not limited) to ischemic heart disease and hypertension. This condition is defined as failure of the heart to pump blood at a rate commensurate with the requirements of the body. The life-threatening effects of congestive heart failure are congestion, edema, and hypoxia, not only in the heart itself but also in the lungs, kidneys, brain, liver, and other vital organs. Congestive heart failure is often divided into left-sided versus right-sided failure. Left-sided failure most often arises due to the combination of ischemic damage to the myocardium from coronary atherosclerosis plus peripheral hypertension requiring greater contractile force of the left ventricle to maintain cardiac output. Right-sided failure (*cor pulmonale*) can develop as a consequence of intrinsic lung disease (e.g., chronic obstructive pulmonary disease) and heightened blood pressure in the pulmonary circulation or may arise from progressive edematous changes in the lungs due to left-sided heart failure. In either case, the right ventricle encounters increased contractile resistance and is subject to hypertrophy, dilatation, and failure.

Hypertensive Heart Disease occurs when the heart continually pumps against high resistance in the peripheral circulatory system. Resistance to blood flow in the peripheral arteriolar system increases with the constriction of blood vessels (vasoconstriction). The effects of vasoconstriction and increased resistance to blood flow are measured by the blood pressure. Regulation of blood pressure is complex and involves the kidneys and other organs. Hypertension is defined as systolic blood pressure exceeding 140 mm Hg and/or diastolic blood pressure exceeding 90 mm Hg.

As the peripheral resistance to blood flow increases, the heart (particularly the left ventricle) must work harder to maintain cardiac output. This sequence leads to left ventricle hypertophy and dilatation and may cause the pooling of blood in the left ventricular chamber (left-sided congestive heart failure). If there is long-standing high blood pressure in the lungs (pulmonary hypertension), the right ventricle may undergo hypertrophy leading to right-sided congestive heart failure (*cor pulmonale*). Other factors, particularly ischemic heart disease, may contribute to and exacerbate hypertensive heart disease and congestive heart failure.

Rheumatic Heart Disease refers to damage to the heart valves and/or the myocardium caused by a persistent infection with beta hemolytic streptococcal A bacteria. The infectious process typically begins as an acute pharyngitis. Rheumatic fever develops as a sequela to the infection and involves inflammatory immune reactions in the heart and joints.

Inflammatory Heart Disease refers to inflammatory conditions of the heart other than rheumatic heart disease. Inflammatory heart disease encompasses viral myocarditis (viral infection of the myocardium), bacterial endocarditis (bacterial infection of the endocardium, the inner lining of the heart chambers), and pericarditis (infection of the pericardial membranes that surround the heart). Infectious agents may attack the myocardium directly or alternatively and may stimulate an autoimmune inflammatory response in the myocardium. A variety of viruses, bacteria, protozoa, and other microbes may be involved, especially in the immunocompromised patient.

Peripherial Artery Disease is caused by obstruction of the arteries (usually by atherosclerotic plaque) supplying the arms and legs. This condition is often a forerunner of ischemic heart disease due to atherosclerosis.

Aortic Aneurysms are abnormal dilatations of the aorta. These balloon-like outpouchings of the aorta arise primarily due to severe atherosclerosis and hypertension that produce thinning and necrosis of the artery wall. Long-standing aortic aneurysms are highly prone to rupture and discharge of blood into surrounding tissues and body cavities. Such *dissecting aortic aneurysms* are frequently fatal.

Deep Venous Thrombosis refers to obstructive blood clots in peripheral veins of the legs (veins carry blood back to the right atrium of the heart). Thrombotic material can dislodge and travel through the pulmonary arteries to the lungs, resulting in a life-threatening pulmonary embolism.

Congenital Heart Disease refers to malformation of anatomic structures (e.g., septal defects, abnormal heart valves) at birth due to genetic factors or gestational events.

DECLINING MORTALITY FROM CARDIOVASCULAR DISEASE IN DEVELOPED COUNTRIES

Cardiovascular disease is the dominating cause of death and disability throughout the industrialized world as well as in many developing nations. Nevertheless, in developed countries such as the United States, Great Britain, Australia/New Zealand, and western European nations, deaths from CVD have declined dramatically in the past several decades. Declining CVD mortality in the United States is illustrative of this trend (**Figure 2.3**). This declining

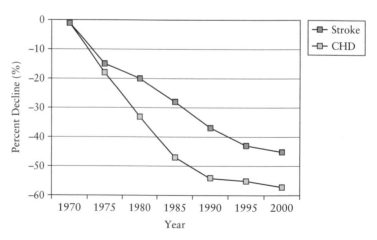

Figure 2.3 Percent Decline in CVD Mortality.

Source: Data from National Heart, Lung and Blood Institute (NHLBI, 2009). *Morbidity and Mortality: 2009 Chart Book on Cardiovascular, Lung and Blood Diseases*. National Institutes of Health, Bethesda, MD.

trend is undoubtedly due to major advances in the prevention and treatment of hypertension, ischemic heart disease, heart failure, and related conditions that predispose to fatal heart attacks and strokes. Indeed, it is estimated that more than half of the deaths due to CVD could be prevented through health promotion and disease prevention activities including cost-effective healthcare policies and individual actions to reduce exposure to major risk factors such as high blood pressure, high cholesterol, obesity, and smoking (Sanderson et al., 2007; Anand and Yusuf, 2011).

UNITED STATES MORTALITY FROM CARDIOVASCULAR DISEASE

Despite the 50% decline in deaths from ischemic heart disease and stroke during the past 40 years, CVD remains the leading cause of death in the United States (as well as most other developed nations). In 2006, CVD claimed 831,272 US lives (34.3% of all deaths) and more than 151,000 CVD victims died before reaching age 65 years. Ischemic/coronary heart disease caused 425,425 deaths in 2006 and is the single leading cause of death in the United States today (Heron et al., 2009).

Prevalent conditions among *living* Americans include high blood pressure (73.6 million), type 2 diabetes mellitus (18 million), prior myocardial infarction (8.5 million), prior stroke (6.4 million), and heart failure (5.8 million). More than one-third of these individuals have two or more forms of CVD, which synergistically increases their risk of developing a secondary catastrophic cardiovascular event,

e.g., fatal myocardial infarction, stroke, or end-stage congestive heart failure (Levy, 1993).

EPIDEMIC OF CONGESTIVE HEART FAILURE IN THE UNITED STATES

One form of CVD that has markedly *increased* rather than decreased in the United States and other developed nations during the past 40 years is congestive heart failure (Bleumink et al., 2004). As shown in **Figure 2.4,** the hospitalization rate for congestive heart failure has increased more than fourfold for adults 65 years and older and more than twofold for younger adults in the United States since 1970 (National Heart, Lung and Blood Institute, 2009). This condition occurs when the heart pumps insufficient blood to meet the metabolic demands of the body. It is effectively diagnosed and monitored by measuring cardiac output as the ejection fraction of the lower heart chambers (ventricles) using electrocardiography and other imaging techniques. The normal adult range for the ejection fraction is 50–70% and congestive heart failure is indicated when the ejection fraction falls below 50%.

Many interactive factors are undoubtedly responsible for the epidemic of congestive heart failure in the United States and other developed nations. Congestive heart failure represents the end stage of a web of pathogenic events of CVD including ischemic/coronary heart disease, atherosclerosis, hypertension, type 2 diabetes, and inflammation (He et al., 2001). Indeed, improvements in the detection and treatment of these conditions have led to a significant increase in overall survival. It is estimated that more than 81 million Americans are living with two or more

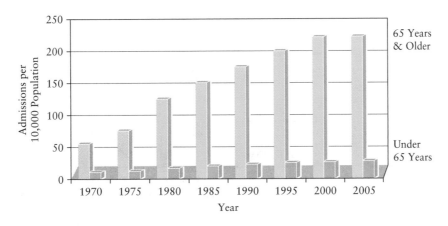

Figure 2.4 Hospitalization Rates for Congestive Heart Failure, 1970–2005, USA.

Source: Data from National Heart, Lung and Blood Institute (NHLBI, 2009). Morbidity and Mortality: 2009 Chart Book on Cardiovascular, Lung and Blood Diseases. National Institutes of Health, Bethesda, MD.

forms of CVD and as more and more patients survive CVD and live longer, their risk of developing congestive heart failure increases. Furthermore, the prevalence of certain risk factors, particularly type 2 diabetes and obesity, has increased in parallel with the rising rates of congestive heart failure.

GENDER AND ETHNIC DIFFERENCES IN CARDIOVASCULAR DISEASE IN THE UNITED STATES

Striking gender and ethnic differences are present in the rates of CVD and its spectrum of component conditions. **Figure 2.5** shows the 2006 US mortality rates for CVD and coronary/ischemic heart disease (CHD) for men and women of African American (AA) and Caucasian American (CA) ethnicity. For each stratum, coronary heart disease constitutes approximately half of the CVD mortality burden. The excess mortality among men compared to women is evident for each ethnic group, e.g., men are at an approximately 40% higher risk of dying from any form of CVD than women. The excess CVD mortality in the African American population is also striking, e.g., in gender-specific comparisons, African Americans have 38% higher CVD mortality than Caucasian Americans. These population disparities reflect not only differences in exposure to the risk factors, but also inadequacies of the healthcare system for the early detection and efficacious treatment of CVD in subpopulations of Americans (Freeman and Payne, 2000).

EPIDEMIOLOGIC TRANSITION OF CARDIOVASCULAR DISEASE

Major causes of death and disability have undergone an *epidemiologic transition* from predominantly nutritional deficiencies and infectious diseases in underdeveloped nations to chronic degenerative diseases such as cardiovascular disease, cancer, and type 2 diabetes in more advanced societies. Yusuf and colleagues divide the international patterns of cardiovascular disease into four distinct stages of the epidemiologic transition: (1) excess rheumatic heart disease and other inflammatory conditions in children and young adults in populations of sub-Saharan Africa, rural Southeast Asia, and South America; (2) excess hypertensive heart disease in young and middle-aged adults in populations of China and urban Asia; (3) rapidly increasing ischemic (coronary) heart disease and cerebrovascular disease in populations of India, Latin America, and Russia; and (4) declining cardiovascular disease among adults in populations of North America, Western Europe, Australia, and New Zealand (Yusuf et al., 2001).

While cardiovascular diseases afflict men and women of all socioeconomic classes in all geographic areas of the world, the prevalence of known CVD risk factors, and corresponding disease rates are highest and on the increase in the developing world. As a consequence, the most populous nations of the world have not yet progressed to stage 4 of the epidemiologic transition. As pointed out by Sanderson

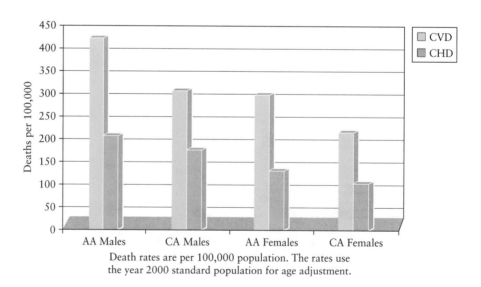

Death rates are per 100,000 population. The rates use the year 2000 standard population for age adjustment.

Figure 2.5 Cardiovascular Disease (CVD) and Coronary Heart Disease (CHD): USA, 2006.

Source: Data from Heron M, Oyert DL, Murphy SL, Xu J, Kochanek KD, Tejada-Vera B (2009). Deaths: Final Data for 2006. *National Vital Statistics Reports* 57, Number 14, 2009.

and colleagues in their review of the global burden of CVD:

> "*Although the mortality rate of cardiovascular diseases and prevalence of major cardiovascular risk factors has generally decreased in economically developed countries, the corresponding mortality rate, and risk prevalence has substantially increased in China, other East Asian societies and now India, which have been undergoing rapid demographic, social and, economic changes.*" (Sanderson et al., 2007)

Futhermore, CVD often strikes middle-aged adults and as a result, families spiral into a cycle of poverty as they lose their primary breadwinners to death or severe disability (Anderson and Chu, 2007). Such premature death and disability reflects a virtual *pandemic* of CVD and if current trends continue, the annual death toll will approach 20 million in the developing world by the year 2020 (WHO, 2005).

RISK FACTORS FOR CARDIOVASCULAR DISEASE

The stages in the epidemiologic transition of cardiovascular diseases have occurred in response to shifts in risk factor profiles for specific cardiovascular conditions. The classical risk factors for CVD include tobacco addiction, hyperlipidemia (*high* low-density lipoprotein cholesterol and *low* high-density lipoprotein cholesterol, diabetes type 2 with hyperglycemia (increased blood glucose), hypertension, and inflammatory conditions of the heart and blood vessels. The inflammatory biomarker, C-reactive protein (CRP), has also been proven to be of value in predicting the development of CVD.

There is also convincing epidemiologic evidence that CVD risk is increased by consuming a diet high in saturated fats, being markedly overweight or obese, and maintaining a sedentary lifestyle with little physical activity. These risk factors tend to cluster in populations thereby synergistically elevating the risk to much higher levels. The time lag effect of risk factors for CVD means that the full effect of past exposure to behavioral risk factors, especially among children, will only be seen in the future. Unless preventive and management efforts are embraced worldwide, the global burden of CVD death and disease will continue to rise (MacKay and Mensah, 2004; Anderson et al., 2010). **Table 2.2** provides a listing of the major and contributing CVD risk factors, each of which is discussed in subsequent chapters.

Table 2.2	Selected Risk Factors for Cardiovascular Disease
Major Risk factors:	
1. Tobacco Addiction	
2. Elevated LDL Cholesterol	
3. Low HDL Cholesterol	
4. High Blood Pressure	
5. Elevated Blood Glucose	
6. Elevated C Reactive Protein	
7. Obesity*	
8. Physical Inactivity*	
9. Dietary Factors*	
Contributing Risk factors:	
1. Low Socioeconomic Status*	
2. Elevated Prothrombotic Factors: Fibrinogen, PAI-1	
3. Markers of Infection or Inflammation	
4. Elevated Homocysteine	
5. Elevated Lipoprotein(a)	
6. Psychological Factors (depression, anger proneness, hostility, stress, acute life-events) and Breakdown in Social Structures (loss of social support and cohesion)*	

*Predisposing risk factors: A predisposing risk factor is presumed to work, at least in part, through impact on other risk factors that act directly. For example, obesity raises blood pressure, causes dyslipidemia, and increases blood glucose. It is likely that some of the contributing risk factors also have direct effects.

PAI indicates plasminogen activator inhibitor.

The global rise in CVD in developing nations reflects increases in the risk factors listed in Table 2.2: heightened consumption of westernized diets, declining physical activity levels, and increased tobacco addiction as a result of industrialization, urbanization, economic development, and market globalization. People of these nations are consuming a more energy-dense, nutrient-poor diet, and are less physically active. Imbalanced nutrition, reduced physical activity, and increased tobacco addiction are the key lifestyle factors. High blood pressure, high blood cholesterol, obesity, and type 2 diabetes are among the major biological risk factors. Unhealthy dietary practices include the high consumption of saturated fats, salt, and refined carbohydrates, and reciprocally, the low consumption of fruits and vegetables, whole grains and nuts, and certain types of unsaturated fats, e.g., omega-3 fatty acids. Futhermore, individuals in the developing world have the "double jeopardy" of increased chronic disease prevalence combined with persistently high rates of infectious diseases, leading to exceedingly high overall morbidity and mortality (Jamison et al., 2006).

PRIMARY PREVENTION OF CARDIOVASCULAR DISEASE

Primary prevention is the avoidance of known CVD risk factors. For example, individuals who never initiate the smoking habit markedly reduce their risk. Other lifestyle changes that have proven beneficial to cardiovascular health include cessation of tobacco use, aerobic exercising for at least 30 minutes daily, maintaining optimal body weight, and consuming a diet low in sodium, carbohydrates, saturated and total fats that is more weighted towards unsaturated fats, fruits, vegetables, whole grains, and omega-3 fatty acids. Compelling evidence indicates that the following strategies listed in **Table 2.3** are effective in preventing CVD and in helping manage the disease.

The most cost-effective methods of reducing CVD rates involve population-wide efforts to reduce modifiable risk factors through multiple economic and educational policies and programs. Food labeling for nutritional content; educational programs to promote decreased consumption of saturated fats, trans-fatty acids, and sodium; targeting and penalizing tobacco use; and campaigns advocating regular aerobic physical activity for weight reduction and control have proven effective in certain populations (Anderson et al., 2010).

TERTIARY PREVENTION OF CARDIOVASCULAR DISEASE

Individuals who have already experienced a cardiovascular event such as a heart attack or stroke are at high risk of suffering recurrence or death. Such individuals have numerous interventions available to them including nonpharmaceutical lifestyle modifications including regular aerobic exercising and dietary changes (e.g., restriction of salt, sugar, refined carbohydrates, and transition of the fatty acid profile to include less saturated fats and more polyunsaturated fats such as omega-3 fatty acids). Safe and effective weight reduction programs typically involve reduced caloric intake and increased fiber in the diet combined with a regular program of aerobic physical activity (Weight Control Information Network, 2010).

Pharmaceutical modalities include aspirin use, blood pressure modification, statin medication for hyperlipidemia, and specific medications to regulate blood glucose. In addition, there are a number of intensive techniques that are used in patients with cardiovascular disease, such as coronary stenting and coronary artery bypass grafting for ischemic heart disease, and thrombolytics for cerebrovascular disease.

Table 2.3	Strategies for the Prevention of Cardiovascular Disease

- Avoid smoking or using any form of tobacco.
- Maintain a healthy weight.
- Practice at least 30 minutes of aerobic physical activity daily.
- Limit energy intake from total fats and shift fat consumption away from saturated fats to unsaturated fats and towards the elimination of trans-fatty acids.
- Increase consumption of omega-3 fatty acids from fish oil or plant sources such as olive oil.
- Consume a diet high in fruits, vegetables, nuts and whole grains, and low in refined grains.
- Avoid excessively salty or sugary foods.
- Limit alcohol consumption to one drink daily.

GLOBAL PREVENTION OF CARDIOVASCULAR DISEASE

Until recently, cardiovascular disease has been largely absent from the international consciousness, overshadowed by public health concerns about HIV/AIDS and other infectious diseases. As recently as 2000, cardiovascular disease was conspicuously absent from the United Nation's Millennium Development Goals. Cardiovascular diseases are largely preventable through public health strategies and evidence-based risk factor interventions. International, national, and community programs are needed to ensure that these interventions reach the individuals most at risk. The World Health Organization has called for a global partnership of nationwide public health campaigns and high-risk intervention strategies (WHO, 2005). Organizations such as the International Cardiovascular Health Alliance (ICHA) are working in underresourced communities to establish and implement effective CVD risk factor intervention programs.

● ● ● REFERENCES

Anand, S.S., & Yusuf, S. (2011). Stemming the global tsunami of cardiovascular disease. *Lancet*, *377*(9765), 529–532.

Anderson, J., Parker, W., Steyn, N.P., Grimsrud, A., Kolbe-Alexander, T., Lambert, E.V., & Mciza, Z. (2010). World Health Organization Global Strategy on Diet, Physical Activity and Health: Interventions on Diet and Physcial Activity: Executive Summary. Geneva, Switzerland: World Health Organization.

Bleumink, G.S., Knetsch, A.M., Sturkenboom, M.C.J.M., et al. (2004). Quantifying the heart failure epidemic: Prevalence, incidence rate, lifetime risk and prognosis of heart failure: The Rotterdam Study. *European Heart Journal*, *25*(18),1614–1619.

Braunwald, E., Zipes, D.P., Libby, P., & Bonow, R. (1997). *Braunwald's Heart Disease: A Textbook of Cariovascular Medicine* (5th ed.). Philadelphia: WB Saunders Company.

Freeman, H., & Payne, R. (2000). Racial injustice in health care. *NEJM*, *342*(14),1045–1047.

He, J., Ogden, L.G., Bazzano, L.A., Vupputuri, S., Loria, C., & Whelton, P.K. (2001). Risk factors for congestive heart failure in US men and women: NHANES I epidemiologic follow-up study. *Arch Intern Med*, *161*(7), 996–1002.

Heron, M., Oyert, D.L., Murphy, S.L., Xu, J., Kochanek, K.D., & Tejada-Vera, B. (2009). Deaths: Final data for 2006. *National Vital Statistics Reports*, *57*, 14.

Jamison, D.T., Breman, J.G., Measham, A.R., et al. (2006). *Disease Control Priorities in Developing Countries* (2nd ed.). Washington, DC: World Bank.

Levy, D. (1993). A multifactorial approach to coronary disease risk assessment. *Clinical and Experimental Hypertension*, *15*(6), 1077–1086.

MacKay, J., & Mensah, G. (2004). *The Atlas of Heart Disease and Stroke*. Geneva, Switzerland: World Health Organization.

National Heart, Lung and Blood Institute (NHLBI). (2009). *Morbidity and Mortality: 2009 Chart Book on Cardiovascular, Lung and Blood Diseases*. Bethesda, MD: National Institutes of Health.

Sanderson, J.E., Mayosi, B., Yusuf, S., Reddy, S., Hu, S., Chen, Z., & Timmis, A. (2007). Global burden of cardiovascular disease. *Heart*, *93*, 1175.

Weight Control Information Network. (2010). National Institute of Diabetes and Digestive and Kidney Diseases (NIDDK). Bethesda, Maryland: US National Institutes of Health and Human Services.

World Health Organization. (2005). Preventing Chronic Diseases: A Vital Investment: WHO global report. Geneva, Switzerland.

World Health Organization. (2009). WHO Disease and Injury Country Estimates. Geneva, Switzerland.

World Health Organization. (2010). World Health Organization Statistical Information System (WHOSIS). Geneva, Switzerland.

Yusuf, S., Reddy, S., Ôunpuu, S., & Anand, S. (2001). Global burden of cardiovascular diseases: Part I: General considerations, epidemiologic transition, risk factors, and impact of urbanization. *Circulation*, *104*, 2746–2753.

3

Epidemiology of Ischemic (Coronary) Heart Disease

DEFINITION OF ISCHEMIC/CORONARY HEART DISEASE

Ischemic heart disease/coronary heart disease[*] refers to a deficiency of blood supply to the heart muscle leading to deprivation of oxygen essential for the proper functioning of the myocardium and related heart tissues and structures. About 98% of the time ischemic heart disease results from atherosclerosis (atherogenesis), a long-term process leading to the development of lipid-laden plaques within blood vessels of the heart and other organs. Such atherosclerotic plaques can cause stenosis (narrowing) and obstruction of the coronary arteries, and they can also rupture, resulting in thrombotic or embolic occlusion of coronary blood vessels. A thrombus refers to the formation of a stationary clot upon rupture of an atherosclerotic plaque within a blood vessel while an embolus refers to a clot that breaks away from its original site of plaque rupture and travels downstream in the blood and occludes a smaller caliber blood vessel.

GLOBAL EPIDEMIOLOGY OF ISCHEMIC/CORONARY HEART DISEASE

Of the more than 17 million deaths caused by cardiovascular disease annually, more than 7.2 million (approximately 42%) are attributable to ischemic heart disease. This condition is nearly always a consequence of long-standing atherosclerosis and the development of atheromatous plaques that occlude the coronary arteries. Ischemic heart disease often culminates in myocardial infarction and sudden cardiac death. The global pattern of disability-adjusted life years (DALY) lost to ischemic heart disease reflects the highest disease burden in many developing nations of the world including Russia, India, North Africa, and the Middle East (**Figure 3.1**). By comparison, lower DALY values are observed in developed nations such as the United States, Canada, Western Europe, Japan, and Australia/New Zealand, where improvements in the healthcare system have produced declines in the mortality and morbidity from ischemic heart disease. Notably, the populations of certain developing countries, e.g., China, have also sustained relatively low rates of ischemic heart disease.

ATHEROGENESIS AND ATHEROSCLEROSIS

Atherosclerosis (atherogenesis) refers to the development of atheromas in the arterial walls of humans and other mammals. Atheromas consist of focal deposits of plaque material that develop just beneath the intima (the enothelial lining) of arteries. These fibrofatty plaques have a lipid core of cholesterol and cholesterol derivatives covered by a fibrous cap of smooth muscle (Robbins and Cotran, 1979).

---

[*] I note at the outset of this chapter that the terms "ischemic heart disease" and "coronary heart disease" are used synonymously. Because reduction in coronary blood flow is virtually always the cause of the lack of oxygenation (ischemia) of the myocardium, the term "coronary heart disease" is favored by some authors. The terms are thus used interchangeably in the text depending upon which one is used by the authors of the referenced work.

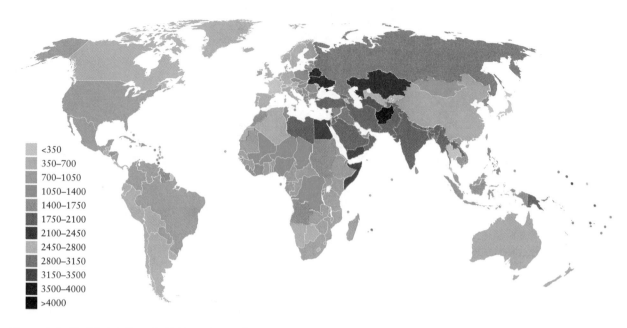

Figure 3.1 Disability-Adjusted Life Years (DALY) for Ischemic Heart Disease, 2004.

Source: Data from World Health Organization. The global burden of disease: 2004 update. Geneva, WHO, 2008. Available at www.who.int /evidence/bod. Age-standardized DALY from ischemic heart disease by country (per 100,000 inhabitants). Disability-adjusted life years (DALYs) are rates per 100,000 people that combine Years of Life Lost (YLL) due to premature mortality in the population and the Years Lost due to Disability (YLD) for incident nonfatal cases of the disease (DALY = YLL + YLD). One DALY represents the loss of one year of healthy life.

Two theories of atherosclerosis have been the subject of long-standing debate among cardiovascular researchers. More than 150 years ago, the famous German pathologist Rudolph Virchow postulated that the accumulation of lipids in arteriolar walls causes atherosclerosis (Virchow, 1856). It is important to note that Virchow also suggested that the disease process involved *inflammation* stimulated by the abnormal subintimal presence of lipids.

Significant evidence supporting the *"lipid hypothesis"* came from a study in 1913 by Nikolai Anitschkow who demonstrated that dietary cholesterol induced the development of atheromatous plaques in the arteries of rabbits (Anitschkow, 1913; Anitschkow and Chatalov, 1913). According to this hypothesis, low-density lipoproteins (LDL) circulating in the blood are oxidized by free radicals to form oxidized LDL that damage the arterial wall and stimulate the influx of macrophages and other immune cells. Lipid laden macrophages (called foam cells) plus extracellular cholesterol and cholesterol derivatives form the core of the plaque beneath the arterial wall. With enlargement and maturation of the plaque over time, smooth muscle cells are stimulated to grow over the plaque to form a fibrous cap (Duff and McMillan, 1951).

A second hypothesis (often called the *"response to injury hypothesis"*) proposes that atherogenesis is an inflammatory disease (Ross and Glomset, 1973 1976). According to this hypothesis, injury to the endothelial lining of the artery stimulates an inflammatory response resulting in smooth muscle proliferation and, subsequently, infiltration of the wound by macrophages and other inflammatory cells. Without resolution, recursive cycles of chronic inflammation ensue, leading to the release of hydrolytic enzymes, cytokines, chemokines, and growth factors that cause further cellular damage and eventually produce focal areas of cell necrosis. As stated by Ross, *"Each characteristic lesion of atherosclerosis represents a different stage in a chronic inflammatory process in the artery; if unabated and excessive, this process will result in an advanced complicated lesion."* (Ross, 1999).

A compromise of these two hypotheses put forth by Steinberg and others is that both mechanisms are intricately involved in the genesis of atherosclerotic plaques, e.g., that hypercholesterolemia and inflammation in atherogenesis are *"two sides of the same coin."* (Steinberg, 2005). This dual hypothesis postulates the following sequence of pathogenesis: (1) hypercholesterolemia (in particular, high LDL) induces adhesion of leukocytes to the arterial endothelium,

(2) circulating monocytes and lymphocytes penetrate into the subendothelial space, (3) oxidized LDL accumulates beneath the endothelium, (4) macrophages are attracted to the developing lesion and become engorged with oxidized LDL to form "*foam cells*," (5) the sustained presence of oxidized LDL and its derivative forms stimulate a vicious cycle of recursive inflammation involving infiltration by macrophages and other immune cells, (6) focal areas of cell necrosis ensue, and (7) smooth muscle cells grow over the lesion producing a fibrous cap. The time sequence of atherogenesis is many years, often decades, first resulting in fibrous streaks in the arterial walls and subsequently progressing to the development of complex atheromas that can obstruct the arterial lumen *per se* or rupture giving rise to thrombotic or embolic occlusion of small caliber arteries (**Figure 3.2**).

OTHER MECHANISMS OF ISCHEMIC/ CORONARY HEART DISEASE

While atherosclerosis is invoked in the genesis of virtually all ischemic/coronary heart disease, other mechanisms may also play an etiologic role, either independently or in combination with the development of atheromatous plaques. For example, hemodynamic reductions in coronary perfusion may result from conditions that damage the aortic valve and compromise coronary filling, such as syphilis and rhuematic heart disease. Since the metabolic needs of the myocardium are high, hypermetabolic states (e.g., vigorous exercise, hyperthyroidism, pregnancy) may also accentuate ischemic disease. In addition, conditions that diminish the oxygen carrying capacity of the blood (e.g., all forms of anemia) may also contribute to imbalance in the supply and demand of oxygen to the myocardium (Robbins and Cotran, 1979).

HISTORICAL PERSPECTIVES OF THE EPIDEMIOLOGY OF ISCHEMIC/CORONARY HEART DISEASE

Prospective epidemiologic investigations conducted in the past half century have contributed significantly to our understanding of the pathogenesis of

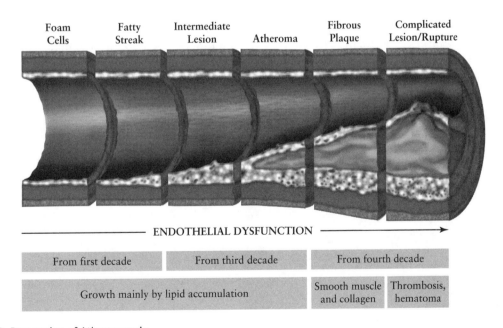

Figure 3.2 Progression of Atherogenesis.

Source: Reproduced from: Matthews, K. A. (2005). Psychological Perspectives on the Development of Coronary Heart Disease. *American Psychologist* 60(8):783–796.

ischemic/coronary heart disease. These include the Seven Countries Study, the Framingham Study, and MONICA, which are discussed in the following paragraphs.

The Seven Countries Study

The Seven Countries Study conducted by Ancel Keys and colleagues examined the effects of diet in an international prospective cohort of 12,763 men, aged 40 to 59 years, in 16 population samples from 7 different countries (Italy, Greece, former Yugoslavia, the Netherlands, Finland, United States, and Japan). All participants were healthy at the time of study entry. Baseline information was collected during 1958–1964 and vital statistics verified at regular intervals over twenty-five years of follow-up. Cardiovascular events and other health outcomes were adjudicated and rates and correlations calculated among and within population samples to determine effects of diet and other potential risk factors (Keys et al., 1967; Keys, 1970; Keys et al., 1980). The study was the first to demonstrate that serum cholesterol is a biomarker of impending coronary heart disease and that the risk increases with intake of saturated fats and decreases with intake of monounsaturated fatty acids (primarily from olive oil). Risk increases were also associated with elevated blood pressure (hypertension), cigarette smoking, sedentary lifestyle, and obesity.

Among the sample populations examined, the cohort from Crete in Greece had the lowest rates of coronary heart disease. The *Mediterranean diet* of this population "*is characterized by abundant plant foods (fruit, vegetables, breads, other forms of cereals, potatoes, beans, nuts, and seeds), fresh fruit as the typical daily dessert,* **olive oil** *as the principal source of fat, dairy products (principally cheese and yogurt), and fish and poultry consumed in low to moderate amounts, zero to four eggs consumed weekly, red meat consumed in low amounts, and wine consumed in low to moderate amounts, normally with meals*" (Keys 1970). Low rates of coronary heart disease were also observed among Japanese men who typically consume a low calorie diet high in fish and rice. Populations consuming diets with higher saturated fats from meat and dairy sources and lower monounsaturated fats had higher adjusted rates of coronary heart disease (**Figure 3.3**).

The Framingham Study

Since 1948, investigators at Harvard University have been following generations of the residents of Framingham, Massachusetts, to better understand the determinants of heart disease. The initial cohort consisted of 5,209 randomly selected members of the adult population of Framingham, 30–62 years of age, who were enrolled for study in 1948. The ongoing study now includes a second generation of 5,124 men and women (offspring of the original cohort), a third generation of 4,095 men and women, and a new spouse cohort that is currently enrolling subjects.

Since 1950, more than 2,000 peer-reviewed scientific articles have been published based upon the Framingham Study. While there have been many research milestones, perhaps the most important finding from the Framingham Study is that coronary heart disease is multifactorial involving both independent effects as well as synergistic interactions of a number of major risk factors including cigarette smoking, hypercholesterolemia, type 2 diabetes mellitus, hypertension, sedentary lifestyle, obesity,

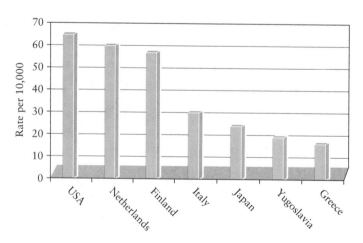

Figure 3.3 Annual Incidence of Coronary Heart Disease in the Seven Countries Study.

Source: Annual incidence of death or myocardial infarct due to coronary heart disease. Data from Keys A (1970). Coronary Heart Disease in Seven Countries. New York, NY: American Heart Association, Monograph No. 29.

dietary factors, and genetic factors. Indeed, a premier accomplishment of Framingham investigators was development of a coronary disease prediction algorithm involving risk factor categories to facilitate accurate risk prediction of coronary heart disease accounting for multiple risk factors. This index is an extremely useful tool for physicians and healthcare workers to instruct patients about their level of risk in order to counsel them on effective preventive and therapeutic interventions.

A series of initial reports based upon the Framingham Study documented significant independent effects of cigarette smoking, hypertension, and hypercholesterolemia in the genesis of ischemic (coronary) heart disease (Dawber and Kannel, 1968; Kannel, Castelli, and McNamara, 1968; Kannel, Castelli, Gordon, and McNamara, 1971; Kannel, Gordon, and Schwartz, 1971). While each of these risk factors independently increases the relative risk of disease by two- to threefold, the interaction of chronic smoking, high blood pressure, and hypercholesterolemia accentuates the risk by more than tenfold in comparison to individuals with no exposure (Levy, 1993). **Figure 3.4** depicts the multifactorial nature of ischemic/coronary heart disease culminating in myocardial infarction or stroke.

The MONICA Project

The MONICA Project (Multinational Monitoring of Trends and Determinants in Cardiovascular Disease) was initiated during the 1980s by the World Health Organization (WHO) in order to monitor the diverse international trends in mortality from cardiovascular disease (CVD) and changes in major CVD risk factors in selected populations. Approximately 15 million men and women aged 35–64 years were targeted for study in 41 MONICA Collaborating Centers around the world. Data collection has been completed after 10 years of follow-up in some population samples and the observed trends in mortality and certain risk factors have been published. MONICA provides a resource for continuing studies of CVD.

Across all sites represented in MONICA, mortality rates from coronary heart disease were, on average, about 4 times higher for men than women, e.g., the median annual mortality rate was 200 per 100,000 for men compared to 50 per 100,000 for women. Among men, relatively high annual mortality rates (>300 per 100,000) were observed in population samples from Finland, Poland, the United Kingdom, and Russia and low rates were observed in populations of China, France, Switzerland, and Italy. Among women, high rates were observed in the UK, Poland, and Russia (> 90 per 100,000) and low rates in Spain, France, Italy, and China (Tunstall-Pedoe et al., 2003).

Over 10 years of follow-up, the age-adjusted mortality from coronary heart disease declined annually by 2.7% in men and 2.1% in women, although there was wide variability among sites. Correspondingly, systolic blood pressure decreased in men and women, cigarette smoking decreased in men but not women, total cholesterol declined slightly in men and women, and survival following coronary events improved in most of the populations sampled. Nevertheless, there was a disturbing upward trend in the overall prevalence of obesity, particularly among men (Tunstall-Pedoe et al., 1999; Evans et al., 2001; Tunstall-Pedoe et al., 2003).

RISK FACTORS FOR ISCHEMIC/CORONARY HEART DISEASE

Major risk factors for ischemic heart disease have been called the *"four horsemen of the apocalypse"*

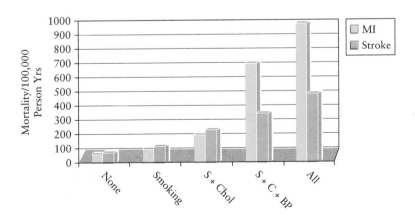

Figure 3.4 Synergy of Multiple Risk Factors: MI and Stroke.

Source: Data from Levy D (1993). A multifactorial approach to coronary disease risk assessment. *Clinical and Experimental Hypertension* 15(6):1077–1086.

(Harris, 1994). They include cigarette smoking, hypertension, elevated cholesterol, and type 2 diabetes mellitus (Grundy et al., 1998). Cholesterol measures are divisible into various fractions, e.g., high-density lipoprotein (HDL) cholesterol, and LDL cholesterol. Recently, a fifth risk factor, elevated C-reactive protein, which appears to be a valid measure of vascular inflammation, has been tested and verified as having significant predictive value for cardiovascular disease including ischemic/coronary heart disease. **Table 3.1** presents a brief listing of important risk factors and biomarkers.

Cholesterol and Ischemic/Coronary Heart Disease

Serum cholesterol has consistently proven to be a valid independent biomarker of impending ischemic heart disease. Early results for men enrolled in the Seven Countries Study suggested that serum cholesterol is linearly related to mortality from coronary heart disease across widely divergent cultures (Keys, 1970; Verschuren et al., 1995).

The Framingham Study provides convincing evidence of the relationship. Lloyd-Jones and colleagues examined the lifetime risk of developing coronary heart disease among 3,269 men and 4,019 women. Estimates of cumulative risk to age 80 years for individuals with baseline serum cholesterol levels at age 40 years of less than 200 mg/dl, 200–239 mg/dl, and 240 mg/dl or greater were 31%, 43%, and 57% for men and 15%, 26%, and 33% for women. The corresponding 10-year cumulative risks were 3%, 5%, and 12% for men and 1%, 2%, and 5% for women, respectively (Lloyd-Jones et al., 2003). Furthermore, the cumulative risk was inversely related to HDL cholesterol.

Table 3.1	Selected Risk Factors for Ischemic Heart Disease

- **Modifiable**
  Dyslipidemia, Hypertension, Smoking, Type 2 Diabetes Mellitus, Inflammation
- **Nonmodifiable**
  Genetics, Increasing Age, Male Gender, Female Menopause
- **Contributing Factors and Biomarkers**
  Obesity, Sedentary Lifestyle, Type A Personality
  Elevated Cholesterol and LDL Cholesterol
  Elevated C-reactive Protein
  Hyperinsulinemia
  Elevated Homocysteine
  Elevated Renin

Stamler and colleagues (Stamler et al., 1986, 1999, 2000) examined the relationship of baseline serum cholesterol to coronary heart disease in three US cohorts of young men and five US cohorts of middle aged men and observed significant dose responses in mortality from coronary heart disease with increasing serum cholesterol in each cohort. For example, in the large Multiple Risk Factor Intervention Trial (MRFIT) involving a cohort of 69,205 young men aged 35–39 years at baseline, the 16-year mortality rate due to coronary heart disease increased from 2.3 per 1,000 for serum cholesterol less than 160 mg/dl to 27.3 per 1,000 for serum cholesterol of 280 mg/dl or greater (adjusted relative risk = 8.1) (Stamler et al., 2000). Findings from the entire MRFIT cohort of 356,222 men aged 35–57 years at baseline and followed more than 25 years show that the mortality from coronary heart disease rises continuously with serum cholesterol level from a reference value of 160 mg/dl irrespective of age and ethnicity and after adjustment for other risk factors such as smoking, diabetes, and hypertension (Stamler and Neaton, 2008).

Clinical Trials of Statins, Cholesterol, and Coronary Heart Disease

In addition to the epidemiologic investigations that initially established elevated blood cholesterol as a risk factor for coronary heart disease, the results of many large clinical trials have provided definitive evidence that reducing cholesterol either by nonpharmacologic methods or by pharmaceutical medications (statins) leads to a significant reduction in the risk. In particular, statins that lower blood cholesterol have been found to significantly reduce the risk of developing coronary heart disease (Lipid Research Clinics Program, 1984; Strandberg et al., 1997; Downs et al., 1998; Bradford et al., 1991) as well as showing profound therapeutic effects in the prevention of recurrent disease (Sever et al., 2005; Nissen et al., 2006). Cholesterol guidelines based upon a consensus statement from the National Cholesterol Education Program (1993) are shown in **Table 3.2**.

Blood Pressure and Ischemic/Coronary Heart Disease

It is well known that elevations in blood pressure increase the risk of developing ischemic/coronary heart disease. Consistent findings have been reported for diverse populations in many studies including the Seven Countries Study and the Framingham Study and based on meta-analyses of data from multiple investigations.

In an early prospective study conducted during 1956–1960, investigators in Great Britain examined

Table 3.2	National Cholesterol Education Program (NCEP)	
Total Cholesterol		
<200 mg/dl	Desirable	
201–239 mg/dl	Borderline Risk	
>239 mg/dl	High Risk	
LDL-Cholesterol		
130 mg/dl	Desirable	
131–159 mg/dl	Borderline Risk	
>159 mg/dl	High Risk	

blood pressure and blood lipids as predictors of ischemic heart disease in a sample of 687 bus drivers and male conductors working on London Transport's central buses. While higher incidence rates were associated with several factors including age, family history, smoking, and obesity, the predominant predictive factors were "high systolic blood pressure" and "elevated plasma cholesterol," each of which was associated with more than a threefold increase in the incidence (Morris et al., 1966).

In a landmark study, Kannel and colleagues examined the relation of blood pressure to coronary heart disease among 2,282 men and 2,845 women in the population sample from Framingham, Massachusetts. Blood pressures were measured at baseline and individuals (who were initially free of coronary disease) were followed over a 14-year period to determine new coronary events. Baseline measures were used to stratify individuals as hypertensive (>160/95 mm Hg), borderline hypertensive (>140/90 mm Hg), or normotensive (<140/90 mm Hg). As shown in **Figure 3.5**, the risk of coronary heart disease increased with advancing blood

pressure for both men and women at all ages of entry into the study (Kannel, Schwartz, and McNamara, 1969; Kannel, 1996).

Using data from six population samples of the Seven Countries Study, van den Hoogen and colleagues examined associations of systolic and diastolic blood pressure with long-term mortality from coronary heart disease. Blood pressures were measured at baseline in 12,031 men initially free of coronary disease and followed over 25 years. Results were consistent for the diverse populations under study (United States, Northern Europe, Inland Europe, Southern Europe, Serbia, and Japan) showing a relative risk of 1.28 for each incremental increase of 10 mm Hg in systolic blood pressure or 5 mm Hg in diastolic blood pressure (van den Hoogen et al., 2000).

In a meta-analysis of diastolic blood pressure, stroke, and coronary heart disease involving 9 major prospective observational studies and 420,000 individuals followed for an average of 10 years, MacMahon and colleagues observed a linear dose response in the risk of coronary heart disease with increasing diastolic blood pressure (**Figure 3.6**).

Cigarette Smoking and Ischemic/Coronary Heart Disease

Cigarette smoking is not only the dominant cause of lung cancer, chronic bronchitis, and emphysema, but addiction to the smoking habit is also one of the major causes of ischemic/coronary heart disease. Many epidemiologic studies have examined the relationship of smoking and coronary heart disease in diverse populations throughout the world including China, India, Canada, Sweden, Japan, Switzerland, China, Great Britain, and the United States. In total, these studies represent more than 30 million person-years of observation, and despite the marked

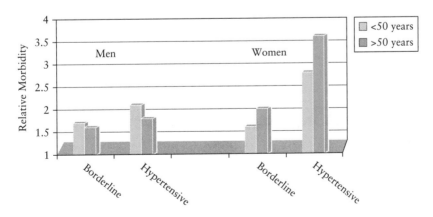

Figure 3.5 Risk of Coronary Heart Disease and Blood Pressure, Framingham Study.

Source: Data from Kannel WB, Schwartz MJ, McNamara PM (1969). Blood pressure and risk of coronary heart disease: The Framingham study. *Dis Chest* 56(1):43–52.

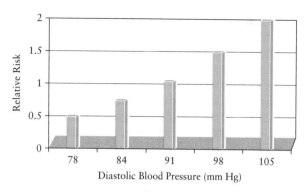

Figure 3.6 Coronary Heart Disease Risk by Diastolic BP Level.

Source: Data from MacMahon S, Peto R, Cutler J, Collins R, Sorlie P, Neaton J, Abbott R, Godwin J, Dyer A, Stamler J (1990). Blood pressure, stroke, and coronary heart disease. Part 1, Prolonged differences in blood pressure: prospective observational studies corrected for the regression dilution bias. *Lancet* 335(8692):765–774.

socioeconomic, genetic, and environmental differences in the populations sampled, the findings are remarkably consistent in demonstrating two- to four-fold increases in the mortality from coronary heart disease for chronic smokers compared to nonsmokers (Reports of the Surgeon General, 1983, 1988, 2004).

Results from three early prospective studies, two in the United States and one in Great Britain, provided strong evidence supporting the etiologic link between cigarette smoking and the development of coronary heart disease.

In 1951, a prospective study of smoking and cause-specific mortality was initiated in cohorts of British physicians (6,194 women and 34,440 men).

After more than 20 years of follow-up, the investigators concluded that cigarette smoking causes lung cancer, chronic obstructive lung disease (emphysema and chronic bronchitis), and heart disease in both men and women (Doll and Peto, 1976; Doll et al., 1980). The relative mortality estimates for ischemic heart disease by level of smoking are shown in **Figure 3.7**. Clearly, the dose response in mortality rates with increasing number of cigarettes smoked per day supports a causal relationship.

In 1954, the United States Public Health Service initiated a prospective study of a cohort of 198,820 male veterans to examine relationships of smoking and other risk factors with chronic diseases including coronary heart disease (Dorn, 1959; Rogot and Murray, 1980). Also in 1954, the American Cancer Society initiated a similar prospective study among a sample of 187,783 men, aged 50–69 years (Hammond, 1960). The results of these two investigations were remarkably similar in demonstrating a dose response relationship between the level of cigarette smoking and mortality due to coronary heart disease (**Figure 3.8**).

Evaluation of two other cohorts provided important confirmation of the causal effect of smoking in the genesis of coronary heart disease. The Framingham Study examined the incidence of coronary heart disease among 2,282 middle-aged men by smoking status. After 10 years of follow-up, the relative risk of developing coronary heart disease was twofold higher among men who smoked up to 20 cigarettes per day and threefold higher among men who smoked more than 20 cigarettes per day compared to nonsmokers (Kannel, 1964). Similar risk increases were observed among cigarette smokers in a

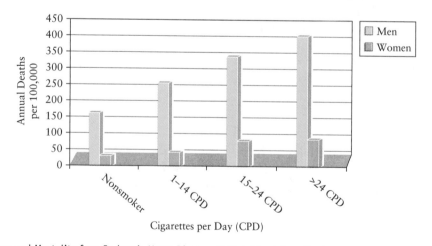

Figure 3.7 Smoking and Mortality from Ischemic Heart Disease, British Physicians Study.

Source: Rates are for individuals aged 65 years or younger. Doll R, Peto R (1976). Mortality in relation to smoking: 20 years' observations on male British doctors. *Br Med J* 2(6051):1525–1536; and Doll et al (1980). Mortality in relation to smoking: 22 years' observations on female British doctors. *Br Med J* 280(6219):967–971.

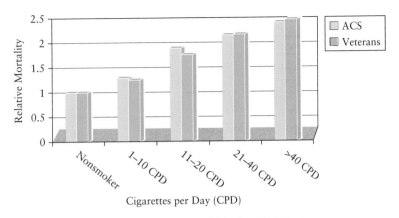

Figure 3.8 Mortality from Coronary Heart Disease by Level of Smoking: Two US Cohorts.

Source: Figure based on data from Dorn HF (1959). Tobacco consumption and mortality from cancer and other diseases. *Public Health Reports* 74:581–593; Hammond EC (1960). Smoking in relationship to heart disease. *Amer J Pub Health Nations Health* 50(3 pt 2):20–26; Rogot E, Murray JL (1980). Smoking and causes of death among US veterans, 16 years of observation. *Public Health Reports* 95(3):213–222.

cohort of 1,838 men from Albany, New York (Doyle et al., 1964).

Risk reductions in coronary heart disease after smoking cessation provide further evidence supporting causality (Report of the Surgeon General, 1990). In a meta-analysis of 20 prospective studies of patients with a diagnosis of coronary heart disease, there was a 36% reduction in the relative risk of mortality for those who quit smoking compared to those who continued to smoke (Critchley and Capewell, 2004). Furthermore, the risk reductions following smoking cessation were consistent regardless of differences between studies in age, gender, country, and time period. Within 2 years of cessation, the risk is reduced by about 50% and after 10 to 15 years of cessation, the risk returns to normal.

In addition to the direct effects of active cigarette smoking, passive smoking also appears to increase the risk. In a meta-analysis of 10 cohort and 8 case control studies, nonsmokers exposed to environmental tobacco smoke had a 25% increase in the relative risk of coronary heart disease (RR = 1.25) compared to nonsmokers with no exposure (He et al., 1999). The relative risk estimates were consistent for cohort studies (RR = 1.21) and case control studies (RR = 1.51) and for men (RR = 1.22) and women (RR = 1.24). Exposure to the highest level of environmental tobacco smoke (from more than 20 cigarettes per day) was associated with the greatest increase in risk (RR = 1.31) consistent with a dose response relationship.

There are multiple biological mechanisms by which cigarette smoking and nicotine addiction elevate the risk of ischemic/coronary heart disease. Nicotine itself is a powerful vasoconstrictor that elevates blood pressure and causes hypertension. As shown in **Figure 3.9**, the first cigarette of the day induces sharp increases in both systolic and diastolic blood pressure (Gropelli et al., 1992).

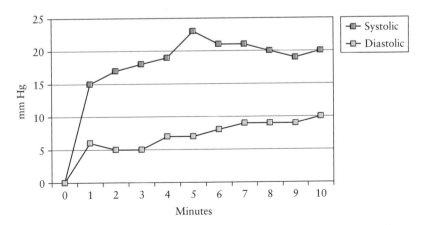

Figure 3.9 Change in Blood Pressure after the First Cigarette of the Day.

Source: Data from Gropelli et al (1992). Persistent blood pressure increase induced by heavy smoking. *J Hypertension* 10:495–499.

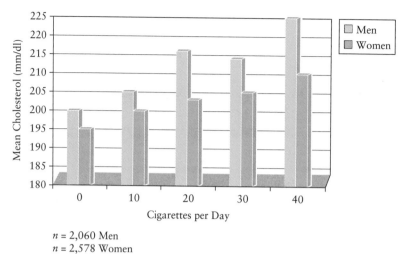

n = 2,060 Men
n = 2,578 Women

Figure 3.10 Total Cholesterol by Cigarettes Smoked.

Source: Data from Muscat JE, Harris RE, Haley NJ, Wynder EL (1991). Cigarette smoking and plasma cholesterol. *Am Heart J* 121(1 Pt 1):141–147.

Tobacco carcinogens, reactive oxygen species (ROS), and other constituents and derivatives of cigarette smoke are highly inflammatory to blood vessels and appear to be cofactors in atherogenesis (Howard et al., 1998). Smoking has also been found to elevate serum cholesterol, possibly through effects on liver metabolism (Muscat et al., 1991) (**Figure 3.10**). Finally, chronic smokers typically develop severe chronic lung diseases such as emphysema and chronic bronchitis and such conditions compromise the oxygenation of hemoglobin, thereby intensifying ischemic conditions in the myocardium and other tissues.

Diabetes and Ischemic/Coronary Heart Disease

Coronary heart disease often follows the diagnosis of type 2 diabetes, particularly in individuals with uncontrolled hyperglycemia and hyperinsulinemia. In the Framingham Study, the risk of developing coronary heart disease was increased nearly threefold in diabetic men and women (Kannel and McGee, 1979; Kannel, 1990) (**Figure 3.11**). Many other studies have reported similar findings. For example, in the Atherosclerosis Risk in Communities (ARIC) Study of 13,446 individuals from 4 US communities, the adjusted relative mortality from coronary heart disease for diabetics compared to nondiabetics was 3.45 for women and 2.52 for men (Folsom et al., 1997). In a meta-analysis of 16 prospective cohort studies involving more than 75,000 individuals, the summary relative mortality due to coronary heart disease for diabetics compared to nondiabetics was 2.58 for women and 1.85 for men (Lee et al., 2000).

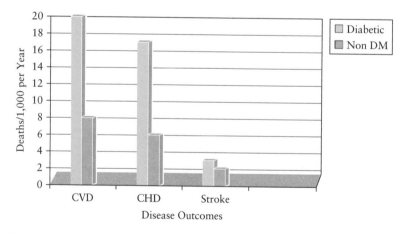

Figure 3.11 CVD Mortality by Diabetic Status, The Framingham Study.

Source: Data from Kannel et al (1990). Diabetes, fibrinogen, and risk of cardiovascular disease: the Framingham experience. *Am Heart J* 120:672–676. CVD = cardiovascular diseases, CHD = coronary heart disease, DM = diabetes mellitus.

Type 2 diabetes mellitus results when insulin fails to stimulate cellular uptake of glucose resulting in hyperglycemia and hyperinsulinemia. In patients with long-term hyperglycemia, nonenzymatic reactions between sugars and proteins form advanced glysolated end products (AGE) that may accumulate in the walls of blood vessels and heighten the process of atherogenesis (Kilhovd et al., 1999; Kiuchi et al., 2001). Hyperinsulinemia has also been observed to increase the risk in some (not all) studies. The Paris Prospective Study examined insulin levels in 7,164 men aged 43–54 years. After more than 10 years of follow-up, the mortality rate due to coronary heart disease was increased by threefold among individuals with the highest levels of fasting glucose (Eschwege et al., 1985). In the Helsinki Policemen Study of 970 men 34–64 years of age and free of coronary disease at baseline, individuals with insulin levels in the highest quintile had triple the risk of suffering a major coronary event (e.g., myocardial infarct) compared to individuals in the lowest quintile over 22 years of follow-up (Pyörälä et al. 1998). In a study of 91 cases and 105 controls from the Quebec Cardiovascular Study, investigators demonstrated an independent effect of baseline hyperinsulinemia whereby the odds of developing ischemic heart disease increased 1.6-fold for each standard deviation increase in the insulin concentration. Nevertheless, the biological mechanism by which hyperinsulinemia increases the risk is controversial and may involve interactions with endocrine factors, visceral obesity, and lipid abnormalities (Després et al., 1996).

Inflammation, C Reactive Protein, and Ischemic/Coronary Heart Disease

Atherogenesis (atherosclerosis) is a long-term disease process that causes the development of atheromatous plaques in blood vessels. When plaque buildup and/or rupture occlude coronary arteries that nourish the myocardium, the end result is ischemic/coronary heart disease, often culminating in myocardial infarction. Since atherogenesis has been described as a progressive inflammatory disease (Ross, 1999), it is perhaps not surprising that a blood marker of inflammation has been consistently linked to the risk of developing coronary heart disease.

Multiple prospective studies have demonstrated that small elevations in blood levels of the acute reactive inflammatory biomarker, C-reactive protein (CRP), accurately predict increasing risk of coronary heart disease (Toss et al., 1997; Ridker, Glynn, and Hennekens, 1998; Ridker et al., 2000, 2003; Koenig et al., 1999; Pai et al., 2004; Cushman et al., 2005). In fact, some studies suggest that C-reactive protein may be a better predictor of impending cardiovascular disease than serum cholesterol (Ridker et al., 2002). Predictive levels of C-reactive protein and corresponding relative risks for cardiovascular events (myocardial infarction or stroke) are shown in **Figure 3.12**.

C-reactive protein is a pentraxin protein that was previously thought to be an acute phase reactant in the innate immune response to acute inflammation or infection. In acute inflammatory conditions, 100-fold to 10,000-fold increases above baseline levels are measurable in the blood. Only recently has the

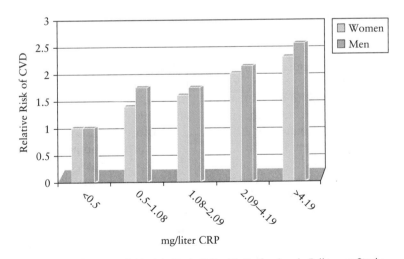

Figure 3.12 CRP & Cardiovascular Risk: Women's Health Study & Health Professionals Follow-up Study.

Source: Data from Ridker et al (2002). Comparison of c-reactive protein and low-density lipoprotein cholesterol levels in the prediction of first cardiovascular events. *New Engl J Med* 347:1557–1565; and Pai et al (2004). Inflammatory markers and the risk of coronary heart disease in men and women. *New Engl J Med* 351(25):2599–2610.

link between relatively small elevations in C-reactive protein and increasing risk of coronary heart disease been observed (Ridker et al., 1998). C-reactive protein apparently has multiple functions including opsonization of bacteria and damaged cells leading to their phagocytosis by macrophages and modulation of the complement system (Marnell, Mold, and Du Clos, 2005). In addition to having predictive value for impending coronary heart disease, increasing levels of blood C-reactive protein have been observed in association with aging (Hung et al., 2008), smoking (Bazzano et al., 2003), hypertension (Sung et al., 2003), type 2 diabetes (Ishikawa et al., 2007), and obesity (Barinas-Mitchell et al., 2001).

Hyperhomocysteinemia and Ischemic/Coronary Heart Disease

Hyperhomocysteinemia (elevated homocysteine in the blood) has recently emerged as a potentially modifiable independent risk factor for atherosclerosis and atherothrombosis involving the coronary and peripheral circulation. In a comprehensive meta-analysis of 57 published studies (3 cohort studies, 12 nested case control studies, and 42 case control studies) involving 5,518 cases with coronary heart disease and 11,068 controls without disease, the summary odds ratio for a 5 μmol/l increase in homocysteine concentration was 1.06 for prospective studies, 1.23 for nested case control studies, and 1.70 for case control studies (Ford et al., 2002). The heterogeneity of estimates between the different types of studies has been attributed to the inclusion of subjects with and without prior cardiovascular disease, and some investigators have suggested that homocysteine is most valuable as a biomarker in high-risk subjects or a prognostic indicator for the progression of preexisting cardiovascular disease (De Bree et al., 2002). However, in a subsequent meta-analysis of 26 prospective studies involving only subjects without known disease and selected to be of fair to good quality, each 5 μmol/l increase in homocysteine level was found to increase the risk of coronary heart disease by approximately 20%, independently of traditional disease risk factors (Humphrey et al., 2008). Nevertheless, it is noteworthy that reduction of homocysteine through intake of B vitamins has *not* consistently been found to prevent coronary heart disease or to have therapeutic benefit (Toole et al., 2004; Bønaa et al., 2006; Ebbing et al., 2008).

Elevations in plasma homocysteine are generally caused by enzymatic defects or vitamin B deficiencies (B_{12}, folate) involved in pathways of homocysteine metabolism. The atherogenic propensity associated with hyperhomocysteinemia has been linked to impaired endothelial function at several levels, including reduced nitric oxide synthesis, enhanced oxidative vascular injury, and increased vascular smooth muscle cell proliferation (Welch and Loscalzo, 1998).

Apolipoproteins and Ischemic/Coronary Heart Disease

Apolipoproteins are proteins that bind to lipids (fats). They form lipoproteins that transport and redistribute dietary fats and cholesterol through the bloodstream to various tissues and cells of the body (Mahley et al., 1985). There are six basic types of apoliproteins and multiple subtypes, all of which are coded by specific genes (Deeb et al., 1986).

Blood levels of specific types of apolipoproteins and lipoproteins can influence the risk of developing coronary heart disease. For example, certain isoforms of apolipoprotein A (ApoA) complex with low density lipoprotein particles to form *lipoprotein(a)*, which appears to influence the risk of coronary heart disease. In a meta-analysis of 27 studies involving 5,436 deaths or nonfatal myocardial infarctions due to coronary heart disease, individuals with lipoprotein(a) levels in the upper tertile had 1.6 times greater risk than individuals with levels in the lowest tertile (Danesh, Collins, and Peto, 2000).

One ApoA isoform, ApoA1, is the major surface component of HDL and is primarily responsible for efflux of cholesterol from tissues to the liver for excretion. High levels of ApoA1 have therefore been found to be cardioprotective in association with removal of cholesterol from arteries whereas low levels increase the risk. In a case control study of 3,510 acute myocardial infarction patients in UK hospitals and 9,805 controls, individuals ApoA1 levels in the lowest tertile had a 2.3-fold increase in the relative risk compared to individuals with levels in the highest tertile (Parish et al., 2009). Furthermore, dysfunctional mutant forms of apoA1 have been found to increase the risk of coronary heart disease (Singh et al., 2007).

Isoforms of apolipoprotein B (ApoB) are the major surface components of LDL that transport cholesterol to target tissues. Two ApoB isoforms are detectable in plasma: ApoB100, which is synthesized in the liver, and ApoB48, which is synthesized in the small intestine (ApoB48 has 48% homology with ApoB100). The liver isoform, ApoB100, is an integral component of very-low-density lipoprotein (VLDL), LDL, and intermediate-density lipoprotein (IDL), all of which transport cholesterol in the blood to target tissues and cells. The level of ApoB100 therefore reflects cholesterol-carrying capacity and has been found to be an accurate biomarker of coronary heart disease (McQueen et al., 2008).

Individuals with high levels of ApoB are at increased risk for the development of atheromatous plaques and subsequent coronary heart disease. In the UK case control study of acute myocardial infarction by Parish and colleagues, individuals with ApoB levels in the highest tertile had a 2.7-fold increase in the risk compared to individuals with levels in the lowest tertile (Parish et al., 2009).

Recent epidemiologic investigations have found the ratio of ApoB to ApoA1 to be a better predictor of coronary heart disease than either biomarker per se. In a nested case control study of 869 incident cases with fatal or nonfatal coronary heart disease and 1,511 controls without disease ascertained from a large European cohort, individuals with ApoB/ApoA1 ratios in the highest quartile had a 2.6-fold increase in the risk (van der Steeg et al., 2007). In a prospective investigation of 9,231 adults from the Danish general population who were asymptomatic at baseline and followed for 8 years, women and men with ApoB in the upper versus the lower tertile had hazard ratios for ischemic heart disease of 1.8 and 1.9, respectively (Benn et al., 2007). Similar results were reported by Parish and colleagues in their case control investigation of acute myocardial infarction in which individuals with ApoB/ApoA1 ratios in the highest tertile had a 3.8-fold increase in the risk (Parish et al., 2009).

INTERHEART is a large international case control study of acute myocardial infarction involving 15,152 incident cases and 14,820 gender- and age-matched controls from 262 partcipating centers in 52 countries througout Africa, Asia, Australia, Europe, the Middle East, and North and South America (Yusuf et al., 2004). Results of the INTERHEART study showed that the ApoB100/ApoA1 ratio was a better predictor than either individual biomarker *per se* and, in fact, was the strongest risk factor for acute myocardial infarction among all those measured. The relative risk for individuals with ApoB100/ApoA1 ratios in the highest quintile was 3.25 after adjustment for all other risk factors (McQueen et al., 2008). Results of these recent studies indicate that ApoB and ApoA1 and their ratio may predict impending coronary heart disease even better than HDL and LDL cholesterol.

Other Molecular Factors in the Pathogenesis of Ischemic/Coronary Heart Disease

Many other molecular factors are undoubtedly involved in determining the ultimate disposition of patients suffering from ischemic heart disease.

Indeed, the vascular response to ischemia is a dynamic process that is contingent upon multiple factors with complex interactions. Often, the patency of blood vessels impacted by atherosclerotic plaque or thrombotic/embolic material depends upon the balance between factors that regulate vasoconstriction versus vasodilatation. Such factors are derived not only from cells of the arterial wall (the endothelium), but also from circulating platelets and other elements of the bloodstream.

Vasoconstrictive factors such as angiotensin II, endothelin, and prostaglandin E_2 are balanced by vasodilatory factors such as nitric oxide, serotonin, and prostacyclin. Platelet activation, aggregation, and clotting are modulated by adenosine diphosphate (ADP), serotonin and thromboxane A_2. Acetylcholine from adrenergic nerves stimulates endothelial nitric oxide synthesis and vasodilatation. The kidneys are instrumental in regulation of vascular tone and rapidly respond to changes in blood flow and blood pressure. Low perfusion stimulates the kidneys to secrete renin, which converts angiotensinogen to a more active form, angiotensin I. Subsequently, angiotensin I is converted to the powerful vasoconstrictor, angiotensin II, by angiotensin-converting enzyme (ACE) in the lungs.

The acute nature of catastrophic cardiovascular events such as heart attack and stroke makes it difficult to accurately quantify biological effects of these molecular factors in the human system. Novel techniques combining molecular biology with epidemiologic methods will be required in order to fully elucidate the exact nature of these mechanisms.

PREVENTION OF ISCHEMIC/CORONARY HEART DISEASE

Ischemic/coronary heart disease is influenced by multiple interactive factors including tobacco addiction, hypertension, dyslipidemia, insulin resistance, glucose intolerance, vascular inflammation, physical inactivity, and obesity. These individual factors rarely occur in isolation and the degree of hazard depends on the number of risk factors present in a given individual. Fortunately, most of these risk factors are modifiable through lifestyle choices, e.g., abstinence from tobacco use, regular aerobic physical exercise, weight control, and consumption of a *heart healthy* diet (Sanderson et al., 2007).

It is, however, readily acknowledged that much controversy exists regarding the most efficacious *heart healthy* diet. Perhaps the key reason for the controversy is that 80–90% of the total cholesterol within the human body is synthesized internally as opposed to being consumed. Since cell structure relies on cholesterol-laden lipid membranes to separate and organize intracellular water, proteins, and nucleic acids, virtually all cells in the body (and particularly liver cells) are fully capable of cholesterol biosynthesis. Thus, modulation of cholesterol, a key factor in atherogenesis, is primarily regulated by biosynthetic and metabolic pathways rather than dietary intake.

Advocates of the Mediterranean diet point to the low rates of coronary heart disease in populations of the coastal regions of southern Italy, Crete, and Greece (Keys, 1970). The Mediterranean diet is characterized by abundant plant foods (fruit, vegetables, whole grain breads, other forms of cereals, potatoes, beans, nuts, and seeds), fresh fruit as the typical daily dessert, olive oil as the principal source of fat, dairy products (principally cheese and yogurt), fish and poultry consumed in low to moderate amounts, zero to four eggs consumed weekly, red meat consumed in low amounts, and wine consumed in low to moderate amounts, normally with meals. In a meta-analysis of 12 prospective studies with a total of 1,574,299 subjects followed for up to 18 years, greater adherence to a Mediterranean diet was associated with significant improvement in health status and significant reductions in overall mortality (9%), mortality from cardiovascular diseases (9%), cancer mortality (6%), and incidence rates of Parkinson's disease and Alzheimer's disease (13%) (Sofi et al., 2008).

Associations of the various types of dietary fats (saturated, polyunsaturated, and monounsaturated) and atherosclerosis are complex and there is hot debate as to which types and what levels are beneficial, neutral, or detrimental to heart health. The United States Deparment of Agriculture (USDA) in its food pyramid promotes a low-fat diet, based largely on its view that fat in the diet is atherogenic (USDA, 2010). The American Heart Association, the American Diabetes Association, and the National Cholesterol Education Program make similar recommendations. In contrast, other investigators recommend a shift to higher levels of monounsaturated and certain polyunsaturated fatty acids (PUFA) substituted for saturated fats in the diet.

Recent evidence supporting the concept that substituting PUFA for saturated fat in the diet is cardioprotective comes from a meta-analysis of 8 randomized clinical trials involving 13,614 subjects randomized to receive either high or low dietary PUFA. After an average follow-up period of 4.25 years, 1,042 subjects developed coronary heart disease and the energy intake from PUFA averaged 14.9% of total calories in the intervention group compared to 5% in the control group. Overall, the risk in the intervention group was reduced by 19% compared to the control group and the risk reduction in coronary heart disease was estimated to be 10% per each 5% *increase* in energy from PUFA (Mozaffarian, Micha, and Wallace, 2010). Furthermore, increasing consumption of PUFA has been found to lower HDL cholesterol (Lewington et al., 2007) and may also improve insulin resistance (Salmeron et al., 2001; Summers et al., 2002) and reduce systemic inflammation (De Caterina, Liao, and Libby, 2000; Pischon et al., 2003; Ferrucci et al., 2006).

It is generally accepted that omega-3 fatty acids are beneficial PUFA whereas trans-fatty acids should be avoided (Willett, Sacks, and Trichopoulous, 1995). Some investigators also advocate lowering the ratio of omega-6 PUFA (linoleic acid) to omega-3 PUFA (linolenic acid) in order to maximize protection against cardiovascular disease and other chronic diseases (Simopoulos, 2008).

Increasingly in developed nations, physicians are recommending daily intake of low dose 81 mg aspirin to reduce the risk of thrombotic cardiovascular events. The epidemiologic evidence supports the judicious use of low dose aspirin for the chemoprevention of both myocardial infarction and stroke. Current guidelines recommend using low dose aspirin in adults at higher risk and over the age of 50 years with the caveat that even low dose aspirin is contraindicated in individuals with known allergies, bleeding diathesis, platelet disorders, and active peptic ulcer disease (Lauer, 2002).

Many randomized clinical investigations have focused on the chemopreventive value of statin drugs in counteracting atherogenesis and reducing the risk of coronary heart disease. In one such trial conducted during a 5-year period in a sample population in Scotland, daily administration of a particular statin (pravastatin) reduced the incidence of coronary death or myocardial infarction by 24% (Ford et al., 2007). Subsequent meta-analyses have confirmed the chemopreventive value of statins against coronary heart disease in subjects *irrespective of the presence of established cardiovascular risk factors.* Meta-analysis of 10 trials enrolling 70,388 men and women *with established cardiovascular risk factors such as diabetes*, statin use reduced the incidence of major coronary events by 30% and cerebrovascular events by 19% (Brugts et al., 2009). A meta-analysis of 20 trials enrolling 63,899 individuals *at relatively low risk* found overall risk reductions of 23% for myocardial infarction, 12% for stroke, and 11% for any cardiovascular-related death (Mills et al., 2008).

Statins are now routinely prescribed to lower cholesterol and prevent atherogenesis.

The association of estrogen replacement therapy (ERT) or estrogen plus progesterone therapy and the risk of developing coronary heart disease has been examined in case-control studies, cohort studies, and more recently in randomized placebo-controlled clinical trials. While risk reductions in coronary heart disease were consistently observed in the case control and cohort studies (Barrett-Connor and Grady, 1998), three randomized clinical trials found just the opposite—that ERT with or without progesterone *increases* the risk (Hulley et al., 1998; Rossouw et al., 2002; Anderson et al., 2004). The discrepant results of the observational epidemiologic studies versus the randomized clinical trials have stimulated much debate regarding the risk versus benefit of ERT in postmenopausal women and controversy still rages as to whether ERT confers cardiovascular benefit or harm (Stevenson, 2009).

Prevention of coronary heart disease as well as all other diseases depends upon the early detection of treatable antecedent conditions through regular physical checkups. Effective anticholesterolemic, antihypertensive, and antidiabetic medications are readily available to maintain serum cholesterol, blood pressure, and blood glucose within normal limits. Sodium (salt) restriction (less than 6 grams of salt per day) is also important for blood pressure control. Weight reduction programs incorporating healthy nutrition and regular exercise regimes have proven successful in reducing obesity and reaching optimal weight.

In summary, keys to the prevention of coronary heart disease include (1) education of the general public to provide a better understanding of the widespread and multifactorial nature of the disease, (2) promotion of simultaneously instituting multiple preventive and treatment strategies as early in life as possible, and (3) adopting aggressive preventive strategies *before* people become symptomatic or suffer a major catastrophic cardiovascular event.

● ● ● **REFERENCES**

Anand, S.S., & Yusuf, S. (2011). Stemming the global tsunami of cardiovascular disease. *Lancet, 377*(9765), 529–532.

Anderson, G.L., Limacher, M., & Assaf, A.R., for the Women's Health Initiative Writing Group. (2004). Effects of conjugated equine estrogen in postmenopausal women with hysterectomy: The Women's Health Initiative randomized controlled trial. *JAMA, 291*(14),1701–1712.

Anitschkow, N.N., & Chatalov, S. (1913). Über experimentelle Cholesterinsteatose und ihre Bedeutung für die Entstehung einiger pathologischer Prozesse. *Zentralbl Allg Pathol, 24*, 1–9.

Anitschkow, N.N. (1913). Über die Veränderungen der Kaninchenaorta bei experimenteller Cholesterinsteatose. *Beitr Pathol Anat, 56*, 379–404.

Barinas-Mitchell, E., Cushman, M., Meilahn, E.N., Tracy, R.P., & Kuller, L.H. (2001). Serum levels of C-reactive protein are associated with obesity, weight gain and hormone replacement therapy in healthy postmenopausal women. *Am J Epidemiol, 153*(11), 1094–1101.

Barrett-Connor, E., & Grady, D. (1998). Hormone replacement therapy, heart disease, and other considerations. *Ann Rev Public Health, 19*, 55–72.

Bazzano, L.A., He, J., Muntner, P., Vupputuri, S., & Whelton, P.K. (2003). Relationship between cigarette smoking and novel risk factors for cardiovascular disease in the United States. *Ann Intern Med, 138*(11), 891–897.

Benn, M., Nordestgaard, B.G., Jensen, G.B., & Tybjaerg-Hansen, A. (2007). Improving prediction of ischemic cardiovascular disease in the general population using apolipoprotein B: The Copenhagen City Heart Study. *Arterioscler Thromb Vasc Biol, 27*(3), 661–670.

Bønaa, K.H., Njølstad, I., Ueland, P.M., et al. (2006). Homocysteine lowering and cardiovascular events after acute myocardial infarction. *New England Journal of Medicine, 354*, 1578–1588.

Bradford, R.H., Shear, C.L., Chremos, A.N., et al. (1991). Expanded clinical evaluation of Lovastatin (EXCEL) study results. I. Efficacy in modifying plasma lipoproteins and adverse event profile in 8,245 patients with moderate hypercholesterolemia. *Arch Intern Med, 151*(1), 43–49.

Brugts, J.J., Yetgin, T., Hoeks, S.E., et al. (2009). The benefits of statins in people without established cardiovascular disease but with cardiovascular risk factors: Meta-analysis of randomised controlled trials. *BMJ, 338*, b2376.

Critchley, J.A., & Capewell, S. (2004). Smoking cessation for the secondary prevention of coronary heart disease. Cochrane Database of Systematic Reviews 2004, Issue 1. Art. No.: CD003041.

Cushman, M., Arnold, A.M., Psaty, B.M., Manolio, T.A., Kuller, L.H., & Burke, G.L. (2005). C-reactive protein and the 10-year incidence of coronary heart disease in older men and women. *Circulation, 112*, 25–31.

Danesh, J., Collins, R., & Peto, R. (2000). Lipoprotein(a) and coronary heart disease. Meta-analysis of prospective studies. *Circulation, 102*(10), 1082–1085.

Dawber, T.R., & Kannel, W.B. (1968). The early diagnosis of coronary heart disease. In: Sharp, C.L.E.H., & Keen, H. (Eds.). *Presymptomatic Detection and Early Diagnosis: A Critical Appraisal* (pp. 257–281). London: Pitman Medical.

De Bree, A., Verschuren, W.M.M., Kromhout, D., Mennen, L.I., & Blom, H.J. (2002). Homocysteine and coronary heart disease: The importance of a distinction between low and high risk subjects. *International Journal of Epidemiology, 31*, 1268–1272.

De Caterina, R., Liao, J.K., & Libby, P. (2000). Fatty acid modulation of endothelial activation. *Am J Clin Nutr, 71*, 213S–223S.

Deeb, S., Failor, A., Brown, B.G., Brunzell, J.D., Albers, J.J., & Motulsky, A.G. (1986). Molecular genetics of apolipoproteins and coronary heart disease. *Cold Spring Harb Symp Quant Biol, 51*, Pt 1, 403–409.

Després, J.P., Lamarche, B., Mauriège, P., Cantin, B., Dagenais, G.R., Moorjani, S., & Lupien, P.J. (1996). Hyperinsulinemia as an independent risk factor for ischemic heart disease. *N Engl J Med, 334*, 952–957.

Doll, R., & Peto, R. (1976). Mortality in relation to smoking: 20 years' observations on male British doctors. *Br Med J, 2*(6051), 1525–1536.

Doll, R., Gray, R., Hafner, B., & Peto, R. (1980). Mortality in relation to smoking: 22 years' observations on female British doctors. *Br Med J, 280*(6219), 967–971.

Dorn, H.F. (1959). Tobacco consumption and mortality from cancer and other diseases. *Public Health Reports, 74*, 581–593.

Downs, J.R., Clearfield, M., Weis, S., et al. (1998). Primary prevention of acute coronary events with Lovastatin in men and women with average cholesterol levels—results of AFCAPS/TexCAPS. *JAMA, 279*(20), 1615–1622.

Doyle, J.T., Dawber, T.R., Kannel, W.B., Kinch, S.H., & Kahn, H.A. (1964). The relationship of cigarette smoking to coronary heart disease: The second report of the combined experience of the Albany, NY, and Framingham, Mass, studies. *JAMA, 190*(10), 886–890.

Duff, G.L., & McMillan, G.C. (1951). Pathology of atherosclerosis. *Am J Med, 11*(1), 92–108.

Ebbing, M., Bleie, Ø., Ueland, P.M., et al. (2008). Mortality and cardiovascular events in patients treated with homocysteine-lowering B vitamins after coronary angiography: A randomized controlled trial. *JAMA, 300*, 795–804.

Evans, A., Tolonen, H., Hense, H.W., Ferrario, M., Sans, S., & Kuulasmaa, K. for the WHO Project. (2001). Trends in coronary risk factors in the WHO MONICA Project. *International J Epidemiology, 30*, S35–S40.

Eschwege, E., Richard, J.L., Thibult, N., Ducimetière, P., Warnet, J.M., Claude, J.R., & Rosselin, G.E. (1985). Coronary heart disease mortality in relation with diabetes, blood glucose and plasma insulin levels. The Paris Prospective Study, ten years later. *Horm Metab Res Suppl, 15*, 41–46.

Ferrucci, L., Cherubini, A., Bandinelli, S., Bartali, B., Corsi, A., et al. (2006). Relationship of plasma polyunsaturated fatty acids to circulating inflammatory markers. *J Clin Endocrinol Metab, 91*, 439–446.

Folsom, A.R., Szklo, M., Stevens, J., Liao, F., Smith, R., & Eckfeldt, J.H. (1997). A prospective study of coronary heart disease in relation to fasting insulin, glucose, and diabetes: The Atherosclerosis Risk in Communities (ARIC) Study. *Diabetes Care, 20,* 935–942.

Ford, I., Murray, H., Packard, C.J., Shepherd, J., Macfarlane, P.W., & Cobbe, S.M., for the West of Scotland Coronary Prevention Study Group. (2007). Long-Term Follow-up of the West of Scotland Coronary Prevention Study. *New Engl J Med, 357,* 1477–1486.

Ford, E.S., Smith, S.J., Stroup, D.F., Steinberg, K.K., Mueller, P.W., & Thacker, S.B. (2002). Homocyst(e)ine and cardiovascular disease: A systematic review of the evidence with special emphasis on case-control studies and nested case-control studies. *Int J Epidemiol, 31,* 59–70.

Gropelli, A., Giorgi, D.M.A., Omboni, S., Parati, G., & Manchia, G. (1992). Persistent blood pressure increase induced by heavy smoking. *J Hypertension, 10,* 495–499.

Grundy, S.M., Gary, J., Balad, G.J., et al. (1998). Primary prevention of coronary heart disease: Guidance from Framingham: A statement for healthcare professionals from the AHA Task Force on Risk Reduction. *Circulation, 97,* 1876–1887.

Hammond, E.C. (1960). Smoking in relationship to heart disease. *Amer J Pub Health Nations Health, 50*(3 pt 2), 20–26.

Harris, R.E. (1994). Approaches to the prevention and treatment of hypertension through lifestyle modification. National Bureau of Information on Coronary Disease. Norwalk, CT: Logical Communications, Inc.

He, J., Vupputuri, S., Allen, K., Prerost, M.R., Hughes, J., & Whelton, P.K. (1999). Passive smoking and the risk of coronary heart disease: A meta-analysis of epidemiologic studies. *N Engl J Med, 340,* 920–926.

Howard, G., Wagenknecht, L.E., Burke, G.L., et al. (1998). Cigarette smoking and progression of atherosclerosis: The Atherosclerosis Risk in Communities (ARIC) Study. *JAMA, 279,* 119–124.

Hulley, S., Grady, D., Bush, T., Furberg, C., Herrington, D., Riggs, B., Vittinghoff, E., for the Heart and Estrogen/Progestin Replacement Study (HERS). (1998). Randomized trial of estrogen plus progestin for secondary prevention of coronary heart disease in postmenopausal women: Heart and Estrogen/progestin Replacement Study (HERS) Research Group. *JAMA, 280,* 605–613.

Humphrey, L.L., Fu, R., Rogers, K., Freeman, M., & Helfand, M. (2008). Homocysteine level and coronary heart disease incidence: A systematic review and meta-analysis. *Mayo Clin Proc, 83*(11), 1203–1212.

Hung, J., Knuiman, M.W., Divitini, M.L., Davis, T., & Beilby, J.P. (2008). Prevalence and risk factor correlates of elevated C-reactive protein in an adult Australian population. *Amer J Cardiol, 101,* 193–198.

Ishikawa, S., Kayaba, K., Gotoh, T., Nakamura, Y., & Kajii, E. (2007). Metabolic syndrome and C-reactive protein in the general population. *Circ J, 72,* 26–31.

Kannel, W.B. (1964). Cigarette smoking and coronary heart disease. *Ann Intern Med, 60,* 1103–1106.

Kannel, W.B., Castelli, W.P., & McNamara, P.M. (1968). Cigarette smoking and risk of coronary heart disease. Epidemiologic clues to pathogenesis. The Framingham Study. *Natl Cancer Inst Monogr, 28,* 9–20.

Kannel, W.B., Schwartz, M.J., & McNamara, P.M. (1969). Blood pressure and risk of coronary heart disease: The Framingham study. *Dis Chest, 56*(1), 43–52.

Kannel, W.B., Gordon, T., & Schwartz, M.J. (1971). Systolic versus diastolic blood pressure and risk of coronary heart disease. The Framingham study. *Am J Cardiol, 27*(4), 335–346.

Kannel, W.B., Castelli, W.P., Gordon, T., & McNamara, P.M. (1971). Serum cholesterol, lipoproteins, and the risk of coronary heart disease. The Framingham study. *Ann Intern Med, 74*(1), 1–12.

Kannel, W.B., & McGee, D.L. (1979). Diabetes and cardiovascular disease. The Framingham study. *JAMA, 241*(19), 2035–2038.

Kannel, W.B., D'Agostino, R.B., Wilson, P.W.F., Belanger, A.J., & Gagnon, D.R. (1990). Diabetes, fibrinogen, and risk of cardiovascular disease: The Framingham experience. *Am Heart J, 120,* 672–676.

Kannel, W.B. (1996). Blood pressure as a cardiovascular risk factor: Prevention and treatment. *JAMA, 275*(20), 1571–1576.

Keys, A., Aravanis, C., Blackburn, H.W., et al. (1967). Epidemiologic studies related to coronary heart disease: Characteristics of men aged 40–59 in seven countries. *Acta Med Scand,* (Suppl to vol. 460), 1–392.

Keys, A. (1970). Coronary Heart Disease in Seven Countries. New York, NY: American Heart Association, Monograph No. 29.

Keys, A., Aravanis, C., Blackburn, H., et al. (1980). *Seven Countries. A Multivariate Analysis of Death and Coronary Heart Disease* (pp. 1–381). Cambridge, MA and London: Harvard University Press.

Kilhovd, B.K., Berg, T.J., Birkeland, K.I., Thorsby, P., & Hanssen, K.F. (1999). Serum levels of advanced glycation end products are increased in patients with type 2 diabetes and coronary heart disease. *Diabetes Care, 22*(9), 1543–1548.

Kiuchi, K., Nejima, J., Takano, T., Ohta, M., Hashimoto, H., & Baxter, G. (2001). Increased serum concentrations of advanced glycation end products: A marker of coronary artery disease activity in type 2 diabetic patients. *Heart, 85*(1), 87–91.

Koenig, W., Sund, M., Fröhlich, M., et al. (1999). C-reactive protein, a sensitive marker of systemic inflammation, predicts future risk of coronary heart disease in initially healthy middle-aged men. Results from the MONICA-Augsburg cohort study 1984–92. *Circulation, 99,* 237–242.

Lauer, M.S. (2002). Aspirin for primary prevention of coronary events. *New Engl J Med, 346*(19), 1468–1474.

Lee, W.L., Cheung, A.G., Cape, D., & Zinman, B. (2000). Impact of diabetes on coronary disease in women and men: A meta-analysis of prospective studies. *Diabetes Care, 23,* 962–968.

Levy, D. (1993). A multifactorial approach to coronary disease risk assessment. *Clinical and Experimental Hypertension, 15*(6), 1077–1086.

Lewington, S., Whitlock, G., Clarke, R., et al. (2007). Blood cholesterol and vascular mortality by age, sex, and blood pressure: A meta-analysis of individual data from 61 prospective studies with 55,000 vascular deaths. *Lancet, 370,* 1829–1839.

Lipid Research Clinics Program. (1984). The lipid research clinics coronary primary prevention trial results I. Reduction in incidence of coronary heart disease. *J Amer Med Assoc, 251*(3), 351–364.

Lloyd-Jones, D.M., Wilson, P.W.F., Larson, M.G., et al. (2003). Lifetime risk of coronary heart disease by cholesterol levels at selected ages. *Arch Intern Med, 163,* 1966–1972.

MacMahon, S., Peto, R., Cutler, J., et al. (1990). Blood pressure, stroke, and coronary heart disease Part 1, Prolonged differences in blood pressure: Prospective observational studies corrected for the regression dilution bias. *Lancet, 335*(8692), 765–774.

Mahley, R.W., Innerarity, T.L., Rall, S.C., & Weisgraber, K.H. (1985). Plasma lipoproteins: apolipoprotein structure and function. *J. Lipid Res, 25*(12),1277–1294.

Marnell, L., Mold, C., & Du Clos, T.W. (2005). C-reactive protein: Ligands, receptors and role in inflammation. *Clin Immunol, 117,* 104–111.

Mills, E.J., Rachlis, B., Wu, P., Devereaux, P.J., Arora, P., & Perri, D. (2008). Primary prevention of cardiovascular mortality and events with statin treatments a network meta-analysis involving more than 65,000 patients. *J Am Coll Cardiol, 52,* 1769–1781.

Morris, J.N., Kaga, A., Pattison, D.C., Gardner, M.J., & Raffle, P.A.B. (1966). Incidence and prediction of ischemic heart disease in London busmen. *Lancet,* Sep 10, 553–559.

Mozaffarian, D., Micha, R., & Wallace, S. (2010). Effects on coronary heart disease of increasing polyunsaturated fat in place of saturated fat: A systematic review and meta-analysis of randomized controlled trials. *PLoS Med, 7*(3), e1000252.

McQueen, M.J., Hawken, S., Wang, X., et al. (2008). Lipids, lipoproteins, and apolipoproteins as risk markers of myocardial infarction in 52 countries (the INTERHEART study): A case-control study. *Lancet, 372*(9634), 224–233.

Muscat, J.E., Harris, R.E., Haley, N.J., & Wynder, E.L. (1991). Cigarette smoking and plasma cholesterol. *Am Heart J, 121*(1 Pt 1), 141–147.

Nissen, S.E., Nicholls, S.J., Sipahi, I., et al. (2006). Effect of very high-intensity statin therapy on regression of coronary atherosclerosis: The ASTEROID trial (PDF). *JAMA, 295*(13), 1556–1565.

Pai, J.K., Pischon, T., Ma, J., et al. (2004). Inflammatory markers and the risk of coronary heart disease in men and women. *New Engl J Med, 351*(25), 2599–2610.

Parish, S., Peto, R., Palmer, A., et al. (2009). The joint effects of apolipoprotein B, apolipoprotein A$_1$, LDL cholesterol, and HDL cholesterol on risk: 3510 cases of acute myocardial infarction and 9805 controls. *Eur Heart J, 17*, 2137–2146.

Pischon, T., Hankinson, S.E., Hotamisligil, G.S., Rifai, N., Willett, W.C., et al. (2003). Habitual dietary intake of n-3 and n-6 fatty acids in relation to inflammatory markers among US men and women. *Circulation, 108*, 155–160.

Pyörälä, M., Miettinen, H., Laakso, M., & Pyörälä, K. (1998). Hyperinsulinemia predicts coronary heart disease risk in healthy middle-aged men: The 22-year follow-up results of the Helsinki Policemen Study. *Circulation, 98*, 398–404.

Report of the Surgeon General. (1983). The Health Consequences of Smoking: Cardiovascular Disease. The Reports of the Surgeon General, 1983: US Department of Health and Human Services (DHHS) Publication No. (PHS) 84-50204.

Report of the Surgeon General. (1988). The health consequences of smoking: Nicotine addiction. A report of the Surgeon General. DHHS pub. no. 88-8406.

Report of the Surgeon General. (1990). The Health Benefits of Smoking Cessation. A Report of the Surgeon General. Atlanta: US Department of Health and Human Services, Public Health Service, Centers for Disease Control, National Center for Chronic Disease Prevention and Health Promotion, Office on Smoking and Health. DHHS Publication No. (CDC) 90-8416.

Report of the Surgeon General. (2004). The Health Consequences of Smoking: What it means to you. Atlanta: US Department of Health and Human Services, Public Health Service, Centers for Disease Control, National Center for Chronic Disease Prevention and Health Promotion, Office on Smoking and Health. DHHS Publication No. (CDC) 90-8416.

Ridker, P.M., Glynn, R.J., & Hennekens, C.H. (1998). C-reactive protein adds to the predictive values of total and HDL cholesterol in determining risk of first myocardial infarction. *Circulation, 97*, 2007–2011.

Ridker, P.M., Nennekens, C.H., Buring, J.E., & Rifai, N. (2000). C-reactive protein and other markers of inflammation in the prediction of cardiovascular disease in women. *New Eng J Med, 3342*(12), 836–843.

Ridker, P.M., Buring, J.E., Cook, N.R., & Rifai, N. (2003). C-reactive protein, the metabolic syndrome, and risk of incident cardiovascular events. *Circulation, 107*, 391–397.

Ridker, P.M., Rifai, N., Rose, L., Buring, J.E., & Cook, N.R. (2002). Comparison of C-reactive protein and low-density lipoprotein cholesterol levels in the prediction of first cardiovascular events. *New Engl J Med, 347*, 1557–1565.

Robbins, S.L., & Cotran, R.S. (1979). *Pathologic Basis of Disease* (2nd Ed.). Philadelphia: WB Saunders Company.

Rogot, E., & Murray, J.L. (1980). Smoking and causes of death among US veterans, 16 years of observation. *Public Health Reports*, 95(3), 213–222.

Ross, R., & Glomset, J.A. (1973). Atherosclerosis and the arterial smooth muscle cell: Proliferation of smooth muscle is a key event in the genesis of the lesions of atherosclerosis. *Science*, *180*, 1332–1339.

Ross, R., & Glomset, J.A. (1976). The pathogenesis of atherosclerosis. *N Engl J Med*, *295*, 369–377.

Ross, R. (1999). Atherosclerosis—An inflammatory disease. *N Engl J Med*, *340*, 115–126.

Rossouw, J.E., Anderson, G.L., Prentice, R.L., for the Women' Health Initiative Writing Group. (2002). Risks and benefits of estrogen plus progestin in healthy postmenopausal women: Principal results From the Women's Health Initiative randomized controlled trial. *JAMA*, *288*(3), 321–333.

Salmeron, J., Hu, F.B., Manson, J.E., Stampfer, M.J., Colditz, G.A., et al. (2001). Dietary fat intake and risk of type 2 diabetes in women. *Am J Clin Nutr*, *73*, 1019–1026.

Sanderson, J.E., Mayosi, B., Yusuf, S., Reddy, S., Hu, S., Chen, Z., & Timmis, A. (2007). Global burden of cardiovascular disease. *Heart*, *93*(10), 1175.

Sever, P.S., Poulter, N.R., Dahlöf, B., et al. (2005). Reduction in cardiovascular events with atorvastatin in 2,532 patients with type 2 diabetes: Anglo-Scandinavian Cardiac Outcomes Trial—lipid-lowering arm (ASCOT-LLA). *Diabetes Care*, *28*(5), 1151–1157.

Simopoulos, A.P. (2008). The importance of the omega-6/omega-3 fatty acid ratio in cardiovascular disease and other chronic diseases. *Exp Biol Med*, (Maywood)*233*, 674–688.

Singh, P., Singh, M., Gaur, S., & Kaur, T. (2007). The ApoAI-CIII-AIV gene cluster and its relation to lipid levels in type 2 diabetes mellitus and coronary heart disease: Determination of a novel susceptible haplotype. *Diab Vasc Dis Res*, *4*(2), 124–129.

Sofi, F., Cesari, F., Abbate, R., Gensini, G.F., & Casini, A. (2008). Adherence to Mediterranean diet and health status: Meta-analysis. *BMJ* (*Clinical research ed.*), *337*, a1344.

Stamler, J., Wentworth, D., Neaton, J.D. for the MRFIT Research Group. (1986). Is relationship between serum cholesterol and risk of premature death from coronary heart disease continuous and graded? Findings in 356,222 primary screenees of the Multiple Risk Factor Intervention Trial (MRFIT). *JAMA*, *256*(20), 2823–2828.

Stamler, J., Stamler, R., Neaton, J.D., et al. (1999). Low-risk factor profile and long-term cardiovascular and noncardiovascular mortality and life expectancy: Findings for 5 large cohorts of young adult and middle-aged men and women. *JAMA*, *282*, 2012–2018.

Stamler, J., Daviglus, M.L., Garside, D.B., Dyer, A.R., Greenland, P., & Neaton, J.D. (2000). Relationship of baseline serum cholesterol levels in 3 large cohorts of younger men to long-term coronary, cardiovascular, and all-cause mortality and to longevity *JAMA*, *284*, 311–318.

Stamler, J., & Neaton, J.D. (2008). The Multiple Risk Factor Intervention Trial (MRFIT)—Importance then and now. *JAMA*, *300*(11), 1343–1345.

Steinberg, D. (2005). Hypercholesterolemia and inflammation in atherogenesis: Two sides of the same coin. *Mol Nutr Food Res*, *49*, 995–998.

Stevenson, J.C. (2009). Hormone replacement therapy and cardiovascular disease revisited. *Menopause Int*, *15*, 55–57.

Strandberg, T.E., Lehto, S., Pyörälä, K., Kesäniemi, A., & Oksa, H. (1997). Cholesterol lowering after participation in the Scandinavian Simvastatin Survival Study (4S) in Finland. *European Heart Journal*, *18*(11), 1725–1727.

Summers, L.K., Fielding, B.A., Bradshaw, H.A., Ilic, V., Beysen, C., et al. (2002). Substituting dietary saturated fat with polyunsaturated fat changes abdominal fat distribution and improves insulin sensitivity. *Diabetologia*, *45*, 369–377.

Sung, K.C., Suh, J.Y., Kim, B.S., et al. (2003). High sensitivity C-reactive protein as an independent risk factor for essential hypertension. *Am J Hypertens*, *16*, 429–433.

Toole, J.F., Malinow, M.R., Chambless, L.E., et al. (2004). Lowering homocysteine in patients with ischemic stroke to prevent recurrent stroke, myocardial infarction, and death: The Vitamin Intervention for Stroke Prevention (VISP) randomized controlled trial. *JAMA, 291,* 565–575.

Toss, H., Lindahl, B., Siegbahn, A., & Wallentin, L. (1997). Prognostic influence of increased fibrinogen and C-reactive protein levels in unstable coronary artery disease. *Circulation, 96,* 4204–4210.

Tunstall-Pedoe, H., Kuulasmaa, K., Mähönen, M., Tolonen, H., Ruokokoski, E., & Amouyel, P. (1999). Contribution of trends in survival and coronary-event rates to changes in coronary heart disease mortality: 10-year results from 37 WHO MONICA project populations. Monitoring trends and determinants in cardiovascular disease. *Lancet, 353*(9164) 1547–1557.

Tunstall-Pedoe, H., Kuulasmaa, K., Tolonen, H., Davidson, M., & Mendis, S. with 64 other contributors for The WHO MONICA Project. (2003). MONICA Monograph and Multimedia Sourcebook. Geneva, Switzerland: World Health Organization.

Summary of the second report of the National Cholesterol Education Program (NCEP). (1993). Expert Panel on Detection, Evaluation, and Treatment of High Blood Cholesterol in Adults (Adult Treatment Panel II). *JAMA, 269,* 3015–3023.

US Department of Agriculture. (2010). MyPyramid .gov. Washington, DC: USDA.

van den Hoogen, P.C.W., Feskens, E.J.M., Nagelkerke, N.J.D., Menotti, A., Nissinen, A., & Kromhout, D., for The Seven Countries Study Research Group. (2000). The relation between blood pressure and mortality due to coronary heart disease among men in different parts of the world. *NEJM, 342*(1), 1–8.

van der Steeg, W.A., Boekholdt, S.M., Stein, E.A., et al. (2007). Role of the Apolipoprotein B–Apolipoprotein A-1 ratio in cardiovascular risk assessment: A case–control analysis in EPIC-Norfolk. *Ann Intern Med, 146,* 640–648.

Verschuren, W.M., Jacobs, D.R., Bloemberg, B.P., et al. (1995). Serum total cholesterol and long-term coronary heart disease mortality in different cultures. Twenty-five-year follow-up of the seven countries study. *JAMA, 274*(2), 131–136.

Virchow, R. (1856). Phlogose und Thrombose im Gefässystem. In: Gesammelte Abhandlungen zur wissenschaftlichen Medizin. Germany: Staatsdruckerei Frankfurt.

Welch, G.N., & Loscalzo, J. (1998). Homocysteine and atherothrombosis. *N Engl J Med, 338,* 1042–1050.

Willett, W.C., Sacks, F., & Trichopoulous, A. (1995). Mediterranean diet pyramid: A cultural model for healthy eating. *Am J Clin Nutr, 61*(6 Suppl), 1402S–1406S.

Yusuf, S., Hawken, S., Ounpuu, S., et al. (2004). Effect of potentially modifiable risk factors associated with myocardial infarction in 52 countries (the INTERHEART study): Case-control study. *Lancet, 364*(9438), 937–952.

Epidemiology of Myocardial Infarction

FUNCTION OF THE HEART

The heart is an extraordinary electrochemical muscular organ that sustains human life by efficiently pumping blood through the circulatory system of the body. The normal heart weighs approximately 250 to 300 grams in adult women and 300 to 350 grams in adult men. The heart consists primarily of striated skeletal muscle called myocardium. The myocardium is specially designed to facilitate rapid flux of sodium and potassium ions between myocardial cells and interstitial fluid that is critical for the polarization and depolarization of contracting cardiac muscle fibers (Robbins and Cotran, 1979).

The human heart efficiently pumps approximately 5 liters of blood through the vascular circulatory system. It pulsates at 70 beats per minute, more than 100,000 times per day without fail over a normal lifespan of more than 80 years. Each heartbeat pumps approximately 60–70 milliliters of blood into the aorta. Thus, on average, red blood cells cycle about once per minute or 1,440 times per day.

Anatomically, the heart is divided into four chambers: the right atrium that receives deoxygenated blood from the superior and inferior vena cava and delivers it to the right ventricle; the right ventricle that receives blood from the right atrium and pumps it through the low pressure pulmonary circulation where carbon dioxide is exchanged for oxygen in the hemoglobin of the red blood cells; the left atrium that receives newly oxygenated blood from the pulmonary arteries and delivers it to the left ventricle; and the left ventricle that pumps blood into the aorta for distribution and delivery to all tissues of the body (Figure 4.1).

Four valves regulate blood flow into and out of the heart chambers: the tricuspid valve that controls blood flow from the right atrium into the right ventricle; the pulmonary valve that controls blood flow from the right atrium into the pulmonary circulation; the mitral valve that regulates blood flow from the left atrium into the left ventricle; and the aortic valve that regulates blood flow from the left ventricle into the aorta (Figure 4.1). The normal two-stage "lub dub" heart sound is due to closure of the atrial valves (closure of the tricuspid and mitral valves causes the "lub" sound) followed by closure of the ventricular valves (closure of the pulmonary and aortic valves causes the "dub" sound).

The regular heartbeat is controlled by electrical impulses synchronously transmitted from the sinoatrial (SA) node to the atrioventricular (AV) node (Figure 4.2). The bundle of His and the Purkinje system of specialized muscle fibers distribute the impulse to the interventricular septum and the left and right ventricles of the myocardium. Depolarization (change of membrane potential from positive to negative) of the atrial myocardium causes the right and left atria to contract first, followed by depolarization and contraction of the right and left ventricles. Sequential contraction of the atria followed by the ventricles facilitates efficient blood perfusion through the lungs and the systemic circulation. Each pulsation of the human heart lasts about eight-tenths of one second, about half of which is a quiescent period that allows the heart muscle to rest between beats.

The heart is nourished by coronary arteries with a characteristic distribution (Figure 4.3). The left anterior descending coronary artery supplies most of the apex of the heart and portions of the left and right ventricles, as well as the interventricular septum. The right coronary artery supplies much of the remaining myocardium, whereas the left circumflex branch supplies a relatively small portion of the left ventricle. Supportive coronary blood flow is supplied by numerous

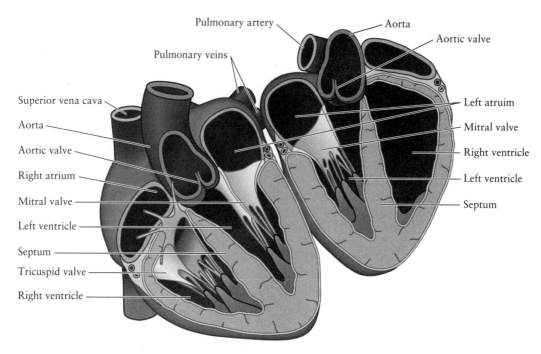

Figure 4.1 Structure of the Human Heart.

capillaries as well as small anastomotic channels between vessels (Robbins and Cotran, 1979).

The *vagus nerve* (the tenth of twelve paired cranial nerves) innervates the human heart and helps to modulate the heart rate. The right branch of the vagus nerve innervates the sinoatrial (SA) node and the left branch innervates the atrioventricular (AV) node. Cholinergic neurotransmitters (acetylcholine)

released by the vagus nerve lower the heart rate and cause vasodilatation whereas adrenergic neurotransmitters (epininephrine or adrenalin) secreted by the adrenal glands stimulate the heart to beat faster and cause vasoconstriction. Cholinergic neurotransmitters such as acetylcholine modulate cell function by activating specific G-protein-coupled cell membrane receptors (e.g., nicotinic and muscarinic

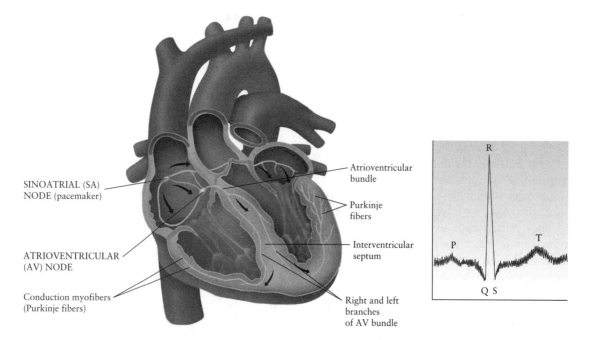

Figure 4.2 Conducting System of the Human Heart.

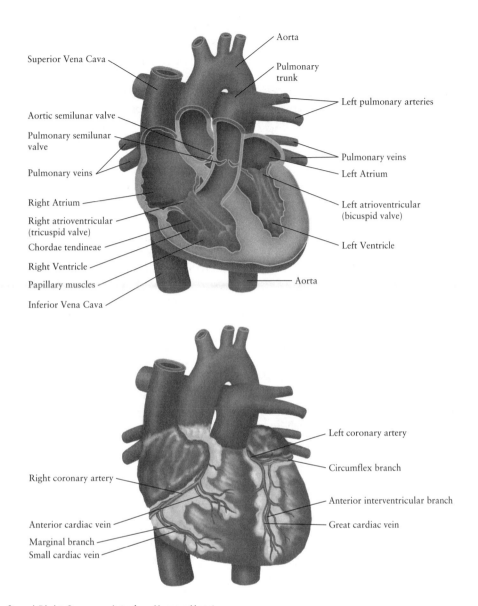

Aorta

Superior Vena Cava

Pulmonary trunk

Left pulmonary arteries

Aortic semilunar valve

Pulmonary semilunar valve

Pulmonary veins

Pulmonary veins

Left Atrium

Right Atrium

Left atrioventricular (bicuspid valve)

Right atrioventricular (tricuspid valve)

Chordae tendineae

Left Ventricle

Right Ventricle

Papillary muscles

Aorta

Inferior Vena Cava

Left coronary artery

Circumflex branch

Right coronary artery

Anterior interventricular branch

Anterior cardiac vein

Great cardiac vein

Marginal branch

Small cardiac vein

Figure 4.3 Left and Right Coronary Arteries, Human Heart.

receptors) whereas adrenergic neurotransmitters such as epinephrine activate a different class of G-protein coupled cell membrane receptors (a and b receptors) (Hoffman and Lefkowitz, 1982; Rosenbaum, Rasmussen, and Kobilka, 2009).

CLINICAL PARAMETERS OF MYOCARDIAL INFARCTION (HEART ATTACK)

Myocardial infarction (MI), commonly known as a heart attack, is the interruption of blood supply to part of the heart causing a portion of the myocardium to die. Myocardial infarcts are most commonly due to occlusion (blockage) of a coronary artery caused by atherosclerosis or following the rupture of a vulnerable

atherosclerotic plaque. The resulting ischemia (restriction in blood supply) and oxygen shortage, if left untreated for a sufficient period of time, can cause *infarction* of the myocardium and often results in death of the patient.

Myocardial infarction presents with sudden chest pain typically radiating to the left arm or left side of the neck in combination with shortness of breath, nausea, vomiting, heart palpitations, sweating, and anxiety. Approximately 25% of myocardial infarctions occur without warning, e.g., in the absence of prior chest pain or other symptoms. More often, the onset of myocardial infarction is gradual over several minutes providing time for emergency treatment. The diagnosis of myocardial infarction is inferred by electrocardiogram abnormalities and confirmed by elevated blood biomarkers of myocardial necrosis such as creatine kinase and troponin (National Heart, Lung and Blood Institute, 2006). Patients with two subtypes of acute myocardial infarctions have been identified based upon electrocardiography: those with elevation of the ST segment of the cardiac rhythm (STEMI) and those without ST elevation (non-STEMI). Elevation of the ST segment indicates thrombotic occlusion of a coronary artery and requires immediate reperfusion therapy with antithombolytic drugs or percutaneous coronary intervention (Alpert et al., 2000). A coronary angiogram allows visualization of narrowing or obstruction of the heart vessels for the immediate institution of potentially lifesaving measures, e.g., angioplasty.

GLOBAL MORTALITY AND MORBIDITY DUE TO MYOCARDIAL INFARCTIONS

According to recent data published by the World Health Organization (WHO) myocardial infarctions cause 7.2 million deaths annually in the world population (Mackay and Mensah, 2004). Of these, approximately 5 million deaths occur in the populations of developing nations at relatively early ages (median age ≈ 50 years). The remaining 2.1 million deaths from myocardial infarctions occur at later ages in populations of developed nations (median age ≈ 65 years). In addition to the deaths from myocardial infarctions, more than 5 million people survive myocardial infarctions every year, the majority in developed nations where emergency care is available (Figure 4.4).

The *Disability-Adjusted Life Years* (DALY = YLL + YDL) is a combined measure of the years of life lost due to premature death (YLL) plus the years of healthy life lost due to severe disability (YDL). Estimated DALY arising due to fatal and nonfatal myocardial infarctions are presented together with coronary heart disease by income level of nations in Figure 4.5. The world pattern of DALY from myocardial infarctions is similar to that for ischemic/coronary heart disease reflecting the huge impact of atherosclerosis and the global epidemiologic transition from infectious/parasitic diseases to chronic diseases. High DALY are evident in populous developing nations such as India, Russia, and Egypt compared to low DALY in the developed nations of North America, Western Europe, South America, China, Japan, Australia, and New Zealand. High DALY are also apparent in the populations of poverty-stricken countries of central Africa such as Sudan, Chad, Ethiopia, and Nigeria. Populations of these nations are not only prone to coronary heart disease and myocardial infarctions, but they also suffer a heavy burden of death and disability from malnutrition plus infectious/parasitic diseases causing life-threatening diarrhea, malaria, HIV/AIDS, and tuberculosis.

TIME TRENDS IN MYOCARDIAL INFARCTION RATES

Several prospective investigations have noted marked declines in the rates of myocardial infarctions in the populations of developed nations. In the US Framingham community-based cohort of

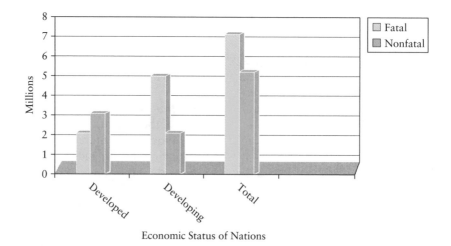

Figure 4.4 Fatal and Nonfatal Myocardial Infarctions, World Population, 2009.

Source: Data from WHO (2010). World Health Statistics 2010. World Health Organization Statistical Information System (WHOSIS), Geneva, Switzerland. Countries are grouped by national annual income per capita: Developed Nations > $10,065, Developing Nations < $10,065.

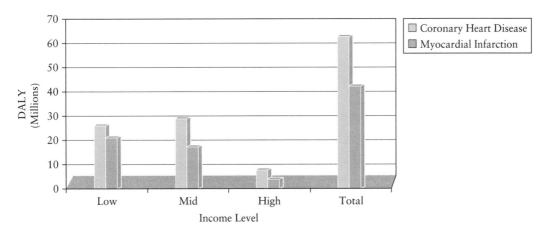

Figure 4.5 Global DALY for Coronary Heart Disease and Myocardial Infarction stratified by Income Level of Nations, 2009.

Source: Data from WHO (2010). World Health Statistics 2010. World Health Organization Statistical Information System (WHOSIS), Geneva, Switzerland. Countries are grouped by national annual income per capita: Low < $826, Middle: $826–$10,065, High > $10,065.

9,824 men and women aged 40–89 years followed for up to 4 decades, incidence rates of acute myocardial infarction diagnosed by electrocardiogram declined by approximately 50% with similar declines in case fatality rates from 1960–1999 (Parikh et al., 2009). These declines were attributed primarily to better control of blood pressure, reduced blood levels of cholesterol, and reduced rates of cigarette smoking among participants. Paradoxically, a slight *increase* was noted in the incidence of myocardial infarctions diagnosed among hospitalized patients, perhaps reflecting increasing use of more sensitive biochemical markers of myocardial necrosis in the diagnosis of myocardial infarction.

In the international MONICA (Multinational Monitoring Trends and Determinants in Cardiovascular Disease) Project, analysis of 37 sample populations from 21 countries after 10 years of follow-up showed average annual declines in coronary heart disease mortality of 4% in both men and women and average annual declines in coronary events (nonfatal myocardial infarction or coronary death) of 2.1% for men and 1.4% for women (Tunstall-Pedoe et al., 1994, 1999). The MONICA investigators attributed the majority of the decline in mortality to factors leading to reduced rates of coronary events rather than improved survival.

In the Atherosclerosis Risk in Communities (ARIC) Study, trends in mortality due to coronary heart disease and the incidence of myocardial infarction among 352,481 adults from 4 US communities were examined from 1987–1994 on the basis of a review of 3,023 deaths due to coronary heart disease and 8,572 hospitalizations for myocardial infarction. During this time period, mortality due to coronary heart disease declined by 28% in men and

31% in women. These reductions were accompanied by declines in case fatality rates and rates of recurrent myocardial infarction as well as improved survival among cases. The ARIC investigators attributed these findings to primary prevention and reductions in risk factors plus improvements in the treatment of coronary heart disease (Rosamond et al., 1998)

Similar to the Framingham Study, the ARIC Study also found no evidence of a decline in the *incidence* of myocardial infarction either in men or women; and in fact, the incidence rates actually *increased* in certain years (Figure 4.6). As pointed out by Levy and Thom, the paradox is explainable in that more sensitive diagnostic tests are routinely being used for hospitalized patients with chest pain, possibly shifting the diagnosis of angina pectoris to myocardial infarction in some patients, thereby increasing the incidence of myocardial infarction (Levy and Thom, 1998).

National statistics from the US National Heart, Lung and Blood Institute confirm that marked declines have occurred in mortality and case fatality due to acute myocardial infarction during the past several decades (Levy and Thom, 1998; National Heart, Lung and Blood Institute, 2009). During the 35-year period from 1970 to 2005, both mortality and case fatality due to acute myocardial infarction declined by more than 70% (Figure 4.7).

RISK FACTORS FOR MYOCARDIAL INFARCTION

Since ischemic/coronary heart disease is the root cause of most myocardial infarctions, certain primary risk factors are synonymous including tobacco addiction,

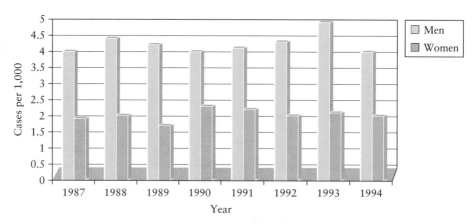

Figure 4.6 Incidence of Nonfatal Myocardial Infarction, USA, 1987–1994.

Source: Data from Rosamond WD, Chambless LE, Folsom AR, Lawton LS, Conwill DE, Clegg L, Wang C-H, Heiss G (1998). Trends in the incidence of myocardial infarction and in mortality due to coronary heart disease, 1987 to 1994. *N Engl J Med* 339:861–867.

hypertension, hyperglycemia (elevated blood glucose), hypercholesterolemia (elevated blood cholesterol), and chronic inflammation. Nevertheless, the abrupt nature of a heart attack also involves other factors.

Heart attack rates are higher in association with intense exertion, either from psychological stress or vigorous physical exercise, especially if the exertion is more intense than usual (Siscovick et al., 1984). Quantitatively, periods of intense exercise and subsequent recovery are associated with an approximate sixfold higher myocardial infarction rate (compared with other more relaxed time frames) for people who are physically very fit. For those in poor physical condition, the rate differential is over 35-fold higher (Mittleman et al., 1993; Willich et al. 1993). Mechanistically, it is suggested that the spiking of blood pressure on extreme physical/psychological exertion may increase the shear stress on atheromas and

the likelihood of plaque rupture (Curfman, 1993). The investigators stress that these findings should not be an impediment to regular aerobic exercise (at least three times weekly for thirty minutes or more) as recommended by the American Heart Association.

Acute severe infection, such as pneumonia, can trigger myocardial infarction. In a study using within-person comparisons, 20,486 individuals with a first myocardial infarction and 19,063 individuals with a first stroke were examined. The risk for myocardial infarction increased fivefold and the risk for stroke increased threefold within a three-day period after diagnosis of a systemic respiratory tract infection. Furthermore, transient risk increases were also observed following urinary tract infections and the risk estimates for recurrent myocardial infarction or stroke subsequent to infection were similar to those for first events. There was no increase in the risk of

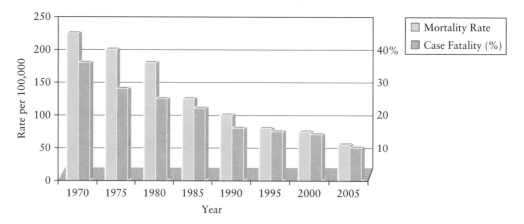

Figure 4.7 Decline in Mortality and Case Fatality due to Myocardial Infarction, USA, 1970–2005.

Source: Data from the National Center for Health Statistics, National Vital Statistics Reports, 2009. Case fatality estimates are for individuals over the age of 65 years, National Heart, Lung and Blood Institute.

myocardial infarction or stroke in the period after influenza, tetanus, or pneumococcal vaccination. The finding that different infectious processes of different organ systems are associated with a significant transient increase in the risk of cardiovascular events lends strong support to the concept that systemic inflammation itself alters the probability of the occurrence of a vascular event (Smeeth et al., 2004).

A more controversial link is that between *Chlamydophila pneumoniae* infection and atherosclerosis. In a nested case control study of 103 patients who suffered sudden cardiac death or a nonfatal myocardial infarction compared to matched controls from the Helsinki Heart Study, the odds ratios were elevated more than twofold among individuals with antibodies to *Chlamydophila pneumoniae* (Saikku et al., 1992). While this intracellular organism has been demonstrated in atherosclerotic plaques, evidence is inconclusive as to whether it can be considered a causative factor. Treatment with antibiotics in patients with proven atherosclerosis has not demonstrated a decreased risk of heart attacks or other coronary vascular diseases (Andraws, Berger, & Brown, 2005).

It is well known that the frequency of heart attacks is increased in the early morning hours upon awakening (Muller et al., 1985; Beamer et al., 1987). Some investigators theorize that this high risk time period may be related to the circadian variation in cortisol production affecting the concentrations of various cytokines and other mediators of inflammation (Fantidis et al., 2002). Other factors potentially underlying this phenomenon include smoking the first cigarette of the day, exercising vigorously, and/or conducting other activities that spike blood pressure in the early morning hours.

Major epidemiologic studies of ischemic/coronary heart disease have elucidated and quantified several individual risk factors and stressed the importance of their multifactorial interactions. These and other selected investigations relevant to the risk of myocardial infarction are discussed in the following paragraphs.

THE INTERHEART STUDY OF ACUTE MYOCARDIAL INFARCTION

Foremost among the studies of myocardial infarction is the INTERHEART Study. INTERHEART is a standardized case-control study that screened all patients admitted to the coronary care unit or equivalent cardiology ward for a first (nonfatal) myocardial infarction at 262 participating centers in 52 countries throughout Africa, Asia, Australia, Europe, the Middle East, and North and South America (Yusuf et al., 2004).

Cases were identified using standardized definitions and enrolled within 24 hours of symptom onset. Matching controls were recruited, resulting in a total of 15,152 incident cases of acute myocardial infarction and 14,820 controls matched by age (± 5 years) and sex but with no history of heart disease. A study questionnaire, translated into 11 languages, was used to collect data on demographic factors (country of origin, first language), socioeconomic status (education, occupation, income), lifestyle (tobacco use, physical activity, dietary patterns), and personal and family history of cardiovascular disease and risk factors (self-reported diabetes and hypertension). Components of the questionnaire were compiled with previously validated questions included in studies of risk factors for cardiovascular disease. Questionnaires were administered by trained staff before the patients left the hospital. Data on medications (prehospital, inhospital, and discharge) and interventions were abstracted from medical charts. Standard physical measurements were recorded in duplicate by the same examiner on each participant: height, weight, waist and hip circumference, and heart rate. A 20-mL sample of nonfasting blood was drawn from each individual and was frozen and stored for biochemical analyses, including total cholesterol, high-density lipoprotein-cholesterol, apolipoproteins B (ApoB), and A1 (ApoA1). The strength of associations between various risk factors and acute myocardial infarction was estimated by odds ratios (OR). The investigators calculated the variation in associations according to geographic region, ethnic origin, gender, and age in order to quantify the impact of each risk factor alone and in combination by the population attributable risk (PAR). For comparison of prevalence across distinct subgroups, e.g., by region, country, or ethnic group, potential differences in age structure of the populations were accounted for by direct standardization of the frequencies to the overall INTERHEART age distribution with a five-level age-stratification factor (<45, 46–55, 56–65, 66–70, >70). Final analyses were carried out for 12,461 cases and 9,459 controls (Yusuf et al., 2004).

Results of INTERHEART

The mean age for the first presentation of acute myocardial infarction was 8–10 years younger in men than women worldwide and 10 years younger in Africa, the Middle East, and South Asia compared

Table 4.1	Interheart Study Results		
Factor	**Controls (%)**	**Cases (%)**	**OR**
poB/poA1	20.0	34.5	3.25
Smoking	26.8	45.2	2.97
Diabetes	7.5	18.5	2.37
High BP	21.9	39.0	1.91
Obesity	33.3	56.3	1.62
Stress	9.4	23.6	2.67
Fruit & Vegetable Diet	42.2	36.8	0.71
Exercise	19.3	14.3	0.86
Alcohol	24.5	24.0	0.91

Source: Data from Yusuf S, Hawken S, Ounpuu S, Dans T, Avezum A, Lanas F, McQueen M, Budaj A, Pais P, Varigos J, Lisheng L; INTERHEART Study Investigators (2004). Effect of potentially modifiable risk factors associated with myocardial infarction in 52 countries (the INTERHEART study): case-control study. *Lancet* 364(9438):937–952.

with other regions of the world. The study identified 9 easily measured risk factors accounting for >90% of the risk of acute myocardial infarction: *smoking, lipids, hypertension, diabetes, obesity, diet, physical activity, alcohol consumption, and psychosocial factors*. Odds ratios estimated from the study are shown in Table 4.1 (Yusuf et al., 2004).

The strongest risk factor detected was the Apolipoprotein B/Apolipoprotein A1 ratio. Apolipoprotein B (Apo-B) is the primary apolipoprotein of low-density lipoproteins (LDL or *bad cholesterol*) in plasma, which is responsible for carrying cholesterol from the liver to tissues. Apolipoprotein A-1 (Apo-A1) is the major protein component of high-density lipoprotein (HDL or *good cholesterol*) in plasma. This protein promotes cholesterol efflux from tissues to the liver for excretion. The relative risk for individuals with ApoB/ApoA1 ratios in the highest quintile was 3.25 after adjustment for all other risk factors (McQueen et al., 2008).

The *Population Attributable Risk* (PAR) takes into consideration both the OR and prevalence of a risk factor to estimate the fraction of the risk that can be attributed to that particular risk factor. Based on the INTERHEART results, 50% of acute myocardial infarctions are attributable to the ApoB/ApoA1 ratio and 36% to current smoking. Thus, these two risk factors, the ApoB/ApoA1 ratio and smoking account for about two-thirds of the risk for developing an acute myocardial infarction in the world population. Five factors (smoking, lipids, hypertension, diabetes, and obesity) accounted for about 80% of the PAR. For all nine risk factors combined, the PAR was significantly greater in younger than in older individuals, but consistent in men and women (90% and

94%, respectively). Abdominal obesity was found to be a stronger risk factor than body mass index (BMI), a result that prompted the investigators to recommend that measurement of waist-to-hip ratio should replace BMI as the preferred indicator of obesity. Finally, the 10-year younger mean age for the first presentation of acute myocardial infarction in Africa, the Middle East, and South Asia compared with other regions of the world implies the onset of an oncoming epidemic and predicts a large increase in cardiovascular disease in these regions in the coming years (Yusuf et al., 2004).

SEVEN COUNTRIES STUDY OF MYOCARDIAL INFARCTION

The Seven Countries Study conducted by Ancel Keys and colleagues examined the effects of diet in an international prospective cohort of 12,763 men, aged 40–59 years, in 16 population samples from 7 different countries (Italy, Greece, former Yugoslavia, the Netherlands, Finland, United States, and Japan). The study was the first to demonstrate that serum cholesterol is a biomarker of impending coronary heart disease and that the risk increases with intake of saturated fats and decreases with intake of monounsaturated fatty acids (primarily from olive oil). Risk increases were also associated with elevated blood pressure (hypertension), cigarette smoking, sedentary lifestyle, and obesity. The investigation elucidated the preventive effects of the Mediterranean diet consisting primarily of daily intake of fruits, vegetables, whole grains, olive oil, fish, and poultry (Keys et al., 1967; Keys, 1970; Keys et al., 1980).

FRAMINGHAM STUDY OF MYOCARDIAL INFARCTION

Since 1948, investigators at Harvard University have been following generations of the residents of Framingham, Massachusetts, to better understand the determinants of heart disease. The initial cohort consisted of 5,209 randomly selected members of the adult population of Framingham, 30–62 years of age, who were enrolled for study in 1948. The ongoing study now includes a second generation of 5,124 men and women (offspring of the original cohort). A series of initial reports based upon the Framingham Study documented significant independent effects of cigarette smoking, hypertension, hyperglycemia, and hypercholesterolemia in the genesis of ischemic/coronary heart disease and myocardial infarction (Kannel, 1964; Dawber and Kannel, 1968; Kannel, Castelli, and McNamara, 1968; Kannel, Schwartz, and McNamara, 1969; Kannel, Gordon, and Schwartz, 1971; Kannel, Castelli, Gordon, and McNamara, 1971; Kannel and McGee, 1979; Kannel et al., 1990; Kannel, 1996). While each of these risk factors independently increases the relative risk of disease by two-to threefold, the interaction of chronic smoking, high blood pressure, hyperglycemia, and hypercholesterolemia accentuates the risk by more than tenfold in comparison to individuals with no exposure (Levy, 1993; Wilson et al., 1998).

Many other epidemiologic investigations have provided consistent evidence confirming the cause and effect relationship of these factors and their synergistic interactions in the pathogenesis of myocardial infarction as well as declining trends in mortality and morbidity rates due to coronary heart disease and myocardial infarction with reductions in these risk factors in past decades. These include the MONICA Project (Tunstall-Pedoe et al., 1994, 1999); the Atherosclerosis Risk in Communities (ARIC) Study (Rosamond et al., 1998); the Copenhagen City Heart Study I and II (Nyboe et al., 1989; Jensen et al., 1991); the Minnesota Heart Survey (McGovern et al., 2001); the Worcester Heart Attack Study (Goldberg et al., 1986, 1999); the Corpus Christi Study (Nichaman et al., 1993); and the Olmstead County Study (Roger et al., 2002).

The sampling design utilized in some US investigations has facilitated comparisons by ethnicity of subpopulations. In the ARIC Study, African American women and men had, respectively, 50% and 80% higher case fatality rates from myocardial infarction or coronary heart disease than Caucasian Americans (White et al., 1999); and in the Corpus Christi Study, Mexican American women and men had 60% and 30% higher rates of hospitalization due to myocardial infarction than non-Hispanic Americans (Nichaman et al., 1993; Goff et al., 1997).

In general, all of these studies provide consistent evidence that most risk factors for atherosclerosis and myocardial infarction are similar. Factors in common include tobacco addiction, diabetes and hyperglycemia (elevated blood glucose), hypercholesterolemia and hyperlipidemia (especially *high* low-density lipoprotein cholesterol coupled with *low* high-density lipoprotein cholesterol), high blood triglycerides, high blood pressure, high C-reactive protein (a measure of inflammation), family history of ischemic heart disease, obesity (body mass index of 30 or more), increased waist to hip ratio, age, male gender, hyperhomocysteinemia, persistent high stress, and alcohol abuse. It is stressed that these risk factors are not mutually exclusive and often cluster together in the same individual to synergistically increase the risk of developing a myocardial infarction.

PRIMARY PREVENTION OF MYOCARDIAL INFARCTION

Since many of its risk factors are modifiable, myocardial infarction is preventable (Kuller et al., 1980; Stamler et al.,1986; Manson et al., 1992). Primary prevention is the reciprocal of exposure to proven risk factors. Avoid tobacco, eat a *heart healthy* diet, maintain blood pressure, blood glucose, and blood lipids (cholesterol) within normal limits, exercise daily, and maintain optimal weight for height.

A key component of prevention for all individuals is to have regular (annual) physical checkups to detect elevations in blood pressure, blood glucose, serum cholesterol, or other irregularities. Effective antihypertensive and antidiabetic medications are readily available to maintain blood pressure and blood glucose within normal limits. Sodium (salt) restriction (less than 6 grams of salt per day) is also important for blood pressure control. Weight reduction programs incorporating healthy nutrition and regular exercise regimes have proven successful in reducing obesity and reaching optimal weight.

Table 4.2 elaborates guidelines for the prevention of cardiovascular disease (including myocardial infarction) according to the American Heart Association. In the paragraphs that follow, the epidemiologic evidence regarding several selected factors (dietary fat, aspirin, statins, and estrogen replacement therapy) is discussed.

Table 4.2	Lifestyle Modification and Cardiovascular Disease

- Avoid Tobacco
- Maintain Serum Cholesterol Within Normal Limits
- Maintain Blood Glucose Within Normal Limits
- Maintain Blood Pressure Within Normal Limits
- Weight Control (Ideal body weight)
- Sodium Reduction (<6 g salt daily)
- Exercise regularly (Aerobic)
- Reduce Fat Intake (<30% calories)
- Alcohol (<1 oz daily)
- Maintain Potassium, Calcium, Magnesium

Source: Data from Manson JE, Tosteson H, Ridker PM, Satterfield S, Hebert P, O'Connor GT, Buring JE, Hennekens CH (1992). The primary prevention of myocardial infarction. *N Engl J Med* 326(21):1406–1416. Mackay J, Mensah G (2004). *Atlas of Heart Disease and Stroke.* World Health Organization, Geneva.

Dietary Fat and Myocardial Infarction

There is much controversy as to what constitutes a *heart healthy* diet. The *Mediterranean diet* has been championed by many investigators as the most prudent *heart healthy* diet. Such a diet is characterized by abundant plant foods (fruit, vegetables, whole grain breads, other forms of cereals, potatoes, beans, nuts, and seeds), fresh fruit as the typical daily dessert, olive oil as the principal source of fat, dairy products (principally cheese and yogurt), and fish and poultry consumed in low to moderate amounts. Notably, in a meta-analysis of 12 prospective studies with a total of 1,574,299 subjects followed for up to 18 years, greater adherence to the *Mediterranean diet* was associated with significant improvement in health status and significant reductions in overall mortality (9%), mortality from cardiovascular diseases (9%), cancer mortality (6%), and incidence rates of Parkinson's disease and Alzheimer's disease (13%) (Sofi et al., 2008).

Dietary transition from saturated fats to polyunsaturated fatty acids (PUFA) has been advocated by some investigators, and it is generally accepted that omega-3 fatty acids are beneficial PUFA whereas transfatty acids should be avoided (Willett et al., 1995). Recent evidence supporting the concept that substituting PUFA for saturated fat in the diet is cardioprotective comes from a meta-analysis of 8 randomized clinical trials involving 13,614 subjects randomized to receive either high or low dietary PUFA. After an average follow-up period of 4.25 years, 1,042 subjects developed coronary heart disease (myocardial infarction or death from coronary heart disease) and the energy intake from PUFA averaged 14.9% of total calories in the intervention group compared to 5% in the control group. Overall, the risk in the intervention group was reduced by 19% compared to the control group and the risk reduction in coronary heart disease was estimated to be 10% per each 5% *increase* in energy from PUFA (Mozaffarian, Micha, and Wallace, 2010).

Increasing consumption of PUFA has been found to lower high-density lipoprotein cholesterol (Lewington et al., 2007) and may also improve insulin resistance (Salmeron et al., 2001; Summers et al., 2002) and reduce systemic inflammation (De Caterina, Liao, and Libby, 2000; Pischon et al., 2003; Ferrucci et al., 2006). Furthermore, specific types of PUFA may offer greater cardioprotection than others (e.g., omega-3 linolenic acid versus omega-6 linoleic acid) and some investigators advocate lowering the ratio of omega-6 PUFA to omega-3 PUFA in order to maximize protection against myocardial infarction and other forms of cardiovascular disease (Simopoulos, 2008).

Aspirin and Myocardial Infarction

The use of low dose (81 mg) aspirin for the primary prevention of myocardial infarction has been examined in numerous studies involving men and women of various cultures. A meta-analysis of four randomized clinical trials found that daily intake confers a reduction of 30% in the rate of myocardial infarction and a 15% reduction in the rate of developing any cardiovascular disease (Sanmuganathan et al., 2001). The authors concluded that the benefit exceeded the risk of gastrointestinal hemorrhage for individuals with a coronary event risk of at least 1.5% per year whereas aspirin had limited value for individuals at lesser risk levels. Ten-year risk can be accurately predicted by the *Framingham Coronary Heart Disease Risk Score Algorithm* (D'Agostino et al., 2001). Current guidelines recommend chemoprevention of myocardial infarction using low dose aspirin in adults at higher risk and over the age of 50 years with the caveat that even low dose aspirin is contraindicated in individuals with known allergies, bleeding diathesis, platelet disorders, and active peptic ulcer disease (Lauer, 2002).

Statins and Myocardial Infarction

The role of statins in reducing serum cholesterol thereby counteracting atherogenesis and reducing the risk of coronary heart disease including myocardial infarction and strokes has been confirmed in a number of randomized clinical trials. In a meta-analysis of 10 studies involving 70,388 subjects *with known cardiovascular risk factors such as diabetes at baseline*, daily statin intake reduced the incidence of major coronary events (myocardial infarction or coronary death) by 30% (Brugts et al., 2009). In a meta-analysis of 20 studies enrolling 63,899 subjects at relatively low risk, daily statin intake reduced the incidence of myocardial infarction by 23% (Mills et al., 2008). In addition to lowering serum cholesterol (and particularly LDL cholesterol), statins may also exert a stabilizing influence on evolving atheromatous plaques thereby diminishing their propensity to rupture and cause a myocardial infarction (Ray and Cannon, 2005). Based on these results, the prescription of statins is now routine in developed countries as an effective chemopreventive strategy to reduce the risk of myocardial infarction and other cardiovascular events.

Estrogen Replacement Therapy and Myocardial Infarction

Estrogen is a powerful hormone that has significant physiological effects related to cardiovascular health. During the premenopausal years during which women produce estrogens via the ovarian axis, cholesterol levels in women average about 10 mg/dl less than men of corresponding age. Correspondingly, women have lower rates of myocardial infarctions and other cardiovascular events than men up until about age 65 years, presumably as a consequence of endogenous estrogen biosynthesis as well as many other factors.

Recent molecular studies suggest that estrogen produces vasodilatation through signal transduction of estrogen receptors in the arterial endothelium resulting in biosynthesis of nitric oxide (Mendelsohn and Karas, 1999). Estrogen replacement therapy (ERT) has been found to lower LDL (*bad*) cholesterol and elevate HDL (*good*) cholesterol, but is also associated with elevations in triglycerides (Espeland et al., 1998).

Estrogen replacement therapy (ERT) is often prescribed to counteract hot flashes and other symptoms of menopause. Administration of estrogen and progesterone are often combined to mimic the female menstrual cycle as a form of hormone replacement therapy (HRT). Millions of women in the United States and throughout the world have received ERT or HRT. Many epidemiologic investigations have focused on the potential role of ERT/HRT in reducing the risk of thrombotic cardiovascular events such as heart attack and stroke. Several meta-analyses of these investigations show good consistency of results and suggest that ERT/HRT for 5 years or more reduces the risk of coronary heart disease (myocardial infarction or sudden cardiovascular death) by 35–50% (Bush, 1990; Stampfer and Colditz, 1991; Grady et al., 1992). Meta-analysis of 25 studies published before 1997 found similar risk reductions for either ERT (30%) or HRT (34%). Albeit, ERT/HRT also appears to increase the risk of developing endometrial cancer and breast cancer (Barrett-Connor and Grady, 1998).

The consistently observed cardioprotective effects of ERT/HRT in observational (nonrandomized) epidemiologic investigations prompted the study of ERT/HRT in randomized clinical trials. Surprisingly, two large placebo-controlled randomized clinical trials, the Heart and Estrogen/Progestin Replacement Study (HERS) and the Women's Health Initiative (WHI), found that ERT/HRT *increased rather than decreased* the risk of thrombotic cardiovascular events (Hulley et al., 1998; Rossouw et al., 2002; Anderson et al., 2004). The discrepant results of the observational epidemiologic studies versus the randomized clinical trials have stimulated much debate regarding the risk versus benefit of ERT/HRT in postmenopausal women.

The Heart and Estrogen/Progestin Replacement Study (HERS) was specifically designed to test the hypothesis that treatment with 0.625 mg/day conjugated equine estrogen (CEE) plus 2.5 mg/day medroxyprogesterone acetate (MPA) would reduce the combined incidence of nonfatal myocardial infarction and/or death from coronary heart disease compared to placebo in postmenopausal women *with prior history of myocardial infarction, coronary revascularization, or angiographic evidence of coronary heart disease*. A total of 2,763 postmenopausal women (age less than 80 years) consented for enrollment and were randomized for study, 1,380 women to the treatment (HRT) arm and 1,383 women to the placebo arm. After an average of 4.1 years of follow-up, there was no difference in the primary outcome of nonfatal myocardial and/or coronary death between the hormone and placebo arms. However, a *post hoc* time-trend analysis revealed a significant 52% *increase* in cardiovascular events (42.5 events/1,000 person-years versus 28.0 events/1,000 person-years) during the first year in the HRT group compared with placebo, with a nonsignificant trend toward fewer events in the treatment arm compared with placebo in later years (23.0/1,000 person-years versus 34.4/1,000 person-years) (Hulley et al., 1998).

The Women's Health Initiative (WHI) was initiated by the National Institutes of Health (NIH) in 1991 (Michels, 2006). The objective of this women's health research initiative was to conduct medical research into some of the major health problems of older women. In particular, randomized controlled trials were designed and funded that address cardiovascular disease, cancer, and osteoporosis. Two of the randomized interventions in WHI involved hormone replacement, a randomized double-blinded placebo-controlled trial of ERT (estrogen replacement alone) versus placebo, and a randomized double-blinded placebo controlled trial of HRT (estrogen plus progestin) versus placebo.

In the HRT versus placebo clinical trial, 8,506 women received equine estrogen plus progestin (MPA) and 8,102 received placebo. After an average follow-up of 5.2 years, the *Data Safety and Monitoring Board* recommended termination of the trial due to increased hazards. Observed hazard ratios (HR) were significantly increased for multiple events: coronary heart disease (HR = 1.29), breast cancer (HR = 1.26), stroke (HR = 1.41), pulmonary embolism (HR = 2.1), and total cardiovascular disease (HR = 1.22) (Rossouw et al., 2002).

In the ERT versus placebo clinical trial, 10,739 postmenopausal women, aged 50–79 years, with prior hysterectomy, were randomized to receive either equine estrogen (n = 5,310) or placebo (n = 5,429). This trial was terminated after 6.8 years of average follow-up due to significantly increased hazards ratios (HR) for multiple events of interest: stroke (HR = 1.39), pulmonary embolism (HR = 1.34), and total cardiovascular disease (HR = 1.12) (Anderson et al., 2004).

The results of these three randomized clinical trials argue against the use of either ERT or HRT for alleged cardioprotection in either healthy postmenopausal women or those with a prior history of myocardial infarction or other forms of coronary heart disease. Obviously, advocates of the administration of exogenous hormones to postmenopausal women can no longer point to a favorable risk versus benefit ratio (Writing Group for WHI, 2002).

It is important to note that subsequent analyses of the WHI trial data sets with stratification by age found that women aged 50–59 years or those who began taking ERT/HRT within five years of menopause had *lower* rates of coronary heart disease compared to women of similar age who received placebo (Manson et al., 2003). Nevertheless, controversy still rages as to whether ERT/HRT has cardiovascular benefit or risk in postmenopausal women (Stevenson, 2009).

Selective Cyclooxygenase-2 (COX-2) Inhibitors and Myocardial Infarction

Nonsteroidal anti-inflammatory drugs (NSAIDs) such as aspirin, ibuprofen, and naproxen relieve pain and inflammation by inhibiting the chief rate-limiting enzymes of prostaglandin biosynthesis: cyclooxygenase-1 and -2 (COX-1 and COX-2). Both COX-1 and COX-2 convert arachidonic acid and certain other fatty acids into prostaglandins. The prostaglandins are short-acting long-chain hydrocarbon molecules that have a bewildering array of cellular effects. The primary inflammatory prostaglandin, PGE-2, is essential for modulating the inflammatory response of the innate immune system.

The cyclooxygenase enzymes, COX-1 and COX-2, are encoded by two separate genes with substantial homology. However, COX-1 continually synthesizes low levels of prostaglandins in most tissues whereas COX-2 is normally silent unless it is induced by inflammatory stimuli. Induction of COX-2 increases the biosynthesis of PGE-2 by 10- to 100-fold in inflamed tissues and so initiates the inflammatory cycle, e.g., vasodilatation, edema and influx of monocytes, macrophages, and lymphocytes of the immune system.

General NSAIDs such as aspirin and ibuprofen nonselectively inhibit both COX-1 and COX-2, and since COX-1 inhibition can lead to gastric irritation and peptic ulcers in some individuals, the development of drugs that selectively inhibit COX-2 became a priority for the pharmaceutical industry. Two such drugs, rofecoxib (Vioxx) produced by Merck and celecoxib (Celebrex) produced by Pfizer, were approved for prescriptive use in 1998 and soon captured a substantial share of the market for arthritis therapy. Both drugs were widely prescribed among patients with arthritic conditions and proved effective in relieving their pain and inflammation.

But the early success of the selective COX-2 inhibitors soon diminished as post-marketing studies appeared in the literature documenting increased rates of thrombotic cardiovascular events, particularly heart attacks, among rofecoxib users (Bombardier et al., 2000). And in dramatic fashion, the results of a double-blinded placebo-controlled randomized clinical trial designed to test rofecoxib for the chemoprevention of colonic polyps revealed a twofold increase in thrombotic cardiovascular events (including myocaridal infarction and stroke) among participants receiving 25 mg of rofecoxib daily (Bresalier et al., 2005). As a consequence of these findings, in September of 2004, Merck removed rofecoxib (Vioxx) from the world market.

Due to concern about a potential adverse cardiovascular class effect of COX-2 inhibitors, the Pfizer COX-2 blocker, celecoxib (Celebrex), has come under extreme scrutiny by the scientific and medical communities (as well as the general public). One highly publicized randomized clinical trial designed to test celecoxib for the chemoprevention of colonic polyps found 2.3-fold and 3.4-fold increases in the composite cardiovascular end point of death from cardiovascular causes, myocardial infarction, stroke, or heart failure among participants receiving daily dosages of 200 mg or 400 mg of celecoxib, respectively (Solomon et al., 2005).

Subsequent to this activity, many investigators have queried available databases to examine the cardiovascular risk of both rofecoxib and celecoxib. Notably, differential effects have been noted for celecoxib compared to rofecoxib. In a meta-analysis of each drug based upon published observational studies, an adverse effect of rofecoxib was confirmed (RR = 2.19 for cardiovascular events, predominantly myocardial infarction) *but not for celecoxib* (RR = 1.06) (McGettigan and Henry, 2006). Furthermore, results of a more comprehensive meta-analysis of celecoxib including 73 published studies also failed to find an effect of celecoxib (Harris, 2009). As shown in Figure 4.8, this investigation included data from 39 short-term randomized clinical trials, 26 observational case control and cohort studies, and 8 long-term randomized clinical trials. From this analysis, the composite estimate of relative risk for celecoxib and thrombotic cardiovascular events (primarily myocardial infarction and stroke) was slightly less than unity (RR = 0.98) and the test for heterogeneity did not approach statistical significance. Thus, based upon the totality of available evidence from randomized clinical trials and observational studies,

celecoxib at 400 mg or less daily shows no association with thrombotic cardiovascular risk.

Secondary Prevention of Myocardial Infarction

The risk of a recurrent myocardial infarction decreases with strict blood pressure management, antiplatelet therapy, regulation of cholesterol and blood glucose, and lifestyle changes: chiefly smoking cessation, regular exercise, limitation of alcohol consumption, and modification of diet. In regard to smoking cessation, counseling should be provided to the patient and family, along with pharmacologic therapy (including nicotine replacement) and formal smoking-cessation programs as appropriate. Counseling on physical activity and weight reduction is also advisable, and all patients recovering from myocardial infarction should be encouraged to exercise for a minimum of 30 minutes, preferably daily but at least 3 or 4 times per week (walking, jogging, cycling, or other aerobic activity). Consensus statements on the secondary prevention of myocardial infarction (with ST elevation) have recently been updated by the American College of Cardiology and the American Heart Association (Antman et al., 2004).

Dietary therapy low in saturated fat, salt, and cholesterol (less than 7% of total calories as saturated fat and less than 200 mg/d cholesterol) should be started after recovery from the initial myocardial

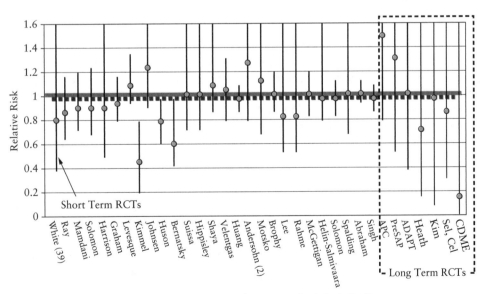

Relative Risk Estimates from 73 Epidemiologic Studies
Combined RR = 0.97, 95% CI = 0.91 – 1.03, No Change in Risk

Figure 4.8 Meta-analysis of Celecoxib (Celebrex) and Cardiovascular Disease.

Source: Reproduced From: Harris RE (2009). Cyclooxygenase-2 (COX-2) blockade in the chemoprevention of cancers of the colon, breast, prostate and lung. *Inflammopharmacology* 17:55–67.

infarction and upon hospital discharge. In addition, evidence from randomized clinical trials shows benefit with increased consumption of omega-3-PUFA, e.g., the *GISSA Prevenzione Trial (Gruppo Italiano per lo Studio della Sopravvivenza nell'Infarto)*, a randomized trial of 11,324 Italian patients surviving myocardial infarction, found that addition of omega-3 PUFA reduced the relative risk of coronary death, nonfatal myocardial infarction, or stroke by 10% (GISSA Prevenzione Trial Investigators, 1999). Total caloric intake should also be balanced with energy output to achieve and maintain a healthy weight.

Blood pressure management using angiotensin-converting enzyme (ACE) inhibiting agents following myocardial infarction has proven extremely effective in reducing the recurrence risk in several randomized clinical trials. In a randomized placebo-controlled double-blinded trial of 2,231 heart failure patients conducted in the United States, those patients who received the ACE-inhibitor, captopril ($n = 1,115$), had 25% less recurrent myocardial infarctions and 37% fewer deaths from cardiovascular events compared to patients receiving placebo ($n = 1,116$) after 42 months average follow-up (Pfeffer et al., 1992).

In addition to antihypertensive medications, sustained therapy for heart arrhythmias using β-adrenergic-antagonist therapy (β-blockers) has also been shown to decrease mortality and morbidity and improve symptoms of cardiac ischemia in certain patients who have survived heart attacks (Yusuf et al., 1985). Furthermore, compared with other modalities, routine administration of β-adrenergic-antagonist therapy has a relatively favorable cost-effectiveness ratio (Goldman et al., 1988, 1991).

Statin therapy has also proven to be beneficial in reducing the risk of subsequent cardiovascular events or death following myocardial infarction. In a large double-blinded placebo-controlled randomized clinical trial involving 3,086 patients from centers in Europe, North and South America, and Austrialia, administration of a statin reduced the incidence of the composite end point (death, nonfatal acute myocardial infarction, cardiac arrest with resuscitation, or recurrent myocardial ischemia) by 16% (Schwartz et al., 2001). Statin therapy administered to reduce even average cholesterol levels has proven beneficial and cost-effective for men and women who have suffered a first myocardial infarction (Goldman et al., 1988; Sacks et al., 1996).

Antiplatelet therapy with low dose aspirin or other antithombolytic agents, e.g., clopidogrel, has been shown in several studies to reduce the recurrence risk (Peters et al., 2003). On the basis of 12 randomized trials involving 18,788 patients with prior myocardial infarction, the Antithrombotic Trialists' Collaboration (2002) reported a 25% reduction in the risk of recurrent infarction, stroke, or vascular death in patients receiving prolonged antiplatelet therapy (36 fewer events for every 1,000 patients treated). No antiplatelet therapy has proved superior to aspirin in this population, and daily doses of aspirin between 80–325 mg appear to be effective (Sagar and Smyth, 1999). Further justification for the use of statins, β-blockers, ACE inhibitors, and antiplatelet drugs to prevent recurrence/death after a first myocardial infarction comes from a large observational study conducted in the United States (Setoguchi et al., 2008). Using data derived from pharmacy assistance programs and Medicare in New Jersey and Pennsylvania between 1995–2004, investigators examined temporal trends in mortality after hospitalization for acute myocardial infarction in 21,484 community-dwelling elderly patients (average age 80 years) who survived at least 30 days after discharge. Results showed that after adjusting for patient demographics, comorbidities, duration of hospitalization, patterns of previous health service use, and clustering of patients within hospitals, the mortality after myocardial infarction decreased significantly by approximately 3% per year. These findings and that from other national and international investigations (Swedberg et al., 1992; Pilote et al., 2000) support the value of implementing proven secondary prevention medications for patients who survive the initial peril of myocardial infarction. Summarizing, there is a large and expanding body of scientific evidence that has validated the importance of using established secondary prevention therapies (aspirin, clopidogrel, statins, β-blockers, and ACE inhibitors) either alone or in combination in reducing long-term death and recurrent myocardial infarction in patients with prior coronary heart disease (Gutstein and Fuster, 1998; Moe and Wong, 2010).

Emergency Services for Acute Myocardial Infarction

Immediate action based upon symptoms of an impending myocardial infarction can prove lifesaving. Ventricular defibrillation can reinstitute the heartbeat in cardiac arrest, and rapid treatment can prevent sustained ischemic damage to the myocardium. Advanced paramedical services include preliminary electrocardiography and administration of oxygen, nitroglycerin, and antithrombolytic agents (aspirin) as appropriate. Reperfusion techniques (e.g., thrombolytic therapy, percutaneous coronary intervention [PCI], or bypass surgery) are central to the modern treatment of acute myocardial infarction (Antman et al., 2004).

● ● ● REFERENCES

Alpert, J.S., Thygesen, K., Antman, E., & Bassand, J.P. (2000). Myocardial infarction redefined—a consensus document of The Joint European Society of Cardiology/American College of Cardiology Committee for the redefinition of myocardial infarction. *J Am Coll Cardiol*, 36(3), 959–969.

Anderson, G.L., Limacher, M., Assaf, A.R., for the Women's Health Initiative Writing Group. (2004). Effects of conjugated equine estrogen in postmenopausal women with hysterectomy: The Women's Health Initiative randomized controlled trial. *JAMA*, 291(14), 1701–1712.

Andraws, R., Berger, J.S., & Brown, D.L. (2005). Effects of antibiotic therapy on outcomes of patients with coronary artery disease: A meta-analysis of randomized controlled trials. *JAMA*, 293(21), 2641–2467.

Antithrombotic Trialists' Collaboration. (2002). Collaborative meta-analysis of randomised trials of antiplatelet therapy for prevention of death, myocardial infarction, and stroke in high risk patients. *BMJ*, 324, 71–86.

Antman, E.M., Anbe, D.T., Armstrong, P.W., et al. (2004). ACC/AHA guidelines for the management of patients with ST-elevation myocardial infarction—executive summary. A report of the American College of Cardiology/American Heart Association Task Force on Practice Guidelines (Writing Committee to revise the 1999 guidelines for the management of patients with acute myocardial infarction). *J Am Coll Cardiol*, 44(3), 671–719.

Barrett-Connor, E., & Grady, D. (1998). Hormone replacement therapy, heart disease, and other considerations. *Ann Rev Public Health*, 19, 55–72.

Beamer, A.D., Lee, T.H., Cook, E.F., et al. (1987). Diagnostic implications for myocardial ischemia of the circadian variation of the onset of chest pain. *Am J Cardiol*, 60(13), 998–1002.

Bombardier, C., Laine, L., Reicin, A., et al. (2000). Comparison of upper gastrointestinal toxicity of rofecoxib and naproxen in patients with rheumatoid arthritis. VIGOR Study Group. *The New England Journal of Medicine*, 343(21), 1520–1528.

Bresalier, R., Sandler, R., Quan, H., et al. (2005). Cardiovascular events associated with rofecoxib in a colorectal adenoma chemoprevention trial. *The New England Journal of Medicine*, 352(11), 1092–1102.

Brugts, J.J., Yetgin, T., Hoeks, S.E., et al. (2009). The benefits of statins in people without established cardiovascular disease but with cardiovascular risk factors: Meta-analysis of randomized controlled trials. *BMJ*, 338, b2376.

Bush, T.L. (1990). The epidemiology of cardiovascular disease in postmenopausal women. *Ann NY Acad Sci*, 592, 263–271.

Curfman, G.D. (1993). Is exercise beneficial—or hazardous—to your heart? *N Engl J Med*, 329, 1730–1731.

D'Agostino, R.B. Sr., Grundy, S., Sullivan, L.M., & Wilson, P. (2001). Validation of the Framingham coronary heart disease prediction scores: Results of a multiple ethnic groups investigation. *JAMA*, 286, 180–187.

Dawber, T.R., & Kannel, W.B. (1968). The early diagnosis of coronary heart disease. In: Sharp, C.L.E.H., & Keen, H. (Eds.). *Presymptomatic Detection and Early Diagnosis: A Critical Appraisal* (pp. 257–281). London: Pitman Medical.

De Caterina, R., Liao, J.K., & Libby, P. (2000). Fatty acid modulation of endothelial activation. *Am J Clin Nutr*, 71, 213S–223S.

Espeland, M.A., Marcovina, S.M., Miller, V., et al. (1998). Effect of postmenopausal hormone therapy on lipoprotein(a) concentration: PEPI Investigators: Postmenopausal Estrogen/Progestin Interventions. *Circulation*, 97, 979–986.

Fantidis, P., Perez De Prada, T., Fernandez-Ortiz, A., et al. (2002). Morning cortisol production in coronary heart disease patients. *Eur. J Clin Invest*, 32(5), 304–308.

Ferrucci, L., Cherubini, A., Bandinelli, S., et al. (2006). Relationship of plasma polyunsaturated fatty acids to circulating inflammatory markers. *J Clin Endocrinol Metab*, 91, 439–446.

GISSA Prevenzione Trial Investigators. (1999). Dietary supplementation with n-3 polyunsaturated fatty acids and vitamin E after myocardial infarction: Results of the GISSI-Prevenzione trial. Gruppo Italiano per lo Studio della Sopravvivenza nell'Infarto miocardico. *Lancet*, 354(9177), 447–455.

Goff, D.C., Nichaman, M.Z., Chan, W., Ramsey, D.J., Labarthe, D.R., & Ortiz, C. (1997). Greater incidence of hospitalized myocardial infarction among Mexican Americans than non-Hispanic whites. The Corpus Christi Heart Project, 1988–1992. *Circulation*, 95(6), 1433–1440.

Goldberg, R.J., Gore, J.M., Alpert, J.S., & Dalen, J.E. (1986). Recent changes in attack and survival rates of acute myocardial infarction (1975 through 1981). The Worcester Heart Attack Study. *JAMA*, 255(20), 2774–2779.

Goldberg, R.J., Yarzebski, J., Lessard, D., & Gore, J.M. (1999). A two-decades (1975 to 1995) long experience in the incidence, in-hospital and long-term case-fatality rates of acute myocardial infarction: A community-wide perspective. *J Am Coll Cardiol*, 33(6), 1533–1539.

Goldman, L., Sia, S.T., Cook, E.F., Rutherford, J.D., & Weinstein, M.C. (1988). Costs and effectiveness of routine therapy with long-term beta-adrenergic antagonists after acute myocardial infarction. *N Engl J Med*, 319, 152–157.

Goldman, L., Weinstein, M.C., Goldman, P.A., & Williams, L.W. (1991). Cost-effectiveness of HMG-CoA reductase inhibition for primary and secondary prevention of coronary heart disease. *JAMA*, 265, 1145–1151.

Grady, D., Rubin, S.M., Petitti, D.B., et al. (1992). Hormone therapy to prevent disease and prolong life in postmenopausal women. *Ann Intern Med*, 117, 1016–1037.

Gutstein, D.E., & Fuster, V. (1998). Pathophysiologic bases for adjunctive therapies in the treatment and secondary prevention of acute myocardial infarction. *Clin Cardiol*, 21, 161–168.

Harris, R.E. (2009). Cyclooxygenase-2 (COX-2) blockade in the chemoprevention of cancers of the colon, breast, prostate and lung. *Inflammopharmacology*, 17, 55–67.

Hoffman, B.B., & Lefkowitz, R.J. (1982). Adrenergic receptors in the heart. *Annu Rev Physiol*, 44, 475–484.

Hulley, S., Grady, D., Bush, T., et al. (1998). Randomized trial of estrogen plus progestin for secondary prevention of coronary heart disease in postmenopausal women: Heart and Estrogen/progestin Replacement Study (HERS) Research Group. *JAMA*, 280, 605–613.

Jensen, G., Nyboe, J., Appleyard, M., & Schnohr, P. (1991). Risk factors for acute myocardial infarction in Copenhagen, II: Smoking, alcohol intake, physical activity, obesity, oral contraception, diabetes, lipids, and blood pressure. *Eur Heart J*, 12(3), 298–308.

Kannel, W.B. (1964). Cigarette smoking and coronary heart disease. *Ann Intern Med*, 60, 1103–1106.

Kannel, W.B., Castelli, W.P., & McNamara, P.M. (1968). Cigarette smoking and risk of coronary heart disease. Epidemiologic clues to pathogenesis. The Framingham Study. *Natl Cancer Inst Monogr*, 28, 9–20.

Kannel, W.B., Schwartz, M.J., & McNamara, P.M. (1969). Blood pressure and risk of coronary heart disease: The Framingham study. *Dis Chest*, 56(1), 43–52.

Kannel, W.B., Gordon, T., & Schwartz, M.J. (1971). Systolic versus diastolic blood pressure and risk of coronary heart disease. The Framingham study. *Am J Cardiol*, 27(4), 335–346.

Kannel, W.B., Castelli, W.P., Gordon, T., & McNamara, P.M. (1971). Serum cholesterol, lipoproteins, and the risk of coronary heart disease. The Framingham study. *Ann Intern Med*, 74(1), 1–12.

Kannel, W.B., & McGee, D.L. (1979). Diabetes and cardiovascular disease. The Framingham study. *JAMA*, 241(19), 2035–2038.

Kannel, W.B., D'Agostino, R.B., Wilson, P.W.F., Belanger, A.J., & Gagnon, D.R. (1990). Diabetes, fibrinogen, and risk of cardiovascular disease: The Framingham experience. *Am Heart J, 120*, 672–676.

Kannel, W.B. (1996). Blood pressure as a cardiovascular risk factor: Prevention and treatment. *JAMA, 275*(20), 1571–1576.

Keys, A., Aravanis, C., Blackburn, H.W., et al. (1967). Epidemiologic studies related to coronary heart disease: Characteristics of men aged 40–59 in seven countries. *Acta Med Scand* (Suppl to vol. 460), 1–392.

Keys, A. (1970). *Coronary Heart Disease in Seven Countries*. New York, NY: American Heart Association, Monograph No. 29.

Keys, A., Aravanis, C., Blackburn, H., et al. (1980). *Seven Countries. A Multivariate Analysis of Death and Coronary Heart Disease* (pp. 1–381). Cambridge, MA and London: Harvard University Press.

Kuller, L., Neaton, J., Caggiula, A., & Falvo-Gerard, L. (1980). Primary prevention of heart attacks: The multiple risk factor intervention trial. *Am J Epidemiol, 112*(2), 185–199.

Lauer, M.S. (2002). Aspirin for primary prevention of coronary events. *New Engl J Med, 346*(19), 1468–1474.

Levy, D. (1993). A multifactorial approach to coronary disease risk assessment. *Clinical and Experimental Hypertension, 15*(6), 1077–1086.

Levy, D., & Thom, T.J. (1998). Death rates from coronary disease—progress and a puzzling paradox. *New Engl J Med, 339*, 915–917.

Lewington, S., Whitlock, G., Clarke, R., et al. (2007). Blood cholesterol and vascular mortality by age, sex, and blood pressure: A meta-analysis of individual data from 61 prospective studies with 55,000 vascular deaths. *Lancet, 370*, 1829–1839.

Mackay, J., & Mensah, G. (2004). *Atlas of Heart Disease and Stroke*. Geneva, Switzerland: World Health Organization.

Manson, J.E., Tosteson, H., Ridker, P.M., et al. (1992). The primary prevention of myocardial infarction. *N Engl J Med, 326*(21), 1406–1416.

Manson, J.E., Hsia, P.H.J., Johnson, K.C., et al. (2003). Estrogen plus progestin and the risk of coronary heart disease. *The New England Journal of Medicine, 349*(6), 523–534.

McGettigan, P., & Henry, D. (2006). Cardiovascular risk and inhibition of cyclooxygenase: A systematic review of the observational studies of selective and nonselective inhibitors of cyclooxygenase 2. *JAMA, 296*(13), 1633–1644.

McGovern, P.G., Jacobs, D.R. Jr., Shahar, E., et al. (2001). Trends in acute coronary heart disease mortality, morbidity, and medical care from 1985 through 1997: The Minnesota heart survey. *Circulation, 104*(1), 19–24.

McQueen, M.J., Hawken, S., Wang, X., et al. (2008). Lipids, lipoproteins, and apolipoproteins as risk markers of myocardial infarction in 52 countries (the INTERHEART study): A case-control study. *Lancet, 372*(9634), 224–233.

Mendelsohn, M.E., & Karas, R.H. (1999). The protective effects of estrogen on the cardiovascular system. *N Engl J Med, 340*, 1801–1811.

Michels, K.B. (2006). The Women's Health Initiative—curse or blessing? *Int J Epidemiol, 35*(4), 814–816.

Mills, E.J., Rachlis, B., Wu, P., Devereaux, P.J., Arora, P., & Perri, D. (2008). Primary prevention of cardiovascular mortality and events with statin treatments: A network meta-analysis involving more than 65,000 patients. *J Am Coll Cardiol, 52*(22), 1769–1781.

Mittleman, M.A., Maclure, M., Tofler, G.H., Sherwood, J.B., Goldberg, R.J., & Muller, J.E. (1993). Triggering of acute myocardial infarction by heavy physical exertion—protection against triggering by regular exertion. *N Engl J Med, 329*, 1677–1683.

Moe, K.T., & Wong, P. (2010). Current trends in diagnostic biomarkers of acute coronary syndrome. *Ann Acad Med Singap*, 39(3), 210–215.

Mozaffarian, D., Micha, R., & Wallace, S. (2010). Effects on coronary heart disease of increasing polyunsaturated fat in place of saturated fat: A systematic review and meta-analysis of randomized controlled trials. *PLoS Med*, 7(3), e1000252.

Muller, J.E., Stone, P.H., Turi, Z.G., et al. (1985). Circadian variation in the frequency of onset of acute myocardial infarction. *N Engl J Med*, 313(21), 1315–1322.

National Heart, Lung and Blood Institute. (2006). Heart Attack Warning Signs. Bethesda, MD: National Institutes of Health.

National Heart, Lung and Blood Institute. (2009). *Morbidity and mortality: 2009. Chartbook on cardiovascular, lung, and blood diseases.* Bethesda, MD: National Institutes of Health.

Nichaman, M.Z., Wear, M.L., Goff, D.C., Jr., & Labarthe, D.R. (1993). Hospitalization rates for myocardial infarction among Mexican-Americans and non-Hispanic whites. The Corpus Christi Heart Project. *Ann Epidemiol*, 3(1), 42–48.

Nyboe, J., Jensen, G., Appleyard, M., & Schnohr, P. (1989). Risk factors for acute myocardial infarction in Copenhagen. I: Hereditary, educational and socioeconomic factors. Copenhagen City Heart Study. *Eur Heart J*, 10(10), 910–916.

Parikh, N.I., Gona, P., Larson, M.G., et al. (2009). Long-term trends in myocardial infarction incidence and case fatality in the National Heart, Lung, and Blood Institute's Framingham Heart Study. *Circulation, 119*, 1203–1210.

Peters, R.J., Mehta, S.R., Fox, K.A., et al. (2003). Effects of aspirin dose when used alone or in combination with clopidogrel in patients with acute coronary syndromes: Observations from the Clopidogrel in Unstable angina to prevent Recurrent Events (CURE) study. *Circulation, 108*(14), 1682–1687.

Pfeffer, M.A., Braunwald, E., Moye, L.A., et al. (1992). Effect of captopril on mortality and morbidity in patients with left ventricular dysfunction after myocardial infarction. Results of the survival and ventricular enlargement trial. The SAVE Investigators. *N Engl J Med*, 327(10), 669–677.

Pilote, L., Lavoie, F., Ho, V., & Eisenberg, M.J. (2000). Changes in the treatment and outcomes of acute myocardial infarction in Quebec, 1988–1995. *CMAJ, 163*, 31–36.

Pischon, T., Hankinson, S.E., Hotamisligil, G.S., et al. (2003). Habitual dietary intake of n-3 and n-6 fatty acids in relation to inflammatory markers among US men and women. *Circulation, 108*, 155–160.

Ray, K.K., & Cannon, C.P. (2005). The potential relevance of the multiple lipid-independent (pleiotropic) effects of statins in the management of acute coronary syndromes. *J Am Coll Cardiol, 46*(8), 1425–1433.

Robbins, S.L., & Cotran, R.S. (1979). *Pathologic Basis of Disease* (2nd Ed.). Philadelphia: WB Saunders.

Roger, V.L., Killian, J., Henkel, M., et al. (2002). Coronary disease surveillance in Olmsted County objectives and methodology. *J Clin Epidemiol, 55*(6), 593–601.

Rosamond, W.D., Chambless, L.E., Folsom, A.R., et al. (1998). Trends in the incidence of myocardial infarction and in mortality due to coronary heart disease, 1987 to 1994. *N Engl J Med, 339*, 861–867.

Rosenbaum, D.M., Rasmussen, S.G.F., & Kobilka, B.K. (2009). The structure and function of G-protein-coupled receptors. *Nature, 459*(7245), 356–363.

Rossouw, J.E., Anderson, G.L., Prentice, R.L., for the Women' Health Initiative Writing Group. (2002). Risks and benefits of estrogen plus progestin in healthy postmenopausal women: principal results From the Women's Health Initiative randomized controlled trial. *JAMA, 288*(3), 321–333.

Sacks, F.M., Pfeffer, M.A., Moye, L.A., et al. (1996). The effect of pravastatin on coronary events after myocardial infarction in patients with average cholesterol levels. Cholesterol and Recurrent

Events Trial investigators. *N Engl J Med*, *335*(14), 1001–1009.

Sagar, A., & Smyth, M.R. (1999). A comparative bioavailability study of different aspirin formulations using on-line multidimensional chromatography. *J Pharm Biomed Anal*, *21*, 383–392.

Saikku, P., Leinonen, M., Tenkanen, L., et al. (1992). Chronic *Chlamydia pneumoniae* infection as a risk factor for coronary heart disease in the Helsinki Heart Study. *Ann Intern Med*, *116*(4), 273–278.

Salmeron, J., Hu, F.B., Manson, J.E., et al. (2001). Dietary fat intake and risk of type 2 diabetes in women. *Am J Clin Nutr*, *73*, 1019–1026.

Sanmuganathan, P.S., Ghahramani, P., Jackson, P.R., Wallis, E.J., & Ramsay, L.E. (2001). Aspirin for primary prevention of coronary heart disease: Safety and absolute benefit related to coronary risk derived from meta-analysis of randomised trials. *Heart*, *85*, 265–271.

Schwartz, G.G., Olsson, A.G., Ezekowitz, M.D., et al. (2001). Effects of atorvastatin on early recurrent ischemic events in acute coronary syndromes: The MIRACL study: A randomized controlled trial *JAMA*, *285*, 1711–1718.

Setoguchi, S., Glynn, R.J., Avorn, J., Mittleman, M.A., Levin, R., & Winkelmayer, W.C. (2008). Improvements in long-term mortality after myocardial infarction and increased use of cardiovascular drugs after discharge: A 10-year trend analysis. *J Am Coll Cardiol*, *51*, 1247–1254.

Simopoulos, A.P. (2008). The importance of the omega-6/omega-3 fatty acid ratio in cardiovascular disease and other chronic diseases. *Exp Biol Med*, (Maywood)*233*, 674–688.

Siscovick, D.S., Weiss, N.S., Fletcher, R.H., & Lasky, T. (1984). The incidence of primary cardiac arrest during vigorous exercise. *N Engl J Med*, *311*, 874–877.

Smeeth, L., Thomas, S.L., Hall, A.J., Hubbgard, R., Farrington, P., & Vallance, P. (2004). Risk of myocardial infarction and stroke after acute infection or vaccination. *New Engl J Med*, *351*, 2611–2618.

Sofi, F., Cesari, F., Abbate, R., Gensini, G.F., & Casini, A. (2008). Adherence to Mediterranean diet and health status: Meta-analysis. *BMJ (Clinical research ed.)*, *337*, a1344.

Solomon, S., McMurray, J., Pfeffer, M., et al. (2005). Cardiovascular risk associated with celecoxib in a clinical trial for colorectal adenoma prevention. *The New England Journal of Medicine*, *352*(11), 1071–1080.

Stamler, J., Wentworth, D., Neaton, J.D., for the MRFIT Research Group. (1986). Is relationship between serum cholesterol and risk of premature death from coronary heart disease continuous and graded? Findings in 356,222 primary screenees of the Multiple Risk Factor Intervention Trial (MRFIT). *JAMA*, *256*(20), 2823–2828.

Stampfer, M.J., & Colditz, G.A. (1991). Estrogen replacement therapy and coronary heart disease: A quantitative assessment of the epidemiologic evidence. *Prev Med*, *1*, 47–63.

Stevenson, J.C. (2009). Hormone replacement therapy and cardiovascular disease revisited. *Menopause Int*, *15*, 55–57.

Summers, L.K., Fielding, B.A., Bradshaw, H.A., et al. (2002). Substituting dietary saturated fat with polyunsaturated fat changes abdominal fat distribution and improves insulin sensitivity. *Diabetologia*, *45*, 369–377.

Swedberg, K., Held, P., Kjekshus, J., Rasmussen, K., Ryden, L., & Wedel, H. (1992). Effects of the early administration of enalapril on mortality in patients with acute myocardial infarction. Results of the Cooperative New Scandinavian Enalapril Survival Study II (CONSENSUS II). *N Engl J Med*, *327*, 678–684.

Tunstall-Pedoe, H., Kuulasmaa, K., Amouyel, P., Arveiler, D., Rajakangas, A.M., & Pajak, A. (1994). Myocardial infarction and coronary deaths in the World Health Organization MONICA Project: Registration procedures, event rates, and case-fatality rates in 38 populations from 21 countries in four continents. *Circulation*, *90*, 583– 612.

Tunstall-Pedoe, H., Kuulasmaa, K., Mähönen, M., Tolonen, H., Ruokokoski, E., & Amouyel, P. (1999). Contribution of trends in survival and coronary-event rates to changes in coronary heart disease mortality: 10-year results from 37 WHO MONICA project populations. Monitoring trends and determinants in cardiovascular disease. *Lancet, 353*(9164), 1547–1557.

White, A.D., Rosamond, W.D., Chambless, L.E., Thomas, N., Conwill, D., Cooper, L.S., & Folsom, A.R. (1999). Sex and race differences in short-term prognosis after acute coronary heart disease events: The Atherosclerosis Risk In Communities (ARIC) study. *Am Heart J, 138*(3 Pt 1), 540–548.

Willett, W.C., Sacks, F., & Trichopoulous, A. (1995). Mediterranean diet pyramid: A cultural model for healthy eating. *Am J Clin Nutr, 61*(6 Suppl), 1402S–1406S.

Willich, S.N., Lewis, M., Lowel, H., Arntz, H.R., Schubert, F., & Schroder, R. (1993). Physical exertion as a trigger of acute myocardial infarction. *N Engl J Med, 329*, 1684–1690.

Wilson, P.W., D'Agostino, R.B., Levy, D., Belanger, A.M., Silbershatz, H., & Kannel, W.B. (1998). Prediction of coronary heart disease using risk factor categories. *Circulation, 97*(18), 1837–1847.

Writing Group for the Women's Health Initiative Investigators. (2002). Risks and benefits of estrogen plus progestin in healthy Postmenopausal women: Principal results from the Women's Health Initiative Randomized Controlled Trial. *JAMA, 288*(3), 321–333.

Yusuf, S., Peto, R., Lewis, J., Collins, R., & Sleight, P. (1985). Beta blockade during and after myocardial infarction: An overview of the randomized trials. *Prog Cardiovasc Dis, 27*(5), 335–371.

Yusuf, S., Hawken, S., Ounpuu, S., et al. (2004). Effect of potentially modifiable risk factors associated with myocardial infarction in 52 countries (the INTERHEART study): Case-control study. *Lancet, 364*(9438), 937–952.

Epidemiology of Stroke (Cerebral Infarction)

ISCHEMIC AND HEMORRHAGIC STROKES

A stroke or cerebral infarction is the rapidly developing loss of brain function due to interruption of the cerebral blood supply and necrosis of neurons in part of the brain. Strokes are diagnosed based on clinical symptoms (e.g., the degree and specificity of acute loss of brain function) plus imaging techniques such as computed tomography (CT) scans and magnetic resonance imaging (MRI). The traditional definition of stroke published by the World Health Organization in 1978 is "a neurological deficit of cerebrovascular cause that persists beyond 24 hours or is interrupted by death within 24 hours." The time frame of 24 hours divides stroke from transient ischemic attack (TIA), the latter referring to a milder form of ischemia in which all neurological symptoms resolve within 24 hours.

Strokes are pathologically categorized into two major types: ischemic strokes and hemorrhagic strokes. Ischemic strokes are those that are caused by interruption of the cerebral blood supply without bleeding whereas hemorrhagic strokes involve rupture of a cerebral blood vessel and leakage of blood into the brain. Approximately 85% of strokes are classified as ischemic and the remainder (about 15%) are hemorrhagic. Hemorrhagic strokes are often further subdivided into intracerebral hemorrhage and subarachnoid hemorrhage. Intracerebral hemorrhage accounts for about 10% of all strokes. This subtype involves the leakage of blood from cerebral vessels directly into the brain. Subarachnoid hemorrhage accounts for about 5% of all strokes and involves the leakage of blood into the subarachnoid space between the arachnoid membrane and the pia mater at the periphery of the brain (Donnan et al., 2008).

Hippocrates (460 to 370 BC) first described the sudden paralysis characteristic of an ischemic stroke (Thompson, 1996). Ischemia (lack of oxygen) of brain tissue rapidly develops when one of the cerebral arteries is occluded by a thrombus (a blood clot) or embolus (detached fragment of a blood clot) or when a cerebral blood vessel ruptures leading to frank hemorrhage of blood into the brain. Brain tissue ceases to function if deprived of oxygen for more than 60 to 90 seconds and after approximately 3 hours, will suffer irreversible injury possibly leading to death (infarction) of the tissue. As a result, the affected area of the brain is unable to function, leading to inability to move one or more limbs on one side of the body, inability to understand or formulate speech, or inability to see one side of the visual field.

The postmortem pathologic examination of brains from patients suffering fatal strokes has provided critical information regarding the distribution of cerebral infarction and the distinction between ischemic and hemorrhagic strokes. The famous German pathologist, Rudolph Virchow, is credited with first describing thromboembolism as a major event in the pathogenesis of stroke (Schiller, 1970).

Ischemic strokes are most often caused by occlusive thrombi in larger blood vessels of the brain such as the internal carotid, the upper vertebral and lower basilar arteries (Fisher, 1975). Occlusive thrombi tend to occur in and around ruptured atheromatous plaques that have developed in the lining (endothelium) of these blood vessels. Emboli that migrate from other sites, e.g., the heart or aorta, and occlude smaller caliber cerebral arteries of the brain can also cause an ischemic stroke.

Various systems have been devised to categorize the subtypes of ischemic stroke based upon clinical symptoms and imaging studies. In one system, the *Trial of Organization 10172 in Acute Stroke Treatment (TOAST)*, ischemic strokes are categorized into five specific etiologic subtypes: (1) thrombus or embolus arising from large artery atherosclerosis, (2) cardioembolism, (3) small vessel occlusion (lacune) associated with diabetes and/or hypertension, (4) other etiology such as coagulopathy, e.g., sickle cell anemia, and (5) undetermined etiology (Adams et al., 1993).

In contrast to ischemic strokes, intracerebral hemorrhagic strokes are more likely to involve embolic occlusion and rupture of smaller cerebral blood vessels. By definition, intracerebral hemorrhagic strokes involve the leakage of blood from cerebral blood vessels directly into the brain. Occlusive emboli are found most frequently at points of arterial bifurcation (branching) or narrowing of the lumens of cerebral blood vessels. Emboli typically arise when a fragment of thrombus is dislodged in the left ventricle of the heart or the aortic arch and travels into a small caliber cerebral artery, often a branch of the middle cerebral artery (Schoene, 1979). Emboli typically arise in the heart as a consequence of atrial fibrillation.

A special subtype of hemorrhagic stroke is caused by subarachnoid hemorrhage. Subarachnoid hemorrhage arises due to leakage of blood from ruptured blood vessels into the subarachnoid space surrounding the brain. Ruptured aneurysms are the cause of 85% of cases of subarachnoid hemorrhage. The collection of blood in the subarachnoid space can cause compression of the brain thereby leading to infarction and stroke. Subarachnoid hemorrhagic strokes have a very high case fatality rate (40–50%) and frequently occur in young adults (van Gijn, Kerr, and Rinkel, 2007).

Hemorrhagic strokes, especially the subarachnoid hemorrhagic subtype, are usually caused by the rupture of aneurysms which are balloon-like dilatations of the walls of diseased blood vessels. Aneurysms most commonly occur in cerebral arteries (cerebral aneurysm) at the base of the brain (the circle of Willis) and in the aorta (aortic aneurysm). As the size of an aneurysm increases, there is an increased risk of rupture, which can result in severe hemorrhage, other complications, or even death.

Hemorrhagic strokes injure and destroy neurons due to physical compression of tissue from the expanding hematoma, ischemia due to loss of blood supply, and direct toxic effects of blood on brain tissue and vasculature. Loss of consciousness, headache, and vomiting tend to occur more often in hemorrhagic stroke than in thrombosis because of the increased intracranial pressure from the leaking blood compressing the brain.

Whether a stroke is classified as ischemic or hemorrhagic, the underlying pathogenesis invariably involves the long-term process of atherogenesis (development of atheromatous plaque in blood vessels). Cerebral infarction (stroke) is one of two major culminating events of this process, the other being heart attack (myocardial infarction). Upon rupture of an atheromatous plaque, platelet activation and initiation of the clotting cascade rapidly ensue resulting in formation of a thrombus or embolus and potential occlusion of cerebral blood vessels, ischemia and infarction (death) of neurons, and significant loss of brain function and/or death. Hypertension is also a primary risk factor, particularly for hemorrhagic stroke.

VASCULAR NETWORK OF THE BRAIN

Oxygenated blood from the left heart travels upward through the carotid and vertebral arteries arising from the aortic arch and is distributed to the brain through a complex network of cerebral arteries, arterioles, and capillaries (**Figure 5.1**). At the base of the brain, the internal carotid and vertebral arteries join to form the arterial circle of Willis, an intricate system with branches that nourish many of the internal structures of the brain.

Approximately 15% of the blood ejected by the left ventricle of the heart is jettisoned upwards into the brain. The cerebral arteries deliver oxygenated blood, glucose, and other nutrients to the brain and the cerebral veins carry deoxygenated blood back to the heart, removing carbon dioxide, lactic acid, and other metabolic products. Although the human brain represents only 2% of the total body weight, it consumes 20% of total body oxygen, and 25% of total body energy. The arterial circulation that nourishes the brain consists of hundreds of branching vessels that become progressively smaller at each bifurcation. The tortuous nature of this arterial network predisposes to stenosis (narrowing) due to atherosclerotic plaque and/or acute occlusion of blood flow by a thrombus or embolism, particularly in and around the junctions where larger vessels bifurcate into smaller caliber vessels.

The lining (endothelium) of very small blood vessels (capillaries) of the brain consists of cells with tight junctions that prevent invasion/contamination by bacteria and other substances in the blood. This is the *blood-brain barrier* first identified by the German bacteriologist and Nobel Laureate, Paul Ehrlich, and his student Edwin Goldman in 1909 (Bradbury, 1979).

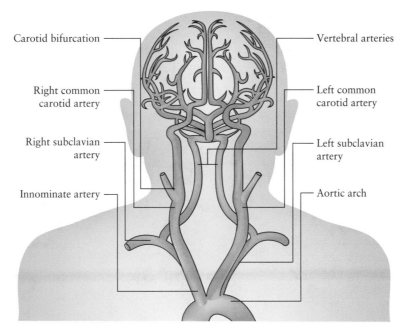

Figure 5.1 Major Cerebral Arteries.

GLOBAL MORTALITY OF STROKE

Strokes afflict more than 15 million people annually in the world population, and approximately one-third (5.5 million) are fatal (Lopez et al., 2006; World Health Organization, 2009, 2010). Stroke ranks second in overall global mortality and has outstripped ischemic heart disease as the leading cause of death in some developing countries, e.g., Hungary, Belgium, and Russia. Annual mortality rates adjusted for age and gender reflect a wide range from less than 50 deaths per 100,000 in nations of North America, Western Europe, and Australia to greater than 250 deaths per 100,000 in nations of Northern and Central Asia, Eastern Europe, Middle Africa, and the South Pacific (**Figure 5.2**). Approximately 85% of the annual deaths from stroke (4.7 million) occur in developing nations where both the incidence and mortality are increasing. The international trends in the mortality from stroke are similar to that for coronary heart disease and cardiovascular disease in general.

Strokes cause both death and disability thus creating a dual health burden. A combined measure of disease health burden that takes into account the years of life lost due to premature death (YLL) plus the years lost due to severe disability (YLD) is the Disability-Adjusted Life Years (DALY = YLL + YLD).

National estimates of the DALYs that are lost due to cerebrovascular disease (primarily stroke) are depicted in Figure 5.3 (Mackay and Mensah, 2004; Johnston, Mendis, and Mathers, 2009). The global DALY pattern is quite similar to that for stroke mortality. The DALYs show a wide range from less than 250 years of life lost annually in certain high income nations (North America, Western Europe, Australia) to levels greater than 2,000 in some middle and low income nations (Eastern Europe, Russia, Central Africa). In general, high income nations have lower DALYs and middle and low income nations have higher DALYs. In a systematic review of mortality and DALY rates, the national per capita income was found to be the strongest predictor of stroke mortality and DALY loss even after adjustment for cerebrovascular disease risk factors (Johnston et al., 2009). This pattern reflects earlier onset of both fatal and nonfatal debilitating strokes in nations with inadequate resources to support effective preventive and therapeutic health services.

DECLINE IN STROKE MORTALITY IN DEVELOPED NATIONS

In developed nations, most notably in North America, Japan, and Western Europe, mortality rates from stroke have declined markedly in the past

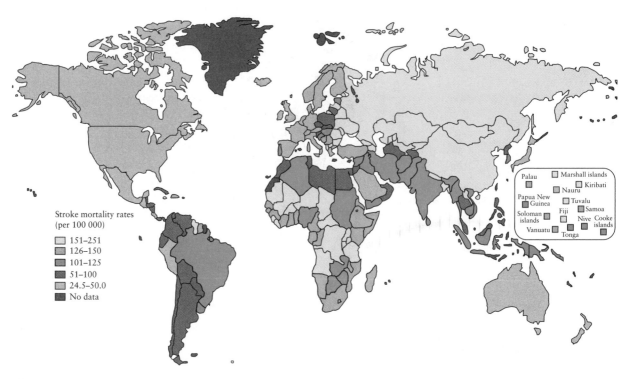

Figure 5.2 Global Mortality from Stroke: 2002.

Source: Reprinted with permission from Johnston SC, Mendis S, Mathers CD (2009). Global variation in stroke burden and mortality: Estimates from monitoring, surveillance, and modeling. *Lancet Neurology* 8(4):345–354.

half-century (Murray and Lopez, 1997; Sudlow and Warlow, 1997; Feigin et al., 2003; Johnston, Mendis, and Mathers, 2009). The declining mortality trends for stroke and coronary heart disease in the United States are depicted in Figure 5.4. These declining trends in mortality are largely attributable to primary prevention (avoidance of smoking and maintaining blood pressure, serum cholesterol and blood glucose within normal limits using both nonpharmacologic and pharmacologic methods) plus secondary

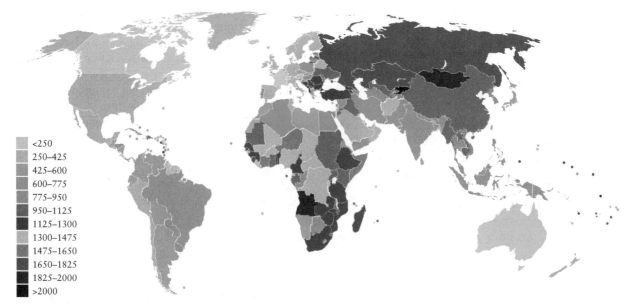

Figure 5.3 Disability-Adjusted Life Years for Cerebrovascular Disease, 2004.

Source: Data from World Health Organization. The global burden of disease: 2004 update. Geneva, WHO, 2008. Available at www.who.int/evidence/bod

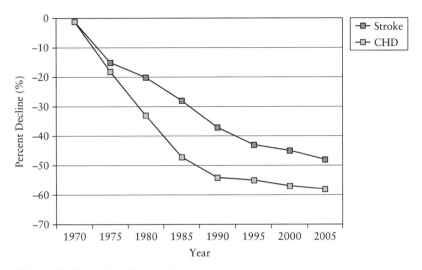

Figure 5.4 Decline in Mortality from Stroke and Coronary Heart Disease: USA, 1970–2005.

Source: Data from National Institutes of Health, Center for Health Statistics, 2009.

prevention (treatment of hypertension, hyperlipidemia, and hyperglycemia and use of antithrombotic/antiplatelet therapy, e.g., low dose aspirin, for individuals with atrial fibrillation) (Straus, Majumdar, and McAlister, 2002). Evidence supporting the value of each of these preventive modalities is discussed in the section of this chapter on stroke prevention.

RACIAL DIFFERENCES IN STROKE MORTALITY IN THE UNITED STATES

Racial disparities in stroke mortality and incidence are similar to that for coronary heart disease

with rates being markedly higher among African Americans compared to Caucasian Americans (Figure 5.5). Various reasons have been proposed to explain this disparity including greater exposure to known risk factors and relatively poor access to both preventive and therapeutic healthcare services. In particular, the high prevalence and inadequate management of hypertension probably account for much of the excess in stroke mortality among African Americans (Kittner et al., 1990; Gillum, 1999).

In 1962, investigators at the Centers for Disease Control and Prevention noted a concentration of high mortality from stroke in certain regions of the

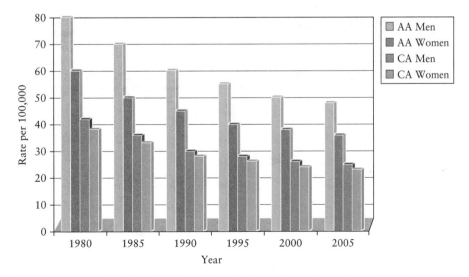

Figure 5.5 Stroke Mortality in African Americans and Caucasian Americans: USA, 1980–2005.

Source: Data from US Center for Health Statistics, National Institutes of Health, 2009. The Stroke Belt, USA.

southeastern United States (Atlantic coastal plain counties of North Carolina, South Carolina, Georgia, and the Mississippi Delta) (Casper et al., 1995). The Stroke Belt in the United States is typically defined to include the states of Alabama, Arkansas, Georgia, Indiana, Kentucky, Louisiana, Mississippi, North Carolina, South Carolina, Tennessee, and Virginia. In 1980 these 11 states had age-adjusted stroke mortality rates more than 10% above the national average (National Heart, Lung and Blood Institute, 1996). Some investigators also include northern Florida as part of the Stroke Belt due to the high mortality from stroke (Siegal et al., 1992).

Several factors have been proposed to explain the high stroke mortality observed in the Stroke Belt. As discussed in the following section on risk factors, stroke is a catastrophic culminating event of multifactorial disease processes. It is therefore likely that the Stroke Belt reflects a web of causative factors such as hypertension, obesity, smoking, lack of exercise, atherosclerosis-prone diets high in fat

and fried foods, and relatively poor access to emergency medical services. One striking feature of the US Stroke Belt is its overlying pattern with US lung cancer mortality (Centers for Disease Control and Prevention, 2004). As shown in Figure 5.6, the Stroke Belt also has high lung cancer mortality, perhaps reflecting the contribution of smoking to both conditions (Peto et al., 2006).

RISK FACTORS FOR STROKE

The INTERSTROKE Study

The INTERSTROKE Study provides an international perspective on the risk factors for stroke (O'Donnell et al., 2010). This investigation was conducted in parallel with the INTERHEART Study of myocardial infarction during 2007 to 2010. INTERSTROKE was designed as a standardized case-control study involving 22 countries worldwide. The investigation

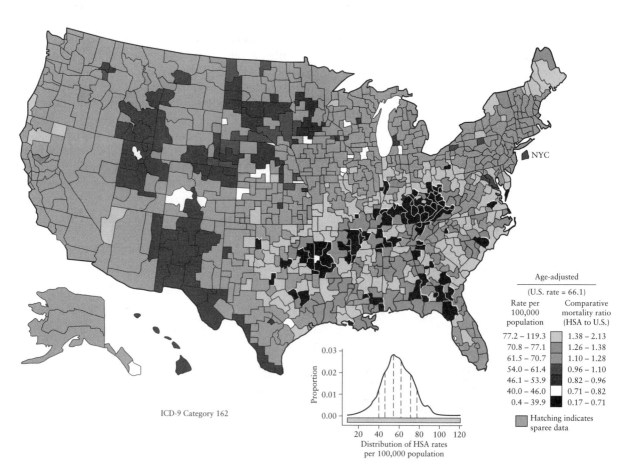

Figure 5.6 Lung Cancer Mortality and the Stroke Belt, 2004, USA.

Source: Centers for Disease Control and Prevention, National Center for Health Statistics, United States Department of Health and Human Services, 2004.

Table 5.1	Risk Factors for Stroke: INTERSTROKE Study, 2010	
Risk Factor	Odds Ratio	Population Attributable Risk
Hypertension	2.6	35%
Current Smoking	2.1	19%
Waist to Hip Ratio	1.7	26%
Unhealthy Diet	1.4	19%
Regular Exercise	0.7	29%
Diabetes Mellitus	1.4	5%
Alcohol Abuse	1.5	4%
Psychological Factors	1.3	5%
Cardiac Disease	1.5	7%
ApoB/ApoA1	1.9	25%

Source: Data from O'Donnell MJ, Xavier D, Liu L, Zhang H, Chin S-L, Melacini PR, Rangarajan S, Islam S, Pais P, McQueen MJ, Mondo C, Damasceno A, Lopez-Jaramillo P, Hankey GJ, Dans AL, Yusoff K, Truelsen T, Diener H-C, Sacco RL, Ryglewicz D, Czlonkowska A, Weimar C, Wang X, Yusuf S on behalf of the INTERSTROKE Investigators (2010). Risk factors for ischemic and intracerebral hemorrhagic stroke in 22 countries (the INTERSTROKE study): A case-control study. *Lancet* 376(9735):112–123.

compared 2,337 cases with acute stroke to 3,000 controls without stroke that were matched to the cases by age and gender. The findings are summarized in Table 5.1.

Collectively, 10 risk factors accounted for almost 90% of the population attributable risk for acute stroke in the INTERSTROKE Study. As expected, the strongest risk factor was hypertension (odds ratio = 2.6); nevertheless, several other factors including smoking, abdominal obesity (measured by high waist to hip ratio), hyperlipidemia (measured by high ApoB/ApoA1 ratio), a dietary risk score, and alcohol abuse were also significant risk factors for both ischemic stroke and hemorrhagic stroke (O'Donnell et al., 2010).

The findings of INTERSTROKE provide international confirmation of a number of modifiable stroke risk factors that were first identified and quantified through many previous epidemiologic investigations. Nonmodifiable risk factors for stroke include the aging process (the risk of acute stroke doubles for each decade of life after age 55 years), gender (men are at higher risk), and hereditary factors (a family history of stroke in one or more first degree relatives [father, mother, sibling] approximately doubles the risk).

Blood Pressure and Stroke

The strongest risk factor for stroke is hypertension, which is clinically definable as systolic blood pressure above 140 mm Hg or diastolic blood pressure above 90 mm Hg. Hypertension is modifiable through both nonpharmacologic modalities as well as by pharmacologic therapy, e.g., taking antihypertensive medications.

Homeostatic regulation of blood pressure is a complex physiological process dependent upon kidney function, vasoactive hormones, the sympathetic and parasympathetic divisions of the autonomic nervous system, the central nervous system and many lifestyle factors such as diet, exercise, physical condition, body mass, and emotional status. Since hypertension is a powerful risk factor in the development of stroke, the risk factors for stroke and hypertension are synonymous. These include smoking, high dietary salt, obesity, elevated blood lipids, diabetes mellitus (particularly type 2 diabetes), sedentary life style, drug abuse (cocaine), and certain emotional factors (high stress or depression).

The evidence that blood pressure is a major causative factor in the genesis of strokes is compelling. In an exhaustive meta-analysis involving more than 1 million subjects from 61 prospective studies published in the scientific literature, the rates of stroke mortality were compared according to systolic and diastolic blood pressure at baseline (Lewington et al., 2002). The authors included all prospective observational studies that collected data on blood pressure, blood cholesterol, date of birth (or age), and sex at baseline, and in which cause of death and date of death (or age at death) for all participants during more than 5,000 person-years of follow-up were available.

As shown in **Figure 5.7**, persons with systolic blood pressure 20 mm Hg less than the reference category (>115 mm Hg) or persons with diastolic blood pressure 10 mm Hg less than the reference category (>75 mm Hg) significantly reduced their risk

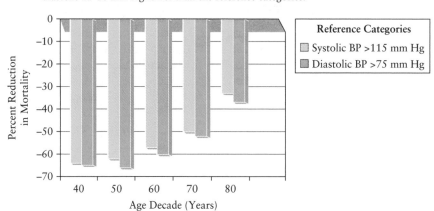

Estimates are for adults of increasing age with systolic BP 20 mm Hg lower or diastolic BP 10 mm Hg lower than the reference categories.

Figure 5.7 Reduction in Stroke Mortality in Adults with Reduced Blood Pressure.

Source: Data from Lewington S, Clarke R, Qizilbash N, Peto R, Collins R, Prospective Studies Collaboration. (2002). Age-specific relevance of usual blood pressure to vascular mortality: A meta-analysis of individual data for one million adults in 61 prospective studies. *Lancet* 360:1903–1913.

of death from stroke. Reductions in mortality were somewhat dependent upon age, e.g., older individuals (70 years and older) reduced their risk by 30–50% whereas younger individuals (less than 70 years) reduced their risk by 50–60% (Lewington et al., 2002). These data, compiled from the existing literature on blood pressure and stroke from prospective investigations, clearly and definitively accentuate the attributes of maintaining blood pressure within normal limits.

Ecological studies are designed to provide estimates of correlations between population-based disease incidence rates (or mortality rates) and exposure rates of potential risk factors. Such correlations do not necessarily imply causality and should be interpreted cautiously as a basis for further etiologic investigations.

Ecological studies show positive correlations between prevalence rates of hypertension and incidence and mortality rates of stroke. In the World Health Organization MONICA Project, blood pressure prevalence estimates for population samples from around the Baltic Sea were found to be positively correlated with the incidence of stroke in men (r = 0.87) and women (r = 0.70) (Stegmayr et al., 1996); subsequently, a further analysis of MONICA data revealed positive correlations for men (r = 0.42) and women (r = 0.56) in 18 population samples from widely diverse geographic regions (Stegmayer et al., 1997). These studies prompted an analysis of 16 MONICA population samples that revealed significant negative correlations between frequencies of effective blood pressure control in hypertensive cases and incidence and mortality rates of stroke (Banegas and Pérez-Regadera, 1998;

Banegas et al., 1998). Finally, hypertension and stroke were also positively correlated (r = 0.78) in an international study of North American and European nations (Wolf-Maier et al., 2003).

Review and meta-analysis of data from clinical trials provide strong evidence that aggressive treatment of elevated blood pressure using antihypertensive medications significantly reduces the risk of acute stroke. For example, a meta-analysis of 398 such trials found a risk reduction of 21% across all studies with adjustment for interindividual variability in response to different classes of antihypertensive medications (Webb et al., 2010).

In an exploration of 3 Japanese cohorts containing a total of 27,172 adults aged 40–69 years in successive time periods from 1963–1994, the incidence of acute stroke after 10 years of average follow-up showed a significant dose response with increasing blood pressure (BP) and even individuals with suboptimal blood pressure (systolic BP between 130–139 mm Hg or diastolic BP between 80–89 mm Hg) were at higher risk than individuals with lesser BP (Imano et al., 2009). These findings suggest that the early management of even mild hypertension with antihypertensive medications is beneficial in the primary prevention of acute stroke.

Lowering elevated blood pressure among first stroke victims by antihypertensive medication has also been found to be effective in the prevention of recurrent strokes. In a meta-analysis of 10 clinical trials, administration of antihypertensive agents to first stroke victims reduced the incidence of recurrent stroke by about 30% (Lakhan and Sapko, 2009).

Cigarette Smoking and Stroke

Smoking has been etiologically linked to stroke in a number of epidemiologic investigations. In an early meta-analysis of data from 32 separate epidemiologic studies (17 cohort studies, 14 case control studies, and one clinical trial), the summary relative risk of stroke associated with cigarette smoking was 1.5 and there was a significant dose response in risk with number of cigarettes smoked, e.g., the summary estimates of relative risk for daily smokers of 1–10, 11–20, and >20 cigarettes were 1.37, 1.45, and 1.82, respectively (Shinton and Beevers, 1989). Estimates by subtype also suggested that the risk of subarachnoid hemorrhage associated with smoking (RR = 2.93) was elevated more so than other subtypes of stroke (RR = 1.43). These results are in close agreement with findings of the large international INTERSTROKE case control study in which heavy smoking also resulted in an approximate twofold increase in the risk of stroke (O'Donnell et al., 2010). Selected prospective cohort studies of smoking and stroke are described in the following paragraphs.

The impact of cigarette smoking on the incidence of stroke was examined in the Framingham Heart Study cohort of 4,255 men and women aged 36–68 years and free of symptoms at baseline. During 26 years of follow-up, 459 strokes were detected in the cohort. After adjustment for age, gender, and other risk factors, the relative risk of stroke among heavy smokers (at least 2 packs per day) was double that of light smokers (less than 10 cigarettes per day). Among individuals who quit smoking during the study, stroke risk decreased to the level of nonsmokers by 5 years after smoking cessation (Wolf et al., 1988).

The Oslo Study was designed as a prospective cohort study of cardiovascular diseases in Norway. The cohort contained 16,173 men aged 40–49 years who were asymptomatic at baseline. After 18 years of follow-up, 85 individuals suffered fatal strokes in the cohort, only 4 of which had never smoked. Daily smokers compared to never smokers had a relative risk of 3.5 and individuals who smoked cigarettes, pipes, and cigars had a relative risk of 6.1. On average, the cases had significantly increased systolic and diastolic blood pressure compared to disease-free individuals (Håheim et al., 1996).

The British Regional Heart Study was designed as a prospective cohort study to examine risk factors for cardiovascular disease in Great Britain. The cohort consisted of 7,735 asymptomatic men aged 40–59 years at baseline randomly drawn from 24 British towns during 1978 to 1980. During 12.5 years of average follow-up, 167 individuals suffered strokes. Current smokers and ex-smokers had relative risks of 3.7 and 1.7, respectively, compared to never smokers and those who smoked pipes or cigars had a relative risk of 2.2. Individuals who quit smoking reduced their risk significantly after five years of smoking cessation (Wannamethee et al., 1995).

Investigators at Harvard studied smoking and stroke in a prospective cohort of 118,539 asymptomatic women aged 30–55 years at baseline. During 8 years of follow-up, 274 strokes were identified and classified by subtype. Compared to never smokers, women who smoked 1–24 cigarettes per day had an age-adjusted relative risk of 2.2 for all subtypes of stroke and those who smoked 25 or more cigarettes per day had a relative risk of 3.7. The risk of subarachnoid hemorrhagic stroke among heavy smokers was increased nearly tenfold. These prospective data support a causal relationship between smoking and stroke in women (Colditz et al., 1988).

As a part of the US Physicians' Health Study (a randomized clinical trial designed to determine the value of aspirin and beta-carotene in preventing cardiovascular disease among 22,022 male physicians), associations between smoking and stroke have been examined in ancillary studies. After 10 years of follow-up, 312 individuals suffered nonfatal strokes. Adjusted relative risks were 1.2 for former smokers, 2.0 for current smokers of less than 20 cigarettes per day, and 2.5 for current smokers of 20 or more cigarettes per day (Robbins et al., 1994).

In a subsequent investigation of the same cohort of US male physicians, investigators examined the risk of specific subtypes of hemorrhagic stroke (subarachnoid hemorrhage and intracerebral hemorrhage). After nearly 18 years of follow-up, 139 hemorrhagic strokes were identified and subclassified by subtype. Compared to never smokers, men smoking less than 20 cigarettes per day had a relative risk of 1.6 (for all subtypes of hemorrhagic stroke) and men smoking 20 or more cigarettes per day had a relative risk of 2.4. The effects of smoking were similar for subtypes of hemorrhagic strokes (Kurth et al., 2003).

Subarachnoid hemorrhagic strokes arise from the leakage of blood from ruptured blood vessels or aneurysms into the subarachnoid space. These lesions often occur in the circle of Willis and its branches.

According to a review of 51 studies from 21 countries, the average annual incidence of subarachnoid hemorrhage is 9.1 per 100,000. Rates were highest in Japan and Finland (>20 per 100,000) and lowest in countries of South and Central America (<5 per 100,000) (de Rooij et al., 2007). Populations at highest risk for subarachnoid hemorrhage have high rates of smoking and hypertension (Stegmayr et al., 1997) and episodic alcohol abuse (Makela et al., 2001).

Feigin and colleagues examined the relationship of smoking to subarachnoid hemorrhage in a meta-analysis of 26 prospective cohort studies involving 306,620 participants in the Asia-Pacific region. This region has active research centers in Japan, China, Taiwan, South Korea, Singapore, and Australia. During a median follow-up of 8.2 years, a total of 236 incident cases of subarachnoid hemorrhage were observed. Current smoking and elevated systolic blood pressure (>140 mm Hg) independently increased the risk of subarachnoid hemorrhage (summary hazard ratios: 2.4 and 2.0, respectively) whereas no significant associations were found for cholesterol, body mass index, or drinking alcohol. For this population, it is estimated that 19% of cases are attributable to systolic blood pressure > 140 mm Hg and 29% of cases are attributable to smoking (Feigin et al., 2005).

In summary, the epidemiologic evidence is compelling that smoking accounts for a substantial portion of the morbidity and mortality due to stroke. Mechanistically, tobacco's addictive agent, nicotine, is a potent vasoconstrictor, and smoking the first cigarette of the day causes an abrupt rise in blood pressure (**Gropelli** et al., 1992; Omvik, 1996). Furthermore, numerous molecular studies have demonstrated that various elements of tobacco smoke including nicotine are highly inflammatory to the lining (endothelium) of blood vessels and are etiologically involved in the genesis of atherosclerotic plaque (Surgeon General's Report, 2004).

Alcohol Abuse and Stroke

The effects of alcohol on the cardiovascular system are dependent upon dose. While some observational studies have found that moderate or light consumption of alcoholic beverages confers a slight risk reduction, other studies of heavy consumption have noted an increase in the risk. To clarify the relationship, Reynolds and colleagues conducted a meta-analysis of alcohol and stroke using data from 35 published case-control and cohort studies. Compared to those who never consumed alcohol, individuals consuming more than 60 grams (about 5 drinks) per day had relative risks of 1.6 for any stroke, 1.4 for ischemic stroke, and 2.2 for hemorrhagic stroke. In contrast, those individuals consuming less than 12 grams of alcohol daily had a slight risk reduction (RR = 0.83). The results suggest that alcohol abuse significantly increases the risk of stroke whereas light drinking may offer slight protection (Reynolds et al., 2003).

Cocaine, Amphetamines, and Stroke

Ischemic and hemorrhagic strokes occasionally occur in temporal association with the use/abuse of illicit drugs. In a case series of 167 stroke patients entered into the Maryland Stroke Data Bank, data were obtained on drug abuse for 116 cases. Eleven of these stroke patients (9.5%) reported a history of recent drug use, and five of these gave a history of cocaine abuse (Sloan et al., 1991).

There is also some evidence that amphetamine use is associated with an increased risk of stroke. In a cross-sectional study of hospital discharge data for young adults treated in Texas hospitals, amphetamine abuse was associated with ischemic stroke (odds ratio = 4.95) and cocaine abuse was associated with both ischemic stroke (OR = 2.03) and hemorrhagic stroke (OR = 2.33). These data suggest the potential danger of stroke with abuse of stimulant drugs (Westover, McBride, and Haley, 2007).

Atrial Fibrillation and Stroke

Atrial fibrillation is the most common cardiac arrhythmia (abnormal heart rhythm). In this condition, the normal electrical impulses that arise in the sinoatrial node of the heart become disorganized leading to fibrillation (quivering) of the heart muscle rather than coordinated contractions. Chronic atrial fibrillation carries an increased risk of stroke. As depicted in **Figure 5.8**, a thrombus in the left ventricular chamber of the heart can be dislodged by atrial fibrillation and migrate into the brain via the internal carotid artery leading to embolic occlusion of a cerebral artery and acute stroke.

Several epidemiologic investigations have found that individuals diagnosed with atrial fibrillation have a markedly increased risk of stroke. **Table 5.2** presents relative risk estimates from four separate studies of atrial fibrillation and stroke: Framingham in the United States (Wolf, Abbott, and Kannel, 1991), the Shibata Study in Japan (Tanaka et al., 1985; Nakayama et al., 1997), the Reykjavik Study in Iceland (Onundarson et al., 1987), and an investigation in Great Britain (Flegel, Shipley, and Rose, 1987).

The data of Table 5.2 reflect greater than five-fold increases in the relative risk of stroke associated with atrial fibrillation for populations of diverse culture living in markedly different environments. Furthermore, some studies suggest that women with atrial fibrillation may be at greater risk than men, e.g., analysis of the Japanese cohort in Shibata after more than 15 years of follow-up revealed a twofold higher stroke risk for women with atrial fibrillation

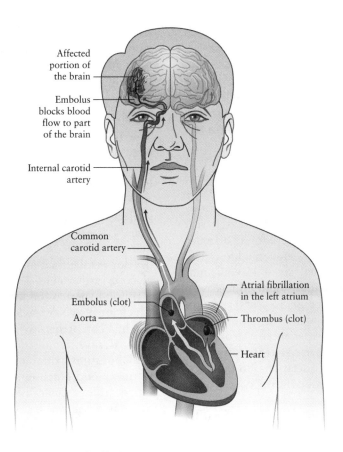

Figure 5.8 Genesis of Acute Stroke by Atrial Fibrillation.

(RR = 10.7) compared to men (RR = 5.2) (Nakayama et al., 1997). These estimates and data from several other studies suggest that about one in three individuals with atrial fibrillation will experience a stroke during their lifetime (Halperin and Hart, 1988). The

Table 5.2	Atrial Fibrillation and Risk of Stroke		
		Stroke Rate	Relative
Study Location	Mean Age	AF	No AF	Risk
Framingham, USA	70	4.1	0.74	5.6
Shibata, Japan	65	5.0	0.90	5.6
Reykjavik, Iceland	52	1.6	0.23	7.2
Whitehall, UK	60	1.8	0.26	6.9

AF = Atrial Fibrillation
Stroke Rate = annual percentage of individuals who developed stroke
Source: Data from Wolf et al. (1991). Atrial fibrillation as an independent risk factor for stroke: The Framingham Study. *Stroke* 22:983–988; Tanaka et al. (1985). Epidemiologic studies of stroke in Shibata, a Japanese provincial city: Preliminary report on risk factors for cerebral infarction. *Stroke* 16:773–780; Onundarson et al. (1987). Chronic atrial fibrillation—Epidemiologic features and 14 year follow-up: A case-control study. *Eur Heart J* 8:521–527; Flegel et al. (1987). Risk of stroke in nonrheumatic atrial fibrillation. *Lancet* 1:526–529; 24. Halperin JL, Hart RG. (1988). Atrial fibrillation and stroke: New ideas, persisting dilemmas. *Stroke* 19:937–941.

value of antithrombotic agents in the prevention atrial fibrillation is discussed below in the section on prevention.

Blood Lipids and Stroke

The INTERSTROKE investigation of stroke risk factors determined that the lipoprotein ratio of ApoB to ApoA1 was a stronger risk factor for stroke than other measures of lipids such as low-density lipoprotein (LDL) cholesterol or total cholesterol (O'Donnell et al., 2010). Consequently, investigators are continuing to explore the association of certain lipoproteins with the risk of cardiovascular disease including stroke. For example, one lipoprotein that specifically binds low-density (bad) cholesterol is lipoprotein(a). A meta-analysis of 27 prospective studies revealed a significant risk increase (RR = 1.6) in coronary heart disease among persons with elevated lipoprotein(a) levels (Danesh, Collins, and Peto, 2000).

The relationship of lipoprotein(a) to stroke was recently examined in a meta-analysis of 31 epidemiologic (Smolders, Lemmens, and Thijs, 2007). In 23 case control studies involving 2,600 strokes, the mean level of lipoprotein(a) was significantly higher in stroke patients than controls and individuals with higher than normal values were at increased risk (odds ratio: 2.37). In 5 prospective cohort studies involving 1,645 strokes, the incidence of stroke was more frequent among individuals in the highest tertile of lipoprotein(a) levels measured at baseline. The authors conclude that elevated lipoprotein(a) is a risk factor for stroke.

Serum cholesterol continues to be of interest as a biomarker of cardiovascular disease risk and its relationship to stroke has been examined in many epidemiologic investigations. The results of these studies are mixed; some showing increased risk with high levels whereas others have found no association. A team of investigators attempted to clarify the association in a meta-analysis of 45 epidemiologic studies involving 450,000 individuals with 5–30 years of follow-up (average: 16 years) and a total of 7.3 million person-years of observation during which 13,397 participants experienced a stroke. The summary estimates of relative risk from this analysis were null reflecting no association of total blood cholesterol to the risk of stroke (Prospective Studies Collaboration, 1995).

Despite these null results, some investigators have noted rising levels of blood cholesterol in many Asian nations and therefore have continuing concern about potential impending increases in the incidence of stroke and other cardiovascular events. To explore this possibility, a team of investigators examined the association of blood cholesterol with incident coronary heart disease and stroke in the Asia-Pacific Region (Asian Pacific Cohort Studies Collaboration, 2003). Meta-analysis was applied to the combined data from 29 prospective cohorts containing 352,033 individuals from sites in China, Japan, Taiwan, South Korea, Singapore, and Australia. During 2 million person-years of follow-up, 4,842 fatalities/events due to cardiovascular disease were recorded. In this investigation, each 1 mmol per liter (38.7 mg per deciliter) increase in total blood cholesterol was associated with a 35% increase in the risk of coronary death and a 25% increase in the risk of fatal or nonfatal ischemic stroke. There was a modest inverse association of cholesterol with hemorrhagic stroke. These results were similar for both Asian and non-Asian cohorts prompting the investigators to suggest that *"rising population-wide levels of cholesterol would be expected to contribute to a substantial increase in the overall burden of cardiovascular diseases in this region"* (Asian Pacific Cohort Studies Collaboration, 2003).

In view of such disparate results, it appears advisable to continue investigation of the association between cholesterol and the risk of stroke. Since many risk factors are involved in the genesis of all cardiovascular diseases including stroke, careful adjustment for confounding will be necessary to elucidate independent effects.

Diabetes Mellitus and Stroke

The rising incidence of diabetes mellitus in the developed world parallels the rising incidence of obesity. Adult-onset or type 2 diabetes is linked with overeating, metabolic overload, and obesity. The relationship of diabetes to the onset of stroke has been the subject of more than 100 epidemiologic investigations. There is compelling evidence that patients with diabetes mellitus are two to three times more likely to develop stroke than individuals with normal blood glucose; furthermore, diabetic individuals commonly manifest hypertension, obesity, and hyperlipidemia, which are also independent risk factors for stroke.

In a comprehensive literature review and meta-analysis, investigators of the Emerging Risk Factors Collaboration examined associations of diabetes, fasting blood glucose, and the risk of stroke and other cardiovascular diseases. The analysis of diabetes-related risk was based on 97 studies; 54 of them contributed to the separate analysis of risk associated with fasting blood glucose. Collectively, they provided 8.5 million person-years of follow-up, with a median time to a first vascular event, fatal or nonfatal, of 10.8 years. The hazard ratios (HR) for ischemic stroke and hemorrhagic stroke were both significantly increased, 2.27 and 1.56, respectively. The risk of coronary heart disease was also increased (HR = 2.0). Elevated levels of fasting blood glucose were also associated with increased risk, e.g., levels exceeding 6.0 mmol per liter (126 mg per deciliter) increased the risk of cardiovascular events by 70%. The investigators point out that the results can be generalized for only those populations of developed high income nations predominantly represented in the studies. Additional studies are needed to quantify the vascular disease burden attributable to diabetes in low and middle-income countries (Emerging Risk Factors Collaboration, 2010).

Obesity and Stroke

Obesity is a potentially important risk factor in the web of causation of stroke as well as most other cardiovascular diseases. A team of investigators in Italy and the United Kingdom conducted a systematic review and meta-analysis of prospective studies addressing the relationship of overweight and obesity to the incidence of ischemic and hemorrhagic stroke. Twenty-five studies were included with 2,274,961 participants and 30,757 events. The body mass index (BMI = kg/m^2) was used to define overweight and obesity. The relative risk for ischemic stroke increased by 22% in overweight individuals (BMI between 25 and 30) and by 64% in obese individuals (BMI of 30 or more). The risk for hemorrhagic stroke showed no increase in overweight individuals and the risk increase in obese individuals (24%) did not quite reach statistical significance. The results suggest that any degree of overweight may increase the risk of ischemic stroke (Strazzullo et al., 2010).

Obesity is integral to several important physiological and biological mechanisms that are known to increase the risk of stroke and other cardiovascular outcomes (Poirier et al., 2006). For example, weight gain increases blood pressure and the majority of hypertensive people are either overweight or obese (Stamler et al., 1978). In addition, obesity has been found to accelerate atherogenesis in young men (McGill et al., 2002) and is associated with dyslipidemia (Brown et al., 2000). Furthermore, obesity in combination with insulin resistance, type 2 diabetes, and elevated triglycerides defines a complex known as the *metabolic syndrome*, which carries a high risk of myocardial infarction and stroke (Eckel, Grundy, and Zimmet, 2005). Excess adiposity is also associated with increased secretion of inflammatory adipokines that may stimulate atherogenesis (Rost et al., 2001). To summarize, obesity increases blood pressure, insulin resistance, and blood lipids and promotes inflammation and atherosclerosis, all of which predispose to stroke.

Inflammation, C-Reactive Protein, and Stroke

Atherogenesis is often characterized as an inflammatory disease (Ross, 1999). Indeed, the inflammatory biomarker, C-reactive protein (CRP), has shown value as a valid predictor of impending coronary heart disease (Ridker et al., 2002).

To clarify the association of CRP with the risk of stroke, investigators in Boston studied the association of plasma CRP levels with the incidence of first ischemic stroke or transient ischemic attack (TIA) in the Framingham Study original cohort. The study included 591 men and 871 women (mean age about 70 years) with no history of stroke or TIA during their clinic examination during 1980 to 1982. The CRP levels were measured using an enzyme immunoassay on previously frozen serum samples. During 12–14 years of follow-up, 196 ischemic strokes and TIAs occurred. Independent of age, men in the highest CRP quartile had a twofold higher risk of ischemic stroke/TIA (RR = 2.0), and women had an almost threefold higher risk (RR = 2.7) compared to

those in the lowest quartile. The trend in the risk of stroke with increasing quartiles of CRP was highly significant. After adjustment for smoking, total/HDL cholesterol, systolic blood pressure, and diabetes, the increase in risk across CRP quartiles remained statistically significant for both men and women. The investigators concluded that elevated plasma CRP levels significantly predict the risk of ischemic stroke and TIA in the elderly (Rost et al., 2001).

PREVENTION OF STROKE

As is true for all cardiovascular diseases, stroke is a multifactorial disease; and as a consequence, preventive strategies must be designed to influence multiple factors in order to be successful. Similar to myocardial infarction, stroke is the culminating event of chronic disease processes that interact in a complex web of causation. Pathogenic mechanisms include hypertension, inflammation, atherogenesis, tobacco addiction, insulin resistance, alcohol abuse, obesity, and atrial fibrillation. All of these risk factors are potentially modifiable through appropriate lifestyle choices and/or therapeutic modalities.

Lifestyle decisions believed to have a favorable impact on stroke prevention include avoidance of tobacco use in any form; maintaining optimal body weight (BMI between 20–25) through exercise and healthy eating; limiting salt intake to less than 6 grams daily; limiting alcohol intake to no more than one drink daily; eating a diet with at least five servings of fruits and vegetables daily; eating fish and other sources of omega-3 polyunsaturated fatty acids on a regular basis (at least twice per week); exercising daily (e.g., brisk walking for 30 minutes); maintaining blood pressure, blood glucose, and blood cholesterol within normal limits through careful monitoring and pharmacologic therapy if needed; chemoprevention of thrombosis with low dose aspirin; and management of atrial fibrillation, hypertension, diabetes, and hyperlipidemia by appropriate sustained therapeutic care.

Diet and Stroke Prevention

Diet has been studied extensively in the prevention of stroke with mixed results. Ancel Keys and his colleagues found that the Mediterranean diet had the greatest benefit in the prevention of cardiovascular and cerebrovascular diseases including stroke (Keys et al., 1980). Furthermore, several other epidemiologic studies have found that increasing consumption of fruits and vegetables is associated with a decreased risk of stroke. Investigators at St. George University in London conducted a meta-analysis of eight studies consisting of nine independent cohorts in order to more precisely quantify the relationship of stroke and intake of fruits and vegetables (He, Nowson, and MacGregor, 2006). Their analysis included dietary data on 257,551 individuals followed on average for 13 years with detection of 4,917 stroke events. Compared to individuals who consumed less than 3 servings of fruits and vegetables daily, individuals consuming 3–5 servings had an 11% risk reduction and individuals consuming more than 5 servings had a 26% risk reduction. Estimates were consistent for both ischemic and hemorrhagic stroke and the authors suggest that daily consumption of 5 or more servings of fruits and vegetables has preventive value.

Various mechanisms have been advanced to explain the beneficial impact of consuming abundant fruits and vegetables in the diet. Fruits and vegetables are rich sources of potassium, folate, fiber, antioxidants (vitamin C, betacarotene, and flavonoids), and anti-inflammatory agents, all of which appear to have favorable effects in helping to maintain optimal blood pressure, blood lipids, and blood glucose.

Investigators at Harvard examined relationships of certain dietary factors (fish and omega-3 fatty acids) and the risk of stroke in the Nurse's Health Study. This prospective cohort study enrolled women aged 34–59 years who were disease free at baseline and agreed to complete a food frequency questionnaire and be followed to determine cardiovascular and other disease outcomes. A total of 79,839 eligible women were followed for up to 14 years (1,086,261 person-years) during which 574 incident strokes were detected. Women who ate fish five or more times per week significantly reduced their risk of stroke (RR = 0.48) compared to those who ate none, and there was a significant inverse dose response of decreasing risk with increasing consumption. Furthermore, women consuming high levels of omega-3 polyunsaturated fatty acids also lowered their risk (RR = 0.72). Stratification of the data by stroke subtypes revealed risk reductions for ischemic stroke but not for hemorrhagic stroke (Iso et al., 2001).

Investigators at Boston University conducted a meta-analysis of prospective studies to further examine the association of fish consumption to risk of stroke. Nine cohorts were identified in eight studies that provided relative risk estimates. Compared with individuals who consumed little or no fish, those who consumed fish at least 5 times per week reduced their risk by 31% (RR = 0.69) and even consumption levels of once per week resulted in a significant protective effect (RR = 0.87). Stratification of data by subtype of stroke revealed significant risk reductions for ischemic stroke but not for hemorrhagic stroke (He et al., 2004).

Fish are the main dietary source of long-chain omega-3 polyunsaturated fatty acids (PUFA), and these compounds have been shown to have favorable effects on blood pressure, arrhythmias, lipid profile, platelet aggregation, and endothelial function (Nestel, 1990; Harris, 1997). One principal mechanism by which fish consumption could benefit the cardiovascular system is reduction of inflammatory prostaglandins. Omega-3 and other complex polyunsaturated fatty acids are not readily transformed into arachidonic acid, the chief substrate of the inflammatory cascade. Intake of fish and other omega-3 polyunsaturated fatty acids could therefore reduce atherogenesis by inhibiting the inflammatory cascade (Dyerberg et al., 1978).

Salt and Stroke Prevention

The level of salt intake in the diet has significant impact on blood pressure and consequently influences the risk of stroke. Strazzullo and colleagues (2009) conducted a comprehensive meta-analysis of 19 independent cohort samples from 13 studies involving 177,025 participants, over 11,000 vascular events and follow-up of 3.5–19 years. They found that high salt intake (greater than 6 grams of salt per day) was associated with a 23% increase in the incidence of acute stroke.

Conversely, reduction in salt intake is advisable to reduce blood pressure for stroke protection. Strong evidence for this inverse association comes from the international INTERSALT Study involving 10,172 men and women aged 20–59 years enrolled for study in 52 centers from around the world (Intersalt Cooperative Research Group, 1988). The INTERSALT investigation was specifically designed to examine the relationship between blood pressure and 24-hour urinary excretion of electrolytes (sodium and potassium). Regression analysis revealed a significant linear relationship between sodium excretion and blood pressure whereby each 100 mmol reduction in sodium excretion independently reduced systolic blood pressure by 9 mm Hg. The results of INTERSALT also demonstrated that high urinary potassium is associated with lower (more optimal) blood pressure whereas high body mass and alcohol abuse significantly increase blood pressure.

Anticoagulation Drugs and Stroke Prevention

It has been estimated that one in three individuals who manifest atrial fibrillation will experience a stroke in their lifetime (Halperin and Hart, 1988). Atrial fibrillation is the most frequently diagnosed arrhythmia and in the United States population alone, 2.3 million people are affected. The prevalence of atrial fibrillation increases with age, approaching

10% in people older than 80 years. Management of atrial fibrillation includes many modalities: pharmacologic therapy aimed to keep patients in sinus rhythm and to control rate, electrical cardioversion, catheter ablation, as well as anticoagulation to prevent thromboembolic disease.

Oral anticoagulants such as warfarin or aspirin have been the mainstay of stroke prevention in patients with atrial fibrillation for more than half a century. A number of randomized clinical trials have been conducted to assess and compare the value of such drugs. In a meta-analysis of data from 5 completed trials, treatment of atrial fibrillation with warfarin reduced the risk of stroke by 84% in women and 60% in men (the total risk reduction was 68%). By comparison, treatment with aspirin produced lesser effects (15% risk reduction for the 75 mg dosage and 44% reduction for the 325 mg dosage). No increases were noted in the frequency of bleeding episodes for either drug. These findings support the value of antithrombotic (warfarin) therapy in stroke prevention for patients with atrial fibrillation (Atrial Fibrillation Investigators, 1994).

Additional studies have been conducted to evaluate the effectiveness and safety of warfarin administration to patients with atrial fibrillation in clinical practice. For example, a US study of 11,526 patients with atrial fibrillation who were treated in usual care settings in Northern California found a 51% reduction in the risk of thromboembolism among those treated with warfarin compared to those not receiving warfarin (Go et al., 2003). Furthermore, several randomized studies have shown that immediate aspirin therapy followed by warfarin therapy is an effective approach for the prevention of recurrence after a first stroke or ischemic attack (Hart, Palacio, and Pearce, 2002).

Statins in Stroke Prevention

As already discussed in this chapter, there is controversy regarding the association of serum cholesterol and stroke. Some studies suggest that elevated levels increase the risk (Asia-Pacific Cohort Studies Collaboration, 2003) whereas others do not (Prospective Studies Collaboration, 1995). Nevertheless, there appears to be consistency of evidence supporting the role of statin use to reduce stroke risk in patients with hyperlipidemia.

Investigators at Leiden University Medical Center in the Netherlands examined HMG-CoA reductase inhibitors* and the risk of stroke in a meta-analysis of 13 randomized clinical trials that enrolled 20,438 participants. A total of 181 strokes were observed in patients randomized to treatment with an HMG-CoA reductase inhibitor and 261 strokes in patients randomized to placebo. Treatment with an HMG-CoA reductase inhibitor led to an overall risk reduction of 31% (odds ratio = 0.69) (Blauw et al., 1997).

More recently, investigators in London conducted a meta-analysis to evaluate the impact of statin therapy on the risk of death in general, and the risk of stroke, specifically, among more than 121,000 study volunteers that participated in 42 clinical research trials. Among the volunteers taking statin drugs, death from any cause was reduced by 12% and the relative risk of stroke (all types) was reduced by 16%. Risk reductions were proportional to the magnitude of LDL cholesterol reduction achieved after initiation of statin therapy. Furthermore, analysis by subtype of stroke revealed that the risk of only ischemic "nonhemorrhagic" strokes was reduced by statin therapy. Ischemic strokes generally result from atherosclerosis of the carotid arteries and intracerebral arteries that supply the brain with blood. The incidence of "hemorrhagic" strokes, which usually result from poorly controlled high blood pressure, was not reduced by statin therapy (O'Regan et al., 2008).

The combined data suggest that statin therapy prevents ischemic stroke and reinforces the value of cholesterol reduction in reducing the risk of cardiovascular disease. Clearly, judicious administration of statins for cholesterol reduction is a valuable component of multifactorial strategies for the prevention of stroke, myocardial infarction, and other forms of coronary heart disease.

Surgical Intervention

Surgical procedures such as carotid endarterectomy or carotid angioplasty can be used to remove significant atherosclerotic narrowing (stenosis) of the carotid artery (the primary conduit for blood supply to the brain). Evidence of benefit comes from the analysis of pooled data from two randomized clinical trials involving 5,893 patients (the European Carotid Surgery Trial and the North American Symptomatic Carotid Endarterectomy Trial). For patients with greater than 50% stenosis of carotid arteries, endarterectomy reduced the 5-year risk of stroke from 20% to 5% (Rothwell et al., 2004).

---

*The enzyme HMG-CoA reductase (3-hydroxy-3-methyl-glutaryl-CoA reductase) is the rate-limiting enzyme of the mevalonate pathway, the metabolic pathway that produces cholesterol in humans and other mammals. This enzyme is the primary target of the cholesterol-lowering drugs known collectively as the statins.

● ● ● REFERENCES

Adams, H.P., Bendixen, B.H., Kappelle, L.J., et al. (1993). Classification of subtype of acute ischemic stroke. Definitions for use in a multicenter clinical trial. TOAST. Trial of Org 10172 in Acute Stroke Treatment. *Stroke, 24*(1), 35–41.

Asia-Pacific Cohort Studies Collaboration. (2003). Cholesterol, coronary heart disease, and stroke in the Asia Pacific region. *International Journal of Epidemiology, 32*, 563–572.

Atrial Fibrillation Investigators. (1994). Risk factors for stroke and efficacy of antithrombotic therapy in atrial fibrillation. Analysis of pooled data from five randomized controlled trials. *Arch Intern Med, 154*(13), 1449–1557.

Banegas J.R., & Pérez-Regadera, A.G. (1998). Hypertension control as an indicator of the geographical variation of stroke. *Stroke, 29*, 867–868.

Banegas, J.R., Rodriguez-Artalejo, F., de la Cruz, T.J.J., et al. (1998). Blood pressure in Spain: Distribution, awareness, control, and benefits of a reduction in average pressure. *Hypertension, 32*, 998–1002.

Blauw, G.J., Lagaay, M., Smelt, A.H.M., & Westendorp, R.G.J. (1997). A meta-analysis of randomized, placebo-controlled, double-blind trials with HMG-CoA reductase inhibitors. *Stroke, 28*, 946–950.

Bradbury, M. (1979). *The concept of a blood-brain barrier.* New York: John Wiley and Sons Ltd.

Brown, C.D., Higgins, M., Donato, K.A., et al. (2000). Body mass index and the prevalence of hypertension and dyslipidemia. *Obes Res, 8*, 605–619.

Casper, M.L., Wing, S., Anda, R.F., Knowles, M., & Pollard, R.A. (1995). The shifting stroke belt. Changes in the geographic pattern of stroke mortality in the United States, 1962 to 1988. *Stroke, 26*(5), 755–760.

Centers for Disease Control and Prevention. (2004). National Center for Health Statistics, United States Department of Health and Human Services.

Colditz, G.A., Bonita, R., Stampfer, M.J., et al. (1988). Cigarette smoking and risk of stroke in middle-aged women. *N Engl J Med, 318*(15), 937–941.

Danesh, J., Collins, R., & Peto, R. (2000). Lipoprotein(a) and coronary heart disease. Meta-analysis of prospective studies. *Circulation, 102*(10), 1082–1085.

de Rooij, N.K., Linn, F.H., van der Plas, J.A., et al. (2007). Incidence of subarachnoid haemorrhage: A systematic review with emphasis on region, age, gender and time trends. *Journal of Neurology, Neurosurgery, and Psychiatry, 78*(12), 1365–1372.

Donnan, G.A., Fisher, M., Macleod, M., & Davis, S.M. (2008). Stroke. *Lancet, 371*(9624), 612–1623.

Dyerberg, J., Bang, H.O., Stoffersen, E., Moncada, S., & Vane, J.R. (1978). Eicosapentaenoic acid and prevention of thrombosis and atherosclerosis? *Lancet, 2*, 117–119.

Eckel, R.H., Grundy, S.M., & Zimmet, P.Z. (2005). The metabolic syndrome. *Lancet, 365*, 1415–1428.

Emerging Risk Factors Collaboration. (2010). Diabetes mellitus, fasting blood glucose concentration, and risk of vascular disease: A collaborative meta-analysis of 102 prospective studies. *Lancet, 375*, 2215–2222.

Feigin, V.L., Lawes, C.M., Bennett, D.A., & Anderson, C.S. (2003). Stroke epidemiology: A review of population-based studies of incidence, prevalence, and case fatality in the late 20th century. *Lancet Neurol, 2*, 43–53.

Feigin, V., Parag, V., Lawes, C.M., et al. (2005). Smoking and elevated blood pressure are the most important risk factors for subarachnoid hemorrhage in the Asia-Pacific region: An overview of 26 cohorts involving 306,620 participants. *Stroke, 36*, 1360–1365.

Fisher, C.M. (1975). Anatomy and pathology of the cerebral vasculature. *Modern Concepts in Cerebrovascular Disease, 1*, 41.

Flegel, K.M., Shipley, M.J., & Rose, G. (1987). Risk of stroke in nonrheumatic atrial fibrillation. *Lancet, 1,* 526–529.

Gillum, R.F. (1999). Stroke mortality in blacks: Disturbing trends. *Stroke, 30,* 1711–1715.

Go, A.S., Hylek, E.M., Chang, Y., et al. (2003). Anticoagulation therapy for stroke prevention in atrial fibrillation: How well do randomized trials translate into clinical practice? *JAMA, 290*(20), 2685–2692.

Gropelli, A., Giorgi, D.M.A., Omboni, S., Parati, G., & Manchia, G. (1992). Persistent blood pressure increase induced by heavy smoking. *J Hypertension, 10,* 495–499.

Håheim, L.L., Holme, I., Hjermann, I., & Leren, P. (1996). Smoking habits and risk of fatal stroke: 18 years follow up of the Oslo Study. *J Epidemiol Community Health, 50*(6), 621–624.

Halperin, J.L., & Hart, R.G. (1988). Atrial fibrillation and stroke: New ideas, persisting dilemmas. *Stroke, 19,* 937–941.

Harris, W.S. (1997). n-3 fatty acids and serum lipoproteins: Human studies. *Am J Clin Nutr, 65*(suppl 5), 1645S–1654S.

Hart, R.G., Palacio, S., & Pearce, L.A. (2002). Atrial fibrillation, stroke, and acute antithrombotic therapy: Analysis of randomized clinical trials. *Stroke, 33,* 2722–2727.

He, F.J., Nowson, C.A., & MacGregor, G.A. (2006). Fruit and vegetable consumption and stroke: Meta-analysis of cohort studies. *Lancet, 367*(9507), 320–326.

He, K., Song, Y., Daviglus, M.L., et al. (2004). Fish consumption and incidence of stroke: A meta-analysis of cohort studies. *Stroke, 35,* 1538–1542.

Imano, H., Kitamura, A., Sato, S., et al. (2009). Trends for blood pressure and its contribution to stroke incidence in the middle-aged Japanese population: The Circulatory Risk in Communities Study (CIRCS). *Stroke, 40*(5), 1571–1577.

Intersalt Cooperative Research Group. (1988). Intersalt: An international study of electrolyte excretion and blood pressure. Results for 24 hour urinary sodium and potassium excretion. *BMJ, 297*(6644), 319–328.

Iso, H., Rexrode, K.M., Stampfer, M.J., Manson, J.E., Colditz, G.A., Speizer, F.E., & Hennekens, C.H. (2001). Intake of fish and omega-3 fatty acids and risk of stroke in women. *JAMA, 285,* 304–312.

Johnston, S.C., Mendis, S., & Mathers, C.D. (2009). Global variation in stroke burden and mortality: Estimates from monitoring, surveillance, and modelling. *Lancet Neurology, 8*(4), 345–354.

Keys, A., Aravanis, C., Blackburn, H., et al. (1980). *Seven Countries. A Multivariate Analysis of Death and Coronary Heart Disease* (pp. 1–381). Cambridge, MA and London: Harvard University Press.

Kittner, S.J., White, L.R., Losonczy, K.G., et al. (1990). Black-white differences in stroke incidence in a national sample. The contribution of hypertension and diabetes mellitus. *JAMA, 264,* 1267–1270.

Kurth, T., Kase, C.S., Berger, K., Schaeffner, E.S., Buring, J.E., & Gaziano, M. (2003). Smoking and the risk of hemorrhagic stroke in men. *Stroke, 34,* 1151–1155.

Lakhan, S.E., & Sapko, M. (2009). Blood pressure lowering treatment for preventing stroke recurrence: A systematic review and meta-analysis. *International Archives of Medicine, 2,* 30.

Lewington, S., Clarke, R., Qizilbash, N., Peto, R., Collins, R., & Prospective Studies Collaboration. (2002). Age-specific relevance of usual blood pressure to vascular mortality: A meta-analysis of individual data for one million adults in 61 prospective studies. *Lancet, 360,* 1903–1913.

Lopez, A.D., Mathers, C.D., Ezzati, M., Jamison, D.T., & Murray, C.J. (2006). Global and regional burden of disease and risk factors, 2001: Systematic analysis of population health data. *Lancet, 367,* 1747–1757.

Mackay, J., & Mensah, G. (2004). *Atlas of Heart Disease and Stroke.* Geneva, Switzerland: World Health Organization.

Makela, P., Fonager, K., Hibell, B., et al. (2001). Episodic heavy drinking in four Nordic countries: A comparative survey. *Addiction, 96*, 1575–1588.

McGill, H.C. Jr., McMahan, C.A., Herderick, E.E., Zieske, A.W., Malcom, G.T., Tracy, R.E., & Strong, J.P., & Pathobiological Determinants of Atherosclerosis in Youth (PDAY) Research Group. (2002). Obesity accelerates the progression of coronary atherosclerosis in young men. *Circulation, 105*, 2712–2718.

Murray, C.J., & Lopez, A.D. (1997). Mortality by cause for eight regions of the world: Global Burden of Disease Study. *Lancet, 349*(9061), 1269–1276.

Nakayama, T., Date, C., Yokoyama, T., Yoshiike, N., Yamaguchi, M., & Tanaka, H. (1997). A 15.5-year follow-up study of stroke in a Japanese provincial city: The Shibata Study. *Stroke, 28*, 45–52.

National Heart, Lung and Blood Institute. (1996). Stroke Belt Initiative. Bethesda, MD: National Institutes of Health.

National Heart, Lung and Blood Institute. (2009). Bethesda, MD: Center for Health Statistics, National Institutes of Health.

Nestel, P.J. (1990). Effects of n-3 fatty acids on lipid metabolism. *Annu Rev Nutr, 10*, 49–167.

O'Donnell, M.J., Xavier, D., Liu, L., et al. (2010). Risk factors for ischaemic and intracerebral haemorrhagic stroke in 22 countries (the INTERSTROKE study): A case-control study. *Lancet, 376*(9735), 112–123.

O'Regan, C., Wu, P., Arora, P., Perri, D., & Mills, E.J. (2008). Statin therapy in stroke prevention: A meta-analysis involving 121,000 patients. *Am J Med, 121*(1), 24–33.

Omvik, P. (1996). How **smoking** affects blood pressure. *Blood Press, 5*, 71–77.

Onundarson, P.T., Thorgeirsson, G., Jonmundsen, E., Sigfusson, N., & Hardarson, T. (1987). Chronic atrial fibrillation—Epidemiologic features and 14 year follow-up: A case-control study. *Eur Heart J, 8*, 521–527.

Peto, R., Lopez, A.D., Boreham, J., et al. (2006). Mortality from smoking in developed countries 1950–2000: Indirect estimates from National Vital Statistics. London: Oxford University Press.

Poirier, P., Giles, T.D., Bray, G.A., Hong, Y., Stern, J.S., Pi-Sunver, X.P., & Eckel, R.H. (2006). Obesity and cardiovascular disease: Pathophysiology, evaluation, and effect of weight loss. Arteriosclerosis, thrombosis, and vascular biology. *Journal of the American Heart Association, 26*, 968–976.

Prospective Studies Collaboration. (1995). Cholesterol, diastolic blood pressure, and stroke: 13,000 strokes in 450,000 people in 45 prospective cohorts. Prospective studies collaboration. *Lancet, 346*(8991–8992), 1647–1653.

Reynolds, K., Lewis, B., Nolen, J.D., Kinney, G.L., Sathya, B., & He, J. (2003). Alcohol consumption and risk of stroke: A meta-analysis. *JAMA, 289*(5), 579–588.

Ridker, P.M., Rifai, N., Rose, L., Buring, J.E., & Cook, N.R. (2002). Comparison of C-reactive protein and low-density lipoprotein cholesterol levels in the prediction of first cardiovascular events. *New Engl J Med, 347*, 1557–1565.

Robbins, A.S., Manson, J.E., Lee, I.M., Satterfield, S., & Hennekens, C. (1994). Cigarette smoking and stroke in a cohort of US male physicians. *Annals of Internal Medicine, 120*(6), 458–462.

Rost, N.S., Wolf, P.A., Kase, C.S., et al. (2001). Plasma Concentration of C-reactive protein and risk of ischemic stroke and transient ischemic attack: The Framingham Study. *Stroke, 32*, 2575–2579.

Ross, R. (1999). Atherosclerosis—an inflammatory disease. *N Engl J Med, 340*, 115–126.

Rothwell, P.M., Eliasziw, M., Gutnikov, S.A., Warlow, C.P., & Barnett, H.J. (2004). Endarterectomy for symptomatic carotid stenosis in relation to clinical subgroups and timing of surgery. *Lancet, 363*(9413), 915–924.

Schiller, F. (1970). Concepts of stroke before and after Virchow. *Med Hist, 14*(2), 115–131.

Schoene, W.C. (1979). The nervous system. In: Robbins, S.L., Cotran, (Eds.). *Pathologic Basis of Disease* (2nd ed.). Philadelphia:WB Saunders Company.

Siegel, P.Z., Wolfe, L.E., Wilcox, D., & Deeb, L.C. (1992). North Florida is part of the stroke belt. *Public Health Rep*, 107(5), 540–543.

Shinton, R., & Beevers, G. (1989). Meta-analysis of relation between cigarette smoking and stroke. *BMJ*, 298, 789–794.

Sloan, M.A., Kittner, S.J., Rigamonti, D., & Price, T.R. (1991). Occurrence of stroke associated with use/abuse of drugs. *Neurology*, 41(9), 1358–1364.

Smolders, B., Lemmens, R., & Thijs, V. (2007). Lipoprotein (a) and stroke: A meta-analysis of observational studies. *Stroke*, 38, 1959–1964.

Stamler, R., Stamler, J., Riedlinger, W.F., Algera, G., & Roberts, R.H. (1978). Weight and blood pressure. Findings in hypertension screening of 1 million Americans. *J Am Med Assoc*, 240, 1607–1610.

Stegmayr, B., Harmsen, P., Rajakangas, A.M., Rastenyté, D., Sarti, C., Thorvaldsen, P., & Tuomilehto, J. (1996). Stroke around the Baltic Sea: Incidence, case fatality and population risk factors in Denmark, Finland, Sweden, and Lithuania. *Cerebrovasc Dis*, 6, 80–88.

Stegmayr, B., Asplund, K., Kuulasmaa, K., et al. (1997). Stroke incidence and mortality correlated to stroke risk factors in the WHO MONICA Project. An ecological study of 18 populations. *Stroke*, 28, 1367–1374.

Straus, S.E., Majumdar, S.R., & McAlister, F.A. (2002). New evidence for stroke prevention: Scientific review. *JAMA*, 288(11), 1388–1396.

Strazzullo, P., D'Elia, L., Bakwin-Kandala, N., & Cappuccio, F.P. (2009). Salt intake, stroke, and cardiovascular disease: Meta-analysis of prospective studies. *BMJ*, 339, b4567.

Strazzullo, P., D'Elia, L., Cairella, G., Garbagnati, F., Cappuccio, F.P., & Scalfi, L. (2010). Excess body weight and incidence of stroke: Meta-analysis of prospective studies with 2 million participants. *Stroke*, 41, e418–e426.

Sudlow, C.L., & Warlow, C.P. (1997). Comparable studies of the incidence of stroke and its pathological types: Results from an international collaboration. International Stroke Incidence Collaboration. *Stroke*, 28491–28499.

Surgeon General's Report. (2004). *The health consequences of smoking: A report of the surgeon general*. Washington, DC: Office of the Surgeon General, US Department of Health and Human Services.

Tanaka, H., Hayashi, M., Date, C., et al. (1985). Epidemiologic studies of stroke in Shibata, a Japanese provincial city: Preliminary report on risk factors for cerebral infarction. *Stroke*, 16773–16780.

Thompson, J.E. (1996). The evolution of surgery for the treatment and prevention of stroke. The Willis Lecture. *Stroke*, 27(8), 1427–1434.

van Gijn, J., Kerr, R.S., & Rinkel, G.J. (2007). Subarachnoid haemorrhage. *Lancet*, 369(9558), 306–318.

Wannamethee, S.G., Shaper, A.G., Whincup, P.H., & Walker, M. (1995). Smoking cessation and the risk of stroke in middle-aged men. *JAMA*, 274(2), 155–160.

Webb, A.J.S., Fischer, U., Mehta, Z., & Rothwell, P.M. (2010). Effects of antihypertensive drug class on interindvidual variation in blood pressure and risk of stroke: A systematic review and meta-analysis. *Lancet*, 375(9718), 906–915.

Westover, A.N., McBride, S., & Haley, R.W. (2007). Stroke in young adults who abuse amphetamines or cocaine: A population-based study of hospitalized patients. *Archives of General Psychiatry*, 64(4), 495–502.

Wolf-Maier, K., Cooper, R.S., Banegas, J.R., et al. (2003). Hypertension prevalence and blood pressure levels in 6 European countries, Canada, and the United States. *JAMA*, 289, 2363–2369.

Wolf, P.A., D'Agostino, R.B., Kannel, W.B., Bonita, R., & Blanger, A.J. (1988). Cigarette smoking as a risk factor for stroke: The Framingham Study. *JAMA, 259*(7), 1025–1029.

Wolf, P.A., Abbott, R.D., & Kannel, W.B. (1991). Atrial fibrillation as an independent risk factor for stroke: The Framingham Study. *Stroke, 22,* 983–988.

World Health Organization. (1978). Cerebrovascular Disorders (Offset Publications).

Geneva, Switzerland: World Health Organization.

World Health Organization. (2009). WHO Disease and Injury Country Estimates. Geneva, Switzerland: World Health Organization.

World Health Organization. (2010). World Health Organization Statistical Information System (WHOSIS). Geneva, Switzerland: World Health Organization.

Epidemiology of Hypertension

CLINICAL DEFINITION OF HYPERTENSION

The following statement from collaborating investigators at the US National Center for Health Statistics, the Centers for Disease Control, Johns Hopkins University, the National Heart, Lung and Blood Institute, and the University of Texas at Houston summarizes important points regarding hypertension (Burt et al., 1995):

"High blood pressure is one of the most important modifiable risk factors for cardiovascular disease. It is an extremely common finding in the community and a risk factor for myocardial infarction, stroke, congestive heart failure, end-stage renal disease, and peripheral vascular disease. Pharmacological treatment of hypertension has been shown to decrease the risk of cardiovascular disease complications, including stroke, coronary heart disease, and renal insufficiency. Nonpharmacological intervention provides an effective means to lower blood pressure and has been emphasized increasingly as a useful method for both prevention and treatment of high blood pressure."

The diagnosis of hypertension is made when an individual's blood pressure is chronically elevated above certain threshold levels. Clinically, hypertension is defined by the American Heart Association as systolic blood pressure equal to or greater than 140 mm Hg or diastolic blood pressure equal to or greater than 90 mm Hg (**Table 6.1**). Systolic blood pressure is the arterial pressure (at the level of the brachial artery in the upper arm) during contraction of the heart whereas diastolic blood pressure is the arterial pressure between contractions when the heart is at rest.

There is controversy regarding optimal blood pressure since the risk of certain cardiovascular conditions (e.g., stroke, myocardial infarction, congestive heart failure, arterial aneurysm, and renal failure) may be elevated at lower levels than 140/90 mm Hg. A consensus statement from the *Seventh Report of the Joint National Committee on Prevention, Detection, Evaluation, and Treatment of High Blood Pressure* has defined systolic levels between 130 to 139 mm Hg or diastolic levels between 80 to 89 mm Hg as being suboptimal and prehypertensive (Chobanian et al., 2003).

Table 6.1	Classification of Blood Pressure	
Classification	**Systolic Pressure (mm Hg)**	**Diastolic Pressure (mm Hg)**
Normal	90–119	60–79
Prehypertensive	130–139	80–89
Hypertensive	≥140	≥90

Blood pressure is measured as the elevation of mercury (Hg) in millimeters (mm) in a closed class column system (sphygmomanometer). Pressures are measured as resistance to blood flow by inflating a cuff placed around the upper arm at the level of the heart in an individual at rest in a sitting position with the arm supported.

Source: Data from Chobanian AV, Bakris GL, Black HR, et al. (2003). Seventh report of the Joint National Committee on Prevention, Detection, Evaluation, and Treatment of High Blood Pressure. *Hypertension* 42(6):1206–1252.

GLOBAL EPIDEMIOLOGY OF HYPERTENSION

Approximately one-quarter of the world's adult population (more than 1 billion people) were afflicted with hypertension at the turn of the 21st century, and if current trends continue, the prevalence is projected to increase to about 29% (more than 2 billion people) by 2025 (Kearney et al., 2005).

These estimates are based upon a comprehensive analysis of available data on blood pressure from 18 national, 3 multisite, and 9 regional studies by a team of investigators at Tulane University School of Public Health and Tropical Medicine, USA, and the University of Oxford, UK (Kearney et al., 2005). Countries and regions represented in the study included Korea (Kim et al., 1994), Taiwan (Pan et al., 2001; InterASIA Collaborative Group, 2003), South Africa (Steyn et al., 2001), Cameroon (Mbanya et al., 1998), West Africa (Cooper et al., 1997), Tanzania (Edwards et al., 2000), Zimbabwe (Mufunda et al., 2000), China (Gu et al., 2002), Turkey (Sonmez et al., 1999), Egypt (Ibrahim et al., 1995), Venezuela (Sulbaran et al., 2000), Paraguay (Ramirez et al., 1995), Mexico (Arroyo et al., 1999), India (Gupta and Sharma, 1994; Gupta et al., 1995; Singh et al., 1997a; Singh et al., 1997b; Malhotra et al., 1999), United States (National CVD Database; Burt et al., 1995; Wolz et al., 2000), Canada (Joffres et al., 1997), Spain (Banegas et al., 1998), England (Primatesta, Brookes, and Poulter, 2001), Germany (Thamm, 1999), Greece (Stergion et al., 1999), Italy (Giampaoli et al., 2001), Scandinavian countries near the Baltic Sea (Stegmayr et al., 1996), Australia (Bennett and Magnus, 1994), Japan (Baba et al., 1991), and Slovakia (Riecansky and Egnerova, 1991).

Overall, 26.4% of the world's adult population (over the age of 20 years) manifested hypertension (26.6% of men and 26.1% of women). Approximately one-third of hypertensive cases were detected in economically developed countries and the remaining two-thirds in developing countries. Relatively high prevalence levels (exceeding 30%) were observed for men and women combined in Western European and Scandinavian nations (Germany, Italy, Spain, and Sweden), Japan, former socialistic economies (Russia), and nations in Latin America and the Caribbean (Mexico, Paraguay, and Venezuela); moderate levels (between 20–30%) were observed in North America (United States and Canada), the Middle East (Egypt and Turkey), sub-Saharan Africa, India, Australia, and China; and low levels (less than 20%) were observed in nations of Southeast Asia (Taiwan, Korea, and Thailand). Populations of urban areas tended to have higher levels than rural areas, e.g., the prevalence of hypertension in rural areas of western India was significantly less than in urban areas (31% versus 22%). Less-developed nations had a lower overall prevalence of hypertension than economically developed nations (22.9% versus 37.3%). Nevertheless, the authors point out that rates of hypertension are increasing more rapidly in populations of developing nations; and since these populations are larger, the burden of hypertension and related cardiovascular and renal diseases is projected to increase worldwide over the next decade (Kearney et al., 2005).

Though the cumulative prevalence of hypertension was similar for men and women, gender differences were noted in the age-specific prevalence patterns of hypertension (Kearney et al., 2005). As shown in **Figure 6.1**, men had the higher prevalence

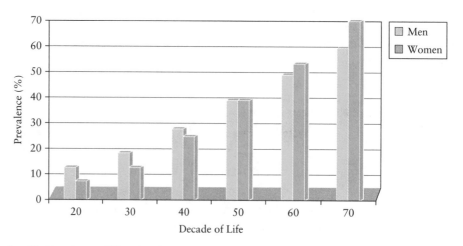

Figure 6.1 Age-Specific Prevalence of Hypertension.

Source: Data from Kearney PM, Whelton M, Reynolds K, Muntner P, Whelton PK, He J (2005). Global burden of hypertension: Analysis of worldwide data. *Lancet* 365(9455):217–223.

until age 50, after which the prevalence for women was greater. Potential reasons for the age differential in the prevalence of hypertension between men and women include (1) a protective effect of endogenous estrogens in women during the premenopausal years and (2) the effect of increased longevity and survivorship among women in the later decades of life.

As discussed in separate chapters of this text, epidemiologic studies provide convincing evidence that hypertension is etiologically linked to the pathogenesis of thromboembolic cardiovascular events such as stroke and myocardial infarction (Fiebach et al., 1989; MacMahon et al., 1990; Stamler, Stamler, and Neaton, 1993) as well as renal insufficiency and failure (Whelton et al., 1992). Successful intervention to curb global increases in these conditions will therefore require intensive multifactorial nonpharmacologic strategies targeting the modifiable risk factors of hypertension as well as effective pharmacologic management of blood pressure for hypertensive individuals.

A variety of risk factors, many of which are modifiable, play an interactive role in the development of hypertension including age, race, gender, body mass index (BMI), excess dietary salt, tobacco addiction, high alcohol intake, and dietary potassium and calcium deficiencies (Whelton, 1994; Australian Institute of Health and Welfare, 2011). Intensive nonpharmacologic intervention is thus essential for the primary prevention of developing high blood pressure (Working Group on Primary Prevention of Hypertension, 1993). Risk factors for hypertension are discussed in greater detail later in this chapter.

Effective intervention to combat hypertension demands incorporation of community-based blood pressure screening programs to identify those patients with elevated blood pressure (Joint National Committee on Detection, Evaluation, and Treatment of High Blood Pressure, 1993). Pharmacologic therapy for the management of hypertension has proven effective in improving cardiovascular and renal function and reducing the risk of myocardial infarction, stroke, and renal failure (Shulman et al, 1989; Collins et al., 1990; Hebert et al., 1993). A variety of antihypertensive medications have been shown to safely and effectively reduce blood pressure and sustain levels within normal limits for patients diagnosed with hypertension (Burt et al., 1995).

ECOLOGICAL PATTERNS OF HYPERTENSION

Marked differences have been observed in the prevalence rates of hypertension among populations, even those of highly developed nations. For example, surveys of European populations consistently show higher levels than in North American populations, a finding based upon combined analysis of national cross-sectional surveys conducted in the 1990s in Germany, Finland, Sweden, England, Spain, Italy, Canada, and the United States (Wolf-Maier et al., 2003). As shown in **Figure 6.2**, the prevalence of hypertension in the European populations sampled ranged from 38–55% compared to 28% in the United States and Canada.

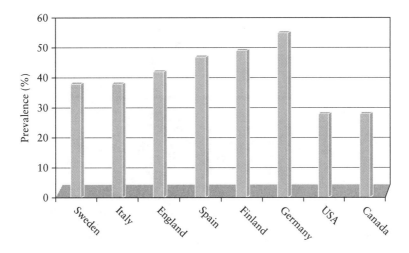

Figure 6.2 The Prevalence of Hypertension in Europe versus North America.

Source: Data from National surveys conducted during the 1990s. Wolf-Maier K, Cooper RS, Banegas JR, Giampaoli S, Hense H, Joffres M, Kastarinen M, Poulter N, Primatesta P, Rodriguez-Artalejo F, Stegmayr B, Thamm M, Tuomilehto J, Vanuzzo D, Vescio F (2003). Hypertension and blood pressure levels in 6 European countries, Canada, and the US. *JAMA*, 289:2363–2369.

In a subsequent study designed to examine the impact of treatment strategies in European versus North American populations, 66% and 49% of individuals previously diagnosed with severe hypertension (defined as blood pressure >160/95 mm Hg) in the United States and Canada, respectively, had controlled blood pressure levels (within normal limits) compared to only 23–38% of individuals in European populations (Wolf-Maier et al., 2004). The investigators emphasize the need for improved pharmacologic management of high blood pressure in order to reduce the risk of cardiovascular and renal diseases.

National prevalence rates of hypertension have been found to be highly correlated with mortality and incidence rates of cardiovascular diseases, particularly stroke. In the World Health Organization MONICA Project, blood pressure prevalence estimates for population samples from around the Baltic Sea showed *positive* correlations with the incidence rates of stroke in men (r = 0.87) and women (r = 0.70) (Stegmayr et al., 1996); and subsequently, *positive* correlations were also observed (r = 0.42 for men and r = 0.56 for women) in an analysis of 18 MONICA population samples from diverse geographic regions (Stegmayr et al., 1997). These results prompted further analysis of data on 16 population samples from MONICA that demonstrated a *negative* correlation between the frequency of effective control of blood pressure in individuals with hypertension and the incidence of stroke (Banegas and Pérez-Regadera, 1998). Hypertension and stroke were also *positively* correlated (r = 0.78) in the international comparison study of North American and European nations (Wolf-Maier et al., 2004). The etiologic link between hypertension and stroke is discussed in greater detail.

HYPERTENSION IN THE US STROKE BELT

The Stroke Belt in the United States is comprised of 11 states including Alabama, Arkansas, Georgia, Indiana, Kentucky, Louisiana, Mississippi, North Carolina, South Carolina, Tennessee, and Virginia. In 1980, these 11 states had age-adjusted stroke mortality rates more than 10% above the national average (National Heart Lung and Blood Institute, 1996). As shown in **Figure 6.3**, most of these states are represented in the cluster of states in the southeastern United States with the highest prevalence rates of hypertension (Centers for Disease Control, 2007). Obviously, there is significant overlap in the distributions of hypertension and stroke.

ETHNICITY AND HYPERTENSION IN THE UNITED STATES

An interdisciplinary team of US investigators studied hypertension by gender and ethnicity in a cross-sectional survey of 9,901 adults in the third US National Health and Nutrition Examination Survey, 1988–1994, NHANES III (Burt et al., 1995). The study included in-home and clinic examinations for the measurement of blood pressure. Based on this survey, 24% of the US adult population was found

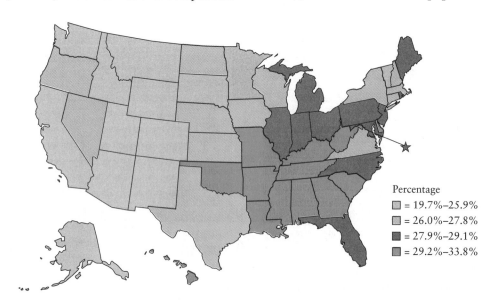

Figure 6.3 Hypertension and the Stroke Belt in the USA, 2007.

Source: Data from Centers for Disease Control (2007). Division for Heart Disease and Stroke Prevention. Department of Health and Human Services.

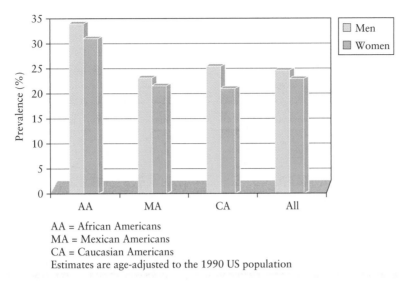

AA = African Americans
MA = Mexican Americans
CA = Caucasian Americans
Estimates are age-adjusted to the 1990 US population

Figure 6.4 Prevalence of Hypertension by Ethnicity in the USA: NHANES III Data, 1988–1991.

Source: Data from Burt VL, Whelton P, Roccella EJ, et al. (1995). Prevalence of hypertension in the US adult population. Results from the Third National Health and Nutrition Examination survey, 1988–91. *Hypertension* 25:305–313.

to be hypertensive (24.7% of men and 23.4% of women). However, there were large differences in the age-adjusted prevalence estimates by ethnicity (**Figure 6.4**). African Americans had markedly higher levels (32.4%) than Caucasian Americans (23.3%) and Mexican Americans (22.6%).

Various reasons have been proposed to explain the higher predisposition of African Americans to the development of hypertension. Racial differences may be due, at least in part, to genetic differences in the regulation of dietary sodium by the kidneys. Furthermore, *Endothelin-1*, a powerful local vasoconstrictor, appears to be secreted at higher levels in the blood vessels of African Americans compared to other ethnic groups (see the section of this chapter on genetics and hypertension for discussion of these mechanisms).

As shown in Figure 6.4, the age-adjusted prevalence estimates from NHANES III were slightly higher for men than women of each ethnic group, although differences were small. As noted above, women appear to have some protection against the development of hypertension and related vascular conditions during their premenopausal years, which may account for the small differences in the age-adjusted estimates.

Overall, 69% of hypertensive individuals in NHANES III were aware of their condition prior to measurement and 53% were taking an antihypertensive agent. Nevertheless, only 35% of Mexican Americans with high blood pressure were receiving treatment and 25% or less of treated individuals were achieving adequate control of their blood pressure, irrespective of ethnicity.

TIME TRENDS OF HYPERTENSION IN THE UNITED STATES

A subsequent analysis of NHANES data compared blood pressure data for samples of US adults aged 18 years or older ascertained during 1988–1994 (n = 16,351) and approximately 10 years later during 1999–2004 (n = 14,430). Analysis and evaluation of these data focused on changes in blood pressure during the interim and the potential factors responsible (Cutler et al., 2008).

As shown in **Figure 6.5**, the age-standardized prevalence of hypertension increased from 24.4–28.9% among the US adult population during 1988–1994 to 1999–2004, an increase of 4.5% in the 10-year period. Perhaps surprisingly, a larger increase was observed in women (5.6%) than men (3.2%), and the final prevalence estimates for men and women sampled during 1999–2004 were similar (28.8% for men and 28.5% for women). In regression models, increases in body mass and obesity accounted for a significant fraction of the increase in hypertension, particularly among men. In women, age was the most important factor, presumably because of their greater longevity and the development of hypertension relatively late in life. While individuals of

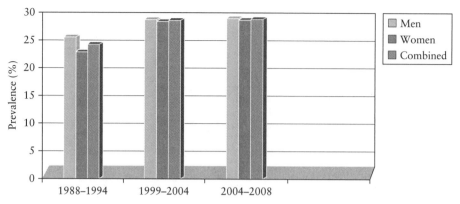

Estimates are age-adjusted to the 2000 USA population

Figure 6.5 Trends in the Prevalence of Hypertension in the USA, NHANES, 1988–2002.

Source: Data from National Health and Nutrition Survey. Cutler JA, et al (2008). Trends in the hypertension prevalence, awareness, treatment, and control rates in United States adults between 1988–1994 and 1999–2004. *Hypertension* 52(5):818–827; Egan et al., 2010.

all ethnic groups demonstrated improved awareness, treatment, and control of their blood pressure, nearly 40% of hypertensive individuals were unaware of their condition at the time of measurement and 65% of hypertensive individuals did not achieve adequate blood pressure control with treatment. The authors point out that these trends are expected to translate into higher rates of cardiovascular and renal diseases in certain US subpopulations (Cutler et al., 2008).

Investigators in the United States are continuing to examine the NHANES databases to assess progress in treating and controlling hypertension. Analysis of blood pressure data for cross-sectional samples of US adults obtained for successive 2-year intervals during 1999–2008 reveals that the overall prevalence of hypertension has stabilized at approximately 29%. The proportion of hypertensive patients who were treated and had controlled blood pressure increased to 50.1% in the most recent survey during 2007 and 2008 (Egan et al., 2010).

TIME TRENDS OF HYPERTENSION IN INDIA

India provides an interesting contrast to developed nations as a model for longitudinal studies of hypertension in a large developing nation with both rural and urban populations. The prevalence rates of severe hypertension (> 160/95 mm Hg) have trended upwards in both urban and rural populations of India since the middle of the 20th century, but the levels remained relatively low: less than 15% in urban populations and less than 5% in rural populations (Gupta and Sharma, 1994; Gupta et al., 1995, 1996; Gupta, 1999).

Albeit, surveys of hypertension defined by revised criteria (> 140/90 mm Hg) for the period 1995–2002 reflect markedly higher prevalence rates, particularly for urban populations. Pooling of epidemiologic studies shows that hypertension is present in about 25% of urban subjects and 10% of rural subjects in India. Furthermore, prevalence rates exceeding 40% have been observed for both men and women in certain urban populations (Gupta, 2004). The accelerating rates of hypertension and related conditions in India are representative of other developing nations around the globe.

PHYSIOLOGICAL CONTROL OF BLOOD PRESSURE

Blood pressure regulation in the human body is complex and dependent upon multiple factors including cardiac output, total blood volume, blood viscosity, and resistance of blood vessels (arteries) to blood flow. Blood pressure can be numerically expressed as *Blood Pressure = Cardiac Output √ Peripheral Resistance*. Consequently, assessment of blood pressure is essential in determining the viability of heart function and the integrity of blood vessels.

Multiple physiological, cellular, and molecular processes are important for maintaining normal blood pressure. In particular, normal kidney function is vital for blood pressure control and patients with renal disease often develop hypertension due to hyperactivity of the *renin-angiotensin system*. The central nervous system can elicit rapid changes in blood pressure by stimulating the release of epinephrine (adrenalin), a powerful vasoconstrictor, from the adrenal glands in the *"fight or flight"* response to stress or a perceived environmental threat. The autonomic nervous system can also elicit minute to minute changes in blood pressure in response to environmental stimuli through the *baroreceptor reflex* described below. Furthermore, locally acting agents with vasoconstricting or vasodilating effects are important for the maintenance of vascular tone. Regulatory mechanisms of arterial blood pressure are broadly subdivided into *short-term* and *long-term* regulation.

The central nervous system responds rapidly to environmental stimuli by activation of the *"fight or flight"* response. Firing of adrenergic nerve cells and release of epinephrine (adrenalin) into the bloodstream by the adrenal glands immediately increases the heart rate, contracts blood vessels, dilates air passages, and intensifies awareness.

The autonomic nervous system helps regulate *short-term* changes in blood pressure through the *baroreceptor reflex*. The baroreceptor reflex refers to immediate changes in arterial blood pressure in response to signals sent from baroreceptors located in the carotid arteries and the arch of the aorta to the medulla of the brain stem. Stimulus of the heart, arteries, and veins by nerve impulses from the medulla adjust arterial blood pressure by altering the speed and force of contractions of the heart and modulating the resistance of peripheral blood vessels to blood flow by vasoconstriction or vasodilatation.

The *renin-angiotensin system* is primarily responsible for the *long-term* regulation of blood pressure and blood volume. Classically, juxtaglomerular cells in the *kidney* monitor the dynamics of blood flow and in response to low blood pressure and flow secrete the enzyme renin, which in turn cleaves the peptide angiotensinogen converting it into angiotensin I, which is inactive. Angiotensin I is converted to angiotensin II in the *lungs* by angiotensin-converting enzyme (ACE). Angiotensin II is a powerful vasoconstrictor throughout the body and is the main effector molecule of the renin-angiotensin system (Paul et al., 2006).

In response to elevated levels of angiotensin II (or potassium) in the blood, the adrenal cortex secretes a steroidal hormone called aldosterone. Aldosterone stimulates retention of sodium and excretion of potassium by the kidney, thereby increasing blood volume and arterial blood pressure. Aldosterone acts on the distal convoluted tubule and the cortical collecting duct in the kidneys, causing them to reabsorb more sodium and water from the urine in exchange for potassium. Aldosterone also acts on the central nervous system to increase thirst and appetite for salt.

Maintenance of vascular tone is also dependent upon vasoconstrictive and vasodilator substances that are locally secreted by the endothelial cells that line blood vessels. Endothelin-1 is a polypeptide with potent vasoconstrictive activity (Yanagisawa, Kurihara, and Kimura, 1988). This protein rapidly elicits smooth muscle cell contraction and infusion of endothelin-1 in humans increases blood pressure and total peripheral resistance of blood vessels (Haynes et al., 1994).

Nitric oxide is a potent vasodilator that is continuously secreted by endothelial cells of the arterial lining in response to changes in blood pressure and blood flow disturbances. Nitric oxide plays an important role in maintaining normal blood pressure and adequate blood flow and its homeostatic effects are diminished in hypertensive persons. Nitric oxide also inhibits platelet adhesion and aggregation and suppresses migration and proliferation of vascular smooth muscle cells.

ESSENTIAL HYPERTENSION

Hypertension is divided into two subtypes: *essential hypertension* and *secondary hypertension*. Most individuals (about 95%) have *essential hypertension,* which means that no specific cause has been identified. Individuals with *secondary hypertension* have a specific underlying cause that has elevated their blood pressure (see discussion of this subtype in the following section).

Essential hypertension develops due to the interaction of multiple factors in a *web of causation*. While exact causes are difficult to establish in the majority of individual patients, the evidence confirming the multifactorial nature of essential hypertension is overwhelming. Two major risk factors stand out: obesity and chronic alcohol abuse. Nevertheless, many other factors undoubtedly contribute to the pathogenesis of essential hypertension including tobacco addiction, excess dietary sodium (salt), low dietary potassium, vitamin D deficiency, excess of certain dietary fats, sedentary lifestyle, psychological factors (stress or depression), and genetic predisposition. Each of these risk factors is discussed in a following section of this chapter.

SECONDARY HYPERTENSION

Hypertension that develops from a known cause (often a hormonal disorder) is called *secondary hypertension*. Secondary hypertension accounts for only about 5% of all cases of hypertension. Various hormonal disorders are known to cause secondary hypertension (Robbins and Cotran, 1979). Selected disorders are described in the following paragraphs.

Cushing's syndrome is caused by excess circulating cortisol due to either long-term administration of synthetic forms of cortisol (such as prednisone or dexamethasone) or oversecretion of cortisol by the adrenal glands as a result of pituitary-hypothalamic dysfunction. Cortisol has properties similar to aldosterone and therefore causes sodium retention and increased blood volume leading to hypertension (Whitworth et al., 1995). The syndrome is also characterized by a variety of other phenotypic abnormalities including truncal obesity, moon facies, diabetes mellitus, osteoporosis, polycythemia, skin striae, and immunosuppression.

Hyperthyroidism often produces an increase in the *systolic blood pressure* by promoting vasoconstriction and accelerating the heart rate and the force of heart contractions. These effects are due to unbridled secretion of thyroid hormones by the thyroid gland that stimulate specific receptors present in the myocardium and vasculature (Brent, 1994). Conversely, *hypothyroidism* occasionally produces an increase in the *diastolic blood pressure*, possibly due to increased resistance in peripheral blood vessels.

Conn's syndrome is due to hypersecretion of aldosterone by the adrenal glands (often by an adrenal adenoma). Elevated aldosterone causes hypertension through effects on the kidney including sodium retention, potassium wasting, and increased blood volume. In Conn's syndrome, there is *decreased* secretion of renin by the kidneys.

Acromegaly (gigantism) is due to excess circulating growth hormone often due to a pituitary adenoma. The association with hypertension is manifest in about 50% of individuals with acromegaly. Growth hormone has been found to have mineralocorticoid activity and excess levels lead to retention of sodium and increased blood volume.

Pheochromocytomas are rare neuroendocrine tumors that usually arise in the adrenal glands. Their overproduction of catecholamines (adrenalin) stimulates the heart and cardiovascular system resulting in severe hypertension in patients with these tumors.

HYPERTENSION OF PREGNANCY (PRE-ECLAMPSIA)

Hypertension in pregnant women is known as *pre-eclampsia*. If untreated, pre-eclampsia can progress to a life-threatening condition called *eclampsia*, which is the development of protein in the urine, generalized swelling (edema), and seizures. Pre-eclampsia occurs in up to 10% of first pregnancies, usually in the 3rd trimester after the 32nd week. Some women develop pre-eclampsia as early as 20 weeks, although this is rare. The condition is much more common in women who are pregnant for the first time and its frequency drops significantly in second pregnancies. Pre-eclampsia can also occur up to 6 weeks postpartum (Robbins and Cotran, 1979).

The cause of pre-eclampsia remains elusive and most likely involves the interaction of multiple variables. Placental ischemia (lack of oxygen) appears to be a common feature. One proposed scenario is that pre-eclampsia arises from rejection of the placenta by the maternal immune system which in turn leads to compromised placental perfusion and the release of inflammatory, vasoconstrictive, and prothrombotic prostaglandins (Moffett and Hiby, 2007). Glomerular filtration is reduced in the kidneys and there is marked retention of salt and water accompanied by increased irritability of the central nervous system. Vitamin deficiencies, obesity, and gestational diabetes have also been observed in association with pre-eclampsia (Ilekis, Reddy, and Roberts, 2006).

RISK FACTORS FOR ESSENTIAL HYPERTENSION

Epidemiologic investigations conducted over the past half century have identified and quantified several major risk factors for cardiovascular conditions including hypertension. International collaborations have made many of these studies possible. Pertinent findings from selected studies are presented in the following paragraphs.

Obesity and Hypertension

In the INTERSALT study, the relationship between body mass index, $BMI = ht \ (kg)/wt^2(m)$, and blood pressure was studied in 10,079 men and women, aged 20–59 years of age, sampled from 52 centers around the world. The BMI was significantly associated with both systolic and diastolic blood pressure, independent of age, alcohol intake, smoking, and sodium and potassium urinary excretion. Based upon regression analysis, each 10 kg increase in body weight increased systolic and diastolic blood pressure by 3 mm Hg and 2.2 mm Hg, respectively (Dyer and Elliott, 1989). The investigators of INTERSALT estimate that about 30% of cases of hypertension are attributable to obesity (defined as BMI of at least 30) and the attributable risk may be as high as 60%

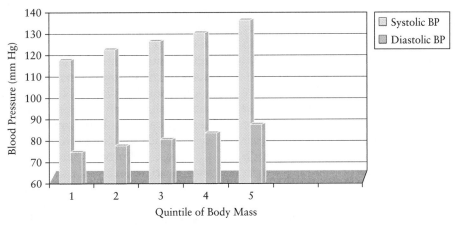

Estimates are age-adjusted to the 2000 US population.

Figure 6.6 Body Mass Index and Blood Pressure, USA.

Source: Data from NHANES II. Aneja A, El-Atat F, McFarlane SI, Sowers JR (2004). Hypertension and obesity. *Recent Progress in Hormone Research* 59:169–205.

in younger individuals under 45 years of age (Dyer, Elliott, and Shipley, 1990).

Many other epidemiologic studies have revealed a strong graded relationship between obesity and hypertension. Data from the NHANES show the striking linear relationship between body mass index and rising blood pressure in the American adult population (**Figure 6.6**). In regression models corrected for age, a BMI gain of 1.7 kg/m^2 in men or 1.25 kg/m^2 in women corresponds to an increase in systolic blood pressure of 1 mm Hg (Kissebah and Krakower, 1994).

The Nurses' Health Study involving 82,473 women revealed that a 5-kg weight gain after age 18 was associated with a 60% higher relative risk of developing hypertension (Huang et al., 1998) compared to those women who gained 2 kg or less. Those who gained 25 kg or more increased their risk more than fivefold. Similar increases in blood pressure and the development of hypertension with increasing body mass have been observed in other populations (Wilsgaard, Schirmer, and Arnesen, 2000) as well as in children (He et al., 2000). In the Framingham cohort, obesity independently accounted for 78% and 65% of essential hypertension in men and women, respectively (Kannel, Garrison, and Dannenberg, 1993).

Nonpharmacologic reduction in weight has been found to reduce blood pressure. In a meta-analysis of 25 randomized controlled trials published between 1966–2002 with a total of 4,874 participants, a net weight reduction of 5.1 kg through energy restriction, increased physical activity, or both, reduced systolic blood pressure by 4.4 mm Hg and diastolic blood pressure by 3.6 mm Hg. Greater blood pressure reductions were observed in subjects who loste more weight.

These results provide clear evidence that dietary modification and exercise are effective in reducing both weight and blood pressure (Neter et al., 2003).

Various weight reduction medications are now on the market and some have been evaluated in randomized placebo-controlled clinical trials. An international team of investigators recently examined effects of three agents in a meta-analysis. Thirty trials of 1 to 4 years, duration met the inclusion criteria: 10 evaluated *orlistat* (n = 10,631 participants), 10 evaluated *sibutramine* (n = 2,623 participants), and 4 evaluated *rimonabant* (n = 6,365 participants). Compared to placebo, significant average weight reductions were observed for each medication: 2.9 kg for orlistat, 4.2 kg for sibutramine, and 4.7 kg for rimonabant. Notably, orlistat and rimonabant also significantly *reduced* blood pressure whereas sibutramine actually *increased* blood pressure. An excess of other adverse events, e.g., gastrointestinal distress and mood disorders, were observed with treatment possibly diminishing the value of these medications (Rucker et al., 2007).

The *epidemiology of obesity* is discussed further. The following statement excerpted from a review by Aneja and colleagues provides a lucid synopsis of the pathogenic link between obesity and hypertension.

"It is becoming clear that the adipocyte is not merely an inert organ for storage of energy but that it also secretes a host of factors that interact with each other and may result in elevated blood pressure. Of particular importance is the putative role of leptin in the causation of hypertension via an activation of the sympathetic nervous system and a direct effect on the

kidneys, resulting in increased sodium reabsorption leading to hypertension. Obesity per se may have structural effects on the kidneys that may perpetuate hypertension, leading to an increased incidence of end-stage renal disease that results in further hypertension. Adipose tissue may elaborate angiotensin from its own local renin-angiotensin system. The distribution of body fat is considered important in the genesis of the obesity-hypertension syndrome, with a predominantly central distribution being particularly ominous. Weight loss is the cornerstone in the management of the obesity-hypertension syndrome. It may be achieved with diet, exercise, medications, and a combination of these measures. Anti-obesity medications that are currently undergoing clinical trials may play a promising role in the management of obesity and may also result in lowering of blood pressure. Antihypertensives are considered important components in the holistic approach to the management of this complex problem." Statement from Aneja, A., El-Atat, F., McFarlane, S.I., Sowers, J.R. (2004). *Hypertension and obesity*. Recent Progress in Hormone Research, 59, 169–205.

Salt and Hypertension

One of the primary objectives of the international INTERSALT study was to elucidate the relationship between urinary electrolytes and blood pressure. Associations of 24-hour urinary sodium and potassium were explored in more than 10,000 adults from 52 centers worldwide. Regression models indicated that each 100 mmol increase in urinary sodium *increased* systolic and diastolic blood pressure by 6 mm Hg and 2.5 mm Hg, respectively. Conversely, each 100 mmol increase in urinary potassium *decreased* systolic and diastolic blood pressure by 2 mm Hg and 1 mm Hg, respectively. Adjustment for body mass decreased the magnitude of these estimates by up to 50%. These results support recommendations for a combined approach to the prevention of hypertension including lower sodium and higher potassium intakes plus weight reduction to prevent and control obesity (Dyer et al., 1994).

Effects of dietary salt reduction on blood pressure have been investigated in a number of randomized clinical trials. In a recent meta-analysis of trials of 4 or more weeks' duration, 24-hour urinary sodium and blood pressure were examined from 17 trials enrolling 734 hypertensive patients and 11 trials enrolling 2,220 normotensive patients. Among hypertensive

patients, reducing urinary sodium by 100 mmol per day (equivalent to 6 grams of salt) produced a 7.1 mm Hg decrease in systolic blood pressure. Among normotensive subjects, the corresponding decrease in systolic blood pressure with reduced sodium was 3.6 mm Hg. These results demonstrate the significant impact of salt restriction in reducing blood pressure for both hypertensive and normotensive individuals (He and MacGregor, 2002).

These and many other epidemiologic investigations clearly link chronic excessive salt intake and salt retention to the genesis of hypertension. Nevertheless, the precise mechanisms by which salt retention increases blood pressure and causes hypertension remain unresolved. Much depends on the level of hydration in individual patients. With dehydration, sodium retention in the kidneys leads to hyperosmolality of blood, which may induce osmol receptors that cause vasoconstriction (Brooks, Haywood, and Johnson, 2005). In individuals who are sufficiently hydrated, sodium retention increases blood volume due to osmosis, thus increasing vascular resistance. It has recently been discovered that elevated plasma sodium induces secretion of the adrenocortical hormone, ouabain, which has multiple effects that raise blood pressure, e.g., inhibition of the Na+ pump plus cardiotonic and vasotonic effects (Blaustein et al., 2006).

Alcohol and Hypertension

Alcohol consumption has been linked to the development of hypertension in a number of epidemiologic investigations. The association was first reported by Lian who found that heavy wine drinking among French servicemen elevated the risk of hypertension (>160/100 mm Hg) by threefold compared to moderate drinking.

In a cross-sectional survey conducted in the United States (the *Lipids Research Clinics Prevalence Study*), prevalence relationships between alcohol consumption and systolic and diastolic blood pressure were examined in 2,482 men and 2,301 women aged 20 years or older sampled from 9 North American populations. In men, the relationship between alcohol and hypertension was linear. Men who consumed 30 ml or more of alcohol per day were 1.5 to 2 times more likely to have hypertension than nondrinkers. In women, the prevalence relationship between alcohol consumption and hypertension was U-shaped: heavy drinkers and individuals who abstained from alcohol were about twice as likely to have hypertension compared to moderate drinkers. As a possible explanation for the increased prevalence of hypertension among women who reported no alcohol consumption, women in this category had higher levels of obesity than other subgroups. Regression analysis indicated that consuming 30 ml of alcohol per day increased systolic blood pressure by 2 to 6 mm Hg. Effects of alcohol on blood pressure were independent of age, gender, obesity, smoking, regular exercise, education, and hormone replacement therapy in women (Criqui et al., 1982).

As a part of the INTERSALT study, alcohol intake and blood pressure were studied among 4,844 men and 4,837 women aged 20–59 years ascertained from 50 centers worldwide. Overall, higher levels of alcohol consumption were associated with higher blood pressures in both men and women. Men who consumed at least 500 ml of alcohol per week had average systolic and diastolic blood pressures that were 4.6 and 3.0 mm Hg higher than nondrinkers, and women who consumed at least 300 ml of alcohol per week had average systolic and diastolic blood pressures that were 3.9 and 3.1 mm Hg higher than nondrinkers. The observed effects of alcohol on blood pressure were independent of body mass and urinary excretion of sodium and potassium. Based on these results, the INTERSALT investigators recommended that individuals at high risk by virtue of their heavy drinking should be targeted for intervention (Marmot et al., 1994).

Since blood pressure is highly labile and subject to acute effects of alcohol and other factors, the influence of time elapsed since last ingestion has come under consideration. In a cross sectional study, 1,089 Brazilian adults from Porto Alegre were studied to assess effects of the time elapsed between the last ingestion of alcohol and the time of blood pressure measurement. Positive associations were observed between the amount of alcohol consumed, increasing blood pressure, and the presence of hypertension (defined as blood pressure equal to or exceeding 160/95 mm Hg). Compared to nondrinkers, consumption of 30 g of alcohol per day produced average increases of 1.5 and 2.3 mm Hg in systolic and diastolic blood pressure in men, and 2.1 and 3.2 mm Hg in women. The prevalence of hypertension was nearly threefold higher among those ingesting more than 30 g of alcohol per day (odds ratio = 2.9). Furthermore, the time elapsed between the last ingestion of alcohol and time of blood pressure measurement was independently associated with the prevalence of hypertension, e.g., men who drank alcohol within 13–23 hours of blood pressure measurement were 2.6 times more likely to be hypertensive compared to those with longer intervals. These results suggest that alcohol has a time-dependent impact on blood pressure that may be

related to the level of consumption and drug pharmacology (Moreira et al., 1998).

In another study designed to examine blood pressure changes related to patterns of alcohol consumption, current alcohol consumption outside of meals was explored as a risk factor in 2,609 men and women from western New York. Notably, individuals who consumed alcohol separately from meals exhibited significantly higher relative risks than those who consumed alcohol during mealtime (Stranges et al., 2004). This result lends some support to a potential benefit of consuming a small amount of alcohol with meals (Klatsky, 2004).

The U-curve relationship of alcohol consumption and hypertension that has been observed in some studies is a source of controversy in the scientific literature. There appears to be consensus that heavy alcohol consumption increases blood pressure and the risk of hypertension, but the impact of light to moderate consumption is not as clear, with some studies reporting a decline in risk and others not. A team of investigators at Harvard reexamined the question in prospective analysis of 28,848 women from the Women's Health Study and 13,455 men from the Physician's Health Study who were free of hypertension at baseline. During 10.9 and 21.8 years of average follow-up, 8,680 women and 6,012 men developed hypertension (defined as systolic pressure equal to or exceeding 140 mm Hg or diastolic pressure equal to or exceeding 90 mm Hg). In women, the dose-response pattern was a J-shaped curve wherein light to moderate drinking slightly decreased the risk and heavy drinking or complete abstinence increased the risk. In men, the dose-response curve was linear, reflecting only increasing risk with increasing alcohol intake. The threshold for increased risk emerged at 1 drink per day for men (RR = 1.26) whereas the threshold for women occurred at 3 drinks per day (multivariate-adjusted RR = 1.84). Results therefore add to the evidence that heavy alcohol consumption significantly increases the risk of hypertension and lend support to the existence of differential effects of alcohol in men and women (Sesso et al., 2008).

Randomized clinical trials have been conducted to examine effects of reducing alcohol intake on blood pressure. In a meta-analysis of 15 randomized controlled trials enrolling 2,234 participants consuming 3 to 6 alcoholic drinks per day, alcohol reduction resulted in significant decreases in average systolic and diastolic blood pressures (3.3 and 2.0 mm Hg, respectively). Greater reductions in blood pressure were noted for individuals with higher blood pressures at baseline. Results support effective intervention to reduce alcohol consumption as an important lifestyle modification for the prevention and treatment of hypertension, particularly among heavy drinkers (Xin et al., 2001; Tomson and Lip, 2006).

Mechanisms by which alcohol increases blood pressure remain under study and have not been resolved (Clark, 1985; Klatsky, 2004). Alcohol metabolism is complex, involving first pass metabolism in the stomach and secondary metabolism in the liver. Compared to men, women have lower average total body water than men, a higher proportion of fat, and lower levels of alcohol-metabolizing enzymes, both in the stomach and in the liver (Frezza et al., 1990). These features are associated with higher blood levels of alcohol in women at comparable amounts of ingestion. Nevertheless, as pointed out already, women appear to have a higher threshold than men for the hypertensive effects of alcohol, e.g., four drinks per day versus one drink per day based on one recent study (Sesso et al., 2008).

One mechanistic link between alcohol and blood pressure that is of special interest involves the induction of *hypoglycemia* by alcohol consumption. Recent animal studies have shown that alcohol induces redistribution of blood flow within the pancreas, leading to markedly increased insulin secretion by the pancreatic *islets of Langerhans*, thus resulting in lowered blood sugar and hypoglycemia (Huang and Sjöholm, 2007). In 1939, Kraines and Gellhorn reported that hypoglycemia increases the blood pressure in psychiatric patients by stimulating the sympathetic nervous system (Kraines and Gellhorn, 1939). More recent studies have confirmed that hypoglycemia stimulates the sympathetic nervous system as well as the adrenal glands causing release of epinephrine and thereby elevating blood pressure (Sommerfeld et al., 2007; Feldman-Billard et al., 2010). Thus, it seems likely that alcohol-induced hypoglycemia may be at least partially responsible for the observed increase in blood pressure and hypertension among heavy drinkers.

Tobacco and Hypertension

Multiple epidemiologic investigations have consistently demonstrated that smoking is a key risk factor in the genesis of cardiovascular diseases including coronary heart disease, myocardial infarction, and stroke. Nevertheless, epidemiologic studies *do not* provide consistent evidence that smoking increases the risk of developing hypertension. Furthermore, blood pressure measured in the physician's office has been found to be similar for smokers compared to nonsmokers, a paradoxical finding in view of the acute vasoconstrictive impact of nicotine (Gropelli et al., 1992; Omvik, 1996).

To resolve this paradox, investigators from the Cardiovascular Disease and Hypertension Center at New York Hospital/Cornell Medical Center conducted a case-control study to compare the blood pressures of 59 untreated hypertensive individuals who smoked at least 2 packs of cigarettes per day (cases) with 118 untreated hypertensive individuals who were nonsmokers (controls). The controls were group-matched to the cases by age, sex, and race. While blood pressures measured in an office setting were similar, ambulatory measurements of systolic blood pressure taken throughout the day were significantly higher for smokers than nonsmokers (145 mm Hg versus 140 mm Hg). The average difference in ambulatory systolic blood pressure between smokers and nonsmokers was greatest among individuals over the age of 50 years (153 mm Hg versus 142 mm Hg). Blood pressure levels returned to normal levels during sleep for both groups (approximately 120/80 mm Hg). These results show that hypertensive smokers have higher ambulatory blood pressure during the waking hours than hypertensive nonsmokers, consistent with their higher risk for the development of cardiovascular disease (Mann et al., 1991).

More recently, the causal link between smoking and the development of hypertension has been validated in follow-up studies of normotensive individuals who were assigned a risk score (e.g., the *Framingham Risk Prediction Score*) based on several factors including smoking status. In the Framingham Heart Study, risk scores were determined for 1,717 participants 20–69 years of age based upon their age, sex, systolic and diastolic blood pressure, parental history of hypertension, body mass index, and cigarette smoking. During 3.8 years of average follow-up time, 726 new cases of hypertension (>140/90 mm Hg) were detected in the cohort. In regression models, risk scores were highly correlated with increasing blood pressure and current smoking was a significant individual predictor of the development of hypertension (Parikh et al., 2008).

Further testing of the *Framingham Risk Prediction Score* was conducted in a European cohort of 2,704 London-based civil servants aged 35–68 years. Each participant was evaluated and assigned a risk score based on age, sex, body mass index, and smoking status at the beginning of each of three 5-year intervals. A total of 2,043 incident cases of hypertension were detected in the three 5-year follow-up data cycles. As in the Framingham cohort, the risk score proved to be a valid tool for the prediction of hypertension in this cohort, and current smoking was the strongest individual predictor of hypertension (Kivimäki et al., 2009).

Insulin Resistance, Diabetes Mellitus, and Hypertension

Diabetes mellitus is a major chronic disease caused by dysfunctional regulation and metabolism of blood glucose. It arises either from (1) inadequate secretion of insulin by cells of the *islets of Langerhans* in the pancreas (type 1 diabetes mellitus) or (2) ineffectiveness of insulin in transporting glucose into cells of the body for energy (type 2 diabetes mellitus). Type 1 diabetes is more common in children and accounts for a relatively small percentage of cases (approximately 5%) whereas type 2 diabetes usually arises in adults and is much more prevalent, accounting for approximately 95% of cases. The *epidemiology of diabetes mellitus* is covered later.

Type 2 diabetes arises because the cells of the body become resistant to the usual effects of insulin in stimulating glucose uptake for energy. Ineffectual glucose uptake in the presence of insulin is appropriately called *"insulin resistance."* In type 2 diabetes, since the cells of the body are insulin resistant, glucose remains in the blood, and blood glucose levels become inordinately high, a condition known as *hyperglycemia.* Furthermore, pancreatic cells may attempt to compensate for high levels of blood glucose by secreting more insulin, a condition known as *hyperinsulinemia.*

The clinical definition of diabetes is when the *fasting blood glucose* (blood glucose measured after 8 hours without food) exceeds 125 mg per dl. Insulin resistance is defined as a *prediabetic* state in which the fasting blood glucose level is between 110–125 mg per dl. Diabetes and insulin resistance are often confirmed by a *glucose tolerance test* in which blood glucose levels are measured following an oral loading dose of glucose. Persistence of elevated blood glucose above 200 mg per dl for more than 2 hours indicates diabetes and a level between 140–200 mg per dl indicates insulin resistance.

In 1966, Welborn and colleagues studied 19 patients with essential hypertension and found that their plasma insulin levels were significantly elevated compared to normotensive controls (Welborn et al., 1966). This was the first of many investigations that have examined insulin and insulin resistance as risk factors for the development of hypertension. Selected studies of population samples from around the globe are discussed in the following paragraphs.

In the United States, Dr. Gerald Reaven and colleagues assessed insulin levels and other factors in 33 obese women aged 27–77 years of age and found that fasting serum insulin level was the strongest predictor of systolic and diastolic blood pressure (Lucas et al., 1985). In Israel, Modan and colleagues studied hypertension and glucose intolerance in 2,475 adults randomly sampled from a central population registry. They found increased rates of hypertension with impaired glucose tolerance (rate ratio = 1.48) as well as in patients with type 2 diabetes (rate ratio = 2.26).

In Italy, insulin resistance was measured in 13 young adults (mean age = 38) with severe essential hypertension and 11 normotensive control subjects matched by age and weight. Total insulin-induced glucose uptake was markedly impaired among the hypertensive individuals (3.8 versus 6.3 mg per minute per kg body weight) (Ferrannini et al., 1987). In an Italian case-control study of 41 patients with essential hypertension and 41 normotensive control subjects, 45% of hypertensive patients had abnormal glucose tolerance tests compared to 10% of normotensive subjects (Zavaroni et al., 1992).

Investigators in Sweden studied relationships of glucose metabolism, insulin resistance, obesity, and hypertension in 143 newly diagnosed hypertensive patients. Insulin resistance and hyperinsulinemia were associated with hypertension in both obese and nonobese individuals compared to normotensive individuals (Pollare, Lithell, and Berne, 1990).

The Insulin Resistance Atherosclerosis Study (IRAS) was designed to prospectively examine insulin resistance and other risk factors for hypertension in US cohorts of differing ethnicities. Participants included 564 non-Hispanic Caucasian Americans, 505 Hispanic Americans, and 403 African Americans aged 40–69 years. Study results reflect increased prevalence rates of hypertension with progressively higher degrees of impaired glucose tolerance for each cohort and across all cohorts: 30% for normal subjects, 39% for prediabetic individuals, and 46% for individuals with type 2 diabetes mellitus (**Figure 6.7**). Multivariate regression analysis of nondiabetic subjects revealed independent effects of gender (male), body mass index, insulin resistance, and fasting blood glucose on the development of hypertension. Nevertheless, among diabetic subjects, insulin resistance was not a significant predictor of hypertension (Saad et al., 2004).

While these investigations implicate insulin resistance and impaired glucose uptake as significant risk factors in the development of hypertension, not all patients with essential hypertension manifest insulin resistance. Clearly, a significant fraction of hypertensive patients, perhaps up to 50%, manifest hyperinsulinemia and/or insulin resistance; whereas the remaining half does not (Reaven, 1988; Landberg, 1995). The findings demonstrate the complexity of interactions involving glucose regulation and blood pressure, and related physiological mechanisms.

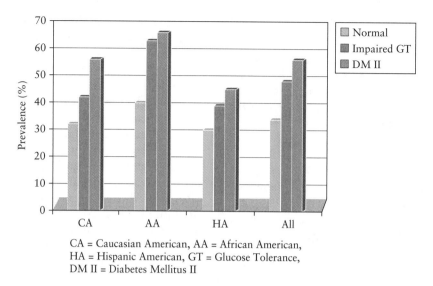

CA = Caucasian American, AA = African American,
HA = Hispanic American, GT = Glucose Tolerance,
DM II = Diabetes Mellitus II

Figure 6.7 Prevalence of Hypertension by Glucose Intolerance and Ethnicity.

Source: Data from Saad MF, Rewers M, Selby J, Howard G, Jinagouda S, Fahmi S, Zaccaro D, Bergman RN, Savage PJ, Haffner SM. (2004). Insulin resistance and hypertension: The Insulin Resistance Atherosclerosis Study. *Hypertension* 43:1–8.

As pointed out by Dr. Gerald Reaven in his discussion of hypertension, insulin resistance, diabetes, and coronary heart disease:

> *"Hyperglycemia develops in insulin-resistant individuals when they no longer are able to secrete the large amount of insulin necessary to overcome insulin resistance. Similarly, it seems likely that hypertension only develops when some unknown compensatory response (or responses) is no longer able to overcome the metabolic changes associated with insulin resistance and compensatory hyperinsulinemia that favor an increase in blood pressure."*
>
> *Statement from Reaven GM (2003). Insulin resistance, hypertension and coronary heart disease.* Journal of Clinical Hypertension, *5(4), 269–274.*

THE METABOLIC SYNDROME (SYNDROME X)

Dietary Calcium and Hypertension

The discovery that dietary calcium may influence blood pressure was first reported by McCarron and colleagues in the 1980s (McCarron, 1985). These early studies demonstrated that low dietary calcium was associated with hypertension and that per capita calcium consumption by US adults was inversely related to the probability of being hypertensive. The initial investigation was a small pilot study comparing 44 normotensive control subjects with 46 cases with essential hypertension. Dietary assessement revealed significantly less daily calcium consumption in the cases compared to controls (668 mg versus 886 mg) (McCarron, Morris, and Cole, 1982).

Subsequently, a number of other epidemiologic studies and clinical trials also found an association between low dietary calcium and hypertension, and reciprocally, beneficial effects of supplemental calcium in reducing blood pressure. In a meta-analysis of 40 randomized clinical trials conducted during 1966–2003 and involving a total of 2,492 participants, calcium supplementation of 1,200 mg per day produced average reductions of 1.86 mm Hg and 0.99 mm Hg in systolic and diastolic blood pressures, respectively. Greater reductions (1.63 and 1.30 mm Hg) were noted for individuals with low dietary calcium at baseline (< 800 mg daily) (van Mierlo et al., 2006). Nevertheless, there was considerable heterogeneity among studies in the response to supplemental calcium and some studies did not discern an effect (Trumbo and Ellwood, 2007). It has been suggested that lack of adjustment for baseline factors, e.g., levels of dietary calcium, vitamin D, and blood pressures among participants, may be responsible for the heterogeneity of effect among studies (McCarron and Reusser, 1999).

One notable example of a "null study" is the randomized double-blinded placebo-controlled trial of calcium and vitamin D supplementation in the US Women's Health Initiative (WHI). In this study,

36,282 postmenopausal women were randomly assigned to receive 1,000 mg of elemental calcium plus 400 international units (IU) of vitamin D daily or placebo in double-blind fashion. Over a median follow-up time of 7 years, there were no significant differences in systolic or diastolic blood pressures between the treatment and placebo groups. Furthermore, among 17,122 normotensive women at baseline, the hazard ratio for the incidence of hypertension for the treatment arm of the study was virtually unchanged after 7 years of follow-up (HR = 1.01). Stratified analysis of data according to baseline factors (race, blood pressure, low dietary calcium, and vitamin D) *did not* reveal effects for subgroups of interest (Margolis et al., 2008). These results provide no evidence that supplemental calcium plus vitamin D reduces blood pressure or the incidence of hypertension in postmenopausal women, regardless of baseline status.

GENETICS OF HYPERTENSION

Certain genetic syndromes have been found to cause hypertension. As might be expected, the ones best described involve dysfunction of sodium transport in the kidney. Liddle's syndrome is due to a rare mutant gene that causes constitutive activation of the sodium transport channel in the renal tubules of the kidney. Patients with Liddle's syndrome develop severe intractable hypertension at an early age (often during infancy) due to their high sodium retention (Shimkets et al., 1994). Gordon's syndrome is caused by a rare mutant gene that disturbs the sodium-chloride transport channel in the distal renal tubules resulting in enhanced chloride and sodium retention thereby causing hypertension by the third decade of life (Gordon et al., 1970).

African Americans have higher rates of hypertension than Caucasian Americans (Burt et al., 1995), which has been attributed to their heightened retention of sodium (salt) by the renin-angiotensin system (Luft et al., 1991; Weinberger, 1993). Specific genes encode vital components of the renin-angiotensin system including renin, angiotensinogen, angiotensin converting enzyme (ACE), and angiotensin receptors, and recent genetic association studies have searched for effects of alleles of these genes among relatives with familial hypertension.

In a recent study involving 192 African American families, single-nucleotide polymorphisms of genes encoding renin and the angiotensin receptor (*AGTR-1*) were found to be significantly associated with the development of essential hypertension (Zhu et al.,

2003). These results take on added significance since the primary effector molecule of the renin-angiotensin system, *angiotensin II*, has been found to increase expression of the gene that encodes endothelin-1, a potent local vasoconstrictive protein secreted by the endothelium of blood vessels (Hong et al., 2004).

Differences in endothelin-1 have been observed in association with the higher rates of hypertension among African Americans compared to other ethnic groups. In a clinical study designed to examine blood levels of endothelin-1 among hypertensive subjects, African American men and women with hypertension were found to have considerably higher endothelin-1 levels than Caucasians with hypertension (Ergul et al., 1996). In other studies, normotensive African American men had twofold higher levels than age-matched Caucasian men (Evans et al., 1996) and African American adolescents had higher levels than Caucasians (Treiber et al., 2000). In view of these findings, the influence of genes that regulate the renin-angiotensin system as well as vasoactive substances within blood vessels may play a role in elevating the susceptibility to hypertension among African Americans.

PREVENTION OF HYPERTENSION

The degree to which hypertension can be prevented in a given patient depends on a number of individual factors including age, gender, current blood pressure level, sodium/potassium balance, body mass, alcohol consumption, smoking, exercise pattern, cholesterol and glucose control, and psychological factors such as stress and depression. A prolonged assessment in which repeated measurements of blood pressure are taken provides the most accurate method of detecting a significant rise in blood pressure above normal. Individuals who manifest systolic blood pressure of 130–139 mm Hg or diastolic blood pressure of 80–89 mm Hg should be considered as *prehypertensive*. Lifestyle changes are recommended to lower blood pressure *before* the initiation of prescription drug therapy. The following guidelines for implementing lifestyle changes are recommended by the British Hypertension Society (**Table 6.2**).

In consideration of nonpharmacologic approaches to blood pressure control, it is noteworthy that dietary modification has been shown to have significant benefit for prehypertensive and hypertensive patients. The *Dietary Approaches to Stop Hypertension* (*DASH*) study was specifically designed to assess the impact on blood pressure of a *combination diet* rich in fruits, vegetables, and

Table 6.2	Nonpharmacologic Guidelines to Reduce Blood Pressure

- Weight reduction and regular (daily) aerobic exercise
- Reducing dietary sugar
- Reducing sodium (salt) in the diet to less than six grams
- Additional dietary changes beneficial to reducing blood pressure, e.g., the DASH diet (dietary approaches to stop hypertension), which is rich in fruits and vegetables and low-fat or fat-free dairy products
- Increasing dietary potassium and calcium
- Abstaining from or discontinuing tobacco use
- Limiting alcohol consumption to one drink daily
- Reducing stress and depression
- Maintaining blood levels of cholesterol and glucose within normal limits

Source: Data from Saad MF, Rewers M, Selby J, Howard G, Jinagouda S, Fahmi S, Zaccaro D, Bergman RN, Savage PJ, Haffner SM. (2004). Insulin resistance and hypertension: the Insulin Resistance Atherosclerosis Study. *Hypertension* 43:1–8.

low-fat dairy products with reduced saturated and total fat. The study randomized 459 adults with systolic blood pressure less than 160 mm Hg and diastolic blood pressure between 80–95 mm Hg into a treatment arm ($n = 230$) to receive the DASH diet and a control arm ($n = 229$) without dietary modification. At 8 weeks of follow-up, the combination DASH diet reduced systolic and diastolic blood pressures by 5.5 and 3.0 mm Hg, respectively, compared to the control diet. Among participants with hypertension (blood pressure exceeding 140/90 mm Hg), the DASH diet produced even greater reductions in average blood pressure (11.4 and 5.5 mm Hg, respectively). The DASH Study investigators concluded that a diet rich in fruits, vegetables, and low-fat dairy foods with reduced saturated and total fat can substantially lower blood pressure in both prehypertensive and hypertensive individuals (Appel et al., 1997).

● ● ● REFERENCES

Aneja, A., El-Atat, F., McFarlane, S.I., & Sowers, J.R. (2004). Hypertension and obesity. *Recent Progress in Hormone Research*, 59, 169–205.

Appel, L.J., Moore, T.J., Obarzanek, E., Vollmer, W.M., Svetkey, L.P., Sacks, F.M.,... DASH Collaborative Research Group. (1997). A clinical trial of the effects of dietary patterns on blood pressure. *N Engl J Med*, 336, 1117–1124.

Arroyo, P., Fernandez, A., Loria, A., et al. (1999). Hypertension in urban Mexico: The 1992–93 national survey of chronic diseases. *J Hum Hypertens*, 13, 671–675.

Australian Institute of Health and Welfare (2011). Risk Factor Prevalence Data.

Baba, S., Pan, W.H., Ueshima, H., et al. (1991). Blood pressure levels, related factors, and hypertension control status of Japanese and Americans. *J Hum Hypertens*, 5, 317–332.

Banegas, J.R., Rodriguez-Artalejo, F., de la Cruz. T.J.J., Guallar-Castillon, P., Calero, J., & del Rey, C.J. (1998). Blood pressure in Spain: Distribution, awareness, control, and benefits of a reduction in average pressure. *Hypertension*, 32, 998–1002.

Banegas, J.R., & Pérez-Regadera, A.G. (1998). Hypertension control as an indicator of the geographical variation of stroke. *Stroke, 29*, 867–868.

Bennett, S.A., & Magnus, P. (1994). Trends in cardiovascular risk factors in Australia. Results from the National Heart Foundation's Risk Factor Prevalence Study, 1980–1989. *Med J Aust, 161*, 519–527.

Blaustein, M.P., Zhang, J., Chen, L., & Hamilton, B.P. (2006). How does salt retention raise blood pressure? *Am J Physiol Regul Integr Comp Physiol*, 290(3), R514–R523.

Brent, G.A. (1994). Mechanisms of disease: The molecular basis of thyroid hormone action. *New Eng J Med*, 331, 847–853.

Brooks, V.L., Haywood, J.R., & Johnson, A.K. (2005). Translation of salt retention to central activation of the sympathetic nervous system in hypertension. *Clinical and Experimental Pharmacology and Physiology*, 32, 426–432.

Burt, V.L., Whelton, P., Roccella, E.J., et al. (1995). Prevalence of hypertension in the US adult population. Results from the Third National Health and Nutrition Examination survey, 1988–91. *Hypertension*, 25, 305–313.

Centers for Disease Control. (2007). Division for Heart Disease and Stroke Prevention. Department of Health and Human Services.

Chobanian, A.V., Bakris, G.L., Black, H.R., Cushman, W.C., Green, L.A., Izzo, J.L. Jr., Jones, D.W., Materson, B.J., Oparil, S., Wright, J.T. Jr., Roccella, E.J. (2003). Seventh report of the Joint National Committee on Prevention, Detection, Evaluation, and Treatment of High Blood Pressure. *Hypertension, 42*(6), 1206–1252.

Clark, L.T. (1985). Alcohol-induced hypertension: Mechanisms, complications, and clinical implications. *J Natl Med Assoc, 77*(5), 385–389.

Collins, R., Peto, R., MacMahon, S., Hebert, P., Fiebach, N.H., Eberlein, K.A., Godwin, J., Qizilbash, N., Taylor, J.O., Hennekens, C.H. (1990). Blood pressure, stroke, and coronary heart disease, part II: Short-term reductions in blood pressure: Overview of randomised drug trials in their epidemiological context. *Lancet, 335*, 827–838.

Cooper, R., Rotimi, D., Ataman, S., et al. (1997). The prevalence of hypertension in seven populations of West African origin. *Am J Public Health, 87*, 160–168.

Criqui, M.H., Mebane, I., Wallace, R.B., Heiss, G., Holdbrook, M.J. (1982). Multivariate correlates of adult blood pressures in nine North American populations: The lipid research clinics prevalence study. *Preventive Medicine, 11*, 391–402.

Cutler, J.A., Sorlie, P.D., Wolz, M., Thom, T., Fields, L.E., & Roccella, E.J. (2008). Trends in the hypertension prevalence, awareness, treatment, and control rates in United States adults between 1988–1994 and 1999–2004. *Hypertension, 52*(5), 818–827.

Dyer, A.R., & Elliott, P. (1989). The INTERSALT study: Relations of body mass index to blood pressure. INTERSALT Co-operative Research Group. *J Hum Hypertens, 3*(5), 299–308.

Dyer, A.R., Elliott, P., & Shipley, M.J. (1990). Body mass index versus height and weight in relation to blood pressure: Findings for the 10,079 persons in the INTERSALT study. *Am J Epidemiol, 131*, 589–596.

Dyer, A.R., Elliott, P., Shipley, M., Stamler, R., & Stamler, J. (1994). Body mass index and associations of sodium and potassium with blood pressure in INTERSALT. *Hypertension, 23*, 729–736.

Edwards, R., Unwin, N., Mugus, F., et al. (2000). Hypertension prevalence and care in an urban and rural area of Tanzania. *J Hypertens, 18*(2000), 145–152.

Ergul, S., Parish, D.C., Puett, D., & Ergul, A. (1996). Racial differences in plasma endothelin-1 concentrations in individuals with essential hypertension. *Hypertension, 28*, 652–655.

Evans, R.R., Phillips, B.G., Singh, G., Bauman, J.L., & Gulati, A. (1996). Racial and gender differences in endothelin-1. *Am J Cardiol, 78*, 486–488.

Feldman-Billard, S., Massin, P., Meas, T., Guillausseau, P.J., & Héron, E. (2010). Hypoglycemia-induced blood pressure elevation in patients with diabetes. *Arch Intern Med, 170*(9), 829–831.

Ferrannini, E., Buzzigoli, G., Bonadonna, R., Giorico, M.A., Oleggini, M., Graziadei, L.,… Bevilacqua, S. (1987). Insulin resistance in essential hypertension. *N Engl J Med, 317*, 350–357.

Fiebach, N.H., Hebert, P.R., Stampfer, M.J., Colditz, G.A., Willett, W.C., Rosner, B.,… Hennekens, C.H. (1989). A prospective study of high blood pressure and cardiovascular disease in women. *Am J Epidemiol, 130*, 646–654.

Frezza, M., di Padova, C., Pozzato, G., Terpin, M., Baraona, E., & Lieber, C.S. (1990). High blood alcohol levels in women. The role of decreased gastric alcohol dehydrogenase activity and first-pass metabolism. *N Engl J Med, 322*(2), 95–99.

Giampaoli, S., Palmieri, L., Dima, F., Pilotto, L., Vescio, M.F., & Vanuzzo, D. (2001). Socioeconomic aspects and cardiovascular risk factors: Experience at the Cardiovascular Epidemiologic Observatory. *Ital Heart J, 2*, 294–302.

Gordon, R., Geddes, R., Pawse, C., & O'Halloran, M. (1970). Hypertension and severe hyperkalaemia associated with suppression of renin and aldosterone and completely reversed by dietary sodium restriction. *Australasian Annals of Medicine, 19*(4), 287–294.

Gropelli, A., Giorgi, D.M.A., Omboni, S., Parati, G., Manchia, G. (1992). Persistent blood pressure increase induced by heavy smoking. *J Hypertension, 10,* 495–499.

Gu, D., Reynolds, K., Wu, X., et al. (2002). Prevalence, awareness, treatment, and control of hypertension in China. *Hypertension, 40,* 920–927.

Gupta, R., & Sharma, A.K. (1994). Prevalence of hypertension and subtypes in an Indian rural population: Clinical and electrocardiographic correlates. *J Hum Hypertens, 8,* 823–829.

Gupta, R., Guptha, S., Gupta, V.P., & Prakash, H. (1995). Prevalence and determinants of hypertension in the urban population of Jaipur in western India. *J Hypertens, 13,* 1193–1200.

Gupta, R., AI-Odat, N.A., & Gupta, V.P. (1996). Hypertension epidemiology in India: Meta-analysis of fifty-year prevalence rates and blood pressure trends. *J Human Hypertens, 10,* 465–472.

Gupta, R. (1999). Hypertension in India: Definition, prevalence and evaluation. *J Indian Med Assoc, 97,* 74–80.

Gupta, R. (2004). Trends in hypertension epidemiology in India. *Journal of Human Hypertension, 18,* 73–78.

Haynes, W.G., Hand, M.F., Johnstone, H.A., Padfield, P.L., & Webb, D.J. (1994). Direct and sympathetically mediated venoconstriction in essential hypertension. *J Clin Invest, 94,* 1359–1364.

He, F.J., & MacGregor, G.A. (2002). Effect of modest salt reduction on blood pressure: A meta-analysis of randomized trials. Implications for public health. *J Hum Hypertens, 16*(11), 761–770.

He, Q., Ding, Z.Y., Fong, D.Y., & Karlberg, J. (2000). Blood pressure is associated with body mass index in both obese and normal children. *Hypertension, 36,* 165 –170.

Hebert, P., Moser, M., Mayer, J., Glynn, R.J., & Hennekens, C.H. (1993). Recent evidence on drug therapy of mild to moderate hypertension and decreased risk of coronary heart disease. *Arch Intern Med, 153,* 578–581.

Hong, J.H., Chan, P., Kiu, J.C., et al. (2004). Angiotensin II induces endothelin-1 gene expression via extracellular signal-related kinase pathway in rat aortic smooth muscle cells. *Cardiovasc Res, 61*(1), 159–168.

Huang, Z., Willett, W.C., Manson, J.E., et al. (1998). Body weight, weight change and the risk of hypertension in women. *Ann Intern Med, 128,* 81–88.

Huang, Z., & Sjöholm, Å. (2007). Ethanol acutely stimulates islet blood flow, amplifies insulin secretion, and induces hypoglycemia via nitric oxide and vagally mediated mechanism. *Endocrinology, 149*(1), 232–236.

Ibrahim, M.M., Rizk, H., Appel, L.J., et al. (1995). Hypertension prevalence, awareness, treatment, and control in Egypt. Results from the Egyptian National Hypertension Project (NHP). NHP Investigative Team. *Hypertension, 26,* 886–890.

Ilekis, J.V., Reddy, U.M., & Roberts, J.M. (2006). Review Article: Pre-eclampsia—a pressing problem: An executive summary of a National Institute of Child Health and Human Development Workshop. *Reproductive Sciences, 14*(6), 508–523.

InterASIA Collaborative group. (2003). Cardiovascular risk factor levels in urban and rural Thailand: The International Collaborative Study of Cardiovascular Disease in Asia (InterASIA). *Eur J Cardiovasc Prev Rehabil, 10,* 249–257.

Joffres M.R., Ghadirian, P., Fodor, J.G., Petrasovits, A., Chockalingam, A., & Hamet, P. (1997). Awareness, treatment, and control of hypertension in Canada. *Am J Hypertens, 10,* 1097–1102.

Joint National Committee on Detection, Evaluation, and Treatment of High Blood Pressure. (1993). The fifth report of the Joint National Committee on the Detection, Evaluation, and Treatment of High Blood Pressure. *Arch Intern Med, 153,* 154–183.

Kannel, W.B., Garrison, R.J., & Dannenberg, A.L. (1993). Secular blood pressure trends in normotensive persons. *Am Heart J, 12,* 1154–1158.

Kearney, P.M., Whelton, M., Reynolds, K., Muntner, P., Whelton, P.K., & He, J. (2005). Global burden of hypertension: Analysis of worldwide data. *Lancet, 365*(9455), 217–223.

Kim, J.S., Jones, D.W., Kim, S.J., & Hong, Y.P. (1994). Hypertension in Korea: A national survey. *Am J Prev Med, 10,* 200–204.

Kissebah, A.H., & Krakower, G.R. (1994). Regional adiposity and morbidity. *Physiol Rev, 74,* 761–811.

Kivimäki, M., Batty, D., Singh-Manoux, A., Ferrie, J.E., Tabak, A.G., Jokela, M., . . . Shipley, M.J. (2009). Validating the Framingham Hypertension Risk Score. *Hypertension, 54,* 496–501.

Klatsky, A.L. (2004). Alcohol-associated hypertension: When one drink makes a difference. *Hypertension, 4,* 805–806.

Kraines, S.H., & Gellhorn, E. (1939). The effects of insulin hypoglycemia on the blood pressure response to oxygen deficiency in man. *American Journal of Psychiatry, 95*(5), 1067–1075.

Landberg, L. (1995). Obesity-related hypertension and the insulin resistance syndrome. *Trans Am Clin Climatol Assoc, 106,* 69–76.

Laurent, S. (2004). Guidelines from the British Hypertension Society. *BMJ, 328,* 593–594.

Lian, C.L. (1915). L'alcoholisme, caused hypertension arterielle. *Bulletin de l'Academie de Medicine, 74,* 525–528.

Lucas, C.P., Estigarribia, J.A., Darga, L.L., & Reaven, G.M. (1985). Insulin and blood pressure in obesity. *Hypertension, 7,* 702–706.

Luft, F.C., Miller, J.Z., Grim, C.E., Fineberg, N.S., Christian, J.C., Daugherty, S.A., & Weinberger, M.H. (1991). Salt sensitivity and resistance

of blood pressure. Age and race as factors in physiological responses. *Hypertension,* 1991 Jan;17(1 Suppl), I102–I108.

MacMahon, S., Peto, R., Cutler, J., Collins, R., Sorlie, P., Neaton, J.,...Stamler, J. (1990). Blood pressure, stroke, and coronary heart disease, part I: Prolonged differences in blood pressure: Prospective observational studies corrected for the regression dilution bias. *Lancet, 335,* 765–774.

Malhotra, P., Kumari, S., Kumar, R., Jain, S., & Sharma, B.K. (1999). Prevalence and determinants of hypertension in an un-industrialized rural population of North India. *J Hum Hypertens, 13,* 467–472.

Mann, S.J., James, G.D., Wang, R.S., & Pickering, T.G. (1991). Elevation of ambulatory systolic blood pressure in hypertensive smokers. *JAMA, 265*(17), 2226–2228.

Margolis, K.L., Ray, R.M., Van Horn, L., Manson, J.E., Allison, M.A., Black, H.R., . . . Torner, J.C., for the Women's Health Initiative Investigators. (2008). Effect of calcium and vitamin D supplementation on blood pressure. *Hypertension, 52,* 847–855.

Marmot, M.G., Elliott, P., Shipley, M.J., Dyer, A.R., Ueshima, H.U., Beevers, D.G.,... Stamler, J. (1994). Alcohol and blood pressure: The INTERSALT study. *British Medical Journal, 308,* 1263–1267.

Mbanya, J.C., Minkoulou, E.M., Salah, J.N., & Balkau, B. (1998). The prevalence of hypertension in rural and urban Cameroon. *Int J Epidemiol, 27,* 181–185.

McCarron, D.A., Morris, C.D., & Cole, C. (1982). Dietary calcium in human hypertension. *Science, 217*(4556), 267–269.

McCarron, D.A. (1985). Is calcium more important than sodium in the pathogenesis of essential hypertension. *Hypertension, 7,* 607–627.

McCarron, D.A., & Reusser, M.E. (1999). Finding consensus in the dietary calcium blood pressure debate. *Journal of the American College of Nutrition, 18*(90005), 398S–405S.

Modan, M., Halkin, H., Almog, S., Lusky, A., Eshkol, A., Shefi, M.,…Fuchs, Z. (1985). Hyperinsulinemia: A link between hypertension, obesity and glucose intolerance. *J Clin Invest, 75,* 809–817.

Moffett, A., & Hiby, S.E. (2007). How does the maternal immune system contribute to the development of pre-eclampsia? *Placenta, 28*(Suppl A), S51–S56.

Moreira, L.B., Fuchs, F.D., Moraes, R.S., Bredemeier, M., & Duncan, B.B. (1998). Alcohol intake and blood pressure: The importance of time elapsed since last drink. *Journal of Hypertension, 16,* 175–180.

Mufunda, J., Scott, L.J., Chifamba, J., et al. (2000). Correlates of blood pressure in an urban Zimbabwean population and comparison to other populations of African origin. *J Human Hypertens, 14,* 65–73.

National Heart, Lung and Blood Institute. (1996). *Stroke Belt Initiative.* Washington, DC: National Institutes of Health.

Neter, J.E., Stam, B.E., Kok, F.J., Grobbee, D.E., & Geleijnse, J.M. (2003). Influence of weight reduction on blood pressure: A meta-analysis of randomized controlled trials. *Hypertension, 42,* 878–884.

Omvik, P. (1996). How smoking affects blood pressure. *Blood Press, 5*(2), 71–77.

Pan, W.H., Chang, H.Y., Yeh, W.T., Hsiao, S.Y., & Hung, Y.T. (2001). Prevalence, awareness, treatment and control of hypertension in Taiwan: Results of Nutrition and Health Survey in Taiwan (NAHSIT) 1993–1996. *J Hum Hypertens, 15,* 793–798.

Parikh, N.I., Pencina, M.J., Wang, T.J., Benjamin, E.J., Lanier, K.J., Levy, D.,…Vasan, R.S. (2008). A risk score for predicing near–term incidence of hypertension: The Framingham Heart Study. *Annals of Internal Medicine, 148*(2), 102–110.

Paul, M., Poyan Mehr, A., & Kreutz, R. (2006). Physiology of local renin-angiotensin systems. *Physiol Rev, 86*(3), 747–803.

Pollare, T., Lithell, H., & Berne, C. (1990). Insulin resistance is a characteristic feature of primary hypertension independent of obesity. *Metabolism, 39,* 167–174.

Primatesta, P., Brookes, M., & Poulter, N.R. (2001). Improved hypertension management and control: Results from the health survey for England 1998. *Hypertension, 38,* 827–832.

Ramirez, M.O., Pino, C.T., Furiasse, L.V., Lee, A.J., & Fowkes, F.G. (1995). Paraguayan National Blood Pressure Study: Prevalence of hypertension in the general population. *J Hum Hypertens, 9,* 891–897.

Reaven, G.M. (1988). Role of insulin resistance in human disease. *Diabetes, 37,* 1595–1607.

Reaven, G.M. (2003). Insulin resistance, hypertension and coronary heart disease. *Journal of Clinical Hypertension, 5*(4), 269–274.

Riecansky, I., & Egnerova, A. (1991). Cardiovascular program in Slovakia—Results achieved over the years 1978–1989. *Bratisl Lek Listy, 92,* 203–218.

Robbins, S.L., & Cotran, R.S. (1979). *Pathologic Basis of Disease.* Philadelphia: WB Saunders Company.

Rucker, D., Padwal, R., Li, S.K., Cuioni, C., & Lau, D.C.W. (2007). Long term pharmacotherapy for obesity and overweight: Updated meta-analysis. *BMJ, 335,* 1194–1199.

Saad, M.F., Rewers, M., Selby, J., Howard, G., Jinagouda, S., Fahmi, S.,…Haffner, S.M. (2004). Insulin resistance and hypertension: The Insulin Resistance Atherosclerosis Study. *Hypertension, 43,* 1–8.

Sesso, H.D., Cook, N.R., Buring, J.E., Manson, J.E., & Gaziano, J.M. (2008). Alcohol consumption and the risk of hypertension in women and men. *Hypertension, 51,* 1080–1087.

Shimkets, R.A., Warnock, D.G., Bositis, C.M., et al. (1994). Liddle's syndrome: Heritable human hypertension caused by mutations in the beta subunit of the epithelial sodium channel. *Cell, 79*(3), 407–414.

Shulman, N.B., Ford, C.E., Hall, W.D., Blaufox, M.D., Simon, D., Langford, H.G., & Schneider, K.A. (1989). Prognostic value of serum creatinine and effect of treatment of hypertension on renal function: Results from the Hypertension Detection and Followup Program. *Hypertension*, *13*(suppl I), I-80–I-93.

Singh, R.B., Beegom, R., Ghosh, S., et al. (1997a). Epidemiological study of hypertension and its determinants in an urban population of North India. *J Hum Hypertens*, *11*, 679–685.

Singh, R.B., Sharma, J.P., Rastogi, V., Niaz, M.A., & Singh, N.K. (1997b). Prevalence and determinants of hypertension in the Indian social class and heart survey. *J Hum Hypertens*, *11*, 51–56.

Sommerfield, A.J., Wilkinson, I.B., Webb, D.J., & Frier, B.M. (2007). Vessel wall stiffness in type 1 diabetes and the central hemodynamic effects of acute hypoglycemia. *Am J Physiol Endocrinol Metab*, *293*(5), E1274–E1279.

Sonmez, H.M., Basak, O., Camci, C., et al. (1999). The epidemiology of elevated blood pressure as an estimate for hypertension in Aydin, Turkey. *J Hum Hypertens*, *13*, 399–404.

Stamler, J., Stamler, R., & Neaton, J.D. (1993). Blood pressure, systolic and diastolic, and cardiovascular risks: U.S. population data. *Arch Intern Med*, *153*, 598–615.

Stegmayr, B., Harmsen, P., Rajakangas, A.M., Rastenyté, D., Sarti, C., Thorvaldsen, P., & Tuomilehto, J. (1996). Stroke around the Baltic Sea: Incidence, case fatality and population risk factors in Denmark, Finland, Sweden and Lithuania. *Cerebrovasc Dis*, *6*, 80–88.

Stegmayr, B., Asplund, K., Kuulasmaa, K., Rajakangas, A., Thorvaldsen, P., & Tuomilehto, J. (1997). Stroke incidence and mortality correlated to stroke risk factors in the WHO MONICA Project: An ecological study of 18 populations. *Stroke*, *28*, 1367–1374.

Stergiou, G.S., Thomopoulou, G.C., Skeva, I.I., & Mountokalakis, T.D. (1999). Prevalence, awareness, treatment, and control of hypertension in Greece: The Didima study. *Am J Hypertens*, *12*, 959–965.

Steyn, K., Gaziano, T.A., Bradshaw, D., Laubscher, R., & Fourie, J. (2001). South African Demographic and Health Coordinating Team. Hypertension in South African adults: Results from the Demographic and Health Survey, 1998. *J Hypertens*, *19*, 1717–1725.

Stranges, S., Wu, T., Dorn, J.M., Freudenheim, J.L., Muti, P., Farinaro, E.,...Trevisan, M. (2004). Relationship of alcohol drinking pattern to the risk of hypertension: A population-based study. *Hypertension*, *44*, 813–819.

Sulbaran, T., Silva, E., Calmon, G., & Vegas, A. (2000). Epidemiologic aspects of arterial hypertension in Maracaibo, Venezuela. *J Hum Hypertens*, *14*, S6–S9.

Thamm, M. (1999). Blood pressure in Germany: Current status and trends. *Gesundheitswesen*, S90–S93.

Tomson, J., & Lip, G.Y.H. (2006). Alcohol and hypertension: An old relationship revisited. *Alcohol and Alcoholism*, *41*(1), 3–4.

Treiber, F.A., Jackson, R.W., Davis, H., et al. (2000). Racial differences in Endothelin-1 at rest and in response to acute stress in adolescent males. *Hypertension*, *35*, 72–725.

Trumbo, P.R., & Ellwood, K.C. (2007). Supplemental calcium and risk reduction of hypertension, pregnancy-induced hypertension, and preeclampsia: An evidence-based review by the US Food and Drug Administration. *Nutr Rev*, *65*, 78–87.

van Mierlo, L.A., Arends, L.R., Streppel, M.T., et al. (2006). Blood pressure response to calcium supplementation: A meta-analysis of randomized controlled trials. *J Hum Hypertens*, *20*(8), 571–580.

Weinberger, M.H. (1993). Racial differences in renal sodium excretion: Relationship to hypertension. *Am J Kidney Dis*, *21*(4), 41–45.

Welborn, T.A., Breckenridge, A., Rubinstein, A.H., et al. (1966). Serum-insulin in essential hypertension and in peripheral vascular disease. *Lancet, 1*, 1136–1137.

Whelton, P.K. (1994). Epidemiology of hypertension. *Lancet, 334*, 101–106.

Whelton, P.K., Perneger, T.V., Klag, M.J., & Brancati, F.L. (1992). Epidemiology and prevention of blood pressure-related renal disease. *J Hypertens, 10*(suppl 7), S77–S84.

Whitworth, J.A., Brown, M.A., Kelly, J.J., & Williamson, P.M. (1995). Mechanisms of cortisol-induced hypertension in humans. *Steroids, 60*(1), 76–80.

Wilsgaard, T., Schirmer, H., & Arnesen, E. (2000). Impact of body weight on blood pressure with a focus on sex differences: The Tromso Study, 1986–1995. *Arch Intern Med, 160*(18), 2847–2853.

Wolf-Maier, K., Cooper, R.S., Banegas, J.R., Giampaoli, S., Hense, H., Joffres, M.,…Vescio, F. (2003). Hypertension and blood pressure levels in 6 European countries, Canada, and the US. *JAMA, 289*, 2363–2369.

Wolf-Maier, K., Cooper, R.S., Kramer, H., Banegas, J.R., Giampaoli, S., Joffres, M.R.,…Thamm, M. (2004). Hypertension treatment and control in five European countries, Canada and the United States. *Hypertension, 43*, 10–17.

Wolz, M., Cutler, J., Roccella, E.J., Rohde, F., Thom, T., & Burt, V. (2000). Statement from the National High Blood Pressure Education Program: Prevalence of hypertension. *Am J Hypertens, 13*, 103–104.

Working Group on Primary Prevention of Hypertension. (1993). Report of the National High Blood Pressure Education Program Working Group on Primary Prevention of Hypertension. *Arch Intern Med, 153*, 186–208.

Xin, X., He, J., Frontini, M.G., Ogden, L.G., Motsamai, O.I., & Whelton, P.K. (2001). Effects of alcohol reduction on blood pressure. *Hypertension, 38*, 1112–1117.

Yanagisawa, M., Kurihara, H., & Kimura, S. (1988). A novel potent vasoconstrictor peptide produced by vascular endothelial cells. *Nature, 332*, 411–415.

Zavaroni, I., Mazza, S., Dall'Aglio, E., et al. (1992). Prevalence of hyperinsulinaemia in patients with high blood pressure. *J Intern Med, 231*, 235–240.

Zhu, X., Chang, Y.P.C., Yan, D., Weder, A., Cooper, R., Luke, A.,…Chakravarti, A. (2003). Associations between hypertension and genes in the renin-angiotensin system. *Hypertension, 41*, 1027–1034.

7

Pathogenesis of Cancer

BIOLOGICAL BASIS OF CANCER

Cancer is the unchecked growth and spread of abnormal cells in the body. Cancers (malignant neoplasms) can arise from virtually any tissue and are usually named by the anatomic site of origin. Examples include breast cancer, prostate cancer, colon cancer, and lung cancer, the four cancers responsible for the majority of cancer deaths in many developed nations such as the United States. Cancer cells have the ability to divide continuously, invade other tissues, and spread (metastasize) to other organs through the blood and lymph. These primary features (uncontrolled cell division, invasion of contiguous tissue, and metastasis) distinguish cancerous growths from benign cellular growths, the latter being self-limiting with no ability to invade tissue or metastasize.

Cancer is further defined according to the cell of origin based upon microscopic examination by pathologists. Adenocarcinomas arise from the cuboidal epithelial cells that line the ducts of glandular tissue (adenocarcinomas of the breast, prostate, colon, or lung). Squamous cell carcinomas arise from the flat pavement cells that line various organs (squamous cell carcinomas of the upper airways, esophagus, or uterine cervix). Sarcomas arise from connective tissue (fibrosarcoma) or bone (osteosarcoma). Adenocarcinomas, squamous cell carcinomas, and sarcomas are solid tumors as opposed to cancerous growths of immune cells that arise in the bone marrow (leukemias) or the lymph nodes (lymphomas) and circulate in the blood or the lymphatic system.

EVOLUTION OF CANCER

Solid cancerous growths (tumors) often develop from cells of the epithelial lining of solid organs, and less often from dividing cells of muscle, bone, and the central nervous system. The evolution of solid tumors is thought to be a long-term process spanning many years and often decades.

The hematopoietic (blood) cancers (leukemias, lymphomas) arise from lymphocytes, granulocytes, or other dividing cells of the bone marrow and the lymphatic system. Leukemias and lymphomas develop much more rapidly than solid tumors, perhaps over the span of a few months or even weeks. The following paragraphs provide a brief description of some of the cell types that appear during the evolution of cancer (Robbins and Cotran, 1979; Kumar et al., 2007).

Dysplasia (Premalignant lesions)

The evolution of a solid cancerous tumor proceeds through a continuum of steps, the first of which is the development of dysplasia wherein normal cells (**Figure 7.1**) undergo morphological changes of the nucleus and cytoplasm.

Dysplasia is a distinct benign growth that arises from the epithelial cells lining various organs. In dysplasia, the cell nucleus becomes prominent, the cytoplasm appears swollen and vacuolated, and the cells exhibit increased rates of cell division and disordered maturation (**Figure 7.2**).

Dysplasia invariably precedes the development of cancer, and dysplastic lesions that serve as

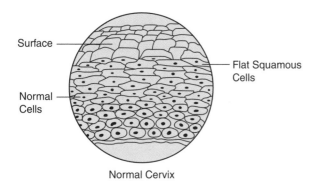

Figure 7.1 Normal Epithelium of the Uterine Cervix. *Source:* Courtesy of Paul D. Indman, MD, All Rights Reserved. 15195 National Avenue, Suite 201, Los Gatos, CA 95032

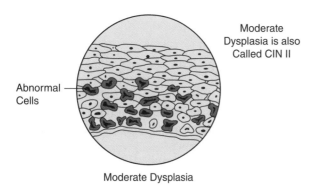

Figure 7.2 Moderate Dysplasia of Epithelium of the Uterine Cervix. *Source:* Courtesy of Paul D. Indman, MD, All Rights Reserved. 15195 National Avenue, Suite 201, Los Gatos, CA 95033

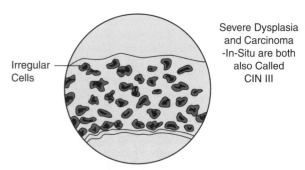

Figure 7.3 Carcinoma in Situ (CIS) of the Uterine Cervix. *Source:* Courtesy of Paul D. Indman, MD, All Rights Reserved. 15195 National Avenue, Suite 201, Los Gatos, CA 95034

precursors of cancer can be detected at a number of anatomic sites. Examples of premalignant lesions include actinic keratosis of the skin, leukoplakia of the oral cavity, Barrett's esophagus, fibrocystic disease with atypia of the breast, adenomatous polyps of the colon, dysplasia of the prostate, and intraepithelial neoplasia of the uterine cervix. Fortunately, all such dysplastic lesions do not have the ability to invade or metastasize and they are curable by surgical excision or other methods of ablation. Clearly, the early detection and treatment of such lesions is an important component of effective cancer control.

Carcinoma in Situ (CIS)

When cancerous solid tumors arise, they are at first confined to their original location and have not broken through the basement membranes into surrounding tissues. A confined neoplasm of the epithelial cell layer is thus called "*carcinoma in situ*" (*CIS*). Such *in*

situ lesions represent a defined step in cancer evolution. They exhibit all of the features of malignancy except invasiveness and metastasis; namely, the cells of *in situ* neoplasms manifest unchecked mitosis and proliferation, maturation failure and resistance to death, and disordered organization of the cell population. And yet, the *in situ* neoplasm is theoretically curable by excision since it has not spread beyond its original location and is in containment by the basement membrane (**Figure 7.3**).

Invasive Cancer

In contrast to *in situ* neoplasms, invasive cancers have broken through the basement membranes to spread beyond their original location into contiguous tissues (**Figure 7.4**). This is a critical step in the evolution of cancer since surgical excision may no longer be effective as a form of cancer therapy. The breach of the basement membranes by cancer cells requires acquisition of certain new functions, e.g., the secretion of enzymes that degrade basement membranes.

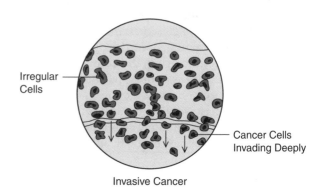

Figure 7.4 Invasive Cancer of the Uterine Cervix. *Source:* Courtesy of Paul D. Indman, MD, All Rights Reserved. 15195 National Avenue, Suite 201, Los Gatos, CA 95035

Metastatic Cancer

Metastatic disease represents the final step in the evolution of cancer. Cancer cells first invade contiguous tissues, and then spread through lymphatic channels and blood vessels to other anatomic sites. Cancer causes death by metastasizing (spreading) to vital organs such as the liver, brain, and spine. It is within these vital organs that the cancer cells overwhelm the normal cellular constituency and produce collapse of their life-sustaining functions. Early detection prior to the development of invasive cancer and metastasis is therefore vitally important to the successful treatment and survival of cancer patients. The entire process of cancer development often goes unheeded and undetected by the human immune system; hence the term "silent killer" has been aptly applied to describe cancer in its various forms.

● ● ● REFERENCES

1. Robbins, S.L., & Cotran, R.S. (1979). Pathologic basis of disease (2nd ed.). Philadelphia, PA: WB Saunders Company.

2. Kumar, V., Abbas, A.K., Fausto, N., & Mitchell, R.N. (2007). *Robbins basic pathology* (8th ed.) (pp. 718–721). Philadelphia, PA: Saunders Elsevier.

8

Theories of Carcinogenesis

SOMATIC MUTATION THEORY OF CANCER

Cancerous growths result from a complex process known collectively as carcinogenesis. Because a variety of genetic (DNA) mutations have been identified through molecular studies of cancerous tissues (Fearon and Vogelstein, 1990) the process of carcinogenesis is considered by many to result from the accumulation of two or more somatic mutations that impact upon control of the cell cycle or other features of neoplastic development (Knudson, 2001). Somatic mutations are base pair changes in DNA that occur during the human lifespan in cells of the body in contrast to mutations that are "inherited" from parents through the germ line. The theory is thus called the *somatic mutation theory of cancer*. It is based upon the premise that cancer arises from a single somatic cell and that tumor progression and development involves the accumulation of multiple DNA mutations with cell replication over time. It is postulated (but not proven) that with each successive mutation, the evolving clone of cancer cells acquires new properties that favorably impact upon growth, invasion of contiguous tissues, and eventually metastasis to other anatomic sites.

While the somatic mutation theory of cancer is the dominant paradigm of carcinogenesis, the emerging molecular evidence is not entirely consistent with this model. For example, many cancers arise without evidence of accumulating somatic mutations, and studies of precancerous and cancerous tissues often fail to disclose either chromosomal aberrations or mutated tumor suppressor genes and oncogenes (Soto and Sonnenschein, 2004). Furthermore, mutational events that are identified in cancerous tissues may have occurred late in tumor development

as the result of cancer development rather than the cause (Lijinsy, 1989; Prehn, 1994; Loeb, Loeb, and Anderson, 2003).

EPIGENETIC THEORY OF CANCER

The existing scientific evidence is inconsistent with the hypothesis that cancer always arises from a single "mutated" cell and progresses due to accumulation of subsequent mutations that confer a survival advantage to cancer cells. An alternative hypothesis, the *epigenetic theory of cancer*, proposes that cancer develops due to activation or deactivation of certain genes that have a major impact upon mechanisms of cell survival and cell division, *but in the absence of mutations that alter the DNA sequence* (Verma, Maruvada, and Srivastara, 2004; Momparler, 2003). Any process that modifies the expression of genes that control major mechanisms of cancer development (e.g., mitosis, apoptosis, angiogenesis, mutagenesis, immunosuppression, and metastasis) could obviously fuel the process of cancer development.

In the epigenetic theory there is no change in the underlying base pair sequence of the DNA. Rather, nongenetic factors of the cellular microenvironment cause genes to be expressed differently. Epigenetic programming involves chemical reactions such as the addition or removal of methyl groups ($CH3$) or acetyl groups ($NH2$) to/from DNA or histones that alter the conformation of the DNA and determine whether genes are expressed or suppressed.

The best known example of programmed epigenetic changes in human biology is the process of *cellular differentiation* that occurs during *embryogenesis*. During embryogenesis, a single fertilized egg with a fixed genotype undergoes continuous mitosis and cell differentiation leading to cell lineages consisting of billions of cells with extraordinarily diverse phenotypes (e.g., neurons, blood vessels, muscles, bones, epithelium, etc.). Cell differentiation produces such phenotypic diversity through programmed activation and inactivation of different sets of genes. Thus, differentiated cells in multicellular organisms express only the genes that are necessary for their own phenotypic activity. Furthermore, once a cell lineage becomes fully differentiated and mature, its inherent epigenetic pattern of genetic expression is usually preserved over multiple generations of cell division throughout the human lifespan. Nevertheless, certain molecular factors are capable of disrupting the normal epigenetic phenotype of a cell population giving rise to mechanisms that initiate and promote the development of malignant tumors. Molecular factors responsible for the genesis of specific forms of cancer will be addressed later.

INFLAMMOGENESIS OF CANCER

One microenvironmental process capable of inducing untoward epigenetic changes in gene expression leading to cancer development is *"chronic inflammation."* More than a century ago the famous German pathologist, Rudolph Virchow, suggested that chronic inflammation leads to cancer development by increasing uncontrolled cellular proliferation (Virchow, 1863; Balkwill and Mantovani, 2001). In 1992, molecular biologists discovered that the process of inflammation is primarily under the control of an inducible gene called cylcooxygenase-2 (COX-2) (Herschman, 2002). The COX-2 gene is normally silent in noninflamed tissue but is readily "turned on" by a variety of inflammatory environmental stimuli known to cause cancer including tobacco smoke, reactive oxygen species (ROS), polyunsaturated fatty acids, radiation, certain infectious bacteria and viruses, hypoxia, endotoxins, and many other agents (Harris, 2007). Overwhelming molecular evidence has linked induction of the COX-2 gene and overexpression of certain molecules of inflammation (called prostaglandins) to all of the essential features of carcinogenesis (mutagenesis, mitogenesis, angiogenesis, reduced apoptosis, metastasis, and immunosuppression). Indeed, carcinogenesis often evolves as a progressive series of highly specific cellular and molecular changes in response to induction of constitutive overexpression of COX-2 and the prostaglandin cascade in the *"inflammogenesis of cancer."*

• • • REFERENCES

Balkwill, F., & Mantovani, A. (2001). Inflammation and cancer: Back to Virchow? *Lancet, 357,* 539–545.

Fearon, E.R., & Vogelstein, B.A. (1990). A genetic model for colorectal tumorigenesis. *Cell, 61*(5), 759–767.

Harris, R.E. (2007). COX-2 and the inflammogenesis of cancer. *Subcellular Biochemistry, 42,* 193–212.

Herschman HR (2002). Historical aspects of COX-2. Cloning and haracterization of the cDNA, Protein and Gene. In *COX-2 blockade in cancer prevention and therapy* (Ed. Harris RE). Humana Press, Totowa, New Jersey.

Knudson, A.G. (2001). Two genetic hits (more or less) to cancer. *Nat Rev Cancer, 1*(2), 157–162.

Lijinsy, W. (1989). A view of the relation between carcinogenesis and mutagenesis. *Environ Mol Mutagen, 14,* Suppl 16, 78–84.

Loeb, L.A., Loeb, K.R., & Anderson, J.P. (2003). Multiple mutations and cancer. *Proc Natl Acad Sci USA, 100,* 776–781.

Momparler, R.L. (2003). Cancer epigenetics. *Oncogene, 22*(42), 6479–6483.

Prehn, R.T. (1994). Cancers beget mutations versus mutations beget cancers. *Cancer Research, 54*(5), 5296–5300.

Soto, A.M., & Sonnenschein, C. (2004). The somatic mutation theory of cancer: Growing problems with the paradigm? *Biosessays, 26*(10), 1097–1107.

Verma, M., Maruvada, P., & Srivastara, S. (2004). Epigenetics and cancer. *Crit Rev Clin Lab Sci, 41,* 5–6.

Virchow, R. (1863). Aetiologie der neoplastischen Geschwulst/Pathogenie der neoplastischen Geschwulste. In: *Die Krankhaften Geschwulste* (pp. 57–101). Berlin: Verlag von August Hirschwald.

Global Epidemiology of Cancer

GLOBAL CANCER MORTALITY

The metastatic spread of cancer to vital organs of the body can result in massive tissue destruction, loss of life-sustaining functions, and, ultimately, the untimely death of the human host. Worldwide, cancer causes more than 7.7 million deaths per year, about 13% of the 60 million annual deaths from all causes. Across all age groups, cancer currently ranks second behind heart disease as a leading cause of global death (Stewart and Kleihues, 2003; Boyle and Levin, 2008; World Health Organization, 2006).

The deadliest cancers differ in men and women. More than 4.3 million men die every year from cancer in the world population (American Cancer Society, 2007). More than 1 million men die from lung cancer and other malignancies of the respiratory tract (larynx, trachea), and nearly 2 million die from malignancies of the gastrointestinal tract (stomach, liver, esophagus, colon/rectum, pancreas, and oral cavity). An additional 10% of male cancer deaths are caused by malignancies of the genitourinary tract (prostate, kidneys, bladder) (**Figure 9.1**).

More than 3.3 million women die from cancer every year in the world population (American Cancer Society, 2007). Breast cancer causes the most deaths (more than 465,000) followed closely by lung cancer (more than 376,000). Gastrointestinal cancers (e.g., stomach, liver, esophagus and pancreas) together account for about one million deaths and malignancies of the genitourinary tract (e.g., uterine, cervix, and ovaries) cause another 450,000 deaths (**Figure 9.2**).

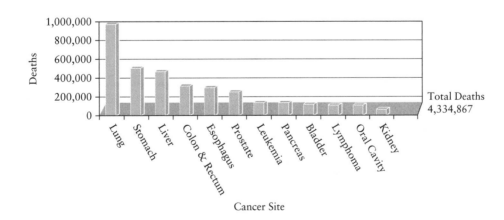

Figure 9.1 Male Cancer Deaths Worldwide, 2007.

Source: Data from American Cancer Society (2007). Global Cancer Facts and Figures, 2007.

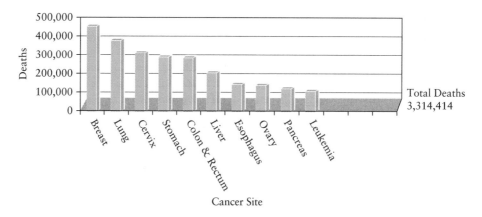

Figure 9.2 Cancer Deaths Worldwide, Women, 2007.

Source: Data from American Cancer Society (2007). Global Cancer Facts and Figures, 2007.

CANCER MORTALITY IN DEVELOPING VERSUS DEVELOPED NATIONS

Profiles of cancer mortality differ dramatically in developing versus developed nations (**Figure 9.3**). Among men living in developing nations, the total number of deaths due to either liver cancer or stomach cancer is more than 3.5 times higher than in developed nations, reflecting high rates of infection by liver viruses (HBV and HCV) and stomach bacteria, e.g., *Helicobacter pylori*, plus contamination of food supplies by molds that produce highly carcinogenic *aflatoxins*. Reciprocally, deaths from colorectal cancer or prostate cancer occur more frequently in developed nations partly due to intake of diets high in fat and calories and low in fiber, fruits, and vegetables. Malignancies associated with tobacco smoking (lung cancer) cause the most male deaths in all populations.

Among women living in developing nations, cancer of the uterine cervix causes the greatest number of deaths, principally due to lack of screening for premalignant dysplastic lesions of the cervical mucosa. Breast cancer is a frequent cause of death in both developing and developed nations and rising rates of smoking among women worldwide have resulted in increasing numbers of female lung cancer deaths in all populations. Death from stomach cancer occurs frequently in all populations whereas death from liver cancer or esophageal cancer occurs more frequently in developing nations. Cancers of the colon and rectum, pancreas, and ovaries cause relatively more deaths in developed nations (**Figure 9.4**).

Industrial nations with the highest overall cancer mortality rates include the United States, Italy, European countries (Germany, Netherlands, France, United Kingdom), Australia, and Canada.

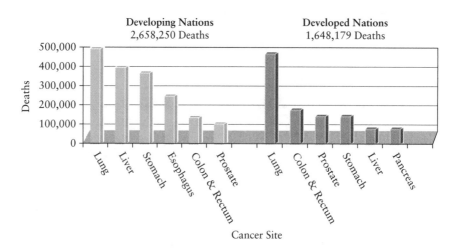

Figure 9.3 Cancer Deaths in Developing Versus Developed Nations, Men, 2007.

Source: Data from American Cancer Society (2011). Cancer Facts and Figures, 2011.

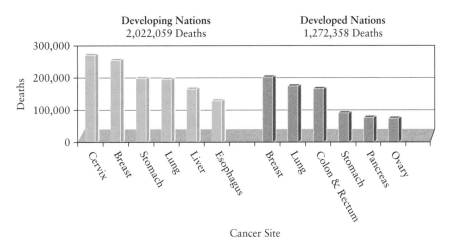

Figure 9.4 Cancer Deaths in Developing Versus Developed Nations, Women, 2007.

Source: Data from American Cancer Society (2011). Cancer Facts and Figures, 2011.

Developing countries with the lowest cancer mortality rates were in Northern Africa, Southern Asia (India), and Eastern Asia (China) (American Cancer Society, 2007). Across all age groups and populations, cancer currently ranks second behind heart disease as a leading cause of global death.

According to data compiled by the American Cancer Society in 2007, the lifetime probability of developing any form of cancer is nearly twice as high in economically developed countries compared to developing countries in both men (14.8% vs. 8.5%) and women (13.1% vs. 8.1%). In contrast, the risk of dying from cancer before age 65 is similar for developed and developing countries (7.2% vs. 6.1% in men and 4.8% vs. 4.9% in women). These differences in cancer incidence and mortality relate to variations in the types of major cancers and to the relative availability of early detection and treatment services in economically developed versus developing countries. Furthermore, the populations residing in developed countries are, on average, older, with a larger proportion of more susceptible individuals due to the aging process.

CANCER MORTALITY IN THE UNITED STATES

Despite the declaration of war on cancer by President Richard Nixon in 1971, cancer incidence and mortality continue to increase in the United States. Shortly after this presidential declaration, the US National Cancer Institute established the Surveillance, Epidemiology, and End Results (SEER) program in

order to monitor the impact of cancer in the United States. Data collection by member tumor registries of SEER began January 1, 1973. The SEER program currently collects and publishes cancer incidence and survival data from 18 population-based cancer registries covering approximately 26% of the US population including all ethnic groups. The SEER registries routinely collect data on patient demographics, primary tumor site, tumor morphology and stage at diagnosis, first course of treatment, and follow-up for vital status. The SEER program is the only comprehensive source of population-based information in the United States that includes stage of cancer at the time of diagnosis and patient survival data (SEER, 2005).

As we enter the 21st century, approximately 1.5 million new cases of invasive cancer are being diagnosed annually in the United States (excluding carcinomas *in situ*, and basal and squamous cell carcinomas of the skin) and more than 565,000 Americans die of the disease (about 1,500 people each day). Lung cancer is the leading cause of cancer deaths in both men and women (Horner et al., 2009; American Cancer Society, 2011).

In **Figures 9.5** and **9.6**, chronological trends in cancer mortality are shown for US men and women for the period 1930–2005 (American Cancer Society, 2011). Among men, more than half of cancer deaths are due to cancers of the lung and bronchus, prostate, colon, and rectum. While lung cancer mortality has declined slightly since about 1990, the male death rates from this malignancy are still more than double that of any other anatomic site. In 1987, prostate cancer surpassed colorectal cancer as the second

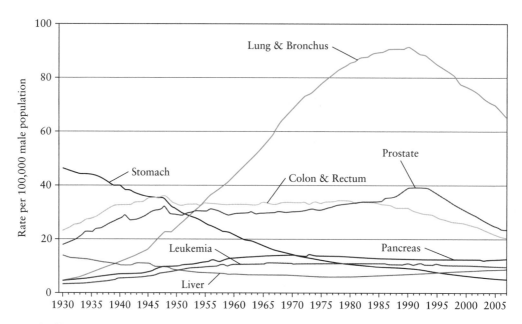

Figure 9.5 Longitudinal Pattern of Cancer Mortality in US Men, 1930–2007.

Source: Reprinted With Permission: American Cancer Society, Atlanta, GA. American Cancer Society (2011). Cancer Facts and Figures.

leading cause of cancer deaths in men. During the past decade, the mortality rates for both prostate and colorectal cancer show evidence of a gradual decline. Mortality rates for other malignancies have remained fairly constant, with the exception of the rates for stomach cancer which have declined dramatically beginning in about 1930, similar to the pattern for women (Figure 9.5) (American Cancer Society, 2011).

Among women, cancers of the lung and bronchus, breast, and colon and rectum account for more than half of all cancer deaths. In 1987, lung cancer surpassed breast cancer as the leading cause of cancer death in women. Since 1950, lung cancer mortality

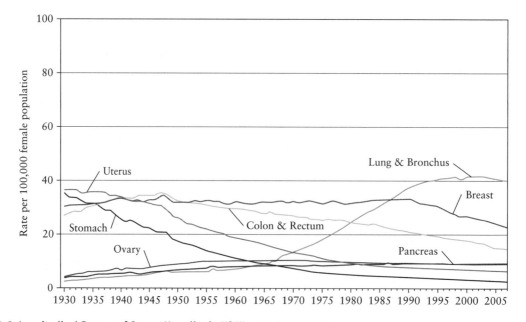

Figure 9.6 Longitudinal Pattern of Cancer Mortality in US Women, 1930–2007.

Source: Reprinted With Permission: American Cancer Society, Atlanta, GA. American Cancer Society (2011). Cancer Facts and Figures.

among American women has increased by more than 600% and it now accounts for about 25% of all female cancer deaths. Breast cancer mortality remained remarkably constant throughout the 20th century but appears to be declining slightly in recent years. Mortality rates for cervical cancer and stomach cancer steadily declined from high to low levels during the same time period. Colorectal cancer mortality has also gradually declined since the 1950s from rates above 30 per 100,000 to rates now lower than 20 deaths per 100,000 (Figure 9.6) (American Cancer Society, 2011).

Cancer mortality and incidence rates vary considerably by race and by gender. In particular, men have about 30% higher cancer death rates than women, and African American men have the highest death rates from cancers of the lung and bronchus, prostate, and colon and rectum compared to any of the other racial or ethnic groups in the United States.

• • • REFERENCES

American Cancer Society. (2007). *Global cancer facts and figures, 2007*. Atlanta, GA: American Cancer Society.

American Cancer Society. (2011). *Cancer facts and figures, 2010*. Atlanta, GA: American Cancer Society.

Horner, M.J., Ries, L.A.G., Krapcho, M., Neyman, N., Aminou, R., Howlader, N., . . . Edwards, B.K. (Eds.). (2009). *SEER cancer statistics review, 1975–2006*. Bethesda, MD: National Cancer Institute.

Surveillance, Epidemiology, and End Results (SEER). (2005). National Cancer Institute. NIH Publication No. 05-4772. Bethesda, MD: Surveillance, Epidemiology, and End Results.

Stewart, B.W., & Kleihues, P. (Eds.). (2003). *IARC world cancer report*. International Association of Cancer Research (IARC) Publications, Lyon, France.

Boyle, P., & Levin, B. (Eds.). (2008). *IARC world cancer report*. International Association of Cancer Research (IARC) Publications, Lyon, France.

World Health Organization. (2006). *Cancer*. World Health Organization. Geneva, Switzerland.

10

Major Environmental Cancer Risk Factors

TOBACCO AND CANCER

Tobacco smoking is the most important cancer risk factor. The World Health Organization reports that during the 20th century approximately 50 million people died from tobacco-associated cancers (WHO, 2006; WHO, 2008). Recent estimates from the International Association for Cancer Research suggest that approximately 50% of regular chronic smokers eventually succumb to tobacco-related cancer and most die prematurely (International Agency for Cancer Research, 2004; Parkin et al., 2005; Peto et al., 2006). Cigarette smoking causes about 30% of all cancer deaths, making tobacco smoke the single most lethal source of carcinogens.

Compared to individuals who avoid the smoking habit, chronic smokers have a 10–40-fold increased risk of developing lung cancer. Worldwide, approximately 90% of lung cancers in both men and women are attributable to cigarette smoking. Chronic tobacco use also markedly increases the risk of cancer development at many other anatomic sites including the oral cavity, larynx, pharynx, nasal cavity, esophagus, stomach, kidney, urinary bladder, pancreas, liver, and uterine cervix (**Figure 10.1**). Smoking has also been implicated in the development of certain types of leukemias, e.g., acute myelocytic leukemia.

The rise in female smoking prevalence is a critical public health concern. In the United States, more women now die from smoking-induced lung cancer than from breast cancer and in some Nordic countries such as Iceland and Denmark, more women die from lung cancer than men. In several European countries, up to 50% of young women are regular smokers, and

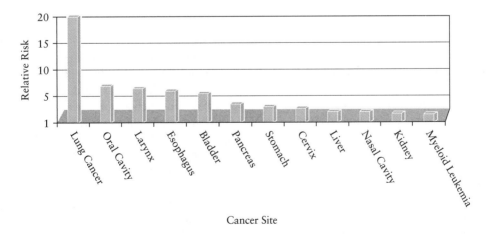

Figure 10.1 Chronic Tobacco Use and Cancer Risk.

Source: Data from WHO, 2008; Peto R, Lopez AD, Boreham J, Thun M (2006). Mortality from smoking in developed countries 1950–2000: Indirect estimates from National Vital Statistics. Oxford University Press. Accessed at: http://www.ctsu.ox.ac.uk/~tobacco/. October 28, 2011.

such high rates will inevitably produce an incredible burden of lung cancer and other smoking-related diseases in women for decades to come.

Cigarette smoke contains three major classes of human carcinogens (polycyclic aromatic hydrocarbons, nitrosamines, and heterocyclic amines), all of which initiate tumors by causing DNA mutations, plus a variety of compounds that promote tumor growth and development. The interested reader is referred to a thorough review of tobacco carcinogenesis that discusses the carcinogens of tobacco smoke, carcinogen uptake and metabolism, and mechanisms by which tobacco carcinogens cause DNA mutations and DNA damage due to the formation of free radicals and reactive oxygen species (Hecht, 1999). Furthermore, cigarette smoke contains powerful stimulants of inflammation and sustained overexpression of inflammatory prostaglandins that upregulate most (if not all) of the molecular mechanisms involved in the genesis and metastasis of malignant neoplasms.

Other types of tobacco exposure have also been linked to the development of malignant neoplasms. Pipe and cigar smoking, chewing tobacco, and snuff dipping are all causes of oral cavity cancer, and chronic involuntary (passive) inhalation of tobacco smoke is a risk factor for cancer of the lung, particularly in women. In counseling individuals about the risk of tobacco use, it is important to keep in mind that tobacco is not only a major risk factor for cancer, but also for a variety of other chronic life-threatening diseases including cardiovascular disease, myocardial infarction, stroke, chronic bronchitis, emphysema, and asthma.

DIET AND CANCER

Only diet rivals tobacco smoke as a cause of cancer, accounting for a comparable number of deaths throughout the world each year. In developed nations, animal (saturated) fat and certain polyunsaturated fatty acids (PUFA) are associated with cancers of the breast, prostate, and lower gastrointestinal tract (colon and rectum). In developed nations, high fat diets are linked to the pathogenesis of colorectal cancer, prostate cancer, breast cancer, endometrial cancer, and several other malignancies. In developing nations, diets contaminated by inflammatory and carcinogenic substances often lead to the development of stomach cancer, esophageal cancer, or liver cancer.

The *westernized Diet* of many affluent nations is characterized by intake of excessive calories from fat, refined carbohydrates, sugar, and animal pro-

tein. The westernized diet combined with a sedentary lifestyle can quickly lead to energy imbalance associated with a multitude of chronic diseases such as obesity, type II diabetes, cardiovascular disease, arterial hypertension, and cancer. Obesity due to metabolic overload and lack of exercise has been linked to a number of malignancies in the United States and other developed nations including colorectal cancer, postmenopausal breast cancer, prostate cancer, endometrial cancer, ovarian cancer, kidney cancer, biliary cancer, and certain forms of esophageal cancers.

Certain types of polyunsaturated fats show differential effects on cancer development. For example, the inflammatory n-6 polyunsaturated fatty acid (linoleic acid), which is abundant in the American westernized diet, has been linked to tumor initiation, promotion, and metastasis of colon cancer, breast cancer, endometrial cancer, ovarian cancer and prostate cancer whereas the anti-inflammatory n-3 polyunsaturated fatty acid (linolenic acid) which is prominent in marine diets shows antitumor effects.

Gastric esophageal reflux disease or GERD is a distressing condition of the esophagus that is associated with obesity in the populations of developed nations. In GERD, reflux of stomach acid into the lower esophagus produces morphological changes and dysplasia of the squamous cell lining, a condition known as *Barrett's esophagus*. If left untreated, Barrett's esophagus can progress to invasive esophageal cancer, a highly lethal form of malignancy.

Among non-nutrient food additives, salt is a causal risk factor for stomach cancer, and the decline in stomach cancer mortality throughout the world is largely due to the replacement of salt as a food preservative by refrigeration and other techniques. Nevertheless, many developing nations continue to consume diets high in sodium, thereby resulting in high incidence and mortality rates of stomach cancer.

Aflatoxins are naturally occurring mycotoxins produced by many species of the fungus, *Aspergillus*, most notably *Aspergillus flavus*, and *Aspergillus parasiticus*. Molds that produce aflatoxins grow on whole grains such as corn, rice, and wheat, as well as on peanuts, almonds, walnuts, sunflower seeds, and spices such as black pepper and coriander. Aflatoxins can contaminate food and food products during processing, storage, or transport when conditions are favorable for mold growth.

Aflatoxin exposure occurs by the ingestion of contaminated foods. On entering the body, aflatoxins are metabolized by the liver into highly carcinogenic epoxides. Chronic exposure to aflatoxins produces liver cancer, a leading cause of death in populations of Southern China, Southeast Asia, and the eastern coastal regions of Africa. Furthermore, aflatoxins and hepatitis viruses (HBV and HCV) interact synergistically in the pathogenesis of liver cancer.

Regular exposure to irritants, spices, and hot beverages produces chronic inflammation of the squamous cell lining of the esophagus and produces dysplastic lesions. With continued exposure, such dysplastic changes often progress to esophageal cancer, which is frequently fatal. The practice of ingesting hot spicy beverages is commonplace in many cultures of the Far East and the Middle East where esophageal cancer is a leading cause of cancer death.

Consumption of alcoholic beverages is also a major risk factor for malignancies of certain anatomic sites including the oral cavity, the esophagus, the liver, and the pancreas. Alcohol abuse in conjunction with chronic cigarette smoking synergistically increases the risk of developing cancer at these anatomic sites.

Links between diet and cancer may have as much to do with what is *not* in the diet as with what is. For example, low fiber coupled with high fat predisposes to colorectal cancer and perhaps other forms of cancer as well. Since many fruits and vegetables contain antioxidants that neutralize free radicals and lessen carcinogenesis, a lack of fruits and vegetables may contribute to many different types of cancers.

INFECTION AND CANCER

In developing countries, more than 20% of malignancies and related deaths are caused by infectious agents that cause cervical cancer, liver cancer, stomach cancer, and certain other malignancies. Three pathogens account for a large proportion of the cancer burden in the populations of China, Asia, and Africa: hepatitis viruses (HBV and HCV) that cause liver cancer, sexually transmitted human papillomavirus (HPV) strains 16 and 18 that cause cervical cancer, and the food contaminant, *Helicobacter pylorus*, that causes stomach cancer.

In many regions of Central America, Southeast Africa, and India, where HPV infection rates are high and cervical screening programs are nonexistent, cervical cancer ranks first as a cause of cancer death. These populations also have high rates of HIV disease which predisposes to chronic HPV infection and the development of invasive cervical cancer. Today, more than 80% of all cervical cancer deaths occur in developing countries.

In populations of Eastern and Middle Africa where sexually transmitted diseases (STDs) remain rampant, Kaposi's sarcoma due to HIV infection has become the leading cause of cancer death. In the wetlands of China, India, and the Middle East, parasitic infections by schistosome worms are responsible for high rates of bladder cancer.

In sharp contrast to developing countries, chronic infections account for less than 10% of all malignancies in more developed nations. Stomach cancer has declined in many nations due to replacement of irritating preservatives by refrigeration and ready access to fresh fruits and vegetables and other food products that are uncontaminated by *Helicobacter pylorus*. Early cytological detection of cervical cancer by the Pap test has led to impressive reductions in cervical cancer mortality. Liver cancer rates have also declined in many nations including China and Thailand due to effective immunization programs to prevent viral hepatitis and improved storage conditions of staple foods to reduce aflatoxin exposure. Well-designed vaccination programs may prove effective in preventing other cancers arising from known infectious agents, e.g., it is likely that vaccination against high-risk HPV strains may help prevent cervical cancer development.

• • • REFERENCES

International Agency for Cancer Research (2004). IARC Monographs on the Evaluation of Carcinogenic Risks to Humans. Volume 83, Tobacco Smoke and Involuntary Smoking. Lyon, France.

Hecht, S.S. (1999). Tobacco smoke carcinogens and lung cancer. *J National Cancer Institute*, 91(14),1194–1210.

Parkin, M.D., Bray, F., Ferlay, J., & Pisani, P. (2005). Global Cancer Statistics, 2002. *CA Cancer J Clin*, 55, 74–108.

Peto, R., Lopez, A.D., Boreham, J., et al. (2006). *Mortality from smoking in developed countries 1950–2000: Indirect estimates from National Vital Statistics.* Oxford University Press, United Kingdom.

World Health Organization (WHO). (2006). *Cancer.* World Health Organization, Geneva, Switzerland.

World Health Organization (WHO). (2008). *WHO Report on the global tobacco epidemic, 2008: The MPOWER package.* Geneva, Switzerland: World Health Organization.

11

Global Cancer Prevention and Control

Prevention of disease, including cancer, is often categorized into primary prevention, secondary prevention, and tertiary prevention. Primary prevention refers to avoidance of exposure to disease-causing risk factors. Secondary prevention refers to screening for the detection of antecedent conditions that predispose to disease and are curable by effective treatment or detection of disease at an early stage when effective treatment is likely to restore health. Tertiary prevention involves behavioral changes that limit the progression of disease and improve the quality of life after diagnosis.

A statement from the World Cancer Report, 2008, published by the International Association of Cancer Research (IARC), succinctly captures the essential objectives of effective cancer control:

"The aim of cancer control is a reduction in both the incidence of the disease and the associated morbidity and mortality, as well as improved life for cancer patients and their families. In addition to substantial opportunities for primary prevention, the World Cancer Report also emphasizes the potential of early detection, treatment, and palliative care. It urges all countries to establish comprehensive national cancer control programs, aimed at reducing the incidence of the disease and improving the quality of life for cancer patients and their families. In developing countries in particular, where a large proportion of cancers are detected late in the course of the disease, efforts to achieve earlier diagnosis and delivery of adequate palliative care and pain relief deserve urgent attention." (Boyle & Levin, 2008)

Despite intensive medical and public health efforts, cancer has now surpassed cardiovascular disease as the leading cause of death in people under age 85 years in highly developed nations such as the United States (Parkin et al., 2005). While some progress has been made in cancer therapy, particularly in the treatment of leukemia in children, conventional methods of surgery, chemotherapy, and radiotherapy have not impacted greatly on the general morbidity and mortality due to many forms of cancer in adults. It is also important to realize that as developing countries succeed in achieving lifestyles similar to Europe, North America, Australia, New Zealand, and Japan, their populations will encounter much higher cancer rates, particularly cancers of the lung, breast, colon, prostate, and other malignancies that tend to appear later in life.

As pointed out by Dr. Moon Chen Jr. in his review of cancer prevention and control for Asian and Pacific Islanders: *"In order to achieve the full benefit of cancer prevention, attention must be directed to the unique cultural, linguistic, and behavioral attributes of Asian and Pacific Islander Americans."* It is essential that this concept be extended to all target populations. In the words of Dr. Chen: *"Effective cancer prevention and control initiatives must incorporate scientific validity, linguistic appropriateness, and cultural competence."* (Chen, 1998)

PRIMARY CANCER PREVENTION

At the core of all cancer prevention and control strategies are the following key elements of primary prevention: abstinence from tobacco and smoking cessation, limiting alcohol intake, regular exercise,

Table 11.1	Major Environmental Cancer Risk Factors	
Risk Factor	**Cancer Sites**	**Prevention**
Tobacco Use	Lung, Pharynx, Larynx, Uterine Cervix, Bladder	Abstinence & Cessation
Obesity, High Fat & High Calorie Diet, Sedentary Lifestyle	Breast, Prostate, Colon, Kidney, Ovary	Exercise, Weight Control & Healthy Diet with Daily Fruits & Vegetables
Alcohol Abuse	Oral Cavity, Esophagus, Pancreas, Liver & Biliary	Limit Alcohol Intake to One Drink or Less Daily
HPV STD	Uterine Cervix, Oral Cavity, Penis	Avoid Exposure, Vaccination
Hepatitis Virus	Liver & Biliary	Avoid Exposure, Vaccination
Helicobacter pylori & High Salt Intake	Stomach, Lower Esophagus	Antibiotic, Limit Salt Intake
Radiation	Skin (Melanoma)	Limit Sun Exposure
Infectious Disease	Lymphoma, Leukemia	Good Personal Hygiene, Antibiotics & Antivirals

maintaining optimum weight, eating a healthy diet with daily fruits and vegetables, limiting salt intake, avoidance of sexually transmitted diseases such as HPV strains 16 and 18 and HIV, avoidance of exposure to hepatitis viruses such as HBV and HCV, vaccination against HPV and HBV, avoidance or early treatment of parasitic infections such as schistosomiasis, avoidance of excessive exposure to sunlight and other sources of radiation such as radon, infection control by good personal hygiene and judicious use of antibiotics and antiviral drugs, avoidance of known chemical carcinogens such as asbestos (occupational hazard), arsenic (water contaminant), aflatoxins (food contaminant) and dioxin (environmental contaminant) (**Table 11.1**). Albeit, the listing in Table 11.1 is far from inclusive and will require continual updating to keep pace with the identification of other carcinogenic factors present in the environment.

SECONDARY CANCER PREVENTION

Premalignant lesions and conditions that herald the development of cancer can usually be treated with a much higher likelihood of success than cancer itself. Effective cancer control therefore includes comprehensive cancer screening for the timely diagnosis and effective treatment of cellular lesions that could progress to invasive cancer. Proven screening methodologies with good sensitivity and specificity include mammograms for carcinoma *in situ* (CIS) of the breast, Papanicolaou (Pap) tests for cervical dysplasia, endoscopies for Barrett's esophagus and stomach ulcers, dental examination for oral leukoplakia, colonoscopy for colorectal

adenomas and prostate specific antigen (PSA), and ultrasound for noninvasive adenocarcinoma of the prostate gland. All of these lesions, if detected early, can be cured by limited surgical resection. Refinements in tissue imaging such as magnetic resonance (MR) and computed tomography (CT) have also led to improvements in the early detection of tumors.

Well-designed population screening programs coupled with skilled surgical excision or ablation of premalignant lesions have already been tremendously successful in reducing the mortality rates of certain cancers in developed nations. Currently, only about half of cancer patients in these populations eventually die from their disease. This differs markedly from developing nations wherein 80% of cancer victims already have late-stage (incurable) tumors when they are diagnosed.

These findings point up the need for development of much better early detection programs in many nations. Such screening modalities must be accurate, safe, inexpensive, and acceptable to the general public. Secondary prevention also mandates regular (annual) physical examinations for identification and treatment of chronic symptomatic medical conditions in individuals with inherent cancer risk factors such as chronic smoking and nicotine addiction, alcohol abuse, COPD, obesity, GERD, and chronic infections such as hepatitis and HIV disease.

TERTIARY PREVENTION

Tertiary prevention emphasizes beneficial behavioral changes that limit disease progression and subsequent disability for patients *after* they have been diagnosed with cancer. Fundamental tertiary preventive practices include smoking cessation, limiting alcohol intake, regular exercise, improved diet, maintenance of optimum weight, and compliance with prescribed treatment regimens. Pain control and palliative care should be implemented when necessary. The ultimate goal of tertiary prevention is to improve the quality of life among cancer survivors and their families.

CANCER EDUCATION

Global cancer control polices have been adopted by the World Health Organization (WHO), the International Agency on Cancer Research (IARC), the American Cancer Society (ACS), the National Cancer Institute (NCI), and many other national and international health organizations. Nevertheless, there is an urgent need for all countries to establish comprehensive national cancer control programs with the objective of reducing cancer incidence and mortality through prevention.

Educational programs should be designed and implemented where they are needed in order to create a high degree of disease awareness regarding the risk factors and early symptoms of cancer and to disseminate accurate information on the cost, safety, and accuracy of cancer screening tests and the availability and effectiveness of cancer treatment modalities. In developing countries in particular, where a large proportion of cancers are detected late in the course of the disease, efforts to achieve earlier diagnosis and delivery of adequate treatment, palliative care, and pain relief deserve immediate attention.

Comprehensive programs of cancer prevention and control must also incorporate effective and carefully evaluated school education programs for early health promotion and disease prevention. Finally, it is imperative that such programs provide continued support of cancer research with particular focus on the molecular biology and molecular genetics of cancer in order to identify etiologic mechanisms of carcinogenesis that translate to effective interventions for the eradication of the disease.

● ● ● REFERENCES

Chen, M. (1998). Cancer prevention and control among Asian and Pacific Islander Americans. *Cancer*, 83(S8), 1856–1864.

Parkin, M.D., Bray, F., Ferlay, J., & Pisani, P. (2005). Global cancer statistics, 2002. *CA Cancer J Clin*, 55, 74–108.

Peto, R., Lopez, A.D., Boreham, J., et al. (2006). *Mortality from smoking in developed countries 1950–2000: Indirect estimates from National Vital Statistics*. Oxford University Press, United Kingdom.

World Health Organization (2006). *Cancer*. World Health Organization, Geneva, Switzerland.

Boyle, P., & Levin, B. (Eds.). (2008). *World cancer report*. Lyon, France: International Agency for Cancer Research (IARC), Lyon, France.

World Health Organization (2008). *WHO Report on the global tobacco epidemic, 2008: The MPOWER package*. Geneva, Switzerland: World Health Organization.

Epidemiology of Lung Cancer

GLOBAL LUNG CANCER MORTALITY

Lung cancer, the deadliest of all malignancies, causes 1.18 million deaths annually; more than double that of any other form of cancer. Approximately 1.35 million new cases of lung cancer are diagnosed each year (nearly 1 million men and 350,000 women) and nearly 90% die from the disease, most within only a few months of diagnosis.

The death toll from lung cancer in the 20th century exceeded 25 million and already in the 21st century, 10 million more have died from lung cancer. Based on the current trajectory of smoking patterns around the globe, it is estimated that 250 million people will die from lung cancer and other smoking-related cancers in the 21st century (Proctor, 2001).

Tobacco smoking is the dominant etiologic factor of lung cancer and is responsible for approximately 87% of cases. The highest rates of lung cancer therefore occur in nations with the highest prevalence rates of chronic smoking such as North America and Europe (**Figure 12.1**) (IARC, 2002). Albeit, in evaluating the global lung cancer mortality map in Figure 12.1, it must be kept in mind that lung cancer develops over a long period of time, perhaps decades from initiation until diagnosis. The world lung

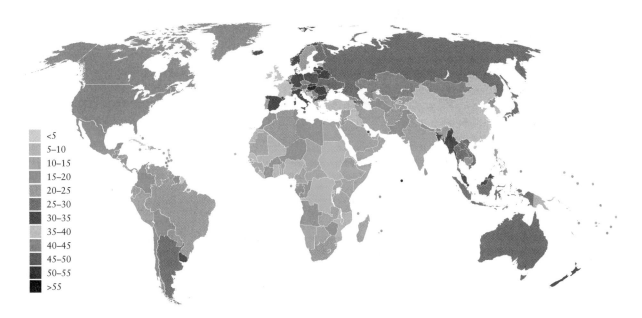

	<5
	5–10
	10–15
	15–20
	20–25
	25–30
	30–35
	35–40
	40–45
	45–50
	50–55
	>55

Figure 12.1 Global Lung Cancer Mortality, 2004.

Source: Data from World Health Organization. The global burden of disease: 2004 update. Geneva, WHO, 2008. Available at www.who.int/evidence/bod.

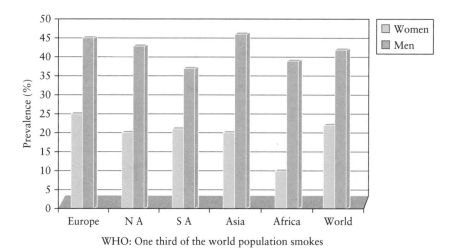

Figure 12.2 Smoking Prevalence: A Global Problem.

Source: Data from World Health Organization. WHO Report on the Global Tobacco Epidemic, 2008: The MPOWER Package. Geneva, Switzerland: World Health Organization; 2008.

cancer mortality rates of today are therefore the consequence of many years of past smoking exposure. Indeed, young people throughout the world are taking up the smoking habit with alarming alacrity (up to 50% in populous countries such as India, China, and Russia), and, unless reversed, this unfortunate trend will have devastating health consequences in generations to come. The following statement from officials of the American Cancer Society succinctly describes the global marketing expansion of tobacco throughout the world by the tobacco industry.

> *"Globally, the data are very clear in indicating that the tobacco epidemic has now expanded to and become more focused in the world's low- and middle-income countries, due largely to the expansion of the multinational tobacco industry's marketing efforts in Eastern Europe, Asia, Africa, and Latin America" (Glenn et al., 2010)*

A particularly disturbing global trend is the rising prevalence of chronic smoking among women, which has produced sharp increases in lung cancer incidence and mortality rates among women. For example, since 1950, women in the United States have experienced a 600% increase in lung cancer mortality. Recent estimates for the 193 member nations of the World Health Organization suggest that 1 in 3 adults smoke in the world population (**Figure 12.2**) and that 5.4 million people die annually from lung cancer and other smoking-related diseases such as heart disease, chronic obstructive pulmonary disease (COPD), stroke, and several other cancers (**Figure 12.3**).

RISK FACTORS FOR LUNG CANCER

Cancer of the lung is the most common cause of cancer-related death among men and women. In developed countries, 25–30% of all cancer deaths are due to lung cancer and more people die from lung cancer than breast cancer, prostate cancer, and colon cancer combined. Notable features of lung cancer in the US population are as follows:

- Mortality has increased by 600% in women since 1950
- Lung cancer causes 28% of all cancer deaths
- More people die each year from lung cancer than breast, prostate, and colon cancer combined

CIGARETTE SMOKING AND LUNG CANCER

The dominant risk factor for lung cancer is cigarette smoking. Early epidemiologic studies by Ernst Wynder and colleagues in the United States and Richard Doll and Bradford Hill in Great Britain clearly demonstrated the etiologic link between cigarette smoking and cancer of the lung (Wynder and Graham, 1950; Doll and Hill, 1950). As shown by the data published by Wynder in 1950, the risk for cancer of the lung increases 10–40-fold with increasing smoking intensity for the major cell types (**Figure 12.4**).

The cause and effect pattern of smoking and lung cancer is clearly visible on examination of ecologic

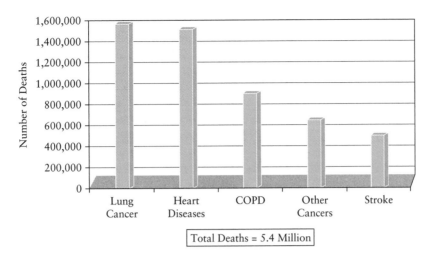

Figure 12.3 Worldwide Deaths Attributable to Cigarette Smoking, 2009.

Source: Data from World Health Organization. WHO Report on the Global Tobacco Epidemic, 2008: The MPOWER Package. Geneva, Switzerland: World Health Organization; 2008.

time trend data in the United States (**Figure 12.5**). In the early years of the 20th century, lung cancer occurred infrequently and was considered a reportable disease in most medical research journals (Wynder and Stellman, 1977). Nevertheless, the rates began to increase after the advent of smoking in the 1930s and henceforth, lung cancer incidence and mortality have continually climbed, reaching epidemic proportions during mid-century and overwhelming other forms of cancer as the leading cause of cancer death. Note the close parallelism of lung cancer mortality and cigarette use in the United States that has persisted since 1930. The time interval between the exposure curve and the mortality curve reflects an approximate average development time of 20 years or more for lung carcinogenesis. Overall, cigarette smoking accounts for 85–90% of all lung cancer risk in the United States and most other developed countries.

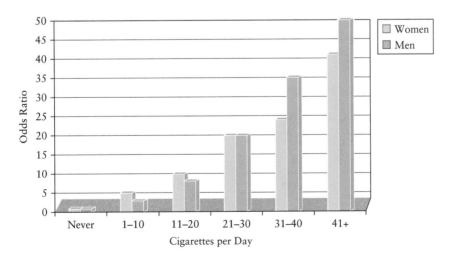

Figure 12.4 Odds Ratios for Lung Cancer by Amount Smoked.

Source: Odds ratios were derived from the original data of Wynder and Graham, 1950. Data From: Wynder EL, Graham EA (1950). Tobacco smoking as a possible etiologic factor in bronchiogenic carcinoma. *JAMA* 143:329–336.

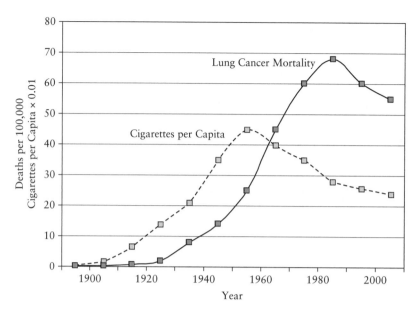

Figure 12.5 Lung Cancer Mortality and Cigarettes Per Capita, 1900–2005, USA.

Source: Data from American Cancer Society, USA (annual mortality rates are the average for men and women), and the US National Center for Health Statistics (annual cigarettes per capita x 0.01).

TRANSITION IN LUNG CANCER HISTOLOGY

Major changes have occurred in the profile of histologic cell types of lung cancer being diagnosed during the past several decades. Specifically, rates of adenocarcinoma of the lung have increased dramatically with corresponding decreases in squamous cell and small (oat) cell carcinoma (**Figure 12.6**).

Concurrent with the changing histologic profile of lung cancer, the composition of American cigarettes has also changed dramatically in recent decades. Filter brands now dominate the market and currently comprise over 85% of all cigarettes manufactured in the United States. This trend is reflected by decreases in the average tar and nicotine yields per cigarette. Among smokers in the United States, about 96% of women and 92% of men smoke filter cigarettes. Despite this transition to "low yield" cigarettes, smokers tend to inhale deeper and compensate by smoking more cigarettes, which may account for the drastic increase in lung adenocarcinoma among cigarette smokers in recent years (Augustine, Harris,

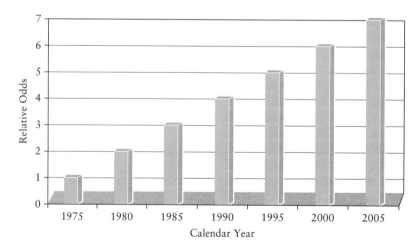

Figure 12.6 Relative Odds of Adenocarcinoma versus Squamous Cell Carcinoma of the Lung.

Source: Data from James Cancer Hospital, Columbus, Ohio, USA.

and Wynder, 1989). As pointed out by Wynder and Muscat (1995):

"Smokers of low-yield (filtered) cigarettes compensate for the low delivery of nicotine by inhaling the smoke more deeply and by smoking more intensely; such smokers may be taking up to 5 puffs/min with puff volumes up to 55 ml. Under these conditions, the peripheral lung is exposed to increased amounts of smoke carcinogens that are suspected to lead to lung adenocarcinoma."

There is also evidence from epidemiologic studies that women have a greater predisposition to smoking-induced lung carcinogenesis than men (Zang and Wynder, 1992; Harris et al., 1993; and Risch et al., 1993). The results of these studies indicate that the risk of lung cancer, particularly adenocarcinoma, is approximately twofold higher in women who smoke than in men of the same age who smoke the same amount. While it has been suggested that the greater susceptibility of women may relate to estrogens or estrogen receptors in the lung epithelium, the biological basis of the observed differential gender predisposition to tobacco carcinogenesis remains to be clarified.

TOBACCO CARCINOGENESIS

Tobacco smoke is a complex mixture of more than 5,000 gases and compounds, many of which are carcinogenic (Rodgman and Perfetti, 2009). While nicotine is the addictive component of tobacco smoke, multiple carcinogens are also present with the potential to induce cancer-causing mutations in critical genes. Three major classes of carcinogens are present in tobacco smoke: polycyclic aromatic hydrocarbons, nitrosamines, and heterocyclic amines (National Toxicology Program, 2005). The metabolism of carcinogens is complex, involving activation versus detoxification by liver enzymes. The carcinogens of tobacco smoke, their uptake and metabolism, and mechanisms by which they cause DNA mutations and DNA damage have been thoroughly reviewed elsewhere (Hecht, 1999).

In addition to the carcinogens of tobacco smoke, multiple other chemical compounds are present that are highly inflammatory to lung tissue. One of the most damaging and inflammatory of the substances in tobacco smoke is the tobacco residue called *tar*. Tar is the common name given to the particulate matter of tobacco smoke less the nicotine and water content. Essentially, tar is a complex mixture of thousands of compounds resulting from the combustion of tobacco and tobacco resins. It is estimated that the lungs of a chronic smoker of 20 or more cigarettes per day for 40 years are exposed to 8–10 kilograms of tar (Harris et al., 1993). Tar is by nature a sticky substance that is difficult if not impossible for the lungs to clear. Adherence to the cilia slows their wave-like motions and eventually stifles their ability to cleanse the airways. With the accumulation of tar in the smoker's lungs, chronic inflammation is inevitable, which in turn stimulates the critical mechanisms of cancer development: mutagenesis, mitogenesis, angiogenesis, inhibition of apoptosis, immunosuppression, and eventually metastasis (Harris, 2007).

LUNG CANCER RISK FACTORS OTHER THAN TOBACCO

Factors that are synergistic with cigarette smoking in heightening the risk of lung cancer include exposure to asbestos fibers, inhalation of radon daughter products, and certain chemical exposures related to specific occupations, e.g., arsenic, cadmium, lead, dioxins, etc. Other factors such as genetic predisposition and diet may also modify the risk of lung cancer. In particular, exposures that lead to chronic inflammation in lung tissues have been found to increase the risk.

Radon Gas and Lung Cancer

Radon is a colorless and odorless gas generated by the breakdown of radioactive radium, the decay product of uranium that is found in rocks and soil of the Earth's crust. Radiation decay products can reach the lungs by inhalation where they are capable of ionizing DNA to produce mutations that could lead to carcinogenesis and the development of lung cancer. In an early ecological study of lung cancer in Maine, estimates of radon levels in domestic water supplies were found to be significantly correlated with county rates of lung cancer across the state (Hess, Weiffenbach, and Norton, 1983). In several studies of uranium miners, exposure to radon particles appeared to increase the risk of lung cancer (Hornung and Meinhardt, 1987; Samet and Hornung, 1990).

Evidence supporting an etiologic link between radon and lung cancer was strengthened by results of the Iowa Radon Study, which evaluated residential exposures among women and found a significant dose response in lung cancer risk with cumulative radon exposures exceeding 4 picocuries per liter (Field et al., 2000). In 1994, the United States Environmental Protection Agency (EPA) issued a warning that radon *could be* the second most frequent cause of lung cancer after cigarette smoking, responsible for up to 21,000 lung cancer deaths per year in the United

States (Lubin et al., 1994). Nevertheless, the EPA estimates are based upon linear extrapolation of high radon exposure in miners to much lower levels of exposure. Currently, the totality of scientific evidence suggests that radon exposure poses an independent risk, albeit small compared to that of tobacco. Furthermore, although not proven, chronic exposure to both tobacco smoke and radon could synergistically elevate the risk of lung cancer. Radon levels vary greatly by locality and the composition of the underlying soil and rocks. This makes the accurate evaluation of radon exposure to individuals extremely difficult and studies sufficiently powered to detect effects of low levels of exposure and interactions are lacking.

Asbestos and Lung Cancer

Asbestos causes mesothelioma, a malignancy of the pleura surrounding the lung. The etiologic link between mesothelioma and asbestos exposure is well established through the studies of Selikoff and colleagues (Selikoff, Hammond, and Churg, 1968). Inhaled asbestos fibers migrate to the periphery of the lung where they become entrapped and cause recursive inflammatory insult and carcinogenesis. Furthermore, there is a synergistic effect between tobacco smoking and asbestos in the development of primary lung cancer. It is estimated that asbestos workers with a history of chronic smoking have a lung cancer risk that is eight times higher than smokers who have not been exposed to asbestos. In addition, asbestos-exposed male smokers have roughly 50 times the lung cancer risk of unexposed men who do not smoke (Berry, Newhouse, and Turok, 1972).

In developed countries such as Great Britain and the United States, where asbestos has traditionally been widely used in construction and building, asbestos exposure is estimated to account for 2–3% of lung cancer deaths. A number of global committees have reviewed the cancer-causing potential of common occupational substances such as asbestos. For example, the International Agency for Research on Cancer (IARC) and the International Union Against Cancer (UICC) have identified many workplace materials including asbestos that are possible lung carcinogens (McCulloch and Tweedale, 2008).

Wood Smoke and Lung Cancer

Wood smoke contains a mixture of harmful chemical substances in the form of gases and particulate matter such as carbon monoxide, ozone, nitrous oxides, sulfur dioxide, volatile organic compounds, dioxin, potential carcinogens, and inhalable particles.

Certain of these compounds such as benzo[a]pyrene and other polycyclic aromatic hydrocarbons are not only irritating and toxic but are also potent carcinogens. It has been estimated that residential wood combustion may account for up to 75% of the exposure to particle-associated organics and account for a significant fraction (up to 20%) of the cancer risk in the upper respiratory tract of nonsmokers (Lewtas et al., 1992).

Exposure to wood smoke may increase the risk of lung cancer via a mechanism similar to that of tobacco. Delgado and colleagues (2005) studied blood samples from patients with and without lung cancer and found that wood smoke exposure in nonsmokers significantly increased the expression of genes that control cell division such as p53, similar to the effects of tobacco exposure. Based on results, they suggested that wood smoke exposure is a possible risk factor for the development of lung cancer in nonsmokers.

Air Pollution and Lung Cancer

The role of air pollution in the genesis of lung cancer was examined in a prospective cohort study of more than 1 million American men and women conducted by investigators at the American Cancer Society. Air pollution was measured as the concentration of particulate matter in ambient air. Study results showed that each 1% increase in the concentration of particles in the air produced a 14% increase in the risk of developing a lung cancer (Krewski et al., 2005; Pope et al., 2002). Lung cancer risk was highest for inhalation of ultrafine particles (less than 2.5 micrometers in diameter) that penetrate further into the lungs (Valavanidis, Fiotakis, and Vlachogianni, 2008).

Dioxins and Lung Cancer

Dioxins and structurally related dioxin-like compounds are environmentally and biologically persistent and induce a spectrum of disease processes. Dioxins are produced by industrial processes, including incineration, chlorine bleaching of paper and pulp, and the manufacture of some pesticides, herbicides, and fungicides. Dioxin strongly absorbs to sediments and soils and persists for decades. Common sources of dioxin included backyard burning of trash, wood stoves, wood-fired commercial boilers, municipal waste incinerators, and pulp and paper mill discharges. Humans are exposed through diet and close proximity to contaminated environments.

In a follow-up study of the population of Seveso, Italy that was exposed to dioxin after an industrial accident that occurred in 1976, lung cancer mortality among men in high-exposure zones was significantly increased (RR = 1.3, 95% CI = 1.0–1.7) (Bertazzi et al., 2001). Dioxins are metabolized by liver enzymes CYP-1A1 and CYP-1B1 into compounds with carcinogenic potential in lung cells and other tissues (MacPherson et al., 2009). Results support continued evaluation of dioxin as a lung carcinogen and underscore the need to also study interactions with tobacco and other risk factors.

Arsenic and Lung Cancer

Arsenic occurs naturally in soil and bedrock and is also used in pressure-treated wood and as an ingredient in pesticides. Long-term exposure to low levels of arsenic in drinking water has been linked to human health risks associated with cancer at multiple sites including the lung, bladder, and skin. DiPaolo and Casto (1979) first demonstrated the malignant transformation of mammalian cells by inorganic arsenic and, subsequently, many other studies have confirmed that arsenic exposure is both mutagenic and carcinogenic in humans (Barrett et al., 1989; Roy and Saha, 2002).

In a 50-year study of a population exposed to arsenic-contaminated drinking water in Chile, Marshall and colleagues (2007) found that toxic arsenic exposure greatly increased lung cancer risk when exposure occurred *in utero* or early in life. The investigators stated that "the impact of arsenic in drinking water on this large population is without precedent for environmental causes of human cancer, and it points to the public health priority of ensuring that arsenic concentrations in drinking water are controlled worldwide."

Environmental Tobacco Smoke (ETS) and Lung Cancer

Over the last several years, much research has focused on the dangers of exposure to environmental tobacco smoke (ETS) or secondhand smoke. Such exposure is also known as passive smoking, or involuntary smoking due to breathing in the tobacco smoke from nearby smokers.

Second hand tobacco smoke arises from the dilution of sidestream smoke from smoldering cigarettes and from the residues of mainstream smoke exhaled by active smokers. More than 4,000 chemicals have been identified in ETS and many of them are carcinogenic including arsenic, benzene, beryllium, cadmium, nickel, chromium, ethylene oxide, polonium, and dioxin (National Toxicology Program, 2005). Furthermore, the ETS inhaled by nonsmokers has higher levels of nitrosamines and smaller particle sizes, leading to easier deposition within the bronchial tree. Specifically, smaller ETS particles are more likely

to reach and be held in the lungs, where they dissolve more readily than larger particles. Therefore, the pattern of deposition of smoke particles in the respiratory tract differs between active and passive smokers.

It is estimated that approximately one-third of lung cancer in nonsmokers results from passive exposure to secondhand cigarette smoke (EPA, 1992; IARC, 2002). Furthermore, ETS has been found to increase the risk of developing heart disease and myocardial infarction in adults and is also linked to various conditions in children, including sudden infant death syndrome, ear infections, and asthmatic attacks. Clearly, there is no safe level of exposure to ETS (DHHS, 2006).

Within the United States, many state and local governments have passed laws prohibiting smoking in public facilities such as schools, hospitals, airports, and bus terminals. Increasingly, state and local governments are also requiring private workplaces, including restaurants and bars, to be smoke free. At the national level, several laws restricting smoking have also been passed, e.g., federal US law bans smoking on domestic airline flights, most international flights, interstate buses and trains, and in federal buildings and facilities. Internationally, several nations, including France, Ireland, New Zealand, Norway, and Uruguay, have also implemented laws requiring workplaces, bars, and restaurants to be smoke free (DHHS, 2000; DHHS, 2006).

Diet and Lung Cancer

For many years, an unresolved puzzle that has faced epidemiologists is the discrepant lung cancer rates in Japan versus the United States. Despite the fact that the prevalence of chronic cigarette smoking among Japanese men is approximately twice that of American men, their lung cancer rates are substantially lower. For example, an early international case-control study of smoking and lung cancer in Japan and the United States found that the relative risk of lung cancer development among chronic smokers is tenfold higher in US men compared to Japanese men (Wynder, Taioli, and Fujita, 1992). This phenomenon is known as the *Japanese smoking paradox*.

Though considerable research has addressed potential causes of the Japanese smoking paradox, a completely satisfactory explanation has not been forthcoming. Wynder and colleagues suggested that several factors may be involved: Japanese smokers are exposed to lower concentrations of carcinogens in their cigarettes (tobacco blends used in formulating cigarettes differ in the United States and Japan, and most Japanese cigarettes are made with charcoal filters that more effectively filter out nitrates and nitrosamines); Japanese men begin smoking at a later age than American men (2–3 years on average); Japanese men consume less alcohol than American men; and perhaps most importantly, the Japanese consume markedly less fat in their diet compared to Americans. Each of these factors could contribute to enhanced protection against carcinogenesis by tobacco smoke among Japanese compared to American smokers (Wynder, Taioli & Fujita, 1992; Stellman et al., 2001; Takahashi, et al., 2008).

Another important dietary difference between Japan and the United States is in fish consumption. In fact, Japan has one of the highest annual levels of fish consumption in the world (70 kg per capita), which is more than fourfold higher than the US level (16 kg per capita) (Josupeit, 2003; EPA, 2002). To examine the role of diet in lung cancer development, Takezaki and colleagues conducted a case-control study within Japan and found that consumption of cooked or raw fish reduced the risk of lung cancer in both men and women by about 50%. Since eating fresh fish provides an excellent source of complex polyunsaturated fatty acids that are known to have potent anti-inflammatory effects, it is possible that regular fish consumption by Japanese smokers inhibits or delays lung carcinogenesis by tobacco smoke (Takezaki et al., 2001).

Viruses and Lung Cancer

It is well known that chronic lung infections due to certain viruses cause lung cancer in animals, e.g., the jaagsiekte sheep retrovirus (JSRV) causes pulmonary adenocarcinoma in sheep (Leroux et al., 2007). Albeit, the role of viral infections in human lung cancer development has not been definitively proven. Certain viruses have been implicated in lung carcinogenesis by virtue of their presence in lung cancer specimens, e.g., human papillomavirus strains, JC virus, simian virus 40, BK virus, and cytomegalovirus have been found in cancerous lung tissues (Giuliani et al., 2007; Cheng et al., 2001) . However, it is highly likely that an acute viral infection present at the time of lung cancer diagnosis is an effect of the lowered susceptibility of such patients rather than the cause of a protracted course of carcinogenesis over many years.

Genetics and Lung Cancer

Sir Ronald Aylmer Fisher, the renowned "Father of Statistics," invented many of the maximum likelihood statistical methods that are still being used in hypothesis testing and the analysis of data. He also founded the field of quantitative genetics, developed methods for genetic linkage analysis, and proposed the concept of additive genetic variance for genes with small effects. Despite his genius for statistics and genetics, Fisher strongly opposed the conclusions of Ernst Wynder, Richard Doll, and Bradford Hill in the early 1950s that smoking caused lung cancer. Fisher compared the correlations in their papers to the "import of apples and the rise of divorce" in order to show that "correlation does not prove causation." In his view, the cause of lung cancer was largely attributable to genetic factors. However, his analysis of the causal association between lung cancer and smoking was flawed by an unwillingness to examine the entire body of available data and to consider the interaction between the dominant causal agent (smoking) and genotype. It has also been pointed out that Dr. Fisher was employed as a consultant by the tobacco firms and that he himself was a smoker, thereby raising the specter of bias and casting huge doubt on the value of his arguments against the early epidemiologic findings (Stolley, 1991).

In recent years, linkage studies of multigenerational familial aggregations of lung cancer and genome-wide association studies (GWAS) have identified a number of genetic polymorphisms and mutant forms of genes that regulate key mechanisms of lung carcinogenesis. Most of these candidate genes modify effects of exposure to tobacco smoke, thereby increasing the susceptibility or resistance to tobacco carcinogenesis. Effects have been observed for genes that regulate the cell cycle and cell division (K-ras, p53, p16), genes that control DNA repair enzymes (BER, NER), genes that control the inflammatory cascade and cellular response to the plethora of highly inflammatory elements in tobacco smoke (COX-2), and genes that modulate phase I and phase II liver enzymes (CYP-1A1, CYP-1B1) resulting in heightened activation or dysfunctional metabolism of carcinogenic compounds in tobacco smoke, including polycyclic aromatic hydrocarbons (PAHs), nitrosamines, and aromatic amines (Schwartz et al., 2007; Aviel-Ronen et al., 2006). Tobacco smoke may also stimulate epigenetic events that induce or suppress gene expression without changing the DNA base pair sequence, such as DNA methylation, histone deacetylation, and phosphorylation, and these changes in gene expression may in turn influence susceptibility to lung carcinogenesis.

Cyclooxygenase-2 (COX-2), Inflammation, and Lung Cancer

More than a century ago, the German pathologist Rudolf Virchow (Virchow, 1863) suggested that chronic inflammation leads to cancer development by increasing cellular proliferation. In 1989, an inducible enzyme called cyclooxygenase-2 (COX-2) that initiates the inflammatory cascade was discovered in the laboratories of Dr. Phil Needleman at Monsanto Corporation in St. Louis (Raz, Wyche, and Needleman, 1989; Fu et al., 1990; Masferrer et al., 1990). In 1991, the human version of the COX-2 gene was cloned in the laboratories of Dr. Harvey Herschman at UCLA (Fletcher et al., 1992). Several investigators working in different laboratories were instrumental in the discovery and ultimate cloning of COX-2 (Herschman, 2002).

The COX-2 gene is normally silent in noninflamed tissues, but when stimulated by inflammatory factors (such as those found in tobacco smoke), COX-2 transcription is triggered, leading to the enzymatic conversion of arachidonic acid into molecules called prostaglandins that are highly inflammatory. Discovery of the inducible COX-2 gene that initiates the inflammatory cascade rekindled interest in the causal link between inflammation and cancer.

Since discovery of the inducible COX-2 gene, a huge volume of cohesive scientific evidence from molecular, animal, and human investigations supports the hypothesis that continuous aberrant induction of COX-2 and up-regulation of the prostaglandin cascade by chronic exposure to a wide variety of inflammatory agents promotes the development of cancer, including cancer of the lung. Indeed, there is evidence that chronic exposure to many highly inflammatory constituents of cigarette smoke plays a significant role in lung carcinogenesis, and reciprocally, that blockade of the process has strong potential for cancer prevention and therapy (Harris, 2002; Harris, Beebe-Donk, & Alshafie, 2007; Harris, 2007).

LUNG CANCER DIAGNOSIS, TREATMENT, AND SURVIVAL

Despite intensive medical efforts involving surgical resection, chemotherapy, and radiation therapy, the survival of patients with pathologically confirmed lung cancer has remained dismally low (10–15% five-year survival) and virtually unchanged for decades (**Figure 12.7**, NCI). The primary reason for the failure of treatment protocols to improve survival is the lack of early detection of lung tumors. Standard chest X-rays and most other imaging techniques have shown little value in detecting lung tumors prior to their invasion of the blood, lymphatics, contiguous tissue, and more distant anatomic sites. One relatively new imaging technique, spiral computed tomography, was recently evaluated in a large multicenter screening program involving 31,567 asymptomatic men and women 40 years of age and older, all of whom were at risk for lung cancer because of a history of cigarette smoking or other environmental exposures. Results demonstrated identification of 412 (85%) of 484 lung cancer cases with small clinical stage I lesions having a projected 10-year survival rate of 85% (Henschke et al., 2006). However, other centers have not been able to replicate this result (Bach et al., 2007).

PRIMARY PREVENTION OF LUNG CANCER

The primary prevention of lung cancer depends to a large extent on the prevention of cigarette smoking among adolescents and young adults. The National Cancer Institute (NCI), the National Heart, Lung

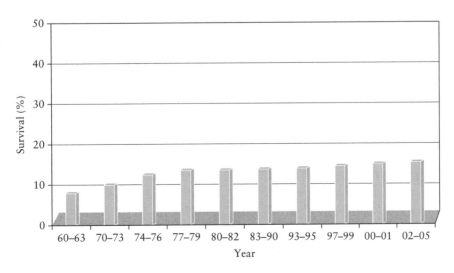

Figure 12.7 Lung Cancer Survival, USA.

Source: Data from US National Institutes of Health. National Cancer Institute: SEER Cancer Statistics Review, 1973–2006.

and Blood Institute (NHLBI), and many other public health agencies have developed presentations and other resources designed to disseminate accurate information to elementary-age school children on the dangers of implementing the smoking habit. Such programs appear to have had some beneficial impact in reducing prevalence rates of smoking in adolescents from 30–40% to 20–25% in the United States over the past 20 years. Paradoxically, the tobacco industry has also sponsored tobacco prevention programs for kids. Nevertheless, most efforts by the tobacco industry are intended to diminish media interventions for tobacco control and oppose national, state, and county tobacco control ballot initiatives and referenda (National Cancer Institute, 2008).

In June of 2009, the United States Senate approved bill H.R. 1256/S. 982, known as the Family Smoking Prevention and Tobacco Control Act. The new law grants the US Food and Drug Administration (FDA) the authority to regulate tobacco products by eliminating tobacco marketing for kids, requiring health warnings and a complete listing of contents on the packaging of cigarettes and other tobacco products, and requiring changes in tobacco products, such as removal or reduction of harmful ingredients. Despite these public health efforts, a huge segment of the world population continues to smoke, as evidenced by recent data from the World Health Organization suggesting that 1 in 3 adults continues to smoke (WHO, 2008), and as a consequence of this addictive habit, 5.4 million people are dying annually from tobacco-related diseases such as lung cancer, heart disease and stroke, chronic obstructive pulmonary disease (COPD), and other forms of cancer (see Figures 12.2 and 12.3 above).

NONSTEROIDAL ANTI-INFLAMMATORY DRUGS (NSAIDS) AND LUNG CANCER

In 1988, Richard Peto and colleagues reported the results of a randomized prospective study of daily aspirin use among 5,139 British physicians. The study was designed to determine if 500 mg of aspirin daily would reduce the incidence of and mortality from stroke, myocardial infarction, or other vascular conditions. In the study, 3,429 of the enrolled subjects were randomly assigned to receive aspirin and 1,710 were randomly assigned to avoid taking any aspirin or aspirin products. After 6 years of follow-up, the results provided little evidence of protective benefit of aspirin against vascular diseases. However, the observed death rate from lung cancer was 7.4 per 10,000 person-years in the group treated with aspirin and 11.6 per 10,000 person-years in the control

group (relative mortality = 0.64) (Peto et al., 1988). Many subsequent investigations have also observed significant protective effects of aspirin and other NSAIDs against the development of lung cancer. For example, in a case-control study of lung cancer and NSAIDs, Harris and colleagues observed a risk reduction of 60% (OR = 0.40) with use of selective COX-2 inhibitors, and comparable risk reductions with regular use of ibuprofen (OR = 0.40) or aspirin (OR = 0.53). Notably, the comparison group in the study consisted of controls that smoked but did not have lung cancer (Harris et al., 2007). In a meta-analysis of 18 studies of lung cancer and NSAIDs, the combined relative risk estimate for regular NSAID use was RR = 0.72 with no evidence of heterogeneity among studies (Harris, 2009).

SMOKING CESSATION AND LUNG CANCER

The 1990 Report of the United States Surgeon General is devoted to the health benefits of smoking cessation. Smoking cessation has major and immediate health benefits for men and women of all ages. Though there is typically a small weight gain with smoking cessation with some adverse psychological impact, the health benefits of smoking cessation far exceed any risks.

On average, former smokers live longer than continuing smokers, and the benefits of quitting extend to those who quit at older ages. For example, persons who quit smoking before age 50 have one-half the risk of dying in the next 15 years compared to continuing smokers. Furthermore, women who stop smoking before or early during pregnancy reduce their risk of having a low birth weight baby.

Smoking cessation reduces the risk of heart attack and stroke by 50% within the first year after quitting and also rapidly improves pulmonary function in patients with established chronic obstructive pulmonary disease (COPD by reducing respiratory symptoms such as cough, sputum production and wheezing, and enhancing immune defense mechanisms against respiratory infections such as bronchitis and pneumonia.

Sustained smoking cessation produces a gradual decrease in the risk of developing lung cancer as well as other tobacco-related cancers (Higgins and Wynder, 1988). Paradoxically, there is a slight increase in the risk of lung cancer diagnosis within the first few years after quitting smoking, which is apparently related to the modified growth characteristics of existing lung tumors that enhances their detection (**Figure 12.8**).

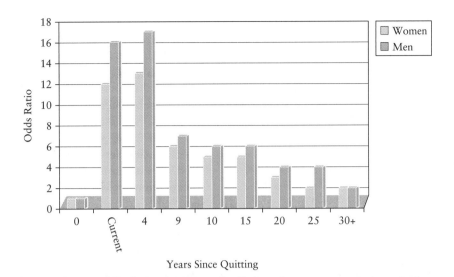

Figure 12.8 Odds Ratios for Lung Cancer by Years of Smoking Cessation.

Source: Data from Higgins IT, Wynder EL (1988). Reduction in risk of lung cancer among ex-smokers with particular reference to histologic type. *Cancer* 62:2397–2401.

● ● ● **REFERENCES**

Augustine, A., Harris, R.E., & Wynder, E.L. (1989). Compensation as a risk factor for lung cancer in smokers who switch from nonfilter to filter cigarettes. *Am J Public Health*, 79(2), 188–191.

Aviel-Ronen, S., Blackhall, F.H., Shepherd, F.A., & Tsao, M.S. (2006). K-ras mutations in non-small-cell lung carcinoma: A review. *Clin Lung Cancer*, 8(1), 30–38.

Bach, P.B., Jett, J.R., Pastorino, U., Tockman, M.S., Swensen, S.J., & Begg, C.B. (2007). Computed tomography screening and lung cancer outcomes. *JAMA*, 297, 953–961.

Barrett, J.C., Lamb, P.W., Wang, T.C., & Lee, T.C. (1989). Mechanisms of arsenic-induced cell transformation. *Biol Trace Elem Res*, 21, 421–429.

Berry, G., Newhouse, M.L., & Turok, M. (1972). Combined effect of asbestos and smoking on mortality from lung cancer and mesothelioma in factory workers. *Lancet ii*, 476–479.

Bertazzi, P.A., Consonni, D., Bachetti, S., Rubagotti, M., Baccarelli, A., Zocchetti, C., & Pesatori, A.C. (2001). Health effects of dioxin exposure: A 20-year mortality study. *American J Epidem*, 153(11), 1031–1044.

Cheng, Y.W., Chiou, H.L., Sheu, G.T., et al. (2001). The association of human papillomavirus 16/18 infection with lung cancer among nonsmoking Taiwanese women. *Cancer Research (American Association for Cancer Research)*, 61(7), 2799–2803.

Delgado, J., Martinez, L.M., Sanchez, T.T., Ramirez, A., Iturria, C., & Gonzalez-Avila, G. (2005). Lung cancer pathogenesis associated with wood smoke exposure. *Chest*, 128, 124–131.

DiPaolo, J.A., & Casto, B.C. (1979). Quantitative studies of in vitro morphological transformation of Syrian hamster cells by inorganic metal salts. *Cancer Res*, 39(3), 1008–1013.

Doll, R., & Hill, A.B. (1950). Smoking and carcinoma of the lung. preliminary report. *British Medical Journal*, 2, 739–748.

Field, R.W., Steck, D.J., Smith, B.J., Brus, C.P., Fisher, E.L., Neuberger, J.S.,...Lynch, C.F. (2000). Residential radon gas and lung cancer: The Iowa Radon Lung Cancer Study. *American J Epidem*, 151, 1091–1152.

Fletcher, B.S., Kujubu, D.A., Perrin, D.M., & Herschman, H.R. (1992). Structure of the mitogen-inducible TIS10 gene and demonstration that the TIS10-encoded protein is a functional prostaglndin G/H synthase. *J Biolo Chem, 267*, 4338–4344.

Fu, J., Masferrer, J.L., Seibert, K., Raz, A., & Needleman, P. (1990). The induction and suppresssion of prostaglandin H2 synthase (cyclooxygenase) in human monocytes. *J Biol Chem, 265*, 16737–16740.

Glynn, T., Seffrin, J.R., Brawley, O.W., Grey, N., & Ross, H. (2010). The globalization of tobacco use: 21 Challenges for the 21st century. *CA Cancer J Clin, 60*, 50–61.

Giuliani, L., Jaxmar, T., Casadio, C., et al. (2007). Detection of oncogenic viruses (SV40, BKV, JCV, HCMV, HPV) and p53 codon 72 polymorphism in lung carcinoma. *Lung Cancer, 57*(3), 273–281.

Harris, R.E., Zang, E.A., Anderson, J.I., & Wynder, E.L. (1993). Race and sex differences in lung cancer risk associated with cigarette smoking. *Intl J Epidemiol, 22*(4), 592–599.

Harris, R.E. (2002). COX-2 blockade in cancer prevention and therapy: Widening the scope of impact. In: R.E. Harris (Ed.), *COX-2 blockade in cancer prevention and therapy* (pp. 341–365). Totowa, NJ: Humana Press.

Harris, R.E., Beebe-Donk, J., & Alshafie, G.A. (2007). Reduced risk of human lung cancer by selective cyclooxygenase-2 (COX-2) blockade: Results of a case control study. *International Journal of Biological Sciences, 3*(5), 328–334.

Harris, R.E. (2007). COX-2 and the inflammogenesis of cancer. *Subcellular Biochemistry, 42*, 193–212.

Harris, R.E. (2009). Cyclooxygenase-2 (Cox-2) blockade in the chemoprevention of cancers of the colon, breast, prostate, and lung. *Inflammopharmacology, 17*, 1–13.

Hecht, S.S. (1999). Tobacco smoke carcinogens and lung cancer. *J National Cancer Institute, 91*(14), 1194–1210.

Henschke, C.I., Yankelevitz, D.F., Libby, D.M., Pasmantier, M.W., Smith, J.P., Meittinen, O.S., & the International Early Lung Cancer Action Program Investigators. (2006). Survival of patients with Stage I lung cancer. *New England Journal of Medicine, 355*(17), 1763–1771.

Herschman, H.R. (2002). Historical aspects of COX-2. In R.E. Harris (ed.), *COX-2 blockade in cancer prevention and therapy* (pp. 13–32). Totowa, NJ: Humana Press.

Hess, C.T., Weiffenbach, C.V., & Norton, S.A. (1983). Environmental radon and cancer correlations in Maine. *Health Phys, 45*(2), 339–348.

Higgins, I.T., & Wynder, E.L. (1988). Reduction in risk of lung cancer among ex-smokers with particular reference to histologic type. *Cancer, 62*, 2397–2401.

Hornung, R.W., & Meinhardt, T.J. (1987). Quantitative risk assessment of lung cancer in U.S. uranium miners. *Health Phys, 52*(4), 417–430.

International Agency for Research on Cancer. (2002). *Tobacco Smoke and Involuntary Smoking.* Lyon, France: International Agency for Research on Cancer.

Josupeit, H. (2003). Global overview of fish consumption (2005). *Options Méditerranéennes, CIHEAM*, Centre International des Hautes.

Krewski, D., Burnett, R., Jerrett, M., Pope, C.A., Rainham, D., Calle, E.,…Thun, M. (2005). Mortality and long-term exposure to ambient air pollution: Ongoing analyses based on the American Cancer Society cohort. *J Toxicol Environ Health, 68*(13–14), 1093–1099.

Lewtas, J., Lewis, C., Zweidinger, R., Stevens, R., & Cupitt, L. (1992). Sources of genotoxicity and cancer risk in ambient air. Review. *Pharmacogenetics, 2*(6), 288–296.

Leroux, C., Girard, N., Cottin, V., Greenland, T., Mornex, J.F., & Archer, F. (2007). Jaagsietkte sheep retrovirus (JSRV): From virus to lung cancer in sheep. *Vet Res, 38*(2), 211–228.

Lubin, J.H., Boice, J.D., Edling, C., et al. (1994). Radon and lung cancer risk: A joint analysis of 11 underground miner studies. Rockville, MD:

National Institutes of Health (NIH publication no. 94–3644).

MacPherson, L., Lo, R., Ahmed, S., Pansoy, A., & Matthews, J. (2009). Activation function 2 mediates dioxin-induced recruitment of estrogen receptor alpha to CYP1A1 and CYP1B1. *Biochem Biophys Res Commun, 385*(2), 263–268.

Marshall, G., Ferreccio, C., Yua, Y., Bates, M.N., Steinmaus, C., Selvin, S., . . . Smith, A.H. (2007). Fifty-year study of lung and bladder cancer mortality in Chile related to arsenic in drinking water. *Journal of the National Cancer Institute, 99*(12), 920–928.

Masferrer, J.L., Zweifel, B.S., Seibert, K., & Needleman, P. (1990). Selective regulation of cellular cyclooxygenase by dexamethasone and endotoxin in mice. *J Clin Invest, 86*, 1375–1379.

McCulloch, J., & Tweedale, G. (2008). The challenge of mesothelioma and Irving J. Selikoff. In *Defending the indefensible: The global asbestos industry and its fight for survival*. Oxford University Press, United Kingdom.

National Cancer Institute. (2008). Tobacco Monograph 19: *The role of the media in promoting and reducing tobacco use*. US Department of Health and Human Services, National Institutes of Health, Washington, D.C.

National Toxicology Program. (2005). *Report on carcinogens* (11th ed.). United States Department of Health and Human Services, Public Health Service, National Toxicology Program, Research Triangle Park, North Carolina.

Peto, R., Gray, R., Collins, R., Wheatley, K., Hennekens, C., Jamrozik, K., . . . Norton, S. (1988). Randomised trial of prophylactic daily aspirin in British male doctors. *Br Med J (Clin Res Ed), 296*(6618), 313–316.

Pope, C.A. III, Burnett, R.T., Thun, M.J., Calle, E.E., Krewski, D., Ito, K., & Thurston, G.D. (2002). Lung cancer, cardiopulmonary mortality, and long-term exposure to fine particulate air pollution. *Journal of the American Medical Association, 287*(9), 1132–1141.

Proctor, R.N. (2001). Tobacco and the global lung cancer epidemic. *Nature Reviews Cancer, 1*, 82–86.

Raz, A., Wynche, A., & Needleman, P. (1989). Temporal and pharmacologic division of fibroblast cylcooxygenase expression into transcriptional and translational phases. *Proc Natl Acad Sci USA, 86*, 1657–1661.

Risch, H.A., Howe, G.A., Jain, M., Burch, J.D., Holowaty, E.J., & Miller, A.B. (1993). Are female smokers at higher risk than male smokers? A case-control analysis by histologic type. *Am J Epidemiol, 138*(5), 281–293.

Rodgman, A., & Perfetti, T.A. (2009). *The chemical components of tobacco and tobacco smoke.* London, England: CRC Press, Taylor & Francis Groud.

Roy, P., & Saha, A. (2002). Metabolism and toxicity of arsenic: A human carcinogen. *Current Science, 82*(1), 38–45.

Samet, J.M., & Hornung, R.W. (1990). Review of radon and lung cancer risk. *Risk Anal, 10*(1), 65–75.

Schwartz, A.G., Prysak, G.M., Bock, C.H., & Cote, M.L. (2007). The molecular epidemiology of lung cancer. *Carcinogenesis, 28*(3), 507–518.

Selikoff, I.J., Hammond, E.C., & Churg, J. (1968). Asbestos exposure, smoking and neoplasia. *JAMA, 204*, 104–110.

Stellman, S.D., Takezaki, T., Wang, L., Chen, Y., Citron, M.L., Djordjevic, M.V., Harlap, S., Muscat, J.E., Neugut, A.I., Wynder, E.L., Ogawa, H., Tajima, K. Aoki, K. (2001). Smoking and lung cancer risk in American and Japanese men: An international case-control study. *Cancer Epidemiol Biomarkers Prev, 10*, 1193–1199.

Stolley, P.D. (1991). When genius errs: RA Fisher and the lung cancer controversy. *American Journal of Epidemiology, 133*(5), 416–425.

Takahashi, I., Matsuzaka, M., Umeda, T., Yamai, K., Nishimura, M., Danjo, K., Kogawa, T., Saito, K., Sato, M. Nakaji, S. (2008). Differences in the influence of tobacco smoking on lung cancer between Japan and the USA: Possible explanations for the "smoking paradox" in Japan. *Public Health, 122*(9), 891–896.

Takezaki, T., Hirose, K., Inoue, M., Hamajima, N., Yatabe, Y., Mitsudomi, T.,...Tajima, K. (2001). Dietary factors and lung cancer risk in Japanese: With special reference to fish consumption and adenocarcinomas. *Br J Cancer, 84*(9), 1199–1206.

National Cancer Institutes (2006). *SEER cancer statistics review, 1973–2006.* Washington, DC: US National Institutes of Health, Washington, DC.

United States Department of Health and Human Services. (2006). *The health consequences of involuntary exposure to tobacco smoke: A report of the surgeon general.* Rockville, MD: United States Department of Health and Human Services.

United States Environmental Protection Agency. (1992). *Respiratory health effects of passive smoking (also known as exposure to secondhand smoke or environmental tobacco smoke—ETS).* Washington, DC: United States Environmental Protection Agency.

United States Environmental Protection Agency. (2002). *Estimated per capita fish consumption in the United States.* Washington, DC: United States Environmental Protection Agency.

United States Department of Health and Human Services. (2000). *Healthy people 2010: Understanding and improving health* (2nd ed.). Washington, DC: U.S. Government Printing Office.

Valavanidis, A., Fiotakis, K., & Vlachogianni, T. (2008). Airborne particulate matter and human health: Toxicological assessment and importance of size and composition of particles for oxidative damage and carcinogenic mechanisms. *J Environ Sci Health C Environ Carcinog Ecotoxicol Rev, 26*(4), 339–362.

Virchow, R. (1863). Aetiologie der neoplastischen Geschwulst/Pathogenie der neoplastischen Geschwulste. In: *Die Krankhaften Geschwulste* (pp. 57–101). Berlin: Verlag von August Hirschwald.

World Health Organization. (2008). *WHO Report on the global tobacco epidemic, 2008: The MPOWER package.* Geneva, Switzerland: World Health Organization.

Wynder, E.L., & Graham, E.A. (1950). Tobacco smoking as a possible etiologic factor in bronchiogenic carcinoma. *JAMA, 143,* 329–336.

Wynder E.L., & Stellman, S.D. (1977). The comparative epidemiology of tobacco-related cancers. *Cancer Res, 37,* 4608–4622.

Wynder, E.L., Taioli, E., & Fujita, Y. (1992). Ecologic study of lung cancer risk factors in the U.S. and Japan, with special reference to smoking and diet. *Jpn J Cancer Res, 83,* 418–423.

Wynder, E.L., & Muscat, J.E. (1995). The changing epidemiology of smoking and lung cancer histology. *Environ Health Perspect, 103*(Suppl 8), 143–148.

Zang, E.A., & Wynder, E.L. (1992). Cumulative tar exposure. A new index for estimating lung cancer risk among cigarette smokers. *Cancer, 70*(1), 69–76.

Epidemiology of Oral Cavity Cancer

GLOBAL EPIDEMIOLOGY OF ORAL CAVITY CANCER

Oral cavity cancer causes nearly 110,000 deaths annually in the world population and at least 68,000 of these deaths occur in developing nations. Globally, nearly two-thirds of cases occur in men; however, the male-to-female ratio varies considerably according to the risk factors in specific populations. In most populations, there is a predominance of male cases due primarily to the higher prevalence of chronic tobacco and alcohol exposure among men; nevertheless, the changing patterns of exposure to certain risk factors, particularly sexually transmitted infection of the oral cavity by human papillomaviruses, have markedly reduced the rate differences in men and women in certain populations (American Cancer Society, 2007).

The global pattern of mortality due to oropharyngeal cancer is shown in **Figure 13.1**. High incidence and mortality rates of oral cavity cancer are observed in developing nations such as India, Pakistan, Southeast Asia, and Melanesia (the southern coastal islands of Southeast Asia). The region with the highest incidence in the world is Melanesia (31.5 per 100,000 men and 20.2 per 100,000 women). In these

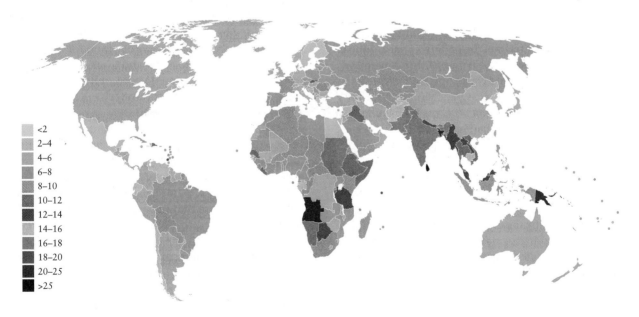

	<2
	2–4
	4–6
	6–8
	8–10
	10–12
	12–14
	14–16
	16–18
	18–20
	20–25
	>25

Figure 13.1 Oropharyngeal Cancer Mortality, 2004.

Source: Data from Death and DALY estimates for 2004 by cause for WHO Member States (Persons, all ages). World Health Organization, 2009. Adapted from File: Mouth and Oropharynx Cancers World Map - Death - WHO2004.svg.

populations, it is customary for both men and women to chew a mixture of tobacco, areca nut, and betel leaf called "betel quid," which has potent carcinogenic properties (Parkin et al., 2005). Also, in certain rural populations of Southern India, *reverse smoking* of tobacco rolled into cigars (called chutta) is particularly popular among women and can lead to the development of cancer of the hard palate (Gupta, Mehta, and Pindborg, 1984). As a consequence of such practices, the rates of oral cavity cancer are high in both men and women of developing nations and the male/female mortality ratio is approximately 1.6:1 (American Cancer Society, 2007).

In developed nations, the rates of oral cavity cancer are lower than in developing nations but males have inordinately higher rates than females and the male/female mortality ratio is approximately 6:1 (American Cancer Society, 2007). This gender difference reflects the higher prevalence of specific risk factors among men, most often the chronic exposure of the oral mucosa to both tobacco and alcohol. Rates are high in men of Western Europe (11.3 per 100,000), Southern Europe, and Australia and New Zealand (10.2 per 100,000). The high rate of oral cancer in Australia is partially due to lip cancer caused by solar irradiation.

PREMALIGNANT LESIONS OF THE ORAL CAVITY

Cancer of the oral cavity may begin as a dysplastic lesion such as leukoplakia (a white patch) or erythroplakia (a red patch) or any other nonhealing sore that persists in the mouth for a matter of weeks. Leukoplakia and erythroplakia are caused by chronic exposure to tobacco, alcohol, certain HPV strains (HPV 16), *Candida albicans* (particularly in immunosuppressed individuals with HIV disease), or any combination of these exposures, all of which are risk factors for the development of oral cavity cancer. These lesions usually precede the diagnosis of invasive cancer by 5–10 years. Progression of precancerous lesions to invasive oral cavity cancer can thus be interrupted by their early detection and complete surgical excision. Regular dental care and careful visual inspection of the oral cavity for such lesions is obviously paramount for cancer prevention.

ORAL CAVITY CANCER RISK FACTORS

Oral cavity neoplasms typically occur between the age of 40–70 years and predominate in men (the male

to female ratio is 2:1). In general, the risk factors for oral cavity cancer include conditions that chronically irritate and inflame the gums, tongue, oral mucosa, and lips. These include chronic alcohol consumption, chronic cigarette smoking, nutritional deficits of iron and vitamin B, chronic use of smokeless tobacco (snuff and chewing tobacco), poor dental hygiene, and certain antecedent nutritional deficiencies, particularly vitamin B deficits. Recent epidemiologic studies in developed countries also suggest that long-term use of alcohol-containing mouthwash is a risk factor. Constant exposure to these alcohol-containing rinses, even in the absence of smoking and drinking, is associated with a significant increase in the development of oral cancer (Kabat and Wynder, 1989).

An important new finding regarding the pathogenesis of oral cavity cancer is its link to sexually transmitted HPV infections. This independent etiologic factor is discussed in a following section.

SYNERGISM OF ALCOHOL AND TOBACCO

The two well-established major risk factors predisposing to oral cavity cancer are alcohol and tobacco. Many independent studies have shown elevated risk in heavy drinkers and heavy smokers (or users of smokeless tobacco) and strongly indicate a synergistic effect between these two risk factors in promoting squamous cell carcinoma of the oral cavity. As an example, an epidemiologic investigation by Blot and colleagues (1988) determined that chronic smoking and drinking had independent odds ratios of 5.8 and 7.4, respectively, whereas the odds ratio for the combination of chronic smoking and drinking increased the odds ratio more than 35-fold, reflecting a multiplicative synergistic effect (Blot et al., 1988; Kabat and Wynder, 1989) (**Figure 13.2**).

While it is well known that tobacco smoke and tobacco juice contain powerful carcinogens and inflammatory substances that are linked to carcinogenesis, the mechanism by which alcohol promotes oral cavity cancer remains elusive. Animal studies do not clearly indicate that pure alcohol acts as a direct carcinogen. Rather, the studies seem to indicate that alcohol may promote the transport of other carcinogens through the cell membrane either as a solvent or by acting on the cell membrane directly. Other possible mechanisms include the induction of microsomal enzymes in the liver that promote the formation of polycyclic aromatic hydrocarbons and/or benzopyrene, interference with DNA repair mechanisms, and epigenetic effects on DNA methylation resulting in epigenetic deregulation of tumor suppressor genes

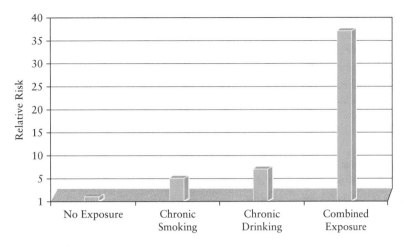

Figure 13.2 Oral Cavity Cancer: Synergism of Tobacco and Alcohol.

Source: Data from Blot WJ, McLaughlin JK, Winn DM, Austin DF, Greenberg RS, Preston-Martin S, Bernstein L, Schoenberg JB, Stemhagen A, Fraumeni JF (1988). Smoking and drinking in relation to oral and pharyngeal cancer. *Cancer Res* 48:3282–3287.

(Poschl and Seitz, 2004). Furthermore, alcohol may be a vehicle for the induction of contaminating carcinogens into the oral cavity, i.e., various alcoholic beverages may contain nitroso compounds, phenols, or a variety of polycyclic aromatic hydrocarbons. Chronic alcohol consumption may also promote nutritional deficiency simply by substituting empty calories and reducing the dietary consumption of important micronutrients and minerals such as vitamins A and B and iron. Heavy alcohol consumption coupled with poor nutrition may therefore result in immunosuppression, which may also increase the predisposition to oral cavity cancer (Testino and Borro, 2009).

HUMAN PAPILLOMAVIRUS (HPV) AND ORAL CAVITY CANCER

It has recently been shown that chronic infection with high risk strains of human papillomavirus (e.g., HPV 16) is an independent risk factor for the development of oral cavity cancer (Gillison et al., 2000; D'Souza et al., 2007). However, the demographic profile of HPV 16-infected patients who develop oral cavity cancer differs markedly from that of patients whose cancer developed from chronic exposure to tobacco and alcohol. In the latter group, the disease is typically diagnosed after age 60, the ratio of African Americans to Caucasians is 2:1, and the ratio of men to women is nearly 3:1. With HPV 16-related disease, chronic exposure to tobacco and alcohol may be absent, the age at diagnosis is much earlier, 20–50 years, the male-to-female ratio is close to 1:1, and tumors develop on the tonsils and base of the tongue. Notably, HPV 16

and and HPV 18 are the same viruses responsible for the vast majority of cervical cancers and HPV is the most common sexually transmitted infection in the United States and elsewhere. Furthermore, infection by high-risk HPV strains is preventable by vaccination (Kenter et al., 2009).

OTHER RISK FACTORS FOR ORAL CAVITY CANCER

The Plummer-Vinson syndrome (iron deficiency anemia, dysphagia, and atrophy of the oral cavity mucosa) is associated with predisposition to oral cavity cancer. Other conditions that may be associated with oral cavity neoplasms include sprue (malabsorption of wheat germ) and scurvy (deficiency in vitamin C). Pipe smoking and cigar smoking, sunburn, and other excessive exposure to ultraviolet radiation are noted risk factors for development of squamous cell carcinomas of the lip, in particular the lower lip.

Rare malignant neoplasms of the oral cavity include cancers of the salivary glands including the parotid glands and submandibular glands. These are typically glandular carcinomas with mixed histologic features. A salivary gland carcinoma mixed with marked lymphocytic invasion is called a Warthin's tumor. The risk of salivary gland cancer is increased by ionizing radiation, e.g., in atomic bomb survivors and after radiotherapy (Boukheris et al., 2009), but other risk factors have not been identified.

Malignant melanomas may also present initially in the oral cavity. Risk factors for oral cavity malignant melanomas include certain genetic syndromes, i.e., the Peutz-Jeghers syndrome and Addison's disease, both of which lead to melanotic pigmentation of the oral cavity mucosa (Boardman et al., 1998).

• • • REFERENCES

American Cancer Society. (2007). *Global cancer facts and figures, 2007*. American Cancer Society, Atlanta, Georgia.

Blot, W.J., McLaughlin, J.K., Winn, D.M., Austin, D.F., Greenberg, R.S., Preston-Martin, S.,... Fraumeni, J.F. (1988). Smoking and drinking in relation to oral and pharyngeal cancer. *Cancer Res, 48*, 3282–3287.

Boardman, L.A., Thibodeau, S.N., Schaid, D.J., et al. (1998). Increased risk for cancer in patients with the Peutz-Jeghers syndrome. *Ann Intern Med, 128*(11), 896–899.

Boukheris, H., Curtis, R.E., Land, C.E., & Dores, G.M. (2009). Incidence of carcinoma of the major salivary glands according to the WHO classification, 1992 to 2006: A population-based study in the United States. *Cancer Epidemiol. Biomarkers Prev, 18*, 2899–2906.

D'Souza, G., Kreimer, A.R., Viscidi, R., Pawlita, M., Fakhry, C., Koch, W.M.,...Gillison, M.L. (2007). *New England Journal of Medicine, 356*(19), 1944–1956.

Gillison, M.L., Koch, W.M., Capone, R.B., et al. (2000). Evidence for a causal association between human papillomavirus and a subset of head and neck cancers. *J Natl Cancer Inst, 92*, 709–720.

Gupta, P.C., Mehta, F.S., & Pindborg, J.J. (1984). Mortality among reverse chutta smokers in south India. *Br Med J (Clin Res Ed), 289*(6449), 865–866.

Kabat, G.C., & Wynder, E.L. (1989). Type of alcoholic beverage and oral cancer. *Int J Cancer, 43*, 190–194.

Kenter, G.G., Welters, M.J., Valentijn, A.R., et al. (2009). Vaccination against HPV-16 oncoproteins for vulvar intraepithelial neoplasia. *N Engl J Med, 361*, 1838–1847.

Parkin, M.D., Bray, F., Ferlay, J., & Pisani, P. (2005). Global cancer statistics, 2002. *CA Cancer J Clin, 55*, 74–108.

Poschl, G., & Seitz, H.K. (2004). Alcohol and cancer. *Alcohol, 39*, 155–165.

Testino, G., & Borro, P. (2009). Carcinogenesis and alcohol. *Mediterr J Nutr Metab, 2*, 89–91.

WHO. (2009). *WHO Disease and injury country estimates. Death and DALY estimates for 2004 by cause for WHO Member States (Persons, all ages)*. Geneva, Switzerland: World Health Organization.

14

Epidemiology of Esophageal Cancer

GLOBAL EPIDEMIOLOGY OF ESOPHAGEAL CANCER

More than 432,000 people die annually from esophageal cancer (300,000 men and 142,000 women) making it the sixth most common cause of cancer deaths in the world population. Slightly less than 5.8% of all cancer deaths are due to this malignancy. In developing countries, esophageal cancer ranks fourth in cancer mortality among men (247,000 deaths) and sixth among women (129,000 deaths) (American Cancer Society, 2007). Once diagnosed, invasive cancer of the esophagus does not respond well to treatment and has very poor survival (only 16% of cases in the United States and 10% of cases in Europe survive at least 5 years) (Parkin et al., 2005).

Esophageal cancer displays some of the most striking international epidemiologic characteristics of all diseases. In the United States, the incidence rates per 100,000 are 4.1 for Caucasian men and 1.2 for women. The corresponding rates for African American men and women are threefold higher, 15.6 and 3.6, respectively.

In sharp contrast, the incidence is considerably higher in certain areas of the world. For example, in northern Iran, the incidence rates are 115 for males and 131 for females; a female preponderance. Iranian women are affected almost 100 times more often than American women (Day, 1975). As depicted in **Figure 14.1**, the *esophageal cancer belt* extends from

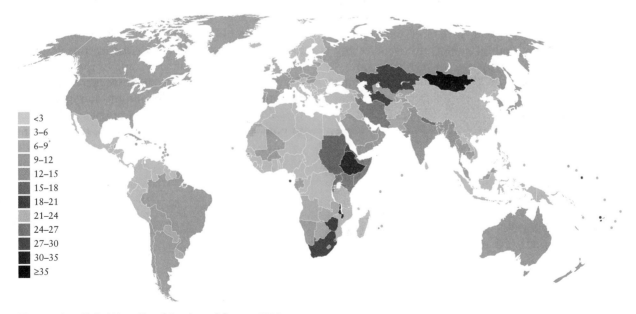

	<3
	3–6
	6–9
	9–12
	12–15
	15–18
	18–21
	21–24
	24–27
	27–30
	30–35
	≥35

Figure 14.1 Global Mortality of Esophageal Cancer, 2004.

Source: Data from Death and DALY estimates for 2004 by cause for WHO Member States (Persons, all ages). World Health Organization, 2009. Adapted from File: Esophageal Cancer World Map - Death - WHO2004.svg.

northeastern China to the Middle East, and in certain populations of this region (e.g., northern Iran and certain provinces in eastern China) the cumulative lifetime risk of esophageal cancer is nearly 25%.

PATHOGENESIS OF ESOPHAGEAL CANCER

Esophageal cancer is usually diagnosed during the sixth or seventh decade of life. Male cases far outnumber female cases in most regions; for example, the male-to-female ratio is 7:1 in Eastern Europe. Historically, the majority of esophageal tumors have been squamous cell carcinomas arising from the squamous cell epithelium in the middle or upper third of the esophagus. However, in recent decades, there has been a marked increase in the incidence of adenocarcinomas of the lower esophagus near the gastroesophageal junction, particularly among men of the United States, the United Kingdom, and other developed nations (Eslick, 2009). Indeed, adenocarcinomas of the lower esophagus are now diagnosed more often than squamous cell carcinomas in the United States, the United Kingdom, and Western European nations (Umar and Fleischer, 2008).

Adenocarcinomas of the lower esophagus arise by a sequence of metaplastic and dysplastic changes in the esophageal epithelium known as Barrett's esophagus (Barrett, 1957). Such changes arise due to chronic gastroesophageal reflux of acidic stomach fluid into the normally basic environment of the lower esophagus. Barrett's esophagus is therefore a premalignant lesion that must be aggressively treated to halt its progression to invasive esophageal cancer, a condition that is life threatening. Effective screening strategies have been proposed for high-risk populations using endoscopy with mucosal iodine staining and biopsy to identify severe dysplastic lesions and carcinomas *in situ* that are curable by radical mucosectomy (Dong et al., 2002).

RISK FACTORS FOR ESOPHAGEAL CANCER

The risk factors for esophageal cancer differ according to histologic subtype (squamous cell carcinoma versus adenocarcinoma) and anatomic location in the esophagus (**Table 14.1**). Among the environmental risk factors for both histologic types, chronic alcoholism and cigarette smoking contribute most heavily to the development of esophageal cancer. This malignancy is 25 times more common among heavy drinkers than among controls. Habitual smokers of cigarettes also have a 6–7-fold increased frequency of esophageal cancer after adjustment for alcohol consumption (Wynder and Mabuchi, 1973).

RISK FACTORS FOR SQUAMOUS CELL CARCINOMAS OF THE ESOPHAGUS

In the esophageal cancer belt of the Middle East and China, most of the cases are squamous cell carcinomas that are related to tobacco and alcohol addiction. However, recent epidemiologic studies have identified additional major risk factors that independently and synergistically elevate the risk. In northern Iran and other populations in the Middle East and India, the cultural practice of consuming steaming hot black tea at temperatures exceeding 70°C beginning early in life coupled with nutritional deficiencies in essential vitamins (beta-carotene, folate, vitamin C, vitamin E) are associated with the extraordinarily high rates observed (Islami et al., 2009).

Epidemiologic investigations conducted in the high-risk populations of northern China have also identified multiple factors other than tobacco and alcohol that synergistically enhance the development of squamous cell carcinoma of the esophagus (Yang, 1980). The web of causative factors includes mycotic (fungal) contamination of food and water, fungal conversion of secondary amines and nitrites to potent carcinogens (nitrosamines), fungal toxins

Table 14.1	Esophageal Cancer Epidemiology	
Characteristic	**Squamous Cell Carcinoma**	**Adenocarcinoma**
Age (Years)	60–70	50–60
Anatomic Site	Middle and Upper	Lower
Risk Factors	Alcohol & Tobacco, Betel Quid, Mycotic Contamination, Nutritional Deficits, Hot Beverages	Alcohol, Tobacco, GE Reflux (GERD), Obesity
GE: Gastroesophageal Junction; GERD: Gastroesophageal Reflux Disease		

(aflatoxins), and nutritional deficiencies in certain vitamins and minerals (selenium, molybdenum) (Chu and Li, 1994).

In Africa, the observed high rates of squamous cell esophageal cancer, particularly in men, are attributed to a web of causative risk factors involving chronic smoking and alcohol consumption, diets poor in fresh fruits and vegetables, and consumption of foods contaminated with *Fusarium verticilloides* (Day, 1975; Dlamini and Bhoola, 2005). During the 20th century there was a gradual transition of the staple diet of South African from sorghum to maize (corn) associated with the rising rates of this malignancy. Fusarium fungi grow readily on maize, producing fumonisins that reduce nitrates to nitrites and produce nitrosamines that may induce and promote esophageal carcinogenesis (Hendricks and Parker, 2008).

RISK FACTORS FOR BARRETT'S ESOPHAGUS AND ESOPHAGEAL ADENOCARCINOMA

As noted above, Barrett's esophagus is a premalignant lesion that develops proximal to the gastroesophageal junction primarily due to reflux of acidic stomach fluid into the lower esophagus. If left untreated, Barrett's esophagus can progress through a sequence of cellular metaplastic and dysplastic changes leading to the development of invasive adenocarcinoma of the esophagus. Patients with Barrett's esophagus have a 25- to 30-fold increased risk of developing invasive adenocarcinoma of the esophagus compared to the general population (Umar and Fleischer, 2008; Wong and Fitzgerald, 2005). The major risk factors for the development of Barrett's esophagus include obesity and gastroesophageal reflux disease (GERD), chronic tobacco and alcohol addiction, and nutritional deficiencies related to lack of intake of fresh fruits and vegetables. It is estimated that 10% of individuals with GERD develop Barrett's esophagus.

The bacterium, *Helicobacter pylori*, is a common contaminant of the stomach that can cause stomach ulcers and gastric adenocarcinoma. Gastric infection by *H. pylori* can be treated with antibiotics plus proton pump inhibiting drugs to counteract excessive secretion of stomach acid. Paradoxically, people who have had such treatment to rid the stomach of *H. pylori* are more prone to develop adenocarcinoma of the esophagus. The biological explanation is that certain strains of *H. pylori* reduce stomach acid, which makes the stomach fluids less harmful to the esophagus (in people with reflux). Thus, *H. pylori* infection, while causing precancerous and cancerous

lesions in the stomach *per se*, may actually protect against the development of Barrett's esophagus and esophageal cancer (Blaser and Atherton, 2004; Delaney and McColl, 2005).

GENETIC RISK FACTORS FOR ESOPHAGEAL CANCER

Genetic polymorphisms of certain tumor suppressor genes that modulate cell division may also contribute to the genesis of esophageal cancer. Bani-Hani and colleagues (2000) found genetic polymorphisms in cyclin D1 and p53 that increased the risk by sixfold and threefold, respectively, and Reid and colleagues (2001) observed a 16-fold increase in the risk of esophageal cancer with loss of heterozygosity in p53.

Genetic syndromes involving malformations in esophageal structure also increase the risk of developing cancer of the esophagus. Achalasia due to dysfunction of the gastrointestinal sphincter interrupts the passage of food from the esophagus into the stomach and elevates the risk of esophageal cancer by 15-fold. The Plummer-Vinson syndrome consists of iron deficiency anemia coupled with muscle atrophy, dysphagia, and the formation of esophageal rings or webs in the upper esophagus. This syndrome is associated with the development of squamous cell carcinomas proximal to the upper esophageal webs (Wynder et al., 1957).

PREVENTION OF ESOPHAGEAL CANCER

The primary prevention of esophageal cancer obviously involves avoiding exposure of the esophagus to alcohol, tobacco, boiling hot beverages, and other caustic substances. In developing nations, intake of moldy grains and other foods or beverages fermented from moldy grain should be avoided. International efforts are now being directed to the obesity pandemic in order to reduce the burden of obesity-related diseases.

Multiple epidemiologic studies have examined the potential role of aspirin and other nonsteroidal anti-inflammatory drugs (NSAIDs) in the prevention of esophageal cancer. In a recent meta-analysis of these studies, Corley and colleagues (2003) determined that regular use of NSAIDs was associated with a 40% reduction in the risk of esophageal cancer. The NSAIDs are known to reduce inflammation by inhibiting the cyclooxygenase enzymes, COX-1 and COX-2, that are responsible for the synthesis of prostaglandins of the inflammatory cascade. It is

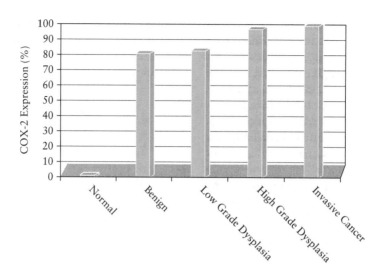

Figure 14.2 COX-2 in Progression of Barrett's Esophagus to Cancer.

Source: Data from Harris RE (2007). COX-2 and the inflammogenesis of cancer. *Subcellular Biochemistry* 42:193–212.

therefore notable that the inducible inflammatory gene, cyclooxygenase-2 (COX-2), which is silent in normal esophageal mucosa, becomes markedly overexpressed throughout the progression of Barrett's esophagus to esophageal cancer (Harris, 2007) (**Figure 14.2**).

In high-risk populations, endoscopic screening for Barrett's esophagus or other dysplastic changes in the esophageal mucosa coupled with ablative treatment have proven effective in preventing the development of esophageal cancer (Spechler, 2001; Dong et al., 2002). Treatments found effective include administration of proton pump inhibitors (Yeh et al., 2003) and ablation by radiofrequency energy (Shaheen et al., 2009). Patients with Barrett's esophagus or other premalignant lesions should thus seek immediate treatment to prevent progression to esophageal cancer.

● ● ● REFERENCES

American Cancer Society. (2007). *Global cancer facts and figures, 2007*. Atlanta, GA: American Cancer Society.

Bani-Hani, K., Martin, I.G., Hardie, L.J., Mapstone, N., Briggs, J.A., Forman, D., et al. (2000). Prospective study of cyclin D1 overexpression in Barrett's esophagus: Association with increased risk of adenocarcinoma. *J Natl Cancer Inst, 92*, 1316–1321.

Barrett, N. (1957). The lower esophagus lined by columnar epithelium. *Surgery, 41*(6), 881–894.

Blaser, M.J., & Atherton, J.C. (2004). *Helicobacter pylori* persistence: Biology and disease. *J Clin Invest, 113*, 321–333.

Corley, D.A., Kerlikowske, K., Verma, R., & Buffler, P. (2003). Protective association of aspirin/NSAIDs and esophageal cancer: A systematic review and meta-analysis. *Gastroenterology, 124*, 47–56.

Chu, F.S., & Li, G.Y. (1994). Simultaneous occurrence of fumonisin B1 and other mycotoxins in moldy corn collected from the People's Republic of China in regions with high incidences of esophageal cancer. *Appl Environ Microbiol, 60*(3), 847–852.

Corley, D.A., Kerlikowske, K., Verma, R., & Buffler, P. (2003). Protective association of aspirin/NSAIDs and esophageal cancer: A systematic review and meta-analysis. *Gastroenterology, 124*, 47–56.

Day, N.E. (1975). Some aspects of the epidemiology of esophageal cancer. *Cancer Research, 35*, 3304–3307.

Delaney, B., & McColl, K. (2005). Review article: *Helicobacter pylori* and gastro-oesophageal reflux disease. *Aliment Pharmacol Ther, 22,* Suppl 1, 32–40.

Dong, Z., Tank, P., Li, L., & Wang, G. (2002). The strategy for esophageal cancer control in high-risk areas of China. *Japanese Journal of Clinical Oncology, 32,* 10–12.

Dlamini, Z., & Bhoola, K. (2005). Esophageal cancer in African blacks of Kwazulu Natal, South Africa: An epidemiological brief. *Ethn Dis, 15*(4), 786–789.

Eslick, G.D. (2009). Epidemiology of esophageal cancer. *Gastroenterology Clinics, 38*(1), 17–25.

Hendricks, D., & Parker, M.I. (2008). Oesophageal cancer in Africa. *IUBMB Life, 53*(4–5), 263–268.

Harris, R.E. (2007). COX-2 and the inflammogenesis of cancer. *Subcellular Biochemistry, 42,* 193–212.

Islami, F., Pourshams, A., Nasrollahzadeh, D., Kamangar, F., Fahimi, S., Shakeri, R.,…Boffetta, P. (2009). Tea drinking habits and oesophageal cancer in a high risk area in northern Iran: population based case-control study. *BMJ, 338,* b929.

Parkin, M.D., Bray, F., Ferlay, J., & Pisani, P. (2005). Global cancer statistics, 2002. *CA Cancer J Clin, 55,* 74–108.

Reid, B.J., Prevo, L.J., Galipeau, P.C., Sanchez, C.A., Longton, G., Levine, D.S., & Rabinovitch, P.S. (2001). Predictors of progression in Barrett's esophagus II: Baseline 17p (p53) loss of heterozygosity identifies a patient subset at increased risk for neoplastic progression. *American Journal of Gastroenterology, 96,* 2839–2848.

Shaheen, N.J., Sharma, P., Overholt, B., et al. (2009). Radiofrequency ablation in Barrett's esophagus with dysplasia. *New England Journal of Medicine, 360,* 2277–2288.

Spechler, S.J. (2001). Screening and surveillance for complications related to gastroesophageal reflux disease. *Am J Med, 111,* Suppl 8A, 130–136.

Umar, S.B., & Fleischer, D.E. (2008). Esophageal cancer: Epidemiology, pathogenesis and prevention. *Nat Reviews Clin Pract Gastroenterol Hepatol, 5,* 517–526.

Wong, A., & Fitzgerald, R.C. (2005). Epidemiologic risk factors for Barrett's esophagus and associated adenocarcinoma. *Clin Gastroentero Hepatol, 3*(1), 1–10.

WHO Disease and injury country estimates. (2009). *Death and DALY estimates for 2004 by cause for WHO Member States (Persons, all ages).* Geneva, Switzerland: World Health Organization.

Wynder, E.L., Hultberg, S., Jacobsson, F., & Bross, I.J. (1957). Environmental factors in cancer of the upper alimentary tract. A Swedish study with special reference to Plummer-Vinson (Paterson-Kelly) syndrome. *Cancer, 10,* 470–482.

Wynder, E.L., & Mabuchi, K. (1973). Etiological and environmental factors in esophageal cancer. *Journal of the American Medical Association, 226,* 1546–1548.

Yeh, R.W., Gerson, L.B., & Triadafilopoulos, G. (2003). Efficacy of esomeprazole in controlling reflux symptoms, intraesophageal, and intragastric pH in patients with Barrett's esophagus. *Dis Esophagus, 16*(3), 193–198.

Yang, C.S. (1980). Research on esophageal cancer in China: A review. *Cancer Research, 40,* 2633–2644.

CHAPTER

15

Epidemiology of Stomach Cancer

GLOBAL EPIDEMIOLOGY OF STOMACH CANCER

Stomach cancer is the fourth most commonly diagnosed malignancy worldwide and the second leading cause of cancer death ranking only behind lung cancer. Nearly 1.1 million cases are diagnosed every year and more than 800,000 deaths are caused by stomach cancer. About 70% of the cases and deaths occur in developing countries. The highest incidence and death rates occur in China and Mongolia, Eastern Asia, the Andean regions of South America, Eastern Europe, and Mali and Zaire in Africa (**Figure 15.1**).

Mortality rates of stomach cancer are declining worldwide and in many nations the declines have been dramatic. In the United States, death rates from stomach cancer have declined by nearly 90% in men and women since 1930 (**Figure 15.2**).

A similar pattern has emerged in Japan, the nation with the highest stomach cancer mortality in the world in 1950 (nearly 100 deaths per 100,000 in men) (**Figure 15.3**). Since then, mortality rates from stomach cancer have declined by nearly 70% in Japanese men and 90% in women (Tajima, Kuroishi, and Oshima, 2004; Inoue and Tsugane, 2005). In Switzerland and neighboring European countries,

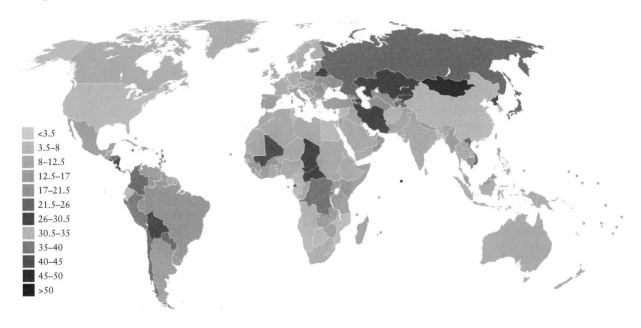

	<3.5
	3.5–8
	8–12.5
	12.5–17
	17–21.5
	21.5–26
	26–30.5
	30.5–35
	35–40
	40–45
	45–50
	>50

Figure 15.1 Global Mortality of Stomach Cancer, 2004.

Source: Data from World Health Organization. The global burden of disease: 2004 update. Geneva, WHO, 2008. Available at www.who.int/evidence/bod.

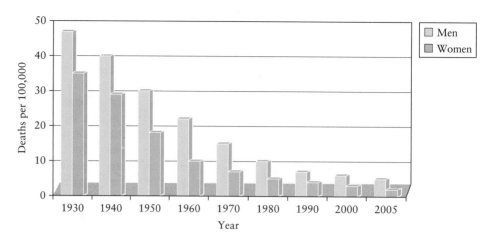

Figure 15.2 Stomach Cancer Mortality Rates, USA.

Source: Data from American Cancer Society, 2009. Cancer Statistics. Mortality rates are age-adjusted to the US population of 2000.

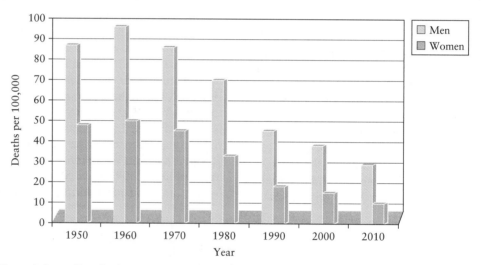

Figure 15.3 Stomach Cancer Mortality in Japan: 1950–2010.

Source: Data from Inoue M, Tsugane S (2005). Epidemiology of gastric cancer in Japan. *Postgrad Med J* 81:419–424. Rates are age-adjusted to the Japanese population of 1985.

stomach cancer mortality has fallen by 60% within one generation (Crew and Neuget, 2006).

STOMACH CANCER PREVENTION: EPIDEMIOLOGY OF AN UNPLANNED TRIUMPH

Howson, Hiyama, and Wynder (1986) described the decline in stomach cancer incidence and mortality among developed countries within the past 50 years as the "*epidemiology of an unplanned triumph.*" The major reason for the decline in stomach cancer in developed countries is the rapid and widespread escalation of refrigeration since 1900. Expansion of industrial refrigeration has meant fresher produce for the consumer and in turn has resulted in higher per capita intake of vitamins A, C, and E, which protect against gastric carcinogenesis. Furthermore, the increase in refrigeration has reduced the need for salting and pickling, two traditional means of food preservation associated with increased gastric cancer risk.

Considerable experimental evidence suggests that high salt concentration enhances gastric carcinogenesis. High salt consumption damages the stomach mucosa and can induce severe gastritis, heightening the predisposition to nitrosamines and other carcinogens. Chronic atrophic gastritis and its associated lesion, intestinal metaplasia, are the precursor conditions most closely linked to increased gastric cancer risk (Joosens et al., 1996).

Due to the widespread use of refrigeration, fish and meat can be readily preserved without salting. Reductions in the incidence and mortality rates are therefore particularly impressive in Nordic countries in which fish consumption is traditionally high, e.g., Iceland. In populations that still prefer salty food, e.g., Portugal and Brazil (salted cod, bacalao), Japan and Korea (salted pickles and salad), stomach cancer rates remain high but have also declined significantly in recent years (Howson et al., 1986).

Another important reason for the reduction in stomach cancer mortality is that improved food sanitation through better techniques of processing, handling, and refrigeration has reduced exposure to the infectious microbe, *Helicobacter pylori*, particularly among children. This bacterium is known to cause chronic stomach inflammation, and bacterial infiltrates of the organism are commonly found associated with gastric adenocarcinoma and its precursor lesions. Studies combining methods of epidemiology and microbiology clearly suggest that *Helicobacter pylori* should be considered as a major causal factor of gastric carcinoma (Kelley and Duggan, 2003).

An additional factor contributing to this trend is the availability in many countries of fresh fruit and vegetables throughout the year. In the gastrointestinal tract, any chronic tissue damage with necrosis and regeneration carries an increased cancer risk, e.g., consumption of very hot beverages (squamous cell carcinoma of the esophagus), gastroesophageal reflux (adenocarcinoma of the esophagus), chronic gastritis induced by *H. pylori* infection (stomach cancer), Crohn's disease (cancer of the small intestines), and ulcerative colitis (colon cancer).

Certain nitroso compounds are carcinogenic in animal models and can induce glandular stomach adenocarcinomas resembling human gastric cancer. Conceivably, nitrosamides can be formed in the human stomach through an interaction between nitrite and suitable substrates. From 1925–1981, the content of nitrates and nitrites in cured meats in the United States decreased by 75% while gastric cancer mortality rates declined by two-thirds (Howson et al., 1986).

Cigarette smoking and other forms of tobacco addiction are also significant risk factors for the development of stomach cancer. A recent comprehensive review and meta-analysis of the available data found a twofold increase in the risk of stomach cancer among male chronic smokers (Ladeiras-Lopes et al., 2008). There is also consistent evidence that tobacco addiction in combination with chronic

alcohol consumption synergistically heighten the risk by fivefold (Sjödahl et al., 2007).

Ecological studies have shown an inverse association between gastric cancer risk and socioeconomic status. These observations led to the hypothesis that high carbohydrate intake at an early age predisposes to increased gastric cancer risk. However, intracountry and time-trend comparisons have shown little association between carbohydrate intake and gastric cancer risk (Larsson, Bergkvist, and Wolk, 2006). Some studies suggest that the dietary glycemic load, a measure of the impact of total carbohydrate intake on blood sugar, is linked to the risk of stomach cancer (Augustin et al., 2003). Albeit, other studies do not support the view that a high starch diet and related measures such as the glycemic index or glycemic load enhance predisposition to gastric carcinoma (Lazarevic, Nagomi, & Jermic, 2009).

HELICOBACTER PYLORI AND STOMACH CANCER

In 1984, two Australian scientists, Drs. Barry J. Marshall and J. Robin Warren, made the remarkable discovery that a bacterium naturally inhabits the strong acid environment in the stomachs of patients with gastritis and stomach ulcers (Marshall and Warren, 1984). The bacterium was named *Helicobacter pylorus* due to its spiraled flagella that make it highly motile and able to avoid the severe acidity of the stomach fluids. In recognition of this remarkable discovery, Marshall and Warren were awarded the 2005 Nobel Prize for Medicine and Physiology.

Subsequent investigations have found that *H. pylorus* contaminates the stomachs of approximately 50% of humans (Pounder and Ng, 1995). The bacterium appears to be readily transmitted by oral-oral and oral-fecal routes, and infection is associated with conditions of poor sanitation (Brown, 2000).

Persistent colonization of the stomach by *H. pylori* results in chronic gastritis, an inflammatory condition of the stomach lining. The severity of the inflammation underlies the genesis of *H. pylori*-related diseases including peptic ulcer, duodenal ulcer, and stomach cancer (Shiotani and Graham, 2002). Specifically, certain strains of *H. pylori* that are seropositive for the CagA antigen are highly inflammatory and carcinogenic and are often present in specimens of gastric ulcers and gastric carcinomas (NIH Consensus Statement, 2004). Molecular epidemiologic studies have determined that severe chronic atrophic gastritis due to infection by CagA-positive strains of *H. pylori* increases the risk of gastric cancer by more than tenfold (Palli et al., 2007). Perhaps the most compelling evidence supporting *H. pylori* as the major etiologic factor in the genesis of gastric cancer comes from a prospective study of 1,526 Japanese participants in which gastric cancers developed in 2.9% of infected individuals and in none of the non-infected individuals (Uemura et al., 2001).

It is also important to realize that chronic *H. pylori* infection interacts synergistically with other factors in the progression of carcinogenesis in the gastric mucosa. Such interactions are particularly evident in certain regions of China and Mongolia where consumption of salted and smoked foods is common-place and conditions are ideal for the transmission of *H. pylori* infections, e.g., crowded living conditions, family size, sharing a bedroom, low socioeconomic status, low educational level, poor sanitation, and infrequent hand washing (Yang, 2006). High rates of smoking and alcohol consumption further exacerbate the risk. This web of causative factors is responsible for the high rates of stomach cancer in China and the staggering fact that more than 50% of stomach cancer deaths worldwide occur in this region.

Interactions involving multiple strains of *H. pylorus* and other infectious and parasitic agents have also been explored. For example, certain regions of Africa with high rates of stomach cancer (e.g., Mali and Zaire) are also prone to multiple gastrointestinal infections and mosquito-borne malarial infections that could further compromise host immunity thereby promoting more severe *H. pylorus* infections (Blaser, 1993; Blaser and Atherton, 2004).

HISTOLOGIC AND ANATOMIC SUBTYPES OF STOMACH CANCER

More than 90% of gastric cancers are adenocarcinomas which are divisible pathologically and anatomically into two subtypes: (1) poorly differentiated or *diffuse* adenocarcinomas arising near the cardia (just distal to the gastroesophageal junction) and (2) well-differentiated or *intestinal* adenocarcinomas that arise elsewhere in the corpus of the stomach (noncardia adenocarcinomas) (Crew and Neuget, 2006).

Well-differentiated (*intestinal*) noncardia adeno-carcinomas of the stomach are thought to develop primarily as a consequence of environmental factors such as chronic *H. pylori* infection, particularly due to CagA positive strains, resulting in chronic severe atrophic gastritis that progresses to invasive cancer. Synergism of *H. pylori* with other environmental factors including high salt diets, nutritional deficits, and

chronic tobacco and alcohol exposure can exacerbate the risk. The noncardia intestinal subtype of gastric cancer predominates in high-risk regions of the world and its rates have declined dramatically in many developed nations, primarily due to refrigeration replacing salt preservation of fish and meat, better access to fresh fruits and vegetables, improved sanitation, reductions in tobacco and alcohol addiction, and effective antibiotic therapy for *H. pylorus* infections.

In contrast to the decline in noncardia *intestinal* gastric cancer, the rates of diffuse gastric adenocarcinomas arising near the cardia are increasing in many developed nations, particularly among Caucasian males. The increasing incidence of the diffuse type of adenocarcinomas arising near the cardia of the stomach is related to obesity and other conditions that predispose to gastroesophageal reflux disease (GERD) and Barrett's esophagus (Crew and Neuget, 2006). It has been hypothesized that ablation of colonization of the stomach by *H. pylorus* has accentuated the development of these conditions in some developed populations (Blaser and Atherton, 2006).

GENETIC PREDISPOSITION TO STOMACH CANCER

Evidence for a genetic predisposition to gastric cancer comes from both epidemiologic studies and reports of multigenerational pedigrees with excess cases of gastric cancer among relatives. Systematic case-control and cohort analyses of gastric cancer patients have shown that the risk of gastric cancer in first-degree relatives of index cases (probands) is increased two to threefold.

Mutations, polymorphisms, and epigenetic changes in the expression of certain genes have been implicated in gastric carcinogenesis, particularly for the diffuse type of adenocarcinoma that arises in the cardia near the gastroesophageal junction. Familial clusters of hereditary diffuse gastric carcinoma have been discovered. Such families manifest key germline mutations in the CDH1 gene that encodes E-cadherin, an important calcium-dependent cell adhesion molecule (Lynch et al., 2005).

Excess cases of gastric cancer have also been observed in families with the adenomatous polyposis coli (APC) gene that predisposes to familial adenomatous polyposis (FAP), and in families with hereditary nonpolyposis colorectal cancer (also called the Lynch syndrome), which is due to mutated mismatch DNA repair genes (Lynch et al., 2005). Other genetic and familial factors are also known to influence gastric cancer risk. Blood group A has been reported to be more prevalent among gastric cancer cases than among controls and appears to be associated with the development of the diffuse type of disease. Patients with pernicious anemia are also at increased risk for the development of gastric cancer. Pernicious anemia is due to the lack of intrinsic factor and failure to absorb vitamin B_{12} (Bevan and Houlston, 1999).

PREVENTION OF STOMACH CANCER

Present knowledge suggests that gastric carcinoma is caused by interactions between carcinogens and inflammatory factors derived from chronic *H. pylori* infection, nitrate/nitrite-rich diets, and gastric mucosa irritation and damage by salt or other factors such as tobacco and alcohol. Salt restriction (less than 6 grams per day), avoidance of processed meats, abstinence from tobacco, and limitation of alcohol intake are all important for prevention and control.

Notably, infection by the bacterium, *Helicobacter pylori*, causes chronic stomach inflammation that can initiate and promote cancerous lesions. Elimination of the bacterium through antibiotic therapy is therefore paramount for the prevention and control of gastric cancer. For example, a recent intervention study in high-risk rural populations in the province of Nariño in the Andes Mountains of Colombia demonstrated that administration of antibiotics for *H. pylori* produced regression of precancerous gastric lesions (Correa et al., 2000). In the same study, supplemental administration of vitamin C or beta-carotene also showed benefit, suggesting that both disease initiation and progression may be counteracted by sufficient year-round ingestion of fresh fruits and vegetables.

• • • REFERENCES

American Cancer Society. (2009). *Cancer statistics*. American Cancer Society, Atlanta, Georgia.

Augustin, L.S.A., Gallus, S., Negri, E., & La Vecchia, C. (2004). Glycemic index, glycemic load and risk of gastric cancer. *Annals of Oncology, 15*(4), 581–584.

Bevan, S., & Houlston, R.S. (1999). Genetic predisposition to gastric cancer. *Q J Med, 92,* 5–10.

Blaser, M.J. (1993). Malaria and the natural history of *Helicobacter pylori* infection [letter]. *Lancet, 342,* 551.

Blaser, M.J., & Atherton, J.C. (2004). *Helicobacter pylori* persistence: Biology and disease. *J Clin Invest, 113,* 321–333.

Brown, L.M. (2000). *Helicobacter pylori*: Epidemiology and routes of transmission. *Epidemiol Rev, 22*(2), 283–297.

Correa, P., Fontham, E.T.H., Bravo, J.C., Bravo, L.E., Ruiz, B., Zarama, G.,...Mera, R. (2000). Chemoprevention of gastric dysplasia: Randomized trial of antioxidant supplements and anti-*Helicobacter pylori* therapy. *Journal of the National Cancer Institute, 92*(23), 1881–1888.

Crew, K.D., & Neuget, A.I. (2006). Epidemiology of gastric cancer. *World J Gastroenterol, 12*(3), 354–362.

Howson, C.P., Hiyama, T., & Wynder, E.L. (1986). The decline in gastric cancer: Epidemiology of an unplanned triumph. *Epidemiol Rev, 8,* 1–27.

Inoue, M., & Tsugane, S. (2005). Epidemiology of gastric cancer in Japan. *Postgrad Med J, 81,* 419–424.

Joosens, J.V., Hill, M.J., Elliott, P., Stamler, R., Stamler, J., Lesaffre, E., Dyer, A., Nichols, R., Kesteloot, H., et al. (1996). Dietary salt, nitrate and stomach cancer mortality in 24 countries. *Int J Epidem, 25*(3), 494–504.

Kelley, J.R., & Duggan, J.M. (2003). Gastric cancer epidemiology and risk factors. *J Clin Epidemiol, 56,* 1–9.

Ladeiras-Lopes, R., Pereira, A.K., Nogueira, A., Pinheiro-Torres, T., Pinto, I., Santos-Pereira, R., & Lunet, N. (2008). Smoking and gastric cancer: Systematic review and meta-analysis of cohort studies. *Cancer Causes Control, 7,* 689–701.

Larrson, S.C., Bergkvist, L., Wolk, A. (2006). Glycemic load, glycemic index and carbohydrate intake in relation to risk of stomach cancer: A prospective study. *International Journal of Cancer, 118*(12), 3167–3169.

Lazarevic, K., Nagomi, A., & Jermic, M. (2009). Carbohydrate intake, glycemic index, glycemic load and risk of gastric cancer. *Cent Eur J Public Health, 17*(2), 75–78.

Lynch, H.T., Grady, W., Suriano, G., & Huntsman, D. (2005). Gastric cancer: New genetic developments. *J Surg Oncol, 90*(3),114–133.

Marshall, B.J., & Warren, J.R. (1984). Unidentified curved bacilli in the stomach of patients with gastritis and peptic ulceration. *Lancet, 1*(8390), 1311–1315.

NIH Consensus Statement. (2004). *Helicobacter pylori* in peptic ulcer disease. *NIH Consensus Statement Online, 12*(1),1–23.

Palli, D., Masala, G., Del Giudice, G., Plebani, M., et al. (2007). CagA+ *Helicobacter pylori* infection and gastric cancer risk in the EPIC-EURGAST study. *Int J Cancer, 120*(4), 859–867.

Pounder, R.E., & Ng, D. (1995). The prevalence of *Helicobacter pylori* infection in different countries. *Aliment Pharmacol Ther*, 9 Suppl 2, 33–39.

Shiotani, A., & Graham, D.Y. (2002). Pathogenesis and therapy of gastric and duodenal ulcer disease. *Med Clin North Am, 86*(6), 1447–1466.

Sjödahl, K., Lu, Y., Nilsen, T.I., Ye, W., Hveem, K., Vatten, L., & Lagergren, J. (2007). Smoking and alcohol drinking in relation to risk of gastric cancer: A population-based, prospective cohort study. *Int J Cancer, 120*(1),128–132.

Tajima, K., Kuroishi, T., & Oshima, A., (eds.). (2004). *Monograph on cancer research, No. 51. Cancer mortality and morbidity statistics. Japan and the world.* Tokyo: Japanese Cancer Association/Karger.

Uemura, N., Okamoto, S., Yamamoto, S., Matsumura, N., Yamaguchi, S., Yamakido, M., Taniyama, K.,...Schlemper, R.J. (2001). *Helicobacter pylori* infection and the development of gastric cancer. *N Engl J Med, 345*, 784–789.

WHO. (2009). *WHO Disease and injury country estimates. Death and DALY estimates for 2004 by cause for WHO Member States (Persons, all ages).* World Health Organization, Geneva, Switzerland.

Yang, L. (2006). Incidence and mortality of gastric cancer in China. *World J Gastroenterol, 12*(1), 17–20.

CHAPTER

16

Epidemiology of Colorectal Cancer

GLOBAL EPIDEMIOLOGY OF COLORECTAL CANCER

Colorectal (large bowel) cancer is diagnosed in nearly 1.2 million individuals and causes more than 600,000 deaths annually in the world population (American Cancer Society, 2007). This disease is the third leading cause of cancer deaths among men (319,000 deaths annually) and the fourth leading cause of cancer deaths among women (284,000 deaths annually). Colorectal cancer is more common in developed countries (341,000 deaths annually) compared to developing countries (250,000 deaths annually). In

developed countries, colorectal cancer mortality ranks second behind only lung cancer, whereas in developing nations, it ranks sixth. The male to female ratio of colorectal cancer deaths for developed nations (1.06) is slightly lower than for developing nations (1.22). Survival rates over 5 years after diagnosis show wide international variability ranging from 30% in India to 65% in the United States (Parkin et al., 2005).

Figure 16.1 depicts the extreme international variability in colorectal cancer mortality rates. Colorectal cancer is the second most frequently diagnosed malignancy in affluent societies but remains

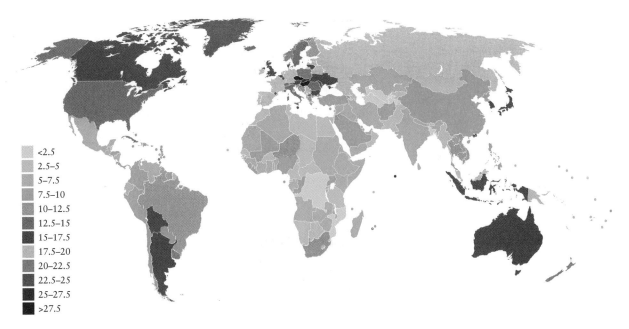

	<2.5
	2.5–5
	5–7.5
	7.5–10
	10–12.5
	12.5–15
	15–17.5
	17.5–20
	20–22.5
	22.5–25
	25–27.5
	>27.5

Figure 16.1 Global Colorectal Cancer Mortality, 2004.

Source: Data from World Health Organization. The global burden of disease: 2004 update. Geneva, WHO, 2008. Available at www.who.int/evidence/bod.

relatively uncommon in many developing countries. Regions with high incidence and mortality rates include North America, Northern and Western Europe including Greenland, Northern Asia (Russia), Australia, and New Zealand, and the southernmost nations of South America and Africa. Low rates are observed in the nations of Central Africa, Central America, and Southern Asia. Nevertheless, colorectal cancer incidence rates are increasing in economically transitioning countries (Center and Jemal, 2009).

PATHOGENESIS OF COLORECTAL CANCER

As with most other solid cancerous tumors, colorectal cancer evolves over a period of years and even decades. Approximately 65–70% of large bowel cancers develop in the descending sigmoid colon and rectum and the remainder develop in the transverse and ascending portions of the colon (**Figure 16.2**). More than 95% of colorectal cancers are adenocarcinomas and many of them secrete mucin. Carcinomas of the sigmoid colon and rectum often grow in an annular fashion producing so-called *napkin-ring*

constriction and obstruction of the bowel. Carcinomas of the ascending colon tend to extend along the bowel wall and are much less likely to cause obstruction. Colorectal cancer often develops as a sequential series of steps beginning with focal dysplasia and hyperplasia of the epithelial lining and progressing to the formation of adenomatous and villous polyps, carcinoma *in situ*, and ultimately invasive cancer (Kumar et al., 2009). It is notable that colon carcinogenesis invariability progresses in the presence of inflammation (Harris, 2007).

RISK FACTORS FOR COLORECTAL CANCER

Comprehensive scientific evidence suggests that colorectal cancer is largely influenced by a number of lifestyle factors. The risk of colorectal cancer development is increased by diets high in fat and low in fiber, sedentary lifestyle, obesity, alcohol and tobacco addiction, and deficiencies in vitamin D, calcium, and possibly selenium. Genetic syndromes involving mutant mismatch repair genes and tumor suppressor genes account for only a small percentage of cases. The

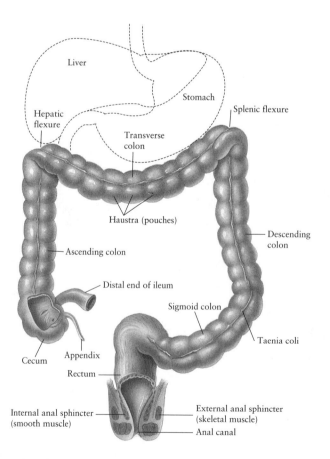

Figure 16.2 Distribution of Large Bowel Cancer.

following sections discuss each of these risk factors individually.

Dietary Fat and Colorectal Cancer

The wide geographical variation in the rates of colorectal cancer is most likely a consequence of differences in diet. Ernst Wynder and colleagues initially postulated that colon cancer development is linked to high intake of dietary fat that upsets the balance of gut flora (Wynder et al., 1969). This hypothesis was based upon the historic low rates of colorectal cancer in Japan compared to high rates in the United States corresponding to their low and high fat diets, respectively. Many subsequent epidemiologic investigations have consistently found that the risk of colorectal cancer increases with high intake of saturated fat and animal fat, and reciprocally that the risk is reduced with increased intake of fish and fish oil (Lipkin et al., 1999; Boyle and Langman, 2000). For example, Willett and colleagues found that American women who ate beef, pork, or lamb daily had a 2.5-fold higher risk compared to women reporting little consumption (Willett et al., 1999). In an investigation conducted in 24 European nations, increasing the intake of omega-3 fatty acids from fish and fish oil conferred significant protection against colon cancer development, even in populations consuming diets high in total fats (Caygill and Hill, 1995). Animal studies are in general agreement with the epidemiologic evidence in finding that a high amount of omega-6 fatty acids from beef, corn oil, or lard in the diet enhances chemically-induced tumor development in laboratory animals, and reciprocally that increasing the intake of omega-3 fatty acids from fish, fish oil, and olive oil decreases carcinogenesis (Reddy and Maeura, 1984).

Marked increases in the rates of colorectal cancer in some developing countries have also been linked to higher levels of fat intake. A striking example is the Japanese population wherein rates have risen from the lowest to the highest in the world in the past 50 years in close parallel with the increase in per capita fat calories (**Figure 16.3**). Furthermore, in studies of migrants from low-risk to high-risk regions, the rates of colon cancer show dramatic increases after a single generation, suggesting that the risk for tumor development in the large bowel increases rapidly with transition to a high fat diet (Wynder et al., 1991; Yu et al., 1991).

Mechanistically, it is theorized that diets high in fat promote secretion of bile acids from the liver and biliary tree. These bile acids are dehydrogenated by anaerobic bacteria of the colon (clostridia and bacteroides) to form the carcinogenic metabolites, deoxycholic acid, and lithocholic acid. In addition, diets high in fat typically contain sterols which have mitogenic activity. A key high-risk enzyme is β-glucuronidase, which is responsible for hydrolysis of sterol-conjugates so that they may be recirculated (Lipkin et al., 1999).

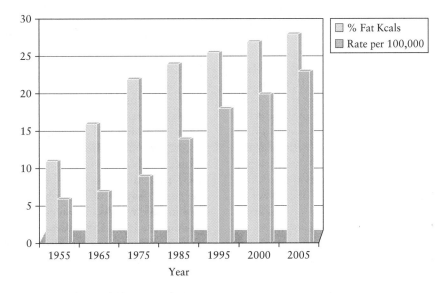

Figure 16.3 Colon Cancer Mortality and Dietary Fat in Japan, 1955–2005.

Source: Data from Cancer Statistics in Japan, 2010. Center for Cancer Control and Information Services, National Cancer Center, Japan. Wynder EL, Fujita Y, Harris RE, Hirayama T, Hiyama T (1991). Comparative epidemiology of cancer between the United States and Japan. A second look. *Cancer* 67(3):746–763. Matsumura Y (2001). Emerging trends of nutrition: transition and trade-offs. Nutrition trends in Japan. *Asia Pacific J Clin Nutr* 10(Suppl.):S40–S47. Mortality rates are age-adjusted to the Japanese population of 2000.

Dietary Fiber and Colorectal Cancer

Denis Burkitt is primarily responsible for formulating the high fat/low fiber hypothesis of colon cancer (Burkitt, 1971). This hypothesis is based upon the low incidence of colon cancer and other intestinal diseases in the African countries where Burkitt conducted his surgical practice. In populations consuming a high fiber, low fat diet, Burkitt observed virtually none of the large bowel diseases that are commonplace in westernized societies such as hemorrhoids, diverticulosis, diverticulitis, ulcerative colitis, Cohn's disease, and colorectal cancer. His recommendations for prevention of colon cancer specify high levels of intake throughout life (40 grams of fiber daily with a high proportion of bran) (Burkitt, 1973; Burkitt et al., 1974).

While many early epidemiologic investigations consistently supported the *Burkitt hypothesis* that high fiber intake reduces the risk of colorectal cancer (Greenwald, Lanza, and Eddy, 1987; Trock, Lanza, and Greenwald, 1990; Levin and Dozois, 1991), some recent epidemiologic investigations have failed to show protective effects of dietary fiber (Fuchs et al., 1999; Nakaji et al., 2001). A pooled analysis of 13 prospective cohort studies determined that the age-adjusted relative risk of colorectal cancer was significantly reduced by high intake of fiber (RR = 0.84), but that adjustment for a large profile of other factors dissipated the effect (Park et al., 2005). On the other hand, Howe and colleagues conducted a meta-analysis of 13 case control studies and found that the highest level of fiber intake reduced the risk of colorectal cancer by 50% (Howe et al., 1992). Furthermore, results from the large *European Prospective Investigation into Cancer and Nutrition* (EPIC) show that colon cancer risk declines by about 9% per quintile increase in fiber intake (multivariate adjusted RR = 0.58 for the highest versus lowest quintile) (Bingham et al., 2003; Bingham et al., 2005). It is important to note that in most of these studies, particularly those that did not show protection, the type of fiber was not considered and the highest level of fiber consumption was far below the 40 gram daily threshold recommended by Denis Burkitt.

Several preclinical trials have also examined the impact of dietary fiber in animal models of colorectal carcinogenesis. The results suggest that colorectal protection depends on the type and level of fiber and that wheat bran inhibits tumor development more consistently than other sources of fiber (Reddy, 1995). The totality of evidence from studies of colon cancer in animals and humans remains compatible with Burkitt's original hypothesis that diets high in fiber, particularly wheat bran fiber, provide significant protection against the development of colorectal cancer.

Protective mechanisms of fiber within the large bowel can be broadly divided into that for soluble and insoluble fiber. Increasing the level of insoluble fiber increases fecal bulk, thereby reducing transit time and diluting the concentration of toxic and carcinogenic compounds. Soluble fiber binds to bile acids and bile salts that may irritate the colorectal mucosa; furthermore, soluble fiber is fermented to single-chain fatty acids such as butyrate that maintain homeostasis of cell proliferation and apoptosis (Wong et al., 2006; Anderson et al., 2009).

Alcohol, Tobacco, and Colorectal Cancer

Chronic alcohol abuse is etiologically linked to colorectal carcinogenesis (Cho et al., 2004; Su and Arab, 2004; Mizoue et al., 2008). Analysis of data from the National Health and Nutrition Examination Survey (NHANES) in the United States showed a 70% increase in colorectal cancer among individuals who consumed one or more drinks of alcoholic beverages daily (Su and Arab, 2004). In a pooled analysis of 8 prospective cohort studies performed in 5 countries, Cho and colleagues (Cho et al., 2004) found that the risk increased by 40% at the highest level of alcohol consumption (>45 grams of alcohol daily). Mizoue and colleagues analyzed data from 5 Japanese studies and estimated that one-quarter of all colorectal cancers in Japan are attributable to alcohol consumption above 23 grams daily (Mizoue et al., 2008).

Chronic tobacco addiction has also been linked to colorectal cancer development. The epidemiologic evidence shows that chronic smokers have a two- to threefold increased incidence of premalignant adenomas of the colon compared to nonsmokers (Giovannucci, 2001a). In a meta-analysis of 106 studies, Botteri and colleagues concluded that smoking significantly increases both the incidence and mortality of colorectal cancer (Botteri et al., 2008). The existing evidence therefore supports the addition of colorectal cancer to the list of tobacco-associated malignancies.

Various mechanisms may be responsible for the effects of alcohol and tobacco on colorectal carcinogenesis. One mechanism involves the combination of chronic alcohol consumption and folate deficiency. As ethanol enters the large bowel, it is metabolized into acetaldehyde by anaerobic microbes; acetaldehyde in turn rapidly degrades folate. Since folate is essential for normal DNA synthesis and repair, its rapid degradation by acetaldehyde could readily lead to DNA instability and carcinogenesis in the colorectal mucosa (Duthie, 1999; Homann, Tillonen, and Salaspuro, 2000).

Alcohol consumption may also delay peristalsis in the large bowel and increase transit time and exposure to carcinogens and other toxic substances. Carcinogens from tobacco can reach the colorectal mucosa through the gastrointestinal tract or the circulatory system and may accentuate mutagenesis, inflammation, and carcinogenesis, particularly in the distal colon (Zisman et al., 2006). There is also speculation that tobacco and alcohol may synergistically heighten the risk of colorectal cancer.

Vitamin D, Calcium, and Colorectal Cancer

As initially noted by Garland and Garland (1980), there is a gradient of colorectal cancer rates with latitude, e.g., the rates become higher in populations that are more distant from the equator. On careful examination, the current pattern of global colorectal cancer mortality reflects a similar gradient (see Figure 16.1). This observation has given rise to the hypothesis that colon cancer development may be related to the lack of vitamin D due to decreased exposure to sunlight in populations more distant from the equator. Activated vitamin D is necessary for the absorption of dietary calcium, an important mineral for the maintenance of physiologic homeostasis in the human body, particularly the regulation and control of cell division and the cell cycle in proliferating cell populations such as the colorectal mucosa.

Higher levels of vitamin D and calcium intake have been found to reduce the risk of colorectal cancer in several epidemiologic studies (Gorham et al., 2005). For example, the relationship of vitamin D and cancer mortality was examined in the Third National Health and Nutrition Examination Survey (NHANES III). Baseline levels of serum 25-hydroxylated vitamin D were measured in 16,818 participants aged 17 years and older with follow-up from 1988–2000. While there was no overall effect on cancer mortality, individuals with serum vitamin D levels of 80 nmol/L or higher at baseline experienced a 72% reduction in colorectal cancer mortality compared to individuals with levels lower than 50 nmol/L, P trend = .02 (Freedman et al., 2007).

Despite the beneficial impact of vitamin D and calcium observed in epidemiologic studies, a randomized clinical trial involving postmenopausal women of the Women's Health Initiative (WHI) failed to show any benefit. In this study, daily supplementation of calcium and vitamin D for 7 years had no effect on the incidence of colorectal cancer. The long latency associated with the development of colorectal cancer and the limited 7-year duration of the trial may have contributed to this null finding (Wactawski-Wende, Morley Kotchen, and Anderson, 2006).

Insulin, Insulin-like Growth Factors, and Colon Cancer

High levels of circulating insulin and insulin-like growth factors (IGF) have been found to increase the risk of developing colorectal cancer (Giovannucci, 2001b). Insulin is secreted by the beta cells in the *islets of Langerhans* of the pancreas and is the chief hormone that regulates blood glucose. The IGF are polypeptide hormones that share sequence homology with insulin. They are synthesized in the liver and other organs in response to growth hormone from the pituitary gland. While the main function of IGF is to regulate human growth and development, they also stimulate cell proliferation and angiogenesis and inhibit apoptosis in the colorectal mucosa.

Individuals who manifest clinical conditions associated with high levels of insulin and IGF-1 such as *type 2 diabetes mellitus*, the *metabolic syndrome*, and *acromegaly* are at increased risk for the development of colorectal cancer. Furthermore, phenotypic and lifestyle factors associated with hyperinsulinemia (physical inactivity, high body mass index, central adiposity) and high IGF-1 levels (tall stature) and dietary patterns that stimulate insulin resistance or secretion, including high consumption of sucrose, various sources of starch, a high glycemic index, and high intake of certain types of fat, also increase the risk (Giovannucci et al., 1996; Giovannucci, 2001b; Terry, Miller, and Rohan, 2002; Giovannucci, 2007). It is clear that components of the IGF axis (IGF-1, IGF-2, IGF cell membrane receptors, and binding molecules) constitute an important molecular interface with exposures that initiate and promote colorectal carcinogenesis.

Ulcerative Colitis, Crohn's Disease, and Colorectal Cancer

Chronic inflammatory conditions of the intestinal tract also predispose to the development of colorectal cancer. Ulcerative colitis is characterized by chronic inflammation and ulceration of the epithelial lining of the colon plus other extra-colonic lesions. The primary site of attack is usually in the descending (left) colon. About 1% of colorectal cancer patients have a history of chronic ulcerative colitis. The risk of developing colorectal cancer varies inversely with the age of onset of the colitis and directly with the extent of colonic involvement and the duration of active disease. It is estimated that 40–50% of individuals with long-standing ulcerative colitis eventually develop colon cancer (Kumar et al., 2009).

Crohn's disease, a granulomatous inflammatory condition of the intestinal tract, also increases the risk of colorectal cancer development but to a lesser extent than ulcerative colitis. Many investigators have noted many similarities in ulcerative colitis and Crohn's disease. Both diseases appear to have an autoimmune basis and are characterized by similar alterations in the IGF axis (Street et al., 2004). Quite possibly these conditions represent different immune and tissue responses to one or more highly inflammatory etiologic factors.

Genetics of Colorectal Cancer

The investigation of a large multigenerational kindred by Aldred Scott Warthin in the early 1900s identified a hereditary form of colorectal cancer. Warthin documented 33 relatives with colorectal cancer or endometrial cancer among 70 members of the pedigree. Hereditary nonpolyposis colorectal cancer (HNPCC) was later named the *Lynch syndrome* after Henry T. Lynch who documented two large kindreds with this autosomal dominant syndrome (Lynch et al., 1966). Lynch and colleagues initially designated HNPCC as the cancer family syndrome (Lynch et al., 1977; Lynch, Lynch, and Harris, 1977).

The cause of HNPCC is an inherited (germline) mutation in at least one of a set of genes that normally repair DNA, the mismatch repair genes. In 1993 the first of the HNPCC genes (*MSH2*) was discovered on chromosome 2 by a team of international investigators (Aaltonen et al., 1993). Soon after, *MLH1* was discovered on chromosome 3 (Aaltonen et al., 1994). It was determined that mutations in these 2 genes accounted for 90% of the known HNPCC families. Carriers of either mutant gene have a lifetime colon cancer risk approaching 100%. The Lynch syndrome accounts for a small percentage of all colorectal cancer cases, perhaps 1–3%.

In 1951, Eldron J. Gardner published a report of a large Utah family containing many relatives with diffuse polyps of the colon and intestinal tract and multiple relatives with colorectal cancer (Gardner, 1951). Gardner's syndrome is a rare form of familial adenomatous polyposis (FAP) characterized by the presence of multiple polyps in the colon together with tumors outside the colon. In Gardner's syndrome, the extracolonic tumors may include osteomas of the skull, thyroid cancer, epidermoid cysts, fibromas, sebaceous cysts, and desmoid tumors.

Familial adenomatous polyposis and Gardner's syndrome are caused by an autosomal dominant germline mutation in the adenomatous polyposis coli (APC) gene located on chromosome 5q21 (band q21 on chromosome 5) (Leppert et al., 1987). The APC gene is a *tumor suppressor gene* that regulates cell adhesion, cell migration, and apoptosis in the colorectal epithelium. Mutations of the APC gene inactivate its protein function leading to initiation and promotion of colorectal carcinogenesis. Inactivation of both copies of the APC is required to initiate polyp development (Fearon and Vogelstein, 2003).

The countless polyps in the colon of FAP patients predispose to the development of colon cancer with 100% probability unless the colon is removed. The onset of polyps occurs during the teenage years and the average age at diagnosis of colon cancer is 35–40 years. Polyps can also grow in the stomach, duodenum, spleen, kidneys, liver, mesentery, and small bowel. In a small number of cases, polyps have also appeared in the cerebellum. Extracolonic cancers related to FAP commonly appear in the thyroid, liver, and kidneys.

Cooking Methods and Colorectal Cancer

Certain cooking methods can lead to carcinogenic compounds that reach the large bowel. For example, heterocyclic amines are formed on the surface of high-protein foods such as meat or fish on exposure to high-temperature cooking processes such as frying or boiling, and particularly to charcoal broiling. Furthermore, mutagens other than heterocyclic amines in meats cooked at high temperature (e.g., pyridines and quinoxalines) may also play a role in increasing the risk of distal adenomas and colorectal tumors (Wu et al., 2006).

Nonsteroidal Anti-Inflammatory Drugs (NSAIDs): Chemoprevention of Colorectal Cancer

The results of many epidemiologic studies provide strong evidence that regular intake of nonsteroidal anti-inflammatory drugs (NSAIDs) such as aspirin and ibuprofen reduces the risk of colorectal cancer development. In a meta-analysis of the published estimates, significant risk reductions were observed in 28 of 32 studies and regular use of NSAIDs produced a 43% reduction in the risk (**Figure 16.4**; Harris, 2009). In randomized clinical trials, regular aspirin use has also been found to decrease the risk of colonic adenomas, the precursors of most colon cancers (Baron et al., 2003).

Molecular studies show that inflammatory biomarkers are often expressed throughout the progression of colorectal carcinogenesis. Most impressive is the overexpression of the inducible cyclooxygenase-2 (COX-2) enzyme, which is responsible for prostaglandin biosynthesis in the inflammatory cascade (Harris, 2007).

In a recent case control study of colon cancer, Harris and colleagues compared effects of over-the-counter NSAIDs with prescription drugs that selectively inhibit COX-2. Their results suggest that both over-the-counter NSAIDs and selective COX-2 inhibitors produce significant reductions in the risk of colon cancer, underscoring their strong potential for colon cancer chemoprevention (Harris, Beebe-Donk, and Alshafie, 2008).

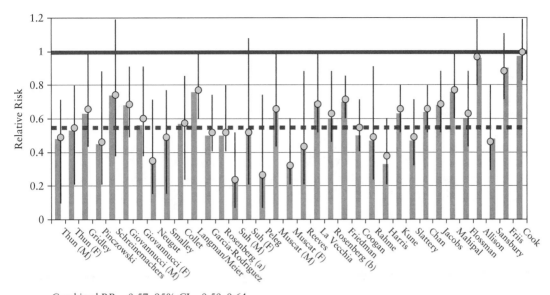

Combined RR = 0.57, 95% CI = 0.50–0.64

Figure 16.4 Colon Cancer and NSAIDs.

Source: Reproduced from Harris RE (2009). Cyclooxygenase-2 (COX-2) blockade in the chemoprevention of cancers of the colon, breast, prostate, and lung. *Inflammo-pharmacology* 17:1–13.

Exogenous Estrogens and Colorectal Cancer

Although postmenopausal hormone replacement therapy (HRT) has been found to increase the risk of developing cardiovascular disease, breast cancer, and endometrial cancer, there is consistent evidence from epidemiologic studies that HRT *reduces* the risk of colorectal cancer (MacLennan, MacLennan, and Ryan, 1991). A meta-analysis of 18 studies determined that current HRT use resulted in a 34% decrease in the risk (Nelson et al., 2002). This finding is supported by the results of a randomized clinical trial in the Women's Health Initiative (WHI) in which the incidence of colorectal cancer was 44% less in women receiving HRT (estrogen plus progesterone) compared to those receiving a placebo (Chlebowski et al., 2004).

SCREENING FOR COLORECTAL CANCER

In recent decades, rates of colorectal cancer have gradually increased in populations of developing nations in association with their transition to diets with higher fat and lower fiber content and lifestyle changes that heighten predisposition. In contrast, colorectal mortality rates have gradually declined in highly developed nations such as the United States (American Cancer Society, 2007).

The declining trends in colorectal cancer death rates differ for US men and women (**Figure 16.5**).

In women, rates began to decline in mid-century and have decreased by more than 50%. In men, rates began to decline during 1970–1980 and have decreased by about 40%. Several factors may have contributed to these declines, including greater awareness, increased screening, more efficacious treatment, improvement in diet, reduction in risk factors, and possibly greater use of chemopreventive agents such as NSAIDs. It is notable that these declines have occurred in the face of concurrent epidemics of obesity and related conditions such as diabetes type 2.

A recent study suggests that the declining pattern of colorectal mortality in the United States is most compatible with a relatively large contribution from screening and a smaller but demonstrable impact of risk factor reductions and improved treatments (Edwards et al., 2009). Colonoscopy has gained greater acceptance in the general population and is the most reliable method of screening for the early detection of adenomatous polyps and cancer of the large bowel. In addition, visual determination of the exact location and size of existing tumors is an invaluable tool in planning and implementing definitive surgical resection. Colonoscopic imaging coupled with effective surgery has produced 5-year survival rates greater than 90% for patients whose tumors have not progressed beyond the bowel wall (National Cancer Institute, 2007).

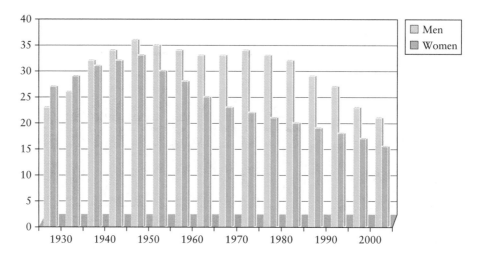

Figure 16.5 Colorectal Cancer Mortality, USA: 1930–2005.

Source: Data from American Cancer Society (2006). Cancer Facts and Figures, 2006.

● ● ● REFERENCES

Aaltonen, L.A., Peltomiki, P., Leach, F.S., Sistonen, P., Pylkkanen, L., Mecklin, J.P., Jirvinen, H., et al. (1993). Clues to the pathogenesis of familial colorectal cancer. *Science, 260*, 812–816.

Aaltonen, L.A., Peltomiki, P., Mecklin, J.P., Jirvinen, H., Jass, J.R., Green, J.S., Lynch, H.T., et al. (1994). Replication errors in benign and malignant tumors from hereditary nonpolyposis colorectal cancer patients. *Cancer Res, 54*, 1645–1648.

American Cancer Society. (2007). *Global cancer facts and figures, 2007.* American Cancer Society.

Anderson, J.W., Baird, P., Davis, R.H., et al. (2009). Health benefits of dietary fiber. *Nutr Rev, 67*(4), 188–205.

Baron, J.A., Cole, B.F., Sandler, R.S., et al. (2003). A randomized trial of aspirin to prevent colorectal adenomas. *N Engl J Med, 348*, 891–899.

Bingham, S.A., Day, N.E., Luben, R. et al. (2010). Dietary fibre in food and protection against colorectal cancer in the European Prospective Investigation into Cancer and Nutrition (EPIC): an observational study. Lancet, 361, 1496–1501.

Bingham, S.A., Norat, T., Moskal, A., et al. (2005). Is the association with fiber from foods in colorectal cancer confounded by folate intake? Cancer Epidemiol Biomarkers Prev, 14, 1552–1556.

Botteri, E., Iodice, S., Bagnardi, V., Raimondi, S., Lowenfel, A.B., & Maisonneuve, P. (2008). Smoking and colorectal cancer: A meta-analysis. *JAMA, 300*(23), 2765–2778.

Boyle, P., & Langman, J.S. (2000). ABC of colorectal cancer. *BMJ, 321*(7264), 805–808.

Burkitt, D.P. (1971). Epidemiology of cancer of the colon and rectum. *Cancer, 28*, 3–13.

Burkitt, D.P. (1973). Epidemiology of large bowel disease: The role of fibre. *Proceedings of the Nutrition Society, 32*, 145–149.

Burkitt, D.P., Walker, A.R.P., & Painter, N.S. (1974). Dietary fiber and disease. *J Am Med Assoc, 229*, 1068–1072.

Caygill, C.P., & Hill, M.J. (1995). Fish, n-3 fatty acids and human colorectal and breast cancer mortality. *Eur J Cancer Prev, 4*, 329–332.

Center, M.M., & Jemal, A.E. (2009). International trends in colorectal cancer incidence rates. *Cancer Epidemiol Biomarkers Prev, 18*(6), 1688–1694.

Chlebowski, R.T., Wactawski-Wende, J.W., Ritenbaugh, C., Hubbell, F.A., Ascensao, J., Rebecca, J.,…White, E. (2004). Estrogen plus progestin and colorectal cancer in postmenopausal women. *New England Journal of Medicine, 350*(10), 991–1004.

Cho, E., Smith-Warner, S.A., Ritz, J., et al. (2004). Alcohol intake and colorectal cancer: A pooled analysis of 8 cohort studies. *Ann Intern Med, 140*(8), 603–613.

Duthie, S. (1999). Folic acid deficiency and cancer: Mechanisms of DNA instability. *British Medical Bulletin, 55,* 578–592.

Edwards, B.K., Ward, E., Kohler, B.A., Eheman, C., Zauber, A.G., Anderson, R.N.,…Ries, L.A.G. (2009). Annual report to the nation on the status of cancer, 1975–2006, featuring colorectal cancer trends and impact of interventions (risk factors, screening, and treatment) to reduce future rates. *Cancer, 116*(3), 544–573.

Fearon, E.R., & Vogelstein, B. (2003). Tumor suppressor gene defects in human cancer. In *Cancer medicine* (6th ed.). Decker, Inc.

Freedman, D.M., Looker, A.C., Chang, S.C., & Graubard, B.L. (2007). Prospective study of serum vitamin D and cancer mortality in the United States. *Journal of the National Cancer Institute, 99*(21), 1594–1602.

Fuchs, C.S., Giovannucci, E.L., Colditz, G.A., Hunter, D.J., Stampfer, M.J., Rosner, B., Speizer, F.E., & Willett, W.C. (1999). Dietary fiber and the risk of colorectal cancer and adenoma in women. *N Engl J Med, 340*(3), 169–176.

Gardner, E.J. (1951). A genetic and clinical study of intestinal polyposis, a predisposing factor for carcinoma of the colon and rectum. *Am J Hum Genet, 3,* 167–176.

Garland, C.F., & Garland, F.C. (1980). Do sunlight and vitamin D reduce the likelihood of colon cancer? *Int J Epidemiol, 9,* 227–231.

Giovannucci, E. (2001a). An updated review of the epidemiological evidence that cigarette smoking increases risk of colorectal cancer. *Cancer Epidemiol Biomarkers Prev, 10,* 725–731.

Giovannucci, E. (2001b). Insulin, insulin-like growth factors and colon cancer: A review of the evidence. *J Nutr, 131,* 3109–3120.

Giovannucci, E. (2007). Metabolic syndrome, hyperinsulinemia, and colon cancer: A review. *Amer J Clin Nutrition, 86*(3), 836–842.

Giovannucci, E., Colditz, G.A., Stampfer, M.J., & Willett, W.C. (1996). Physical activity, obesity and risk of colorectal cancer in women (United States). *Cancer Causes Control, 7,* 253–263.

Gorham, E.D., Garland, C.F., Garland, F.C., et al. (2005). Vitamin D and prevention of colorectal cancer. *J Steroid Biochem Mol Biol, 97,* 179–194.

Greenwald, P., Lanza, E., & Eddy, G.A. (1987). Dietary fibre in the reduction of colon cancer risk. *Journal of the American Dietetic Association, 87,* 1178–1188.

Harris, R.E. (2007). COX-2 and the inflammogenesis of cancer. *Subcellular Biochemistry, 42,* 193–212.

Harris, R.E. (2009). Cyclooxygenase-2 (COX-2) blockade in the chemoprevention of cancers of the colon, breast, prostate, and lung. *Inflammopharmacology, 17,* 1–13.

Harris, R.E., Beebe-Donk, J., & Alshafie, G.A. (2008). Similar reductions in the risk of human colon cancer by selective and non-selective cyclooxygenase-2 (COX-2) inhibitors. *BMC Cancer, 8*(237).

Homann, N., Tillonen, J., & Salaspuro, M. (2000). Microbially produced acetaldehyde from ethanol may increase the risk of colon cancer via folate deficiency. *Int J Cancer, 86,* 169–173.

Howe, G.R., Benito, E., Castellato, R., Cornee, J., Esteve, J., et al. (1992). Dietary intake of fiber and decreased risk of cancers of the colon and rectum: Evidence from the combined analysis of 13 case-control studies. *J Natl Cancer Inst, 84,* 1887–1896.

Kumar, V., Abbas, A.K., Fausto, N., & Astor, J. (2009). *Robbins and Cotran pathologic basis of disease* (8th ed.). Philadelphia: W.B. Saunders.

Leppert, M., Dobbs, M., Scambler, P., O'Connell, P., Nakamura, Y., Stauffer, D., Woodward, S., Burt, R., Hughes, T., Gardner, E., et al. (1987). The gene for familial polyposis coli maps to the long arm of chromosome 5. *Science, 238*(4832), 1411–1413.

Levin, K.E., & Dozois, R.R. (1991). Epidemiology of large bowel cancer. *World J Surg, 15*(5), 562–567.

Lipkin, M., Reddy, B., Newmark, H., & Lamprecht, S.A. (1999). Dietary factors in human colorectal cancer. *Annu Rev Nutr, 19*, 545–586.

Lynch, H.T., Shaw, M.W., Magnuson, C.W., Larsen, A.L., & Krush, A.J. (1966). Hereditary factors in cancer: A study of two large midwestern kindreds. *Arch Intern Med, 117*(2), 206–212.

Lynch, H.T., Guirgis, H.A., Lynch, P.M., & Harris, R.E. (1977). Familial cancer syndromes: A survey. *Cancer, 39*(4 Suppl), 1867–1881.

Lynch, H.T., Lynch, P.M., & Harris, R.E. (1977). Proximal colon cancer in familial carcinoma of the colon exclusive of familial polyposis coli. *Lancet, 1*(8025), 1306–1307.

MacLennan, S.C., MacLennan, A.H., & Ryan, P. (1991). Colorectal cancer and oestrogen replacement therapy: A meta-analysis of epidemiological studies. *Med J Aust, 162*, 491–493.

Matsumura, Y. (2001). Emerging trends of nutrition: Transition and trade-offs. Nutrition trends in Japan. *Asia Pacific J Clin Nutr, 10*(Suppl.), S40–S47.

Mizoue, T., Inoue, M., Wakai, K., et al. (2008). Alcohol drinking and colorectal cancer in Japanese: A pooled analysis of results from five cohort studies. *American Journal of Epidemiology, 167*(12), 1397–1406.

Nakaji, S., Shimoyama, T., Umeda, T., Sakamoto, J., Katsura, S., Sugawara, K., & Baxter, D. (2001). Dietary fiber showed no preventive effect against colon and rectal cancers in Japanese with low fat intake: An analysis from the results of nutrition surveys from 23 Japanese prefectures. *BMC Cancer, 1*, 1–14.

National Cancer Center, Japan. (2010). *Cancer statistics in Japan, 2010.* Japan: Center for Cancer Control and Information Services, National Cancer Center, Japan.

National Cancer Institute. (2007). *Colon cancer PDQ: Treatment options for colon cancer.* National Cancer Institute.

Nelson, H.D., Humphrey, L.L., Nygren, P., Teutsch, S.M., & Allen, J.D. (2002). Postmenopausal hormone replacement therapy: Scientific review. *JAMA, 288*(7), 872–881.

Park, Y., Hunter, D.J., Spiegelman, D., Bergkvist, L., Berrino, F., et al. (2005). Dietary fiber intake and risk of colorectal cancer: A pooled analysis of prospective cohort studies. *JAMA, 294*, 2849–2857.

Parkin, M.D., Bray, F., Ferlay, J., & Pisani, P. (2005). Global cancer statistics, 2002. *CA Cancer J Clin, 55*, 74–108.

Reddy, B.S. (1995). Nutritional factors and colon cancer. *Crit Rev Food Sci Nutr, 35*, 175–190.

Reddy, B.S., & Maeura, Y. (1984). Tumor promotion by dietary fat in azoxymethane induced colon carcinogenesis in female F344 rats: Influence of amount and source of dietary fat. *J Natl Cancer Inst, 72*, 746–750.

Street, M.E., de'Angelis, G., Camacho-Hübner, C., Giovannelli, G., Ziveri, M.A., Bacchini, P.L.,… Savage, M.O. (2004). Relationships between serum IGF-1, IGFBP-2, interleukin-1beta and interleukin-6 in inflammatory bowel disease. *Horm Res, 61*(4), 159–164.

Su, L.J., & Arab, L. (2004). Alcohol consumption and risk of colon cancer: Evidence from the national health and nutrition examination survey I epidemiologic follow-up study. *Nutr Cancer, 50*(2), 111–119.

Terry, P.D., Miller, A.B., & Rohan, T.E. (2002). Obesity and colorectal cancer risk in women. *Gut, 51*, 191–194.

Trock, B., Lanza, E., & Greenwald, P. (1990). Dietary fiber, vegetables, and colon cancer: Critical review and meta-analysis of epidemiological studies. *JNCI, 82*, 650–661.

Wactawski-Wende, J., Morley Kotchen, J., & Anderson, G.L. (2006). Calcium plus vitamin D supplementation and the risk of colorectal cancer. *New England Journal of Medicine, 354*(7), 684–696.

Willett, W.C., Stampfer, M.J., Colditz, G.A., Rosner, B.A., & Speizer, F.E. (1990). Relation of meat, fat, and fiber intake to the risk of colon cancer in a prospective study among women. *N Engl J Med*, 323, 1664–1672.

Wong, J.M., de Souza, R., Kendall, C.W., Emam, A., & Jenkins, D.J. (2006). Colonic health: Fermentation and short chain fatty acids. *J Clin Gastroenterol*, 40(3), 235–243.

Wu, K., Giovannucci, E., Byrne, C., Platz, E.A., Fuchs, C., Willett, W.C., & Sinha, R. (2006). Meat mutagens and risk of distal colon adenoma in a cohort of U.S. men. *Cancer Epidemiol Biomarkers Prev*, 15(6), 1120–1125.

Wynder, E.L., Kajitani, T., Ishikawa, S., Dodo, H., Takano, A., et al. (1969). Environmental factors of cancer of the colon and rectum. II. Japanese epidemiological data. *Cancer*, 23, 1210–1220.

Wynder, E.L., Fujita, Y., Harris, R.E., Hirayama, T., & Hiyama, T. (1991). Comparative epidemiology of cancer between the United States and Japan: A second look. *Cancer*, 67(3), 746–763.

Yu, H., Harris, R.E., et al. (1991). Comparative epidemiology of cancers of the colon, rectum, prostate and breast in Shanghai, China versus the United States. *Intl J Epidemiol*, 20(1), 76–81.

Zisman, A.L., Nickolov, A., Brand, R.E., Gorchow, A., & Roy, H.K. (2006). Associations between the age at diagnosis and location of colorectal cancer and the use of alcohol and tobacco. *Archives of Internal Medicine*, 166, 629–634.

Epidemiology of Pancreatic Cancer

GLOBAL EPIDEMIOLOGY OF PANCREATIC CANCER

Pancreatic cancer is diagnosed in more than 250,000 individuals and causes nearly 260,000 deaths annually in the world population (American Cancer Society, 2007). This malignancy is the eighth leading cause of cancer deaths among men (137,000 deaths annually) and the ninth leading cause of cancer deaths among women (122,000 deaths annually). Pancreatic cancer is more common in developed countries (151,000 deaths annually) compared to developing countries (109,000 deaths annually). In developed countries, pancreatic cancer mortality ranks fifth among the leading causes of death from cancer, whereas in developing nations, it ranks tenth. The male to female ratio of pancreatic cancer deaths for developed nations (1.07) is lower than for developing nations (1.44). Regardless of gender, pancreatic cancer is usually fatal and survival rates one year after diagnosis are less than 20% even in developed nations such as the United States. Without treatment, survival after diagnosis is only 3 to 5 months (Parkin et al., 2004.

Figure 17.1 depicts the international variability in pancreatic cancer mortality rates. Regions with high incidence and mortality rates include affluent industrialized nations in North America, Northern

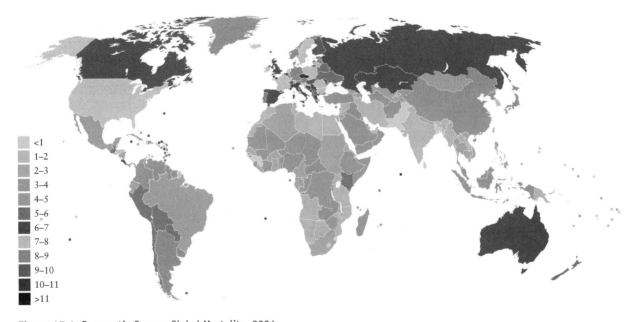

Legend:
<1
1–2
2–3
3–4
4–5
5–6
6–7
7–8
8–9
9–10
10–11
>11

Figure 17.1 Pancreatic Cancer: Global Mortality, 2004.

Source: Data from World Health Organization. The global burden of disease: 2004 update. Geneva, WHO, 2008. Available at www.who.int/evidence/bod.

and Western Europe including Greenland, Northern Asia (Russia), Australia, and New Zealand, and the southernmost nations of South America. Low rates are observed in Africa and Southern Asia. As initially pointed out by Dr. Ernst Wynder, the international mortality rates of pancreatic cancer are positively correlated with per capita consumption of dietary fat, presumably from meat and dairy products (Wynder, 1975). Nevertheless, as with other forms of cancer that currently occur more often in developed nations, pancreatic cancer incidence rates are increasing in economically transitioning countries whereas in developed countries such as the United States the rates appear to be stable or slightly declining (Parkin, 2004).

PATHOGENESIS OF PANCREATIC CANCER

The pancreas is a dual functioning gland located deep in the abdomen just behind the stomach. Numerous pancreatic ducts communicate with the main (central) pancreatic duct that merges with the common bile duct to form the *ampulla of Vater* that empties into the duodenum (the upper small intestine). The anatomy of the pancreas is shown in **Figure 17.2**.

The pancreas functions as both an endocrine and an exocrine gland. Specialized endocrine cells of the *islets of Langerhans* are instrumental in the secretion of insulin and glucagon to maintain tight control of blood glucose. In contrast, specialized exocrine cells (called acinar cells) secrete powerful digestive enzymes (e.g., trypsin, lipase, and amylase) as well as alkaline fluid into the pancreatic ducts that eventually drain into the main pancreatic duct and the duodenum (upper small intestine). The digestive enzymes include trypsin, lipase, and amylase that break down protein, fats, and carbohydrates, respectively. Pancreatic fluids mix with bile from the liver in the ampulla of Vater prior to reaching the duodenum (the upper small intestine). A layer of specialized columnar epithelium circumferentially lines the pancreatic ducts as well as the main pancreatic duct.

Most pancreatic cancers (approximately 99%) are adenocarcinomas that arise from the epithelial cells that line the ducts of the exocrine pancreas. The majority of this chapter is devoted to "carcinoma of the pancreas," which implies carcinoma arising from the epithelial lining of the exocrine portion of the pancreas. Only a small fraction (perhaps 1–2%) of pancreatic tumors arise from the acinar cells of the pancreas or cells within the islets of Langerhans. These relatively rare tumors are discussed in a later section of this chapter.

Pancreatic cancer rates increase exponentially during the latter decades of the life span. Most cases are diagnosed after the age of 50 years with peak rates occurring in the age range of 65–70 years. Furthermore, the majority of cases involve the head of the pancreas (60–70%) rather than the body or tail of the gland (30–40%) (Robbins and Cotran, 1979). Since developing pancreatic tumors are difficult to palpate and there are no valid biomarkers of impending disease, it is believed that the genesis of these malignancies spans many years. Recent cellular and molecular studies suggest that pancreatic cancer develops over time by a progression of steps in the epithelial lining of the pancreatic ducts, from dysplasia to *in situ* carcinoma and ultimately invasive cancer.

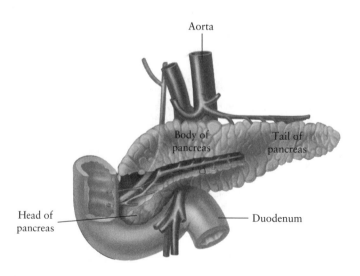

Figure 17.2 Anatomy of the Human Pancreas.

TOBACCO SMOKING AND PANCREATIC CANCER

Tobacco smoking is a recognized risk factor for the development of pancreatic cancer. Wynder and colleagues first observed a significant dose response in the risk of pancreatic cancer with increasing number of cigarettes per day in chronic smokers (Wynder, Mabuchi, and Maruchia, 1973). As shown in **Figure 17.3**, the risk increased nearly fivefold for smokers of two or more packs per day compared to never smokers. Subsequently, many epidemiologic investigations have confirmed the etiologic impact of smoking tobacco in the development of this deadly malignancy. In a comprehensive meta-analysis of 82 studies conducted in 4 continents, chronic cigarette smoking increased the risk of developing pancreatic cancer by 74% compared to never smoking (summary RR = 0.74, 95% confidence interval = 1.61–1.87) and the risk elevation persisted 10 years after smoking cessation (Iodice et al., 2008). Results were highly consistent for case control studies (RR = 1.77) and cohort studies (RR = 1.70). The risk was also elevated for pipe or cigar smokers (RR = 1.47, 95% CI = 1.17–1.83). Furthermore, the risk remained significantly elevated for a period of at least 10 years among individuals who had quit the smoking habit. The public health implications of these results are enormous, e.g., for populations with a smoking prevalence of 30%, the proportion of pancreatic cancer attributable to smoking is approximately 20%, and since recent global estimates suggest that 1 in 3 adults smoke (WHO, 2009), it is evident that at least one-fifth of all pancreatic cancers are preventable by avoidance of the smoking habit.

Carcinogens from inhaled tobacco smoke can reach the pancreas through the circulatory system or through the bile. In particular, nitrosamines are activated in the liver and detoxified by liver enzymes of the cytochrome P-450 system (e.g., *CYP1A2*) or *n*-acetyl transferase enzymes. Recall that bile is secreted by the liver through the common cystic duct into the ampulla of Vater in the head of the pancreas. Notably, carcinogenic nitrosamines and their metabolites have been found in human bile (Hecht, 1998). Conceivably, some individuals may be genetically deficient in essential detoxification enzymes and as a consequence be at high risk for the development of pancreatic cancer due to sustained exposure to inhaled or ingested carcinogens (Lowenfels and Maisonneuve, 2006). Indeed, in a recent case control investigation of genetic polymorphisms and pancreatic cancer, heavy smoking individuals genetically null for the glutathione-S-transferase enzyme, *GSTT1*, had markedly increased risk estimates compared to nonsmokers with normal *GSTT1* (Duell et al., 2002). Estimated odds ratios (OR) in the study were OR = 5.0, 95% confidence interval = 1.8–14.5 for women, and OR = 3.2, 95% CI = 1.3–8.1 for men.

ALCOHOL AND PANCREATIC CANCER

The role of alcohol in the development of pancreatic cancer appears to be related to the dose and duration of alcohol consumption. The risk is increased by two- to threefold in heavy drinkers, e.g., consuming four or more drinks per day (Olson et al., 1989; Ye et al., 2002) and the risk increase is higher per level of intake for certain ethnic groups, e.g., risk

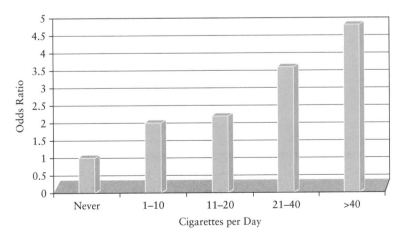

Figure 17.3 Risk of Pancreatic Cancer and Cigarette Smoking in Men.

Source: Data from Wynder EL, Mabuchi K, and Maruchia N (1973). Epidemiology of cancer of the pancreas. *J Natl Cancer Inst* 50:645–667.

estimates for African American women are higher than for Caucasians (Silverman et al., 1995). A recent pooled analysis of 14 prospective studies found that consumption of at least 30 grams of alcohol daily (about 2 drinks) produced only a modest elevation in the risk (summary RR = 1.22, 95% CI = 1.03–1.45) whereas consumption of lesser amounts had no effect (Genkinger et al., 2009). Furthermore, some investigators caution that observed risk increases may be due to confounding with smoking (Zatonski et al., 1993; Ye et al., 2002). Nevertheless, there is no doubt that chronic alcohol abuse is a major cause of chronic pancreatitis, which in turn predisposes to the development of pancreatic cancer. The association of chronic pancreatitis and pancreatic cancer is discussed in a later section of this chapter.

RISK OF PANCREATIC CANCER: COMBINED EFFECT OF TOBACCO AND ALCOHOL

Talamini and colleagues recently published results of a case control study that examined both independent and combined effects of tobacco smoking and alcohol consumption in the development of pancreatic cancer. They compared 326 cases with incident pancreatic cancer to 652 hospital controls matched on age and gender without neoplastic disease. All subjects were ascertained and interviewed in hospitals in northern Italy during the period 1991–2008. Results revealed independent effects of tobacco smoking (OR = 2.04 for 20 or more pack years) and heavy alcohol consumption (OR = 2.03 for 21–34 drinks per week and OR = 3.42 for 35 or more drinks per week). The risk increased more than fourfold for chronic smokers and heavy drinkers (OR = 4.3) compared to never smokers who consumed less than 7 drinks per week. The authors suggest that the effects of tobacco and alcohol are additive, and together they account for approximately one-third of pancreatic cancer in Italy (Talamini et al., 2010).

DIETARY FAT AND PANCREATIC CANCER

Fat and red meat consumption have been linked to the development of pancreatic cancer in a number of epidemiologic studies (Wynder, 1975; Durbec et al., 1983; Raymond et al., 1987; Mills et al., 1988; Bueno de Mesquita et al., 1990; Farrow and Davis, 1990; Ghadirian et al., 1991; Stolzenberg-Solomon et al., 2002; Chan, Wang, and Holly, 2007; Zhang, Zhao, and Berkel, 2005; Nöthlings et al., 2005; Larsson et al., 2006); however, results have not been

consistent among all studies (Michaud et al., 2003; Lin et al., 2006).

The US National Institutes of Health American Association of Retired Persons (AARP) Diet and Health Study was designed to provide definitive evidence on dietary factors and the development of a variety of chronic diseases including pancreatic cancer (Schatzkin et al., 2001). Using the NIH-AARP database, Thiébaut and colleagues recently examined the association between dietary fat and pancreatic cancer. Their investigation is based upon the NIH-AARP cohort of 308,736 men and 216,737 women aged 51–70 years who completed a 124-item food frequency questionnaire in 1995–1996. Important findings of this study are summarized below (Thiébaut et al., 2009).

Over an average follow-up of 6.3 years, 865 men and 472 women were diagnosed with exocrine pancreatic cancer (45.0 and 34.5 cases per 100,000 person-years, respectively). After multivariable adjustment and combination of data for men and women, pancreatic cancer risk was directly related to the intakes of total fat (highest versus lowest quintile, 46.8 vs. 33.2 cases per 100,000 person-years, hazard ratio (HR) = 1.23, 95% CI = 1.03–1.46, P trend = 0.03), saturated fat (51.5 vs. 33.1 cases per 100,000 person-years, HR = 1.36, 95% CI = 1.14–1.62, P trend <0.001), and monounsaturated fat (46.2 vs. 32.9 cases per 100,000 person-years, HR = 1.22, 95% CI = 1.02–1.46, P trend = 0.05) but not polyunsaturated fat. The associations were strongest for saturated fat from animal food sources (52.0 vs. 32.2 cases per 100,000 person-years, HR = 1.43, 95% CI = 1.20–1.70, P trend <0.001); specifically, intakes from red meat and dairy products were both statistically significantly associated with increased pancreatic cancer risk (HR = 1.27 and 1.19, respectively).

Of further note regarding findings of the NIH-AARP study of pancreatic cancer is that there were no consistent associations with polyunsaturated, saturated, or monounsaturated fats from plant food sources. Though there was no association with total intake of polyunsaturated fats (PUFA) in this large comprehensive study; it is important to note that the high intake of dietary arachidonic acid (20:4), an n-6 PUFA obtained primarily from animal foods, was significantly associated with the risk of developing pancreatic cancer (HR = 1.33, 95% CI = 1.12–1.59, P trend <0.002). The investigators concluded that high intake of dietary fat of animal origin, particularly from red meat and dairy food sources, increases the risk of developing pancreatic cancer (Thiébaut et al., 2009).

Various hypotheses have been advanced to explain the link between high dietary fat and the development of pancreatic cancer. It is well known that diets with high fat content stimulate bile secretion by the liver, which in turn increases the gastrointestinal exposure to cholesterol, bile acids, and their metabolites. There is considerable experimental evidence that bile acids promote the development of gastrointestinal tumors both *in vivo* (Reddy, Weisburger, and Wynder, 1978; Reddy, 1981; Hill, 1991) and *in vitro* (Kaibara, Yurugi, and Koga, 1984). Recent evidence also suggests that bile acids promote carcinogenesis by up-regulating cyclooxygenase-2 (COX-2) and prostaglandin production (Zhang et al., 1998; Shirvani et al., 2000; Glinghammar and Rafter, 2001). Furthermore, bile acids have been found to induce COX-2 in pancreatic cancer cell lines (Tucker et al., 2004). These findings plus the significant effects of dietary fat and, specifically, arachidonic acid (the primary substrate of COX-2 in the inflammatory cascade) observed in the NIH-AARP Dietary Study (Thiébaut et al., 2009), suggest that up-regulation of COX-2 and excess production of prostaglandins may have an important role in the development of pancreatic cancer. This general process (called inflammogenesis) induces and promotes essential features of carcinogenesis (mutagenesis, mitogenesis, angiogenesis, reduced apoptosis, metastasis, and immunosuppression) (Harris, 2007).

CHRONIC PANCREATITIS AND PANCREATIC CANCER

Chronic pancreatitis refers to persistent inflammation of the pancreas, irrespective of the cause. This condition is clearly a risk factor for the development of pancreatic cancer. In an international multicenter historical cohort study of 2,015 patients diagnosed with chronic pancreatitis, 56 new cases of pancreatic cancer developed over a mean follow-up period of 7.4 years, an incidence rate more than sixteen times the expected rate (standardized incidence ratio = 16.5, 95% CI = 11.1–23.7) (Lowenfels et al., 1993). The cumulative risk after twenty years of follow-up was 4.0% (95% CI = 2.0–5.9) and the risk increase was independent of gender, country of origin, and type of pancreatitis.

The main cause of chronic pancreatitis among adults is chronic alcohol abuse. More than 70% of adult patients diagnosed with chronic pancreatitis have a long-term history of frequently drinking excessive amounts of alcoholic beverages. The majority of such patients report daily consumption of at least 150 grams of alcohol for more than 5 years (Nair, Lawler, and Miller, 2007). The presence of gallstones (cholelithiasis) also predisposes affected individuals to the development of chronic pancreatitis. These 2 conditions, chronic alcohol abuse and cholelithiasis, account for about 90% of chronic pancreatitis in the United States. Autoimmune pancreatitis accounts for an additional 5–6% of cases (Finkelberg et al., 2006).

The pathophysiology of chronic pancreatitis has been characterized through detailed studies of alcoholic pancreatitis in both animals and humans (Witt et al., 2007). Alcohol is directly toxic to pancreatic tissue and chronic exposure causes significant cell damage, necrosis, and inflammation (a process known as *necroinflammation*). In addition, the alcohol-induced destruction and destabilization of the epithelial lining of the pancreatic ducts permits the release of powerful digestive enzymes thereby predisposing the gland to *autodigestion*. The progressive cascade of pathogenic events in chronic alcoholic pancreatitis involves chronic inflammation, cell necrosis, release of digestive enzymes, cell autodigestion, formation of reactive oxygen species, collagen deposition, fibrosis, and scarring of the pancreatic tissues. The inflammatory pathophysiology of chronic pancreatitis clearly provokes multiple mechanisms of carcinogenesis such as mitogenesis, mutagenesis, and angiogenesis (Harris, 2007).

Chronic pancreatitis induced by chronic cholelithiasis (gallstone formation) appears to follow a similar course (Yan and Li, 2006). Gallstones that travel down the common bile duct and become lodged in the ampulla of Vater can cause obstruction in the outflow of pancreatic digestive fluids. Backflow of these digestive fluids into the pancreas predisposes the ductal epithelium to autodigestion. The end result is persistent necroinflammation that progresses to chronic pancreatitis.

GERMLINE MUTATIONS AND PANCREATIC CANCER

Various germline mutations have been identified that heighten the risk of developing pancreatic cancer. For example, hereditary pancreatitis is an autosomal dominant genetic condition caused by a mutation in the gene that encodes the powerful digestive enzyme, trypsinogen. Carriers of the mutant gene produce abnormal trypsinogen that is resistant to autolysis, thereby causing autodigestion of the pancreas, necroinflammation, and chronic pancreatitis. Such individuals have a 40% lifetime risk of developing pancreatic cancer (Whitcomb, 1999).

Cystic fibrosis is an autosomal recessive genetic condition caused by a deleterious mutation in the transmembrane conductance regulator gene (*CFTR*) located on the long arm of chromosome 7. The protein encoded by *CFTR* is essential for normal function of the chloride ion channel of cell membranes and homeostatic regulation of concentrations of electrolytes in sweat, digestive enzymes, and mucus. The extremely viscid mucinous secretions characteristic of this condition result in cystic dilatation, necroinflammation, and fibrosis within the pancreas, lungs, and other organs, hence the name cystic fibrosis. Chronic pancreatitis develops early in patients with cystic fibrosis with a consequent fivefold increase in the risk of early onset pancreatic cancer (Maisonneuve, Marshall, and Lowenfels, 2007). Cystic fibrosis is one of the more common genetic conditions among Caucasians, occurring in one of every 3,200 newborns. The median life expectancy for individuals with cystic fibrosis is only 30–35 years. Familial breast/ovarian cancer is often caused by a heritable mutation in either of two tumor suppressor genes, *BRCA-1* or *BRCA-2*. Females who inherit mutant alleles of *BRCA-1* or *BRCA-2* are not only at high risk for developing breast cancer and/or ovarian cancer, but they are also at increased risk for the development of other tumors, including pancreatic cancer. Both *BRCA-1* and *BRCA-2* are tumor suppressor genes that are essential for precise DNA replication in cell division. Mutant forms of a third gene (called *PAL-B2* because it interacts with *BRCA-2*) also increase pancreatic cancer risk as well as breast cancer risk (Chen et al., 2008).

The Familial Atypical Mole and Melanoma (FAMM) syndrome is a rare genetic disorder giving rise to multiple dysplastic pigmented moles of the skin that can progress to malignant melanoma. There is also an increase in the risk of developing pancreatic cancer. One form of the FAMM syndrome is caused by a mutation in the gene that encodes *p16*, an important cell cycle regulating protein (Hussussian et al., 1994).

Peutz–Jeghers syndrome is a rare autosomal dominant disorder characterized by the development of benign hamartomatous polyps in the gastrointestinal tract and hyperpigmented macules on the lips and oral mucosa (Boardman et al., 1998). This syndrome is caused by a mutant tumor suppressor gene known as *STK11* located on chromosome 19. Mutations in this gene result in an altered serine/threonine protein kinase that markedly increases the risk of gastrointestinal tumors including pancreatic cancer (Jenne et al., 1998).

The Lynch syndrome (hereditary nonpolyposis colorectal colon cancer, HNPCC) is characterized by a high lifetime risk for the development of colon cancer. The cause of HNPCC is an inherited (germline) mutation in at least one of a set of genes that normally repair DNA, the mismatch repair genes. This genetic disorder also carries an increase in the risk of developing pancreatic cancer.

SOMATIC MUTATIONS IN PANCREATIC CANCER

Somatic mutations involving base pair changes in DNA occasionally occur in specific cells of specific tissues of the human body. The phenotypic effects of such mutations persist in the lineage of the cell of origin.

The *K-ras* gene product communicates signals from outside the cell to the nucleus, a process known as *signal transduction*. Somatic mutations of the *K-ras* gene can lead to its permanent activation thereby causing inappropriate signaling inside the cell even in the absence of extracellular stimuli. Because K-ras signal transduction stimulates cell division, its deregulation may result in heightened cell proliferation and malignant transformation (Goodsell, 1999).

Somatic mutations of K-ras have been observed in up to 90% of certain malignancies such as colon cancer, lung cancer, and pancreatic cancer (Almoguera et al., 1988). Somatic mutations of K-ras have also been detected in pre-malignant lesions of these organs (Moskaluk, Hruban, and Kern, 1997). Molecular studies also suggest that mutational activation of K-ras coupled with disabling mutations in tumor suppressor genes such as *p53* and *p16* accentuate carcinogenesis (Pellegata et al., 1994; Moskaluk et al., 1997; Ghaneh, Costello, and Neoptolemos, 2007). Although specific mutagenic stimuli of persistent K-ras mutations have not yet been clearly identified (Crous-Bou et al., 2009), most factors that are associated with the development of pancreatic cancer (e.g., tobacco, alcohol, bile acids, reactive oxygen species, and inflammatory factors) do have significant mutagenic potential. Clearly, the oncogenic activation of K-ras is likely to play a key role in the initiation and promotion of pancreatic ductal adenocarcinoma.

EPIGENETICS OF PANCREATIC CANCER

Epigenetics refers to the study of changes in the expression of genes without any alteration in the base pair sequence of the DNA. Down-regulation of genetic expression has generally been linked to DNA methylation as opposed to up-regulation, which may be a result of DNA acetylation.

Since pancreatic cancer often develops subsequent to *chronic pancreatitis* and *necroinflammation*, it is notable that the inducible cyclooxygenase-2 (COX-2) gene that encodes the chief regulatory enzyme of the inflammatory cascade is markedly over-expressed in a high percentage of pancreatic adenocarcinomas; and furthermore, positive immunostaining for COX-2 is localized to malignant epithelial cells whereas COX-2 staining is negative in noncancerous pancreatic tissues (Tucker et al., 1999). In addition, studies of pancreatic cancer cell lines show that bile acids effectively upregulate the inducible COX-2 gene (Tucker et al., 2004). These findings suggest that bile acids could promote pancreatic cancer by up-regulation of the inducible COX-2 gene.

OBESITY, DIABETES MELLITUS TYPE 2, AND PANCREATIC CANCER

Twin epidemics of obesity and diabetes mellitus type 2 have emerged in many populations throughout the world. Both conditions are independently associated with the development of pancreatic cancer and obesity is associated with the onset of diabetes.

An early meta-analysis of 20 epidemiologic studies determined a twofold elevation in the risk of pancreatic cancer among individuals with a 5-year history of diabetes mellitus type 2 (Everhart and Wright, 1995). In a more recent meta-analysis of 36 epidemiologic studies (17 case-control and 19 cohort studies involving 9,220 cases), the adjusted summary odds ratio was 1.83 (95% CI = 1.66–1.89) (Huxley et al., 2005). These results support a modest causal association of type 2 diabetes in the genesis of pancreatic cancer.

A major problem with studies of the association of pancreatic cancer and diabetes is that since both conditions evolve in the same organ over a period of many years, it is difficult to determine the causal pathway. The question becomes: does diabetes predispose to pancreatic cancer or the reverse? Drawing conclusions regarding the role of diabetes in causing pancreatic cancer is thus subject to a form of bias known as *reverse causality bias*. In fact, more than 70% of pancreatic cancer cases present with glucose intolerance (Schwarts et al., 1978; Gullo et al., 1994).

The issue of *reverse causality* in regard to pancreatic cancer and diabetes has been discussed in some detail by various investigators. Currently, there is no general consensus as to a cause and effect relationship between these conditions. One argument *against* such a relationship is the fact that rates of pancreatic cancer have remained constant or declined in many nations even though prevalence rates of obesity and type 2 diabetes have increased dramatically. Nevertheless, in subjects with long-standing type 2 diabetes, the pancreas is exposed to hyperinsulinemia for years, and since cultures of pancreatic cancer cells have been found to express insulin receptors, it is conceivable that hyperinsulinemia could serve as a promoter of pancreatic cancer (Wang et al., 2003).

ISLET CELL TUMORS

Islet cell tumors of the pancreas arise from endocrine cells in the *Islets of Langerhans*. While such tumors may involve any of the hormone-producing islet cells (alpha cells produce glucagon, beta cells produce insulin, delta cells produce somatostatin, PP cells produce pancreatic polypeptide, and epsilon cells produce ghrelin), most are beta cell tumors (also called insulinomas) since the beta cells elaborate insulin. Insulinomas are clinically characterized by attacks of hyperinsulinism and hypoglycemia. Islet cell tumors are a component of the *Zollinger-Ellison syndrome* defined by the triage of recalcitrant peptic ulcer, hypersecretion of gastrin (gastrinoma) and pancreatic islet cell tumor. Islet cell tumors also occur in the *Multiple Endocrine Neoplasia syndrome* (MEN I) which may include adenomas of the pituitary gland, the thyroid and parathyroid glands, and the adrenal cortex in combination with peptic ulcer. Most islet cell tumors are benign (less than 10% are malignant carcinomas). Malignant islet cell tumors constitute only about 1% of all cases of pancreatic cancer (Robbins and Cotran, 1979). Germline and somatic mutations and epigenetic suppression of multiple tumor suppressor genes that regulate nucleosome remodeling have been linked to the development of these rare pancreatic tumors (Elsässer, Allis, and Lewis, 2011).

PREVENTION OF PANCREATIC CANCER

There are currently no proven methods of preventing the development of pancreatic cancer. Nor are there satisfactory tests or imaging procedures that can be used to screen the population for early lesions of the pancreas. Nevertheless, there are steps that can be taken to reduce the risk. These include complete avoidance of tobacco and alcohol; maintenance of healthy weight through regular exercise; eating a diet rich in fruits, vegetables, and whole grains; and maintenance of blood glucose within normal limits.

● ● ● **REFERENCES**

Almoguera, C., Shibata, D., Forrester, K., Martin, J., Arnheim, N., & Perucho, M. (1988). Most human carcinomas of the exocrine pancreas contain mutant c-K-*ras* genes. *Cell, 53,* 549–554.

American Cancer Society. (2007). Global Cancer Facts and Figures, 2007. Atlanta, Georgia.

Boardman, L.A., Thibodeau, S.N., Schaid, D.J., et al. (1998). Increased risk for cancer in patients with the Peutz-Jeghers syndrome. *Ann Intern Med, 128*(11), 896–899.

Bueno de Mesquita, H.B., Moerman, C.J., Runia, S., & Maisonneuve, P. (1990). Are energy and energy-providing nutrients related to exocrine carcinoma of the pancreas? *Int J Cancer, 46*(3), 435–444.

Chan, J.M., Wang, F., & Holly, E.A. (2007). Pancreatic cancer, animal protein and dietary fat in a population-based study, San Francisco Bay Area, California. *Cancer Causes Control, 18*(10), 1153–1167.

Chen, P., Liang, J., Wang, Z., Zhou, X., Chen, L., Li, M.,…Wang, H. (2008). Association of common PALB2 polymorphisms with breast cancer risk: A case-control study. *Clin Cancer Res, 14*(18), 5931–5937.

Crous-Bou, M., Parta, M., Morales, E., Lopez, T., Carrato, A., Puigdome'nech, E., Readl, F.X., & PANKRAS II Study Group. (2009). Past medical conditions and K-ras mutations in pancreatic ductal adenocarcinoma: A hypothesis-generating study. *Cancer Causes Control, 20,* 591–599.

Duell, E.J., Holly, E.A., Bracci, P.M., Liu, M., Wiencke, J.K., & Kelsey, K.T. (2002). A population-based, case control study of polymorphisms in carcinogen-metabolizing genes, smoking, and pancreatic adenocarcinoma risk. *J Natl Cancer Inst, 94*(4), 297–306.

Durbec, J.P., Chevillotte, G., Bidart, J.M., Berthezene, P., & Sarles, H. (1983). Diet, alcohol, tobacco and risk of cancer of the pancreas: A case-control study. *Br J Cancer, 47*(4), 463–470.

Elsässer, S.J., Allis, C.D., & Lewis, P.W. (2011). New epigenetic drivers of cancers. *Science, 331*(6021),1145–1146.

Everhart, J., & Wright, D. (1995). Diabetes mellitus as a risk factor for pancreatic cancer. A meta-analysis. *J Amer Med Assoc, 273*(20), 1605–1609.

Farrow, D.C., & Davis, S. (1990). Diet and the risk of pancreatic cancer in men. *Am J Epidemiol, 132*(3), 423–431.

Finkelberg, D.L., Sahani, D., Deshpande, V., & Brugge, W.R. (2006). Autoimmune pancreatitis. *N Engl J Med, 355,* 2670–2676.

Genkinger, J.M., Spiegelman, D., Anderson, K.E., et al. (2009). Alcohol intake and pancreatic cancer risk: A pooled analysis of fourteen cohort studies. *Cancer Epidemiology, Biomarkers & Prevention, 18*(3), 765–776.

Ghadirian, P., Simard, A., Baillargeon, J., Maisonneuve, P., & Boyle, P. (1991). Nutritional factors and pancreatic cancer in the Francophone community in Montreal, Canada. *Int J Cancer, 47*(1), 1–6.

Ghaneh, P., Costello, E., & Neoptolemos, J.P. (2007). Biology and management of pancreatic cancer. *Gut, 56*(8), 1134–1152.

Glinghammar, B., & Rafter, J. (2001). Colonic luminal contents induce cyclooxygenase 2 transcription in human colon carcinoma cells. *Gastroenterology, 120,* 401–410.

Goodsell, D.S. (1999). The molecular perspective: The ras oncogene. *Oncologist, 4*(3), 263–264.

Gullo, L., Pezzilli, R., & Morselli-Labate, A.M., Italian Pancreatic Cancer Study Group. (1994). Diabetes and the risk of pancreatic cancer. *N Engl J Med, 331,* 81–84.

Harris, R.E. (2007). COX-2 and the inflammogenesis of cancer. *Subcellular Biochemistry, 42,* 193–212.

Hecht, S.S. (1998). Biochemistry, biology, and carcinogenicity of tobacco-specific N-nitrosamines. *Chem Res Toxicol, 6,* 559–603.

Hill, M.J. (1991). Bile acids and colorectal cancer: Hypothesis. *Eur J Cancer Prev, 2,* 69–74.

Hussussian, C.J., Struewing, J.P., Goldstein, A.M., Higgins, P.A., Ally, D.S., Sheahan, M.D., et al. (1994). Germ line p16 mutations in familial melanoma. *Nat Genet, 8*(1), 15–21.

Huxley, R., Ansary-Moghaddam, A., Berrington de González, A., Barzi, F., & Woodward, M. (2005). Type-II diabetes and pancreatic cancer: A meta-analysis of 36 studies. *Br J Cancer*, 92(11), 2076–2083.

Iodice, S., Gandini, S., Maisonneuve, P., & Lowenfels, A.B. (2008). Tobacco and the risk of pancreatic cancer: A review and meta-analysis. *Langenbeck's Archives of Surgery*, 393(4), 535–545.

Jenne, D.E., Reimann, H., Nezu, J., Friedel, W., Loff, S., Jeschke, R.,...Zimmer, M. (1998). Peutz-Jeghers syndrome is caused by mutations in a novel serine threonine kinase. *Nat Genet*, 18, 38–43.

Kaibara, N., Yurugi, E., & Koga, S. (1984). Promoting effect of bile acids on the chemical transformation of C3H/10T1/2 fibroblasts *in vitro*. *Cancer Res*, 44, 5482–5485.

Larsson, S.C., Hakanson, N., Permert, J., & Wolk, A. (2006). Meat, fish, poultry and egg consumption in relation to risk of pancreatic cancer: A prospective study. *Int J Cancer*, 118, 2866–2870.

Lin, Y., Kikuchi, S., Tamakoshi, A., Yagyu, K., Obata, Y., et al. (2006). Dietary habits and pancreatic cancer risk in a cohort of middle-aged and elderly Japanese. *Nutr Cancer*, 56, 40–49.

Lowenfels, A.B., Maisonneuve, P., Cavallini, G., Ammann, R.W., Lankisc, P.G., Andersen, J.R.... Domellof, L., for The International Pancreatitis Study Group. (1993). Pancreatitits and the risk of pancreatic cancer. *New Engl J Med*, 328(20), 1433–1437.

Lowenfels, A.B., & Maisonneuve, P. (2006). Epidemiology and risk factors for pancreatic cancer. *Best Pract Res Clin Gastroenterol*, 20(2), 197–209.

Maisonneuve, P., Marshall, B.C., & Lowenfels, A.B. (2007). Risk of pancreatic cancer in patients with cystic fibrosis. *Gut*, 56, 1327–1328.

Michaud, D.S., Giovannucci, E., Willett, W.C., Colditz, G.A., & Fuchs, C.S. (2003). Dietary meat, dairy products, fat, and cholesterol and pancreatic cancer risk in a prospective study. *Am J Epidemio*, 157(12), 1115–1125.

Mills, P.K., Beeson, W.L., Abbey, D.E., Fraser, G.E., & Phillips, R.L. (1988). Dietary habits and past medical history as related to fatal pancreas cancer risk among Adventists. *Cancer*, 61(12), 2578–2585.

Moskaluk, C.A., Hruban, R.H., & Kern, S.E. (1997). p16 and K-ras gene mutations in the intraductal precursors of human pancreatic adenocarcinoma. *Cancer Research*, 57, 2140–2143.

Nair, R.J., Lawler, L., & Miller, M.R. (2007). Chronic pancreatitis. *Am Fam Physician*, 76(11), 1679–1688.

Nöthlings, U., Wilkens, L.R., Murphy, S.P., Hankin, J.H., Henderson, B.E., & Kolonel, L.N. (2005). Meat and fat intake as risk factors for pancreatic cancer: The Multiethnic Cohort Study. *J Natl Cancer Inst*, 97(19), 1458–1465.

Olsen, G.W., Mandel, J.S., Gibson, R.W., Wattenberg, L.W., & Schuman, L.M. (1989). A case-control study of pancreatic cancer and cigarettes, alcohol, coffee and diet. *American Journal of Public Health*, 79(8), 1016–1019.

Parkin, D.M. (2004). International variation. *Oncogene*, 23, 6329–6340.

Pellegata, N.S., Sessa, F., Renault, B., Sonato, M., Leone, B.E., Solcia, E., & Ranzani, N. (1994). K-ras and p53 gene mutations in pancreatic cancer: Ductal and nonductal tumors. *Cancer Research*, 54, 1556–1560.

Raymond, L., Infante, F., Tuyns, A.J., Voirol, M., & Lowenfels, A.B. (1987). Alimentationet cancer du pancréas [Diet and cancer of the pancreas]. *Gastroenterol Clin Biol*, 11(6–7), 488–492.

Reddy, B.S. (1981). Diet and excretion of bile acids. *Cancer Res*, 41, 3766–3788.

Reddy, B.S., Weisburger, J.H., & Wynder, E.L. (1978). Colon cancer: Bile salts as tumor promoters. In Slaga, T.J., Sivak, A., and Boutwell, R.K. (Eds.), *Carcinogensis, Vol. 2. Mechanisms of tumor promotion and carcinogenesis* (pp. 1453–1464). New York: Raven Press.

Robbins, S.L., & Cotran, R.S. (1979). *Pathologic basis of disease*. 2nd Edition, W.B. Saunders, Philadelphia.

Schatzkin, A., Subar, A.F., Thompson, F.E., Harlan, L.C., Tangrea, J., Hollenbeck, A.R., Hurwitz, P.E., Coyle, L., Schussler, N., Michaud, D.W., Freedman, L.S., Brown, C.C., Midthune, D., & Kipnis, V. (2001). Design and serendipity in establishing a large cohort with wide dietary intake distributions: The National Institutes of Health–American Association of Retired Persons Diet and Health Study. *Am J Epidemiol 154*(12), 1119–1125.

Schwarts, S.S., Zeidler, A., Moossa, A.R., Kuku, S.F., & Rubenstein, A.H. (1978). A prospective study of glucose tolerance, insulin, C-peptide, and glucagon responses in patients with pancreatic carcinoma. *Dig Dis, 23*, 1107–1114.

Shirvani, V.N., Ouatu-Lascar, R., Kaur, B.S., et al. (2000). Cyclooxygenase 2 expression in Barrett's esophagus and adenocarcinoma: *Ex vivo* induction by bile salts and acid exposure. *Gastroenterology, 118*, 487–496.

Silverman, D.T., Brown, L.M., Hoover, R.N., et al. (1995). Alcohol and pancreatic cancer in blacks and whites in the United States. *Cancer Research, 55*(21), 4899–4905.

Stolzenberg-Solomon, R.Z., Pietinen, P., Taylor, P.R., Virtamo, J., & Albanes, D. (2002). Prospective study of diet and pancreatic cancer in male smokers. *Am J Epidemiol, 155*(9), 783–792.

Talamini, R., Polesil, J., Gallus, S., Dal Maso, L., Zucchetto, A., Negri, E.,...La Vecchia, C. (2010). Tobacco smoking, alcohol consumption and pancreatic cancer risk: A case-control study in Italy. *European Journal of Cancer, 46*(2), 370–376.

Thiébaut, A.C.M., Jiao, L., Silverman, D.T., Cross, A.J., Thompson, F.E., Subar, A.F.,...Stolzenberg-Solomon, R.Z. (2009). Dietary fatty acids and pancreatic cancer in the NIH-AARP Diet and Health Study. *J Natl Cancer Inst, 101*, 1001–1011.

Tucker, O.N., Dannenberg, A.J., Yang, E.K., Zhang, F., Teng, L., Daly, J.M.,...Fahey, T.J. III (1999). Cyclooxygenase-2 expression is upregulated in human pancreatic cancer. *Cancer Research, 59*, 987–990.

Tucker, O.N., Dannenberg, A.J., Yang, E.K., & Fahye, T.J. (2004). Bile acids induce cyclooxygenase-2 expression in human pancreatic cancer cell lines. *Carcinogenesis, 25*(3), 419–423.

Wang, F., Herrington, M., Larrson, J., & Permert, J. (2003). The relationship between diabetes and pancreatic cancer. *Molecular Cancer, 2*(4), doi:10.1186/1476-4598-2-4.

Whitcomb, D. (1999). Hereditary pancreatitis: New insights into acute and chronic pancreatitis. *Gut, 45*(3), 317–322.

Witt, H., Apte, M.V., Keim, V., & Wilson, J.S. (2007). Chronic pancreatitis: Challenges and advances in pathogenesis, genetics, diagnosis, and therapy. *Gastroenterology, 132*, 1557–1573.

WHO (2009). Report on the Global Tobacco Epidemic, 2009. World Health Organization, Geneva, Switzerland.

Wynder, E.L. (1975). An epidemiological evaluation of the causes of cancer of the pancreas. *Cancer Res, 35*(8), 2228–2233.

Wynder, E.L., Mabuchi, K., & Maruchia, N. (1973). Epidemiology of cancer of the pancreas. *J Natl Cancer Inst, 50*, 645–667.

Yan, M.X., & Li, Y.Q. (2006). Gallstones and chronic pancreatitis: The black box in between. *Postgrad Med J, 82*, 254–258.

Ye, W., Lagergren, J., Weiderpass, E., Nyrén, O., Adami, H.O., & Ekbom, A. (2002). Alcohol abuse and the risk of pancreatic cancer. *Gut, 51*(2), 236–239.

Zatonski, W.A., Boyle, P., Przewozniak, K., Maisonneuve, P., Drosik, K., & Walker, A.M. (1993). Cigarette smoking, alcohol, tea and coffee consumption and pancreas cancer risk: A case-control study from Opole, Poland. *International Journal of Cancer, 53*(4), 601–607.

Zhang, F., Subbaramaiah, K., Altorki, N., & Dannenberg, A.J. (1998). Dihydroxy bile acids activate the transcription of cyclooxygenase-2. *J Biol Chem, 273*, 2424–2428.

Zhang, J., Zhao, Z., & Berkel, H.J. (2005). Animal fat consumption and pancreatic cancer incidence: Evidence of interaction with cigarette smoking. *Ann Epidemiol, 15*(7), 500–508.

Epidemiology of Primary Liver Cancer

INTRODUCTION

There are two separate and distinctly different forms of primary liver cancer. Hepatocellular carcinoma arises from the cells of the liver *per se* (called hepatocytes) whereas cholangiocarcinoma (biliary cancer) arises from the epithelial lining of the gallbladder or the biliary ducts. Hepatocellular carcinoma is much more common than biliary cancer, accounting for approximately 93% of all primary liver cancers. Since each type has its own set of epidemiologic parameters, hepatocellular carcinoma and cholangiocarcinoma are discussed individually in the following sections of this chapter.

HEPATOCELLULAR CARCINOMA

Global Epidemiology of Hepatocellular Carcinoma

Hepatocellular carcinoma is the fifth most common malignancy in the world (more than 711,000 new cases are diagnosed annually) and the third most common cause of death due to cancer (American Cancer Society, 2007). This malignancy has an extremely poor prognosis and nearly as many people die from the disease (approximately 662,000 annually) as are diagnosed (WHO, 2009). Most hepatocellular carcinomas are nonresectable at the time of diagnosis and the disease is usually fatal within 3–6 months.

Rates are highest in sub-Saharan Africa, Eastern and Southeastern Asia, and Melanesia (South Pacific islands north of Australia) (**Figure 18.1**). More than 84% of new cases occur in developing countries in areas where oncogenic liver viruses (particularly hepatitis B virus and hepatitis C virus) are endemic. Chronic exposure to alfatoxins from moldy grains and chronic alcohol abuse are independent risk factors that can synergistically interact with oncogenic hepatitis viruses to markedly heighten the risk of developing hepatocellular carcinoma. The burden of hepatocellular carcinoma is particularly extreme in China where more than half of new cases are diagnosed. Hepatocellular carcinoma develops two to three times more frequently in men than women (Parkin et al., 2005).

Global Patterns of Hepatocellular Carcinoma

Hepatocellular carcinoma shows two main epidemiologic patterns, the predominant one being in China, sub-Saharan Africa, Southeast Asia, and the Amazon Basin. In these regions, liver viruses are endemic and the initial infection usually occurs during the perinatal period. In the populations of these regions, hepatocellular carcinomas are diagnosed early in life, sometimes during adolescence, and the peak incidence occurs before the age of 50.

A less common pattern of late onset is evident in North America and Western Europe. In the populations of these regions, the onset of hepatocelluar carcinoma occurs late in life, usually after the age of 60. This pattern is primarily a consequence of sustained damage to liver cells from chronic alcohol abuse or late onset viral hepatitis.

In the United States, the annual age-adjusted incidence rates of invasive liver cancer increased by more than twofold in women during 1975–2007 (from 1.6 to 3.6 cases per 100,000) and by nearly threefold in men (from 3.9 to 10.7 cases per 100,000). Consistent with their higher rates of chronic exposure to alcohol and liver viruses, incidence rates among African American men and women exceed Caucasians by about 75% (Alterkruse et al., 2010).

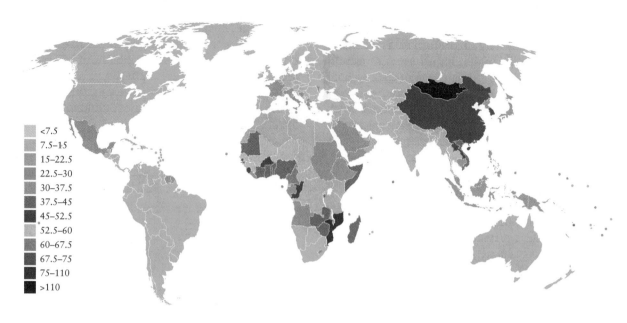

	<7.5
	7.5–15
	15–22.5
	22.5–30
	30–37.5
	37.5–45
	45–52.5
	52.5–60
	60–67.5
	67.5–75
	75–110
	>110

Figure 18.1 Global Liver Cancer Mortality, 2004.

Source: Data from World Health Organization. The global burden of disease: 2004 update. Geneva, WHO, 2008. Available at www.who.int/evidence/bod.

Pathogenesis of Hepatocellular Carcinoma

Hepatocellular carcinoma is initiated and promoted by sustained recursive damage to hepatocytes due to infection by oncogenic liver viruses, chronic exposure to alfatoxins, chronic alcohol abuse, or a combination of these factors. Though the exact sequence of events may differ from person to person, the cellular mechanisms involved include early fatty change (the appearance of lipid-containing vacuoles in hepatocytes), chronic inflammation and cell necrosis (termed necroinflammation), wound healing and regeneration of hepatocytes, and late stage fibrosis leading to the eventual formation of fibrotic nodules (cirrhosis of the liver).

The cellular processes of necroinflammation and wound healing incite several mechanisms of cancer development (mutagenesis, cell proliferation, angiogenesis, dysfunctional apoptosis, immunosuppression, and metastasis). Hepatocelluar carcinoma may develop with or without liver cirrhosis, e.g, chronic viral hepatitis alone may produce cancer in a non-cirrhotic liver. Cirrhosis (scarring) of the liver is invariably associated with chronic alcohol abuse and severe cirrhosis of the liver markedly increases the risk of developing primary liver cancer, particularly in individuals suffering from chronic active hepatitis. The fibrotic nodules characteristic of alcoholic liver cirrhosis may occur in either a micronodular pattern or as large macronodules of coalesced foci of micronodules (Robbins and Cotran, 1979).

Liver Viruses and Hepatocellular Carcinoma

Two liver viruses, hepatitis B virus (HBV) and hepatitis C virus (HCV), account for 75% of the new cases of liver cancer worldwide and 85% of cases in developing countries (Parkin et al., 1999). In high-risk areas where HBV and HCV are endemic, 10–20% of young individuals become chronic carriers of HBV or HCV. Among those who suffer from chronic viral hepatitis, the annual incidence rates per 100,000 range from 400–800 for men and 120–180 for women (Nguyen, Law, and Dore, 2009). Among such individuals, the cumulative risk of developing hepatocellular carcinoma by age 65 years is nearly 33% in men and 10% in women.

The relative risk of developing liver cancer is increased by more than 20-fold for those chronically infected with either HBV or HCV compared to non-infected individuals and more than 100-fold for those infected by both viruses (Donato, Boffetta, and Puoti, 1998). Based upon current estimates of the attributable fraction for each virus, approximately 50–55% of hepatocellular carcinomas are caused by HBV and 20–25% by HCV (Kirk, Bah, and Montesano, 2006). Since HBV causes far more infections than HCV, particularly in the younger generations, the global pattern of chronic HBV infections roughly simulates the global distribution of liver cancer (Hou, Liu, and Gu, 2005). It is important to note that HBV and HCV have both been classified as human carcinogens by the International Agency for Research on Cancer (IARC, 1994).

Hepatitis B Virus (HBV) and Hepatocellular Carcinoma

Baruch Blumberg and colleagues discovered the hepatitis B virus (HBV) by its novel *Australia antigen* in the serum of a patient with leukemia (Blumberg, Alter, and Visnich, 1965). Blumberg later developed the diagnostic test and vaccine for HBV and in 1976 was awarded the Nobel Prize in Medicine for these achievements (Blumberg, 2002). Dane first identified hepatitis B virus (HBV) in the serum of hepatitis patients using electron microscopy (Dane, 1970). A few years later, the genome of HBV was sequenced (Galibert et al., 1979) and antibody testing of viral antigens developed (Bonino et al., 1987).

Hepatitis B virus is highly endemic in developing regions of the world that are heavily populated such as Southeast Asia, China, sub-Saharan Africa, and the Amazon Basin. In these high-risk regions, up to 95% of the population shows past or present serological evidence of HBV infection and a significant fraction (15–20%) become chronic carriers of the HBV surface antigen (HBsAg) (Kirk et al., 2004). The global distribution of hepatocellular carcinoma correlates with the geographic prevalence of chronic carriers of HBV, who number nearly 400 million worldwide (**Figure 18.2**).

Epidemiologic studies have demonstrated that there is a consistent and specific causal association between chronic HBV infection and hepatocellular carcinoma. In a landmark study, Beasley and colleagues followed 22,707 male Taiwanese health workers for more than a decade with nearly complete follow-up. Incidence rates of hepatocellular carcinoma among carriers of the HBV surface antigen (HBsAg) were approximately 100 times higher than noncarriers (495 vs. 5 per 100,000 per year) (Beasley et al., 1981). In a meta-analysis of 32 studies, Donato and colleagues determined that the overall risk of developing hepatocellular carcinoma was increased by approximately 20-fold for individuals positive for the HBV surface antigen (HBsAg) and with no evidence of coinfection by HCV (Donato et al., 1998). Nevertheless, relative risk estimates from case-control and cohort studies show wide variability, ranging from 5–100, presumably due to genotypic differences in HBV strains (Yu and Chen, 1994). Furthermore, the risk estimates vary depending on the presence/absence of other risk factors, e.g., HCV infection, chronic alcohol abuse, and alfatoxin exposure. These risk factors and combinations of risk factors involving HBV are discussed in the following sections of this chapter.

Hepatitis B virus is spread through contact with infected body fluids and the only natural host is human. Blood is the most important vehicle for transmission, but other body fluids have also been implicated, including semen, breast milk, and saliva. In regions of the world where HBV is endemic, most HBV infections occur during infancy or early childhood. Vertical transmission from mother to baby can occur at the time of childbirth when the newborn passes through the birth canal or later, e.g.,

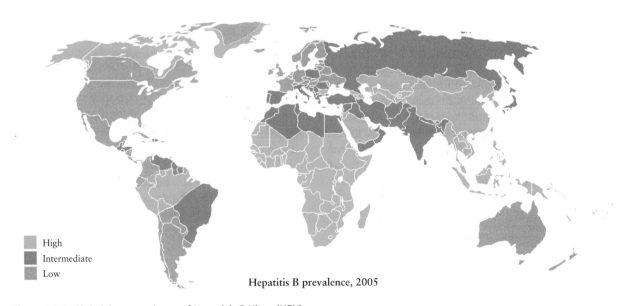

High
Intermediate
Low

Hepatitis B prevalence, 2005

Figure 18.2 Global Seroprevalence of Hepatitis B Virus (HBV).

Source: Data from CDC Travelers' Health Yellow Book. (2012). Chapter 3: Infectious Diseases Related to Travel; Hepatitis B. Available at http://wwwnc.cdc.gov/travel/yellowbook/2012/chapter-3-infectious-diseases-related-to-travel/hepatitis-b.htm. Accessed October 28, 2011.

through contaminated saliva or breast milk. High rates of child-to-child transmission have also been documented in certain populations. Most acute HBV infections are asymptomatic and therefore left untreated. Since babies and young children may not have fully developed immune systems, once infected they are far more susceptible to persistence of the virus than adults. Therefore, acute HBV infections acquired during the perinatal period or early in childhood often progress to chronic infections that persist for many years (Shapiro, 1993).

Antibodies against the HBV surface antigen (HBsAg) develop in exposed individuals after an incubation period of a few weeks. Individuals who remain HBsAg positive for at least 6 months are considered to be hepatitis B carriers (Shapiro, 1993; Zuckerman, 1996). In young individuals who become chronic carriers of HBV, the rates of liver cancer begin to rise during adolescence and reach peak values by age 50 (Parkin et al., 2005).

Transmission of HBV in adults occurs through unprotected sexual contact with an infected individual or by using contaminated needles and syringes for the intravenous injection of illicit drugs. The virus can also be transmitted by transfusion with contaminated blood or blood products in countries without effective screening programs for donor blood. Nevertheless, immunocompetent adults who become infected by HBV usually clear the virus without treatment and less than 1% of individuals who become infected during adulthood will develop chronic hepatitis B.

The genome of HBV is made of circular DNA, but it is unusual because the DNA is not fully double-stranded. Furthermore, HBV replicates by reverse transcriptase, similar to the RNA viruses. At least four serotypes and eight genotypic strains of HBV have been identified. The process of carcinogenesis induced by chronic HBV infection involves interaction of the HBV genotype with the host immune system and infiltration of infected foci of hepatocytes by cytotoxic (killer) T lymphocytes (Zuckerman, 1996). Integration of the viral genome into the host DNA is a prominent feature of carcinogenesis that may induce overexpression of oncogenes and dysfunction of tumor suppressor genes (Kew, 1996).

While all strains of HBV appear to be capable of sustaining long-term infections associated with liver damage, cirrhosis, and carcinogenesis, molecular epidemiologic studies suggest that there are genotypic differences in the pathogenesis of cirrhosis, carcinogenicity, and response to therapy. For example, individuals who carry genotype C are likely to have antibodies against the viral precore antigen, HBeAg, which is indicative of a high viral load and increased

cirrhosis and carcinogenesis (Cao, 2009). In a prospective study of 11,893 men conducted in Taiwan (Yang et al., 2002), investigators observed a much higher incidence rate of hepatocellular carcinoma among men positive for both HBsAg and HBeAg (1,169 cases per 100,000 person years, relative risk = 60.2) compared to men positive for HBsAg alone (324 cases per 100,000 person years, relative risk = 9.6). Other studies also suggest that viral load and viral replication are important determinants of liver cirrhosis and cancer risk in individuals suffering from chronic HBV infection (Chen, 2006; Iloeje, 2007). Furthermore, therapeutic trials show that individuals infected by genotypes A or B respond better to interferon therapy than individuals with other HBV genotypes (Cao, 2009). As will be discussed below, effective vaccines that target the viral envelope (HBsAg) are now available that provide long-term immunity against HBV infection as well as protection against liver carcinogenesis (Vandamme and Van Herck, 2007).

Hepatitis C Virus (HCV) and Hepatocellular Carcinoma

The studies of Harvey J. Alter and colleagues at the US National Institutes of Health during the 1970s demonstrated that most patients who developed hepatitis following transfusion were not infected by either hepatitis A or B viruses (Alter, 1995; Alter, 1997). Subsequently, in the laboratories of Michael Houghton, a novel virus named hepatitis C virus (HCV) was identified in patients with non-A, non-B hepatitis (Choo et al., 1989; Kuo et al., 1989). Screening methods for detecting HCV in donor blood have markedly reduced the risk of post-transfusion hepatitis (Tanaka et al., 1994).

Hepatitis C virus is endemic in many parts of the world, particularly in those nations with impoverished populations, poor living conditions, and substandard sanitation. In these nations, seropositive rates range from 10–15% and high rates of transmission have no doubt persisted for centuries. Recent estimates suggest that HCV has infected nearly 200 million people worldwide and infects 3–4 million more people per year (WHO, 2009). The seroprevalence of HCV is highest in certain countries of Africa, Asia, and South America (**Figure 18.3**). Egypt has the highest seroprevalence (approximately 20%), which may have resulted from a now discontinued mass campaign of parenteral treatment of schistosomiasis (infection by an endemic parasitic worm) (Frank et al., 2000).

The hepatitis C virus is transmitted by exposure to contaminated blood. In developed countries such as the United States, most infections were once

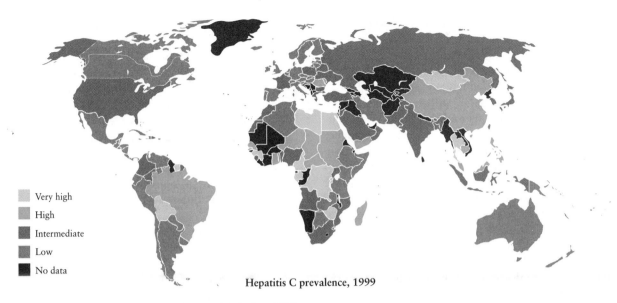

Hepatitis C prevalence, 1999

Very high
High
Intermediate
Low
No data

Figure 18.3 Global Seroprevalence of Hepatitis C Virus (HCV).

Source: Data from CDC Travelers' Health Yellow Book. (2012). Chapter 3: Infectious Diseases Related to Travel; Hepatitis C. Available at http://wwwnc.cdc.gov/travel/yellowbook/2012/chapter-3-infectious-diseases-related-to-travel/hepatitis-c.htm. Accessed October 28, 2011.

caused by transfusions with contaminated blood or blood products; fortunately, accurate methods of screening the blood supply have been developed and are in use; as a consequence, there has not been a documented post-transfusion-related case of hepatitis C in the United States for more than a decade. Currently, the primary route of HCV transmission in the United States is by intravenous injection of illicit drugs using contaminated needles (Campbell et al., 2006).

In less developed countries, the primary sources of HCV infection are unsterilized injection equipment and transfusion of inadequately screened blood and blood products. Vertical transmission from an infected mother to her child can occur during the birthing process, particularly when the mother is coinfected by the human immunodeficiency virus (HIV).

Sexual contact with an HCV-infected individual is believed to be an inefficient method of transmission; nevertheless, circumstances and any untoward events causing exposure to contaminated blood could facilitate transmission. Prison inmates are at high risk of being infected either by injecting drugs using contaminated needles or by sexual transmission, e.g., a survey conducted in California found that 82% of subjects diagnosed with hepatitis C had previously been incarcerated (McGovern et al., 2006).

The hepatitis C virus is a small single-stranded RNA virus (50 nanometers in diameter). Like HBV and other liver viruses, HCV has a tropism for the liver where it tends to persist in the cytoplasm of hepatocytes. Six major genotypes of HCV have been identified and host responses to acute HCV infection are variable. The virus can be detected in the blood by polymerase chain reaction (PCR) within 1–3 weeks after infection and antibodies against HCV usually develop within 15 weeks. The acute phase of infection lasts up to 6 months and is treatable with antiviral drugs plus interferon. Chronic hepatitis C, defined as infection persisting for more than 6 months, is much more resistant to therapy (Caruntu and Benea, 2006).

The natural course of chronic hepatitis C varies considerably from one person to another. Nevertheless, HCV usually persists in the hepatocytic cell population of the liver, even in immunocompetent individuals who become infected. It is estimated that 60–70% of infected adults will develop chronic hepatitis C. Furthermore, over a period of 10–30 years, 20–30% of chronically infected individuals progress to liver cirrhosis and some develop hepatocellular carcinoma. Without treatment, it is estimated that more than 50% of patients with chronic hepatitis C will develop cirrhosis of the liver (NIH, 2002). Concomitant alcohol abuse and/or coinfection with HIV are cofactors that hasten progression of liver cirrhosis. Males also tend to have more rapid disease progression than females.

Chronic hepatitis C and progressive liver cirrhosis may lead to loss of liver function and accumulation of ammonia and other toxic substances, jaundice, hepatic encephalopathy, ascites, portal hypertension, and bleeding varices. Chronic infection by HCV and subsequent cirrhosis of the liver resulting in liver failure is the leading reason for liver transplantation in the United States.

A meta-analysis of 32 studies that examined hepatocellular carcinoma and chronic hepatitis due to HBV and/or HCV provides convincing evidence that chronic infection by either virus alone markedly increases the risk of developing this malignancy and that chronic coinfection by both viruses further increases the risk (Donato et al., 1998). Two distinct patterns of risk are evident (**Figure 18.4**). In nations where HBV is highly endemic (sub-Saharan Africa, China, Taiwan, South Korea, and Vietnam), HBV risk exceeds HCV risk and the markedly increased risk due to coinfection with both viruses is consistent with synergism. A different pattern is apparent in Japan and Mediterranean nations where *HCV* is more prominent. In these populations, HCV risk exceeds HBV risk but the risk due to coinfection is more consistent with an additive model.

Coinfection with HIV and HCV: Liver Cirrhosis and Hepatocellular Carcinoma

Approximately 30% of HIV-infected patients in the United States are also infected with the hepatitis C virus. The increasing rates of HIV and HCV coinfection have arisen due to blood-borne transmission of both viruses in association with high-risk behavior, e.g., IV drug use and unprotected sex with multiple partners. Even though overall survival has improved for HIV-infected individuals due to highly active antiretroviral therapy (HAART), it has been demonstrated in clinical studies that patients coinfected with HIV and HCV have more rapid progression of liver cirrhosis and are at increased risk of liver failure and hepatocellular carcinoma compared to those infected by only HCV (Giordano et al., 2003; Ding et al., 2009). In a recent meta-analysis, Chen and colleagues observed that coinfected individuals have increased mortality primarily due to liver disease that is unrelated to HIV disease progression (Chen et al., 2009). Indeed, hepatocellular carcinoma has become the leading cause of non-AIDS-related death among coinfected individuals (Wilcox, 2009).

Aflatoxins and Hepatocellular Carcinoma

Aflatoxins are mycotoxins produced by certain species of the fungus *Aspergillus*, most notably *Aspergillus flavus* and *Aspergillus parasiticus*. When conditions of high humidity and heat prevail, these fungi readily colonize and contaminate grain before harvest and during storage. A wide variety of crops are frequently affected including cereals (maize, sorghum, pearl millet, rice, wheat), oilseeds (peanut, soybean, sunflower, cotton), spices (chili peppers, black pepper, coriander, turmeric, ginger), and tree nuts (almond, pistachio, walnut, coconut, brazil nut). Humans are exposed to aflatoxins by consumption of moldy grains (Williams et al., 2004). Exposure rates are highest in populations with high rates of hepatocellular carcinoma, particularly in the nations of sub-Saharan Africa and in certain provinces of southern China (Montesano, Hainaut, and Wild, 1997).

Aflatoxins are toxic and potent carcinogens in the liver where they are metabolized to form reactive (highly mutagenic) epoxides. Among the many

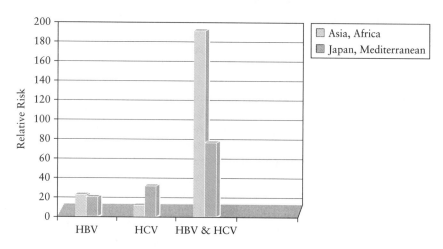

Figure 18.4 Relative Risk of Hepatocellular Carcinoma by HBV and HCV Seropositivity.

Source: Data from Donato F, Boffetta P, Puoti MA (1998). Meta-analysis of epidemiological studies on the combined effect of Hepatitis B and C virus infections in causing hepatocellular carcinoma. *Int J Cancer* 75:347–354.

different forms of aflatoxins that have been identified, aflatoxin B_1, which is produced by both *Aspergillus flavus* and *Aspergillus parasiticus*, is considered the most toxic. Recent molecular studies have found that aflatoxin B_1 can specifically mutate and hence deactivate *p53*, a tumor suppressor gene that is critical for control of cell division (Montesano et al., 1997; Stern et al., 2001).

Chronic exposure to aflatoxins independently increases the risk of developing hepatocellular carcinoma. Early epidemiologic investigations using urinary metabolites of aflatoxins as biomarkers of exposure determined five- to sixfold increases in the risk with exposure to metabolites of aflatoxin B_1 (Ross et al., 1992; Wang et al., 1996). Furthermore, aflatoxin exposure in combination with chronic hepatitis B or C has been found to synergistically increase hepatocarcinogenesis. It is estimated that chronic exposure to aflatoxins plus concomitant liver infection by HBV increases the risk of developing hepatocellular carcinoma by up to 60-fold (Yeh et al., 1989; Groopman, 1993; Sylla et al., 1999).

Alcohol Abuse, Cirrhosis of the Liver, and Hepatocellular Carcinoma

Cirrhosis of the liver is characterized by replacement of necrotic liver tissue by fibrosis, scar tissue, and regenerative nodules. The most common causes of this devastating condition are chronic alcohol abuse and chronic hepatitis due to HBV and/or HCV infection. Alcoholic cirrhosis of the liver develops in 10–20% of individuals who drink heavily, usually for a decade or more. The process is accelerated when alcohol abuse is combined with chronic hepatitis.

Heavy chronic alcohol consumption (greater than 80 grams daily for more than a decade) is estimated to increase the risk of developing hepatocellular carcinoma by more than fivefold, and if severe alcoholic liver cirrhosis develops, the risk approaches 1% per year (Morgan, Mandayam, and Jamal, 2004). Furthermore, chronic alcohol abuse in combination with chronic hepatitis C doubles the risk compared to hepatitis C alone, and even in the absence of liver cirrhosis and hepatitis, alcohol abuse increases the risk of hepatocellular carcinoma by more than fourfold (Chiesa et al., 2000). Alcohol is the primary risk factor for hepatocellular carcinoma in populations of many developed nations such as the United States and Italy.

Other Risk Factors for Hepatocellular Carcinoma

Acute and chronic hepatic porphyrias are inherited genetic disorders in heme biosynthesis that predispose to the development of hepatocellular carcinoma.

Heme is the oxygen-binding component of hemoglobin in red blood cells and it is also a key element of many enzymes of the P-450 system in the liver. This enzyme family is important in converting potentially harmful substances such as alcohol, drugs, and carcinogens to inactive metabolites destined for excretion. Thus, the pathogenesis of hepatocellular carcinoma in genetic carriers of this heme disorder may be due to inadequate detoxification and persistence of harmful substances in the liver.

In patients with acute hepatic porphyria, the calculated risk of hepatocellular carcinoma is increased 61-fold compared to normal individuals (Kauppinen and Mustajoki, 1988); furthermore, the risk increase appears to be several fold higher in women who carry this genetic disorder compared to men (Andant et al., 1998). Both active and latent genetic carriers of acute hepatic porphyrias are at risk and patients with acute hepatic porphyria should be monitored for hepatocellular carcinoma.

Several other risk factors appear to modify the risk of developing hepatocellular carcinoma. These include cigarette smoking, obesity and certain comorbid conditions such as hemochromatosis (excess deposition of iron in the liver and other organs), and Wilson's disease (excess deposition of copper in the liver). Also, vinyl chloride, a compound used in the plastics industry, can cause a rare form of liver cancer called *hepatic angiosarcoma* that appears many years after exposure (Baxter, 1976; Chuang, La Vecchia, and Boffetta, 2009).

Prevention of Hepatocellular Carcinoma

Primary prevention of the majority of liver cancer cases worldwide is now feasible, thanks to the development of a vaccine against HBV. This has been shown to be effective in preventing infection in childhood. A dramatic demonstration of the results of community vaccination is already available from Taiwan, where HBV immunization of newborns was introduced in 1984; for children aged 6–9 years in birth cohorts receiving vaccination, there was a dramatic decrease in the incidence of liver cancer (Chang et al., 1997; Thomas and Zhu, 2005).

EPIDEMIOLOGY OF CHOLANGIOCARCINOMA

Cholangiocarcinoma is a relative rare malignancy that arises from the epithelial lining of the gallbladder or bile ducts that drain bile from the liver into the small intestine. The annual incidence is highest in certain regions of Southeast Asia which is attributable to endemic liver parasites. The annual incidence in northern Thailand was estimated at 135 per 100,000 in men and 43 per 100,000 in women compared to only 1–2 cases per 100,000 in the United States (Green et al., 1991). Without complete resection, this tumor has an extremely poor prognosis.

In certain regions of Asia, chronic colonization with the liver flukes *Opisthorchis viverrini* (found in Thailand, Laos, and Malaysia) or *Clonorchis sinensis* (found in Japan, Korea, and Vietnam) markedly heighten the risk of developing cholangiocarcinoma (Watanapa, 1996; Watanapa and Watanapa, 2002). The highest annual incidence rates (334 and 104 per 100,000 for males and females, respectively) were observed in the northern Thailand province of *Khon Kaen* where *Opisthorchis viverrini* is endemic (Green et al., 1991). In an epidemiologic study in Pusan, Korea, infection by *Clonorchis sinensis* was associated with a threefold increase in the risk (Shin et al., 1996).

The life cycle of liver flukes involves a larva stage in snails and an encysted larval stage (metacercaria) in fish. Human infection results from the consumption of uncooked (raw) freshwater fish contaminated with the metacercarial form of the parasite (Markell and Voge, 1976).

In developed countries such as the United States, the most common risk factor for the development of cholangiocarcinoma is the presence of primary sclerosing cholangitis, an inflammatory disease of the bile ducts that arises in patients with ulcerative colitis. Epidemiologic investigations suggest that up to 30% of individuals with sclerosing cholangitis may eventually develop cholangiocarcinoma (Rosen et al., 1991). Other risk factors identified by some investigators include chronic alcohol abuse, hepatitis, cirrhosis, HIV disease, congenital liver abnormalities (choledochal cysts), hepatolithiasis (liver stones), and cholelithiasis (gallstones).

Thorotrast, a radiologic contrast medium, was widely used throughout the world from 1920–1950. This ionizing compound has a half-life of 400 years and is retained in the liver where it caused the eventual development of cholangiocarcinoma in some patients many years after their exposure. Thorotrast was banned from use in the United States in the 1950s due to its carcinogenicity (Zhu, Lauwers, and Tanabe, 2004).

Multiple studies have documented a steady increase in the incidence of intrahepatic cholangiocarcinoma over the past several decades; increases have been seen in North America, Europe, Asia, and Australia (Patel, 2001; Patel, 2002). The reasons for the increasing occurrence of cholangiocarcinoma are unclear; improved diagnostic methods may be partially responsible, but the prevalence of potential risk factors for cholangiocarcinoma such as HBV and HCV infections have also been increasing in some populations during this time frame. In a recent meta-analysis of case control studies of cholangiocarcinoma, the odds ratios were highest for individuals chronically infected with liver flukes (summary OR = 4.8) but also consistently elevated for individuals with hepatitis B (summary OR = 2.6) or hepatitis C (summary OR = 1.8) (Shin et al., 2010).

● ● ● REFERENCES

Alter, M.J. (1995). Epidemiology of hepatitis C in the West. *Semin Liver Dis, 15,* 5–14.

Alter, M.J. (1997). Epidemiology of Hepatitis C. *Hepatology,* 3(Suppl 1), 62S–65S.

Alterkruse, S.F., Kosary, C.L., Krapcho, M., Neyman, N., Aminou, R., Waldron, W., Ruhl, J., Howlader, N., Tatalovich, B.K., Cho, H., Mariotto, A., Eisner, M.P., Lewis, D.R., Cronin, K., Chen, H.S., Feuer, E.J., Stinchcomb, D.G., & Edwards, B.K. (2010). SEER Cancer Statistics Review, 1975–2007. *Surveillance Epidemiology and End Results.* National Cancer Institute. National Institutes of Health, Bethesda MD.

Andant, C., Puy, H., Faivre, J., & Deybach, J.C. (1998). *NEJM, 338,* 1853–1854.

American Cancer Society. (2007). Global Cancer Facts and Figures, 2007. Atlanta, Georgia.

Baxter, P.J. (1976). Epidemiological studies of PVC manufacturers and fabricators, and primary angiosarcoma of the liver. *Proc R Soc Med,* 69(4), 297–299.

Beasley, R.P., Huang, L.Y., Lin, C., & Chien, C. (1981). Hepatocellular carcinoma and HBV: A prospective study of 22,707 men in Taiwan. *Lancet,* 2, 1129–1133.

Blumberg, B.S. (2002). Baruch Blumberg—hepatitis B and beyond. Interviewed by Pam Das. *The Lancet infectious diseases,* 2(12), 767–771.

Blumberg, B.S., Alter, H.J., & Visnich, S. (1965). A "new" antigen in leukemia sera. *JAMA,* 252(2), 252–257.

Bonino, F., Chiaberge, E., Maran, E., & Piantino, P. (1987). Serological markers of HBV infectivity. *Annali dell'Istituto superiore di sanita,* 24(2), 217–223.

Campbell, J., Hagan, H., Latka, M., Garfein, R., Golub, E., Coady, M.,…Thomas, D., Strathdee, S. (2006). High prevalence of alcohol use among hepatitis C virus antibody positive injection drug users in three US cities. *Drug Alcohol Depend*, 81(3), 259–265.

Cao, G.W. (2009). Clinical relevance and public health significance of hepatitis B virus genomic variations. *World Journal of Gastroenterology: WJG*, 15(46), 5761–5769.

Caruntu, F.A., & Benea, L. (2006). Acute hepatitis C virus infection: Diagnosis, pathogenesis, treatment. *Journal of Gastrointestinal and Liver Diseases: JGLD*, 15(3), 249–256.

Chang, M.H., Chen, C.J., Lai, M.S., Hsu, H.M., Wu, T.C., Kong, M.S., for the Taiwan Childhood Hepatoma Study Group. (1997). Universal hepatitis B vaccination in Taiwan and the incidence of hepatocellular carcinoma in children. *New England Journal of Medicine*, 336(26), 1855–1859.

Chen, C.J., Yang, H.I., Su, J., et al. (2006). Risk of hepatocellular carcinoma across a biological gradient of serum hepatitis B virus DNA level. *JAMA*, 295(1), 65–73.

Chen, T.Y., Ding, E.L., Seage Iii, G.R., & Kim, A.Y. (2009). Meta-analysis: Increased mortality associated with hepatitis C in HIV-infected persons is unrelated to HIV disease progression. *Clin Infect Dis*, 49(10), 1605–1615.

Chiesa, R., Donato, F., Tagger, A., Favret, M., Ribero, M.L., Nardi, G.,…Callea, F. (2000). Etiology of hepatocellular carcinoma in Italian patients with and without cirrhosis. *Cancer Epidemiol Biomarkers Prev*, 9, 213–216.

Choo, Q., Kuo, G., Weiner, A., Overby, L., Bradley, D., & Houghton, M. (1989). Isolation of a cDNA clone derived from a blood-borne non-A, non-B viral hepatitis genome. *Science*, 244(4902), 359–362.

Chuang, S.-C., La Vecchia, C., & Boffetta, P. (2009). Liver cancer: Descriptive epidemiology and risk factors other than HBV and HCV infection. *Cancer Letters*, 286, 9–14.

Dane, D. (1970). Virus-like particles in serum of patients with Australia-antigen-associated hepatitis. *Lancet*, 295, 695–698.

Ding, L.P., Gui, X.E., Zhang, Y.X., Gao, S.C., & Yang, R.R. (2009). Impact of human immunodeficiency virus infection on the course of hepatitis C virus infection. A meta-analysis. *World J Gastroent*, 28(3), 996–1008.

Donato, F., Boffetta, P., & Puoti, M.A. (1998). Meta-analysis of epidemiological studies on the combined effect of Hepatitis B and C virus infections in causing hepatocellular carcinoma. *Int J Cancer*, 75, 347–354.

Frank, C., Mohamed, M., Strickland, G., Lavanchy, D., Arthur, R., Magder, L.,…Sallam, I. (2000). The role of parenteral anti-schistosomal therapy in the spread of hepatitis C virus in Egypt. *Lancet*, 355(9207), 887–891.

Galibert, F., Mandart, E., Fitoussi, F., Tiollais, P., & Charnay, P. (1979). Nucleotide sequence of the hepatitis B virus genome (subtype ayw) cloned in E. Coli. *Nature*, 281(5733), 646.

Giordano, T.P., Kramer, J.R., Souchek, J., Richardson, P., & El Serag, H.B. (2004). Cirrhosis and hepatocellular carcinoma in HCV-infected veterans with and without hepatitis C virus: A cohort study, 1992–2001. *Arch Intern Med*, 164, 2249–2254.

Green, A., Uttaravichien, T., Bhudhisawasdi, V., Chartbanchachai, W., Elkins, D.B., Marieng, E.O.,…Haswell-Elkins, N. (1991). Cholangiocarcinoma in northeast Thailand. A hospital-based study. *Trop Geogr Med*, 43(1–2), 193–198.

Groopman, J.D. (1993). Molecular dosimetry methods for assessing human aflatoxin exposure. In D.L. Easton & J.D. Groopman (Eds.), *The toxicology of aflatoxins: Human health, veterinary and agricultural signficance* (pp. 259–279). London: Academic Press.

Hou, J., Liu, Z., & Gu, F. (2005). Epidemiology and prevention of hepatitis B virus infection. *Int J Med Sci*, 2, 50–57.

International Agency for Research on Cancer. (1994). IARC monographs on the evaluation of carcinogenic risks in humans. *International Agency for Research on Cancer, 59*, 1994.

Iloeje, U.H., Yang, H.I., Jen, C.L., et al. (2007). Risk and predictors of mortality associated with chronic hepatitis B infection. *Clin Gastroenterol Hepatol, 5*(8), 921–931.

Kauppinen, R., & Mustajoki, P. (1988). Acute hepatic porphyria and hepatocellular carcinoma. *Br J Cancer, 57*(1), 117–120.

Kew, M.C. (1996). Hepatitis B and C viruses and hepatocelluar carcinoma. *Clin Lab Med, 16*, 395–406.

Kirk, G.D., Bah, E., & Montesano, R. (2006). Molecular epidemiology of human liver cancer: Insights into etiology, pathogenesis and prevention from The Gambia, West Africa. *Carcinogenesis, 27*(10), 2070–2082.

Kirk, G.D., Lesi, O.A., Mendy, M., Akano, A.O., Sam, O., Goedert, J.J.,…Montesano, R. (2004). The Gambia Liver Cancer Study: Infection with hepatitis B and C and the risk of hepatocellular carcinoma in West Africa. *Hepatology, 39*(1), 211–219.

Kuo, G., Choo, Q., Alter, H., Gitnick, G., Redeker, A., Purcell, R.,…Stevens, C. (1989). An assay for circulating antibodies to a major etiologic virus of human non-A, non-B hepatitis. *Science, 244*(4902), 362–364.

Markell, E.K., & Voge, M. (1976). *Medical parasitology*, 4th Edition. W.B. Saunders Company, Philadelphia, Pennsylvania.

McGovern, B., Wurcel, A., Kim, A., Schulze zur Wiesch, J., Bica, I., Zaman, M.,…Lauer, G. (2006). Acute hepatitis C virus infection in incarcerated injection drug users. *Clin Infect Dis, 42*(12), 1663–1670.

Montesano, R., Hainaut, P., & Wild, C.P. (1997). Hepatocellular carcinoma: From gene to public health. *J Natl Cancer Inst, 898*, 1844–1851.

Morgan, T.R., Mandayam, S., & Jamal, M.M. (2004). Alcohol and hepatocellular carcinoma. *Gastroenterology, 127*(5 Suppl 1), S87–S96.

Nguyen, V.T.T., Law, M.G., & Dore, G.J. (2009). Hepatitis B-related hepatocellular carcinoma: Epidemiological characteristics and disease burden. *J Viral Hepat, 16*(7), 453–463.

NIH Consensus Statement on Management of Hepatitis C. (2002). NIH consensus statement. *Sci Statements, 19*(3), 1–46.

Parkin, D.M., Pisani, P., Muñoz, N., & Ferlay, J. (1999). The global health burden of infection associated cancer. In R.A. Weiss, V. Beral, & R. Newton (Eds.), *Infections and human cancer. Cancer surveys, 33*, 5–33.

Parkin, M., Bray, F., Ferlay, J., & Pisani, P. (2005). Global cancer statistics, 2002. *CA Cancer J Clin, 55*, 74–108.

Patel, T. (2001). Increasing incidence and mortality of primary intrahepatic cholangiocarcinoma in the United States. *Hepatology, 33*(6), 1353–1357.

Patel, T. (2002). Worldwide trends in mortality from biliary tract malignancies. *BMC Cancer, 2*, 10.

Robbins, S.L., & Cotran, R.S. (1979). Pathologic Basis of Disease. 2nd Edition. W.B. Saunders, Philadelphia.

Rosen, C., Nagorney, D., Wiesner, R., Coffey, R., & LaRusso, N. (1991). Cholangiocarcinoma complicating primary sclerosing cholangitis. *Ann Surg, 213*(1), 21–25.

Ross, R.K., Yuan, J.M., Yu, M.C., Wogan, G.N., Qian, G.S., Tu, J.T.,…Henderson, B.E. (1992). Urinary aflatoxin biomarkers and risk of hepatocellular carcinoma. *Lancet, 339*(8799), 943–946.

Shapiro, C.N. (1993). Epidemiology of hepatitis B. *The Pediatric Infectious Disease Journal, 12*(5), 433–437.

Shin, H., Lee, C., Park, H., Seol, S., Chung, J., Choi, H., Ahn, Y., & Shigemastu, T. (1996). Hepatitis B and C virus, *Clonorchis sinensis* for the risk of liver cancer: A case-control study in Pusan, Korea. *Int J Epidemiol, 25*(5), 933–940.

Shin, H.R., Oh, J.K., Masuyer, E., Curado, M.P., Bouvard, V., Fang, Y.Y., Wiangnon, S., Sripa, B., & Hong, S.T. (2010). Epidemiology of cholangiocarcinoma: An update focusing on risk factors. *Cancer Sci, 101*(3), 579–585.

Stern, M.C., Umbach, D.M., Yu, M.C., London, S.J., Zhang, Z.Q., & Taylor, J.A. (2001). Hepatitis B, aflatoxin B(1), and p53 codon 249 mutation in hepatocellular carcinomas from Guangxi, People's Republic of China, and a meta-analysis of existing studies. *Cancer Epidemiol Biomarkers Prev, 10*(6), 617–625.

Sylla, A., Diallo, M.S., Castegnaro, J.J., & Wild, C.P. (1999). Interactions between hepatitis B virus infection and exposure to aflatoxins with the development of hepatocellular carcinoma: A molecular epidemiological approach. *Mutat Res, 428*, 187–196.

Tanaka, H., Hiyama, T., Tsukuma, H., Okubo, Y., Yamano, H., Kitada, A., & Fujimoto, I. (1994). Prevalence of second generation antibody to hepatits C antibody among voluntary blood donors in Osaka, Japan. *Cancer Causes Control, 5*, 409–413.

Thomas, M., & Zhu, A. (2005). Hepatocellular carcinoma: The need for progress. *J Clin Oncol, 23*(13), 2892–2899.

Vandamme, P., & Van Herck, K. (2007). A review of the long-term protection after hepatitis A and B vaccination. *Travel Medicine and Infectious Disease, 5*(2), 79–84.

Wang, L.Y., Hatch, M., Chen, C.J., Levin, B., You, S.L., Lu, S.N.,…Santella, R.M. (1996). Aflatoxin exposure and risk of hepatocellular carcinoma in Taiwan. *Int J Cancer, 67*(5), 620–625.

Watanapa, P. (1996). Cholangiocarcinoma in patients with opisthorchiasis. *Br J Surg, 83*(8), 1062–1064.

Watanapa, P., & Watanapa, W. (2002). Liver fluke-associated cholangiocarcinoma. *Br J Surg, 89*(8), 962–970.

Wilcox, R.D. (2009). Hepatocelluar carcinoma and HIV: Is there an association? *HIV Clinician, 21*(4), 11–12.

Williams, J.H., Phillips, T.D., Jolly, P.E., Stiles, J.K., Jolly, C.M., & Aggarwal, D. (2004). Human aflatoxicosis in developing countries: A review of toxicology, exposure, potential health consequences, and interventions. *Am J Clin Nutr, 80*(5), 1106–1122.

WHO. (2009). Death and DALY estimates for 2004 by cause for WHO Member States (Persons, all ages). World Health Organization, Geneva, Switzerland.

Yang, H.I., Lu, S.N., Liaw, Y.F., You, S.L., Su, C.A., Wang, L.Y.,…for the Taiwan Community-Based Cancer Screening Project Group. (2002). Hepatitis B e Antigen and the risk of hepatocellular carcinoma. *New Engl J Med, 347*(3), 168–174.

Yeh, F.S., Yu, M.C., Mo, C.C., Luo, S., Tong, M.J., & Henderson, B.E. (1989). Hepatitis B virus, aflatoxins, and hepatocelluar carcinoma in southern Guangxi, China. *Cancer Research, 49*, 2506–2509.

Yu, M.W., & Chen, C.J. (1994). Hepatitis B and C viruses in the development of hepatocellular carcinoma. *Crit Rev Oncol Hematol, 17*, 71–91.

Zhu, A., Lauwers, G., & Tanabe, K. (2004). Cholangiocarcinoma in association with Thorotrast exposure. *J Hepatobiliary Pancreat Surg, 11*(6), 430–433.

Zuckerman, A.J. (1996). Hepatitis viruses. In: S. Baron et al. (Eds.), *Baron's medical microbiology* (4th ed.). Texas: University of Texas Medical Branch.

19

Epidemiology of Breast Cancer

GLOBAL IMPACT OF BREAST CANCER

Breast cancer strikes 1.3 million women and results in 465,000 deaths annually throughout the world. It is the most commonly diagnosed cancer and the second leading cause of cancer death among women (only lung cancer causes more deaths). Breast cancer incidence is highly variable among populations ranging from low rates of 19 per 100,000 women in China, Africa, and India to high rates exceeding 80 cases per 100,000 in Scandinavian and European countries, the United States, and Great Britain (**Table 19.1**). Among developed countries, the United States has the highest annual incidence rates of breast cancer, exceeding 100 cases per 100,000. The lifetime risk of breast cancer for American women is approximately 1 in 8 compared to a lifetime risk of only 1 in 66 for Chinese women.

Breast cancer mortality rates show a narrower range than incidence rates, ranging from 5.5 deaths per 100,000 Chinese women to 27.8 deaths per 100,000 Danish women. The incidence and mortality rates of breast cancer tend to be higher for women in developed countries compared to those in underdeveloped countries (**Figure 19.1**).

BREAST CANCER DETECTION, STAGING, AND SURVIVAL

Mammography is a radiographic imaging process using low-dose X-rays to assist in the detection and diagnosis of breast cancer. The goal of mammography as a screening tool is to detect breast tumors early in their growth and development so they can be completely excised by qualified breast surgeons.

Screening mammography together with effective biopsy, accurate pathologic evaluation, and surgical excision of breast tumors have been shown to reduce the mortality from breast cancer by approximately 30% in women over the age of 50 years. Because of the difficulty in discriminating normal active mammary glands from abnormal neoplastic growths in women

Table 19.1	Annual Incidence and Mortality Rates of Breast Cancer per 100,000 Women	
Nation	**Incidence**	**Mortality**
China	18.7	5.5
Africa (Zimbabwe)	19.0	14.1
India	19.1	10.4
Japan	32.7	8.3
Brazil	46.0	14.1
Singapore	48.7	15.8
Italy	74.4	18.9
Switzerland	81.7	19.8
Australia	83.2	18.4
Canada	84.3	21.1
Netherlands	86.7	27.5
United Kingdom	87.2	24.3
Sweden	87.8	17.3
Denmark	88.7	27.8
France	91.9	21.5
United States	101.1	19.0

Source: Data from J. Ferlay, F. Bray, P. Pisani and D.M. Parkin. GLOBOCAN 2002. Cancer Incidence, Mortality and Prevalence Worldwide. IARC Cancer Base No. 5, version 2.0. IARC Press, Lyon, 2004.

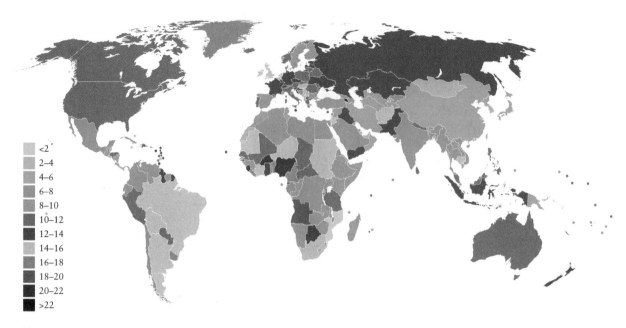

Figure 19.1 Global Breast Cancer Mortality, 2004.

Source: Data from World Health Organization. The global burden of disease: 2004 update. Geneva, WHO, 2008. Available at www.who.int/evidence/bod.

during their reproductive years, there is controversy about the value of screening for breast cancer by mammography in premenopausal women (before age 50). Currently, the American National Cancer Institute recommends that women initiate biannual screening for breast cancer by mammography at age 40–49, whereas after age 50 screening is recommended on an annual basis. Other imaging techniques such as ultrasound, magnetic resonance imaging (MRI), and positron emission tomography (PET) are now being widely used by physicians to assist in the evaluation and diagnosis of breast tumors. Breast self-examination (BSE) and physician examination are also considered essential components of regular breast care.

PATHOLOGY OF BREAST CANCER

Tumor staging refers to the microscopic evaluation of tissue by a pathologist to assess size, exact anatomic location, growth, and spread of a cancerous lesion. It is important to realize that while imaging procedures are important for the identification of suspicious lesions, the ultimate diagnosis of breast cancer (or any other malignant neoplasm) must be confirmed by microscopic examination of cancerous tissue (obtained by biopsy) by a qualified pathologist.

Breast cancer survival is highest when tumors are detected prior to breaching the basement membrane upon which most solid tumors develop and invading

contiguous tissues or lymph nodes (Carcinoma *in situ*, stage I) whereas survival is lowest with late detection after tumors have spread (metastasized) to other sites (**Table 19.2**). Early stage breast cancer is effectively "cured" by complete surgical excision with clear margins (no evidence of spread beyond the surgical margins) whereas later stage disease is much more resistant to therapy and is conventionally treated by a combination of treatment modalities including chemotherapy, radiation therapy, and hormonal therapy and immunomodulation.

MECHANISMS OF BREAST CARCINOGENESIS

Breast cancer arises from the epithelial cells that line the ductal and glandular structures of the mammary gland. Breast carcinogenesis is most probably due to excess stimulation of these cells by estrogen. Estrogen is a powerful mitogen that stimulates cell proliferation by activating estrogen receptors of the cell surface membrane. Sustained excessive estrogen stimulation may lead to heightened proliferation and atypia of the mammary epithelium, which are believed to be forerunners of breast cancer.

Breast cancer primarily occurs in women, although occasionally breast tumors do develop in men, particularly in association with Klinefelter's syndrome, where there is an extra X chromosome in the karyotype (XXY) or by ingestion of synthetic

Table 19.2	Breast Cancer Survival by Stage at Detection	
Stage at Diagnosis	Description of Stage at Diagnosis	Five-Year Survival (%)
0	Carcinoma *in situ* (no invasion)	100%
I	Tumor < 2 cm with no lymphatic spread)	100%
IIA	Tumor ≥ 2 cm with no lymphatic spread	92%
IIB	Spread to axillary lymph nodes	81%
IIIA	Spread to axillary and other lymph nodes	67%
IIIB	Spread to lymph nodes and opposite breast	54%
IV	Widespread metastatic cancer	20%

Source: Data from American Cancer Society (2005). Cancer Facts and Figures, 2005.

estrogens such as diethylstibesterol that has been used for the treatment of cancer of the prostate.

Several theories have been proposed to explain breast carcinogenesis. Perhaps the best known of these theories relates breast cancer risk to the sustained stimulus of estrogen over many years. The "estrogen-stimulus" theory of breast cancer postulates that the risk is enhanced with a sustained continuum of estrogen cycles unbroken by pregnancy or other mechanisms of estrogen ablation such as ovariectomy. As discussed below, both endogenous and exogenous factors may potentially increase estrogen stimulus of the mammary gland in association with breast cancer development.

A derivative of the estrogen-stimulus hypothesis is the "estrogen window" hypothesis (Korenman, 1980). This postulate states that human breast cancer is induced by environmental carcinogens in a susceptible mammary gland, and that susceptibility is due to unopposed estrogen stimulation early in life during the onset of puberty (menses) and later in life with the onset of menopause. By this theory, susceptibility to induction of breast cancer declines with establishment of normal luteal phase progesterone secretion and becomes very low during pregnancy.

RISK FACTORS FOR BREAST CANCER

Several risk factors have been identified that increase a woman's chance of developing breast cancer. Nevertheless, cause and effect cannot be established in most individual cases. The classical risk factors of breast cancer were first established in an early case-control study of breast cancer cases and matched controls conducted in 1923 by Dr. Janet Elizabeth Lane-Claypon in the United Kingdom. Dr. Lane-Claypon compared 500 women with breast cancer (cases) to 500 women of similar age with no history

of cancer (controls) in the first documented epidemiologic case-control study (Winkelstein, 2006). Her groundbreaking study was the first to elucidate the well-known profile of classical breast cancer risk factors including familial and genetic predisposition, early menses, delayed reproductive history, nulliparity, absence of lactation, late menopause, and the natural process of aging.

During the reproductive years, estrogens are produced by the ovaries, whereas after menopause the source of circulating estrogens is biosynthesis in fat and muscle cells catalyzed by the enzyme aromatase. The risk of premenopausal breast cancer increases two- to threefold with either nulliparity or "late" first pregnancy (after age 30). Parous women who do not breastfeed are also at increased risk.

Genetic Predisposition to Breast Cancer

A strong family history (breast cancer in a first-degree or second-degree relative) increases the risk of breast cancer by three- to fivefold. Genetic or familial predisposition is identifiable for approximately 5–10% of women diagnosed with breast cancer. Hallmarks of familial predisposition to breast cancer include early age of onset, an excess of bilateral disease, and breast cancer in familial association with other malignancies such as ovarian cancer and endometrial cancer.

Two heritable genetic mutations have been identified that predispose to familial breast and ovarian cancer, *BRCA-1* and *BRCA-2*. The *BRCA-1* gene was discovered in 1990 by King and colleagues and is located on the long arm of chromosome 17 (Hall et al., 1990). Subsequently, a second breast cancer gene, *BRCA-2*, was identified on the long arm of chromosome 13 (Wooster et al., 1994). A mutation in either *BRCA* gene predisposes heterozygous female carriers to both breast cancer and, to a lesser extent, ovarian cancer. The lifetime risk of breast cancer among women who carry a single mutation in either *BRCA-1* or *BRCA-2* is approximately 85%, whereas the lifetime ovarian cancer risk for women with a *BRCA-1* mutation is 54%, compared to 24% for women with a *BRCA-2* mutation (King et al., 2003).

Both *BRCA-1* and *BRCA-2* are tumor suppressor genes that upon transcription form proteins essential for the repair of double-stranded DNA breaks (Boulton, 2006). Mutated *BRCA* genes result in proteins that do not function properly in DNA repair, thereby promoting accumulation of genetic errors and carcinogenesis.

Breast cancer has also been observed in individuals with Cowden's disease and Sipple syndrome, two very rare genetic conditions caused by germline autosomal dominant mutations (Eng, 1998). Cowden's disease is caused by a mutated tumor suppressor gene called *PTEN* located on chromosome 11 that normally helps regulate cell division and cell senescence (apoptosis). Mutations in the *PTEN* gene cause the development of small benign papules of the skin and mucous membranes (called hamartomas) and often result in thyroid lesions such as goiter, follicular adenomas, and thyroid cancer, as well as breast cancer, uterine cancer, and renal cancer. Sipple syndrome is caused by a variant of a proto-oncogene called *RET* located on chromosome 10 that regulates an important cellular growth factor (transforming growth factor beta or TGF-β). Carriers of the *RET* mutation develop malignancies of the endocrine system (specifically medullary thyroid cancer, pheochromocytoma, and occasionally breast cancer) (Lima and Smith, 1971).

Estrogen Replacement Therapy and Postmenopausal Breast Cancer

Approximately 75% of breast cancers are diagnosed in women after they undergo menopause. A number of investigations have examined the association between hormone replacement therapy and postmenopausal breast cancer risk, and most have reported a modest increase in breast cancer risk with estrogen alone but a greater risk for estrogen plus progestin. For example, in the *Million Women Study* conducted in the United Kingdom, current use of estrogen alone increased the risk of invasive breast cancer by 30% compared to a twofold risk increase with current use of estrogen plus progestin (Beral, 2003). Similar results were observed in the randomized clinical trial of estrogen plus progestin and the prospective observational cohort of postmenopausal women of the *Women's Health Initiative* (WHI) in the United States. The WHI results showed that breast cancer risk doubled after about five years of using estrogen plus progestin but

declined soon after discontinuation of hormone therapy (Chlebowski et al., 2009).

Results of studies of hormone replacement therapy involving only estrogen are less clear with some studies finding an increase in the risk of breast cancer whereas others report either no effect or a decrease in the risk. In the WHI clinical trial of conjugated equine estrogen (CEE) versus placebo for women who had undergone hysterectomy prior to enrollment, the risk of invasive breast cancer was *reduced* by 23% in women who received CEE (Anderson et al., 2004). However, 40% of the women in the trial also reported having bilateral oophorectomies prior to enrollment, and an alternative explanation of results is that discontinuation of estrogen replacement among oophorectomized women in the placebo arm may have heightened their risk by removing feedback inhibition of estrogen biosynthesis in breast tissues.

Several studies show consistency in observing an interaction between body mass and estrogen replacement therapy (ERT) in elevating the risk of breast cancer in postmenopausal women (Kaufman et al., 1991; Palmer et al., 1991; Colditz et al., 1992; Stanford et al., 1995; Harris et al., 1996). Specifically, lean women who receive ERT after menopause have been found to be at significantly higher risk than heavier women (**Figure 19.2**). One possible explanation for this is that lean women who receive ERT may have relatively higher concentrations of exogenous estrogens per unit of breast tissue thereby increasing carcinogenesis.

Body Mass and Postmenopausal Breast Cancer

Body mass index (BMI) shows differential effects on premenopausal versus postmenopausal breast cancer risk. Before menopause, BMI shows little association with risk, whereas after menopause, the risk of breast cancer increases two- to threefold among women with high BMI, presumably due to heightened estrogen biosynthesis through conversion of other steroids to estrogen by the enzyme aromatase in adipose tissue. The elevated risk of postmenopausal disease is most evident among women who gain excessive weight throughout the reproductive years and have no exposure to exogenous estrogens after menopause (Harris, Namboodiri, and Wynder, 1992).

Dietary Fat and Breast Cancer

From an etiologic perspective, it is of interest that rates of breast cancer are changing in populations which historically have been at low risk whereas the rates have remained relatively constant in populations at higher risk. For example, breast cancer mortality rates among Japanese, Indian, and Chinese

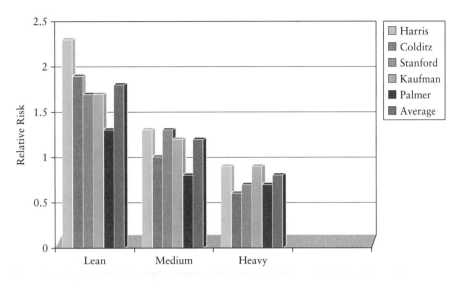

Figure 19.2 Estrogen Replacement Therapy and Breast Cancer Risk by Body Mass.

Source: Data from Harris RE, Namboodiri KK, Farrar WB, Solano SM, Wynder EL (1996). Hormone replacement therapy and breast cancer risk. *JAMA* 275(15):1158.

women have increased approximately threefold in the past 2 decades whereas the United States, United Kingdom, and European (French) rates have remained constant or slightly declined (**Figure 19.3**). Concurrently, the Japanese, Indian, and Chinese diets have also changed dramatically with higher intakes of fat and calories. However, other risk factors may also be involved since birth rates are declining, age at first pregnancy is being delayed, and nulliparity is increasing in these populations.

A well-known but controversial hypothesis of breast cancer etiology is known as the *dietary fat hypothesis*. An extension of this hypothesis states

that breast cancer development is due to intake of certain types of essential polyunsaturated fatty acids (PUFA) that increase inflammation and estrogen biosynthesis and thus promote breast cancer development (Harris, 2002). Karmali and colleagues first observed the divergent effects of n-6 versus n-3 PUFA in animal models of breast carcinogenesis. Their studies clearly show that proinflammatory n-6 fatty acids such as linoleic acid promote tumor development and metastasis whereas anti-inflammatory n-3 fatty acids such as linolenic acid are inhibitory (Karmali et al., 1993).

Important supportive evidence for the dietary fat hypothesis of breast cancer comes from chronological

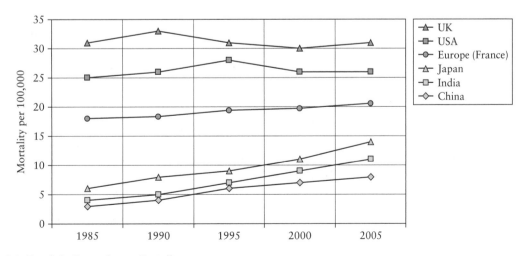

Figure 19.3 Trends in Breast Cancer Mortality.

Source: Data from American Cancer Society; National Vital Statistics, Japan; Center for Health Information and Statistics, China; Office for National Statistics, UK; French National Institute for Health and Medical Research; WHO Mortality Data.

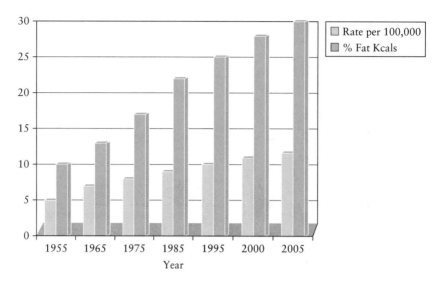

Figure 19.4 Breast Cancer Mortality and Dietary Fat, Japan: 1955–2005.

Source: Data from Harris RE. Epidemiology of breast cancer and nonsteroidal anti-inflammatory drugs: extension of the dietary fat hypothesis of breast cancer. In: COX-2 Blockade in Cancer Prevention and Therapy, edited by Harris RE. Humana Press, Totowa, NJ, 2002, 57-68; Minami et al (2004). The increase of female breast cancer incidence in Japan: emergence of birth cohort effect. *Int J Cancer* 108(6):901-906; Kawamura T, Sobue T (2005). Comparison of breast cancer mortality in five countries: France, Italy, Japan, the UK and the USA from the WHO Mortality Database (1960–2000). *Jpn J Clin Oncol* 35(12):758–759; Saika K, Sobue T (2009). Epidemiology of breast cancer in Japan and the US. *Jap Med Assoc J* 52(1):39–44.

studies of Japanese women. Over the past half century, the age-adjusted breast cancer mortality rate among Japanese women has increased more than twofold, rising from less than 5 deaths per 100,000 in 1950 to nearly 12 deaths per 100,000 in 2006 (Saika and Sobue, 2009; Kawamura and Sobue, 2005). Notably, this gradual increase in breast cancer mortality among Japanese women closely parallels a threefold increase in per capita fat consumption over the same time period (**Figure 19.4**). In 1950, less than 10% of kilocalories were derived from fat, whereas in 2005, the level had risen to nearly 30% (Harris, 2002; Minami et al., 2004).

While the correlated time trends of breast cancer rates and per capita dietary changes in certain populations support a role for dietary fat, analytic (case control and cohort) studies of diet and breast cancer have yielded inconsistent results, perhaps due to the difficulty of accurately assessing dietary exposure on an individual basis. As a consequence, there is controversy among epidemiologists regarding the role of dietary fat or other dietary factors in the genesis of breast cancer.

Oral Contraceptives and Premenopausal Breast Cancer

Oral contraceptive (OC) use has been found to influence the development of breast cancer in premenopausal women but not postmenopausal women (Mills

et al., 1989; Romieu, Berlin, and Colditz, 1990). In a meta-analysis of 34 studies, OC use was found to increase the risk of premenopausal breast cancer in parous women (OR = 1.29) and nulliparous women (OR = 1.24), and the association was stronger when OCs were used before the first full-term pregnancy (OR = 1.44) (Kahlenborn et al., 2006). Conceivably, the OC content of estrogen and progestin heightens cancer risk by inducing hyperplasia of the breast epithelium in some premenopausal women.

Other Breast Cancer Risk Factors

Some investigations have noted a weak association between moderate alcohol consumption and breast cancer risk (Willett, Stampfer, and Colditz, 1989). Nevertheless, the results of independent studies are mixed and this too is a controversial issue in breast cancer epidemiology (Harris and Wynder, 1988; Wynder and Harris, 1989).

Certain endogenous conditions may also modulate the development of cancer of the breast. Fibrocystic disease with hyperplasia and/or atypia appears, in some instances, to antedate the development of cancer of the breast. In case-control studies, this condition elevates the risk of breast cancer by about two- to threefold.

Thyroid dysfunction has also been observed in association with breast cancer in some studies (Smyth, 1997). In particular, hypothyroidism may elevate breast cancer risk in certain individuals. The physiologic basis for this is presumptively the anti-estrogenic effect of thyroxin; that is, when thyroxin levels are diminished, estrogen levels rise, thereby enhancing breast cancer risk.

It is noteworthy that the highest risk target organ for development of breast cancer is the contralateral (opposite) breast of a woman who has already manifested unilateral disease. In addition, the familial breast cancer patient has a markedly enhanced risk for development of malignancy in the contralateral breast (about 50% over 20 years, postmastectomy) (Harris, Lynch, and Guirgis, 1978).

Many studies in biochemical epidemiology have been performed with the objective of identifying a biochemical marker of breast cancer risk. The various subtypes of estrogens (estradiol, estrone, and estriol) and their ratios, androgens and other steroids, polypeptide hormones such as prolactin, and various indices of these parameters have been tried; however, no single parameter or index of parameters have been developed that accurately predict an individual's risk for developing cancer of the breast.

PREVENTION OF BREAST CANCER

Breast cancer specimens ascertained by biopsy or surgical procedures (mastectomy) are routinely subjected to laboratory analysis of estrogen receptors (ER) and progesterone receptors (PR). Breast tumors

that are positive for ER/PR may respond to hormone therapy by administration of antiestrogenic compounds such as tamoxifen. Tamoxifen is now being offered to women treated for early stage breast cancer for protection against the development of second primary cancer in the contralateral breast.

Large independent clinical trials have been performed to examine the preventive activity of tamoxifen. While a US trial showed beneficial effects (Fisher et al., 1998), the results of two European trials were negative (Veronesi et al., 1998; Powles et al., 1998). In a fourth randomized clinical trial conducted in European centers, tamoxifen administration reduced the incidence of breast cancer by 32% compared to the control group, but despite this benefit, there was a significant *excess* of deaths in the tamoxifen group (25 vs. 11 deaths, P <0.03) (Cuzik et al., 2002). Nevertheless, the US FDA approved tamoxifen for use as a preventive agent in high-risk women. This action tends to disregard adverse side effects of the drug including increased risks of endometrial cancer, ER negative breast cancer, colon cancer, pulmonary embolus, and other thrombotic events.

Many epidemiologic studies have noted a significant preventive effect of nonsteroidal anti-inflammatory drugs (NSAIDs) against breast cancer. A meta-analysis of these investigations suggests that the risk of breast cancer is reduced by approximately 25% with regular use of common over-the-counter NSAIDs such as aspirin and ibuprofen (**Figure 19.5**) (Harris, 2009). Studies in molecular epidemiology

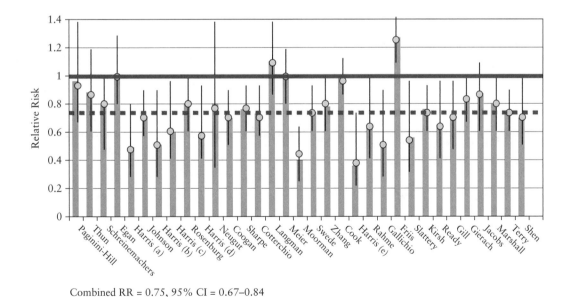

Combined RR = 0.75, 95% CI = 0.67–0.84

Figure 19.5 Breast Cancer and NSAIDs.

Source: Reproduced from Harris RE (2009). Cyclooxygenase-2 (COX-2) blockade in the chemoprevention of cancers of the colon, breast, prostate, and lung. *Inflammo-pharmacology* 17:1–13.

and in animals suggest that this effect is manifest primarily due to blockade of cyclooxygenase isozymes of the inflammatory cascade, particularly the inducible isoform, cyclooxygenase-2 (Harris, 2007).

SUMMARY OF BREAST CANCER EPIDEMIOLOGY

Breast cancer is a multifactorial disease promoted by sustained heightened exposure to endogenous or exogenous estrogens. Rates of breast cancer vary widely and are higher in developed countries such as the United States and United Kingdom and lower in developing countries such as India and China. Breast cancer risk appears to increase with high intake of essential polyunsaturated fats that promote inflammation and estrogen biosynthesis. Reproductive risk factors include early menses, nulliparity, late first pregnancy, absence of lactation, and late menopause, all of which increase exposure to endogenous estrogens. Estrogen replacement therapy (ERT) and high body mass increase breast cancer risk in postmenopausal women. Identifiable genetic factors account for only a small fraction of breast cancer cases. Studies in cancer control show that annual screening with mammography after age 50 is effective in detecting early breast lesions when they can be surgically excised with a high probability of long-term survival. Breast cancer prevention may be aided by taking synthetic or natural compounds with anti-inflammatory or antiestrogenic activity. Additional studies in molecular epidemiology are needed to more clearly delineate the way in which breast cancer risk factors interact to impact the natural history of this disease.

● ● ● REFERENCES

Anderson, G.L., Limacher, M., Assaf, A.R., et al. (2004). Effects of conjugated equine estrogen in postmenopausal women with hysterectomy: The Women's Health Initiative randomized controlled trial. *JAMA, 291*(14), 1701–1712.

Beral, V., & Million Women Study Collaborators. (2003). Breast cancer and hormone-replacement therapy in the Million Women Study. *Lancet, 362*(9382), 419–427.

Boulton, S.J. (2006). Cellular functions of the BRCA tumour-suppressor proteins. *Biochemical Society Transactions, 34*(5), 633–645.

Chlebowski, R.T., Kuller, L.H., Prentice, R.L., Stefanick, M.L., Manson, J.E., Gass, M., et al. (2009). Breast cancer after use of estrogen plus progestin in Postmenopausal Women. *N Engl J Med, 360*(6), 573–587.

Colditz, G.A., Stampfer, M.J., Willett, W.C., et al. (1992). Type of postmenopausal hormone use and risk of breast cancer: 12 year follow-up from the Nurses' Health Study. *Cancer Causes Control, 3*, 433–439.

Cuzick, J., Forbes, J., Edwards, R., Baum, M., Cawthorn, S., Coates, A., et al. (2002). First results from the International Breast Cancer Intervention Study (IBIS-I): A randomised prevention trial. *Lancet, 360*(9336), 817–824.

Eng, C. (1998). Genetics of Cowden syndrome: Through the looking glass of oncology. *Int J Oncol, 12*(3), 701–710.

Ferlay, J., Bray, F., Pisani, P., & Parkin, D.M. (2002). GLOBOCAN 2002. (2004). *Cancer incidence, mortality, and prevalence worldwide.* IARC Cancer Base No. 5, version 2.0. Lyon, France: IARC Press.

Fisher, B., Costantino, J.P., Wickerham, D.L., Redmond, C.K., Kavanah, M., Cronin, W.M., et al. (1998). Tamoxifen for prevention of breast cancer: Report of the National Surgical Adjuvant Breast and Bowel Project P-1 Study. *J Natl Cancer Inst, 90*, 1371–1388.

Hall, J.M., Lee, M.K., Newman, B., Morrow, J.E., Anderson, L.A., Huey, B., & King, M.C. (1990). Linkage of early-onset familial breast cancer to chromosome 17q21. *Science, 250*(4988), 1684–1689.

Harris, R.E., Lynch, H.T., & Guirgis, H.A. (1978). Familial breast cancer: Risk to the contralateral breast. *J Natl Cancer Inst, 60*, 955–960.

Harris, R.E., & Wynder, E.L. (1988). Breast cancer and alcohol consumption: A study in weak associations. *J Am Med Assoc, 259*(19), 2867–2871.

Harris, R.E., Namboodiri, K.K., & Wynder, E.L. (1992). Breast cancer risk: Effects of estrogen replacement therapy and body mass. *J Natl Cancer Inst, 84*, 1575–1582.

Harris, R.E., Namboodiri, K.K., Farrar, W.B., Solano, S.M., & Wynder, E.L. (1996). Hormone replacement therapy and breast cancer risk. *JAMA, 275*(15), 1158.

Harris, R.E. (2002). Epidemiology of breast cancer and nonsteroidal anti-inflammatory drugs: Extension of the dietary fat hypothesis of breast cancer. In R.E. Harris (Ed.), *COX-2 Blockade in cancer prevention and therapy* (pp. 57–68). Totowa, NJ: Humana Press.

Harris, R.E. (2007). COX-2 and the inflammogenesis of cancer. *Subcellular Biochemistry, 42*, 193–212.

Harris, R.E. (2009). Cyclooxygenase-2 (COX-2) blockade in the chemoprevention of cancers of the colon, breast, prostate, and lung. *Inflammo-pharmacology, 17*, 1–13.

Kahlenborn, C., Modugno, F., Potter, D.M., & Severs, W.B. (2006). Oral contraceptive use as a risk factor for premenopausal breast cancer: A meta-analysis. *Mayo Clin Proc, 81*(10), 1290–1302.

Karmali, R.A., Adams, L., & Trout, J.R. (1993). Plant and marine n-3 fatty acids inhibit experimental metastasis of rat mammary adenocarcinoma cells. *Pros Leuk Essential Fatty Acids, 48*, 309–314.

Kaufman, D.W., Palmer, J.R., de Mouzon, J., Rosenberg, L., Stolley, P.D., Warshauer, E., Zauber, A.G., & Shapiro, S. (1991). Estrogen replacement therapy and the risk of breast cancer: Results from the case-control surveillance study. *Am J Epidemiol, 134*, 1375–1385.

Kawamura, T., & Sobue, T. (2005). Comparison of breast cancer mortality in five countries: France, Italy, Japan, the UK, and the USA from the WHO Mortality Database (1960–2000). *Japan J Clin Oncol, 35*(12), 758–759.

King, M.C., Marks, J.H., Mandell, J.B., & New York Breast Cancer Study Group. (2003). Breast and ovarian cancer risks due to inherited mutations in BRCA1 and BRCA2. *Science, 302*(5645), 643–646.

Korenman, S.G. (1980). Oestrogen window hypothesis of the aetiology of breast cancer. *Lancet, i*, 700–701.

Lima, J.B., & Smith, P.D. (1971). Sipple's syndrome (pheochromocytoma and thyroid carcinoma) with bilateral breast carcinoma. *Am J Surg, 1*(6), 732–735.

Mills, P.K., Beeson, L., Phillips, R.L., et al. (1989). Prospective study of exogenous hormone use and breast cancer in Seventh-day Adventists. *Cancer, 64*, 591–597.

Minami, Y., Tsubono, Y., Nishino, Y., Ohuchi, N., Shibuya, D., & Hisamichi, S. (2004). The increase of female breast cancer incidence in Japan: Emergence of birth cohort effect. *Int J Cancer, 108*(6), 901–906.

Palmer, J.R., Rosenberg, L., Clarke, E.A., et al. (1991). Breast cancer risk after estrogen replacement therapy: Results from the Toronto Breast Cancer Study. *Am J Epidemiol, 134*, 1386–1395.

Powles, T., Eeles, R., Ashley, S., Easton, D., Chang, J., Dowsett, M., et al. (1998). Interim analysis of the incidence of breast cancer in the Royal Marsden Hospital tamoxifen randomised chemoprevention trial. *Lancet, 352*, 98–101.

Romieu, I., Berlin, J.A., & Colditz, G. (1990). Oral contraceptives and breast cancer. Review and meta-analysis. *Cancer, 66*(11), 2253–2263.

Saika, K., & Sobue, T. (2009). Epidemiology of breast cancer in Japan and the US. *Jap Med Assoc J, 52*(1), 39–44.

Smyth, P.P. (1997). The thyroid and breast cancer: A significant association? *Ann Med, 3*, 189–191.

Stanford, J.L., Weiss, N.S., Voight, L.F., Daling, J.R., Habel, L.A., & Rossing, M.A. (1995). Combined estrogen and progestin hormone replacement therapy in relation to risk of breast cancer in middle-aged women. *J Am Med Assoc, 274*, 137–142.

Veronesi, U., Maisonneuve, P., Costa, A., Sacchini, V., Maltoni, C., Robertson, C., et al. (1998). Prevention of breast cancer with tamoxifen: Preliminary findings from the Italian randomised trial among hysterectomised women. Italian Tamoxifen Prevention Study. *Lancet, 352*, 93–97.

Willett,W.C., Stampfer, M.J., & Colditz, G.A. (1989). Does alcohol consumption influence the risk of developing breast cancer? Two Views (15a). In V.T. DeVita Jr., S. Hellman, & S.A. Rosenberg (Eds.), *Important advances in oncology, 1989* (pp. 267–281). Philadelphia: JB Lippincott Company.

Winkelstein Jr., W. (2006). Janet Elizabeth Lane-Claypon: A forgotten epidemiologic pioneer. *Epidemiology, 17*(6), 705.

Wooster, R., Neuhausen, S.L., Mangion, J., Quirk, Y., Ford, D., Collins, N.,…Stratton, M.R. (1994). Localization of a breast cancer susceptibility gene, BRCA2, to chromosome 13q12–13. *Science, 265*(5181), 2088–2090.

Wynder, E.L., & Harris, R.E. (1989). Does alcohol consumption influence the risk of developing breast cancer? Two Views (15b). In V.T. DeVita Jr., S. Hellman, & S.A. Rosenberg (Eds.), *Important advances in oncology, 1989* (pp. 267–281). Philadelphia: JB Lippincott Company.

20

Epidemiology of Ovarian Cancer

GLOBAL EPIDEMIOLOGY OF OVARIAN CANCER

Worldwide, ovarian cancer is diagnosed in more than 230,000 women annually and causes more than 150,000 deaths. This malignancy accounts for approximately 4% of all female cancers and about 2.5% of cancer deaths in women. Most of the new cases (80–90%) are diagnosed either during or after menopause and the peak incidence occurs during the fifth decade of life (American Cancer Society, 2009; National Cancer Institute, USA, 2009).

The global pattern of ovarian cancer mortality is similar to that of breast cancer (**Figure 20.1**). High rates are found among Caucasian women living in industrialized nations such as the United States, Canada, Europe, Israel, Scandinavia, Australia, and New Zealand. In addition, women residing in Greenland and certain regions of South America, e.g., Chile, Brazil, and Argentina, have high mortality rates of ovarian cancer.

Ovarian cancer develops silently over a period of many years without clinically detectable signs or symptoms. At the time of diagnosis, more than

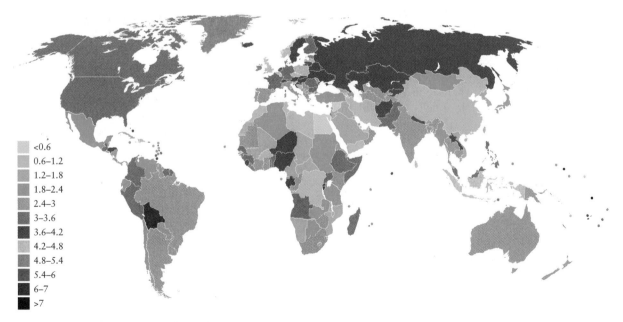

	<0.6
	0.6–1.2
	1.2–1.8
	1.8–2.4
	2.4–3
	3–3.6
	3.6–4.2
	4.2–4.8
	4.8–5.4
	5.4–6
	6–7
	>7

Figure 20.1 Ovarian Cancer: Global Mortality, 2004.

Source: Data from World Health Organization. The global burden of disease: 2004 update. Geneva, WHO, 2008. Available at www.who.int/evidence/bod.

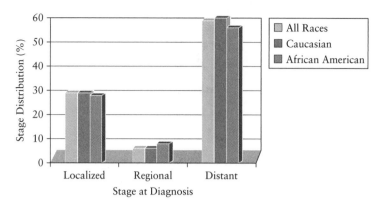

Figure 20.2 Ovarian Cancer: Stage at Diagnosis.

Source: Data from Howlader et al (eds) (2011). SEER Cancer Statistics Review, 1975–2008, National Cancer Institute. Bethesda, MD.

70% of ovarian cancers have spread to lymph nodes, surrounding tissues of the peritoneum, or beyond (**Figure 20.2**). As a consequence of the failure to detect ovarian cancers at an early stage when treatment is more likely to be of benefit to the patient, ovarian cancer generally has an extremely poor prognosis. Worldwide, the 5-year survival of ovarian cancer is only about 30% (Parkin et al., 2005).

PATHOGENESIS OF OVARIAN CANCER

Ovarian physiology is complex. The gland is covered by surface epithelium and the inner core (the cortex) consists of multiple cell types. Follicles within the cortex contain the oocytes (eggs), granulosa cells, and theca cells. Granulosa cells surround and nourish the oocytes in response to follicular stimulating hormone (FSH) secreted by the pituitary gland. Theca cells respond to luteinizing hormone (LH) and synthesize androgens that are subsequently aromatized to estrogens by the granulosa cells. On ovulation, the remnant of the follicle (the corpus luteum) secretes progesterone as well as estrogen (Merck Online Medical Library: Female Reproductive System).

Ovarian cancer usually arises from the epithelial cells at the surface of the ovary. Dr. Mahmoud Fathalla originally proposed that the genesis of this malignancy is likely related to incessant ovulation and repetitive disruption and wound healing of the surface epithelium coincident with the menstrual cycle during the reproductive years (Fathalla, 1971). Incessant ovulation could sustain exposure of the ovarian epithelium to hormones and growth factors secreted by the ovarian cortex (Scully, 1995) as well as increasing the inflammatory microenvironment of cytokines and prostaglandins leading to cell damage and oxidative stress (Ness and Cottreau, 1999).

In support of the incessant ovulation model, several epidemiological studies have determined that the number of successive ovulatory cycles uninterrupted by pregnancy, lactation, and/or contraception increases the risk of ovarian cancer (Risch, Marrett, and Howe, 1994). The natural repetitive cyclic process of ovulation may thus increase the chance of spontaneous somatic mutations and/or epigenetic changes that alter the expression of tumor suppressor genes and oncogenes in favor of carcinogenesis.

Albeit, the incessant ovulation model does not explain the increased risk of ovarian cancer in women who are infertile due to anovulation (absence of ovulation). Such women may be at risk due to excessive stimulation of the ovary by gonadotropic hormones secreted by the pituitary gland, namely, follicular stimulating hormone (FSH) and luteinizing hormone (LH). Ovulation and ovarian secretion of estrogen and progesterone during the menstrual cycle depend upon normal functioning of the hypothalamic-pituitary-ovarian axis; reciprocally, abnormalities in this system may result in anovulation, loss of hormonal feedback control, and hypersecretion of gonadotropins (**Figure 20.3**). Indeed,

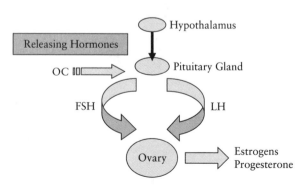

Figure 20.3 The Hypothalmic-Pituitary-Ovarian Axis.

as a woman undergoes menopause, the diminished ovarian secretion of estrogen and progesterone results in loss of feedback inhibition thereby resulting in marked elevations in FSH and LH secreted by the pituitary gland (Chakravarti et al., 1976). These perimenopausal events (diminished ovarian hormones and excess pituitary gonadotropins) are temporally related to the onset of ovarian cancer in the postmenopausal years (Helzlsouer et al., 1995; Choi et al., 2007). Furthermore, gonadotropin levels in ovarian cyst and peritoneal fluid appear to be associated with ovarian cancer incidence (Kramer, Leeker, and Jager, 1998) and cell membrane receptors for FSH are overexpressed in a high percentage of ovarian carcinomas as well a preneoplastic lesions of the ovarian surface epithileum (Zheng et al., 2000; Choi et al., 2004). Upregulation of FSH in particular appears to be related to the growth, survival, and metastasis of ovarian cancer cells and may involve other growth factors mediated by a complex array of intracellular signaling pathways (Choi et al., 2007). Finally, it has been hypothesized that ovarian cancer is etiologically linked to the excessive production of androgens and diminished levels of progesterone that upset the balance of the ovarian hormonal milieu resulting in carcinogenesis (Risch, 1998).

RISK FACTORS FOR OVARIAN CANCER

Several risk factors have been identified that increase a woman's chance of developing ovarian cancer. Since the ovarian epithelium contains many of the same cell membrane receptors as the ductal epithelium of the mammary gland, the reproductive risk factor profile for ovarian cancer is similar to that of breast cancer. These risk factors include familial and genetic predisposition plus reproductive events that increase the cumulative months of ovulation, rupture of the ovarian surface epithelium, and exposure to hormones of the menstrual cycle (early menses, delayed reproductive history, nulliparity, absence of lactation, late menopause, and the natural process of aging).

Reciprocally, reproductive factors such as pregnancy, lactation, and oral contraceptive use that interrupt the menstrual cycle have consistently been observed to be protective. These factors are discussed in greater detail in a following section of this chapter.

Genetic Predisposition to Ovarian Cancer

A strong family history (ovarian cancer in a first-degree or second-degree relative) increases the risk of ovarian cancer by three- to fivefold. Genetic or familial predisposition is identifiable for approximately 5–10% of women diagnosed with ovarian cancer. Hallmarks of familial predisposition to ovarian cancer include early age of onset, an excess of bilateral disease, and ovarian cancer in familial association with other malignancies such as breast cancer, endometrial cancer, and colorectal cancer.

Two heritable genetic mutations have been identified that predispose to familial breast and ovarian cancer, BRCA-1 and BRCA-2. The BRCA-1 gene was discovered in 1990 by King and colleagues and is located on the long arm of chromosome 17 (Hall et al., 1990). Subsequently, a second breast cancer gene, BRCA-2, was identified on the long arm of chromosome 13 (Wooster et al., 1994). A mutation in either BRCA gene predisposes heterozygous female carriers to both breast cancer and, to a lesser extent, ovarian cancer. The lifetime risk of breast cancer among women who carry a single mutation in either BRCA-1 or BRCA-2 is approximately 85%, whereas the lifetime ovarian cancer risk for women with a BRCA-1 mutation is 54% compared to 24% for women with a BRCA-2 mutation (King et al., 2003).

Both BRCA-1 and BRCA-2 are tumor suppressor genes that upon transcription form proteins essential for the repair of double-stranded DNA breaks (Boulton, 2006). Mutated BRCA genes result in proteins that do not function properly in DNA repair, thereby promoting accumulation of genetic errors and carcinogenesis. Population studies have identified high gene frequencies of BRCA-1 and BRCA-2 among women of Ashkenazi Jewish descent and high frequencies of BRCA-1 among women of Greenlander origin (Harboe et al., 2009).

Another genetic condition that predisposes to ovarian cancer is hereditary nonpolyposis colorectal cancer (HNPCC), also called the Lynch syndrome (named after Henry T. Lynch who characterized the genetic and clinical features of HNPCC). The cause of HNPCC is an inherited (germline) mutation in at least one of a set of genes that normally repair DNA, the mismatch repair genes. In 1993, the first of the HNPCC genes (MSH2) was discovered on chromosome 2 by a team of international investigators (Aaltonen et al., 1993). Soon after, MLH1 was discovered on chromosome 3 (Aaltonen et al., 1994). Mutations in these 2 genes account for approximately 90% of the known HNPCC families. The Lynch syndrome accounts for a small percentage of all colorectal cancer cases, perhaps 1–3%. Women in HNPCC families are also at increased risk of developing cancers of the uterine lining (endometrium), colon, ovary, and stomach (Offit and Kauff, 2006).

Fertility Agents and Ovarian Cancer

Results of several case-control studies suggest a link between the use of fertility drugs and the development of ovarian cancer. In general, fertility drugs, e.g., clomiphene citrate, stimulate the secretion of FSH and LH by the pituitary gland in order to help stimulate ovulation. In a meta-analysis of 12 studies, Whittemore and colleagues found that infertile women who had taken any form of fertility drugs were 2.7 times more likely to develop ovarian cancer than women who had never taken these medications (Whittemore, Harris, and Itnyre, 1992). It is important to point out that there was no increase in cancer risk among the women who used fertility drugs and subsequently became pregnant. Nevertheless, a subsequent study by Rossing and colleagues also found more than a twofold increase in the risk of ovarian cancer among women who had used clomiphene citrate for at least one year (Rossing et al., 1994). Controversy remains regarding the exact nature of the increased risk and it is difficult to reconcile whether it is due to use of the fertility agent or the underlying pathologies of infertility (Holschneider and Berek, 2000).

Polycystic ovary syndrome (also called Stein-Leventhal syndrome) is a relatively common female endocrine disorder affecting approximately 5–10% of women of reproductive age. This syndrome is a leading cause of female infertility that develops when the ovaries are stimulated to produce excessive amounts of male hormones (androgens), particularly testosterone, either through the release of excessive luteinizing hormone (LH) by the anterior pituitary gland or through high levels of insulin in the blood (hyperinsulinemia) (Carmina, 2004). One small case control study observed a 2.5-fold increase in the risk of ovarian cancer in women with polycystic ovary syndrome (Schildkraut et al., 1996); however, this finding has not been confirmed in prospective studies (Coulam, Annegers, and Kranz, 1983; Pierpoint et al., 1998).

Other Risk Factors of Ovarian Cancer

Many other potential risk factors have been examined in epidemiologic investigations of ovarian cancer. One factor that has received considerable attention in the media is perineal dusting with talcum powder, a practice that has been observed to increase the risk of ovarian cancer by some investigators (Cramer et al., 1999). A meta-analyses of 16 case-control studies determined a modest increase in the risk (the summary relative risk was 1.3), but also reflected heterogeneity among studies (Huncharek, Geschwind, and Kupelnick, 2003).

Furthermore, the biological basis of talc carcinogenicity remains controversial since inhaled talc in mining and milling operations has not been found to be associated with the development of pulmonary tumors (Muscat and Huncharek, 2008).

Ecological studies of ovarian cancer and dietary factors have noted positive correlations between milk consumption, lactase persistence (a measure of lactose digestion), and the incidence of ovarian cancer (Rose, Boyar, and Wynder, 1986; Cramer, 1989). However, analytic studies have yielded conflicting results, some finding a positive association of lactose intake with ovarian cancer development and others finding no association (Risch, Jain, Marrett, and Howe, 1994; Larsson, Bergkvist, and Wolk, 2004). It has been hypothesized that galactose, a component sugar of the disaccharide lactose, might increase the risk of ovarian cancer either by direct toxicity to the oocytes or by inducing high concentrations of gonadotropins, thereby stimulating the proliferation of the ovarian surface epithelium (Harlow et al., 1991).

Findings from both case-control and cohort epidemiologic studies suggest there is a dose-response relationship between body mass index and the risk of developing ovarian cancer, particularly among postmenopausal women. In a large prospective study of 94,525 women aged 50–71 years, Leitzmann and colleagues observed that obesity increased the risk of ovarian cancer by 80% in postmenopausal women with no history of hormone replacement therapy (Lietzmann et al., 2009). In a meta-analysis of 28 epidemiologic studies, Olsen and colleagues found significant increases in the risk of developing ovarian cancer with obesity (summary relative risk = 1.3) or being overweight (summary relative risk = 1.2) (Olsen et al., 2007); however, there is lack of agreement regarding the timing of the development of ovarian cancer in relation to adiposity (Schouten et al., 2008). In general, the epidemiologic findings support the hypothesis that long-term adiposity enhances aromatase-catalyzed estrogen biosynthesis that in turn increases the genesis of ovarian cancer.

The use of exogenous hormones (estrogen replacement therapy [ERT]) has been studied extensively in relation to various forms of cancer, including ovarian cancer. In a meta-analysis of 19 case-control studies and 8 cohort studies, the risk increase was approximately 20% in ever users versus never users and the risk increased with the duration of use (Zhou et al., 2008). A recent prospective study of nearly 1 million women in the United Kingdom found that current ERT users were about 20% more likely to develop and die from ovarian cancer than never users (Beral et al., 2007). Biologically, the ovarian surface epithelium has cell member receptors that are responsive to estrogen and it is conceivable that ERT may stimulate cell proliferation and other cellular events related to carcinogenesis through modulation of estrogen receptors.

It has been hypothesized that circulating androgens may be involved in the development of ovarian cancer (Risch, 1998). Futhermore, in one study, the synthetic male hormone danazol has been linked to the development of ovarian cancer (Cottreau et al., 2003). Danazol is sometimes prescribed to women who suffer from endometriosis, a condition associated with dysplasia and bleeding of the endometrium. Albeit, there is consistent evidence that endometriosis is a risk factor for the development of ovarian cancer, e.g., a pooled analysis of 8 case-control studies found a summary relative risk of 1.7 (Ness et al., 2002) and a large cohort study of Swedish women found a 1.3-fold increase in the risk of ovarian cancer among women with endometriosis (Melin, Sparén, and Bergqvist, 2007). Since the use of danazol is confounded by the presence of endometriosis, additional studies will be required to determine whether this drug truly increases the risk of ovarian cancer.

PROTECTIVE REPRODUCTIVE FACTORS AND OVARIAN CANCER

Interruption of the menstrual cycle by a first pregnancy early in the reproductive years or by sustained use of oral contraceptives has been found to be protective against the development of ovarian cancer in a number of studies. For example, in a multicenter population-based case control study of 436 cases and 3,833 controls, the estimated relative risks of epithelial ovarian cancer were 0.6 for women who had ever been pregnant, 0.6 for women who had ever breast fed, and 0.5 for women who had ever used oral contraceptives, and there was a strong trend in decreasing risk with increasing cumulative months of pregnancy (Gwinn et al., 1990). Overall, women with multiple children have risk reductions in the range of 40–60% compared to nulliparous women (Adami et al., 1994; Risch, Marrett, and Howe, 1994; Hankinson et al., 1995). Lactation also confers a slight additional reduction in the risk of ovarian cancer (Rosenblatt and Thomas, 1993).

During the reproductive years estrogens are produced by the ovaries, whereas after menopause estrogen biosynthesis is catalyzed by the enzyme aromatase in fat and muscle cells. Some investigations have therefore focused on the differential impact of reproductive factors on the risk of developing ovarian

cancer in the premenopausal years versus the postmenopausal years. In a large study of 896 cases and 967 controls, Moorman and colleagues observed that interruption of the menstrual cycle by either pregnancy or oral contraception conferred protection, but the effect tended to diminish with age during the postmenopausal years (Moorman et al., 2008).

ORAL CONTRACEPTIVES AND OVARIAN CANCER

A number of epidemiologic investigations have observed significant reductions in the risk of ovarian cancer in women who used oral contraceptives (Franceschi et al., 1991; Gross and Schlesselman, 1994; Schlesselman, 1995; Narod et al., 1998). Recently, a comprehensive meta-analysis of 45 epidemiologic studies comparing 23,257 cases with 87,303 controls determined that the use of oral contraceptives reduced the risk by as much as 29% per 5 years of use (Collaborative Group on Epidemiological Studies of Ovarian Cancer, 2008). Furthermore, the rates of ovarian cancer appear to be declining in some countries as a consequence of widespread oral contraceptive use. For example, the incidence of ovarian cancer has declined by 30% and mortality rates have declined by 25% since 1975 when oral contraceptive pills were approved for use by premenopausal women in America (**Figure 20.4**). Oral contraceptives interfere with the pituitary hormones, follicular stimulating hormone (FSH), and luteinizing hormone (LH), thereby reducing proliferation of epithelial cells at the surface of the ovary and diminishing their potential for carcinogenesis.

SCREENING FOR OVARIAN CANCER

No screening tools have proven successful in detecting ovarian cancer at an early stage (*in situ* or localized, stage I) when it can be effectively treated by complete surgical excision. As a consequence, more than 70% of these tumors are diagnosed after they have metastasized to contiguous tissue and/or nearby lymph nodes. The overall survival is poor with 5-year survival well less than 50%, even in developed countries such as the United States. Elevated levels of a small antigenic protein called CA-125 secreted by ovarian cancer cells are usually present and measurable at the time of diagnosis; however, this biomarker has only shown value in monitoring cancer regression or progression and thus far has not proven useful for screening and early detection (Bast et al., 1981; Bast et al., 1998).

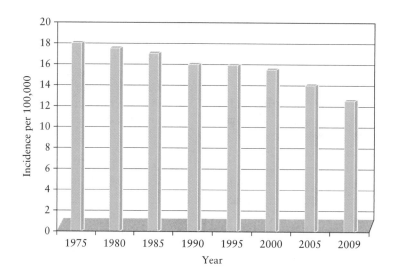

Figure 20.4 Ovarian Cancer Incidence in Caucasian Women, 1975–2009, USA.

Source: Data from American Cancer Society, Cancer Facts and Figures, Statistics for 2009; Howlader et al (eds) (2011). SEER Cancer Statistics Review, 1975–2008, National Cancer Institute. Bethesda, MD.

● ● ● **REFERENCES**

Aaltonen, L.A., Peltomiki, P., Leach, F.S., Sistonen, P., Pylkkanen, L., Mecklin, J.P., Jirvinen, H., et al. (1993). Clues to the pathogenesis of familial colorectal cancer. *Science, 260,* 812–816.

Aaltonen, L.A., Peltomiki, P., Mecklin, J.P., Jirvinen, H., Jass, J.R., Green, J.S., Lynch, H.T., et al. (1994). Replication errors in benign and malignant tumors from hereditary nonpolyposis colorectal cancer patients. *Cancer Res, 54,* 1645–1648.

Adami, H.O., Hsieh, C.C., Lambe, M., et al. (1994). Parity, age at first childbirth, and risk of ovarian cancer. *Lancet, 344*(8932), 1250–1254.

American Cancer Society. (2009). Cancer facts and figures. American Cancer Society.

Bast, R.C., Feeney, M., Lazarus, H., Nadler, L.M., Colvin, R.B., & Knapp, R.C. (1981). Reactivity of a monoclonal antibody with human ovarian carcinoma. *J Clin Invest, 68*(5), 1331–1337.

Bast, R.C., Xu, F.J., Yu, Y.H., Barnhill, S., Zhang, Z., & Mills, G.B. (1998). CA 125: The past and the future. *Int J Biol Markers, 13*(4), 179–187.

Beral, V., Million Women Study Collaborators, Bull, D., Green, J., & Reeves, G. (2007). Ovarian cancer and hormone replacement therapy in the Million Women Study. *Lancet, 369*(9574), 1703–1710.

Boulton, S.J. (2006). Cellular functions of the BRCA tumour-suppressor proteins. *Biochemical Society Transactions, 34*(5), 633–645.

Carmina, E. (2004). Diagnosis of polycystic ovary syndrome: From NIH criteria to ESHRE-ASRM guidelines. *Minerva Ginecol, 56*(1), 1–6.

Chakravarti, S., Collins, W.P., Forecast, J.D., Newton, J.R., Oram, D.H., & Studd, J.W. (1976). Hormonal profiles after the menopause. *Br Med J, 2,* 784–787.

Choi, J.H., Choi, K.C., Auersperg, N., & Leung, P.C. (2004). Overexpression of follicle-stimulating hormone receptor activates oncogenic pathways in preneoplastic ovarian surface epithelial cells. *J Clin Endocrinol Metab, 89,* 5508–5516.

Choi, J.H., Wong, A.S.T., Huang, H.F., & Leung, P.C.K. (2007). Gonadotropins and ovarian cancer. *Endocrine Reviews, 28*(4), 440–461.

Collaborative Group on Epidemiological Studies of Ovarian Cancer. (2008). Ovarian cancer and oral contraceptives: Collaborative reanalysis of data from 45 epidemiological studies including 23,257 women with ovarian cancer and 87,303 controls. *Lancet, 371,* 303–314.

Cottreau, C.M., Ness, R.B., Modugno, F., Allen, G.O., & Goodman, M.T. (2003). Endometriosis and its treatment with Danazol or Lupron in relation to ovarian cancer. *Clinical Cancer Research, 9*, 5142–5144.

Coulam, C.B., Annegers, J.F., & Kranz, J.S. (1983). Chronic anovulation syndrome and associated neoplasia. *Obstetrics and Gynecology, 61*, 403–407.

Cramer, D.W. (1989). Lactase persistence and milk consumption as determinants of ovarian cancer risk. *American J Epidemiology, 130*(5), 904–910.

Cramer, D.W., Liberman, R.F., Titus-Ernstoff, L., Welch, W.R., Greenberg, E.R., Baron, J.A., & Harlow, B.L. (1999). Genital talc exposure and risk of ovarian cancer. *Int J Cancer, 81*, 351–356.

Fathalla, M.F. (1971). Incessant ovulation—A factor in ovarian neoplasia? *Lancet, 2*(7716), 163.

Franceschi, S., Parazzini, F., Negri, E., et al. (1991). Pooled analysis of 3 European case-control studies of epithelial ovarian cancer: III. Oral contraceptive use. *Int J Cancer, 49*, 61–65.

Gross, T.P., & Schlesselman, J.J. (1994). The estimated effect of oral contraceptive use on the cumulative risk of epithelial ovarian cancer. *Obstet Gynecol, 83*, 419–424.

Gwinn, M.L., Lee, N.C., Rhodes, P.H., Layde, P.M., & Rubin, G.L. (1990). Pregnancy, breast feeding, and oral contraceptives and the risk of epithelial ovarian cancer. *J Clin Epidemiol, 43*(6), 559–568.

Hall, J.M., Lee, M.K., Newman, B., Morrow, J.E., Anderson, L.A., Huey, B., & King, M.C. (1990). Linkage of early-onset familial breast cancer to chromosome 17q21. Science, *250*(4988), 1684–1689.

Hankinson, S.E., Colditz, G.A., Hunter, D.J., et al. (1995). A prospective study of reproductive factors and risk of epithelial ovarian cancer. *Cancer, 76*, 284–290.

Harboe, T.L., Eiberg, E.H., Kern, E.P., Ejlertsen, B., Nedergaard, E.L., Timmermans-Wielenga, V., Nielsen, I.M., & Bisgaard, M.L. (2009). A high frequent BRCA1 founder mutation identified in the Greenlandic population. *Familial Cancer, 8*, 413–419.

Harlow, B.L., Cramer, D.W., Geller, J., Willett, W.C., Bell, D.A., & Welch, W.R. (1991). The influence of lactose consumption on the association of oral contraceptive use and ovarian cancer risk. *Am J Epidemiol, 134*, 445–453.

Helzlsouer, K.J., Alberg, A.J., Gordon, G.B., et al. (1995). Serum gonadotropins and steroid hormones in the development of ovarian cancer. *JAMA, 274*, 1926–1930.

Holschneider, C.H., & Berek, J.S. (2000). Ovarian cancer: Epidemiology, biology and prognostic factors. *Seminars in Surgical Oncology, 19*, 3–10.

Huncharek, M., Geschwind, J.F., & Kupelnick, B. (2003). Perineal application of cosmetic talc and risk of invasive epithelial ovarian cancer: A meta-analysis of 11,933 subjects from sixteen observational studies. *Anticancer Res, 23*, 1955–1960.

King, M.C., Marks, J.H., Mandell, J.B., & New York Breast Cancer Study Group. (2003). Breast and ovarian cancer risks due to inherited mutations in BRCA1 and BRCA2. *Science, 302*(5645), 643–646.

Kramer, S., Leeker, M., & Jager, W. (1998). Gonadotropin levels in ovarian cyst fluids: A predictor of malignancy? *Int J Biol Markers, 13*, 165–168.

Larsson, S.C., Bergkvist, L., & Wolk, A. (2004). Milk and lactose intakes and ovarian cancer risk in the Swedish Mammography Cohort. *American J Clinical Nutrition, 80*(5), 1353–1357.

Leitzmann, M.F., Koebnick, C., Danforth, K.N., Brinton, L.A., Moore, S.C., Hollenbeck, A.R.,… Schatzkin, A., Lacey, J.V. Jr. (2009). Body mass index and risk of ovarian cancer. *Cancer, 155*(4), 812–822.

Melin, A., Sparén, P., & Bergqvist, A. (2007). The risk of cancer and the role of parity among women with endometriosis. *Hum Reprod, 22*(11), 3021–3026.

Moorman, P.G., Calingaert, B., Palmieri, R.T., Iversen, E.S., Bentley, R.C., Halabi, S.,..., Berchuck, A., Schildkraut, J.M. (2008). Hormonal risk factors for ovarian cancer in premenopausal and postmenopausal women. *American Journal of Epidemiology, 167*(9), 1059–1069.

Muscat, J.E., & Huncharek, M.S. (2008). Perineal talc use and ovarian cancer: A critical review. *European Journal of Cancer Prevention, 17,* 139–146.

Narod, S.A., Risch, H., Moslehi, R., et al. (1998). Oral contraceptives and the risk of hereditary ovarian cancer. *New Engl J Med, 339,* 424–428.

National Cancer Institute, USA. (2009). Cancer statistics, 2009. National Cancer Institute.

Ness, R.B., & Cottreau, C. (1999). Possible role of ovarian epithelial inflammation in ovarian cancer. *J Natl Cancer Inst, 91,* 1459–1467.

Ness, R.B., Cramer, D.W., Goodman, M.T., Kruger Kjaer, S., & Mallin, K. (2002). Infertility, fertility drugs, and ovarian cancer: A pooled analysis of case–control studies. *Am J Epidemiol, 155,* 217–224.

Offit, K., & Kauff, N.D. (2006). Reducing the risk of gynecologic cancer in the Lynch syndrome. *New Engl J Med, 354*(3), 293–295.

Olsen, C.M., Green, A.C., Whiteman, D.C., Sadeghi, S., Kolahdooz, F., & Webb, P.M. (2007). Obesity and the risk of epithelial ovarian cancer: A systematic review and meta-analysis. *Eur J Cancer, 43,* 690–709.

Parkin, M.D., Bray, F., Ferlay, J., & Pisani, P. (2005). Global cancer statistics, 2002. *CA Cancer J Clin, 55,* 74–108.

Pierpoint, T., McKeigue, P.M., Isaacs, A.J., Wild, S.H., & Jacobs, H.S. (1998). Mortality of women with polycystic ovary syndrome at long-term follow-up. *Journal of Clinical Epidemiology, 51,* 581–586.

Risch, H.A., Marrett, L.D., & Howe, G.R. (1994). Parity, contraception, infertility, and the risk of epithelial ovarian cancer. *Am J Epidemiol, 140,* 585–597.

Risch, H.A., Jain, M., Marrett, L.D., & Howe, G.R. (1994). Dietary lactose intake, lactose intolerance, and the risk of epithelial ovarian cancer in southern Ontario (Canada). *Cancer Causes Control, 5,* 540–548.

Risch, H.A. (1998). Hormonal etiology of epithelial ovarian cancer, with a hypothesis concerning the role of androgens and progesterone. *J Natl Cancer Inst, 90,* 1774–1786.

Rose, D.P., Boyar, A.P., & Wynder, E.L. (1986). International comparisons of mortality rates for cancer of the breast, ovary, prostate, and colon, and per capita food consumption. *Cancer, 58,* 2363–2371.

Rosenblatt, K.A., & Thomas, D.B. (1993). Lactation and the risk of epithelial ovarian cancer. The WHO Collaborative Study of Neoplasia and Steroid Contraceptives. *Int J Epidemiol, 22,* 192–197.

Rossing, M.A., Daling, J.R., Weiss, N.S., Moore, D.E., & Self, S.G. (1994). Ovarian tumors in a cohort of infertile women. *N Engl J Med, 331,* 771–776.

Schildkraut, J.M., Schwingl, P.J., Bastos, E., Evanoff, A., & Hughes, C. (1996). Epithelial ovarian cancer risk among women with polycystic ovary syndrome. *Obstet Gynecol, 88*(4 Pt 1), 554–559.

Schlesselman, J.J. (1995). Net effect of oral contraceptive use on the risk of cancer in women in the United States. *Obstet Gynecol, 85*(5 Pt 1), 793–801.

Schouten, L.J., Rivera, C., Hunter, D.J., Spiegelman, D., Adami, H.O., Arslan, A., et al. (2008). Height, body mass index, and ovarian cancer: A pooled analysis of 12 cohort studies. *Cancer Epidemiol Biomarkers Prev, 17,* 902–912.

Scully, R.E. (1995). Pathology of ovarian cancer precursors. *J Cell Biochem Suppl*, *23*, 208–218.

Whittemore, A.S., Harris, R., & Itnyre, J. (1992). Characteristics relating to ovarian cancer risk: Collaborative analysis of 12 US case-control studies. II. Invasive epithelial ovarian cancers in white women. *Am J Epidemiol*, *136*, 1184–1203.

Wooster, R., Neuhausen, S.L., Mangion, J., Quirk, Y., Ford, D., Collins, N., et al. (1994). Localization of a breast cancer susceptibility gene, BRCA2, to chromosome 13q12–13. *Science*, *265*(5181), 2088–2090.

Zheng, W., Lu, J.J., Luo, F., Zheng, Y., Feng, Y., Felix, J.C., Lauchlan, S.C., & Pike, M.C. (2000). Ovarian epithelial tumor growth promotion by follicle-stimulating hormone and inhibition of the effect by luteinizing hormone. *Gynecol Oncol*, *76*, 80–88.

Zhou, B., Sun, Q., Cong, R., Gu, H., Tang, N., Yang, L., & Wang, B. (2008). Hormone replacement therapy and ovarian cancer risk: A meta-analysis. *Gynecol Oncol*, *108*(3), 641–651.

Epidemiology of Cervical Cancer

GLOBAL IMPACT OF CERVICAL CANCER

Cancer of the uterine cervix is the second most common cancer diagnosed among women worldwide. Based upon projections from the American Cancer Society, more than 555,000 new cases are diagnosed annually and nearly 310,000 women die from the disease (ACS, 2007). More than 473,000 of the new cases (about 85%) are diagnosed in women living in developing countries where cervical cancer is the leading cause of cancer death (more than 270,000 deaths per year). Cervical cancer is much less common in developed countries, affecting 87,500 women and accounting for approximately 40,000 deaths per year.

The highest incidence and mortality rates are observed in sub-Saharan African, Melanesia, Latin American and the Caribbean, South Central Asia (India), and Southeast Asia (**Figure 21.1**). The public health burden due to cervical cancer in these nations reflects the virtual absence of screening programs for the detection and treatment of precancerous lesions of the uterine cervix. For example, in India where screening is still largely absent, approximately 132,000 women are diagnosed with invasive cervical cancer resulting in more than 74,000 deaths annually (Singh, 2005).

The women of most developed nations and certain other nations such as China have relatively low

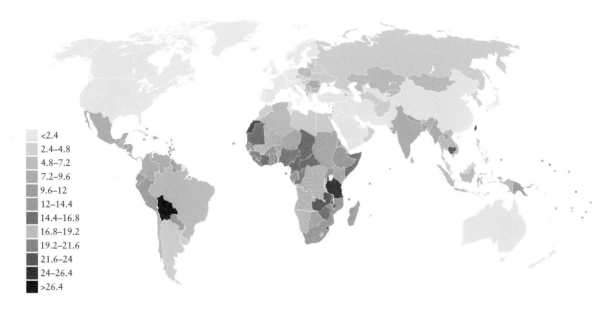

| <2.4 |
| 2.4–4.8 |
| 4.8–7.2 |
| 7.2–9.6 |
| 9.6–12 |
| 12–14.4 |
| 14.4–16.8 |
| 16.8–19.2 |
| 19.2–21.6 |
| 21.6–24 |
| 24–26.4 |
| >26.4 |

Figure 21.1 Global Cervical Cancer Mortality, 2004.

Source: Data from World Health Organization. The global burden of disease: 2004 update. Geneva, WHO, 2008. Available at www.who.int/evidence/bod.

rates. The incidence and mortality rates of cervical cancer have declined dramatically among women of developed countries since the introduction and widespread use of screening for cervical dysplasia in the mid-20th century (Ferlay et al., 2002).

EARLY DETECTION OF CERVICAL DYSPLASIA

The early detection and appropriate treatment of premalignant conditions of the cervical mucosa, e.g., cervical dysplasia, reflects a major triumph of modern medicine over a life-threatening disease process. In the early decades of the 20th century, cancer of the cervix was the leading cause of cancer mortality among American women. Since 1955, mortality due to cervical cancer has declined by 74%, and today cancer of the cervix ranks 14th in female cancer mortality, accounting for approximately 4,000 deaths per year in the United States (Jemal et al., 2009).

The dramatic reduction in cervical cancer among women of developed nations is due largely to the effectiveness of the Papanicolaou-Traut cytological test (Papanicolaou and Traut, 1943). The *Pap test*, which was introduced in the United States around 1950, provides a quick, safe, affordable, and accurate means of detecting precancerous dysplastic lesions of the cervix that can be "cured" by simple surgery or other ablative techniques. It is important to note that *in situ* cervical cancer is 100% curable by appropriate surgical excision. Furthermore, advanced stage cervical cancer that has not spread beyond the cervix is 80–90% curable by appropriate surgery. The importance of cervical screening coupled with appropriate therapy is underscored by differences in cervical cancer mortality in populations with high versus low screening rates. Public health programs to inform and educate the population as to the efficacy of cervical screening by appropriate implementation

of Papanicolaou cytological testing at an early age are therefore imperative. Evaluation of the Pap smear has also resulted in critical information regarding carcinogenesis, and in fact, more is known about the natural history of cervical cancer than any other malignancy.

Though the Pap test has produced substantial declines in cervical cancer incidence and mortality, it is noteworthy that marked disparities persist among the subpopulations within certain nations, perhaps due to excess risk, lack of screening, and limited healthcare access (Sherman et al., 2005). For example, among US women, the mortality rate for African Americans is still nearly twice that of Caucasians (Howlader et al., 2011) (**Figure 21.2**).

PATHOGENESIS OF CERVICAL CANCER

Cancer of the uterine cervix almost always originates at the squamocolumnar junction at the cervical os in the transitional area between the cervix and the vagina. It is at this border that the columnar epithelium of the cervix transforms into the squamous cell epithelium of the vagina. The vast majority (95%) of cervical cancers are of the squamous cell variety; however, a few adenocarcinomas evolve from the cervical glands, and in fact some of the cervical malignancies are of the mixed variety, i.e., adenosquamous carcinomas (Kumar et al., 2007).

Carcinoma of the cervix arises in a series of stepwise epithelial changes ranging from progressively more severe dysplasia to *carcinoma in situ* and ultimately invasive carcinoma (**Figure 21.3**). While carcinoma of the cervix may occur at any age following puberty, the peak incidence is about 30–40 years of age for *in situ* lesions and 40–50 years of age for invasive cancer.

Several questions remain regarding the risk factors associated with cervical carcinoma and cervical dysplasia. One feature of mild cervical dysplasia is

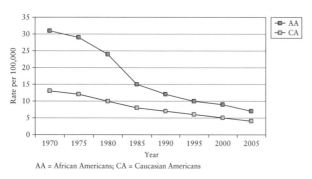

AA = African Americans; CA = Caucasian Americans

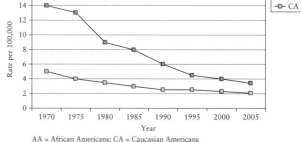

AA = African Americans; CA = Caucasian Americans

Figure 21.2 Cervical Cancer Incidence and Mortality, USA.

Source: Data from Howlader et al (eds) (2011). SEER Cancer Statistics Review, 1975–2008, National Cancer Institute. Bethesda, MD.

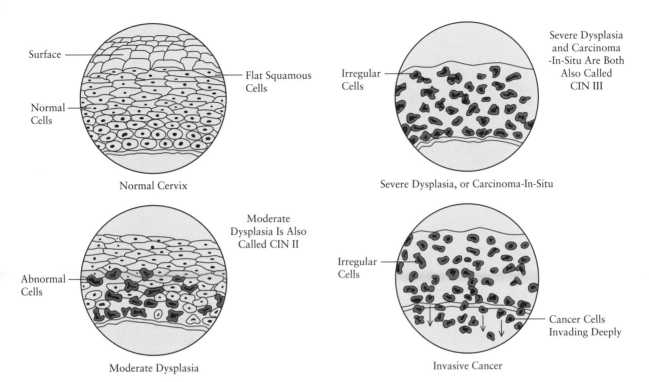

Figure 21.3 Progression of Cervical Neoplasia.

Source: Courtesy of Paul D. Indman, MD. All rights reserved. 15195 National Avenue, Suite 201, Los Gatos, CA 95032.

the tendency for a large percentage of cases to spontaneously remiss. That is, individuals with mild dysplasia when followed over time may spontaneously undergo resolution. While the reason for this is unknown, it is certainly a subject worthy of study by prospective epidemiologic methods.

RISK FACTORS FOR CERVICAL CANCER

Results of early epidemiologic studies of cervical cancer strongly suggested that the disease was related to the sexual transmission of an oncogenic agent, most probably a virus, from male to female at an early age. Factors that were consistently observed to increase the risk included early age at first intercourse and high parity, multiple sexual partners, contact with "high-risk"(promiscuous) male sexual partners, and cigarette smoking. Observed differences in risk for certain subpopulations of women were also related to sexual behavior, including the higher incidence of cervical cancer in lower socioeconomic groups, the higher incidence in married women which increases with the number of marriages and children, the rarity of cervical cancer in virgins and nuns, and the high incidence in prostitutes. Although herpes simplex virus type II (HSV II) was once suspected as the

etiologic agent, it is now believed that infection by certain strains of human papillomavirus (HPV) is the most important risk factor in the genesis of cervical malignancies.

Human Papillomavirus (HPV) and Cervical Cancer

It is now quite clear that oncogenic subtypes of human papillomavirus (HPV-16 and HPV-18) are necessary agents in the pathogenesis of cervical cancer (Walboomers et al., 1999). The link between cervical cancer and HPV infection was first suggested by Harald zur Hausen in Germany (zur Hausen, 1976). Professor zur Hausen and colleagues demonstrated the presence of HPV strains 16 and 18 in cancerous tissues from cervical cancer patients (Dürst et al., 1983; Boshart et al., 1984). Strong etiologic evidence came from an epidemiologic case-control study in which HPV DNA was detected by hybridization techniques in 75–100% of patients with cervical condylomas, precancerous cervical dysplasia, and invasive cervical carcinoma (Muñoz et al., 1992). Although there is an overlap in HPV strains, strains 6 and 11 are found most frequently in benign condylomas (vulvar condyloma acuminatum) whereas oncogenic HPV strains such as 16, 18, and 31 are more often present in carcinoma of the cervix (**Figure 21.4**). Cancer develops when the DNA from the oncogenic

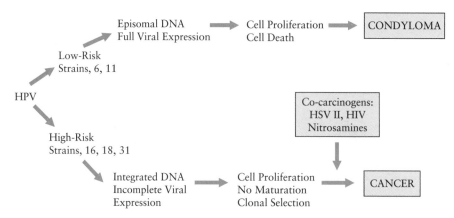

Figure 21.4 Model of Cervical Cancer and HPV Infection.

strains becomes integrated with the DNA of infected cervical cells leading to overexpression of certain viral genes (E6 and E7) that in turn inactivate tumor suppressor genes such as *P53* and *Rb* (Münger and Howley, 2002).

Molecular epidemiologic studies also indicate that HPV infection coupled with low-dose nitrosamines in the cervical mucosa of cigarette smokers may accentuate carcinogenesis (Gunnell et al., 2006). It has also been shown that HPV strains 16 and 18 (but not 6 and 11) interact with the *ras* oncogene in causing transformed tumorigenic foci in cultured cervical cells (Prokopakis et al., 2002). Furthermore, male partners of women with cervical cancer have been found to exhibit lesions of the genitalia harboring high-risk strains HPV-16 and HPV-18. Certain strains of HPV are also suspected as oncogenic agents in a variety of other squamous cell tumors or proliferative lesions of the skin and mucous membranes.

Immunosuppression and Cervical Cancer

Immunosuppression places women at high risk for infection by oncogenic strains of HPV, thereby increasing the risk of cervical cancer (Stentella et al., 1998). Indeed, women who are seropositive for the human immunodeficiency virus (HIV) are at extremely high risk for development of cervical cancer. Apparently this is due to a synergistic interaction between HIV and onocogenic HPV strains. Antecedent infection by HIV compromises the immune system and predisposes sexually active women to co-infection by strains of HPV that cause cervical cancer.

Visual Inspection for Detection of Cervical Neoplasia

Direct visual inspection of the uterine cervix after staining with acetic acid or Lugol's iodine has proven very effective in the detection of precancerous lesions (Sherris et al., 2009). Direct visual inspection procedures eliminate the need for transport of specimens and laboratory testing, require very little equipment, and provide women with immediate test results. A range of medical professionals including doctors, nurses, and professional midwives can effectively perform the procedure, provided they receive adequate training and supervision. Furthermore, such screening tests have been shown to perform equal to or better than cervical cytology in accurately identifying precancerous lesions. A major advantage of direct visual inspection is that women can be screened and treated in a single visit. One efficacious treatment option is cryotherapy (freezing), a relatively simple and inexpensive method by which cervical lesions can be immediately removed by the primary care physician (Denny et al., 2005).

HPV VACCINATION

Two effective vaccines have now been developed and are approved for use against high-risk HPV strains in the United States and Europe (McNeil, 2006). In randomized clinical trials, Gardasil (Merck) prevented infection by HPV types 6, 11, 16, and 18 in up to 98% of those vaccinated; and Cervarix (GlaxoSmithKline) prevented infections by HPV strains 16 and 18 in 92% of recipients over a 4-year follow-up period. These vaccines are only effective if administered to young females prior to HPV exposure. Unfortunately, their relatively high cost may prohibit widespread HPV vaccination programs in impoverished nations. Furthermore, vaccination should not be considered a replacement for screening since the known oncogenic HPV strains only account for about 70% of cervical cancer overall.

● ● ● **REFERENCES**

American Cancer Society. (2007). *Global cancer facts and figures, 2007*. American Cancer Society, Atlanta, Georgia.

Boshart, M., Gissmann, L., Hans Ikenberg, H., Kleinheinz, A., Wolfram Scheurlen, W., & zur Hausen, H. (1984). A new type of papilloma virus DNA, its presence in genital cancer biopsies and in cell lines derived from cervical cancer. *The EMBO Journal, 3*(5), 1151–1157.

Denny, L., Kuhn, L., De Souza, M., Pllack, A.E., Dupree, W., & Wright, T.C. Jr. (2005). Screen-and-treat approaches for cervical cancer prevention in low-resource settings: A randomized controlled trial. *Journal of the American Medical Association, 294*(17), 2173–2181.

Dürst, M., Gissmann, L., Ikenberg, H., & zur Hausen, H. A papillomavirus DNA from a cervical carcinoma and its prevalence in cancer biopsy samples from different geographic regions. *Proc Natl Acad Sci USA, 80*(12), 3812–3815.

Ferlay, J., Bray, F., Pisani, P., & Parkin, D.M. (2002). GLOBOCAN 2002. *Cancer incidence, mortality, and prevalence worldwide*. IARC Cancer Base No. 5, version 2.0. Lyon, France: IARC Press.

Gunnell, A.S., Tran, T.N., Torrång, A., Dickman, P.W., Sparén, P., Palmgren, J., & Ylitalo, N. (2006). Synergy between cigarette smoking and human papillomavirus type 16 in cervical cancer in situ development. *Cancer Epidemiol Biomarkers Prev, 15*(11), 2141–2147.

Howlader, N., Noone, A.M., Krapcho, M., Neyman, N., Aminou, R., Waldron, W., Altekruse, S.F., Kosary, C.L., Ruhl, J., Tatalovich, Z., Cho, H., Mariotto, A., Eisner, M.P., Lewis, D.R., Chen, H.S., Feuer, E.J., Cronin, K.A., Edwards, B.K. (eds) (2011). SEER Cancer Statistics Review, 1975–2008, National Cancer Institute. Bethesda, MD.

Jemal, A., Siegel, R., Ward, E., Hao, Y., Xu, J., & Thun, M.J. (2009). Cancer statistics, 2009. *CA Cancer J Clin, 59*, 225–249.

Kumar, V., Abbas, A.K., Nelson, F., & Mitchell, R.N. (2007). *Robbins basic pathology* (8th ed., pp. 718–721). Elsevier, Amsterdam, The Netherlands.

McNeil, C. (2006). Who invented the VLP cervical cancer vaccines? *J. Natl. Cancer Inst, 98*(7), 433.

Münger, K., & Howley, P.M. (2002). Human papillomavirus immortalization and transformation functions. *Virus research, 89*(2), 213–228.

Muñoz, N., Bosch, F.X., de Sanjose, S., et al. (1992). The causal link between human papillomavirus and invasive cervical cancer: A population-based case-control study in Colombia and Spain. *Int J Cancer, 52*, 743–749.

Papanicolaou, G.N., & Traut, H.F. (1943). *Diagnosis of uterine cancer by the vaginal smear*. New York: Commonwealth Fund.

Prokopakis, P., Sourvinos, G., Koumantaki, Y., Koumantakis, E., & Spandidos, D.A. (2002). K-ras mutations and HPV infection in cervicitis and intraepithelial neoplasias of the cervix. *Oncol Rep, 9*, 129–133.

Sherman, M.E., Wang, S.S., Carreon, J., & Devesa, S.S. (2005). Mortality trends for cervical squamous and adenocarcinoma in the United States. Relation to incidence and survival. *Cancer, 103*, 1258–1264.

Sherris, J., Wittet, S., Kleine, A., Sellors, J., Luciani, S., Sankaranarayanan, R., & Barone, M.A. (2009). Evidence-based alternative cervical cancer screening approaches in low-resource settings. *International Perspectives on Sexual and Reproductive Health, 35*(3), 147–152.

Singh, N. (2005). HPV and cervical cancer: Prospects for prevention through vaccination. *Indian J Med Pediatric Oncology, 26*(1), 20–23.

Stentella, P., Frega, A., Ciccarone, M., Cipriano, L., Tinari, A., Tzantzoglou, S., & Pachì, A. (1998). HPV and intraepithelial neoplasia recurrent lesions of the lower genital tract: Assessment of the immune system. *Eur J Gynaecol Oncol, 19*(5), 466–469.

Walboomers, J.M., Jacobs, M.V., Manos, M.M., et al. (1999). Human papillomavirus is a necessary cause of invasive cervical cancer worldwide. *J Pathol, 189*, 12–19.

zur Hausen, H. (1976). Condylomata acuminata and human genital cancer. *Cancer Res, 36*, 530.

Epidemiology of Prostate Cancer

GLOBAL EPIDEMIOLOGY OF PROSTATE CANCER

Carcinoma of the prostate is the second most common form of cancer in men and the sixth leading cause of cancer deaths worldwide. Based upon projections by the American Cancer Society, more than 780,000 cases of prostate cancer are diagnosed annually and more than 250,000 die from metastatic disease (American Cancer Society, 2009).

In developed countries, prostate cancer is diagnosed more often than any other form of male cancer (nearly 567,000 cases) and is the third leading cause of death from cancer in men (144,000 deaths annually). Disease survival in developing countries is high and the ratio of incidence to mortality is 0.25, which is primarily due to screening of asymptomatic men by prostate specific antigen (PSA) and the early detection of small latent carcinomas of the prostate. Invasive prostate cancer is diagnosed less often in developing countries (195,000 cases) but tumors are usually detected late in development resulting in a twofold higher incidence-to-mortality ratio (0.55) and more than 106,000 deaths annually. As a consequence of disparities in screening, mortality rates are probably a better guide to the risk of invasive disease in different populations.

There is marked variability in the international mortality rates of prostate cancer. Mortality rates are high in the Caribbean, Southern and Central Africa, Northern and Central regions of South America, Northern and Western Europe, and Australia/New Zealand. Rates are low in populations of Asia and North Africa (**Figure 22.1**). Furthermore, certain ethnic groups within countries have exceedingly high mortality rates, e.g., African Americans living in the United States have the highest age-adjusted death rates from prostatic cancer in the world (annual rate >70 deaths per 100,000). Their rate is more than double that of Caucasian or Hispanic Americans (less than 35 deaths per 100,000) (**Figure 22.2**). These population differences suggest that prostate cancer is conditioned by environmental influences, particularly in view of the increased rates in Japanese and Chinese migrants to the United States. By comparison, native Chinese and Asian men have annual mortality rates of less than 5 deaths per 100,000 (Parkin et al., 2005).

AGE-SPECIFIC RISK OF PROSTATE CANCER

The incidence of invasive cancer of the prostate increases dramatically in men over the age of 50. The disease is rare until age 50 after which the risk increases exponentially (**Table 22.1**). The lifetime risk of developing invasive disease is approximately 1 in 6 among US Caucasian men (ACS, 2009).

In addition to the clinically overt forms of prostate cancer, there is an even more frequent biologic form of prostate cancer that is discovered as an incidental finding either at postmortem examination or in a surgical specimen removed for other reasons, e.g., in the treatment of benign prostatic hypertrophy (BPH). In almost all of these incidental findings, the lesions are small and comprised only of microscopic foci of malignant cells. This form of prostatic cancer is called *occult* or *latent* prostate cancer.

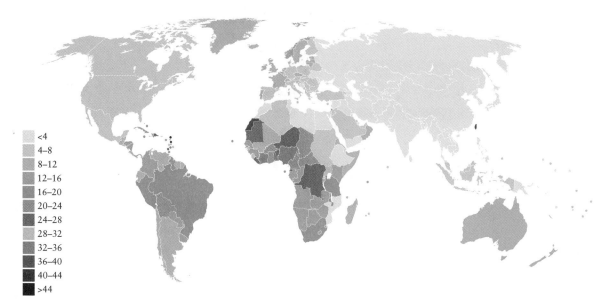

Figure 22.1 Global Prostate Cancer Mortality, 2004.

Source: Data from World Health Organization. The global burden of disease: 2004 update. Geneva, WHO, 2008. Available at www.who.int/evidence/bod.

In postmortem studies of unselected men, occult prostate cancer can be identified in about 10% of subjects between 50–59 years of age, rising to a prevalence of 40–50% in those over the age of 70. It is noteworthy that in the vast majority of these subjects (95%) these occult lesions were absolutely unsuspected and clinically asymptomatic (Robbins and Cotran, 1979).

PATHOGENESIS OF PROSTATE CANCER

Prostate cancer arises from the epithelial lining of the prostatic ducts which channel prostatic fluids into the ejaculatory ducts of the prostate gland. Histologically, nearly all cancerous tumors are adenocarcinomas that display prominent glandular features.

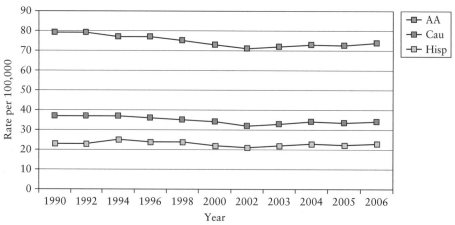

AA = African American; Cau = Caucasian; Hisp = Hispanic

Figure 22.2 Prostate Cancer Mortality in the United States.

Source: Data from American Cancer Society (2009), Cancer Facts and Figures, 2009.

Table 22.1	Cumulative Risk of Invasive Prostate Cancer
Age 45 Years	1 in 2,500
Age 50	1 in 476
Age 55	1 in 120
Age 60	1 in 43
Age 65	1 in 21
Age 70	1 in 9
Age 75	1 in 7
Lifetime	1 in 6

Source: Data from American Cancer Society (2009), Cancer Facts and Figures, 2009.

The prostate gland is roughly divisible into a central region that is responsive to estrogen and a more peripheral region that is stimulated by androgens. Benign prostatic hyperplasia (BPH) is an extremely common disorder that affects men over the age of 50. The hyperplastic nodules of BPH typically arise from the inner regions of the prostate gland, perhaps due to the balance between androgens and estrogens. There is long-standing controversy regarding the development of cancer from the common condition known as benign prostatic hyperplasia (Robbins and Cotran, 1979).

Dihydrotestosterone (DHT), the active form of testosterone, mediates prostatic epithelial cell division through interactions with androgen receptors (AR) on the cell membrane. While nodular hyperplasia tends to develop centrally in the prostate, prostate cancer usually arises in the posterior lobe and peripheral zones of the prostate gland (McNeal, 1981). For this reason, most experts do not believe that nodular hyperplasia is a precursor lesion of prostate cancer. Rather, microscopic carcinomas appear to arise from focal areas of dysplasia in the peripheral zones of the prostate gland (McNeal, 1993). Subsequently, over a period of many years these very small lesions increase in size and acquire invasive potential.

MOLECULAR BIOLOGY OF PROSTATE CANCER

The pathogenesis of prostate cancer and benign prostatic hyperplasia (BPH) are both related to the endocrine system. Androgens acting through androgen receptors (AR) on the cell membranes of prostatic epithelium play critical roles in prostate development and growth as well as the pathogenesis of BPH and prostate cancer (Zhu, 2005). Studies over the years have demonstrated that there are two natural potent androgens acting at the same AR in mammals, including humans (Zhu, Katz, and Imperato-McGinley, 1998). Although testosterone is the primary androgen synthesized and secreted by the testes, dihydrotestosterone (DHT) converted from testosterone by the enzyme 5α-reductase (5αRD) is the main androgen in the prostate. Two forms of 5α-reductase have been identified: 5αRD-1 and 5αRD-2 (Russell and Wilson, 1994). Cellular effects of both of these enzymes are mediated by their activation of AR in prostatic tissues.

Early studies by Rose and colleagues demonstrated higher levels of the active metabolite of testosterone, dihydrotestosterone (DHT), in prostatic fluid of cases with prostate cancer compared to controls with other urologic conditions (Rose et al., 1984). International metabolic epidemiologic studies by Ross and colleagues revealed that US African Americans have higher average serum levels of testosterone than US Caucasians (Ross et al., 1986) and that native Japanese and Chinese men have significantly lower average 5α-reductase activity than either US African Americans or US Caucasians (Ross et al., 1992). These differences suggested a hormonal basis for the high prostate cancer rates observed in African American men compared to the relatively low rates in Asian men.

More recently, molecular studies have shown that prostate cancer tissues overexpress both the 5αRD-1 and 5αRD-2 isozymes whereas BPH tissues overexpress only the 5αRD-2 isozyme. It has also been demonstrated in animal studies that both forms of 5α-reductase can be markedly upregulated by high intake of dietary fat (Cai et al., 2006). This observation provides an important mechanistic link between dietary fat intake and the genesis of prostate cancer (see section below on dietary fat and prostate cancer). Furthermore, the molecular link between 5α-reductase activity and prostate carcinogenesis has motivated the development and investigation of drugs such as finasteride that inhibit 5α-reductase.

FINASTERIDE AND PROSTATE CANCER

In 1993, a large placebo-controlled randomized clinical trial, the Prostate Cancer Prevention Trial (PCPT), was initiated to determine if the 5α-reductase inhibitor finasteride could prevent prostate cancer. The study enrolled 18,882 men aged 55 years and older randomized to receive either finasteride (5 mg daily) or placebo. About 4% of participants were African American men. After 7 years of follow up, 18% of men receiving finasteride developed prostate cancer compared to 24% in the placebo group, a risk reduction of 25%. However, the men who did develop prostate cancer while receiving finasteride were more likely to have high-grade tumors with high metastatic potential. Furthermore, the men taking finasteride reported significantly more sexual side effects (impotence) than men on placebo. Final results were based upon analysis of 9,060 participants, only about half the men who initially enrolled in the study (Thompson et al., 2003).

DIETARY FAT AND PROSTATE CANCER

Ecological correlation studies show a strong positive correlation between diets high in fat and calories with prostate cancer incidence and mortality. Within countries, chronological trends in prostate cancer rates tend to follow in close parallel with per capita trends in dietary fat intake. For example, prostate cancer rates in Japanese men have increased nearly fivefold over a 50-year period since 1955, seemingly in response to the rising level of fat in the Japanese diet (**Figure 22.3**).

West and colleagues examined associations of prostate cancer with dietary intakes of fat, protein, carbohydrate, and certain vitamins and minerals in a population-based case control study in Utah. Dietary data were ascertained from 358 cases and 679 controls

group-matched by age and county of residence. For older cases with aggressive tumors, significant associations were observed for the highest versus lowest quartiles of intake of total fat (OR = 2.9), saturated fat (OR = 2.2), monounsaturated fat (OR = 3.6), polyunsaturated fat (OR = 2.7), and total energy (OR = 2.5). Results suggest that dietary fat increases the risk of aggressive prostate cancer in elderly men (West et al., 1991).

Giovannucci and colleagues examined the association of dietary fat and prostate cancer in a prospective cohort of 51,529 US men aged 40–75 years in the *Health Professionals Follow-Up Study*. After 5 years, men reporting fat intake in the highest quintile experienced a 79% increase in the risk of invasive prostate cancer compared to men in the lowest quintile. Notably, fat derived from consumption of red meat produced a 2.6-fold increase in the risk (Giovannucci et al., 1993).

Neuhouser and colleagues examined the association of prostate cancer and various dietary factors in a prospective cohort of 12,025 US men followed over an 11-year period. In men with a family history of prostate cancer, high intake of essential n-6 polyunsaturated fatty acids produced a 2.6-fold increase in the risk of invasive disease (Neuhouser et al., 2007).

Animal studies support an important etiologic link between prostate cancer development and intake of specific types of dietary fat. Zhu and colleagues found that feeding young rats a diet high in α-linoleic

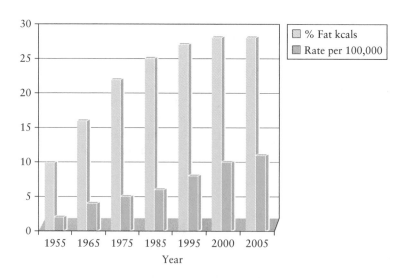

Figure 22.3 Prostate Cancer Mortality and Dietary Fat, Japan: 1955–2005.

Source: Data from Cancer Statistics in Japan, 2010; Center for Cancer Control and Information Services, National Cancer Center, Japan; Wynder EL, Fujita Y, Harris RE, Hirayama T, Hiyama T (1991). Comparative epidemiology of cancer between the United States and Japan: a second look. *Cancer* 67(3):746–763; Matsumura Y (2001). Emerging trends of nutrition: transition and trade-offs. Nutrition trends in Japan. *Asia Pacific J Clin Nutr* 10(Suppl.):S40–S47.

acid from corn oil induced high levels of plasma DHT and 5αRD-2 expression in the prostate gland, thus suggesting a potential molecular mechanism for dietary fat stimulation of prostate growth and pathogenesis (Cai, Imperato-McGinley, and Zhu, 2006). Their studies also suggest that insulin-like growth factor (IGF-1) increases with intake of dietary fat and may be involved in mediating the effects of androgens in the prostate gland.

Using a transgenic model of prostate cancer, Aaronson and colleagues identified strong tumor promotion by essential n-6 polyunsaturated fats from corn oil (α-linoleic acid) that are common in the American diet (Kobayashi et al., 2008). Mechanistically, n-6 polyunsaturated fatty acids are readily converted by the cyclooxygenase and lipoxygenase pathways to eicosanoids, such as prostaglandin E2, leukotrienes, and hydroxyl derivatives of fatty acids. These inflammatory eicosanoids have long been implicated in the pathogenesis of cancer and are believed to play important roles in tumor promotion, progression, and metastasis. Reciprocally, essential n-3 polyunsaturated fatty acids such as gamma-linolenic acid that inhibit the inflammatory cascade have been found to inhibit conversion of testosterone to its active metabolite, DHT (Rose and Connolly, 1991; Pham and Ziboh, 2002).

The differential effects of n-6 versus n-3 fatty acids on androgen metabolism suggest an important etiological link between the balance of essential fatty acids in the diet and prostate carcinogenesis. As discussed above, international studies reflect marked differences in the rates of prostate cancer. African Americans have the highest rates and Asian men the lowest, but Asian men who migrate to the United States transition to higher rates after a single generation (Parkin et al., 2005). This pattern correlates with the 5α-reductase activity among ethnic groups. There is high 5α-reductase activity in African Americans and low activity in Asian men, and furthermore, Asian males who live in North America have higher 5α-reductase activity when compared to males in their home countries (Ross et al., 1992). As pointed out by Yuan-Shan Zhu and Julianne Imperato-McGinley (2009), *"These data indicate that differences in 5α-reductase activity may be ethnically and environmentally determined and may be related to differences in prostate cancer development."* Indeed, the totality of evidence indicates that the *"westernized lifestyle,"* which incorporates high fat/high calorie diets and, in particular, high levels of inflammatory n-6 fatty acids, enhances the risk for malignant transformation of the prostate gland.

NONSTEROIDAL ANTI-INFLAMMATORY DRUGS (NSAIDS) AND PROSTATE CANCER

In the past 2 decades, traditional nonsteroidal anti-inflammatory drugs (NSAIDs) with cyclooxygenase-2 (COX-2) blocking activity have consistently shown potential in the chemoprevention of several forms of malignant neoplasms, including prostate cancer. In a meta-analysis of 17 epidemiologic studies, regular intake of aspirin, ibuprofen, or other over-the-counter NSAIDs was found to reduce the risk of prostate cancer by 27% (Harris, 2009).

Such effects are manifest primarily through COX-2-dependent molecular mechanisms. For example, NSAIDs reduce COX-2-catalyzed formation of specific inflammatory prostaglandins (particularly PGE-2) that promote key cellular processes in cancer development including mutagenesis, mitogenesis, angiogenesis, deregulation of apoptosis, immunosuppression, and metastasis (Harris, 2007).

GENETICS OF PROSTATE CANCER

Prostatic cancer also shows a strong familial component. In studies by Meikle and Stanish (1982), brothers of cases had four times higher cumulative rates of prostate cancer than brothers-in-law or males of the general population, thereby reflecting existence of genetic factors that increase the risk of neoplastic development in the prostate gland. Logically, discovery of mutations and genetic polymorphisms that influence prostate carcinogenesis might be expected in components of the androgen axis that regulate testosterone, dihydrotestosterone, 5α-reductase, and the androgen receptors. One such mutation has already been discovered in African American men with a family history of prostate cancer, a genetic defect in the receptor for the male hormone androgen (testosterone) that may contribute to the development of prostate cancer and its progression (Hu et al., 2010).

NUTRITIONAL SUPPLEMENTS AND PROSTATE CANCER

The findings of a number of observational studies plus two randomized clinical trials indicated that supplemental intake of selenium and vitamin E might be effective in preventing the development of prostate cancer. In 2001, a large randomized placebo controlled clinical trial, the *Selenium and Vitamin E Cancer Prevention Trial (SELECT)*, was initiated to determine whether selenium, vitamin E, or both could prevent prostate cancer. A total of 35,533 men aged 55 years and older were recruited for study from 427 participating sites in the United States, Canada, and Puerto Rico. After more than 5 years of follow up, supplemental selenium or vitamin E, alone or in combination, produced no effect on the risk of developing invasive prostate cancer (Lippman et al., 2008).

PROSTATE CANCER AND SEXUAL ACTIVITY

Another factor that may impact on prostate cancer risk is sexual activity. Declining activity with age may relate to changing ratios of testosterone and estrogen which in turn may stimulate enhanced proliferation of prostatic glandular epithelium.

SCREENING FOR PROSTATE CANCER

Screening for prostate cancer using serum prostate specific antigen (PSA) gained favor in the United States and other developed countries during the 1990s. It is estimated that 20 million PSA tests are performed annually in North America and possibly 20 million more outside of North America (De Angelis et al., 2007). A high level of serum PSA (>4 nanograms per ml) when coupled with digital rectal examination (DRE), ultrasonography, and directed biopsy of suspicious prostatic tissue can be effective in identifying men with invasive disease confined to the prostate gland that can be completely surgically excised without recurrence. Nevertheless, PSA screening is controversial since prostate cancer often develops so slowly that it will never lead to symptoms during a man's lifetime. Furthermore, prostatectomy for removal of a cancerous prostate gland often produces major debilitating side effects such as urinary incontinence, erectile dysfunction, and impotence. The major consideration for any screening protocol is to weigh the benefits of early detection and lifesaving treatment against the risk of harm from unnecessary intervention.

Results of two large randomized clinical trials of PSA screening have now been published. The *European Randomized Study of Screening for Prostate Cancer* evaluated PSA testing versus no screening among 182,000 men ages 50–74 years. After 9 years of follow up, the results did show 20% fewer deaths in the treated group; however, the study also found that a large number of men were treated unnecessarily, resulting in a high rate of major side effects (Schröder et al., 2009). Another randomized study of 76,693 men in the United States compared PSA plus DRE to "usual care" in the detection and treatment of prostate cancer. After 7 years of follow up, there were actually 13% fewer deaths in the "usual care" group (Andriole et al., 2009).

After careful review of the scientific evidence, the US Prevention Task Force concluded that the data were insufficient to recommend screening for men under 75 and that men 75 and older should not be screened (US Preventive Task Force, 2008). Rather, clinicians are now advised to use a process of shared decision-making with each patient that includes candid discussion about the potential risks and benefits of screening. A telling statement from the investigator who initially discovered PSA, Dr. Richard J. Ablin, underscores the controversial nature of routinely screening asymptomatic men for prostate cancer using the PSA test. Dr. Ablin states *"I never dreamed that my discovery four decades ago would lead to such a profit-driven public health disaster. The medical community must confront reality and stop the inappropriate use of PSA screening. Doing so would save billions of dollars and rescue millions of men from unnecessary, debilitating treatments"* (Albin, 2010).

ZINC AND SURVIVAL OF PROSTATE CANCER

Zinc is an essential mineral with known antioxidant and anti-inflammatory effects. Zinc is an important cofactor in DNA repair, apoptosis, and cellular immunity. Notably, the concentration of zinc is higher in prostate tissue than any other tissue in the human body. Recently, Epstein and colleagues examined the level of dietary zinc as a potential predictor of survival among 525 Swedish men diagnosed with invasive prostate cancer during 1989–1995. Swedish men have one of the highest annual mortality rates from prostate cancer in the world (22 deaths per 100,000). After a median follow-up time of 6.4 years, 218 cases (42%) had died of prostate cancer. Zinc intake was estimated based upon its average content in grains, meat, dairy products, fruits, and vegetables consumed by the individual patients. Results revealed that high dietary zinc intake (>15.6 mg per day) was associated with a reduced risk of death due to prostate cancer (hazard ratio = 0.64), whereas zinc intake was not associated with mortality from other causes. The protective effect of high dietary zinc was stronger among men diagnosed with localized tumors (hazard ratio = 0.24). These results suggest that high intake of dietary zinc may have therapeutic benefit in men diagnosed with prostate cancer, particularly among those with localized tumors at the time of diagnosis (Epstein et al., 2011).

● ● ● REFERENCES

Ablin, R.J. (2010, March 10). The great prostate mistake. *New York Times.*

American Cancer Society. (2009). Cancer facts and figures. American Cancer Society.

Andriole, G.L., et al. (2009). Mortality results from a randomized prostate-cancer screening trial. *NEJM, 360*(13), 1310–1319.

Cai, L.Q., Imperato-McGinley, J., & Zhu, Y.S. (2006). Regulation of prostate 5α-reductase-2 gene expression and prostate weight by dietary fat and caloric intake in the rat. *Prostate, 66,* 738–748.

Center for Cancer Control and Information Services. (2010). Cancer statistics in Japan, 2010. Japan: Center for Cancer Control and Information Services, National Cancer Center.

De Angelis, G., Rittenhouse, H.G., Mikolajczyk, S.D., Blair Shamel, L., & Semjonow, A. (2007). Twenty years of PSA: From prostate antigen to tumor marker. *Rev Urol, 9*(3),113–123.

Epstein, M.M., Kasperzyk, J.L., Andrén, O., Giovannucci, E.L., Wolk, A., Håkansson, N.,… Mucci, L.A. (2011). Dietary zinc and prostate cancer survival in a Swedish cohort. *Am J Clin Nutr, 93*(3), 586–593.

Giovannucci, E., Eric, B., Rimm, E.B., Colditz, G.A.,…Stampfer, M.J., Ascherio, A.,…Willett, W.C. (1993). A prospective study **of dietary fat** and risk **of prostate cancer.** *Journal of the National Cancer Institute, 85*(19), 1571–1579.

Harris, R.E. (2007). COX-2 and the inflammogenesis of cancer. *Subcellular Biochemistry, 42,* 193–212.

Harris, R.E. (2009). Cyclooxygenase-2 (COX-2) blockade in the chemoprevention of cancers of the colon, breast, prostate and lung. *Inflammopharmacology, 17,* 1–13.

Horton, R., Pasupuletti, V., & Antonipillai, I. (1993). Androgen induction of steroid 5 alpha-reductase may be mediated via insulin-like growth factor-I. *Endocrinol, 133,* 447–451.

Hu, S.Y., Liu, T., Liu, Z., Ledet, E., Velasco-Gonzalez, C., Mandal, D.M., & Koochekpour, S. (2010). Identification of a novel germline missense mutation of the androgen receptor in African American men with familial prostate cancer. *Asian Journal of Andrology*, 2010.

Kobayashi, N., Barnard, R.J., Said, J., Hong-Gonzalez, J., Corman, D.M., Ku, M.,…Aronson, W.J. (**2008**). Effect of low-fat diet on development of prostate cancer and Akt phosphorylation in the Hi-Myc transgenic mouse model. *Cancer Res, 68*(8), 3066–3073.

Lippman, S.M., Klein, E.A., Goodman, P.J., Lucia, M.S., Thompson, I.M., Ford, L.G.,…Coltman, C.A. Jr. (2008). Effect of selenium and vitamin E on risk of prostate cancer and other cancers: The Selenium and Vitamin E Cancer Prevention Trial (SELECT). *JAMA, 301*(1), 39–51.

Matsumura, Y. (2001). Emerging trends of nutrition: Transition and trade-offs. Nutrition trends in Japan. *Asia Pacific J Clin Nutr, 10*(Suppl.), S40–S47.

McNeal, J. (1981). Normal and pathologic anatomy of prostate. *Urology, 17*(Suppl 3), 11–16.

McNeal, J. (1993). Prostatic microcarcinomas in relation to cancer origin and the evolution to clinical cancer. *Cancer, 71,* 984–91.

Meikle, A.W., & Stanish, W.M. (1982). Familial prostatic cancer risk and low testosterone. *J Clin Endocrinol Metab, 54,* 1104–1108.

Neuhouser, M.L., Barnett, M.J., Kristal, A.R., Ambrosone, C.B., King, I., Thornquist, M., & Goodman, G. (2007). n-6 PUFA increase and dairy foods decrease prostate cancer risk in heavy smokers. *J Nutr, 137,* 1821–1827.

Parkin, M.D., Bray, F., Ferlay, J., & Pisani, P. (2005). Global cancer statistics, 2002. *CA Cancer J Clin, 55,* 74–108.

Pham, H., & Ziboh, V.A. (2002). 5 alpha-reductase-catalyzed conversion of testosterone to dihydrotestosterone is increased in prostatic adenocarcinoma cells: Suppression by 15-lipoxygenase metabolites of gamma-linolenic and eicosapentaenoic acids. *J Steroid Biochem Mol Biol, 82*(4–5), 393–400.

Robbins, S.L., & Cotran, R.S. (1979). *Pathologic basis of disease.* 2nd Edition, W.B. Saunders, Philadelphia.

Rose, D.P., Laaksa, K., Satarouta, M., & Wynder, E.L. (1984). Hormone levels in prostatic fluid in healthy Fins and prostate cancer patients. *Eur J Cancer Clin Oncol, 20,* 1317–1324.

Rose, D.P., & Connolly, J.M. (1991). Effects of fatty acids and eicosanoid synthesis inhibitors on the growth of two human prostate cancer cell lines. *Prostate, 18*(3), 243–254.

Ross, R., Bernstein, L., Judd, H., Hanisch, R., Pike, M., & Henderson, B. (1986). Serum testosterone levels in healthy young black and white men. *J Natl Cancer Inst, 76*(1), 45–48.

Ross, R.K., Bernstein, L., Lobo, R.A., Shimizu, H., Stanczyk, F.Z., Pike, M.C., & Henderson, B.E. (1992). 5-alpha-reductase activity and risk of prostate cancer among Japanese and US white and black males. *Lancet, 339*(8798), 887–889.

Russell, D.W., & Wilson, J.D. (1994). Steroid 5 alpha-reductase: Two genes/two enzymes. *Ann Rev Biochem, 63,* 25–61.

Schröder, F.H., et al. (2009). Screening and prostate cancer mortality in a randomized European study. *NEJM, 360*(13), 1320.

Thompson, I.M., Goodman, P.J., Tangen, C.M., et al. (2003). The influence of finasteride on the development of prostate cancer. *N Engl J Med, 349,* 215–224.

US Preventive Services Task Force. (2008). Screening for prostate cancer: US Preventive Services Task Force recommendation statement. *Ann. Intern Med, 149*(3), 185–191.

West, D.W., Slattery, M.L., Robison, L.M., Fench, T.K., & Mahoney, A.W. (1991). Adult dietary intake and prostate cancer risk in Utah: A case-control study with special emphasis on aggressive tumors. *Cancer Causes and Control, 2,* 85–94.

World Health Organization. (2009). *Death and DALY estimates for 2004 by cause for WHO Member States (Persons, all ages).* World Health Organization.

Wynder, E.L., Fujita, Y., Harris, R.E., Hirayama, T., & Hiyama, T. (1991). Comparative epidemiology of cancer between the United States and Japan: A second look. *Cancer, 67*(3), 746–763.

Zhu, Y.S. (2005). Molecular basis of steroid action in the prostate. *Cellscience Rev, 1,* 27–55.

Zhu, Y.S., Katz, M.D., & Imperato-McGinley, J. (1998). Natural potent androgens: Lessons from human genetic models. *Bailliere's Clin. Endocrinol Metab, 12,* 83–113.

Zhu, Y.S., & Imperato-McGinley, J. (2009). 5α-reductase isozymes and androgen actions in the prostate. *NY Acad Sci, 1155,* 43–56.

Epidemiology of Urinary Bladder Cancer

GLOBAL EPIDEMIOLOGY OF URINARY BLADDER CANCER

Worldwide, approximately 408,000 new cases of urinary bladder cancer are diagnosed each year and 165,000 die from the disease (American Cancer Society, 2009). Bladder cancer develops about 3.3 times more frequently in men than women. Rates are highest in African nations and Eastern Mediterranean regions, particularly Egypt, where squamous cell bladder cancer arises due to chronic infection by the parasitic worm *Schistosoma hematobium* (**Figure 23.1**). Rates of transitional cell carcinoma of the bladder urothelium are highest in Western Europe and other countries where the prevalence of smoking is high, particularly among men (Parkin et al., 2005).

PATHOGENESIS OF URINARY BLADDER CANCER

In developed countries of North America, Europe, and Australia, most bladder cancers (approximately 95%) are transitional cell carcinomas that arise from the epithelial cell lining of the bladder (called the urothelium). The progression of carcinogenesis appears similar to other forms of cancer with epithelial cell

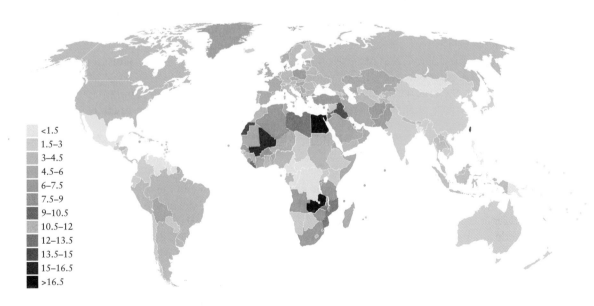

<1.5
1.5–3
3–4.5
4.5–6
6–7.5
7.5–9
9–10.5
10.5–12
12–13.5
13.5–15
15–16.5
>16.5

Figure 23.1 Global Mortality: Bladder Cancer, 2004.

Source: Data from World Health Organization. The global burden of disease: 2004 update. Geneva, WHO, 2008. Available at www.who.int/evidence/bod.

origin. The urothelium undergoes a stepwise progression of changes from mild to severe dysplasia that results in the formation of *noninvasive papillary carcinoma in situ* and ultimately invasive cancer that penetrates the basement membrane. The evolutionary progression of carcinogenesis in the urinary bladder is believed to occur over many years, usually 2 to 3 decades. Often, transitional cell carcinomas of the urinary bladder show multiple cancerous foci at the time of diagnosis, a phenomenon known as *field cancerization.*

In developing nations of Africa and Southern Asia, the predominant histological type of bladder cancer is squamous cell carcinoma, which arises due to chronic infection by the parasitic worm *Schistosoma hematobium.* Chronic infection of the bladder by these parasites (called *bilharziasis*) causes sustained local inflammation, irritation, and subsequent reparative hyperplasia and squamous metaplasia in which the normal urothelial cells are replaced by squamous cells. These changes in the bladder mucosa eventually progress to squamous cell carcinoma (Robbins and Cotran, 1979).

RISK FACTORS FOR URINARY BLADDER CANCER

Tobacco Use and Urinary Bladder Cancer

The dominant risk factor for transitional cell urinary bladder cancer is cigarette smoking, which accounts for about two-thirds of new cases in men and one-third of new cases in women. Epidemiologic cohort and case-control studies have consistently observed two- to threefold increases in the relative risk of developing transitional cell bladder cancer among chronic smokers compared to nonsmokers, as well as dose response relationships with the number of cigarettes smoked and duration of smoking. Cigarette smoking shows similar effects for men and women as well as for individuals with different ethnic backgrounds (Bofetta, 2008).

Urinary bladder carcinogenesis associated with smoking is primarily the result of aromatic amines and arylamines present in cigarette smoke that reach the bladder mucosa, e.g, benzidine, 4-aminobiphenyl, 2-naphthylamine, and 4-chloro-ortho-toluidine (Patrianakos and Hoffman, 1979). Molecular investigations show that these compounds are ultimately biotransformed (activated) in the acidic environment of the bladder to form potent DNA-reactive carcinogens (Vineis et al., 1990). Detoxification enzymes compete with activating enzymes for these procarcinogens to facilitate their excretion in the urine.

Genetic differences in these enzymes are discussed in the *Genetic Factors and Urinary Bladder Cancer* section.

Interestingly, individuals who smoke black (air-cured) tobacco are at a two- to threefold higher risk than smokers of blonde (flue-cured) tobacco, a difference attributable to the higher levels of highly carcinogenic arylamines in black tobacco (Vineis, 1994). The common practice of smoking black tobacco may thus explain the high rates of bladder cancer observed among men in Spain, Italy, the Netherlands, and Uruguay.

Notably, cigarette smoking also independently increases the risk of developing squamous cell carcinoma of the bladder and may in fact interact synergistically with other risk factors (Fortuny et al., 1999). As discussed below, chronic schistosomiasis infection is the key risk factor for development of squamous cell carcinoma of the urinary bladder.

Schistosomiasis and Urinary Bladder Cancer

Squamous cell carcinomas of the bladder occur frequently in conjunction with infection by the trematode *Schistosoma haematobium.* The parasite is endemic in the Nile River but is also found throughout Africa, in certain parts of Southeast Asia, and on the islands of Cyprus and in Southern Portugal. It has been estimated that 85% of Egyptians become infected with this parasite in their lifetimes, which comprises for the astounding fact that bladder cancer accounts for 30% of all malignant neoplasms in Egypt (el Mawla, el-Bolkainy, and Khaled, 2001).

Schistosome worms mature in the liver and migrate to the plexus of blood vessels which nourish the bladder and pelvic organs. The female worms may deposit their eggs in the walls of the bladder, uterus, prostate, or other pelvic organs. This parasitic infection can result in chronic inflammation of the bladder urethelium, which may ultimately produce squamous metaplasia and carcinoma.

The schistosomes are diecious, and the two sexes mature and reproduce in the vascular system. The eggs are laid in small blood vessels that are then liberated into the lumen of the intestines or the urinary bladder. Schistosome eggs subsequently hatch when they reach fresh water and the newborn form of the worm (the miracidium) swims in search of an appropriate snail host. After infestation of the snail, the miracidium develops into another form called the cercariae, which is liberated into the fresh water again and capable of penetrating the skin of swimmers and bathers. Upon penetration of human skin, the parasite reaches the circulation and the liver and the cycle repeats itself.

Molecular studies also suggest that bladder carcinogenesis associated with chronic schistosomiasis may be promoted by coinfection with certain viruses and bacteria, particularly in immunocompromised patients. For example, oncogenic strains of human papillomavirus (HPV-16, HPV-18, and HPV-52) have been found in cancerous urothelial tissues of such patients (Boucher and Anderson, 1997).

Environmental Risk Factors for Urinary Bladder Cancer

A number of environmental and occupational factors increase the risk of bladder cancer. These include occupational exposure to arylamines such as 2-naphthylamine, 4-aminobiphenyl, benzidine, and other compounds and intermediates in the synthesis of azo-dyes and pigments used in the textile, printing, plastic, rubber, and cable industries. Long-term exposure to these compounds among workers in these industries increases the risk of bladder cancer by about 50%.

Workers in aluminum production, auramine O (yellow), and magenta dye manufacturing and coal gasification may also be at increased risk because of sustained exposure to a variety of chemicals that reach the bladder mucosa including polycyclic aromatic hydrocarbons, polychlorinated biphenyls, formaldehyde, and solvents. The uncertainty surrounding the hazards posed by these occupations is partly attributable to the difficulty of measuring past exposure to specific chemical agents.

Pharmacologic Agents and Urinary Bladder Cancer

The analgesic medication phenacetin was once widely used in European nations until the drug was linked to cancers of the renal pelvis and urinary bladder (Johansson and Wahlqvist, 1977; Hoover and Fraumeni, 1981). A case control investigation found more than a sixfold increase in the risk of bladder cancer development due to heavy phenacetin ingestion among women (Piper, Tonascia, and Matanoski, 1985). Phenacetin compounds were removed from the US market in 1983 and have now been discontinued worldwide.

Certain chemotherapeutic agents used in cancer therapy also increase the risk of developing bladder cancer. For example, cyclophosphamide, an alkylating agent used to treat advanced malignancies, has been linked to bladder cancer development. This agent has strong immunosuppressive side effects and sometimes causes a disease known as hemorrhagic cystitis. This condition is associated with cellular atypia and a tenfold increase in the risk of developing transitional

cell carcinoma of the urinary bladder (Hoover and Fraumeni, 1981).

Fluid Intake, Arsenic, and Urinary Bladder Cancer

It is important to ingest plenty of water and fluids (drinking eight to ten 8-ounce glasses of water per day is recommended) to continually flush the renal system and protect against diseases of the urinary tract including bladder cancer. In a 10-year prospective cohort study of 47,909 men, the risk of bladder cancer was reduced by about 50% among men who consumed, on average, 84 ounces of fluids daily compared to those consuming 43 ounces (Michaud et al., 1999). Nevertheless, certain contaminants of drinking water including chlorination disinfection by-products, nitrates, and arsenic have been linked to bladder carcinogenesis (Cantor, 1997).

A 50-year longitudinal study documented marked increases in bladder and lung cancer mortality related to ingestion of arsenic-contaminated drinking water by the population residing in Northern Chile. Observed cancer rates were highest 10–20 years after peak concentrations of arsenic were detected in the drinking water, suggesting a long latency period. Peak rates of bladder cancer were elevated by 6-fold in men and nearly 14-fold in women. Cancer rates declined dramatically following installation of water treatment plants to eliminate arsenic from the drinking water (Smith et al., 1998; Marshall et al., 2007).

Genetic Factors and Urinary Bladder Cancer

The relative risk of bladder cancer is influenced by the smoking habit as well as genetically determined enzymes that either activate or detoxify arylamines that enter the human system via tobacco smoke or contaminated environments. For example, first-degree relatives of patients with bladder cancer have a twofold increased risk of developing the disease compared to the general population, whereas there is a fivefold increase in the risk for individuals with a positive family history who are also chronic smokers.

Exposure to arylamines (e.g., from tobacco smoke or the environments of certain occupations) is known to increase the risk of bladder cancer. The metabolism of arylamines occurs in the liver and the urinary bladder through specific enzymatic reactions. The first step takes place in the liver where nitrogen oxidation of arylamines is catalyzed by enzymes of the P450 system. Subsequently in the bladder, the N-hydroxylamines can either be detoxified and excreted or activated to form potent DNA-reactive carcinogens.

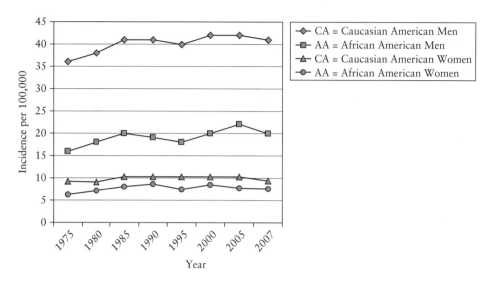

Figure 23.2 Incidence of Urinary Bladder Cancer, USA, 1975–2005.

Source: Data from Howlader et al (eds) (2011). SEER Cancer Statistics Review, 1975–2008, National Cancer Institute. Bethesda, MD.

The enzyme arylamine N-acetyltransferase 2 (NAT2) is involved in the detoxification of various bladder carcinogens, including carcinogenic arylamines (Vineis et al., 1990). A specific dominant mutation in the *NAT2* gene results in slow metabolism of arylamines. Consequently, individuals with the *NAT2* slow-acetylation mutation are at higher risk of developing bladder cancer than those without the mutation (Vineis et al., 1990; Risch et al., 1995). Furthermore, a synergistic interaction is present involving the *NAT2* slow-acetylation mutation and heavy smoking which translates to a greatly increased risk of developing bladder cancer in individuals with both these risk factors compared to nonsmokers who do not carry the *NAT2* mutation (Marcus, Vineis, and Rothman, 2000).

Other enzymatic reactions also modulate the potential carcinogenicity of arylamines in the urinary bladder. Notably, levels of the ubiquitous enzyme beta-glucuronidase are present in the bladder. At urine PH 5.6, this enzyme is capable of splitting various urinary conjugates into carcinogenic elements. The glutathione-*S*-transferase M1 (GSTM1) null genotype also increases the risk of bladder cancer, although it apparently has no interaction with smoking status (Yu et al., 1995).

Ethnic Variation in Urinary Bladder Cancer

In the United States, the annual incidence of bladder cancer is twice as high in Caucasian American men as African American men (41 vs. 20 per 100,000 in 2007) and 24% higher in Caucasian American women compared to African American women (9.4 vs. 7.6 per 100,000 in 2007) (SEER, 2007). These ethnic differences have persisted for decades (**Figure 23.2**) and they pertain primarily to transitional cell bladder cancer that is related to cigarette smoking and other sources of exposure to arylamines (Risch et al., 1995).

The persistently higher incidence rates of bladder cancer in Caucasians versus African Americans in the United States prompted investigations of genetic polymorphisms of smoking and NAT2 in these populations. In a study restricted to smokers, Richie and colleagues demonstrated that the frequency of slow NAT2 acetylators was twofold higher in Caucasians than African Americans (64% vs. 36%). Furthermore, Caucasians smoked an average of 8 cigarettes per day *more* than African American smokers. These observations (high smoking-related arylamine exposure coupled with slow genetically regulated NAT2 acetylation and delayed detoxification in Caucasians) provide a genetic by environmental basis for the ethnic divergence in the incidence rates of bladder cancer (Muscat et al., 2008).

Albeit, despite their relatively low incidence rates of bladder cancer, African Americans typically have more advanced disease at the time of diagnosis and poor survival compared to Caucasians (Underwood et al., 2009). Thus, racial disparity continues to exist in bladder cancer presentation and survival in the United States (Underwood et al., 2009).

• • • REFERENCES

American Cancer Society. (2009). Cancer facts and figures. American Cancer Society, Atlanta, Georgia.

Boffetta, P. (2008). Tobacco smoking and risk of bladder cancer. *Scand J Urol Nephrol Suppl*, 42(S218), 45–54.

Boucher, N.R., & Anderson, J.B. (1997). Human papillomavirus and bladder cancer. *Int Urogynecol J*, 8, 354–357.

Cantor, K.P. (1997). Drinking water and cancer. *Cancer Causes Control*, 8(3), 292–308.

el-Mawla, N.G., el-Bolkainy, M.N., & Khaled, H.M. (2001). Bladder cancer in Africa: Update. *Semin Oncol*, 28(2), 174–178.

Fortuny, J., Kogevinas, M., Chang-Claude, J., González, C.A., Hours, M., Jöckel, K.H.,… Boffetta, P. (1999). Tobacco, occupation and non-transitional-cell carcinoma of the bladder: An international case-control study. *Int J Cancer*, 80(1), 44–46.

Hoover, R., & Fraumeni, J.F. Jr. (1981). Drug-induced cancer. *Cancer*, 47, 1071.

Johansson, S., & Wahlqvist, L. (1977). Tumours of urinary bladder and ureter associated with abuse of phenacetin-containing analgesics. *Acta Pathol Microbiol Scand [A]*, 85, 768–774.

Marcus, P.M., Vineis, P., & Rothman, N. (2000). NAT2 slow acetylation and bladder cancer risk: A meta-analysis of 22 case–control studies conducted in the general population. *Pharmacogenetics*, 10, 115–122.

Marshall, G., Catterina Ferreccio, C., Yuan, Y., Bates, M.N., Steinmaus, C., Selvin, S.,…Smith, A.H. (2007). Fifty-year study of lung and bladder cancer mortality in Chile related to arsenic in drinking water. *J Natl Cancer Inst*, 99, 920–928.

Michaud, D.S., Spiegelman, D., Clinton, S.K., Rimm, E.B., Curhan, G.C., Willett, W.C., & Giovannucci, E.L. (1999). Fluid intake and the risk of bladder cancer in men. *New Eng J Med*, 340, 1390–1397.

Muscat, J.E., Pittman, B., Kleinman, W., Lazarus, P., Steven, D., Stellman, S.D., & Richie, J.P. Jr. (2008). Comparison of CYP1A2 and NAT2 phenotypes between black and white smokers. *Biochemical Pharmacology*, 76(7), 929–937.

Parkin, D.M., Bray, F., Ferlay, J., & Pisani, P. (2005). Global cancer statistics, 2002. *CA Cancer J Clin*, 55, 74–108.

Patrianakos, C., & Hoffman, D. (1979). Chemical studies of tobacco smoke. LXIV. On the analysis of aromatic amines in cigarette smoke. *J Anal Chem*, 3, 150–154.

Piper, J.M., Tonascia, J., & Matanoski, G.M. (1985). Heavy phenacetin use and bladder cancer in women aged 20 to 49 years. *N Engl J Med*, 313(5), 292–295.

Robbins, S.L., & Cotran, R.S. (1979). *Pathologic basis of disease*. Philadelphia: WB Saunders Company.

Risch, A., Wallace, D.M.A., Bathers, S., et al. (1995). Slow N-acetylation genotype is a susceptibility factor in occupational and smoking related bladder cancer. *Hum Mol Genet*, 4, 231–236.

Scélo, G., & Brennan, P. (2007). The epidemiology of bladder and kidney cancer. *Nature Clinical Practice Urology*, 4, 205–217.

SEER Cancer Statistics Review (1975–2007). *Surveillance epidemiology and end results*, United States: National Cancer Institute.

Smith, A.H., Goycolea, M., Haque, R., & Biggs, M.L. (1998). Marked increase in bladder and lung cancer mortality in a region of Northern Chile due to arsenic in drinking water. *Am J Epidemiol*, 147, 660– 669.

Underwood, W. III, Dunn, R., Williams, C., & Lee, C. (2009). Gender and geographic influence on the racial disparity in bladder cancer mortality in the US. *Journal of the American College of Surgeons*, 202(2), 284–290.

Vineis, P. (1994). Epidemiology of cancer from exposure to arylamines. *Environmental Health Perspectives, 102*(Supplement 6), 7–10.

Vineis, P., Caporaso, N., Tannenbaum, S.R., Skipper, P.L., Glogowski, J., Bartsch, H.,… Kadlubar, F. (1990). Acetylation phenotype, carcinogen-hemoglobin adducts, and cigarette smoking. *Cancer Research, 50*, 3002–3004.

Yu, M.C., Ross, R.K., Chan, K.K., Henderson, B.E., Skipper, P.L., Tannenbaum, S.R., & Coetzee, G.A. (1995). Glutathione *S*-transferase M1 genotype affects aminobiphenyl–hemoglobin adduct levels in white, black, and Asian smokers and nonsmokers. *Cancer Epidemiol Biomarkers Prev, 4*, 861–864.

CHAPTER

24

Epidemiology of Kidney Cancer

GLOBAL EPIDEMIOLOGY OF KIDNEY CANCER

Kidney cancer causes significant morbidity and mortality worldwide. In 2008, 271,000 new cases were detected (168,000 men and 103,000 women) and 116,000 deaths were attributed to kidney cancer (72,000 men and 44,000 women). Furthermore, both the incidence and mortality have increased steadily in the past 2 decades, particularly among men (**Figure 24.1**) (Parkin, Pisani, and Ferlay, 1999a, 1999b; Parkin et al., 2005; Ferlay et al., 2010). While the rising incidence rates may be partially attributable to improvements in imaging techniques, better

detection does *not* explain the worldwide increase in mortality (Hollingsworth et al., 2006).

GLOBAL PATTERN OF KIDNEY CANCER

There is considerable geographic variability in both the incidence and mortality rates of kidney cancer. North American and Scandanavian populations have the highest reported rates and Asian and African populations have the lowest. In 2002, the annual incidence rates in populations of more developed nations, approximately 10 per 100,000 for men and 5 per 100,000 for women, were fivefold higher than

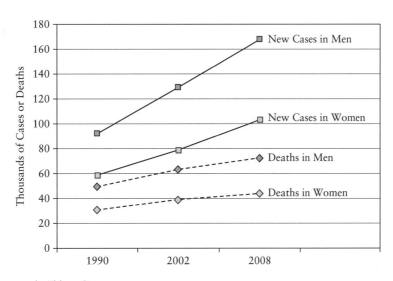

Figure 24.1 Global Increase in Kidney Cancer.

Source: Data from Parkin DM, Pisani P, Ferlay J (1999). Global cancer statistics. *CA Cancer J Clin* 49 (1):33–64; Parkin DM, Bray F, Ferlay J, Pisani, P (2005). Global cancer statistics, 2002. *CA Cancer J Clin* 55:74–108; Ferlay J, Shin H-R, Forman D, Mathers C, Parkin DM (2010). Esimates of worldwide burden of cancer in 2008. *Int J Cancer* 127(12):2893–2917.

corresponding rates in less developed nations, 2 per 100,000 for men and 1 per 100,000 for women (Ferlay et al., 2002; Weikart and Ljungberg, 2010). While such differences may partially reflect specific effects of lifestyle and environmental exposures, it is likely that they are largely attributable to underreporting due to lack of diagnostic imaging and detection in underdeveloped nations.

KIDNEY CANCER MORTALITY

Historically, the classic triad of clinical signs (flank pain, hematuria, and palpable mass) in a patient usually led to the detection of a large tumor of the kidney at a late stage of development. Such tumors had often metastasized to other anatomic sites by the time they were diagnosed, making treatment difficult and prognosis poor.

In the current practice of medicine, kidney tumors are often detected incidentally at a relatively early stage of development during imaging studies of the abdomen for other conditions. As with all forms of cancer, early detection of kidney cancer is essential for successful therapy and prolonged patient survival. Kidney tumors detected at an early stage often respond well to treatment and, as a consequence, survival rates have improved and mortality rates have stabilized or declined in many developed nations of the world (Pantuck, Zisman, and Belldegrun, 2001). Nevertheless, in less developed nations without sophisticated methods of early detection, the upward trend in mortality is continuing.

TYPES OF KIDNEY CANCER

Renal cell carcinoma, arising from epithelial cells that line the renal tubules, is the most common type of kidney cancer, accounting for approximately 85–90% of all malignant kidney tumors. Since these cells normally secrete a variety of vasoactive and regulatory hormones (e.g., renin, erythropoietin, antidiuretic hormone), such tumors often manifest symptoms of hypertension, polycythemia, and other metabolic disturbances.

Transitional cell carcinomas, arising from epithelial cells at the junction of the renal pelvis and the ureter, constitute 5–10% of malignant kidney tumors. Microscopically, transitional cell carcinomas of the renal pelvis are similar to urothelial carcinomas of the urinary bladder. Transitional epithelial cells are intermediate between flat squamous cells and tall columnar cells. This type of epithelium lines the collecting ducts in the renal pelvis, the ureters, and the urinary bladder (Robbins and Cotran, 1979).

Wilms' tumor (named after the German surgeon Max Wilms, who first described it) accounts for about 5% of malignant kidney tumors. This tumor occurs almost exclusively in children under the age of 10 years, usually before the age of 5. Wilms' tumors are comprised of mixed stromal and epithelial cells with abortive configurations of renal glomeruli and tubules. As discussed in the following sections of this chapter, Wilms' tumor most often arises in children with heritable genetic susceptibility, in contrast to the adult forms of kidney cancer that are predominantly associated with exposure to certain environmental risk factors (Robbins and Berg, 1979; Kim and Chung, 2006).

PATHOLOGIC SUBTYPES OF RENAL CELL CARCINOMA

Histological examination of renal cell carcinomas reveals four distinct subtypes: clear cell, papillary, chromophobe, and collecting duct tumors. Clear cell tumors make up about 85% of all renal cell carcinomas. They arise from the proximal tubules of the kidney and are genetically characterized by deletions and other abnormalities of the short arm of chromosome 3. An important finding in the field of cancer genetics is that the genetic abnormalities of clear cell tumors of the kidney invariably involve the *von Hippel Lindau gene*. The remaining subtypes consist of papillary carcinomas (~10%), chromophobe tumors (~5%), and collecting duct (*Bellini*) tumors (<1%), all of which have been found in association with a variety of chromosomal abnormalities.

RISK FACTORS FOR RENAL CELL CARCINOMA

The web of causation of renal cell carcinoma includes three major risk factors that are modifiable: cigarette smoking, obesity, and hypertension. While epidemiologic studies have clearly established that each of these factors has an etiologic link with renal cell carcinoma, the underlying physiologic mechanisms and interactions remain to be elucidated. Specific dietary factors and certain other environmental factors have also shown effects in some studies, although the evidence supporting their role has been inconsistent. A notable finding from molecular analyses of renal cell tumors (clear cell subtype) is the presence of abnormalities in the von Hippel Lindau gene, a tumor suppressor gene with pleiotropic (multiple) effects on tumor growth and development (Pascual and Borque, 2008).

Gender Differences in Kidney Cancer

Renal cell carcinoma occurs in a male:female ratio of approximately 1.6:1 in most populations studied. A recent analysis of the US Surveillance, Epidemiology, and End Results (SEER) database also shows that men present with significantly larger and higher-grade tumors than women, and women have a slightly higher 5-year survival rate than men (69% for women vs. 65% for men) (Aron et al., 2008). Though the exact reasons for these differences have not been clarified, it is probable that men have higher levels of exposure to tobacco and other toxic compounds than women, and women are traditionally more health conscious than men.

Smoking and Renal Cell Carcinoma

There is compelling evidence to support a causal link between cigarette smoking and the development of renal cell carcinomas. Hunt and colleagues examined this association in a meta-analysis of 24 epidemiologic investigations: 19 case-control studies of 8,032 cases and 13,800 controls, and 5 cohort studies of 1,326 cases among 1,457,754 participants. Combined estimates of relative risk (RR) for ever smokers compared to never smokers were RR = 1.38 for all subjects, RR = 1.54 for men, and RR = 1.22 for women. Furthermore, there were significant dose responses in the risk with increasing intensity of smoking in both men and women (**Figure 24.2**), and significant risk reductions were evident in former

smokers. The investigators concluded that cigarette smoking is clearly implicated in the etiology of renal cell carcinoma (Hunt et al., 2005). It is also noteworthy that two case-control studies suggest there may be an association between exposure to environmental smoke and the risk of developing renal cell carcinoma, although further studies will be needed to confirm this (Hu and Ugnat, 2005; Theis et al., 2008).

Obesity and Renal Cell Carcinoma

Numerous epidemiologic investigations suggest there is an association between obesity and the risk of developing renal cell carcinoma. In a recent meta-analysis of 32 studies involving 11,950 male cases and 6,592 female cases, the combined estimates of relative risk were elevated for overweight (BMI: 25–30, RR = 1.4) and obese (BMI: 30–40, RR = 1.9) subjects compared to those of normal weight (BMI: 20–25). Risk elevations were similar for obese men (RR = 1.8) and obese women (RR = 2.1), and each unit of BMI increase above BMI: 25 produced a risk increase of approximately 7%. These results are in agreement with an earlier meta-analysis and suggest that obese people have a near twofold increase in the risk of developing renal cell carcinomas compared to those of normal weight (Ward et al., 2010).

Hypertension and Renal Cell Carcinoma

Regulation of blood pressure is an important kidney function, and as such, hypertension has been extensively examined as a risk factor for the development of renal cell carcinoma. As discussed in the following paragraphs, several recent epidemiologic studies of

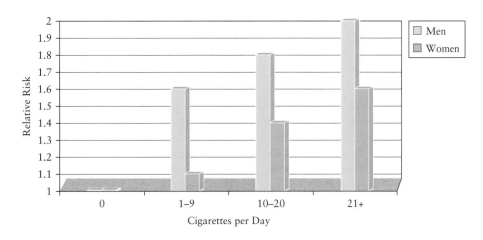

Figure 24.2 Renal Cell Carcinoma and Cigarette Smoking.

Source: Data from Hunt JD, van der Hel OL, McMillan GP, Boffetta P, Brennan P (2005). Renal cell carcinoma in relation to cigarette smoking: meta-analysis of 24 studies. *Int J Cancer* 114:101–108.

hypertension and renal cell carcinoma in different populations show reasonable consistency in revealing an association; nevertheless, whether hypertension is a cause or an effect of this malignancy remains a topic of high controversy.

Chow and colleagues examined the health records of 363,992 Swedish men who underwent at least one physical examination during 1971–1992 and were followed until death or the end of the study in 1995. Cases of kidney cancer (759 with renal cell carcinoma and 136 with transitional cell carcinoma of the renal pelvis) were identified through cross-linkage of data with the nationwide *Swedish Cancer Registry*. Results revealed that obesity and hypertension independently increased the risk of developing renal cell carcinoma but not transitional cell carcinoma, whereas smoking was a risk factor for both forms of kidney cancer (Chow et al., 2000).

Choi and colleagues examined the association between death from kidney cancer and baseline hypertension in a large cohort of 576,562 Korean men who were studied during 1992–2001. Hypertension was found to significantly increase the risk (RR = 2.43), and the risk was particularly high among cigarette smokers (RR = 8.18) (Choi et al., 2005).

Flaherty and colleagues examined hypertension, thiazide use, BMI, weight change, and smoking as risk factors for renal cell carcinoma in prospective cohorts being followed in the United States. The study population included 118,191 women enrolled in the US *Nurses' Health Study* and 48,953 men enrolled in the *Health Professionals Follow-Up Study*. Analysis was based upon 155 incident cases reported during 24 years of follow-up for women and 110 incident cases reported during 12 years of follow-up for men. With adjustment for other variables, hypertension significantly increased the risk of cancer development in both women (RR = 1.9) and men (RR = 1.8). Risk increases were also noted for obesity and chronic smoking, but there was no increase with thiazide use (Flaherty et al., 2005).

Vatten and colleagues conducted a prospective cohort study of blood pressure and renal cell carcinoma in 36,728 women and 35,688 men from Norway. Compared to normotensive individuals, women with elevated blood pressure (systolic blood pressure exceeding 150 mm Hg) had twice the risk of developing renal cell carcinoma (RR = 2.0). However, results were inconsistent for men (Vatten et al., 2007).

Weikart and colleagues examined blood pressure and renal cell carcinoma in the *European Prospective Investigation into Cancer and Nutrition (EPIC)*. Blood pressure was measure in 296,638 men and women recruited in 8 European countries during 1992–1998. Information on the use of antihypertensive medications was available for 254,935 of these individuals. During an average follow-up of more than 6 years, 250 cases of renal cell carcinoma were detected. Elevated blood pressure (systolic blood pressure exceeding 160 mm Hg) was found to be an independent risk factor (RR = 2.48). Risk estimates did not differ by gender or type of antihypertensive medication, and individuals taking antihypertensive medications were not found to be at increased risk unless blood pressure was poorly controlled (Weikart et al., 2008).

Corrao and colleagues conducted a meta-analysis of 18 studies that examined the association of renal cell carcinoma with hypertension and use of antihypertension medications. The pooled estimate of risk for hypertension was significantly increased (OR = 1.62). Risk increases were also noted for use of antihypertensive medications although effects were attenuated with adjustment for other factors (Corrao et al., 2007).

What is clear from these studies is that hypertension is independently associated with a significant increase in the risk of developing renal cell carcinoma in both men and women. What is as yet unclear is the sequence of pathogenesis. Does malignant transformation induce changes in renin and other vasoactive substances in the kidney that increase blood pressure, or does an increase in the blood pressure cause malignant transformation?

Diabetes Mellitus and Kidney Cancer

Since type 2 diabetes is etiologically linked to chronic diseases of the kidney (nephrosis and nephritis), it is logical to examine the association between diabetes and kidney cancer. Investigators at the *Karolinski Institute* in Sweden recently examined this association by meta-analysis of nine prospective cohort studies involving patients from Europe, Asia, and North America. Across all studies, individuals with diabetes were at increased risk for the development of kidney cancer compared to those without diabetes (combined RR = 1.42). However, there was statistically significant heterogeneity among studies, and the association with diabetes was stronger in women (RR = 1.70) than men (RR = 1.26). Additional studies designed to assess the time interval between the onset of diabetes and development of kidney cancer are needed to provide definitive evidence of a causal link (Larrson and Wolk, 2010).

GENETIC ABNORMALITIES IN RENAL CELL CARCINOMA

Renal cell carcinomas occasionally occur in a familial setting in association with certain genetic abnormalities. However, only a small fraction of cases (about 4%) report a positive family history of kidney cancer (Lipworth et al., 2009). Familial cases often develop multifocal and/or bilateral tumors at a relatively early age. Among the heritable cancer syndromes, the most important are the *von Hippel Lindau (VHL) syndrome* and *Birt-Hogg-Dube syndrome*.

von Hippel Lindau Syndrome and Renal Cell Carcinoma

The von Hippel Lindau syndrome is a rare autosomal dominant cancer syndrome with a prevalence rate of about 1 in 36,000 individuals. This syndrome is caused by a mutant tumor suppressor gene called the von Hippel Lindau (*VHL*) gene. Approximately one-third of patients who carry a mutant form of the *VHL* gene develop renal cell carcinoma (clear cell type). Other clinical characteristics include retinal angiomas, hemangioblastomas of the central nervous system, islet cell pancreatic tumors, and pheochromocytomas of the adrenal glands. The syndrome is named after the physicians who first described its clinical signs in afflicted patients. The German ophthalmologist Eugen von Hippel first described the angiomas of the eye (von Hippel, 1904), and the Swedish pathologist Arvid Lindau first described the angiomas of the cerebellum and spine (Lindau, 1927).

The *VHL* gene, which is located on the short arm of chromosome 3, regulates the transcription of other genes that encode proteins critical for cell division and function such as *hypoxia-inducible factor (HIF)*, *vascular endothelial growth factor (VEGF)*, *platelet-derived growth factor (PDGF)*, and *transforming growth factors (TGF-a and TGF-b)*. Mutations in the *VHL* gene accelerate tumor initiation, growth, and development.

von Hippel Lindau Gene and Sporadic Renal Cell Carcinoma

It has recently been discovered that mutations of the *VHL* gene are common not only in the von Hippel Lindau syndrome but also in sporadic (nonfamilial) cases of clear cell renal carcinoma. In a study of 187 Japanese patients with malignancy, 108 tumor samples were found to have *VHL* abnormalities (98 with *VHL* mutations and 10 with *VHF* hypermethylation)

(Yao et al., 2002). And in a more recent study of 205 clear cell tumors ascertained from patients in Central Europe, investigators found *VHL* abnormalities in 91% of cases (82.4% with *VHL* mutations and 8.3% with *VHL* hypermethylation). These studies suggest that most clear cell tumors of the kidney arise in association with genetic or epigenetic modifications of a single gene, the *VHL* gene (Nickerson et al., 2008). Indeed, the *VHL* gene has potential as a biomarker, a prognostic indicator, and/or a target for molecular therapy.

Birt-Hogg-Dube Syndrome

Birt-Hogg-Dube syndrome is a rare autosomal dominant syndrome that has been identified in about 50 families worldwide. This syndrome is characterized by renal cancer, renal and pulmonary cysts, and benign tumors of the hair follicles (Birt, Hogg, and Dubé, 1977). It is caused by mutations in the *folliculin gene (FLCN)*, a tumor suppressor gene located on the short arm of chromosome 17 (Toro et al., 2008).

OCCUPATIONAL EXPOSURES AND RENAL CELL CARCINOMA

A few epidemiologic investigations have examined exposure to toxic compounds and the risk of developing renal cell carcinomas. Mandel and colleagues conducted an international case-control study involving 1,732 incident cases of renal cell carcinoma and 2,309 controls from centers in Australia, Denmark, Germany, Sweden, and the United States. Significant associations were found for occupational exposures to asbestos (RR = 1.4), cadmium (RR = 2.0), petroleum products (RR = 1.6), and dry-cleaning solvents (RR = 1.4) (Mandel et al., 1995). Synergism involving environmental exposures have also been noted in some studies. For example, in an early case-control study of cadmium exposure and renal cancer, the combination of cadmium exposure and cigarette smoking was found to increase the risk more than fourfold (Kolonel, 1976).

Development of renal cell carcinoma has been found in association with somatic genetic mutations in the *VHL* tumor suppressor gene. As already discussed, the *VHL* gene functions by controlling steps in the cell cycle and, if mutated, cell proliferation continues unabated. Brauch and colleagues studied 151 cases of renal cell carcinoma (clear cell type), 44 of whom had long-term occupational exposure to trichloroethylene, an industrial solvent, and 107 cases without exposure.

Somatic mutations were detected in tumor specimens from 33 of the 44 (75%) cases exposed to trichloroethylene, whereas such mutations were totally absent in tumors from the 107 nonexposed cases. Results suggest that exposure to trichloroethylene may trigger mutational events in the *VHL* gene that are associated with the development of renal cell carcinoma (Brauch et al., 1999).

ACQUIRED CYSTIC KIDNEY DISEASE AND RENAL CELL CARCINOMA

Acquired cystic kidney disease develops in approximately 50% of patients who are maintained on chronic hemodialysis and peritoneal dialysis for kidney failure. A major complication of this condition is the development of renal cell carcinoma. Follow-up studies of patients with acquired cystic kidney disease suggest that their risk of developing renal cell carcinoma is 50-fold higher than in the general population. Careful surveillance of dialysis patients by periodic ultrasonography and computerized tomography is recommended for the early detection of such tumors (Brennan et al., 1991; Truong et al., 1995).

ANALGESICS AND RENAL CELL CARCINOMA

Though some studies have found an association between renal cell carcinoma and heavy or long-term use of analgesics, others have not. Chow studied associations in 440 cases of renal cell carcinoma, spouses of 151 cases, and 691 control subjects. No significant excess risk was observed with regular use of aspirin, acetaminophen, or combinations of these agents. The investigators concluded that the use of analgesics is not likely to pose a significant risk for the development of renal cell carcinoma (Chow et al., 2000).

RISK FACTORS FOR TRANSITIONAL CELL CARCINOMA OF THE RENAL PELVIS

The profile of risk factors associated with the development of transitional cell carcinomas of the renal pelvis is essentially the same as for transitional cell carcinomas of the urinary bladder.

The dominant risk factor is chronic exposure to tobacco smoke, which has been found to elevate the risk two- to threefold compared to nonsmokers (Bofetta, 2008). Carcinogenesis associated with smoking is primarily the result of aromatic amines and arylamines present in cigarette smoke that reach the mucosal lining of the renal pelvis, ureters, and urinary bladder.

A number of environmental and occupational factors increase the risk including occupational exposure to arylamines such as 2-naphthylamine, 4-aminobiphenyl, benzidine, and other compounds and intermediates in the synthesis of azo-dyes and pigments used in the textile, printing, plastic, rubber, and cable industries. Long-term exposure to these compounds among workers in these industries increases the risk by about 50% (Vineis, 1994).

The analgesic medication phenacetin was once widely used in European nations until the drug was linked to cancers of the renal pelvis and urinary bladder (Johansson and Wahlqvist, 1977; Hoover and Fraumeni, 1981). A case control investigation found more than a sixfold increase in the risk of bladder cancer development due to heavy phenacetin ingestion among women (Piper, Tonascia, and Matanoski, 1985). Phenactin compounds were removed from the US market in 1983 and have now been discontinued worldwide (Chow et al., 1994).

• • • REFERENCES

Aron, M., Nguyen, M.M., Stein, R.J., & Gill, I.S. (2008). Impact of gender in renal cell carcinoma: An analysis of the SEER database. *European Urology, 54*(1), 133–142.

Birt, A.R., Hogg, G.R., & Dubé, W.J. (1977). Hereditary multiple fibrofolliculomas with trichodiscomas and acrochordons. *Arch Derm, 113*(12), 1674–1677.

Boffetta, P. (2008). Tobacco smoking and risk of bladder cancer. *Scand J Urol Nephrol Suppl, 42*(S218), 45–54.

Brauch, H., Weirich, G., Hornauer, M.A., Störkel, S., Wöhl, T., & Brüning, T. (1999). Trichloroethylene exposure and specific somatic mutations in patients with renal cell carcinoma. *J Natl Cancer Inst, 91*(10), 854–861.

Brennan, J.F., Stilmant, M.M., Babayan, R.K., & Siroky, M.B. (1991). Acquired renal cystic disease: implications for the urologist. *Br J Urol, 67*(4), 342–348.

Choi, M.Y., Jee, S.H., Sull, J.W., & Nam, C.M. (2005). The effect of hypertension on the risk for kidney cancer in Korean men. *Kidney Int, 67*(2), 647–652.

Chow, W.H., McLaughlin, J.K., Linet, M.S., Niwa, S., & Mandel, J.S. (1994). Use of analgesics and risk of renal cell cancer. *Int J Cancer*, 59(4), 467–470.

Chow, W.H., Gridley, G., Fraumeni, J.F. Jr., & Järvholm, B.N. (2000). Obesity, hypertension, and the risk of kidney cancer in men. *N Engl J Med*, 343(18), 1305–1311.

Chow, W.H., Dong, L.M., & Devesa, S.S. (2010). Epidemiology and risk factors for kidney cancer. *Nature Reviews Urology*, 7, 245–257.

Corrao, G., Scotti, L., Bagnardi, V., & Sega, R. (2007). Hypertension, antihypertensive therapy and renal-cell cancer: A meta-analysis. *Curr Drug Saf*, 2(2), 125–133.

Ferlay, J., Bray, F., Pisani, P., & Parkin, D.M. (2002). GLOBOCAN 2002. (2004). *Cancer incidence, mortality, and prevalence worldwide.* IARC Cancer Base No. 5, version 2.0. Lyon, France: IARC Press.

Ferlay, J., Shin, H.R., Forman, D., Mathers, C., & Parkin, D.M. (2010). Esimates of worldwide burden of cancer in 2008. *International Journal of Cancer*, 127(12), 2893–2917.

Flaherty, K.T., Fuchs, C.S., Colditz, G.A., Stampfer, M.J., Speizer, F.E., Willett, W.C., & Curhan, G.C. (2005). A prospective study of body mass index, hypertension, and smoking and the risk of renal cell carcinoma (United States). *Cancer Causes Control*, 16(9), 1099–1106.

Hollingsworth, J.M., Miller, D.C., Daignault, S., & Hollenbeck, B.K. (2006). Rising incidence of small renal masses: A need to reassess treatment effect. *J Natl Cancer Inst*, 98, 1331–1334.

Hoover, R., & Fraumeni, J.F. Jr. (1981). Drug-induced cancer. *Cancer*, 47(5 Suppl), 1071–1080.

Hu, J., & Ugnat, A.M. (2005). Active and passive smoking and risk of renal cell carcinoma in Canada. *Eur J Cancer*, 41, 770–778.

Hunt, J.D., van der Hel, O.L., McMillan, G.P., Boffetta, P., & Brennan, P. (2005). Renal cell carcinoma in relation to cigarette smoking: Meta-analysis of 24 studies. *Int J Cancer*, 114, 101–108.

Johansson, S., & Wahlqvist, L. (1977). Tumours of urinary bladder and ureter associated with abuse of phenacetin-containing analgesics. *Acta Pathol Microbiol Scand*, [A]85, 768–774.

Kim, S., & Chung, D.H. (2006). Pediatric solid malignancies: Neuroblastoma and Wilms' tumor. *Surg Clin North Am*, 86(2), 469–487.

Kolonel, L.N. (1976). Association of cadmium with renal cancer. *Cancer*, 37, 1782–1787.

Larsson, S.C., & Wolk, A. (2010). Diabetes mellitus and incidence of kidney cancer: A meta-analysis of cohort studies. *Diabetologia*, 54(5), 1013–1018

Lindau, A. (1927). Zur Frage der Angiomatosis Retinae und Ihrer Hirncomplikation. *Acta Ophthal*, 4, 193–226.

Lipworth, L., Tarone, R.E., Lund, L., & McLaughlin, J.K. (2009). Epidemiologic characteristics and risk factors for renal cell cancer. *Clinical Epidemiology*, 2009(1), 33–43.

Mandel, J.S., McLaughlin, J.K., Schlehofer, B., Mellemgaard, A., Helmert, U., Lindblad, P., et al. (1995). International renal-cell cancer study. IV. Occupation. *Int J Cancer*, 61(5), 601–605.

Nickerson, M.L., Jaeger, E., Shi, Y., Durocher, J.A., Mahurkar, S., Zaridze, D., et al. (2008). Improved identification of von Hippel-Lindau gene alterations in clear cell renal tumors. *Clin Cancer Res*, 14(15), 4726–4734.

Parkin, D.M., Pisani, P., & Ferlay, J. (1999a). Estimates of the worldwide incidence of 25 major cancers in 1990. *Int J Cancer*, 80(6), 827–841.

Parkin, D.M., Pisani, P., & Ferlay, J. (1999b). Global cancer statistics. *C A Cancer J Clin*, 49(1), 33–64.

Parkin, D.M., Bray, F., Ferlay, J., & Pisani, P. (2005). Global cancer statistics, 2002. *CA Cancer J Clin*, 55, 74–108.

Pantuck, A.J., Zisman, A., & Belldegrun, A.S. (2001). The changing natural history of renal cell carcinoma. *J Urol*, 166(5), 1611–1623.

Pascual, D., & Borque, A. (2008). Epidemiology of kidney cancer. *Adv Urol, 2008*, doi:10.1155 /2008/782381.

Piper, J.M., Tonascia, J., & Matanoski, G.M. (1985). Heavy phenacetin use and bladder cancer in women aged 20 to 49 years. *N Engl J Med, 313*(5), 292–295.

Robbins, S.L., & Cotran, R.S. (1979). *Pathologic basis of disease*. 2nd Edition. Philadelphia, W.B. Saunders.

Theis, R.P., Dolwick Grieb, S.M., Burr, D., Siddiqui, T., & Asal, N.R. (2008). Smoking, environmental tobacco smoke and risk of renal cell cancer: A population-based case–control study. *BMC Cancer, 8*, 387.

Toro, J.R., Wei, M.H., Glenn, G.M., Weinreich, M., Toure, O., Vocke, C.,...Linehan, W.M. (2008). *BHD* mutations, clinical and molecular genetic investigations of Birt–Hogg–Dubé syndrome: A new series of 50 families and a review of published reports. *J Med Genet, 45*(6), 321–331.

Truong, L.D., Krishnan, B., Cao, J.T., Barrios, R., & Suki, W.N. (1995). Renal neoplasm in acquired cystic kidney disease. *Am J Kidney Dis, 26*(1), 1–12.

Vatten, L.J., Trichopoulos, D., Holmen, J., & Nilsen, T.I. (2007). Blood pressure and renal cancer risk: The HUNT Study in Norway. *Br J Cancer, 97*(1), 112–114.

Vineis, P. (1994). Epidemiology of cancer from exposure to arylamines. *Environmental Health Perspectives, 102*(Suppl 6), 7–10.

Von Hippel, E. (1904). Ueber eine sehr seltene Erkrankung der Netzhaut. *Albrecht von Graefes Arch Ophthal, 59*, 83–106.

Ward, J., Yeung, A.A., Routledge, C.E., & Zeegers, M. (2010). BMI and renal cell carcinoma: A meta-analysis. United Kingdom: University of Birmingham.

Weikert, S., Boeing, H., Pischon, T., Weikert, C., Olsen, A., Tjonneland, A.,...Riboli, E. (2008). Blood pressure and risk of renal cell carcinoma in the European prospective investigation into cancer and nutrition. *Am J Epidemiol, 167*(4), 438–446.

Weikert, S., & Ljungberg, B. (2010). Contemporary epidemiology of renal cell carcinoma: Perspectives of primary prevention. *World J Urol, 28*(3), 247–252.

Yao, M., Yoshida, M., Kishida, T., Nakaigawa, N., Baba, M., Kobayashi, K.,...Kondo, K. (2002). VHL tumor suppressor gene alterations associated with good prognosis in sporadic clear-cell renal carcinoma. *J Natl Cancer Inst, 94*(20), 1569–1575.

Epidemiology of Sarcoma

INTRODUCTION

Sarcomas are tumors of connective tissue. These tumors are derived from mesenchymal cells that normally mature into skeletal muscle, smooth muscle, fat, fibrous tissue, bone, and cartilage. They are broadly classified as sarcomas of soft tissue or bone. Sarcomas are named after the cell of origin; those that arise in fat are called liposarcomas, those derived from fibrous tissues are fibrosarcomas, and those that develop in bone are osteosarcomas. Other subtypes include leiomyosarcomas of smooth muscle, rhabdomyosarcomas of skeletal muscle, synovial sarcomas of joint capsule tissues, angiosarcomas of blood vessels, gastrointestinal sarcomas of the gut, chondrosarcomas of cartilage, and Ewing sarcoma of the long bones. Tumors derived from tissues of the peripheral nervous system are also included with the soft tissue sarcomas, including malignant nerve sheath tumors (schwannomas) and neurofibromas (Skubitz, 2007).

GLOBAL EPIDEMIOLOGY OF SARCOMA

Data on sarcomas of bones and soft tissues are conspicuously absent from the global data on cancer routinely reported by the World Health Organization. While some information is available on Kaposi sarcoma, a tumor derived from blood vessels that is associated with immunosuppression and the epidemic of HIV disease, little is known about the geographic distribution of the more common forms of sarcoma, namely, those arising from bone, fat, muscle, and fibrous tissues. Relevant epidemiologic data on these tumors are abstracted primarily from the *United States Surveillance Epidemiology and End Results (SEER)* tumor registry and the *European Automated Childhood Cancer Information System (ACCIS)* database.

SARCOMA IN THE UNITED STATES POPULATION

In the United States population of approximately 310 million people, more than 13,000 individuals are diagnosed with sarcomas every year (2,650 with bone tumors and 10,500 with soft tissue tumors). The annual age-adjusted incidence rates of bone tumors in the US population are about 10 per million in men and 8 per million in women, markedly less than the rates for soft tissue sarcomas (38 per million in men and 27 per million in women). Nevertheless, among children and adolescents under the age of 20 years, bone sarcomas and soft tissue sarcomas have relatively similar rates (about 9 per million for bone tumors and 11 per million for soft tissue tumors, respectively) and each type accounts for a significant fraction of all pediatric malignancies.

As shown in **Figure 25.1**, the US age distribution of bone sarcomas differs dramatically from that of soft tissue sarcomas. Nearly 30% of bone sarcomas are diagnosed during childhood and adolescence (under 20 years of age) after which there is a general decline in the number of new cases. The incidence of these tumors peaks during times of rapid growth and development of bones, between ages 10 and 15 years for both boys and girls.

In contrast to bone sarcomas, soft tissue sarcomas are diagnosed at a relatively constant rate

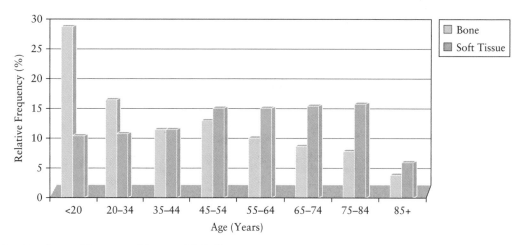

Figure 25.1 New Cases of Sarcomas of Bone and Soft Tissue, USA, 2006.

Source: Data From Altekruse SF, Kosary CL, Krapcho M, Neyman N, Aminou R, Waldron W, Ruhl J, Howlader N, Tatalovich Z, Cho H, Mariotto A, Eisner MP, Lewis DR, Cronin K, Chen HS, Feuer EJ, Stinchcomb DG, Edwards BK (2010). SEER Cancer Statistics Review, 1975–2007, National Cancer Institute. Bethesda, MD, USA.

throughout the lifespan (**Figure 25.1**). This pattern reflects a mixture of age distributions for the various subtypes of soft tissue sarcomas. For example, rhabdomyosarcomas tend to grow and develop more rapidly and are usually detected before the age of 20 years, whereas liposarcomas, leiomyomas, and gastrointestinal sarcomas are detected more often in adults (Darling, 2007; Altekruse et al., 2010).

In the United States population, nearly 1,500 men and women die from bone tumors and nearly 4,000 die from soft tissue tumors every year. Similar to the pattern of incidence rates, the overall age-adjusted annual mortality rates for bone tumors (5 per million in men and 4 per million in women) are much lower

than the rates for soft tissue tumors (14 per million in men and 11 per million in women); whereas the pediatric mortality rates are relatively similar (3.5 per million for bone tumors and 4.4 per million for soft tissue tumors). The US distributions of age at death for bone tumors and soft tissue tumors are compared in **Figure 25.2**. The death curve for bone tumors is bimodal with approximately 29% of deaths occurring in pediatric patients or young adults under the age of 35 years followed by an exponential rise with age and a later peak at 75–84 years. In contrast, the death curve for soft tissue tumors rises gradually with age and peaks late in life with more than 40% of deaths occurring in the age interval 65–84 years.

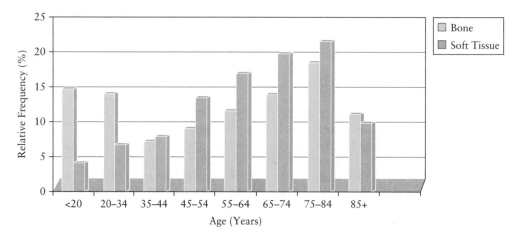

Figure 25.2 Deaths from Sarcomas of Bone and Soft Tissue, USA, 2006.

Source: Data From Altekruse SF, Kosary CL, Krapcho M, Neyman N, Aminou R, Waldron W, Ruhl J, Howlader N, Tatalovich Z, Cho H, Mariotto A, Eisner MP, Lewis DR, Cronin K, Chen HS, Feuer EJ, Stinchcomb DG, Edwards BK (2010). SEER Cancer Statistics Review, 1975–2007, National Cancer Institute. Bethesda, MD, USA.

It is clear from the preceding discussion that key epidemiologic features of bone tumors and soft tissue sarcomas differ dramatically for pediatric versus adult populations. In addition to the distributional differences already noted, the histological types of sarcomas that predominate among pediatric patients are replaced by other types among adult patients. Due to these striking distinctions, pediatric and adult sarcomas are discussed separately in the following sections of this chapter.

EPIDEMIOLOGY OF PEDIATRIC SARCOMAS

Bone Sarcomas in Children and Adolescents

Bone tumors account for slightly more than 6% of all pediatric malignancies. Stiller and colleagues reported rates of pediatric bone tumors among European children during 1978–1997 using the Automated Childhood Cancer Information System (ACCIS) database. Rates were similar for boys and girls up to 14 years of age (5.5 cases per million) whereas in the older adolescent age group, ages 15–19 years, boys had higher rates than girls (19.3 vs. 10.7 cases per million). Combining the rates for these age categories yields estimates of 9.2 cases per million in boys, 6.9 per million in girls, and 8.0 per million for all individuals under 20 years of age. In the European database of 5,572 pediatric bone tumors, 52% were classified as osteosarcoma, 34% as Ewing sarcoma, and 6%

as chondrosarcoma. No significant time trends were detected (Stiller et al., 2006).

Data from the Surveillance Epidemiology and End Results (SEER) tumor registry in the United States reflect rates of pediatric bone tumors that are similar to the European rates. For the time period 1975–1995, the annual incidence of bone tumors was 8.7 per million for individuals under the age of 20 years and boys had higher annual rates than girls (9.4 vs. 7.9 cases per million). As in Europe, no significant time trends were observed in the US annual rates. **Figure 25.3** shows the age distribution of bone tumors diagnosed among US children. Clearly, onset peaks at age 15 years, coinciding with the growth spurt during adolescence (Gurney, Swensen, and Bulterys, 1999; Gurney et al., 1999).

Of the approximate 700 bone tumors diagnosed among children and adolescents in the United States every year, about 56% are classified as osteosarcoma, 34% as Ewing sarcoma, and 6% as chondrosarcoma. Osteosarcomas arise most often in the metaphyseal zones near the extremities of elongating long bones (femur, tibia, and humerus) whereas Ewing sarcoma is more likely to develop in the marrow of bones of the central axis (pelvis, rib cage, ischium, sternum). Osteosarcoma occurs at approximately the same rate in African American and Caucasian children whereas the rate of Ewing sarcoma is about six times higher in Caucasians. The relative paucity of Ewing sarcoma in children of African descent is consistent in populations other than the United States (Parkin et al., 1988).

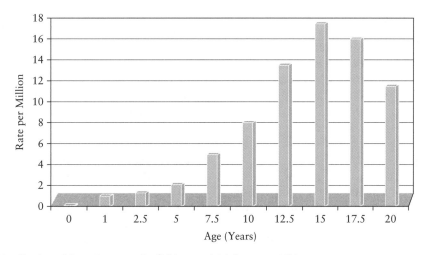

Figure 25.3 Age Distribution of Bone Sarcomas in Children and Adolescents, USA.

Source: Data From Gurney JG, Swensen AR, Bulterys M (1999). Malignant bone Tumors. Ries LAG, Smith MA, Gurney JG, Linet M, Tamra T, Young JL, Bunin GR (eds). Cancer Incidence and Survival among Children and Adolescents: United Sates SEER program 1975-1995, National Cancer Institute, SEER Program. NIH Pub No 99-4649. Bethesda, 1999. pp. 99–110.

Subtypes of Pediatric Bone Sarcomas

Osteosarcoma

Osteosarcoma is the most common primary malignant tumor of bone among children and adolescents, accounting for 3–4% of all malignancies in individuals less than 20 years of age. Approximately 400 cases are diagnosed each year in the United States, most (~75%) in children and adolescents. Osteosarcomas are characterized by the production of immature bone (osteoid) by the malignant cells. The most common anatomic sites of origin are the femur, tibia, and humerus bones (Robbins and Cotran, 1979).

Ewing Sarcoma

Nearly a century ago, James Ewing first described the pathologic features of the tumor that bears his name (Ewing, 1921). *Ewing sarcoma* is characterized as an undifferentiated tumor of the diaphyses of long bones of the extremities. In contrast to osteosarcoma, Ewing sarcoma is sensitive to radiation. As discussed in the following section, such tumors are now identified by karyotypic studies that reveal the presence of reciprocal chromosomal translocations involving the *Ewing sarcoma gene* (*EWSR-1*) on chromosome 22. Ewing sarcomas also occasionally arise in soft tissues. Ewing sarcoma is the second most common bone tumor among children and adolescents, accounting for more than one-third of bone sarcomas and about 2% of all malignancies in individuals less than 20 years of age. Although the peak incidence of Ewing sarcoma occurs during adolescence, molecularly confirmed cases have been discovered in adults as old as 80 years (Robbins and Cotran, 1979).

Chondrosarcoma

Chondrosarcomas account for about 6% of bone tumors that occur in children and adolescents. These cartilaginous tumors occur more often in adults and are discussed in a later section of this chapter.

CYTOGENETICS OF PEDIATRIC BONE SARCOMAS

Certain types of bone sarcomas have similar (non-random) patterns of chromosomal translocations and aberrations. For example, nearly all cases of Ewing sarcoma demonstrate one of several reciprocal chromosomal translocations involving break points within the Ewing *sarcoma gene* (*EWSR-1*) located on the long arm of chromosome 22. Such translocations create *chimeric fusion proteins* with

oncogenic potential. About 95% of the *EWSR-1* translocations reposition a portion of the *EWSR-1* gene in close proximity to the *Friend leukemia integration* (*FLI-1*) locus on chromosome 11. The *FLI-1* gene encodes a protein involved in the regulation of cellular proliferation and differentiation. The chimeric fusion proteins encoded by *EWSR-1* and *FLI-1* reciprocal translocations stimulate tumorigenesis of bone (Ewing sarcoma) and translocations of the *EWSR-1* gene to other loci have also been found in association with other types of sarcomas (myxoid liposarcoma). It is likely that these proteins act as *transcription activators*, deregulating genes associated with cell signaling, proliferation, angiogenesis, apoptosis, tissue invasion, and metastasis; consequently, they provide potential targets for molecular therapy (Ladanyi, 1995; Delaney et al., 2010).

Unlike Ewing sarcoma, osteosarcomas *do not* consistently manifest specific chromosomal translocations or molecular defects. Rather, they tend to have a complex karyotype. Nevertheless, osteosarcomas do develop in association with certain *rare* genetic anomalies. Specifically, osteosarcomas are a component of the profile of malignancies that develop in *hereditary retinoblastoma*, the *Li-Fraumeni syndrome*, and the *Rothmund-Thomson* syndrome.

Hereditary retinoblastoma is caused by a genetic mutation in the *Retinoblastoma gene* (*Rb1*). When the mutant *Rb1* gene is present, carriers invariably develop retinoblastoma either in one or both eyes. Treatment usually involves enucleation of the afflicted eye combined with external beam radiotherapy. Abramson and colleagues studied 817 patients who were treated for bilateral retinoblastoma during childhood. Among survivors, the cumulative risk of subsequently developing a second primary malignancy was found to cumulate at about 1% per year, reaching 53% at 50 years of age. Among the 180 second primary tumors reported, 60 were bone tumors, 36 of which developed in the skull and facial bones and 24 in bones of the extremities outside of the field of radiation. Soft tissue sarcomas of the head and neck (*n* = 60) and brain tumors (*n* = 12) also developed at high rates among survivors (Abramson and Frank, 1998). Other studies suggest that the onset of osteosarcoma following radiotherapy occurs earlier in bones within the field of radiation, possibly due to radiation-induced mutations in the second (normal) *Rb1* gene (Chauveinc et al., 2001). There is controversy as to whether the development of osteosarcoma in retinoblastoma survivors is due to the *Rb1* gene defect, radiotherapy for retinoblastoma, or the combination of both factors.

The *Li-Fraumeni syndrome* carries a high risk for sarcomas, brain tumors, breast cancer, leukemia, lymphoma, and adrenal cortical carcinoma. This syndrome is caused by a genetic mutation in either of two tumor suppressor genes, *P53 or CHEK2*. Individuals who inherit a defective *P53* or *CHEK2* gene have an approximate 85% lifetime risk of developing one or more of the malignancies characteristic of the Li-Fraumeni syndrome. Among women with the syndrome, the lifetime risk approaches 100% due to their inordinately high risk of developing premenopausal breast cancer (Li et al., 1998).

The *Rothmund-Thomson syndrome* is an extraordinarily rare genetic disorder caused by an autosomal recessive gene defect in the *helicase gene* (*RECQL-4*) located on the long arm of chromosome 8. DNA helicases are enzymes that unwind DNA and are involved in many basic cellular processes (DNA replication, transcription, translation, recombination, DNA repair, and ribosome biogenesis). Homozygous carriers of two mutant copies of the gene have early photosensitivity and develop a skin rash known as *poikiloderma*, juvenile cataracts, and skeletal anomalies. Most individuals with this syndrome develop osteosarcomas early in life (Leonard et al., 1996; Wang et al., 2003).

SOFT TISSUE SARCOMAS IN CHILDREN AND ADOLESCENTS

Soft tissue sarcomas account for approximately 7.4% of all childhood tumors. In the United States, the annual incidence of soft tissue sarcomas in individuals under 20 years of age is 11 per million. Annual rates are about 20% higher in boys than girls (12.2 versus 10.3 per million). Of the approximate 900 soft tissue sarcomas that develop in children and adolescents in the United States every year, about 41% are rhabdomyosarcomas of skeletal muscle and 24% are sarcomas of fibrous tissues. Other types such as histiocytomas, synovial sarcomas, and liposarcomas occur less frequently. **Figure 25.4** shows the age distribution of soft tissue tumors diagnosed in the US pediatric population. The early peak in the age distribution of soft tissue sarcomas is due to the early onset of rhabdomyosarcomas followed by a nadir and then escalating rates of fibrosarcoma, synovial sarcoma, and other forms. Rare cases of congenital fibrosarcoma have also been reported. No notable ethnic differences have been observed in the pediatric rates of the various histologic subtypes of soft tissue sarcomas. Nor have there been trends in the annual rates over the past several decades.

Subtypes of Pediatric Soft Tissue Sarcomas

Rhabdomyosarcoma

Rhabdomyosarcoma is the most common pediatric solid tumor, accounting for more than half of soft tissue sarcomas and approximately 4% of all malignancies among individuals under 20 years of age. Rhabdomyosarcomas arise from primitive cells that are the precursors of striated skeletal muscle. They predominantly arise in soft tissues of the head, neck, and genitourinary tract and the extremities. These tumors are divisible into two main histologic types, *embryonal rhabdomyosarcoma* and *alveolar rhabdomyosarcoma*.

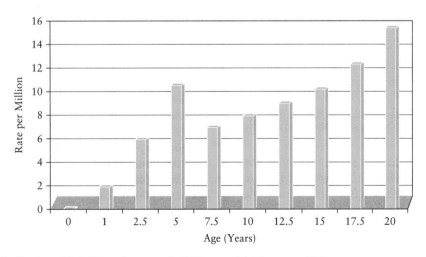

Figure 25.4 Age Distribution of Soft Tissue Sarcomas in Children and Adolescents, USA.

Source: Data From Gurney JG, Young JL Jr, Roffers SD, Smith MA, Bunin GR (1999). Soft tissue sarcomas. Ries LAG, Smith MA, Gurney JG, Linet M, Tamra T, Young JL, Bunin GR (eds). Cancer Incidence and Survival among Children and Adolescents: United Sates SEER program 1975–1995, National Cancer institute, SEER Program. NIH Pub No 99–4649. Bethesda, 1999. pp. 111–122.

In embryonal rhabdomyosarcomas, which are more common in children, the malignant cells resemble embryonal cells of a typical embryo at 6–8 weeks of development. In alveolar rhabdomyosarcomas, which are more common in older children and teenagers, the malignant cells resemble pulmonary alveolar cells of the embryo at 10–12 weeks of development.

Fibrosarcoma

Fibrosarcomas are diagnosed more often in adults, but they also occur among children and adolescents and account for 20–30% of bone tumors among individuals under 20 years of age. Tumors in this category arise from fibroblasts, the precursor cells of collagen-rich connective tissues. Fibrosarcomas are most often discovered in the soft connective tissues of the trunk and extremities, but they also occasionally develop from fibroblasts of the long bones (Cordon-Cardo, 1997).

Rare cases of fibrosarcoma discovered at birth or shortly thereafter have been reported in the literature. Such *congenital fibrosarcomas* usually involve the extremities and are characterized by sheets of anaplastic spindle-shaped tumor cells and abundant deposition of collagen. They are slow growing and while they invade other contiguous tissues, including bone, they do not readily metastasize to distant anatomic sites (Balsaver, Butler, and Martin, 1967; Exelby et al., 1973).

Synovial Sarcoma

Synovial sarcomas account for about 15–20% of soft tissue tumors in children and adolescents. These tumors arise most often in the soft tissues near the large joints of the arm (elbow) and leg (knee), but can also occur at many other anatomic sites. Histologically, the tumors are comprised of two cell types, spindle cells and epithelial cells, and consequently, these tumors reflect a *biphasic* pattern of growth. Synovial sarcomas are characterized by a *signature chromosomal translocation* involving chromosome 18 and the X chromosome, which is discussed in the following section.

Alveolar Soft-Part Sarcoma

Alveolar soft-part sarcoma is a very rare type of soft tissue sarcoma that arises mainly in children and adolescents. These tumors are usually slow growing but tend to be highly angiogenic. They are characterized by intensive ingrowth of new blood vessels (angiogenesis), thereby facilitating dissemination of tumor cells into the bloodstream. Tumor cells often metastasize to the lungs and the brain. Alveolar soft-part sarcomas most often arise in muscles and soft tissues of the thigh or leg, but can also develop from connective tissues at other anatomic sites. Histologically, the tumor cells grow in a pattern resembling pulmonary alveolar cells, leading to the name "alveolar soft-part sarcoma" (Christopherson, Foote, and Stewart, 1952).

Cytogenetics of Pediatric Soft Tissue Sarcomas

As with pediatric bone sarcomas, the various forms of soft tissue sarcomas that are diagnosed in children and adolescents are characterized by certain cytogenetic abnormalities. *Rhabdomyosarcomas* often show deletions of the short arm of chromosome 11 and loss of tumor suppressor genes, or reciprocal translocations involving the *FKHR* gene on chromosome 13 and the *PAX* genes on chromosomes 1 and 2. The *FKHR* gene regulates transcription and the *PAX* genes help regulate cell differentiation during embryogenesis. The chimeric fusion protein (called *FOX01*) encoded by the translocated gene has oncogenic potential resulting in the development of rhabdomyosarcomas consisting of cells with characteristics of pulmonary alveolar cells (Barr, 1997).

Some fibrosarcomas also involve reciprocal translocations of specific genes on specific chromosomes that result in the expression of chimeric fusion proteins with oncogenic potential. For example, congenital fibrosarcomas that are present at birth are characterized by a translocation gene product of the *ETV6* gene on chromosome 12 and the *NTRK3* gene on chromosome 13. These genes are intricately involved in the regulation of DNA mitosis and cell differentiation (Knezevich et al., 1998).

Synovial sarcoma is also characterized by the presence of a chimeric fusion protein that results from a reciprocal translocation. In this tumor, the *SYT* gene of the long arm of chromosome 18 is translocated in close proximity to one of three closely related genes (*SSX1*, *SSX2*, or *SSX4*) located on the X chromosome. The *SYT* gene is a transcription activator whereas the *SSX* genes are transcription repressors. The resulting chimeric fusion protein can produce one of two patterns of growth in the development of synovial sarcomas, a monophasic pattern of spindle cell growth, or a biphasic pattern involving both spindle cells and epithelial cells (Clark et al., 1994).

Karyotypic and molecular studies have also revealed a characteristic reciprocal translocation and fusion protein in *alveolar soft-parts sarcoma*. The translocation involves chromosome 17 and the X chromosome, creating fusion of the *TFE3* and *ASPA* genes and the corresponding chimeric fusion protein that enhances transcription of other genes with oncogenic potential (Ladanyi et al., 2001).

In summary, reciprocal chromosomal translocations constitute the majority of specific genetic alterations associated with *pediatric sarcomas*. As noted for both pediatric sarcomas of bone and soft tissues, many specific reciprocal chromosomal translocations have been identified and the chimeric fusion proteins encoded by the translocated genes characterized. It is likely that these proteins act as *transcription activators*, deregulating genes associated with sarcoma development. Thus, in addition to providing specific and sensitive diagnostic markers, such molecules provide potential targets for therapy with monoclonal antibodies (Ladanyi and Bridge, 2000; Ladanyi, 1995).

EPIDEMIOLOGY OF ADULT SARCOMAS

While some reciprocal chromosomal translocations and genetic aberrations have been identified in adult sarcomas, most such tumors *do not* manifest characteristic genetic anomalies. As with other adult forms of cancer, adult sarcomas are characterized by several critical interrelated biological mechanisms including overexpression of oncogenes and/or underexpression of tumor suppressor genes due to mutagenic and/or epigenetic effects, sustained uncontrolled cell division, angiogenesis, dysregulated apoptosis, immunosuppression, and metastatic spread, and invasive potential of tumor cells. Dysregulation of the inflammatory cascade may be an important trigger and promoter of all of these biological mechanisms.

Bone Sarcomas in Adults

Subsequent to adolescence, the relative frequency of primary bone tumors gradually declines throughout the lifespan (**Figure 25.1**). There are four main subtypes of adult sarcomas of bone: osteosarcoma, chondrosarcoma, Ewing sarcoma, and giant cell sarcoma. Each subtype is discussed separately.

Osteosarcoma

Though about 75% of *osteosarcomas* are diagnosed in children and adolescents, such tumors are occasionally discovered in adults. Among adult cases, males exceed females (a 35% male excess was observed in one series of 47 cases diagnosed after 40 years of age) and tumors most often involve the lower limbs (55% of cases) or the axial skeleton (38% of cases) (Carsi and Rock, 2002).

Unlike other tumors of bone, osteosarcomas are characterized by the formation of osteoid matrix by tumor cells (Robbins and Cotran, 1979). Characteristic cytogenetic or molecular aberrations have not been discovered in studies of osteosarcoma tissues. However, as already discussed in the section of this chapter on pediatric bone tumors, osteosarcomas are a component of the profile of malignancies that develop in rare genetic syndromes such as *hereditary retinoblastoma*, the *Li-Fraumeni syndrome*, and the *Rothmund-Thomson syndrome*.

Chondrosarcoma

Chondrosarcomas are tumors that produce hyaline cartilage. Most chondrosarcomas (80–90% of cases) arise *de novo* in older adults in the sixth or seventh decade of life without any evidence of premalignancy. Such tumors predominantly arise in and around the pelvis and scapula, although any site of cartilage formation may be involved (Azzarelli et al., 1986). Though chondrosarcomas do not ordinarily manifest specific cytogenetic abnormalities, one rare subtype, *extraskeletal myxoid chondrosarcoma*, is defined by the presence of a fusion gene between the orphan nuclear receptor *CHN1/NR4A3* and one of several partners, most commonly the Ewing sarcoma gene, *EWSR-1*.

About 10–20% of chondrosarcomas develop in young adults due to malignant transformation of benign neoplasms within bones (*osteochondromas*) or exterior to bones (*enchondromas*). Certain hereditary conditions such as *Olier disease* (multiple enchondromatosis) or *Maffucci syndrome* (multiple enchondromas and hemangiomas) predispose to the development of chondrosarcoma (Robbins and Cotran, 1979).

Hereditary multiple exostoses is a rare genetic disorder in which multiple bony spurs (also known as exostoses or osteochondromas) develop on the bones of a child. Approximately 90% of cases with this disorder are due to inheritance of either of two mutated tumor suppressor genes, *EXT1* or *EXT2*. These genes normally encode protein components of heparan sulfate proteoglycans that are essential for normal cartilage development, and mutant forms cause uncontrolled proliferation and lack of differentiation of chondrocytes, sometimes resulting in the development of chondrosarcoma.

Ewing Sarcoma

Ewing sarcoma rarely develops in adults over the age of 25 years. Nevertheless, adult cases that have been reported in the literature invariably demonstrate one of the reciprocal translocations of the Ewing sarcoma gene (*EWSR-1*) that characterize pediatric cases. Such tumors diagnosed in adults show a propensity for rapid metastatic spread and poor survival (Baldini et al., 1999).

Giant Cell Tumor of Bone

Giant cell tumors of bone, also known as *osteoclastomas*, constitute about 5% of adult bone tumors. These tumors are characterized by the presence of large (giant) multinucleated osteoclasts (cells that resorb bone matrix) admixed with spindle-shaped fibroblasts. Giant cell tumors are usually benign but can be locally aggressive. They most commonly arise in the epiphyses (growth plates) of long bones with diagnosis in the third or fourth decade of life (Robbins and Cotran, 1979; Mendenhall et al., 2006).

Normal osteoclasts are large cells in bone that contain 15–20 closely packed nuclei and cytoplasm with abundant vacuoles and vesicles. The primary function of osteoclasts is to resorb bone matrix. It is notable that osteoclasts are derived from mononuclear cells (macrophages) of the blood rather than progenitor cells of bone (Walker, 1972, 1973).

Osteoclast formation requires a ligand called *RANKL* (*receptor activator for nuclear factor κB ligand*) that activates the *receptor for nuclear factor κB* (*RANK*). Activation of nuclear factor κB by RANKL induces the differentiation and maturation of osteoclasts from mononuclear cells (macrophages) in hematopoietic tissues. Tight homeostatic regulation of these molecules is critical for normal osteoclast development and activity, as overexpression of RANKL has been found associated with the development of giant cell tumors of bone (Mendenhall et al., 2006; Thomas and Skubitz, 2009).

Soft Tissue Sarcomas in Adults

Soft tissue sarcomas occur with regular frequency, albeit low, throughout the lifespan (**Figure 25.1**). Subtypes are classified by the cell and/or anatomic site of origin: liposarcoma (adipoctyes), leiomyosarcoma (smooth muscle), gastrointestinal stromal tumors (intestinal stroma), and angiosarcoma (blood or lymphatic vessels). *Malignant fibrous histiocytomas* are heterogeneous sarcomas consisting of histiocytic cells and fibroblasts. *Kaposi sarcoma*, a malignancy arising from lymphatic endothelium, is named after Moritz Kaposi (1837–1902), a Hungarian dermatologist who first described its features and symptoms (Kaposi, 1872).

Liposarcoma

Lipomas are *benign* tumors composed of adipose tissue that arise most often in the subcutaneous tissues of the neck, trunk, and extremities. They are the most common form of soft tissue tumor with an estimated prevalence of about 1%. Lipomas have no metastatic potential, distinguishing them from liposarcomas, which are malignant neoplasms that can invade other tissues. Lipomas are typically diagnosed in adults ages 40–60 years of age, but occasionally they are discovered in children (Robbins and Cotran, 1979).

Whether lipomas are *premalignant* tumors is controversial, as malignant transition of lipoma to liposarcoma has not been definitively demonstrated in humans. Nevertheless, liposarcomas are clearly derived from adipocytes (fat cells) and are often comprised of cell populations containing both normal and malignant adipocytes.

Liposarcomas are the most common histological type of sarcoma found in adults. These malignant tumors comprise more than 20% of all adult sarcomas. In contrast to lipomas which usually develop in subcutaneous fat, liposarcomas typically arise in deep-seated fat of muscle or other tissues. Liposarcomas are extraordinarily heterogeneous and can be histologically characterized by the mixtures of cells they contain. For example, myxoid liposarcoma is characterized by malignant adipocytes in various stages of differentiation (Robbins and Cotran, 1979).

Leiomyosarcoma

Uterine fibroids (*uterine leiomyomas*) *are the most common of all tumors in women*. These benign tumors are typically discovered during the reproductive years with a prevalence of about 30%. They originate from cells in the smooth muscle layer of the uterus (the myometrium). Most uterine fibroid tumors are asymptomatic and harmless, but they can enlarge and cause pain, discomfort, and urinary incontinence, in which case they are usually surgically excised by hysterectomy (Wallach and Vlahos, 2004).

The malignant version of leiomyoma is *leiomyosarcoma*. These malignant tumors can arise from smooth muscle anywhere in the body, most commonly in the uterus, stomach and intestinal tract, blood vessels, and skin. Leiomyosarcomas comprise 5–10% of all soft tissue sarcomas in adults. Whether benign leiomyomas undergo malignant transformation to leiomyosarcoma is controversial. Nevertheless, cases have been reported in which malignant transformation has apparently been observed over time (Indraccolo, Luchetti, and Indraccolo, 2008). It is noteworthy that uterine leiomyomas are often surgically removed, thereby negating the chance of malignant transformation.

Gastrointestinal Stromal Tumors (GIST)

Sarcomas arising from connective (mesenchymal) tissues in the wall of the stomach or other gastrointestinal organs are called *gastrointestinal stromal tumors* (*GIST*). Tran and colleagues recently utilized the US SEER database to characterize distributional features of GIST in the US population during 1992–2000. During this time period, 1,458 cases were reported, 54% in men and 46% in women. Tumors were distributed throughout the gastrointestinal tract, 51% in the stomach, 36% in the small intestine, 7% in the colon, 5% in the rectum, and 1% in the esophagus. Estimates of the annual age-adjusted incidence rates were 8.3 per million in men, 5.7 per million in women, and 6.8 per million overall. As shown in **Figure 25.5**, GIST is predominantly a malignancy of old age and is rarely diagnosed before the age of 40 years. Peak onset occurs in the eighth decade of life (Tran, Davila, and El-Serag, 2005).

Gastrointestinal stromal tumors (GIST) apparently arise from the *interstitial cells of Cajal*, cells that serve as electrical pacemakers and generate spontaneous electrical slow waves and smooth muscle contractions (peristalsis) in the wall of the gastrointestinal tract (Connolly, Gaffney, and Reynolds, 2003; Sanders, Koh, and Ward, 2006). Such cells have morphological characteristics similar to fibroblasts and express specific tyrosine kinase receptors on their cell membranes that control differentiation and maturation (Lorincz et al., 2008).

Angiosarcoma

Angiosarcoma is an uncommon subtype of soft tissue sarcoma that can arise from the endothelial cells that line blood vessels (hemangiosarcoma) or lymphatic vessels (lymphangiosarcoma). These tumors occasionally develop in the scalp or face of older adults or in patients who have undergone radiation therapy for dermatitis or other conditions. An association with lymphedema, a complication of mastectomy for breast cancer, has also been noted. In addition, angiosarcoma of the liver has been etiologically linked to at least three chemical carcinogens: arsenic in arsenical pesticides, thorotrast (a radioactive contrast medium used prior to 1950), and polyvinyl chloride, an alkylating agent and gas used in the manufacture of plastic. Important studies of environmental risk factors for adult sarcomas are discussed later in this chapter (Robbins and Cotran, 1979).

Malignant Fibrous Histiocytoma

Malignant fibrous histiocytoma is a rare type of soft tissue sarcoma that is discovered most often in the elderly, usually between the ages of 50 and 70 years. Histologically, such tumors consist of a mixture of histocytes (cells derived from tissue macrophages or monocytes) and fibroblasts (cells of mesenchymal lineage). Based upon early pathologic investigations, this tumor was initially characterized as the most common sarcoma in late adult life (O'Brien and Stout, 1964). However, in more recent studies, the majority of such tumors have been reclassified as poorly differentiated liposarcomas or leiomyosarcomas. In a population-based study of malignant

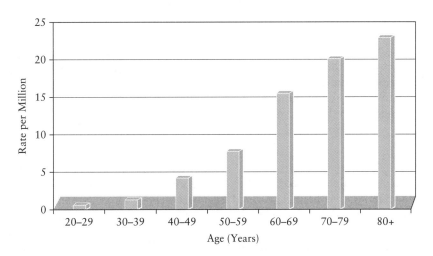

Figure 25.5 Age-Specific Incidence of Gastrointestinal Stromal Tumors (GIST), USA, 1992-2006.

Source: Data From Tran T, Davila JA, El-Serag HB (2005). The epidemiology of malignant gastrointestinal stromal tumors: an analysis of 1,458 cases from 1992 to 2000. *The American Journal of Gastroenterology* 100:162–168.

fibrous sarcoma in Sweden, the annual incidence rate was estimated at only 4.2 per million (Rööser et al., 1991).

Dermatofibrosarcoma Protuberans

Dermatofibrosarcoma protuberans is a rare form of fibrosarcoma that arises from the dermis (the layer of skin between the epidermis and subcutaneous tissue). This tumor can infiltrate contiguous tissues but rarely metastasizes to distant sites. Dermatofibrosarcoma protuberans is cytogenetically defined by a translocation of chromosomes 17 and 22 in which a collagen promoter gene (*COL1A1*) is juxtaposed to the platelet-derived growth factor (*PDFG*) gene resulting in constitutive production of PDGF. This scenario creates an autocrine loop in which PDGF stimulates PDGF receptors of tumor cells, promoting their perpetual growth and survival. Monoclonal antibodies directed against the PDGF receptor have shown some benefit in the treatment of patients with this tumor (Patel et al., 2008).

Desmoid Tumor

Desmoid tumors are benign slow-growing tumors without metastatic potential. Histologically, these tumors resemble fibrosarcomas. While most cases are sporadic, desmoid tumors develop in about 10–15% of patients with *familial adenomatous polyposis* or *Gardner's syndrome* (*adenomatous polyposis coli*) in which multiple adenomatous polyps and malignant adenocarcinomas develop in the colon. As already discussed, this syndrome is caused by inheritance of an autosomal dominant mutant *APC* gene on chromosome 5.

An investigative team in London conducted a meta-analysis of desmoid tumors among patients with familial adenomatous polyposis (*FAP*). Desmoid tumors developed in 559 (12%) of 4,625 *FAP* patients. Peak onset was in the second and third decades and 80% of tumors were diagnosed by age 40 years. Having a family history of desmoid tumors conferred a sevenfold increase in the risk, suggesting the existence of modifier genes (Sinha et al., 2010).

Cytogenetics of Soft Tissue Adult Sarcomas

Though not as common as in pediatric sarcomas, nonrandom genetic abnormalities have been discovered in some soft tissue sarcomas in adults. For example, translocation of the *CCAAT-enhanced binding protein* (*CEBP*) gene on chromosome 12 to chromosome 16 is characteristic of *myxoid liposarcoma*. The *CEBP* gene encodes a factor that is critical for normal differentiation of adipocytes and its translocation creates a chimeric fusion protein that interferes with differentiation and leads to cancer development (Turc-Carel et al., 1986; Adelmant, Bilbert, and Freytag, 1998). A second molecular transcription factor, *peroxisome proliferator-activator receptor gamma* (*PPAR-γ*), is also often over-expressed in malignant liposarcoma cells (Tontonoz et al., 1997). Cytogenetic studies of liposarcomas have also revealed the presence of ring or giant-marker chromosomes derived from the short arm of chromosome 12 with amplification of specific oncogenes in this region (Coindre et al., 2003).

The existing scientific literature reflects highly variable and inconsistent cytogenetic and molecular genetic changes in *leiomyosarcoma*. Wang and colleagues reviewed karyotypes of 100 leiomyosarcomas and found no consistent aberrations at the chromosomal level. Since the most frequent chromosomal deletions were detected in the long arms of chromosome 10 and 13, regions where tumor suppressor genes *PTEN* and *Rb* reside, the investigators concluded that loss of function of tumor suppressor genes and/or activation of oncogenes associated with such changes are likely involved in the development of leiomyosarcoma (Wang et al., 2001).

Approximately 95% of *gastrointestinal stromal tumors* (*GIST*) have been found to carry mutant forms of an important tyrosine kinase receptor gene called c-*KIT*. The c-*KIT* receptor facilitates differentiation and maturation of stem cells into hematopoietic cells and several other cell lineages. It was first identified in the laboratories of the German biochemist, Axel Ullrich (Yarden et al., 1987). Mutations in c-*KIT* cause overexpression of tyrosine kinase receptors in the cell membrane resulting in unregulated phosphorylation and disruption of communication pathways inside the cell. Constitutive expression of mutant forms of c-*KIT* therefore lead to malignant transformation and the development of GIST (as well as testicular seminoma, malignant melanoma, and myeloid leukemia). Notably, a monoclonal antibody directed against the c-*KIT* protein has been found effective in the treatment of GIST (Joensuu et al., 2001; Edling and Hallberg, 2007).

Cytogenetic studies of *angiosarcomas* reflect considerable heterogeneity and no consistent pattern of chromosomal or genetic aberrations. Literature reports based on limited sample sizes have revealed karyotypes with gains or losses of many different chromosomal regions without a common chromosomal profile (Baumhoer et al., 2005). One recent study reported a reciprocal chromosomal translocation involving chromosomes 1 and 21 in a 79-year-old woman with a primary bone angiosarcoma. While the biological significance of this translocation is unclear, it could possibly involve abnormal expression of the gene for colony stimulating factor (*CSF-1*) which is located on chromosome 1 (Dunlap et al., 2009).

Some genetic syndromes are associated with the development of soft tissue sarcoma in adults. *Neurofibromatosis type 1*, or *von Recklinghausen disease*, is a rare autosomal dominant condition caused by mutation in the *NF1* gene located on chromosome 17. The *NF1* gene encodes the protein neurofibromin, which is essential for the development of fibrous nerve sheaths. Patients with this genetic disorder have a high incidence of benign schwannomas and neurofibromas as well as an increased risk of developing malignant peripheral nerve sheath tumors (malignant schwannomas and neurofibrosarcomas).

Neurofibromatosis type 2, also a rare autosomal dominant disorder, is caused by mutation in the *NF2* gene located on chromosome 22 which is essential for development of myelin nerve sheaths. This syndrome is associated with the development of meningiomas as well as schwannomas of cranial nerves, especially the vestibular nerve.

Gardner syndrome is an autosomal dominant disorder caused by by mutation of the *adenomatous polyposis coli* (*APC*) gene located on the long arm of chromosome 5. Carriers of the mutant APC gene develop multiple polyps throughout the colon and without total colectomy, the probability of transformation to colon cancer is virtually 100%. Approximately 15–20% of afflicted individuals also develop other extracolonic tumors such as osteomas, fibromas, desmoid tumors, and thyroid cancer (Gardner, 1951; Johnson et al., 1972; Markowitz and Bertagnolli, 2009).

Environmental Risk Factors for Adult Sarcoma

Ionizing Radiation

There is consistent evidence that radiation exposure increases the risk of developing both bone and soft tissue sarcomas. The association was first observed by the German physician, Dr. A. Beck, who commented on the unusually high incidence of sarcomas in patients who had previously been irradiated for tuberculosis arthritis (Beck, 1922). Subsequently in the United States, Martland and Humphreys (1929) reported finding 42 bone sarcomas in 1,468 female watch-dial painters exposed to radioactive luminous paint, an incidence proportion of 2.8%. Several more reports of excess rates of bone sarcomas soon appeared in the literature, most notably a report from investigators at Memorial Sloan-Kettering Hospital in New York City describing 50 cases of radiation-induced osteogenic sarcoma identified during 1931–1970 (Arlen et al., 1971).

Post-radiation sarcomas arise more often in bones than soft tissues, perhaps due to the greater absorption of radioactivity by bone (Robinson, Neugut, and Wylie, 1988). Nevertheless, excess rates of soft tissue sarcomas have been observed subsequent to certain types of radiotherapy. For example, investigators in Sweden observed a 90% excess of soft tissue sarcomas among 122,991 women treated for breast cancer from 1958–1992 (standardized incidence ratio = 1.9). Furthermore, 63% of the reported sarcomas developed in the exposed region of the irradiated breast or the ipsilateral arm. Among the 116 sarcomas detected, there were 40 angiosarcomas and 76 sarcomas of other subtypes. In substudies of these tumors, angiosarcomas were found to develop in association with lymphedema of the ipsilateral axilla and arm (Karlsson et al., 1998).

Chemical and Occupational Exposures

Some epidemiologic studies have noted increases in the risk of developing soft tissue or bone sarcomas among individuals with certain occupational exposures, e.g., sawdust and wood dust, cutting oils (solvents), arsenicals, phenoxyherbicides, chlorophenols, and dioxins. However, results are inconsistent from study to study, which is most likely due to the use of occupation as a proxy for exposure to broad classes of chemicals and the lack of precise information on the type, concentration, and duration of specific chemical exposures. Furthermore, inconsistencies in study results may also reflect different disease etiologies for sarcoma subtypes (Hoppin et al., 1999).

Various implant materials, including chromium, nickel, cobalt, titanium, and polyethylene, are also suspected risk factors, though epidemiological evidence for causation is lacking. It is obvious that more precise measures of environmental exposures are needed in order to accurately quantify the risk.

Angiosarcoma of the liver is an unfortunate human model for both radiation and chemical carcinogenesis. This rare tumor has been found in excess among workers exposed to polyvinyl chloride as a solution or gas where plastics are manufactured, patients exposed to thorotrast (a radioactive contrast medium used in the past for imaging studies), and individuals exposed to arsenic in arsenical pesticides. Selected studies are discussed here.

Between September 1967 and December 1973, 4 cases of angiosarcoma of the liver were diagnosed among men employed in the polyvinyl chloride polymerization section of the BF Goodrich manufacturing plant near Louisville, Kentucky, United States.

This section of the plant began operations in 1938. It employed 270 persons and produced polyvinyl chloride as well as a variety of copolymers by polymerization of vinyl chloride monomers. All 4 men had worked continuously in the section for at least 14 years prior to onset of illness and had worked directly in various phases of the polymerization process. None of the patients gave histories of prolonged alcohol use or exposure to hepatotoxins outside the workplace. In particular, none had ever had exposure to thorium dioxide (thorotrast) or to arsenic, two materials known specifically to induce hepatic angiosarcoma (Creech and Johnson, 1974).

Subsequent studies in Australia, Italy, Germany, and the United Kingdom also revealed that polyvinyl chloride workers were at increased risk for the development of hepatic angiosarcoma (Mundt et al., 2000). In 1983, a team of international investigators charted the latency periods from time of exposure to vinyl chloride monomers or thorotrast (a radioactive contrast medium also known to increase the risk of developing hepatic angiosarcoma) to time of death due to angiosarcoma of the liver. Exposure to thorotrast occurred during 1928–1955 and exposure to polyvinyl chloride occurred during 1940–1970. Among 101 men exposed to thorotrast who later died from liver angiosarcoma, the median latency period from exposure to death was 22 years. Among 95 men exposed to polyvinyl chloride who later died from liver angiosarcoma, the median latency period was substantially longer at 29 years. The investigators suggest that their results reflect different mechanisms of radiation versus chemical carcinogenesis (Spirtas et al., 1983).

Boffetta and colleagues conducted a meta-analysis of cancer mortality and exposure to polyvinyl chloride using data from eight published studies, two multicenter cohorts, and six smaller studies. They found an increase in the standardized mortality ratio due to soft tissue sarcoma (SMR = 2.52), the predominant cell type being angiosarcoma. Their results also showed a significant increase in mortality due to primary liver cancer (SMR = 2.96), although there was significant heterogeneity among studies (Boffetta et al., 2003).

All known cases of angiosarcoma that have developed from exposure to vinyl chloride monomers were in workers who were regularly exposed to very high levels for many years. Most of these workers cleaned accretions in reactors, a practice that has now been replaced by automated high-pressure water jets. Other epidemiologic studies have demonstrated that the risk of developing hepatic angiosarcoma is also significantly increased with exposure to thorium dioxide (thorotrast) or arsenical pesticides (Falk et al., 1979, 1981).

Rous Sarcoma Virus

In the early 1900s, Dr. Peyton Rous reported a series of experiments with chicken sarcoma at the Rockefeller University in New York City. He found that by injecting *cell free extracts derived from chicken sarcoma* into healthy Plymouth Rock chickens, he could transfer the tumor from one chicken to another. Rous found that extracts of tumors that passed through a Berkefeld filter (which did not allow passage of bacteria) could transfer the sarcoma to other chickens. This was the first demonstration of an oncogenic virus and heralded the beginning of the field of cancer virology. Rous was awarded the Nobel Prize for his discoveries in 1966 (Rous, 1910, 1911; Rous and Huggins, 1966).

Later studies revealed that the transmissable *Rous sarcoma virus* (*RSV*) was a retrovirus containing RNA rather than DNA and that the transforming region of the virus was an oncogene (named *SRC* for *sarcoma*) (Crawford and Crawford, 1961; Stehelin et al., 1977; Oppermann et al., 1979). During the 1970s, J. Michael Bishop and Harold Varmus directed a series of studies showing that the *SRC* gene encodes a constitutively active form of the enzyme, tyrosine kinase, that stimulates carcinogenesis, a discovery for which they received the Nobel Prize in 1989 (Bishop and Varmus, 1989). Although the Rous sarcoma virus (RSV) that causes sarcomas in chickens was the first tumor virus found to cause solid tumors, the only virus now known to cause sarcoma in humans is *human herpes virus 8* (*HHV-8*), which causes the development of *Kaposi sarcoma*.

Kaposi Sarcoma

Kaposi sarcoma is a tumor that sometimes develops in individuals who are severely immunocompromised. It was originally described in 1872 by Dr. Moritz Kaposi, a Hungarian dermatologist practicing at the University of Vienna (Kaposi, 1872). Before the epidemic of AIDS in the 1980s, Kaposi sarcoma was practically unheard of in populations of developed nations. Only rare cases were reported, most occurring in organ transplant patients who received cyclosporin or other immunosuppressive drugs to prevent transplant rejection. But following the onset of the AIDS epidemic, the incidence of Kaposi sarcoma increased more than a thousandfold in those subgroups at high risk for HIV. The main subgroups are homosexual and bisexual men, intravenous drug abusers, and sexually promiscuous men and women.

Due to its prevalence in individuals who are immunodeficient, Kaposi sarcoma became widely known as one of the defining conditions of the *acquired immunodeficiency syndrome* (*AIDS*) during the 1980s. The etiologic agent of AIDS is the *human immunodeficiency virus* (*HIV*) and AIDS is now appropriately called *HIV disease*. Although associated with HIV disease, Kaposi sarcoma is actually caused by another virus, human herpes virus 8 (HHV-8).

Discovery of Human Herpes Virus 8 (HHV-8)

In 1994, Yuan Chang, Patrick Moore, and Ethel Cesarman at Columbia University in New York isolated a novel herpes virus from the tumor cells of a Kaposi sarcoma. They later sequenced the virus and identified it as the eighth human herpes virus; hence it was given the name, HHV-8. This virus has since been found in all Kaposi sarcomas tested and is considered the cause of the disease. In infected lymphatic endothelial cells, HHV-8 incorporates genes from the host DNA into its own DNA, thus avoiding detection and destruction by the immune system. This process leads to active proliferation and immortalization of infected cells resulting in the development of Kaposi sarcoma (Chang et al., 1994; Moore and Chang, 1995; Cesarman et al., 1995).

Pathologic Features of Kaposi Sarcoma

Despite its name, Kaposi sarcoma does not arise from connective tissue and is therefore not a true sarcoma. Rather, Kaposi sarcoma arises from the endothelial cells that line lymphatic vessels. The tumor is characterized by the formation of vascular channels engorged with red blood cells giving it a dark red papular appearance. Such papules may be solitary or multifocal.

The tumor cells of Kaposi sarcoma are spindle-shaped cells characteristic of fibroblasts in connective tissue. Detection of proteins such as *latency-associated nuclear antigen* (*LANA*) that are specific for HHV-8 in tumor cells confirms the diagnosis of Kaposi sarcoma (Moore et al., 1996). Kaposi sarcoma is typically found on the skin, but metastatic spread to other sites is common, especially the mouth, the gastrointestinal tract, and the respiratory tract. Kaposi sarcoma is associated with significant morbidity and mortality worldwide (Parkin et al., 2005).

Transmission of HHV-8

Herpes viruses can be transmitted by intimate sexual contact and by transplantation of contaminated organs. In sub-Saharan Africa where high rates of HHV-8 prevail, Kaposi sarcoma is the most common of all cancers. As with other herpes viral infections,

☐ <0.6   ▨ <3.7   ▧ <10.1   ▣ <22.0   ▦ <74.9

Figure 25.6 Incidence of Kaposi Sarcoma in African Men.

Source: Data From Parkin DM, Bray F, Ferlay J, Pisani, P (2005). Global Cancer Statistics, 2002. *CA Cancer J Clin* 55:74–108. Figure reprinted by permission: GLOBOCAN, 2002, International Agency for Cancer Research.

HHV-8 may persist in a dormant state for many years, only to be reactivated by conditions of severe immunosuppression such as HIV disease. Active HHV-8 infection specifically initiates and promotes malignant transformation of the lymphatic endothelium in the genesis of Kaposi sarcoma. Seropositivity rates for HHV-8 coincide closely with the high rates of this tumor in sub-Saharan Africa (**Figure 25.6**). Coinfection by HIV is also prominent in these same African populations. It is noteworthy that there are marked ethnic differences in the rates of Kaposi sarcoma. For example, individuals of Asian descent rarely develop the disease, even those with HIV infection. Such ethnic disparities may reflect differences in the rates of HIV and HHV-8 coinfection (Parkin et al., 2005).

Subtypes of Kaposi Sarcoma

Several subtypes of Kaposi sarcoma have been defined. The main ones are listed below.

- *Classic Kaposi sarcoma* is a rare and relatively indolent form affecting elderly men from the Mediterranean coastal region or of Eastern European descent.
- *Endemic Kaposi sarcoma* is a moderately aggressive form found predominantly in young individuals from sub-Saharan Africa. It is *not* associated with HIV disease.

- *Transplant-related Kaposi sarcoma* is a rare form that develops in organ transplant patients who receive powerful immunosuppressive drugs such as cyclosporin.
- *AIDS-related Kaposi sarcoma* is a highly aggressive form and one of the defining components of AIDS (HIV disease).

Impact of AIDS on Kaposi Sarcoma

A team of investigators spearheaded by Denis Burkitt investigated the geographical distributions of Kaposi sarcoma, non-Hodgkin's lymphoma, and Burkitt's lymphoma in populations of sub-Saharan Africa prior to the AIDS epidemic. High cumulative rates of Kaposi sarcoma (exceeding 6 per 1,000 in men ages birth–64 years) were found in equatorial Africa whereas the rates were low (nearly zero) in Northern and Southern regions. Rates were up to 10-fold higher in men than women, and in certain populations, such as Uganda and Zaire, the estimated cumulative rates of Kaposi sarcoma (approximately 15 per 1,000) were similar to that for common malignancies of the Western world, e.g., colon cancer. These rates are hundreds of times higher than rates of Kaposi sarcoma reported for the populations of England and the United States in the pre-AIDS era. The authors noted the discovery of the etiologic viral agent of Kaposi sarcoma (HHV-8) in 1994, and suggested that the geographic and gender-related distribution of Kaposi sarcoma "may possibly mirror the

distribution of the virus prior to the advent of AIDS" (Cook-Mosaffari et al., 1998).

Before the epidemic of AIDS, Kaposi sarcoma was rare in Western countries, comprising only 0.3% of all cancers in men and 0.1% in women in the United States and Europe. During the 1970s, the cumulative (lifetime) incidence rates averaged less than 0.5 per 100,000 in men and less than 0.1 per 100,000 in women of the US population. Cases were occasionally discovered in older people of Mediterranean or Eastern European descent, often with a family history of the disease, and immunosuppressed organ transplant recipients (Biggar et al., 1984; Parkin et al., 2005).

Following onset of the HIV epidemic, rates of Kaposi sarcoma increased dramatically among men in developed nations. In the United States, the annual incidence rates peaked in 1989 at 9.6 per 100,000 (**Figure 25.7**). Since that time, rates have declined to pre-AIDS levels, presumably in response to effective combined chemotherapy for HIV disease by *highly active anti-retroviral therapy* (*HAART*) (Stebbing and Portsmouth, 2003).

Remarkably, the AIDS epidemic has had negligible impact on the rates of Kaposi sarcoma in the US female population (**Figure 25.7**). While this may reflect their relatively low rates of HIV and HHV-8 coinfection, another possibility is that there are other risk factors to which women are not ordinarily exposed. For example, use of amyl-nitrites has been explored as a cofactor in the development of

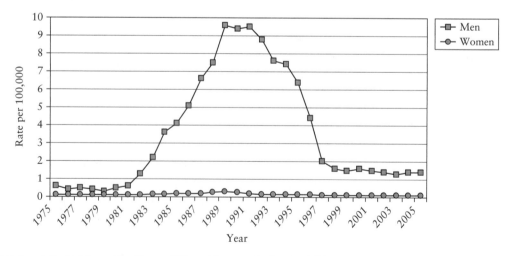

Figure 25.7 Age-Adjusted Annual Incidence of Kaposi Sarcoma by Gender, USA, 1975–2005.

Source: Data From Altekruse SF, Kosary CL, Krapcho M, Neyman N, Aminou R, Waldron W, Ruhl J, Howlader N, Tatalovich Z, Cho H, Mariotto A, Eisner MP, Lewis DR, Cronin K, Chen HS, Feuer EJ, Stinchcomb DG, Edwards BK (2010). SEER Cancer Statistics Review, 1975–2007, National Cancer Institute. Bethesda, MD, USA.

Kaposi sarcoma among AIDS patients (Fung and Tran, 2006).

In central Africa, post-AIDS rates of Kaposi sarcoma have continued to increase in populations with high endemic rates and little access to effective therapy, such as Uganda, Malawi, Zimbabwe, and Swaziland. Indeed, Kaposi sarcoma is now the most common cancer in men and the second most common cancer in women in many nations of sub-Saharan Africa (Parkin et al., 2005).

CYCLOOXYGENASE-2 (COX-2) IN SARCOMAS

As in many other forms of cancer, the over expression of cyclooxygenase-2 (COX-2) has been found to be a prominent feature of pediatric sarcomas. At the University of Cincinnati in the United States, Dickens and colleagues evaluated COX-2 expression in a series of 59 pediatric sarcomas using immunohistochemical analysis and cDNA microarray analysis. Tumor specimens included rhabdomyosarcoma, osteosarcoma, and Ewing sarcoma. Expression of COX-2 was detected in 83% of tumors by immunohistochemistry and in 89% of tumors by microarray analysis. In samples of normal osteocytes from nonmalignant bone and muscle tissues, no COX-2 expression was detected. The investigators suggest that COX-2 inhibitors should be tested in the treatment of pediatric sarcomas (Dickens et al., 2002).

At Helsinki University in Finland, Lassus and colleagues evaluated COX-2 expression by immunohistochemistry in 103 specimens of adult soft tissue sarcomas. They found COX-2 expression in 50 of the 103 tumors (49%) and in all 10 biphasic synovial sarcomas in the sample. They noted that COX-2 was expressed primarily by epithelial cells and in cells proximal to necrotic areas. The investigators concluded that COX-2 expression is associated with epithelial differentiation and tumor necrosis (Lassus et al., 2005).

At the University of Naples in Italy, Rossiello and colleagues evaluated cyclooxygenase-1 (COX-1) and COX-2 in tissues of Kaposi sarcoma using immunohistochemistry and Western blot analysis. They investigated 35 cases of classic Kaposi sarcoma and 27 cases of epidemic Kaposi sarcoma. The results revealed that both COX-1 and COX-2 were overexpressed by tumor cells of all cases; and furthermore, COX overexpression was detected in early and late stages of tumor progression, suggesting that the COX enzymes are involved in the pathogenesis of Kaposi sarcoma (Rossiello et al., 2007).

PREVENTION AND TREATMENT OF SARCOMA

In developed nations, most cases of Kaposi sarcoma are diagnosed in patients with HIV/AIDS. Taking measures to avoid HIV infection could therefore prevent the vast majority of Kaposi sarcoma cases in these populations. Currently there is no effective vaccine against either HIV or HHV-8. Consequently, prevention depends on reducing the chance of infection by avoiding unprotected sex with HIV carriers and abstaining from injecting recreational drugs since hypodermic needles may be contaminated.

In the past, transfusions of contaminated blood and clotting factors were responsible for some HIV infections. As a result of improved HIV testing at blood banks, there is now a very low risk of HIV infection from blood products in the United States and most developed nations. In some poorer countries, blood products are not tested well, leading to a higher risk of HIV infection with transfusion.

Since only a few modifiable risk factors are known for other types of sarcomas, population-based preventive strategies are generally absent. Exposure to excess radiation should be avoided and care should be taken to minimize exposure to environmental pollutants such as polyvinyl chloride, sawdust and wood dust, cutting oils (solvents), arsenicals, phenoxyherbicides, chlorophenols, and dioxins. It is also advisable to consider surgical removal of benign lesions that have the potential for malignant transformation, in particular, lipomas and leiomyomas.

The development of optimal treatment strategies for sarcoma is complicated by the large number of subtypes, the heterogeneity in their biological behavior, and the small number of patients with particular subtypes enrolled in trials. However, exciting new research has identified molecular markers for some sarcomas, particularly those in children, and such molecules are natural targets for therapy with monoclonal antibodies.

• • • REFERENCES

Abramson, D.H., & Frank, C.M. (1998). Second nonocular tumors in survivors of bilateral retinoblastoma: A possible age effect on radiation-related risk. *Ophthalmology*, *105*(4), 573–580.

Adelmant, G., Bilbert, J.D., & Freytag, S.O. (1998). Human translocation liposarcoma-CCAAT/ Enhancer Binding Protein (C/EBP) homologous protein (TLS-CHOP) oncoprotein prevents adipocyte differentiation by directly interfering with C/EBPβ function. *The Journal of Biological Chemistry, 273,* 15574–15581.

Altekruse, S.F., Kosary, C.L., Krapcho, M., Neyman, N., Aminou, R., Waldron, W., Edwards, B.K. (2010). SEER Cancer Statistics Review, 1975–2007, Bethesda, MD: National Cancer Institute.

Arlen, M., Higinbotham, N.L., Huvos, A.G., Marcove, R.C., Miller, T., & Shah, I.C. (1971). Radiation-induced sarcoma of bone. *Cancer, 28,* 1087–1099.

Azzarelli, A., Gennari, L., Quagliuolo, V., Bonfanti, G., Cerasoli, S., & Bufalino, R. (1986). Chondrosarcoma: 55 unreported cases: Epidemiology, surgical treatment and prognostic factors. *Eur J Surg Oncol, 12*(2), 165–168.

Baldini, E.H., Demetri, G.D., Fletcher, C.D., Foran, J., Marcus, K.C., & Singer, S. (1999). Adults with Ewing's sarcoma/primitive neuroectodermal tumor: Adverse effect of older age and primary extraosseous disease on outcome. *Ann Surg, 230*(1), 79–86.

Balsaver, A.M., Butler, J.J., & Martin, R.G. (1967). Congenital fibrosarcoma. *Cancer, 20,* 1607–1616.

Bancroft, L.W., Kransdorf, M.J., Peterson, J.J., & O'Connor, M.I. (2006). Benign fatty tumors: Classification, clinical course, imaging appearance, and treatment. *Skeletal Radiol, 35*(10), 719–733.

Barr, F.G. (1997). Molecular genetics and pathogenesis of rhabdomyosarcoma. *J Pediatr Hematol Oncol, 19,* 483–491.

Baumhoer, D., Gunawan, B., Becker, H., & Füzesi, L. (2005). Comparative genomic hybridization in four angiosarcomas of the female breast. *Gynecol Oncol, 97,* 348–352.

Beck, A. (1922). Zur Frage des Rontgensarkoms, zugleich ein Beitrag zur Pathogenese des Sarkoms. *Munchener Med Wochenschr, 69,* 623–625.

Biggar, R.J., Horm, J., Fraumeni, J.F. Jr., Greene, M.H., & Goedert, J.J. (1984). Incidence of Kaposi's sarcoma and mycosis fungoides in the United States including Puerto Rico, 1973–81. *J Natl Cancer Inst, 73*(1), 89–94.

Bishop, J.M., & Varmus, H.E. (1989). The Nobel Prize in Physiology or Medicine.

Boffetta, P., Matisane, L., Mundt, K.A., & Dell, L.D. (2003). Meta-analysis of studies of occupational exposure to vinyl chloride on relation to cancer mortality. *Scand J Work Environ Health, 29,* 220–229.

Carsi, B., & Rock, M.G. (2002). Primary osteosarcoma in adults older than 40 years. *Clin Orthop Relat Res, 397,* 53–61.

Cesarman, E., Chang, Y., Moore, P.S., Said, J.W., & Knowles, D.M. (1995). Kaposi's sarcoma-associated herpesvirus-like DNA sequences in AIDS-related body-cavity-based lymphomas. *N Engl J Med, 332*(18), 1186–1191.

Chang, Y., Cesarman, E., Pessin, M.S., Lee, F., Culpepper, J., Knowles, D.M., & Moore, P.S. (1994). Identification of herpesvirus-like DNA sequences in AIDS-associated Kaposi's sarcoma. *Science, 266,* 1865–1869.

Chauveinc, L., Mosseri, V., Quintana, E., Desjardins, L., Schlienger, P., Doz, F., & Dutrillaux, B. (2001). Osteosarcoma following retinoblastoma: Age at onset and latency period. *Ophthalmic Genet, 22*(2), 77–88.

Christopherson, W.M., Foote, F.W., & Stewart, F.W. (1952). Alveolar soft part sarcomas: Structurally characteristic tumors of uncertain histogenesis. *Cancer, 5,* 100–111.

Clark, J., Rocques, P.J., Crew, A.J., Gill, S., Shipley, J., Chan, A.L.,...Cooper, C.S. (1994). Identification of novel genes, SYT and SSX, involved in the t(X;18)(p11.2;q11.2) translocation found in human synovial sarcoma. *Nat Genet, 7,* 502–508, 1994.

Coindre, J.M., Mariani, O., Chibon, F., Maira, O., Somerhausen, N.A., Favre-Guilevin, E.,...Aurias, A. (2003). Most malignant fibrous histiocytomas developed in the retroperitoneum are dedifferentiated liposarcomas: A review of

25 cases initially diagnosed as malignant fibrous histiocytoma. *Mod Pathol*, *16*(3), 256–262.

Connolly, E., Gaffney, E., & Reynolds, J. (2003). Gastrointestinal stromal tumors. *Br J Surg*, *90*, 1178–1186.

Cook-Mozaffari, P., Newton, R., Beral, V., & Burkitt, D.P. (1998). The geographical distribution of Kaposi's sarcoma and of lymphomas in Africa before the AIDS epidemic. *Br J Cancer*, *78*(11), 1521–1528.

Cordon-Cardo, C. (1997). Sarcomas of the soft tissues and bone. In V.T. DeVita, Jr. (Ed.), *Cancer principles and practice of oncology* (pp. 1731–1782). New York: Lippincott-Raven Publishers.

Crawford, L.V., & Crawford, E.M. (1961). The properties of Rous sarcoma virus purified by density gradient centrifugation. *Virology*, *13*, 227–232.

Creech, J.L. Jr., & Johnson, M.N. (1974). Angiosarcoma of the liver in the manufacture of polyvinyl chloride. *J Occup Med*, *16*, 150–151.

Darling, J. (2007). A different view of sarcoma statistics. *Electronic Sarcoma Update Newsletter, ESUN*, *4*(6), Liddy Shriver Sarcoma Initiative, 2007.

Delaney, T.F., Hornicek, F.J., Lessnick, S.L., & Mankin, H.J. (2010). Epidemiology, pathology, and molecular genetics of the Ewing sarcoma family of tumors. *UpToDate*, Version 18.3, September, 2010.

Dickens, D.S., Kozielski, R., Khan, J., Forus, A., & Cripe, T.P. (2002). Cyclooxygenase-2 expression in pediatric sarcomas. *Pediatr Dev Pathol 5*(4), 356–364.

Dunlap, J.B., Magenis, R.E., Davis, C., Himoe, E., & Mansoor, A. (2009). Cytogenetic analysis of a primary bone angiosarcoma. *Cancer Genetics and Cytogenetics*, *194*(1), 1–3.

Edling, C.E., & Hallberg, B. (2007). c-Kit-a hematopoietic cell essential receptor tyrosine kinase. *Int J Biochem Cell Biol*, *39*(11), 1995–1998.

Ewing, J. (1921). Diffuse endothelioma of bone. *Proceedings of the New York Pathological Society*, *21*, 17–24.

Exelby, P.R., Knapper, W.H., Huvos, A.G., & Beattie, E.J. Jr. (1973). Soft-tissue fibrosarcoma in children. *Journal of Pediatric Surgery*, *8*(3), 415–420.

Falk, H., Telles, N.C., Ishak, K.G., Thomas, L.B., & Popper, H. (1979). Epidemiology of thorotrast-induced hepatic angiosarcoma in the United States. *Environmental Research*, *18*(1), 65–73.

Falk, H., Caldwell, G.G., Ishak, K.D., Thomas, L.B., & Popper, H. (1981). Arsenic-related hepatic angiosarcoma. *American Journal of Industrial Medicine*, *2*(1), 43–50.

Fung, H.L., & Tran, D.C. (2006). Effects of inhalant nitrites on VEGF expression: a feasible link to Kaposi's sarcoma? *J Neuroimmune Pharmacol*, *1*(3), 317–322.

Gardner, E.J. (1951). A genetic and clinical study of intestinal polyposis, a predisposing factor for carcinoma of the colon and rectum. *Am J Hum Genet*, *3*(2), 167–176.

Gurney, J.G., Swensen, A.R., & Bulterys, M. (1999). Malignant bone tumors. L.A.G. Ries, M.A. Smith, J.G. Gurney, M. Linet, T. Tamra, J.L. Young, & G.R. Bunin (Eds). *Cancer incidence and survival among children and adolescents: United States SEER program 1975–1995* (NIH Pub No 99-4649. 1999) (pp. 99–110). Bethesda, MD: National Cancer Institute, SEER Program.

Gurney, J.G., Swensen, A.R., & Bulterys, M. (1999). Malignant bone tumors. L.A.G. Ries, M.A. Smith, J.G. Gurney, M. Linet, T. Tamra, J.L. Young, & G.R. Bunin (Eds). *Cancer incidence and survival among children and adolescents: United States SEER program 1975–1995* (NIH Pub No 99-4649. 1999) (pp. 111–122). Bethesda, MD: National Cancer Institute, SEER Program.

Hoppin, J.A., Tolbert, P.E., Flanders, W.D., Zhang, R.H., Daniels, D.S., Ragsdale, B.D., & Brann, E.A. (1999). Occupational risk factors for sarcoma subtypes. *Epidemiology*, *10*(6), 300–306.

Indraccolo, U., Luchetti, G., & Indraccolo, S.R. (2008). Malignant transformation of uterine leiomyomata. *Eur J Gynaecol Oncol, 29*(5), 543–534.

Joensuu, H., Roberts, P.J., Sarlomo-Rikala, M., Andersson, L.C., Tervahartiala, P., Tuveson, D.,…Demetri, G.D. (2001). Effect of the tyrosine kinase inhibitor STI571 in a patient with a metastatic gastrointestinal stromal tumor. *N Engl J Med, 344*(14), 1052–1056.

Johnson, J.G., Gilbert, E., Zimmermann, B., & Watne, A.L. (1972). Gardner's syndrome, colon cancer, and sarcoma. *Journal of Surgical Oncology, 4*(4), 354–362.

Kaposi, M. (1872). Idiopathisches multiples pigmentsarkom der haut. *Arch Dermatol Syph, 4,* 265–273.

Karlsson, P., Holmberg, E., Samuelsson, A., Johansson, K.A., & Wallgren, A. (1998). Soft tissue sarcoma after treatment for breast cancer–A Swedish population-based study. *Eur J Cancer, 34*(13), 2068–2075.

Knezevich, S.R., Garnett, M.J., Pysher, T.J., Beckwith, J.B., Grundy, P.E., & Sorensen, P.H. (1998). ETV6-NTRK3 gene fusions and trisomy 11 establish a histogenetic link between mesoblastic nephroma and congenital fibrosarcoma. *Cancer Res, 58,* 5046–5048.

Ladanyi, M. (1995). The emerging molecular genetics of sarcoma translocations. *Diagn Mol Pathol, 4*(3), 162–173.

Ladanyi, M., & Bridge, J.A. (2000). Contribution of molecular genetic data to the classification of sarcomas. *Hum Pathol, 31,* 532–538.

Ladanyi, M., Lui, M.Y., Antonescu, C.R., Krause-Boehm, A., Meindl, A., Argani, P.,…Bridge, J. (2001). The der(17)t(X;17)(p11;q25) of human alveolar soft part sarcoma fuses the TFE3 transcription factor gene to ASPL, a novel gene at 17q25. *Oncogene, 20*(1), 48–57.

Lassus, P., Ristimaki, A., Huuhtanen, R., Tukiainen, E., Asko-Seljavaara, S., Andersson, L.C.,…Bohling, T. (2005). Cyclooxygenase-2 expression in human soft-tissue sarcomas is related to epithelial differentiation. *Anticancer Research, 25,* 2669–2674.

Leonard, A., Craft, A.W., Moss, C., & Malcolm, A.J. (1996). Osteogenic sarcoma in the Rothmund-Thomson syndrome. *Med Pediatr Oncol, 26*(4), 249–253.

Li, F.P., Fraumeni, J.F. Jr., Mulvihill, J.J., Blattner, W.A., Dreyfus, M.G., Tucker, M.A., & Miller, R.W. (1998). A cancer family syndrome in twenty-four kindreds. *Cancer Research, 48*(18), 5358–5362.

Lorincz, A., Redelman, D., Horvath, V.J., Bardsley, M.R., Chen, H., & Ordog, T. (2008). Progenitors of interstitial cells of Cajal in the postnatal murine stomach. *Gastroenterology, 134,* 1083–1093.

Markowitz, S.D., & Bertagnolli, M.M. (2009). Molecular basis of colorectal cancer. *N Engl J Med, 361*(25), 2449–2460.

Martland, H., & Humphries, R.E. (1929). Osteogenic sarcoma in dial painters using luminous paint. *Arch Pathol, 7,* 406–417.

Mendenhall, W.M., Zlotecki, R.A., Scarborough, M.T., Gibbs, P.C., & Mendenhall, N.P. (2006). Giant cell tumor of bone. *American Journal of Clinical Oncology, 29*(1), 96–99.

Moore, P.S., & Chang, Y. (1995). Detection of herpesvirus-like DNA sequences in Kaposi's sarcoma in patients with and without HIV infection. *N Engl J Med, 332*(18), 1181–1185.

Moore, P.S., Gao, S.J., Dominguez, G., Cesarman, E., Lungu, O., Knowles, D.M.,…Chang, Y. (1996). Primary characterization of a herpesvirus agent associated with Kaposi's sarcoma. *The Journal of Virology, 70*(1), 549–558.

Mundt, K.A., Dell, L.D., Austin, R.P., Luippold, R.S., Noess, R., & Bigelow, C. (2000). Historical cohort study of 10,109 men in the North American vinyl chloride industry, 1942–1972. Update of cancer mortality to 31 December. *Occup Environ Med, 57,* 774–781.

O'Brien, J.E., & Stout, A.P. (1964). Malignant fibrous xanthomas. *Cancer, 17,* 1445–1455.

Oppermann, H., Levinson, A.D., Varmus, H.E., Levintow, L., & Bishop, J.M. (1979). Uninfected vertebrate cells contain a protein that is closely related to the product of the avian sarcoma virus transforming gene (src). *Proc Natl Acad Sci USA*, 76(4), 1804–1808.

Parkin, D.M., Stiller, C.A., Draper, G.J., & Bieber, C.A. (1988). The international incidence of childhood cancer. *Int J Cancer*, 42, 511–520.

Parkin, D.M., Bray, F., Ferlay, J., & Pisani, P. (2005). Global cancer statistics, 2002. *CA Cancer J Clin*, 55, 74–108.

Patel, K.U., Szabo, S.S., Hernandez, V.S., Prieto, V.G., Abruzzo, L.V., Lazar, A.J.F., & López-Terrada, D. (2008). Dermatofibrosarcoma protuberans COL1A1-PDGFB fusion is identified in virtually all dermatofibrosarcoma protuberans cases when investigated by newly developed multiplex reverse transcription polymerase chain reaction and fluorescence in situ hybridization assays. *Hum Pathol*, 39(2), 184–193.

Robbins, S.L., & Cotran, R.S. (1979). *Pathologic basis of disease* (2nd ed.). Philadelphia: WB Saunders Company.

Robinson, E., Neugut, A.I., & Wylie, P. (1988). Clinical aspects of postirradiation sarcomas. *J Natl Cancer Inst*, 80, 233–240.

Rööser, B., Willén, H., Gustafson, P., Alvegård, T.A., & Rydholm, A. (1991). Malignant fibrous histiocytoma of soft tissue. A population-based epidemiologic and prognostic study of 137 patients. *Cancer*, 67(2), 499–505.

Rossiello, L., Ruocco, E., Signoriello, G., Micheli, P., Rienzo, M., Napoli, C., & Rossiello, R. (2007). Evidence of COX-1 and COX-2 expression in Kaposi's sarcoma tissues. *European Journal of Cancer*, 43(8), 1232–1241.

Rous, P. (1910). A transmissable avian neoplasm. *J Exp Med*, 12, 696–705.

Rous, P. (1911). A sarcoma of the fowl transmissible by an agent separable from the tumor cells. *J Exp Med*, 13, 397–399.

Rous, P., & Huggins, C.B. (1966). The Nobel Prize in Physiology or Medicine.

Sanders, K., Koh, S., & Ward, S. (2006). Interstitial cells of cajal as pacemakers in the gastrointestinal tract. *Annu Rev Physiol*, 68, 307–343.

Sinha, A., Tekkis, P.P., Gibbons, D.C., Phillips, R.K., & Clark, S.K. (2010). Risk factors predicting desmoid occurrence in patients with familial adenomatous polyposis: A meta-analysis. *Colorectal Dis*, no. doi:10.1111/j.1463–1318.2010.

Skubitz, K.M. (2007). Sarcoma. *Mayo Clinic Proceedings*, 82(11), 1409–1432.

Spirtas, R., Beebe, G., Baxter, P., Dacey, F., Faber, M., Falk, H., van Kaick, G., & Stafford, J. (1983). Angiosarcoma as a model for comparative carcinogenesis. *Lancet*, 322(8347), 456.

Stebbing, J., & Portsmouth, B. (2003). How does HAART lead to the resolution of Kaposi's sarcoma? *J Antimicrob Chemother*, 51(5), 1095–1098.

Stehelin, D., Fujita, D.J., Padgett, T., Varmus, H.E., & Bishop, J.M. (1977). Detection and enumeration of transformation-defective strains of avian sarcoma virus with molecular hybridization. *Virology*, 76(2), 675–684.

Stiller, C.A., Bielack, S.S., Jundt, G., & Steliarova-Foucher, E. (2006). Bone tumours in European children and adolescents, 1978–1997. Report from the Automated Childhood Cancer Information System project. *Eur J Cancer*, 42(13), 2124–2135.

Thomas, D.M., & Skubitz, T. (2009). Giant-cell tumour of bone. *Current Opinion in Oncology*, 21, 338–344.

Tontonoz, P., Singer, S., Forman, B.M., Sarraf, P., Fletcher, J.A., Fletcher, C.D.,…Spiegelman, B.M. (1997). Terminal differentiation of human liposarcoma cells induced by ligands for peroxisome proliferator-activated receptor gamma and the retinoid X receptor. *Proc Natl Acad Sci USA*, 94(1), 237–241.

Tran, T., Davila, J.A., & El-Serag, H.B. (2005). The epidemiology of malignant gastrointestinal stromal tumors: An analysis of 1,458 cases from 1992 to 2000. *The American Journal of Gastroenterology*, *100*, 162–168.

Turc-Carel, C., Limon, J., Dal Cin, P., Rao, U., Karakousis, C., & Sandberg, A.A. (1986). Cytogenetic studies of adipose tissue tumors. II. Recurrent reciprocal translocation t(12:16)(q13;p11) in myxoid liposarcomas. *Cancer Genetics and Cytogenetics*, *23*(4), 291–299.

Walker, D.G. (1972). Congenital osteopetrosis in mice cured by parabiotic union with normal siblings. *Endocrinology*, *91*(4), 916–920.

Walker, D.G. (1973). Osteopetrosis cured by temporary parabiosis. *Science*, *180*(88), 875.

Wallach, E.E., & Vlahos, N.F. (2004). Uterine myomas: An overview of development, clinical features, and management. *Obstet Gynecol*, *104*, 393–406.

Wang, R., Lu, Y.J., Fisher, C., Bridge, J.A., & Shipley, J. (2001). Characterization of chromosome aberrations associated with soft-tissue leiomyosarcomas by twenty-four-color karyotyping and comparative genomic hybridization analysis. *Genes Chromosomes Cancer*, *31*, 54–64.

Wang, L.L., Gannavarapu, A., Kozinetz, C.A., Moise, L., Levy, M.L., Lewis, R.A.,...Zackai, E.H. (2003). Association between osteosarcoma and deleterious mutations in the RECQL4 gene in Rothmund-Thomson syndrome. *J Natl Cancer Inst*, *95*(9), 669–674.

Yarden, Y., Kuang, W.J., Yang-Feng, T., Coussens, L., Munemitsu, S., Dull, T.J.,...Ullrich, A. (1987). Human proto-oncogene c-kit: a new cell surface receptor tyrosine kinase for an unidentified ligand. *EMBO J*, *6*(11), 3341–3351.

Epidemiology of Malignant Melanoma

GLOBAL EPIDEMIOLOGY OF MALIGNANT MELANOMA

Malignant melanoma of the skin is diagnosed in 160,000 individuals worldwide and causes 41,000 deaths annually. This potentially fatal form of skin cancer is detected slightly more frequently in women than in men (the male to female ratio is 0.97); nevertheless, mortality is 20% higher in men. Malignant melanoma is most common in Caucasian populations living in sunny climates. High mortality and incidence rates are observed in Caucasian populations of Australia/New Zealand, South Africa, Northern Chile and Colombia in South America, certain regions of North America, and Northern Europe (Parkin et al., 2005).

Survival from malignant melanoma is nearly 100% if diagnosed prior to invasion of the dermis and metastatic spread (Balch et al., 2001). Overall, 5-year survival is 91% in the United States and 81% in Europe. Females have better survival than males, probably because the site distribution permits earlier diagnosis of noninvasive lesions that can be surgically removed prior to metastasis. Survival in developing countries is relatively poor (approximately 40%), in part due to late diagnosis and limited access to therapy, but also because melanomas often develop on the soles of the feet and thus go undetected until invasion and metastasis has occurred (Buzaid, 2004).

The global pattern of malignant melanoma reflects the interactions of susceptible genotypes and phenotypes with cumulative exposure to ionizing radiation from the sun. Due to heavy diffuse melanin skin pigmentation that forms a protective barrier against cumulative radiation damage, populations living nearest the equator are *not* at the highest risk for development of melanoma. Rather, individuals without substantial melanin pigment in the epidermis are most susceptible to cumulative damage due to ultraviolet rays and the development of this potentially fatal malignancy of the skin. The highest mortality rates are observed among the fair-skinned populations of Australia, South Africa, and certain regions of South America, and progressively lesser rates are found depending upon the degree of skin pigmentation coupled with the level of sun exposure (**Figure 26.1**). Furthermore, several investigators have suggested that the depletion of the ozone layer and the absence of cloud cover increase exposure to the sun and therefore heighten the risk, e.g., the Caucasian populations of Australia and New Zealand have the highest mortality, presumably as a consequence of the thinning ozone layer in the Southern Hemisphere over the past several decades (Carver, 1998).

Rapid increases in incidence and mortality have recently been observed in both sexes in many countries, even where rates were formerly low, such as Japan. In the Nordic countries, for example, the rate of increase since 1980 has averaged approximately 30% every 5 years (Parkin et al., 2005). Similar increases are evident in the US population where the incidence of malignant melanoma has more than tripled in men and women during the past 3 decades (Altekruse et al., 2009) (**Figure 26.2**).

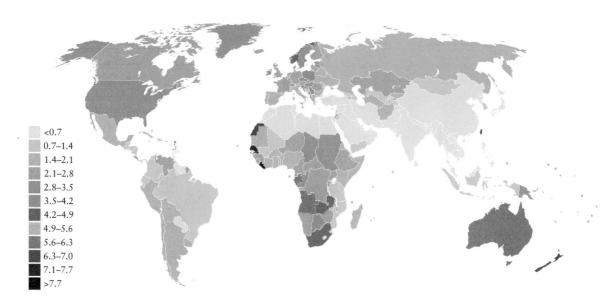

Figure 26.1 Global Mortality: Malignant Melanoma, 2004.

Source: Data from World Health Organization. The global burden of disease: 2004 update. Geneva, WHO, 2008. Available at www.who.int/evidence/bod

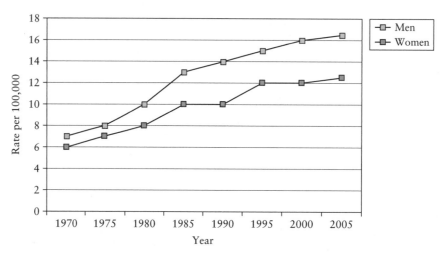

Figure 26.2 Chronologic Trends of Malignant Melanoma among Men and Women in the United States: SEER, 1970–2005.

Source: Data from Altekruse SF, Kosary CL, Krapcho M, Neyman N, Aminou R, Waldron W, Ruhl J, Howlader N, Tatalovich Z, Cho H, Mariotto A, Eisner MP, Lewis DR, Cronin K, Chen HS, Feuer EJ, Stinchcomb DG, Edwards BK (eds). SEER Cancer Statistics Review, 1975–2007, National Cancer Institute. Bethesda, MD, 2009.

PATHOGENESIS OF MALIGNANT MELANOMA

The cell of origin of malignant melanoma is the melanocyte which resides in the basal layer of the epidermis. In this location, melanocytes are in contact with keratinocytes of the epidermis. Melanocytes synthesize melanin, a brownish-black pigment that is distributed to surrounding keratinocytes through dendritic projections (Gilchrest et al., 1999). The melanocyte

population rests upon a fibrous basement membrane that separates the epidermis from the dermis. When malignant melanoma first develops, the basement membrane forms a protective barrier that keeps the tumor cells confined (*in situ*). However, malignant melanocytes are unusual in their ability to breach the basement membrane and invade the underlying dermis (**Figure 26.3**). The high metastatic potential of malignant melanoma is responsible for its significant impact on cancer mortality.

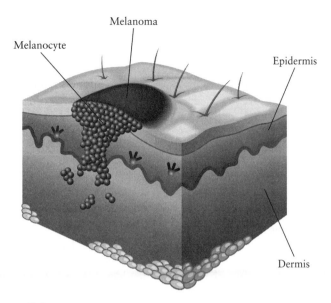

Figure 26.3 Cutaneous Malignant Melanoma.
Source: © rob3000/ShutterStock, Inc.

Damage to melanocytes caused by ultraviolet radiation is central to the pathogenesis of malignant melanoma (Gilchrest et al., 1999). For example, patients with *xeroderma pigmentosum* have a genetically inherited defect in the repair of DNA photoproducts induced by ultraviolet radiation (Cleaver, 1968) and individuals with this condition are at greatly increased risk of developing malignant melanoma as well as squamous cell and basal cell carcinomas of the skin (Lambert, Kuo, and Lambert, 1995).

Both ultraviolet A (wavelength: 320–400 nanometers) and ultraviolet B radiation (wavelength: 270–320 nanometers) have deleterious effects on the DNA of melanocytes and other cells of the skin. Ultraviolet B radiation induces the formation of pyrimidine dimers that if incorrectly repaired cause DNA mutations (Freeman et al., 1989). Ultraviolet A radiation causes oxidative damage to DNA that is also potentially mutagenic (Pathak, 1991; Meyskens, Farmer, and Anton-Culver, 2004).

Melanin serves *photoprotective* functions in the skin: it absorbs ultraviolet photons and reactive oxygen species generated by the interaction of photons with cell membrane lipids and other cellular components (Pathak, 1995). Within cells, melanin forms a *supranuclear protective cap* about the nucleus, thereby shielding the nuclear DNA from damaging ultraviolet radiation (Kobayashi et al., 1998). The photoprotective property of melanin is illustrated by the phenomenon of tanning in response to ultraviolet radiation. Tanning is due to enhanced proliferation of melanocytes accompanied by increased synthesis and transfer of melanin to surrounding keratinocytes (Gilchrest et al., 1998).

Numerous studies suggest that repeated intense exposure to ultraviolet radiation leads to the accumulation of cancer-causing mutations in melanocytes. As discussed below, a number of genetic mutations have already been identified that cause dysfunction in melanin biosynthesis and dissemination, cell adhesion and communication, mechanisms of DNA repair, and regulation of the cell cycle.

In addition to the potential for inducing mutagenic changes in the DNA of melanocytes, ultraviolet radiation also causes inflammation and immunosuppression in the skin, both of which may play a role in carcinogenesis as well as the metastatic spread of cancer (Gilchrest et al., 1999). Several molecular studies have noted overexpression of cyclooxygenase-2 (COX-2), the chief regulatory enzyme of the inflammatory cascade, in the progression of malignant melanoma from dysplasia to invasive cancer (Denkart et al., 2001; Goulet et al., 2003). In fact, some investigators have observed chemopreventive effects of nonsteroidal anti-inflammatory drugs against melanoma development (Harris, Namboodiri, and Beebe-Donk, 2001) and selective anti-inflammatory COX-2 inhibiting agents such as celecoxib have shown significant therapeutic value in clinical trials of patients with metastatic malignant melanoma (Hakim et al., 2006).

Even low-dose ultraviolet B exposure can damage the Langerhans cells (circulating immune cells found in the epidermis) and produce significant immunosuppression (Tang and Udey, 1991). Thus, failure of the immune system to recognize and destroy malignant cells may also play a significant role in the expansion and promotion of clones of malignant melanocytes (Cruz and Bergstresser, 1989).

A key feature in the progression of malignant melanoma is the unusual capacity of cancerous melanocytes to metastasize throughout the body. Homeostasis of the melanocytic population depends on many features of the cellular milieu in the dermis and epidermis of the skin. In particular, keratinocytes in the epidermis keep melanocytic proliferation in check and the basement membrane prevents melanocytes from migrating into the dermis. Melanocytes that become cancerous often lose important molecules called cadherins that modulate cell to cell adhesion and communication. Though signature mutations of malignant melanoma have not yet been identified, the metastatic potential of this form of cancer appears to be the result of complex epigenetic and genetic phenomena that result in the silencing of tumor suppression genes (e.g., p16, K-ras, E-cadherin, p53, etc.) and the activation of oncogenes that stimulate cell division (*BRAF, EGFR*), angiogenesis (*VEGF*), deregulation of apoptosis (telomerase), and metastasis (*C-MET*) (Rákosy et al., 2007; Soubrane et al., 2006; Rudolph et al., 2000; Satyamoorthy and Herlyn, 2002). Recent molecular investigations have identified mutations of the *BRAF* gene in up to 80% of malignant melanomas (Davies et al., 2002). Mutant *BRAF* protein stimulates deregulation of important mechanisms of carcinogenesis in melanocytes, e.g., cell division and apoptosis, and has been proposed as a molecular target for the therapy of malignant melanoma (Garber, 2009).

GENERAL RISK FACTORS FOR MALIGNANT MELANOMA

The primary risk factor for the development of malignant melanoma is excessive exposure to ultraviolet rays from the sun. Many epidemiologic investigations have also demonstrated that the risk increases with lighter pigmentation of the skin by melanin. Individuals with lightly pigmented skin are at the highest risk and individuals with darkly pigmented skin are at the lowest risk. Other phenotypic factors also increase the risk, including inability to tan, light eye color, red hair, and extensive freckling. Futhermore, the risk increases with the number of pigmented (melanocytic) nevi (see discussion below).

While the risk of malignant melanoma development is clearly linked to cumulative exposure to the sun, the risk is heightened further by intense, intermittent exposure causing multiple sunburns, particularly during childhood and adolescence.

In contrast to other types of skin cancer, malignant melanoma frequently occurs in areas of the body that are intermittently exposed to the sun, such as the back in men and the lower legs in women, with relative sparing of more frequently exposed sites such as the face, hands, and forearms (Gilchrest et al., 1999). Furthermore, malignant melanoma is more likely to develop in persons with predominantly indoor occupations whose exposure to the sun is limited to weekends and vacations (Holman, Armstrong, and Heenan, 1986). Indeed, the marked increase in the incidence of malignant melanoma in recent decades may reflect the effects of intense intermittent exposures in individuals who vacation in sunny climates during the winter months (Westerdahl et al., 1992). The risk of malignant melanoma is specifically increased with exposures that induce sunburn, e.g., a history of five or more severe sunburns during adolescence more than doubles the risk (Weinstock, 1996).

Pigmented Nevi and Malignant Melanoma

As pointed out in a review of melanoma epidemiology by Margaret Tucker, there are two broad categories of pigmented nevi, common and dysplastic, which carry different risks of melanoma development (Tucker, 2009). Dysplastic nevi, which carry a far greater risk, are characterized by size greater than 5 mm at largest diameter, a flat surface, irregular asymmetric shape, indiscriminate borders, and variability in the degree of pigmentation. In a meta-analysis of 46 epidemiologic studies, Gandini and colleagues examined dose responses in melanoma risk associated with the number of common or dysplastic nevi. Individuals with more than 100 common nevi had a relative risk of 6.4 compared to individuals with less than 15 common nevi, whereas even the presence of one solitary dysplastic nevus doubled the risk and having 10 or more dysplastic nevi produced a 12-fold increase in the risk (Gandini et al., 2005).

Genetic Predisposition to Malignant Melanoma

Approximately 10% of melanoma cases diagnosed in the United States report that one or more relatives are also affected (Greene, 1998; Tucker, 2009). In case control studies, individuals with a positive family history have roughly a twofold increased risk compared to individuals with no family history.

The familial atypical mole and melanoma (FAMM) syndrome is a rare genetic disorder giving rise to multiple dysplastic pigmented moles of the skin that invariably progress to malignant melanoma. Genetic linkage studies of members of families with the FAMM syndrome have identified two major susceptibility genes, *CDKN2A* and *CDK4*, both of which are inherited in an autosomal dominant pattern. Carriers of either mutant gene are at 100% risk of developing malignant melanoma during their lifetimes (Greene, 1998).

One form of the FAMM syndrome is caused by a mutation in *CDKN2A*, the gene that encodes p16, an important cell cycle regulating protein (Hussussian et al., 1994). The *CDKN2A* gene is located on the short arm of chromosome 9 (9p21). This gene normally codes for the tumor suppressor protein, p16, which is essential for the regulation of cell division (Monzon et al., 1998). Mutant forms of *CDKN2A* encode dysfunctional p16 protein that leads to loss of control of cell division and enhanced proliferation of melanocytes.

A second form of the FAMM syndrome is caused by a mutation in the *CDK4* gene, which maps to the long arm of chromosome 12 (12q13). This gene also codes for an oncogenic protein that is important for the regulation of cell division of melanocytes. Mutations in *CDK4* are very rare and have been detected in only a few families (Greene, 1998).

Individuals who carry certain polymorphisms or mutant alleles of a gene called *MC1R* (melanocortin receptor) are also at increased risk for the development of malignant melanoma. The *MC1R* gene plays an important role in melanin biosynthesis and pigmentation of the skin and hair. Mutant forms of *MC1R* are extremely common and may result in a highly susceptible phenotype: red hair, fair skin, numerous freckles, and inability to tan.

UV Radiation from Tanning Beds

In 2009, the International Agency for Research on Cancer (IARC) released a report that categorized tanning beds as "*carcinogenic to humans.*" This classification is based upon analysis of more than 20 epidemiological studies indicating that people who begin using tanning devices before age 30 are 75% more likely to develop melanoma (WHO, 2009).

Ozone Holes and Malignant Melanoma

The stratospheric ozone layer resides approximately 10–30 miles above the earth and acts as a protective shield against the sun's harmful ultraviolet rays, particularly UVB rays (wavelengths of 270–315 nanometers). The natural ozone shield has been gradually depleted by the atmospheric release of man-made chemicals such as chlorofluorocarbons (freons) and bromofluorocarbons (halons) that spark the catalytic destruction of ozone. Ozone destruction is most prominent around the polar regions of the earth leading to "ozone holes" and penetration of the earth's atmosphere by UVB rays. Excessive exposure to UVB rays is linked to the development of malignant melanoma as well as other conditions, e.g., cataracts (Norval et al., 2007). Such windows of UVB exposure appear to coincide roughly with the high mortality rates of malignant melanoma in the Southern Hemisphere of the world (**Figure 26.1**).

PREVENTION OF MALIGNANT MELANOMA

The primary prevention of malignant melanoma is dependent upon minimizing exposure to intensive ultraviolet radiation from the sun, tanning beds, and other sources of radiation. Avoidance of intense sun exposure during peak times of the day, wearing protective clothing, and using sunscreen lotions can offer protection (Autier, 2005).

National and community programs of secondary prevention have also proven to be highly effective. The American Academy of Dermatology recommends annual inspection of the skin by a certified dermatologist for the detection and surgical removal of dysplastic pigmented nevi and other suspicious lesions prior to their progression to malignancy (American Academy of Dermatology, 2010). A special surgical technique called "Mohs surgery," wherein repeated circumferential sections of tumor are removed and microscopically examined until cancer-free margins are evident, has been shown to be effective in treating *in situ* cutaneous malignant melanoma (Bene, Healy, and Coldiron, 2008).

● ● ●   REFERENCES

Altekruse, S.F., Kosary, C.L., Krapcho, M., Neyman, N., Aminou, R., Waldron, W.,… Edwards, B.K. (Eds.). (2009). SEER Cancer Statistics Review, 1975–2007, Bethesda, MD: National Cancer Institute.

American Academy of Dermatology. (2010). National Skin Cancer Screening Program, USA. American Academy of Dermatology.

Autier, P. (2005). Cutaneous malignant melanoma: Facts about sunbeds and sunscreen. *Expert Rev Anticancer Ther*, 5(5), 821–833.

Balch, C., Buzaid, A., Soong, S., Atkins, M., Cascinelli, N., Coit, D., …Thompson, J. (2001). Final version of the American Joint Committee on Cancer staging system for cutaneous melanoma. *J Clin Oncol*, 19(16), 3635–3648.

Bene, N.I., Healy, C., & Coldiron, B.M. (2008). Mohs micrographic surgery is accurate 95.1% of the time for melanoma in situ: A prospective study of 167 cases. *Dermatologic Surgery*, 34(5), 660–664.

Buzaid, A. (2004). Management of metastatic cutaneous melanoma. *Oncology (Williston Park)*, 18(11), 1443–1450.

Carver, G. (1998). *Part III. The science of the ozone hole.* Cambridge [?]: University of Cambridge, Center for Atmospheric Science.

Cleaver, J.E. (1968). Defective repair replication of DNA in xeroderma pigmentosum. *Nature, 218*, 652–656.

Cruz Jr., P.D., Paul, R., & Bergstresser, P.R. (1989). Ultraviolet radiation, Langerhans' cells and skin cancer: Conspiracy and failure. *Arch Dermatol, 125*(7), 975–979.

Davies, H., Bignell, G.R., Cox, C., Stephens, P., Edkins, S., Clegg, S., …Futreal, P.A. (2002). Mutations of the BRAF gene in human cancer. *Nature, 417*, 949–954.

Denkert, C., Köbel, M., Berger, S., Siegert, A., Leclere, A., Trefzer, U., & Hauptmann, S. (2001). Expression of cyclooxygenase 2 in human malignant melanoma. *Cancer Res, 61*(1), 303–308.

Freeman, S.E., Hacham, H., Gange, R.W., Maytum, D.J., Sutherland, J.C., & Sutherland, B.M. (1989). Wavelength dependence of pyrimidine dimer formation in DNA of human skin irradiated *in situ* with ultraviolet light. *Proc Natl Acad Sci USA, 86*, 5605–5609.

Gandini, S., Sera, F., Cattaruzza, M.S., Pasquini, P., Abeni, D., Boyle, P., & Melchi, C.F. (2005). Meta-analysis of risk factors for cutaneous melanoma: I. Common and atypical naevi. *Eur J Cancer, 41*(1), 28–44.

Garber, K. (2009). Cancer research. Melanoma drug vindicates targeted approach. *Science, 326*(5960), 1619.

Gilchrest, B.A., Park, H.Y., Eller, M.S., & Yaar, M. (1998). The photobiology of the tanning response. In: J.J. Nordlund, R.E. Boissy, V.J. Hearing, R.A. King, & J.P. Ortonne (Eds.), *The pigmentary system: Physiology and pathophysiology* (pp. 359–372). New York: Oxford University Press.

Gilchrest, B.A., Eller, M.S., Geller, A.C., & Yaar, M. (1999). The pathogenesis of melanoma induced by ultraviolet radiation. *New Engl J Med, 340*(17), 1341–1348.

Goulet, A.C., Einsphar, J.G., Alberts, D.S., Beas, A., Burk, C., Bhattacharyya, A., …Nelson, M.A. (2003). Analysis of cyclooxygenase 2 (COX-2) expression during malignant melanoma progression. *Cancer Biol Ther, 2*(6), 713–718.

Greene, M.H. (1998). The genetics of hereditary melanoma and nevi. *Cancer, 86*(11), 2464–2477.

Hakim, R., Poggi, R., Pantaleo, M., Benedetti, G., Brandi, G., Zannetti, G.,…Biasco, G. (2006). Phase II study of temozolomide and celecoxib in the treatment of metastatic melanoma. *Journal of Clinical Oncology, 24*(18S), 18015.

Harris, R.E., Namboodiri, K.A., & Beebe-Donk, J. (2001). Inverse association of malignant melanoma and non-steroidal anti-inflammatory drugs (NSAIDs) in women. *Oncology Reports, 8*, 655–657.

Holman, C.D.J., Armstrong, B.K., & Heenan, P.J. (1986). Relationship of cutaneous malignant melanoma to individual sunlight-exposure habits. *J Natl Cancer Inst, 76*, 403–414.

Hussussian, C.J., Struewing, J.P., Goldstein, A.M., Higgins, P.A., Ally, D.S., Sheahan, M.D.,… Dracopoli, N.C. (1994). Germline p16 mutations in familial melanoma. *Nat Genet, 8*(1), 15–21.

Kobayashi, N., Nakagawa, A., Muramatsu, T., Yamashin, Y., Shiral, T., Hashimoto, M.W.,… Mori, T. (1998). Supranuclear melanin caps reduce ultraviolet induced DNA photoproducts in human epidermis. *J Invest Dermatol, 110,* 806–810.

Lambert, W.C., Kuo, H.R., & Lambert, M.W. (1995). Xeroderma pigmentosum. *Dermatol Clin, 13,* 169–209.

Meyskens, F.L. Jr., Farmer, P.J., & Anton-Culver, H. (2004). Etiologic pathogenesis of melanoma: A unifying hypothesis for the missing attributable risk. *Clin Cancer Res, 10*(8), 2581–2583.

Monzon, J., Liu, L., Brill, H., Goldstein, A.M., Tucker, M.A., From, L., …Lassam, N.J. (1998). CDKN2A mutations in multiple primary melanomas. *New Engl J Med, 338*(13), 879–887.

Norval, M., Cullen, A.P., de Gruijl, F.R., Longstreth, J., Takizawa, Y., Lucas, R.M.,…van der Leun, J.C. (2007). The effects on human health from stratospheric ozone depletion and its interactions with climate change. *Photochem Photobiol Sci, 6*(3), 232–251.

Parkin, M., Bray, F., Ferlay, J., & Pisani, P. (2005). Global cancer statistics, 2002. *CA Cancer J Clin, 55,* 74–108.

Pathak, M.A. (1991). Ultraviolet radiation and the development of non-melanoma and melanoma skin cancer: Clinical and experimental evidence. *Skin Pharmacol, 4,* Suppl 1, 85–94.

Pathak, M.A. (1995). Functions of melanin and protection by melanin. In L. Zeise, M.R. Chedekel, T.B. Fitzpatrick (Eds.), *Melanin: Its role in human photoprotection* (pp. 125–134). Overland Park, Kansas: Valdenmar Publishing.

Rákosy, Z., Vízkeleti, L., Ecsedi, S., Vokó, Z., Bégány, A., Barok, M., Krekk, Z.,…Balázs, M. (2007). EGFR gene copy number alterations in primary cutaneous malignant melanomas are associated with poor prognosis. *International Journal of Cancer, 121*(8), 1729–1737.

Rudolph, P., Schubert, C., Tamm, S., Heidorn, K., Hauschild, A., Michalska, I.,…Parwaresch, R. (2000). Telomerase activity in melanocytic lesions: A potential marker of tumor biology. *Amer J Path, 156,* 1425–1432.

Satyamoorthy, K., & Herlyn, M. (2002). Cellular and molecular biology of human melanoma. *Cancer Biology and Therapy, 1*(1), 12–15.

Soubrane, C., Mouawad, R., Sultan, V., Spano, J., Khayat, D., & Rixe, O. (2006). Soluble VEGF-A and lymphangiogenesis in metastatic malignant melanoma patients. *Journal of Clinical Oncology, 24*(18S), 8049.

Tang, A., & Udey, M.C. (1991). Inhibition of epidermal Langerhans cell function by low dose ultraviolet B radiation. Ultraviolet B radiation selectively modulates ICAM-1 (CD54) expression by murine Langerhans cells. *The Journal of Immunology, 146*(10), 3347–3355.

Tucker, M. (2009). Melanoma epidemiology. *Hematol Oncol Clin N Am, 23,* 383–395.

Weinstock, M.A. (1996). Controversies in the role of sunlight in the pathogenesis of cutaneous melanoma. *Photochem Photobiol, 63,* 406–410.

Westerdahl, J., Olsson, H., Ingvar, C., Brandt, L., Jonsson, P.E., & Moller, T. (1992). Southern travelling habits with special reference to tumour site in Swedish melanoma patients. *Anticancer Res, 12,* 1539–1542.

WHO International Agency for Research on Cancer Monograph Working Group. (2009). A review of human carcinogens—Part D: Radiation. *The Lancet Oncology, 10*(8), 751–752.

Epidemiology of Lymphoma

INTRODUCTION

The World Health Organization categorizes lymphomas into three broad groups: non-Hodgkin's lymphoma, Hodgkin's lymphoma, and multiple myeloma. Non-Hodgkin's lymphomas show considerable heterogeneity and are divisible into those arising from B cells or T cells. This chapter focuses primarily on the epidemiology of non-Hodgkin's lymphoma with brief sections devoted to Hodgkin's lymphoma and multiple myeloma.

Lymphomas are malignancies that can arise in the lymphocytes of lymphoid tissue anywhere in the body, most commonly within lymph nodes. These tumors are broadly classified as Hodgkin's lymphoma, non-Hodgkin's lymphoma, or multiple myeloma. Hodgkin's lymphoma, which is distinguishable by the presence of multi-nucleated *Reed-Sternberg cells*, constitutes 10–15% of all lymphomas (Reed, 1902). Multiple myeloma, a neoplasm of plasma cells, constitutes 15–20% of lymphomas. The remaining 65–75% of lymphomas, the non-Hodgkin's lymphomas, arise at various stages in the maturation of B lymphocytes or T lymphocytes. According to classification schemes currently used in clinical practice, non-Hodgkin's lymphomas can be subdivided into a bewildering array of subtypes. In most populations, 80–90% of non-Hodgkin's lymphomas are derived from the B-cell lineage (Harris et al., 1999).

Lymphomas are cohesive malignancies (solid tumors) comprised primarily of lymphocytes. Their origin, usually in lymph nodes, may involve an arrest in differentiation of immature lymphocytes, or alternatively, retrodifferentiation of mature lymphocytes. In either case, there is sustained unrelenting proliferation of the transformed cells. As with other malignancies, the initiation, growth, development, and metastatic spread of lymphomas involves various cellular and genetic processes including mutagenesis, mitogenesis, angiogenesis, aberrant apoptosis, immunosuppression, and metastasis.

Lymphocytes arise from hematopoietic stem cells of the bone marrow. The B lymphocytes mature and differentiate in the lymph nodes whereas T lymphocytes do so in the thymus gland. The different types of lymphocytes display specific cell surface receptors and have characteristic morphological features and distinct functions in the immune system. For example, the maturation, differentiation, and proliferation of T lymphocytes spawn at least three distinct subpopulations: antigen-presenting T cells (also called helper T cells), suppressor T cells, and killer T cells.

With appropriate stimulation by helper T cells, mature B lymphocytes differentiate into plasma cells that secrete antibodies directed against specific antigens recognized as foreign to the human immune system. Malignancies of plasma cells are called *myelomas* and since neoplasms of plasma cells usually involve multiple anatomic sites throughout the skeletal system and sometimes soft tissues, the condition is commonly called *multiple myeloma*.

GLOBAL BURDEN OF LYMPHOMA

Lymphomas (including non-Hodgkin's lymphoma, Hodgkin's lymphoma, and multiple myeloma) were responsible for more than 250,000 deaths worldwide in 2002, approximately 0.45% of all deaths. Annual mortality rates varied widely and were highest in the

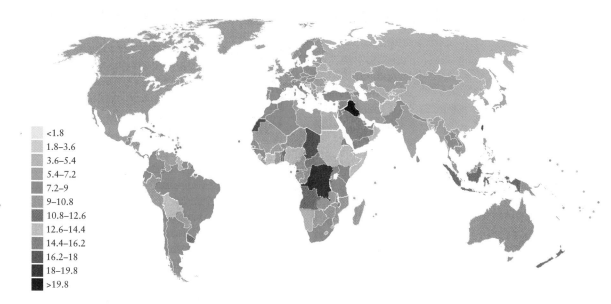

Figure 27.1 Global Lymphoma Mortality, 2004.

Source: Data from World Health Organization. The global burden of disease: 2004 update. Geneva, WHO, 2008. Available at www.who.int/evidence/bod.

populations of central Africa (18 per 100,000) and lowest in China and Eastern Asia (2 per 100,000) (Parkin et al., 2005). In African populations where mortality is high, the available healthcare resources are generally inadequate for effective treatment. Nevertheless, relatively high death rates from lymphoma are also evident in the populations of most developed nations (**Figure 27.1**).

GLOBAL PATTERNS AND TRENDS OF NON-HODGKIN'S LYMPHOMA

The global number of deaths due to non-Hodgkin's lymphoma has steadily increased during the past 2 decades: 126,000 deaths in 1990, 172,000 deaths in 2002, and 191,000 deaths in 2008 (Parkin, Pisani, and Ferlay, 1999a, 1999b; Parkin et al., 2005; WHO, 2008; Ferlay et al., 2010). However, the global annual *age-adjusted* mortality rates have been relatively stable during this time period, averaging approximately 3.4 per 100,000 in men and 2.2 per 100,000 in women. Likewise, the global annual age-adjusted incidence rates have also stabilized at 6.1 per 100,000 in men and 4.2 per 100,000 in women.

The rising absolute number of deaths from non-Hodgkin's lymphoma without substantial concomitant changes in the age-adjusted rates may be largely due to increasing longevity of the world population. This phenomenon has resulted in more individuals living to later ages when the risk of death from lymphoma is highest. As shown in **Figure 27.2**, lymphoma onset rises with age and nearly 75% of deaths occur after the age of 65 years (Altekruse et al., 2010).

Investigators at the World Health Organization reported there were 355,000 new cases of non-Hodgkin's lymphoma worldwide in 2008. This figure represents an approximate 60% increase since 1990 when 221,000 new cases were reported (Parkin, Pisani, and Ferlay, 1999a, 1999b; Parkin et al., 2005; Ferlay et al., 2010). Notably, the worldwide pattern of non-Hodgkin's lymphoma reflects an inverse association with socioeconomic status. The highest annual incidence rates have been reported for the Caucasian population of the United States (19 per 100,000), and the lowest for the populations of Thailand and China (3 per 100,000). High rates have also been observed in some populations residing in the tropical zone of Africa, partly due to the high incidence of Burkitt's lymphoma, a particularly aggressive form of B-cell lymphoma that develops primarily in children. Of further note is that T cell lymphomas are most common in Japan and the Caribbean (Shipp, Mauch, and Harris, 1997). However, caution is advised in drawing epidemiologic conclusions based on the wide variability in international rates as many nations do not have population-based cancer registries and reporting may therefore be incomplete.

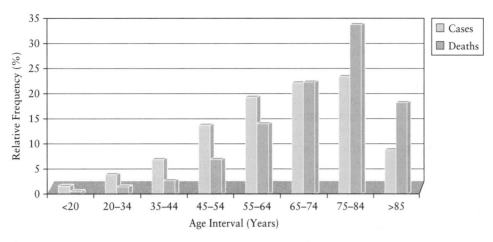

Figure 27.2 Age-Specific Frequencies of New Cases and Deaths: Non-Hodgkin's Lymphoma.

Source: Data from Surveillance Epidemiology and End Results (SEER) Cancer Statistics Review, 1975–2007, National Cancer Institute, Bethesda, Maryland, USA.

NON-HODGKIN'S LYMPHOMA IN THE UNITED STATES

In nations with population-based cancer registries, marked increases have been observed in the annual incidence rates of non-Hodgkin's lymphoma during the latter decades of the 20th century. For example, in the United States the incidence doubled for both men and women during 1970–1995 (**Figure 27.3**). The rising incidence rates during this time period were consistent in men and women of all ethnicities and age groups except for the very young (Devesa and Fears, 1992). Subsequently, during 1995–2010 the rates have stabilized and appear to have declined slightly (Altekruse et al., 2010).

Several factors have contributed to the increasing trends in non-Hodgkin's lymphoma in populations of the United States and other developed nations. In particular, escalations in the incidence among young adult males and (to a lesser extent) females occurred following the onset of the *acquired immunodeficiency syndrome* (*AIDS*) epidemic in 1981 (Hartge, Devesa, and Fraumeni, 1994). With discovery of the *human immunodeficiency virus* (*HIV*), which is considered the causative agent of AIDS, this syndrome is currently referred to as *HIV disease* (Gallo et al., 1983; Barré-Sinoussi et al., 1983).

Other factors that have contributed to the rising incidence of non-Hodgkin's lymphoma include improvements in the detection and reporting of

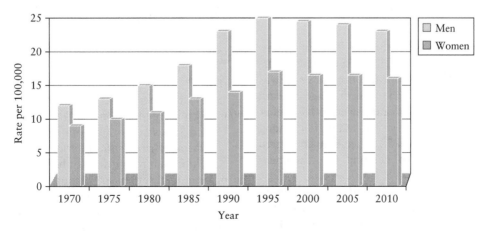

Figure 27.3 Incidence Rates of Non-Hodgkin's Lymphoma, USA, 1970–2010.

Source: Data from Surveillance Epidemiology and End Results (SEER) Cancer Statistics Review, 1975–2007, National Cancer Institute, Bethesda, Maryland, USA.

lymphomas, and refinements in the classification system of lymphoproliferative disorders, resulting in the diagnosis of relatively more cases of non-Hodgkin's lymphoma. For example, certain extra-nodal lymphoproliferative conditions and T-cell neoplasms are now recognized and classified as non-Hodgkin's lymphoma. Although stomach and skin remain the most common extra-nodal sites, primary disease in the brain has sharply increased (Groves et al., 2000). Furthermore, the incidence of non-Hodgkin's lymphoma is also increased among cancer patients treated by chemotherapy and among subjects undergoing heart or kidney transplants, all of whom experience immunosuppression (Banks, 1992; Müller et al., 2005). Despite these coincident trends, a large portion of the increase in non-Hodgkin's lymphoma during the latter 20th century remains to be explained.

As shown in Figure 27.3, the annual incidence of non-Hodgkin's lymphoma in the United States increased until about 1995, but then subsequently declined. This pattern coincides with a decline in the development of HIV disease due to primary preventive measures and/or use of highly active antiretroviral therapy that inhibits progression of HIV infection to active disease (Eltom et al., 2002). Nevertheless, the incidence of non-Hodgkin's lymphoma *not* related to HIV disease is continuing to increase, particularly among *older* men and women. It is well known that old age is accompanied by decreased immune function (immunosuppression) and higher susceptibility to infection, conditions that may heighten the risk of developing lymphoma as well as other malignancies (Fisher and Fisher, 2004; Müller et al., 2005).

GENDER AND ETHNIC DIFFERENCES IN NON-HODGKIN'S LYMPHOMA

In the US population, more than 21,000 individuals died from non-Hodgkin's lymphoma each year during 2003–2007. The age-adjusted *mortality* rate was 6.9 per 100,000 per year and the median age at death was 75 years of age. Death rates were 60% higher for men than women (8.7 vs. 5.5) and higher among Caucasians (9.1 in men and 5.7 in women) compared to other ethnicities (5.8 in men and 4.1 in women) (Altekruse et al., 2010).

During 2003–2007, the age-adjusted *incidence* rate of non-Hodgkin's lymphoma (NHL) was 19.6 per 100,000 per year. Incidence rates were 43% higher in men than women (23.6 vs. 16.5, respectively), and higher in Caucasians (24.6 in men and

17.2 in women) than other ethnic groups (16.2 in men and 12.1 in women). American Indians and Alaska natives had the lowest rates (12.5 in men and 10.6 in women) (Altekruse et al., 2010).

RISK FACTORS FOR NON-HODGKIN'S LYMPHOMA

Multiple viruses and bacteria have been found in association with the development of non-Hodgkin's lymphoma (Fisher and Fisher, 2004; Müller et al., 2005; Alexander et al., 2007a; Melbye, Ekström Smedby, and Trichopoulos, 2008). These infectious agents appear to be associated with two principal biological phenomena involved in the genesis of this malignancy: immunosuppression and antigenic stimulation. Immunosuppression can be incited not only by microbes, but also by powerful drugs routinely used in transplant therapy. Indeed, the combination of drug-induced immunosuppression and heightened antigenic stimulation through reactivation of latent Epstein-Barr virus (EBV) infection appears to markedly accelerate lymphomagenesis. Selected microbes and conditions and their effects on the pathogenesis of non-Hodgkin's lymphoma are discussed in the following sections.

Genetics of Non-Hodgkin's Lymphoma

Family studies suggest that genetic susceptibility has a modest influence on the development of non-Hodgkin's lymphoma. For example, the presence of one or more first degree relatives (parents, siblings, and offspring) afflicted with a hematopoietic malignancy has been found to increase the risk of developing non-Hodgkin's lymphoma by two to fourfold (Linet and Pottern, 1992; Zhu et al., 1998). Nevertheless, it is not clear whether familial clustering is truly attributable to genetic predisposition or rather to similar environmental exposures. Furthermore, familial lymphomas account for less than 5% of all cases, and it is unlikely that hereditary factors *per se* played a substantial role in the increasing trend in non-Hodgkin's lymphoma in the United States and other populations.

Primary congenital immunodeficiency is a rare condition that results in the absence of specific types of immunoglobulins in the immune system. This disorder arises due to point mutations in the genes controlling immunoglobulin formation, most of which are located on chromosomes 2, 14, and 22. When congenital immunodeficiency is present, the risk of developing lymphoma is high, up to 25% by the age of 25 years. This condition also shortens the lifespan considerably, as most afflicted patients die before the age of 50 years. Certain other genetic syndromes also increase the risk of developing lymphoma. These include *ataxia-telangiectasia*, a condition marked by DNA repair defects and impaired cell-mediated immunity; *Wiscott-Aldridge syndrome*, a rare X-linked condition characterized by eczema, thrombocytopenia (low platelets), immunodeficiency, and bloody diarrhea; and the *X-linked lymphoproliferative syndrome* characterized by fatal or near-fatal infectious mononucleosis due to EBV and immunoglobulin deficiency in childhood (Filipovich et al., 1992).

Lymphomas are genetically characterized by the presence of chromosomal translocations, which are usually *balanced reciprocal recombinations* that involve a switch of DNA between two chromosomes. Such chromosomal rearrangements are *not* heritable and are thought to occur during immune reactions against various infectious agents, particularly EBV. Rearrangements often involve the immunoglobulin genes of B-cells or the receptor genes of T-cells (Tycko and Sklar, 1990). At the molecular level, such translocations induce neoplastic development by either activating tumor oncogenes or inactivating tumor suppressor genes. The most common translocations found in non-Hodgkin's lymphomas involve juxtaposition of genes that regulate transcription to regions of chromosome 14 that control promotion and enhancement elements of highly active immunoglobulin genes. In studies of lymphoma karyotypes, chromosomal translocations have been detected in up to 90% of non-Hodgkin's lymphomas (Offit et al., 1991; Grogan and Miller, 1995; Ye, 2000; Vega and Medeiros, 2003).

HIV Disease and Non-Hodgkin's Lymphoma

Following the onset of the AIDS epidemic and discovery of HIV in the early 1980s, population registries were established in many countries in order to monitor the number of new cases and evaluate the impact of widespread efforts to control the epidemic. Analysis of the HIV/AIDS registry data has helped elucidate important clues regarding the genesis of non-Hodgkin's lymphoma.

In 1999, a team of Italian investigators reported findings on the association of lymphoma and HIV disease based on registry data from the United States, Europe, and Australia. The study involved the analysis of datasets developed by linking registries of AIDS patients with population-based cancer registries. During 1988–1997, AIDS surveillance data from 17 Western European countries revealed

that more than 7,000 cases involved non-Hodgkin's lymphoma as the *AIDS-defining illness*, and during the 1990s, non-Hodgkin's lymphoma was the AIDS-defining condition in approximately 5% of cases. Among adults with HIV/AIDS, the relative risks for non-Hodgkin's lymphoma ranged from 15 for low-grade disease (confined to one lymph node) to 400 for high-grade disease (affecting multiple nodes and/or sites). The relative risk of Hodgkin's lymphoma among individuals with HIV/AIDS was also increased (RR = 10). The extraordinarily high risk for the development of non-Hodgkin's lymphoma among individuals who are HIV-seropositive has led to its recognition as an AIDS-defining condition (Franceschi, Dal Maso, and La Vecchia, 1999; Dal Maso and Franceschi, 2003).

The HIV-associated non-Hodgkin's lymphomas are invariably derived from B lymphocytes, and more than 80% originate at extranodal sites, most commonly in the brain and central nervous system. These lymphomas usually present as high grade malignancies with 60–70% being metastatic at the time of diagnosis. An Australian case control study identified the duration of immunosuppression and the degree of B-cell stimulation as primary risk factors (Gurlich et al., 2000). While sequences of the HIV genome have never been found incorporated in the DNA of lymphoma cells, it is notable that EBV is often present in tumor tissues and/or the cerebral spinal fluid of patients. It has thus been suggested that interactions involving coinfection with EBV and/or other viruses predispose to the development of non-Hodgkin's lymphoma through immunosuppression and impairment of cell-mediated immunity in patients with HIV disease (Cinque et al., 1993; Biggar et al., 2001).

Immunosuppression and Non-Hodgkin's Lymphoma

Immunosuppression has consistently been found to be a strong risk factor in the development of non-Hodgkin's lymphoma. Individuals with drug-induced immunodeficiency for the purpose of suppressing post-transplant organ rejection, treating autoimmune conditions, or resulting from sustained chemotherapy for cancer are among those at high risk. Enormous increases in relative risk (more than 100-fold) have been observed in organ transplant patients who receive sustained aggressive immunosuppressive regimens (Opelz and Henderson, 1993). As with HIV/AIDS patients, active infection with EBV is a common finding in post-transplant patients (Purtilo, 1980; Cleary et al., 1984; Kinlen, 1992). Furthermore, a striking feature of some post-transplant patients who receive aggressive therapy is the short interval from the time of transplant to the diagnosis of malignancy, often within 6 months (Swinnen et al., 1990). Such rapidly evolving tumors have a predilection for the brain and are associated with sustained immunosuppression and active EBV infection (Palackdharry, 1994).

Molecular studies suggest that three host factors interact to increase the risk of developing non-Hodgkin's lymphoma in immunosuppressed individuals: active EBV infection, defects in immunoregulation and production of inflammatory cytokines, and genetic defects precipitating abnormal immunoglobulin and T-cell receptor gene rearrangement. Both congenital and acquired immunodeficiencies appear to have common features that predispose to chronic antigenic stimulus of B lymphocytes and the development of non-Hodgkin's lymphoma (Filipovich et al., 1992).

Autoimmune Disease and Non-Hodgkin's Lymphoma

The risk of developing non-Hodgkin's lymphoma is also increased in patients with autoimmune conditions such as *rheumatoid arthritis*, *systemic lupus erythematosus*, *Sjogren's syndrome*, and *celiac disease* (Kamel et al., 1995; Pettersson et al., 1992; Harris et al., 1967). While such conditions are conventionally treated with immunosuppressive drugs, persistent inflammation appears to have a dominant etiologic role in the genesis of lymphoma. For example, Baecklund and colleagues demonstrated a 25-fold increase in the risk of developing non-Hodgkin's lymphoma among patients with highly inflammatory rheumatoid arthritis compared to a similar group with low inflammation, after adjustment for treatment (Baecklund et al., 1998).

Epstein Barr Virus (EBV) and Burkitt's Lymphoma

EBV is a member of the herpes family of viruses. The virus is ubiquitous in the human population. Following infection in childhood, EBV persists in a dormant state as an episomal plasmid in B lymphocytes in 80–90% of adults. When the first exposure to EBV occurs in adolescence, up to 50% of individuals manifest *infectious mononucleosis*. If an EBV-positive individual experiences sustained immunosuppression (as in HIV disease or post-transplant immunosuppressive therapy), the EBV plasmid can transform into active virus and resume proliferation in B lymphocytes. Such activity markedly heightens the risk of developing non-Hodgkin's lymphoma (Fisher and Fisher, 2004; Müller et al., 2005; Alexander et al., 2007a).

In populations residing in the tropical zone of Africa, a form of childhood B-cell lymphoma called *Burkitt's lymphoma* is endemic. This tumor typically arises in the jawbones. Burkitt's lymphoma is named after the British investigator Denis Burkitt who studied its epidemiology and etiology in the children of New Guinea and sub-Saharan Africa. Burkitt's lymphoma develops in children in these geographic regions with a startlingly high incidence rate, accounting for up to 25% of all childhood malignancies (Burkitt, 1958, 1983).

In pathologic studies of Burkitt's lymphoma ascertained from the endemic areas of Africa and New Guinea, EBV is detected in nearly 100% of cases. Epstein and colleagues first detected EBV in a lymphoma specimen taken from a child in New Guinea, providing the first example of a tumor-related virus (Epstein, Achong, and Pope, 1967). Most cases also have a medical history of malaria and have been found to have elevated levels of antibodies against both EBV and the malarial parasite, *Plasmodium falciparum* (Carpenter et al., 2008). Burkitt initially noted the geographic clustering of EBV and malarial infection and suggested that the convergence of these two infectious agents in the same host predisposes to the development of B-cell lymphoma (Burkitt, 1971, 1983).

A defining cytogenetic feature of nearly all cases of Burkitt's lymphoma is the presence of a chromosomal translocation involving the *c-myc* gene. The *c-myc* gene, which is normally located on the long arm of chromosome 8, encodes a protein that is essential for the regulation of transcription and expression of many other genes. Translocations of the *c-myc* gene to positions in close proximity to the heavy chain immunoglobulin loci on chromosome 14 have been found in approximately 80% of cases of Burkitt's lymphoma, and translocations of *c-myc* to immunoglobulin loci on chromosomes 2 and 12 are present in the remaining 20% of cases. These *c-myc* translocations result in hyperactivity of immunoglobulin genes and over-proliferation of B-cells, leading to the development of lymphoma. Transformation to malignancy involves the perpetual proliferation of B lymphocytes involving dysregulation of mitosis, differentiation, apoptosis, and cell adhesion (Blum, Lozanski, and Byrd, 2004; Ferry, 2006).

It is obvious from the preceding discussion that the pathogenesis of Burkitt's lymphoma is complex, often involving the interaction of at least three factors: EBV infection, malarial infection, and chromosomal translocation involving the *c-myc* gene. A stepwise process has been proposed in which EBV and malaria may depress the regulatory function of T cells leading to unbridled proliferation of B-cells with the *c-myc* translocation (de Thé, 1993).

The clinical variants of Burkitt's lymphoma include endemic, sporadic, and immunodeficiency-related disease. Endemic Burkitt's lymphoma occurs in young African children, ages 4–7 years, with a male to female ratio of 2:1. The incidence is about 13 per 100,000 in children of endemic areas such as New Guinea and sub-Saharan Africa, more than 50 times higher than in US children. The tumors characteristically involve the jawbone but can also arise in the gastrointestinal and/or urogenital tract (Ferry, 2006). EBV is present in nearly all cases and high levels of antibodies against both EBV and *Plasmodium falciparum* have been found to increase the risk by fivefold (Carpenter et al., 2008). As initially suggested by Denis Burkitt, the immunosuppressive effect of chronic malarial infection predisposes the host to EBV-induced proliferation and malignant transformation of B lymphocytes (Burkitt, 1983).

Sporadic Burkitt's lymphoma occasionally develops in children without geographic or temporal clustering. The gastrointestinal tract, particularly around the ileocecal valve, is the most common anatomic site of involvement. EBV is present in only 10–30% of sporadic tumors (Ferry, 2006).

Immunodeficiency-associated Burkitt's lymphoma occurs in association with HIV/AIDS, organ transplant, and congenital immunodeficiency. Burkitt's lymphoma accounts for 30–40% of non-Hodgkin's lymphoma in patients with HIV disease and is estimated to be 1,000 times more common in such patients than in the general population. Analogous to malaria, HIV infection and other immunosuppressive conditions lead to EBV-induced proliferation and malignant transformation of B lymphocytes (Ferry, 2006).

Human T-Cell Lymphotrophic Virus (HTLV-1) and Lymphoma

In 1974, Japanese investigators discovered a rare form of T-cell leukemia in two Japanese adults (Yodoi, Takatsuk, and Masuda, 1974). Further investigation soon identified a cluster of 16 patients with lymphoma or leukemia arising from T lymphocytes in the population living on the islands off the southern coast of Japan (Takatsuki et al., 1977; Uchiyama et al., 1977). Shortly thereafter in the laboratories of Dr. Robert Gallo at the US National Institutes of Health, an RNA retrovirus was identified in malignant T-cells of tumor specimens and named *human T-cell lymphotrophic virus* (*HTLV-1*) (Poiesz et al., 1980). In studies conducted by Japanese investigators, T-cell-specific antibodies were detected in 76 of 80 patients (95%) with T-cell leukemia/lymphoma and 26% of healthy adults from endemic areas (Hinuma et al., 1981; Yoshida, Miyoshi, and Hinuma, 1982).

Subsequent epidemiologic investigations have confirmed the presence of high seroprevalence rates of HTLV-1 in populations of Southern Japan (30%), the Caribbean (7%), New Guinea (5%), and Central Africa (3%). In endemic regions, adult T-cell lymphomas and leukemias account for more than 50% of all lymphoid malignancies (Manns and Blattner, 2003).

Seropositivity for HTLV-1 develops early in life as a consequence of vertical transmission from mother to child during delivery or breastfeeding. The virus can also be transmitted sexually and through transfusion of contaminated blood. With sustained infection beginning in childhood, the cumulative lifetime risk of developing T-cell lymphoma/leukemia approaches 5% (Cleghorn et al., 1995). Carriers of HTLV-1 apparently manifest progressive immunosuppression and uncontrolled proliferation of infected helper T cells that can eventually lead to the development of adult T-cell lymphoma or leukemia (Takatsuki, 2005).

Helicobacter pylori and Non-Hodgkin's Lymphoma

Helicobacter pylori (*H. pylori*) is a flagellated bacterium that infects the gastric mucosa. This unusual bacterium was discovered by Australian investigators Barry Marshall and Robin Warren in 1982, and in recognition, they were awarded the 2005 Nobel Prize in Physiology or Medicine (Marshall and Warren, 2005). It is estimated that more than 50% of the world's population harbor *H. pylori* in their upper gastrointestinal tract (Pounder and Ng, 1995).

Since its discovery, numerous investigations have examined linkages between *H. pylori* and human disease. Chronic colonization of the gastric mucosa by *H. pylori* is associated with chronic gastritis and the development of peptic ulcer disease, gastric adenocarcinoma, and gastric lymphoma arising in mucous-associated lymphoid tissue (gastric MALT lymphoma) (Isaacson and Spencer, 1995; Kusters, van Vliet, and Kuipers, 2006).

The evidence linking chronic *H. pylori* infection to the genesis of gastric lymphoma is compelling. In a study conducted in London, Wotherspoon and colleagues detected *H. pylori* in 101 of 110 cases with primary gastric MALT lymphoma, and suggested that infection-induced gastritis provides the background lymphoid tissue in which non-Hodgkin's lymphoma develops (Wotherspoon et al., 1991).

At Stanford University in California, Parsonnet and colleagues conducted a *nested* case control study to evaluate the potential role of *H. pylori* in the development of non-Hodgkin's gastric lymphoma. (In a nested study design, the cases accrue over time in a specific cohort after collection of baseline data and matched controls are ascertained from the same cohort.) The investigators compared baseline *H. pylori* seropositivity in 33 patients who developed gastric non-Hodgkin's lymphoma to controls matched 4:1 to the cases on age, gender, and time of serum collection. Results revealed more than a sixfold increase in the risk of developing gastric lymphoma related to baseline *H. pylori* seropositivity. The median interval between serum collection for *H. pylori* testing and onset of gastric lymphomas was 14 years, suggesting a long-term process of carcinogenesis (Parsonnet et al., 1994).

Subsequent *in vitro* experiments have demonstrated that malignant B cells proliferate only after T-cell-specific activation by *H. pylori* (Hussell et al., 1993), and in clinical studies, antibiotic therapy directed against *H. pylori* infection produced regression of low-grade gastric lymphoma (Wotherspoon et al., 1993). These findings support a model of chronic *H. pylori* infection, chronic inflammation, and T-cell-modulated antigenic stimulation of B-cell proliferation in the pathogenesis of gastric MALT lymphoma (Wotherspoon, 1998).

Human Herpes Virus 8

Human herpes virus 8 (HHV-8), also called *Kaposi's sarcoma-associated herpes virus* (KSHV), was discovered by Yuan Chang, Patrick Moore, and colleagues at Columbia University in 1994 (Chang et al., 1994). This virus has been detected in the majority of patients with primary effusion lymphoma, a rare B-cell lymphoma seen almost exclusively in HIV-positive patients (Cesarman et al., 1995). Such patients often present with dual EBV and HHV-8 infection; therefore, delineation of the etiologic role of each virus is difficult. Primary effusion lymphomas appear to involve monoclonal expansion of viral-infected cells (Judde et al., 2000).

Hepatitis C Virus and Non-Hodgkin's Lymphoma

Approximately 300 million people worldwide are infected with *hepatitis C virus* (HCV), a single-strand RNA virus. The seroprevalence of HCV is high in certain populations of Asia and Africa (3%) and low in most developed countries (1%). Although not known to be oncogenic, HCV has immunomodulatory effects and has been shown to replicate in peripheral blood mononuclear cells.

While HCV is a major etiologic factor in the development of hepatocellular carcinoma, its role in the development of non-Hodgkin's lymphoma is less clear. Early molecular studies detected anti-HCV antibodies in sera and HCV RNA sequences in biopsy specimens from some patients with B-cell non-Hodgkin's lymphoma (Luppi et al., 1996; Silvestra et al., 1996). A systematic review of HCV seroprevalence among non-Hodgkin's lymphoma patients revealed high rates in some populations (Southern and Eastern Europe, Japan, and Southern United States) but not in others (Northern Europe, Northern United States, Canada, and certain Asian countries) (Negri et al., 2004). Nevertheless, in a pooled analysis of 48 studies of B-cell non-Hodgkin's lymphoma, HCV infection was present in 13% of 5,542 patients, and based upon meta-analysis of 10 studies that included estimates of the odds ratio (OR), the overall risk was increased more than 10-fold (combined OR = 10.8) (Gisbert et al., 2003). In a subsequent meta-analysis of 23 studies of HCV and non-Hodgkin's lymphoma, HCV-seropositive subjects were nearly six times more likely to develop non-Hodgkin's lymphoma than seronegative subjects (combined OR = 5.7) (Matsuo et al., 2004).

Despite the increase in lymphoma risk with HCV exposure suggested by meta-analyses, it is noteworthy that some studies do not reflect an association between HCV and non-Hodgkin's lymphoma. For example, in a prospective study of 48,420 persons in northern California, serological evidence of HCV infection was totally absent in all 57 patients who developed non-Hodgkin's lymphoma (Rabkin et al., 2002). And in Thailand, a nation with a relatively high prevalence of HCV, no link was found between HCV infection and non-Hodgkin's lymphoma (Udomsakdi-Auewarakul et al., 2000). Furthermore, in a US study of 304,411 adults with AIDS, standardized incidence ratios of non-Hodgkin's lymphoma by grade were inversely related to the prevalence rates of HCV infection (Engels et al., 2002). These disparities among study results may have multiple causes including genetic, cultural, and/or environmental differences in populations; variation in HCV strains; and the different methods used for the diagnosis of lymphoma and/or assessment of HCV seropositivity (Alexander et al., 2007a).

Simian Virus 40 (SV40) and Non-Hodgkin's Lymphoma

Millions of people worldwide were inadvertently exposed to live *simian virus 40* (*SV40*) between 1955 and 1963 through immunization with SV40-contaminated polio vaccines. This virus is known to induce malignancies in laboratory animals including primary brain cancer, bone cancer, mesothelioma, and lymphoma. Recent molecular studies have shown that SV40 DNA is present in a significant fraction (~40%) of tumor specimens from patients with non-Hodgkin's lymphoma (Shivapurkar et al., 2002; Vilchez et al., 2002).

Butel and colleagues studied SV40 seropositivity in malignant lymphoid tissues from 156 patients with non-Hodgkin's lymphoma (76 HIV-positive patients and 78 HIV-negative patients), in nonmalignant lymphoid samples from 107 patients without tumors, and in colorectal tumors from 54 patients. Polymerase chain reaction and Southern blot hybridization techniques were used to detect the DNA sequences of SV40. Specific SV40 DNA sequences were detected in 64 (42%) specimens from lymphoma patients compared to none of the nonmalignant lymphoid specimens or colorectal tumors (Butel et al., 2003). Furthermore, a recent retrospective study in Japan demonstrated a fourfold increase in the odds of detecting SV40 sequences in large B-cell lymphomas (19%) compared to controls (4.7%), suggesting that SV40 may be a candidate etiologic factor for lymphoma (Nakatsuka et al., 2003).

The findings of SV40 DNA sequences in human lymphoma prompted population-based studies in Denmark and the United States that compared cancer incidence rates in cohorts of children with and without exposure to the (allegedly) contaminated Salk polio vaccine. Fortunately, these studies found no increase in cancer rates associated with exposure (Carroll-Pankhurst et al., 2001; Engels et al., 2003).

Not all studies have found an association between SV40 and lymphoma. For example, a Spanish study that used enzyme immunoassay to detect antibodies to SV40 in sera from 520 patients with non-Hodgkin's lymphoma and 587 matched controls actually found a higher frequency of SV40 seropositivity among the controls than cases (9.5% versus 5.9%) (de Sanjose et al., 2003). In addition, a molecular study that assessed the oncogenic protein of SV40 found no significant difference in its frequency between lymphoid specimens of 85 cases of non-Hodgkin's lymphoma and 95 matched controls (Engels et al., 2004). Given these contrasting results, it seems advisable to clarify the differences in studies of SV40 DNA sequences and seropositivity through additional investigations.

Other Pathogens and Non-Hodgkin's Lymphoma

Borrelia burgdorferi is a small spirochete that can be transmitted to humans by the bite of an infected tick. Systemic human infection with this microorganism (*borreliosis*) causes skin rash, arthritis, and neurologic deficits, a clinical picture commonly referred to as Lyme disease. Recently, infection with *Borrelia burgdorferi* has been linked to lymphoproliferative conditions, which have been known to evolve into primary cutaneous B-cell lymphomas. The majority of these observations have come from European countries, with little evidence of such an association in North America (Garbe et al., 1991; Willemze et al., 1997; Cerroni et al., 1997; Jelic and Filipovic-Ljeskovic, 1999).

Mantle cell lymphoma, a B-cell malignancy arising in the mantle zone of lymph nodes, has also been found in association with borreliosis. Schöllkopf and colleagues conducted a Danish-Swedish case-control study of 3,055 patients with non-Hodgkin's lymphoma and 3,187 population controls to evaluate the association of lymphoma subtypes with *Borrelia burgdorferi*. History of tick bite or *Borrelia* infection was ascertained through personal interviews and enzyme-linked immunosorbent assay serum analyses for antibodies against *B burgdorferi*. Self-reported history of *B burgdorferi* infection (OR = 2.5) and seropositivity for anti-*Borrelia* antibodies (OR = 3.6) were both found to increase the risk of mantle cell lymphoma, suggesting that *Borrelia burgdorferi* infection predisposes to the development of this malignancy (Schöllkopf et al., 2008).

Other infectious agents have also been found in association with B-cell lymphomas. *Mediterranean lymphoma* is an unusual B-cell lymphoma that arises in small intestinal *mucosa-associated lymphoid tissue (MALT)*. Early-stage disease regresses with antibiotic treatment, suggesting a bacterial etiology. In a recent small series, 5 of 7 tumor specimens of Mediterranean lymphoma tested positive for the intestinal bacteria, *Campylobacter jejuni* (Lecuit et al., 2004).

Ocular adnexal lymphoma, a rare form of lymphoma that arises in the conjunctival membranes of the eye socket, also shows an association with an infectious microbe. In a molecular study of ocular adnexal lymphoma samples, 32 of 40 tumors (80%) carried *Chlamydia psittaci* DNA, whereas all specimens were negative for *Chlamydia trachomatis* and *Chlamydia pneumoniae*. This observation suggests that *Chlamydia psittaci* infection predisposes to the development of ocular adnexal lymphoma (Ferreri et al., 2004).

Clearly, the number of pathogens involved in the genesis of immunoproliferative lymphoid neoplasms is growing. As a rule, these infectious agents appear to enhance the initiation and promotion of malignancy by antigenic stimulation of B cells coupled with immunosuppression of T cells.

Pesticide and Insecticide Exposures in Non-Hodgkin's Lymphoma

Several cohort and case control studies have evaluated exposure to pesticides, insecticides, and/or herbicides as risk factors in the development of non-Hodgkin's lymphoma. In general, nonsignificant findings have been reported.

For example, Blair and colleagues studied a US cohort of 52,393 licensed pesticide applicators and 32,345 spouses and found *no* significant associations between lymphoma mortality with the number of years handling pesticides or any other measure of exposure. The overall mortality due to non-Hodgkin's lymphoma in the cohort showed no difference from the general population (standardized mortality ratio = 1.0) (Blair et al., 2005). A number of other cohort studies also evaluated the risk of developing non-Hodgkin's lymphoma among persons employed in occupations involving potential exposure to pesticides, herbicides, and/or insecticides. Albeit, studies of occupational cohorts of farmers, pesticide-manufacturing workers, and pesticide applicators from Italy, Iceland, Sweden, Norway, Canada, and Australia have yielded mixed and generally nonsignificant results (Alexander et al., 2007a).

Meta-analyses of published studies of agricultural workers reflect the inconsistency in results. In an analysis of 14 studies that evaluated cancer risk among farmers, the combined estimate of non-Hodgkin's lymphoma risk was not significant (Blair et al., 1992). Subsequently, a meta-analysis of 36 studies found a weak positive association overall (RR = 1.10); however, there was significant heterogeneity among studies and the directional change in risk differed for case-control studies (RR = 1.19) and cohort studies (RR = 0.95) (Khuder, Schaub, and Keller-Byrne, 1998).

Thus, while a few studies suggest there may be an increased risk of non-Hodgkin's lymphoma in occupations with heightened exposure to pesticides and related compounds, technical difficulties inherent in assessment of the intensity and duration of exposure limit any interpretation of causality. Studies that infer exposure based upon occupation

or job title have many limitations, most notably the lack of detailed information regarding exposure to specific environmental factors for each individual. Furthermore, complete information on other potential exposures or confounding factors is often missing or not collected. Results of these studies therefore reflect a general lack of consistent evidence to support an etiologic link between pesticide/herbicide/insecticide exposure and the development of non-Hodgkin's lymphoma (Fisher and Fisher, 2004; Müller et al., 2005; Alexander et al., 2007a).

Other Chemical Exposures and Non-Hodgkin's Lymphoma

Studies of chemical workers have also failed to delineate consistent associations with non-Hodgkin's lymphoma. Studies of workers potentially exposed to petroleum products, solvents, trichloroethylene, asbestos, occupational dusts, and other chemicals have generally been negative or inconclusive. Thus, as with pesticides and herbicides, epidemiologic investigations have not clearly identified specific occupational exposures to specific chemicals that increase the risk of developing non-Hodgkin's lymphoma (Figgs, Dosemeci and Blair,1995; Alexander et al., 2007a).

Hair Dye and Non-Hodgkin's Lymphoma

Hair dyes contain compounds that are mutagenic and carcinogenic in animals. Numerous human studies have therefore evaluated the relationship between exposure to these compounds and the risk of developing malignant neoplasms including non-Hodgkin's lymphoma. Based on a meta-analysis of 14 studies, Takkouche and colleagues reported a significant increase in the risk among ever users of hair dye compared to never users (combined RR = 1.23). However, there was significant heterogeneity among studies and the risk estimate derived from case control studies (RR = 1.27) was higher than cohort studies (RR = 1.10). Thus, differential recall between cases and controls may have contributed to the elevated risk estimates in the case control studies. Furthermore, dose-response relationships have not been consistently observed between lymphoma risk and the duration of use (Takkouche, Etminan, and Montes-Martinez, 2005).

Ultraviolet Radiation and Non-Hodgkin's Lymphoma

Zheng and colleagues speculated that sun exposure might increase the risk of developing non-Hodgkin's lymphoma on the following grounds: the incidence of non-Hodgkin's lymphoma has increased in parallel with that of cutaneous melanoma, antecedent skin cancer increases the risk of developing non-Hodgkin's lymphoma, sun exposure has immunosuppressive effects, and the risk of non-Hodgkin's lymphoma increases with immunosuppression (Zheng et al., 1992). In support of this hypothesis, Cartwright and colleagues reported a significant positive correlation between the incidence rates of non-Hodgkin's lymphoma and nonmelanocytic skin cancer among nine cancer registries worldwide (Cartwright, McNally, and Staines, 1994).

In opposition to this hypothesis, three case control studies of non-Hodgkin's lymphoma and sun exposure found significant *inverse* relationships (Armstrong and Kricker, 2007). Thus, the data on *individual sun exposure* and risk of non-Hodgkin's lymphoma are more consistent with a *protective* than a causal effect of sun exposure. Furthermore, in a geographic study of annual mortality rates reported during 1970–1989 for economic regions within the United States, the mortality rates due to non-Hodgkin's lymphoma showed a significant *inverse* association with average levels of UV exposure whereas the rates for melanoma increased with exposure (Hartge et al., 1996).

Since these studies were not powered to examine lymphoma subtypes, it is noteworthy that some molecular investigations have found indirect evidence linking sun exposure to the development of *cutaneous* non-Hodgkin's lymphomas. For example, McGregor and colleagues examined the type and frequency of *p53* gene mutations in a series of 55 cases of primary cutaneous lymphoma and found 14 separate *p53* mutations with a mutation spectrum characteristic of DNA damage caused by ultraviolet B radiation. These mutations were most evident in the progression of a type of cutaneous T-cell lymphoma known as *mycosis fungoides* (McGregor et al., 1999). Well-designed epidemiologic studies that are powered to examine lymphoma by subtype should help resolve the present conflicting results on sun exposure and non-Hodgkin's lymphoma.

Tobacco, Alcohol, and Non-Hodgkin's Lymphoma

Tobacco and tobacco metabolites are known to be carcinogenic; however, there is little scientific evidence to support an association between tobacco use and the development of non-Hodgkin's lymphoma. Zahm and colleagues examined smoking and non-Hodgkin's lymphoma in a combined analysis of data from three population-based case control studies conducted in four midwestern states in the United States. Data on smoking and other variables were available for 1,177 cases and 3,625 controls. Overall, there was no association between smoking and the risk of developing non-Hodgkin's lymphoma (odds ratio = 1.0) and no clear dose-response relationships were evident (Zahm et al., 1997).

In a subsequent meta-analysis, Morton and colleagues examined the association between cigarette smoking and subtypes of non-Hodgkin's lymphoma using data collected through the *International Lymphoma Epidemiology Consortium* (*InterLymph*). The database included information on smoking and other variables for 6,594 cases and 8,892 controls ascertained in nine case control studies conducted in the United States, Europe, and Australia. Overall, smoking was associated with only a slight increase in the risk (odds ratio = 1.07). Among subtypes of non-Hodgkin's lymphoma, only follicular lymphoma was associated with current smoking (OR = 1.31); however, the test for trend with pack-years of smoking was not significant. Risk estimates for other subtypes ranged from 0.79–1.11 and were nonsignificant (Morton et al., 2005a). These and many other epidemiologic investigations do not provide consistent evidence that tobacco exposure has a role in the genesis of non-Hodgkin's lymphoma.

A number of studies have detected a weak *inverse* association between alcohol consumption and the risk of developing non-Hodgkin's lymphoma. Morton and colleagues examined the relationship in a pooled analysis of nine case control studies conducted in the United States, Great Britain, Sweden, and Italy. Data on alcohol intake and other variables were available for 6,492 cases and 8,683 controls. Overall, the results suggested that people who drank alcohol had a slightly lower risk than nondrinkers (OR = 0.83) and current drinkers had a lower risk (OR = 0.73) than former drinkers (OR = 0.95). The investigators suggest the need for additional investigations to determine whether confounding by lifestyle factors or immunomodulatory effects by alcohol are responsible for this association (Morton et al., 2005b).

Dietary Factors and Non-Hodgkin's Lymphoma

Nutritional studies of non-Hodgkin's lymphoma reflect mixed results for most dietary factors investigated. One possible exception is fish consumption, which shows a weak *inverse* association with the risk of developing non-Hodgkin's lymphoma in several studies. For example, in an American study of 1,418 cases and 4,202 controls, intake in the highest quartile compared to the lowest quartile reduced the risk by 29% (Fritschi et al., 2004). Nevertheless, observed risk reductions do not reach statistical significance in all studies (Fernandez et al., 1999) and additional investigations are needed to clarify if high fish consumption has preventive value.

Blood Transfusions and Non-Hodgkin's Lymphoma

Interest in blood transfusion and its relation to non-Hodgkin's lymphoma spiked after three prospective cohort studies reported increases in the risk of developing non-Hodgkin's lymphoma following transfusion. Cerhan and colleagues initially investigated this association in a prospective cohort of 37,337 older women in Iowa. Baseline information was collected in 1986 and after 5 years of follow-up, a total of 68 cases of non-Hodgkin's lymphoma were detected. Women who reported ever receiving a blood transfusion were at increased risk of developing non-Hodgkin's lymphoma (RR = 2.2) (Cerhan et al., 1993). In a subsequent study of the same cohort of women after 12 years of follow-up resulting in detection of 229 cases of non-Hodgkin's lymphoma, a significant risk increase was again observed (RR = 1.6) among women reporting a history of blood transfusion (Cerhan et al., 2001).

Shortly after publication of the initial findings from the Iowa cohort, Blomberg and colleagues reported similar increases in the risk of developing non-Hodgkin's lymphoma associated with a history of blood transfusion in two Swedish cohorts (Blomberg et al., 1993); and Memon and Doll found greater than a twofold increase in mortality due to non-Hodgkin's lymphoma among subjects who had received perinatal transfusions in a cohort of 13,000 Britons (Memon and Doll, 1994). Moreover, several biological mechanisms seemed plausible to explain transfusion-related lymphoma development including oncogenic virus transmission, transfusion-induced immunosuppression, and engraftment of malignant lymphoma cells from donors (Chow and Holly, 2002).

Nevertheless, five subsequent case control studies have since revealed inconsistent results with only one showing a significant positive association. Thus, the association between blood transfusion and development of non-Hodgkin's lymphoma remains to be clarified. As has been pointed out, future studies should be designed to collect more detailed information on the exposure variable, including the type and amount of transfusion products received by each subject. Similarly, such studies should be powered to facilitate risk estimates for lymphoma subtypes (Chow and Holly, 2002).

Breast Implants and Non-Hodgkin's Lymphoma

Anaplastic large cell lymphoma is a *rare* T-cell lymphoma typically seen in children and young adults. Such tumors are seldom detected in breast tissues. Nevertheless, published case reports of primary anaplastic large cell lymphoma arising in the fibrous capsules of breast implants have produced speculation that breast prostheses may increase the risk of developing this rare tumor (Bishara, Ross, and Sur, 2009).

To determine if the risk of developing anaplastic large cell lymphoma is related to breast implants, investigators in Amsterdam conducted a matched case control study among women in the Netherlands. Cases and controls were ascertained from the population-based nationwide pathology registry. Eleven cases were identified who had been diagnosed with primary anaplastic large cell lymphoma of the breast during 1990–2006. Cases were age-matched to controls with other histologic types of breast lymphomas in an overall ratio of about 3:1. Among the 11 cases, 5 had received breast prostheses for cosmetic purposes 1– 23 years prior to diagnosis, whereas among the 35 control patients, only one had received a breast implant. The odds ratio linking the development of anaplastic large cell lymphoma to breast prostheses was markedly increased and statistically significant (OR = 18.2, P < 0.01). While these preliminary findings suggest an association between breast implants and the subsequent development of anaplastic large cell lymphoma of the breast, even women with implants have an exceedingly low *absolute risk* (de Jong et al., 2008).

EPIDEMIOLOGY OF HODGKIN'S LYMPHOMA

Hodgkin's lymphoma is a B-cell lymphoma that is defined by the presence of morphologically altered immune cells called Reed-Steinberg cells. In nations with population-based tumor registries, Hodgkin's lymphoma accounts for less than 15% of all lymphomas (Altekruse et al., 2010).

The disease is named after Thomas Hodgkin, who first described elemental clinical features of lymphoid malignancies in 1832 (Hodgkin, 1832). The Reed-Sternberg cell is named after Dorothy Reed and Carl Sternberg who discovered it in the malignant lymphoid tissues of patients with Hodgkin's lymphoma more than a century ago (Reed, 1902; Sternberg, 1898). These giant multinucleate tumor cells sometimes have the unusual appearance of "owl eyes" peering out from the microscopic field due to the presence of a double nucleus (Robbins and Cotran, 1979).

Because of the coexpression of markers of several different cell types in Hodgkin's lymphoma tissues, the cellular origin of Reed-Sternberg cells remained enigmatic for many decades. Nevertheless, isolation of these cells by microscopic laser dissection and gene amplification by polymerase chain reaction has clarified their derivation through the presence of immunoglobulin gene rearrangements. Thus, nearly a century after their discovery, Reed-Sternberg cells have been definitely characterized as transformed lymphocytes arising from B cells in the germinal centers of lymph nodes (Küppers et al., 1994; Kanzler et al., 1996; Bräuninger et al., 1997).

Worldwide, approximately 67,000 new cases of Hodgkin's lymphoma were diagnosed in 2008 and 30,000 died from the disease (Ferlay et al., 2010). Comparatively, 59,000 cases were diagnosed in 1990 and 26,000 cases died (Parkin Pisani, and Ferlay, 1999a, 1999b).

Based on data from the Surveillance Epidemiology and End Results (SEER) program of the United States National Cancer Institute, 8,490 new cases of Hodgkin's lymphoma were diagnosed in 2010 and 1,320 individuals died from the disease. The highest annual incidence rates were observed among Caucasians (3.2 per 100,000 in men and 2.5 per 100,000 in women) and the lowest among Asian/Pacific Islanders (1.5 per 100,000 in men and 1.1 per 100,000 in women). During the time period 1998–2007, incidence rates increased among US men and women by about 2% per year. Nevertheless, during the same period mortality rates declined and 5-year survival rates now exceed 90% for patients who are diagnosed without distant metastasis (Altekruse et al., 2010).

Classical Hodgkin's lymphoma always arises in lymph nodes and is classified into four subtypes. The most common of these is the *nodular sclerosing* type in which the affected lymph nodes are largely replaced by fibrotic tumor nodules. The second most common is the *mixed cellularity* subtype in which affected lymph nodes are infiltrated by inflammatory cells without fibrosis. Lymphocyte-rich and lymphocyte-depleted subtypes are rare forms (Robbins and Cotran, 1979).

Recent molecular studies show that the malignant cells of Hodgkin's lymphomas often carry incapacitating mutations of the immunoglobulin genes (Küppers et al., 1994; Kanzler et al., 1996; Bräuninger et al., 1997). Furthermore, approximately 40% of Hodgkin's lymphomas are positive for EBV, and EBV-positive tumors typically carry mutations that induce aberrant signal transduction and render immunoglobulin genes ineffectual. These molecular findings suggest that viral proteins may induce mutational events in tumor suppressor genes and/or interfere with apoptosis and other processes that restrict cancer development (Bräuninger et al., 2006; Melbye, Ekström Smedby, and Trichopoulos, 2008).

Genetic studies have found markedly higher concordance rates of Hodgkin's lymphoma among monozygous (identical) twins than dizygous twins, and risk increases have been observed in association with several antigens of the *human leukocyte antigen (HLA)* locus. While these studies suggest that genetic variability at the HLA locus may influence the development of Hodgkin's lymphoma, it is noteworthy that familial Hodgkin's disease accounts for less than 5% of cases (Cartwright and Watkins, 2004).

Unlike non-Hodgkin's lymphoma, which shows an exponential increase in age-specific incidence, Hodgkin's lymphoma has a bimodal age of onset distribution with an early peak (15–34 years of age) and a late peak (over 55 years of age). For example, in the United States during 2003–2007, 44% of cases were diagnosed before age 35 years and 28% were diagnosed at 55 years or older. Similarly, the distribution of deaths by age also shows an early peak at 20–34 years and a late peak at 75–84 years (**Figure 27.4**) (Altekruse et al., 2010).

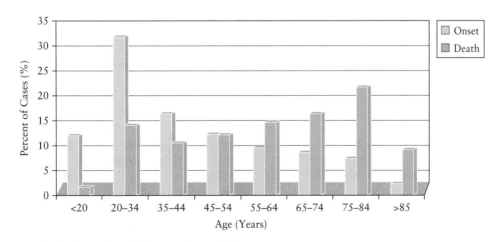

Figure 27.4 Age Distributions of Hodgkin's Lymphoma, USA.

Source: Data from Altekruse SF, Kosary CL, Krapcho M, Neyman N, Aminou R, Waldron W, Ruhl J, Howlader N, Tatalovich Z, Cho H, Mariotto A, Eisner MP, Lewis DR, Cronin K, Chen HS, Feuer EJ, Stinchcomb DG, Edwards BK (2010). SEER Cancer Statistics Review, 1975–2007, National Cancer Institute. Bethesda, MD, USA.

Despite differences in their age distributions, the profile of factors that increase the risk of developing Hodgkin's lymphoma is similar to that of non-Hodgkin's lymphoma. Risk factors include male gender, family history, recent history of infectious mononucleosis or active infection with EBV, a weakened immune system due to HIV disease or use of immunosuppressive drugs, and the presence of somatic mutations and/or gene rearrangements that cause dysfunction of immunoglobulins.

EPIDEMIOLOGY OF MULTIPLE MYELOMA

Multiple myeloma, also known as *plasma cell myeloma*, is a malignancy of plasma cells, which are B lymphocytes that produce antibodies. In this disease, collections of neoplastic plasma cells accumulate in bones and the bone marrow causing bone lesions and interfering with the production of normal blood cells. Since *multiple* anatomic sites are usually involved in the same patient, the name multiple myleoma is appropriate. Characteristic signs and symptoms include hypercalcemia, renal failure, anemia, and bone lesions (Raab et al., 2009).

Multiple myeloma develops from B lymphocytes that have migrated from the germinal centers of lymph nodes to other tissues. It is thus classified as a type of lymphoma. Cytogenetic features of multiple myeloma are similar to other B-cell lymphomas. Chromosomal translocations involving the immunoglobulin genes of chromosomes 2, 14, and 22 are often involved in the transformation of normal B cells to myeloma cells. For example, translocations and gene rearrangements involving the heavy chain immunoglobulin locus on chromosome 14 are found in approximately 50% of cases (Kyle and Rajkumar, 2004).

As with other forms of lymphoma, both the incidence and mortality of rates of multiple myeloma are increasing throughout the world. In 2008, 102,000 new cases were diagnosed and 72,000 died compared to 57,000 cases and 45,000 deaths in 1990 (Ferlay et al., 2010; Parkin, Pisani, and Ferlay, 1999a, 1999b). These increases are at least partly due to increasing longevity, since diagnosis is rare prior to age 40 years, and nearly 95% of cases are diagnosed in individuals 65 years and older.

Striking ethnic differences are evident in US rates of multiple myeloma. In particular, African American men and women have the highest reported annual rates of multiple myeloma in the world (14.3 cases per 100,000 in men and 10.0 cases per 100,000 in

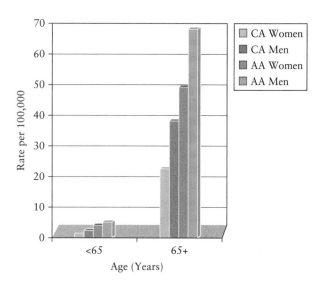

Figure 27.5 Annual Incidence of Multiple Myeloma by Age, Gender, and Race, USA.

Source: Data from Altekruse SF, Kosary CL, Krapcho M, Neyman N, Aminou R, Waldron W, Ruhl J, Howlader N, Tatalovich Z, Cho H, Mariotto A, Eisner MP, Lewis DR, Cronin K, Chen HS, Feuer EJ, Stinchcomb DG, Edwards BK (2010). SEER Cancer Statistics Review, 1975–2007, National Cancer Institute. Bethesda, MD, USA.

women); more than double the rates found among Caucasians (6.7 per 100,000 in men and 4.1 per 100,000 in women) (**Figure 27.5**).

In search of an explanation for the high multiple myeloma rates among African Americans, studies were designed to elucidate possible genetic susceptibility. These early studies targeted the *human leukocyte antigen (HLA)* locus on chromosome 6; and in 1983, Leech and colleagues identified an HLA gene (*HLA-Cw2*) associated with excess risk among African American cases (Leech et al., 1983; Leech, Brown, and Scharifeld, 1985). Subsequently, a larger study was conducted to further evaluate associations between myeloma risk and genotypes of the HLA locus. The study examined frequencies of HLA-Cw2 and several other HLA antigens in 46 African American cases and 88 controls, and 85 Caucasian cases and 122 controls. Findings revealed that the presence of HLA-Cw2 significantly increased the risk in both African Americans (RR = 5.7) and Caucasians (RR = 2.6), suggesting that HLA-Cw2 may contribute to the increased incidence among African Americans (Pottern et al., 1992).

As with other types of lymphoma, significant increases in the risk of developing multiple myeloma have been observed among patients with AIDS and certain other infectious conditions. Risk increases have been noted in cohorts of AIDS patients in the United States, Puerto Rico, and Australia (Goedert et al., 1998; Grulich et al., 1999); and in a national Swedish cohort, the risk of multiple myeloma was significantly increased among individuals with hepatitis C infection (Duberg et al., 2005). In other studies, risk increases have been reported among relatives of myeloma patients, and a modest relationship has been observed between obesity and myeloma development (Alexander et al., 2007b).

Monocloncal gammopathy of undetermined significance (MGUS) refers to the presence of a high concentration of a specific monoclonal immunoglobulin protein in the blood. Such monoclonal proteins are sometimes called *paraproteins*. Patients with MGUS have been found to have a markedly increased risk of developing multiple myeloma.

In a series of 241 patients diagnosed with MGUS at the Mayo Clinic, 94 patients (39%) developed myeloma during 25 years of follow-up (Kyle et al., 2004). In a larger series of 1,384 patients with MGUS, 115 patients progressed to multiple myeloma in 11,009 years of follow-up, and the relative risk of developing multiple myeloma was increased by 25-fold compared to the general population. These patients developed multiple myeloma or a related disorder at a rate of 1% per year and the initial concentration of serum monoclonal protein was found to be a significant predictor of progression (Kyle et al., 2002). The prevalence rates of MGUS in population surveys have a pattern similar to the incidence rates of multiple myeloma in the US population: African Americans have twofold higher rates than Caucasians (8.4% vs. 3.6%) and men have higher rates than women (4.0% vs. 2.7%) (Cohen et al., 1998; Kyle et al., 2006).

In a landmark study of MGUS, Landgren and colleagues followed 77,469 adults enrolled in the nationwide population-based *Prostate, Lung, Colorectal, and Ovarian (PLCO) Cancer Screening Trial*. During the study, 71 subjects developed multiple myeloma from whom serum samples had been collected 2–10 years prior to diagnosis. Notably, MGUS was present in 100% of patients at least 2 years prior to the diagnosis of multiple myeloma, and the concentration of monoclonal protein was found to be a significant predictor of progression. Based on these results, the investigators concluded that, "*monoclonal gammopathy of undetermined significance (MGUS) is a premalignant plasma-cell proliferative disorder associated with a life-long risk of progression to multiple myeloma*" (Landgren et al., 2009).

WALDENSTRÖM'S MACROGLOBULINEMIA

Waldenström's macroglobulinemia is a rare condition characterized by a monoclonal gammopathy of immunoglobulin M (IgM) plus infiltration of the bone marrow by plasma cells derived from a single clone of B lymphocytes (Robbins and Cotran, 1979). This condition was named after the Swedish physician, Jan Gosta Waldenström, who first described two patients with the condition in 1944 (Waldenström, 1944). Though similar in some respects to myeloma, Waldenström's macroglobulinemia rarely causes bone lesions and is now classified as a form of low grade non-Hodgkin's lymphoma.

A team of investigators at the US National Cancer Institute investigated associations between Waldenström's macroglobulinemia and chronic immunostimulatory conditions in a cohort of 4 million male veterans who received health care in Veteran's Administration (VA) hospitals during 1969–1996. Data on each subject were ascertained from computerized medical records maintained in the VA medical system. During an average follow-up of 12 years, a total of 361 cases of Waldenström's macroglobulinemia were identified, yielding an age-standardized incidence of 0.34 cases per 100,000 person-years. Disease risk was significantly elevated in individuals with autoimmune conditions (RR = 2.2), hepatitis (RR = 3.4), HIV disease (RR = 12.1), or *rickettsiosis* (RR = 3.4), a zoonotic infection transmitted by ticks and fleas. These results suggest that chronic immune stimulation plays an important role in the etiology and pathogenesis of Waldenström's macroglobulinemia (Koshiol et al., 2008).

In addition to chronic immune stimulation, the majority of patients with Waldenström's macroglobulinemia have been found to carry chromosomal defects. Deletion of the long arm of chromosome 6 (*6q deletion*) is the most commonly observed cytogenetic abnormality. In a US study, bone marrow samples from 38 patients were examined by *fluorescence in situ hybridization (FISH)*, and 6q deletions were detected in 21 (55%) of the 38 specimens (Schop et al., 2006). Subsequently, in a larger international study of 102 patients, 6q deletions were detected in 54% of bone marrow specimens and found to be associated with a worsened prognosis (Ocio et al., 2007).

In summary, the general epidemiologic features of Waldenström's macroglobulinemia are similar to other forms of lymphoma. The trisomic combination of immunosuppression, chronic antigenic stimulation, and specific chromosomal aberrations stimulate the terminal differentiation of plasma cells that subsequently invade and proliferate uncontrollably in the bone marrow.

MODELS OF PATHOGENESIS OF LYMPHOMA

Biological mechanisms responsible for the genesis of lymphoma are variable and complex, and while some events and interactions have been elucidated, much remains to be discovered. In many patients, lymphomagenesis appears to involve chronic antigenic stimulation by one or more infectious agents in combination with chromosomal translocations, somatic mutations, gene rearrangements and/or epigenetic changes that cause dysregulation and/or hyperactivity of immunoglobulin genes. While the exact sequence of molecular events is unknown, the end result is the perpetual proliferation of lymphocytes characteristic of lymphoid malignancy. Imbalance in the function of T and B lymphocytes appears to be an important stimulus. For example, drug-induced immunosuppression of T cells in conjunction with active EBV infection and B-cell response has been found to rapidly accelerate the genesis of lymphoma in post-transplant patients and those with HIV disease. The complex nature of lymphomagenesis is perhaps best illustrated by endemic Burkitt's lymphoma, a B-cell malignancy that involves a trisomy of risk factors, e.g., chronic EBV and malarial infection in combination with chromosomal translocation of the *c-myc* oncogene to a position in close proximity to one of the immunoglobulin loci (de Thé, 1993; Küppers, 2005; Ferry, 2006).

PREVENTION OF AIDS-RELATED LYMPHOMA

Primary prevention of AIDS-related lymphomas depends largely upon avoiding HIV infection (Thun et al., 2010). Preventive behaviors include sexual abstinence, monogamous sex with an uninfected partner, regular condom use, and abstinence from injection drug use. Similar precautions are recommended for individuals who are HIV positive to prevent infecting others and avoid other sexually transmitted and blood-borne diseases. Screening of high-risk individuals to identify HIV-seropositivity is therefore imperative for control of AIDS and AIDS-related conditions including lymphoma.

Tertiary Prevention of Lymphoma in AIDS Patients

Key measures of immunosuppression and disease progression in patients with AIDS include the CD4 and CD8 lymphocyte counts and the viral load. In particular, severe immunosuppression reflected by a very low CD4 count is a major risk factor for the development of AIDS-related lymphoma.

In recent years, a variety of antiretroviral drugs have been developed for the treatment of patients with AIDS, and in randomized clinical trials conducted in several countries, antiretroviral drugs taken in combination have proved superior to single drug regimens in reducing the HIV viral load and improving the CD4 lymphocyte count. Such multidrug therapy is called *high activity antiretroviral therapy (HAART)*. Furthermore, following the introduction of HAART, the incidence of AIDS-related lymphoma has dramatically declined.

An example of the chemopreventive value of HAART against lymphoma development comes from the *Swiss HIV Cohort Study*. In this investigation, 12,959 people with HIV disease were followed during 1984–2006 to assess the long-term impact of HAART compared to single drug regimens. For the entire cohort, 429 cases of non-Hodgkin's lymphoma were detected in 75,222 person-years of observation. Patients receiving HAART contributed 36,787 person years in the study. The annual incidence of non-Hodgkin's lymphoma in the cohort peaked during pre-HAART years, 1993–1995 (13.6 per 1,000 person-years) and reached a nadir during post-HAART years, 2002–2006 (1.8 per 1,000 person-years). After adjustment for age, baseline CD4 count, and other variables, HAART was found to reduce the risk of developing non-Hodgkin's lymphoma by 76% (hazard ratio = 0.74). Furthermore, the reduction in risk has been sustained up to 10 years after initiation of HAART, even among patients with a low baseline CD4 count. These findings support the efficacy of HAART regardless of immune impairment at initiation of treatment. The investigators concluded that *"although it was already clear that HAART prevents [non-Hodgkin's lymphoma] through improvement of immune status, this study shows that HAART avoids the majority of [non-Hodgkin's lymphoma], even among the most severely immunosuppressed individuals."* (Polesel, Clifford, Rickenbach, Dal Maso, Battegay,…the Swiss HIV Cohort Study, 2008).

SUMMARY

Rates of non-Hodgkin's lymphoma, Hodgkin's lymphoma, and multiple myeloma have risen steadily in the past 3 decades. These upward trends reflect increases in three immunological states: immunosuppression due to primary or acquired immunodeficiency, chronic antigenic stimulation, and disruption of normal lymphocyte function and proliferation.

Rates of lymphoma are high in patients with acquired immunosuppression due to HIV infection, in post-transplant patients treated with immunosuppressive drugs, and in patients with autoimmune conditions or cancer who received immunosuppressive chemotherapy. Heightened antigenic stimulation often involves active infection by ubiquitous microbes such as EBV and *H. pylori* in a genetically susceptible host. Genetic errors in immunoglobulin genes due to somatic mutations and gene rearrangements are characteristic of many lymphomas, and such mutations have been found to induce aberrant signal transduction and render immunoglobulin genes ineffectual. Exposure to other exogenous factors such as agrichemicals, aniline dyes, ultraviolet radiation, and allogeneic blood transfusions may also heighten the risk.

Prevention involves avoidance or elimination of factors known to cause immunodeficiency and/or that inordinately heighten the antigenic response. Screening high risk groups for the presence of HIV and *H. pylori* are advisable measures for lymphoma control. As pointed out in a recent review of non-Hodgkin's lymphoma, "*Interdisciplinary collaborations are needed to investigate the broad scope of factors that may alter individual susceptibility and promote lymphoid malignancies*" (Fisher and Fisher, 2004).

THERAY OF LYMPHOMA

Results of recent clinical trials suggest that the addition of monoclonal antibodies to regimes of conventional chemotherapeutic agents has significantly improved survival of patients with non-Hodgkin's lymphoma. A variety of monoclonal antibodies are under study, many of which target cell membrane receptors of lymphocytes. One example is rituximab which specifically targets the CD20 receptors of B lymphocytes. Addition of rituxamab to conventional therapeutic regimens significantly improves survival in patients with CD20 positive B-cell lymphoma (Plosker and Figgitt, 2003).

• • • REFERENCES

Alexander, D.D., Mink, P.J., Adami, H.O., Chang, E.T., Cole, P., Mandel, J.S., & Trichopoulos, D. (2007a). The non-Hodgkin lymphomas: A review of the epidemiologic literature. *Int J Cancer*, 120(S12), 1–39.

Alexander, D.D., Mink, P.J., Adami, H.O., Cole, P., Mandel, J.S., Oken, M.M., & Trichopoulos, D. (2007b). Multiple myeloma: A review of the epidemiologic literature. *Int J Cancer*, 120(S12), 40–61.

Altekruse, S.F., Kosary, C.L., Krapcho, M., Neyman, N., Aminou, R., Waldron, W.,… Edwards, B.K. (2010). SEER Cancer Statistics Review, 1975–2007. Bethesda, MD: National Cancer Institute.

Armstrong, B.K., & Kricker, N. (2007). Sun exposure and non-Hodgkin lymphoma. *Cancer Epidemiol Biomarkers Prev*, 16(3), 396–400.

Baecklund, E., Ekbom, A., Sparén, P., Feltelius, N., & Klareskog, L. (1998). Disease activity and risk of lymphoma in patients with rheumatoid arthritis: Nested case-control study. *Br Med J*, 317, 180–181.

Banks, P.M. (1992). Changes in diagnosis of non-Hodgkin's lymphomas over time. *Cancer Res*, 52, 5453s.

Barré-Sinoussi, F., Chermann, J.C., Rey, F., Nugeyre, M.T., Chamaret, S., Gruest, J.,…Montagnier, L. (1983). Isolation of a T-lymphotropic retrovirus from a patient at risk for acquired immune deficiency syndrome (AIDS). *Science*, 220, 868–870.

Biggar, R.J., Frisch, M., Engels, E.A., & Goedert, J.J. (2001). Risk of T-cell lymphomas in persons with AIDS. *J Acquir Immune Defic Syndrome*, 26, 371–376.

Bishara, M.R., Ross, C., & Sur, M. (2009). Primary anaplastic large cell lymphoma of the breast arising in reconstruction mammoplasty capsule of saline filled breast implant after radical mastectomy for breast cancer: An unusual case presentation. *Diagn Pathol*, 2(4), 11.

Blair, A., Sandler, D.P., Tarone, R., Lubin, J., Thomas, K., Hoppin, J.A.,…Alavania, M.C. (2005). Mortality among participants in the agricultural health study. *Ann Epidemiol*, 15, 279–285.

Blair, A., Zahm, S.H., Pearce, N.E., Heineman, E.F., & Fraumeni, J.F. (1992). Clues to cancer etiology from studies of farmers. *Scand J Work Environ Health, 18,* 209–215.

Blomberg, J., Möller, T., Olsson, H., Anderson, H., & Jonsson, M. (1993). Cancer morbidity in blood recipients—Results of a cohort study. *Eur J Cancer, 29A,* 2101–2105.

Blum, K.A., Lozanski, G., & Byrd, J.C. (2004). Adult Burkitt leukemia and lymphoma. *Blood, 104,* 3009–3020.

Bräuninger, A., Küppers, R., Strickler, J.G., Wacker, H.H., Rajewsky, K., & Hansmann, M.L. (1997). Hodgkin's and Reed–Sternberg cells in lymphocyte predominant Hodgkin's disease represent clonal populations of germinal center-derived tumor B cells. *Proc Natl Acad Sci USA, 94,* 9337–9342.

Bräuninger, A., Schmitz, R., Bechtel, D., Renné, C., Hansmann, M.L., & Küppers, R. (2006). Molecular biology of Hodgkin's and Reed/Sternberg cells in Hodgkin's lymphoma. *International Journal of Cancer, 118*(8), 1853–1861.

Burkitt, D. (1958). A sarcoma involving the jaws in African children. *The British Journal of Surgery, 46*(197), 218–223.

Burkitt, D.P. (1971). Epidemiology of Burkitt's lymphoma. *Proc R Soc Med, 64*(9), 909–910.

Burkitt, D.P. (1983). The discovery of Burkitt's lymphoma. *Cancer, 51,* 1777–1786.

Butel, J.S., Vilchez, R.A., Jorgensen, J.L., & Kozinetz, C.A. (2003). Association between SV40 and non-Hodgkin's lymphoma. *Leuk Lymphoma, 44*(Suppl 3), S33–S39.

Carpenter, L.M., Newton, R., Casabonne, D., Ziegler, J., Mbulaiteye, S., Mbidde, E.,...Beral, V. (2008). Antibodies against malaria and Epstein-Barr virus in childhood Burkitt lymphoma: A case-control study in Uganda. *International J Cancer, 122*(6), 1319–1323.

Carroll-Pankhurst, C., Engels, E.A., Strickler, H.D., Goedert, J.J., Wagner, J., & Mortimer, E.A. Jr. (2001). Thirty-five year mortality following receipt of SV40-contaminated polio vaccine during the neonatal period. *Br J Cancer, 85*(9), 1295–1297.

Cartwright, R., McNally, R., & Staines, A. (1994). The increasing incidence of non-Hodgkin's lymphoma (NHL): The possible role of sunlight. *Leuk Lymphoma, 14,* 387–394.

Cartwright, R.A., & Watkins, G. (2004). Epidemiology of Hodgkin's disease: A review. *Hematological Oncology, 22,* 11–26.

Cerhan, J.R., Wallace, R.B., Folsom, A.R., Potter, J.D., Munger, R.G., & Prineas, R.J. (1993). Transfusion history and cancer risk in older women. *Ann Intern Med, 119,* 8–15.

Cerhan, J.R., Wallace, R.B., Dick, F., Kemp, J., Parker, A.S., Zheng, W.,...Folsom, A.R. (2001). Blood transfusions and risk of non-Hodgkin's lymphoma subtypes and chronic lymphocytic leukemia. *Cancer Epidemiol Biomarkers Prev, 10*(4), 361–368.

Cerroni, L., Zochling, N., Putz, B., & Kerl, H. (1997). Infection by *Borrelia burgdorferi* and cutaneous B-cell lymphoma. *J Cutan Pathol, 24,* 457–461.

Cesarman, E., Chang, Y., Moore, P.S., Said, J.W., & Knowles, D.M. (1995). Kaposi's sarcoma-associated herpesvirus-like DNA sequences in AIDS-related body-cavity-based lymphomas. *N Engl J Med, 332*(18), 1186–1191.

Chang, Y., Cesarman, E., Pessin, M.S., Lee, F., Culpepper, J., Knowles, D.M., & Moore, P.S. (1994). Identification of herpesvirus-like DNA sequences in AIDS-associated Kaposi's sarcoma. *Science, 266*(5192), 1865–1869.

Chow, E.J., & Holly, E.A. (2002). Blood transfusions and non-Hodgkin's lymphoma. *Epidemiol Rev, 24*(2), 269–279.

Cinque, P., Brytting, M., Vago, L., Castagna, A., Parravicini, C., Zanchetta, N.,...Linde, A. (1993). Epstein-Barr virus DNA in cerebrospinal fluid from patients with AIDS-related primary lymphoma of the central nervous system. *Lancet, 342*(8868), 398–401.

Cleary, M.L., Chao, J., Warnke, R., & Sklar, J. (1984). Immunoglobulin gene rearrangement as a diagnostic criterion of B-cell lymphoma. *Proc Natl Acad Sci USA, 81*, 593–597.

Cleghorn, F.R., Manns, A., Falk, R., Hartge, P., Hanchard, B., Jack, N.,…Blattner, W. (1995). Effect of human T-lymphotropic virus type I infection on non-Hodgkin's lymphoma incidence. *Journal of the National Cancer Institute, 87*(13), 1009–1014.

Cohen, H.J., Crawford, J., Rao, M.K., Pieper, C.F., & Currie, M.S. (1998). Racial differences in the prevalence of monoclonal gammopathy in a community-based sample of the elderly. *Am J Med, 104*, 439–444.

Dal Maso, L., & Franceschi, S. (2003). Epidemiology of non-Hodgkin lymphomas and other haemolymphopoietic neoplasms in people with AIDS. *Lancet Oncol, 4*(2), 110–119.

de Jong, D., Vasmel, W.L.E., de Boer, J.P., Verhave, G., Barbé, E., Casparie, M.K., & van Leeuwen, F.E. (2008). Anaplastic large-cell lymphoma in women with breast implants. *JAMA, 300*(17), 2030–2035.

de Sanjose, S., Shah, K.V., Domingo-Domenech, E., Engels, E.A., Fernandez, D.S.,…Viscidi, R.P. (2003). Lack of serological evidence for an association between simian virus 40 and lymphoma. *Int J Cancer, 104*, 522–524.

de Thé, G. (1993). The etiology of Burkitt's lymphoma and the history of the shaken dogmas. *Blood Cells, 19*, 667–673.

Devesa, S.S., & Fears, T. (1992). Non-Hodgkin's lymphoma time trends, United States and international data. *Cancer Res, 52*, 5432s–5440s.

Duberg, A.S., Nordstrom, M., Torner, A., Reichard, O., Strauss, R., Janzon, R., Back, E., & Ekdahl, K. (2005). Non-Hodgkin's lymphoma and other nonhepatic malignancies in Swedish patients with hepatitis C virus infection. *Hepatology, 41*, 652–659.

Eltom, M.A., Jemal, A., Mbulaiteye, S.M., Devesa, S.S., & Biggar, R.J. (2002). Trends in Kaposi's sarcoma and non-Hodgkin's lymphoma incidence in the United States from 1973 through 1998. *J Natl Cancer Inst, 94*(16), 1204–1210.

Engels, E.A., Frisch, M., Lubin, J.H., Gail, M.H., Biggar, R.J., & Goedert, J.J. (2002). Prevalence of hepatitis C virus infection and risk for hepatocellular carcinoma and non-Hodgkin lymphoma in AIDS. *J Acquir Immune Defic Syndr, 31*, 536–541.

Engels, E.A., Katki, H.A., Nielsen, N.M., Winther, J.F., Hjalgrim, H., Gjerris, F.,…Frisch, M. (2003). Cancer incidence in Denmark following exposure to poliovirus vaccine contaminated with simian virus 40. *J Natl Cancer Inst, 95*(7), 532–539.

Engels, E.A., Chen, J., Hartge, P., Cerhan, J.R., Davis, S., Severson, R.K.,…Viscidi, R.P. (2005). Antibody responses to simian virus 40 T antigen: A case-control study of non-Hodgkin lymphoma. *Cancer Epidemiol Biomarkers Prev, 14*(2), 521–524.

Epstein, M.A., Achong, B.G., & Pope, J.H. (1967). Virus in cultured lymphoblasts from a New Guinea Burkitt lymphoma. *Br Med J, 2*(5547), 290–291.

Ferlay, J., Shin, H.R., Forman, D., Mathers, C., & Parkin, D.M. (2010). Estimates of worldwide burden of cancer in 2008. *International Journal of Cancer, 127*(12), 2893–2917.

Fernandez, E., Chatenoud, L., La Vecchia, C., Negri, E., & Franceschi, S. (1999). Fish consumption and cancer risk. *Am J Clin Nutr, 70*(1), 85–90.

Ferreri, A.J., Guidoboni, M., Ponzoni, M., De Conciliis, C., Dell'Oro, S., Fleischhauer, K.,…Dolcetti, R. (2004). Evidence for an association between *Chlamydia psittaci* and ocular adnexal lymphomas. *J Nat Cancer Inst, 96*(8), 586–594.

Ferry, J.A. (2006). Burkitt's lymphoma: Clinicopathologic features and differential diagnosis. *The Oncologist, 11*(4), 375–383.

Figgs, L.W., Dosemeci, M., & Blair, A. (1995). United States non-Hodgkin's lymphoma surveillance by occupation 1984–1989: A twenty-four state death certificate study. *American Journal of Industrial Medicine, 27*, 817–835.

Filipovich, A.H., Mathur, A., Kamat, D., & Shapiro, R.S. (1992). Primary immunodeficiencies: Genetic risk factors for lymphoma. *Cancer Res, 52,* 5465s–5467s.

Fisher, S.G., & Fisher, R.I. (2004). The epidemiology of non-Hodgkin's lymphoma. *Oncogene, 23,* 6524–6534.

Franceschi, S., Dal Maso, L., & La Vecchia, C. (1999). Advances in the epidemiology of HIV-associated non-Hodgkin's lymphoma and other lymphoid neoplasms. *Int J Cancer, 83*(4), 481–485.

Fritschi, L., Ambrosini, G.L., Kliewer, E.V., & Johnson, K.C.; Canadian Cancer Registries Epidemiologic Research Group. (2004). Dietary fish intake and risk of leukaemia, multiple myeloma, and non-Hodgkin lymphoma. *Cancer Epidemiol Biomarkers Prev, 13*(4), 532–537.

Gallo, R.C., Sarin, P.S., Gelmann, E.P., Robert-Guroff, M., Richardson, E., Kalyanaraman, V.S.,...Popovic, M. (1983). Isolation of human T-cell leukemia virus in acquired immune deficiency syndrome (AIDS). *Science, 220*(4599), 865–867.

Garbe, C., Stein, H., Dienemann, D., & Orfanos, C.E. (1991). *Borrelia burgdorferi*-associated cutaneous B cell lymphoma: Clinical and immunohistologic characterization of four cases. *J Am Acad Dermatol, 24,* 584–590.

Gisbert, J.P., García-Buey, L., Pajares, J.M., & Moreno-Otero, R. (2003). Prevalence of hepatitis C virus infection in B cell non-Hodgkin's lymphoma: Systematic review and meta-analysis. *Gastroenterology, 125,* 1723–1732.

Goedert, J.J., Cote, T.R., Virgo, P., Scoppa, S.M., Kingma, D.W., Gail, M.H.,...Biggar, R.J. (1998). Spectrum of AIDS-associated malignant disorders. *Lancet, 351,* 1833–1899.

Grogan, T., & Miller, T. (1995). *Cancer Treatment* (pp. 979–1005), C.M. Haskell (Ed.). Philadelphia: WB Saunders.

Groves, F.D., Linet, M.S., Travis, L.B., & Devesa, S.S. (2000). Cancer surveillance series: Non-Hodgkin's lymphoma incidence by histologic subtype in the United States from 1978 through 1995. *J Natl Cancer Inst, 92,* 1240–1251.

Grulich, A.E., Wan, X., Law, M.G., Coates, M., & Kaldor, J.M. (1999). Risk of cancer in people with AIDS. *AIDS, 13,* 839–843.

Grulich, A.E., Wan, X., Law, M.G., Milliken, S.T., Lewis, C.R., Garsia, R.J.,...Kaldor, J.M. (2000). B-cell stimulation and prolonged immune deficiency are risk factors for non-Hodgkin's lymphoma in people with AIDS. *AIDS, 14,* 133–140.

Harris, N.L., Jaffe, E.S., Diebold, J., Flandrin, G., Muller-Hermelink, H.K., Vardiman, J., Lister, T.A., & Bloomfield, C.D. (1999). World Health Organization classification of neoplastic diseases of the hematopoietic and lymphoid tissues: Report of the Clinical Advisory Committee meeting-Airlie House, Virginia, November 1997. *Journal of Clinical Oncology, 17*(12), 3835–3849.

Harris, O.D., Cooke, W.T., Thompson, H., & Waterhouse, J. A.H. (1967). Malignancy in adult coeliac disease and idiopathic steatorrhoea. *American Journal of Medicine, 42,* 899–912.

Hartge, P., Devesa, S.S., & Fraumeni, J.F. Jr. (1994). Hodgkin's and non-Hodgkin's lymphomas. *Cancer Surv, 19–20,* 423–453.

Hartge, P., Devesa, S.S., Grauman, D., Fears, T.R., & Fraumeni, J.F. Jr. (1996). Non-Hodgkin's lymphoma and sunlight. *J Natl Cancer Inst, 88,* 298–300.

Hinuma, Y., Nagata, K., Hanaoka, M., Nakai, M., Matsumoto, T., Kinoshita, K.I.,...Miyoshi, I. (1981). Adult T-cell leukemia: Antigen in an ATL cell line and detection of antibodies to the antigen in human sera. *Proc Natl Acad Sci USA, 78*(10), 6476–6480.

Hodgkin, T. (1832). On some morbid experiences of the absorbent glands and spleen. *Med Chir Trans, 17,* 69–97.

Hussell, T., Isaacson, P.G., Crabtree, J.E., & Spencer, J. (1993). The response of cells from low-grade B-cell gastric lymphomas of mucosa-associated lymphoid tissue to *Helicobacter pylori*. *Lancet, 342,* 571–574.

Isaacson, P.G., & Spencer, J. (1995). The biology of low grade MALT lymphoma. *J Clin Pathol, 48*(5), 395–397.

Jelic, S., & Filipovic-Ljeskovic, I. (1999). Positive serology for Lyme disease borrelias in primary cutaneous B-cell lymphoma: A study in 22 patients: Is it a fortuitous finding? *Hematol Oncol, 17,* 107–116.

Judde, J.G., Lacoste, V., Briere, J., Kassa-Kelembho, E., Clyti, E., Couppie, P.,…Gessain, A. (2000). Monoclonality or oligoclonality of human herpesvirus 8 terminal repeat sequences in Kaposi's sarcoma and other diseases. *J Natl Cancer Inst, 92,* 729–736.

Kamel, O.W., van de Rijn, M., Hanasono, M.M., & Warnke, R.A. (1995). Immunosuppression-associated lymphoproliferative disorders in rheumatic patients. *Leukemia Lymph, 16,* 363.

Kanzler, H., Küppers, R., Hansmann, M.L., & Rajewsky, K. (1996). Hodgkin's and Reed–Sternberg cells in Hodgkin's disease represent the outgrowth of a dominant tumor clone derived from (crippled) germinal center B cells. *J Exp Med, 184,* 1495–1505.

Khuder, S.A., Schaub, E.A., & Keller-Byrne, J.E. (1998). Meta-analyses of non-Hodgkin's lymphoma and farming. *Scand J Work Environ Health, 24,* 255–261.

Kinlen, L. (1992). Immunosuppressive therapy and acquired immunological disorders. *Cancer Res, 52,* 5474s–5476s.

Koshiol, J., Gridley, G., Engels, E., McMaster, M., & Landgren, O. (2008). Chronic immune stimulation and subsequent Waldenström macroglobulinemia. *Archives of Internal Medicine, 168*(17), 1903–1909.

Küppers, R., Rajewsky, K., Zhao, M., Simons, G., Laumann, R., Fischer, R., & Hansmann, M.L. (1994). Hodgkin's disease: Hodgkin's and Reed–Sternberg cells picked from histological sections show clonal immunoglobulin gene rearrangements and appear to be derived from B cells at various stages of development. *Proc Natl Acad Sci USA, 91,* 10962–10966.

Küppers, R. (2005). Mechanisms of B-cell lymphoma pathogenesis. *Nat Rev Cancer, 5*(4), 251–262.

Kyle, R.A., Therneau, T.M., Rajkumar, S.V., Offord, J.R., Larson, D.R., Plevak, M.F., & Melton, L.J. III (2002). A long-term study of prognosis in monoclonal gammopathy of undetermined significance. *N Engl J Med, 346,* 564–569.

Kyle, R.A., Therneau, T.M., Rajkumar, S.V., Larson, D.R., Plevak, M.F., & Melton, L.J. III. (2004). Long-term follow-up of 241 patients with monoclonal gammopathy of undetermined significance: The original Mayo Clinic series 25 years later. *Mayo Clin Proc, 79,* 859–866.

Kyle, R.A., & Rajkumar, S.V. (2004). Multiple myeloma. *N Engl J Med, 351*(18), 1860–1873.

Kyle, R.A., Therneau, T.M., Rajkumar, S.V., Larson, D.R., Plevak, M.F., Offord, J.R.,… Melton, L.J. III (2006). Prevalence of monoclonal gammopathy of undetermined significance. *N Engl J Med, 354,* 1362–1369.

Landgren, O., Kyle, R.A., Pfeiffer, R.M., Katzmann, J.A., Caporaso, N.E., Hayes, R.B., …Rajkumar, S.V. (2009). Monoclonal gammopathy of undetermined significance (MGUS) consistently precedes multiple myeloma: A prospective study. *Blood, 113*(22), 5412–5417.

Lecuit, M., Abachin, E., Martin, A., Poyart, C., Pochart, P., Suarez, F.,…Lortholary, O. (2004). Immunoproliferative small intestinal disease associated with *Campylobacter jejuni*. *N Engl J Med, 350,* 239–248.

Leech, S.H., Bryan, C.F., Elston, R.C., Rainey, J., Bickers, J.N., & Pelias, M.Z. (1983). Genetic studies in multiple myeloma: Association with HLA-Cw5. *Cancer, 51,* 1408–1411.

Leech, S.H., Brown, R., & Scharifeld, M.S. (1985). Genetic studies in multiple myeloma: Immunoglobulin allotype associations. *Cancer, 5,* 1473–1476.

Linet, M.S., & Pottern, L.M. (1992). Familial aggregation of hematopoietic malignancies and risk of non-Hodgkin's lymphoma. *Cancer Res, 52S,* 5468–5473.

Luppi, M., Longo, G., Ferrari, M.G., Barozzi, P., Marasca, R., Morselli, M., Valenti, C., Mascia, T., Vandelli, L., Vallisa, D., Cavanna, L., & Torelli, G. (1998). Clinico-pathological characterization of hepatitis C virus-related B-cell non-Hodgkin's lymphomas without symptomatic cryoglobulinemia. *Ann Oncol, 9,* 495–498.

Manns, A., & Blattner, W.A. (2003). The epidemiology of the human T-cell lymphotrophic virus type I and type II: Etiologic role in human disease. *Transfusion, 31*(1), 67–75.

Marshall, B.J., & Warren, R.J. (2005). The Nobel Prize in Physiology or Medicine, 2005.

Matsuo, K., Kusano, A., Sugumar, A., Nakamura, S., Tajima, K., & Mueller, N.E. (2004). Effect of hepatitis C virus infection on the risk of non-Hodgkin's lymphoma: A meta-analysis of epidemiological studies. *Cancer Sci, 95,* 745–752.

McGregor, J.M., Crook, T., Fraser-Andrews, E.A., Rozycka, M., Crossland, S., Brooks, L., & Whittaker, S.J. (1999). Spectrum of p53 gene mutations suggests a possible role for ultraviolet radiation in the pathogenesis of advanced cutaneous lymphomas. *J Invest Dermatol, 112*(3), 317–321.

Melbye, M., Ekström Smedby, K., & Trichopoulos, D. (2008). Non-Hodgkin lymphoma. In: *Textbook of cancer epidemiology* (Chapter 27). H.O. Adami, D. Hunter, & D. Trichopoulos (Eds.). Oxford: Oxford University Press.

Melbye, M., Hjalgrim, H., & Adami, H.O. (2008). Hodgkin's lymphoma. In: *Textbook of cancer epidemiology* (Chapter 26). H.O. Adami, D. Hunter, & D. Trichopoulos (Eds.). Oxford: Oxford University Press.

Memon, A., & Doll, R. (1994). A search for unknown blood-borne oncogenic viruses. *Int J Cancer, 58,* 366–368.

Morton, L.M., Hartge, P., Holford, T.R., Holly, E.A., Chiu, B.C., Vineis, P.,…Zheng, T. (2005a). Cigarette smoking and risk of non-Hodgkin lymphoma: A pooled analysis from the International Lymphoma Epidemiology Consortium (InterLymph). *Cancer Epidemiol Biomarkers Prev, 14,* 925–933.

Morton, L.M., Zheng, T., Holford, T.R., Holly, E.A., Chiu, B.C., Costantini, A.S.,…InterLymph Consortium. (2005b). Alcohol consumption and risk of non-Hodgkin lymphoma: A pooled analysis. *Lancet Oncol, 6,* 469–476.

Müller, A.M.S., Ihorst, G., Mertelsmann, R., & Engelhardt, M. (2005). Epidemiology of non-Hodgkin's lymphoma (NHL): Trends, geographic distribution, and etiology. *Ann Hematol, 84,* 1–12.

Nakatsuka, S., Liu, A., Dong, Z., Nomura, S., Takakuwa, T., Miyazato, H., & Aozasa, K. (2003). Simian virus 40 sequences in malignant lymphomas in Japan. *Cancer Research, 63,* 7606–7608.

Negri, E., Little, D., Boiocchi, M., La Vecchia, C., & Franceschi, S. (2004). B-cell non-Hodgkin's lymphoma and hepatitis C virus infection: A systematic review. *Int J Cancer, 111,* 1.

Ocio, E.M., Schop, R.F.J., Gonzalez, B., Van Wier, S.A., Hernandez-Rivas, J.M.,… Fonseca, R. (2007). 6q deletion in Waldenström macroglobulinemia is associated with features of adverse prognosis. *British Journal of Haematology, 136*(1), 80–86.

Offit, K., Wong, G., Filippa, D.A., Tao, Y., & Chaganti, R.S. (1991). Cytogenetic analysis of 434 consecutively ascertained specimens of non-Hodgkin's lymphoma: Clinical correlations. *Blood, 77*(7), 1508–1515.

Opelz, G., & Henderson, R. (1993). Incidence of non-Hodgkin lymphoma in kidney and heart transplant recipients. *Lancet, 342*(8886–8887), 1514–1516.

Palackdharry, C.S. (1994). The epidemiology of non-Hodgkin's lymphoma: Why the increased incidence? *Oncology, 8*(8), 67–73; discussion 73–78.

Parkin, D.M., Pisani, P., & Ferlay, J. (1999a). Estimates of the worldwide incidence of 25 major cancers in 1990. *Int J Cancer, 80*(6), 827–841.

Parkin, D.M., Pisani, P., & Ferlay, J. (1999b). Global cancer statistics. *C A Cancer J Clin, 49*(1), 33–64.

Parkin, D.M., Bray, F., Ferlay, J., & Pisani, P. (2005). Global Cancer Statistics, 2002. *CA Cancer J Clin, 55*, 74–108.

Parsonnet, J., Hansen, S., Rodriguez, L., Gelb, A.B., Warnke, R.A., Jellum, E., …Friedman, G.D. (1994). *Helicobacter pylori* infection and gastric lymphoma. *N Engl J Med, 330*, 1267–1271.

Pettersson, T., Pukkala, E., Teppo, L., & Friman, C. (1992). Increased risk of cancer in patients with systemic lupus erythematosus. *Ann Rheum Dis, 51*(4), 437–439.

Plosker, G.L., & Figgitt, D.P. (2003). Rituximab: A review of its use in non-Hodgkin's lymphoma and chronic lymphocytic leukaemia. *Drugs, 63*(8), 803–843.

Poiesz, B.J., Ruscetti, F.W., Gazdar, A.F., Bunn, P.A., Minna, J.D., & Gallo, R.C. (1980). Detection and isolation of type C retrovirus particles from fresh and cultured lymphocytes of a patient with cutaneous T-cell lymphoma. *Proc Natl Acad Sci USA, 77*, 7415–7419.

Polesel, J., Clifford, G., Rickenbach, M., Dal Maso, L., Battegay, M., Bouchardy, C.,…the Swiss HIV Cohort Study. (2008). Non-Hodgkin's lymphoma incidence in the Swiss HIV Cohort Study before and after highly active antiretroviral therapy. *AIDS, 22*(2), 301–306.

Pottern, L.M., Gart, J.J., Nam, J.M., Dunston, G., Wilson, J., Greenberg, R.,…Schwartz, A.G. (1992). HLA and multiple myeloma among black and white men: Evidence of a genetic association. *Cancer Epidemiol Biomarkers Prev, 1*(3), 177–182.

Purtilo, D.T. (1980). Epstein–Barr virus-induced oncogenesis in immune-deficient individuals. *Lancet, 1*, 300–303.

Raab, M.S., Podar, K., Breitkreutz, I., Richardson, P.G., & Anderson, K.C. (2009). Multiple myeloma. *Lancet, 374*(9686), 324–339.

Rabkin, C.S., Tess, B.H., Christianson, R.E., Wright, W.E., Waters, D.J., Alter, H.J., & Van Den Berg, B.J. (2002). Prospective study of hepatitis C viral infection as a risk factor for subsequent B-cell neoplasia. *Blood, 99*, 4240–4242.

Reed, D. (1902). On the pathological changes in Hodgkin's disease, with special reference to its relation to tuberculosis. *Johns Hopkins Hosp Rep, 10*, 133–196.

Robbins, S.L., & Cotran, R.S. (1979). Pathologic basis of disease (2nd ed.) Philadelphia: WB Saunders Company.

Schöllkopf, C., Melbye, M., Munksgaard, L., Smedby, K.E., Rostgaard, K., Glimelius, B.,…Hjalgrim, H. (2008). *Borrelia* infection and risk of non-Hodgkin lymphoma. *Blood, 111*(12), 5524–5529.

Schop, R.F., Van Wier, S.A., Xu, R., Ghobrial, I., Ahmann, G.J., Greipp, P.R.,…Fonseca, R. (2006). 6q deletion discriminates Waldenström macroglobulinemia from IgM monoclonal gammopathy of undetermined significance. *Cancer Genet Cytogenet, 169*(2), 150–153.

Shipp, M.A., Mauch, P.M., & Harris, N.L. (1997). *Cancer principles & practice of oncology* (Vol. 3) (pp. 2165–2220). V. DeVita Jr., S. Hellman, and S.A. Rosenberg (Eds.). Philadelphia, New York: Lippincott-Raven.

Shivapurkar, N., Harada, K., Reddy, J., Scheuermann, R.H., Xu, Y., McKenna, R.W.,…Gazdar, A.F. (2002). Presence of simian virus 40 DNA sequences in human lymphomas. *Lancet, 359*, 851–852.

Silvestri, F., Pipan, C., Barillari, G., Zaja, F., Fanin, R., Infanti, L., Russo, D., Falasca, E., Botta, G.A., & Baccarani, M. (1996). Prevalence of hepatitis C virus infection in patients with lymphoproliferative disorders. *Blood, 87*(10), 4296–4301.

Sternberg, C. (1898). Uber eine eigenartige unter dem Bilde der Pseudoleukamie verlaufende Tuberculose des lymphatischen Apparates. *Ztschr Heilk, 19*, 21–90.

Swinnen, L., Costanzo-Nordin, M.R., Fisher, S.G., O'Sullivan, E.J., Johnson, M.R., Heroux, A.L.,…Fisher, R.I. (1990). Increased incidence of lymphoproliferative disorder after immunosuppression with the monoclonal antibody OKT3 in cardiac-transplant recipients. *N Engl J Med, 323*(25), 1723–1728.

Takatsuki, K., Uchiyama, T., Sagawa, K., & Yodoi, J. (1977). Adult T cell leukemia in Japan. In S. Seno, F. Takaku, & S. Irino (Eds.), *Topics in hematology* (pp. 73–77). Amsterdam: Excerpta Medica.

Takatsuki, K. (2005). Discovery of adult T-cell leukemia. *Retrovirology, 2*, 16.

Takkouche, B., Etminan, M., & Montes-Martinez, A. (2005). Personal use of hair dyes and risk of cancer: A meta-analysis. *JAMA, 293*, 2516–2525.

Thun, M.J., DeLancey, J.O., Center, M.M., Jemal, A., & Ward, E.M. (2010). The global burden of cancer: Priorities for prevention. *Carcinogenesis, 31*(1), 100–110.

Tycko, B., & Sklar, J. (1990). Chromosomal translocations in lymphoid neoplasia: A reappraisal of the recombinase model. *Cancer Cells, 2*(1), 1–8.

Uchiyama, T., Yodoi, J., Sagawa, K., Takatsuki, K., & Uchino, H. (1977). Adult T-cell leukemia: Clinical and hematologic features of 16 cases. *Blood, 50*, 481–492.

Udomsakdi-Auewarakul, C., Auewarakul, P., Sukpanichnant, S., & Muangsup, W. (2000). Hepatitis C virus infection in patients with non-Hodgkin lymphoma in Thailand. *Blood, 95*, 3640–3641.

Vega, F., & Medeiros, L.J. (2003). Chromosomal translocations involved in non-Hodgkin lymphomas. *Arch Pathol Lab Med, 127*(9), 1148–1160.

Vilchez, R.A., Madden, C.R., Kozinetz, C.A., Halvorson, S.J., White, Z.S., Orgensen, J.L.,... Butel, J.S. (2002). Association between simian virus 40 and non-Hodgkin lymphoma. *Lancet, 359*, 817–823.

Waldenstrom, J. (1944). Incipient myelomatosis or "essential" hyperglobulinemia with fibrinogenopenia—a new syndrome? *Acta Med Scand, 117*, 216–247.

Willemze, R., Kerl, H., Sterry, W., Berti, E., Cerroni, L., Chimenti, S.,...Meijer, C.J.L.M. (1997). EORTC classification for primary cutaneous lymphomas: A proposal from the Cutaneous Lymphoma Study Group of the European Organization for Research and Treatment of Cancer. *Blood, 90*, 354–371.

World Health Organization. (2008). *World cancer report 2008*. Lyon, France: IARC.

Wotherspoon, A.C., Ortiz-Hidalgo, C., Falzon, M.R., & Isaacson, P.G. (1991). *Helicobacter pylori*-associated gastritis and primary B-cell gastric lymphoma. *Lancet, 338*, 1175–1176.

Wotherspoon, A.C., Doglioni, C., Diss, T.C., Pan, L., Moschini, A., de Boni, M., & Isaacson, P.G. (1993). Regression of primary low-grade B-cell gastric lymphoma of mucosa-associated lymphoid tissue type after eradication of *Helicobacter pylori*. *Lancet, 342*, 575–577.

Wotherspoon, A.C. (1998). *Helicobacter pylori* infection and gastric lymphoma. *British Medical Bulletin, 54*(1), 79–85.

Ye, B.H. (2000). Role of BCL-6 in the pathogenesis of non-Hodgkin's lymphoma. *Cancer Invest, 18*, 356–365.

Yodoi, J., Takatsuki, K., & Masuda, T. (1974). Letter: Two cases of T-cell chronic lymphocytic leukemia in Japan. *N Engl J Med, 290*(10), 572–573.

Yoshida, M., Miyoshi, I., & Hinuma, Y. (1982). Isolation and characterization of retrovirus from cell lines of human adult T-cell leukemia and its implication in the disease. *Proc Natl Acad Sci USA, 79*(6), 2031–2035.

Zahm, S.H., Weisenburger, D.D., Holmes, F.F., Cantor, K.P., & Blair, A. (1997). Tobacco and non-Hodgkin's lymphoma: Combined analysis of three case-control studies (United States). *Cancer Causes Control, 8*, 159–166.

Zheng, T., Mayne, S.T., Boyle, P., Holford, T.R., Liu, W.L., & Flannery, J. (1992). Epidemiology of non-Hodgkin lymphoma in Connecticut. 1935–1988.

Zhu, K., Levine, R.S., Gu, Y., Brann, E.A., Hall, I., Caplan, L.S., & Baum, M.K. (1998). Non-Hodgkin's lymphoma and family history of malignant tumors in a case-control study (United States). *Cancer Causes Control, 9*, 77–82.

28

Epidemiology of Leukemia

INTRODUCTION

Leukemias arise in the bone marrow from cell lineages that form the immune cells that circulate in the blood. The three basic types of immune cells are myelocytes, lymphocytes, and monocytes. Leukemias are therefore broadly categorized as either myelocytic, lymphocytic, or monocytic. A further classification is based on whether disease follows a rapidly fatal course in a matter of weeks if left untreated (acute leukemia) or persists over a period of years (chronic leukemia).

The term *leukemia*, which means *white blood*, was first used by the famous German pathologist Rudolph Virchow, in describing the predominance of circulating white blood cells versus red blood cells that often exists in patients with leukemia. As pointed out by Stanley Robbins and Ramzi Cotran in their classic text, leukemias are best characterized by diffuse replacement of bone marrow by proliferating leukemic cells, abnormal forms of malignant cells circulating in the blood, and infiltrates of leukemic cells in various anatomic sites such as the liver, spleen, lymph nodes, and elsewhere (Robbins and Cotran, 1979).

Standard nomenclature for the leukemias is given in **Table 28.1**. The six basic types are acute and chronic forms of lymphocyte leukemia, myelocytic leukemia, and monocytic leukemia. Each can be further subdivided according to the morphology of the cell of origin and staining characteristics of cells. For example, when cells are routinely stained with hematoxylin and eosin dye, the cells are identifiable as neutrophils (neutral stain), basophils (blue stain), or eosinophils (red stain). Cell types can also be molecularly characterized by the presence of cell membrane receptors. Such receptors are used to differentiate T and B lymphocytic leukemias. Rare forms of leukemia have also been identified such as histiocytic or hairy-cell leukemia (derived from monocytes and macrophages) and erthroleukemia in which the majority of tumor cells are of erythropoietic lineage (Wintrobe, 2004).

Table 28.1	Classification of Leukemias
Type of Leukemia	**Common Characteristics**
Acute Lymphocytic Leukemia (ALL)	Predominant type in children, usually B cell origin; T cell origin is rare
Chronic Lymphocytic Leukemia (CLL)	Predominant type in adults, usually B cell origin; T cell origin is rare
Acute Myelocytic Leukemia (AML)	Occurs in young adults, usually myelocyte (granulocyte) origin
Chronic Myelocytic Leukemia (CML)	Adult leukemia of granulocytes due to translocation (Philadelphia chromosome)
Acute Monocytic Leukemia	Less common adult leukemia of monocyte origin
Chronic Monocytic Leukemia	Rare adult leukemia of monocyte origin

Source: Data from Robbins and Cotran, 1979; Wintrobe MM (2004). Wintrobe's Clinical Hematology. (Editors) Greer et al (11th Edition), Hagerstown, MD, Lippincott Williams and Wilkins. pp. 2465–2466.

HEMATOPOIESIS

Immune cells of the blood are continuously being formed in the bone marrow. They originate from progenitor (stem) cells and undergo tightly regulated differentiation into the various lineages of immune cell populations. It is estimated that more than *one trillion* new cells are produced daily to maintain homeostasis in the peripheral circulation. Hematopoietic stem cells reside in the bone marrow and have the unique ability to differentiate into all of the mature cell types that circulate in the blood (**Figure 28.1**). There are differences of opinion regarding the cell of origin of monocytes, which are not shown in the diagram. The conventional view is that monocytes arise from myeloid precursors; however, some studies suggest that monocytes are derived from stem cells that are distinct from the myeloid lineage. Macrophages (also called phagocytes) develop from circulating monocytes that migrate into tissues of the body (Wintrobe, 2004; Dale, Boser, and Liles, 2008).

Production of red and white blood cells is regulated with extreme precision in the human body. A plethora of growth factors, hormones, and transcription factors are involved in the differentiation and maturation of progenitor cells. For example, erythropoietin secreted by the kidney stimulates the formation of red blood cells and thrombopoietin stimulates the formation of blood platelets.

In children, hematopoiesis occurs in the marrow of the long bones such as the femur and tibia. In adults, it occurs mainly in the pelvis, cranium, vertebrae, and sternum. Differentiation and maturation of progenitor cells begins in the bone marrow and continues throughout the life cycle of immune cells. Cells of the immune system enter the blood and lymphatic systems through an extensive plexus of fenestrated capillaries that anastomose with the bone marrow. Lymphocytes differentiate into T lymphocytes in the thymus whereas the final maturation of B lymphocytes occurs in the lymph nodes.

PATHOGENESIS OF LEUKEMIA

Leukemia refers to immature immune cells in the bone marrow that are undergoing uncontrolled proliferation. Without treatment, the expanding clone of leukemic cells replaces other cell populations in the bone marrow, blood, and lymph. Cytogenetic/genetic analyses of leukemia tissues often reveal the presence of reciprocal chromosomal translocations, chromosomal deletions, and/or DNA point mutations. Reciprocal exchanges of DNA between chromosomes can form hybrid genes that encode chimeric fusion proteins that deregulate critical cellular processes such as mitosis, apoptosis, and angiogenesis. Chromosomal deletions can silence tumor suppressor genes that regulate these

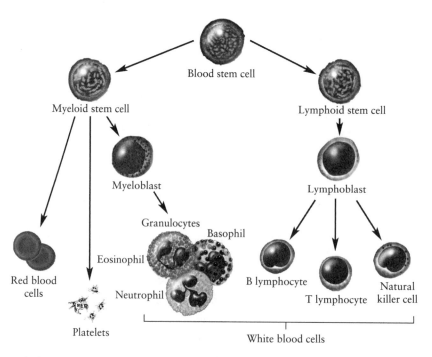

Figure 28.1 Hematopoiesis.

Source: © 2007 Terese Winslow, U.S. Govt. has certain rights.

same processes. Point mutations may also be involved as well as epigenetic modifications in the expression of proto-oncogenes or tumor suppressor genes. Such genetic errors can be acquired at any time during the life span, and some undoubtedly occur during early growth and development, perhaps even "in utero" during embryogenesis. Inherited genetic defects are uncommon. Various models have been proposed suggesting that two or more DNA errors are required to form a leukemic clone of cells. Endogenous hormones may also play a role in leukemogenesis, particularly cortisol, which culls populations of immature immune cells by inducing apoptosis (Wintrobe, 2004).

GLOBAL EPIDEMIOLOGY OF LEUKEMIA

Figure 28.2 shows the global pattern of leukemia mortality in 2004 based upon data collected by the World Health Organization (WHO). The highest annual mortality rates were found in Iraq and Afghanistan, whose populations have been ravaged by war and strife in recent years. High rates are also evident in Turkey and Saudi Arabia. In those populations where mortality is exceptionally high, the available healthcare resources are generally inadequate for effective treatment. Nevertheless, relatively high death rates from leukemia are also evident in the populations of many developed nations including the

United States. According to the latest WHO data, leukemias in children and adults cause more than 257,000 deaths every year, approximately 0.35% of all deaths (WHO, 2008; Ferlay et al., 2010).

The global number of deaths due to leukemia has steadily increased during the last two decades: 184,000 deaths in 1990, 219,000 deaths in 2002, and 257,000 deaths in 2008. However, the global annual *age-adjusted* mortality rates have been relatively stable during this time period averaging approximately 4.3 per 100,000 in men and 3.1 per 100,000 in women. Likewise, the global annual age-adjusted incidence rates have also stabilized at 5.9 per 100,000 in men and 4.3 per 100,000 in women (Parkin, Pisani, and Ferlay, 1999a, 1999b; Parkin et al., 2005; WHO, 2008; Ferlay et al., 2010).

The rising absolute number of leukemia cases and deaths without substantial concomitant changes in the age-adjusted rates is largely due to increasing longevity of the world population. This phenomenon has resulted in more individuals living to later ages when the risk of death from leukemia is highest. **Figure 28.3** shows the age distribution of new cases and deaths based upon data from the United States collected during 2003–2007 (43,050 cases and 21,840 deaths). Leukemia onset shows an early peak during childhood and then rises throughout the life span with more than 70% of deaths occurring after the age of 65 years (Altekruse et al., 2010).

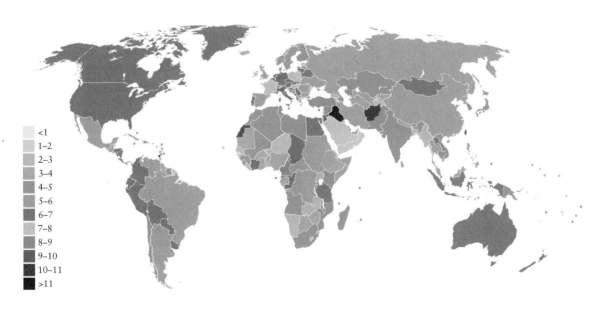

Figure 28.2 Global Leukemia Mortality, 2004.

Source: Data from World Health Organization. The global burden of disease: 2004 update. Geneva, WHO, 2008. Available at www.who.int/evidence/bod.

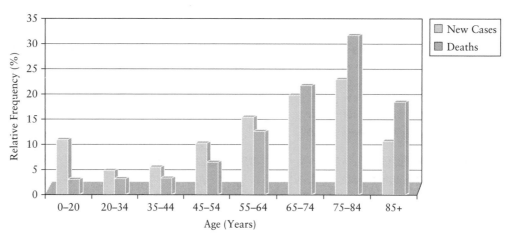

Figure 28.3 Age-Specific Frequencies of New Cases and Deaths: Leukemia.

Source: Data from Altekruse SF, Kosary CL, Krapcho M, Neyman N, Aminou R, Waldron W, Ruhl J, Howlader N, Tatalovich Z, Cho H, Mariotto A, Eisner MP, Lewis DR, Cronin K, Chen HS, Feuer EJ, Stinchcomb DG, Edwards BK (2010). SEER Cancer Statistics Review, 1975–2007, National Cancer Institute. Bethesda, MD, USA.

TRENDS IN LEUKEMIA INCIDENCE AND SURVIVAL

A team of Italian investigators examined trends in the age-standardized annual mortality rates from leukemia based on death certificate data collected by the World Health Organization during 1960–1997. Data were available for the European Union (consisting of 27 member nations) and other developed regions of the world. In the European Union, the peak rates for children up to 14 years of age were observed in 1960–1964, after which mortality decreased more than 70%, reaching a nadir of 1.2 per 100,000 in males and 0.9 per 100,000 in females in 1995–1997. Substantial decreases in mortality were also noted for young and middle-aged adults, ages 15–44 years (40%) and 45–59 years (25%), but not for older age groups. The observed decline in leukemia mortality over the 35-year calendar period corresponds to nearly 250,000 saved lives. Leukemia mortality rates in the United States and Japan started from different values, but trends were similar to those of the European Union in the late 1990s, indicating that the impact of therapeutic advancements has been comparable in developed areas of the world. In Eastern Europe, however, the declines in leukemia mortality occurred later and were appreciably smaller (Levi et al., 2000).

Investigators at the University of Minnesota examined time trends in the annual age-specific incidence rates of different types of leukemia in the United States population during 1973–1998. Their analysis was based upon 66,404 leukemia cases identified by the *Surveillance, Epidemiology and End Results (SEER)* program of the US National Cancer Institute. In analyses by subtype of leukemia, significant increases were observed for acute lymphocytic leukemia in all age groups except individuals over 65 years of age. Among children and adolescents under 20 years of age, the annual incidence rate of acute lymphocytic leukemia increased by 1.1% per year. Notably, 5-year survival improved by about 15% in younger age groups, presumably as a consequence of improved regimens of chemotherapy; however, there was little improvement in survival for older individuals, and survival actually worsened for elderly African Americans (Xie et al., 2003).

PEDIATRIC LEUKEMIA: TRENDS IN INCIDENCE AND MORTALITY

Approximately 11% of all cases of leukemia are diagnosed in children and adolescents under the age of 20 years. The profile of pediatric leukemia is distinctly different from that in adults. *Acute lymphocytic leukemia* accounts for approximately 75% of cases among children and adolescents younger than 15 years of age, and more than 80% of cases for children younger than 10 years of age. In contrast, the relative frequency of acute lymphocytic leukemia declines dramatically with age and other types account for 75% of leukemias diagnosed after the age of 50 years.

Figure 28.4 shows the age-specific annual incidence of childhood leukemia in US children and

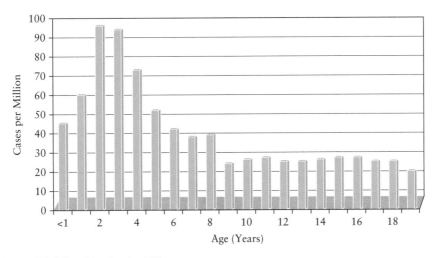

Figure 28.4 Incidence of Childhood Leukemia, USA.

Source: Data from Smith MA, Gloeckler-Ries LA, Gurney JG, Ross JA (1999). Leukemia. Ries LAG, Smith MA, Gurney JG, Linet M, Tamra T, Young JL, Bunin GR (eds). Cancer Incidence and Survival among Children and Adolescents: United States SEER Program 1975–1995, National Cancer Institute, SEER Program. NIH, Pub. No. 99-4649. Bethesda, MD, 1999. pp. 17–34.

adolescents up to 19 years of age. There is a sharp peak for ages 2–3 years (96 cases per million), after which the incidence declines. The incidence of the predominant subtype in children, acute lymphocytic leukemia, also peaks in 2-year-olds at 83 per million (Smith et al., 1999).

In developed nations, the annual death rate from leukemia in children has fallen by more than 50% in the past 3 decades. This favorable downward trend in mortality has occurred even though the incidence of childhood leukemia has *increased* more than 30% over the same time period (Smith et al., 2010). For example, during 1975–1995, the incidence among US children under age 15 years increased steadily

by about 0.9% per year as the mortality rate fell by 2.4% per year (Ries et al., 1998; Ries, 1999; Smith et al., 1999). Similar trends have been noted in Europe; for example, during 1970–1999, the incidence of childhood leukemia increased by an average of 1.4% per year while the overall mortality rate declined by nearly 60% (Shah and Coleman, 2007). Declines in mortality have been noted for boys and girls of all ages. Trends in the incidence rates for US children under 15 years of age are shown for the period 1975–2010 in **Figure 28.5**.

The falling leukemia mortality in children of developed nations reflects a marked increase in survival due to rapid detection coupled with improved

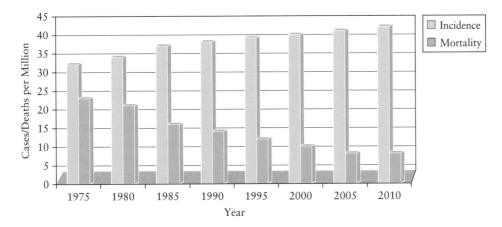

Figure 28.5 Incidence and Mortality Trends in Pediatric Leukemia, USA, 1975–2010.

Source: Data from Ries LAG (1999). Childhood Cancer Mortality. Ries LAG, Smith MA, Gurney JG, Linet M, Tamra T, Young JL, Bunin GR (eds). Cancer Incidence and Survival among Children and Adolescents: United States SEER Program 1975–1995, National Cancer Institute, SEER Program. NIH, Pub. No. 99-4649. Bethesda, MD, 1999. pp. 165–170. Smith MA, Seibel NL, Seibel NL, Altekruse SF, Ries LAG, Melbert DL, O'Leary M, Smith FO, Reaman GH (2010). Outcomes for children and adolescents with cancer: challenges for the twenty-first century. *Journal of Clinical Oncology* 28(15):2625–2634.

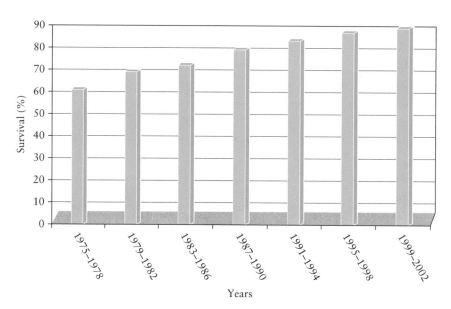

Figure 28.6 Acute Lymphocytic Leukemia: Five-Year Survival in Children, 1975–2002.

Source: Data from Smith MA, Seibel NL, Seibel NL, Altekruse SF, Ries LAG, Melbert DL, O'Leary M, Smith FO, Reaman GH (2010). Outcomes for children and adolescents with cancer: challenges for the twenty-first century. *Journal of Clinical Oncology* 28(15):2625–2634.

therapy. In the United States, 5-year survival for children who developed acute lymphocytic leukemia increased from 61% in 1975–1978 to 89% in 1999–2002 (**Figure 28.6**). As stated by Malcolm Smith and colleagues at the US National Cancer Institute, "*the improvement in survival for children with acute lymphocytic leukemia over the past 35 years is one of the great success stories of clinical oncology*" and reflects the therapeutic benefit of combination chemotherapy, radiation therapy, and bone marrow transplantation (Smith et al., 2010).

Despite the obvious benefit of early detection and effective therapy in some parts of the world, survival remains poor for the children who develop leukemia in less developed nations. For example, 5-year survival for children stricken with leukemia who live in the Philippines is only 33% compared to nearly 90% for afflicted children of the same ethnicity in the United States. Such differences highlight the deficiencies in pediatric cancer care and the need for major improvements in diagnostic and treatment facilities in developing countries (Redaniel et al., 2010).

PEDIATRIC LEUKEMIA: RISK FACTORS

Leukemia is the most common cancer in children and has been intensively investigated using molecular, genetic, clinical, and epidemiologic techniques. Nevertheless, with the exception of ionizing radiation, rare genetic syndromes, and certain chemotherapeutic drugs that are implicated in a small fraction of cases, causal factors for most cases are obscure and the etiology remains enigmatic.

Gender and Ethnic Differences of Childhood Leukemia

Marked gender and ethnic differences have been noted in the incidence rates of pediatric acute lymphocytic leukemia. For children under 15 years of age, boys have about 1.2 times higher risk than girls, and Caucasians have about 2 times higher risk than African Americans. Such differences are not spurious, as they have persisted for several decades (Harris et al., 1987; Smith et al., 1999).

Reasons for these gender and ethnic differences are speculative. The recently proposed *adrenal hypothesis* relates the higher leukemia risk in children of higher socioeconomic classes to their relatively low exposure to infectious viruses and bacteria during the early years of life. Presumably, the risk of acute lymphocytic leukemia is *reduced* when childhood infections during infancy induce the hypothalamic-pituitary-adrenal axis to secrete high levels of plasma cortisol. Corticosteroids are known to regulate the maturation and proliferation of B lymphocytes by stimulating apoptosis, and high levels may eliminate leukemic cells and/ or progenitor B lymphocytes with leukemogenic potential. Furthermore, early infection and heightened cortisol secretion may favor the maturation and proliferation of T lymphocytes that secrete *anti-inflammatory* rather than *proinflammatory* cytokines, thereby reducing the risk of leukemogenesis (Schmiegelow et al., 2008).

Familial Associations of Childhood Leukemia

Some studies have noted an association between childhood leukemia and the presence of autoimmune conditions among relatives. A team of investigators in Paris designed a case-control study to assess the relationship between childhood leukemia and a family history of autoimmune conditions such as type 1 diabetes mellitus, thyroid disease, and rheumatoid arthritis. Family histories of autoimmune disease in first and second degree relatives were ascertained for 279 incident cases of acute leukemia and 285 controls matched by age, gender, and ethnicity. The study revealed a significant association between familial autoimmune disease and the risk of leukemia (OR = 1.7). The relationship was stronger for autoimmune thyroid conditions such as *Grave's disease* or *Hashimoto's thyroiditis* (OR = 3.5) but diminished for other types of thyroid diseases (goiter or adenoma). These results suggest that a family history of autoimmune thyroid disease may be associated with childhood acute leukemia (Perillat-Menegaux et al., 2003).

Investigators at the University of Montreal in Quebec explored genetic polymorphisms of the P-450 enzyme system to determine potential associations of xenobiotic-metabolizing enzymes and the risk of developing childhood leukemia. They compared polymorphisms among 177 children with acute lymphocytic leukemia to 304 controls matched by age and gender. The results revealed increased odds ratios for individuals carrying the null polymorphism of the *Glutathione-S transferase gene* (*GSTM-1*) (OR = 1.8) or the *CYP-1A1-2A* allele (OR = 1.7). Furthermore, the odds of disease was stronger for individuals carrying both genotypes (OR = 3.3). The investigators suggest that these findings have biological plausibility in that the CYP-1A1-2A enzyme activates polycyclic aromatic compounds that are not metabolized for excretion by individuals with the null GSTM-1 genotype (Krajinovic et al., 1999).

Genetic Syndromes and Childhood Leukemia

The risk of developing acute lymphocytic leukemia is increased in subjects with certain rare genetic syndromes and conditions. These include Down syndrome, Bloom syndrome, Shwachman syndrome, ataxia-telangieactasia, neurofibromatosis, and Fanconi anemia.

Down syndrome (*trisomy 21*) markedly increases the risk of developing acute leukemia. The syndrome is named after the British physician John Langdon Down, who first described it in 1866 (Down, 1866). The genetic anomaly identified as an extra 21st chromosome was discovered by the French pediatrician/cytogeneticist Jérôme Lejeune in 1959 (Lejeune, 1959).

Down syndrome is a chromosomal condition caused by the presence of an extra copy of genetic material on the 21st chromosome, either in whole (trisomy 21) or in part (when due to translocations). In addition to its characteristic phenotypic, mental, and cognitive features, Down syndrome carries a high risk for development of leukemia. In particular, the risk of acute lymphoblastic leukemia is elevated at least 10-fold and the risk of acute myelogenous leukemia is increased at least 50-fold in patients with Down syndrome, perhaps due to overexpression of proto-oncogenes on the extra 21st chromosome (Hasle, Clemmensen, and Mikkelsen, 2000).

Bloom syndrome (congenital telangiectatic erythema) is a rare autosomal recessive disorder characterized by telangiectasia (clusters of small cutaneous dilated blood vessels or spider veins), photosensitivity, growth deficiency of prenatal onset, variable degrees of immunodeficiency, and increased susceptibility to various forms of cancer including leukemia. The New York dermatologist David Bloom first described the syndrome in 1954 (Bloom, 1954). Approximately 20% of patients with Bloom syndrome develop specific malignancies (acute leukemia, lymphoma, and/or gastrointestinal adenocarcinoma). Cancer risk in such patients is increased 150–300 times compared to the general population (German, 1993).

Bloom syndrome is caused by a mutation of a tumor suppressor gene designated *BLM* (*short for Bloom*), traced to the long arm of chromosome 15. The protein encoded by the normal gene has DNA helicase activity and functions in the maintenance of genomic stability. Mutant forms of *BLM* increase the exchange of DNA during mitosis (sister chromatid exchange) and chromosomal instability, which are presumably responsible for the characteristic phenotypic abnormalities and cancer predisposition (Cheok et al., 2005).

Shwachman–Bodian-Diamond syndrome is a rare autosomal recessive disorder caused by a mutated gene, *SBDS*, on the long arm of chromosome 7. The *SBDS* gene appears to help regulate RNA metabolism and ribosomal assembly of proteins in the cell. Individuals homozygous for the mutant *SBDS* gene typically manifest exocrine pancreatic dysfunction, skeletal anomalies, anemia, neutropenia, and progressive bone marrow failure that may transform to acute myelogenous leukemia (Bodian, Sheldon, and Lightwood, 1964; Shwachman et al., 1964; Popovic et al., 2002).

Ataxia-telangiectasia is a rare autosomal recessive disorder caused by a mutant gene (called *ATM*) located on the long arm of chromosome 11 that is critical for regulating checkpoints during cell division and repairing errors in DNA replication. This condition is characterized by lack of coordination and cognitive control, immune deficiency, and telangiectasia (clusters of small dilated blood vessels) particularly in the sclera of the eye. Patients who are homozygous recessive for the *ATM* mutation have an approximate risk of 1% per year of developing either leukemia or lymphoma (Canman and Lim, 1998).

Neurofibromatosis type 1 (von Recklinghausen's disease) is a rare autosomal dominant disorder characterized by the development of multiple fibromas (neurofibromas) of the skin, brain, and other anatomic sites. The rare disorder was first described by the German physician Friedrech von Recklinghausen in 1882. The syndrome is due to a mutant autosomal dominant gene called *NF1* located on the long arm of chromosome 17. The mutant gene encodes a protein called neurofibromin that regulates cell division of fibrous nerve sheaths (Boyd, Korf, and Theos, 2009).

In addition to causing neurofibromas, mutant forms of *NF1* also increase the risk of developing leukemia and lymphoma. Stiller and colleagues at Oxford quantified the risk among 58 subjects with neurofibromatosis type 1 based on data ascertained from the National Registry of Childhood Tumors in Great Britain. Over the 17-year study period, 12 cases of acute lymphocytic leukemia (RR = 5.4), 5 cases of non-Hodgkin's lymphoma (RR = 10.0), and 5 cases of myelomonocytic leukemia (RR = 221) were detected among the 58 patients with neurofibromatosis type 1 (Stiller, Chessells, and Fitchett, 1994). These results suggest that the *NF1* gene has pleiotropic impact on the regulation of hematopoiesis.

Fanconi Anemia

Fanconi anemia is a rare autosomal recessive genetic disorder named after the Swiss pediatrician Guido Fanconi, who initially described it (Fanconi, 1927). Fanconi anemia is caused by mutations in any one of 13 different genes that encode proteins involved in the regulation of DNA repair during replication. One of these genes is the well-known breast cancer susceptibility gene, *BRCA-2*. Up to 75% of patients have congenital defects, commonly short stature, and developmental disabilities and abnormalities at various anatomic sites. Approximately 20% of patients develop some form of cancer, the most common of which is *acute myelocytic leukemia*, and 90% suffer myelodysplasia with bone marrow failure by the age

of 40 years. The median age at death for patients with Fanconi anemia is about 40 years (D'Andrea, 2010).

Drugs and Childhood Leukemia

Certain chemotherapeutic agents have been found to heighten the risk of leukemia development in children and adults. For example, the compound *epipodophyllotoxin* (etoposide and teniposide) has been linked to the development of acute myeloid leukemia. This compound interferes with the function of *topoisomerases*, enzymes that unwind and wind DNA for transcription and replication. Investigators at St. Jude Children's Research Hospital in Memphis, Tennessee, examined the effects of epipodophyllotoxin therapy among 734 consecutive children with acute lymphoblastic leukemia who attained completed remission and received continuation (maintenance) treatment according to specific schedules of epipodophyllotoxin administration. After 6 years of follow-up, secondary acute myelocytic leukemia was diagnosed in 21 of the 734 patients, yielding a cumulative risk of 3.8%. Within subgroups receiving higher dosages of epipodophyllotoxin, the cumulative risk increased to more than 12%. In comparative groups not treated with epipodophyllotoxin, the highest cumulative risk was 1.6%. The results indicate that maintenance therapy with epipodophyllotoxin stimulates leukomogenesis of myelocytic cells (Pui et al., 1991).

Radiation and Childhood Leukemia

The *Life Span Study* was initiated in 1950 to monitor the impact of radiation exposure among survivors of the atomic bomb explosions in Japan during World War II. As of the year 2000, 204 leukemia deaths had occurred among 49,204 survivors who received a bone marrow radiation dose of at least 0.005 Gy, constituting an excess of 94 cases (46%) attributable to radiation from the atomic bomb explosions. The dose response pattern in excess number of observed deaths reflects a nonlinear pattern; however, even at low doses in the range of 0.2 to 0.5 Gy, the leukemia risk is elevated (**Figure 28.7**). Risk increases have been noted for acute lymphocytic leukemia in children and acute and chronic myelocytic leukemia in adults, but not other types (Preston et al., 1994, 2004).

A recent population-based study found a marked increase in the rates of leukemia among children in Southern Iraq during the period 1993–2007. Investigators from the University of Basrah in Iraq and the University of Washington in Seattle analyzed leukemia registry data collected at Ibn Ghazwan Hospital in Basrah to evaluate leukemia trends since 1993. Annual

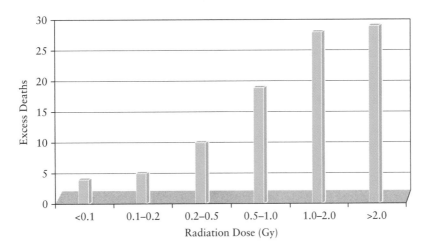

Figure 28.7 Dose Response of Excess Leukemia Deaths and Radiation Exposure among Atomic Bomb Survivors.

Source: Data from Smith MA, Seibel NL, Seibel NL, Altekruse SF, Ries LAG, Melbert DL, O'Leary M, Smith FO, Reaman GH (2010). Outcomes for children and adolescents with cancer: challenges for the twenty-first century. *Journal of Clinical Oncology* 28(15):2625–2634.

leukemia incidence rates were estimated from 698 cases diagnosed in children aged 14 years or younger. The annual incidence (cases per 100,000) increased dramatically during the period of study, from 2.6 in 1993 to 6.9 in 2007, peaking at 12.2 in 2006. Estimates for the final 3 years of the study are more than double the rates in the European Union or the United States (Hagopian et al., 2010). These results have led to speculation that heightened exposure to chemical warfare agents since 2003, in particular benzene and depleted uranium dust, may be responsible for the increased incidence of childhood leukemia, although additional investigations will be needed to definitively establish an etiologic link (Greiser and Hoffman, 2010).

Seasonal Onset of Acute Lymphocytic Leukemia

Acute lymphocytic leukemia is characterized by quick onset with rapid transition from good health to life-threatening disease, particularly in children. Typically, a newfound bleeding diathesis leads to the diagnosis by discovery of lymphoblasts in the peripheral blood and bone marrow. Due to its acute nature, onset of this form of leukemia has been examined for seasonal periodicity by a number of investigators, in the hope of elucidating etiologic factors.

Investigators at the University of Nebraska examined month-of-onset of successive cases of acute lymphocytic leukemia diagnosed during 1971–1980 in the Midwestern United States. They detected significant peaks in early winter and late summer coinciding with peak rates of influenza and hay fever from ragweed pollen, respectively (Harris and Al-Rashid, 1984). Subsequently, these same investigators examined all cases of acute lymphocytic leukemia reported

in the US *Surveillance Epidemiology and End Results* (*SEER*) database during 1973–1980 and found that in 8 of 9 SEER locations, the pattern of onset fit a trimodal pattern with peaks in winter, spring, and summer, coinciding with seasonal elevations in the rates of allergenic and infectious diseases which are capable of promoting lymphocytic proliferation and transformation (Harris et al., 1987).

Investigators in the United Kingdom found a 40% excess of acute lymphocytic leukemia cases diagnosed in summer months compared to winter months based upon analysis of data from the East Anglian Cancer Registry collected during 1971–1994. Seasonal patterns were not evident for other forms of leukemia. The authors suggest the data are most compatible with an infectious etiology of acute lymphocytic leukemia (Badrinath, Day, and Stockton, 1997).

Despite these results, many other investigators have *not* found evidence of seasonality in the onset of acute lymphocytic leukemia. In an attempt to resolve the question, Gao and colleagues conducted an extensive analysis of reported data on 27,000 cases from 11 countries over a wide range of latitudes. Though there was evidence of seasonal peaks and valleys in certain populations, no consistent pattern of seasonality emerged by latitude and the investigators concluded that seasonal influences are not likely to be of major etiologic importance (Gao, Chia, and Machin, 2007).

Cytogenetics of Pediatric Leukemia

Cytogenetic abnormalities are characteristic of pediatric acute lymphocytic leukemia. Karyotypic studies of the chromosomes reveal translocations, inversions, or deletions of chromosomes in the lymphoblasts of approximately 90% of cases. Approximately 40% of karyotypes are pseudodiploid (46 chromosomes with structural or numeric abnormalities), 35–45% are hyperdiploid (47 or more chromosomes), less than 10% are hypodiploid (fewer than 46 chromosomes), and 10–15% are diploid (46 chromosomes without detectable abnormalities) (Pui, Relling, and Downing, 2004).

Reciprocal translocations are the most common structural chromosomal aberrations found in acute lymphocytic leukemia. The first translocation discovered in pediatric acute lymphocytic leukemia was t(9;22), a reciprocal translocation involving juxtaposition of the *BCR* gene on chromosome 9 to the promoter region of the *ABL* gene on chromosome 22. The altered chromosome 22 produced by this translocation is called the *Philadelphia chromosome* since it was discovered by investigators at the University of Pennsylvania and the Fox-Chase Cancer Research Institute in Philadelphia (Nowell and Hungerford, 1960). The resulting hybrid gene, *BCR-ABL*, encodes a chimeric fusion protein that stimulates the intracellular *RAS* signal transduction pathway leading to uncontrolled proliferation of lymphocytes and myelocytes. The Philadelphia chromosome, which is found in about 5% of pediatric acute lymphocytic leukemia cases, is the defining genetic signature of chronic myelocytic (granulocytic) leukemia in adults (Kurzrock et al., 2003).

An exciting development in leukemia research was the discovery of the *TEL-AML1* fusion gene created by the t(12;21) translocation, which is found in approximately 25% of cases of acute lymphocytic leukemia. The *TEL* gene appears to repress transcription of the *AML1* gene thereby inhibiting normal differentiation of B lymphocytes (Golub et al., 1995). In addition to somatic rearrangements of the *TEL* gene, germline *TEL* mutations have also been discovered in pediatric acute lymphocytic leukemia that are associated with a relatively poor prognosis (Rubnitz et al., 1997; Rubnitz et al., 2008).

The t(1;19) translocation is detected in 15–25% of pediatric acute leukemia cases. This translocation fuses the *E2A* gene on chromosome 19 with the *PBX1* gene on chromosome 1, producing a hybrid gene that encodes a chimeric fusion protein, *E2A-PBX1*, that serves as a transcription activator of several other genes (Pui et al., 1994).

The most common *chromosomal deletion* found in pediatric acute lymphocyte leukemia involves loss of a portion of the short arm of chromosome 9. Such deletions are found in about 11% of cases and are associated with poor survival (Heerema et al., 1999).

In 35–45% of young patients with acute lymphocytic leukemia, tumor cells manifest extra chromosomes (*hyperdiploidy*) without apparent structural abnormalities. Chromosome 21 is the most frequently detected "extra" chromosome (*Down syndrome* or *trisomy 21*). In addition, about 5% of patients manifest *hypodiploid* karyotypes characterized by the loss of certain chromosomes. An important finding is that the chromosomal pattern detected in the karyotype of children with leukemia is often an accurate predictor of survival. For example, patients with normal or hyperdiploid karyotypes respond better to treatment and have longer survival than those with translocations, deletions, or hypodiploidy (Bloomfield et al., 1986).

Genome-wide association studies of single nucleotide polymorphisms and targeted genetic polymorphism studies have also identified germline (inherited) mutations associated with the development and progression of pediatric acute lymphocytic leukemia. These include point mutations in the *TEL* gene and the *ARID5B* gene, both of which regulate transcription in embryonic development and during cell growth and differentiation (Rubnitz et al., 2008; Healy et al., 2010).

ADULT LEUKEMIA

The relative incidence of myelocytic leukemia compared to lymphocytic leukemia increases with age and is the prominent form of leukemia in adults. In adults over the age of 50 years, approximately 60% of leukemias arise from myelocytes and 40% from lymphocytes. Leukemias diagnosed in adults (20 years or older) account for nearly 90% of all cases.

The genesis of myelocytic leukemia is similar to lymphocytic leukemia. Progenitor (stem) cells in the bone marrow appear to become *frozen* at a particular stage of differentiation, giving rise to a proliferative clone of leukemic cells (myeloblasts). The expanding clone of leukemic cells interrupts normal hematopoiesis leading to neutropenia, anemia, and thrombocytopenia. Epidemiologic features of the major subtypes of adult leukemias are discussed in the following paragraphs.

Acute Myelocytic Leukemia

Acute myelocytic (myelogenous) leukemia accounts for about 25% of adult leukemias. Several subtypes of this form of leukemia have been defined based upon cellular morphology, the degree of maturation, staining characteristics, and cytogenetic findings. Following an early peak during the first year of life, the incidence of acute myelocytic leukemia remains low until age 40 years, after which it increases exponentially with age. Most cases are diagnosed after age 60 years and the median onset is about 65 years of age (**Figure 28.8**) (Gurney et al., 1995).

Worldwide, acute myelocytic leukemia causes nearly 65,000 deaths per year, approximately 25% of all deaths attributable to leukemia. The incidence is highest in developed countries such as the United States, Australia, and nations in Western Europe. In the United States, nearly 12,000 men and women were diagnosed with acute myelocytic leukemia in 2006 and the average age-adjusted annual incidence during 1975–2003 was 3.4 per 100,000. No significant time trends have been noted in the past few decades (Ries et al., 2003; American Cancer Society, 2005). The higher rates in developed countries partially reflect greater longevity since the elderly are at greatest risk (Figure 28.8).

Acute myeloctyic leukemia shows a clear male predominance. For example, the 2006 age-adjusted rate in US men (4.6 per 100,000) was about 50% higher than in women (3.0 per 100,000). The annual mortality rate was also higher in men (3.5 per 100,000) than women (2.2 per 100,000). Survival dramatically declines with later onset of acute myelocytic leukemia. The 5-year survival for individuals diagnosed before age 50 years is 50% compared to only 5% for individuals diagnosed at 65 years or older (Altekruse et al., 2010).

Risk Factors for Acute Myelocytic Leukemia

Acute myelocytic leukemia is the most common type of all leukemias; yet the known risk factors account for only a small fraction of cases. One relatively common feature of this disease is the presence of cytogenetic abnormalities, which are found in up to 80% of cases. These include translocations, trisomic conditions, and other chromosomal deletions and aberrations.

The most common translocations found in acute myelocytic leukemia are t(8;21) and t(15;17). Both translocations create chimeric fusion proteins that promote leukemogenesis of immature myeloctyes by deregulating nuclear binding factors and gene expression (Lavau and Dejean, 1994; McNeil et al., 1999). Significant advances have been made in the treatment of acute myelocytic leukemia with the introduction of new chemotherapeutic regimens that target specific cytogenetic markers of leukemia subtypes (Bloomfield et al., 1998).

In addition to chromosomal aberrations, some point mutations and epigenetic alterations have also been found in association with leukemia development. In England, Bowen and colleagues examined allelic frequencies of genes encoding carcinogen-metabolizing enzymes of the P-450 enzyme system among 447 cases of acute myelocytic leukemia using polymerase chain reaction technology. They found that a variant form of the *CYP1A1* gene was associated with an increase in risk (OR = 2.36). The investigators suggest that the *CYP1A1-2B* allele may predispose to the development of certain subtypes of acute myelocytic leukemia by catalyzing the formation of carcinogenic polycyclic aromatic hydrocarbons or other reactive compounds (Bowen et al., 2003).

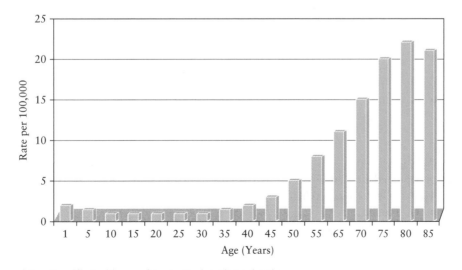

Figure 28.8 Annual Age-Specific Incidence of Acute Myelocytic Leukemia.

Source: Data from Deschler B, Lübbert M (2006). Acute myeloid leukemia: epidemiology and etiology. *Cancer* 107:2099–2107.

Epigenetic silencing of tumor suppressor genes and/or amplification of proto-oncogenes may also contribute to leukemogenesis. For example, hypermethylation of the *p15-INK4B* gene, a negative cell cycle regulator of myelocytes, has been identified in a significant fraction of cases (Christiansen, Andersen, and Pedersen-Bjergaard, 2003).

As with other forms of leukemia, the risk of developing acute myelocytic leukemia is increased by radiation exposure. The most notable example is among survivors of the atomic bomb explosions in Japan who were found to have a 4-fold increase in the risk with a peak 5–7 years after exposure (Preston et al., 1994). Excess rates of acute myelocytic leukemias have also been observed secondary to therapeutic radiation exposure (Kossman and Weiss, 2000).

Excess rates of acute myelocytic leukemia have been observed secondary to intensive chemotherapy for other forms of cancer. For example, alkylating agents such as cyclophosphamide and topoisomerase inhibitors such as **epipodophyllotoxin** have both been reported to significantly increase the risk (Le Beau et al., 1986a, 1986b; Pui et al., 1991). A team of Swedish investigators examined the rate of secondary leukemia in a cohort of 115 patients who received chemotherapy for other malignancies. In patients primarily treated with alkylating agents, the risk increased by approximately 1% per year over 8 years of follow-up, and in those receiving both alkylating agents and topoisomerase inhibitors, the risk increased more than 100-fold. These investigators point out that secondary development of acute myeloctyic leukemia "*has become the most serious long-term complication of cancer therapy*" (Pedersen-Bjergaard et al., 1993).

Certain chemicals have also been implicated as risk factors for acute myelocytic leukemia including benzene, embalming fluids (formalin), ethylene oxides, and herbicides (Savitz and Andrews, 1997; Deschler and Lübbert, 2006). Furthermore, chronic cigarette smoking has been found to increase the risk of certain subtypes of acute myelocytic leukemia (Pogoda et al., 2002).

Myelodysplastic Syndrome (Preleukemia)

It has long been recognized that individuals who develop acute myelocytic leukemia often manifest a prodromal period of anemia, myelocytic dysplasia, and abnormal erythropoiesis (red blood cell production). The first description of *preleukemia* was published in 1953 by Block and colleagues, who characterized the transformation of myelodysplasia to acute myelocytic leukemia among 12 patients (Block, Jacobson, and Bethard, 1953). In 1976, a French-American-British (FAB) team of physicians and researchers defined refractory anemia in combination with myelocytic dysplasia as the *myelodysplastic syndrome*.

It is now recognized that the myelodysplastic syndrome actually consists of a diverse collection of hematological conditions characterized by various degrees of anemia, dysplasia of myeloid cells, neutropenia, and other symptoms. *Myeloid dysplasia* refers to abnormal differentiation and maturation of myeloid progenitor (stem) cells resulting in alterations in their size, shape, organization, and function. Often, myeloid dysplasia is accompanied by excessive proliferation (hyperplasia) of deranged myelocytes.

Myeloid dysplasia is invariably associated with anemia due to ineffectual erythropoiesis and the lack of production of functional red blood cells. Over time, the disease worsens and patients develop refractory anemia, neutropenia, and thrombocytopenia. In about 30% of cases, the condition eventually transforms into acute myelocytic leukemia.

In recent years, cytogenetic, morphological, and clinical data have been reassessed to create more accurate prognostic categories of the myelodysplastic syndrome. In general, patients are classified according to the type and severity of cytopenia, the fraction of myeloblasts in the bone marrow, the appearance of multiple cytogenetic aberrations, and the likelihood of developing acute myelocytic leukemia within one year. In the most severe form, patients have refractory anemia and pancytopenia, 21–30% of cells in the bone marrow are myeloblasts, and the chance of transformation to acute myelocytic leukemia is very high, about 40% per year (Greenberg et al., 1997).

The incidence and prevalence rates of myelodysplastic disease have not been accurately quantified in most populations. This paucity of epidemiologic data reflects the absence of population-based screening and early detection programs, plus inconsistencies in the diagnosis and classification of disease. Nevertheless, small regional studies have provided some initial estimates and suggest that the incidence is increasing, particularly among the elderly. In a study conducted in the population of Düsseldorf in Germany during 1986–1990, the annual incidence for all ages was 3.9 per 100,000 in men and 4.3 per 100,000 in women. The peak rates occurred after 70 years of age, 33.9 per 100,000 in men, and 18.0 per 100,000 in women. Among 1,759 cases, 82% were diagnosed after age 50 years and the median age of onset was 71 years. Studies in other centers found similar patterns of onset as well as increasing numbers of cases, largely reflecting improvements in geriatric disease detection and medical care (Aul, Giagounidis, and Germing, 2001).

Certain cytogenetic abnormalities are regularly found in myeloblasts of patients with the myelodysplastic syndrome. The most common abnormality is deletion of the long arm of chromosome 5 (also called 5q- syndrome), initially discovered in 1974 (Van den Berghe et al., 1974). More recent studies have identified genes encoding colony stimulating factors and receptors (GM-CSF, CSF-1, FMS) and interleukin genes (IL-3, IL-4, IL-5) that regulate hematopoiesis which are lost in the 5q- syndrome (Bunn, 1986; Le Beau et al., 1986a, 1986b; van Leeuwen et al., 1989). A number of cytogenetic findings have been linked to the prognosis of myelodysplastic disease and/or conversion to acute myelocytic leukemia. For example, cases with single abnormalities of the long arm of chromosome 1 experience poor survival, those with trisomy 8 have a high risk of malignant transformation, whereas patients with deletions in the short arm of chromosome 12 show relatively good survival. Clinical studies of cases reveal that cytogenetic features, the proportion of bone marrow myeloblasts, and hemoglobin and blood platelet levels are the main prognostic factors of survival and transformation to acute leukemia (Solé et al., 2000).

The risk factors for myeloid dysplasia are synonymous with those for acute myelocytic leukemia: exposure to ionizing radiation, benzene-containing compounds, alkylating agents and topoisomerase inhibitors used in cancer therapy, and immunosuppressive drugs used in organ transplantation (Aul, Giagounidis, and Germing, 2001).

Chronic Myelocytic (Granulocytic) Leukemia

Chronic myelocytic (granulocytic) leukemia is defined by the presence of the Philadelphia chromosome, which is caused by a reciprocal translocation involving juxtaposition of the BCR gene on chromosome 9 to the promoter region of the ABL gene on chromosome 22, designated t(9;22). The resulting hybrid gene, BCR-ABL, encodes a chimeric fusion protein that stimulates the intracellular RAS signal transduction pathway leading to uncontrolled proliferation of myelocytes and other immune cells (Kurzrock et al., 2003). The Philadelphia chromosome was introduced earlier in the section of this chapter on pediatric leukemia since it was first discovered in cells of a pediatric leukemia by investigators in Philadelphia (Nowell and Hungerford, 1960).

Chronic myelocytic leukemia is characterized by increased proliferation of granulocytes of all types in the bone marrow. Basophils and eosinophils are virtually always increased. Presence of the Philadelphia chromosome identified by cytogenetic or genetic analysis of tumor cells validates the diagnosis (Savage et al., 1997). This form of leukemia may persist in a chronic phase for many years, but eventually terminates in a blast crisis with widespread metastatic spread of myeloblasts and lymphoblasts and short survival (Kantarjian et al., 1988).

Chronic myeloctyic leukemia is most commonly diagnosed in middle-aged and older adults and accounts for approximately 15–20% of adult leukemias. The only definitive risk factor for this form of leukemia is ionizing radiation. Among survivors of the atomic bomb blasts in Japan who have been followed for more than half a century, the cumulative incidence of chronic myelocytic leukemia is about sevenfold higher than the general population (Preston et al., 1994).

Radiotherapy has also been linked to the development of chronic myelocytic leukemia. Preston-Martin and colleagues conducted a case-control study of radiation exposure in 136 cases diagnosed in Los Angeles hospitals during 1979–1985 and 136 neighborhood controls. Odds ratios (OR) were estimated by the cumulative level of bone marrow exposure to radiotherapy. Results revealed a dose response in the risk with increasing radiation dose maximizing at OR = 2.4 for the highest cumulative dose (at least 2,000 mrads) (Preston-Martin et al., 1989).

Chronic Lymphocytic Leukemia

Chronic lymphocytic leukemia is typified by excess proliferation of small but well differentiated (mature) lymphocytes in the bone marrow and peripheral blood. In most cases, the vast majority (98%) of malignant lymphocytes are B cells. Leukemic cells are, on average, smaller but otherwise morphologically similar to normal lymphocytes. Furthermore, the cells from most patients have membrane receptors, antigens, and immunoglobulins that are characteristic of mature B lymphocytes. However, they are functionally deficient and incapable of mounting an immune response. Hence, patients with chronic lymphocytic leukemia are predisposed to a variety of infectious conditions.

Chronic lymphocytic leukemia is a disease of older adults with nearly 90% of cases diagnosed after the age of 55 years. The condition often takes years to progress and patients are usually monitored for clinical and hematologic changes before initiation of treatment. Albeit, transformation of the chronic form to an acute blast crisis carries a high risk of death.

In the United States population, approximately 15,000 new cases were diagnosed in 2010 and more than 4,000 deaths were attributed to chronic lymphocytic leukemia. Annual incidence rates per 100,000 were higher in men than women (5.7 vs. 3.0) and were highest in Caucasians (6.1 in men and 3.2 in women) and lowest in Asian and Pacific Islanders (1.3 in men and 0.7 in women). Annual death rates were also highest in Caucasians (2.1 in men and 1.0 in women) and lowest in Asian and Pacific Islanders (0.4 in men and 0.1 in women). Five-year survival approaches 80% for Caucasians but is less than 70% for African Americans (Altekruse et al., 2010).

Certain populations in Europe have been found to have high incidence and prevalence rates of chronic lymphocytic leukemia. For example, relatively high rates have been reported for Ashkenazi Jews in Israel compared to other ethnic groups (Bartal et al., 1978). The relative importance of genetic and environmental factors is currently being explored in comparative studies of different ethnic groups. However, in a recent investigation of 302 cases of B-cell chronic lymphocytic leukemia, ethnicity *per se* had no discernable effects on the biological and clinical behavior of the disease (Shvidel et al., 1998).

Chronic Lymphocytic Leukemia: Risk Factors

Familial history is one of the strongest risk factors for the development of chronic lymphocytic leukemia. Studies of monozygous and dizygous twins, siblings, and pedigrees with multiple generations have established that close relatives of probands (index cases) are at high risk. For example, in a Swedish study of 14,336 first degree relatives of 5,918 probands with chronic lymphocytic leukemia and 28,876 first degree relatives of 11,778 control subjects, first degree relatives of the probands were found to have a 7.5-fold increase in the risk of also developing chronic lymphocytic leukemia (Goldin et al., 2004). Genome-wide association studies and linkage studies are currently being conducted to elucidate the genes responsible for the increase in familial risk of chronic lymphocytic leukemia (Goldin and Caporaso, 2007).

Chromosomal abnormalities are well documented in chronic lymphocytic leukemia. The most common of these is an interstitial deletion of the long arm of chromosome 13 which has been found in approximately 50% of cases. Other common cytogenetic findings include specific deletions of the long arm of chromosome 11 (20%), trisomy 12 (15%), specific deletions of the long arm of chromosome 6 (10%), and specific deletions of the short arm of chromosome 17 (5%) (Stilgenbauer, Dohner, and Lichter, 1993). Such nonrandom chromosomal deletions and aberrations may confer selective advantage

to B lymphocytes by inactivation of tumor suppressor genes, or conversely, by amplifying the expression of proto-oncogenes.

Point mutations and epigenetic changes that alter gene expression without changing the nucleotide sequence may also be involved in the genesis of chronic lymphocytic leukemia. For example, hypermethylation and epigenetic silencing of the *death associated protein kinase (DAPK1)* gene, which regulates apoptosis, has been noted in a large kindred affected with chronic lymphocytic leukemia (Plass et al., 2007).

Despite compelling evidence that ionizing radiation causes most forms of leukemia, including *acute lymphocytic leukemia*, most studies of *chronic lymphocytic leukemia* have not detected risk increases with radiation exposure. These results have led some expert committees to conclude that ionizing radiation is not a significant risk factor for chronic lymphocytic leukemia (UNSCEAR, 2000). However, it has also been pointed out that methodological difficulties such as lack of statistical power and limited duration of follow-up have hampered efforts to detect an association (Richardson et al., 2005).

Data are limited on the association of specific chemical exposures and the development of chronic lymphocytic leukemia. Though some individual studies suggest risk increases associated with certain occupational exposures (agrichemicals, petroleum, rubber), there is little consistency of results from study to study (Linet et al., 2007).

Agent Orange has been linked to the genesis of several lymphoproliferative disorders, including chronic lymphocytic leukemia. The compound was widely used during the Vietnam War as a defoliant. It is a 50:50 mixture of two phenoxyl herbicides, 2,4-dichlorophenoxyacetic acid (2,4-D) and 2,4,5-trichlorophenoxyacetic acid (2,4,5-T). Agent Orange was manufactured by US chemical companies and given its name because it was shipped to Vietnam in orange-striped 55 gallon barrels. The 2,4,5-T used to produce Agent Orange was later discovered to be contaminated with 2,3,7,8-tetrachlorodibenzodioxin, an extremely toxic dioxin compound.

Investigators at The Ohio State University examined computerized patient treatment files collected by the Veteran's Administration Hospital system to estimate incidence rates of various malignancies among the 3.7 million US veterans treated in VA hospitals during 1970–1982. During this period, 31,835 hematopoeitic and lymphatic cancers were diagnosed in the VA user sample. Compared to the general US population, the VA sample showed risk increases in lymphocytic leukemia (RR = 1.54), granulocytic leukemia (RR = 1.23), and monocytic leukemia (RR = 1.51). Risk increases were also noted for Hodgkin's disease (RR = 1.93), non-Hodgkin's lymphoma (RR = 1.20), and multiple myeloma (RR = 1.51). Notably, the risk of developing either leukemia or lymphatic cancer was approximately 70% higher among Vietnam-era veterans than other veterans in the sample (Namboodiri and Harris, 1991).

In 2002, the United States Institute of Medicine issued an update in a series of consensus reports examining the impact of chemical defoliants, including Agent Orange, on human health. The combined evidence was found sufficient to support an association between exposure to herbicides sprayed during the Vietnam War and the risk of developing chronic lymphocytic leukemia in veterans who served in Vietnam. Other Institute of Medicine consensus reports document significant associations between herbicide exposure and the development of Hodgkin's lymphoma or non-Hodgkin's lymphoma in Vietnam War veterans (Institute of Medicine, 2003).

Chronic Lymphocytic Leukemia: Survival

A devastating event in patients with chronic lymphocytic leukemia is the abrupt conversion of a chronic, relatively indolent disease into an acute decompensated accelerated phase with a marked increase in lymphoblasts in both the bone marrow and the peripheral circulation. As with other forms of leukemia, the blast crisis of chronic leukemia is associated with short survival, often just a few weeks. As described in the next few paragraphs, certain genetic and cytogenetic markers have been found to predict accelerated progression of chronic lymphocytic leukemia and transition into a blast crisis.

Though it seems paradoxical, a *less favorable* clinical course of chronic lymphocytic leukemia is *inversely* correlated with the presence of somatic mutations in the gene that encodes the heavy-chain variable region of immunoglobulins. Patients with the *non-mutated immunoglobulin gene* have a more aggressive course and shorter survival than patients with mutated genes (Van Bockstaile, Verhasselt, and Philippe, 2009).

Recent molecular investigations have identified an important protein, ZAP-70, that also has prognostic significance in chronic lymphocytic leukemia. The ZAP-70 protein is a tyrosine kinase encoded by a gene located on the long arm of chromosome 2. It is an integral component in cell signaling by T lymphocytes; however, the gene can also be expressed in B lymphocytes. Notably, patients who are *positive* for ZAP-70 progress about twice as rapidly as patients who are

negative (Orchard et al., 2006). Gene expression profiles and clinical studies show that ZAP-70 positivity is highly correlated with the nonmutated immunoglobulin subtype, suggesting that both biomarkers influence adverse survival by the same biological mechanism (Klein et al., 2001; Rosenwald et al., 2001).

In general, the appearance of multiple chromosomal aberrations in leukemic cells, e.g., chromosomal deletions and trisomy, has been found to herald poor prognosis and an impending blast crisis in patients with chronic lymphocytic leukemia. Nevertheless, there is a lack of consistency of results from different centers, and additional investigations are needed to clarify the prognostic value of genetic and cytogenetic biomarkers.

Hairy Cell Leukemia

Hairy cell leukemia is an uncommon hematological malignancy characterized by the accumulation of abnormal B lymphocytes in the bone marrow and peripheral circulation. Hairy cell leukemia is rare with an annual incidence of 3 cases per million in US men and 0.6 cases per million in women. It is usually classified as a sub-type of chronic lymphoid leukemia. Fewer than 2,000 new cases are diagnosed annually in North America and Western Europe combined. Hairy cell leukemia was first identified and pathologically characterized by Bertha Bouroncle and colleagues at Ohio State University in 1958 (Bouroncle, Wiseman, and Doan, 1958; Wintrobe, 2004).

Due to the rare nature of this form of leukemia, only limited data are available regarding its genesis. Nevertheless, at least 12 cases of familial hairy cell leukemia have been published and afflicted relatives have been found to have certain HLA haplotypes in common (Gramatovici et al., 1993). The role of the HLA locus in the genesis of hairy cell leukemia is as yet undetermined (Villemagne et al., 2005; Cannon et al., 2008).

In 2003, the Institute of Medicine announced there was sufficient evidence in the published literature to support an association between exposure to herbicides (such as Agent Orange) and the development of chronic B-cell leukemia, including hairy cell leukemia (Institute of Medicine, 2003).

Monocytic Leukemia

Monocytic leukemia arises from the monocytic lineage of immune cells. Monocytes are produced in the bone marrow from hematopoietic stem cell precursors called monoblasts. Monocytes circulate in the bloodstream for one to three days and then migrate into tissues throughout the body. In the tissues, monocytes mature into different types of *macrophages* at different anatomical locations. The diagnosis of *acute monocytic leukemia* is confirmed when more than 20% of immune cells of the bone marrow are myeloblasts (Wintrobe, 2004; Dale, Boser, and Liles, 2008).

As in other forms of leukemia, there is an increased risk of monocytic leukemia in subjects with rare genetic disorders that impact cell division, DNA repair, apoptosis, and angiogenesis. These include Down syndrome, Fanconi anemia, Bloom syndrome, ataxia-teleangieactasia, and neurofibromatosis. Environmental risk factors for monocytic leukemia are similar to those for myelocytic leukemia and include exposure to ionizing radiation, pesticides and herbicides, alkylating agents, and topoisomerase inhibitors.

Most cases of monocytic leukemia are diagnosed in adults, usually after the age of 50 years. The disease usually presents as an acute leukemia and may develop after exposure to ionizing radiation, herbicides and pesticides, or certain chemotherapeutic agents, particularly epipodophyllotoxins and anthracyclines (Wintrobe, 2004). *Chronic monocytic leukemia* is extraordinarily rare and only a small number of cases have been reported in the literature (Bearman et al., 1981).

Monocytic leukemia is characterized by specific chromosomal abnormalities. The most common of these involve deletions of portions of the long arm of chromosome 11 or a reciprocal translocation, t(9:11), involving chromosomes 9 and 11. These genetic rearrangements involve the *MLL* locus that encodes a methyltransferase involved in regulation of transcription (Dewald et al., 1983; Guenther et al., 2005). A second translocation, t(8;16), found in some monocytic leukemia cases creates a transfusion protein that promotes leukemogenesis of immature monocytes and myeloctyes by deregulating nuclear binding factors and gene expression (Borrow et al., 1996). In addition, mutations and duplications have been observed in the *Flt3* tumor suppressor gene in approximately 40% of cases (Lui et al., 2007).

Monocytic leukemia does occasionally occur in children who are most often less than 2 years of age. The incidence in US children under the age of 15 years ranges from 4.8–6.6 cases per million. However, in children with Down syndrome (trisomy 21), the relative risk of monocytic leukemia is increased 150-fold for ages 1–4 years (Hasle, Clemmensen, and Mikkelsen, 2000).

● ● ● **REFERENCES**

Altekruse, S.F., Kosary, C.L., Krapcho, M., Neyman, N., Aminou, R., Waldron, W.,… Edwards, B.K. (2010). SEER Cancer Statistics Review, 1975–2007, Bethesda, MD: National Cancer Institute., USA.

American Cancer Society. (2005). *Cancer facts and figures, 2005*. Atlanta, GA: American Cancer Society.

Aul, C., Giagounidis, A., & Germing, U. (2001). Epidemiological features of myelodysplastic syndromes: Results from regional cancer surveys and hospital-based statistics. *Int J Hematol, 73*(4), 405–410.

Badrinath, P., Day, N.E., & Stockton, D. (1997). Seasonality in the diagnosis of acute lymphocytic leukaemia. *Br J Cancer, 75*(11), 1711–1773.

Bartal, A., Bentwich, Z., Manny, N., & Izak, G. (1978). Ethnical and clinical aspects of chronic lymphocytic leukemia in Israel. *Acta Hematol, 60*, 161–171.

Bearman, R.M., Kjeldsberg, C.R., Pangalis, G.A., & Rappaport, H. (1981). Chronic monocytic leukemia in adults. *Cancer, 48*, 2239–2255.

Block, M., Jacobson, L.O., & Bethard, W.F. (1953). Preleukemic acute human leukemia. *JAMA, 152*, 1018–1028.

Bloom, D. (1954). Congenital telangiectatic erythema resembling lupus erythematosus in dwarfs; probably a syndrome entity. *AMA Am J Dis Child, 88*(6), 754–758.

Bloomfield, C.D., Goldman, A.I., Alimena, G., Berger, R., Borgstrom, G.H., Brandt, L.,…Garson, O.M. (1986). Chromosomal abnormalities identify high-risk and low-risk patients with acute lymphoblastic leukemia. *Blood, 67*(2), 415–420.

Bloomfield, C.D., Lawrence, D., Byrd, J.C., Carroll, A., Pettenati, M.J., Tantravahi, R.,…Mayer, R.J. (1998). Frequency of prolonged remission duration after high-dose cytarabine intensification in acute myeloid leukemia varies by cytogenetic subtype. *Cancer Res, 58*(18), 4173–4179.

Bodian, M., Sheldon, W., & Lightwood, R. (1964). Congenital hypoplasia of the exocrine pancreas. *Acta Paediatr, 53*, 282–293.

Borrow, J., Stanton, V.P. Jr., Andresen, J.M., Becher, R., Behm, F.G., Chaganti, R.S.K.,…Housman, D.E. (1996). The translocation t(8;16)(p11;p13) of acute myeloid leukaemia fuses a putative acetyltransferase to the CREB–binding protein. *Nature Genetics, 14*, 33–41.

Bouroncle, B.A., Wiseman, B.K., & Doan, C.A. (1958). Leukemic reticuloendotheliosis. *Blood, 13*, 609–630.

Bowen, D.T., Frew, M.E., Rollinson, S., Roddam, P.L., Dring, A., Smith, M.T.,…Morgan, G.J. (2003). CYP1A1*2B (Val) allele is overrepresented in a subgroup of acute myeloid leukemia patients with poor-risk karyotype associated with NRAS mutation, but not associated with FLT3 internal tandem duplication. *Blood, 101*, 2770–2774.

Boyd, K.P., Korf, B.R., & Theos, A. (2009). Neurofibromatosis type 1. *J Am Acad Dermatol, 61*(1), 1–14.

Bunn, H.F. (1986). 5q- and disordered haematopoiesis. *Clin Haematol, 15*(4), 1023–1035.

Canman, C.E., & Lim, D.S. (1998). The role of ATM in DNA damage responses and cancer. *Oncogene, 17*(25), 3301–3308.

Cannon, T., Mobarek, D., Wegge, J., & Tabbara, I.A. (2008). Hairy cell leukemia: Current concepts. *Cancer Invest, 26*(8), 860–865.

Cheok, C.F., Bachrati, C.Z., Chan, K.L., Ralf, C., Wu, L., & Hickson, I.D. (2005). Roles of the Bloom's syndrome helicase in the maintenance of genome stability. *Biochem Soc Trans, 33*, 1456–1459.

Christiansen, D.H., Andersen, M.K., & Pedersen-Bjergaard, J. (2003). Methylation of p15INK4B is common, is associated with deletion of genes on chromosome arm 7q and predicts a poor prognosis in therapy-related myelodysplasia and acute myeloid leukemia. *Leukemia, 17*(9), 1813–1819.

D'Andrea, A.D. (2010). Susceptibility pathways in Fanconi's anemia and breast cancer. *N Engl J Med, 362*(20), 1909–1919.

Dale, D.C., Boser, L., & Liles, W.C. (2008). The phagocytes: Neutrophils and monocytes. *Blood, 112*(4), 935–945.

Deschler, B., & Lübbert, M. (2006). Acute myeloid leukemia: Epidemiology and etiology. *Cancer, 107*, 2099–2107.

Dewald, G.W., Morrison-DeLap, S.J., Schuchard, K.A., Spurbeck, J.L., & Pierre, R.V. (1983). A possible specific chromosome marker for monocytic leukemia: Three more patients with t(9;11)(p22;q24) and another with t(11;17)(q24;q21), each with acute monoblastic leukemia. *Cancer Genetics and Cytogenetics, 8*(3), 203–212.

Down, J.L.H. (1866). Observations on an ethnic classification of idiots. *Clinical Lecture Reports, London Hospital, 3*, 259–262.

Fanconi, G. (1927). Familiäre, infantile perniciosähnliche Anämie (perniziöses Blutbild und Konstitution). *Jahrbuch für Kinderheilkunde und physische Erziehung, Wien, 117*, 257–280.

Ferlay, J., Shin, H.R., Forman, D., Mathers, C., & Parkin, D.M. (2010). Esimates of worldwide burden of cancer in 2008. *International Journal of Cancer, 127*(12), 2893–2917.

Gao, F., Chia, K.S., & Machin, D. (2007). On the evidence for seasonal variation in the onset of acute lymphoblastic leukemia (ALL). *Leukemia Research, 31*(10), 1327–1338.

German, J. (1993). Bloom syndrome: A mendelian prototype of somatic mutational disease. *Medicine (Baltimore), 72*(6), 393–406.

Goldin, L., Pfeiffer, R.M., Li, X., & Hemminki, K. (2004). Familial risk of lymphoproliferative tumors in families of patients with chronic lymphocytic leukemia: Results from the Swedish Family-Cancer Database. *Blood, 104*, 1850–1854.

Goldin, L.R., & Caporaso, N.E. (2007). Family studies in chronic lymphocytic leukaemia and other lymphoproliferative tumours. *British Journal of Haematology, 139*(5), 774–779.

Golub, T.R., Barker, G.F., Bohlander, S.K., Hiebert, S.W., Ward, D.C., Bray-Ward, P.,...Gilliland, D.G. (1995). Fusion of the TEL gene on 12p13 to the AML1 gene on 21q22 in acute lymphoblastic leukemia. *Proc Natl Acad Sci USA*, 92(11), 4917–4921.

Gramatovici, M., Bennett, J.M., Hiscock, J.G., & Grewal, K.D. (1993). Three cases of familial hairy cell leukemia. *American Journal of Hematology*, 42(4), 337–339.

Greenberg, P., Cox, C., LeBeau, M.M., Fenaux, P., Morel, P., Sanz, G.,...Bennett, J. (1997). International scoring system for evaluating prognosis in myelodysplastic syndromes. *Blood*, 89(6), 2079–2088.

Greiser, E., & Hoffman, W. (2010). Questionable increase of childhood leukemia in Basrah, Iraq. *Am J Public Health*, 100(9), 1556–1557.

Guenther, M.G., Jenner, R.G., Chevalier, B., Nakamura, T., Croce, C.M., Canaani, E., & Young, R.A. (2005). Global and Hox-specific roles for the MLL1 methyltransferase. *Proc Natl Acad Sci USA*, 102(24), 8603–8608.

Gurney, J.G., Severson, R.K., Davis, S., & Robison, L.L. (1995). Incidence of cancer in children in the United States. Sex-, race-, and 1-year age-specific rates by histologic type. *Cancer*, 75, 2186–2195.

Hagopian, A., Lafta, R., Hassan, J., Davis, S., Mirick, D., & Takaro, T. (2010). Trends in childhood leukemia in Basrah, Iraq, 1993–2007. *Am J Public Health*, 100(6), 1081–1087.

Harris, R.E., & Al-Rashid, R.A. (1984). Seasonal variation in the incidence of childhood acute lymphocytic leukemia in Nebraska. *Nebr Med J*, 69, 192–198.

Harris, R.E., Harrell, F.E. Jr., Patil, K.D., & Al-Rashid, R. (1987). The seasonal risk of pediatric/juvenile acute lymphocytic leukemia in the USA. *J Chronic Dis*, 40, 915–924.

Hasle, H., Clemmensen, I.H., & Mikkelsen, M. (2000). Risks of leukaemia and solid tumours in individuals with Down's syndrome. *Lancet*, 355(9199), 165–169.

Healy, J., Richer, C., Bourgey, M., Kritikou, E.A., & Sinnett, D. (2010). Replication analysis confirms the association of *ARID5B* with childhood B-cell acute lymphoblastic leukemia. *Haematologica*, 95(9), 1608–1611.

Heerema, N.A., Sather, H.N., Sensel, M.G., Liu-Mares, W., Lange, B.J., Bostrom, B.C.,...Uckun, F.M. (1999). Association of chromosome arm 9p abnormalities with adverse risk in childhood acute lymphoblastic leukemia: A report from the Children's Cancer Group. *Blood*, 94(5), 1537–1544.

Institute of Medicine. (2003). *Veterans and Agent Orange: Update 2002*. Washington, DC: Institute of Medicine of the National Academies, United States National Academy of Science.

Kantarjian, H., Dixon, D., Keating, M., Talpaz, M., Walters, R., McCredie, K., & Freireich, E. (1988). Characteristics of accelerated disease in chronic myelogenous leukemia. *Cancer*, 61(7), 1441–1446.

Klein, U., Tu, Y., Stolovitzky, G.A., Mattioli, M., Cattoretti, G., Husson, H.,...Dalla-Favera, R. (2001). Gene expression profiling of B cell chronic lymphocytic leukemia reveals a homogeneous phenotype related to memory B cells. *Journal of Experimental Medicine*, 194, 1625–1638.

Kossman, S.E., & Weiss, M.A. (2000). Acute myelogenous leukemia after exposure to strontium-89 for the treatment of adenocarcinoma of the prostate. *Cancer*, 88, 620–624.

Krajinovic, M., Labuda, D., Richer, C., Karimi, S., & Sinnett, D. (1999). Susceptibility to childhood acute lymphoblastic leukemia: Influence of CYP1A1, CYP2D6, GSTM1, and GSTT1 genetic polymorphisms. *Blood*, 93(5), 1496–1501.

Kurzrock, R., Kantarjian, H.M., Druker, B.J., & Talpaz, M. (2003). Philadelphia chromosome-positive leukemias: From basic mechanisms to molecular therapeutics. *Ann Intern Med*, 138(10), 819–830.

Lavau, C., & Dejean, A. (1994). The t(15;17) translocation in acute promyelocytic leukemia. *Leukemia*, 8(10), 1615–1621.

Le Beau, M.M., Pettenati, M.J., Lemons, R.S., Diaz, M.O., Westbrook, C.A, Larson, R.A.,...Rowley, J.D. (1986a). Assignment of the GM-CSF, CSF-1, and FMS genes to human chromosome 5 provides evidence for linkage of a family of genes regulating hematopoiesis and for their involvement in the deletion (5q) in myeloid disorders. *Cold Spring Harb Symp Quant Biol*, *51*(Pt 2), 899–909.

Le Beau, M.M., Albain, K.S., Larson, R.A., Vardiman, J.W., Davis, E.M., Blough, R.R.,...Rowley, J.D. (1986b). Clinical and cytogenetic correlations in 63 patients with therapy-related myelodysplastic syndromes and acute nonlymphocytic leukemia: Further evidence for characteristic abnormalities of chromosomes no. 5 and 7. *J Clin Oncol*, *4*, 325–345.

Lejeune, J. (1959). Le mongolisme. Premier example d'aberration autosomique humaine. *Ann Genet*, *1*, 41–49.

Levi, F., Lucchini, F., Negri, E., Barbui, T., & La Vecchia, C. (2000). Trends in mortality from leukemia in subsequent age groups. *Leukemia*, *14*(11), 1980–1985.

Linet, M.S., Schubauer-Berigan, M.K., Weisenburger, D.D., Richardson, D.B., Landgren, O., Blair, A.,...Dores, G.M. (2007). Chronic lymphocytic leukaemia: An overview of aetiology in light of recent developments in classification and pathogenesis. *Br J Haematol*, *139*(5), 672–686.

Liu, H., Yu, H., Jia, H.Y., Zhang, W., & Guo, C.J. (2007). Detection of FLT3 gene mutation in hematologic malignancies and its clinical significance. *Zhongguo Shi Yan Xue Ye Xue Za Zhi*, *15*(4), 709–713.

McNeil, S., Zeng, C., Harrington, K.D., Hiebert, S., Lian, J.B., Stein, J.L.,...Stein, G.S. (1999). The t(8;21) chromosomal translocation in acute myelogenous leukemia modifies intranuclear targeting of the AML1/CBFa2 transcription factor. *PNAS*, *96*(26), 14882–14887.

Namboodiri, K.K., & Harris, R.E. (1991). Hematopoietic and lymphoproliferative cancer among male veterans using the Veterans Administration Medical System. *Cancer*, *68*(5), 1123–1130.

Nowell, P., & Hungerford, D. (1960). A minute chromosome in chronic granulocytic leukemia. *Science*, *132*, 1497.

Orchard, J., Ibbotson, R., Best, G., Parker, A., & Oscier, D. (2006). ZAP-70 in B cell malignancies. *Leuk Lymphoma*, *46*(12), 1689–1698.

Parkin, D.M., Pisani, P., & Ferlay, J. (1999a). Estimates of the worldwide incidence of 25 major cancers in 1990. *Int J Cancer*, *80*(6), 827–841.

Parkin, D.M., Pisani, P., & Ferlay, J. (1999b). Global cancer statistics. *CA Cancer J Clin*, *49*(1), 33–64.

Parkin, D.M., Bray, F., Ferlay, J., & Pisani, P. (2005). Global cancer statistics, 2002. *CA Cancer J Clin*, *55*, 74–108.

Pedersen-Bjergaard, J., Philip, P., Larsen, S.O., Andersson, M., Daugaard, G., Ersbøll, J.,...Osterlind, K. (1993). Therapy-related myelodysplasia and acute myeloid leukemia. Cytogenetic characteristics of 115 consecutive cases and risk in seven cohorts of patients treated intensively for malignant diseases in the Copenhagen series. *Leukemia*, *7*(12), 1975–1986.

Perillat-Menegaux, P., Clave, J., Auclerc, M.F., Baruchel, A., Leverger, G., Nelken, B.,...Hémon, D. (2003). Family history of autoimmune thyroid disease and childhood acute leukemia. *Cancer Epidemiol Biomarkers Prev*, *12*(1), 60–63.

Plass, C., Byrd, J.C., Raval, A., Tanner, S.M., & De La Chapelle, A. (2007). Molecular profiling of chronic lymphocytic leukaemia: Genetics meets epigenetics to identify predisposing genes. *British Journal of Haematology*, *139*, 744–752.

Pogoda, J.M., Preston-Martin, S., Nichols, P.W., & Ross, R.K. (2002). Smoking and risk of acute myeloid leukemia: Results from a Los Angeles County case-control study. *Am J Epidemiol*, *155*, 546–553.

Popovic, M., Goobie, S., Morrison, J., Ellis, L., Ehtesham, N., Richards, N.,...Rommens, J.M. (2002). Fine mapping of the locus for Shwachman–Diamond syndrome at 7q11, identification of shared disease haplotypes, and exclusion of TPST1 as a candidate gene. *Eur J Hum Genet*, *10*(4), 250–258.

Preston, D.L., Kusumi, S., Tomonaga, M., Izumi, S., Ron, E., Kuramoto, A., Kamada, N.,… Mabuchi, K. (1994). Cancer incidence in atomic bomb survivors. Part III. Leukemia, lymphoma and multiple myeloma, 1950–1987. *Radiat Res*, *137*(2 Suppl), S68–S97.

Preston, D.L., Pierce, D.A., Shimizu, Y., Cullings, H.M., Fujita, S., Funamoto, S., & Kodama, K. (2004). Effect of recent atomic bomb survivor dosimetry changes on cancer mortality risk estimates. *Radiation Research, 162*, 377–389.

Preston-Martin, S., Thomas, D.C., Yu, M.C., & Henderson, B.E. (1989). Diagnostic radiography as a risk factor for chronic myeloid and monocytic leukaemia (CML). *Br J Cancer, 59*(4), 639–644.

Pui, C.H., Ribeiro, R.C., Hancock, M.L., Rivera, G.K., Evans, W.E., Raimondi, S.C.,…Crist, W.M. (1991). Acute myeloid leukemia in children treated with epipodophyllotoxins for acute lymphoblastic leukemia. *N Engl J Med, 325*, 1682–1687.

Pui, C.H., Raimondi, S.C., Hancock, M.L., Rivera, G.K., Ribeiro, R.C., Mahmoud, H.H.,…Behm, F.G. (1994). Immunologic, cytogenetic, and clinical characterization of childhood acute lymphoblastic leukemia with the t(1;19) (q23; p13) or its derivative. *Clin Oncol, 12*(12), 2601–2606.

Pui, C.H., Relling, M.V., & Downing, J.R. (2004). Acute lymphoblastic leukemia. *N Engl J Med, 350*, 1535–1548.

Redaniel, M.T., Laudico, A., Miraol-Lumague, M.R., Alcasabas, A.P., Pulte, D., & Brenner, H. (2010). Geographic and ethnic differences in childhood leukaemia and lymphoma survival: Comparisons of Philippine residents, Asian Americans and Caucasians in the United States. *British Journal of Cancer, 103*, 149–154.

Richardson, D.B., Wing, S., Schroeder, J., Schmitz-Feuerhake, I., & Hoffmann, W. (2005). Ionizing radiation and chronic lymphocytic leukemia. *Environmental Health Perspectives, 113*, 1–5.

Ries, L.A.G., Kosary, C.L., Hankey, B.F., Miller, B.A., Clegg, L., & Edwards, B.K. (Eds.). (1998). *SEER cancer statistics review 1973–1996*. National Cancer Institute.

Ries, L.A.G. (1999). Childhood cancer mortality. In L.A.G. Ries, M.A. Smith, J.G. Gurney, M. Linet, T. Tamra, J.L. Young, & G.R. Bunin (Eds.). *Cancer incidence and survival among children and adolescents: United States SEER program 1975–1995* (pp. 165–170). Bethesda, MD: National Cancer Institute, SEER Program. NIH, Pub. No. 99-4649.

Ries, L.A.G., Kosary, C.L., Hankey, B.F., Miller, B.A., Clegg, L., & Edwards, B.K. (Eds.). (2003). *SEER cancer statistics review, 1975–2000*. Bethesda, MD: National Cancer Institute.

Robbins, S.L., & Cotran, R.S. (1979). *Pathologic basis of disease* (2nd Edition). Philadelphia: W.B. Saunders Company.

Rosenwald, A., Alizadeh, A.A., Widhopf, G., Simon, R., Davis, R.E., Yu, X.,…Staudt, L.M. (2001). Relation of gene expression phenotype to immunoglobulin mutation genotype in B cell chronic lymphocytic leukemia. *Journal of Experimental Medicine, 194*, 1639–1647.

Rubnitz, J.E., Downing, J.R., Pui, C.H., Shurtleff, S.A., Raimondi, S.C., Evans, W.E.,…Behm, F.G. (1997). TEL gene rearrangement in acute lymphoblastic leukemia: A new genetic marker with prognostic significance. *J Clin Oncol, 15*(3), 1150–1157.

Rubnitz, J.E., Wichlan, D., Devidas, M., Shuster, J., Linda, S.B., Kurtzberg, J.,…Children's Oncology Group. (2008). Prospective analysis of TEL gene rearrangements in childhood acute lymphoblastic leukemia: A Children's Oncology Group study. *J Clin Oncol, 26*(13), 2186–2191.

Savage, D.G., Szydlo, R.M., & Goldman, J.M. (1997). Clinical features at diagnosis in 430 patients with chronic myeloid leukaemia seen at a referral centre over a 16-year period. *Br J Haematol, 96*(1), 111–116.

Savitz, D.A., & Andrews, K.W. (1997). Review of epidemiologic evidence on benzene and lymphatic and hematopoietic cancers. *Am J Ind Med, 31*, 287–295.

Schmiegelow, K., Vestergaard, T., Nielsen, S.M., & Hjalgrim, H. (2008). Etiology of common childhood acute lymphoblastic leukemia: The adrenal hypothesis. *Leukemia, 22*, 2137–2141.

Shah, A., & Coleman, M.P. (2007). Increasing incidence of childhood leukaemia: A controversy re-examined. *Br J Cancer, 97*(7), 1009–1012.

Shvidel, L., Shtarlid, M., Klepfish, A., Sigler, E., & Berrebi, A. (1998). Epidemiology and ethnic aspects of B cell chronic lymphocytic leukemia in Israel. *Leukemia, 12,* 1612–1617.

Shwachman, H., Diamond, L.K., Oski, F.A., & Khaw, K.T. (1964). The syndrome of pancreatic insufficiency and bone marrow dysfunction. *J Pediatr, 65,* 645–663.

Smith, M.A., Gloeckler-Ries, L.A., Gurney, J.G., & Ross, J.A. (1999). Leukemia. In L.A.G. Ries, M.A. Smith, J.G. Gurney, M. Linet, T. Tamra, J.L. Young, G.R. Bunin (Eds). *Cancer incidence and survival among children and adolescents: United States SEER program 1975–1995* (pp. 17–34). Bethesda, MD: National Cancer Institute, SEER Program. NIH, Pub. No. 99-4649.

Smith, M.A., Seibel, N.L., Seibel, N.L., Altekruse, S.F., Ries, L.A.G., Melbert, D.L.,… Reaman, G.H. (2010). Outcomes for children and adolescents with cancer: Challenges for the twenty-first century. *Journal of Clinical Oncology, 28*(15), 2625–2634.

Solé, F., Espinet, B., Sanz, G.F., Cervera, J., Calasanz, M.J., Luño, E.,…Woessner, S. (2000). Incidence, characterization and prognostic significance of chromosomal abnormalities in 640 patients with primary myelodysplastic syndromes. *British Journal of Haematology, 108,* 346–356.

Stilgenbauer, S., Dohner, H., & Lichter, P. (1993). Genomic aberrations in B-cell chronic lymphocytic leukemia, Chap 16. In B. Cheson (Ed.), *Chronic lymphocytie leukemia, CLL* (2nd ed., pp. 353–376). New York: Marcel Dekker.

Stiller, C.A., Chessells, J.M., & Fitchett, M. (1994). Neurofibromatosis and childhood leukaemia/ lymphoma: A population-based UKCCSG study. *Br J Cancer, 70*(5), 969–972.

UNSCEAR. (2000). United Nations Scientific Committee on the Effects of Atomic Radiation. Sources and effects of ionizing radiation. Annex I. Epidemiological evaluation of radiation-induced cancer (pp. 297–431). New York, NY: UNSCEAR.

Van Bockstaele, F., Verhasselt, B., & Philippe, J. (2009). Prognostic markers in chronic lymphocytic leukemia: A comprehensive review. *Blood Rev, 23*(1), 25–47.

Van den Berghe, H., Cassiman, J.J., David, G., Fryns, J.P., Michaux, J.L., & Sokal, G. (1974). Distinct haematological disorder with deletion of long arm of no. 5 chromosome. *Nature, 251*(5474), 437–438.

van Leeuwen, B.H., Martinson, M.E., Webb, G.C., & Young, I.G. (1989). Molecular organization of the cytokine gene cluster, involving the human IL-3, IL-4, IL-5, and GM-CSF genes, on human chromosome 5. *Blood, 73,* 1142–1148.

Villemagne, B., Bay, J.O., Tournilhac, O., Chaleteix, C., & Travade, P. (2005). Two new cases of familial hairy cell leukemia associated with HLA haplotypes A2, B7, Bw4, Bw6. *Leukemia Lymph, 46*(2), 243–245.

Wintrobe, M.M. (2004). *Wintrobe's clinical hematology* (11th ed.) J.G. Greer, J. Foerster, J.N. Lukens, G.M. Rodgers, F. Paraskevas (Eds.). (pp. 2465–2466). Hagerstown, MD: Lippincott Williams and Wilkins.

World Health Organization. (2008). *World cancer report.* Geneva: WHO.

Xie, Y., Davies, S.M., Xiang, Y., Robison, L.L., & Ross, J.A. (2003). Trends in leukemia incidence and survival in the United States (1973–1998). *Cancer, 97*(9), 2229–2235.

29

Epidemiology of Brain Tumors with Special Reference to Gliomas

GLOBAL EPIDEMIOLOGY OF BRAIN TUMORS

Based upon sequential reports from the World Health Organization, the incidence and mortality of malignant tumors of the brain and nervous system are rising. Since 1990, reported new cases and deaths have increased more than 80% in both men and women (**Figure 29.1**). Corresponding to the increasing numbers of cases and deaths, the annual age-standardized incidence and mortality rates have both increased approximately 30% in the past two decades. These increases are due in large part to the widespread use of advanced neuroimaging (computerized tomography and magnetic resonance imaging) and other diagnostic techniques (stereotactic biopsy) resulting in earlier and more accurate detection of brain tumors (Parkin, Pisani, and Ferlay, 1999a,

1999b; Parkin et al., 2002; GLOBOCAN, 2002; Parkin et al., 2005; Ferlay et al., 2010).

Global annual incidence rates are higher in men than women (3.9 versus 3.0 per 100,000), and higher in developed countries (5.8 per 100,000 in men and 4.1 per 100,000 in women) than developing countries (3.0 per 100,000 in men and 2.1 per 100,000 in women) (Ferlay et al., 2010; Bondy et al., 2008). Schwartzbaum and colleagues reported a fourfold difference in the incidence of primary malignant brain tumors between countries with a high incidence, e.g., Canada, Australia, New Zealand, Denmark, Finland, and the United States, and countries with a low incidence, such as India and the Philippines. Such differences are difficult to interpret since diagnostic practices, access to and quality of care, and completeness of reporting differ

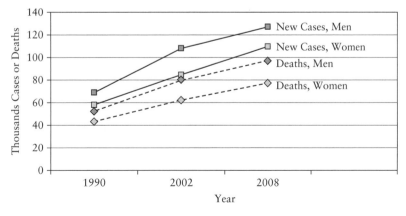

Figure 29.1 Global Trends in Malignant Tumors of the Brain and Nervous System.

Source: Data from Parkin DM, Pisani P, Ferlay J (1999). Global Cancer Statistics, 1990. *CA Cancer J Clin* 49(1):33–64. Parkin DM, Bray F, Ferlay J, Pisani, P (2005). Global Cancer Statistics, 2002. *CA Cancer J Clin* 55:74–108. Ferlay J, Shin H-R, Forman D, Mathers C, Parkin DM (2010). Estimates of worldwide burden of cancer in 2008. *International Journal of Cancer* 127(12):2893–2917.

widely worldwide. (Schwartzbaum et al., 2006; Fisher et al., 2007).

BRAIN TUMORS IN THE UNITED STATES

Based upon recent data from the *Surveillance Epidemiology and End Results (SEER)* program of the US National Cancer Institute and the *Central Brain Tumor Registry of the United States (CBTRUS)*, approximately 22,000 new cases of primary malignant brain tumors are diagnosed every year in the US population and more than 13,000 deaths are attributed to such tumors. During the past two decades, the age-adjusted annual incidence rate in the US population declined slightly from 7.0 cases per 100,000 in 1990 to 6.5 cases per 100,000 during 2003–2007 (CBTRUS, 2008; Horner et al., 2009; Altekruse et al., 2010).

Annual incidence and mortality rates are higher for US men (7.6 and 5.6 per 100,000) than women (5.5 and 3.5 per 100,000). However, survival differs dramatically by histology and age. For example, patients with aggressive malignant gliomas such as *glioblastoma multiforme* have very poor survival (only about 3% survive 5 years) whereas patients with low-grade gliomas have 5-year survival rates exceeding 70%. A disturbing fact is that brain cancer is the leading cause of cancer mortality in people under the age of 35 years (Bondy et al., 2008).

As shown in **Figure 29.2**, the relative frequencies of newly diagnosed cases of malignant brain tumors and attributable deaths both show early peaks during adolescence. A disturbing fact is that brain cancer is the leading cause of cancer mortality among people under the age of 35 years. As discussed in a separate section of this chapter, the histological profile of pediatric brain tumors differs markedly from that in adults. Following the early peak, incidence and mortality accelerate rapidly with age among adults (CBTRUS, 2008; Horner et al., 2009; Altekruse et al., 2010).

CLASSIFICATION OF BRAIN TUMORS

As pointed out by Stanley Robbins and Ramzi Cotran in their classic textbook of pathology, "*the term brain tumor should be restricted only to neoplasms arising from any of the constituent cells within brain substance, neuroglial cells, neurons, cells of the blood vessels and connective tissues*" (Robbins and Cotran, 1979). It is also important to note that metastatic tumors from other primary anatomic sites account for 25–30% of all intracranial tumors.

The classification of primary brain tumors is based upon the cell of origin. Tumors arising from glial cells (neuroglia) are called gliomas, those arising from neurons are called neuromas or neuroblastomas, and tumors arising from meningeal cells are called meningiomas. The most common types of primary brain tumors that develop in adults are gliomas, meningiomas, pituitary gland tumors, acoustic neuromas, and lymphomas (**Table 29.1**). These 5 cell types constitute approximately 90% of all primary brain tumors, with gliomas and meningiomas accounting for approximately two-thirds of all tumors that arise in the brain.

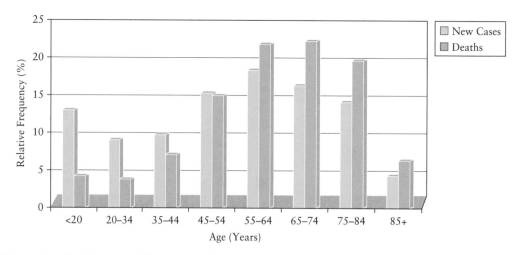

Figure 29.2 Age-Specific Frequency of New Cases and Deaths: Malignant Tumors of the Brain and Nervous System.

Source: Data from Altekruse SF, Kosary CL, Krapcho M, Neyman N, Aminou R, Waldron W, Ruhl J, Howlader N, Tatalovich Z, Cho H, Mariotto A, Eisner MP, Lewis DR, Cronin K, Chen HS, Feuer EJ, Stinchcomb DG, Edwards BK (2010). SEER Cancer Statistics Review, 1975–2007, National Cancer Institute. Bethesda, MD, USA.

Gliomas account for more than one-third of primary brain tumors in adults. Gliomas develop from neuroepithelial cells. There are several types of gliomas. One type, the *astrocytoma*, arises from star-shaped cells called astrocytes and can grow anywhere in the brain or spinal cord. In adults, astrocytomas most often arise in the cerebrum, the largest part of the brain that fills most of the upper skull. *Glioblastoma multiforme* is an especially aggressive form of astrocytoma. Gliomas are diagnosed about twice as frequently in men compared to women.

Meningiomas also account for more than one-third of adult brain tumors. Meningiomas develop from the meninges, the protective membrane covering the brain directly underneath the skull. *These tumors are usually benign and grow very slowly.* Indeed, meningiomas *rarely* metastasize to other tissues, and symptoms such as headache, visual impairment, and focal seizures are due to compression of surrounding tissues by the expanding tumor in the confined intracranial vault. In contrast to gliomas, which predominate in men, meningiomas are diagnosed about twice as frequently in women compared to men. As discussed in the section on risk factors, gliomas and meningiomas have distinctly different sets of risk factors.

Schwannomas are *benign* tumors that develop from *Schwann cells* in the peripheral nervous system. Schwann cells are named after the German physiologist, Theodor Schwann, who first described them in 1838 (Aszmann, 2000). These cells produce the *myelin* that covers and protects the peripheral or cranial nerve fibers connected with the brain. Acoustic neuromas are a type of schwannoma that arise from the Schwann cells that wrap around the acoustic nerve between the brain and the ear. Acoustic neuromas account for most of the brain tumors that arise in and around the cranial nerves.

Tumors arising from tissues and structures within the bony compartment called the *sella turcica* in the center of the brain are called *sellar tumors*. Sellar tumors usually develop from the pituitary gland. Less common types of primary brain tumors include primary lymphomas that develop from collections of lymphocytes within the brain, vascular tumors, germ cell tumors, sarcomas, and tumors of the pineal gland.

CELL OF ORIGIN OF GLIOMA

Glioma is a cancer that arises from the glial cells (glia) of the brain. These cells were first described by the famous German pathologist Rudolph Virchow, who named them *nervenkitt* (nerve glue) or *glia*

Table 29-1	Profile of Brain Tumors	
Classification of Primary Brain Tumors		**Relative Frequency (%)**
Neuroepithelial Tumors (Glioma)		33
Meningeal Tumors (Meningioma)		34
Sellar Tumors (Pituitary Gland)		12
Nerve Tumors (Acoustic Neuroma)		9
Embryonal Tumors (Medulloblastoma)		1
Lymphomas		3
Other or Unclassified		9
Total		100

Source: Data From: Centralized Brain Tumor Registry of the United States (CBTRUS), 2004–2006. Total sample size = 158,088 tumors.

(Virchow, 1846, 1854). Glial cells outnumber neurons by about 9:1, but most are unable to generate action potentials or communicate by electrical signaling. Glia are crudely divisible by size into macroglia and microglia.

Macroglia are further categorized as astrocytes and oligodendrocytes. Astrocytes nurture and support neurons, and their tentacle-like processes encircle and envelop the synapses between nerve cells, supplying energy and oxygen necessary for the transmission of nerve impulses. Astrocytes also modulate the neuronal influx and efflux of important ions such as calcium, sodium, potassium, and chloride, and serve as a conduit for waste disposal. As such, they are often juxtaposed between cerebral blood vessels and neurons, and they provide biochemical support to endothelial cells of the blood-brain barrier (**Figure 29.3**).

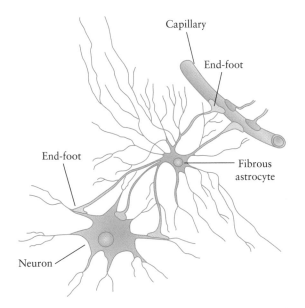

Figure 29.3 Astrocyte of the Brain.

Oligodendrocytes are macroglia that produce and secrete myelin, the insulatory material of neurons. A single oligodendrocyte can extend its tentacle-like processes to scores of axons, wrapping a sheath of myelin around each axon.

Small glial cells (microglia) protect the brain against invading microbes through immunosurveillance and innate immune reactions, and they assist in wound healing following traumatic injury to neurons. Microglia develop from hematopoietic stem cells rather than the neuroepithelium (Kimelberg, Jalonen, and Walz, 1993; Purves et al., 2008; Pollard and Earnshaw, 2008).

Glia were once believed to be relatively passive cells whose only purpose was to support the function of neurons. Nevertheless, in recent years, certain macroglia (particularly astrocytes) have been found to act in a partnering role with neurons in the processes of signal transduction and neurotransmission. Specifically, astrocytes are now known to play a very active role in modulating signal propagation and synaptic action by controlling the uptake of neurotransmitters at or near the synaptic cleft, and some are even capable of secreting neurotransmitters. For example, astrocytes are activated by elevated levels of calcium ions and have been found to secrete the neurotransmitter, glutamate, as partners in the neuronal response to excitation (Araque et al., 1999; Santello and Volterra, 2008).

Since cancer involves uncontrolled cell division, it is important to realize that glia *do* retain the ability to undergo cell division in adulthood, whereas neurons do not. Following injury due to trauma or stroke, there is often profound proliferation of glial cells (gliosis) at or near the site of injury.

Types of Gliomas

Glioma tumors are further classified by glial cell type into astrocytomas, glioblastoma multiforme, oligodendrogliomas, ependymomas, and mixed gliomas. *Glioblastoma multiforme* is the most common and most aggressive type of glioma. Patients diagnosed with glioblastoma have a median survival time of less than one year. Approximately 50–60% of gliomas are classified as glioblastoma. These tumors develop from cells of the cerebral white matter and tend to grow rapidly and become very large before producing symptoms that lead to diagnosis. The cell of origin of glioblastoma multiforme has long been the subject of controversy and debate. The current view is that glioblastoma arises from pluripotent neural progenitor (stem) cells in the subventricular zone of the mature brain (Quigley, Post, and Ehrlich, 2007).

Astrocytomas account for 20–30% of all gliomas. These tumors arise from astrocytes or their precursor cells. As their name implies, astrocytes are star-shaped cells that perform multiple functions including support of endothelial cells of the blood-brain barrier, provision of nutrients and energy to neurons and maintenance of their ionic balance, and repair of nerve tissues following traumatic injury. The cytoplasm of astrocytes is densely populated with mitochondria and other organelles. These cells are highly branched and their cellular processes envelope the synapses of nerve cells to facilitate transport of glucose for energy and ions (principally calcium) to stimulate neurotransmission. Furthermore, astrocytes have recently been found capable of communicating with neurons by calcium-modulated release of the neurotransmitter, glutamate (Santello and Volterra, 2008).

Ependymomas account for about 6% of all gliomas. They arise from the layer of neuroepithelial cells that line both the hollow cavities of the brain and the canal containing the spinal cord. Within the brain, ependymomas most often arise from the floor of the fourth ventricle, situated in the lower back portion of the brain.

Oligodendrogliomas account for less than 5% of all gliomas. They arise from the oligodendrocytes, glial cells that are primarily responsible for laying down myelin around axons of neurons.

Microglia are the predominant immune cells of the brain that normally function in a protective role against foreign microbes and agents. Paradoxically, these cells are often abundant in and around developing gliomas, particularly astrocytomas, and they may release growth-promoting factors that actually accelerate tumor development and progression (Graeber, Scheithauer, and Kreutzberg, 2002).

Risk Factors for Glioma

Gliomas account for about 75% of all *malignant* brain tumors that develop in adults (this figure excludes meningiomas which are invariably benign). Only a few risk factors for glioma have been identified and corroborated through independent investigation. Established risk factors include exposure to high-dose ionizing radiation, chronic immunosuppression, and certain rare genetic syndromes. Studies of other factors including nonionizing radiation from cellular telephones, viral and microbial agents, household chemicals, nutritional factors, and certain environmental toxins have thus far yielded equivocal results (Schwartzbaum et al., 2006; Fisher et al., 2007).

Gender Difference in Gliomas

Gliomas are detected about 1.5 times more often in men than in women, and reciprocally, meningiomas develop about 1.5 times more often in women. These gender differences may reflect the influence of hormones. To clarify associations of reproductive factors and glioma risk in women, Whelan and colleagues conducted a case control study of 371 female glioma cases ascertained from hospitals and clinics in four Midwestern states and 527 controls randomly selected from licensed drivers and Health Care Finance Administration enrollees. All cases were confirmed by pathology. Compared with women who never breast fed, women who breast fed for 18 months or more were at increased risk (OR = 1.8), and women who used estrogen replacement therapy had a decreased glioma risk compared to nonusers (OR = 0.7). These results suggest that estrogens may provide a modest degree of protection against the development of malignant gliomas (Huang et al., 2004).

Radiation Exposure and Brain Tumors

There is consistent evidence from a number of prospective epidemiologic investigations showing that *high exposure* to ionizing radiation increases the risk of developing glioma and other tumors of the brain. Sources of radiation include therapeutic and diagnostic medical procedures, occupational exposures as in uranium mining and radiology, atmospheric testing of nuclear weapons, natural sources, industrial accidents, and atomic bomb explosions.

In a study of mortality among US physicians over a 50-year period, Matanoski and colleagues found two to threefold increases in brain cancer mortality among cohorts of radiologists from the 1920s and 1930s compared to cohorts of other physicians (Matanoski et al., 1975). Subsequent studies have also noted increases in the incidence of brain tumors among physicians and radiologists (Andersen et al., 1999; Yoshinaga et al., 2004).

A team of investigators characterized the incidence of brain tumors among atomic bomb survivors in Hiroshima and Nagasaki as a function of radiation dose. Tumors diagnosed between 1958 and 1995 among 80,160 atomic bomb survivors were ascertained using the Hiroshima and Nagasaki tumor registries, medical records, and death certificates. Malignant neoplasms were confirmed by pathology. Results revealed a significant dose response in risk with increasing radiation exposure (each additional sievert of radiation increased the risk by 20%). The investigators concluded that even moderate doses of radiation (< 1 sievert) increase the risk of developing nervous system tumors (United Nations, 2000; Preston et al., 2002).

A number of epidemiologic studies provide strong evidence that childhood exposure to ionizing radiation for the treatment of benign diseases increases the risk of developing a brain tumor later in life. In a study conducted in New York City, a cohort of 2,224 children given X-ray treatment and a matched cohort of 1,380 given topical medications for ringworm of the scalp (*tinea capitis*) during 1940–1959 were followed over nearly 4 decades to determine the comparative incidence of brain tumors. The average dose of ionizing radiation administered was 1.4 Gy. Sixteen intracranial tumors were detected in the irradiated cohort (7 brain cancers, 4 meningiomas, and 5 acoustic neuromas) compared to 1 acoustic neuroma in the control cohort. The standardized incidence ratio for brain cancer was 3.0 and the irradiated children also had excess incidence rates of other tumors including basal cell carcinomas of the skin and tumors of the thyroid and parotid glands (Shore, Albert, and Pasternack, 1976; Shore et al., 2003).

In Israel, a team of investigators studied the relationship between radiotherapy in childhood for *tinea capitis* and the development of tumors of the brain and nervous system. A total of 10,834 children received ionizing radiation between 1948 and 1960 and were followed for 30 years or more. Sixty neural tumors developed in the cohort of irradiated children, a rate of 1.8 per 10,000 person-years of follow-up. Compared with a matched population control group of 10,834 nonirradiated subjects and a second control group of 5,392 nonirradiated siblings of the irradiated children, the cumulative risk of neural tumors was increased more than eightfold (RR = 8.4) (**Figure 29.4**). Risk increases were noted for meningiomas (RR = 9.5), gliomas (RR = 2.6), and nerve sheath tumors (RR = 18.8). The investigators found significant risk increases at exposure levels of 1–2 Gy and they were also able to demonstrate a significant dose response in the risk with increasing exposure to ionizing radiation (Ron et al., 1988). In a subsequent investigation of these same cohorts after a median follow-up of 40 years, similar risk increases and dose responses were observed, prompting the investigators to conclude *"that brain and meninges tissues are highly sensitive to radiation carcinogenesis"* (Sadetzki et al., 2005).

Investigators in Sweden examined the risk of brain tumors in 2 cohorts containing a total of 28,008 children who received ionizing radiation therapy for *hemangioma* (a benign tumor of blood vessels). The average dose of radiation was low (7 cGY) but there was wide variation in exposure

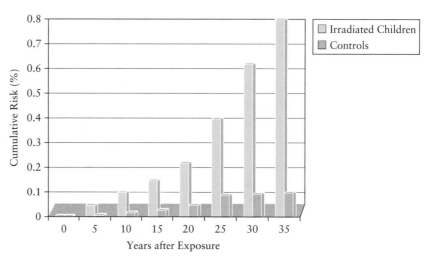

Figure 29.4 Cumulative Risk of Neural Tumors after Radiation for Tinea Capitis.

Source: Data from Ron E, Modan B, Boice JD Jr, Alfandary E, Stovall M, Chetrit A, Katz L (1988). Tumors of the brain and nervous system after radiotherapy in childhood. *N Engl J Med* 319(16):1033–1039.

(up to 11.5 Gy). These cohorts were followed using the Swedish Cancer Register for detection of intracranial tumors during the period 1958–1993. For both cohorts, a total of 86 individuals developed brain tumors compared to 61 expected, yielding a standardized incidence ratio of 1.42. The excess relative risk increased by 2.7 per unit (Gy) of radiation exposure suggesting a cause and effect dose-response relationship between the absorbed dose of ionizing radiation and brain tumor development. The findings also suggested that the risk was higher with exposure to ionizing radiation during infancy (Karlsson et al., 1998).

The development of a new primary neoplasm has long been recognized as a possible late effect of curative therapy involving ionizing radiation in combination with chemotherapy for an original childhood cancer. The *Childhood Cancer Survivor Study* (CCSS) is a large, retrospective cohort study of long-term survivors of childhood cancer. Participants were ascertained from 26 centers in the United States or Canada. To quantify the relative impact of radiation, chemotherapy, and other factors, Neglia and colleagues conducted a nested case control study of secondary primary neoplasms of the brain and nervous system in the CCSS cohort of 14,361 5-year survivors of childhood cancers (leukemia or primary brain tumors). Each patient with a second primary was matched to four control subjects who had not developed a second primary by age, gender, and time since the original cancer diagnosis. Detailed information on the dose of ionizing radiation and the types and dosages of chemotherapeutic

agents were ascertained from the medical records and conditional logistic regression was used to estimate odds ratios. A total of 40 gliomas and 66 meningiomas were detected in the cohort. The median interval from the original diagnosis to detection was shorter for gliomas (9 years) than meningiomas (17 years). Radiation exposure was associated with increased risk of glioma (OR = 6.78) and meningioma (OR = 9.94) and there was a significant dose response in risk with increasing dosage of ionizing radiation. After adjustment for radiation dose, chemotherapeutic agents were *not* found to be associated with the risk of developing a subsequent primary brain tumor. The investigators concluded that exposure to radiation therapy is the most important risk factor for the development of a new primary brain tumor. They also noted that irradiation during infancy carries the highest risk for the development of a subsequent glioma (Neglia et al., 2006).

Mobile Phones and Brain Tumors

Due to the increasing use of mobile phones (more than 4.3 billion users worldwide in 2009), several expert groups have expressed concerns about the health and safety of low-level exposure to radio frequency electromagnetic fields (GSM, 2009). As a consequence, an international case control study, INTERPHONE, was launched to investigate possible associations between mobile phone use and the development of brain tumors. The study included interviews with 2,708 cases of glioma, 2,409 cases of meningioma, and matched controls ascertained from

13 countries. The results actually showed that regular mobile phone use was associated with a *decrease* in the odds ratios for both glioma (OR = 0.81) and meningioma (OR = 0.79). Odds ratios were less than 1.0 for all deciles of lifetime number of phone calls and nine deciles of cumulative call time. However, in the 10th decile of *recalled* cumulative call time (51,640 hours), the OR was significantly increased for glioma (OR = 1.40) but not for meningioma (OR = 1.15). However, the investigators state that *"there were implausible values of reported use in this group."* While they could not rule out an effect at the highest exposure level, biases and error prevented a causal interpretation (INTERPHONE, 2010).

Several investigators have analyzed subsets of the INTERPHONE database. For example, investigators in Sweden examined detailed information on mobile phone use among 371 cases of glioma and 273 cases of meningioma compared to 574 control subjects matched by age, gender, and residential area. For regular mobile phone use, the odds ratios were reduced for both glioma (OR = 0.8) and meningioma (OR = 0.7) and no increases in risk were observed for any type or anatomic location of brain tumor after more than 10 years of exposure. The authors concluded that *"the data do not support the hypothesis that mobile phone use is related to an increased risk of glioma or meningioma"* (Lönn et al., 2005).

Other investigators examined the use of mobile phones and the risk of *acoustic neuromas* because of proximity of the ipsilateral acoustic nerve to the handset. In a case control study conducted in 4 Nordic countries and the United Kingdom, 678 cases of acoustic neuroma were compared to 3,553 controls. In the pooled dataset, there was no overall association between regular mobile phone use and the risk of acoustic neuroma (OR = 0.9); furthermore, subgroup analyses by duration of use, lifetime cumulative hours of exposure, total number of calls made, and type of mobile phone failed to reveal significant associations. Interestingly, the risk of acoustic neuroma development on the *same* side of the head as reported phone use was increased with use for 10 years or more (OR = 1.8); but reciprocally, the risk to the *opposite* side decreased by a corresponding amount, making interpretation difficult (Schoemaker et al., 2005).

It is important to note that case control studies are prone to differential reporting bias whereby the cases (with disease) may report differently than the controls (without disease). Thus, in case control studies of self-reported environmental exposures that are perceived by the general public to present a health risk, such bias may artificially increase the risk.

Allergy, Asthma, and Glioma

In 1990, Hochberg and colleagues conducted a case control study of 160 patients with brain tumors ascertained from hospitals in Boston, Providence, and Baltimore. Controls were 128 healthy persons who were friends of the cases. Their results suggested an inverse association between the development of glioblastoma and susceptibility to allergies (OR = 0.60).

Subsequently, several other epidemiologic studies examined the association between allergic conditions such as asthma and the development of brain tumors, and the majority of these investigations also found an inverse association (Schwartzbaum et al., 2003). To quantify the risk and check for heterogeneity among studies, Linos and colleagues identified eight observational studies that examined associations between atopic diseases (asthma, eczema, hay fever, or allergy) and glioma or meningioma, and performed a meta-analysis by pooling estimates according to the inverse of their variances. Their analysis involved 3,450 patients with gliomas and 1,070 patients with meningiomas. Pooled estimates revealed that the risk of glioma development was significantly reduced for each atopic condition (RR = 0.61 for allergy, RR = 0.68 for asthma, and RR = 0.69 for eczema). There was no association between atopic disease and the risk of meningioma. The investigators concluded that there is a strong inverse association between atopic disease and the development of glioma that is not likely explainable by methodological bias (Linos et al., 2007).

More recently, Chen and colleagues identified four additional published studies for inclusion in a meta-analysis to evaluate the association between allergic conditions and glioma risk. Their analysis was based on 12 studies (10 case control and 2 cohort studies) containing 6,408 glioma patients and a total of 61,090 participants. Compared to subjects without allergies, those with reported allergic conditions had a 40% reduced risk of glioma (pooled OR = 0.60). The risk reductions were consistent for specific conditions (OR = 0.70 for asthma, OR = 0.69 for eczema, and OR = 0.78 for hay fever).

Though the results of these meta-analyses show consistency of effects, it has been pointed out that in most of the studies, spouses or close relatives were often called upon to provide information about the medical histories of patients with brain tumors, and as a consequence, the inverse association with allergic conditions may be an artifact of general underreporting of asthmatic conditions for cases. In a novel investigation, Schwartzbaum and colleagues attempted to rule out such reporting bias by examining the distributions of asthma and allergy-related genetic polymorphisms in 111 patients with *glioblastoma multiforme* and 421 controls. Similar to other studies, their results revealed that *self-reported* history of allergic conditions reduced the risk of glioma development (OR = 0.64). But what is most important about this study is that the risk was independently modified by single nucleotide polymorphisms related to asthma susceptibility (*interleukin-4 receptor a* and *interleukin-13*) and these genetic effects could not have been influenced by reporting bias. Specifically, genetic polymorphisms that heighten asthma risk were found to reduce the risk of glioma development, and vice versa. For example, interleukin-4 receptor a polymorphisms, which are known to decrease the risk of asthma, were found to increase the risk of glioma (OR = 1.61), and an interleukin 13 polymorphism that is known to increase the risk of asthma was found to decrease glioma risk (OR = 0.56). The investigators suggest that since germ line mutations were used as biomarkers of susceptibility to asthma and allergic conditions, these results cannot be attributed to recall bias. As such, these findings tend to validate the inverse associations between adult glioma and self-reported histories of allergies that have been consistently observed in epidemiologic research over the past 20 years (Schwartzbaum et al., 2005; Schwartzbaum et al., 2006).

Nonsteroidal Anti-inflammatory Drugs (NSAIDs) and Glioma

Evidence from epidemiologic and experimental studies suggests that use of *nonsteroidal anti-inflammatory drugs (NSAIDs)* reduces the risk of a number of malignant neoplasms including cancers of the colon, breast, prostate, and lung (Harris, 2009). These results prompted an investigation of the association between use of aspirin and other NSAIDs and risk of adult *glioblastoma multiforme*. The association was evaluated among 236 incident cases and 401 population-based controls frequency-matched on age, gender, and ethnicity from the *San Francisco Bay Area Adult Glioma Study*. Cases (or proxies) and controls were interviewed in person between 1997–2000. Cases with glioblastoma multiforme reported less use of at least 600 pills of all types of NSAIDs combined during the 10-year prediagnostic period than did controls (OR = 0.53). Findings were consistent for aspirin (OR = 0.51), ibuprofen (OR = 0.41), and naproxen or other NSAIDs (OR = 0.34). Eliminating participants who initiated NSAID use within 2 years of diagnosis yielded similar results. These findings show an inverse association between

NSAID use and the risk of developing glioblastoma multiforme. The authors suggest the need for further studies to determine whether NSAIDs might be effective in the inhibition of glioma development or progression (Sivak-Sears et al., 2004).

UNITED STATES STUDY OF BRAIN TUMORS

The National Cancer Institute of the United States recently coordinated a comprehensive study of adult brain tumors to identify and quantify the risk factors. The study included 782 brain tumor cases and 799 controls ascertained from medical centers in Phoenix, Arizona, Brigham and Women's Hospital in Boston, and Western Pennsylvania Hospital in Pittsburgh. Cases included 489 patients with gliomas, 197 patients with meningiomas, and 96 patients with acoustic neuromas. The controls were ascertained from the same hospitals with matching to the cases on gender, race, age, and location of residence. Data were collected by research nurses using standardized questionnaires. Furthermore, blood samples were collected to explore associations of genetic mutations and polymorphisms with the development of brain tumors.

The study found no evidence of higher brain tumor risk among people who use handheld cellular phones compared to those who did not use them. The risk of developing brain tumors did not increase with increasing years of use or average minutes of use per day, nor did brain tumors among cellular phone users occur more often than expected on the side of the head on which people reported using their phone. There was no evidence for an increased risk of any of the three major categories of tumors (glioma, meningioma, or acoustic neuroma) among persons who used cellular telephones 60 or more minutes per day, or regularly for up to 5 years (Inskip et al., 2001).

There was evidence that people with a history of allergies or autoimmune diseases were at reduced risk for developing glioma. Allergies evaluated included asthma, eczema, hay fever, and allergies to medicine, insects, food, and chemicals. Autoimmune diseases included rheumatoid arthritis, lupus erythematosus, multiple sclerosis, diabetes, and pernicious anemia. The reduced risk associated with history of allergies was specific for gliomas (OR = 0.67), as there was no significant association between history of allergies and risk of meningioma or acoustic neuroma. History of autoimmune disease, however, was associated with a reduced risk of both glioma (OR = 0.49) and meningioma (OR = 0.59). The exact nature of the immunological basis for these associations remains to be determined (Brenner et al., 2002).

Investigators also examined associations between the incidence of brain tumors and polymorphisms in glutathione *S*-transferase and the cytochrome P450 system, two families of genes involved in the metabolism of solvents that may play a role in the development of brain tumors. One polymorphism of GSTP1 was found associated with an 80% increase in glioma risk, but results for other polymorphisms were indeterminate (De Roos et al., 2003).

GENETIC ANOMALIES AND BRAIN TUMORS

A few genetic syndromes have been found that heighten the risk of developing a brain tumor. These include *neurofibromatosis* 1 and 2, *tuberous sclerosis, retinoblastoma, Li-Fraumeni syndrome, Turcot's syndrome*, and *Cowden syndrome*. These genetic syndromes are caused by heritable mutations in certain tumor suppressor genes that are critical to the processes of normal cell division and function. Furthermore, certain brain tumors such as *retinoblastoma* and *oligodendroglioma* are also characterized by specific gene mutations or chromosomal deletions.

Neurofibromatosis Types 1 and 2

Neurofibromatosis type 1 (von Recklinghausen's disease) is a rare autosomal dominant disorder first described by the German physician Friedrech von Recklinghausen in 1882. This condition is characterized by the development of multiple fibromas (neurofibromas) of the skin, brain, and other anatomic sites. Some patients also develop gliomas of the optic nerve. The syndrome is due to a mutant autosomal dominant gene called *NF1* located on the long arm of chromosome 17. The gene encodes a protein called neurofibromin that regulates cell division of fibrous nerve sheaths. Mutant forms of *NF1* result in the development of neurofibromas (Boyd, Korf, and Theos, 2009).

Neurofibromatosis type 2 is a rare autosomal dominant disorder caused by a mutation of a tumor suppressor gene called *NF2* located on the long arm of chromosome 22. The gene encodes a protein called *merlin* that is essential for the formation of the myelin sheaths of nerves. Mutant forms of *NF2* result in the development of *schwannomas* of the vestibular branch of the eighth cranial nerve as well as tumors of other cranial nerves. Furthermore, approximately 50% of *NF2* mutant carriers develop meningiomas (Asthagiri et al., 2009).

Li-Fraumeni syndrome

Li-Fraumeni syndrome is a rare autosomal dominant hereditary disorder (Li and Fraumeni, 1969). The syndrome is linked to germ line mutations of the *p53 tumor suppressor gene* located on the short arm of chromosome 17. Such mutations can be inherited or arise *de novo* early in embryogenesis or in one of the parent's germ cells (Varley, 2003). Patients who carry the *p53* mutant gene are at risk for a wide range of malignancies including breast cancer, brain tumors, acute leukemia, soft tissue and bone sarcomas, and adrenal cortical carcinoma. A genetic variant of the Li-Fraumeni syndrome may be due to a mutation of another gene called *CHEK2* located on the long arm of chromosome 22 (Bell et al., 1999). Mutant forms of *CHEK2* lead to dysfunctional DNA repair during cell division, thereby increasing the risk of certain malignancies. However, there is controversy about whether *CHEK2* mutations cause a similar profile of cancer as *p53* mutations in the Li-Fraumeni syndrome (Evans, Birch, and Narod, 2008).

Turcot's Syndrome

Turcot's syndrome is a rare genetic disorder characterized clinically by the concurrence of a primary brain tumor and multiple colorectal adenomas. The condition is caused by mutations in the *APC* gene located on chromosome 5 or mismatch repair genes on chromosomes 2 and 3. The *APC* gene plays a critical role in a number of cellular processes, and the mismatch repair genes are responsible for the detection and repair of errors that occur during DNA replication. Mutant forms of these genes cause adenomatous polyps of the colon and medulloblastomas of the cerebellum (Hamilton et al., 1995). Mutations of the *APC* gene and the mismatch repair genes also cause *familial adenomatous polyposis (FAP)* and other hereditary colon cancer syndromes.

Tuberous Sclerosis

Tuberous sclerosis is a rare genetic disorder that causes development of nonmalignant fibromas in the brain and other anatomic sites including the kidneys, heart, eyes, lungs, and skin. This condition is caused by mutations in either of two tumor suppressor genes, *TSC1* or *TSC2*, located on chromosomes 9 and 16, respectively. These genes encode two proteins, *hamartin* and *tuberin*, that regulate cell proliferation and differentiation. Mutant forms of *TSC1* and *TSC2* result in the development of giant cell astrocytomas, fibrous cortical tumors in the brain, and subependymal tumors in the walls of the ventricles of the brain (Yates, 2006).

Cowden Syndrome

Cowden syndrome (also known as *multiple hamartoma syndrome*) is a rare autosomal dominant inherited disorder characterized by multiple tumor-like growths called hamartomas and an increased risk of certain forms of cancer. The characteristic hamartomas of Cowden syndrome are small, noncancerous growths that are most commonly found on the skin and mucous membranes (such as the lining of the mouth and nose), but they can also occur in the intestinal tract and other parts of the body. This syndrome is caused by a mutant gene known as *PTEN* located on the long arm of chromosome 10. The *PTEN* gene encodes a protein known as *phosphatase and tensin homolog* that helps regulate normal cell division and growth. Mutant forms of *PTEN* result in the development of hamartomas and increase the risk of developing thyroid cancer, breast cancer, and endometrial cancer. In addition, individuals with Cowden syndrome sometimes develop slow-growing benign tumors of the cerebellum (Eng, 1998).

Retinoblastoma

Retinoblastoma is a rare malignant tumor that arises from the retinal cells of the eye. Retinoblastomas are caused by mutations of the *retinoblastoma gene* (*Rb1*) located on the short arm of chromosome 13. This gene encodes a tumor suppressor protein that regulates DNA replication during cell division. Mutations in *Rb1* cause retinoblastoma of the eye, and occasionally, malignant tumors of the pineal gland (Du and Pogoriler, 2006; Parsam et al., 2009).

Oligodendroglioma

Oligodendrogliomas are believed to originate from the oligodendrocytes of the brain or their precursor cells. These tumors constitute less than 5% of all malignant brain tumors. A common genetic structural deformity found in oligodendroglioma is codeletion of chromosomal arms 1p and 19q. In fact, this striking feature is considered to be the "genetic signature" of oligodendroglioma. In a recent study, 1p loss was present in 35 of 42 tumors (83%), 9q loss was present in 28 of 39 tumors (72%), both 1p and 9q losses were present in 27 of 39 tumors (69%), and at least one deletion was present in all tumors. Such deletions may silence the expression of important tumor suppressor genes such as the *CAMTA1* gene, a transcription regulator on chromosome 1 (Barbashina et al., 2005).

Cellular Signaling Pathways and Brain Tumors

Genetic alterations found associated with the development of brain tumors tend to disrupt cellular signaling pathways that regulate key processes of carcinogenesis such as cell division, DNA repair, angiogenesis, and apoptosis. Expression of growth factors such as epidermal growth factor (*EGFR*), protein kinase activators (*RAS*), vascular endothelial growth factor (*VEGF*), and/or inactivation of tumor suppressor genes such as *p53*, *Rb1*, and *PTEN* are currently under intense investigation to elucidate mechanisms of carcinogenesis. Elucidation of such mechanisms could obviously reveal targets for effective molecular therapy.

As pointed out in this book and by many other investigators, inflammation is a powerful contributing factor to the development of cancer, including brain tumors (Harris, 2009; Kaluz and Van Meir, 2011). For example, *glioblastoma multiforme* tissues are characterized by the presence of immune cell infiltrates and the expression of inflammatory cytokines. In a study of the immunohistochemistry of 47 glioblastomas, 35 tumors (74.4%) stained positive for COX-2, the rate-limiting enzyme of the prostaglandin inflammatory cascade, and tumors with a high rate of proliferation tended to have greater COX-2 expression (Prayson et al., 2002).

Many studies have implicated *hypoxia* (lack of oxygen) and sustained activation of *hypoxia inducible factor* (*HIF-1*) as key events in carcinogenesis. It is therefore noteworthy that *HIF-1* can be induced by factors other than hypoxia, primarily proinflammatory mediators such as interleukin-1b and NF-κB. According to one model of glioblastoma development, activation of *HIF-1* is sustained by an autocrine loop that involves the protein kinase (*RAS*) cascade and amplified expression of interleukin-1b (Sharma et al., 2010; Kaluz and Van Meir, 2011).

RISK FACTORS FOR MENINGIOMAS

Intracranial meningiomas account for more than one-third of all brain tumors. Though most meningiomas are benign (~95%), their expansion in the closed cranial vault can produce serious neurological symptoms and even death.

Meningiomas arise from cells of the meninges, the membranous tissue that covers the surface of the brain beneath the skull. Meningeal membranes also line the ventricles of the brain and cover certain structures and glands within the brain such as the pineal gland and the thalamus. The exact cell of origin is thought to be the arachnoid cap cell, a progenitor (stem) cell of mature meningeal tissue (Bondy et al., 2008).

Meningiomas are diagnosed roughly twice as often in women compared to men. In the United

States, the age-adjusted rates of meningioma are 8.4 per 100,000 in women and 3.6 per 100,000 in men. In contrast to gliomas, which can occur in children, meningiomas are infrequently diagnosed before the age of 20 years, and the age-specific incidence rises steadily throughout the adult life span (**Figure 29.5**).

As with malignant gliomas of the brain, ionizing radiation is the major environmental risk factor for meningioma. A number of studies have consistently found that exposure to high doses of ionizing radiation markedly elevates the risk of developing meningioma. For example, in the well-known cohort study of 10,834 Israeli children who received ionizing radiation to the scalp for the treatment of tinea capitis (ringworm) during 1948–1960, the risk of subsequent development of meningioma over 40 years of follow-up was increased nearly tenfold (RR = 9.5). The mean latency period from radiation exposure to detection was 36 years, reflecting the extremely slow growth of most meningiomas (Ron et al., 1988; Sadetzki et al., 2005). It is also notable that multiple sources of radiation have been found to increase the risk of meningioma development, including radiation therapy for certain intracranial malignancies such as lymphoma and leukemia (Neglia et al., 2006), and full mouth dental X-rays (Longstreth et al., 2004).

The excess female risk for meningioma compared to males has been linked to reproductive factors and hormone (estrogen) exposure. Women have more than a threefold higher incidence than men during the reproductive years, and a few epidemiological studies have linked exogenous estrogens to the relatively high female risk. In the *Nurse's Health Study*, current use of exogenous estrogens was found to increase the risk in both premenopausal women (RR = 2.48) and postmenopausal women (RR = 1.86) (Jhawar et al., 2003). In the INTERPHONE case control study of brain tumors, an increased risk of meningioma was observed among postmenopausal women who had ever received hormone replacement therapy (OR = 1.7) (Wigertz et al., 2008); and in a retrospective cohort study of the US Mayo Clinic database, the incidence of meningioma among women who received hormone replacement therapy was more than twofold higher than women with no exposure (865 vs. 366 per 100,000, adjusted OR = 2.2) (Blitshteyn, Crook, and Jaeckle, 2008). To clarify the effects of estrogen and other hormones on the pathogenesis of meningioma, it is suggested that future studies incorporate information on both hormonal exposures and the molecular expression of hormone receptors in meningial tumor tissues (Wiemels, Wrensch, and Claus, 2010).

While epidemiologic studies have consistently found that allergic conditions reduce the risk of developing *glioma*, it is unclear whether these conditions influence *meningioma* development. To help clarify the issue, Schoemaker and colleagues conducted a pooled analysis of two population-based case control studies of meningioma and allergic conditions. The analysis included 475 cases and 1,716 controls ascertained during 2001–2004 in the United Kingdom. The analysis revealed that meningioma risk was significantly reduced by individual allergic conditions including asthma (OR = 0.85), hay fever

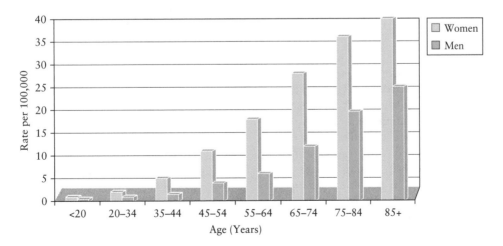

Figure 29.5 Age-Specific Incidence of Meningioma: USA, 2002–2006.

Source: Data from CBTRUS (2009–2010) CDTRUS Statistical Report: Primary brain and central nervous system tumors diagnosed in eighteeen states in 2002–2006. Central Brain Tumor Registry of the United States, Hinsdale, Ill. Wiemels J, Wrensch M, Claus EB (2010). Epidemiology and etiology of meningioma. *J Neurooncol* 99(3):307–314.

(OR = 0.81), and eczema (OR = 0.72). Interestingly, the risk reductions were greatest among children with allergic conditions (OR ~0.50) whereas the estimates of risk were close to unity for adults.

Familial clustering of meningioma is uncommon, although some studies suggest that relatives of affected cases are at increased risk. For example, Malmer and colleagues examined the risk to relatives of index cases of meningioma (probands) ascertained through the Swedish National Cancer Registry and found a twofold increase in the risk among first degree relatives compared to unrelated spouses (OR = 2.2) (Malmer, Henriksson, and Gronberg, 2003). In a similar analysis incorporating data from both the Swedish and Norwegian Registry databases, Hemminiki and colleagues also found an increase in meningioma risk among offspring of probands (OR = 1.6) (Hemminki et al., 2009). While these results suggest the existence of genetic factors that heighten susceptibility to meningioma development, at present, no linkage and/or segregation studies of familial meningioma have been reported (Wiemels, Wrensch, and Claus, 2010).

As already noted, the currently available evidence suggests that certain risk factors for meningioma are similar to those for breast cancer, e.g., exposure to exogenous estrogens. Furthermore, several studies have demonstrated that breast cancer and meningioma develop in the same patient more often than expected. For example, in a study of second primary tumors that developed among women with either a first primary breast cancer or meningioma, the risk was increased for breast cancer after meningioma (RR = 1.54), and reciprocally, for meningioma after breast cancer (RR = 1.64). The investigators concluded that shared risk factors may account for this association (Custer, Koepsell, and Mueller, 2002).

In a recent genome-wide association study designed to examine single nucleotide polymorphisms (SNPs) in genes that regulate DNA repair, several polymorphisms were identified that were significantly associated with meningioma. Notably, three of these genetic variants were located in a gene called *BRIP1* that is also associated with breast cancer. The *BRIP1* gene interacts with the breast cancer gene, *BRCA1*, in the repair of DNA double-strand breaks. This finding suggests that the association between meningioma and breast cancer may be due to shared genetic susceptibility (similar polymorphisms in DNA repair genes) in addition to shared environmental risk factors (estrogen replacement therapy) (Bethke et al., 2008).

PITUITARY TUMORS

Pituitary gland tumors account for about 15% of intracranial tumors in adults and 11% in children. These tumors are usually benign but can secrete excessive amounts of prolactin or growth hormone. Furthermore, enlargement of the pituitary gland in the confined bony compartment in the center of the brain, the *sellica turcica*, can produce compressive injury and also result in substantial morbidity. The etiology of pituitary tumors is largely unknown.

Schoemaker and colleagues conducted a population-based case-control study to examine potential risk factors for pituitary tumors in England. Data on medical and reproductive history, female hormones, and cigarette smoking were collected by personal interview from 299 cases and 630 controls aged 18–59 years. Tumor risk was reduced in subjects reporting a past diagnosis of hay fever (OR = 0.7) but not asthma or eczema. Among women, certain features of menopause were found to increase the risk. Women who underwent surgical menopause within 1 year of diagnosis or experienced menopause before the age of 40 years were found to be at markedly increased risk (OR = 6.7 and OR = 7.5, respectively). The effect of early menopause remained when evaluating menopausal status 10 years before diagnosis. The risk was also increased among women who delivered their first child before the age of 20 years compared with nulliparous women (OR = 3.4). No significant associations were observed for ever use of oral contraceptives, hormone replacement therapy, cigarette smoking, past head injury, or past diagnosis of epilepsy. This study suggests an elevated risk of pituitary tumors in relation to surgically induced menopause, early postmenopausal age, and young age at first childbirth, and possibly a reduced risk with allergic conditions such as hay fever. Reasons for these associations need further investigation, but among women, abrupt or early changes in the hormonal milieu appear to play a role in the genesis of pituitary tumors (Schoemaker and Swerdlow, 2009).

An international team of researchers based in Finland examined three clusters of familial pituitary adenomas using chip-based technologies to characterize germ line mutations. Within these families, mutant forms of the *aryl hydrocarbon receptor interacting protein (AIP) gene* were identified by linkage and segregation analysis in those individuals who developed pituitary adenomas. The aryl hydrocarbon receptor activates certain genes of the P450 system involved in a variety of metabolic pathways including xenobiotic and drug metabolism. In a series of pituitary adenomas ascertained from cases in Northern Finland, the investigators found that 2 *AIP* mutations accounted for 16% of all pituitary adenomas and 40% of pituitary adenomas diagnosed in patients under the age of 35 years. Based on these results, they suggest that inherited tumor susceptibility due to low penetrance genes, such as *AIP*, may be more common than previously thought (Vierimaa et al., 2006).

PRIMARY LYMPHOMA OF THE BRAIN

Immunosuppressed patients have an inordinately high risk of developing a primary lymphoma of the brain. Patients with progressive HIV infection complicated by EBV reactivation and post-transplant patients receiving powerful immunosuppressive drugs are at greatest risk.

BRAIN TUMORS IN CHILDREN

The profile of brain tumors that occur in children and adolescents up to 19 years of age differs markedly from that in adults. More than 70% of childhood tumors are malignant gliomas arising from astrocytes, oligodendrocytes, ependymoma cells, or primitive neuroectoderm cells. Pituitary tumors account for about 11% of childhood tumors and are more commonly found in late adolescence. Meningiomas, which account for about 34% of adult brain tumors, comprise only about 4% of childhood brain tumors. The remaining histological types (neuroblastomas, nerve sheath tumors, germ cell tumors) each account for less than 5% of childhood tumors (CBTRUS, 2010).

Medulloblastomas are derived from progenitor (stem) cells of the neuroectoderm and are often referred to as *primitive neuroectodermal tumors* (*PNET*). Medulloblastomas are one type of PNET that are found near the midline of the cerebellum. These tumors are more common in children under the age of 5 years. They tend to grow rapidly and often block drainage of the cerebral spinal fluid causing symptoms associated with increased intracranial pressure. Medulloblastoma cells can spread (metastasize) to other areas of the central nervous system, especially around the spinal cord.

Nonrandom patterns of chromosomal deletions and aberrations have been discovered in several histologic types of childhood brain tumors. These findings suggest that the loss or inactivation of tumor suppressor genes are critical events in tumorigenesis. For example, deletions and aberrations involving chromosome 17 are characteristic cytogenetic findings in medulloblastoma cells. Elucidation of key cellular events that are disrupted by such genetic changes is critical to finding molecular targets for effective therapeutic intervention (Biegel, 1999).

In the United States, the annual incidence of childhood brain tumors jumped from 2.3 cases per 100,000 in 1975 to 3.2 cases per 100,000 in 1985, and since that time the rates have remained relatively stable. Malcolm Smith and colleagues at the National Cancer Institute attributed this rapid increase to improved detection of brain tumors with the advent of magnetic resonance imaging (MRI) during the early 1980s. There have also been refinements in the pathological classification of brain tumors due to improved neurosurgical techniques for obtaining biopsy specimens of brain tumors (Smith et al., 1998).

As pointed out by an Ohio pediatrician, Dr. Arthur Varner: "*In the report by Smith et al., the authors' conclusion is that the increasing incidence of brain tumors in children is best explained by a "jump model" with the optimum point of change being around 1985, the time of rapidly increasing availability of magnetic resonance imaging. The authors discount environmental factors, since the change seemed to occur rapidly*" (Smith et al., 1998; Varner, 1999). Nevertheless, as noted by Dr. Varner, an abrupt change in drug use among children *did occur* at that time, namely, a large fraction of parents switched their children from pediatric aspirin to acetaminophen due to concern about aspirin as a potential cause of Reye's syndrome, and this led to a rapid and substantial decline in the use of pediatric aspirin in the early 1980s. According to US marketing data for the period 1979–1985, annual purchases of pediatric aspirin declined from 600 million pills in 1979 to less than 200 million pills in 1985, coincident with a marked increase in sales of acetaminophen products (Arrowsmith et al., 1987). Varner states that "*the anti-inflammatory effects of aspirin, as opposed to acetaminophen, may have been an unrecognized protective factor in the development of brain tumors, as has been demonstrated for other cancers.*" Indeed, it is now well known that aspirin and other NSAIDs have chemopreventive activity against many solid tumors through inhibition of the COX-2 prostaglandin inflammatory cascade, whereas acetaminophen is *not* a COX-2 inhibitor (Harris, 2009). Furthermore, recent molecular studies have shown that the tumor cells of high-grade gliomas and medulloblastomas diagnosed in children markedly overexpress COX-2 and related inflammatory cytokines (Bodey, Siegel, and Kaiser, 2006).

THERAPEUTIC APPROACHES TO GLIOMA AND OTHER BRAIN TUMORS

Diagnosis of Brain Tumors

Brain tumors can present clinically by a myriad of neurological signs and symptoms such as headache, nausea, vomiting, altered consciousness, visual disturbances, impaired hearing, loss of smell, emotional changes, paralysis, and other losses of function. Radiologically, these neoplasms present as masses with partial contrast enhancement due to limited disruption of the blood-brain barrier. Noninvasive, high-resolution techniques, such as computed tomography (CT) scans and especially magnetic resonance imaging (MRI) have enhanced the detection of brain tumors. Histologically, malignant tumors are classified and staged based upon the morphology and staining characteristics of tumor cells, nuclear atypia, and mitotic activity.

Prognosis of Malignant Brain Tumors

In general, the prognosis for a patient diagnosed with a malignant brain tumor such as glioma is quite poor. Of 10,000 Americans diagnosed each year with malignant gliomas, only about 50% are alive 1 year after diagnosis, and survival drops to less than 25% after 2 years. Glioblastoma has a 14-month median survival after diagnosis. Tumor histology and grade are important prognostic factors. For example, patients diagnosed with anaplastic astrocytoma typically survive 3 or more years.

Van Meir and colleagues have recently published an excellent review of exciting new advances in neuro-oncology with emphasis on malignant glioma. They state that

> *"new discoveries are being made in basic and translational research, which are likely to improve this situation further in the next 10 years. These include agents that block one or more of the disordered tumor proliferation signaling pathways, and that overcome resistance to already existing treatments. Targeted therapies such as antiangiogenic therapy with antivascular endothelial growth factor antibodies (bevacizumab) are finding their way into clinical practice. Large-scale research efforts are ongoing to provide a comprehensive understanding of all the genetic alterations and gene expression changes underlying glioma formation. These have already refined the classification of glioblastoma into four distinct molecular entities that may lead to different treatment regimens. The role of cancer stem-like cells is another area of active investigation. There is definite hope that by 2020, new cocktails of drugs will be available to target the key molecular pathways involved in gliomas and reduce their mortality and morbidity, a positive development for patients, their families, and medical professionals alike" (Van Meir et al., 2010).*

● ● ● REFERENCES

Altekruse, S.F., Kosary, C.L., Krapcho, M., Neyman, N., Aminou, R., Waldron, W.,… Edwards, B.K. (2010). *SEER cancer statistics review, 1975–2007*. Bethesda, MD: National Cancer Institute.

Andersen, A., Barlow, L., Engeland, A., Kjærheim, K., Lynge, E., & Pukkala, E. (1999). Work-related cancer in the Nordic countries. *Scand J Work Environ Health, 25*(suppl 2), 1–116.

Araque, A., Parpura, V., Sanzgiri, R.P., & Haydon, P.G. (1999). Tripartite synapses: Glia, the unacknowledged partner. *Trends in Neuroscience, 22*(5), 208–215.

Arrowsmith, J.B., Kennedy, D.L., Kuritsky, J.N., & Faich, G.A. (1987). National patterns of aspirin use and Reye's syndrome reporting, United States, 1980 to 1985. *Pediatrics, 79*, 858–863.

Asthagiri, A.R., Parry, D.M., Butman, J.A., Kim, H.J., Tsilou, E.T., Zhuang, Z., & Lonser, R.R. (2009). Neurofibromatosis type 2. *Lancet, 373*(9679), 1974–1986.

Aszmann, O.C. (2000). The life and work of Theodore Schwann. *Journal of Reconstructive Microsurgery* (United States), *16*(4), 291–295.

Barbashina, V., Salazar, P., Holland, E.C., Rosenblum, M.K., & Ladanyi, M. (2005). Allelic losses at 1p36 and 19q13 in gliomas: Correlation with histologic classification, definition of a 150-kb minimal deleted region on 1p36, and evaluation of CAMTA1 as a candidate tumor suppressor gene. *Clin Cancer Res, 11*(3), 1119–11128.

Bell, D.W., Varley, J.M., Szydlo, T.E., Kang, D.H., Wahrer, D.C., Shannon, K.E.,…Haber, D.A. (1999). Heterozygous germ line hCHK2 mutations in Li-Fraumeni syndrome. *Science, 286*, 2528–2531.

Bethke, L., Murray, A., Webb, E., Schoemaker, M., Muir, K., McKinney, P.,...Houlston, R. (2008). Comprehensive analysis of DNA repair gene variants and risk of meningioma. *J Natl Cancer Inst, 100,* 270–276.

Biegel, J.A. (1999). Cytogenetics and molecular genetics of childhood brain tumors. *Oncology, 1,* 139–151.

Blitshteyn, S., Crook, J.E., & Jaeckle, K.A. (2008). Is there an association between meningioma and hormone replacement therapy? *J Clin Oncol, 26,* 279–282.

Bodey, B., Siegel, S.E., & Kaiser, H.E. (2006). Cyclooxygenase-2 (COX-2) overexpression in childhood brain tumors. *In Vivo, 20*(4), 519–525.

Bondy, M.L., Scheurer, M.E., Malmer, B., Barnholtz-Sloan, J.S., Davis, F.G., Il'yasova, D.,...Brain Tumor Epidemiology Consortium. (2008). Brain tumor epidemiology: Consensus from the Brain Tumor Epidemiology Consortium. *Cancer, 1,* 113(7 Suppl), 1953–1968.

Boyd, K.P., Korf, B.R., & Theos, A. (2009). Neurofibromatosis type 1. *J Am Acad Dermatol, 61*(1), 1–14.

Brenner, A.V., Linet, M.S., Fine, H.A., Shapiro, W.R., Selker, R.G., Black, P.M., & Inskip, P.D. (2002). History of allergies and autoimmune diseases and risk of brain tumors in adults. *Int J Cancer, 99,* 252–259.

Central Brain Tumor Registry of the United States (CBTRUS). (2008). *Statistical report: Primary brain tumors in the United States, 2000–2004.* Hinsdale, Ill.: Central Brain Tumor Registry of the United States.

CBTRUS. (2010). *CDTRUS Statistical report: Primary brain and central nervous system tumors diagnosed in eighteen states in 2002–2006.* Hinsdale, Ill.: Central Brain Tumor Registry of the United States.

Chen, C., Xu, T., Chen, J., Zhou, J., Yan, Y., Lu, Y., & Wu, S. (2010). Allergy and risk of glioma: A meta-analysis. *Eur J Neurol,* DOI:10.1111/j.1468-1331.2010.03187.x.

Custer, B.S., Koepsell, T.D., & Mueller, B.A. (2002). The association between breast carcinoma and meningioma in women. *Cancer, 94,* 1626–1635.

De Roos, A.J., Rothman, N., Inskip, P.D., Linet, M.S., Shapiro, W.R., Selker, R.G.,...Bell, D.A. (2003). Genetic polymorphisms in GSTM1, -P1, -T1 and CYP2E1 and the risk of adult brain tumors. *Cancer Epidemiol Biomarkers Prev, 12,* 14–27.

Du, W., & Pogoriler, J. (2006). Retinoblastoma family genes. *Oncogene, 25*(38), 5190–5200.

Eng, C. (1998). Genetics of Cowden syndrome: Through the looking glass of oncology. *Int J Oncol, 12*(3), 701–710.

Evans, D.G., Birch, J.M., & Narod, S.A. (2008). Is *CHEK2* a cause of the Li–Fraumeni syndrome? *J Med Genet, 45,* 63–64.

Ferlay, J., Shin, H.R., Forman, D., Mathers, C., & Parkin, D.M. (2010). Estimates of worldwide burden of cancer in 2008. *International Journal of Cancer, 127*(12), 2893–2917.

Fisher, J.L., Schwartzbaum, J.A., Wrensch, M., & Wiemels, J.L. (2007). Epidemiology of brain tumors. *Neurol Clin, 25,* 867–890.

GLOBOCAN. (2002). *Worldwide incidence and mortality of cancer, 2002.* Lyon, France: IARC Press.

Graeber, M.B., Scheithauer, B.W., & Kreutzberg, G.W. (2002). Microglia in brain tumors. *Glia, 40*(2), 252–259.

GSM Association Market Data Summary. (2009). Global System for Mobile Communciations (GSM) Association.

Hamilton, S.R., Liu, B., Parsons, R.E., Papadopoulos, N., Jen, J., Powell, S.M.,...Kinzler, K.W. (1995). The molecular basis of Turcot's syndrome. *N Engl J Med, 332,* 839–847.

Harris, R.E. (2009). Cyclooxygenase-2 (COX-2) blockade in the chemoprevention of cancers of the colon, breast, prostate, and lung. *Inflammopharmacology, 17,* 1–13.

Hemminki, K., Tretli, S., Sundquist, J., Johannesen, T.B., & Granstrom, C. (2009). Familial risks in nervous-system tumours: A histology-specific analysis from Sweden and Norway. *Lancet Oncol, 10*, 481–488.

Hochberg, F., Toniolo, P., Cole, P., & Salcman, M. (1990). Non-occupational risk indicators of glioblastoma in adults. *J Neurooncol, 8*, 55–60.

Horner, M.J., Ries, L.A.G., Krapcho, M., Neyman, N., Aminou, R., Howlader, N.,...Edwards, B.K. (Eds). (2009). *SEER cancer statistics review, 1975–2006*. Bethesda, MD: National Cancer Institute.

Huang, K., Whelan, E.A., Ruder, A.M., Ward, E.M., Deddens, J.A., Davis-King, K.E.,...Brain Cancer Collaborative Study Group. (2004). Reproductive factors and risk of glioma in women. *Cancer Epidemiol Biomarkers Prev, 13*(10), 1583–1588.

Inskip, P.D., Tarone, R.E., Hatch, E.E., Wilcosky, T.C., Shapiro, W.R., Selker, R.G.,...Linet, M.S. (2001). Cellular telephone use and brain tumors. *N Engl J Med, 344*, 79–86.

INTERPHONE Study Group. (2010). Brain tumour risk in relation to mobile telephone use: Results of the INTERPHONE international case–control study. *International Journal of Epidemiology, 39*(3), 1–20.

Jhawar, B.S., Fuchs, C.S., Colditz, G.A., & Stampfer, M.J. (2003). Sex steroid hormone exposures and risk for meningioma. *J Neurosurg, 99*, 848–853.

Kaluz, S., & Van Meir, E.G. (2011). At the crossroads of cancer and inflammation: Ras rewires an HIF-driven IL-1 autocrine loop. *J Mol Med, 89*, 91–94.

Karlsson, P., Holmberg, E., Lundell, M., Mattsson, A., Holm, L.E., & Wallgren, A. (1998). Intracranial tumors after exposure to ionizing radiation during infancy: A pooled analysis of two Swedish cohorts of 28,008 infants with skin hemangioma. *Radiat Res, 150*, 357–364.

Kimelberg, H.K., Jalonen, T., & Walz, W. (1993). Regulation of the brain microenvironment: Transmitters and ions (pp. 193–222).

In: S. Murphy (Ed.). *Astrocytes: Pharmacology and function*. San Diego, CA: Academic Press.

Li, F.P., & Fraumeni, J.F. (1969). Soft-tissue sarcomas, breast cancer, and other neoplasms. A familial syndrome? *Ann Intern Med, 71*(4), 747–752.

Linos, E., Raine, T., Alonso, A., & Michaud, D. (2007). Atopy and risk of brain tumors: A meta-analysis. *J Natl Cancer Inst, 99*, 1544–1550.

Longstreth, W.T., Jr., Phillips, L.E., Drangsholt, M., Koepsell, T.D., Custer, B.S., Gehrels, J.A., & Belle, G. (2004). Dental X-rays and the risk of intracranial meningioma: A population-based case–control study. *Cancer, 100*, 1026–1034.

Lönn, S., Ahlbom, A., Hall, P., Feychting, M., & the Swedish Interphone Study Group. (2005). Long-term mobile phone use and brain tumor risk. *American Journal of Epidemiology, 161*(6), 526–535.

Malmer, B., Henriksson, R., & Gronberg, H. (2003). Familial brain tumours—genetics or environment? A nationwide cohort study of cancer risk in spouses and first-degree relatives of brain tumour patients. *Int J Cancer, 106*, 260–263.

Matanoski, G.M., Seltser, R., Sartwell, P.E., Diamond, E.L., & Elliott, E.A. (1975). The current mortality rates of radiologists and other physician specialists: Specific causes of death. *Am J Epidemiol, 101*, 199–210.

Neglia, J.P., Robison, L.L., Stovall, M., Liu, Y., Packer, R.J., Hammond, S.,...Inskip, P.D. (2006). New primary neoplasms of the central nervous system in survivors of childhood cancer: A report from the Childhood Cancer Survivor Study. *J Natl Cancer Inst, 98*(21), 1528–1537.

Parkin, D.M., Pisani, P., & Ferlay, J. (1999a). Estimates of the worldwide incidence of 25 major cancers in 1990. *Int J Cancer, 80*(6), 827–841.

Parkin, D.M., Pisani, P., & Ferlay, J. (1999b). Global cancer statistics, 1990. *CA Cancer J Clin, 49*(1), 33–64.

Parkin, D.M., Whelan, S.L., Ferlay, J., Teppo, L., & Thomas, D.B. (2002). Cancer in five continents (vol. 5). Lyon, France: IARC Press.

Parkin, D.M., Bray, F., Ferlay, J., & Pisani, P. (2005). Global cancer statistics, 2002. *CA Cancer J Clin, 55*, 74–108.

Parsam, V.L., Kannabiran, C., Honavar, S., Vemuganti, G.K., & Ali, M.J. (2009). A comprehensive, sensitive and economical approach for the detection of mutations in the RB1 gene in retinoblastoma. *J Genet, 88*(4), 517–527.

Pollard, W., & Earnshaw, W.C. (2008) *Cell biology.* Philadelphia, PA: Saunders Elsevier.

Prayson, R.A., Castilla, E.A., Vogelbaum, M.A., & Barnett, G.H. (2002). Cyclooxygenase-2 (COX-2) expression by immunohistochemistry in glioblastoma multiforme. *Ann Diagn Pathol, 6*(3), 148–153.

Preston, D.L., Ron, E., Yonehara, S., Kibuke, T., Fjuii, H., Kishikawa, M.,…Mabuchi, K. (2002). Tumors of the nervous system and pituitary gland associated with atomic bomb radiation exposure. *J Natl Cancer Inst, 94*, 1555–1563.

Purves, D., Augustine, G.J., Fitzpatrick, D., Hall, W.C., LaMantia, A., McNamara, J.O., & White, L.E. (2008). *Neuroscience.* Sunderland, MA: Sinauer Associates, Inc.

Quigley, M.R., Post, C., & Ehrlich, G. (2007). Some speculation on the origin of glioblastoma. *Neurosurg Rev, 30*, 16–21.

Robbins, S.L., & Cotran, R.S. (1979). *Pathologic basis of disease* (2nd Ed.). Philadelphia: W.B. Saunders Company.

Ron, E., Modan, B., Boice, J.D. Jr., Alfandary, E., Stovall, M., Chetrit, A., & Katz, L. (1988). Tumors of the brain and nervous system after radiotherapy in childhood. *N Engl J Med, 319*(16), 1033–1039.

Sadetzki, S., Chetrit, A., Freedman, L., Stovall, M., Modan, B., & Novikov, I. (2005). Long-term follow-up for brain tumor development after childhood exposure to ionizing radiation for tinea capitis. *Radiat Res, 163*, 424–432.

Santello, M., & Volterra, A. (2008). Synaptic modulation by astrocytes via Ca(2+)-dependent glutamate release. *Neuroscience, 158*(1), 253–259.

Schoemaker, M.J., Swerdlow, A.J., Ahlbom, A., Auvinen, A., Blaasaas, K.G., Cardis, E.,…Tynes, T. (2005). Mobile phone use and risk of acoustic neuroma: Results of the Interphone case–control study in five North European countries. *British Journal of Cancer, 93*, 842–848.

Schoemaker, M.J., & Swerdlow, A.J. (2009). Risk factors for pituitary tumors: A case-control study. *Cancer Epidemiol Biomarkers Prev, 18*(5), 1492–1500.

Schwartzbaum, J., Fonsson, F., Ahlbom, A., Preston-Martin, S., Lönn, S., Söderberg, K.C., & Feychting M. (2003). Cohort studies of association between self-reported allergic conditions, immune-related diagnoses and glioma and meningioma risk. *International Journal of Cancer, 106*(3), 423–428.

Schwartzbaum, J., Ahlbom, A., Malmer, B., Lönn, S., Brookes, A.J., Doss, H.,…Feychting, M. (2005). Polymorphisms associated with asthma are inversely related to glioblastoma multiforme. *Cancer Res, 65*, 6459–6465.

Schwartzbaum, J.A., Fisher, J.L., Aldape, K.D., & Wrensch, M. (2006). Epidemiology and molecular pathology of glioma. *Nature Clinical Practice Neurology, 2*, 494–503.

Sharma, V., Dixit, D., Koul, N., Mehta, V., & Sen, E. (2010). Ras regulates interleukin-1β-induced HIF-1α transcriptional activity in glioblastoma. *J Mol Med, 89*(1), 1–14.

Shore, R.E., Albert, R.E., & Pasternack, B.S. (1976). Follow-up study of patients treated by X-ray epilation for tinea capitis: Resurvey of post-treatment illness and mortality experience. *Arch Environ Health, 31*(1), 21–28.

Shore, R.E., Moseson, M., Harley, N., & Pasternack, B.S. (2003). Tumors and other diseases following childhood x-ray treatment for ringworm of the scalp (tinea capitis). *Health Phys, 85*(4), 404–408.

Sivak-Sears, N.R., Schwartzbaum, J.A., Miike, R., Moghadassi, M., & Wrensch, M. (2004). Case-control study of use of nonsteroidal antiinflammatory drugs and glioblastoma multiforme. *Am J Epidemiol, 159*, 1131–1139.

Smith, M.A., Freidlin, B., Ries, L.A., & Simon, R. (1998). Trends in reported incidence of primary malignant brain tumors in children in the United States. *Journal of the National Cancer Institute, 90*(17), 1269–1277.

United Nations. (2000). *Scientific Committee on the Effects of Atomic Radiation Sources and effects of ionizing radiation: UNSCEAR 2000 report to the general assembly, with scientific annexes.* New York, NY: United Nations.

Van Meir, E.G., Hadjipanayis, C.G., Norden, A.D., Shu, H.K., Wen, P.Y., & Olson, J.J. (2010). Exciting new advances in neuro-oncology: The avenue to a cure for malignant glioma. *CA Cancer J Clin, 60*, 166–193.

Varley, J.M. (2003). Germline TP53 mutations and Li-Fraumeni syndrome. *Hum Mutat, 21*(3), 313–320.

Varner, A. (1999). Letter to the editor: Re: Trends in reported incidence of primary malignant brain tumors in children in the United States. *Journal of the National Cancer Institute, 91*(11), 973.

Vierimaa, O., Georgitsi, M., Lehtonen, R., Vahteristo, P., Kokko, A., Raitila, A.,…Aaltonen, L.A. (2006). Pituitary adenoma predisposition caused by germ line mutations in the AIP gene. *Science, 312*, 1228–1230.

Virchow, R. (1846). Ueber das granulirte aussehen der wandungen der gehirnventrikel. *Allg Z Psychiat, 3*, 242–250.

Virchow, R. (1854). Ueber das ausgebreitete Vorkommen einer dem Nervenmark analogen substanz in den tierischen Geweben. *Virchows Arch Pathol Anat, 6*, 562.

Wiemels, J., Wrensch, M., & Claus, E.B. (2010). Epidemiology and etiology of meningioma. *J Neurooncol, 99*(3), 307–314.

Wigertz, A., Lonn, S., Hall, P., Auvinen, A., Christensen, H.C., Johansen, C.,…Feychting, M. (2008). Reproductive factors and risk of meningioma and glioma. *Cancer Epidemiol Biomarkers Prev, 17*, 2663–2670.

Yates, J.R. (2006). Tuberous sclerosis. *Eur J Hum Genet, 14*(10), 1065–1073.

Yoshinaga, S., Mabuchi, K., Sigurdson, A.J., Doody, M.M., & Ron, E. (2004). Cancer risks among radiologists and radiologic technologists: Review of epidemiologic studies. *Radiology, 233*, 313–321.

Epidemiology of Chronic Obstructive Pulmonary Disease

ANATOMY AND FUNCTION OF THE LUNGS

The human lungs are paired organs that perform the cardinal function of exchanging carbon dioxide in the blood for oxygen in inspired air. The left lung is divided into two lobes and the right lung into three lobes. Together, they contain approximately 1,500 miles of airways and 300–500 million alveoli where the carbon dioxide and oxygen exchange occurs. The total surface area of adult human lungs is approximately 70 square meters (roughly the same area as one side of a tennis court). If all of the capillary vessels that envelop the alveoli were unwound and laid end to end, they would extend for more than 600 miles (Robbins and Cotran, 1979; Weinberger, 2004).

Inspired air is conducted into the lungs through the trachea, the bronchi, and the bronchioles (**Figure 30.1**). This *conducting zone* is not involved in gas exchange and is reinforced with cartilage to maintain patency for the inhalation and exhalation of air. Its function is to warm the inspired air to 37°C and humidify the air. Small projections known as *cilia* effectively cleanse inspired air by wave-like motions that propel foreign material back into the larger bronchi and trachea where the cough reflex completes the expulsion. Furthermore, mucus-secreting cells and immune cells line the airways and help protect the lungs by trapping viruses, bacteria, pollen, dust, and other foreign material (Robbins and Cotran, 1979; Weinberger, 2004).

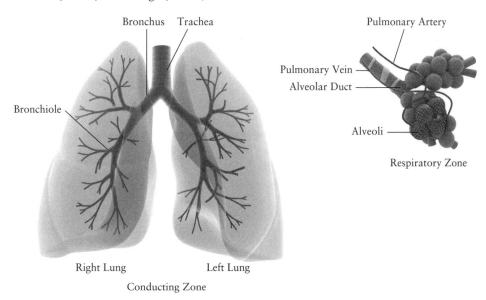

Figure 30.1 Diagram of Human Lungs.

Source: © Sebastian Kaulitzki/ShutterStock, Inc.

Exchange of gases occurs in the *respiratory zone*, which consists of respiratory bronchioles, the alveolar ducts, and the alveoli (**Figure 30.1**). The alveolar epithelium is a continuous layer of cells consisting of two principal cell types: *Type I pneumocytes* that cover 95% of the alveolar surface and granular *Type II pneumocytes* that secrete *pulmonary surfactant* (the major lubricant in the lungs) and are involved in repairing damage to the alveoli. Type I pneumocytes interface with the endothelial cells lining the pulmonary capillaries to facilitate the diffusion of carbon dioxide and oxygen across the alveolar-capillary membrane (Robbins and Cotran, 1979; Weinberger, 2004).

Total lung capacity ranges between 4 and 6 liters and is contingent upon age, height, weight, and gender. On average, females have 20–25% less capacity than males. The typical adult resting respiratory rate is 10–20 breaths per minute, and with each breath about 500 milliliters of air are exchanged (the *tidal volume*). Nevertheless, the lungs have a tremendous reserve volume and the amount of air that can be exchanged by *forced* inspiration and expiration is about 4 liters (the *vital capacity*). The average human breathes approximately 11,000 liters of air containing 2.31 liters of oxygen per day (Robbins and Cotran, 1979; Weinberger, 2004).

DIAGNOSIS OF CHRONIC OBSTRUCTIVE PULMONARY DISEASE (COPD)

Chronic obstructive pulmonary disease (COPD) actually refers to the presence of either of two conditions, emphysema or chronic bronchitis, which may exist simultaneously or separately in a given individual. The diagnosis of COPD is initially suggested by chronic repeated episodes of dyspnea (shortness of breath), wheezing, and coughing with or without mucous production.

In emphysema uncompromised by chronic bronchitis, the patient is typically barrel-chested and dyspneic with obviously prolonged expiration due to air trapping in the lungs. Significant weight loss is a common presenting symptom. Such patients remain well oxygenated and are thus referred to as *pink puffers*. Pathologically, the lungs are characterized by permanent enlargement of the air spaces distal to the terminal bronchioles accompanied by significant destruction of the alveolar walls (Robbins and Cotran, 1979; Weinberger, 2004).

Chronic bronchitis is clinically defined as persistent cough with sputum production for at least 3 months in at least 2 consecutive years. This condition in its pure form involves chronic bacterial or viral infection and inflammation of the lungs. Patients characteristically are obese and may be *cyanotic* and *hypercapnic* due to lack of oxygen and excess carbon dioxide in the blood, respectively. Due to the bluish tinge of skin and lips from cyanosis and fluid retention from congestive right heart failure (*cor pulmonale*), such patients are referred to as *blue bloaters*. The classic signs and symptoms of patients with emphysema versus chronic bronchitis are compared in **Table 30.1**.

The diagnosis of COPD is confirmed using spirometry, a test that measures the ratio of the forced expiratory volume of air in 1 second by the patient (FEV1) to the forced vital capacity of the lungs (FVC). Ratios less than 0.70 are diagnostic of COPD. Radiographic images of the lungs may aid in the diagnosis, and biopsy specimens are sometimes ascertained to microscopically assess the degree of alveolar destruction in emphysema. The stages of COPD based upon post-spirometry values measured after administration of a bronchodilator (e.g., a beta 2 agonist) are shown in **Table 30.2**.

Table 30.1	Emphysema versus Chronic Bronchitis
Pink Puffer	**Blue Bloater**
No Bronchitis	Bronchitis, Cough, Mucous, Infection
Barrel Chest	No Barrel Chest
Early Dyspnea	Late Dyspnea
Hyperventillation	Cyanosis
Adequate Oxygenation	Hypercapnia
Hunched Over	Cor Pulmonale, CHF
Weight Loss	Obesity

Table 30.2	Stages of COPD	
Stage of COPD	**Symptoms**	**Spirometry**
Stage I: Mild	SOB, Cough	FEV1/FVC <0.70 FEV1 <80%
Stage II: Moderate	SOB, Cough, Sputum	FEV1/FVC <0.70 FEV1 <80%
Stage III: Severe	SOB, Fatigue, Cough, Sputum	FEV1/FVC <0.70 FEV1 <50%
Stage IV: Very Severe	SOB, Cyanosis, Respiratory Failure	FEV1/FVC <0.70 FEV1 <30%

It is important to realize that emphysema and chronic bronchitis are often superimposed in the same patient. Indeed, the coexistence of both conditions in the same individual is the rule rather than the exception. However, chronic bronchitis is diagnosed according to clinical parameters (productive cough for 3 months in 2 consecutive years). Consequently, chronic bronchitis is easier to diagnose giving rise to higher prevalence rates. Nevertheless, pathologic studies of biopsy specimens from COPD patients with stage III or stage IV disease invariably reflect the presence of components of *both* emphysema and chronic bronchitis (Robbins and Cotran, 1979; Weinberger, 2004).

AGE DISTRIBUTION OF COPD

The onset of COPD (chronic bronchitis and/or emphysema) increases exponentially with age in both men and women. The age-specific prevalence of COPD estimated from a random sample of the general population of England ($n = 10,750$) is shown in **Figure 30.2**. Note that after age 55 years the prevalence in men is approximately double that in women, e.g., 12% of men over 75 years have COPD compared to 6% in women (Nacul, Soljak, and Meade, 2007). This marked gender difference primarily reflects the greater rates of smoking among men (as discussed in the section on COPD risk factors). The age distribution of COPD differs markedly from that of asthma, which is similar for men and women and actually declines in the later years of life.

GLOBAL BURDEN OF COPD

Chronic obstructive pulmonary disease (COPD) causes nearly 3 million deaths annually in the world population. Overall, COPD ranks fifth in cause-specific mortality and is projected to climb even higher in the coming years. The vast majority of deaths from COPD (nearly 90%) occur in developing countries. In developed countries, COPD currently ranks third in mortality, behind only cardiovascular disease and cancer (WHO, 2008a).

Most patients suffer from COPD for many years with severe disability and diminished quality of life. The rapidly rising prevalence, morbidity, and mortality due to COPD, particularly in developing countries, are generating enormous healthcare costs worldwide.

Estimates of the disability adjusted life years for COPD are shown by country in **Figure 30.3** (*DALY = YLL + YDL, where YLL = years of life lost due to death and YDL = years of life lost due to severe disability*). High DALY rates are present in nations of Eastern Europe and Southern Asia (China and India) where smoking rates are high, particularly among men. Other exposures, e.g., pollution from burning biomass for heat and cooking, play a major role in the populations of developing countries (see discussion of risk factors for COPD).

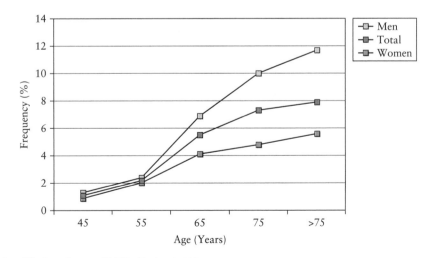

Figure 30.2 Age-Specific Prevalence of COPD, England, 2005.

Source: Data from Nacul LC, Soljak M, Meade T (2007). Model for estimating the population prevalence of chronic obstructive pulmonary disease: cross sectional data from the Health Survey for England. *Population Health Metrics* 5(8):1478–1482.

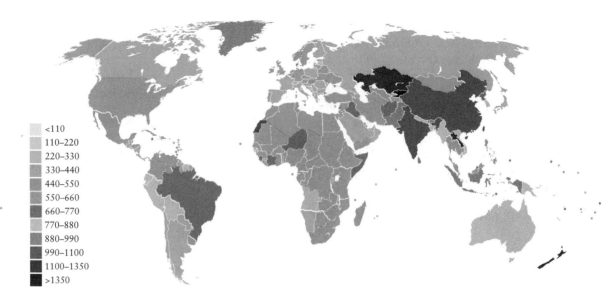

Figure 30.3 Disability Adjusted Life Years for COPD: 2004.

Source: Data from World Health Organization. The global burden of disease: 2004 update. Geneva, WHO, 2008. Available at www.who.int /evidence/bod

TRENDS IN MORTALITY RATES OF COPD: UNITED STATES AND THE UNITED KINGDOM

Mortality rates of COPD appear to be changing in certain populations of the world. In the United States and the United Kingdom, COPD mortality in men has declined, whereas in women the rates have increased (**Figure 30.4**). The predominant risk factor for COPD development is cigarette smoking. These trends in COPD mortality are thus largely explainable by the declining rates of smoking in men versus increasing rates in women. Nevertheless, there is some evidence suggesting that women may have heightened susceptibility to cigarette smoke or other sources of lung pollution compared to men. Further investigations are needed to better understand and quantify the potential role of occupational and environmental exposures in contributing to the rising prevalence of COPD among women (Sørheim et al., 2010).

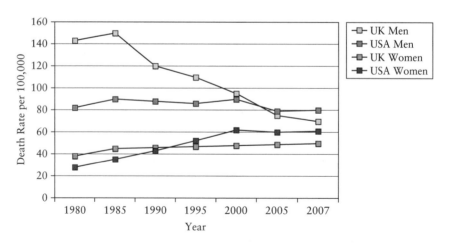

Figure 30.4 COPD Mortality Trends, USA and UK, 1980–2007.

Source: World Health Organization. Global surveillance, prevention and control of chronic respiratory diseases; a comprehensive approach. Geneva, WHO, 2009.

PATHOGENESIS OF COPD

Chronic obstructive pulmonary disease (COPD) is initiated by inflammation, usually due to chronic exposure of the airways to tobacco smoke (**Figure 30.5**). Inflammation triggers chemotaxis and infiltration of the bronchioles and alveoli by macrophages and neurophils. These cells of the innate immune system secrete cytokines and degrasive enzymes such as collagenase, elastase, and matrix metalloproteinases that in turn biodegrade elastin, collagen, and other proteins leading to the loss of alveolar wall integrity and enlargement of the alveolar air spaces. These features are the pathological hallmarks of *emphysema*.

Tobacco smoke also stimulates metaplastic and dysplastic changes in the mucous secreting cells (goblet cells) that line the bronchioles. Hypersecretion of mucous by goblet cells coupled with infiltration of the bronchioles by mononuclear leukocytes (white blood cells) leads to occlusion, infection, and narrowing of the airways. These features are the pathological hallmarks of *chronic bronchitis*.

It is estimated that in at least half of COPD cases, these processes are triggered by exposure to the thousands of noxious chemicals in tobacco smoke and the deposition of tobacco residue (tar) in the lungs (Marsh et al., 2006). Inflammation ensues with the influx of inflammatory cells leading to the pathologic changes characteristic of both emphysema and chronic bronchitis. Additionally, increased oxidative stress caused by the free radicals in tobacco smoke and the oxidants released by cells of the immune system produce necrosis and apoptosis of exposed cells. Both emphysematous destruction and small airway inflammation are often found in combination in individual patients, leading to the spectrum that is known as COPD. When emphysema is moderate or severe, loss of elastic recoil, rather than bronchiolar disease, is the mechanism of airflow limitation. In contrast, when emphysema is mild and chronic bronchitis is the dominant component of disease, bronchiolar abnormalities are most responsible for the deficit in lung function.

Tobacco Use and COPD

The predominant etiologic agent in the genesis of both emphysema and chronic bronchitis is cigarette smoking (or any other form of smoking tobacco). Nevertheless, there is substantial international variation in death rates possibly reflecting smoking behavior, type and processing of tobacco, pollution, climate, respiratory management, and genetic factors.

In order to examine the prevalence of COPD in developing and middle income nations, an international team of investigators from five participating centers in Latin America initiated the Latin American Project for the Investigation of Obstructive Lung Disease (PLATINO). Centers in major metropolitan cities of Brazil, Chile, Mexico, Uruguay, and Venezuela contributed patients for the study. A total of 5,315 adults aged 40 years or older were sampled with approximately similar numbers of individuals representing each site. The presence of COPD was defined as lung function less than 70% of normal based upon spirometry. Prevalence estimates of COPD ranged from 7.8% in Mexico to 19.7% in Uruguay. The investigators suggested that the high COPD prevalence in the Uruguay sample may be related to not only high rates of smoking but also high altitude and the lower oxygen content of ambient air. They also noted that the health burden of COPD was greater than previously realized (Menezes et al., 2005).

Halbert and colleagues conducted a review and meta-analysis of studies reporting prevalence estimates of COPD. Their study included population-based prevalence estimates of COPD, chronic bronchitis, and/or emphysema reported during 1990–2004. A total of 101 estimates based upon sample populations from 28 different countries were ascertained from 67 published reports for analysis. The pooled estimates of prevalence were 7.6% for COPD ($n = 37$ studies), 6.4% for chronic bronchitis ($n = 38$ studies), and 1.8% for emphysema (8 studies). Restriction of data to only cases confirmed by spirometry yielded a prevalence estimate of 8.9%. Subgroup analyses showed that the prevalence rates were highest in smokers (15.4%) and individuals over 65 years of age (14.2%). Rates were also higher in men than women (9.8% vs. 5.6%) and higher in urban populations compared to rural or mixed populations (10.2% vs. 6.4%). The investigators noted the presence of significant heterogeneity among the

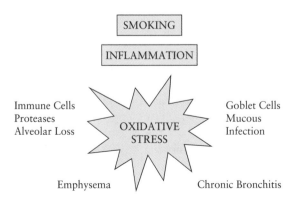

Figure 30.5 Pathogenesis of COPD.

reported estimates that was incompletely explained by sampling differences in age and smoking (Halbert et al., 2006).

Recently, the Global Obstructive Lung Disease Initiative (GOLD) was initiated by the World Health Organization (WHO) in collaboration with the Global Alliance Against Respiratory Diseases (GARD) in order to raise awareness of the increasing burden of COPD, implement programs of prevention to decrease morbidity and mortality, and promote further COPD research (GOLD, 2007). Subsequently, the Burden of Obstructive Lung Disease (BOLD) initiative was developed by GOLD primarily to estimate the worldwide prevalence of COPD and its risk factors using standardized methods (Buist et al., 2005). These methods were developed in conjunction with the Latin American Project for the Investigation of Obstructive Lung Disease (PLATINO) conducted in five Latin American countries (Menezes et al., 2005).

An early report based upon 12 participating centers in the BOLD initiative examined the prevalence of COPD among 9,425 adults aged 40 years or more. Centers representing China, Turkey, Austria, South Africa, Iceland, Germany, Poland, Norway, Canada, the United States, Australia, and the Phillipines were included in the study. At least 600 participants were recruited per center and the diagnosis of COPD was confirmed by spirometry. Logistic regression analysis was use to estimate adjusted odds ratios (OR) for COPD associated with 10-year age increments and 10-pack-year increments of smoking. The prevalence of stage II or higher COPD was 11.8% in men, 8.5% in women, and 10.1% overall. The risk of COPD increased by 94% for each 10-year age increment and the smoking-related risk of COPD increased by 28% in women and 16% in men for each 10-pack-year increment of smoking. Heterogeneity of smoking effects were observed in women but not in men, leading the investigators to suggest the need to study factors other than smoking in order to implement primary and secondary policies of prevention (Buist et al., 2007).

The *Obstructive Lung Disease in Northern Sweden (OLIN) Study* was designed to determine the cumulative incidence of COPD in cohorts of subjects with respiratory symptoms. Two methods of COPD diagnosis were compared, the British Thoracic Society (BTS) criteria and the Global Initiative for Chronic Obstructive Lung Disease (GOLD) criteria. The GOLD criterion uses a lower threshold of lung dysfunction (FEV1/FVC <0.70) for detection of COPD than the BTS criterion (FEV1/FVC <0.70 and FVE1 <80% of normal). The final cohort included 1,109 men and women from Northern Sweden who completed technically adequate spirometric pulmonary function tests. The 10-year cumulative incidence was 8.2% by BTS criteria and 13.5% by GOLD criteria. The incidence of COPD increased with age and intensity of smoking but did not differ by gender or heredity (familial predisposition). The odds ratios for chronic smokers compared to never smokers did not differ appreciably for the BTS (OR = 5.4) and GOLD criteria (OR = 4.6). Results using the more liberal GOLD criteria indicate that 50% of chronic smokers eventually develop COPD (Lundbäck et al., 2003; Lindberg et al., 2005).

As part of the Copenhagen Heart Study in Denmark, a population sample of 8,045 men and women aged 30–60 years with normal lung function at baseline were followed for 25 years to determine changes in lung function by spirometry and mortality due to COPD. Among chronic smokers, 36% developed COPD compared to only 8% among nonsmokers. The odds ratio for developing clinically significant (stage II or higher) COPD was 6.3 for continuous smokers compared to never smokers. Smoking cessation during the follow-up period markedly decreased the risk of developing COPD, e.g., approximately 12% of early quitters developed COPD. During the follow-up period, 100 of the 109 deaths from COPD occurred among individuals who were smokers (Løkke et al., 2006).

The Rotterdam Study was designed to examine the incidence of COPD and the risk associated with aging and smoking in a prospective cohort of men and women in the Netherlands. In the study cohort, 7,983 participants aged 55 years or older at baseline were followed on average for 11 years. During 70,209 person-years of observation, 648 incident cases of COPD were detected by spirometry reports. The diagnosis of COPD was based upon spirometry values indicative of at least stage II disease (FEV1/FVS <0.70 and FEV1 <80% of normal value). The incidence of COPD for the entire cohort was 9.2 cases per 1,000 person-years. Crude incidence rates were higher in men than women (14.4 vs. 6.2 per 1,000 person-years) and higher in smokers than never smokers (12.8 vs. 3.9 per 1,000 person-years). As shown in **Figure 30.6**, age-gender-adjusted estimates of the hazard ratio (relative risk) increased dramatically with pack-years of smoking, e.g., 10-pack-years of smoking increased the risk nearly fourfold and 50-pack-years of smoking increased the risk nearly ninefold. These results underscore the etiologic link between smoking and the development of COPD. Nevertheless, as the authors point out:

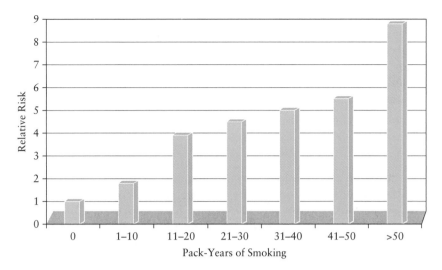

Figure 30.6 Dose Response of the Relative Risk of COPD by Pack-Years of Smoking: The Rotterdam Study.

Source: Data from van Durme YM, Verhamme KM, Stijnen T, van Rooij FJ, Van Pottelberge GR, Hofman A, Joos GF, Stricker BH, Brusselle GG (2009). Prevalence, incidence, and lifetime risk for the development of COPD in the elderly: the Rotterdam study. *Chest* 135:368–377.

"Incident COPD cases were also detected among male and especially female never-smokers, indicating that—besides active smoking—other environmental exposures such as passive smoking, occupational exposures, and (outdoor and indoor) air pollution might contribute to the development of COPD" (van Durme et al., 2009).

Environmental Tobacco Smoke and COPD

A limited number of epidemiologic studies have examined the risk of developing COPD in individuals exposed to environmental tobacco smoke (ETS). Jaakkola reviewed the results of three case-control studies and three cohort studies, all of which found significant increases in the risk of developing COPD in elderly nonsmoking individuals who reported chronic exposure to ETS (Jaakkola, 2006). Estimates of relative risk for the highest exposure levels ranged from 1.7 to 5.6 and 4 of the studies found a significant dose response in COPD risk with increasing duration of ETS exposure. The biological effects of ETS are similar to mainstream smoke and individuals with chronic heavy exposure should be considered at increased risk for the development of COPD.

Indoor Air Pollution and COPD

Recent estimates from the World Health Organization suggest that nearly 3 billion people, almost half of the world population, are continually exposed to biomass smoke from the combustion of solid fuels such as wood and coal (WHO, 2006). In many regions of Africa, Central America, and Asia, the vast majority of rural homes use solid fuel as the primary cooking and heating fuel. Because of their routine cooking and other domestic activities, women in these households tend to have far greater exposure to indoor air pollution than men.

Epidemiologic evidence has accrued regarding the risk of COPD associated with chronic exposure to biomass smoke. Kurmi and colleagues conducted a review and meta-analysis of 23 epidemiologic investigations in order to quantify the risk associated with indoor air pollution. These studies included population samples from China, Turkey, Saudi Arabia, Spain, Columbia, and Mexico. Despite heterogeneity among study designs and population samples, chronic exposure to biomass smoke significantly increased the risk of developing COPD (OR = 2.8) and chronic bronchitis (OR = 2.3) compared to no exposure. Chronic indoor exposure to wood smoke conferred the highest risk (OR = 4.5) although chronic exposure to biomass smoke from other types of fuel (coal, charcoal, straw, dung) also produced significant risk increases (Kurmi et al., 2010).

In a separate meta-analysis, Hu and colleagues analyzed data from 15 studies including population samples from China, India, Nepal, Turkey, Pakistan, Saudi Arabia, Spain, Brazil, Columbia, Bolivia, and Mexico. Overall, chronic exposure to biomass smoke significantly increased the risk of developing COPD in both women (OR = 2.7) and men (OR = 4.3) and in cigarette smokers (OR = 4.4) and nonsmokers

(OR = 2.5). The higher risk in men was consistent with their higher rates of smoking. Risk increases were observed after about 5 years of exposure and increased with duration of exposure. Estimates were not influenced by ethnicity, e.g., similar increases were observed for Asian and non-Asian populations (Hu et al., 2010).

Air Pollution and COPD

In their comprehensive textbook on the pathogenesis of disease, Stanley Robbins and Ramzi Cotran provide an excellent discussion of air pollution and the lung disorders collectively called *pneumoconiosis*. Numerous studies have shown that air contaminants that are present in the atmospheric environment of the industrialized world are capable of provoking lung dysfunction and respiratory ailments including COPD. Hundreds of millions of tons of air pollutants are discharged each year from the combustion of gasoline and fossil fuels, in both developed and developing nations. As quoted from Robbins and Cotran on environmental pathology: "*To be found in city air are variable mixtures of carbon, sulfur, and nitrogen oxides; organic residues containing tars and aldehydes (some of which may be potentially carcinogenic); the vaporized metals and acids emitted by industry and gasoline engines; and all manner of organic and inorganic dust.*" The authors go on to point out that "*cigarette smoking potentiates or exaggerates the effects of air contamination*" (Robbins and Cotran, 1979).

Repeated inhalation of coal dust or other carbon particles leads to the deposition of these materials throughout the respiratory bronchioles and alveolar spaces producing carbon pigmentation of the lungs known as *pulmonary anthracosis*. Many other small particles that enter the airways, both organic and inorganic, can also lead to pneumoconiosis, e.g., silicosis is a particularly severe form of pneumoconiosis resulting from the inhalation of silica dust.

In general, pneumoconiosis is characterized by the accumulation of such particles within the macrophages of the lungs accompanied by irritation, inflammation, and the release of destructive enzymes and reactive oxygen species that result in cell necrosis and, subsequently, pulmonary fibrosis. These same processes are integral to the development of chronic bronchitis, emphysema, and COPD. Hence, rates of COPD are high among those individuals exposed to high levels of coal dust, silica dust, and other types of air pollution.

The etiologic role of coal mine dust in the pathogenesis of debilitating pneumoconiosis and *black lung disease* is a well-known phenomenon. Albeit, exposure to coal dust also heightens the risk of COPD. Studies of the relation between COPD and exposure to respirable coal mine dust have been carried out in Britain, the United States, Italy, and Germany (Coggon and Taylor, 1998).

In an investigation of coal miners versus telecommunications workers in South Wales, more of the miners reported symptoms of chronic bronchitis than controls (31% vs. 5%) and 20% of the miners had lower than normal forced expiratory volumes compared to 10% of controls. Differences were apparent for both smokers and nonsmokers (Lloyd, Gauld, and Soutar, 1986).

Lewis and colleagues compared spirometry measures of FEV1 (forced expiratory lung volume in one second) in 1,286 coal miners with 567 men in other occupations sampled from the East Midlands of England. After adjustment for age, height, and smoking, the mean FEV1 was 155 ml lower in the miners, suggesting that they were developing higher rates of COPD (Lewis et al., 1996).

An important body of work on coal miners and COPD was conducted in the British Pneumoconiosis Field Research (PFR) program conducted by the Institute of Occupational Medicine. This series of investigations was based on data for more than 30,000 miners at 24 collieries in Great Britain. In an analysis of 3,380 of these miners who either smoked cigarettes or were nonsmokers, the cumulative exposure to coal dust over 10 years was assessed and related to the risk of 4 end points: FEV1 <80%; symptoms of chronic bronchitis; symptoms of chronic bronchitis and FEV1 <80%; and FEV1 <65%. In both smokers and nonsmokers, odds ratios for all end points increased by approximately twofold with high cumulative exposure to coal dust (Marine, Gurr, and Jacobsen, 1988).

The US National Study of Coal Workers' Pneumoconiosis (SCWP) examined risk factors for COPD including coal dust exposure in miners from 31 nationally distributed collieries. Data were collected on chest radiographs, spirometric measures of lung function, details of clinical symptoms, and smoking habits of the miners. In a study of 7,139 miners, linear regression was used to relate pulmonary function to cumulative coal dust exposure. After adjustment for age, height, mine location, and smoking, exposure to coal dust was associated with significantly lower FEV1 values (Attfield and Hodous, 1992).

Italian investigators reported the results of an 11-year follow-up study of Sardinian coal miners. Analysis of 909 miners who had worked in the mines for more than 2 years revealed declining

FEV1 function and more frequent onset of chronic bronchitis with increasing exposure to coal dust (Carta et al., 1996).

Oxman and colleagues described a study of 544 miners who worked in a colliery at Recklinghausen in Germany. Analysis of cross-sectional data revealed a significant negative association between coal dust exposure and FEV1 (Oxman et al., 1993).

Due to their increased exposure to silica dust, gold miners have been studied to assess their risk of developing COPD and silicosis. Such studies have examined the level of silica dust and the severity of COPD in postmortem lung specimens. In a review of studies of South African gold miners, the incidence of chronic bronchitis was found to increase with increasing exposure to silica dust, and individuals in jobs with high exposure to silica dust for 20 years or more exhibited significantly more extensive lung damage from emphysema than individuals with low exposure (Hnizdo and Vallyathan, 2003).

In general, findings from SCWP and PFR and other studies of miners are similar in demonstrating increased rates of COPD and significant loss of pulmonary function in miners who are chronically exposed to coal mine dust or silica dust. Clearly, occupational mining dust is an important cause of COPD.

As opposed to studies of high-risk groups such as miners who are exposed to inordinately high levels of occupational dust, investigations of the health effects of air pollution in the general population are more complex due to difficulties in obtaining accurate measures of exposure to relatively low levels of contamination over long periods of time. Two US studies, the *Harvard Six Cities Study* and the *American Cancer Society Study*, have attempted to examine the contribution of air pollution to overall morbidity and mortality.

The Harvard Six Cities Study was designed to evaluate effects of air pollution on the mortality among cohorts of adults sampled from Watertown, Massachusetts; Kingston and Harriman, Tennessee; Steubenville, Ohio; Portage, Wyocena, and Pardeeville, Wisconsin; and Topeka, Kansas. A total of 8,111 adults 25–74 years of age were followed for 14–16 years to determine associations of mortality with the level of air pollution. Each participant reported their age, gender, weight, height, education level, smoking history, occupational exposures, and medical history at baseline. Concentrations of total suspended particulate matter, sulfur dioxide, ozone, and suspended sulfates were measured in each community at a centrally located air-monitoring station. Based on proportional hazards (Cox) general linear regression, smoking had the strongest association with mortality. Nevertheless, after adjustment for smoking and other health risk factors, the city-specific all-cause mortality rates were positively associated with the average levels of air pollutants (hazard ratio = 1.26). Increasing levels of air pollution, particularly involving fine particulates and sulfates, were associated with higher mortality from lung cancer and cardiopulmonary disease (Dockery et al., 1993).

The American Cancer Society Study examined effects of particulate air pollution using ambient air pollution data from 151 US metropolitan areas and risk factor information for 552,138 adults who resided in these areas. Participants in the study completed a risk factor questionnaire to ascertain detailed information on age, gender, smoking, and other risk factors. Exposure to sulfate and fine particulate air pollution (primarily from fossil fuel combustion) was estimated from national databases. Relationships of air pollution to all-cause mortality and mortality from lung cancer and cardiopulmonary disease were examined by multivariate analysis controlling for smoking and other risk factors. All-cause mortality in the most polluted areas was 15% higher than in the least polluted areas and exposure to high levels of particulate air pollution significantly increased mortality due to lung cancer and cardiopulmonary disease (Pope et al., 1995).

Subsequent analyses of the data from the Harvard Six Cities Study and the American Cancer Society Study of air pollution and mortality were conducted by a team of investigators in order to check the original findings. Collectively, this *reanalysis* of the data from these two studies confirmed the original results and provided evidence that exposure to high concentrations of sulfur dioxide in addition to fine particulates and sulfates heightens the mortality risk (Krewski et al., 2003).

The exhaust from motor vehicles is a significant source of air pollution, contributing nitrogen oxides, carbon monoxide, benzene, and other volatile organic compounds to the ambient air near high-traffic roadways. Evidence is emerging from epidemiologic investigations linking exposure to motor vehicle exhaust near high-volume traffic roads with adverse health effects including COPD. Novel experimental designs are necessary to accrue such evidence as illustrated by the following investigation.

Lindgren and colleagues conducted a geographical study of COPD and traffic-related air pollution in Southern Sweden. Exposures were measured as the volume of traffic per minute and the concentration of nitrogen oxide compounds in ambient air. Cases were identified by self-report in a sample of

9,319 individuals aged 18–77 years. Individuals were linked by geocoded residential addresses to a Swedish road database and an emission database of nitrogen oxide concentrations in ambient air for the region. The study found that living within 100 meters of a high-traffic road (>10 cars per minute) significantly increased the risk of COPD (OR = 1.64). There was also a significant positive dose response of the level of nitrogen oxide concentration and COPD risk (OR = 1.55 for the highest concentration) (Lindgren et al., 2009).

α_1 Antitrypsin Deficiency and COPD

The best documented genetic risk factor for COPD is α_1 antitrypsin deficiency, a relatively rare condition that is present in only 1–2% of patients with mild to moderate COPD. Nevertheless, up to 50% of patients over 40 years of age with severe (stage IV) COPD have been found to have α_1 antitrypsin deficiency. As pointed out by Graham Devereux in his review of COPD: "*Detection of such cases identifies family members who will require genetic counseling and patients who might be suitable for future potential treatment with α_1 antitrypsin replacement*" (Devereux, 2006).

The glycoprotein α_1 antitrypsin is responsible for inhibiting collagenase, elastase, and other proteases derived from leukocytes, particularly in the aveoli of the lungs. If α_1 antitrypsin is deficient or absent, there is uncontrolled degradation of alveolar proteins such as elastase and collagen resulting in the accelerated development of emphysema.

The inheritance pattern of alleles is codominant, and since the gene for α_1 antitrypsin is highly polymorphic, some rare genotypes (e.g., ZZ) result in extremely low concentrations of active α_1 antitrypsin (10–20% of normal) whereas other genotypes may result in intermediate levels. With severe α_1 antitrypsin deficiency, progression of COPD can be rapid, particularly in combination with cigarette smoking (Robbins and Cotran, 1979; Devereux, 2006).

UNDERDIAGNOSIS OF COPD

A number of studies suggest that COPD is often underdiagnosed, particularly among those individuals with mild disease. Two sets of criteria have been used by clinicians to confirm the presence of COPD: the British Thoracic Society (BTS) and the Global Initiative for Chronic Obstructive Lung Disease (GOLD) criteria. The GOLD criteria shown earlier in **Table 30.2** uses a lower threshold of lung dysfunction (FEV1/FVC <0.70) for detection of COPD than the BTS criterion (FEV1/FVC <0.70 and FVE1 <80% of normal). Consequently, application of the GOLD criteria detects higher incidence and prevalence rates of COPD.

The *Obstructive Lung Disease in Northern Sweden (OLIN) Study* was designed to compare the BTS and GOLD guidelines for COPD detection in cohorts of subjects ascertained from Northern Sweden. Subjects enrolled for study already had clinical respiratory symptoms, e.g., persistent cough, wheezing, shortness of breath, and sputum production, but had not undergone spirometric testing. Among 1,236 patients, 14% of patients had COPD by the GOLD criterion compared to only 8.2% by the BTS criterion, an absolute difference of more than 5% (Lindberg et al., 2006).

Many other investigations also reveal that COPD is underdiagnosed, particularly among those patients with mild disease. In a review and meta-analysis of data on the diagnosis and prevalence of COPD, Halbert and colleagues noted significant heterogeneity due to differences in diagnostic methodology. Their analysis is based upon 37 prevalence estimates ascertained from 62 published studies. Notably, the application of spirometric criteria resulted in nearly a twofold higher prevalence estimate compared with either patient-reported or physician-diagnosed COPD (9.2% vs. 4.9% and 5.2%, respectively). These findings suggest the need for standardization of diagnostic measures of COPD in subsequent epidemiologic investigations. Spirometric evaluation of patients using the GOLD criteria has been adopted as an epidemiologic case definition by the Burden of Obstructive Lung Disease (BOLD) initiative and the Latin-American Project for the Investigation of Pulmonary Obstruction (PLATINO). Widespread application of a valid and reproducible method of COPD diagnosis is critical to gain a better understanding of the global burden of COPD (Halbert et al., 2006).

POPULATION ATTRIBUTABLE FRACTION: SMOKING AND COPD

The *population attributable fraction (PAF)* is the fraction of a disease that can be attributed to a particular risk factor. The PAF is calculated in various ways, e.g., if the relative risk (*RR*) and the frequency of the risk factor (*p*) are known, then

$$PAF = p(RR - 1) / [p(RR - 1) + 1].$$

If the incidence rate of disease for individuals who are exposed to a risk factor (I_E) and individuals who are not exposed to the risk factor (I_{NE}) are known, then

$$PAF = p(I_E - I_{NE}) / [p(I_E - I_{NE}) + (1 - p) I_{NE}].$$

For example, if the relative risk of COPD among chronic smokers is 5 and the prevalence of chronic smoking is 40%, the population attributable fraction = 61.5%.

Estimates of the fraction of COPD attributable to cigarette smoking vary widely, ranging from 40% to 90% depending on the population under study, the detail of smoking exposure, and the diagnostic criteria that are used. A review of estimates from recent studies suggests that the population attributable fraction (PAF) from smoking may be closer to 50% with up to 20% of cases due to other sources of pollution such as biomass smoke from cooking and heating in poorly ventilated dwellings (Marsh et al., 2006).

It is best to keep in mind that the strength of risk factors and corresponding estimates of PAF may vary widely depending upon the population under study and the exposure frequencies. As an example, in a report based on the Chinese Epidemiologic Survey of COPD in 20,245 adults aged 40 years or older, 86.2% of 1,024 smokers who developed COPD were men, whereas 69.4% of 644 nonsmokers who developed COPD were women. Furthermore, the prevalence of smoking in men (74.3%) was nearly 7 times higher than in women (11.3%). Thus, factors other than cigarette smoke, e.g., smoke from burning coal and biomass in poorly ventilated dwellings, appear to have a significant impact on the development of COPD, particularly among Chinese women (Zhou et al., 2009).

LUNG CANCER AND COPD

The dominant risk factor for both lung cancer and COPD is chronic tobacco smoking. Furthermore, the impaired lung function of COPD patients may also increase their lung cancer risk. Swedish investigators studied the association of COPD and lung cancer in a large cohort of individuals ($n = 176,997$) for whom spirometry measurements were available at baseline. The stage of COPD was determined using the GOLD criteria for spirometric measures of lung function. During 1971–2001, 834 incident cases of lung cancer were detected in the cohort through linkage with the Swedish National Cancer Registry. As shown in **Figure 30.7**, the relative risk of lung cancer is significantly increased in patients with COPD and more severe disease accentuates the risk (Purdue et al., 2007).

PREVENTION OF COPD

As with all smoking-related diseases, the key to primary prevention is complete abstinence from tobacco use. As elaborated earlier in this text, educational efforts must be initiated early in life to prevent young individuals from taking up the smoking habit. Effective educational programs have produced impressive results in some nations, e.g., smoking rates have declined dramatically in certain developed countries such as the United States and the United Kingdom. Furthermore, many countries and local jurisdictions throughout the world have successfully implemented laws requiring indoor workplaces and public places to be smoke free. Nevertheless, it is startling that nearly one-third of adults in the

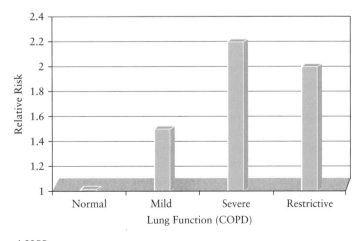

Figure 30.7 Lung Cancer and COPD.

Source: Data from Purdue MP, Gold L, Järvholm B, Alavanja MCR, Ward MH, Vermeulen R (2007). Impaired lung function and lung cancer incidence in a cohort of Swedish construction workers. *Thorax* 62:51–56.

world population continue to smoke tobacco (WHO, 2008b). Recently, an international program of tobacco control titled the *Tobacco Free Initiative (TFI)* was ratified and implemented through the auspices of the World Health Organization to curb the epidemic of tobacco-related diseases throughout the world (WHO, 2009a, 2009c).

A key component of effective COPD prevention is the early detection of mild symptoms when the disease process is reversible and lung function can be restored to normal. A positive development is the adoption of standardized measures of lung function based upon spirometry, e.g., the GOLD criteria for detection and staging of COPD. Certainly, there is strong evidence that smoking cessation effectively reduces the risk of COPD progression in patients with mild disease. In nonsmokers with early symptoms, the source of pollution and lung irritation should be identified and steps taken for remediation.

SMOKING CESSATION IN COPD PATIENTS

Though smoking cessation is the single most important behavioral change to prevent COPD or reduce its progression, intensive intervention involving counseling, pharmacotherapy, or both is usually required to successfully motivate an individual to quit smoking. The *Lung Health Study* was designed to examine the impact of a smoking cessation program in middle-aged patients with asymptomatic airway obstruction (mild COPD). Patients enrolled in the study ($n = 5,887$) were randomized to receive intensive intervention to help them quit smoking versus usual care. Ten clinical centers located in the United States and Canada enrolled patients for study. The intervention was a 10-week smoking cessation program that included a strong physician message and 12 group sessions using behavior modification and nicotine gum, plus either *ipratropium* or a placebo inhaler. The vital status of each patient was followed up to 14.5 years to determine progression/regression of their lung disease and mortality due to cardiovascular disease, lung cancer, or pulmonary disease. After 5 years of follow-up, 21.7% of patients who received the special intervention had stopped smoking compared to 5.4% of patients receiving usual care. After 14.5 years of follow-up, all-cause mortality was reduced by about 15% in the intervention group compared to the usual care group. Notably, the death rate from respiratory diseases other than lung cancer was significantly less in the intervention group than the usual care group (0.56 vs. 1.08 per 1,000 person-years). These results demonstrate that an intensive smoking cessation program can produce significant reduction in all-cause mortality in people with mild to moderate airway obstruction (Anthonisen et al., 2005).

Several randomized trials have focused on effects of smoking cessation interventions to reduce the progression of COPD. Strassmann and colleagues conducted a meta-analysis of 6 such trials to evaluate smoking cessation counseling with or without pharmacotherapy or nicotine replacement among 7,372 COPD patients. Their analysis showed that intervention involving counseling plus nicotine replacement had the greatest effect on prolonged abstinence rates. Compared to usual care, patients receiving treatment were five times more likely to sustain smoking cessation (Strassmann et al., 2009).

CONTROL OF AIR POLLUTION

Chronic exposure to high concentrations of indoor or outdoor air pollution increases the risk of developing COPD. Outdoor pollution is mainly due to the combustion of fossil fuel for heating, industry, and transport. In particular, motor vehicle exhaust is a primary source. Indoor pollution arises from the combustion of biomass (e.g., wood and coal) for cooking and heating.

In many nations, outdoor pollution has been greatly reduced by switching from coal to cleaner burning fuels such as oil and gas and by the elimination of poorly controlled incinerators. Emission of toxic chemicals in motor vehicle exhaust has been reduced through the use of catalytic converters and air injection systems and development of more efficient engines. In many developed countries, progress in improving air quality and reducing motor vehicle emissions has been maintained as a result of national clean air acts (Higgins, 1986).

Control of indoor pollutants is by ventilation, removal of the source of pollution, improved cooking and heating devices, and behavioral adjustments to avoid exposure. In many nations, new laws have been passed and are being strictly enforced to prohibit smoking in public buildings and regulate the content of toxic and polluting substances in building materials.

Special efforts must be taken to reduce lung damage in individuals with extreme occupational exposure to air pollutants, e.g., miners, foundry workers, and textile mill workers. Air quality in these environments can be improved using filtration and purification systems that cleanse the air supply and mobile positive-pressure face mask filters that protect the individual (Kilburn, 1986).

GLOBAL ALLIANCE AGAINST CHRONIC RESPIRATORY DISEASES (GARD)

The World Health Organization (WHO) has launched a comprehensive international program titled the Global Alliance against Chronic Respiratory Disease (GARD). Its purpose is to integrate the collective knowledge of national and international organizations, institutions, and agencies to implement an effective global strategy for the prevention, detection, treatment, and monitoring of chronic respiratory diseases such as COPD and asthma. Detailed discussion of the objectives of GARD, its structure, member nations and organizations, an overview of chronic respiratory diseases, and the proposed framework for action can be found on the WHO GARD website (WHO, 2010).

REFERENCES

Anthonisen, N.R., Skeans, M.A., Wise, R.A., Manfreda, J., Kanner, R.E., Connett, R.E., for the Lung Health Study Research Group. (2005). The effects of a smoking cessation intervention on 14.5-year mortality: A randomized clinical trial. *Ann Intern Med, 142,* 233–239.

Attfield, M.D., & Hodous, T.K. (1992). Pulmonary function of US coal miners related to dust exposure estimates. *Am Rev Respir Dis, 145,* 605–609.

Buist, A.S., Vollmer, W.M., Sullivan, S.D., Weiss, K.B., Lee, T.A., Menezes, A.M.B.,…Burney, P.G.J. (2005). The burden of lung disease initiative (BOLD): Rational and design. *COPY, 2,* 277–283.

Buist, A.S., McBurnie, M.A., Vollmer, W.M., Gillespie, S., Burney, P., Mannino, D.M.,…Nizankowska-Mogilnicka, E., on behalf of the BOLD Collaborative Research Group. (2007). International variation in the prevalence of COPD (The BOLD study): A population-based prevalence study. *Lancet, 370*(9589), 741–750.

Carta, P., Aru, G., Barbieri, M.T., Vataneo, G., & Casula, D. (1996). Dust exposure, respiratory symptoms, and longitudinal decline in lung function in young coal miners. *Occup Environ Med, 53,* 312–319.

Coggon, D., & Taylor, A.N. (1998). Coal mining and chronic obstructive pulmonary disease: A review of the evidence. *Thorax, 53,* 398–407.

Devereux, G. (2006). ABC of chronic obstructive pulmonary disease. Definition, epidemiology, and risk factors. *BMJ, 332*(7550), 1142–1144.

Dockery, D.W., Pope, C.A., Xu, X., Spengler, J.D., Ware, J.H., Fay, M.E.,…Speizer, F.E. (1993). An association between air pollution and mortality in six U.S. cities. *N Engl J Med, 329,* 1753–1759.

Global Initiative for Chronic Obstructive Lung Disease. (2007). *Global strategy for the diagnosis, management, and prevention of chronic obstructive pulmonary disease.* Medical Communications Resources, Inc.

Halbert, R.J., Natoli, J.L., Gano, A., Badamgarav, E., Buist, A.S., & Mannino, D.M. (2006). Global burden of COPD: Systematic review and meta-analysis. *Eur Respir J, 28,* 523–532.

Higgins, I.T.T. (1986). Air pollution. In J.M. Last (Ed.). *Maxcey-Rosenau public health and preventive medicine* (12th ed.). Norwalk, Connecticut: Appleton-Century-Crofts.

Hnizdo, E., & Vallyathan, V. (2003). Chronic obstructive pulmonary disease due to occupational exposure to silica dust: A review of epidemiological and pathological evidence. *Occup Environ Med, 60*(4), 237–243.

Hu, G., Zhou, Y., Tian, J., Yao, W., Li, J., Li, B., & Ran, P. (2010). Risk of COPD from exposure to biomass smoke. *Chest, 138*(1), 20–31.

Jaakkola, M.S. (2006). Environmental tobacco smoke and health in the elderly. *European Respiratory Journal, 19*(1), 172–181.

Kilburn, K.H. (1986). Occupational chronic bronchitis. In J.M. Last (Ed.). *Maxcey-Rosenau public health and preventive medicine* (12th ed.). Norwalk, Connecticut: Appleton-Century-Crofts.

Krewski, D., Burnett, R., Goldberg, M., Hoover, B.K., Siemiatycki, J., Jerrett, M.,…White, W. (2003). Overview of the reanalysis of the Harvard Six Cities Study and American Cancer Society Study of particulate air pollution and mortality. *J Toxicology Environmental Health, 66*(15), 1507–1552.

Kurmi, O.P., Sample, S., Simkhada, P., Smith, W.C.S., & Ayers, J.G. (2010). COPD and chronic bronchitis risk of indoor air pollution from solid fuel: A systematic review and meta-analysis. *Thorax, 65,* 221–228.

Lewis, S., Bennett, J., Richards, K., et al. (1996). A cross sectional study of the independent effect of occupation on lung function in British coal miners. *Occup Environ Med, 53*, 125–128.

Lindberg, A., Jonsson, A.C., Rönmark, E., Lundgren, R., Larsson, L.G., & Lundbäck, B. (2005). Ten-year cumulative incidence of COPD and risk factors for incident disease in a symptomatic cohort. *Chest, 127*(5), 1544–1552.

Lindberg, A., Bjerg, A., Ronmark, E., Larsson, L.G., & Lundback, B. (2006). Prevalence and underdiagnosis of COPD by disease severity and the attributable fraction of smoking. Report from the Obstructive Lung Disease in Northern Sweden Studies. *Respir Med, 100*, 264–272.

Lindgren, A., Stroh, E., Montnémery, P., Nihlén, U., Jakobsson, K., & Axmon, A. (2009). Traffic-related air pollution associated with prevalence of asthma and COPD/chronic bronchitis. A cross-sectional study in Southern Sweden. *International Journal of Health Geographics, 8*(2), 1476–1480.

Lloyd, M.H., Gauld, S.J., & Soutar, C.A. (1986). Respiratory ill health among coal miners and telecommunication workers in South Wales. *Br J Ind Med, 43*, 177–181.

Løkke, A., Lange, P., Scharling, H., Fabricius, P., & Vestbo, J. (2006). Developing COPD: A 25 year follow up study of the general population. *Thorax, 61*, 935–939.

Lundbäck, B., Lindberg, A., Lindström, M., Rönmark, E., Jönsson, E., Larsson, L.G.,… Larsson, K. (2003). Obstructive lung disease in Northern Sweden Studies. Not 15 but 50% of smokers develop COPD? Report from the Obstructive Lung Disease in Northern Sweden Studies. *Respir Med, 97*, 115–122.

Marine, W.M., Gurr, D., & Jacobsen, M. (1988). Clinically important effects of dust exposure and smoking in British coal miners. *Am Rev Respir Dis, 137*, 106–112.

Marsh, S., Aldington, S., Shirtcliffe, P., Weatherall, M., & Beasley, R. (2006). Smoking and COPD: What really are the risks? Eur Respir J, 28, 883–884.

Menezes, A.M., Padilla, R.P., Jardim, J.R., Muino, A., Lopez, M.V., Valdivia, G., de Oca, M.M.,… Victoria, C.G. for the PLATINO Team. (2005). Chronic obstructive pulmonary disease in five Latin American cities (the PLATINO study): A prevalence study. *Lancet, 366*, 1875–1881.

Nacul, L.C., Soljak, M., & Meade, T. (2007). Model for estimating the population prevalence of chronic obstructive pulmonary disease: Cross sectional data from the Health Survey for England. *Population Health Metrics, 5*(8) doi:10.1186/1478-7954-5-8.

Oxman, A.D., Muir, D.C.F., Shannon, H.S., Stock, S.R., Hnizdo, E., & Lange, H.J. (1993). Occupational dust exposure and chronic obstructive pulmonary disease. *Am Rev Respir Dis, 148*, 38–48.

Pope, C.A., Thun, M.J., Namboodiri, M.M., Dockery, D.W., Evans, J.S., Speizer, F.E., & Heath, C.W. (1995). Particulate air pollution as a predictor of mortality in a prospective study of US adults. *Am J Respir Crit Care Med, 151*(3), 669–674.

Purdue, M.P., Gold, L., Järvholm, B., Alavanja, M.C.R., Ward, M.H., & Vermeulen, R. (2007). Impaired lung function and lung cancer incidence in a sohort of Swedish construction workers. *Thorax, 62*, 51–56.

Robbins, S.L., & Cotran, R.S. (1979). *Pathologic basis of disease*. Philadelphia, PA: WB Saunders Company.

Sørheim, I.C., Johannessen, A., Gulsvik, A., Bakke, P.S., Silverman, E.K., & DeMeo, D.L. (2010). Gender differences in COPD: Are women more susceptible to smoking effects than men? *Thorax, 65*, 480–485.

Strassmann, R., Bausch, B., Spaar, A., Kleijnen, J., Braendli, O., & Puhan, M.A. (2009). Smoking cessation interventions in COPD: A network meta-analysis of randomised trials. *European Respiratory Journal, 34*(3), 634–640.

Weinberger, S.E. (2004). *Principles of pulmonary medicine* (4th ed.). Philadelphia: WB Saunders Company.

World Health Organization. (2006). *Fuel for life-household energy and health*. Geneva, Switzerland: World Health Organization.

World Health Organization. (2008a). *The global burden of disease: Update 2004*. Geneva, Switzerland: World Health Organization.

World Health Organization. (2008b). *WHO Report on the global tobacco epidemic, 2008: The MPOWER package*. Geneva, Switzerland: World Health Organization.

World Health Organization. (2009a). *WHO Report on the global tobacco epidemic, 2009*. Geneva, Switzerland: World Health Organization.

World Health Organization. (2009b). *Disease and injury country estimates. Death and DALY estimates for 2004 by cause for WHO Member States (Persons, all ages)*. Geneva, Switzerland: World Health Organization.

World Health Organization. (2009c). *Global surveillance, prevention and control of chronic respiratory diseases; A comprehensive approach*. Geneva, Switzerland: World Health Organization.

World Health Organization. (2010). *Global alliance against chronic diseases, action plan, 2008–2013*. Geneva, Switzerland: World Health Organization.

van Durme, Y.M., Verhamme, K.M., Stijnen, T., van Rooij, F.J., Van Pottelberge, G.R., Hofman, A.,... Brusselle, G.G. (2009). Prevalence, incidence, and lifetime risk for the development of COPD in the elderly: The Rotterdam study. *Chest, 135*, 368–377.

Zhou, Y., Wang, C., Yao, W., Chen, P., Kang, J., Huang, S.,...Ran, P. (2009). COPD in Chinese nonsmokers. *European Respiratory Journal, 33*(3), 509–518.

Epidemiology of Asthma

CLINICAL DIAGNOSIS OF ASTHMA

Asthma is a restrictive inflammatory pulmonary disease that usually first presents during childhood or adolescence. Though this disease has some similarities with other chronic inflammatory lung diseases, asthma has distinct clinical and epidemiologic characteristics that clearly differentiate it from conditions such as chronic bronchitis and emphysema.

In contrast to COPD, which impacts smaller ciliated bronchioles and alveoli in the lower airways, the pathophysiological effects of asthma are usually localized in the upper airways including the trachea, bronchi, and larger bronchioles. These upper airway structures are lined by squamous epithelium that is without cilia. A further distinction from COPD is that asthma onset occurs more often early in life and the prevalence declines in adulthood. Characteristic

patterns of onset are shown for males and females in **Figure 31.1**. As shown, the prevalence is higher in males during childhood and adolescence, but then becomes higher in females during adulthood (Senthilselvan et al., 2003).

Asthma is caused by the recursive abnormal immune response of B lymphocytes to one or more allergenic stimuli, resulting in inflammation and IgE-mediated histamine release by mast cells plus infiltration by eosinophilic immune cells, a combination that causes constriction of the upper airways and restriction of air flow both into and out of the lungs (Robbins and Cotran, 1979; NHLBI, 2007). Early clinical signs include chronic rhinitis and conjunctivitis, coughing, wheezing, shortness of breath, chest tightness, and acute episodes of respiratory distress provoked by allergenic stimuli, infection, respiratory irritants, exposure to cold air, exercise, emotional

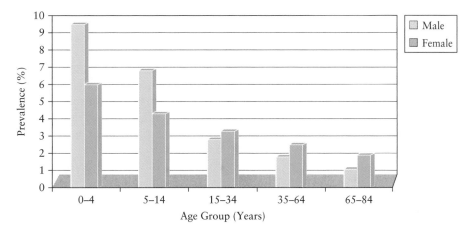

Figure 31.1 Prevalence of Asthma by Age.

Source: Data from Senthilselvan A, Lawson J, Rennie DC, Dosman JA (2003). Stabilization of an Increasing Trend in Physician-Diagnosed Asthma Prevalence in Saskatchewan, 1991 to 1998. *Chest* 124(2):438–448. Rates for 65–84 years were estimated by linear regression.

stress, and drugs (Higgins, 1974). Pathologically, the bronchi and bronchioles are occluded by thick mucous plugs laden with inflammatory eosinophilic cells and containing characteristic crystalline microscopic structures called Curschmann's spirals and Charcot-Leyden crystals (Robbins and Cotran, 1979).

In the asthmatic patient, spirometry testing classically reveals that lung dysfunction is partially reversible by administration of a short-acting beta-agonist such as *albuterol*. Spirometry measures the maximal volume of air forcibly exhaled after maximal inhalation (the forced vital capacity, *FVC*) and the volume of air expired during the first second (*FEV1*). When the prebronchodilation and postbronchodilation spirometry values are compared, improved values of 12% or more plus a normal *FEV1/FVC* ratio suggest the presence of restrictive lung disease, a.k.a., asthma (American Thoracic Society, 1991, 1995; Bye, Kerstein, and Barsh, 1992).

Asthma can also be detected by a *peak flow meter*, a handheld device that measures expiratory air pressure. Classically, peak expiratory flow (*PEF*) that varies by more than 20% before and after bronchodilation indicates the presence of asthma.

Other tests are sometimes used to confirm the diagnosis. The *exhaled nitric oxide test* measures the level of nitric oxide in exhaled air. High levels reflect inflammation in the upper airways and the presence of asthma.

GLOBAL BURDEN OF ASTHMA

Two large multinational studies have been conducted to assess the prevalence of asthma in the world population: the International Study of Asthma and Allergies in Childhood (ISAAC) and the European Community Respiratory Health Survey (ECRHS I and ECRHS II).

The International Study of Asthma and Allergies in Childhood (ISAAC) was initiated in 1991. This ongoing study uses standardized methodology and testing to assess the prevalence and severity of asthma, rhinitis and eczema in children, elucidate risk factors, evaluate the impact of therapy, and provide a framework for future etiological research of these conditions (Asher et al., 1995).

Phase I of the International Study of Asthma and Allergies in Childhood (ISAAC) assessed the prevalence of asthmatic symptoms in young children, ages 6–7 years (*n* = 257,800 subjects from 91 centers in 38 countries) and older children, ages 13–14 years (*n* = 463,801 subjects from 155 centers in 56 countries). Population samples of about 3,000 children were studied from each center. Participating centers in ISAAC represented most regions of the world. The results of phase I of ISAAC revealed wide geographic variation in the rates of asthmatic symptoms, e.g., prevalence estimates for "*wheeze in the last 12 months*" ranged from 2.1–32.2%. The highest estimates in both young and older children were observed in English-speaking and Latin American countries (ISAAC, 1998a). Examination of comorbidity data from phase I of ISAAC also revealed significant positive correlations between prevalence estimates for asthma, rhinoconjunctivitis, and atopic eczema (ISAAC, 1998b).

The initial phase of the European Community Respiratory Health Survey (ECRHS I) was designed to assess the prevalence and geographical variation in asthma, allergy, and allergic sensitization in adults living primarily in European countries. In this large survey, data were collected from about 140,000 adults aged 10–44 years from 22 countries. Clinical procedures included administration of a detailed questionnaire to ascertain information about symptoms and risk factors, administration of a quality of life questionnaire, collection of blood specimens to measure IgE-specific antibodies against common aeroallergens, and lung function testing by spirometry. Asthma prevalence varied widely, ranging from 2.0–11.9%. Prevalence estimates were lower in Eastern and Southern Europe and higher in Western (English-speaking) European nations (Heinrich et al., 2002).

Comparison of the findings of the International Study of Asthma and Allergies in Childhood (ISAAC) and the European Community Respiratory Health Survey (ECRHS) revealed strong positive correlations between the prevalence data from countries represented in both surveys. While there were differences in the absolute levels of prevalence, the geographical patterns from the two studies showed good agreement, thereby validating results (Pearce, Pekkanen, and Beasley, 1999; Pearce, Douwes, and Beasley, 2000).

The Global Initiative for Asthma (GINA) Program was established in 1989 to increase awareness among government and public health officials, healthcare workers, and the general population about the rising global burden of asthma. Recently, GINA commissioned an investigative team headed by Dr. Richard Beasley of New Zealand to examine data from ISAAC and ECRHS and summarize findings (Masoli et al., 2004).

A composite map of the worldwide prevalence of asthma based on the GINA investigation is shown in **Figure 31.2**. Relatively high prevalence estimates

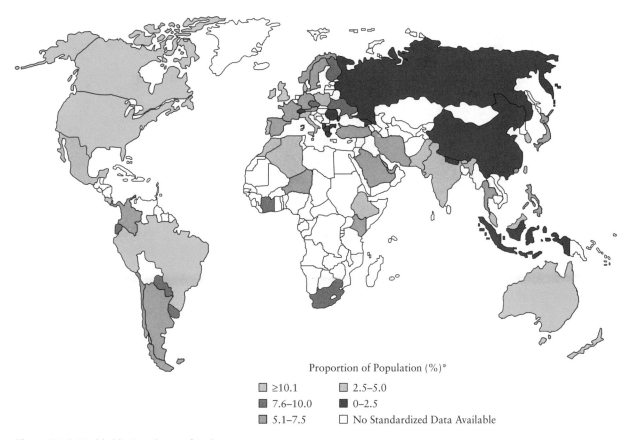

Proportion of Population (%)*

☐ ≥10.1	☐ 2.5–5.0
☐ 7.6–10.0	☐ 0–2.5
☐ 5.1–7.5	☐ No Standardized Data Available

Figure 31.2 Worldwide Prevalence of Asthma.

Source: Reprinted with permission: Masoli M, Fabian D, Holt S, Beasley R, for the Global Initiative for Asthma (GINA) Program (2004). The global burden of asthma: executive summary of the GINA Dissemination Committee Report. *Allergy* 59:469–478.

(> 10%) are apparent in the United States, Canada, Great Britain, Australia, Brazil, and Peru, whereas much lower estimates (< 5%) are noted for the large populations of China, India, and the Russian Federation. Based upon these data, it is estimated that at least 300 million people currently suffer from asthma in the world population (Masoli et al., 2004).

Important conclusions drawn from the GINA investigation include the following: (1) asthma currently affects about 300 million people worldwide, (2) international patterns are not fully explained by current knowledge, (3) the prevalence of asthma is increasing in children and adults, and with increasing urbanization, even steeper increases are projected in the coming decades, (4) persons suffering from asthma do not have access to the appropriate medications in many regions of the world, (5) asthma causes approximately 250,000 deaths per year worldwide, many of which are due to suboptimal long-term medical care and lack of access to emergency services during the final attack of *status asthmaticus*, (6) economic costs of asthma are considerable and significantly more

resources are needed in order to make appropriate long-term pharmacologic therapy available to asthmatic patients, and (7) more resources are also needed to reduce air pollution from smoking, motor vehicle exhaust, and other environmental sources that may exacerbate asthmatic attacks.

A widely used measure of the health burden of disease is the disability-adjusted years of life lost ($DALY = YLL + YDL$ *where YLL = years of life lost due to premature death and YDL = years of life lost due to severe disability*). **Figure 31.3** shows the global DALY rates for asthma (WHO, 2009). Obviously, the geographic pattern of DALY rates differs dramatically from the pattern of prevalence rates in **Figure 31.2**, e.g., DALY rates are highest in nations with low prevalence or that lack standardized data, particularly in Africa. The GINA investigators estimate that 15 million DALY are lost due to asthma each year, which reflects the rising prevalence and inadequate access to long-term therapy and emergency treatment, particularly in underdeveloped countries (Masoli et al., 2004).

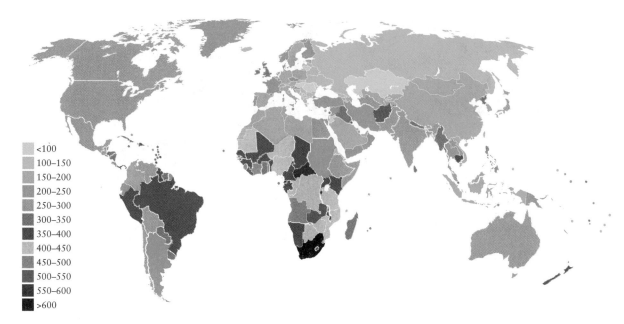

Figure 31.3 Disability-Adjusted Life Years, Asthma, 2004.

Source: Data from World Health Organization. The global burden of disease: 2004 update. Geneva, WHO, 2008. Available at www.who.int/evidence/bod

The findings from the International Study of Asthma and Allergies in Childhood (ISAAC) and the European Community Respiratory Health Survey (ECRHS) suggest that the prevalence of asthma is rising in many countries throughout the world; indeed, there is widespread concern that asthma may reach epidemic proportions in the coming years (Eder and Ege, 2006). However, part of the observed increase may be attributed to greater awareness of asthmatic conditions and higher detection rates in the populations under study. Furthermore, population-based studies have not been conducted in many nations and the global picture is far from complete.

THE HYGIENE HYPOTHESIS OF ASTHMA

In 1989, a brief report was published in the *British Medical Journal* by David P. Strachan that suggested allergic diseases are prevented by infection in early childhood transmitted by unhygienic exposure to older siblings or acquired prenatally from mothers infected by contact with older children. Strachan presented evidence for this hypothesis from a prospective study of 17,414 British children born in 1958 and followed to age 23 years. Prevalence estimates of hay fever during the past 12 months were obtained for the birth cohort when subjects were 11 and 23 years

of age. Prevalence estimates of hay fever by number of older siblings at ages 11 and 23 years are shown in **Figure 31.4**. Clearly, the prevalence of hay fever decreases with increasing number of older siblings. A similar trend was also noted for eczema during the first year of life (declining prevalence with increasing number of older siblings). Strachan interpreted these interesting findings to mean that exposure of younger children to infectious agents already contracted by older children in the family conferred protection against the development of allergic conditions such as eczema, hay fever, and asthma.

Strachan's *hygiene hypothesis* has been the subject of intense immunological and epidemiologic research. The theory has been used to infer that the increased incidence of allergic diseases in industrialized nations is due to decreases in infectious diseases with immunization and antibiotics, decreases in family size, and increases in certain allergenic and inflammatory stimuli.

If it is indeed true that exposure to infectious agents, symbiotic microorganisms (e.g., gut flora or probiotics), and parasites increases resistance to the development of allergic diseases such as eczema, hay fever, and asthma, then the important question becomes, *what is the biological mechanism*?

One proposed mechanism is that early exposure to certain infectious agents induces homeostatic

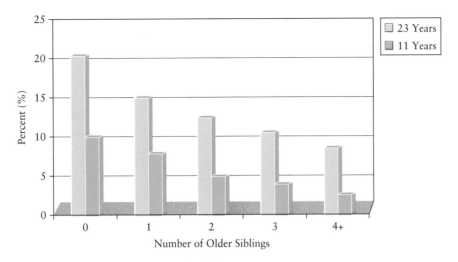

Figure 31.4 Prevalence of Hay Fever by Number of Older Siblings.
Source: Data from Strachan DP (1989). Hay fever, hygiene and household size. *BMJ* 299(6710):1259–1260.

balance between subsets of circulating T lymphocytes. Specifically, early infection may increase the population of T helper lymphocytes of the innate immune system (Th-1 cells) to counterbalance T helper cells of the acquired immune system (Th-2 cells). Alternative mechanisms have also been suggested, e.g., perhaps the developing immune system must receive stimuli from infectious agents, symbiotic bacteria, and parasites in order to develop regulatory T lymphocytes that suppress both the innate and the acquired immune response, thereby reducing inflammation and atopic reactions (Bufford and Gern, 2005). As discussed in the following section, a number of risk factors, including both allergens and infectious agents, have been found to increase the risk of asthma development. The emerging epidemiology indicates important effects of genotype by environment interactions in the pathogenesis of asthma.

RISK FACTORS OF ASTHMA

Combinations of risk factors have been found to significantly heighten the risk of developing asthma. For example, many asthmatic patients report genetic or familial predisposition coupled with environmental exposure to inhaled substances that provoke allergic reactions or irritate the upper airways. Examples of environmental factors that may stimulate asthmatic attacks include indoor allergens (tobacco smoke, house dust mites, pet dander, cockroach allergens, biomass smoke), outdoor allergens (pollen, mold, motor vehicle exhaust), infectious agents (particularly respiratory viruses), chemical irritants in the workplace, cold air, emotional stress, physical exercise, drugs and drug interactions, and certain foods and food additives. Key studies of some of these factors are discussed in the following paragraphs.

Atopy and Asthma

Atopy refers to the production of specific antibodies belonging to the IgE class of immunoglobulins in response to common environmental allergens. Allergenic stimuli induce large B lymphocytes of the immune system (known as plasma cells) to synthesize and release E-type immunogobulins (IgE). In turn, IgE antibodies activate receptors on the cell membranes of mast cells in the upper airways leading to the release of highly inflammatory substances such as histamines and leukotrienes (**Figure 31.5**). Inflamed tissues are infiltrated by macrophages and eosinophilic cells of the immune system that also

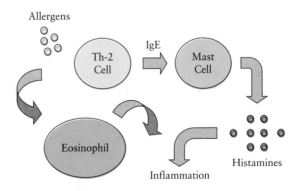

Figure 31.5 The Atopic Inflammatory Response.

elaborate cytokines and actively participate in the inflammatory process (Holgate and Polosa, 2006; NHLBI, 2007). Release of destruction enzymes by these immune cells causes necrosis and shedding of the bronchial epithelium and secretion of mucin resulting in the development of characteristic mucous plugs of the disease (Robbins and Cotran, 1979). Atopy can be assessed by skin prick testing as well as total serum IgE.

Many allergens have been indicted in the genesis of atopic asthma. Sources include pollen, pet dander, dust mites, cockroaches, mice, molds, environmental tobacco smoke, and biomass smoke. However, definitive evidence of cause and effect has been difficult to ascertain. Epidemiologic studies of childhood asthma are complicated by the young age of target populations, profound genetic and environmental differences, and difficulty in accurately measuring exposure to specific allergens using standardized methods. Perhaps as a consequence of these problematic issues, high environmental levels of offending allergens have not been consistently found to increase the risk of asthma development (Pearce, Douwes, and Beasley, 2000). Selected studies are discussed in the following paragraphs.

Sporik and colleagues examined a cohort of 67 British children from 1978–1989 to determine the relation of house dust mite antigen and the development of asthma. During 11 years of follow-up, 17 children developed asthma, 16 of whom were sensitized to dust mite allergens. Among the 50 children who did not develop asthma, 19 were atopic. Among children exposed to high levels of dust mites in the home before age 1 year, the relative risk of asthma development was 4.8. Based on these observations, it was concluded that exposure to house dust mites early in childhood is a strong determinant of subsequent asthma development (Sporik et al., 1990).

The German *Multicenter Allergy Study* was designed to examine exposure to dust mites and cat allergens and asthma development in a prospective birth cohort of 1,314 children enrolled in 5 German cities. Periodic measurements of indoor allergen exposure and specific IgE antibodies to food and inhalant allergens were available for 939 children who were followed to the age of 7 years. The overall prevalence of asthma in the study was 6.1%. The study demonstrated a clear association between allergen exposure during infancy and subsequent sensitization. The association became apparent at the age of 3 years and was stronger at 7 years of age. Furthermore, there was a strong association between immune sensitization and the development of asthma. Nevertheless,

levels of allergen exposure measured in the home at 6 months were *not* associated with asthma development (Lau et al., 2000).

In the *Asthma Multicenter Infant Cohort Study* of 1,000 newborns conducted by investigators in the United Kingdom and Spain, allergens were measured in the homes of 3 month old babies followed by skin prick testing at 6 years of age. Exposure to cat allergens but not dust mites increased sensitization to skin testing (OR = 4.4) and the risk of asthma (OR = 2.6) (Torrent et al., 2007).

Huss and colleagues conducted skin tests in 1,041 children ages 5–12 years with *mild to moderate* asthma to determine allergenic risk factors. They also tested for specific allergens in the home environments. Data were obtained from eight North American cities participating in the *US Childhood Asthma Management Program*. Children living in homes with high levels of dust mites or cockroaches were more likely to have positive skin tests than children with no exposure (OR = 9.0 and 2.2, respectively). Sensitization was also related to serum IgE and the total number of positive skin tests (Huss et al., 2001).

Despite observed inconsistencies in the association between environmental measures of allergy exposure and asthma development, there is consensus that high levels of individual sensitization responses measured by skin prick or IgE level significantly increase the risk. In a review and meta-analysis of available studies on skin prick testing, various measures of testing revealed a striking dose response between the relative risk of asthma and the number of positive tests. As shown in **Figure 31.6**, the risk of asthma increases by more than 10-fold for individuals with 5 or more positive skin test reactions to a variety of common allergens (Pearce, Pekkanen, and Beasley, 1999). A similar though less dramatic dose response has been reported between the risk of asthma and the level of total serum IgE (Burrows et al., 1982; Sears et al., 1991).

The *International Study of Asthma and Allergy in Childhood (ISAAC)* utilized standardized methodology to study asthma and allergy in children, ages 8–12 years, on a global basis. Thirty study centers in 22 countries enrolled subjects from environments reflecting a wide range of living conditions from rural Africa to urban Europe. Data were collected by parental questionnaires ($n = 54,439$), skin prick testing ($n = 31,759$), and measurements of allergen-specific IgE in serum ($n = 8,951$). The prevalence of current "wheeze" varied widely from 0.8% in Ecuador to 25.6% in Brazil and the fraction of individuals with current wheeze attributable to atopy ranged from

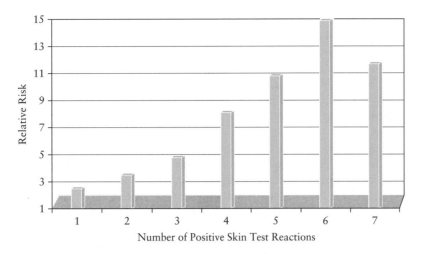

Figure 31.6 Dose Response of Asthma Risk and Positive Skin Test Reactions.

Source: Data from Pearce N, Pekkanen J, Beasley R. (1999). How much asthma is really attributable to atopy? *Thorax* 54:268–272.

0% in Turkey to 93.8% in China. The prevalence of wheeze and fraction of wheeze attributable to atopy (skin test reactivity) were positively correlated with gross national income per capita, e.g., sensitivity rates increased with increasing income per capita. The ISAAC investigators concluded from these results that the link between atopic sensitization and asthmatic symptoms in children differs markedly between populations and increases with economic development (Weinmayr et al., 2007).

While the majority of asthmatic cases are diagnosed in childhood, adult onset constitutes a significant fraction of disease, perhaps up to one-third in some populations. In the *European Community Respiratory Health Survey*, associations of specific types of allergic rhinitis and bronchial hyper-responsiveness were examined in 3,719 *adults* followed over nine years. In subjects with allergic rhinitis, the risk of developing bronchial hyper-responsiveness was markedly increased in individuals sensitized to cat allergens (OR = 7.9) or dust mites (OR = 2.8) (Shaaban et al., 2007).

The totality of current evidence therefore suggests that sensitization to certain allergens plays a significant role in the development of asthma in both children and adults. Nevertheless, as demonstrated by the results of the *International Study of Asthma and Allergy in Childhood (ISAAC)*, there is marked variability among populations in the prevalence of atopic asthma (Weinmayr et al., 2007). Asthma development appears to be a complex, interactive process involving the interaction of a number of environmental and genetic factors (NHLBI, 2007).

Respiratory Viruses and Asthma

Respiratory viruses have been found to influence the development of childhood asthma. In particular, the onset of asthma in children is often preceded by severe infection due to respiratory viruses, particularly respiratory syncytial virus and rhinoviruses.

Early studies linked seasonal viral infections to the subsequent development of asthma (Anderson, Bailey, and Bland, 1981; Aberg, 1989). More recently, Wu and colleagues studied the relationship of winter virus infections during infancy and the development of childhood asthma in over 95,000 US infants born between 1995 and 2000. Subjects were enrolled for study through the Tennessee Medicaid program. The risk of developing asthma tracked with the timing of infant birth and the winter virus peak. Infants born 4 months prior to the winter virus peak had a 29% increase in the odds of developing asthma compared to infants born 12 months prior to the peak. The results suggest that winter viral infection during infancy is a risk factor for the subsequent development of asthma (Wu et al., 2008).

Investigators at the University of Arizona conducted a prospective study of 880 US children who were enrolled at birth and followed for the development of lower respiratory tract infections in the first 3 years of life and then evaluated for the presence or absence of physician-diagnosed asthma at ages 6 and 11 years. At age 6, physician-diagnosed asthma was present in 13.6% of children with a history of early pneumonia compared to 4.6% of subjects with no history of lung infection (OR = 3.3). At 11 years of age, 25.6% of children in the early pneumonia group had developed asthma compared to 11% in the reference group (OR = 2.2). Furthermore, lung function was significantly compromised in the asthmatic group but showed significant improvement with administration of the beta-blocker, *albuterol*. These findings suggest that early childhood pneumonia is an important risk factor for asthma (Castro-Rodríguez et al., 1999).

Sigurs and colleagues studied asthma development in a cohort of 47 Swedish children who were hospitalized with bronchiolitis during infancy due to respiratory syncytial virus (RSV). The rate of asthma development in the RSV bronchiolitis cohort was compared to a matched control group of 93 disease-free infants. All children were evaluated at age 7 years by physical examinations, skin prick tests, and serum IgE tests for common food and pet allergens. The cumulative prevalence of asthma in the RSV group was 30% compared to 3% in the control group. The odds of asthma development in children who were hospitalized for RSV bronchiolitis as infants compared to controls was 12.7. Furthermore, allergenic responses to common foods and allergens were also heightened with RSV exposure (OR = 2.4). These results indicate that early exposure to RSV serves as a strong stimulus for subsequent asthma development (Sigurs et al., 2000).

Jackson and colleagues studied 259 US children from birth–6 years of age to assess the etiology and timing of specific *wheezing* viral respiratory infections in relation to the development of asthma. Viral etiology was determined by multiplex reverse transcriptase polymerase chain reaction in cultured specimens ascertained by nasal lavage. Viral etiologies were identified in 90% of the respiratory infections and the risk of asthma development increased following early infection by respiratory syncytial virus (OR = 2.6), rhinovirus (OR = 9.8), or combined infection (OR = 10). Nearly 90% of children who developed rhinovirus infection with wheezing before 3 years of age subsequently developed asthma by the age of 6 years (Jackson et al., 2008).

Environmental Tobacco Smoke and Asthma

Investigators at the California Environmental Protection Agency conducted a meta-analysis of 37 epidemiologic investigations of environmental tobacco smoke and asthma. Across all studies, maternal smoking increased asthma risk by 60% and household exposure increased the risk by 45% (Dunn and Zeise, 1997; Dunn, Zeise, and Waller, 1997).

These findings provide compelling evidence that environmental tobacco smoke increases the risk of asthma in children (Strachan and Cook, 1998; Cook and Strachan, 1999). Nevertheless, heterogeneity of study designs and lack of control for potential confounders has produced some inconsistencies in the evidence.

Vork and colleagues used meta-regression analysis to synthesize data from 38 epidemiologic studies that adjusted effects of environmental tobacco smoke for history of atopy. Their primary objective was to elucidate consistent patterns of risk by eliminating potential sources of bias and confounding. Increased summary estimates of relative risk were observed for both *prevalent asthma* and *incident asthma* with exposure to environmental tobacco smoke from any source (RR = 1.48 and 1.21, respectively) and from maternal smoking (RR = 1.29 and 1.24, respectively). Stratification of the data by age revealed differences in the relative risk estimates for young children ages 5 years or less (RR = 1.05) versus older children ages 6–18 years (RR = 1.33). These findings suggest that the duration of exposure to environmental tobacco smoking is an important factor in the genesis of asthma (Vork, Broadwin, and Blaisdell, 2007).

Atopy, Environmental Tobacco Smoke, and Asthma

Jaakkola and colleagues examined the joint effect of genetic propensity to asthma and exposure to environmental tobacco smoke in a prospective population-based study of 2,531 children born in Oslo, Norway. Data were collected on health and environmental exposures at the time of birth and after 6, 18, 24, and 48 months of follow-up. Parental atopy was defined as a history of maternal or paternal asthma or hay fever and exposure to environmental tobacco smoke was defined as smokers in the household. Parental atopy independently increased the risk of asthma (OR = 1.67) whereas exposure to environmental tobacco smoke *per se* had no effect. Notably, parental atopy *plus* exposure to environmental tobacco smoke produced a stronger effect than either risk factor alone (OR = 2.68). The results suggest a joint effect of parental atopy and exposure to environmental tobacco smoke in the development of asthma in young children (Jaakkola, Naftad, and Magnus, 2001).

Food Allergy and Asthma

Investigators in Chicago, Illinois, conducted a nested case control study of 201 children with asthma and 366 children of similar age without asthma to determine the relationship between food allergies and physician-diagnosed asthma. Food allergies to common foods (egg, sesame, peanut, soy, milk, shrimp, walnut, codfish, and wheat) were determined following ingestion of specific foods using skin prick testing and serum IgE. Logistic regression was used to estimate odds ratios with adjustment for other factors including sensitization to common aeroallergens. The presence of symptomatic food allergies significantly increased the risk of asthma in younger children (OR = 5.3) and older children (OR = 4.9). Effects of specific allergies to milk, eggs, and peanuts were also statistically significant. The results suggest that symptomatic food allergies significantly increase the risk of asthma development in children (Schroeder et al., 2009). Furthermore, they provide corroboration of earlier findings suggesting that specific allergies (e.g., milk, eggs, and peanuts) enhance the genesis of asthma (Kulig et al., 1998; Leung et al., 2002; Penard-Morand et al., 2005).

Asthma and Obesity

As elaborated elsewhere in this text, obesity is a major cause of morbidity and mortality worldwide. Life-threatening and debilitating sequelae of this condition include cardiovascular disease, diabetes, and malignancy. Furthermore, the obesity epidemic continues to expand, threatening to envelop virtually all populations of the planet. Due to parallel increases in the rates of obesity and asthma over time, scientific interest has recently focused on a potential etiologic link between excess adiposity and the development of asthma.

Several prospective studies have examined the associations between weight gain, obesity, and the development of asthma in children. The *Children's Health Study* enrolled 3,792 school-age children from 12 Southern California communities to examine obesity and asthma. All children were asthma-free at baseline. Participants were examined annually from 1993–1998. Body mass was determined by height and weight measurements and incident cases of asthma were detected based upon symptoms and lung function tests. Over 4 years of follow-up, 288 new cases of asthma were detected in the cohort. The risk of incident asthma was significantly higher among children who were obese (RR = 1.6); overweight boys were at higher risk (RR = 2.06) than overweight girls (RR = 1.25). Effects of excess weight were strongest in those individuals without detectable allergies (RR = 1.77). The authors concluded that increased body weight was associated with increased risk of asthma development, particularly in boys and in nonallergic children (Gilliland et al., 2003).

Flaherman and Rutherford examined obesity and physican-diagnosed asthma in children using meta-analysis. Twelve cohort studies met inclusion criteria for the study. Combined results from four studies revealed that high body mass during middle childhood increased the risk of subsequent asthma development (RR = 1.5). Combined results from nine studies also revealed a modest effect of high birth weight on the risk of developing asthma (RR = 1.2). The results indicate that children with high body weight either at birth or later in childhood are at increased risk for the subsequent development of asthma. The authors suggest several potential mechanisms including diet, gastroesophageal reflux, mechanical effects of obesity, atopy, and hormonal influences (Flaherman and Rutherford, 2006). In addition, adipocytes engorged with triglycerides are induced to secrete a variety of inflammatory cytokines (adipokines) that may influence asthma risk.

Obesity has been determined to be a risk factor for asthma development in adults as well as children. Swedish investigators examined risk factors for incident asthma, including obesity, in a case control study of 309 adults with asthma and a similar number of age- and gender-matched controls. Compared to subjects with optimal body mass (BMI: 20–24.9), obese men and women (BMI > 30) had similar increases in the risk of developing asthma (OR = 3.3 and 3.0, respectively). These estimates retained statistical significance after adjustment for other significant risk factors including hay fever, family history of asthma, allergic sensitization, and smoking (Rönmark et al., 2005).

Beuther and Sutherland explored the relationship between obesity and asthma in adults using meta-analysis. Seven prospective epidemiologic investigations involving 333,102 subjects met inclusion criteria for the study. Compared with normal weight (BMI < 25), being overweight (BMI: 25–29.9) or obese (BMI > 30) increased the odds of incident asthma (OR = 1.38 and 1.92, respectively). Estimates were similar for men and women and there was a significant dose response in the risk with increasing body mass. The investigators concluded that being overweight or obese increases the risk of asthma development in adults (Beuther and Sutherland, 2007).

Asthma and Household Cleaning Products

Some studies have examined the effects of cleaning solutions and sprays used in the home. In the *European Community Respiratory Health Survey*, frequent household exposure to cleaning sprays and solutions more than doubled the relative risk of developing asthma (RR = 2.4) (Zock et al., 2007). Likewise, analysis of the environments of healthcare professionals found increased odds of developing asthma with exposure to aerosolized irritants such as cleaning solvents and there was a significant dose response between reported asthma and the length of time on the job (e.g., OR = 4.1 for > 27 years) (Delclos et al., 2007).

Drug-Induced Asthma

The link between asthma, nasal polyposis, and aspirin sensitivity was first reported by Widal in 1922. Nearly half a century later, Samter and Beers further characterized this condition, which typically involves the progressive development of chronic rhinitis, asthma, nasal polyposis, and hypersensitivity to aspirin in young adults (Samter and Beers, 1968). Reactions to aspirin in such patients can produce severe asthma attacks and episodes of anaphylaxis. The disorder is often called *Samter's triad*.

Investigators in Finland conducted a postal survey of 4,300 Finnish adults, aged 18–64 years, to assess the prevalence of asthma and its risk factors. Respondents included 1,408 men and 1,694 women. The prevalence of reported physician-diagnosed asthma in the sample was 4.6%. Reported aspirin intolerance more than doubled the odds of developing asthma (OR = 2.2). Other significant risk factors included allergic rhinitis (OR = 3.9), nasal polyposis (OR = 3.9), and familial history of asthma (OR = 2.5). Samter's triad was present in 4.3% of subjects who reported they had physician-diagnosed asthma (Hedman et al., 1999).

Published estimates of the prevalence of aspirin sensitivity among asthmatic patients vary widely ranging from 4% to 44%. In a comprehensive review of the literature, Jenkins and colleagues pooled data from 21 randomized clinical trials of asthmatic patients in which sensitivity to asthma was determined by oral provocation testing and by verbal history. Based upon provocation testing, the pooled prevalence of aspirin sensitivity among asthmatic patients was 21% in adults and 5% in children. These values are markedly higher than estimates based on verbal history (3% in adults and 2% in children). These results suggest that many asthmatic patients may be unaware of their sensitivity to aspirin (Jenkins, Costello, and Hodge, 2004).

In a retrospective review of 208 patients who underwent sinus surgery for chronic rhinosinusitis, Samter's triad was present in 10 patients (4.8%). Subgroup analyses showed that aspirin hypersensitivity was present in 25.6% of patients with both nasal polyps and asthma, and 16.9% of patients with asthma (Kim and Kountakis, 2007).

Sensitivity to aspirin, ibuprofen, and other nonsteroidal anti-inflammatory drugs (NSAIDs) may be largely due to their impact on the biosynthesis of prostaglandins versus leukotrienes. The NSAIDs reduce inflammation by specifically inhibiting cyclooxygenase, the rate-limiting enzyme of the prostaglandin cascade, thereby shunting conversion of arachidonic acid to leukotrienes rather than prostaglandins. Exposure of the upper airways to certain leukotrienes, e.g., leukotriene B-4, can produce inflammatory responses that lead to the development of asthma (Leff, 2000).

Vaccination and Childhood Asthma

In recent years, the prevalence of asthma has risen dramatically throughout the world, most notably in developed countries. In the majority of cases, asthma is diagnosed in childhood and adolescence, often during the first 6 years of life. Since childhood immunization is routinely practiced in the industrialized world, the emerging burden of asthma in children has prompted studies of a possible etiologic link with immunization.

To resolve the question, investigators in Israel conducted a meta-analysis of studies of immunization and asthma. The study included seven studies of pertussis vaccination (n = 186,663 children) and five studies of bacillus Calmette-Guérin (BCG) vaccination (n = 41,479 children). Pertussis vaccine is directed against *Bordetella pertussis*, the bacterium that causes whooping cough, and BCG is a vaccine consisting of attenuated human tubercle bacilli. No statistically significant associations were detected in the meta-analysis. Thus, the currently available data from observational studies do not support a link between either BCG or pertussis vaccine and the risk of asthma development in childhood (Balicer et al., 2007).

GENETICS OF ASTHMA

Expression of the asthmatic phenotype depends not only on the environment, but also on the underlying genetic predisposition. It is the combination of these influences that ultimately determines whether asthma develops in a given individual. Therefore, in considering the origins of asthma and the development of effective interventions for prevention and therapy, contributions of genes, environments, and genotype x environment interactions need to be accurately identified and quantified. Genome-wide association studies of single nucleotide polymorphisms (SNPs) and genetic linkage studies of affected relatives within kindreds have been used to explore the human genome for genes that increase susceptibility to asthma and atopy.

A recent review of nearly 500 genetic studies revealed that 25 "true" susceptibility genes have been discovered that increase susceptibility to asthma or atopy in 6 or more populations (Ober and Hoffjan, 2006). Nevertheless, the effects of single genes appear to be small and contingent upon the environment and population studied, thereby reflecting the importance of gene-environment and gene-gene interactions. Simple inheritance patterns of asthma susceptibility genes have not been identified; rather, the inheritance of susceptibility genes and their translation to the asthmatic phenotype is that of a complex polygenic disorder.

The *GABRIEL* Project is a multidisciplinary study initiated in 2006 to identify genetic and environmental causes of asthma in the European community. The project is led by an international team of 164 scientists from 19 countries in Europe, along with other groups in the United Kingdom, Canada, and Australia. Using the latest research techniques across a variety of disciplines, including genetics, epidemiology, and immunology, this team is currently investigating representative population samples of asthmatic patients and control subjects from these locations to identify key factors in the development of asthma.

Members of the GABRIEL Consortium recently conducted a large genome-wide association study of 10,365 cases with physician-diagnosed asthma and 16,110 unaffected controls matched on ancestry. A total of 582,892 single nucleotide polymorphisms (SNPs) were determined for each subject in the study. The study was powered to detect the statistical significance of odds ratios in the range of 1.1–1.2. Small effects of a few genes were found with known biological effects on inflammatory interleukins and their receptors and regulatory T cells of the acquired immune system. Only one genetic locus, *HLA-DR* of the major histocompatibility gene, was found to have a genome-wide association with total serum IgE concentration. The investigators concluded that "*asthma is genetically heterogeneous*" wherein a few common alleles increase genetic susceptibility by influencing components of the adaptive immune system and inflammatory damage to the upper airways (Moffatt et al., 2010).

A novel discovery in the field of asthma research involves the *YKL-40* protein, which belongs to a family of enzymes known as chitinases. These enzymes are produced in humans as an innate immune response to *chitin* exposure. Chitin is a long-chain polysaccharide that serves as an armor or cell wall for fungi and arthropods, including all crustaceans

and insects. Interestingly, chitin is found in insects such as dust mites and cockroaches that are known to provoke allergenic responses, and animal studies have shown that chitinase is a powerful stimulant of allergic reactions and inflammation (e.g., Reese et al., 2007). Subsequently, in human studies of the US *Hutterite* population, subjects with asthma or broncho-hyperresponsiveness were found to have significantly elevated levels of *YKL-40* compared to subjects without asthma (the *Hutterite* population is a small genetically isolated religious community of European descent now residing in South Dakota and other locations in the United States). Further studies of asthma in the *Hutterite* population and in other population samples have revealed that differences in *YKL-40* and asthma susceptibility are genetically determined. Specifically, a variant of the promoter region of the *CHI3L1* gene on chromosome 1 that encodes *YKL-40* significantly increases serum levels of the protein and confers greater susceptibility to asthma and broncho-hyperresponsiveness (Ober et al., 2008). Thus, genetic variation at the *YKL-40* locus may play an important role in determining the risk of asthma development in response to chitin exposure.

PREVENTING ASTHMA PROGRESSION: AVOIDANCE OF ENVIRONMENTAL TOBACCO SMOKE

Chilmonzayk and colleagues examined the association of environmental tobacco smoke, urinary levels of cotinine (a nicotine metabolite), and exacerbations of disease in 199 children with asthma. Serum theophylline levels were used to adjust for confounding due to disease management. Median urinary cotinine levels increased according to reported exposure to environmental tobacco smoke (5.6 ng per ml for no exposure, 13.1 ng per ml for primarily maternal exposure, and 55.8 ng per ml for maternal exposure plus other significant exposure). Children with high exposure to environmental tobacco smoke (based on either reported exposure or the level of urinary cotinine) had approximately twice the risk of experiencing acute exacerbation compared to those with low exposure. Furthermore, spirometry measures of lung function decreased significantly with increasing exposure (Chlmonczyk et al., 1993).

Gerald and colleagues conducted a randomized clinical trial to assess the effects of reducing exposure to environmental tobacco smoke in children with asthma. Children were randomized to receive either supervised asthma therapy with counseling to avoid exposure to environmental tobacco smoke or usual care without counseling. Children whose exposure decreased had fewer hospitalizations and emergency room visits and they were 48% less likely to experience an episode of poor asthma control (Gerald et al., 2009). These results underscore the importance of making sure that asthmatic children avoid any exposure to environmental tobacco smoke.

THERAPY FOR THE ASTHMATIC PATIENT

Though asthma is an incurable condition, symptoms can be controlled reasonably well using inhaled beta-blockers such as *albuterol* for relief of acute attacks and inhaled corticosteroids such as *budesonide* for long-term maintenance therapy. Inhaled corticosteroids are the preferred class of long-term medications to manage persistent asthma in both children and adults. Numerous studies in asthmatic children have established that inhaled corticosteroids reduce the frequency of asthmatic attacks, improve pulmonary function, improve quality of life, enhance exercise tolerance, and reduce hospitalizations (Rachelefsy, 2009).

Treatment protocols should be individualized to proactively monitor and manage symptoms and prevent attacks. In children with asthma, handheld spray devices efficiently deliver regulated aerosolized doses of these drugs into the upper airways in order to prevent asthmatic attacks and maintain air flow. Identification and avoidance of specific triggers of asthmatic attacks is a critical component of asthma management. Such stimuli are variable from person to person and may include smoke, mold, dust mites, pollen, pet dander, exercise, food allergies, respiratory infection, and other environmental factors. The Global Initiative for Asthma (GINA) is an international organization of healthcare professionals and public health officials committed to reducing the burden of asthma worldwide. The recent GINA publication entitled "*Global Strategy for Asthma Management and Prevention*" presents evidence-based guidelines for asthma management and prevention (GINA, 2011).

SUMMARY

According to an Expert Panel Report of the National Heart Lung and Blood Institute,

> "*Asthma is a chronic inflammatory disorder of the airways in which many cell and cellular elements play a role: in particular, mast cells,*

eosinophils, T lymphocytes, macrophages, neutrophils, and epithelial cells. In susceptible individuals, this inflammation causes recurrent episodes of wheezing, breathlessness, chest tightness, and coughing, particularly at night or in the early morning. These episodes are usually associated with widespread but variable airflow obstruction that is often reversible either spontaneously or with treatment. The inflammation also causes an associated increase in the existing bronchial hyperresponsiveness to a variety of stimuli. Reversibility of airflow limitation may be incomplete in some patients with asthma" (National Heart, Lung, Blood Institute, 2007).

Asthma is clearly a multifactorial disease. Several important risk factors have been identified including environmental allergens, respiratory viruses, environmental tobacco smoke, and obesity. Genetic predisposition appears to be polygenic and the transition of susceptible genotype to asthmatic phenotype appears to be highly dependent upon interactions with environmental factors. In the asthmatic patient, allergenic and environmental triggers of exacerbation and attacks must be avoided. Therapeutic approaches are currently available that allow most asthmatic patients to enjoy a high quality of life. Elucidation of causative genotype by environmental interactions in future studies will be of benefit in the prevention and reversal of the asthmatic process.

• • • REFERENCES

Aberg, N. (1989). Birth season variation in asthma and allergic rhinitis. *Clin Exp Allergy*, 19, 643–648.

American Thoracic Society. (1991). Lung function testing: Selection of reference values and interpretive strategies. *Am Rev Respir Dis*, 144, 1202–1018.

American Thoracic Society. (1995). Standardization of spirometry: Update. *Am J Respir Crit Care Med*, 152, 1107–1036.

Anderson, H.R., Bailey, P.A., & Bland, J.M. (1981). The effect of birth month on asthma, eczema, hayfever, respiratory symptoms, lung function, and hospital admissions for asthma. *Int J Epidemiol*, 10, 45–51.

Asher, M.I., Keil, U., Anderson, H.R., Beaslely, R., Crane, J., Martinez, F.,...Stewart, A.W. (1995). International Study of Asthma and Allergies in

Childhood (ISAAC): Rationale and methods. *Eur Respir J, 8,* 483–491.

Balicer, R.D., Grotto, I., Mimouni, M., & Mimouni, D. (2007). Is childhood vaccination associated with asthma? A meta-analysis of observational studies. *Pediatrics, 120*(5), e1269–e1277.

Beuther, D.A., & Sutherland, E.R. (2007). Overweight, obesity, and incident asthma. *Am J Respir Crit Care Med, 175,* 661–666.

Bye, M.R., Kerstein, D., & Barsh, E. (1992). The importance of spirometry in the assessment of childhood asthma. *Am J Dis Child, 146,* 977–978.

Bufford, J.D., & Gern, J.E. (2005). The hygiene hypothesis revisited. *Immunol Allergy Clin North Am, 25*(2), 247–262.

Burrows, B., Halonen, M., Lebowitz, M.D., et al. (1982). The relationship of serum immunoglobulin E, allergy skin tests, and smoking to respiratory disorders. *J Allergy Clin Immunol, 70,* 199–204.

Castro-Rodríguez, J.A., Holberg, C.J., Wright, A.L., Halonen, M., Taussig, L.M.,…Martinez, F.D. (1999). Association of radiologically ascertained pneumonia before age 3 yr with asthma like symptoms and pulmonary function during childhood: A prospective study. *Am J Respir Crit Care Med, 159*(6), 1891–1897.

Chilmonczyk, B.A., Salmun, L.M., Megathlin, K.N., Neveux, L.M., Palomaki, G.E., Knight, G.J.,… Haddow, J.E. (1993). Association between exposure to environmental tobacco smoke and exacerbations of asthma in children. *N Engl J Med, 328,* 1665–1669.

Cook, D.G., & Strachan, D.P. (1999). Health effects of passive smoking-10: Summary of effects of parental smoking on the respiratory health of children and implications for research. *Thorax, 54*(4), 357–366.

Delclos, G.L., Gimeno, D., Arif, A.A., Burau, K.D., Carson, A., Lusk, C., Stock, T., Symanski, E., Whitehead, L.W., Zock, J.P., et al. (2007). Occupational risk factors and asthma among health care professionals. *Am J Respir Crit Care Med, 175,* 667–675.

Dunn, A., & Zeise, L. (Eds.). (1997). *Health effects of exposure to environmental tobacco smoke.* Sacramento, CA: California Environmental Protection Agency.

Dunn, A., Zeise, L., & Waller, K. (1997). Developmental toxicity II: Postnatal manifestations in health effects of exposure to environmental tobacco smoke (pp. 4-1–4-48). A. Dunn, L. Zeise (Eds.). California Environmental Protection Agency.

Eder, W., & Ege, M.J. (2006). The asthma epidemic. *N Engl J Med, 355,* 2226–2235.

Flaherman, V., & Rutherford, G.W. (2006). A meta-analysis of the effect of high weight on asthma. *Arch Dis Child, 91,* 334–339.

Gerald, L.B., Gerald, J.K., Gibson, L., Patel, K., Zhang, S., & McClure, L.A. (2009). Changes in environmental tobacco smoke exposure and asthma morbidity among urban school children. *Chest, 135*(4), 911–916.

Gilliland, F.D., Berhane, K., Islam, T., McConnell, R., Gauderman, W.J., Gilliland, S.S.,…Peters, J.M. (2003). Obesity and the risk of newly diagnosed asthma in school-age children. *Am J Epidemiol, 158*(5), 406–415.

Global Initiative for Asthma (GINA). (2011). Global Strategy for Asthma Management and Prevention. NHLBI/WHO workshop report. National Institutes of Health, National Heart, Lung and Blood Institute, Washington, DC.

Heinrich, J., Richter, K., Frye, C., Meyer, I., Wölke, G., Wjst, M.,…Wichmann, H.E. (2002). European Community Respiratory Health Survey in Adults (ECRHS). *Pneumologie, 56*(5), 297–303.

Hedman, J., Kaprio, J., Poussa, T., & Nieminen, M.M. (1999). Prevalence of asthma, aspirin intolerance, nasal polyposis and chronic obstructive pulmonary diseases in a population-based study. *Int J Epidem, 28,* 717–722.

Higgins, I.T.T. (1974). *Epidemiology of chronic respiratory disease. A literature review.* EPA-650/1-74-007. Washington, DC: Environmental Protection Agency.

Holgate, S.T., & Polosa, R. (2006). The mechanisms, diagnosis, and management of severe asthma in adults. *Lancet, 368*, 780–793.

Huss, K., Adkinson, N.F., Eggleston, P.A., Dawson, C., Van Natta, M.L., & Hamilton, R.G. (2001). House dust mite and cockroach exposure are strong risk factors for positive allergy skin test responses in the Childhood Asthma Management Program. *Journal of Allergy and Clinical Immunology, 107*(1), 48–54.

ISAAC. (1998a). Worldwide variations in the prevalence of asthma symptoms: The International Study of Asthma and Allergies in Childhood (ISAAC). The International Study of Asthma and Allergies in Childhood (ISAAC) Steering Committee. *Eur Respir J, 12*, 315–335.

ISAAC. (1998b). Worldwide variation in prevalence of symptoms of asthma, allergic rhinoconjunctivitis, and atopic eczema: ISAAC. The International Study of Asthma and Allergies in Childhood (ISAAC) Steering Committee. *Lancet, 351*, 1225–1232.

Jaakkola, J.J.K., Naftad, P., & Magnus, P. (2001). Environmental tobacco smoke, parental atopy, and childhood asthma. *Environ Health Perspect, 109*, 579–582.

Jackson, D.J., Gangnon, R.E., Evans, M.D., Roberg, K.A., Anderson, E.L.,...Lemanske, Jr. R.F. (2008). Wheezing rhinovirus illnesses in early life predict asthma development in high-risk children. *Am J Respir Crit Care Med, 178*, 667–672.

Jenkins, C., Costello, J., & Hodge, L. (2004). Systematic review of prevalence of aspirin induced asthma and its implications for clinical practice. *BMJ, 328*(7437), 434–437.

Kim, J.E., & Kountakis, S.E. (2007). The prevalence of Samter's triad in patients undergoing functional endoscopic sinus surgery. *Ear Nose Throat J, 86*(7), 396–399.

Kulig, M., Bergmann, R., Tacke, U., Wahn, U., & Guggenmoos-Holzmann, I. (1998). Long-lasting sensitization to food during the first two years precedes allergic airway disease. The MAS Study Group, Germany. *Pediatr Allergy Immunol, 9*, 61–67.

Lau, S., Illi, S., Sommerfeld, C., Niggemann, B., Bergmann, R., von Mutius, E., & Wahn, U. (2000). Early exposure to house-dust mite and cat allergens and development of childhood asthma: A cohort study. Multicentre Allergy Study Group. *Lancet, 356*, 1392–1397.

Leff, A.R. (2000). Role of leukotrienes in bronchial hyperresponsiveness and cellular responses in airways. *Thorax, 55*, S32–S37.

Leung, T.F., Lam, C.W., Chan, I.H., Li, A.M., & Tang, N.L. (2002). Sensitization to common food allergens is a risk factor for asthma in young Chinese children in Hong Kong. *J Asthma, 39*, 523–529.

Moffatt, M.F., Gut, I.F., Dmeenais, F., Strachan, D.P., Bouzigon, E., Heath, S.,...WOCM for the GABRIEL Consortium. (2010). A large-scale, consortium-based genomewide association study of asthma. *N Engl J Med, 363*, 1211–1221.

Masoli, M., Fabian, D., Holt, S., Beasley, R., for the Global Initiative for Asthma (GINA) Program. (2004). The global burden of asthma: Executive summary of the GINA Dissemination Committee Report. *Allergy, 59*, 469–478.

National Heart, Lung, Blood Institute. (2007). *National Asthma Education and Prevention Program. Expert panel report 3: Guidelines for the diagnosis and management of asthma.* Washington, DC: US Department of Health and Human Services, National Institutes of Health.

Ober, C., & Hoffjan, S. (2006). Asthma genetics 2006: The long and winding road to gene discovery. *Genes and Immunity, 7*, 95–100.

Ober, C., Tan, Z., Sun, Y., Possick, J.D., Pan, L., Nicolae, R.,...Chupp, G.L. (2008). Effect of variation in *CHI3L1* on serum YKL-40 level, risk of asthma, and lung function. *N Engl J Med, 358*, 1682–1691.

Pearce, N., Sunyer, J., Cheng, S., Chinn, S., Bjorksten, B., Burr, M.,...Burney, P. (2000). Comparison of asthma prevalence in the ISAAC and the ECRHS. ISAAC Steering Committee and the European Community Respiratory Health Survey. International Study of Asthma and

Allergies in Childhood. *European Respiratory Journal*, 16(3), 420–426.

Pearce, N., Pekkanen, J., & Beasley, R. (1999). How much asthma is really attributable to atopy? *Thorax*, 54, 268–272.

Pearce, N., Douwes, J., & Beasley, R. (2000). Is allergen exposure the major primary cause of asthma? *Thorax*, 55, 424–431.

Penard-Morand, C., Raherison, C., Kopferschmitt, C., et al. (2005). Prevalence of food allergy and its relationship to asthma and allergic rhinitis in schoolchildren. *Allergy*, 60, 1165–1171.

Rachelefsy, G. (2009). Inhaled corticosteroids and asthma control in children: Assessing impairment and risk. *Pediatrics*, 123(1), 353–366.

Reese, T.A., Liang, H.E., Tager, A.M., Luster, A.D., Van Rooijen, N., Voehringer, D., & Locksley, R.M. (2007). Chitin induces accumulation in tissue of innate immune cells associated with allergy. *Nature*, 447, 92–96.

Robbins, S.L., & Cotran, R.S. (1979). *Pathologic basis of disease* (2nd ed.). Philadelphia: W.B. Saunders Company.

Rönmark, E., Andersson, C., Nyström, L., Forsberg, B., Järvholmand, B., & Lundbäck, B. (2005). Obesity increases the risk of incident asthma among adults. *European Respiratory Journal*, 25(2), 282–288.

Samter, M., & Beers, R.F. (1968). Intolerance to aspirin. Clinical studies and consideration of its pathogenesis. *Ann Intern Med*, 68(5), 975–983.

Schroeder, A., Kumar, R., Pongracic, J.A., Sullivan, C.L., Caruso, D.M., Costello, J.,…Wang, X. (2009). Food allergy is associated with an increased risk of asthma. *Clin Exp Allergy*, 39(2), 261–70.

Sears, M.R., Burrows, B., Flannery, E.M., et al. (1991). Relation between airway responsiveness and serum IgE in children with asthma and in apparently normal children. *N Engl J Med*, 325, 1067–1071.

Senthilselvan, A., Lawson, J., Rennie, D.C., & Dosman, J.A. (2003). Stabilization of an increasing trend in physician-diagnosed asthma prevalence in Saskatchewan, 1991 to 1998. *Chest*, 124(2), 438–448.

Shaaban, R., Zureik, M., Soussan, D., Antó, J.M., Heinrich, J., Janson, C., Künzli, N., Sunyer, J., Wjst, M., Burney, P.G., et al. (2007). Allergic rhinitis and onset of bronchial hyperresponsiveness: A population-based study. *Am J Respir Crit Care Med*, 176, 659–666.

Sigurs, N., Bjarnason, R., Sigurbergsson, F., & Kjellman, B. (2000). Respiratory syncytial virus bronchiolitis in infancy is an important risk factor for asthma and allergy at age 7. *Am J Respir Crit Care Med*, 161(5), 1501–1507.

Sporik, R., Holgate, S.T., Platts-Mills, T.A.E., & Cogswell, J.J. (1990). Exposure to house dust mite allergen (Der p1) and the development of asthma in childhood. A prospective study. *N Engl J Med*, 323, 502–507.

Strachan, D.P. (1989). Hay fever, hygiene and household size. *BMJ*, 299(6710), 1259–1260.

Strachan, D.P., & Cook, D.G. (1998). Parental smoking and childhood asthma: Longitudinal and case-control studies. *Thorax*, 53(3), 204–212.

Torrent, M., Sunyer, J., Garcia, R., Harris, J., Iturriaga, M.V., Puig, C.,…Cullinan, P. (2007). Early-life allergen exposure and atopy, asthma, and wheeze up to 6 years of age. *Am J Respir Crit Care Med*, 176, 446–453.

Vork, K.L., Broadwin, R.L., & Blaisdell, R.J. (2007). Developing asthma in childhood from exposure to secondhand tobacco smoke: Insights from a meta-regression. *Environ Health Perspect*, 115(10), 1394–1400.

Weinmayr, G., Weiland, S.K., Björkstén, B., Brunekreef, B., Büchele, G., Cookson, W.O.C.,…Wong, G.W., and the ISAAC Phase Two Study Group. (2007). Atopic sensitization and the international variation of asthma symptom prevalence in children. *Am J Respir Crit Care Med*, 176, 565–574.

WHO. (2009). *Death and DALY estimates for 2004 by cause for WHO Member States (Persons, all ages)*. Geneva, Switzerland: World Health Organization.

Widal, M.F. (1922). Anaphylaxie et idiosyncraise. *Press Med, 119,* 48–51.

Wu, P., Dupont, W.D., Griffin, M.R., Carroll, K.N., Mitchel, E.F., Gebretsadik, T., & Hartert, T.V. (2008). Evidence of a causal role of winter virus infection during infancy on early childhood asthma. *Am J Respir Crit Care Med, 11,* 1123–1129.

Zock, J.P., Plana, E., Jarvis, D., Antó, J.M., Kromhout, H., Kennedy, S.M.,…, Torén, K., et al. (2007). The use of household cleaning sprays and adult asthma: An international longitudinal study. *Am J Respir Crit Care Med, 176,* 735–741.

Epidemiology of Diabetes Mellitus

Susanne K. Scott & Randall E. Harris

INTRODUCTION

Diabetes mellitus is a complex chronic metabolic disease characterized by high fasting blood glucose. The two major forms of diabetes, type 1 and type 2, arise by different mechanisms. Elevated blood glucose, or hyperglycemia, arises when insulin, a key hormone produced by the beta (β) cells of the *islets of Langerhans* of the pancreas, is either no longer secreted (diabetes type 1) or no longer able to adequately facilitate glucose entry into the cells for energy production (diabetes type 2).

Because of its unprecedented global impact since the early 1980s, diabetes may be incorrectly labeled or considered a contemporary disease. This is largely due to its strong association with prominent features of modern day lifestyle, primarily increasing caloric intake and decreasing physical activity, which have contributed to an equally alarming global increase in the prevalence of obesity. The historical written record that describes the medical condition of diabetes, however, has a cross-cultural lineage spanning thousands of years.

HISTORICAL SUMMARY OF DIABETES MELLITUS

Diabetes mellitus has an ancient recorded history dating to 5th century BC Indian texts. The earliest description of cases included thirst, emaciation, and excessive output of sweet urine (Eknoyan and Nagy, 2005). Ancient Egyptian documents (Buqrat, 460 BC, and Papyrus of Ebers, *circa* 1550 BC)

described excessive urine output, without reference to sweet urine (Ali et al., 2006). The Chinese (Huang Ti's Canon of Medicine, *Nei Ching Su Wen*, revised during 475–221 BC, and Chang Chung-Ching, 229 AD) described classic diabetes mellitus in much the same way as the Indian Hindus, who most likely observed patients with type 2 diabetes, linking the disease with risk factors such as socioeconomic status ("*the rich*"), excess calories ("*large quantities*"), and simple carbohydrates ("*rice, cereal, sweets*") (Henschen, 1969; Guthrie and Humphreys, 1988; Eknoyan and Nagy, 2005).

While Demetrius of Apameia (*circa* 1st or 2nd century BC) has been credited with coining the term "diabetes," which derives from Greek origins and means "to siphon" (Henschen, 1969), Aretaeus of Cappadocia (*circa* 81–138 AD) first clinically described diabetes (Ali et al., 2006; Kirchoff, Popat, and Maloway, 2008) and wrote of a "cure" in his book entitled *Therapeutics of Chronic Diseases* (Henschen, 1969).

Aretaeus, and later, Galen of Pergamum (*circa* 129–200 AD), whose experiments on dogs showed the kidneys to be the source of urine, considered diabetes to be a rare disease of the kidneys (Gemmill, 1972). Both men, however, never commented on the sweetness of urine, leading one to question whether it was *diabetes insipidus*, commonly caused by antidiuretic hormone (ADH) deficiency, and not *diabetes mellitus* that they were describing (Henschen, 1969). For the half century following Galen, Greek physicians cited Galen's descriptive, theoretical, and etiologic work on diabetes, and contributed new medical literature focusing primarily on treatments that included medicinal herbs, wines, and bloodletting (Christopoulou-Aletra and Papavramidou, 2008).

Early historical writings show that tasting urine was the first diagnostic diabetes test. The early Egyptians, Indians, and Asians noted the sweet taste of urine from patients, and Chang Chung-Ching (229 AD) stated that *the urine was so sweet that the dogs liked it.* Hindu medical textbooks from the 5th century described sweet honey and sugarcane urine of patients (Guthrie and Humphreys, 1988). Theodore Protospatharios (630 AD) recommended examining the residue of heated of urine as a diagnostic test (Henschen, 1969).

Like the Indian Hindus centuries before, the Iranian physician Avicenna (980–1037), the Swiss physician Paracelsus (1493–1541), and the Italian Anatomist Morgagni (1635–1683) all described the urine of patients as tasting sweet. Paracelsus concluded that diabetes was caused by salt deposition in the kidneys, which led to *polydipsia* (excessive thirst) and *polyuria* (excessive urine). He based this on the observation that an unknown white substance remained after evaporating urine from diabetic patients (Pickup and William, 1997; Ali et al., 2006).

In 1674, the English physician Thomas Willis (1621–1675) tasted the urine of afflicted patients and gave the disease the name diabetes *mellitus*, meaning honey sweet (Eknoyan and Nagy, 2005), which he differentiated from *diabetes insipidus* in his classic work, *Pharmaceutice Rationalis*. A century passed before Robert Wyatt in 1774 and Mathew Dobson in 1776 showed that the sweetness in urine was accompanied by sugar in the blood (Eknoyan and Nagy, 2005).

In the 19th and early 20th centuries, the first quantitative clinical and diagnostic tools were developed to test for elevated sugar in the urine (*glycosuria*) and blood (*hyperglycemia*). In addition, French, Italian, German, and American researchers studied and experimented on the liver, digestive system, and pancreas. Diabetologist Apollinaire Bouchardat (1806–1886) noticed the disappearance of glycosuria among food-rationed diabetics in Paris during the Franco-Prussian War. He subsequently treated diabetic patients with fasting and low carbohydrate diets. Bouchardat also observed that weight reduction and exercise improved metabolism and he is credited with developing the paradigm of patient education and personal responsibility for diabetic control (Chast, 2000). The discovery of insulin in 1921 by Canadian scientists Frederick Banting, Charles Best, John James Rickard Macleod, and James Collip forever transformed type 1 diabetes from a rare and fatal disease to one where prolonged survival was possible (Gale, 2002).

ROLE OF INSULIN IN DIABETES

Carbohydrate is the preferred source of energy for the human body. Glucose, a monosaccharide, is the basic unit of complex carbohydrates and is the primary sugar metabolized for energy. The cellular use of carbohydrate for energy depends upon multiple factors including the digestive breakdown of complex carbohydrates to glucose, the absorption of glucose through the small intestine, and the transport of glucose via the portal circulation to the cells that use it. Glucose uptake occurs first in the liver where excess glucose is packaged and stored in limited quantities as glycogen, before systemic distribution to the rest of the tissues of the body.

Insulin is synthesized and secreted by the beta (β) cells of the endocrine pancreas within specialized areas called the *islets of Langerhans*. Insulin release into the bloodstream is rapidly triggered in response to increased blood glucose, for example, after a carbohydrate-rich meal. In turn, insulin induces glucose uptake for energy production in muscle cells and storage in fat cells.

Glucose enters most cells of the body through facilitated diffusion via a family of transmembrane proteins called glucose transporters (Gould and Holman, 1993). Some cells, specifically those of striated muscle (myocytes) and fat (adipocytes), require insulin to facilitate glucose uptake, whereas others such as neurons, retinal cells, red blood cells, and kidney cells do not. Insulin-stimulated cellular uptake of glucose is initiated when insulin binds to insulin-specific receptors located within the plasma membrane of target cells (Shepard and Kahn, 1999).

Glucose transporter 4 (GLUT-4) is the gateway for insulin-mediated cellular glucose uptake (Sheperd and Kahn, 1999). Once insulin binds with the insulin receptor, a cascade of physiologic intracellular signaling events unfolds, including translocation of GLUT-4 from a nonactivated state within cytoplasmic vesicles to insertion within the plasma membrane, where cellular uptake of glucose then proceeds (Kandror and Pilch, 1996; Pessin et al., 1999; Czech and Corvera, 1999). The process is depicted in **Figure 32.1**.

Diabetes mellitus is a disease state of persistent inappropriate excess blood glucose (hyperglycemia) caused by the inability of *endogenous* insulin to adequately mediate glucose uptake for the target cells that require it. Reasons for inadequate insulin action may include lack of insulin production by the β-cells of the pancreas (insulin insufficiency) and reduced, downregulated, or dysregulated insulin receptor signaling (insulin resistance).

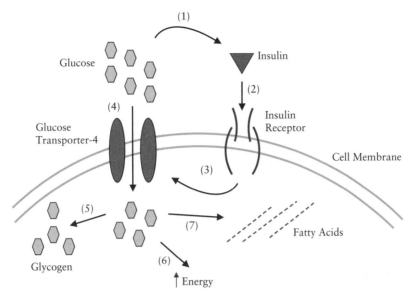

Figure 32.1 Effects of Insulin on Glucose Uptake and Metabolism.

DIAGNOSIS OF DIABETES

Several blood glucose tests are available and recommended for the diagnosis of diabetes. A diagnosis is made when the blood glucose exceeds a clinically identified threshold level or diagnostic cut point for the particular test in use (**Table 32.1**). A repeat confirmatory *same-test* is recommended on a subsequent day for a definitive diagnosis (American Diabetes Association, 2010).

Fasting Plasma Glucose Test

The fasting plasma glucose test is currently considered the diagnostic test of choice over other available tests, such as the hemoglobin A1c and the two-hour postload plasma glucose test, primarily due to the ease, convenience, speed, patient acceptability, cost, reproducibility, and reduced intraindividual variation of the test. According to the American Diabetes

Association, the fasting blood glucose is also able to predict microvascular complications to a similar degree as the complex and more expensive 2-hour post-load plasma glucose tolerance test (American Diabetes Association, 2010). As the name implies, a minimal overnight 8-hour fast is required prior to the test, and a diagnosis of diabetes is made when the fasting blood glucose is 126 mg/dL or greater.

Oral Glucose Tolerance Test

The oral glucose tolerance test is considered the *gold standard* of diagnostic tests for diabetes; however, it is more complex and expensive than other tests, and also requires fasting for at least 8 hours prior to testing (National Institute of Diabetes and Digestive and Kidney Diseases, NIDDK, 2008). To obtain the glucose tolerance for a patient, the fasting blood glucose is measured at baseline, and a standard dose of glucose is then given (75 grams) and plasma glucose is measured 2 hours later. A fasting level of 126 mg/dL or higher and a post-load level of 200 mg/dL is diagnostic of diabetes.

Random Blood Test

A random blood glucose test may be used as a screening test if diabetic symptoms are present. This test assumes a nonfasted state and therefore allows for higher glucose values. A test result of 200 mg/dL or higher warrants further testing using one of the clinically recommended diagnostic blood glucose tests (NIDDK, 2008).

Table 32.1	Diagnostic Tests for Diabetes		
Diagnostic Test	**Normal**	**Pre-diabetes**	**Diabetes**
Fasting Glucose (mg/dL)	<100	100–125	>126
Glucose Tolerance (mg/dL)	<140	140–199	>200
Random Blood Test (mg/dL)	<140	140–199	>200
Hemoglobin A1c	<6.0%	6.0–6.5%	>6.5%

Hemoglobin A1c Test (HbA1c)

Hemoglobin A1c (HbA1c) is the newest blood test recommended for diagnosing diabetes (American Diabetes Association, 2010). It assesses average glucose levels over a 2- to 3-month period. Fasting is not required for the test. Traditionally, HbA1c is used by diabetics to monitor blood glucose levels. In this capacity, the level of HbA1c can be used as an indicator of treatment effectiveness. A diagnosis of diabetes is made when the HbA1c is 6.5% or higher. The HbA1c test quantifies the percentage of hemoglobin (the oxygen carrying molecule of the red blood cell) that has been bound by glucose within the 120-day life span of the red blood cell (Kilpatrick, 2000). The nonenzymatic binding of glucose to hemoglobin is called *glycosylation* or *glycation*. The higher the blood glucose, the higher the level of glycated hemoglobin (Gomero, 2008).

TYPES OF DIABETES

There are two major types of diabetes mellitus (type 1 and type 2), which are differentiated, in large part, by their underlying etiologies. In type 1 diabetes, the pancreas no longer produces insulin, primarily due to autoimmune destruction of the β-cells. Type 1 diabetes is therefore characterized as *insulin dependent*. It develops primarily in children and accounts for about 5–10% of all diabetics.

In classic type 2 diabetes, insulin is still produced and secreted, but because of *insulin resistance* of target cells coupled with relative *insulin insufficiency*, blood glucose is not adequately controlled. Type 2 diabetes develops primarily in adults and accounts for 90–95% of all diabetics. Conditions that lead to ineffective insulin action are likely influenced by various combinations of underlying genetic, inherited, congenital, acquired, and/or environmental factors.

A third type, gestational diabetes, is diagnosed during pregnancy (Homko, 2010). Pregnancy increases the metabolic workload of the maternal pancreas and heightens both insulin resistance and insulin insufficiency.

Other etiologic forms of diabetes are due to rare genetic defects of the β-cells and defects in insulin action, signaling, or secretion. Diabetes can also be caused by diseases of the exocrine pancreas such as cystic fibrosis, endocrinopathies (e.g., Cushing syndrome), certain infections (e.g., congenital rubella and cytomegalovirus), certain medications (chemotherapeutics and glucocorticoids), as well as rare autoimmune disorders and genetic syndromes, such as Down syndrome or Prader-Willi syndrome (NIDDK, 2010).

GLOBAL PANDEMIC OF DIABETES MELLITUS

The beginning of the 21st century marked a profound increase in the global burden of diabetes, which is now described as a pandemic (Narayan et al., 2006). While heightened levels of obesity and greater longevity are clearly important determinants of this worldwide phenomenon, the web of causation is complex and involves multiple factors including fetal and childhood growth and development, maternal biology and influence, genetics, nutrition, urbanization, automation, perceptions of weight gain, changes in food costs, greater access to foods high in fat and calories, and proclivity to lack of exercise through a sedentary lifestyle. As pointed out by Dr. Lucy Candib in her essay on diabetes and obesity in vulnerable populations,

> *"The strategy with the most powerful long-term effect in curtailing the escalation is reduction in the prevalence of obesity. [Nevertheless] The merger of many interacting forces conjoined in creating this global phenomenon calls for explanatory models and ways of thinking that go beyond traditional singular notions of causality"* (Candib, 2007).

GLOBAL PREVALENCE OF DIABETES

Diabetes mellitus is currently the most frequently diagnosed of noncommunicable diseases and the fastest-growing chronic disease in the world (Sudagani and Hitman, 2005; Gupta and Kumar, 2008). According to survey data from the 216 member nations and territories of the International Diabetes Federation (IDF), more than 285 million people had diabetes in 2010, a 67% increase from the estimated 171 million people with diabetes in 2000 (IDF Diabetes Atlas, 2010).

Across *all* age groups, the worldwide prevalence of diabetes more than doubled in the first decade of the 21st century, rising from 2.8% in 2000 to 6.4% in 2010 (IDF Diabetes Atlas, 2010). The greatest increase in prevalence has occurred among the elderly, rising from <5% in 1970 to nearly 15% in 2010 for adults 65 years or older (**Figure 32.2**).

The global pandemic of diabetes is largely due to type 2 diabetes that predominantly strikes in adulthood. In 1995, survey data from 188 member nations of the World Health Organization (WHO) revealed that 4.0% of adults ages 20 years or older had diabetes (King, Aubert, and Herman, 1998). In 2010, IDF investigators analyzed survey data from 216 member

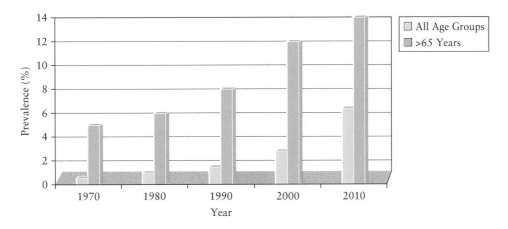

Figure 32.2 Global Trends in the Prevalence of Diabetes.

Source: Data from World Health Organization, 1970–2010. IDF Diabetes Atlas, 4th Edition.

nations and territories and found that 6.6% of adults ages 20–79 years had diabetes (IDF Atlas, 2010). In that same year, an independent team of investigators found a similar prevalence of 6.4% based on analysis of population surveys from 91 countries (Shaw, Sicree, and Zimmit, 2010).

These data reflect an alarming 4% annual increase in the worldwide prevalence of adult diabetes over the past 15 years. If this steep trajectory continues, the worldwide number of diabetics is expected to exceed 400 million by 2025, effectively doubling the absolute number of diabetics within a 30-year period (Wild et al., 2004; Hossain, Kawar, and El Nahas, 2007; Shaw, Sicree, and Zimmit, 2010).

In the year 2000, the prevalence was highest (>60 cases per 1,000) in developed countries of North America and Western Europe and lowest (<15 cases per 1,000) in developing countries of Southeast Asia and Central Africa (**Figure 32.3**). This pattern is similar to that of obesity and energy consumption. Nations in which the prevalence is high have a greater burden of obesity (>30%) and higher levels of energy intake per capita (>3,200 kcals per day); reciprocally, nations in which the prevalence is low have less obesity (<15%) and consume less energy (<2,800 kcals per day).

The international survey data also show wide variation in the prevalence of adult diabetes among

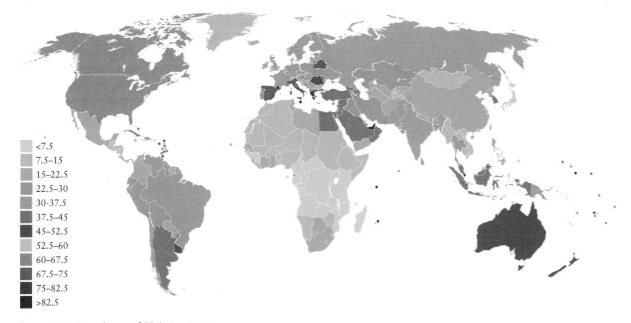

Figure 32.3 Prevalence of Diabetes, 2004.

Source: Data from World Health Organization. The global burden of disease: 2004 update. Geneva, WHO, 2008. Available at www.who.int/evidence/bod.

countries. Most notably, the Republic of Naura, an island nation in Micronesia in the Southwest Pacific, had the highest prevalence in 2010 (nearly 31%) while the Republic of Rwanda, located in the East-Central African highlands, had the lowest (about 1%). The prevalence was also high (>15%) in several other island nations of Micronesia and in nations bordering the Persian Gulf such as the United Arab Emirates and Saudi Arabia (IDF Diabetes Atlas, 2010). The data suggest that diabetes is uncommon in developing countries where a traditional lifestyle has been preserved, whereas communities that have undergone westernization and urbanization are at higher risk (Hossain, Kawar, and El Nahas, 2007).

The accelerating worldwide prevalence of diabetes has occurred in concert with changes in population dynamics and demography. In particular, more people are living beyond the age of 65 years when the diabetic risk is high (Wild et al., 2004), and many nations are experiencing urbanization, or the migration of their populations from rural areas to cities (Candib, 2007). In particular, the increasing prevalence of type 2 diabetes is closely linked to the upsurge in obesity (Sobngwi et al., 2004; Hossain, Kawar, and El Nahas, 2007).

DISTRIBUTION OF DIABETES BY GENDER AND AGE

Investigators from the University of Edinburgh, Scotland, recently compiled data from population samples in more than 40 countries to estimate the age-gender specific prevalence of diabetes. The importance of age is illustrated in **Figure 32.4**. The prevalence

increases exponentially by age reaching a maximum of approximately 14% in adults 80 years and older. Prevalence estimates by age are similar for men and women, becoming slightly higher (about 1%) in elderly women compared to men. The observed gender difference late in life is most likely due to the combined effects of more elderly women than men in most populations and the increasing prevalence of diabetes in the upper age brackets (Wild et al., 2010).

GLOBAL DEATHS ATTRIBUTABLE TO DIABETES

In the year 2000, the World Health Organization (WHO) reported that the global death toll from diabetes was 2.9 million, approximately 5.2% of all-cause mortality. It is important to realize that this estimate is based upon the underlying causes of death abstracted from death certificates. Since diabetes is a major risk factor for other life-threatening events such as heart attack and stroke and since vital statistics based on death certificates are not available in some underdeveloped nations, many investigators believe that the number of deaths attributable to diabetes based on vital statistics may be grossly underestimated.

To correct for potential under-reporting, WHO investigators Gojka Roglic and Nigel Unwin used census data for the world population of 2000 together with cause-specific mortality rates reported by WHO and estimates of the risk of death in diabetics versus nondiabetics derived from the literature to recalculate the deaths attributable to diabetes. They found that in 2000, 3.2 million people died from

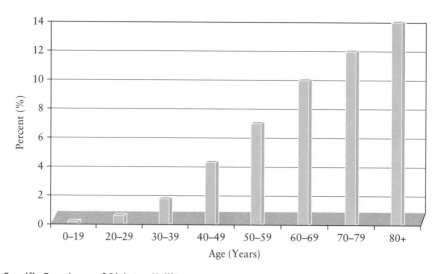

Figure 32.4 Age-Specific Prevalence of Diabetes Mellitus.

Source: Data from Wild S, Roglic G, Green A, Sicree R, King H. (2004). Global prevalence of diabetes. Estimates for the year 2000 and projections for 2030. *Diabetes Care* 27:1047–1053.

diabetes, approximately 6% of all-cause mortality for that year. Their estimates, which are approximately 10% higher than those based on death certificates, are likely to be a more accurate reflection of the death toll from diabetes (Roglic and Unwin, 2005).

In a subsequent investigation using similar methods, Roglic and Unwin calculated the number of deaths attributable to diabetes among adults ages 20–79 years for the world population of 2010 and populations residing in selected countries and geographic regions. They estimated that 3.96 million deaths were attributable to diabetes in 2010, or approximately 6.8% of all-cause global mortality. The highest number of deaths attributable to diabetes occurred in countries with the largest populations: approximately 1 million deaths in India, 575,000 in China, 231,000 in the United States, and 182,000 in the Russian Federation. Estimates of relative mortality attributable to diabetes varied widely among regions, ranging from 6% in Africa to 15.7% in North America. Estimates were also calculated for 2007 and compared with those for 2010. In the 3-year time span, the overall number of deaths attributable to diabetes increased by 5.5%. The largest increases in relative mortality were found in North America (29%), Southeast Asia (12%), and the Western Pacific (11%). The results indicate that diabetes is a leading cause of premature death worldwide, and the death toll is expected to rise further, particularly in developing countries where the prevalence is increasing and access to health care is limited (Roglic and Unwin, 2010).

DISABILITY ADJUSTED LIFE YEARS FOR DIABETES

The disability adjusted life years ($DALY$) lost from diabetes measures the years of life lost due to premature death (YLL) plus the years lost to severe disability (YLD), $DALY = YLL + YLD$. National estimates of DALYs due to diabetes reported by WHO are shown in **Figure 32.5**. High DALYs are evident in many developing nations of Africa, the Middle East, Asia, the Southwest Pacific, Central America, and South America. In nations with high DALYs, (>600 per 100,000), populations are migrating from rural areas to cities (urbanization) leading to lifestyle modifications (high caloric diet and sedentary lifestyle) favoring positive energy balance, excessive weight gain, and the genesis of type 2 diabetes (Sobngwi et al., 2004). Of the 4 million annual deaths attributable to diabetes, nearly two-thirds occur in developing countries where 80% of the world population lives. It is in these nations that the general lack of access to effective sustained therapy for diabetes results in not only premature death, but also high disability.

BURDEN OF DIABETES IN THE UNITED STATES

The prevalence of diabetes across all age groups has risen more than sevenfold in the United States in the past half century, from less than 1% in 1960 to

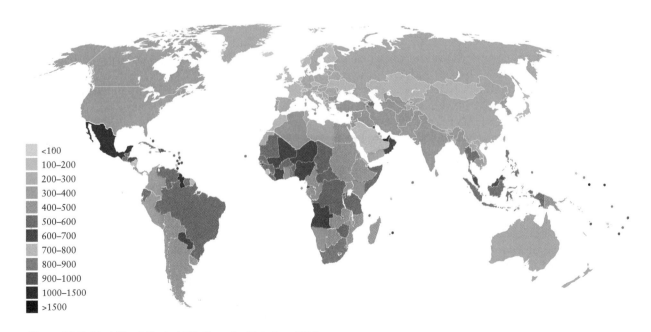

Legend:
- <100
- 100–200
- 200–300
- 300–400
- 400–500
- 500–600
- 600–700
- 700–800
- 800–900
- 900–1000
- 1000–1500
- >1500

Figure 32.5 Disability Adjusted Life Years for Diabetes, 2004.

Source: Data from World Health Organization. The global burden of disease: 2004 update. Geneva, WHO, 2008. Available at www.who.int/evidence/bod.

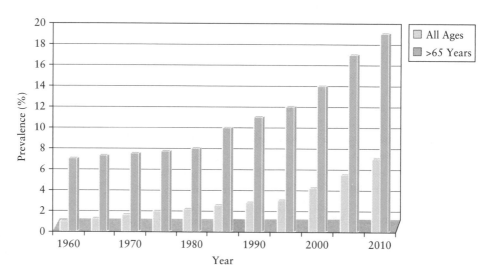

Figure 32.6 Prevalence of Diabetes in the United States, 1960–2010.

Source: Data from US National Health and Nutrition Survey (NHANES), 1960–2010; Centers for Disease Control and Prevention (2010). National Center for Chronic Disease Prevention and Health Promotion, Division of Diabetes Translation.

approximately 7% in 2010 (**Figure 32.6**). Sequential analysis of data from the nationwide *Behavioral Risk Factor Surveillance System* (*BRFSS*) revealed that among adults ages 18 years or older, 7.3% had diabetes in 2000 compared to 4.9% in 1990, an increase of nearly 50% in the decade. In 1990, the prevalence was 6% or greater in 4 states, whereas in 2008 the prevalence was 6% or greater in 49 of 52 participating states and territories. The greatest absolute increase occurred among the elderly; for example, the prevalence of diabetes increased from approximately 8% to nearly 20% for adults 65 years and older during 1980–2010 (Mokdad et al., 2000, 2001; CDC, 2010).

Investigators at the National Institute of Diabetes and Digestive and Kidney Disease (NIDDK) found a similar trend among adults based upon analysis of data from the National Health and Nutrition Examination Surveys (NHANES) of 1988–2006. They examined the prevalence of diabetes diagnosed by elevated hemoglobin A1c (6.5% or higher) among probability samples of US adults ages 20 and over, and also estimated the fraction of diabetics who remained undiagnosed. The age-standardized prevalence of *physician-diagnosed* diabetes increased from 5.3% to 7.6% (43%) during this time span, whereas the prevalence of *undiagnosed* diabetics declined from 2.1% to 1.6%. While gender differences were not apparent, standardized estimates of prevalence were nearly twice as high in Hispanics and African Americans as in Caucasians.

Investigators at the Centers for Disease Control (CDC) used data from the National Health Interview Surveys of 1984–2000 to project the lifetime risk of diabetes by age, gender, and ethnicity for the cohort born in 2000 in the United States. The estimated lifetime risk of developing diabetes was 32.8% in men and 38.5% in women. Hispanic men and women had the highest lifetime risks, 45.4% and 52.5%, respectively. In addition, the life span of a person diagnosed with diabetes at age 40 was found to be 11 years shorter (for men) and 14 years shorter (for women) than disease-free individuals (Narayan et al., 2003).

Overall, these results underscore the continuing rise in the incidence and prevalence of diabetes among US adults in this century, particularly among Hispanics and African Americans; they also suggest that nearly 20% of diabetics remain undiagnosed (Cowie et al., 2010). Clearly, diabetes has reached epidemic proportions in the US population.

MORTALITY FROM DIABETES IN THE UNITED STATES

Concurrent with the dramatic increase in the prevalence of diabetes in the United States during the past 3 decades, the death toll has also accelerated. According to vital statistics abstracted from death certificates in 2005, diabetes contributed to more than 233,000 deaths and was directly responsible for more than 75,000 deaths. The relative mortality (percentage of all deaths) due to diabetes in that year was 3.1% (Kung et al., 2008). By comparison, 25 years earlier, in 1980, diabetes was responsible for nearly 36,000 deaths and the relative mortality was

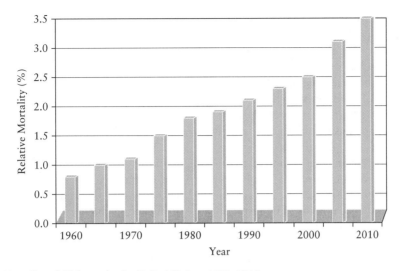

Figure 32.7 Relative Mortality of Diabetes in the United States, 1960–2010.

Source: Data from US National Health and Nutrition Survey (NHANES), 1960–2010; Centers for Disease Control and Prevention (2010). National Center for Chronic Disease Prevention and Health Promotion, Division of Diabetes Translation.

1.8% (Rogot et al., 1985). Proportionate estimates of relative mortality reflect at least a fourfold increase in deaths from diabetes since 1960 (**Figure 32.7**).

A number of studies suggest that diabetes is likely to be under-reported as the main cause of death or a contributing factor on death certificates. Investigators at the Centers for Disease Control used data from the 1986 *National Mortality Followback Survey* to estimate the frequency that diabetes was recorded on the death certificates of diabetics. They examined death certificates of 2,766 decedents who were diabetic in life and found that diabetes was recorded on 38.2% of certificates and 9.6% as the underlying cause of death. The investigators concluded that diabetes is usually *not* listed on the death certificate and is more likely to be recorded for older patients with long-standing disease or comorbid conditions (Bild and Stevenson, 1992).

A research team from the University of Michigan examined the frequency of reported diabetes on the death certificates of 540 decedents with known diabetes. Subjects were enrolled in the *Translating Research into Action for Diabetes Study* (TRIAD), a multicenter prospective study of nearly 12,000 participants with diabetes. Diabetes was recorded on 39% of death certificates and as the underlying cause of death for only 10% of decedents. The investigators concluded that vital statistics based on death certificates markedly underestimate the prevalence of diabetes among decedents (McEwen et al., 2006).

Investigators at the University of California in San Diego examined reporting of diabetes on the death certificates of 3,209 decedents who were enrolled in

the *Rancho Bernardo* cohort in 1972–1974 and followed to 2003. Of those who died, 378 had a history of diabetes but only 168 (44%) had diabetes reported anywhere on the death certificate. Diabetes was approximately twice as likely to be reported on the death certificates of diabetics who died of cardiovascular causes compared with other causes, reflecting increased recognition that diabetes is a major cardiovascular risk factor (Cheng et al., 2008).

POPULATION-BASED MODELS OF DIABETES

In type 1 diabetes, the pancreas no longer produces insulin, primarily due to autoimmune destruction of the β-cells. With classical type 2 diabetes, insulin is still produced and secreted, but because of insulin resistance of target cells coupled with relative insulin insufficiency, blood glucose is not adequately controlled. All conditions that lead to ineffective insulin action are likely influenced by various combinations of underlying genetic, congenital, acquired, and/or environmental factors and their interactions. In addition, the temporal sequence of these conditions and the cause and consequence pathways to the onset of diabetes add to the heterogeneity and complexity surrounding the pathogenesis of diabetes.

Etiologic complexities of diabetes are illustrated by a brief summary of hypothetical population-based models that seek to explain the origin of the global pandemic of diabetes. The *thrifty genotype hypothesis* of Neel implicates the evolutionary selection of "*thrifty genes,*" which facilitate efficient storage of fat during times of nutritional abundance, and which helped hunter-gatherer populations survive times of famine and food scarcity (Neel, 1962). Neel postulated that the genetic selection that served human populations so well in the past have been "*rendered detrimental by progress.*" In other words, an abundance of food and calories that are perpetually available will inevitably lead to obesity and obesity-related chronic diseases, such as type 2 diabetes.

Various mechanisms have been advanced to explain the link between excess caloric intake, obesity, and type 2 diabetes. Adipose tissue clearly plays a central role in pathogenesis since it is the chief reservoir for the storage of body fat and an essential regulatory organ in maintaining energy homeostasis. The "energy storage capacity" of adipose tissue is restricted by the size, number, and metabolic integrity of adipocytes. Several investigators therefore suggest that type 2 diabetes is the result of the inability of the adipocyte population to expand and undergo sufficient cellular differentiation to accommodate excess calories (Leonhardt et al., 1972; Danforth, 2000; Scott et al., 2010). A corollary to the *energy storage capacity hypothesis* is that unremitting caloric surplus is complicated by the failure of adipocytes to maintain protection against lipotoxicity. Protective factors include enhanced proliferation of adipocytes (lipogenesis) and secretion of protective adipokines such as leptin and adiponection. Leptin has been found to suppress appetite and induce fatty acid oxidation thereby reducing toxicity from the accumulation of fat, ceramide, and cholesterol in skeletal muscle, liver, and other tissues, and adiponection has anti-inflammatory, pro-angiogenic, and anti-apoptotic properties. Conversely, when the energy storage capacity of the adipocyte population is surpassed, protection against lipotoxicity is severely compromised due to secretion of excessive inflammatory adipokines such as resistin coupled with rising concentrations of circulating triglycerides and fatty acids. These are key factors in the development of not only insulin resistance, but also β-cell insufficiency and depletion due to the heightened demand for insulin (Frühbeck et al., 2001; Willett, Manson, and Liu, 2002; Bays, Mandarino, and DeFronzo, 2004; Petersen and Shulman, 2006; Unger and Scherer, 2010).

Other models have been proposed in which nutritional conditions in the prenatal and postnatal environments influence the later development of type 2 diabetes. The *thrifty phenotype hypothesis*, also known as the *fetal origins hypothesis*, proposes that poor nutritional conditions during fetal development lead to intrauterine growth restriction and produce phenotypic changes such as low birth weight and body size, lowered metabolism, and altered glucose-insulin metabolism that are adapted for nutritional scarcity later in life (Hales and Barker, 1992; Barker, 1997). If, during postnatal growth and development of the child, the nutritional environment then becomes plentiful, inappropriate (accelerated) growth trajectory may occur, thereby resulting in the development of chronic health conditions later in life.

A variation of the fetal origins hypothesis is the theory of *metabolic programming* in which adaptation of the fetus to nutritional stress at a sensitive period of development leads to permanent changes in physiology and metabolism (Lucas, 1991). Animal studies have shown that maternal malnutrition during fetal development results in permanent effects in the offspring, including reduced pancreatic islet vascularization, size and function, and heightened insulin resistance, lending some support to the concept of metabolic programming (Patel, Srinivasan, and Aalinkeel, 2000).

Human studies also suggest that long-term postnatal development may be modified by metabolic experiences *in utero*. For example, Silverman and colleagues found that the offspring of diabetic mothers are more likely to become obese and develop impaired glucose tolerance than controls (Silverman et al., 1995, 1998). Dabelea and colleagues compared siblings born before and after their mother developed diabetes in 19 families ascertained from the Pima Indian Tribe residing in Arizona. This special population has one of the highest rates of type 2 diabetes in the world. The study revealed that siblings born *after* their mothers were diagnosed with diabetes were three times more likely to develop type 2 diabetes and have higher body mass than siblings born before. Results suggest that the diabetic intrauterine environment conveys a high risk for the development of diabetes and obesity to offspring (Dabelea et al., 2000).

Obviously, these proposed models and mechanisms are not mutually exclusive and may interact to heighten the risk of developing insulin resistance and glucose intolerance. Such models provide a template for continuing investigation of the genetic, endocrine, metabolic, and morphological changes that underlie the etiopathogenesis of type 2 diabetes.

THE HEALTH IMPACT OF DIABETES

Diabetes has been found to increase the risk of developing a variety of comorbid conditions. Compared to nondiabetic subjects, diabetics have two- to fourfold higher rates of ischemic heart disease, stroke, and hypertension and five- to tenfold higher rates of blindness, kidney disease, neuropathy, and amputation. When comparing people with and without diabetes, the death rate among men is almost double (1.9), while among women it is 2.6 (Lee et al., 2000). Furthermore, persons with diabetes suffer disproportionately from physical and cognitive disability, and have twice the risk of developing dementia in old age compared to nondiabetics (Engelgau et al., 2004).

Although diabetes is among the top 10 leading causes of death in the United States and the fastest growing noncommunicable disease in the world, the onset of type 2 diabetes can often go undetected for years before a medical diagnosis is made (Gregg et al., 2004; Harris et al., 1992). In many developing countries, up to 90% of people with adult-onset diabetes are undiagnosed. In China, roughly 6 out of 10 diabetics are undiagnosed. Lack of public awareness and diagnostic opportunities are cited as reasons for the high percentage of undiagnosed diabetes in poor and developing countries (IDF Diabetes Atlas, 2010). Even in developed countries such as the United States, up to 30% of diabetes cases are undiagnosed (Gregg et al., 2004). This is because hyperglycemia, similar to hypertension, often lacks clinical signs and symptoms. The following paragraphs discuss the pathogenesis of conditions that commonly arise in diabetics and which contribute significantly to their high rates of morbidity and mortality.

DIABETIC KETOACIDOSIS

Diabetic ketoacidosis is a life-threatening phenomenon that occurs in individuals with severe hyperglycemia (blood glucose levels exceeding 250 mg/dL). Most patients who develop ketoacidosis have poorly controlled type 1 (insulin-dependent) diabetes mellitus, and about one-fifth of cases are first-time presenters with newly diagnosed disease. Nevertheless, varying degrees of ketoacidosis has been increasingly recognized among patients with type 2 diabetes. Poor patient education is an important determinant of this catastrophic event (Kitabchi and Wall, 1999; Kitabchi et al., 2006; Eledrisi et al., 2006).

Ketoacidosis results from an extension of normal physiological mechanisms that compensate for starvation. Normally, in the fasting state, there is a transition of metabolism from glycolysis (breakdown of glycogen) to lipolysis (breakdown of fat) for energy. Free fatty acids are released by adipocytes (fat cells) and transported to the liver bound to albumin. There they are broken down into acetate which is transformed into ketoacids (acetoacetate and beta-hydroxybutyrate). The ketoacids are then exported from the liver to peripheral tissues (notably brain and muscle) where they can be oxidized. Diabetic ketoacidosis represents a derangement of the above mechanism in diabetics with markedly elevated levels of blood glucose (hyperglycemia). Despite vast amounts of circulating glucose, it cannot be used as an energy source owing to lack of insulin. Ketogenic pathways are thus maximally activated and the supply of ketones exceeds peripheral utilization. Ketone bodies are acidic and high concentrations lower blood pH leading to ketoacidosis. During ketosis, a relatively small amount of acetone is produced, thus giving the breath of ketotic patients a typical "fruity" smell. The high blood glucose also induces profound osmotic diuresis and dehydration resulting in deficits in key electrolytes such as sodium, potassium, chloride, phosphate, magnesium, and calcium.

Case fatality rates among patients who develop diabetic ketoacidosis vary widely, ranging from 1% to 10%. Such variation is likely due to patients presenting at different stages of the process and/or differences in management. Causes of death in such patients include acute myocardial infarction, stroke, septic shock, profound acidosis of arterial blood, and cerebral edema. Patient management involves suppression of ketosis by administration of insulin, fluid resuscitation, and restoration of electrolyte balance in the blood, plus treatment of any coexisting conditions (Kitabchi and Wall, 1999; Kitabchi et al., 2006; Eledrisi et al., 2006).

MICROVASCULAR COMPLICATIONS OF DIABETES

Undetected or uncontrolled type 2 diabetes often results in silent pathology that can do irreparable damage at the *microvascular* (small blood vessel) level, causing irreversible consequences to health and quality of life such as diabetic retinopathy and blindness, diabetic nephropathy and kidney failure, and/or diabetic neuropathy and amputation (Moss, Klein, and Klein, 1991; Fowler, 2008). Primary pathogenic mechanisms include increased intracellular oxidative stress, increased proinflammatory activity, and the accelerated formation of advanced glycation end-products (AGEs), which are a class of complex reactive compounds that alter the structural properties of tissue proteins (Brownlee, 2005; Hatfield and Mulfinger, 2005). Unlike most cells that can control the concentration of intracellular glucose, susceptible cell types, specifically capillary endothelieal cells in the retina, mesangial cells in the renal glomeruli, and neurons/schwann cells in the periperheral nerves, are unprotected from extracellular glycemic exposure (Brownlee, 2005). Population-based studies have shown that by the time type 2 diabetes is diagnosed, over 20% of patients already have diabetic retinopathy and 10% have nephropathy (Klein et al., 1988; Harris, 1992). Diabetes is, in fact, a leading cause of these devastating conditions and they account for much of the economic burden associated with the disease (WHO Expert Consultation, 2004).

MACROVASCULAR COMPLICATIONS OF DIABETES

Extended duration of undiagnosed or uncontrolled hyperglycemia increases the risk for macrovascular (large blood vessel) complications (Stratton et al., 2001; Younis et al., 2003; Fowler, 2008). For example, there is a twofold increase in overall premature mortality, a fourfold increase in deaths due to cardiovascular disease (CVD), and a fourfold increase in stroke deaths among diabetics compared to nondiabetics (USPTFS, 2008). In addition, CVD is the primary cause of death among both type 1 and type 2 diabetics, eventually killing one out of every two patients (Wingard and Barrett-Conner, 1995; Fowler, 2008).

While persistent hyperglycemia *per se* has been implicated in the microvascular complications of diabetes, mechanisms related to atherogenesis and the development of atherosclerotic plaque in blood vessels are typically invoked to explain the macrovascular complications of diabetes. For example, both *in vitro* and *in vivo* (animal) studies suggest that insulin-resistant adipocytes (fat cells) increase the *free fatty acid flux* by releasing large quantities of free fatty acids into the blood that are subsequently oxidized in the mitochondria of the vascular endothelium resulting in overproduction of reactive oxygen species (Brownlee, 2005; Petersen and Shulman, 2006). Indeed, endothelial injury resulting from increased oxidative stress is one of the primary triggers in the *response to injury hypothesis of atherogenesis* (Ross and Glomset, 1976; Ross, 1999; Libby, 2002; Libby, Ridker, and Hansson, 2009).

The *response to injury hypothesis* of atherogenesis proposes that initial injury (mechanical, chemical, oxidative, immune reactive, infectious) to the endothelial cells causes their release of cytokines and other proinflammatory and vasoactive compounds (Ross and Glomset, 1976; Ross, 1999). These molecular events initiate a complex inflammatory cascade leading to the formation and development of atherosclerotic plaque (atherogenesis). For example,

expression of *vascular cellular adhesion molecule-1* (*VCAM-1*) by endothelial cells mediates the adhesion of monocytes, lymphocytes, and other immune cells to the vascular epithelium in the early stages of atherogenesis (Ley and Huo, 2001). Sustained atherogenesis and the development of atherosclerotic plaque in blood vessels is the underlying cause of the majority of deaths from cardiovascular diseases.

It is important to realize that hyperglycemia and insulin resistance often go unrecognized for many years in adults and, as a consequence, the presence of microvascular and macrovascular complications is a near certainty when type 2 diabetes is finally diagnosed (Sheehy et al., 2010). In contrast, the prominent clinical signs and symptoms of type 1 diabetes usually lead to a prompt diagnosis, and with effective treatment (insulin replacement) and glycemic control, the risk of long-term sequelae can be ameliorated (Moore et al., 2009). Albeit, diabetic children are more sensitive to insulin deficiency than adults and are thus at higher risk for the rapid and catastrophic development of ketoacidosis, which is associated with significant mortality, even in countries with well-developed healthcare systems (Dahlquist and Kallen, 2005).

EPIDEMIOLOGY OF TYPE 1 DIABETES

Type 1 diabetes, previously called *insulin-dependent diabetes mellitus* or *juvenile-onset diabetes*, is characterized by a lack of endogenous insulin production. It is the major form of diabetes in children and young adults and accounts for 5–10% of all diabetics. In patients without insulin, glucose is not able to enter into the cells that require insulin-mediated glucose uptake. This can lead to dangerously high levels of blood glucose and life-threatening *diabetic ketoacidosis* (metabolic acidosis caused by the by-products of fatty acid oxidation accumulating in the blood). Because glucose is available for energy but cannot be used by the cells that require insulin's action, the phrase *starvation amidst plenty* has been linked with type 1 diabetes. Type 1 diabetes is diagnosed with a recommended blood sugar test, coupled with autoantibody assessment, and/or the presence of classic signs and symptoms such as *ketonuria* (ketones in the urine), excessive thirst, persistent hunger, unexplained weight loss, and excessive urination.

There are two subforms of type 1 diabetes. *Type 1a* is caused by autoimmune destruction of the β-cells of the pancreas, confirmed by the presence of β-cell autoantibodies, while *Type 1b* is nonautoimmune pancreatic β-cell destruction that is *idiopathic* or of unknown origin. Serum autoantibodies reactive against the pancreatic β-cells are detectable in approximately 90% of patients diagnosed with type 1 diabetes. The process of autoimmune destruction occurs in the genetically susceptible and has a rather long latency period, as a large proportion of β-cells must be destroyed before signs and symptoms of type 1 diabetes occurs (American Diabetes Association, 2010; Eisenbarth and McCulloch, 2010).

Rising Incidence of Type 1 Diabetes

The global incidence of type 1 diabetes has increased markedly in the past 50 years, especially among children under 5 years of age (Krolewski et al., 1987; Bingley and Gale, 1989; Onkamo et al., 1999; Eurodiabe ACE Study Group, 2000; Gale, 2002; Gillespie et al., 2004; Patterson et al., 2009). Significant increases have been documented in Finland, England, Norway, Israel, Austria, and several other countries. In Finland, which has one of the world's highest rates, the annual incidence has more than tripled since 1953, from 12 per 100,000 to current levels of approximately 40 per 100,000 (Tuomilehto et al., 1995; Patterson et al., 2009). Globally, the average annual rate of increase is approximately 3%. Furthermore, there are no signs that the trend is abating. According to the International Diabetes Federation, 76,000 children under the age of 15 developed type 1 diabetes in 2010, and 480,000 children are currently living with the disease, approximately 115,000 in Southeast Asia, 110,000 in Europe, and 95,000 in North America (**Figure 32.8**)

(McCarty and Zimmet, 1994; Sudagani and Hitman, 2005; IDF Diabetes Atlas, 2010).

In a recent worldwide study covering the period 1990–1999, investigators of the *Diabetes Mondiale Project* (*DIAMOND*) examined the incidence of type 1 diabetes in children up to 15 years of age from 114 populations in 112 centers and 57 countries. A total of 43,013 cases were diagnosed in study populations containing a total of 84 million children. For the decade, the average annual increase in the incidence of type 1 diabetes was 2.8%. The observed rate of increase was slightly higher during 1995–1999 compared to 1990–1994 (3.4% vs. 2.4%). High rates of increase were notable in Europe (3.2%), Asia (4.0%), and North America (5.3%). Annual rates varied widely by nation from 0.1 per 100,000 in China and Venezuela to 39.9 per 100,000 in Finland. The US annual rate was approximately 17 per 100,000. Based on these results, the investigators concluded that "*the constantly increasing incidence of type 1 diabetes over such a short period of time cannot be explained by shifts in genetic susceptibility alone,*" and they stressed the need to search for causative agents in the environment or genetic by environmental interactions (Karvonen et al., 2000; DIAMOND, 2006).

Epidemiologic studies also indicate that the greatest increase in incidence is occurring in previously low-prevalence geographic areas. For example, Patterson and colleagues examined trends in the incidence of type 1 diabetes during 1989–2003 in 20 population-based registries in 17 European countries.

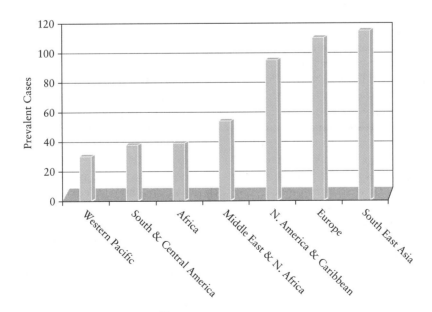

Figure 32.8 Prevalent Cases of Type 1 Diabetes Mellitus.

Source: Data from World Health Organization, 1970–2010. IDF Diabetes Atlas, 4th Edition.

Estimates were based upon 29,311 new cases diagnosed in children before their 15th birthday. The overall annual increase in the incidence of type 1 diabetes during this time period was 3.9%. Greater rates of increase were observed in younger age groups, 5.4% for ages 0–4 years, 4.3% for ages 5–9 years, and 2.9% for ages 10–14 years. The median annual rate was approximately 11 per 100,000, but rates varied widely, from 5.2 per 100,000 in Poland to 39.9 per 100,000 in Finland. Other Scandanavian countries also had high annual rates, e.g., 25.8 per 100,000 in Sweden and 21.1 per 100,000 in Norway; however, the former communist bloc countries in Eastern Europe, specifically Poland, Romania, the Czech Republic, and Slovakia have experienced the most rapid rates of increase. By 2020, the total number of new annual cases of type 1 diabetes in Europe is expected to rise to 24,400 from the 15,000 new cases estimated in 2005, with incident cases doubling among children under 5 years of age. Among youngsters under age 15, the number of existing European cases in 2020 is expected to rise to 160,000 from 94,000 (Patterson et al., 2009).

In the search for causative agents responsible for the rise in type 1 diabetes in the past half-century, many environmental factors have been studied which could trigger autoimmune responses responsible for the destruction of pancreatic β-cells of the islets of Langerhans. Enteric viruses, dietary proteins such as those found in milk or wheat, reduced exposure to sunshine or reduced intake of vitamin D, organic pollutants and other toxins, perinatal exposures to toxic contaminants, and increasing obesity levels among children have all been implicated as possible environmental triggers; nevertheless, definitive proof of causation remains elusive (Gale, 2002, 2005).

A number of hypotheses have been proposed to explain the rise in type 1 diabetes. The *hygiene hypothesis*, initially proposed to explain the concurrent patterns of asthma and allergy (Strachan, 1989), suggests that exposure to a wide range of infectious agents in childhood is necessary for successful maturation of the innate immune system; and in the absence of such exposure, cell-mediated immunity becomes more robust, thereby predisposing to type 1 diabetes and other autoimmune diseases. According to this hypothesis, improved hygienic conditions during childhood may have contributed to the rising incidence of type 1 diabetes (Kolb and Elliot, 1994). The *accelerator hypothesis* initially proposed by Wilkin suggests that metabolic overload of pancreatic β-cells brought about by accelerated growth during childhood, insulin resistance, and fat accumulation leads to their destruction through apoptosis and autoimmune reactions (Wilkin, 2001; Fourlanos, Harrison, and Colman, 2008).

There is also speculation and some evidence suggesting that environmental changes have induced a transition to earlier onset in a relatively constant pool of genetically susceptible individuals resulting in an increase in the incidence of type 1 diabetes in younger but not older age groups (Gale, 2002, 2005). Nevertheless, application of a population-based genetic model involving increasing penetrance of alleles conferring susceptibility through environmental changes was found incompatible with the Finnish data on type 1 diabetes (Pitkäniemi et al., 2004).

Risk Factors for Type 1 Diabetes

Risk factors for type 1 diabetes include genetic propensity and family history, environmental and/or dietary factors or triggers, ethnoracial distribution, and geography. Albeit, definitive linkages between these factors and molecular mechanisms of pathogenesis have not been fully clarified and remain under intense study.

Genetics of Type 1 Diabetes

A modest genetic risk of developing type 1 diabetes has been confirmed by twin studies and family studies. Disease concordance rates are several-fold higher in monozygous (identical) twins than dizygous twins (maximum concordance estimates, 70% vs. 13%, respectively). Furthermore, among monozygous twin pairs with only one twin affected, the nondiabetic twins show a high prevalence (up to 76%) of anti-islet β-cell autoantibodies. However, the absolute risk attributable to genetics *per se* is small since only 10–15% of cases have an affected first degree relative and the risk to offspring with an affected parent or sibling is less than 10% (Warram, Krolewski, and Kahn, 1988; Redondo et al., 1999; American Diabetes Association, 2010).

Multiple polymorphisms of genes in both the major and nonmajor histocompatibility complexes located on chromosome 6 have been found to influence the risk of type 1 diabetes. For example, certain alleles of the major histocompatibilty complex (also called human leukocyte antigen, HLA) appear to modulate the risk. Specifically, HLA-DR3/4 and HLA-DQ8 have been found to significantly increase progression to type 1 diabetes (Piettropaolo and Trucco, 2003; Barker et al., 2004). Such alleles presumably encode antigens that predispose to autoimmune destruction of β-cells in the pancreas by killer T lymphocytes. The prevalence of susceptibility genes varies by ethnic origin and this may explain, in part, why type 1 diabetes is common in some countries such as Finland and Sardinia, but relatively rare in countries such as China and Mexico (Eisenbarth and McCulloch, 2010).

Environmental Factors and Type 1 Diabetes

In addition to genetic and familial predisposition, viral exposures, particularly to mumps, Coxsackie virus B, Epstein-Barr virus, congenital rubella syndrome, and cytomegaloviruses have been implicated as possible triggers for β-cell autoimmunity, but it is unclear whether they are necessary or sufficient to cause type 1 diabetes (Dorman, LaPorte, and Songer, 2003). Such triggers may contribute directly to immune activation by inciting cross-reactivity against pancreatic islet proteins bearing a similar structure or indirectly by inciting the production of proinflammatory cytokines that injure pancreatic islet tissue (Gregory et al., 2010). Dietary factors in early life have also been hypothesized to influence the development of type 1 diabetes, particularly cow's milk (Yoon, 1990). One proposed mechanism is that early introduction of β lactoglobulin in cow's milk triggers antibodies that interfere with T cell regulation and induce immune reactions against the pancreatic β-cells (Goldfarb, 2008).

The wide geographic variation in type 1 diabetes has been well documented by large prospective studies and surveillance surveys (IDF Diabetes Atlas, 2010). Moreover, some studies also show seasonal variation in the onset of type 1 diabetes (Levy-Marchal, Patterson, and Green, 1995; Ye et al., 1998; Eurodiab ACE Study Group, 2000; McKinney, 2001). For example, a large study of 31,091 cases from 105 centers worldwide found significant seasonality in the diagnosis of type 1 diabetes in 42 of the locations. The incidence among children, particularly boys ages birth–14 years, was typically higher in the winter months and lower in the summer depending on geographic location and latitude (Moltchanova et al., 2009). These results suggest there may be significant variability in the environmental triggers of type 1 diabetes, perhaps related to certain viral or bacterial infections being more prevalent in the winter months.

Ethnic Disparities in Type 1 Diabetes

Although epidemiologic features of type 1 diabetes, such as gender distribution and peak age at onset, are relatively similar across populations, the global variation in the incidence of type 1 diabetes is greater than any other chronic disease that affects children (Dohrman, LaPorte, and Songer, 2003). For example, children in Finland and Sardinia are nearly 400 times more likely to develop diabetes than children in the People's Republic of China. Profound changes have also been observed in migrant populations, e.g., the incidence of type 1 diabetes is 4 times greater among Chinese children living in Hong Kong compared with those who live in China (Yang et al., 1998).

Marked ethnic differences are also apparent in the United States. Whereas Asians, Hispanics, and African Americans are at relatively high risk for type 2 diabetes, Caucasians have the highest risk for the development of type 1 diabetes. Multiple factors (e.g., genetic susceptibility, family history, and certain environmental triggers) may contribute to the increased risk for developing type 1 diabetes among Caucasians (Lambert et al., 2004).

Type 1 Diabetes in Sardinia

One notable epidemiologic observation is the high incidence of type 1 diabetes in Sardinia (an island 120 miles off the west coast of Italy) compared to continental Italy. In fact, Sardinia has one of the highest incidence rates in the world (approximately 39 cases per 100,000 among children under 15 years of age) which is nearly 7 times higher than in comparable regions on the west coast of Italy (Casu et al., 2004). Sardinia is therefore a *hot spot* for the development of islet cell autoimmunity and type 1 diabetes and, as a consequence, epidemiologic studies of the Sardinian population have intensified.

Recent studies of Sardinian children have focused on an increasing trend in the prevalence of obesity and related conditions. In a sample of 1,000 children ages 6–10 years attending primary schools in the capital city, Cagliari, the observed prevalence of obesity increased by age and lower socioecomic status. The prevalence of obesity was 23% at age 10 compared to 14% at age 6; and in the lowest socioeconomic class, the prevalence was 26.5% in boys and 23.6% in girls. The authors concluded that obesity is becoming a serious social health problem among the youth of Sardinia (Sanna, Soro, and Calo, 2006).

Cambuli and colleagues studied insulin resistance and other clinical features of 104 obese children ascertained from a pediatric obesity clinic in Cagliari, Sardinia, in comparison to 54 children of normal weight. At baseline, the overweight and obese children had significantly *higher* blood levels of insulin, triglycerides, and leptin, and significantly *lower* levels of HDL-cholesterol and adiponectin than normal weight children. The average insulin resistance of the overweight and obese children was nearly twofold higher than normal weight children. Furthermore, after one year of intervention (diet and exercise), values for overweight/obese children who lost weight tended to normalize. In particular, baseline levels of adiponectin in the overweight/obese children increased by nearly threefold following intervention. The results indicate that dietary and physical intervention has benefit for overweight and obese children and suggest that adiponectin has potential as a biomarker of metabolic overload (Cambuli et al., 2008).

Other factors may also be at work in causing the increased incidence of type 1 diabetes among the children of Sardinia. For example, the time frame of major reductions in parasitic diseases and the eradication of polio, malaria, and tuberculosis in Sardinia coincide closely with increases in atopic and immunomediated diseases (type 1 diabetes, multiple sclerosis, Crohn's disease, celiac disease) (Casu et al., 2004). These trends are consistent with the *hygiene hypothesis*, which proposes that the absence of immunogenic stimuli early in life may heighten the risk of developing autoimmune diseases (Strachan, 1989). Furthermore, the Sardinian population has been described as a *genetic isolate* and certain genes that predispose to diabetes or other autoimmune conditions may have reached high frequencies due to natural selection and/or inbreeding.

Type 1 Diabetes and Multiple Sclerosis in Sardinia

In addition to having high rates of type 1 diabetes, the Sardinian population also has higher incidence and prevalence rates of multiple sclerosis than other European and Italian populations (Rosati et al., 1996). Since both conditions involve autoimmune reactions (destruction of neurons in multiple sclerosis and pancreatic β-cells in diabetes), they may have genetic and/or environmental risk factors in common.

Morrosu and colleagues at the University of Cagliari therefore designed studies to elucidate familial and genetic associations between type 1 diabetes and multiple sclerosis in the Sardinian population. They first conducted a cohort study to examine the incidence of type 1 diabetes in 1,090 individuals with multiple sclerosis and their parents (*n* = 2,180) and siblings (*n* = 3,300). All participants were ascertained at the Multiple Sclerosis Clinic in Cagliari. Type 1 diabetes developed five times more often in patients with multiple sclerosis than in the general population, and the presence of familial multiple sclerosis increased the odds of developing type 1 diabetes more than threefold (OR = 3.4). In a subsequent investigation, the same investigators compared *human leukocyte antigen* (HLA) genotypes in 1,052 patients

with type 1 diabetes, 1,049 patients with multiple sclerosis, and 1,917 control subjects. Susceptibility to both disorders was associated with common variants of the *HLA-DRB1* and *HLA-DQB1* loci, but coinheritance of these alleles could only partially explain the increase in diabetes among patients with multiple sclerosis. The results suggest that in the high-risk Sardinian population, HLA and non-HLA genetic factors and/or unknown environmental factors contribute significantly to the association of both type 1 diabetes and multiple sclerosis (Marrosu et al., 2002; Marrosu et al., 2004).

Obesity and Type 1 Diabetes Mellitus

The role of obesity in the pathogenesis of type 1 diabetes is controversial. To clarify the presence and strength of the association, Veberteen and colleagues conducted a meta-analysis of BMI and type 1 diabetes. They identified 8 case-control studies and 1 cohort study involving 2,658 cases for analysis. Of the nine studies, seven reported finding a significant association between a measure of increased body mass and type 1 diabetes. Overall, the odds of developing type 1 diabetes increased by twofold in obese children compared to normal weight children (OR = 2.03) and the risk increased by 1.25 per unit increase in BMI. The authors concluded that "*our systematic review indicates a likely association between childhood obesity, or higher BMI, and subsequent increased risk of childhood-onset type 1 diabetes*" (Veberteen et al., 2011).

Birth Weight and Type 1 Diabetes

Finnish children reportedly have the highest incidence of type 1 diabetes in the world, exceeding 40 cases per 100,000 in the 1990s. Recently, investigators at the National Public Health Institute in Helsinki examined incidence trends in type 1 diabetes during 1980–2005. During this time period, 10,737 children under 15 years of age were diagnosed with type 1 diabetes, and the average age-standardized incidence was 42.9 cases per 100,000 per year. Notably, the incidence more than doubled in the 25-year period, from 31.4 per 100,000 in 1980 to 64.2 per 100,000 in 2005. The greatest rate of increase (4.7% per year) occurred in children under 5 years of age (Harjutsalo, Sjöberg, and Tuomilehto, 2008). The frequency of overweight or obese children ages 5–15 years also increased during the same time period, from 9.5% in the mid-1980s to 20% in 2005. It is also noteworthy that the average birth weight in Finland actually *declined* during this time, suggesting that early postnatal weight gain may play a more significant role in the genesis of type 1 diabetes (Kautiainen et al., 2002; Salo, 2006).

Birth weight and weight gain during the first postnatal year have been examined as risk factors for type 1 diabetes in a number of epidemiologic studies. To clarify their effects, Harder and colleagues conducted a meta-analysis of 12 published studies of birth weight and type 1 diabetes involving 2,398,150 children, 7,491 of whom had type 1 diabetes. Results indicate that each 1,000 g increase in birth weight increases the risk by 7%. Furthermore, patients with type 1 diabetes gained significantly more weight during the first year of life than controls. The authors concluded that birth weight and particularly early weight gain are significant risk factors for the development of type 1 diabetes (Harder et al., 2009).

Accelerator Hypothesis of Type 1 Diabetes

Though the existing epidemiologic evidence supports a positive association between childhood obesity and type 1 diabetes, definitive proof of cause and effect is lacking. The *accelerator hypothesis* of Wilkin proposes that type 1 and type 2 diabetes are both triggered by insulin resistance that heightens apoptosis (programmed death) and immune-mediated destruction of the β-cells of the pancreas (Wilkin, 2001). Conceivably, excessive weight gain during the early years of life and particularly during the pubertal growth spurt could heighten the vulnerability of hyperfunctioning β-cells to such processes.

Nevertheless, some studies have failed to find an association between insulin resistance and obesity in type 1 diabetics. In a clinical investigation of premenopausal women, Greenfield and colleagues compared insulin resistance and other factors in 10 women with type 1 diabetes to 10 women without disease who were matched to the cases on body mass index. Though insulin sensitivity was significantly reduced in the diabetic women compared to controls, the two groups had similar levels of lipids, androgens, energy expenditure, physical activity, blood pressure, and abdominal adiposity. Thus, the study, albeit small, demonstrated insulin resistance among premenopausal women with type 1 diabetes that appeared to be unrelated to abdominal obesity, lipids, or androgens (Greenfield, Samaras, and Chisholm, 2002).

Furthermore, genetic linkages have *not* been substantiated by studies using specific markers of type 1 and type 2 diabetes. For example, in a genetic study of single nucleotide polymorphisms covering 12 gene regions associated with type 2 diabetes among 7,606 type 1 diabetics and 8,218 controls without diabetes, there were no convincing genetic linkages between type 1 and type 2 diabetes or interactions of these regions with other factors including autoantibody status and the major HLA class II genotypes (Raj et al., 2009).

Treatment for Type 1 Diabetes

Though there is no treatment that can cure type 1 diabetes, insulin replacement by daily injection or other methods can effectively maintain blood glucose levels within normal limits (McCulloch, 2010). Timing and dosing of exogenous insulin in relation to dietary patterns and activity levels are necessary to avoid hyperglycemia and life-threatening diabetic ketoacidosis and dangerously low blood glucose levels called *hypoglycemia* that can lead to diabetic coma. For the type 1 diabetic, lifelong daily insulin replacement and glucose monitoring are required to maintain proper blood glucose levels and minimize the complications that can arise from hyperglycemia or hypoglycemia.

PREDIABETES

Prediabetes is defined as impaired fasting glucose and/or impaired glucose tolerance. In this condition, blood glucose is higher than normal, but not high enough to be diagnosed with type 2 diabetes. It is likely to be a metabolic state, where in order to maintain normal blood glucose levels, the pancreatic β-cells secrete excess insulin in response to increasing insulin resistance (Wang et al., 2010). A fasting plasma glucose test between 100 mg/dL and 126 mg/dL indicates the prediabetic state of *impaired fasting glucose*. If the oral glucose tolerance test is used, a 2-hour 75 g post-load plasma glucose level between 140 mg/dL and 200 mg/dL is indicative of prediabetes and *impaired glucose tolerance*. According to the American Diabetes Association, a hemogloblin A1c test of 5.7–6.4% reflects an increased risk for developing type 2 diabetes and is also categorized as a prediabetic state (ADA, 2010). An estimated 344 million adults were living with impaired glucose tolerance in 2010, a worldwide prevalence of 7.9% (IDF Diabetes Atlas, 2010). A number of studies conducted in a wide range of populations provide clear evidence that prediabetes is a significant risk factor for the development of type 2 diabetes and microvascular and macrovascular disease.

A recent example comes from the *Strong Heart Study*, a population-based longitudinal study of American Indians. In this investigation, 1,677 subjects who were nondiabetic at baseline were followed over a median of 7.8 years to determine the effects of prediabetes and other risk factors on the relative risk of developing type 2 diabetes. Compared to men and women with normal glucose tolerance, diabetes incidence was more than twofold higher among gender-stratified prediabetics, even after adjusting for age, body mass index, waist circumference, albuminuria, smoking, family history of diabetes, and quartiles of physical activity. Overall, the incidence of diabetes among individuals with either impaired fasting glucose and/or impaired glucose tolerance was 66.1 per 1,000 person-years, 2.35-fold higher than normotensive individuals. The investigators concluded that prediabetic status is an independent predictor of conversion to type 2 diabetes (Wang et al., 2010).

Gerstein and colleagues examined the association of prediabetes with type 2 diabetes in a meta-analysis of prospective cohort studies published from 1979–2004 (comprised of 30,000 individuals and representing a broad range of ethnicities and countries). Estimates of the annual incidence of type 2 diabetes among prediabetics ranged from 5% to 10%. Overall, the annual incidence of type 2 diabetes was 7.0% for individuals with impaired fasting glucose, 6.1% for individuals with impaired glucose tolerance, and 14% for those with both conditions. Compared to normotensive individuals, the relative risk was fivefold higher in subjects with impaired fasting glucose, sevenfold higher in subjects with impaired glucose tolerance, and more than twelvefold higher in subjects with both conditions. These results indicate that impaired fasting glucose and/or impaired glucose tolerance are predictive of impending type 2 diabetes and suggest that dysglycemia is progressive and time-dependent (Gerstein et al., 2007).

TYPE 2 DIABETES

In type 2 diabetes (also called *non-insulin-dependent diabetes* or *adult-onset diabetes*), which represents approximately 90–95% of all cases of diabetes, insulin is still produced and secreted by the pancreas but its impact on glucose uptake is ineffectual. Elevated blood glucose occurs when there is a mismatch between the amount of insulin that is produced and secreted by the β-cells of the pancreas and the amount needed to maintain normal blood glucose levels. This mismatch is caused by target tissue insulin resistance, relative insulin insufficiency, or both (NIDDK, 2008).

Although insulin resistance can be caused by genetic syndromes, primary target cell defects, autoantibodies to insulin, or accelerated insulin degradation (Reaven, 1995), the most common cause of insulin resistance is relative weight gain or obesity. Excess energy beyond the body's capacity to store it appears to attenuate insulin-mediated cellular glucose uptake and to suppress energy uptake, initially within muscle cells (which have limited glycogen storage capacity) and later within the primary site of excess energy storage, the adipocytes (which have abundant storage capacity for excess calories from protein, carbohydrate, and alcohol that are converted and stored as triacylglycerol). Diminished energy uptake likely occurs through physiologic decreases in the number of insulin receptors and down-regulation or inhibition of target cell insulin receptor signaling (Olatunbosun and Dagogo-Jack, 2010).

Risk Factors for Type 2 Diabetes

The known major risk factors for type 2 diabetes include family history, age, ethnicity, obesity, and prediabetes. Family history generally reflects genetic propensity as well as the shared environment, cultural practices, and behaviors of family members. Family history is one of the strongest predictors of type 2 diabetes. The risk of developing diabetes is doubled if one first degree relative (parent or sibling) has the disease and is increased over fourfold if two or more first degree relatives have the disease (Valdez et al., 2007). Nevertheless, the profound increase in diabetes incidence and prevalence within the past several decades rules out a genetic basis for the excess burden of the disease, and points to insidious environmental factors that most likely play a permissive role in the etiology of diabetes.

Genetics of Type 2 Diabetes

The β₃ *adrenoreceptor gene* on the short arm of chromosome 8 encodes a protein that modulates fat metabolism and thermogenesis (conversion of energy to heat). This gene is expressed primarily in fat and muscle cells. One specific mutation of the β₃ adrenoreceptor gene called *TRP64ARG* is almost four times more common in Pima Indians living in Arizona than Caucasians of European descent, and nearly twice as common in other groups at high risk for diabetes such as African Americans and Mexican Americans (Walston et al., 1995). Notably, the Arizona Pimas have one of the highest rates of type 2 diabetes in the world (as discussed in the section of this chapter on dietary fat and type 2 diabetes). The mutated TRP64ARG gene (which involves a single amino acid substitution of arginine for tryptophan) has been found to enhance lipolysis in adipose tissue and reduce thermogenesis in muscle, and has also been associated with heightened insulin resistance in obese and high-risk subgroups (Zhan and Ho, 2005). Thus, the high gene frequency of the TRP64ARG mutation may be partially responsible for the extraordinarily high rates of type 2 diabetes in the Pima Indians of Arizona as well as heightened rates in other high-risk populations.

Other genes have also been identified that increase the risk of insulin resistance and development of type 2 diabetes. The *calpain-10 gene (CAPN10)* located on the long arm of chromosome 2 encodes a protease that influences both insulin secretion and insulin action, and single nucleotide polymorphisms of this gene have been noted that increase insulin resistance and the risk of developing type 2 diabetes in several populations (Lynn et al., 2002).

A syndrome known as *maturity onset of diabetes in the young (MODY)* shows autosomal dominant inheritance and is characterized by onset of type 2 diabetes *without* β-cell autoantibodies in one or more family members under the age of 25 years. Gene variants of *hepatocyte nuclear factor* genes (*HNF-1α, HNF-4α, and HNF-1β*), the *glucokinase* gene (*GCK*), and the *peroxisome proliferator-activated receptor-g* gene (*PPARg*) have been linked to this syndrome.

These genetic variants may contribute significantly to the risk of type 2 diabetes conferring insulin resistance of liver, muscle, and fat and/or deficiencies in insulin secretion. It is likely that in the near future additional studies of the human genome will lead to the discovery of many more gene variants that influence the risk of type 2 diabetes. As pointed out by Hansen and Pederson in their review of the genetics of type 2 diabetes, "*the results of these efforts are likely to be the platform for major progress in the*

development of personalized antidiabetic drugs with higher efficacy and few side effects" (Hansen and Pederson, 2005).

Obesity and Type 2 Diabetes

Obesity is the strongest modifiable predictor of type 2 diabetes. Maintaining a healthy weight or losing a moderate amount of excess weight have both been shown to improve metabolic health (Truesdale, Stevens, and Cai, 2005; Klein et al., 2004; Willett, Dietz, and Colditz, 1999; Tremblay et al., 1999; NHLBI, 1998; Colditz et al., 1995). In the *Health Professionals Follow-up Study*, a team of US investigators prospectively examined associations between changes in body weight and body fat distribution measured during 1986–1996 and the subsequent development of diabetes during 1996–2000 among 22,171 men ages 40–75 years. Results showed that weight gain was monotonically related to the risk of diabetes, with an average risk increase of 7.3% per kg of weight gain. Compared to men with stable weight, those who gained at least 6 kg more than doubled their risk of developing diabetes (RR = 2.1); and reciprocally, those who lost at least 6 kg reduced their risk by 50%. Similar results were seen using waist circumference to evaluate body mass. Of all cases of incident diabetes in the cohort, 56% were attributable to a weight gain of 7 kg or greater, whereas only 20% of cases were attributable to a 2.5 cm increase in waist circumference (Koh-Banerjee et al., 2004).

The cause and effect relationship between obesity and type 2 diabetes is dramatically illustrated for US men and women in **Figure 32.9**. Relative risk estimates are abstracted from the *US Health*

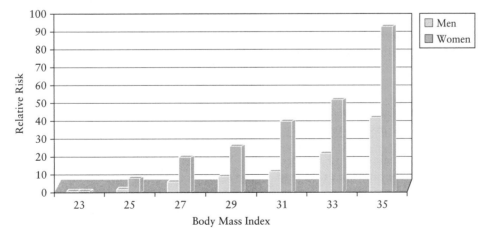

Figure 32.9 Dose Repsponse in the Risk of Type 2 Diabetes by BMI.

Source: Data from Chan JM, Rimm EB, Colditz GA, Stampfer MJ, Willett WC (1994). Obesity, fat distribution, and weight gain as risk factors for clinical diabetes in men. *Diabetes Care* 17(9): 961–969. Colditz GA, Willett WC, Rotnitzky A, Manson JE (1995). Weight gain as a risk factor for clinical diabetes mellitus in women. *Ann Intern Med* 122:481–486.

Professionals Follow-up Study for men (Chan et al., 1994) and the *Nurses Health Study* for women (Colditz et al., 1995). Compared with a BMI of 21, the relative risk of developing type 2 diabetes rises exponentially with increasing BMI. The relative risk rises to more than 40 for gravidly obese men and more than 90 for gravidly obese women, and furthermore, multifold risk elevations are notable even for modest increases in body mass.

Obesity disproportionately affects African Americans, Hispanics, American Indians, and Pacific Islanders, all of whom are at higher risk for developing type 2 diabetes compared to Caucasians. Asians, on the other hand, also have a higher risk for type 2 diabetes than Caucasians, but at a lower BMI and fat mass compared to other ethnoracial groups (Shai et al., 2006). This may be due to their decreased storage capacity. For example, Mott and colleagues evaluated body fat and age in a sample of healthy New York City volunteers ($n = 1,324$) of 4-ethnic groups, ages 20 and older. Using a 4-compartment model of body composition which included measures of body volume, total body water, total body bone mineral mass, and body weight, Asian men and women had mean lower fat mass at every decade of age compared to Caucasians, African Americans, and Puerto Ricans. In another study, Pan et al. consistently found higher prevalence rates of hypertension, diabetes, and hyperuricemia in Taiwanese compared to African Americans or Caucasians by level of BMI (Pan et al., 2004).

Dietary Factors and Diabetes Risk

Dietary factors have also been found to influence the risk of developing type 2 diabetes. In particular, the glycemic index, glycemic load, type of fat, type of carbohydrate, dietary fiber, magnesium, and an emerging potential risk factor, high fructose corn syrup, have all been investigated in experimental and epidemiologic studies.

Glycemic Index and Type 2 Diabetes   The glycemic index is a measure of postprandial increase in blood glucose due to intake of a specific food relative to that induced by glucose *per se*. Use of the glyemic index in evaluating risk of diabetes, and perhaps just as important, its clinical application in diabetes management, has proven to be reproducible. Numerous studies have also shown that the glycemic index is predictable in the context of mixed meals, which was an early criticism (Wolever et al., 1994).

The glycemic index was developed in 1981 by David Jenkins and associates at St. Michael's Hospital in Toronto, Canada. Jenkins realized that carbohydrate exchange lists do not account for the physiological effects of foods and that the type of carbohydrate as well as other dietary factors influence postprandial glycemia. Jenkins and his team sought a valid measure of the conversion of carbohydrates to glucose that could be effectively used in the dietary management of diabetes to maintain good glucose control (Jenkins et al., 1981).

Using groups of 5–10 normal weight, nondiabetic men and women, Jenkins introduced 62 individual foods and glucose (controlling for total carbohydrate quantity by standardizing to 50 grams) in random order, after overnight fasts, and using specified mean protocols. Subsequent glucose tolerance tests were conducted and the glycemic index value for each food was calculated as the area under the 2-hour blood glucose response curve expressed as a percentage of the appropriate mean glucose tolerance test value (Jenkins et al., 1981). In simple terms, "*glycemic index is a concept that ranks foods on the basis of their acute glycemic impact (relative to glucose = 100)*" (Brand-Miller, 1994).

Dietary studies have revealed wide variability in the glycemic index based on the type of carbohydrate. In general, simple carbohydrates (e.g., sugars) have higher values than complex carbohydrates (starches). However, there are numerous exceptions to these general rules and many factors can influence the glycemic index of food including variety, processing, and preparation, as well as the precise mixture of liquid, fat, protein, fiber, and carbohydrate ingested. Inverse relationships have been observed between the glycemic indices of foods and their content of fat, protein, and dietary fiber. Some experts in the field of human nutrition advise that while the glycemic index is a valid and useful concept, application and interpretation in dietary studies are "*deceptively complex*" (Wolever et al., 1997).

A modification of the *glycemic index* that takes into account the amount of carbohydrate ingested is called the *glycemic load*. The glycemic load of food adjusts the glycemic index of carbohydrate for the content of carbohydrate the food contains based on the formula, *glycemic load = glycemic index × total carbohydrate content (grams)/(100)*. Several large prospective cohort studies have found positive associations between the glycemic index or the glycemic load and the risk of type 2 diabetes.

Jenkin's glycemic index and the related measurement, the glycemic load, have been widely used in epidemiologic and clinical investigations. In 1997, an expert committee of the Food and Agricultural Organization and the World Health Organization endorsed the use of the glycemic index to classify carbohydrate-rich foods and help guide food choices (Foster-Powell, Holt, and Brand-Miller, 2002). Nevertheless, considerable controversy exists as to the value of the glycemic index or the glycemic load in predicting the development of certain conditions such as type 2 diabetes and/or guiding dietary choices in patients with disease.

Hodge and colleagues examined associations of type 2 diabetes with the glycemic index and other dietary factors in a prospective cohort of 36,787 men and women aged 40–69 years from Melbourne, Australia. During four years of follow-up, 365 cases were identified among 31,641 participants. High levels of the dietary glycemic index were found to increase the risk (OR = 1.32 per 10 unit increase). Risk increases were also observed for high intakes of white bread (OR = 1.37 for the highest versus lowest quartiles) and starch (OR = 1.47 per 100 grams per day) whereas risk reductions were observed for higher intakes of magnesium, total carbohydrates, and sugars. These associations were attenuated with adjustment for measures of obesity. Intake of fiber was not associated with diabetes in the study. The investigators concluded that reducing the glycemic index by decreasing intake of white bread while maintaining a high carbohydrate diet may reduce the risk of developing type 2 diabetes (Hodge et al., 2004).

Collaborators from the Shanghai Cancer Institute in China and Vanderbilt and UCLA in the United States studied associations of the glycemic index and glycemic load with type 2 diabetes in a cohort of 64,227 Chinese women with no history of diabetes at baseline. After 4.6 years (297,755 person years) of follow-up, 1,608 incident cases of type 2 diabetes were detected. Relative risk estimates for the highest versus the lowest quintile were 1.21 for the glycemic index, 1.34 for the glycemic load, 1.28 for carbohydrate intake, and 1.78 for rice intake. The investigators concluded that high intake of foods with a high glycemic index or a high glycemic load, especially rice, the main carbohydrate source in the target population, increased the risk of developing type 2 diabetes (Villegas et al., 2007).

Krishnan and colleagues examined associations of the glycemic index and cereal fiber with type 2 diabetes among 59,000 women of the *Black Women's Health Study* who were disease-free at baseline. During 8 years of follow-up, 1,938 cases of type 2 diabetes were detected. Women with a high glycemic index (highest quintile) had an increase in the relative risk (RR = 1.23) whereas those with a high intake of cereal fiber had a decrease in risk (RR = 0.82). Associations were strongest for leaner women with BMI <25, RR = 1.91 for high glycemic index,

and RR = 0.41 for high cereal fiber intake. The investigators concluded that increasing cereal fiber in the diet may be effective in reducing the risk of type 2 diabetes (Krishnan et al., 2007).

Barclay and colleagues conducted a systematic review and meta-analysis of 37 prospective cohort studies of associations of the glycemic index and the glycemic load with type 2 diabetes and other chronic diseases. The adjusted relative risks in comparisons of the highest with the lowest quintiles were RR = 1.40 for the glycemic index and RR = 1.27 for the glycemic load. Furthermore, significant increases in risk associated with high glycemic indices were also noted for other chronic diseases including coronary heart disease (RR = 1.25) and gallbladder disease (RR = 1.26). Mechanisms by which high glycemic index diets contribute to the development of type 2 diabetes include insulin resistance of target cells due to persistent glycemic exposure and accelerated pancreatic β-cell insufficiency due to a chronically higher insulin demand per quantity of carbohydrate (Barclay et al., 2008).

Dietary Fiber and Type 2 Diabetes   Some epidemiologic studies have found that certain types of dietary fiber protect against the development of type 2 diabetes. Selected investigations plus a meta-analysis of dietary fiber and diabetes are discussed in the following paragraphs.

Meyer and colleagues conducted a cohort study of total dietary fiber, soluble dietary fiber, carbohydrates, fruits, and vegetables, refined grains, magnesium, and the glycemic index in 35,988 older women from Iowa. During 6 years of follow-up, 1,141 cases of type 2 diabetes were reported. Strong inverse associations were observed for high versus low intakes of whole grain (RR = 0.79), total dietary fiber (RR = 0.78), and magnesium (RR = 0.67). Intakes of total carbohydrates, refined grains, fruits and vegetables, and soluble fiber and the glycemic index were unrelated to diabetes risk. The authors concluded that *"these data support a protective role for grains (particularly whole grains), cereal fiber, and dietary magnesium in the development of diabetes in older women"* (Meyer et al., 2000).

Stevens and colleagues studied associations of the glycemic index, the glycemic load, and types of dietary fiber with type 2 diabetes among 12,251 adults aged 45–64 years enrolled in the *Atherosclerosis Risk in Communities (ARIC)* observational cohort. After 9 years of follow-up, a total of 1,447 cases of type 2 diabetes were reported. A significant risk reduction was observed for high versus low intake of cereal fiber among Caucasians (RR = 0.75) but the reduction among African Americans (RR = 0.86) did not reach statistical significance. The authors concluded that cereal fiber may have a protective role against type 2 diabetes in Caucasians and suggested the need for more studies in African Americans (Stevens et al., 2002).

A team of investigators in Helsinki conducted a cohort study of fiber and whole grain intake among 2,286 men and 2,030 women, ages 40–69 years, ascertained through the *Finland Nationwide Health Registry*. During the 10-year follow-up period, type 2 diabetes was diagnosed in 54 men and 102 women. In comparisons of highest versus lowest quartiles, risk reductions were observed for consumption of whole grain (RR = 0.65) and cereal fiber (RR = 0.39) (Montonen et al., 2003).

Schulze and colleagues conducted a prospective cohort study of dietary fiber, magnesium, and type 2 diabetes among 9,702 men and 15,365 women, ages 35–65 years, enrolled in the *European Prospective Investigation of Cancer and Nutrition, Potsdam*. During 176,117 person-years of follow-up, they observed 844 incident cases of type 2 diabetes. High intake of cereal fiber was inversely associated with the risk of diabetes (RR = 0.72 for highest vs. lowest quintile) whereas no associations were found for vegetable fiber, fruit fiber, or magnesium. Furthermore, in a meta-analysis of nine cohort studies, high cereal fiber intake was also found to reduce the risk (combined RR = 0.67 for the highest versus lowest quintile) but there were no significant effects of fruit or vegetable fiber. The authors also conducted a meta-analysis of eight studies of magnesium and type 2 diabetes, in which they found a significant overall risk reduction for high versus low intake (combined RR = 0.77) (Schulze et al., 2007).

Dietary fiber consists of both soluble and insoluble forms. Soluble fiber has been shown to inhibit macronutrient absorption, reduce postprandial glucose responses, and beneficially influence blood lipids (Torsdottir et al., 1991; Weickert and Pfeiffer, 2008). Nevertheless, it is primarily insoluble (cereal) fiber that has consistently been found associated with reduced diabetes risk (Weickert et al., 2005). The biological mechanism by which insoluble fiber protects against diabetes is unknown; however, in a small dietary intervention study, the administration of insoluble cereal fiber to overweight and obese women was found to improve insulin sensitivity (Weickert et al., 2006).

Magnesium and Type 2 Diabetes   As noted in the above discussion, several epidemiologic studies of type 2 diabetes have included investigation of effects of magnesium intake. Furthermore, a meta-analysis

of 8 studies by Schulze and colleagues found an overall risk reduction of 23% with high magnesium intake (Schulze et al., 2009). One notable investigation of magnesium and type 2 diabetes involved 85,060 women enrolled in the *Nurses Health Study* and 42,872 men enrolled in the *Health Professionals' Follow-up Study*. After 18 years of follow-up in women and 12 years of follow-up in men, 4,085 female cases and 1,333 male cases of type 2 diabetes were documented. After adjusting for age, BMI, physical activity, family history of diabetes, smoking, alcohol consumption, and history of hypertension and hypercholesterolemia, the relative risk of type 2 diabetes among those in the highest compared to the lowest quintile of total magnesium intake was similarly reduced in both women (RR = 0.66) and men (RR = 0.67). Furthermore, the risk reductions retained statistical significance after further adjustment for dietary variables including glycemic load, polyunsaturated fat, trans fat, cereal fiber, and processed meat in multivariate models, and the estimates were stable for subgroups of BMI, physical activity, and family history of diabetes. These findings suggest that magnesium has significant chemopreventive activity against the development of type 2 diabetes and prompted the authors to state that *"this study supports the dietary recommendation to increase consumption of major food sources of magnesium such as whole grains, nuts, and green leafy vegetables"* (Lopez-Ridaura et al., 2004).

Several mechanisms have been proposed to explain the beneficial effects of magnesium in protecting against the development of type 2 diabetes. Intracellular magnesium is a critical cofactor for several enzymes in carbohydrate metabolism, and deficiencies may trigger insulin resistance by interfering with intracellular insulin signalling (Tosiello, 1996; Takaya, Higashino, and Kobayashi, 2004).

Dietary Fat and Type 2 Diabetes   Dietary fat has also been implicated as a potential risk factor for type 2 diabetes. However, it is difficult to separate effects of dietary fat *per se* from effects that are related to obesity and increased BMI, which are powerful risk factors in the development of type 2 diabetes (see **Figure 32.9**).

In nutritional studies, it is important to stratify the types of fat, as specific fatty acids appear to have differential effects on the genesis of type 2 diabetes. Furthermore, results may differ substantially for men and women and for ethnically distinct populations. Obviously, such studies are limited by the survey instrument, the imprecision of self-reported dietary questionnaires, and the interrelatedness of the various dietary factors, especially dietary fat and total calories. Indeed, marked inconsistencies in reported findings on dietary fat as well as other components of diet have led to substantial controversy regarding the benefit or detriment of certain combinations of dietary fat and carbohydrates for the prevention and/or therapy of type 2 diabetes. Selected studies of this controversial issue are described in the following paragraphs.

International correlation and comparative studies show that populations consuming diets with a higher proportion of fat have higher prevalence rates of type 2 diabetes (Feskens et al., 1995; Fujimoto, 1996). However, such population comparisons have limited value in testing for cause and effect and are subject to the *ecological fallacy* whereby within-population heterogeneity is not taken into account.

A few longitudinal and cohort studies have examined the association of dietary fat and the incidence of diabetes. In the *Zutphen Study* conducted in the Netherlands, fat and cholesterol intake were studied in 394 nondiabetic men, ages 50–70 years, during 1960–1970. Diabetic status was confirmed in 1970 by oral glucose tolerance tests. Positive associations were noted between abnormal glucose tolerance and the intake of saturated fat and cholesterol whereas negative associations were observed for the intake of pectin and sugar products (Feskens and Kromhout, 1990).

The Pima Indians of Arizona have the highest reported incidence and prevalence rates of type 2 diabetes in the United States. In 1978, the age-gender adjusted incidence of diabetes was 26.5 per 1,000, nearly 20-fold higher than US Caucasian populations. Adult Pima Indians typically develop diabetes early in adulthood (mean onset is 36 years), which puts them at extraordinarily high risk of developing major complications including hypertension, kidney failure, and cardiovascular disease (Knowler et al., 1978). The *traditional diet* of the Mexican Pima Indians consists of 8–12% fat, 70–80% carbohydrate, and 12–18% protein. In contrast, the *modern day diet* of Pima Indians who migrated to Arizona has changed dramatically and is comprised of approximately 50% carbohydrate, 40% fat, and 10% protein (Arizona Department of Health Services, 2004).

In a longitudinal study conducted during 1982–1992, 200 healthy nondiabetic subjects from the Pima Indian population of Arizona were evaluated for diabetes yearly using oral glucose tolerance tests. Among the 87 women and 113 men, type 2 diabetes developed in 38 subjects (24 women and 14 men). The average follow-up time for these subjects was 5.3 years. Percentage of body fat and waist-to-hip

circumference were strong predictors of developing type 2 diabetes, increasing the risk by 8-fold and 12-fold, respectively, in comparisons of the 90th and 10th percentiles. Low glucose sensitivity (abnormal glucose tolerance) was the strongest single risk factor for the development of type 2 diabetes (RR = 31.1) and the effects of obesity were attenuated in models containing measures of insulin resistance. Based on these results, the authors suggest that insulin resistance and glucose tolerance worsens as a result of increasing obesity, aging, and/or other factors (Lillioja et al., 1993).

Additional studies have compared lifestyles and rates of diabetes in the Pima Indians of Arizona versus Mexico. This comparison evaluates the impact of a dramatic change in diet in populations with roughly equivalent gene pools. Ravussin and colleagues traveled to a remote mountainous area of northwestern Mexico to assess the clinical characteristics of 19 women (mean age, 36 years) and 16 men (mean age, 48 years) of the Mexican Pima Indian tribe. Measurements of weight, height, body fat, blood pressure, plasma glucose, cholesterol, and hemoglobin A1c were taken for comparison with matched controls of the Arizona Pima population. The matching ratio of Arizona Pimas to Mexican Pimas was 10:1. Arizona Pimas were 40% heavier (90.2 vs. 64.2 kg) with 34% higher BMI (33.4 vs. 24.9) and plasma cholesterol (174 vs. 146 mg/dL) than Mexican Pimas. Only 2 of 19 women (11%) and 1 of 16 men (6%) in the sample of Mexican Pimas had diabetes, contrasting with prevalences of 37% and 54% in men and women of the Arizona Pimas. Based on these findings, the authors suggest, "*despite a similar potential genetic predisposition to these conditions, a traditional lifestyle, characterized by a diet including less animal fat and more complex carbohydrates and by greater energy expenditure in physical labor, may protect against the development of diabetes and related diseases*" (Ravussin and Smith, 2002).

The *Colorado San Luis Valley Study* was designed to examine the diets of 1,317 Mexican Americans and the development of diabetes and glucose intolerance. All subjects were disease-free at baseline. Levels of dietary fat and carbohydrate in 70 individuals who developed type 2 diabetes and 171 individuals who developed glucose intolerance were compared to 1,076 control subjects who remained disease free during 4 years of follow-up. Diabetic status was established by an oral glucose tolerance test for each subject. The odds ratios for a 40 g per day increase in fat intake were 1.51 for type 2 diabetes and 1.62 for glucose intolerance, suggesting that high-fat, low carbohydrate diets increase the risk of developing type 2 diabetes (Marshall, Hamman, and Baxter, 1991).

In the *Nurse's Health Study*, associations of types of dietary fat with the risk of type 2 diabetes were examined among 84,302 women aged 34–59 years at baseline. During 14 years of follow-up, 2,507 cases of type 2 diabetes were documented. In multivariate models that adjusted for energy intake, percentages of energy from protein and specific fatty acids and BMI, intakes of total fat, saturated fat, and monounsaturated fat were *not* associated with diabetes risk. However, for a 5% increase in energy from polyunsaturated fat, the risk *decreased* by 37% (RR = 0.67), and for a 2% increase in energy from trans fat, the risk *increased* by 39% (RR = 1.39). The findings suggest that in women, trans fatty acids increase the risk and polyunsaturated fatty acids are protective, while other types of fat are neutral (Salmeron et al., 2001).

In the *Heath Professional's Follow-Up Study*, associations of dietary fats and meat intake with the risk of type 2 diabetes were examined among 42,504 men aged 40–75 years at baseline. The results revealed increased risks for high intake of total fat (RR = 1.27) and saturated fat (RR = 1.34). However, these risks disappeared after adjustment for BMI. There were no associations of diabetes risk with oleic acid, trans fatty acid, long chain n-3 polyunsaturated fat, or a-linolenic acid. Frequent consumption of processed meat was associated with an increase in the risk (RR = 1.46) and high intake of linoleic acid reduced the risk in some subgroups. These findings implicate high intake of processed meat as a risk factor and suggest that the effects of fat intake in men may not be independent of body mass (van Dam et al., 2002).

A number of randomized dietary intervention studies have been conducted to compare the impact of various nutritional approaches for patients with type 2 diabetes. Two basic dietary therapies have been compared in such studies, diets low in saturated fat and high in carbohydrates versus diets high in monounsaturated fat. In a recent meta-analysis of nine such studies, diets high in monounsaturated fat produced significantly greater net reductions in fasting plasma triaglycerol (19%) and very low density lipoprotein cholesterol (22%) than low saturated fat, high carbohydrate diets. Findings suggest that compared with a high-carbohydrate diet, a diet rich in monounsaturated fat improves the glycemic and lipoprotein profiles and provides significant benefit for diabetic patients (Garg, 1998).

High Fructose Corn Syrup and Type 2 Diabetes   High fructose corn syrup has recently attracted attention as a potential risk factor in the development of type 2

diabetes, possibly through its effects on weight gain and obesity. For example, during the time period 1970–1990, the consumption of high fructose corn syrup increased more than 1,000%, far exceeding the changes in intake of any other food or food groups. High fructose corn syrup, which is a mixture of primarily fructose and sucrose (usually 55% and 42%, respectively), is currently the sole caloric sweetener of soft drinks, and its increasing use has occurred in close parallel with the rising prevalence of obesity and type 2 diabetes in the United States (Bray, Nielsen, and Popkin, 2004).

Although the data are sparse, recent short-term studies suggest that overconsumption of fructose-laden sweeteners may have a detrimental impact on glucose metabolism. Swarbrick and colleagues investigated the metabolic effects of consuming fructose-sweetened beverages for ten weeks in seven overweight or obese women under energy-balanced conditions. The intervention diet supplied 25% of energy from fructose. Fructose consumption significantly increased blood concentrations of fasting glucose, postprandial triacylglycerol (the storage form of fat), and apolipoprotein-B (the integral protein of the low density lipoprotein that transports cholesterol to tissues) while decreasing insulin response (Swarbrick et al., 2008).

In a small clinical trial, Stanhope and colleagues administered fructose or glucose in beverages providing 25% of energy requirements over ten weeks to overweight or obese men and women. Fifteen subjects received fructose and 17 subjects received glucose. Although both groups had similar weight gains during the study, visceral adipose volume was significantly increased *only* in the fructose-treated group. Also, fructose increased hepatic *de novo* lipogenesis and postprandial triglyceride levels as well as blood concentrations of apolipoprotein-B and LDL-cholesterol. Furthermore, fasting plasma glucose and insulin levels *increased* whereas insulin sensitivity *decreased* with fructose but not glucose consumption. Based on these results, the authors suggest that high dietary fructose specifically increases lipogenesis, promotes dyslipidemia, decreases insulin sensitivity, and increases visceral adiposity in overweight or obese adults (Stanhope et al., 2009). This is perhaps one of the first studies to show selective adipose deposition based on the type of monosaccharide.

These early studies therefore suggest that consuming a high level of fructose (e.g., by drinking beverages sweetened with high fructose corn syrup) may increase the risk of developing insulin resistance and type 2 diabetes. Unlike glucose, fructose does not stimulate insulin secretion or leptin release, and since these hormones are critical in the regulation of food intake and body weight, sweeteners with high levels of fructose may promote increased energy uptake and weight gain (Bray, Nielsen, and Popkin, 2004). Nevertheless, additional well-designed long-term studies are needed to confirm these early observations.

Ethnic Disparities in Type 2 Diabetes

Type 2 diabetes disproportionately affects Asians, Hispanics, Native Americans, Pacific Islanders, and African Americans (NIDDK, 2008; IDF Diabetes Atlas, 2010). As discussed earlier in the section on risk factors, obesity increases the risk of diabetes and is the strongest modifiable predictor of type 2 diabetes. Nevertheless, diabetes risk is modified by ethnicity, and paradoxically, Asians, although phenotypically leaner on average than members of most other ethnic groups, have been found to be at high risk for developing type 2 diabetes at relatively low levels of body mass (Lauderdale and Rathouz, 2000).

For example, Shai and colleagues found that ethnicity significantly modified the effects of body mass on the risk of diabetes in a multiethnic cohort study conducted as a part of the US *Nurses' Health Study*. They studied associations between measures of body mass (BMI and BMI gain) and the risk of diabetes in 78,419 middle-aged female nurses who were healthy at baseline and followed for up to 20 years during 1980–2000. Compared to Caucasians, the BMI and age-adjusted relative risks for type 2 diabetes were 34% and 86% higher among Hispanics and African Americans, respectively. The relative risk, however, was 126% higher among Asian women, who also exhibited the *lowest* mean baseline BMI and *lowest* mean BMI gain. For each 5 kg weight gain, the risk of diabetes increased by 84% for Asians, 38% for African Americans, 37% for Caucasians, and 4% for Hispanics. Controlling for additional factors including energy and alcohol intake, exercise, and smoking status did not appreciably alter the relative risks (Shai et al., 2006).

Similar results have been observed by other investigators and there is general consensus that Asian men and women have higher risks of developing type 2 diabetes at lower BMIs than other ethnoracial groups (Bei-Fan, 2003; Deurenberg-Yap and Deurenberg, 2003; Misra, 2003; Pan et al., 2004). Although Asians have a very low prevalence of obesity, they are still at higher risk for developing type 2 diabetes compared to Caucasians, and Asians are at highest risk for type 2 diabetes at any given level of BMI, compared to Caucasian Americans, African Americans, and Hispanic Americans (Shai et al., 2006). The physiological basis for this ethnic differential in risk may relate to body composition and the distribution of body fat. For example, some studies suggest that persons of Asian origin have a higher percentage of body fat and/or a higher level of visceral or abdominal fat at the same level of BMI than control subjects of other ethnicities (Tanaka, Horimai, and Katsukawa, 2003; Deurenberg-Yap and Deurenberg, 2003).

In the United States, obesity and diabetes statistics have become *less* transparent with respect to certain minority groups. Specifically, the aggregation of data for Asian and Pacific Islander populations in government reports and some epidemiologic studies conceals important differences in the prevalence of obesity (Harrison et al., 2005; NIDDK, 2008). This is probably an attempt to overcome statistical problems associated with small sample sizes. At issue is a significant underestimation of the prevalence of obesity among Pacific Islanders, shown clearly in a recent study of childhood obesity among Asians and Pacific Islanders. In this study of children ages 9–17 years old, the obesity prevalence among the aggregated Asian/Pacific Islander group was 13%. However, once the data were disaggregated, the Asian obesity prevalence was 12.1%, while among the Pacific Islanders, the prevalence was threefold higher at nearly 36% (Shabbir et al., 2010). As in children, adult Pacific Islanders (to include Native Hawaiian, Guamanian, Samoan, Tahitian, and others) exhibit one of the highest obesity levels of all ethnic groups, while Asians, which include Southeast Asian subgroups, Asian Indian, Chinese, Japanese, Korean, and Filipino, have the lowest (WHO, 2004).

Although Asians are purported to represent approximately 95% of the entire Asian/Pacific Islander category, the relative proportions of Asians and Pacific Islanders for any particular study may differ. Aggregating Asian and Pacific Islander data makes it difficult to identify the relative contribution of obesity (or other risk factors) to the risk of diabetes for each group, and to adequately compare estimates across studies or evaluate trends over time. Obviously, aggregating data across ethnic groups or BMI categories results in diabetes statistics that fail to discern important differences in the burden of disease. Rather than aggregating these two highly dissimilar populations, oversampling of each may provide more accurate and precise estimates per group and improve public health analytic and intervention efforts (Brown and Rother, 2010).

THE METABOLIC SYNDROME (SYNDROME X)

The recognition of constellations of clinical entities that predispose individuals to subsequent more gravid conditions has become increasingly important in developing effective multidisciplinary therapeutic strategies. Such is the case for the *metabolic syndrome* or *syndrome X*. According to the National Cholesterol Education Program's Adult Treatment Panel III Report, the constellation of symptoms defining the metabolic syndrome consists of abdominal obesity (increased waist circumference), atherogenic dyslipidemia (increased triglycerides and decreased HDL-cholesterol), hypertension, insulin resistance (impaired glucose uptake in the presence of normal or elevated insulin levels), a proinflammatory state (elevated C-reactive protein), and a prothrombotic state (increased plasminogen activator inhibitor). The clinical diagnosis is made when any three of these conditions exist in the same individual (Grundy et al., 2004).

Certain components of the metabolic syndrome were described by Dr. Gerald Phillips of Columbia University in New York. His definition included glucose intolerance, hyperinsulinemia, hypercholesterolemia, hypertriglyceridemia, and hypertension in association with obesity, aging, and an elevation in the ratio of estrogen to testosterone (Phillips, 1977). Dr. Gerald Reaven of Stanford University described a similar constellation of symptoms and ascribed the predominant underlying condition to be "insulin resistance" (Reaven, 1988).

There is debate regarding whether obesity and/or insulin resistance cause the metabolic syndrome or if they are consequences of other metabolic abnormalities. One pathogenic sequence involves the development of obesity and excess adiposity; subsequently, adipocytes that have reached their threshold of fat storage respond by secreting inflammatory substances called adipokines that interfere with the insulin-driven glucose transport system (Unger, 2003; Unger and Scherer, 2010). A number of markers of systemic inflammation, including C-reactive protein, are often increased in individuals with the metabolic syndrome, as are fibrinogen, interleukin 6 (IL–6), and tumor necrosis factor-alpha (TNFα). Two prominent adipokines that may be involved in insulin resistance are leptin and resistin, both of which have been observed to increase in association with obesity and insulin resistance (Degawa-Yamauchi et al., 2003). However, other investigators have not observed this association and in fact have noted *decreased* levels of resistin associated with obesity (Nagaev and Smith, 2001). Additional studies will be needed to clarify the role of specific adipokines in the pathogenesis of insulin resistance.

In 2002, members of the *National Cholesterol Education Program Expert Panel on Detection, Evaluation and Treatment of High Blood Cholesterol in Adults* analyzed data from the *Third Nutrition Examination Survey (NHANES III)* to determine the prevalence and other characteristics of the metabolic syndrome. Estimates of prevalence were obtained from a cross-sectional survey of a nationally representative sample of 8,814 men and women of the United States collected during 1988–1994. The age-adjusted prevalence of the metabolic syndrome for this time frame was 23.7%. Estimates were similar for men and women but varied by ethnicity, e.g., Mexican Americans had a higher prevalence (31.9%) than Caucasian Americans (23.8%) or African Americans (21.9%). The prevalence increased with age to levels greater than 40% for individuals aged 60 years or older. Extrapolating to data from the 2000 US census, the investigators estimated that approximately 47 million adults in the US met the criteria for the metabolic syndrome during 1988–1994 (Ford, Giles, and Dietz, 2002).

In a subsequent analysis of NHANES data ($n = 3,423$) for the time period 2003–2006, approximately 34% of US adults met the criteria for the metabolic syndrome. Prevalence estimates increased with age reaching levels higher than 50% for men and women 60 years and older. The survey reflects a marked increase (from 24% to 34%) in the prevalence of the metabolic syndrome among US adults during the past two decades; currently, it is estimated that nearly one-third of US adults (66 million) are afflicted by the metabolic syndrome (Ervin, 2009).

Estimates from the United States, Western Europe, Japan, Australasia, and elsewhere suggest that 75% of patients with prediabetes and 86% of patients diagnosed with type 2 diabetes also have the metabolic syndrome (Grundy, 2006). In fact, some investigators suggest that without treatment, virtually all patients with the syndrome will progress to type 2 diabetes. A number of studies have shown that the metabolic syndrome as well as its individual components are predictive of the development of type 2 diabetes (Hanson et al., 2002; Laaksonen et al., 2002; Lorenzo et al., 2003; Hanley et al., 2005). But whether the syndrome itself is a better predictor than the sum of its individual components is controversial and remains under study.

The metabolic syndrome also increases the risk of developing coronary heart disease, myocardial infarction, and stroke. In an analysis of 10,357 adults participating in the Third National Health and Nutrition Survey (NHANES), presence of the metabolic syndrome doubled the risk of myocardial infarction (OR = 2.0) and stroke (OR = 2.2) in both men and women (Ninomiya et al., 2004).

In the international INTERHEART Study, 26,903 subjects from 52 centers worldwide were classified according to criteria of the International Diabetes Federation (IDF) into cases with the metabolic syndrome and controls not meeting the criteria. Presence of the metabolic syndrome more than doubled the risk of myocardial infarction (OR = 2.2) and estimated risk increases were similar by region and ethnic group. Overall, the metabolic syndrome accounted for approximately 17% of the risk of developing myocardial infarction (Mente et al., 2010).

In a meta-analysis of 21 prospective studies, individuals with the metabolic syndrome compared to those without had increases in mortality from any cause (RR = 1.35), cardiovascular disease (RR = 1.74), coronary heart disease (RR = 1.53), and stroke (RR = 1.76) (Galassi, Reynolds, and He, 2006). While the underlying physiology and even the defining clinical components of the metabolic syndrome remain subjects of hot debate, it is undeniable that the complex of obesity, insulin resistance, hypertension, hyperlipidemia, and impaired glucose metabolism known as the *metabolic syndrome* markedly heightens the risk of type 2 diabetes and catastrophic thrombotic cardiovascular outcomes such as myocardial infarction and stroke.

GESTATIONAL DIABETES

Gestational diabetes mellitus refers to hyperglycemia that arises during pregnancy. The condition is detected in approximately 200,000 pregnant women annually in the United States, or about 7.5% of pregnancies (IDF Diabetes Atlas, 2010; Homko, 2010; IADPSG, 2010). Gestational diabetes disproportionately occurs in ethnic groups at high risk for developing type 2 diabetes, such as women of Hispanic, Asian, American Indian/Pacific Islander, and African American origin (Lawrence et al., 2008, Dabelea et al., 2005).

Although the *prevalence* of gestational diabetes has remained stable from 1999 to 2005 in the United States, there are indications that the *incidence* has risen. For example, Lawrence and colleagues noted that among all the deliveries at Kaiser Permanente hospitals in Southern California, 10% involved

women with pre-existing diabetes in 1999, which doubled to 21% by 2005 (Lawrence et al., 2008). Congenital malformations, spontaneous abortion, and *macrosomia* (excessive birth weight) are three major pregnancy complications associated with pregestational diabetes. In addition to fetal risk, the health consequences of diabetes, retinopathy, nephropathy, neuropathy, and cardiovascular disease, are all accentuated by pregnancy (Leary, Pettitt, and Jovanivic, 2008). Women with a history of gestational diabetes mellitus are at two- to threefold elevated risk for developing type 2 diabetes (Kim, Newton, and Knopp, 2002).

TYPE 2 DIABETES IN CHILDREN AND ADOLESCENTS

Type 2 diabetes is becoming more common in children and adolescents, and in some ethnic pediatric populations, it is more common than type 1 diabetes (American Diabetes Association, 2010). Obesity is the primary risk factor for type 2 diabetes and the global increases in the prevalence of overweight and obese individuals over the past 60 years are inexorably linked to the increase in type 2 diabetes. Calorically dense and nutritionally poor food and drink choices coupled with increased sedentary behaviors and decreases in physical activity are implicated as the primary behavioral culprits. Environmental factors are thought to influence behaviors in children. These include parental lifestyle and guidance, the built environment, safety factors, school policies on physical education, access to healthier food choices, value-driven trends in the cost:size ratio of energy-dense fast foods, and inappropriate marketing to children.

DOUBLE DIABETES

Differentiating type 1 from type 2 diabetes is complicated by an entity known as *double diabetes,* also coined 1.5 diabetes, type 3 diabetes, LADY (latent autoimmune diabetes in youth), or LADA (latent autoimmune diabetes in adulthood) (Pozzilli and Buzzetti, 2007; Kroner, 2009). This *hybrid* form of diabetes can present clinically as type 2 diabetes, but observed markers of autoimmunity to pancreatic β-cells are also evident. Double diabetes can also present clinically as type 1 diabetes with either a concomitant underlying insulin resistance syndrome, or acquired insulin resistance due to a long-term chronic positive energy balance coupled with tight exogenous insulin-mediated glucose control. Indeed, 20–30% of type 1 diabetic patients receiving insulin replacement therapy subsequently become overweight or obese thereby predisposing them to insulin resistance (Moore et al., 2009; Nadeau, 2010; McCulloch, 2010).

ECONOMIC IMPACT OF DIABETES

The predicted healthcare burden and profound economic implications of the long-term management of diabetes is staggering and unsustainable. Worldwide, the annual estimated cost is $490 billion in US dollars (IDF Diabetes Atlas, 2010). After adjusting for age and gender differences, the average US medical expenditure among diabetics living in the United States in 2007 was 2.3 times higher than what expenditures would have been in the absence of diabetes, at a total cost of $174 billion dollars annually (USPTFS, 2008). In addition, nearly one out of five healthcare dollars in the United States is spent on the care of diabetic patients (Permutt, Wasson, and Cox, 2005). Clearly, the cost of effective treatment and management has outstripped the resources of healthcare systems worldwide, underscoring the critical need for more cost-effective strategies for the primary, secondary, and tertiary prevention of diabetes and its complications.

PREVENTION OF DIABETES MELLITUS

For all individuals and particularly those at high risk for developing type 2 diabetes (those overweight or obese, or who have prediabetes or a strong family history of diabetes), the American Diabetes Association recommends specific lifestyle practices that include sustained weight control through restriction of caloric intake and regular daily physical exercise (American Diabetes Association, 2010). Specific dietary strategies include reduction of saturated fat to less than 7% of calories, avoidance of trans fats, limiting alcohol consumption to a maximum of two drinks daily, frequent consumption of whole grain products and monounsaturated fat, daily intake of at least 14 g of fiber, monitoring of carbohydrates, limiting consumption of foods with a high glycemic index, limiting intake of sweetened beverages and desserts (particularly those with high levels of fructose), and monitoring of total average daily calories consumed. Blood lipids, blood pressure, blood glucose, and other vital signs should be checked by a physician on a regular basis and maintained within normal limits.

A remarkable and disturbing statistic is that nearly 25% of people with type 2 diabetes in the United States are undiagnosed. Indeed, adult-onset disease is often not detected until clinically overt complications are present. Fortunately, relatively simple tests are available to detect preclinical disease (prediabetes) and effective nonpharmacologic interventions have proven effective in preventing the progression of prediabetes to diabetes. (Pan et al., 1997; Tuomilehto et al., 2001; Diabetes Prevention Program Research Group, 2002). Clearly, well-designed population screening programs coupled with effective lifestyle changes and therapy could substantially reduce the overwhelming health burden of type 2 diabetes (Norris et al., 2008).

Type 2 diabetes is characterized by insulin resistance and reduced energy storage capacity of adipocytes and progressive deterioration in beta-cell function and mass. These metabolic disturbances may be reversible by therapeutic intervention, particularly during the early stage of disease. Interventions found to maintain insulin sensitivity and energy storage capacity of adipocytes and preserve or rejuvenate beta-cells include short-term intensive insulin therapy and judicious use of drugs with both adipogenic and anti-apoptotic effects, such as the thiazolidinediones (Rosen and MacDougald, 2006; Wajchenberg, 2007).

Type 2 diabetes is characterized by progressive deterioration in β-cell function and mass. The reduction of β-cell mass is attributable to accelerated apoptosis which can often be reversed by early therapeutic intervention, particularly during the early stage of disease. Interventions found to preserve or rejuvenate β-cells include short-term intensive insulin therapy and administration of anti-apoptotic drugs, such as the thiazolidinediones (Wajchenberg, 2007).

Widespread clinical testing of asymptomatic low-risk individuals is currently *not* recommended for type 1 diabetes. However, annual physical examinations should include a check of blood glucose in addition to observation of clinically overt signs and risk factors. Children who develop type 1 diabetes most often present with acute symptoms and markedly elevated blood glucose levels and most cases are quickly diagnosed and treated.

Approximately 7% of all pregnancies in the United States are complicated by gestational diabetes (200,000 cases annually). Because the risks to the mother and the neonate are significant, screening for diabetes is warranted based on the presence of any one of the following risk factors: obesity, prior history of disease, delivery of a large-for-gestational-age baby, presence of glycosuria, diagnosis of polycystic ovarian syndrome, and family history of type 2 diabetes.

TERTIARY PREVENTION OF MICROVASCULAR/MACROVASCULAR COMPLICATIONS OF DIABETES

Diabetes is a chronic illness that requires continuing medical care and ongoing patient management, education, and support to prevent acute complications and to reduce the risk of long-term complications. The cornerstone of tertiary prevention for diabetic patients is maintenance of blood glucose levels within normal limits by a combination of insulin replacement, antidiabetic agents, diet, and exercise. Self-monitoring of blood glucose is the major component of effective maintenance therapy, allowing patients to manage individual responses to medications and assess whether glycemic targets are being achieved. Hemoglobin A1c reflects the average glycemia over several months and has strong predictive value for diabetic complications. Hemoglobin A1c testing should therefore be performed routinely in all patients with diabetes, at initial assessment, and then as a part of continuing care. In overweight and obese diabetic patients, weight loss has been shown to reduce insulin resistance. Thus, weight loss through an individualized program of diet and exercise is recommended for all overweight or obese patients (American Diabetes Association, 2010).

Morbidly obese diabetic individuals who are unable to lose weight through diet and exercise are prime candidates for bariatric (weight loss) surgery. Follow-up studies of patients who elect to have this surgery show that most achieve substantial weight loss plus markedly improved control of blood glucose, blood lipids and blood pressure (Buchwald et al., 2004; Dixon et al., 2008). Furthermore, weight loss surgery has also been found effective in preventing the development of insulin resistance in non-diabetic individuals who are morbidly obese (Sjostrom et al., 2000).

Regular eye examinations are critical to prevent vision loss due to retinopathy among diabetics. The prevalence of retinopathy increases with duration of disease, affecting up to 80% of patients who have lived with diabetes for 10 or more years (Kertes and Johnson, 2007).

Routine foot examinations and proper daily foot care are important for the diabetic patient, as vascular and neurologic damage to the extremities can lead to amputation (McCulloch, 2010). As a result of diabetic neuropathy, wound healing is severely impaired largely due to the inability to mount an effective immune response. Multiple factors, including decreased cell and growth factor responses lead to diminished peripheral blood flow and decreased local angiogenesis (Brem and Tomic-Canic, 2007). Even the slightest injury can result in sepsis and the subsequent need to amputate. Diabetic foot ulcers are a leading cause of lower-leg amputations, preceding 84% of all diabetes-related amputations and affecting 15% of people with diabetes (Reiber, Boyko, and Smith, 1995).

Sustained glucose control is essential for the prevention of dangerous episodes of hyperglycemia and ketoacidosis or hypoglycemia and diabetic coma, and to interrupt the development of long-term microvascular and macrovascular complications that increase the risk of retinopathy, neuropathy, nephropathy, and atherogenesis leading to catastrophic events such as blindness, limb amputation, kidney failure, coronary heart disease, myocardial infarction, and stroke.

SUMMARY

Diabetes mellitus is a complex heterogeneous metabolic condition whereby hyperglycemia is the defining characteristic. The two major forms of diabetes are type 1 and type 2. The global incidence and prevalence of diabetes has risen profoundly within the past 50 years among children and adults, and both type 1 and type 2 diabetes dramatically increase the risk for irreversible health consequences such as blindness, kidney failure, and amputation as well as premature cardiovascular mortality. The long-term economic and financial healthcare burden required to manage the health consequences of this devastating disease is unsustainable.

Type 1 diabetes constitutes approximately 5–10% of all cases of diabetes and is predominately the result of autoimmune destruction of the β-cells of the pancreas, leading to little or no insulin production. Without daily, lifetime exogenous insulin, either through injection or pump, glucose cannot enter the cells that require insulin's action, leading to severe hyperglycemia. A disease with a long latency period, type 1 diabetes has no known cure and has been increasing in annual incidence. Type 1 diabetes *does not* have a strong basis for primary prevention or screening, as genetic susceptibility, family history, and unknown environmental triggers interact to induce the onset of disease. Excess postnatal weight gain and obesity, and certain alleles of the HLA locus (HLA-DR3/4 and HLA-DQ8) have been reported to increase the risk. Linkages with other autoimmune conditions have been found in certain populations; for example, Sardinian children have high rates of both type 1 diabetes and multiple sclerosis.

Susceptible Caucasians are at highest risk for developing type 1 diabetes; however, geography, seasonality, and latitude appear to modify the risk.

Type 2 diabetes constitutes approximately 90–95% of all cases of diabetes and is currently considered a global pandemic as both the incidence and prevalence have risen sharply within the past several decades. Developing countries with large populations are partly responsible for the increasing global burden of diabetes as urbanization and westernization are leading to lifestyle factors that are driving increasing levels of obesity. The strongest predictors of type 2 diabetes are family history, age, ethnicity, and obesity. Family history is the strongest *nonmodifiable* predictor of type 2 diabetes; however, obesity is the strongest *modifiable* predictor and has therefore been a primary target for public health prevention efforts. It is noteworthy that obesity produces marked increases in the risk (relative risk estimates for gravid obesity exceed 90 in women and 40 in men). Some gene variants have been identified that increase the risk of type 2 diabetes by down-regulating the secretion and action of insulin, and future studies of the human genome are likely to elucidate genetic targets for effective antidiabetic therapy. Diets with a high glycemic index and high levels of saturated fat and trans fat have also been reported to increase the risk, whereas diets high in polyunsaturated fat, monounsaturated fat, and magnesium appear to decrease the risk.

The *metabolic syndrome* is diagnosed by a constellation of clinical signs and symptoms including abdominal obesity, hyperlipidemia (triglycerides and cholesterol), hypertension, elevated C-reactive protein, and insulin resistance. The syndrome markedly elevates the risk of developing type 2 diabetes, and in fact the majority of afflicted subjects are either prediabetic or already have type 2 diabetes. The metabolic syndrome also significantly increases the risk of developing thrombotic cardiovascular conditions, e.g., coronary heart disease, myocardial infarction, and stroke.

The primary mechanism by which obesity causes classic obesity-related type 2 diabetes is through insulin resistance in striated muscle and fat cells. When these cells reach their storage capacity and are no longer able to store additional excess energy, a host of regulatory signaling proteins are secreted that stimulate decreases in the activities of insulin receptors, insulin signaling, lipoprotein lipase, and Glut-4 translocation. The β-cells of the pancreas produce and secrete even more insulin to compensate. Blood glucose can increase silently over many years without producing clinical symptoms. Afflicted individuals typically pass through a prediabetic state of elevated blood glucose and general metabolic dysregulation that may include hyperinsulinemia, dyslipidemia, and hypertension. Eventually, the amount of insulin that is produced and secreted can no longer maintain glucose levels within normal limits.

In the United States, type 2 diabetes disproportionately affects minority groups such as Hispanics, African Americans, American Indians, and Pacific Islanders, who have relatively high obesity levels. Paradoxically, Asians, who are phenotypically leaner than other ethnoracial groups, are at high risk for developing type 2 diabetes despite much lower levels of obesity, as defined by the BMI. A higher body fat percentage and/or higher visceral fat or abdominal fat per unit BMI are often cited as the primary reasons for this observation. Emerging hypotheses implicate a lower overall adipocyte energy storage capacity, which would stimulate metabolic regulatory feedback mechanisms at a lower level of weight gain, resulting in insulin resistance and reduced glucose uptake at lower obesity levels. This explanation provides a biologic rationale for the public health recommendation to avoid inappropriate weight gain and the observation that moderate weight loss of approximately 10% results in improvements in metabolic health n individuals with elevated body mass. Albeit, persons who are clinically obese may need to lose more than 10% excess weight in order to achieve metabolic homeostasis.

● ● ● ● **REFERENCES**

Ali, H., Anwar, M., Ahmed, T., & Chand, N. (2006). Diabetes mellitus from antiquity to present scenario and contribution of Greco-Arab physicians. *JISHIM*, 5, 46–50.

American Diabetes Association. (2010). Standards of medical care in diabetes—2010. *Diabetes Care*, 33, S11–S61.

Arizona Department of Health Services. (2004). *Health status profile of American Indians in Arizona (2004)*. Arizona Bureau of Public Health Services.

Barclay, A.W., Petocz, P., McMillan-Price, J., et al. (2008). Glycemic index, glycemic load, and chronic disease risk—A meta-analysis of observational studies. *Amer J Clin Nutr*, 87, 627–736.

Barker, D.J.P. (1997). Maternal nutrition, fetal nutrition, and disease in later life. *Nutrition*, 13, 807.

Barker, J.M., Barriga, K.J., Yu, L., et al. (2004). Prediction of autoantibody positivity and progression to type 1 diabetes: Diabetes Autoimmunity Study in the Young (DAISY). *J Clin Endocrinol Metab*, 89(08), 3896–3902.

Bays, H., Mandarino, L., & DeFronzo, R.A. (2004). Role of the adipocyte, free fatty acids, and ectopic fat in pathogenesis of type 2 diabetes mellitus: Peroxisomal proliferator-activated receptor agonists provide a rational therapeutic approach. *J Clin Endocrinol Metab*, 89, 463–478.

Bei-Fan, Z., the Cooperative Meta-analysis Group on Obesity in China. (2003). Predictive values of body mass index and waist circumference for risk factors of certain related diseases in Chinese adults: Study on optimal cut-off points of body mass index and waist circumference in Chinese adults. *Asia Pacific Journal of Clinical Nutrition*, 11(S8), S685–S693.

Bild, D.E., & Stevenson, J.M. (1992). Frequency of recording of diabetes on US death certificates: Analysis of the 1986 National Mortality Followback Survey. *Journal of Clinical Epidemiology*, 45(3), 275–281.

Bingley, P.J., & Gale, E.A.M. (1989). Rising incidence of IDDM in Europe. *Diabetes Care*, 12, 289–295.

Brand-Miller, J. (1994). The importance of the glycemic index in diabetes. *Am J Clin Nutr*, 59, 747S–752S.

Bray, G.A., Nielsen, S.J., & Popkin, B.M. (2004). Consumption of high-fructose corn syrup in beverages may play a role in the epidemic of obesity. *Am J Clin Nutr*, 79(4), 537–543.

Brem, H., & Tomic-Canic, M. (2007). Cellular and molecular basis of wound healing in diabetes. *J Clin Invest*, 117(05), 1219–1222.

Brown, R.J., & Rother, K.I. (2010). Type 1 and type 2 diabetes in five race and ethnic populations: The SEARCH for Diabetes in Youth Study. *Curr Cardio Risk Rep*, 4, 175–177.

Brownlee, M. (2005). The pathobiology of diabetic complications. A unifying mechanism. *Diabetes*, 54(06), 1615–1625.

Cambuli, V.M., Musiu, C., Incani, M., Paderi, M., Serpe, R., Marras, V.,...Baroni, M.G. (2008). Assessment of adiponectin and leptin as biomarkers of positive metabolic outcomes after lifestyle intervention in overweight and obese children. *Journal of Clinical Endocrinology & Metabolism*, 93(8), 3051–3057.

Candib, L.M. (2007). Obesity and diabetes in vulnerable populations: Reflection on proximal and distal causes. *Ann Fam Med*, 5, 541–556.

Casu, A., Pascutto, C., Bernardinelli, L., the Sardinian IDDM Epidemiology Study Group, & Songini, M. (2004). Type 1 diabetes among sardinian children is increasing. The Sardinian diabetes register for children aged 0–14 years (1989–1999). *Diabetes Care*, 27(7), 1623–1629.

Centers for Disease Control. (2010). Division of Diabetes Translation. National Diabetes Surveillance System.

Chan, J.M., Rimm, E.B., Colditz, G.A., Stampfer, M.J., & Willett, W.C. (1994). Obesity, fat distribution, and weight gain as risk factors for clinical diabetes in men. *Diabetes Care*, 17(9), 961–969.

Chast, F. (2000). Apollinaire Bouchardat, pharmacist, nutritionist. *Ann Pharm Fr*, 58(6 Suppl), 435–442.

Cheng, W.S., Wingard, D.L., Kritz-Silverstein, D., & Barrett-Connor, E. (2008). Sensitivity and specificity of death certificates for diabetes: As good as it gets? *Diabetes Care*, 31(2), 279–284.

Christopoulou-Aletra, H., & Papavramidou, N. (2008). "Diabetes" as described by Byzantine writers from the fourth to the ninth century AD: The Graeco-Roman influence. *Diabetologia*, 51, 892–896.

Colditz, G.A., Willett, W.C., Rotnitzky, A., & Manson, J.E. (1995). Weight gain as a risk factor for clinical diabetes mellitus in women. *Ann Intern Med*, 122, 481–486.

Cowie, C.C., Rust, K.F., Byrd-Holt, D.D., Gregg, E.W., Ford, E.S., Geiss, L.S.,...Fradkin, J.E. (2010). Prevalence of diabetes and high risk for diabetes using A1C criteria in the US population in 1988–2006. *Diabetes Care*, 33(3), 562–568.

Czech, M.P., & Corvera, S. (1999). Signaling mechanisms that regulate glucose transport. *J Biol Chem*, 274(4), 1865–1868.

Dabelea, D., Hanson, R.L., Lindsay, R.S., Pettit, D.J., Imperatore, G., Gabir, M.M., Roumain, J., Bennett P.H., & Knowler, W.C. (2000).

Intrauterine exposure to diabetes conveys risk for type 2 diabetes and obesity. A study of discordant sibship. *Diabetes, 49,* 2208–2211.

Dabelea, D., Snell-Bergeon, J.K., Hartsfield, C.L., et al. (2005). Increasing prevalence of gestational diabetes mellitus (GDM) over time and by birth cohort: Kaiser Permanente of Colorado GDM screening program. *Diabetes Care, 28,* 579–584.

Dahlquist, G., & Kallen, B. (2005). Mortality in childhood-onset type 1 diabetes. *Diabetes Care, 28*(10), 2384–2387.

Danforth, E. (2000). Failure of adipocyte differentiation causes type II diabetes? *Nature Genetics, 26,* 13.

Degawa-Yamauchi, M., Bovenkerk, J.E., Juliar, B.E., Watson, W., Kerr, K., Jones, R., Zhu, Q., & Considine, R.V. (2003). Serum resistin (FIZZ3) protein is increased in obese humans. *J Clin Endocrinol Metab, 88*(11), 5452–5455.

Deurenberg-Yap, M., & Deurenberg, P. (2003). Is a re-evaluation of WHO body mass index cut-off values needed? The case of Asians in Singapore. *Nutr Rev, 62,* S80–S87.

Diabetes Prevention Program Research Group. (2002). Reduction in the incidence of type 2 diabetes with lifestyle intervention or metformin. *New Engl J Med 346,* 393–403.

DIAMOND Project Group. (2006). Incidence and trends of childhood type 1 diabetes worldwide, 1990–1999. *Diabet Med, 23,* 857–866.

Dixon, J.B., O'Brien, P.E., Playfair, J., et al. (2008). Adjustable gastric banding and conventional therapy for type 2 diabetes. A randomized controlled trial. *JAMA 299,* 316–323.

Dorman, J.S., LaPorte, R.E., & Songer, T.J. (2003). Epidemiology of type 1 diabetes. In *Type 1 diabetes. Etiology and treatment.* Totowa, NJ: Human Press.

Eisenbarth, G.S., & McCulloch, D.K. (2010). Pathogenesis of type 1 diabetes mellitus. In UpToDate®. Accessed: July 2010.

Eknoyan, G., & Nagy, J. (2005). A history of diabetes mellitus or how a disease of the kidneys evolved into a kidney disease. *Adv Chron Kid Dis, 12*(02), 223–229.

Eledrisi, M.S., Alshanti, M.S., Shah, M.F., Brolosy, B., & Jaha, N. (2006). Overview of the diagnosis and management of diabetic ketoacidosis. *American Journal of Medical Science, 331*(5), 243–251.

Engelgau, M.M., Geiss, L.S., Saaddine, B.M., Gregg, E.W., Tierney, E.F., Rios-Burrows, N.,... Narayan, K.M.V. (2004). The evolving diabetes burden in the United States. *Annals of Internal Medicine, 140*(11), 945–950.

Ervin, R.B. (2009). Prevalence of metabolic syndrome among adults 20 years of age and over, by sex, age, race and ethnicity, and body mass index: United States, 2003–2006. *National Health Statistics Reports, 13.* Hyattsville, MD: National Center for Health Statistics.

Eurodiab ACE Study Group. (2000). Variation and trends in incidence of childhood diabetes in Europe. *Lancet, 355,* 873–876.

Feskins, E.J.M., & Kromhout, D. (1990). Habitual dietary intake and glucose tolerance in euglycemic men: The Zutphen Study. *Int J Epidemiol, 19,* 953–959.

Feskens, E.J.M., Virtanen, S.M., Rasanen, L., Tuomilehto, J., Stengard, J., Pekkanen, J.,... Kromhout, D. (1995). Dietary factors determining diabetes and impaired glucose tolerance. A 20-year follow-up of the Finnish and Dutch cohorts of the Seven Countries Study. *Diabetes Care, 18,* 1104–1112.

Ford, E.S., Giles, W.H., & Dietz, W.H. (2002). Prevalence of the metabolic syndrome among US adults: Findings from the third National Health and Nutrition Examination Survey. *JAMA, 287,* 356–359.

Foster-Powell, K., Holt, S.H.A., & Brand-Miller, J.C. (2002). International table of glycemic index and glycemic load values. *Amer J Clin Nutr, 76,* 5–56.

Fourlanos, S., Harrison, L.C., & Colman, P.G. (2008). The accelerator hypothesis and increasing incidence of type 1 diabetes. *Curr Opin Endocrinol Diabetes Obes, 15*(4), 321–325.

Fowler, M.J. (2008). Microvascular and macrovascular complications of diabetes. *Clin Diab, 26,* 77–82.

Frühbeck, G., Gomez-Ambrosi, J., Muruzabai, F.J., & Burrell, M.A. (2001). The adipocyte: A model for integration of endocrine and metabolic signaling in energy metabolism regulation. *AJP–Endo and Metab, 280*, E827–E847.

Fujimoto, W.Y. (1996). Overview of non-insulin-dependent diabetes mellitus (NIDDM) in different population groups. *Diabetic Med, 13*(suppl 6), S7–S10.

Galassi, A., Reynolds, K., & He, J. (2006). Metabolic syndrome and risk of cardiovascular disease: A meta-analysis. *Am J Med, 119*(10), 812–819.

Gale, E.A.M. (2002). The rise of childhood type 1 diabetes in the twentieth century. *Diabetes, 51*, 3353–3361.

Gale, E.A.M. (2005). Spring harvest? Reflections on the rise of type 1 diabetes. *Diabetologia, 48*(12), 2445–2450.

Garg, A. (1998). High-monounsaturated-fat diets for patients with diabetes mellitus. *Am J Clin Nutr, 67*(Suppl), 577S–582S.

Gemmill, C.L. (1972). The Greek concept of diabetes. *Bull NY Acad Med, 48*(08), 1033–1036.

Gerstein, H.C., Santaguida, P., Raina, P., Morrison, K.M., Galion, C., Hunt, D.,…Booker, L. (2007). Annual incidence and relative risk of diabetes in people with various categories of dysglycemia: A systematic overview and meta-analysis of prospective studies. *Diab Res Clin Pract, 78*, 305–312.

Gillespie, K.M., Bain, S.C., Barnett, A.H., et al. (2004). The rising incidence of childhood type 1 diabetes and reduced contribution of high-risk HLA haplotypes. *Lancet, 364*, 1699–1700.

Goldfarb, M.F. (2008). Relation of time of introduction of cow milk protein to an infant and risk of type 1 diabetes mellitus. *J Proteome Research, 7*, 2165–2167.

Gomero, A., McDade, T., Williams, S., et al. (2008). Dried bloodspot measurement of glycosylated hemoglobin (HbA1c) in wave 1 of the National Social Life and Aging Project. NORC and the University of Chicago.

Gould, G.W., & Holman, G.D. (1993). The glucose transporter family: Structure, function, and tissue-specific expression. *Biochem J, 295*, 329–341.

Greenfield, J.R., Samaras, K., & Chisholm, D.J. (2002). Insulin resistance, intra-abdominal fat, cardiovascular risk factors, and androgens in healthy young women with type 1 diabetes mellitus. *Journal of Clinical Endocrinology & Metabolism, 87*(3), 1036–1040.

Gregg, E.W., Cadwell, B.L., Cheng, Y.J., et al. (2004). Trends in the prevalence and ratio of diagnosed to undiagnosed diabetes according to obesity levels. *Diab Care, 27*, 2806–2812.

Gregory, J.M., Lilley, J.S., Misfeldt, A.A., Buscariollo, D.L., Russell, W.E., & Moore, D.J. (2010). Incorporating type 1 diabetes prevention into clinical practice. *Clinical Diabetes, 28*(2), 61–70.

Grundy, S.M., Brewer, H.B., Cleeman, J.I., Smith, S.C., Lenfant, D., for the Conference Participants. (2004). Definition of metabolic syndrome: Report of the National, Heart, Lung, and Blood Institute/ American Heart Association conference on scientific issues related to definition. *Circulation, 109*, 433–438.

Grundy, S.M. (2006). Metabolic syndrome: Connecting and reconciling cardiovascular and diabetes worlds. *J Am Coll Cardiol, 47*(6), 1093–1100.

Gupta, R., & Kumar, P. (2008). Global diabetes landscape—Type 2 diabetes mellitus in South Asia: Epidemiology, risk factors, and control. *Insulin, 3*(02), 78–94.

Guthrie, D.W., & Humphreys, S.S. (1988). Diabetes urine testing: An historical perspective. *Diabetes Educ, 14*(06), 521–526.

Hales, C.N., & Barker, D.J.P. (1992). Type 2 (non-insulin dependent) diabetes mellitus: The thrifty phenotype hypothesis. *Diabetologia, 35*, 1235–1239.

Hanley, A.J.G., Karter, A.J., Williams, K., Festa, A., D'Agostino, R.B., Wagenknecht, L.E., & Haffner, S.M. (2005). Prediction of type 2 diabetes mellitus with alternative definitions of the metabolic syndrome: The Insulin Resistance Atherosclerosis Study. *Circulation, 112*, 3713–3721.

Hansen, L., & Pedersen, O. (2005). Genetics of type 2 diabetes mellitus: Status and perspectives. *Diabetes Obes Metab, 7*(2), 122–135.

Hanson, R.L., Imperatore, G., Bennett, P.H., & Knowler, W.C. (2002). Components of the "metabolic syndrome" and incidence of type 2 diabetes. *Diabetes, 51,* 3120–3127.

Harder, T., Roepke, K., Diller, N., Stechling, Y., Dudenhausen, J.W., & Plagemann, A. (2009). Birth weight, early weight gain, and subsequent risk of type 1 diabetes: Systematic review and meta-analysis. *Am J Epidemiol, 169*(12), 1428–1436.

Harjutsalo, V., Sjöberg, L., & Tuomilehto, J. (2008). Time trends in the incidence of type 1 diabetes in Finnish children: A cohort study. *Lancet, 31*(9636), 1777–1782.

Harris, M.I., Klein, R., Welborn, T.A., et al. (1992). Onset of NIDDM occurs at least 4–7 years before clinical diagnosis. *Diab Care, 15,* 815–819.

Harrison, G.G., Kagawa-Singer, M., Foerster, S.B., et al. (2005). Seizing the moment: California's opportunity to prevent nutrition-related health disparities in low-income Asian American population. *Cancer, 104,* 2962–2968.

Hatfield, J., & Mulfinger, L. (2005). Review: Advanced glycation end products (AGEs) in hyperglycemic patients. *JYI, 13*(04).

Henschen, F. (1969). On the term diabetes in the works of Aretaeus and Galen. *Med History, 13*(02), 190–192.

Hodge, A.M., English, D.R., O'Dea, K., & Giles, G. (2004). Glycemic index and dietary fiber and risk of type 2 diabetes. *Diabetes Care, 27,* 2701–2706.

Homko, C.J. (2010). Gestational diabetes: Can we reach consensus? *Curr Diab Rep, 10,* 252–254.

Hossain, P., Kawar, B., & El Nahas, M. (2007). Obesity and diabetes in the developing world: A growing challenge. *N Engl J Med, 356*(03), 213–215.

IADPSG Consensus Panel. (2010). International Association of Diabetes and Pregnancy Study Groups: Recommendations on the diagnosis and classification of hyperglycemia in pregnancy. *Diabetes Care, 33*(03), 676–682.

International Diabetes Federation (IDF) Diabetes Atlas. (2006). Prevalence estimates of diabetes mellitus (DM), 2006. Brussels, Belgium.

International Diabetes Federation (IDF) Diabetes Atlas. (2010). Prevalence estimates of diabetes mellitus (DM), 2010. Brussels, Belgium.

Jenkins, D.J.A., Wolever, T.M.S., Taylor, R.H., Barker, H., Fielden, H., Baldwin, J.M.,... Goff, D.V. (1981). Glycemic index of foods: A physiologic basis for carbohydrate exchange. *Amer J Clin Nutr, 34,* 362–366.

Kandror, K.V., & Pilch, P.F. (1996). Compartmentalization of protein traffic in insulin sensitive cells. *Am J Physiol, 271,* E1–E14.

Karvonen, M., Viik-Kajander, M., Moltchanova, E., Libman, I., LaPorte, R., Tuomilehto, J., for the Diabetes Mondiale (DIAMOND) Project Group. (2000). *Diabetes Care, 23,* 1516–1526.

Kautiainen, S., Rimpelä, A., Vikat, A., & Virtanen, S.M. (2002). Secular trends in overweight and obesity among Finnish adolescents in 1977–1999. *Int J Obes Relat Metab Disord, 26,* 544–552.

Kertes, P.J., & Johnson, T.M. (2007). *Evidence-based eye care.* Philadelphia, PA: Lippincott Williams & Wilkins.

Kilpatrick, E.S. (2000). Glycated haemoglobin in the year 2000. *J Clin Path, 53*(5), 335–339.

Kim, C., Newton, K.M., & Knopp, R.H. (2002). Gestational diabetes and the incidence of type 2 diabetes. A systematic review. *Diabetes Care, 25*(10), 1862–1868.

King, H., Aubert, R.E., & Herman, W.H. (1998). Gobal burden of diabetes: 1995–2025. *Diabetes Care, 21,* 1414–1431.

Kirchof, M., Popat, N., & Malowany, J. (2008). A historical perspective of the diagnosis of diabetes. *UWOMJ, 78*(01), P7–P9.

Kitabchi, A.E., & Wall, B.M. (1999). Management of diabetic ketoacidosis. *Am Fam Physician, 60*(2), 455–464.

Kitabchi, A.E., Umpierrez, G.E., Murphy, M.B., & Kreisberg, R.A. (2006). Hyperglycemic crises in adult patients with diabetes: A consensus statement from the American Diabetes Association. *Diabetes Care*, 29(12), 2739–2748.

Klein, R., Klein, B.E., Moss, S., & Demets, D.L. (1988). Proteinuria in diabetes. *Arch Intern Med*, 148, 181–187.

Klein, S., Sheard, N.F., Pi-Sunyer, X., Daly, A., Wylie-Rosett, J., Kulkarni, K., & Clark, N.G. (2004). Weight management through lifestyle modification for the prevention and management of type 2 diabetes: Rationale and strategies. *Am J Clin Nutr*, 80(2), 257–263.

Knowler, W.C., Bennett, P.H., Hamman, R.F., & Miller, M. (1978). Diabetes incidence and prevalence in Pima indians: A 19-fold greater incidence than in Rochester, Minnesota. *Am J Epidemiol*, 108(6), 497–505.

Koh-Banerjee, P., Wang, Y., Hu, F.B., Spiegelman, D., Willett, W.C., & Rimm, E.B.(2004). Changes in body weight and body fat distribution as risk factors for clinical diabetes in US men. *Am J Epidemiol*, 159, 1150–1159.

Kolb, H., & Elliott, R.B. (1994). Increasing incidence of IDDM a consequence of improved hygiene? *Diabetologia*, 37(7), 729.

Krishnan, S., Rosenberg, L., Singer, M., Hu, F.B., Djoussé, L., Cupples, L.A., & Palmer, J.R. (2007). Glycemic index, glycemic load, and cereal fiber intake and risk of type 2 diabetes in US black women. *Arch Intern Med*, 167, 2304–2309.

Krolewski, A.S., Warram, J.H., Rand, L.I., & Kahn, C.R. (1987). Epidemiologic approach to the etiology of type 1 diabetes and its complications. *N Engl J Med*, 317, 1390–1398.

Kroner, Z. (2009). The relationship between Alzheimers disease and diabetes: Type 3 diabetes? *Alt Med Rev*, 14(04), 373–379.

Kung, H.C., Hoyert, D.L., Xu, J., & Murphy, S. (2008). Deaths: Final data for 2005. *National Vital Statistics Report*, 56(10), 1–121.

Laaksonen, D.E., Lakka, H.M., Niskanen, L.K., Kaplan, G.A., Salonen, J.T., & Lakka, T.A. (2002). Metabolic syndrome and development of diabetes mellitus: Application and development of recently suggested definitions of the metabolic syndrome in a prospective cohort study. *Am J Epidemiol*, 156, 1070–1077.

Lambert, P.A., Gillespie, K.M., Thompson, G., et al. (2004). Absolute risk of childhood-onset type 1 diabetes defined by human leukocyte antigen class II genotype: A population-based study in the United Kingdom. *J Clin Endo Metab*, 89(08), 4037–4043.

Lauderdale, D.S., & Rathouz, P.J. (2000). Body mass index in a US national sample of Asian Americans: Effects of nativity, years since immigration and socioeconomic status. *Int J Obes Relat Metab Disord*, 24(09), 1188–1194.

Lawrence, J.M., Contreras, R., Chen, W., et al. (2008). Trends in the prevalence of pre-existing diabetes and gestational diabetes mellitus among a racially/ethnically diverse population of women, 1999–2005. *Diabetes Care*, 31, 899.

Leary, J., Pettitt, D.J., & Jovanivic, L. (2010). Gestational diabetes guidelines in a HAPO world. *Best Practice & Research Clinical Endocrinology & Metabolism*, 24(4), 673–685.

Lee, W.L., Cheung, A.M., Cape, D., & Zinman, D. (2000). Impact of diabetes on coronary artery disease in women and men: A meta-analysis of prospective studies. *Diab Care*, 23(07), 962–968.

Leonhardt, W., Hanefeld, M., Schneider, H., & Haller, H. (1972). Human adipocyte volumes: Maximum size, and correlation to weight index in maturity onset-diabetes. *Diabetologia*, 8, 287–291.

Levy-Marchal, C., Patterson, C., & Green, A. (1995). Variation by age group and seasonality at diagnosis of childhood IDDM in Europe. The EURODIAB ACE Study Group. *Diabetologia*, 38, 823–830.

Ley, K., & Huo, Y. (2001). VCAM-1 is critical in atherosclerosis. *J Clin Invest*, 107(10), 1209–1210.

Libby, P. (2002). Inflammation in atherosclerosis. *Nature*, 420(6917), 868–874.

Libby, P., Ridker, P.M., & Hansson, G.K. (2009). Inflammation in atherosclerosis. *J Am Coll Cardio, 54,* 2129–2138.

Lillioja, S., Mott, D.M., Spraul, M., Ferraro, R., Foley, J.E., Ravussin, E.,...Bogardus, C. (1993). Insulin resistance and insulin secretry dysfunction as precursors of non-insulin-dependent diabetes mellitus: Prospective studies of Pima Indians. *N Engl J Med, 329,* 1988–1992.

Lopez-Ridaura, R., Willett, W.C., Rimm, E.B., Liu, S., Stampfer, M.J., Manson, J.E., & Hu, F.B. (2004). Magnesium intake and risk of type 2 diabetes in men and women. *Diabetes Care, 27*(1), 134–140.

Lorenzo, C., Okoloise, M., Williams, K., Stern, M.P., Haffner, S.M., the San Antonio Heart Study. (2003). The metabolic syndrome as predictor of type 2 diabetes: The San Antonio Heart Study. *Diabetes Care, 26,* 3153–3159.

Lucas, A. (1991). Programming by early nutrition in man. In G.R. Bock & J. Whelan (Eds.), *The childhood environment and adult disease* (pp. 38–55). Chichester, United Kingdom: Wiley.

Lynn, S., Evans, J.C., White, C.H., Frayling, T.M., Hattersley, A.T., Turnbull, D.M.,...Walker, M. (2002). Variation in the calpain-10 gene affects blood glucose levels in the British population. *Diabetes, 51*(1), 247–250.

Marrosu, M.G., Cocco, E., Lai, M., Spinicci, G., Pischedda, M.P., & Contu, D. (2002). Patients with multiple sclerosis and risk of type 1 diabetes mellitus in Sardinia, Italy: A cohort study. *Lancet, 359,* 1461–1465.

Marrosu, M.G., Motzo, C., Murru, R., Lampis, R., Costa, G., Zavattari, P.,...Cucca, F. (2004). The co-inheritance of type 1 diabetes and multiple sclerosis in Sardinia cannot be explained by genotype variation in the HLA region alone. *Hum Mol Genet, 13*(23), 2919–2924.

Marshall, A., Hamman, R.F., & Baxter, J. (1991). High-fat, low-carbohydrate diet and the etiology of non-insulin-dependent diabetes mellitus: The San Luis Valley Diabetes Study. *Am J Epidemiol, 134,* 590–603.

McCarty, D., & Zimmet, P. (1994). *Diabetes from 1994 to 2010: Global estimates and projections.* Melbourne: International Diabetes Institute.

McCulloch, D.K. (2004). Classification of diabetes mellitus and genetic diabetic syndromes. In: *UpToDate*®.

McCulloch, D.K. (2010). Screening for diabetes mellitus. In: *UpToDate*®.

McEwen, L.N., Kim, C., Haan, M., Ghosh, D., Mangione, C.M., Safford, M.M.,...Triad Study Group. (2006). Diabetes reporting as a cause of death: Results from the Translating Research into Action for Diabetes (TRIAD) study. *Diabetes Care, 29*(2), 247–253.

McKinney, P.A. (2001). Seasonality of birth in patients with childhood type 1 diabetes in 19 European regions. *Diabetologia, 44,* B67–B74.

Mente, A., Yusuf, S., Islam, S., McQueen, M.J., Tanomsup, S., Onen, C.L.,...Anand, S.S., for the INTERHEART Investigators. (2010). Metabolic syndrome and risk of acute myocardial infarction: A case-control study of 26,903 subjects from 52 countries. *J Am Coll Cardiol, 55,* 2390–2398.

Meyer, K.A., Kushi, L.H., Jacobs, D.R. Jr., Slavin, J., Sellers, T.A., & Folsom, A.R. (2000). Carbohydrates, dietary fiber, and incident type 2 diabetes in older women. *Am J Clin Nutr, 71,* 921–930.

Misra, A. (2003). Revisions of cutoffs of body mass index to define overweight and obesity are needed for the Asian-ethnic groups (Debate). *Int J Obes, 27,* 1294–1296.

Mokdad, A.H., Ford, E.S., Bowman, B.A., Nelson, D.E., Engelgau, M.M., Finicor, F., & Marks, J.S. (2000). Diabetes trends in the US: 1990–1998. *Diabetes Care, 23*(9), 1278–1283.

Mokdad, A.H., Bowman, B.A., Ford, E.S., Vinicor, F., Marks, J.S., & Koplan, J.P. (2001). The continuing epidemics of obesity and diabetes in the United States. *JAMA, 286*(10), 1195–1200.

Moltchanova, E.V., Schreier, N., Lammi, N., et al. (2009). Seasonal variation of diagnosis of type 1 diabetes in children worldwide. *Diab Med, 26*(07), 673–678.

Montonen, J., Kneckt, P., Järvinen, R., Aromaa, A., & Reunanen, A. (2003). Whole-grain and fiber intake and incidence of type 2 diabetes. *Am J Clin Nutr, 77*, 622–629.

Moore, D.J., Gregory, J.M., Kumah-Crystal, Y.A., & Simmons, J.H. (2009). Mitigating micro- and macro-vascular complications of diabetes in adolescence. *Vasc Health and Risk Mgmt, 5*, 1015–1031.

Moss, S.E., Klein, R., & Klein, B.E. (1991). Cause-specific mortality in a population-based study of diabetes. *Am J Public Health*, 1158–1162.

Mott, J.W., Wang, J., Thornton, J.C., Allison, D.B., Heymsfield, S.B., & Pierson Jr., R.N. (1999). Relation between body fat and age in 4 ethnic groups. *Am J Clin Nutr, 69*(5), 1007–1013.

Nadeau, K.J., Regensteiner, J.G., Bauer, T.A., Brown, M.S., Dorosz, J.L., Hull, A.,…Reusch, J.E. (2010). Insulin resistance in adolescents with type 1 diabetes and its relationship to cardiovascular function. *J Clin Endocrinol Metab, 95*(2), 513–521.

Nagaev, I., & Smith, U. (2001). Insulin resistance and type 2 diabetes are not related to resistin expression in human fat cells or skeletal muscle. *Biochem Biophys Res Commun, 285*(2), 561–564.

Narayan, K.M., Boyle, J.P., Thompson, T.J., Sorensen, S.W., & Williamson, D.F. (2003). Lifetime risk of diabetes mellitus in the United States. *JAMA, 290*(14), 1884–1890.

Narayan, K.M., Zhang, P., Kanaya, A.M., et al. (2006). Diabetes: The pandemic and potential solutions. In *Disease control priorities in development countries* (2nd ed., pp. 591–603). New York: Oxford University Press.

National Heart, Lung, and Blood Institute. (1998). *National Institute of Diabetes and Digestive and Kidney Diseases. Clinical guidelines on the identification, evaluation, and treatment of overweight and obesity in adults. The evidence report* (pp. 1–228). Bethesda, MD: NIH.

National Institute of Diabetes and Digestive and Kidney Diseases. (2008). *US Department of Health and Human Services, National Institutes of Health. National Diabetes Statistics, 2007 fact sheet*. Bethesda, MD: National Institutes of Health.

Neel, J.V. (1962). Diabetes mellitus: A "thrifty" genotype rendered detrimental by "progress"? *Am J Human Genetics, 14*, 353–362.

Ninomiya, J.K., L'Italien, G., Criqui, M.H., Whyte, J.L., Gamst, A., & Chen, R.S. (2004). Association of the metabolic syndrome with history of myocardial infarction and stroke in the Third National Health and Nutrition Examination Survey. *Circulation, 109*(1), 42–46.

Norris, S.L., Kansagara, D., Bougatsos, C., Nygren, P., & Fu, R. (2008). Screening for type 2 diabetes mellitus: Update of 2003 Systematic Evidence Review for the U.S. Preventive Services Task Force [Internet]. Rockville, MD: Agency for Healthcare Research and Quality (US); 2008 Jun. Report No.: 08-05116-EF-1.

Olatunbosun, S.T., & Dagogo-Jack, S. (2010). Insulin resistance. *Medscape eMedicine*.

Onkamo, P., Vaananen, S., Karvonen, M., et al. (1999). Worldwide increase in incidence of type 1 diabetes—The analysis of the data on published incidence trends. *Diabetologia, 42*, 1395–1403.

Pan, W.H., Flegal, K.M., Chang, H.Y., Yeh, W.T., Yeh, C.J., & Lee, W.C. (2004). Body mass index and obesity-related metabolic disorders in Taiwanese and US whites and blacks: Implications for definitions of overweight and obesity for Asians. *Am J Clin Nutr, 79*, 31–39.

Pan, X.R., Li, G.W., Hu, Y.H., et al. (1997). Effects of diet and exercise in preventing NIDDM in people with impaired glucose tolerance: The Da Qing IGT and Diabetes Study. *Diabetes Care 20*, 537–544.

Patel, M.S., Srinivasan, M., & Aalinkee, R. (2000). Metabolic programming by nutrition during early development. *Indian Journal of Experimental Biology, 38*(9), 849–855.

Patterson, C.C., Dahlquist, G.G., Gyürüs, E., Green, A., Soltész, G., and the EURODIAB Study Group. (2009). Incidence trends for childhood type 1 diabetes in Europe during 1989–2003 and predicted new cases 2005–20: A multicenter prospective registration study. *Lancet, 373*, 2027–2033.

Permutt, M.A., Wasson, J., & Cox, N. (2005). Genetic epidemiology of diabetes. *J Clin Invest, 115*(06), 1431–1439.

Pessin, J.E., Thurmond, D.C., Elmendorf, J.S., et al. (1999). Molecular basis of insulin-stimulating GLUT4 vesicle trafficking. *J Biol Chem, 274*(05), 2593–2596.

Petersen, K.F., & Shulman, G.I. (2006). Etiology of insulin resistance. *AJM, 119*, 10S–16S.

Phillips, G.B. (1977). Relationship between serum sex hormones and glucose, insulin, and lipid abnormalities in men with myocardial infarction. *Proc Natl Acad Sci USA, 74*, 1729–1733.

Pickup, J., & William, G. (1997). *Textbook of diabetes* (2nd ed.). London: Blackwell Science.

Piettropaolo, M., & Trucco, M. (2003). Genetics of type 1 diabetes. In *Type 1 diabetes. Etiology and treatment*. Totowa, NJ: Humana Press.

Pitkäniemi, J., Onkamo, P., Tuomilehto, J., & Arjas, E. (2004). Increasing incidence of Type 1 diabetes—Role for genes? *BMC Genetics, 5*, 5.

Pozzilli, P., & Buzzetti, R. (2007). A new expression of diabetes: Double diabetes. *Trends Endo Metab, 18*(02), 52–57.

Raj, S.M., Howson, J.M., Walker, N.M., Cooper, J.D., Smyth, D.J., Field, S.F.,…Todd, J.A. (2009). No association of multiple type 2 diabetes loci with type 1 diabetes. *Diabetologia, 52*, 2109–2116.

Ravussin, E., Valencia, M.E., Esparza, J., Bennett, P.H., & Schulz, L.O. (1994). Effects of a traditional lifestyle on obesity in Pima Indians. *Diabetes Care, 14*, 1067–1074.

Ravussin, E., & Smith, S.R. (2002). Increased fat intake, impaired fat oxidation, and failure of fat cell proliferation result in ectopic fat storage, insulin resistance, and type 2 diabetes mellitus. *Ann NY Acad Sci, 967*, 363–378.

Reaven, G.M. (1988). Banting lecture 1988. Role of insulin resistance in human disease. *Diabetes, 37*, 1595–1607.

Reaven, G.M. (1995). Pathophysiology of insulin resistance in human disease. *Physio Rev, 75*(03), 473–486.

Redondo, M.J., Rewers, M., Yu, L., et al. (1999). Genetic determination of islet cell autoimmunity in monozygotic twin, dizygotic twin, and non-twin siblings of patients with type 1 diabetes: Prospective twin study. *BMJ, 318*, 698–702.

Reiber, G.E., Boyko, E.J., & Smith, D.G. (1995). Lower extremity foot ulcers and amputations in diabetes. In M.I. Harris & M.P. Stern (Eds.), *Diabetes in America* (pp. 409–428). Bethesda, MD: US Government Printing Office.

Roglic, G., & Unwin, N. (2005). Global mortality attributable to diabetes: Time for a realistic estimate. *Diabetes Voice, 50*(1), 33–34.

Roglic, G., & Unwin, N. (2010). Mortality attributable to diabetes: Estimates for the year 2010. *Diabetes Research and Clinical Practice, 87*, 15–19.

Rogot, E., Sorlie, P., Johnson, N.J., Glover, C.S., & Makus, D. (1985). Mortality by cause of death among selected census sample cohorts for 1979–1981. *1985 proceedings of the Section on Survey Research Methods*. American Statistical Association.

Rosati, G., Aiello, I., Pirastru, M.I., Mannu, L., Sanna, G., Sau, G.F., & Sotgiu, S. (1996). Epidemiology of multiple sclerosis in northwestern Sardinia: Further evidence for higher frequency in Sardinians compared to other Italians. *Neuroepidemiology, 15*, 10–19.

Rosen, E.D., & MacDougald, O.A. (2006). Adipocyte differentiation from the inside out. *Molecular Cell Biology 7*, 885–896.

Ross, R., & Glomset, J.A. (1976). The pathogenesis of atherosclerosis. *N Engl J Med, 295*, 369–377.

Ross, R. (1999) Atherosclerosis—An inflammatory disease. *N Engl J Med, 340*, 115–126.

Salmeron, J., Hu, F.B., Manson, J.E., Stampfer, M.J., Colditz, G.A., Rimm, E.B., & Willett, W.C. (2001). Dietary fat intake and risk of type 2 diabetes in women. *Amer Soc Clin Nutr, 76*, 1019–1026.

Salo, M. (2006). Obesity among children—A large amount of work together. *Duodecim, 122,* 1211–1212.

Sanna, E., Soro, M.R., & Calo, C. (2006). Overweight and obesity prevalence in urban Sardinian children. *Anthropologischer Anzeiger, 64,* 333–344.

Schulze, M.B., Schulz, M., Heidemann, C., Schienkiewitz, A., Hoffmann, K., & Boeing, H. (2007). Fiber and magnesium intake and incidence of type 2 diabetes. A prospective study and meta-analysis. *Arch Intern Med, 167*(9), 956–965.

Scott, S.K., Rabito, F.A., Butler, N.N., & Harris, R.E. (2004). *The energy storage capacity hypothesis.* (PhD dissertation).

Shabbir, S., Kwan, D., Wang, M.C., et al. (2010). Asians and Pacific Islanders and the growing childhood epidemic. *Ethnicity and Disease, 20,* 129–135.

Shai, I., Jiang, R., Manson, J.E., Stampfer, M.J., Willett, W.C., Colditz, G.A., & Hu, F.B. (2006). Ethnicity, obesity, and risk of type 2 diabetes in women: A 20-year follow-up study. *Diabetes Care, 29*(7), 1585–1590.

Shaw, J.E., Sicree, R.A., & Zimmet, P.Z. (2010). Global estimates of the prevalence of diabetes for 2010 and 2030. *Diabetes Res Clin Pract, 87*(1), 4–14.

Sheehy, A.M., Flood, G.E., Tuan, W.J., et al. (2010). Analysis of guidelines for screening diabetes mellitus in an ambulatory population. *Mayo Clin Proc, 85,* 27–35.

Sheperd, P.R., & Kahn, B.B. (1999). Glucose transporters and insulin action—Implications for insulin resistance and diabetes mellitus. *NEJM, 341*(04), 248–257.

Silverman, B.L., Metzger, B.E., Cho, N.H., & Loeb, C.A. (1995). Impaired glucose tolerance in adolescent offspring of diabetic mothers. *Diabetes Care, 18,* 611–617.

Silverman, B.L., Rizzo, T.A., Cho, N.H., & Metzger, B.E. (1998). Long-term effects of the intrauterine environment: The Northwestern University Diabetes in Pregnancy Center. *Diabetes Care, 21*(Suppl. 2), B142–B149.

Sjostrom, D.C., Peltonen, M., Wedel, H., & Sjostrom, L. (2000). Differentiated long-term effects of intentional weight loss on diabetes and hypertension. *Hypertension 36,* 10–25.

Sobngwi, E., Mbanya, J.C., Unwin, N., et al. (2004). Exposure over the life course to an urban environment and its relation with obesity, diabetes, and hypertension in rural and urban Cameroon. *IJE, 33*(04), 769–776.

Stanhope, K.L., Schwarz, J.M., Keim, N.L., Griffen, S.C., Bremer, A.A., Graham, J.L.,...Havel, P.J. (2009). Consuming fructose-sweetened, but not glucose-sweetened beverages increases visceral adiposity and lipids and decreases insulin sensitivity in overweight/obese humans. *J Clin Invest, 119,* 1322–1334.

Stevens, J., Ahn, K., Juhaeri, J., Houston, D., Steffan, L., & Couper, D. (2002). Dietary fiber intake and glycemic index and incidence of diabetes in African American and White adults: The ARIC Study. *Diabetes Care, 25,* 1715–1721.

Strachan, D.P. (1989). Hay fever, hygiene and household size. *BMJ, 299*(6710), 1259–1260.

Stratton, I.M., Kohner, E.M., Aldington, S.J., et al. (2001). UKPDS 50: Risk factors for incidence and progression of retinopathy in type II diabetes over 6 years from diagnosis. *Diabetologia, 44,* 156–163.

Sudagani, J., & Hitman, G.A. (2005). Diabetes mellitus: Etiology and epidemiology. In *Encyclopedia of human nutrition* (pp. 535–542). London, UK: Elsevier.

Swarbrick, M.M., Stanhope, K.L., Elliott, S.S., Graham, J.L., Krauss, R.M., Christiansen, M.P.,...Havel, P.J. (2008). Consumption of fructose-sweetened beverages for 10 weeks increases postprandial triacylglycerol and apolipoprotein-B concentrations in overweight and obese women. *Br J Nutr, 100*(5), 947–952.

Takaya, J., Higashino, H., & Kobayashi, Y. (2004). Intracellular magnesium and insulin resistance. *Magnes Res, 17*(2), 126–136.

Tanaka, S., Horimai, C., & Katsukawa, F. (2003). Ethnic differences in abdominal visceral fat accumulation between Japanese, African–Americans, and Caucasians: A meta-analysis. *Acta Diabetologica, 40*(1), S302–S304.

Torsdottir, I., Alpsten, M., Holm, G., et al. (1991). A small dose of soluble alginate fiber affects postprandial glycemia and gastric emptying in humans with diabetes. *J Nutr, 121*, 795–799.

Tosiello, L. (1996). Hypomagnesemia and diabetes mellitus: A review of clinical implications. *Arch Intern Med, 156*, 1143–1148.

Tremblay, A., Doucet, E., Imbeault, P., et al. (1999). Metabolic fitness in active reduced-obese individuals. *Obes Res, 7*, 556–563.

Truesdale, K.P., Stevens, J., & Cai, J. (2005). The effect of weight history on glucose and lipids. *A J Epid, 161*, 1133–1143.

Tuomilehto, J., Virtala, E., Karvonen, M., Lounamaa, R., Pitkaniemi, J., Reunanen, A.,…Toivanen, L. (1995). Increase in incidence of insulin-dependent diabetes mellitus among children in Finland. *Int J Epidemiol, 24*, 984–992.

Tuomilehto, J., Lindstrom, J., Eriksson, J.G., et al. (2001). Prevention of type 2 diabetes mellitus by changes in lifestyle among subjects with impaired glucose tolerance. *New Engl JMed, 344*, 343–350.

Unger, R.H. (2003). The physiology of cellular liporegulation. *Ann Review Physiol, 65*, 333–347.

Unger, R.H., & Scherer, P.E. (2010). Gluttony, sloth and the metabolic syndrome: A roadmap to liptoxicity. *Trends Endocrinol Metab, 21*(6), 345–354.

United States Preventive Services Task Force. (2008). *Screening for type 2 diabetes mellitus in adults.* Agency for Health Care Research and Quality, US Department of Health and Human Services.

Valdez, R., Yoon, P.W., Liu, T., & Khoury, M. (2007). Family history and prevalence of diabetes in the US population: The six year results from the National Health and Nutrition Examination Survey (1999–2004). *Diabetes Care, 30*(10), 2517–2522.

van Dam, R.M., Willett, W.C., Rimm, E.B., Stampfer, M.J., & Hu, F.B. (2002). Dietary fat and meat intake in relation to risk of type 2 diabetes in men. *Diabetes Care, 25*, 417–424.

Verbeeten, K.C., Elks, C.E., Daneman, D., & Ong, K.K. (2011). Association between childhood obesity and subsequent Type 1 diabetes: A systematic review and meta-analysis. *Diabet Med, 28*(1), 10–18.

Villegas, R., Liu, S., Gao, Y.T., Yang, G., Li, H., Zheng, W., & Shu, X.O. (2007). Prospective study of dietary carbohydrates, glycemic index, glycemic load, and incidence of type 2 diabetes mellitus in middle-aged chinese women. *Arch Intern Med, 167*(21), 2310–2316.

Wajchenberg, B.L. (2007). β-cell failure in diabetes and preservation by clinical treatment. *Endo Rev, 28*, 187–218.

Walston, J., Silver, K., Bogardus, C., Knowler, W.C., Celi, F.S., Austin, S.,…Shuldiner, A.R. (1995). Time of onset of non-insulin-dependent diabetes mellitus and genetic variation in the β_3-adrenergic–receptor gene. *N Engl J Med, 333*, 343–347.

Wang, H., Shara, N.M., Calhoun, D., Umans, J.G., Lee, E.T., & Howard, B.V. (2010). Incidence rates and predictors of diabetes in those with prediabetes: The Strong Heart Study. *Diab Metab Res Rev, 26*, 378–385.

Warram, J.H., Krolewski, A.S., & Kahn, C.R. (1988). Determinants of IDDM and perinatal mortality in children of diabetic mothers. *Diabetes, 37*, 1328–1334.

Weickert, M.O., Mohlig, M., Koebnick, C., Holst, J.J., Namsolleck, P., Ristow, M.,…Pfeiffer, A.F.H. (2005). Impact of cereal fibre on glucose-regulating factors. *Diabetologia, 48*, 2343–2353.

Weickert, M.O., Möhlig, M., Schöfl, C., Arafat, A.M., Otto, B., Viehoff, H.,…Spranger, A.F.H. (2006). Cereal fiber improves whole-body insulin sensitivity in overweight and obese women. *Diabetes Care, 29*(4), 775–780.

Weickert, M.O., & Pfeiffer, A.F.H. (2008). Metabolic effects of dietary fiber consumption and prevention of diabetes. *J Nutr, 138*, 439–442.

WHO Expert Consultation. (2004). Appropriate body mass index for Asian populations and its implications for policy and intervention strategies. *Lancet, 363,* 157–163.

Wild, S., Roglic, G., Green, A., Sicree, R., & King, H. (2004). Global prevalence of diabetes. Estimates for the year 2000 and projections for 2030. *Diabetes Care, 27,* 1047–1053.

Wilkin, T.J. (2001). The accelerator hypothesis: Weight gain as the missing link between Type I and Type II diabetes. *Diabetologia, 44,* 914–922.

Willett, W.C., Dietz, W.H., & Colditz, G.A. (1999). Guidelines for healthy weight. *N Engl J Med, 341,* 427–434.

Willett, W., Manson, J., & Liu, S. (2002). Glycemic index, glycemic load and risk of type 2 diabetes. *Am J Nutrition, 76*(1), 274S–280S.

Wingard, D.L., & Barrett-Conner, E. (1995). Heart disease and diabetes. In M.I. Harris, C.C. Cowie, M.P. Stern, E.J. Boyko, G.E. Reiber & P.H. Bennett (Eds.), *Diabetes in America* (2nd ed., pp. 429–488). Bethesda, MD: National Institutes of Health.

Wolever, T.M.S., Katzman-Relle, L., Jenkins, A.L., Vuksan, V., Josse, R.G., & Jenkins, D.J.A. (1994). Glycaemic index of 102 complex carbohydrate foods in patients with diabetes. *Nutrition Research, 14,* 651–669.

Wolever, T.M. (1997). The glycemic index: Flogging a dead horse? *Diabetes Care, 20*(3), 452–456.

World Health Organization. (2004). Diabetes action now: An initiative of the World Health Organization.

World Health Organization. (2009). Fact sheet No. 312.

Yang, W., Lu, J., Weng, J., et al. (2010). Prevalence of diabetes among men and women in China. *NEJM, 362,* 1090–1101.

Yang, Z., Wang, K., Li, T., et al. (1998). Childhood diabetes in China. *Diabetes Care, 21,* 525–529.

Ye, J., Chen, R.G., Ashkenazi, I., & Laron, Z. (1998). Lack of seasonality in the month of onset of childhood IDDM (0.7–15 years) in Shanghai, China. *J Pediatr Endo Metab, 11,* 461–464.

Yoon, J.W. (1990). The role of viruses and environmental factors in the induction of diabetes. *Curr Top Microbiol Immunol, 164,* 95.

Younis, N., Broadbent, D.M., Vora, J.P., & Harding, S.P. (2003). Liverpool Diabetic Eye Study: Incidence of sight-threatening retinopathy in patients with type 2 diabetes in the Liverpool Diabetic Eye Study: A cohort study. *Lancet, 361,* 195–200.

Zhan, S., & Ho, S.C. (2005). Meta-analysis of the association of the Trp64Arg polymorphism in the b3 adrenergic receptor with insulin resistance. *Obesity Research, 13,* 1709–1719.

33

Epidemiology of Obesity

Susanne K. Scott & Randall E. Harris

INTRODUCTION

The global epidemic of obesity is one of the most significant public health threats of the 21st century. Fueled primarily by excess calories and physical inactivity, the dramatic increase in overweight and obesity of the past several decades is considered the major cause for the parallel rise in incident and prevalent diabetes (WHO, 2003; International Diabetes Federation, 2006). Obesity, which is a strong, independent, and modifiable predictor of type 2 diabetes, is also associated with numerous other serious chronic diseases and health conditions such as cardiovascular diseases; some cancers; musculoskeletal, gastrointestinal, respiratory, dermatologic, and reproductive disorders; social stigma; and psychological distress. As William Wadd aptly wrote in his 1816 book on obesity, *"Corpulence is not only a disease itself, but the harbinger of others"* (Wadd, 1816).

Even more disturbing than increasing obesity in adults is the alarming rise in the prevalence of childhood and adolescent overweight and obesity. Increasing obesity levels in children have contributed to a much earlier onset of obesity-related diseases, diseases that were previously diagnosed only in older adults (Freedman et al., 1999, 2007; Ebbeling, Pawling, and Ludwig, 2002; Hung-Kwan et al., 2008). Moreover, childhood obesity tracks robustly into adulthood, which means that once a child becomes obese, it is likely that obesity will persist throughout the life course. Early onset of obesity and the health sequelae that follow have profound economic implications. The long-term medical management of obesity and related diseases, especially beginning in youth, is expected to overwhelm

healthcare systems, devastate personal income and earnings, and threaten national budgets, as medical costs rise to unsustainable levels (WHO, 2005).

Although the trend of increasing obesity prevalence in the United States may have abated somewhat in children (Ogden, Carroll, and Flegal, 2008) and among some adults since 1999 (Ogden et al., 2007a; Flegal et al., 2010), obesity levels continue to skyrocket in other parts of the world, particularly in poor developing countries known more for problems of hunger and infectious diseases (Prentice, 2006; Misra and Khurana, 2008). Globalization and urbanization are considered primary factors responsible for the changes in physical activity levels and the *"nutrition transition"* that has altered traditional dietary patterns in countries with emerging economies (Drewnowski and Popkin, 2009; Caballero, 2007; Satia, 2010; Economic Research Service, 2010). This is leading to a persistent positive energy balance, inappropriate weight gain, and increasing obesity levels that are contributing to an increase in worldwide chronic disease rates. Although the primary causes and consequences of obesity have been clearly articulated in the literature, prevention efforts remain the single most significant challenge in the fight against obesity.

CLASSIFICATION OF OVERWEIGHT AND OBESITY IN ADULTS

The World Health Organization (WHO) defines obesity as excessive body fat which has accumulated to the point where health is negatively affected (WHO, 1998). The body mass index (BMI), which is a ratio of the weight in kilograms to the square of the height in meters, $BMI = kg/(m^2)$, is the global metric used for measuring and classifying levels of adiposity and associated obesity-related chronic disease risk among adults. Obesity in children is measured differently using percentile cut points based upon standardized growth charts for boys and girls. The burden of childhood obesity is discussed below in a separate section of this chapter.

Body mass was originally described as the *Quételet index* in 1832, until the metric was renamed the body mass index (BMI) in 1972 by Ancel Keys (Keys et al., 1972). The Quételet index was named after Adolphe Quételet, a Belgian mathematician and statistician who in 1835 concluded that other than during developmental growth spurts, "*the weight increases as the square of the height*" (Quételet, 1835). The Framingham Heart Study was one of the first epidemiologic studies to show that the Quételet index was consistent with measures of relative weight (Eknoyan, 2006, 2008). Keys followed up with his own study, correlating various relative weight indices with subcutaneous fat thickness (skinfold thickness) among 7,424 healthy men in 12 cohorts across five countries, confirming the validity of the Quételet index (Keys et al., 1972).

Quételet's interest in developing a weight index was not related to obesity or health matters, but rather to describe and index anthropometric characteristics of "normal man" for statistical purposes. The Metropolitan Life Insurance Company (MLIC), however, was interested in identifying normal relative body weight, primarily because of the increased death claims of their obese policy holders (Ekoynan, 2008; Medico-Actuarial Mortality Investigation, 1912). Metropolitan Life Insurance actuaries (using MLIC policy-holders and with questionable validity) developed the first standard weight tables (Kuczmarski and Flegal, 2000). These tables were based on tertiles of weight at a given height and were labeled according to small, medium, and large body frames. Sex-specific average weight within those tertiles were classified as "ideal" in the 1940s, and then later, in 1959, were presented as "desirable" (MLIC, 1942, 1943, 1959). For insurance decisions, undesirable weight was considered 20–25% below the average, while morbid obesity was 70–100% above the average within each tertile (Ekoynan, 2008).

In 1984, the body mass index (BMI) with a cut point of ≥ 28 was used to report the first prevalence estimates of overweight status among males, ages 25–74, in *Health United States*, the official annual report on the health of the nation. For women, a different weight-height index was used, but this alternative formula (height in meters, raised to the power 1.5)

was soon discredited. Over the next decade, BMI cut points for overweight evolved, and by 1997, the WHO BMI criteria, which had added obesity cut points, was first applied to US data. In 1998, the BMI-disease risk classification system (currently in use) was developed, derived in part from epidemiologic studies that consistently showed an association of increasing BMI with increasing morbidity and mortality (NIH, 1985; Lee, Manson, and Hennekens, 1993; Manson et al., 1995; Allison et al., 1999). The current BMI criteria are given in **Table 33.1**.

In 2004, the WHO reported that the universal BMI criteria for overweight and obesity were not suitable for Asian populations (WHO, 2004). This was based primarily on studies which revealed that Asians, as a whole, were at risk for obesity-related chronic diseases at a much lower BMI than other ethnic groups (Bei-Fan, 2002; Misra, 2003). Although the WHO report acknowledged the vast diversity in geography, culture, ethnicity, level of urbanization, as well as the social and economic conditions of people classified under the umbrella term of "Asian," the common thread among the subgroups was a lower mean and median BMI than that observed in non-Asian populations (WHO, 2004).

For example, in a study of body mass index and cardiovascular risk factors in a rural Chinese population, Hu and colleagues found that, in 1993, the 90th percentile of the BMI distribution was only 23.5 in men and 24.5 in women living in the rural Anquing region of China (Hu et al., 2000). These data and others (Popkin et al., 1995; Werkman et al., 2000; Lin et al., 2002; Moon et al., 2002; Ito et al., 2003; Razak et al., 2007) have provided the rationale for those who have recommended that Asian regions develop lower *Asian-specific* BMI cut points (Bei-Fan, 2002; Yuji, 2002; Misra, 2003). It has also

Table 33.1	Weight Classification and Disease Risk by Body Mass Index (BMI)		
Weight Classification	Obesity Class	BMI (kg/m^2)	Risk of Disease
Underweight		<18.5	Elevated
Normal Weight		18.5<25	Baseline
Overweight		25<30	Elevated
Obese	I	30<35	High
Obese	II	35<40	Very High
Morbidly Obese	III	40+	Extremely High

Source: Data from the Evidence Report 1998. National Institutes of Health. *Obes Res* 6:51S–209S.

been the basis for the WHO to develop additional international BMI cut points (23, 27.5, 32.5, and 37.5) along the continuum of BMI, to be used for public health action (WHO, 2004).

LIMITATIONS OF THE BODY MASS INDEX (BMI)

Although the BMI is currently the universally accepted obesity metric, providing a gross approximation of total body fat for the majority of people, it is not without several well-described limitations, the first being that it does not really measure body fat. The BMI is a measure of a person's weight adjusted for height (Kuczmarski and Flegal, 2000; WHO, 2004). In a two compartment model of body composition, the BMI is a standardized measure of fat mass and fat-free mass, the latter of which is comprised of bone, muscle, and all other proteins and tissues. The BMI does not differentiate between the two. Thus, people with increased muscle mass, such as bodybuilders, are likely to be misclassified as overweight or obese, whereas fat mass could be underestimated for those who have lost lean mass due to infirmity, sedentary lifestyle, or increasing age (Kuczmarski and Flegal, 2000).

A second limitation is that BMI does not measure the distribution of body fat and may not accurately reflect levels of intra-abdominal fat and associated health risks in different individuals and populations. Indeed, it is often visceral or abdominal fat rather than peripheral or subcutaneous fat which is implicated in elevating the risk of developing certain chronic diseases (Frayn, 2000; Bergman et al., 2006).

Third, BMI cut points do not show within-interval variation in morbidity, which could be substantial (Stommel and Schoenborn, 2010). Even among the obese, there is a portion of the population that is healthy (Brochu et al., 2001). For instance, in a nationally representative sample of US hospital discharge records of morbidly obese patients in 2002, 76% of the discharge records did not report a diagnosis of diabetes (Scott et al., 2006).

Fourth, since disease risk per BMI level varies by ethnicity, the use of universal BMI cut points may not be appropriate across populations (Stevens, Jianwen, and Jones, 2002; Stevens, 2003a, 2003b). The adult BMI cut points for being overweight or obese are derived primarily from studies of Caucasians, but these may be inaccurate for other ethnic groups (WHO, 1998, 2000, 2004). For example, comparative studies have consistently shown that, on average, Asians have higher percentages of body fat than Caucasians at corresponding levels of BMI

(Deurenberg, Deurenberg-Yap, and Guricci, 2002; Abate et al., 2004; Chung et al., 2005; Kagawa et al., 2006).

Despite a host of methodological concerns related to obesity metrics, the BMI is currently the accepted standard global obesity measure. It remains an appealing epidemiologic and clinical measurement tool primarily due to the simplicity, inexpense, ease, the accuracy and reliability of measuring height and weight, and because of the positive correlation with body fat and obesity-related diseases (Spiegelman et al., 1992; Gallagher et al., 1996; Hubbard, 2000; Kuczmarski and Flegal, 2000). The BMI also provides a standard definition of obesity to use for national and international surveillance and ecologic comparisons (Flegal et al., 2010). It is important to note, however, that due to increasing heterogeneity of societies as well as the development and use of a variety of revised and modified BMI charts for adults and children (e.g., Asian-specific BMI charts and revised WHO growth standards), secular and ecologic comparisons using the BMI could be hindered (Jackson et al., 2007; Hung-Kwan et al., 2008). In future studies, use of the BMI may be best suited for within-population surveillance to track and compare obesity trends within relatively homogeneous groups.

GLOBAL BURDEN OF ADULT OBESITY

The World Health Organization (WHO) has established a global surveillance program to track the worldwide pandemic of obesity and obesity-related diseases and monitor the progress of intervention and prevention strategies. Data on BMI from population surveys conducted in member nations of the WHO have been compiled to estimate the number and prevalence of overweight and obese individuals in the world population (WHO, 1998).

The most recent global data reflect persisting upward trends in the numbers of overweight and obese adults and clearly indicate that the worldwide obesity pandemic is continuing unabated in the 21st century. In 2000, there were approximately 750 million overweight and 300 million obese adults, ages 15 years or older (WHO, 2000); whereas 5 years later in 2005, 1 billion adults were overweight and more than 400 million were obese (WHO, 2005). Thus, obesity is increasing at an annual rate of about 6.6%, which is at least five times greater than the current annual world population growth rate of 1.3%. The WHO has projected that by 2015, 1.6 billion adults will be overweight, with more than 700 million classified as obese, more than doubling the worldwide burden of these conditions within the first 15 years of the 21st century (WHO, 2009a).

Kelly and colleagues reported similar results using a slightly higher age threshold (20 years or older) to define adulthood. Their estimates were compiled from published population surveys of 106 nations representing 88% of the world population. In 2005, 937 million adults (23.2%) were overweight and 396 million (9.8%) were obese. The prevalence of obesity was higher in women (11.2%) than men (7.7%). If global secular trends continue, by the year 2030, approximately 2.2 billion people will be overweight and 1.1 billion people will be obese (Kelly et al., 2008).

GLOBAL PREVALENCE OF ADULT OBESITY

Global patterns of obesity are shown for men and women in **Figure 33.1** and **Figure 33.2**, respectively. National prevalence estimates of obesity by gender are based upon WHO surveys conducted during 2004 using a cut point of BMI > 30 to define obesity.

Prevalence estimates range from less than 5% in Vietnam, India, China, Japan, Korea, the Philippines, Pakistan, and several African nations, to greater than 60% in Polynesian populations residing in the islands of the South Pacific (WHO, 2009a). Gender-specific estimates are 2–3-fold higher in populations of developed nations compared to developing nations. In most countries, the prevalence of obesity in women exceeds that in men by 5–10%. In the United States, the overall prevalence of obesity is approximately 36% in women and 31% in men (Flegal et al., 2010).

The development of obesity is related to an imbalance between calories consumed versus calories expended or *energy input versus energy output.* Notably, the per capita dietary energy supply has increased significantly in nearly all parts of the world during the past five decades, closely paralleling emergence of the global obesity epidemic. Estimates derived from WHO survey data suggest that the world daily per capita energy consumption increased from 2,250–2,750 kilocalories during the period from 1960–2005 (Earth Trends, 2009). National estimates of per capita energy consumption (kilocalories per capita per day) for the period 2001–2003 are depicted in **Figure 33.3**. The world pattern of energy consumption is similar to the global patterns of obesity in men and women (**Figure 33.1** and **Figure 33.2**). These international patterns underscore the etiologic link between total calorie consumption and the development of obesity.

The heightened intake of calories with increasing obesity and disease risk mirrors a global transition

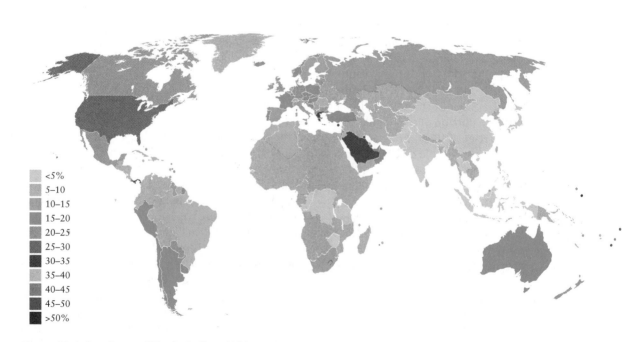

Figure 33.1 Prevalence of Obesity in Men, 2004.

Source: Data from World Health Organization. Global Infobase, International Comparisons: Estimated Obesity (BMI > 30 kg/m²) Prevalence, Males, Aged 15+, 2010. Accessed at: https://apps.who.int/infobase/. October 28, 2011.

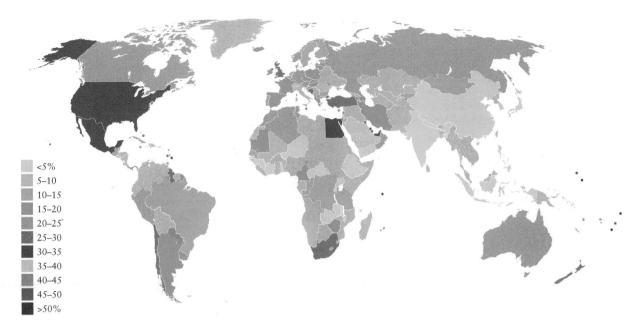

Figure 33.2 Prevalence of Obesity in Women, 2004.

Source: Data from World Health Organization. Global Infobase, International Comparisons: Estimated Obesity (BMI > 30 kg/m^2) Prevalence, Females, Aged 15+, 2010. Accessed at: https://apps.who.int/infobase/. October 28, 2011.

in diet toward increased intake of energy-dense foods that are high in fat and sugars but low in vitamins, minerals, and other micronutrients and a trend toward decreased physical activity due to increasingly sedentary lifestyles, changing modes of transportation, and increasing urbanization (Satia, 2010; Stanhope et al., 2009). These factors are discussed in the following sections of this chapter.

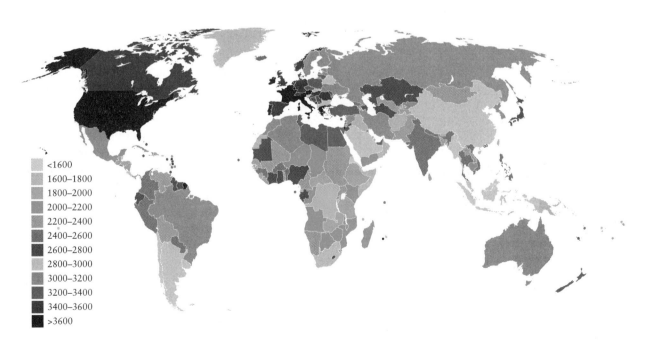

Figure 33.3 World Map of Energy Consumption, 2001–2003.

Source: Data from FAO Statistical Yearbook. (2004). Section D: Consumption. Rome, Italy. Available at ftp://ftp.fao.org/docrep/fao/008/y5473m/y5473m01d.pdf. Accessed October 28, 2011.

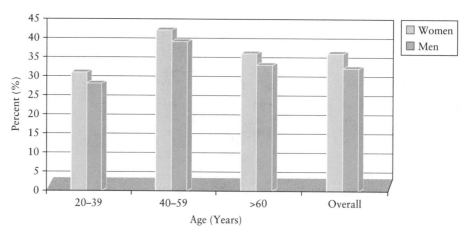

Figure 33.4 Age-Specific Prevalence of Obesity in Men and Women, USA.

Source: Data from National Health and Nutrition Survey (NHANES), 2005-2006. Prevalence estimates are age-adjusted to the US 2000 population.

GENDER DIFFERENCES IN OBESITY

As shown in **Figure 33.1** and **Figure 33.2**, the prevalence of obesity in women exceeds that in men by 5–10% in most of the countries represented. Data for US men and women reflect the higher prevalence of obesity among women at every age (**Figure 33.4**). The gender difference in obesity is widely recognized and has been attributed to evolutionary pressures that predispose women to store excess fat for reproduction and lactation (O'Sullivan, 2008). However, a plethora of other factors may influence gender differences in body mass including body composition, fat distribution, estrogens and androgens, appetite and eating behavior, social and cultural differences, dieting and weight control, exercise patterns, basal metabolism, genes on the X and Y chromosomes, reproductive history, and menopause (Welch and Sowers, 2000; Lovejoy and Sainsbury, 2009).

Recent studies suggest that gender differences in the distribution of body fat are largely determined by differences in sex hormones. In premenopausal women, estrogen may prevent oxidization of fatty acids leading to increased body fat, particularly at puberty and during early pregnancy (O'Sullivan, 2008). In postmenopausal women, abdominal/visceral adiposity increases with the loss of ovarian estrogens (Lovejoy et al., 2008); whereas in men, the gradual decline in circulating androgens with aging predisposes to the accumulation of abdominal fat (Blouin et al., 2005). Furthermore, administration of androgens has been found to reverse abdominal obesity in men (Marin et al., 1993) but not in women

(Lovejoy et al., 1996). Estrogens therefore appear to decrease visceral fat in aging men and women whereas androgens decrease visceral fat in men but have the opposite effect in women (Lovejoy and Sainsbury, 2009).

URBAN VERSUS RURAL DIFFERENCES IN OBESITY

Based upon population studies within nations, the prevalence of obesity is much higher in urban areas than in rural areas, even in low prevalence countries. For example, in China where the overall prevalence of obesity is very low (2.9%), prevalence estimates of 20% or higher have been observed in some urban cities (WHO, 2003).

A research team in Kenya examined changes in body mass in the populations of seven African countries during 1992–2005. Population changes in the prevalence of obesity were assessed for each country over a time span of at least 10 years. Final prevalence estimates for the wealthy were nearly twofold higher than the poor (38% vs. 21%) and during the decade of observation, obesity increased by 35% in urban locales. Notably, the percentage increase among the poorest (50%) was more than sevenfold higher than the richest (7%). These results suggest that obesity is on the rise in developing nations and, as in developed nations, may soon reach epidemic proportions (Ziraba, Fotso, and Ochako, 2009).

In some areas of Africa, obesity has been a longstanding problem. For example, in the Cape Peninsula of South Africa, high obesity levels have persisted among African women since at least 1990 when the prevalence was estimated at 44% (Steyn, 1991). Although Africa is arguably one of the last continents to undergo industrial and market globalization, urban migration patterns have paralleled that of countries with emerging economies. The Population Division of the United Nations predicts that by 2030, half of Africa's total population will live in urban areas, more than tripling the proportion of urban dwellers in 1950 (United Nations, 2006). The implication is that coincident with expanding urbanization, the obesity epidemic emerging in Africa will continue to worsen.

PREVALENCE OF ADULT OBESITY IN THE UNITED STATES

In the United States, the prevalence of obesity has more than doubled since 1960, when only 13.3% of the adult population was classified as obese (**Figure 33.5**). While the *global* prevalence of obesity is expected to double between 2015 and 2030 (WHO, 2009a), obesity trends in the United States may be attenuating. For the past several years, nationally representative sample survey data from the National Health and Nutrition Examination Survey (NHANES) have shown no significant change in the overall prevalence of obesity among adults (Flegal et al., 2010). Nevertheless, almost 70% of people ages 20 and older are overweight or obese, with nearly 34% (almost 73 million people) classified as

obese (Flegal et al., 2010). In addition, the prevalence of obesity in 2008 exceeded 30% in most states, in both sexes, and for most age groups.

DISTRIBUTION OF OBESITY BY AGE, GENDER, AND ETHNICITY IN THE UNITED STATES

The prevalence of obesity is disproportionately higher in certain US age-gender-ethnic groups than others. For example, obesity increases with age in African American women but not other ethnicities (**Figure 33.6**). The prevalence is particularly high (about 60%) in African American women ages 60 and older; roughly double the levels in Caucasian and Hispanic women. In men, the prevalence of obesity is high (about 40%) in young African Americans and middle-aged Caucasians. In men and women of all ages, African Americans have higher levels (44%) than Hispanics (39%) and Caucasians (33%) (Wagner and Heyward, 2000).

Compared to other gender-ethnic groups, the lifestyles of certain African American women appear to predispose them to excessive weight gain and the development of obesity (Gower et al., 2002). The web of causation includes high intake of carbohydrates, sugar and fat in the diet, physical inactivity, high stress, high parity, low vitamin D, lactose intolerance, depression, and perception of body weight (Kumanyika et al., 1991). Furthermore, compared to other groups in weight management programs,

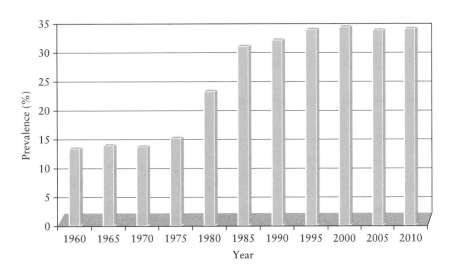

Figure 33.5 Prevalence of Obesity in the United States, 1960–2008.

Source: Data from US National Health and Nutrition Survey (NHANES), 1960-2010. Obesity defined as BMI > 30.

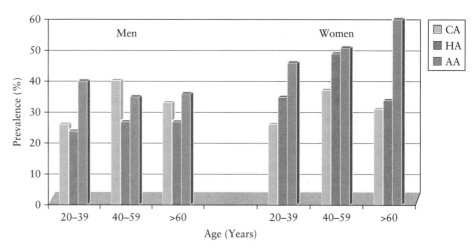

Figure 33.6 Prevalence of Obesity by Gender, Age, and Ethnicity, USA.

Source: Data from US National Health and Nutrition Survey (NHANES), 2005-2006.

African American women are less likely to lose weight and maintain weight loss (Kumanyika, Wilson, and Guliford-Davenport, 1993).

HEALTH CONSEQUENCES OF OBESITY

Obesity exerts deleterious effects on nearly every organ system of the body and is associated with numerous health conditions including type 2 diabetes, cardiovascular diseases (such as coronary heart disease, myocardial infarction, and stroke), gastro-esophageal reflux disease (GERD), obstructive sleep apnea, asthma, gall bladder and fatty liver disease, depression, urinary incontinence, gout, polycystic ovarian syndrome, and osteoarthritis. Selected obesity-related diseases and the overall mortality attributable to obesity are reviewed in the following sections.

Obesity and Total Mortality

Obesity is strongly associated with increased morbidity, mortality, and disability and impaired quality of life (Flegal et al., 2005; 2006; Jia and Lubetkin, 2010). Recent cause-specific mortality data reported by the World Health Organization suggest that overweight and obesity are responsible for 2.8 million deaths annually, ranking 5th among the top 10 leading causes of death worldwide (WHO, 2009a). In the same report, disease burdens attributable to selected risk factors were estimated as the product of the fraction of disease attributed to the risk factor (the population attributable fraction or *PAF*) and

the corresponding total disability-adjusted life years lost (DALY): *Disease Burden = PAF × DALY*. According to these estimates, 44% of the disease burden from diabetes, 23% of the disease burden from ischemic heart disease, and 7–41% of the disease burdens from many forms of cancer are attributable to overweight and obesity (WHO, 2009a).

Studies have consistently shown that obesity is associated with premature death. A recent Danish study followed 5,000 military conscripts ages 20–80 years old and found that men who were obese at age 20 were twice as likely to die prematurely compared to men who were not, and that at any given age thereafter, obesity had a lifelong constant effect on death (the risk remained double) up until 60 years of age. In addition, for each BMI unit above normal, the risk of early death increased by 10% throughout life, with obese men dying approximately 8 years earlier than nonobese men (ICO, 2010).

Investigators at Harvard University evaluated BMI and mortality in a prospective cohort of 115,195 women, ages 30–55, enrolled in the *Nurses Health Study* and free of cardiovascular disease and cancer at baseline. Participants were enrolled in 1976 and followed for 16 years. Compared to women with BMI < 19, obese women (BMI > 32) had 90% higher total mortality, more than fourfold higher cardiovascular mortality (RR = 4.1), and more than twofold higher cancer mortality (RR = 2.1). Results suggested that 53% of deaths among women with a BMI > 29 were attributable to their obesity. In addition, weight gain of 10 kg or more after the age of 18 and a BMI > 22 at age 18 were both predictors of death from cardiovascular disease in middle adulthood. Moreover, the lowest mortality occurred among the leanest women who had remained weight stable since age 18 (Manson et al., 1995).

Investigators at the US National Institutes of Health evaluated BMI and all cause mortality in a cohort of 527,265 men and women, ages 50–71, ascertained through the American Association of Retired Persons (AARP). Participants were enrolled in 1995–1996 and followed for a maximum of 10 years. Among those who had never smoked and who had no preexisting health conditions at baseline, there was a graded increase in the relative risk of all-cause mortality for both men and women as BMI levels rose from 26.5 to more than 40 compared to the reference group with BMI in the range, 23.5–24.9. Morbidly obese men and women (BMI > 40) were more than twice as likely to die as individuals in the reference group (Adams et al., 2006).

Daniel McGee and collaborators in Florida examined relationships of obesity and mortality from all causes, cardiovascular disease and cancer in a meta-analysis of 26 prospective observational studies that included men and women from several racial and ethnic groups. The final database consisted of 74 analytic cohorts consisting of 388,622 individuals. A total of 60,374 individuals died during follow-up. Proportional hazards models were used to examine relationships of BMI categories and mortality. Obesity was associated with increased mortality due to heart disease (RR = 1.57), cardiovascular disease (RR = 1.48), and cancer (RR = 1.07). The total

mortality rate was 22% higher among obese individuals compared to individuals of normal weight (McGee, 2005).

While obesity is associated with an increased risk of early death, people who are obese are also at greater risk for developing major chronic diseases such as type 2 diabetes, cardiovascular diseases, and some cancers. Obesity most likely leads to the onset of most, if not all chronic diseases through direct effects on metabolic dysregulation expressed clinically as hypertension, insulin resistance, hyperinsulinemia, hyperglycemia, dyslipidemia, and low-grade chronic inflammation. Selected obesity-related diseases are discussed in the following sections.

Obesity and Type 2 Diabetes

Obesity and type 2 diabetes are often characterized as the *twin epidemic* or *diabesity* based primarily on their parallel increasing trends in prevalence over the past several decades. Indeed, obesity is considered the strongest modifiable predictor of type 2 diabetes, e.g., recent estimates suggest that nearly 70% of cases in the United States are attributable to overweight and obesity (Eyre et al., 2004; NIDDK, 2008). Prevalence data among older adults, ages 65–74 years, for the United States over the past half-century reflect the close temporal relationship between obesity and diabetes (**Figure 33.7**).

Although the majority of obese people are not diabetic, the risk of type 2 diabetes increases substantially as the BMI increases, particularly within the obese range of BMI (Ogden et al., 2007b;

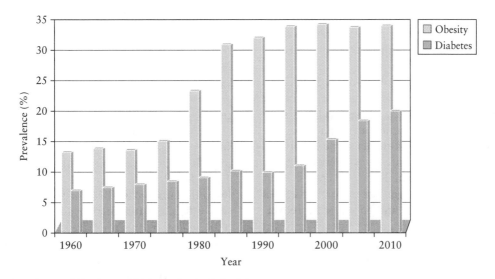

Figure 33.7 Prevalence of Obesity and Diabetes in the United States, 1960–2008.

Source: Data from US National Health and Nutrition Survey (NHANES), 1960-2010; Centers for Disease Control and Prevention (2010). National Center for Chronic Disease Prevention and Health Promotion, Division of Diabetes Translation.

Scott et al., 2006). In a prospective cohort study, researchers at Harvard evaluated diet, lifestyle, and the risk of type 2 diabetes among 84,941 female nurses, ages 30–55 years, enrolled in the Nurses Health Study. The cohort was followed for 16 years (1980–1996). Compared to lean women with BMI < 23, obese women with BMI of 30–35 had a *20-fold* increase in the relative risk of diabetes even after controlling for age, family history of diabetes, menopausal status, postmenopausal hormone therapy, diet, smoking, alcohol intake, and activity levels (Hu et al., 2001).

Haffner and colleagues examined BMI, central obesity (measured by a scapular/tricep skinfold ratio index), fasting glucose, and insulin levels as predictors of *decompensation* in disease progression to incident type 2 diabetes among 474 nondiabetic Mexican Americans. After 8 years of follow-up, 28 nondiabetics developed type 2 diabetes. In univariate analysis, BMI and central obesity were both significantly associated with incident type 2 diabetes, but neither factor retained statistical significance when fasting blood glucose and insulin levels were included in multivariate models. Based on their results, the investigators suggested that obesity may influence the *progression* of hyperglycemia and hyperinsulinemia to type 2 diabetes over a period of many years (Haffner et al., 1990).

While numerous epidemiologic studies have shown that obesity *per se*, as defined by the BMI, is a major risk factor for type 2 diabetes, *weight gain* during adulthood is also strongly associated with the onset of type 2 diabetes, independent of baseline or attained BMI status (Shai et al., 2006; Oguma et al., 2005; Koh-Banerjee et al., 2004; Willett, Dietz, and Colditz, 1999; Colditz et al., 1995; Chan et al., 1994). In addition, the timing and magnitude of adult weight gain may play an important role in determining the age of onset of diabetes.

For example, in a 7-year follow-up study of 7,720 men and 10,371 women enrolled in the *European Prospective Investigation into Cancer and Nutrition (EPIC)-Potsdam Study*, German investigators evaluated BMI history and risk of incident type 2 diabetes. Results revealed that the relative risks were higher for men (RR = 1.25) and women (RR = 1.24) per one unit BMI gain during the younger age interval of 25–40 years than between ages 40 and 55 years. Moreover, high weight gain in the younger age interval resulted in an increased diabetes relative risk for men (RR = 1.5) and women (RR = 4.3) compared to those who were weight stable in early adulthood and who gained weight in later life. Among the younger weight gainers, the average age of onset of diabetes diagnosis also occurred 3–5 years earlier (Schienkiewitz et al., 2006).

Knowler and colleagues conducted a 10-year study of diabetes in a cohort of 3,733 Pima Indians living in Arizona. This special population was found to have one of the highest rates of diabetes in the world (26.5 cases per 1,000 person-years) which was 19-fold higher than a matched US Caucasian population. The incidence increased steadily with increasing body mass measured prior to disease onset, from 0.8 cases per 1,000 person years for individuals with BMI < 20 to 72.2 cases per 1,000 person years for those with BMI > 40. The presence of diabetes in one or both parents also increased the risk. The investigators emphasized the importance of estimating effects of body mass measured prior to disease onset since poorly controlled diabetes can rapidly cause significant weight loss (Knowler et al., 1978, 1979).

Obesity and Cardiovascular Disease

Epidemiologic studies provide unequivocal evidence that obesity is a major risk factor for the development of cardiovascular diseases. Key studies include the US Framingham Study, the Seven Countries Study, the MONICA Project (Multinational Monitoring of trends and determinants in Cardiovascular Disease), the ARIC Study (Atherosclerosis Risk in Communities, USA), the INTERHEART Study, and several others. In brief, obesity (definable as BMI > 30 or waist-to-hip ratio exceeding 1.0 in men or 0.85 in women) significantly elevates the risk of developing coronary heart disease, myocardial infarction, stroke, as well as other forms of cardiovascular disease such as congestive heart failure (Krauss et al., 1998).

Results of a recent meta-analysis are indicative of the major contribution of obesity to the risk of developing coronary heart disease. Investigators in the Netherlands examined obesity and the risk of coronary heart disease in a meta-analysis of 21 prospective cohort studies. Among the 302,296 participants in these studies, 18,000 developed coronary heart disease during follow-up. Estimates of relative risk (RR) were initially adjusted for age, gender, physical activity, and smoking. Compared to normal weight subjects, those who were obese (BMI > 30) were 81% more likely to develop coronary heart disease (RR = 1.81). Results also suggested a modest risk increase for individuals with BMI in the range of 25–29.9 (RR = 1.32). After further adjustment for cholesterol and blood pressure levels, these estimates were reduced (1.49 and 1.17, respectively) but retained statistical significance, leading the authors to conclude that the adverse effects of excess weight on blood pressure and cholesterol may account for a substantial fraction (up to 45%) of the obesity-related risk increase (Bogars et al., 2007).

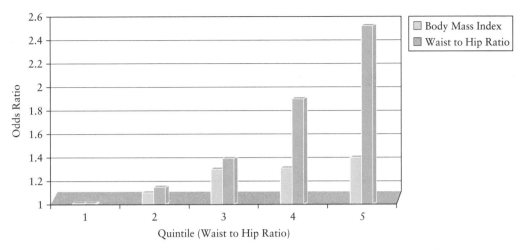

Figure 33.8 Obesity and Myocardial Infarction: Results of INTERHEART.

Source: Data from Yusuf S, Hawken S, Ounpuu S, Bautista L, Franzosi MG, Commerford P, Lang CC, Rumboldt Z, Onen CL, Lisheng L, Tanomsup S, Wangai P Jr, Razak F, Sharma AM, Anand SS; INTERHEART Study Investigators (2005). Obesity and the risk of myocardial infarction in 27,000 participants from 52 countries: a case-control study. *Lancet* 366(9497):1640–1649.

The INTERHEART Study examined obesity and other risk factors for myocardial infarction among 12,461 cases and 13,637 controls ascertained from 52 countries and representing several major ethnic groups. The effects of two measures of obesity were compared, BMI and waist-to-hip ratio. The odds of myocardial infarction increased significantly with each increasing quintile of waist-to-hip ratio (**Figure 33.8**). Men and women in the highest quintile of waist-to-hip ratio were 2.5 times more likely to develop a myocardial infarction compared to those in the lowest quintile. By comparison, those in the highest quintile of BMI were only 1.4 times more likely to suffer a myocardial infarction than those in the lowest quintile. The population attributable fraction estimated from the upper two quintiles of the waist-to-hip ratio was 24.3% compared to only 7.7% for BMI. These results suggest that the waist-to-hip ratio is superior to BMI as a predictor of disease risk (Yusuf et al., 2005).

Yatsuya and colleagues demonstrated that three separate measures of obesity were associated with incident ischemic stroke among 13,549 participants (5,930 men, 7,619 women, 3,694 African Americans, and 9,855 Caucasian Americans) ages 46–64 years enrolled in the US Atherosclerosis Risk in Communities (ARIC) Study. During the follow-up period (1987–2005) a total of 598 individuals suffered ischemic strokes confirmed through hospital discharge records and imaging studies. Using quintiles of BMI, waist circumference, and waist-to-hip ratio, the investigators found that the incidence of

stroke among African Americans was two to three times higher than Caucasian Americans within each obesity quintile. Notably, observed results were similar for all three of the obesity measurements tested. Furthermore, adjustment for hypertension and diabetes markedly attenuated the effects of obesity, suggesting that much of the obesity-related risk of developing a stroke is due to related increases in blood pressure and insulin resistance. Estimates of the population attributable fraction (PAF) due to obesity suggest that 18–20% of the new cases of ischemic stroke are attributable to excess adiposity, which can be measured by BMI > 28.1, waist circumference > 100 cm, or waist-to-hip ratio > 0.95 (Yatsuya et al., 2010).

Obesity and Cancer

According to a report from the American Institute of Cancer Research, more than 100,500 annual cases of cancer and 14–20% of all cancer deaths in the United States can be attributed to excess body fat (World Cancer Research Fund/American Institute for Cancer Research, 2007). The report includes estimates of the percent of cancer cases attributable to obesity (population attributable fractions) for selected cancers based on a review of more than 7,000 publications (**Table 33.2**). The investigators estimate that excess body fat is responsible for approximately 33,000 postmenopausal breast cancers, 21,000 endometrial cancers, 14,000 kidney cancers, 13,000 colorectal cancers, and 12,000 pancreatic cancers per year in the US population.

Table 33.2	Estimated Percent and Number of Cancer Cases Attributed to Obesity in the United States	
Cancer Type	Attributable Fraction	Annual Cases
Endometrium	49%	20,700
Esophagus	35	5,800
Pancreas	28	11,900
Kidney	24	13,900
Gallbladder	21	2,000
Breast	17	33,000
Colon/Rectum	9	13,200
	Total	100,500

Source: Data from World Cancer Research Fund/American Institute for Cancer Research (2007). Food, Nutrition, Physical Activity, and the Prevention of Cancer: A Global Perspective. Washington, DC.

While obesity is a significant risk factor for many cancers, the association of obesity with cancer risk does not affect all subgroups equally. For example, colon cancer risk is higher in obese men than obese women (Pischon, Nothlings, and Boeing, 2007; Calle, 2008), and obesity increases breast cancer risk in postmenopausal women but not premenopausal women (Harris et al., 1992). The increased breast cancer risk in obese postmenopausal women may be due to the fact that adipose tissue [?] is the primary source of estrogens after the menopause.

Hyperinsulinemia, growth factors, sustained low grade inflammation, oxidative stress, and hormonal changes that are associated with excess adiposity are proposed as potential mechanisms that promote the development of cancer (Pischon, Nothlings, and Boeing, 2007; Calle et al., 1999; Calle, 2008). The current body of evidence supports the general recommendation to maintain a healthy weight as part of a comprehensive cancer prevention lifestyle (Byers et al., 2002).

Recent epidemiologic evidence suggests that weight loss can reduce the risk of developing certain malignancies in overweight and obese individuals. The impact of weight loss among young women at high genetic risk for breast cancer was recently demonstrated in a matched pair case control study. The study examined effects of weight loss/gain in 1,073 pairs of genetically susceptible women carrying either the *BRCA1* gene (*n* = 797 pairs) or the *BRCA2* gene (*n* = 276 pairs). Cases with breast cancer were matched to controls by year of birth, mutation (*BRCA1* or *BRCA2*), country of residence and history of ovarian cancer. Results revealed that weight loss of at least

10 pounds between ages 18 and 30 years was associated with a 53% reduction in the risk of subsequently developing breast cancer between the ages of 30 and 49 years (OR = 0.47). Weight gain was not found to significantly influence the subsequent risk of developing breast cancer (Kotsopoulos et al., 2005).

Another study evaluated bariatric surgery (surgical reduction of stomach size for weight loss) among morbidly obese patients and their risk of cancer. Rates of cancer were compared in two observational cohorts of men and women. All patients of both cohorts were morbidly obese (BMI > 40) at baseline. Patients in one cohort received elective bariatric surgery (*n* = 1,035) whereas those in the other did not (*n* = 5,746). The control cohort was developed by matching 5 or 6 control patients to each bariatric case based on the date of first diagnosis of morbid obesity within 2 years, age within 5 years, and gender. Observed average reductions in excess weight and BMI were 62% and 32% in the bariatric cases. After 5 years of follow-up, the observed incidence of cancer in the control cohort was more than four times greater than the bariatric cohort (8.5% vs. 2%). The incidence of breast cancer among women of the control cohort was more than five times greater than the bariatric cohort (6.3% vs. 1.2%). The relative risk in the bariatric cohort (RR = 0.22) is equivalent to an 80% reduction in cancer risk associated with bariatric surgery in the morbidly obese (Christou et al., 2008).

Obesity and Gastroesophageal Reflux Disease (GERD)

Gastroesophageal reflux disease (GERD) is defined by the Brazilian Consensus Conference as "*a chronic disorder related to the retrograde flow of gastroduodenal contents into the esophagus and/or adjacent organs, resulting in a spectrum of symptoms, with or without tissue damage*" (Moraes-Filho et al., 2002). In laymen's terms, GERD is characterized as heartburn or regurgitation two or three times a week (Friedenberg et al., 2008).

Epidemiologic studies have consistently found a positive association between obesity and the development of GERD. Hampel and colleagues at Baylor University in Texas conducted a meta-analysis of nine epidemiologic studies of GERD in which BMI was used to classify individuals as overweight (BMI of 25–30) or obese (BMI > 30). The risk of developing GERD symptoms was significantly elevated for overweight and obese individuals compared to those of normal weight (RR = 1.43 and RR = 1.94, respectively). Risk increases with body mass were also found for comorbid conditions such as erosive esophagitis and esophageal adenocarcinoma, e.g., the risk of developing esophageal cancer was significantly elevated for overweight and obese individuals (RR = 1.52 and RR = 2.78, respectively). The investigators concluded that the risk of developing GERD and related disorders increases with increasing body mass and obesity (Hampel, Abraham, and El-Serag, 2005).

Abdominal or central adiposity is of particular importance in the pathogenesis of GERD and its progression. Complications and comorbid conditions of GERD include erosive esophagitis, Barrett's esophagus (progressive metaplasia and dysplasia of the lower esophagus), and esophageal carcinoma. Epidemiologic studies have consistently shown that specific measures of central obesity, e.g., waist-to-hip ratio or waist circumference, are better predictors of GERD risk and disease progression than BMI. Two examples of such studies are given below.

Investigators in Seoul, Korea, compared BMI and waist circumference as predictors of erosive esophagitis due to gastric reflux in a prospective study of 1,029 subjects. Each subject was examined by endoscopy at baseline and was found to have a normal gastroesophageal junction. Subsequent endoscopic examinations were conducted for study participants after a 3-year interim and 42 subjects had developed erosive esophagitis. In multivariate models, BMI *did not* show statistical significance as a predictor of disease. In contrast, subjects with a waist circumference exceeding 90 cm at baseline were more than seven times more likely (OR = 7.2) to develop erosive esophagitis than subjects with a waist circumference less than 80 cm (Koo et al., 2009).

In a case control study conducted in Seattle, Washington, 193 patients with Barrett's esophagus confirmed by biopsy were compared to 211 population controls without disease. Results showed that central obesity (defined as waist-to-hip ratio in the highest quintile) was associated with a significant increase in the risk of disease. The risk of developing Barrett's esophagus increased more than twofold (OR = 2.4) in subjects with central obesity compared to those with normal girth, and most notably, the risk of advanced disease increased more than fourfold (OR = 4.3) in subjects with central obesity (Edelstein et al., 2007). Comparative models incorporating BMI cut points and waist-to-hip cut points in defining central obesity clearly favor the use of waist-to-hip ratios.

The pathogenesis and progression of GERD in patients with central obesity may be a consequence of several biologically plausible mechanisms. Magnanimous abdominal girth may cause hiatal hernia and excessive reflux of acid from the stomach into the esophagus by increasing intra-abdominal pressure (Fisichella and Patti, 2009; Herbella and Patti, 2010). Also, visceral fat is more metabolically active

than subcutaneous fat or peripheral fat, capable of producing a multitude of bioactive proteins (adipokines), including proinflammatory cytokines such as interleukin 6 and tumor necrosis factor-α (Lundgren et al., 2004; Einstein et al., 2005). Visceral adiposity therefore heightens the proinflammatory acidic environment of GERD, and heightened activity of cytokines, cyclooxygenase-2 (COX-2), prostaglandin E2 (PGE2), and leptin may accelerate the progression of GERD to erosive esophagitis, Barrett's esophagus, and esophageal adenocarcinoma (Ogunwobi, Mutungi, and Peales, 2006; Friedenberg et al., 2008).

Estrogens may also play a role in the development of GERD among the obese. Magnus Nilsson of the Karolinska Hospital, Stockholm, and his associates found a stronger relationship between BMI and GERD among young, severely obese premenopausal women (OR = 6.8) compared with men (OR = 3.3) and postmenopausal women (OR = 4.2) at the same BMI level. Results prompted the investigators to theorize that the association between estrogen and GERD is a nitric oxide mediated reduction in smooth muscle tone at the lower esophageal sphincter. Obese women have increased aromatase-catalyzed estrone production by fatty tissue, lower concentrations of sex hormone binding globulin, and thus a larger proportion of unbound active estradiol. Excess estrogen increases nitric oxide synthesis (the primary relaxing molecule at the lower esophageal sphincter) which leads to reduced sphincter tone and increased acid reflux (Nilsson et al., 2003).

While research indicates that obesity is a major risk factor for the development of GERD, traditional weight loss programs have not shown consistent success in reducing symptoms. Two studies found no changes in reflux parameters or measures of esophageal acid (Kjellin et al., 1996; Fredericksen et al., 2000) whereas one study did observe improved gastroesophageal function due to a dietary exercise-based weight loss program (Fraser-Moodie et al., 1999). Surgically induced weight loss by the *Roux-en-Y gastric bypass procedure* has shown predominantly positive effects in patients with GERD although the majority of studies are case reports (Suter et al., 2003).

Obesity and Obstructive Sleep Apnea

Obstructive sleep apnea is a respiratory condition characterized by repeated episodes of upper airway collapse during sleep. Results of numerous epidemiologic investigations suggest that obesity is a major risk factor for the development of obstructive sleep apnea. The disorder is particularly prominent among men with abdominal (central) obesity (Young, Pappard, and Gottlieb, 2002).

Investigators at the University of Wisconsin in Madison studied a random sample of 603 men and women using overnight polysomnography to determine the frequency of episodes of apnea and hypopnea per hour of sleep (the *apnea-hypopnea index*). Abnormal index values (5 or more episodes per hour) were found in 24% of men and 9% of women. Results suggested that each 1 standard deviation increase in BMI was associated with a four-fold increase in the risk of developing sleep apnea (Young et al., 1993). Investigators at Johns Hopkins University in Baltimore studied sleep disorders in 150 obese men who were otherwise in good health. Estimates of the prevalence of sleep apnea varied from 40–60% depending on the severity of symptoms (Punjaba et al., 2002).

Some studies suggest that the prevalence of sleep apnea is higher in men than women. For example, investigators at Pennsylvania State University studied 200 obese women and 50 obese men using several measures of sleep disturbance in an 8-hour sleep laboratory. They detected obstructive sleep apnea in 20 men (40%) but only 6 women (6%) (Vgontzas et al., 1994).

In a study of data from the 2002 *US National Hospital Discharge Survey* (NHDS), Scott and colleagues examined the prevalence of sleep apnea and other disorders among 3,473 morbidly obese patients, 833 of whom underwent bariatric surgery. Patients electing bariatric surgery had higher prevalence rates of sleep apnea than patients receiving other forms of treatment (24% vs. 11%) and men had higher rates of sleep apnea than women (47.3% vs. 19% among bariatric patients and 17.2% vs. 8.7% among all other patients). These results suggest that severe cases of morbid obesity (those who receive bariatric surgery) have a markedly increased risk of developing obstructive sleep apnea and, furthermore, that men are more susceptible than women (Scott et al., 2006). In a much smaller investigation of sleep disturbances in the morbidly obese, investigators at the University of Helsinki, Finland, studied sleep apnea in 27 morbidly obese patients including 13 men and 14 women. Obstructive sleep apnea was diagnosed in 10 men (78%) but only 1 woman (7%) (Rajala et al., 1991).

On the contrary, other studies have found similar rates of sleep apnea in population samples of men and women, as well as relatively high rates of disease among obese women. A study of sleep disturbances in a Spanish cohort comprised of 1,050 men and 1,098 women found similar prevalence levels of mild sleep apnea (5 or more episodes of apnea/ hypopnea per hour) in men (26%) and women (28%). Notably, the prevalence of sleep apnea became higher in men with increasing severity, e.g., severe sleep apnea (15 or more episodes) was twice as common in men compared to women (14% vs. 7%) (Durán et al., 2001). Investigators in Australia studied sleep disturbances among 108 obese women using overnight ambulatory measures and found that 41 patients (38%) met the threshold criteria for obstructive sleep apnea (Richman et al., 1994). Thus, while increasing obesity may exacerbate the risk more so in men than women, it is clear that obese women should also be considered at high risk for the development of obstructive sleep apnea.

Biological mechanisms by which central obesity predisposes to obstructive sleep apnea include anatomic alterations and/or disturbances in upper airway neuromuscular control. The heightened predisposition in men versus women may be related to androgenic hormonal factors or the predominantly abdominal (central) distribution of body fat in aging men. Central adiposity is likely to cause excess deposition of fat in the head and neck which in turn predisposes to narrowing and closure of the upper airways. In addition, signaling proteins secreted by visceral adipose could diminish neuromuscular control of the airways (Schwartz et al., 1998; Gibson, 2005).

In several epidemiologic studies, both weight gain and weight loss have been shown to influence the risk of developing sleep apnea. For example, in a prospective study of 690 randomly selected employed residents of Wisconsin conducted during 1989–2000, individuals who gained 10% in weight increased their odds of developing mild sleep apnea by 32% compared to those with stable weight, whereas those who lost 10% of their initial body weight decreased their disease odds by 26%. In addition, a 10% increase in weight was associated with a sixfold increase in the odds of developing moderate to severe sleep apnea (Peppard et al., 2000).

Therapeutic effects of moderate weight loss were demonstrated in a study of 15 hypersomnolent patients with moderately severe obstructive sleep apnea. In overweight patients who reduced their weight by 9%, apnea frequency fell and sleep patterns improved (P < 0.01). No improvement occurred among the age-and weight-matched controls who did not lose weight (Smith et al., 1985).

Obstructive sleep apnea has also been shown to improve or resolve as a result of surgically induced weight loss. In a systematic review of 134 extracted bariatric surgical studies worldwide from 1990 to 2003 (56 in North America, 58 in Europe, and 20 throughout the rest of the world) involving a total of 22,094 patients, nearly 20% of patients were diagnosed with sleep disorder breathing (sleep apnea) preoperatively. After surgery, substantial weight loss was attained across all measures of adiposity. Significant reductions were observed in average BMI (14.2 units) and absolute weight (39.7 kg) and obstructive sleep apnea resolved in 85.7% of patients (Buchwald, Avidor, and Braunwald, 2004)

Obesity and Osteoarthritis

Osteoarthritis, also called *degenerative joint disease* is a common progressive disorder usually manifesting in late adulthood principally affecting the weight-bearing joints of the body (knees, hips, and vertebral column). Other joints commonly affected are those subjected to sustained repetitive mechanical stress and trauma over the lifespan such as the distal finger joints and the thumb joint. Osteoarthritis is characterized clinically by pain, inflammation, deformity, and limitation of motion and pathologically by the erosion and destruction of cartilage, sclerosis (scarring), and other pathologic lesions in the joints. Radiographic studies reveal the presence of at least subclinical osteoarthritis in the majority of adults over the age of 65 years. Progressive disease is a leading cause of disability in many populations (Fletcher and Lewis-Fanning, 1945; Mankin, 1974; Robbins and Cotran, 1979; Raynauld et al., 2006).

The strong association between obesity and osteoarthritis of the major weight-bearing joints has been widely verified. Leach and colleagues found that 83% of their female subjects with knee osteoarthritis were obese compared to 42% of the control group (Leach, Baumgard, and Broom, 1973). In the Framingham Study, Felson and colleagues demonstrated that a 5.1 kg loss in body mass over a 10-year period reduced the odds of developing knee osteoarthritis by more than 50% (Felson et al., 1992). In a case-control study of 675 matched pairs conducted in the United Kingdom, Coggon and colleagues determined that the risk of knee osteoarthritis in people with a BMI > 30 was 6.8 times that of normal weight controls (Coggon et al., 2001). Using data from the 1982–1984 US National Health and Nutrition Examination Survey (NHANES I), Ettinger and colleagues examined the effects of comorbid diseases on disability and found that people with a BMI > 30 were 4.2 times more likely to have knee osteoarthritis than leaner people (Ettinger et al., 1994). Taken together, these studies indicate that obesity is a major risk factor for osteoarthritis of weight-bearing joints and associated functional impairment. Physiologic processes related to the increased susceptibility of obese individuals to osteoarthritis include greater joint stress, diminished muscle strength, and increased inflammation (Messier, 2008).

Obesity and Quality of Life

In addition to substantial morbidity and increased risk of premature mortality, obesity is also associated with decreases in the overall quality of life. The *quality-adjusted life years (QALY)* is a population health outcome summary measure that quantifies the impact of both the duration of life and the quality of life for a specific period of time (Zeckhauser and Shepard, 1976; Gold, Stevenson, and Fryback, 2002; Sassi, 2006).

Calculation of the QALY for a particular disease is calculated from the number of years lived without the disease (Y1) and the number of years lived with the disease (Y2). Each year of healthy life is assigned the value of 1.0 whereas subpar health due to disease is assigned a lower value between 0 and 1. Death has a value of zero. Thus, the QALY for obesity would be estimated for a given individual as QALY = Y1 × 1.0 + Y2 × q where Y1 denotes the years lived at normal weight, Y2 denotes the years lived with obesity, and q is the quality of life weighting factor for obesity.

Using data from the 2003–2008 US Behavioral Risk Factor Surveillance System (BRFSS), Jia and Lubetkin calculated the *loss of QALYs* among US adults due to obesity-related morbidity and mortality. Estimates of QALYs lost for US adults were calculated as the sum of QALYs lost due to morbidity and future QALYs lost in expected life years due to premature deaths. Results revealed that the loss of QALYs for all adults more than doubled from 1993–2008, while the prevalence of obesity increased from 14.1–26.7% during the same time frame. In addition, the loss of QALYs among African American women was 31% higher than African American men and approximately 50% higher than Caucasian men or women. A strong positive correlation was found between the percentage of state populations reporting no leisure time activity and the obesity-related QALYs lost ($r = 0.71$). The investigators suggest there is a critical need for effective programs to reduce obesity at local, state, and national levels (Jia and Lubetkin, 2010).

MECHANISMS OF PATHOGENESIS IN OBESITY-RELATED DISEASES

Obesity and excess weight increase the mechanical stress and strain on multiple systems of the human body. Browning and Kram examined differences in biomechanical load between obese and normal-weight individuals during walking. They found that obese individuals exerted 60% greater vertical ground reaction forces compared to normal-weight people (Browning and Kram, 2007). Obesity may also lead to the compression of blood vessels and body organs, thereby creating mechanical resistance and distortion of normal function.

White adipose tissue (WAT), which includes the energy storage fat cells (adipocytes), along with several other cell types (neurons, endothelial cells, stromovascular cells, and immune cells) was once considered an inert tissue primarily responsible for storing or releasing energy as required. Within the past several decades, adipose tissue has been found to play a critical role in whole body metabolic regulation and cellular energy homeostasis. It is now known that adipose tissue is an active endocrine organ that secretes a variety of proinflammatory bioactive proteins, collectively called *adipokines* or *adipocytokines* (Lyon, Law, and Hsueh, 2003). Adipokines such as leptin, resistin, adiponectin, interleukin-6 (IL-6), and tumor necrosis factor-alpha (TNF-α) influence many physiologic processes including body weight homeostasis, insulin resistance, lipid levels, blood pressure, coagulation, inflammation, and atherosclerosis.

Grossly enlarged adipocytes associated with obesity release proinflammatory adipokines that simultaneously promote atherogenesis and insulin resistance (Leonhardt et al., 1972; Weyer et al., 2000; Lonn et al., 2010) (**Figure 33.9**). Resistin and TNF-α downregulate insulin receptors, decrease GLUT-4 translocation to the cellular membrane, inhibit lipoprotein lipase activity, and increase hormone sensitive lipase. Plasminogen activator inhibitor (PAI-1)

and angiotensinogen enhance thrombus (clot) formation and reduce local blood flow, and interleukin-6 (IL-6) and C-reactive protein (CRP) stimulate macrophage infiltration and complement activation. There is also an endocrine response via the synthesis and secretion of leptin, which acts on the hypothalamic-pituitary axis to decrease food intake and increase energy expenditure. The single adipokine that is clearly reduced with obesity is adiponectin, which has anti-inflammatory properties that increase insulin sensitivity and reduce atherogenesis (Fruhbeck et al., 2001; Lyon, Law, and Hsueh, 2003; Kadowaki and Yamauchi, 2005). As pointed out by Lyon, Law, and Hsueh (2003):

> "*Adipose tissue is a dynamic endocrine organ that secretes a number of factors that are increasingly recognized to contribute to systemic and vascular inflammation. Obesity promotes the parallel progression of insulin resistance to type 2 diabetes and endothelial dysfunction to atherosclerosis.*"

OBESITY AND ATHEROGENESIS

The "response to injury hypothesis" proposes that atherogenesis (atherosclerosis) is an inflammatory disease (Ross and Glomset, 1973, 1976). According to this hypothesis, injury to the endothelial lining of the artery stimulates an inflammatory response resulting in smooth muscle proliferation and subsequently, infiltration of the wound by macrophages and other inflammatory cells. Without resolution, recursive cycles of chronic inflammation ensue, leading to the release of hydrolytic enzymes, cytokines, chemokines, and growth factors that cause further cellular damage and eventually produce focal areas of cell necrosis. As stated by Ross, "*Each characteristic lesion of atherosclerosis represents a different stage in a chronic inflammatory process in the artery; if unabated and excessive, this process will result in an advanced complicated lesion*" (Ross, 1999).

In the human system, the presence of excess white adipose tissue (WAT) that is characteristic of obesity has been found to induce a persistent state of low grade inflammation. Excess calories are stored in fat cells (adipocytes) of WAT in the form of triacylglycerol, and in times of caloric restriction, free fatty acids are mobilized and released into the blood. The expansion of WAT with obesity is accompanied by angiogenesis (formation of new blood vessels), increased proliferation of fibroblasts, and infiltration by macrophages. There is also increased secretion of interleukins, inflammatory cytokines, and adipokines.

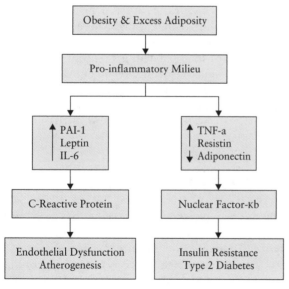

Figure 33.9 Obesity and Adipokines.

Source: Data from Lyon CJ, Law RE, Hsueh WA (2003). Minireview: Adiposity, inflammation, and atherogenesis. *Endocrinology* 144:2195–2200.

Investigations by Fain and colleagues have demonstrated that leptin and adiponectin are primarily secreted by the adipoctyes (fat cells) whereas other inflammatory mediators are released by both fat cells and nonfat cells of the WAT cellular milieu (Fain, 2006). With obesity, elevated levels of circulating autocrine, paracrine, and endocrine factors derived primarily from the excess visceral WAT are capable of inducing sustained inflammation and atherogenesis.

In a review of pathogenic mechanisms of adiposity, Lyon, Law, and Hsueh describe how several proinflammatory cytokines and adipokines contribute to atherogenesis. According to their model of obesity-related atherogenesis, rising levels of adipokines and cytokines including leptin, resistin, TNF-α, interleukin-6 (IL-6), angiotensin II (Ang II), and plasminogen activator inhibitor-1 (PAI-1) initiate endothelial dysfunction through activation of the nuclear transcription factor, nuclear factor kappa beta (NF-κb). A cascade of inflammatory changes in vascular tissue occurs, including the migration and attachment of monocytes to the arterial wall and their subsequent conversion to macrophages. Chronic inflammation ensues as macrophage activation results in the release of hydrolytic enzymes, cytokines, chemokines, and an increase in oxidative stress, which leads to focal necrosis and the eventual formation of atherosclerotic plaque (Lyon, Law, and Hsueh, 2003).

The obesity-related proinflammatory milieu of WAT-derived cytokines and adipokines (particularly IL-6) stimulates the production of *C-reactive protein* (*CRP*) by the liver. C-reactive protein is an *acute phase protein* whose concentration in the blood is increased in both acute and chronic inflammatory states. Its primary physiologic function is to assist complement binding to foreign and damaged cells and enhance phagocytosis by macrophages. Individuals without inflammation usually have CRP levels below 1.0 μg/mL. Patients with bacterial infections, autoimmune diseases, or cancer can have elevated CRP of 100 μg/mL or higher, making CRP a nonspecific marker for inflammation. Despite the lack of specificity, CRP has emerged as one of the most powerful predictors of cardiovascular risk (Yeh and Willerson, 2003).

It has been well established in numerous prospective studies that an elevated serum concentration of CRP (even within a "normal" range of values, 1–5 μg/mL) is a risk factor for cardiovascular disease and has significant predictive value for cardiovascular events (Koenig, 2003; Yeh and Willerson, 2003). Examination of *both* CRP and cholesterol levels is particularly valuable in risk prediction. For example, Ridker and colleagues demonstrated that the combination of elevated levels of CRP (> 2.11 μg/L) and total cholesterol (> mg/dL) was associated with a fivefold increase in the risk of first myocardial infarction, more than double the relative risk for either factor alone. Furthermore, those in the top quintile of *both* CRP and the ratio of total cholesterol to high density lipoprotein exhibited an 8.7-fold increase in risk compared to relative risks of 4.2 and 2.2, respectively, for individual factors (Ridker, Glynn, and Hennekins, 1998). Prospective studies have also demonstrated that CRP is a predictor for cardiovascular morbidity, mortality, and/or recurrent coronary events among individuals with known cardiovascular disease, unstable and stable angina, and prior myocardial infarction (Rifai and Ridker, 2001). In addition to being a biologic marker of inflammation, CRP appears to activate complement in atherosclerotic plaques, thereby increasing the risk of thrombotic complications and vascular damage (Yasojima et al., 2001).

Many epidemiologic studies have found a strong positive association between obesity (body mass) and serum levels of CRP. Hak and coworkers examined relationships of CRP, obesity, common carotid intima-media thickness, and insulin resistance among 186 healthy middle-aged women from the general population. In regression models, BMI and waist circumference were significant predictors of CRP; and CRP was in turn associated with several variables related to insulin resistance and subclinical atherosclerosis including blood pressure, insulin level, high density lipoprotein cholesterol, triglycerides, apolipoprotein A1 (inversely), plasminogen activator inhibitor-1 antigen, and tissue type plasminogen activator antigen. These results suggest that inflammatory mediators derived from adipose and linked to CRP may play an important role in the development of insulin resistance and coronary heart disease (Hak et al., 1999).

Yudkin and colleagues examined correlations of CRP and concentrations of proinflammatory adipokines, interleukin-6 (IL-6), and TNF-α among 107 nondiabetic adults ascertained from a medical practice in London. Statistically significant correlations were observed between CRP, IL-6, and TNF-α. In contrast, correlations of CRP with *Helicobacter pylori*, *Chlamydia pneumoniae*, and cytomegalovirus antibody titers were weak or nonsignificant. Furthermore, CRP was significantly related to insulin resistance, blood pressure, high-density lipoproteins, and markers of endothelial dysfunction, such as von Willebrand factor, tissue plasminogen activator, and cellular fibronectin. These data suggest that chronic bacterial or viral infections are *not* important determinants of low-level chronic inflammation, whereas adipocyte-related inflammatory molecules (CRP, IL-6, and TNF-α) may induce insulin resistance, endothelial dysregulation, and atherogenesis. Results infer a critical molecular link between obesity and increased risk of cardiovascular disease (Yudkin et al., 1999).

Tchernof and colleagues investigated obesity, caloric restriction, weight loss, and CRP in 61 obese postmenopausal Caucasian women in Vermont. Total body fat was measured by dual X-ray absorptiometry and intra-abdominal fat was measured by computerized tomography. Both measures of obesity were significant predictors of plasma CRP. Twenty-five of the women completed a 13-month weight loss protocol involving caloric restriction (1,200 kcals daily) with no change in physical activity levels. Weight loss averaged approximately 15 kg and resulted in a significant decrease in plasma CRP (P < 0.0001). Compared to visceral fat measures, overall body fatness was a better predictor of plasma CRP in multivariate regression analyses (Tchernof et al., 2002).

Plasminogen activator inhibitor-1 (*PAI-1*) is an adipokine that inhibits the breakdown of fibrin clots, thus increasing the risk for thromboembolic events. In molecular studies of adipose from morbidly obese women, Fain and colleagues demonstrated that *visceral adipose tissue* released greater amounts of vascular endothelial growth factor, IL-6, and PAI-1 compared with abdominal subcutaneous tissue (Fain et al., 2004). This finding may help explain the stronger association of abdominal obesity with an increased risk of stroke and other thromboembolic cardiovascular events (Yatsuya et al., 2010; Suk et al., 2003).

Obesity and Insulin Resistance

As lipid-laden adipocytes reach their threshold of fat storage, the white adipose tissue (WAT) releases a variety of pro-inflammatory adipokines and cytokines that contribute to insulin resistance and the development of type 2 diabetes. For example, TNF-α inhibits tyrosine kinase phosphorylation of the insulin receptor, resulting in defects in insulin signaling and ultimately leading to insulin resistance and impaired glucose transport. Contributing to the process, circulating levels of resistin and other inflammatory factors rise and levels of adiponectin fall (resistin increases insulin resistance and inflammation whereas adiponectin improves insulin sensitivity and inhibits vascular inflammation). Without intervention, these inflammatory processes continue unabated, resulting in hyperinsulinemia, hyperglycemia, dyslipidemia, and eventual lipotoxicity and glucotoxicity of nonadipose tissue, including the

β-cells of the pancreas (Unger, 2003). Furthermore, functional deterioration of the pancreatic β cells and insulin insufficiency may contribute to the development of type 2 diabetes (Wajchenberg, 2000).

OVERVIEW OF ADIPOCYTE REGULATORY PROCESSES

Over the past several decades, researchers have developed a better understanding of how adipose tissue helps to regulate energy homeostasis and metabolism. A relatively new obesity-chronic disease paradigm is emerging which is focused on adipose tissue physiology and the role of feedback mechanisms which respond to disruptions in adipocyte homeostasis (Larsen, Toubro, and Astrup, 2003; Scott et al., 2004; Löfgren et al., 2005; Skurk, Alberti-Huber, and Hauner, 2006; Rosen and MacDougald, 2006; Maffeis et al., 2007; Sethi and Vidal-Puig, 2007; Iozzo, 2009; Arner and Spalding, 2010).

Adiposity encompasses fat cell number (cellularity) and fat cell size. Adipose tissue serves important physiologic functions that include protecting vital organs, helping to preserve heat through insulation, and energy storage. *White adipose tissue* (WAT) is the repository or storage vesicle for excess energy in the form of triglycerides (triacylglycerol). White adipose tissue (WAT) acts to buffer energy imbalances when energy intake is not equal to energy output and thus provides a normal dynamic physiologic storage space for excess energy in long-term generally calorically stable environments (Faust and Miller, 1983).

Fat Storage (Lipogenesis)

Excess fat is stored in the adipocytes (fat cells) of WAT by a process known as lipogenesis. When the caloric intake of fat, carbohydrate, and protein is greater than the energy expenditure, the liver converts the excess calories to fat in the form of triglycerides. Triglycerides are transported in the blood from the liver to WAT by lipid carriers called lipoproteins. Chylomicrons carry dietary triglycerides from the breakdown of fat, while very low density lipoproteins (VLDL) carry endogenously formed triglycerides converted from excess glucose (the basic unit of carbohydrates) and amino acids (basic units of protein). Triglyceride molecules are broken down to their constituent parts of fatty acids and glycerol in the cell membrane of adipocytes (fat cells) by the enzyme *lipoprotein lipase*. Fatty acids are then able to enter into the adipocyte where they are repackaged as triacylglycerol and stored (the overall process is called *lipogenesis*). Insulin, produced by the beta (β)-cells of the pancreas, is secreted into the blood in response to elevated blood glucose and is the prime mediator of adipocyte glucose uptake to furnish the energy required for lipogenesis.

Fat Breakdown (Lipolysis)

When long-term energy intake does not meet energy requirements, stored triacylglycerol within adipocytes is broken down by *hormone sensitive lipase* to free fatty acids that are released from the fat cell to be used for energy by tissues of the body (the overall process is called *lipolysis*). Subsequently, the adipocytes become smaller. At a given level of excess energy, adipocyte size is proportionate to the number of fat cells. More fat cells equate to more storage space with which to store excess energy, while fewer fat cells place a greater burden of storage on individual fat cells. Fat cell size can therefore be viewed as a measure of the excess energy that is stored by the body at any given time.

Homeostatic regulation of lipogenesis and lipolysis depends upon the presence of adequate normal functioning WAT. To illustrate, studies of transgenic *lipoatrophic* (fatless) mice, reveal that the absence of fat cells results in severe metabolic dysregulation including hypertriglyceridemia, hyperinsulinemia, hyperglycemia, dyslipidemia, insulin resistance, and type 2 diabetes. In other words, with no fat cells to store excess energy, the fatless mice present clinically as if they were obese. Notably, surgical transplantation of WAT to fatless mice reverses diabetes, normalizes glycemia and insulinemia, and improves blood lipids, demonstrating that the lack of adipose tissue is the cause of the insulin resistance (Gavrilova et al., 2000). The physiologic mechanisms responsible for these effects have not been fully clarified. One hypothesis is that elevated levels of circulating triglycerides and free fatty acids may interfere with insulin-dependent glucose transport in muscle, leading to insulin resistance and type 2 diabetes (Kim and Moustaid-Mousa, 2000).

Secretion of Adipokines by Adipocytes

Adipocytes actively participate in maintaining energy homeostasis by synthesizing and secreting a multitude of autocrine, paracrine, and endocrine signaling proteins such as hormones, complement components, growth factors, and cytokines collectively called adipokines (Bays, Mandarino, and DeFronzo, 2004; Ravussin and Smith, 2002; Fruhbeck et al., 2001; Marques, Hauman, and Martin, 1998). Adipokine levels are strongly influenced by changes in the cellular storage of fat and related gains (or losses) in whole body weight. For example, leptin concentrations

increase as fat cell size increases and *decrease* as fat cell size decreases (Löfgren et al., 2005). The increase in leptin with obesity and increased fat cell size acts to *decrease* food intake and *increase* energy expenditure. Reciprocally, adiponectin levels are *reduced* in obesity and *increase* with weight loss (Fruhbeck et al., 2001; Ziccardi et al., 2002; Löfgren et al., 2005). In this manner, adipocyte signaling proteins appear to work in concert, regulating metabolism and maintaining energy homeostasis both locally and distally.

Fat cells secrete adipokines as a direct response to their energy storage capacity (Kim, 2000; Fruhbeck et al., 2001; Skurk et al., 2006). As excess energy in the form of triacylglycerol is stored in adipocytes, individual fat cells can increase tremendously in size (undergo *hypertrophy*) with the ability to expand twenty-fold in diameter and over one thousand-fold in volume (Hewitt, 1997; Björnheden et al., 2004). However, each cell can only store so much excess energy (as triacylglycerol) and when its storage capacity is surpassed, proinflammatory adipokines are secreted.

The adipocyte response to hypertophy is an *epigenetic phenomenon* leading to the overexpression of specific genes that encode proinflammatory adipokines. One factor that may induce such genetic expression is the physical stress and strain that wounds the plasma membrane of fat-laden cells. Indeed, plasma membrane wounding is considered the principal mechano-sensing event that initiates the inflammatory response (Vlahakis and Hubmayr, 2005; Zeghari, 2000). This may help explain why enlarged fat cells elicit an inflammatory response, while increased numbers of fat cells do not.

Tissue hypoxia associated with increasing fat mass may also play a role. Excess adiposity increases the demand for oxygen to support tissue remodeling and vascularization (Attie and Scherer, 2009). If the oxygen demand of excess adipose tissue exceeds the oxygen supply, hypoxia could induce the expression of genes such as *hypoxia inducible factor-1a* (*HIF-1a*) which triggers *cyclooxygenase-2* (*COX-2*) and the proinflammatory milieu observed with obesity (Yin et al., 2009).

Fat Cell Size, Number, and Turnover in Humans

Many studies have found that a significant loss of weight and fat mass in humans results in a decrease in volume (size) of adipocytes but produces no change in adipocyte number. As an example, the involuntary weight loss associated with cachexia in patients with advanced cancer causes a decrease in adipocyte size but no change in number. Reciprocally, significant weight gain in adults increases adipocyte size but also produces no net change in number. One interpretation of these findings is that weight changes in adulthood are primarily due to increases in adipocyte volume and size rather than number (Arner and Spalding, 2010).

Early investigations of human adipose tissue by Jules Hirsch and Bruce Batchelor at Rockefeller University in New York suggested that all human obesity is characterized by adipocyte hypertrophy and when body weight exceeds 170% of ideal, the maximum cell size increases to approximately twice that of normal cells. But they also found that increasing severity of obesity is correlated with increasing hyperplasia of adipocytes, and that hypercellularity (increased adipocyte number) is characteristic of the early onset of obesity (Hirsch and Batchelor, 1976).

While lipid storage in mature fat cells is undoubtedly of major importance, recent investigations suggest that the number of fat cells is also an important determinant of fat mass. Using an innovative molecular technique, Spalding and colleagues studied the dynamics of fat cell turnover among cohorts of adults in the United States. Fat cell turnover was assessed using measures of ^{14}C integrated into genomic DNA during nuclear testing. Results indicate that the number of fat cells remains constant in lean and obese adults even after marked weight loss, indicating that the number of adipocytes is fixed early in life. Nevertheless, approximately 10% of fat cells die and are replaced annually at all adult ages and levels of body mass index, *vis-à-vis*, approximately 50% of fat cells are replaced every 8 years. Furthermore, neither adipocyte death nor generation rate is altered in early obesity, suggesting that fat cell number is under tight genetic regulation (Spalding et al., 2008).

According to these observations on the rate of human fat cell turnover, individuals with a large number of fat cells have a greater inherent fat storage capacity than individuals with small numbers. It is therefore possible to categorize obesity into two types: hypertrophic obesity (increased adipocyte volume) and hyperplastic obesity (increased adipoctye number). An important finding from *in vitro* and *in vivo* animal studies is that progenitor (stem) cells present in adipose tissue can be stimulated to proliferate and differentiate into mature adipocytes. The data suggest that progenitor cells are recruited to become mature adipocytes at the same rate that adipocytes die. Under normal conditions, the fat mass is therefore in a constant state of flux whereby the adipocyte number remains relatively constant (Arner and Spalding, 2010).

Multiple molecular factors are undoubtedly involved in the differentiation of progenitor stem cells into adipocytes. Recent studies suggest that in the presence of excess energy, fibroblast-like precursor cells are stimulated to differentiate into new adipocytes by activation of the nuclear receptor peroxisome proliferator-activated receptor-gamma (PPAR-γ), a major regulator of adipogenesis (Larsen, Toubro, and Astrup, 2003; Grun and Blumberg, 2006), thereby increasing fat cell number (*hyperplasia*) and expanding energy storage capacity (Rosenbaum and Leibel, 1998; Marques, Hauman, and Martin, 1998; Hube and Hauner, 2000; Danforth, 2000; Hausman, DiGirolamo, and Bartness, 2001; Fruhbeck et al., 2001). In other words, as Rosen and MacDougald (2006) correctly explain: "*adipocytes provide a safe place to store lipids.*"

Brown Adipose Tissue

While the role of WAT is primarily that of energy storage and homeostasis, brown adipose tissue (BAT) is principally involved in classic cold-induced nonshivering thermogenesis for the purpose of producing heat to help regulate body temperature (Cannon and Nedergaard, 2004). Facultative thermogenesis, defined as heat production in response to cold temperature, occurs in skeletal muscle and BAT. Skeletal muscle produces heat via shivering thermogenesis, while nonshivering thermogenesis (characteristic of human newborns) occurs in BAT (Argyropoulos and Harper, 2002).

BAT is abundant in small mammals and hibernating animals and constitutes about 5% of the body weight of human newborn infants. Its presence in newborns is of great importance to avoid hypothermia. Brown fat is highly innervated and vascularized and the cells have abundant mitochondria. Brown fat efficiently produces heat in response to signals from the sympathetic nervous system. In cold temperatures, a special uncoupling protein 1 (UCP1) is activated within the mitochondria, resulting in uncoupling of oxidative phosphorylation and heat production (Lowell, 1998). Brown fat diminishes rapidly during infancy and is negligible in human adults. Adaptive thermogenesis and the dissipation of energy through heat production are possible targets for obesity intervention (Lowell and Spiegelman, 2000).

RISK FACTORS OF OBESITY

The genesis of obesity is multifactorial, involving both modifiable and nonmodifiable risk factors and determinants (**Table 33.3**). For any individual, the development of obesity is a result of the interaction

Table 33.3	Selected Determinants of Obesity		
Modifiable	**Non-Modifiable**	**Environmental**	
Energy Input Excess calories from high fat, high sugar, and energy-dense diet	Gender, aging, ethnicity, genetics, prenatal & postnatal effects, menopause, psychological and physiologic factors	Built Environment Motorized transportation, mechanization, and automation	
Energy Output Sedentary lifestyle with low exercise and low physical activity		Food Policy Marketing, cost, quality, access, and availability	

of behavioral, environmental, sociocultural, and genetic factors that collectively tip the energy balance in favor of excess energy that is stored as fat.

The dramatic global rise in the prevalence of obesity during the past several decades has led some investigators to rule out a genetic basis for the obesity epidemic on the rationale that, collectively, the population gene pool could not have changed significantly in such a short period of time (Stunkard et al., 1986; Heindel, 2003; Christakis and Fowler, 2007; Wardle et al., 2008). The obesity epidemic has therefore, more often been described as resulting from contemporary "obesity-promoting" environmental factors interacting with relatively stable, but underlying genes among those who are susceptible in the population (Flegal and Troiano, 2000). As a consequence, public health and health behavior research and intervention programs have focused primarily on social and environmental determinants, which generally refer to a myriad of multilevel factors that influence, either directly or indirectly, the two predominant behaviors that impact energy balance: dietary intake and physical activity.

In addition to the traditional perspective that energy excess leads to the subsequent development of obesity, emerging factors which have generated interest as potential contributors to the secular increase in obesity include dietary factors, genetic predisposition, demography (age, longevity, gender, ethnicity), maternal influence during the perinatal period, psychological stressors (sleep debt, emotional stress, depression), physiologic factors (adiposity rebound and fat cell dynamics), food marketing strategies and food access, economic advances (urbanization, automation, and mechanization), organic pollutants (endocrine disruptors), assortative mating, and pharmaceuticals that influence weight (Crovetti et al., 1997; Grun and Blumberg, 2006; Keith et al., 2006; Economic Research Service, 2010). Selected risk factors are discussed in the following sections.

Genetics of Obesity

The marked increase in the prevalence of obesity in the last three decades has led some investigators to question the importance of genetics in the etiology of obesity (O'Rahilly and Farooqi, 2006). Though it is well established that obesity runs in families, family members tend to share similar environments and behaviors in their patterns of diet and exercise. Furthermore, in the vast majority of families studied, obesity does not segregate with a mendelian pattern of inheritance. Still, the available evidence clearly reflects significant genetic impact on measures of body mass and obesity. The genetic factors that influence obesity can be classified into three broad categories.

Monogenic forms of obesity are caused by single gene mutations that are extremely rare. Examples include genetic deficiencies in key hormones that regulate appetite and metabolism such as melanocortin and leptin (Farooqi and O'Rahilly, 2005a, 2007).

Syndromic forms of obesity, of which there are approximately 30 rare syndromes, arise from discrete genetic defects or chromosomal abnormalities. Such syndromes are often associated with mental impairment, dimorphic features and developmental abnormalities, e.g., Prader Willi syndrome, Alstrom syndrome, and fragile X syndrome (Farooqi and O'Rahilly, 2005b, 2007).

Polygenic forms of obesity occur as a result of the effects of multiple genes (Ichihara and Yamada, 2008). Studies of obesity in monozygous and dizygous twins, siblings, parents, and their offspring, adoptees and their adoptive parents, and extended pedigrees have consistently revealed a strong genetic and heritable contribution to measures of adiposity, such as BMI, body fat, fat mass, and waist circumference (Stunkard et al., 1986; Segal and Allison, 2002; Wardle et al., 2008).

According to O'Rahilly and Farooqi (2006), *"the heritability of a trait is defined as the per cent of inter-individual variation in that trait that can be explained by inherited factors.*" Notably, genetic studies conducted in different populations and environments have found that 40–70% of the variability in body mass is "heritable" (Wardle et al., 2008). For example, among 25,000 twin pairs born in Sweden between 1886 and 1958, the heritability of BMI was estimated as 70% for men and 66% for women (Stunkard et al., 1986). Nevertheless, since human genotypes cannot be replicated and studied in different environments, such studies are limited in their ability to partition the variability due to genotype by environment, interaction.

Indeed, one explanation for the rapid rise in obesity is the mismatch between today's environment and "thrifty genes" that were selected for in the past under different environmental conditions when food sources were rather unpredictable. This hypothesis was initially proposed in 1962 by geneticist James Neel to explain how genes predisposing to diabetes arose in the population. Neel suggested that genes which predispose to diabetes (the "thrifty genes") were historically advantageous, but they became detrimental in the modern world. In his words they were "*rendered detrimental by 'progress.'*" Thrifty genes are genes that enable individuals to efficiently collect and process food to deposit fat during periods of food abundance which is later used for energy in times of famine. Neel's primary interest was in diabetes, but the idea was soon expanded to encompass obesity. According to the "thrifty genotype" hypothesis, the same genes that helped our ancestors survive occasional famines are now being challenged by environments in which food is plentiful year round (Neel, 1962).

Environmental Factors Contributing to Obesity

Environmental factors can increase the risk of developing obesity by directly or indirectly influencing energy intake and energy expenditure. Two environmental factors have been implicated as major culprits in causing obesity: food marketing strategies (especially to children) and 24-hour availability of cheap, convenient, energy dense, high fat, high sugar, ultra-processed, super-sized, ready-to-eat meals, snacks, and drinks (Hill and Peters, 1998; McGinnis, Gootman, and Kraak, 2006; Bodor et al., 2008).

Compelling evidence to support an association between excess calorie consumption and obesity comes from the research conducted by Nestle and colleagues who analyzed the trend of portion sizes over time. Their results revealed that portion sizes rose dramatically in the 1970s and then skyrocketed in the 1980s, with foods such as french fries, hamburgers, and soft drinks being two to five times larger than their original sizes (Nestle and Young, 2002). In

addition, Rolls and colleagues showed that, within a single meal, total energy intake increases with increased portion size (Rolls, Morris, and Roe, 2002).

The trend of super-sized portions has been primarily economic and value-driven, with consumers wanting "more food for their money" (Hill and Peters, 1998; DiDomenico, 1994), even choosing restaurants based on portion sizes (Carangelo, 1995). Larger portion sizes equate to more calories. A "best value" drink, such as a typical 64 oz. soft drink from any fast food or franchised restaurant, contains almost 800 calories, an amount equivalent to a nearly half the energy requirements for most children and adolescents.

Environmental factors also influence physical activity levels and energy expenditure. For example, the *built environment*, which reflects the land use and transportation patterns of a population, can either facilitate or constrain physical activity (US National Academy of Sciences, 2005). Urban sprawl patterns such as low density land use, single use zoning, and employment dispersion may result in a heavy reliance on motorized methods of transportation and lengthened commute times, as well as lack of opportunities or spaces and places to walk, bicycle, and play safely (Hu, 2008). In addition, neighborhood characteristics such as sidewalks, lighting, perception of safety, streetscapes, traffic calming techniques, and other qualities may play a role in physical activity patterns, as well as characteristics of parks, trails, and playgrounds (Hanson, 2006).

Technological advances in the workplace, specifically mechanization and automation, have reduced physical activity requirements in almost all occupations and many technological conveniences in the home have further reduced energy expenditure from daily living. While energy expenditure from daily living has most certainly declined, so too have the physical activity requirements for school-age teenagers and children. For example, daily enrollment in physical education classes declined among high school students from 45% in 1991 to 25% in 1995 and many public schools have reduced or eliminated structured physically activity altogether (Kahn et al., 1993).

In addition to decreases in physical activity, cross-sectional and longitudinal studies have also linked increased sedentary behaviors, such as television viewing, to childhood adiposity (Dietz and Gortmaker, 1985; Gortmaker et al., 1996; Anderson et al., 1998) as well as video games and computer use. Sedentary behavior can contribute to obesity by competing with more physically active behaviors, thus reducing energy expenditure and by providing the opportunity for passive consumption of snack foods during viewing or as a result of food advertisements (Robinson, 1999; Epstein et al., 2000).

CHILDHOOD OBESITY

Classification of Overweight and Obesity in Children and Adolescents

In the United States, childhood and adolescent overweight and obesity (ages 2–20 years) are defined as the gender-specific 85th and 95th percentiles of *body mass index-for-age*, which corresponds approximately to the respective BMI cut-off points of 25 and 30 for adults. According to the Centers for Disease Control and Prevention (CDC), the revised expanded range of percentiles (3rd–97th) represents the relative position of the child's BMI among children of the same sex and age (Kuzmarski and Flegal, 2000; Kuzmarksi et al., 2002).

In addition to gender-specific BMI-for-age percentile growth charts, there are numerous additional age- and gender-specific growth charts used clinically and in research settings to assess size, growth, nutritional status, and the general health and well-being of infants, children, and adolescents for use in the United States (Kuzmarski and Flegal, 2000). Furthermore, international child growth standards for infants and children from birth to age 5 years, as well as child and adolescent growth standards for children ages 5–19 years, were recently revised and released by the World Health Organization (WHO) in 2006 and 2007 (WHO Multicentre Growth Reference Study Group, 2009).

It is important to note that the US growth reference charts for children were developed based on data derived from the National Health and Nutrition Examination Surveys (NHANES) and represent the age- and gender-specific distribution of body measures in US children, reflecting growth "as is." Cameron and Hawley make the correct distinction that: "*the WHO growth standards are a different tool—they are based on* [multinational] *longitudinal data in which the source sample has been selected according to predefined criteria* (e.g., breastfeeding for 4 months) *and reflect growth not "as is" but growth "as it ought to be"* (Cameron and Hawley, 2010). The WHO reference charts therefore reflect growth under optimal circumstances thought to be conducive to optimal long-term health (Ziegler and Nelson, 2010). The implication is that the charts are not interchangeable and that the differences between them may be large enough to compromise international comparisons of infant, child, and adolescent populations.

The Burden of Childhood Obesity

Globally, over 20 million children 5 years and younger were overweight in 2005, and by the end of 2010, it is estimated that 43 million will be overweight, doubling the prevalence in 5 years (WHO, 2009b). Although current estimates suggest that the rate of obesity in developed countries is double that in developing countries (similar to adult overweight and obesity), in absolute numbers, developing countries have far more children who are affected. For example, it is estimated that there are 35 million overweight/obese preschoolers in developing countries, compared with 8 million in developed countries (de Onis, Borghi, and Blössner, 2010).

In the United States, the steep rise in childhood obesity has paralleled the epidemic rise in adult obesity. For instance, in 1990, not a single state participating in the Behavior Risk Factor Surveillance System (BRFSS) had a prevalence of childhood obesity greater than 15%, and in 10 states, the prevalence was less than 10%. In sharp contrast, by 2010, no state had a prevalence of childhood obesity that was less than 20%, and in 36 states, over a quarter of all children were classified as obese (Centers for Disease Control and Prevention, 2010). According to the 2006 US National Health and Nutrition Examination Survey (NHANES, 2005–2006) nearly 1 in 5 children ages 6–19 years were classified as obese (Ogden, Carroll, and Flegal, 2008), and among 5–10-year-old obese children, 61% had one or more risk factors for heart disease and 27% had 2 or more risk factors (Freedman et al., 2007).

Similar to the disproportionate burden of obesity observed among certain ethnic groups of US adults, childhood obesity is more common among African Americans, Hispanics, and American Indians compared to Caucasians. For example, the prevalence of obesity is higher among adolescent 12–19-year-old African American boys (19%) and Hispanic boys (22%) compared to Caucasians (17%). Similarly, African American adolescent girls had the highest prevalence of obesity (28%) followed by Hispanic girls (20%) and Caucasians (15%) (Ogden, Carroll, and Flegal, 2008).

In a recent survey of 8,550 multiethnic US-born 4-year old children enrolled in the *Early Childhood Longitudinal Study Birth Cohort*, 18.4% of children were classified as obese. The highest prevalence was observed among American Indian/Native Alaskan children (31.2%), more than double the prevalence among Asian children (12.8%). Comparatively, the prevalence of obesity was also high among Hispanics (22.0%) and African Americans (20.8%). Caucasian children also exhibited a higher burden of obesity (15.9%) than Asians (Anderson and Whitaker, 2009).

The distribution of childhood obesity also varies by socioeconomic status. For instance, in a national survey of pre-school children aged 2–4 years, the prevalence of obesity was nearly 16% higher among low-income children (14.6%) than non-Hispanic Caucasian children (12.6%) (MMWR, 2009).

Although not all children and adolescents who are overweight or obese will end up being obese in adulthood, the risk of becoming an obese adult is much higher among children who are overweight or obese compared to those who are not. Whitaker and colleagues studied BMI and obesity in childhood and adulthood in a retrospective cohort of 854 subjects from the northwestern United States. The parents' medical records were also reviewed to determine obesity status. The results clearly show that elevated BMI tracks from childhood to adulthood, even after adjusting for parental obesity (**Figure 33.10**). For example, in children 10 to 15 years old, 10% of those with BMI-for-age < 85th percentile were obese at age 25 compared to 75% of those with a BMI-for-age > 85th percentile and 80% of those with a BMI-for-age > 95th percentile. Thus, overweight and obese children are much more likely than children of normal weight to be obese as adults (Whitaker et al., 1997).

Risk Factors in Early Life and the Development of Later Obesity

Perinatal Influences

A variety of prenatal factors have been studied to determine their impact on the development of obesity

in adulthood. Parent-offspring studies suggest that maternal obesity, diabetes, malnutrition, and other psychological, immunological, and pharmacological stressors during gestation can promote the development of obesity in offspring (Levin, 2006). In a study of 261 women born during 1959–1961, maternal weight, weight gain during pregnancy, and birth weight retained statistical significance as predictors of adult BMI after adjustment for childhood growth and development (Terry, Wei, and Esserman, 2007). Postnatally, maternal diet and health, infant feeding patterns, and adiposity rebound have all been associated with obesity in later life (Ebbeling, Pawlak, and Ludwig, 2002).

Early Adiposity Rebound and Future Health Risk

In early life, the BMI curve is not monotonic, nor is it invariant. Adiposity typically increases during the first year of life, decreases in the second year, and increases again between 2 and 8 years of age (Chivers et al., 2010; Williams and Goulding, 2009). *Adiposity rebound* refers to the age at which the BMI reverses direction at its nadir (lowest point) and increases toward adiposity. Studies have shown that early onset of adiposity rebound (under 5 years of age) is related to obesity in later life, independent of parental obesity and BMI at the time of the rebound (Peneau, Thibault, and Rolland-Cachera, 2009; Lagstrom et al., 2008; Nader et al., 2006; Whitacker et al., 1998). For example, Peneau and colleagues showed that among a sample of severely obese French adolescents, 97% experienced adiposity rebound at a very early median age of 2 years (Peneau, Thibault, and Rolland-Cachera, 2009). In addition, a majority

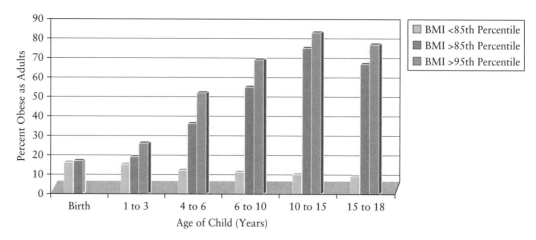

Figure 33.10 Percentage of Overweight Individuals, Birth to Age 18 Years, Who Become Obese at Age 25.

Source: Data from Whitaker RC, Wright JA, Pepe MS, Seidel KD, Dietz WH (1997). Predicting obesity in young adulthood from childhood and parental obesity. *N Engl J Med* 337:869-873.

of children who experienced early adiposity rebound were of normal weight at the time of rebound. This finding has been confirmed in other studies (Williams and Goulding, 2009).

Health Consequences of Childhood Obesity

The health consequences of obesity in children are similar to those observed in obese adults, affecting multiple body systems (Ebbeling, Pawlak, and Ludwig, 2002). Obesity in children increases the risk of hypertension, dyslipidemia, hyperglycemia, hyperinsulinemia, and chronic inflammation (Freedman et al., 1999; Ford et al., 2001; Srinivasan, Myers, and Berenson, 2002). In addition, obese children may be at higher risk for other health conditions such as obstructive sleep apnea, asthma, orthopedic complications, psychological distress, and psychosocial stigma (French, Story, and Perry, 1995; Dietz, 1998; Tauman and Gozal, 2006; Chinn, 2006).

It is estimated that over 50% of overweight 5–10-year-old children have at least one cardiovascular risk factor such as hypertension, dyslipidemia, or hyperinsulinemia (Freedman et al., 1999). Although childhood obesity is associated with earlier onset of obesity-related diseases in adulthood, a study by Pinhas-Hamiel and colleagues showed that the incidence of *adolescent* type 2 diabetes in Cincinnati increased tenfold, from 0.7/100,000 per year in 1982 to 7.2/100.000 per year in 1994 (Pinhas-Hamiel et al., 1996).

PREVENTION OF OBESITY

The principal reason for preventing weight gain and obesity is to reduce the risk of obesity-related diseases. Burke and colleagues estimated the number and proportion of incident cases of type 2 diabetes that could be prevented by targeting each BMI category in the *San Antonio Heart Study*. Results revealed that most cases of type 2 diabetes developed in individuals who were overweight or mildly obese, and that preventing normal weight individuals from becoming overweight would reduce the incidence of type 2 diabetes by 74% in Caucasians and 62% in Mexican Americans. These findings underscore the need to establish comprehensive primary prevention programs to reduce obesity and obesity-related diseases (Burke et al., 2003).

Primary prevention of obesity and associated diseases begins in early life (Berenson et al., 1993; Ebbeling, Pawlak, and Ludwig, 2002). The *US Expert Committee on Childhood Obesity* recommends that pediatricians advise all children and their parents to

Table 33.4	Primary Prevention of Obesity

Dietary Recommendations
- Limit consumption of sugar-sweetened drinks
- Limit portion sizes and restaurant meals, particularly fast food
- Eat recommended servings of fruits and vegetables
- Eat diet with recommended macro- and micro-nutrient content
- Eat breakfast and encourage structured time for meals with family
- For mothers: breastfeed to 6 months and introduce solid foods and maintain breastfeeding to at least 12 months

Physical Activity Recommendations
- Encourage vigorous physical activity of 60 minutes daily
- Limit television, computer, and video games

Source: Data from Barlow SE, Expert Committee (2007). Expert Committee Recommendations Regarding the Prevention, Assessment, and Treatment of Child and Adolescent Overweight and Obesity: Summary Report. *Pediatrics* 120:S164-192.

integrate healthy habits into their lifestyle that may help prevent excessive weight gain and are unlikely to cause harm (Barlow and Expert Committee, 2007). Recommended guidelines for the primary prevention of obesity are shown in **Table 33.4**.

Lemmens and colleagues recently conducted a systematic review of the peer-reviewed literature to evaluate the efficacy of adult obesity prevention programs. The programs reviewed were designed to maintain current weight or prevent weight gain among nonobese adults (BMI < 30) by diet, exercise, or both. The review showed mixed results: four out of nine studies found a positive intervention effect, but there were small absolute weight losses and minimal differences between control and intervention groups. The investigators concluded that the current evidence is too limited to draw firm conclusions on the efficacy of prevention programs in adults (Lemmens et al., 2008).

Nevertheless, there are published reports of successful obesity-prevention programs in adults. In a small randomized study of 30 young women, 18–28 years of age, with at least one severely obese parent, 14 women were randomized to a treatment group receiving an intensive individualized intervention program called *Health Hunters* focusing on food choice, physical activity, and other lifestyle factors, and 16 women were randomized to a control group receiving no intervention. Results were evaluated after one year of follow-up. Compared to the control group (which gained weight), the intervention group displayed significant average *decreases* in body weight, body mass index, waist circumference, and waist-to-hip ratio and a significant *increase* in self-reported physical activity. The investigators concluded that the intervention was effective in high-risk young women with a familial predisposition to the development of obesity (Eiben and Lissner, 2006).

Silverman and colleagues conducted a randomized study designed to evaluate the impact of a lifestyle dietary and physical activity program among middle-aged women known as the *Women's Healthy Lifestyle Project*. A total of 535 premenopausal women ages 44–50 years at baseline were enrolled in the trial. Participants were randomly assigned to receive either a 5-year program of intensive lifestyle intervention or no intervention. After 54 months of observation, 136 of 246 women (55%) in the intervention group were at or below baseline weight compared to 68 of 261 women (26%) in the control group. The average weight loss in the intervention group was 0.1 kg *below* baseline weight whereas the average weight gain in the control group was 2.4 kg *above* baseline weight. The average reduction in waist circumference was also significantly greater in the intervention group than the control group (2.9 cm vs. 0.5 cm). Furthermore, participants receiving lifestyle intervention were consistently more physically active and reported eating fewer calories and less fat than controls. The investigators concluded that in healthy women, weight gain and increased waist circumference are preventable through a sustained dietary and physical activity program focused on weight, body composition, physical activity, diet, and other cardiovascular risk factors (Simkin-Silverman et al., 2003).

The foundation of successful obesity prevention programs is inclusion of effective dietary and physical activity components. The dietary component should be designed to reduce energy intake and improve nutritional content. The physical activity component should be designed to increase daily caloric expenditure and decrease sedentary behavior. Careful monitoring of compliance of participants is essential through detailed reporting of the frequency, intensity, type, and duration of interventions. Periodic measures of weight, body mass, quality of life and other outcomes should be taken to gauge progress. The objective for a given individual may be to reduce weight, prevent weight gain, or maintain current weight. Behavior modification, education, and motivational and psychological counseling may also contribute to success. Structured obesity prevention programs and services may be offered in a variety of settings such as outpatient clinics, schools, worksites, community centers, churches, fitness centers, and neighborhood recreational facilities (United Nations Development Program, 2001; NIH, 1985, 1991, 1992, 1998).

THERAPY OF OBESITY

Therapeutic approaches to obesity include nonpharmacologic programs focused on diet and exercise to reduce weight through manipulation of energy balance, and more recently, administration of pharmacologic antiobesity agents. Current therapies include appetite suppressants and drugs that inhibit the absorption of dietary fat. A wide variety of antiobesity drugs are under investigation, and it is the goal of researchers to develop safe and effective antiobesity drugs analogous to those used to treat other chronic conditions such as hypertension, dyslipidemia, and diabetes (Bays, Mandarino, and DeFronzo, 2004).

An emerging concept is that the development of antiobesity agents must not only reduce fat mass but must also correct fat dysfunction (Bays and Dujovne, 2002; Bays, Mandarino, and DeFronzo, 2004; Bays et al., 2008). For example, agents such as pioglitazone and rosiglitazone that activate the nuclear receptor peroxisome proliferator activated receptor-γ (PPARγ) have shown therapeutic value in reducing proinflammatory adipokines and cytokines and increasing the anti-inflammatory adipokine, adiponectin (Larsen, Toubro, and Astrup, 2003; Lyon, Law, and Hseuh, 2003).

It is also well to keep in mind that obesity and particularly severe obesity are due not only to increased fat cell size (hypertrophy) but also to increased fat cell number (hypercellularity). As pointed out by Arner and Spalding in their review of fat cell turnover:

> "Traditional weight loss regimes, such as diet and exercise, are successful in decreasing adipocyte size, but fail to reduce adipocyte number. Since many obese and almost all severely obese individuals have more than the average number of adipocytes, methods other than diet and exercise alone are needed if one hopes to reduce (and maintain) the fat mass to lean levels. The dynamic and highly regulated turnover of adipocytes in adult humans establishes a new therapeutic target whereby pharmacological intervention may potentially tip the balance in favor of weight loss, or gain, depending on the preferred outcome." (Arner and Spalding, 2010)

Liposuction

Liposuction, also known as lipoplasty, refers to the suctioning of fat from certain areas of the body. The procedure is performed primarily for cosmetic purposes. The value of liposuction in the treatment of obesity is highly controversial.

In a small study of 15 adult women with severe abdominal obesity (BMI~40), liposuction surgery removed an average of 10 kg of subcutaneous body fat (18% of total fat mass) resulting in an average weight loss of more than 6 kg. The women were evaluated at baseline and 10–12 weeks postsurgery. Liposuction did not significantly alter insulin sensitivity, plasma concentrations of C-reactive protein, interleukin-6, tumor necrosis factor-α, adiponectin, or any other risk factors of coronary heart disease including blood pressure, plasma glucose, insulin and lipid concentrations. The investigators concluded that abdominal liposuction did not improve obesity-associated metabolic abnormalities in the short follow-up period (Klein et al., 2004). Seven women in the study were followed for up to four years after surgery to assess long-term effects of liposuction. Post-surgery body composition and weight were unchanged throughout the follow-up period; however, metabolic endpoints (oral glucose tolerance, insulin resistance, blood pressure, plasma triglyceride and cholesterol concentrations) showed no improvement from baseline values. Results suggest that removal of a large volume of subcutaneous abdominal fat by liposuction *does not* improve risk factors for coronary heart disease, despite a long-term reduction in body fat (Mohammed et al., 2008).

Case reports suggest that weight gain after liposuction results in deposition of subcutaneous fat in areas that were not aspirated such as the back and breasts (Yun et al., 2003; van der Lei et al., 2007). Also, there have been several case reports of *fat embolism syndromes* following liposuction and animal studies have proven that removal of subcutaneous fat by liposuction results in systemic fat mobilization and fat embolism (El-Ali and Gourlay, 2006; Mentz, 2008). Additional investigations are needed to determine both the short-term and long-term impacts of high volume liposuction.

Bariatric Surgery

Although primary prevention is the best approach to attenuating the obesity epidemic and controlling, improving, or reversing obesity-related comorbidities, bariatric surgery is the only proven treatment for severe obesity in adults and adolescents (Sugarman et al., 2003; Buchwald, Avidor, and Braunwald, 2004; Dixon et al., 2005). Bariatric surgery is an elective surgical weight loss procedure that reduces the gastric reservoir and limits food intake.

In 1991, the National Institutes of Health Consensus Development Panel recommended that gastric restriction or bypass surgery be considered for severely obese individuals, BMI > 35 with comorbidity or BMI > 40 with or without comorbidity (NIH Conference, 1991). In 1992, a statement from the NIH Health Consensus Development Conference affirmed the superiority of surgical over nonsurgical approaches to weight loss in the severely obese (NIH Consensus Development Conference, 1992), and in 2000, an editorial by Dr. Harvey Sugerman, an internationally known bariatric surgeon, suggested lowering the obesity level guidelines to European standards, recommending surgical management of obesity for those with BMI > 30 and with comorbidity (Sugerman, 2000).

Because of these recommendations and increasing media attention, bariatric surgery has gained considerable popularity as the only treatment to produce sustained weight loss (NIH Consensus Development Conference, 1992). Furthermore, studies of surgical weight loss have demonstrated long-term significant improvements and resolution of type 2 diabetes as well as sustained risk factor reduction of comorbid conditions such as dyslipidemia, hypertension, hyperinsulinemia, glucose intolerance, and adipokine levels (Kral et al., 1977; Salameh, Khoukaz, and Bell, 2010; Trakhtenbroit et al., 2009; Meneghini, 2007; Buchwald, Avidor, and Braunwald, 2004). Additional high quality studies are needed to establish evidence-based criteria for bariatric surgery, as current recommendations are based on consensus (NIH Conference, 1991; NIH Consensus Development Conference, 1992).

SUMMARY

Obesity is dramatically increasing across the globe. Because of the profound rise in obesity within the past several decades, most experts have ruled out a change in genetics as contributing substantially to the obesity epidemic, which only recently was considered to be a by-product of affluence related to Western societies. Instead, increased urbanization worldwide is leading to fundamental changes in physical activity levels and dietary patterns. Multiple structural changes in the environment have led to decreased physical activity, increased sedentary behavior, and ready access to high fat, high sugar, energy dense, and cheap food and drink, and these changes have tipped the global energy balance scale so that long-term energy intake exceeds energy expenditure. Excess energy leads to an increase in energy stored as triacylglycerol within adipocytes of white adipose tissue and subsequently excess weight gain.

Other risk factors include genetic susceptibility, female gender, aging, ethnicity, perinatal factors (maternal obesity), menopause, psychological factors (stress, depression), and physiological factors (adiposity rebound and fat cell dynamics). It is notable that genetic studies have consistently found obesity to be highly heritable. Moreover, though genetic changes do not explain the ongoing obesity epidemic, genotype x environment interactions could certainly have an impact. Conceivably, the rapid global rise in obesity could at least in part be due to the mismatch between today's environment and "thrifty genes" that were selected for in the past under different environmental conditions when food sources were unpredictable.

Obesity exerts deleterious effects on nearly every organ system of the body and is a significant risk factor for type 2 diabetes, cardiovascular diseases (such as coronary heart disease, myocardial infarction, and stroke), gastroesophageal reflux disease (GERD), obstructive sleep apnea, asthma, gallbladder and fatty liver disease, depression, urinary incontinence, gout, polycystic ovarian syndrome, and osteoarthritis. In particular, obesity promotes the parallel progression of insulin resistance to type 2 diabetes and endothelial dysfunction to atherosclerosis. Overall, obesity has become one of the leading causes of premature death and disability in the world.

Adipocytes not only function as a storage repository for excess energy, but they also actively participate in metabolic processes that regulate energy homeostasis. Excess adiposity incites the synthesis of a multitude of autocrine, paracrine, and endocrine bioactive signaling proteins called adipokines. Certain adipokines (resistin and leptin) have proinflammatory properties that promote atherogenesis and insulin resistance whereas others (adiponectin) are anti-inflammatory. Numerous studies indicate that visceral (abdominal) fat is more metabolically active than subcutaneous (peripheral) fat, and that visceral adiposity is primarily responsible for increasing the risk of developing obesity-related diseases.

Based upon studies of fat cell turnover, obesity can be classified into type basic types: hypertrophic obesity (increased fat cell size) and hyperplastic obesity (increased fat cell number). Preventive and therapeutic strategies should be designed to counteract both types.

As with adults, the prevalence of obesity in children has risen dramatically in populations across the globe. Obesity in children increases the risk of hypertension, dyslipidemia, hyperglycemia, hyperinsulinemia, chronic inflammation, and many other health conditions. Childhood obesity tracks to adult obesity, and early rebound adiposity is a significant predictor of adult obesity.

While obesity is still increasing worldwide, recent US survey results indicate that the epidemic may be abating in children, perhaps as a consequence of prevention programs in schools and communities and public health awareness campaigns promoting a lifestyle of healthy eating and regular exercise to maintain ideal body weight. Early health education is the cornerstone of primary prevention. Clearly, comprehensive and sustainable prevention programs should be established in populations around the globe to encourage healthy, nutritious eating habits and physically active lifestyles in order to avoid the development of obesity and obesity-related diseases in future generations.

● ● ● REFERENCES

Abate, N., Chandalia, M., Snell, P.G., & Grundy, S.M. (2004). Adipose tissue metabolites and insulin resistance in non-diabetic Asian Indian men. *J Clin Endocrinol Metab, 89,* 2750–2755.

Adams, K.F., Schatzkin, A., Harris, T.B., Kipnis, V., Mouw, T., Ballard-Barbash, R.,... Leitzmann, M.F. (2006). Overweight, obesity and mortality in a large prospective cohort of persons 50 to 71 years old. *NEJM, 355*(08), 763–778.

Allison, D.B., Fontaine, K.R., Manson, J.E., et al. (1999). Annual deaths attributable to obesity in the United States. *JAMA, 282,* 1530–1538.

Anderson, S.E., & Whitaker, R.C. (2009). Prevalence of obesity among US preschool children in different racial and ethnic groups. *Arch Pediatr Adolesc Med, 163*(04), 344–348.

Anderson, R.E., Crespo, C.J., Bartlett, S.J., et al. (1998). Relationship of physical activity and television watching with body weight and level of fatness among children: Results from the third National Health and Nutrition Examination Survey. *JAMA, 279,* 938–942.

Argyropoulos, G., & Harper, M.E. (2002). Molecular biology of thermoregulation invited review: Uncoupling proteins and thermoregulation. *J Appl Physiol, 92,* 2187–2198.

Arner, P., & Spalding, K.L. (2010). Fat cell turnover in humans. *Biochemical and Biophysical Research Communications, 396,* 100–104.

Attie, A.D., & Scherer, P.E. (2009). Adipocyte metabolism and obesity. *J Lipid Res, 50,* S395–S399.

Barlow, S.E., & Expert Committee. (2007). Expert Committee recommendations regarding the prevention, assessment, and treatment of child and adolescent overweight and obesity: Summary report. *Pediatrics, 120,* S164–S192.

Bays, H.E., & Dujovne, C.A. (2002). Anti-obesity drug development. *Expert Opinion Invest Drugs, 11,* 1189–1204.

Bays, H., Mandarino, L., & DeFronzo, R.A. (2004). Role of the adipocyte, free fatty acids, and ectopic fat in pathogenesis of type 2 diabetes mellitus: Peroxisomal proliferator-activated receptor agonists provide a rational therapeutic approach. *J Clin Endocrinol Metab, 89,* 463–478.

Bays, H.E., Gonzalez-Campoy, J.M., Henry, R.R., et al. (2008). Is adiposopathy (sick fat) an endocrine disease? *Int J Clin Pract, 62,* 1474–1483.

Bei-Fan, Z. (2002). The Cooperative Meta-Analysis Group of Working Group on Obesity in China. Predictive values of body mass index and waist circumference for risk factors of certain related diseases in Chinese adults: Study on optimal cut-off points of body mass index and waist circumference in Chinese adults. *Asia Pac J Clin Nutr, 11*(08), S685–S693.

Berenson, G.S., Srinivasan, S.R., Wattigney, W.A., & Harsha, D.W. (1993). Obesity and cardiovascular risk in children. *Ann NY Acad Sci, 699,* 93–103.

Bergman, R.M., Kim, S.P., Katalano, K.J., et al. (2006). Why visceral fat is bad: Mechanisms of the metabolic syndrome. *Obesity, 14,* 16S–19S.

Björnheden, T., Jakubowicz, B., Levin, M., Odén, B., Edén, S., Sjöström, L., & Lönn, M. (2004). Computerized determination of adipocyte size. *Obes Res, 12*(1), 95–105.

Blouin, K., Despres, J.P., Couillard, C., Tremblay, A., Prud'homme, D., Bouchard, C., & Tchernof, A. (2005). Contribution of age and declining androgen levels to features of the metabolic syndrome in men. *Metabolism, 54,* 1034–1040.

Bodor, J.N., Rose, D., Farley, T.A., Swalm, C., & Scott, S.K. (2008). Neighborhood fruit and vegetable availability and consumption: The role of small food stores in an urban environment. *Public Health Nutr, 11,* 413–420.

Bogers, R.P., Bemelmans, W.J., Hoogenveen, R.T., Boshuizen, H.C., Woodward, M., Knekt, P.,… Shipley, M.J., for the BMI-CHD Collaboration Investigators. (2007). Association of overweight with increased risk of coronary heart disease partly independent of blood pressure and cholesterol levels: A meta-analysis of 21 cohort studies including more than 300,000 persons. *Arch Intern Med, 167*(16), 1720–1728.

Brochu, M., Tchernof, A., Dionee, I.J., et al. (2001). What are the physical characteristics associated with a normal metabolic profile despite a high level of adiposity in postmenopausal women? *J Clin Endocrinol Metab, 86,* 1020–1025.

Browning, R.C., & Kram, R. (2007). Effects of obesity on the biomechanics of walking at different speeds. *Med Sci Sports Exerc, 39*(9), 1632–1641.

Buchwald, H., Avidor, Y., & Braunwald, E. (2004). Bariatric surgery: A systemtatic review and meta-analysis. *JAMA, 292,* 1724–1737.

Burke, J.P., Williams, K., Narayan, K.M., Leibson, C., Haffner, S.M., & Stern, M.P. (2003). A population perspective on diabetes prevention: Whom should we target for preventing weight gain? *Diabetes Care, 26*(7), 1999–2004.

Byers, T., Nestle, M., McTiernan, A., et al. (2002). American Cancer Society guidelines on nutrition and physical activity for cancer prevention: Reducing the risk of cancer with healthy food choices and physical activity. *CA Cancer J Clin, 52,* 92–119.

Caballero, B. (2007). The global epidemic of obesity: An overview. *Epidemiologic Reviews, 29,* 1–5.

Calle, E.E. (2008). Chapter 10: Obesity and cancer. In *Obesity epidemiology.* Oxford, New York: Oxford University Press.

Calle, E.E., Thun, M.J., Petrelli, J.M., et al. (1999). Body mass index and mortality in a prospective cohort of US adults. *NEJM, 341,* 1097–1105.

Cameron, N., & Hawley, N.L. (2010). Should the UK use WHO growth charts? *Paediatrics and Child Health, 20*(04), 151–156.

Cannon, B., & Nedergaard, J. (2004). Brown adipose tissue: Function and physiological significance. *Physiol Rev, 84*, 277–359.

Carangelo, C. (1995). Why are Americans so fat? *Food Management, 30*(4), 63–98.

Centers for Disease Contol and Prevention. (2010). U.S. obesity trends, http://www.cdc.gov/obesity /data/trends.

Chan, J.M., Rimm, E.B., Colditz, G.A., et al. (1994). Obesity, fat distribution and weight gain as risk factors for clinical diabetes in men. *Am J Epidemiol, 17*, 961–969.

Chinn, S. (2006). Obesity and asthma. *Paediatr Respir Rev, 7*, 223–228.

Chivers, P., Hand, B., Parker, H., et al. (2010). Body mass index, adiposity rebound, and early feeding in a longitudinal cohort (Raine study). *IJO, 34*, 1169–1176.

Christakis, N.A., & Fowler, J.H. (2007). The spread of obesity in a large social network over 32 years. *NEJM, 357*, 370–379.

Christou, N.V., Lieberman, M., Sampalis, F., & Sampalis, J.S. (2008). Bariatric surgery reduces cancer risk in morbidly obese patients. *SOARD, 4*, 691–697.

Chung, S., Song, M.Y., Shin, H.D., et al. (2005). Korean and Caucasian overweight premenopausal women have different relationship of body mass index to percent body fat with age. *J Appl Physiol, 99*, 103–107.

Colditz, G.A., Willett, W.C., Rotnitsky, A., & Manson, J.E. (1995). Weight gain as a risk factor for clinical diabetes mellitus in women. *Ann Intern Med, 122*, 481–486.

Coggon, D., Reading, I., Croft, P., McLaren, M., Barrett, D., & Cooper, C. (2001). Knee osteoarthritis and obesity. *Int J Obes Relat Metab Disord, 25*(5), 622–627.

Crovetti, R., Porrini, M., Santangelo, A., & Testolin, G. (1997). The influence of thermic effect of food on satiety. *Europ J Clin Nutr, 52*, 482–488.

Danforth, E. (2000). Failure of adipocyte differentiation causes type II diabetes? *Nature Genetics, 26*, 13.

de Onis, M., Blössner, M., & Borghi, E. (2010). Global prevalence and trends of overweight and obesity among preschool children. *Am J Clin Nutr, 92*(5), 1257–1264.

Deurenberg, P., Deurenberg-Yap, M., & Guricci, S. (2002). Asians are different from Caucasians and from each other in their body mass index/body fat percent relationship. *Obes Rev, 3*, 141–146.

DiDomenici, P. (1994). Portion size: How much is too much. *Restaurants USA, 14*, 18–21.

Dietz, W.H. (1998). Health consequences of obesity in youth: Childhood predictors of adult disease. *Pediatrics, 101*, 518–525.

Dietz, W.H., & Gortmaker, S.L. (1985). Do we fatten our children at the television set? Obesity and television viewing in children and adolescents. *Pediatrics, 75*, 807–812.

Dixon, J.B., Pories, W.J., O'Brien, P.E., Schauer, P.R., & Zimmet, P. (2005). Surgery as an effective early intervention for diabesity: Why the reluctance? *Diabetes Care, 28*(2), 472–474.

Drewnowski, A., & Popkin, B.M. (2009). The nutrition transition: New trends in the global diet. *Nutri Rev, 55*(02), 31–43.

Durán, J., Esnaola, S., Rubio, R., & Iztueta, A. (2001). Obstructive sleep apnea–hypopnea and related clinical features in a population-based sample of subjects aged 30 to 70 yr. *Am J Respir Crit Care Med, 163*, 685–689.

EarthTrends. (2009). Nutrition: Calorie supply per capita. *World Resources Institute.* Retrieved from http://earthtrends.wri.org.

Ebbeling, C.B., Pawlak, D.B., & Ludwig, D.S. (2002). Childhood obesity: Public health crisis, common sense cure. *Lancet, 360*, 473–482.

Edelstein, Z.R., Bronner, D.C., Rosen, M.P., et al. (2007). Central adiposity and risk of Barrett's esophagus. *Gastroenterology, 133*, 403–411.

Eiben, G., & Lissner, L. (2006). Health Hunters—An intervention to prevent overweight and obesity in young high risk women. *IJO (London), 30*, 691–696.

Economic Research Service. (2010). USDA website. Retrieved from http://www.ers.usda.gov/Data /BiotechCrops/ExtentofAdoptionTable1.htm.

Einstein, F.H., Atzmon, G., Yang, X., et al. (2005). Differential responses of visceral and subcutaneous fat depots to nutrients. *Diabetes, 54*, 672–678.

Eknoyan, G. (2008). Adolphe Quetelet (1796–1874)—The average man and indices of obesity. *Nephrol Dial Transplant, 23*(01), 47–51.

Ekoynan, G. (2006). A history of obesity, or how what was good became ugly and then bad. *Adv Chronic Kidney Dis, 13*, 421–427.

El-Ali, K.M., & Gourlay, T. (2006). Assessment of the risk of systemic fat mobilization and fat embolism as a consequence of liposuction: Ex vivo study. *Plast Reconstr Surg, 117*(7), 2269–2276.

Epstein, L.H., Paluch, R.A., Gordy, C.C., et al. (2000). Decreasing sedentary behaviors in treating pediatric obesity. *Arch Pediatr Adolesc Med, 154*, 220–226.

Ettinger, W.H., Davis, M.A., Neuhaus, J.M., & Mallon, K.P. (1994). Long-term physical functioning in persons with knee osteoarthritis from NHANES. I: Effects of comorbid medical conditions. *J Clin Epidemiol, 47*(7), 809–815.

Eyre, H., Kahn, R., Robertson, R.M., and the ACS/ ADA/AHA Collaborative Writing Committee. (2004). Preventing cancer, cardiovascular disease, and diabetes: A common agenda for the American Cancer Society, the American Diabetes Association, and the American Heart Association. *Stroke, 35*(8), 1999–2010.

Fain, J.N., Madan, A.K., Hiler, M.L., Cheema, P., & Bahouth, S.W. (2004). Comparison of the release of adipokines by adipose tissue, adipose tissue matrix, and adipocytes from visceral and subcutaneous abdominal adipose tissues of obese humans. *Endocrinology, 145*, 2273–2282.

Fain, J.N. (2006). Release of interleukins and other inflammatory cytokines by human adipose tissue is enhanced in obesity and primarily due to the nonfat cells. *Vitamins & Hormones, 74*, 443–477.

Farooqi, I.S., & O'Rahilly, S. (2005a). Monogenic obesity in humans. *Ann Rev Med, 56*, 443–458.

Farooqi, I.S., & O'Rahilly, S. (2005b). New advances in the genetics of early onset obesity. *International Journal of Obesity, 29*, 1149–1152.

Farooqi, I.S., & O'Rahilly, S. (2007). Genetic factors in human obesity. *Obesity Reviews, 8*(Suppl 1), 37–40.

Faust, I., & Miller, W.J. (1983). *Hyperplastic growth of adipose tissue in obesity*. New York: Raven Press.

Felson, D.T., Zhang, Y., Anthony, J.M., Naimark, A., & Anderson, J.J. (1992). Weight loss reduces the risk for symptomatic knee osteoarthritis in women. The Framingham Study. *Ann Intern Med, 116*(7), 535–539.

Fisichella, P.M., & Patti, M.G. (2009). Gastroesophageal reflux disease and morbid obesity: Is there a relation? *World J Surg, 33*, 2034–2038.

Flegal, K.M., Carroll, M.D., Ogden, C.L., & Curtin, L.R. (2010). Prevalence and trends in obesity among US adults, 1999–2008. *JAMA, 303*, 235–241.

Flegal, K.M., Graubard, B.I., Williamson, D.F., & Gail, M.H. (2006). Cause-specific excess death associated with underweight, overweight and obesity. *JAMA, 298*, 2028–2037.

Flegal, K.M., Graubard, B.I., Williamson, D.F., & Gail, M.H. (2005). Excess deaths associated with underweight, overweight, and obesity. *JAMA, 293*, 1861–1867.

Flegal, K.M., & Troiano, R.P. (2000). Changes in the distribution of body mass index of adults and children in the US population. *IJO, 24*, 807–818.

Fletcher, E., & Lewis-Faning, E. (1945). Chronic rheumatic diseases: Statistical study of 1000 cases of chronic rheumatism. *Postgraduate Medical Journal, 1945*, 21137.

Ford, E.S., Galuska, D.A., Gillespie, C., et al. (2001). C-reactive protein and body mass index in children: Findings from the third National Health and Nutrition Examination Survey, 1988–1994. *J Pediatr, 138*, 486–492.

Fraser-Moodie, C.A., Norton, B., Gornall, C., et al. (1999). Weight loss has an independent beneficial effect on symptoms of gastro-oesophageal reflux in patients who are overweight. *Scand J Gastroenterol, 34*, 337–340.

Frayn, K.N. (2000). Visceral fat and insulin resistance—Causative or correlative? *British J Nutr, 83*(S1), S871–S877.

Frederiksen, S.G., Johansson, J., Johnsson, F., et al. (2000). Neither low-calorie diet nor vertical banded gastroplasty influence gastro-oesophageal reflux in morbidly obese patients. *Eur J Surg, 166*, 296–300.

Freedman, D.S., Dietz, W.H., Srinivasan, S.R., & Berenson, G.S. (1999). The relation of overweight to cardiovascular risk factors among children and adolescents: The Bogalusa Heart Study. *Pediatrics, 103*, 1175–1182.

Freedman, D.S., Mei, Z., Srinivasan, S.R., et al. (2007). Cardiovascular risk factors and excess adiposity among overweight children and adolescents: The Bogalusa Heart Study. *J Pediatr, 150*, 12–17.

Friedenberg, F.K., Xanthopoulos, M., Foster G.D., & Richter, J.E. (2008). The association between gastroesophageal reflux disease and obesity. *Am J Gastroenterol, 103*, 2111–2122.

French, S.A., Story, M., & Perry, C.L. (1995). Self esteem and obesity in children and adolescents: A literature review. *Obes Res, 3*, 479–490.

Fruhbeck, G., Gomez-Ambrosi, J., Muruzabai, F.J., & Burrell, M.A. (2001). The adipocyte: A model for integration of endocrine and metabolic signaling in energy metabolism regulation. *AJP–Endo and Metab, 280*, E827–E847.

Gallagher, D., Visser, M., Sepulveda, D., et al. (1996). How useful is body mass index for comparison of body fatness across age, sex, and ethnic groups? *Am J Epidemiol, 143*, 228–239.

Gavrilova, O., Marcus-Samuels, B., Graham, D., et al. (2000). Surgical implantation of adipose tissue reverses diabetes in lipoatrophic mice. *J Clin Invest, 105*, 271–278.

Gibson, H.J. (2005). Obstructive sleep apnoea syndrome: Underestimated and undertreated. *Br Med Bull, 72*, 49–65.

Gold, M.R., Stevenson, D., & Fryback, D.G. (2002). HALYs and QALYs and DALYs, oh my: Similarities and differences in summary measures of population health. *Ann Rev Pub Health, 23*, 115–134.

Gortmaker, S.L., Must, A., Sobol, A.M., et al. (1996). Television viewing as a cause of increasing obesity in the United States, 1986–1990. *Arch Pediatr Adolesc Med, 150*, 356–362.

Gower, B.A., Weisner, R.L., Jordan, J.M., et al. (2002). Effects of weight loss on changes in insulin sensitivity and lipid concentrations in premenopausal African American and white women. *Am J Clin Nutr, 76*, 923–927.

Grun, F., & Blumberg, B. (2006). Environmental obesigens: Organotins and endocrine disruption via nuclear receptor signaling. *Endocrinology, 147*, S50–S55.

Hak, E.A., Stehouwer, C.D.A., Bots, M.L., et al. (1999). Associations of C-reactive protein with measures of obesity, insulin resistance, and subclinical atherosclerosis in healthy middle-aged women. *Arterioscler Throm Vasc Biol, 19*, 1986–1991.

Haffner, S.M., Stern, M.P., Mitchell, B.D., et al. (1990). Incidence of type II diabetes in Mexican Americans predicted by fasting insulin, glucose levels, obesity, and body fat distribution. *Diabetes, 39*, 283–288.

Hampel, H., Abraham, N.S., & El-Serag, H.B. (2005). Meta-analysis: Obesity and the risk for gastroesophageal reflux disease and its complications. *Ann Intern Med, 143*, 199–211.

Hanson, S. (2006). Active living research in light of the TRB/IOM report. *Journal of Physical Activity and Health*, 3, S258–S266.

Harris, R.E., Namboodiri, K.K., Wynder, E.L. (1992). Breast cancer risk: Effects of estrogen replacement therapy and body mass. *J Natl Cancer Inst*, 84(20), 1575–1582.

Hausman, D.B., DiGirolamo, D.B., & Bartness, T.J. (2001). The biology of white adipocyte proliferation. *Obes Rev*, 2, 239–254.

Heindel, J.J. (2003). Endocrine disruptors and the obesity epidemic. *Toxicol Sci*, 76(2), 247–249.

Herbella, F.A., & Patti, M.G. (2010). Gastroesophageal reflux disease: From pathophysiology to treatment. *World J Gastroenterol*, 16(30), 3745–3749.

Hewitt, J.K. (1997). The genetics of obesity: What genetic studies told us about the environment. *Behav Genet*, 27, 353–358.

Hills, J.O., & Peters, J.C. (1998). Environmental contributions to the obesity epidemic. *Science*, 280, 1371–1374.

Hirsch, J., & Batchelor, B. (1976). Adipose tissue cellularity in human obesity. *Clin Endocrinol Metab*, 5(2), 299–311.

Hu, F.B. (2008). *Obesity epidemiology*. Oxford, New York: Oxford University Press.

Hu, F.B., Manson, J.E., Stampfer, M.J., et al. (2001). Diet, lifestyle, and the risk of type 2 diabetes in women. *NEJM*, 345, 790–797.

Hu, F.B., Wang, B., Chen, C., et al. (2000). Body mass index and cardiovascular risk factors in a rural Chinese population. *Am J Epidemiology*, 151, 88–97.

Hubbard, V.S. (2000). Defining overweight and obesity: What are the issues? *Am J Clin Nutr*, 72, 1067–1068.

Hube, F., & Hauner, H. (2000). The two tumor necrosis factor receptors mediate opposite effects on differentiation and glucose metabolism in human adipocytes in primary culture. *Endocrinology*, 141, 2582–2588.

Hung-Kwan, S., Nelson, E.A.S., Li, A.M., et al. (2008). Secular changes in height, weight and body mass index in Hong Kong children. *BMC Public Health*. Retrieved from http://www.biomedcentral.com/1471-2458/8/320.

Ichihara, S., & Yamada, Y. (2008). Genetic factors for obesity. *Cell Mol Life Sci*, 65, 1086–1098.

ICO. (2010). The 11th Congress on Obesity news release. Retrieved from http://www.ico2010.org/documents/10.menobeseat20release-final.pdf.

IDF, International Diabetes Federation. (2006). *Diabetes e-Atlas, based on the Diabetes Atlas* (2nd ed.). Brussels, Belgium: International Diabetes Federation.

Iozzo, P. (2009). Viewpoints on the way to the consensus session: Where does insulin resistance start? The adipose tissue. *Diabetes Care*, 32, S169–S173.

Ito, H., Nagasuga, K., Ohshima, A., et al. (2003). Detection of cardiovascular risk factors by indices of obesity obtained from anthropometry and dual-energy X-ray absorbtiometry in Japanese individuals. *J Obes Relat Metab Discord*, 27, 232–237.

Jackson, R.T., Rashed, M., Al-Hamad, N., et al. (2007). Comparison of BMI-for-age in adolescent girls in 3 countries of the Eastern Mediterranean Region. *Eastern Mediterranean Health Journal*, 13, 430–440.

Jia, H., & Lubetkin, E.I. (2010). Obesity-related quality-adjusted life years lost in the U.S. from 1993 to 2008. *American Journal of Preventive Medicine*, 39(03), DOI: 10.1016/j.amepre.2010.03.026.

Kadowaki, T., & Yamauchi, T. (2005). Adiponectin and adiponectin receptors. *Endocrine Reviews*, 26, 439–451.

Kagawa, M., Kerr, D., Uchida, H., & Binns, C.W. (2006). Differences in the relationship between BMI and percentage body fat between Japanese and Australian-Caucasian young men. *British J Nutr*, *95*, 1002–1007.

Kahn, L., Warren, C.W., Harris, W.J., et al. (1993). Youth risk behavior surveillance—United States. *MMWR*, *44*, 1–55.

Kelly, T., Yang, W., Chen, C.S., Reynolds, K., & He, J. (2008). Global burden of obesity in 2005 and projections to 2030. *International Journal of Obesity*, *32*, 1431–1437.

Keys, A., Fidanza, F., Karvonen, M.J., et al. (1972). Indices of relative weight and adiposity. *J Chronic Dis*, *25*, 329–343.

Keith, S.W., Redden, D.T., Katzmarzyk, P.T., et al. (2006). Putative contributors to the secular increase in obesity: Exploring the roads less traveled. *IJO*, *30*, 1585–1594.

Kim, J.K., Gavrilova, O., Chen, Y., Reitman, M.L., & Shulman, G.I. (2000). Mechanism of insulin resistance in A-ZIP/F-1 fatless mice. *J Biol Chem*, *275*(12), 8456–8460.

Kim, S., & Moustaid-Mousa, N. (2000). Secretory endocrine and autocrine/paracrine function of the adipocyte. *J Nutr*, *130*, S3110–S3115.

Kjellin, A., Ramel, S., Rossner, S., et al. (1996). Gastroesophageal reflux in obese patients is not reduced by weight reduction. *Scand J Gastroenterol*, *31*, 1047–1051.

Klein, S., Fontana, L., Young, V.L., Coggan, A.R., Kilo, C., Patterson, B.W., & Mohammed, B.S. (2004). Absence of an effect of liposuction on insulin action and risk factors for coronary heart disease. *N Engl J Med*, *350*, 2549–2557.

Kotsopoulos, J., Olopade, O.I., Ghadirian, P., et al. (2005). Changes in body weight and the risk of breast cancer in *BRCA1* and *BRCA2* mutation carriers. *Breast Cancer Research*, *7*, 833–843.

Knowler, W.C., Bennett, P.H., Hamman, R.F., & Miller, M. (1978). Diabetes incidence and prevalence in Pima Indians, a 19-fold greater incidence than in Rochester, Minnesota. *AJE*, *108*, 497–505.

Knowler, W.C., Pettitt, D.J., Savage, P.J., & Bennett, P.H. (1979). Diabetes incidence in Pima Indians: Contributions of obesity and parental diabetes. *Am J Epidemiol*, *113*(2), 144–156.

Koenig, W. (2003). C-reactive protein and cardiovascular risk: An update on what is going on in cardiology. *Nephro Dial Transplant*, *18*, 1039–1041.

Koh-Banerjee, P., Wang, Y., Hu, F.B., Spiegelman, D., Willett, W.C., & Rimm, E.B. (2004). Changes in body weight and body fat distribution as risk factors for clinical diabetes in US men. *Am J Epidemiol*, *159*, 1150–1159.

Koo, J.S., Lee, S.W., Park, S.M., Jung, S.W., Yim, H.J., Park, J.J.,…Ryu, H.S. (2009). Abdominal obesity as a risk factor for the development of erosive esophagitis in subjects with a normal esophago-gastric junction. *Gut Liver*, *3*(4), 276–284.

Kral, J.G., Bjorntorp, P., Scherstein, T., & Sjostrom, L. (1977). Body composition and adipose tissue cellularity before and after jejuno-ileostomy in severely obese subjects. *Eur J Clin Invest*, *5*, 413–419.

Krauss, R.M., Winston, M., Fletcher, R.N., & Grundy, S.M. (1998). Obesity: Impact on cardiovascular disease. *Circulation*, *98*, 1472–1476.

Kuczmarski, R.J., & Flegal, K.M., (2000). Criteria for definition of overweight in transition: Background and recommendations for the United States. *Am J Clin Nutr*, *72*, 1074–1081.

Kuczmarski, R.J., Ogden, C.L., Guo, S.S., et al. (2002). 2000 CDC growth charts for the United States: Methods and development. National Center for Health Statistics. *Vital Health Stat*, *11*(246), 1–203.

Kumanyika, S.K., Obarzanek, E., Stevens, V.J., Herbert, P.R., & Whelton, P.K. (1991). Weight-loss experience of black and white participants in NHLBI-sponsored clinical trials. *American Journal of Clinical Nutrition*, *53*, 1631S–1638S.

Kumanyika, S., Wilson, J., & Guliford-Davenport, M. (1993). Weight-related attitudes and behaviors of Black women. *Journal of the American Dietetic Association*, 93, 416–422.

Lagstrom, H., Hakanen, M., Niinikoski, H., et al. (2008). Growth patterns and obesity devlopment in overweight or normal-weight 13 year old adolescents: The STRIP Study. *Pediatrics*, 122, e876–e883.

Larsen, T.M., Toubro, S., & Astrup, A. (2003). PPAR-gamma agonists in the treatment of type II diabetes: Is increased fatness commensurate with long-term efficacy? *IJO*, 27, 147–161.

Lee, I.M., Manson, J.E., & Hennekens, C.H. (1993). Body weight and mortality. A 27-year follow-up of middle-aged men. *JAMA*, 270(23), 2823–2828.

Leach, R.E., Baumgard, S., & Broom, J. (1973). Obesity: Its relationship to osteoarthritis of the knee. *Clin Orthop*, 1973, 93271–93273.

Lemmens, V.E.P.P., Oenema, A., Klepp, K.I., Henriksen, H.B., & Brug, J. (2008). A systematic review of the evidence regarding efficacy of obesity prevention interventions among adults. *Obesity Reviews*, 9(5), 446–456.

Leonhardt, W., Hanefeld, M., Schneider, H., & Haller, H. (1972). Human adipocyte volumes: Maximum size, and correlation to weight index in maturity-onset diabetes. *Diabetologia*, 8, 287–291.

Levin, B.E. (2006). Metabolic imprinting: Critical impact of the perinatal environment on the regulation of energy homeostasis. *Philos Trans R Soc Lond B Biol Sci*, 361(1471), 1107–1121.

Lin, W.Y., Lee, L.T., Chen, C.Y., et al. (2002). Optimal cut-off values for obesity: Using simple anthropometric indices to predict cardiovascular risk factors in Taiwan. *Int J Obes Relat Metab Disord*, 26, 1232–1238.

Löfgren, P., Andersson, I., Adolfsson, B.M., Leijonhufvud, K., Hertel, J., Hoffstedt, P., & Arner, P. (2005). Long-term prospective and controlled studies demonstrate adipose tissue hypercellularity and relative leptin deficiency in the post-obese state. *J Clin Endocrinol Metab*, 90, 6207–6213.

Lonn, M., Mehlig, K., Bengtsson, C., & Lissner, L. (2010). Adipocyte size predicts incidence of type 2 diabetes in women. *FASEB J*, 24, 326–331.

Lovejoy, J.C., Bray, G.A., Bourgeois, M.O., Macchiavelli, R., Rood, J.C., Greeson, C., & Partington, C. (1996). Exogenous androgens influence body composition and regional body fat distribution in obese postmenopausal women—A clinical research center study. *J Clin Endocrinol Metab*, 81, 2198–2203.

Lovejoy, J.C., Champagne, C.M., De Jonge, L., Xie, H., & Smith, S.R. (2008). Increased visceral fat and decreased energy expenditure during the menopausal transition. *Int J Obes*, 32, 949–958.

Lovejoy, J.C., & Sainsbury, A. (2009). Sex differences in obesity and the regulation of energy homeostasis. *Obesity Reviews*, 10(2), 154–167.

Lowell, B.B., & Spiegelman, B.M. (2000). Towards molecular understanding of adaptive thermogenesis. *Nature*, 406, 652–659.

Lowell, B.B. (1998). Adaptive thermogenesis: Turning on the heat. *Current Biology*, 8, R517–R520.

Lundgren, M., Buren, J., Ruge, T., et al. (2004). Glucocorticoids down-regulate glucose uptake capacity and insulin signaling proteins in omental but not subcutaneous human adipocytes. *J Clin Endocrinol Metab*, 89, 2989–2997.

Lyon, C.J., Law, R.E., & Hsueh, W.A. (2003). Minireview: Adiposity, inflammation, and atherogenesis. *Endocrinology*, 144, 2195–2200.

Maffeis, C., Silvagni, D., Bonadonna, R., Grezzani, A., Banzato, C., & Tatò, L. (2007). Fat cell size, insulin sensitivity, and inflammation in obese children. *J Pediatr*, 151(6), 647–652.

Manson, J.E., Willett, W.C., Stamfer, M.J., Colditz, G.A., Hunter, J.H., Hankinson, S.E.,…Speizer, F.E. (1995). Body weight and mortality among women. *NEJM*, 333, 677–685.

Mankin, H.J. (1974). The reaction of articular cartilage to injury and osteoarthritis. *New Engl J Med*, 291, 1285–1292.

Marin, P., Holmang, S., Gustafsson, C., Jonsson, L., Kvist, H., Elander, A.,...Bjorntorp, P. (1993). Androgen treatment of abdominally obese men. *Obes Res*, *1*, 245–251.

Marques, B.G., Hauman, D.B., & Martin, R.J. (1998). Association of fat cell size and paracrine growth factors in development of hyperplastic obesity. *Am J Physiol Regul Integr Comp Physiol*, *275*, R1898–R1908.

McGee, D.L. (2005). Body mass index and mortality: A meta-analysis based on person-level data from twenty-six observational studies. *Ann Epidemiol*, *15*, 87–97.

McGinnis, J.M., Gootman, J.A., & Kraak, V.I. (Eds.). (2006). *Food marketing to children and youth: Threat or opportunity*. Washington, DC: National Academies Press.

Medico-Actuarial Mortality Investigation. (1912). Vol. 1. New York: Association of Life Insurance Medical Directors and the Actuarial Society of America.

Meneghini, L.F. (2007). Impact of bariatric surgery on type 2 diabetes. *Cell Biochem Biophys*, *48*, 97–102.

Mentz, H.A. (2008). Fat emboli syndromes following liposuction. *Aesth Plast Surg*, *32*, 737–738.

Messier, S.P. (2008). Obesity and osteoarthritis: Disease genesis and nonpharmacologic weight management. *Rheumatic Diseases Clinics of North America*, *34*(3).

Metropolitan Life Insurance Company. (1959). New weight standards for men and women. *Stat Bull Metropol Life Insur Co*, *40*, 1–4.

Metropolitan Life Insurance Company. (1943). Ideal weights for women. *Stat Bull Metropol Life Insur Co*, *24*, 6–8.

Metropolitan Life Insurance Company. (1942). Ideal weights for men. *Stat Bull Metropol Life Insur Co*, *23*, 6–8.

Misra, A., & Khurana, L. (2008). Obesity and metabolic syndrome in developing countries. *Clin Endo Metabol*, *93*(11), S9–S13.

Misra, A. (2003). Revisions of cutoffs of body mass index to define overweight and obesity are needed for the Asian-ethnic groups. *IJO*, *27*, 1294–1296.

MMWR. (2009). Obesity prevalence among low-income, preschool-aged children—United States, 1998–2008. *Morb Mortal Wkly Rep*, *58*(28), 769–773.

Mohammed, B.S., Cohen, S., Reeds, D., Young, L., & Klein, S. (2008). Long-term effects of large-volume liposuction on metabolic risk factors for coronary heart disease. *Obesity*, *16*(12), 2648–2651.

Moon, O.R., Kim, N.S., Jamg, S.M., et al. (2002). The relationship between body mass index and the prevalence of obesity-related diseases based on 1995 National Health Interview Survey in Korea. *Obes Rev*, *3*, 191–196.

Moraes-Filho, J., Cecconello, I., Gama-Rodrigues, J., et al. (2002). Brazilian consensus on gastroesophageal reflux disease: Proposals for assessment, classification, and management. *Am J Gastroenterol*, *97*, 241–248.

Nader, P.R., O'Brien, M., Houts, R., et al. (2006). Identifying risk for obesity in early childhood. *Pediatrics*, *118*, e594–e601.

National Institutes of Health Consensus Development Panel on the Health Implications of Obesity. (1985). Health implications of obesity: National Institutes of Health consensus development conference statement. *Ann Intern Med*, *103*, 1073–1077.

National Institutes of Health Conference. (1991). Gastrointestinal surgery for severe obesity. Consensus Development Conference Panel. *Ann Intern Med*, Dec, *115*(12), 956–961.

National Institutes of Health Consensus Development Conference. (1992). *Am J Clin Nutr*, *55*, 487S–619S.

National Institutes of Health. (1998). The Evidence Report. *Obes Res*, *6*, 51S–209S.

National Institute of Diabetes and Digestive and Kidney Diseases (NIDDK). (2008). *National diabetes statistics, 2007 fact sheet*. Bethesda, MD: US Department of Health and Human Services, National Institutes of Health.

Neel, J.V. (1962). Diabetes mellitus: A "thrifty" genotype rendered detrimental by "progress"? *Am J Hum Genet, 14,* 353–362.

Nestle, M., & Young, L.R. (2002). The contribution of expanding portion sizes to the obesity epidemic. *AJPH, 92,* 246–249.

Nilsson, M., Johnsen, R., Weimin, Y., et al. (2003). Obesity and estrogen as risk factors for gastroesophageal reflux symptoms. *JAMA, 290,* 66–72.

Ogden, C.L., Carroll, M.D., & Flegal, K.M. (2008). High body mass index for age among US children and adolescents, 2003–2006. *JAMA, 299,* 2401–2405.

Ogden, C.L., Carroll, M.D., McDowell, M.A., & Flegal, K.M. (2007). *Obesity among adults in the United States—No change since 2003–2004.* NCHS data brief no 1. Hyattsville, MD: National Center for Health Statistics.

Ogden, C.L., Yanovski, S.Z., Carroll, M.D., & Flegal, K.M. (2007). The epidemiology of obesity. *Gastroenterology, 132,* 2087–2102.

Oguma, Y., Sesso, H.D., Paffenbarger, R.S., & Lee, I.M. (2005). Weight change and the risk of devloping type 2 diabetes. *Obes Res, 13,* 945–951.

Ogunwobi, O., Mutungi, G., & Peales, I.L. (2006). Leptin stimulates proliferation and inhibits apoptosis in Barrett's esophageal adenocarcinoma cells by cyclooxygenase-2-dependent, prostaglandin-E2-mediated transactivation of the epidermal growth factor receptor and c-Jun NH2-terminal kinase activation. *Endocrinology, 147*(9), 4506–4516.

O'Rahilly, S., & Farooqi, I.S. (2006). Genetics of obesity. *Philos Trans R Soc Lond B Biol Sci, 361*(1471), 1095–1105.

O'Sullivan, A.J. (2008). Does oestrogen allow women to story fat more efficiently? A biological advantage for fertility and gestation. *Obesity Reviews, 10*(2), 168–177.

Peneau, S., Thibault, H., & Rolland-Cachera, M.F. (2009). Massively obese adolescents were of normal weight at the age of adiposity rebound. *Obesity, 17,* 1309–1310.

Peppard, P.E., Young, T., Palta, M., Dempsey, J., Skatrud, J. (2000). Longitudinal study of moderate weight change and sleep-disordered breathing. *JAMA, 284*(23), 3015–3021.

Pischon, T., Nothlings, U., & Boeing, H. (2007). Obesity and cancer. *Proc Nutr Soc, 67,* 128–145.

Pinhas-Hamiel, O., Dolan, L.M., Daniels, S.R., et al. (1996). Increased incidence of non-insulin dependent diabetes mellitus among adolescents. *J Pediatr, 128,* 608–615.

Popkin, B.M., Paeratakul, S., Ge, K., et al. (1995). Body weight patterns among the Chinese: Results from the 1989 and 1991 China Health and Nutrition Survey. *Am J Public Health, 85,* 690–694.

Prentice, A.M. (2006). The emerging epidemic of obesity in developing countries. *IJE, 35,* 93–99.

Punjabi, N.M., Sorkin, J.D., Katzel, L.I., Goldberg, A.P., Schwartz, A.R., & Smith, P.L. (2002). Sleep-disordered breathing and insulin resistance in middle-aged and overweight men. *Am J Respir Crit Care Med, 165,* 677–682.

Quételet, A. (1835). *Sur l'homme et le developpement de ses facultes, ou essai de physique sociale.* Paris: Bachelier.

Rajala, R., Partinen, M., Sane, T., Pelkonen, R., Huikuri, K., & Seppalainen, A.M. (1991). Obstructive sleep apnoea syndrome in morbidly obese patients. *J Intern Med, 230,* 125–129.

Raynauld, J.P., Martel-Pelletier, J., Berthiaume, M.J., Beaudoin, G., Choquette, D., Haraoui, B., et al. (2006). Long-term evaluation of disease progression through the quantitative magnetic resonance imaging of symptomatic knee osteoarthritis patients: Correlation with clinical symptoms and radiographic changes. *Arthritis Research & Therapy, 8*(1).

Ravussin, E., & Smith, S.R. (2002). Increased fat intake, impaired fat oxidation, and failure of fat cell proliferation result in ectopic fat storage, insulin resistance, and type 2 diabetes mellitus. *Ann NY Acad Sci, 967*, 363–378.

Razak, F., Anand, S.S., Shannon, H., Vuksan, V., Davis, B., Jacobs, R., Teo., K.K., McQueen, M., Yusuf, S., for the SHARE Investigators. (2007). Defining obesity cut points in a multiethnic population. *Circulation, 115*, 2111–2118.

Richman, R.M., Elliott, L.M., Burns, C.M., Bearpark, H.M., Steinbeck, K.S., & Caterson, I.D. (1994). The prevalence of obstructive sleep apnoea in an obese female population. *Int J Obes Relat Metab Disord, 18*, 173–177.

Ridker, P.M., Glynn, R.J., & Hennekins, C.H. (1998). C-reactive protein adds to the predictive values of total and HDL cholesterol in determining risk of first myocardial infarction. *Circulation, 97*, 2007–2011.

Rifai, N., & Ridker, P.M. (2001). High sensitive C-reactive protein: A novel and promising marker of coronary heart disease. *Clin Chem, 47*, 401–411.

Robbins, S.L., & Cotran, R.S. (1979). *Pathologic basis of disease*. Philadelphia: WB Saunders Company.

Robinson, T.N. (1999). Reducing children's television viewing to prevent obesity: A randomized controlled trial. *JAMA, 281*, 1561–1567.

Rolls, B.J., Morris, E.L., & Roe, L.S. (2002). Portion size of food affects energy intake in normal-weight and overweight men and women. *Am J Clin Nutr, 76*, 1207–1213.

Rosen, E.D., & MacDougald, O.A. (2006). Adipocyte differentiation from the inside out. *Nat Rev Mol Cell Biol, 7*, 885–896.

Rosenbaum, M., & Leibel, L.L. (1998). The physiology of body weight regulation in children: Relevance to the etiology of obesity in children. *Pediatrics, 101*, 525–539.

Ross, R., & Glomset, J.A. (1973). Atherosclerosis and the arterial smooth muscle cell: Proliferation of smooth muscle is a key event in the genesis of the lesions of atherosclerosis. *Science, 180*, 1332–1339.

Ross, R., & Glomset, J.A. (1976). The pathogenesis of atherosclerosis. *N Engl J Med, 295*, 369–377.

Ross, R. (1999). Atherosclerosis—An inflammatory disease. *N Engl J Med, 340*, 115–126.

Salameh, B.S., Khoukaz, M.T., & Bell, R.L. (2010). Metabolic and nutritional changes after bariatric surgery. *Expert Rev Gastroenterol Hepatol, 4*, 217–223.

Sassi, F. (2006). How to do (or not to do)... Calculating QALYs, comparing QALY and DALY calculations. *Health Policy and Planning, 21*, 402–408.

Satia, J.A. (2010). Dietary acculturation and the nutrition transistion: An overview. *Appl Physiol Nutr Metab, 35*, 219–223.

Schienkiewitz, A., Schulze, M.B., Hoffmann, K., Kroke, A., & Boeing, H. (2006). Body mass index history and risk of type 2 diabetes: Results from the European Prospective Investigation into Cancer and Nutrition (EPIC)-Potsdam Study. *Am J Clin Nutr, 84*, 427.

Schwartz, A.R., O'Donnell, C.P., Baron, J., Schubert, N., Alam, D., Samadi, S.D., & Smith, P.L. (1998). The hypotonic upper airway in obstructive sleep apnea: Role of structures and neuromuscular activity. *Am J Respir Crit Care Med, 157*(4 Pt 1), 1051–1057.

Scott, S.K., Rabito, F.A., Price, P.D., Butler, N.N., Schwartzbaum, J.A., Jackson, B.M.,...Harris, R.E. (2006). Co-morbidity among the morbidly obese: A comparative study of 2002 US hospital patient discharges. *SOARD, 02*, 105–111.

Scott, S.K., Rabito, F.A., Butler, N.N., & Harris, R.E. (2004). *The energy storage capacity hypothesis*. (PhD dissertation).

Segal, N.L., & Allison, D.B. (2002). Twin and virtual twins: Bases of relative body weight revisited. *Int J Obese Metab Disord, 26*(04), 437–441.

Sethi, J.K., & Vidal-Puig, A.J. (2007). Targeting fat to prevent diabetes. *Cell Metab, 5*(5), 323–325.

Shai, I., Jiang, R., Manson, J.E., Stampfer, M.J., Willett, W.C., Colditz, G.A., & Hu, F.B. (2006). Ethnicity, obesity, and risk of type 2 diabetes in women: A 20-year follow-up study. *Diabetes Care, 29*(7), 1585–1590.

Simkin-Silverman, L.R., Wing, R.R., Boraz, M.A., & Kuller, L.H. (2003). Lifestyle intervention can prevent weight gain during menopause: Results from a 5 year randomized controlled trial. *Ann Behav Med, 26,* 212–220.

Skurk, T., Alberti-Huber, C., & Hauner, H. (2006). Relationship between adipocyte size and adipokine expression and secretion. *JCEM, 92,* 1023–1033.

Smith, P.L., Gold, A.R., Meyers, D.A., et al. (1985). Weight loss in mildly to moderately obese patients with obstructive sleep apnea. *Ann Intern Med, 103,* 850–855.

Spalding, K.L., Arner, P.O., Westermark, S., et al. (2008). Dynamics of fat cell turnover in humans. *Nature, 453,* 783–787.

Spiegelman, D., Israel, R.G., Bouchard, C., & Willett, W.C. (1992). Absolute fat mass, percent body fat, and body-fat distribution: Which is the real determinant of blood pressure and serum glucose? *Am J Clin Nutr, 55*(6), 1033–1044.

Srinivasan, S.R., Myers, L., & Berenson, G.S. (2002). Predictability of childhood adiposity and insulin for developing insulin resistance syndrome (syndrome X) in young adulthood: The Bogalusa Heart Study. *Diabetes, 51,* 204–209.

Stanhope, K.L., Schwarz, J.M., Keim, N.L., et al. (2009). Consuming fructose-sweetened, but not glucose-sweetened beverages increases visceral adiposity and lipids and decreases insulin sensitivity in overweight/obese humans. *J Clin Invest, 119,* 1322–1334.

Stevens, J. (2003a). Ethnic-specific revisions of body mass index cutoffs to define overweight and obesity in Asians are not warranted. *IJO, 27,* 1297–1299.

Stevens, J. (2003b). Ethnic-specific cutpoints for obesity vs. country-specific guidelines for action. *IJO, 27,* 287–288.

Stevens, J., Jianwen Cai, J., & Jones, W. (2002). The effect of decision rules on the choice of a body mass index cutoff for obesity: Examples from African American and white women. *Am J Clin Nutr, 75,* 986–992.

Steyn, K. (1991). Risk factors for coronary heart disease in the black population of the Cape Peninsula. *South African Medical Journal, 79,* 480–485.

Stommel, M., & Schoenborn, C.A. (2010). Variations in BMI and prevalence of health risks in diverse racial and ethnic populations. *Obesity,* doi:10.1038/oby.2009.472.

Stunkard, A.J., Sorensen, T.I., Hanis, C., et al. (1986). An adoption study of human obesity. *NEJM, 314*(04), 193–198.

Sugerman, H.J. (2000). The epidemic of severe obesity: The values of surgical treatment. *Mayo Clin Proc, 75,* 669–672.

Sugerman, H.J., Sugerman, E.L., Demaria, E.J., Kellum, J.M., Kennedy, C., Mowery, Y., & Wolfe, L.G. (2003). Bariatric surgery for severely obese adolescents. *J Gastrointest Surg, 7,* 102–107.

Suk, S.H., Sacco, R.L., Boden-Albala, B., et al. (2003). Abdominal obesity and risk of ischemic stroke. *Adv Chronic Kidney Dis, 34,* 1586–1592.

Suter, M., Giusti, V., Heraief, E., Zysset, F., & Calmes, J.M. (2003). Laparoscopic Roux-en-Y gastric bypass: Initial 2-year experience. *Surg Endosc, 17,* 603–609.

Tauman, R., & Gozal, D. (2006). Obesity and obstructive sleep apnea in children. *Paediatr Respir Rev, 7,* 247–259.

Tchernof, A., Nolan, A., Sites, C.K., et al. (2002). Weight loss reduces C-reactive protein levels in obese postmenopausal women. *Circulation, 105,* 564–569.

Terry, M.B., Wei, Y., & Esserman, D. (2007). Maternal, birth, and early-life influences on adult body size in women. *AJE, 166,* 5–13.

Trakhtenbroit, M.A., Leichman, G.J., Algahim, M.F., et al. (2009). Body weight, insulin resistance, and serum adipokine levels two years after two types of bariatric surgery. *Am J Med, 122,* 435–442.

US National Academy of Sciences. (2005). Transportation Research Board Annual Report. Washington, DC: US National Academy of Sciences.

Unger, R.H. (2003). The physiology of cellular liporegulation. *Annual Review of Physiology, 65,* 333–347.

United Nations Development Program. (2001). *Human development report.* New York: Oxford University Press. Published for the United Nations Development Program (UNDP). Retrieved from http://hdr.undp.org/en/media/completenew1.pdf.

United Nations. (2006). *World urbanization prospectus: The 2005 revision.* New York: UN, Dept of Economics and Social Affairs, Population Division.

van der Lei, B., Halbesma, G.J., van Neiuwenhoven, C.A., & van Wingerden, J.J. (2007). Spontaneous breast enlargement following liposuction of the abdominal wall: Does a link exist? *Plast Reconstr Surg, 119,* 1584–1589.

Vgontzas, A.N., Tan, T.L., Bixler, E.O., et al. (1994). Sleep apnea and sleep disruption in obese patients. *Arch Intern Med, 154,* 1705–1711.

Vlahakis, N.E., & Hubmayr, R.D/ (2005). Review: Cellular stress failure in ventilator-injured lungs. *Am J Respir Crit Care Med, 171*(12),1328–1342.

Wadd, W. (1816). *Cursory remarks on corpulence; Or obesity considered a disease with critical examination of ancient and modern opinions, relative to its causes and cure* (3rd ed.). London: J Callow.

Wajchenberg, B.L. (2007). β-cell failure in diabetes and preservation by clinical treatment. *Endocr Rev, 28,* 187–218.

Wajchenberg, B.L. (2000). Subcutaneous and visceral adipose tissue: Their relation to the metabolic syndrome. *Endocr Rev, 21,* 697–738.

Wagner, D.R., & Heyward, V.H. (2000). Measures of body composition in blacks and whites: A comparative review. *American Journal of Clinical Nutrition, 71,* 1392–1402.

Wardle, J., Carnell, S., Haworth, C.M.A., & Plomin, R. (2008). Evidence for a strong genetic influence on childhood adiposity despite the force of the obesogenic environment. *Am J Clin Nutr, 87,* 398–404.

Welch, G.W., & Sowers, M.F.R. (2000). The interrelationship between body topology and body composition varies with age among women. *J Nutr, 130,* 2371–2377.

Werkman, A., Deurenberg-Yap, M., Schmidt, G., & Deurenberg, P. (2000). A comparison between composition and density of the fat-free mass of young adult Singaporean Chinese and Dutch Caucasians. *Ann Nutr Metab, 44,* 235–242.

Weyer, C., Foley, J.E., Bogardus, C., et al. (2000). Enlarged subcutaneous abdominal adipocyte size, but not obesity itself, predicts type II diabetes, independent of insulin resistance. *Diabetologia, 43,* 1498–1506.

Whitaker, R.C., Wright, J.A., Pepe, M.S., Seidel, K.D., & Dietz, W.H. (1997). Predicting obesity in young adulthood from childhood and parental obesity. *N Engl J Med, 337,* 869–873.

Whitaker, R.C., Pepe, M.S., Wright, J.A., Seidel, K.D., & Dietz, W.H. (1998). Early adiposity rebound and the risk of adult obesity. *Pediatrics, 101,* e5.

Willett, W.C., Dietz, W.H., & Colditz, G.A. (1999). Guidelines for a healthy weight. *NEJM, 341,* 427–434.

WHO. (1998). Obesity. *Preventing and managing the global epidemic. Report of a WHO consultation on obesity.* Geneva, Switzerland: World Health Organization.

WHO. (2000). *Preventing and managing the global epidemic. Report of a WHO consultation on obesity.* WHO Technical Report Series No. 894. Geneva: World Health Organization.

WHO. (2003). *Diet, nutrition and the prevention of chronic diseases: A report of the joint WHO/FAO expert consultation.* WHO Technical Report Series 916. Geneva, Switzerland: World Health Organization.

WHO. (2004). Appropriate body mass index (BMI) for Asian populations and its implications on policy and intervention strategies: Report of a

WHO Expert Consultation. *Lancet, 363,* 157–163.

WHO. (2005). *Preventing chronic diseases.* Geneva: World Health Organization.

WHO. (2009a). *Global health risks: Mortality and burden of disease attributable to selected major risks.* Geneva: World Health Organization.

WHO. (2009b). *Population-based prevention strategies for childhood obesity: Report of a WHO forum and technical meeting, Geneva, 15–17, December 2009.* Geneva: World Health Organization.

WHO Multicentre Growth Reference Study Group. (2009). *WHO Child Growth Standards: Growth velocity based on weight, length and head circumference: Methods and development.* Geneva: World Health Organization.

Williams, S.M., & Goulding, A. (2009). Patterns of growth associated with the timing of adiposity rebound. *Obesity, 17,* 335–341.

World Cancer Research Fund/American Institute for Cancer Research. (2007). *Food, nutrition, physical activity, and the prevention of cancer: A global perspective.* Washington, DC: World Cancer Research Fund/American Institute for Cancer Research.

Yasojima, K., Schwab, C., Mcgeer, E.G., et al. (2001). Generation of C-reactive protein and complement components in atherosclerotic plaques. *Am J Pathol, 158,* 1039–1051.

Yatsuya, H., Folsom, A.R., Yamagishi, K., et al. (2010). Race- and sex-specific associations of obesity measures with ischemic stroke incidence in the Atheroslerosis Risk in Communities (ARIC) Study. *Adv Chronic Kidney Dis, 41,* 417–425.

Yin, J., Gao, Z., He, Q., & Ye, J. (2009). Role of hypoxia in obesity-induced disorders of glucose and lipid metabolism in adipose tissue. *Am J Physiol Endocrinol Metab, 296,* E333–E342.

Yeh, E.T.H., & Willerson, J.T. (2003). Coming of age of C-reactive protein. Using inflammatory markers in cardiology. *Circulation, 107,* 307–372.

Young, T., Palta, M., Dempsey, J., Skatrud, J., Weber, S., & Badr, S. (1993). The occurrence of sleep-disordered breathing among middle-aged adults. *N Engl J Med, 328,* 1230–1235.

Young, T., Pappard, P.E., & Gottlieb, D.J. (2002). Epidemiology of obstructive sleep apnea. *American Journal of Respiratory and Critical Care Medicine, 165,* 1217–1239.

Yudkin, J.S., Stehouwer, C.D.A., Emeiss, J.J., et al. (1999). C-reactive protein in healthy subjects: Associations with obesity, insulin resistance, and endothelial dysfunction. A potential role for cytokines originating from adipose tissue? *Arterioscler Thromb Vasc Biol, 19,* 972–978.

Yuji, M. (2002). New criteria for "obesity disease" in Japan. *Circ J, 66,* 987–992.

Yun, P.L., Bruck, M., Felsenfeld, L., & Katz, B.E. (2003). Breast enlargement observed after power liposuction: A retrospective review. *Dermatol Surg, 29,* 165–167.

Yusuf, S., Hawken, S., Ounpuu, S., Bautista, L., Franzosi, M.G., Commerford, P.,... INTERHEART Study Investigators. (2005). Obesity and the risk of myocardial infarction in 27,000 participants from 52 countries: A case-control study. *Lancet, 366*(9497), 1640–1649.

Zeckhauser, R., & Shepard, D.S. (1976). Where now for saving lives? *Law and Contemporary Problems, 40,* 5–45.

Zeghari, N., Vidal, H., Younsi, M., Ziegler, O., Drouin, P., Donner, M. (2000). Adipocyte membrane phospholipids and PPAR-gamma expression in obese women: Relationship to hyperinsulinemia. *Am J Physiol Endocrinol Metab, 279*(4), E736–E743.

Ziccardi, P., Nappo, F., Giugliano, G., et al. (2002). Reduction of inflammatory cytokine concentrations and improvement of endothelial functions in obese women after weight loss over one year. *Circulation, 105,* 804–809.

Ziegler, E.E., & Nelson, S.E. (2010). Growth charts compared. *Nestle Nutr Workshop Ser Pediatr, 65,* 197–210.

Ziraba, A., Fotso, J., & Ochako, R. (2009). Overweight and obesity in urban Africa: A problem of the rich or of the poor? *BMC Public Health, 9,* 465.

34

The Epidemiology of Thyroid Disease

THYROID GLAND: ANATOMY AND FUNCTION

The human thyroid is a butterfly-shaped gland located in the anterior neck inferior to the thyroid cartilage (also known as the *Adam's apple*). The term "thyroid" means "shield," which describes the basic shape of the thyroid cartilage.

The thyroid produces iodine-containing thyroid hormones, the principal ones being triiodothyronine (T_3) and thyroxine (T_4). Triiodothyronine is 2–3 times more potent than thyroxine and considerably more T_4 is produced than T_3 (20:1 ratio). These circulating hormones are essential in regulating the rate of metabolism in the body. Inside the cell, T_3 and T_4 stimulate energy production by the mitochondria and promote glucose catabolism, protein synthesis, lipolysis, and excretion of cholesterol. Thyroid hormones also influence growth and development in early life and participate in a number of essential physiologic functions throughout life, e.g., maintenance of normal cardiac rhythm, muscle tone, and neuronal function in the sympathetic nervous system (Robbins and Cotran, 1979).

The functional unit of the thyroid is the thyroid follicle. The thyroid is comprised of thousands of spherical thyroid follicles, each of which contains a material called colloid that contains iodide (the storage form of iodine) and thyroglobulin (the glycoprotein bound to thyroid hormones). Thyroid hormones are synthesized by cuboidal epithelial cells that line the thyroid follicles. The essential substrates for biosynthesis are the amino acid, tyrosine, and the mineral, iodine. The biosynthesis of thyroid hormones (T_3 and T_4) is regulated by peptide hormones secreted by the hypothalamus and the anterior pituitary gland (**Figure 34.1**). In response to low blood levels of thyroid hormones or neurological signals, the hypothalamus secretes a protein called *thyroid releasing hormone (TRH)* into special blood vessels connected to the pituitary gland which in turn triggers the anterior pituitary to secrete a second protein called *thyroid stimulating hormone (TSH or thyrotropin)* into the blood. In response to TSH, receptors on the cell membranes of thyroid epithelial cells (*thyrotropin receptors*) activate the biosynthetic pathway for the production of thyroid hormones (T_3 and T_4). Thyroid hormones are stored in a glycoprotein called thyroglobulin which is also synthesized in the thyroid epithelium. Thyroid hormones are secreted into the blood from the thyroglobulin (colloid) stored within thyroid follicles. Thyroid hormones (T_3 and T_4) are transported in the blood bound to a carrier protein known as *thyroxine-binding globulin*. The secretion and release of T_3 and T_4 is regulated by blood levels of thyroid hormones, e.g., low levels stimulate the release of active T_3 and T_4.

Special cells of the thyroid gland called C *cells* produce a polypeptide hormone called "*calcitonin*" that helps regulate calcium homeostasis throughout the body. Relatively small *parathyroid glands* (usually four in number) are located at the periphery of the thyroid gland (Figure 34.1). The parathyroid glands synthesize *parathyroid hormone (PTH)*, which together with calcitonin and the active form of vitamin D regulate levels of calcium and phosphorous in the blood, the bones, and most other tissues (Robbins and Cotran, 1979).

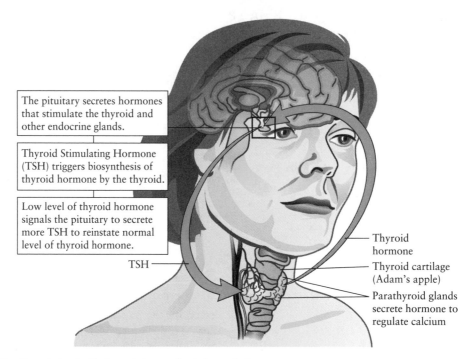

The pituitary secretes hormones that stimulate the thyroid and other endocrine glands.

Thyroid Stimulating Hormone (TSH) triggers biosynthesis of thyroid hormone by the thyroid.

Low level of thyroid hormone signals the pituitary to secrete more TSH to reinstate normal level of thyroid hormone.

TSH

Thyroid hormone

Thyroid cartilage (Adam's apple)

Parathyroid glands secrete hormone to regulate calcium

Figure 34.1 The Hypothalamic-Pituitary-Axis: Feedback Control of the Thyroid Gland.

DISEASES OF THE THYROID GLAND

The most commonly encountered diseases of the thyroid gland involve either an overactive gland (*hyperthyroidism*) or and underactive gland (*hypothyroidism*). Early screening surveys conducted among adults in the United States and Great Britain reflect prevalence rates of thyroid abnormalities of approximately 6% (Tunbridge et al., 1977; Baldwin and Rowitt, 1978). The most prevalent thyroid condition is enlargement of the thyroid gland which is commonly called a "*goiter.*" As discussed in the following sections, goiters fall into two broad categories: *toxic goiters* caused by hyperthyroidism and *nontoxic goiters* caused by hypothyroidism.

Thyroid adenomas (nodules) occasionally arise within the thyroid gland. On pathologic examination, the vast majority of thyroid nodules turn out to be benign. Thyroid cancer is rare but it must be differentiated from all benign lesions. Thyroid neoplasms are discussed later in this chapter.

Hyperthyroidism

Hyperthyroidism refers to an overactive thyroid. Symptoms of hyperthyroidism are due to the overproduction of thyroid hormones (T_3 and T_4) by the thyroid gland. The most common cause of hyperthyroidism is a condition known as *Graves'*

disease (named after the Irish physician Robert J. Graves who first described the condition in 1835 [Weetman, 2000]).

Graves' Disease

Graves' disease, also called *diffuse toxic goiter*, is believed to arise as a consequence of autoimmune reactions. Graves' disease affects approximately 0.5% of the US population and is the underlying cause of up to 80% of all cases of hyperthyroidism. The clinical signs and symptoms of this condition result from excess stimulation of the thyroid gland by autoantibodies resulting in overproduction of T_3 and T_4 hormones. Molecular studies suggest that circulating IgG antibodies bind to and activate thyrotopin receptors of the thyroid epithelium, thus stimulating hypertrophy and hyperplasia of thyroid follicles. This process results in increased production of thyroid hormones, thyroid enlargement, and goiter formation. The peak incidence of Graves' disease is between 20–40 years of age. Symptoms include enlargement of the thyroid gland (goiter), protruding eyes (exopthalmos), palpitations, excess sweating, diarrhea, weight loss, muscle weakness, and unusual sensitivity to heat. Notably, Graves' disease is diagnosed 5–10 times more often in women than men (Weetman, 2000; Brent, 2008). As shown by the age-specific rates for Swedish women and men in **Figure 34.2**, the marked

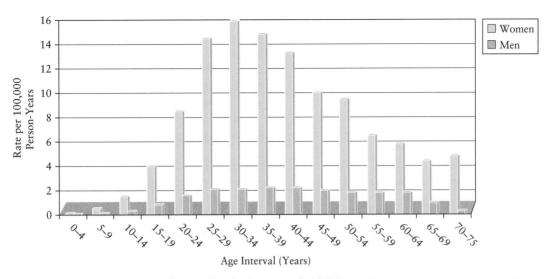

Figure 34.2 Age-Specific Incidence of Graves' Disease by Gender in Sweden, 1987–2007.

Source: Data from Hemminki K, Li X, Sundquist J, Sundquist K (2010). The epidemiology of Graves' disease: evidence of a genetic and an environmental contribution. *Autoimmun* 34(3):J307–J313.

female excess of this condition is evident throughout life (Hemminki et al., 2010).

Genetic studies suggest that Graves' disease has a significant hereditary component. A nationwide population-based study of twins ascertained from the Danish Twin Registry during 1953–1976 revealed a concordance rate of 35% among monozygous twins compared to 3% for dizygous twins. In regression models, genetic factors accounted for 79% of the liability to development of Graves' disease compared to 21% for environmental factors. Based on these findings, the investigators suggested that "*genetic factors play a major role in the etiology of Graves' disease*" (Brix et al., 2001).

A national genetic study of Graves' disease was conducted in Sweden using data from the *Swedish Multigeneration Register* linked to the *Swedish Hospital Discharge Register* for the years 1987–2007. Standard incidence ratios were calculated based on familial relationships of 15,743 patients hospitalized for Graves' disease during this time period. Standard incidence ratios were increased 5-fold in families with an affected sibling and more than 300-fold in families with two affected siblings. The standard incidence ratio in twins was 16.5. The incidence of Graves' disease was also increased in families with other autoimmune conditions such as Addison's disease, type 1 diabetes mellitus, Hashimoto's thyroiditis, pernicious anemia, myasthenia gravis, lupus erythematosus, and scleroderma. Surprisingly, the standard incidence ratio was also increased among spouses of affected

individuals suggesting that environmental factors may also be involved in the genesis of Graves' disease (Hemminki et al., 2010). Interestingly, cigarette smoking has been linked to the development of multiple autoimmune diseases, including rheumatoid arthritis, systemic lupus erythematosus, multiple sclerosis, and Graves' disease (Manji et al., 2006; Costenbader and Karlson, 2006). Notwithstanding, the genetic factors that influence the thyroid autoimmunity involved in Graves' disease clearly outweigh the environmental factors (Jacobson and Tomer, 2007a; 2007b).

The Human Leukocyte Antigen (HLA) Locus and Autoimmune Thyroiditis

Genes of the *human leukocyte antigen (HLA)* play a major role in the immune response to foreign antigens as well as the recognition of *self versus nonself* in immune reactions. The six major genes of the *super HLA locus* are all located on the short arm of chromosome 6 (Levinson, 2006). Specific HLA genes encode cell-surface antigen-presenting proteins that regulate the processing of bacterial antigens by T lymphocytes and the formation of antibodies by B lymphocytes. The profile of cell membrane HLA proteins differentiates *self from nonself* in the immune response and perturbations in the system occasionally result in the formation of antibodies that are directed against self. Such autoantibodies are capable of selectively stimulating and/or destroying certain tissues of the body, thereby causing autoimmune disease.

Two classical forms of thyroiditis are known to have an autoimmune basis, Graves' disease and Hashimoto's thyroiditis (discussed in the following section). Genetic variants at the HLA locus appear to increase susceptibility to both conditions. For example, individuals who carry the *HLA-DR3* allele have been found to be three to four times more likely to develop Graves' disease than noncarriers (Farid, Stone, and Johnson, 1980; Zamani et al., 2000; Jacobsen and Tomer, 2007a), and likewise, *HLA-DR3* has been found to increase the risk of developing Hashomito's thyroiditis more than twofold in some populations (Tandon, Zhang, and Weetman, 1991; Jacobsen, Huber, and Tomer, 2008). It is hypothesized that the HLA-DR3 protein may heighten susceptibility through its special affinity for thyroid antigens thereby creating an autoimmune response directed against the thyroid gland. Furthermore, there is increasing evidence suggesting that interactions between genetic variants of thyroglobulin and the *HLA-DR3* allele enhance susceptibility to the development of Graves' disease (Jacobsen and Tomer, 2007b).

Another candidate gene for conferring susceptibility to the development of autoimmune thyroid disorders is the *cytotoxic T lymphocyte associated antigen-4* (*CTLA-4*). The normal *CTLA-4* gene product helps to regulate the response of T lymphocytes to antigenic stimuli. It apparently provides a negative signal to the T cell thus limiting autoimmune responses and maintaining self-tolerance (Chambers and Allison, 1997). Significant associations have consistently been observed between Graves' disease and certain allelic forms of *CTLA-4*, whereas associations with Hashimoto's thyroiditis are less clear (Chistiakov and Turakulov, 2003).

Other susceptibility genes have also been identified. For example, variants of the gene that encodes *vitamin-D-binding protein* have been linked to the development of Graves' disease. Vitamin-D-binding protein facilitates the transport and release of vitamin D in blood and tissues, and the active form of vitamin D works in concert with calcitonin, parathyroid, and thyroid hormones to regulate calcium and phosphorous homeostasis. Graves' disease combined with low serum vitamin D leads to poor absorption of calcium and related symptoms of muscle wasting, bone resorption, and nervous system dysfunction (Herman-Bonert and Friedman, 2004).

German investigators studied genetic polymorphisms of vitamin-D-binding protein among 561 individuals in families with an offspring affected by either Graves' disease (95 pedigrees) or Hashimoto's thyroiditis (92 pedigrees). They found that allelic variants of vitamin-D-binding protein confer susceptibility to the development of Graves' disease but not Hashimoto's thyroiditis (Pani et al., 2002). In a subsequent genetic case control study of Graves' disease and vitamin-D-binding protein, Polish investigators compared single nucleotide polymorphisms of 332 cases to 185 healthy control subjects. They found a specific polymorphism at codon 420 involving substitution of lysine for threonine that significantly increased the risk of disease and decreased the level of serum vitamin D (Kurylowicz et al., 2006). These results suggest that genetic regulation of vitamin D activity plays a role in thyroid autoimmunity and the development of Graves' disease.

Hashimoto's Thyroiditis

Hashimoto's thyroiditis is a chronic autoimmune disease in which the thyroid gland is gradually destroyed by the body's own immune system. The disorder was first described by the Japanese physician Dr. Hakaru Hashimoto in 1912 (Hashimoto, 1912). It is diagnosed by clinical symptoms plus the presence of autoantibodies against thyroglobulin or other cellular components of the thyroid gland. Pathologic review of thyroidal tissue from patients reveals inflammation and striking infiltration by lymphocytes admixed with plasma cells, necrosis, and derangement of thyroid follicles plus goitrous enlargement of the gland. Without treatment, there is progressive depletion of thyroid follicles accompanied by hypothyroidism and loss of thyroid function (Rapoport, 1991).

Patients often have a family history of thyroid disorders including Graves' disease and/or other autoimmune conditions such as type 1 diabetes, celiac disease, pernicious anemia, Addison's disease, and Sjogren's syndrome. Hashimoto's thyroiditis is typically diagnosed between the ages of 45–65 years and occurs 10–20 times more often in women than men (Vanderpump and Tunbridge, 2002).

Certain genes of the HLA locus confer susceptibility to the development of this disorder, e.g., presence of the *HLA-DR5* gene increases the relative risk more than threefold. As discussed above, the *CTLA-4* gene has also been implicated in the genesis of Hashimoto's thryoiditis (Tomer et al., 1999; Chistiakov, 2005; Yesilkaya et al., 2008).

Grave's disease and Hashimoto's thyroiditis are often treated with oral doses of radioactive iodine, resulting in permanent destruction of cells in the thyroid and rendering them permanently inactive. Another treatment option for these conditions is surgery in which the thyroid gland is partially or fully removed. Patients who undergo thyroid ablation or thyroidectomy receive daily replacement thyroid hormone therapy.

Hypothyroidism

Hypothyroidism refers to an underactive thyroid gland, which results in a deficiency of thyroid hormones (T_3 and T_4). Hypothyroid disorders occur when the thyroid gland is inactive or underactive as a result of improper formation from birth, lack of iodine, or removal or iatrogenic inactivation (ablation) of the thyroid gland. Symptoms of hypothyroidism include abnormal weight gain, fatigue, baldness, temperature intolerance (typically cold), and in some cases thyroid enlargement (*nontoxic goiter*).

Nontoxic goiter, or simply "*goiter*," refers to enlargement of the thyroid gland in conjunction with hypothyroidism. As discussed below, the dominant global cause of goiter is iodine deficiency. Enlargement of the thyroid gland in iodine-deficient children is progressive, initially involving diffuse hyperplasia and later the development of multiple nodules wherein the thyroid follicles are markedly distended by the presence of excess colloid (Robbins and Cotran, 1979). Goiter arising from iodine deficiency is very uncommon in developed countries since iodine is routinely added to salt and other foods for consumption. Indeed, iodized salt has been a prominent feature of the American diet since 1924 (Marine, 1924; McClure, 1935).

The discovery of iodine as an essential mineral for normal function of the thyroid glands and the production of thyroid hormones provides a convincing example of the power of epidemiologic investigation. In 1905, a young physician trained at Johns Hopkins University, David Marine, began his residency training in pathology at Lakeside Hospital on the shores of Lake Erie in Cleveland, Ohio. His interest in thyroid disease was spiked by the high prevalence of goiters in dogs in the area and he began a series of studies to elucidate the cause. Marine observed that dietary supplements of iodine in the form of iodized salt reduced the incidence of goiter in sheep and produced regression of goiters and reversal of hypothyroid symptoms in dogs (Marine, 1907). In pathologic studies, Marine found that large goitrous thyroids from dogs had lower levels of iodine than normal thyroids from healthy dogs (Marine and Williams, 1908). Marine was also called upon to investigate the high rate of "*alleged thyroid carcinomas*" in trout in a fish hatchery in northern Ohio. Pathologic studies revealed that the fish had goiters due to iodine deficiency rather than thyroid carcinomas and Marine demonstrated that goiter development was effectively prevented by the addition of iodine or foods high in iodine content to the trout hatchery water (Marine, 1914).

Marine soon translated these findings to the human population, showing in his clinic that children suffering from simple goiter responded to therapy with sodium iodide. Realizing the devastating problem of goiter in the Great Lakes region, Marine and his colleague, O.P. Kimball, organized and conducted a field intervention study using sodium iodide supplements in the diets of young girls in the Akron, Ohio region. Girls in the 5th–8th grades received 200 mg of sodium iodide for 10 consecutive days and older girls received twice this amount. The dosing regimen was repeated every six months. A total of 2,305 girls received the supplemental iodine compared to 2,190 girls from a nearby region that did not. Results of this field experiment after 30 months of follow-up are summarized in **Table 34.1**.

After 30 months of observation, the chemopreventive value of the treatment with sodium iodide was remarkable. Among participants with normal thyroid glands at the beginning of the study, 347 of 1,257 girls (27.6%) who *did not* receive iodine developed goiters compared to only 2 of 908 girls (0.2%) who *did* receive iodine. Substantial therapeutic effects were also evident. Among participants with enlarged thyroid glands at baseline, *progression* of disease was observed in only 0.2% of treated girls compared to 14.1% of controls, whereas *regression* of disease was observed in 60.3% of treated girls compared to 13.8% of controls. Importantly, no toxic effects of the sodium iodide supplement were detected in the study (Marine and Kimball, 1917; Marine and Kimball, 1920; Marine, 1924). The definitive evidence

Table 34.1	Effects of Sodium Iodide Supplementation in School Girls of Northern Ohio	
Size of Thyroid	**Treatment Group**	**Control Group**
Initially Normal	*N* = 908	*N* = 1,257
Unchanged	906 (99.8%)	910 (72.4%)
Enlarged	2 (0.2%)	347 (27.6%)
Initially Enlarged	*N* = 1,282	*N* = 1,048
Unchanged	506 (39.5%)	755 (72.0%)
Increased	3 (0.2%)	148 (14.1%)
Decreased	773 (60.3%)	145 (13.8%)

Source: Data from Marine D, Kimball OP (1920). The prevention of simple goiter in man: Fourth paper. Arch Intern Med 25:661–672.

from this study was the crowning achievement of Marine's work on iodine deficiency as the causative factor in the development of hypothyroidism and simple goiter.

Cretinism

The health consequences of iodine deficiency often manifest early in life. These include abnormal neuronal development, mental retardation, congenital malformations, and hypothyroidism. Deleterious effects on reproduction such as spontaneous abortion, miscarriage, and infertility are also notable. Later in life, lack of iodine is also associated with intellectual impairment.

Cretinism is an anomaly that is caused by iodine deficiency in the developing fetus. Clinical manifestations of this condition depend upon the gestational timing and severity of iodine and hormonal insufficiency in both the mother and fetus. In the absence of iodine, there is abnormal development and function of the fetal thyroid gland. This devastating condition typically manifests at birth or during infancy and is characterized by hypothyroidism, goiter, mental retardation, deaf-mutism, stunted growth, and other anomalies.

Endemic cretinism was once common in the Alpine populations of Southern Europe due to lack of iodine in their diets. As an example, in Switzerland where the soil contains little iodine, cases of cretinism were once commonplace. In fact, the soils of many inland areas on all continents are iodine deficient, and plants and animals grown there are correspondingly deficient. Populations living in such areas without outside food sources are therefore at high risk for the development of iodine deficiency diseases (Gaitan and Dunn, 1992).

Fortunately, the addition of iodine to table salt has virtually eliminated cretinism in developed countries. Furthermore, early detection of thyroid insufficiency in newborns and administration of thyroxine (T_4) can often be effective in reinstating thyroid function and normal growth and development. Nevertheless, in developing nations without such programs, the lack of dietary iodine remains the leading cause of preventable mental retardation in babies and small children.

GOITROGENIC DIETARY FACTORS AND THYROID DISORDERS

Goitrogens are dietary agents that suppress thyroid function and induce the formation of goiters, particularly in children. The principal goitrogens are *isothiocyanate* and the *isoflavones* (a class of phytoestrogens). These compounds inhibit the activity of *thyroxine peroxidase*, a key enzyme in the formation of thyroid hormones from iodine and tyrosine. Cruciferous vegetables such as broccoli, cauliflower, and cabbage contain high levels of isothiocyanate. Other sources include peanuts, spinach, peaches, and strawberries (Vanderpas, 2006). Soybeans and soy-based products contain high concentrations of isoflavones (Doerge and Sheehan, 2002).

Thiocyanate overload from consumption of cassava root has been found to be goitrogenic in Central Africa, particularly in association with selenium deficiency. The cassava root has low concentrations of iodine and selenium and high concentrations of isothiocyanate. Thilly and colleagues investigated dietary factors and thyroid disorders in children aged 5–7 years from goiter-endemic areas of Central Africa. Low serum levels of thyroxine (T_4) were associated with low selenium and high thiocyanate levels in children residing in regions where cassava is the principal source of carbohydrates in the diet. Furthermore, high rates of cretinism were observed among children with severe iodine and selenium deficiencies in combination with thiocyanate overload (Thilly et al., 1993).

High consumption of soy has also been linked to thyroid disorders in children. Early case reports document goiter development in infants on a soy diet (Hydovitz, 1960). Fort and colleagues studied 59 children with autoimmune thyroid disease, their 76 healthy siblings, and 54 healthy unrelated children. They found that the frequency of feedings with soy-based milk formulas in early life (31%) was significantly higher in children with autoimmune thyroid disease compared to healthy siblings and unrelated children (12%) (Fort, Moses, and Fasano, 1990). Thus, despite some beneficial health effects of soy, the issue of goitrogenic impact remains problematic.

GLOBAL IMPACT OF IODINE DEFICIENCY

Following the pioneering research of David Marine in the early 20th century, confirming evidence of the chemopreventive value of supplemental iodine soon became available from studies in Sweden, Switzerland, and other many other nations. In the United States, iodized table salt containing 100 mg per kg of potassium iodide has been available since 1924. The United States Food and Drug Administration recommend 150 micrograms of iodine per day for both men and women.

Supplementing the diet with iodized salt is a simple cost-effective method of ensuring adequate iodine intake and successful population-based programs have increased around the world with the active encouragement and support of the World Health Organization (Holman and McCartney, 1960). According to recent survey data from the World Health Organization, 164 countries now have iodized salt programs and the percent of households in the developing world that use iodized salt rose from about 20% in 1970 to 70% in 2000. Nevertheless, these estimates also suggest that iodine deficiency impacts approximately 2 billion people worldwide and causes a high burden of disease in many developing nations. For example, in India, it is estimated that 100 million suffer from iodine deficiency, 4 million from goiter, and 500,000 from cretinism. Other pockets of iodine deficiency are evident in the Western Pacific, Southeast Asia, Africa, and the Russian Federation (Andersson et al., 2005). Continuing international efforts should therefore focus on implementing and sustaining iodine supplementation programs in all nations (*The Lancet*, 2008).

NEOPLASMS OF THE THYROID GLAND

Benign Thyroid Adenomas

Solitary thyroid adenomas (nodules) usually arise from the thyroid follicles. Thyroid nodules are relatively common and are detected approximately three times more often in women than men. Treatment is typically by simple excision; however, careful histological examination of tissue is always necessary to rule out malignant transformation. Similar to thyroid cancer (discussed in the next section), the major risk factors for thyroid adenoma include radiation exposure, iodine deficiency or excess, and personal and/or familial history of thyroid disorders.

Investigators in New York monitored the incidence of thyroid adenomas in a cohort of 2,657 infants given X-ray treatment for thymus enlargement and a comparison cohort of 4,833 untreated siblings. Individuals in these cohorts were followed for up to 50 years. The observed rates of thyroid adenoma increased in a linear dose response with the level of radiation. Exposure levels of 6 Gy increased the relative risk more than sixfold (1 Gy is approximately equivalent to 100 rads of ionizing radiation). Other significant risk factors included a personal medical history and/or a family history of thyroid disorders (Shore et al., 1993).

Thyroid Cancer

Malignant tumors of the thyroid gland are rare. Nevertheless, all thyroid nodules must be carefully examined under the microscope to distinguish benign from malignant tumors. Thyroid carcinomas arise from the cuboidal epithelium that lines the thyroid follicles. These cells normally synthesize thyroid hormones (T_3 and T_4) and thryoglobulin. Medullary thyroid carcinomas arise from the parafollicular C cells that normally synthesize parathyroid hormone (PTH).

The annual incidence of thyroid cancer in the United States during 1996–2000 was estimated at 68 cases per million. The female to male ratio of thyroid cancer is approximately 3 to 1 (98 cases per million women compared to 36 cases per million men in the US). Based on recent data from the International Association for Research on Cancer (Parkin et al., 1992) and the US National Cancer Institute (Goodman, Yoshizawa, and Kolonel, 1988), the annual incidence rates are highest in Hawaii (119 per million in women and 45 per million in men) and lowest in Poland (14 per million in women and 4 per million in men).

There is evidence that the incidence of thyroid cancer has increased in some developed countries during the past few decades, e.g., in the United States the incidence rates have doubled since the 1970s (**Figure 34.3**). Since mortality has remained relative constant over the same time period, this trend may largely reflect the increased early detection of small papillary thyroid tumors that were treated by complete surgical resection. Other potential factors include the indiscriminant use of X-rays for the diagnosis and therapy of certain conditions of the head and neck and the obesity epidemic in developed nations.

There is also evidence that the incidence of thyroid malignancies increased markedly in populations exposed to excessive radioactive fallout in Japan following the atomic bombing in World War II and in Russia after the Chernobyl nuclear reactor accident (Boice, 1998, 2006). Furthermore, a recent study suggests the presence of synergism between radiation exposure and iodine deficiency in elevating the risk of developing thyroid cancer (Cardis et al., 2005).

Cardis and colleagues conducted a case control study of thyroid cancer and exposure to radioactive fallout from the Chernobyl nuclear reactor accident in combination with dietary intake of iodine and iodine supplements. Cases and controls were ascertained from Belarus and the Russian Federation population living near the reactor at the time of the accident. Questionnaire data on diet were obtained from 276 patients with pathologically confirmed

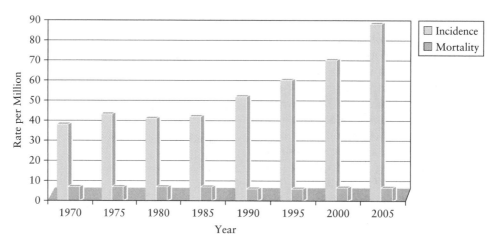

Figure 34.3 Incidence and Mortality of Thyroid Cancer: 1970–2005, USA.

Source: Data from Surveillance Epidemiology and End Results (SEER Data, 1973–2007). US National Institutes of Health, National Cancer Institute, Bethesda, Maryland.

thyroid cancer and 1,300 healthy control subjects matched by age and gender. Radiation exposure was estimated by a comprehensive dose reconstruction program taking into account both inhaled and ingested radioactive particles. The major contribution to dose was from drinking milk contaminated with radioactive iodine isotopes, particularly I^{131}. Dietary iodine and dietary supplements containing potassium iodide were also examined as cofactors in the study. Similar to many other investigations, the overall risk of thyroid cancer increased with increasing dose of radioactivity. Notably, subjects with low iodine intake and 1 Gy of total radiation exposure had high odds ratios ranging from 4.85–8.44, whereas those with similar radiation exposure who took potassium iodide supplements were *not* at increased risk (OR = 1.08). These results indicate that diets deficient in iodine potentiate the risk of radiation-induced thyroid cancer and suggest that iodine supplementation has a protective effect against carcinogenesis (Cardis et al., 2005).

Goodman and colleagues conducted a population-based case control study of thyroid cancer, diet, and other factors in Hawaii, which has one of the highest incidence rates of thyroid cancer in the world. Cases with pathologically confirmed thyroid cancer (51 men and 140 women) were compared to 113 male and 328 female controls matched on age and gender. The risk of thyroid cancer increased with increasing body weight in both men and women. Men and women in the highest quartiles of weight had fivefold and two-fold increases in thyroid cancer risk, respectively, compared to those in the lowest quartiles. Risk increases were also observed among heavier women who used fertility drugs or experienced miscarriages or stillbirths

at first pregnancy. Results suggest a dose response relationship between body weight and thyroid carcinogenesis with potential effect modification due to fertility drugs and/or reproductive failure (Goodman, Yoshizawa, and Kolonel, 1988; Goodman, Kolonel, and Wilkens, 1992). Interestingly, certain inflammatory adipokines secreted by adipocytes (fat cells) in obese individuals have been linked to carcinogenesis (Barb, Pazaitou-Panayiotou, and Mantzoros, 2006; Vona-Davis and Rose, 2007). It is therefore conceivable that the increased storage of fat associated with weight gain could induce adipocytes to secrete inflammatory adipokines that target the thyroid gland.

In another case control study conducted in the Hawaiian population, women with high iodine intake who took fertility drugs or suffered miscarriage or stillbirth at first pregnancy were found to be at exceptionally high risk for the development of thyroid cancer. Women with high iodine intake who suffered a first-pregnancy miscarriage had an odds ratio of 4.8 and women with high iodine intake who used fertility drugs had an odds ratio of 7.3 (Kolonel et al., 1990). These results tend to contradict the more recent findings of Cardis and colleagues who observed protective effects of supplemental potassium iodide. Clearly, additional investigations are needed in order to clarify the impact of radiation, iodine, body mass, female reproduction, and other risk factors on thyroid carcinogenesis in different populations.

Medullary Thyroid Cancer

Medullary thyroid cancer arises from the parafollicular calcitonin-secreting cells of the thyroid gland. While the majority of cases are sporadic (nonfamilial), approximately 25% involve heritable mutations of the *RET* gene, a proto-oncogene located on chromosome 10 (Donis-Keller et al., 1993; Eng, 1999). The *RET* gene encodes a cell membrane receptor called *receptor tyrosine kinase* that activates signal transduction and complex cascades of biochemical reactions involving tyrosine phosphorylation within cells. The exact nature of these reactions depends upon the cell type, e.g., in parafollicular C cells, *RET* signaling induces excess biosynthesis of calcitonin.

Mutations of the *RET* gene or the *MENIN* gene (a tumor suppressor gene located on chromosome 11) cause distinct heritable syndromes known as *multiple endocrine neoplasia (MEN)* (Donis-Keller et al., 1993; Guru et al., 1998). Endocrine tumors of the *MEN* syndromes elaborate a variety of amines and peptides depending upon the tissue of origin. Individuals who manifest *MEN* syndromes are classified into two major groups: *MEN I* (adenomas of the pituitary gland, islet cell tumors of the pancreas, hyperplasia of the parathyroid glands, and peptic ulcers) and *MEN II* (medullary thyroid carcinoma, pheochromocytoma, and occasionally mucocutaneous neuroma). These syndromes show an *autosomal dominant* inheritance pattern (Werner, 1963; Carney, 1998).

Carriers of certain mutated forms of the *RET* gene have a high lifetime risk of developing medullary thyroid carcinoma and pheochromocytoma (a malignant tumor of the adrenal glands). The familial association of medullary thyroid cancer and pheochromocytoma is called the *Sipple syndrome* after the physician who first described it (Sipple, 1961). Early onset, typically between 15–20 years of age, is a prominent characteristic of hereditary medullary thyroid cancer.

Fortunately, early detection of thyroid malignancies coupled with complete excision is often curative. The five-year survival rates for patients with stage I disease exceed 95%. Total thyroidectomy is the definitive surgery followed by replacement of thyroid hormones with thyroxine (T_4).

• • • REFERENCES

Andersson, M., Takkouche, B., Egli, I., Allen, H.E., & de Benoist, B. (2005). Current global iodine status and progress over the last decade towards the elimination of iodine deficiency. *Bull World Health Organ, 83*(7), 518–525.

Baldwin, D.B., & Rowett, D. (1978). Incidence of thyroid disorders in Connecticut. *JAMA, 239*, 742–744.

Barb, D., Pazaitou-Panayiotou, K., & Mantzoros, C.S. (2006). Adiponectin: A link between obesity and cancer. *Expert Opinions in Investigative Drugs, 15*, 917–931.

Boice, J.D. Jr. (1998). Radiation and thyroid cancer: What more can be learned? *Acta Oncol, 37*, 321–324.

Boice, J.D. Jr. (2006). Thyroid disease 60 years After Hiroshima and 20 years after Chernobyl. *JAMA, 295*, 1060–1062.

Brent, G. (2008). Graves' disease. *N Engl J Med, 358*, 2594–2605.

Brix, T.H., Kyvik, K.O., Christensen, K., & Hegedus, L. (2001). Evidence for a major role of heredity in Graves' disease: A population-based study of two Danish twin cohorts. *J Clin Endocrinol Metab, 86*, 930–934.

Cardis, E., Kesminiene, A., Ivanov, V., Malakhova, I., Shibata, Y., Khrouch, V., et al. (2005). Risk of thyroid cancer after exposure to ^{131}I in childhood. *J Natl Cancer Inst, 97*, 724–732.

Carney, J.A. (1998). Familial multiple endocrine neoplasia syndromes: Components, classification, and nomenclature. *J Intern Med, 243*(6), 425–432.

Chambers, C.A., & Allison, J.P. (1997). Co-stimulation in T cell responses. *Current Opinion in Immunology, 9*, 396–404.

Chistiakov, D.A. (2005). Immunogenetics of Hashimoto's thyroiditis. *J Autoimmune Diseases, 2*, 1–10.

Chistiakov, D.A., & Turakulov, R.I. (2003). CTLA-4 and its role in autoimmune thyroid disease. *J Molecular Endocrinology, 31*, 21–36.

Costenbader, K.H., & Karlson, E.W. (2006). Cigarette smoking and autoimmune disease: What can we learn from epidemiology? *Lupus, 15*, 737–745.

Doerge, D.R., & Sheehan, D.M. (2002). Goitrogenic and estrogenic activity of soy isoflavones. *Environ Health Perspect, 110*(suppl3), 349–353.

Donis-Keller, H., Dou, S., Chi, D., Carlson, K.M., Toshima, K., Lairmore, T.C.,...Wells, S.A. Jr.

(1993). Mutations in the RET proto-oncogene are associated with MEN 2A and FMTC. *Hum Mol Genet*, 2(7), 851–856.

Eng, C. (1999). RET proto-oncogene in the development of human cancer. *J Clin Oncol*, 17(1), 380–393.

Farid, N.R., Stone, E., & Johnson, G. (1980). Graves' disease and HLA: Clinical and epidemiologic associations. *Clin Endocrinol (Oxf)*, 13, 535–544.

Fort, P., Moses, N., & Fasano, M. (1990). Breast and soy-formula feedings in early infancy and the prevalence of autoimmune thyroid disease in children. *J Am Coll Nutr*, 9, 164–167.

Gaitan, E., & Dunn, J.T. (1992). Epidemiology of iodine deficiency. *Trends Endocrinol Metab*, 3(5), 170–175.

Goodman, M.T., Yoshizawa, C.N., & Kolonel, L.N. (1988). Descriptive epidemiology of thyroid cancer in Hawaii. *Cancer (Phila.)*, 61, 1272–1281.

Goodman, M.T., Kolonel, L.N., & Wilkens, L.R. (1992). The association of body size, reproductive factors and thyroid cancer. *Br J Cancer*, 66(6), 1180–1184.

Guru, S.C., Manickam, P., Crabtree, J.S., Olufemi, S.E., Agarwal, S.K., & Debelenko, L.V. (1998). Identification and characterization of the multiple endocrine neoplasia type 1 (MEN1) gene. *J Intern Med*, 243(6), 433–439.

Hashimoto, H. (1912). Report on lymphomatous goiter. *'Archiv für klinische Chirurgie,' Berlin*, 97, 219–248.

Hemminki, K., Li, X., Sundquist, J., & Sundquist, K. (2010). The epidemiology of Graves' disease: Evidence of a genetic and an environmental contribution. *Autoimmun*, 34(3), J307–J313.

Herman-Bonert, V., & Friedman, T.C. (2004). *The thyroid gland in cecil essentials of medicine* (6th ed., pp. 593–602). C.C.J. Carpenter, R.C. Griggs, & J. Loscalzo (Eds.) Philadelphia: W.B. Saunders.

Holman, J.C.M., & McCartney, W. (1960). Iodized salt. *Endemic Goitre*, 1960, 411–441, WHO, Geneva, Switzerland.

Hydovitz, J.D. (1960). Occurrence of goiter in an infant on a soy diet. *NEJM*, 262, 351–353.

Jacobson, E.M., Huber, A., & Tomer, Y. (2008). The HLA gene complex in thyroid autoimmunity: From epidemiology to etiology. *J Autoimmun*, 30(1–2), 58–62.

Jacobson, E.M., & Tomer, Y. (2007a). The genetic basis of thyroid autoimmunity. *Thyroid*, 17, 949–961.

Jacobson, E.M., & Tomer, Y. (2007b). The CD40, CTLA-4, thyroglobulin, TSH receptor, and PTPN22 gene quintet and its contribution to thyroid autoimmunity: Back to the future. *J Autoimmun*, 28(2–3), 85–98.

Kolonel, L.N., Hankin, J.H., Wilkens, L.R., Fukunaga, F.H., & Hinds, M.W. (1990). An epidemiologic study of thyroid cancer in Hawaii. *Cancer Causes Control*, 1(3), 223–234.

Kurylowicz, A., Ramos-Lopez, E., Bednarczuk, T., & Badenhoop, K. (2006). Vitamin D-binding protein (DBP) gene polymorphism is associated with Graves' disease and the vitamin D status in a Polish population study. *Exp Clin Endocrinol Diabetes*, 114(6), 329–335.

Levinson, W. (2006). Major histocompatibility complex and transplantation. In *Review of medical microbiology and immunology* (9th ed., pp. 434–439). McGraw Hill, Lange.

Manji, N., Carr-Smith, J.D., Boelaert, K., et al. (2006). Influences of age, gender, smoking, and family history on autoimmune thyroid disease phenotype. *J Clin Endocrinol Metab*, 91, 4873–4880.

Marine, D. (1907). On the occurrence and physiological nature of glandular hyperplasia of the thyroid (dog and sheep), together with remarks on important clinical (human) problems. *Johns Hopkins Bull*, 18, 359–365.

Marine, D. (1914). Further observations and experiments on goitre (so called thyroid carcinoma) in brook trout (*Salvelinus fontinalis*). *J Exp Med*, 19, 70–88.

Marine, D. (1924). Etiology and prevention of simple goiter. *Harvey Lectures Ser*, 19, 96–122, Lippincott Philadelphia, PA.

Marine, D., & Kimball, O.P. (1917). The prevention of simple goiter in man. *J Lab Clin Med, 3,* 40–48.

Marine, D., & Kimball, O.P. (1920). The prevention of simple goiter in man: Fourth paper. *Arch Intern Med, 25,* 661–672.

Marine, D., & Williams, W.W. (1908). The relation of iodine to the structure of the thyroid gland. *Arch Intern Med, 1,* 349–384.

McClure, R.D. (1935). Goiter prophylaxis with iodized salt. *Science (New York, NY), 82*(2129), 370–371.

Pani, M.A., Regulla, K., Segni, M., Hofmann, S., Hüfner, M., Pasquino, A.M., …Badenhoop, K. (2002). A Polymorphism within the vitamin D-binding protein gene is associated with Graves' disease but not with Hashimoto's thyroiditis. *J Clin Endocrinol Metab, 87,* 2564–2567.

Parkin, D.M., Muir, C.S., Whelan, S.L., Gao, Y.T., Ferlay, J., & Powell, J. (1992). Cancer incidence in five continents. VI. IARC Scientific Publ. No. 120. Lyon, France: IARC.

Rapoport, B. (1991). Pathophysiology of Hashimoto's thyroiditis and hypothyroidism. *Annu Rev Med, 42,* 91–96.

Robbins, S.L., & Cotran, R.S. (1979). *Pathologic basis of disease* (2nd ed.). Philadelphia: WB Saunders Company.

Shore, R.E., Hildreth, N., Dvoretsky, P., Pasternack, B., & Andresen, E. (1993). Benign thyroid adenomas among persons X-irradiated in infancy for enlarged thymus glands. *Radiat Res, 134*(2), 217–223.

Sipple, J.H. (1961). The association of pheochromocytoma with carcinoma of the thyroid gland. *American Journal of Medicine, 31,* 163.

Surveillance Epidemiology and End Results (SEER Data, 1973–2007). Bethesda, Maryland: US National Institutes of Health, National Cancer Institute.

Tandon, N., Zhang, L., & Weetman, A.P. (1991). HLA associations with Hashimoto's thyroiditis. *Clin Endocrinol (Oxf), 34,* 383–386.

The Lancet. (2008). Iodine deficiency—Way to go yet. *The Lancet, 372*(9633), 88.

Thilly, C.H., Swennen, B., Bourdoux, P., Ntambue, K., Moreno-Reyes, R., Gillies, J., & Vanderpas, J.B. (1993). The epidemiology of iodine-deficiency disorders in relation to goitrogenic factors and thyroid-stimulating-hormone regulation. *American Journal of Clinical Nutrition, 57,* 267S–270S.

Tomer, Y., Barbesino, G., Greenberg, D.A., Concepcion, E., & Davies, T.F. (1999). Mapping the major susceptibility loci for familial Graves' and Hashimoto's diseases: Evidence for genetic heterogeneity and gene interactions. *J Clin Endocrinol Metab, 84,* 4656–4664.

Tunbridge, W.M.G., Evered, D.C., Hall, R., Appleton, P.A., Brewis, M., Clark, F.,…Smith P.A. (1977). The spectrum of thyroid disease in a community: The Whickham survey. *Clin Endocrinol, 7,* 481–493.

Vanderpump, M.P., & Tunbridge, W.M. (2002). Epidemiology and prevention of clinical and subclinical hypothyroidism. *Thyroid, 12,* 839–847.

Vanderpas, J. (2006). Nutritional epidemiology and thyroid hormone metabolism. *Annu Rev Nutr, 26,* 293–322. http://en.wikipedia.org/wiki/Digital_object_identifier

Vona-Davis, L., & Rose, D.P. (2007). Adipokines as endocrine, paracrine, and autocrine factors in breast cancer risk and progression. *Endocrine-Related Cancer, 14,* 189–206.

Weetman, A.P. (2000). Graves' disease. *N Engl J Med, 343,* 1236–1248.

Werner, P. (1963). Endocrine adenomatosis and peptic ulcer in a large kindred. Inherited multiple tumors and mosaic pleiotropism in man. *Am J Med, 35,* 205–212.

Yesilkaya, E., Koc, A., Bideci, A., Camurdan, O., Boyraz, M., Erkal, O.,…Cinaz, P. (2008). CTLA4 gene polymorphisms in children and adolescents with autoimmune thyroid diseases. *Genetic Testing, 12*(3), 461–464.

Zamani, M., Spaepen, M., Bex, M., Bouillon, R., & Cassiman, J.J. (2000). Primary role of the HLA class II DRB1*0301 allele in Graves disease. *Am J Med Genet, 95*(5), 432–437.

35

Epidemiology of Kidney Disease

ANATOMY AND FUNCTION OF THE KIDNEYS

The human kidneys are paired organs that perform multiple functions that are essential for life. They excrete waste products of metabolism, regulate the body's concentration of water and salt, maintain the acid-base balance of the blood, regulate blood pressure, and secrete important hormones including erythropoietin, renin, and prostaglandins. These physiological functions necessarily require a high degree of structural complexity (Robbins and Cotran, 1979).

Kidneys are bean-shaped organs weighing about 150 grams that are located in the retroperitoneal cavity. Individual renal arteries branching from the abdominal aorta supply blood to the kidneys. The kidneys filter about 17 liters of blood per day producing a derived specialized filtrate of about 1 liter of urine.

Urea is the most abundant of the nitrogen-containing waste products excreted by the kidneys. Urea is formed from ammonia or amino acids by a series of reactions known as the urea cycle, which occurs primarily in the liver. Ammonia arising from the metabolism of amino acids and nitrogen containing compounds is rapidly transported by red bloods cells to the liver where it enters the urea cycle.

Ammonia itself is highly toxic and cannot be filtered by the kidneys. In contrast, its breakdown product, urea, is colorless, odorless, highly soluble in water, and nontoxic in humans. Urea formed in the liver is transported in the blood to the kidneys where it is freely filtered by the glomeruli and becomes a major constituent of urine.

The basic functional unit of the kidney is the nephron (**Figure 35.1**). Each kidney contains up to 1 million nephrons that carry out the essential

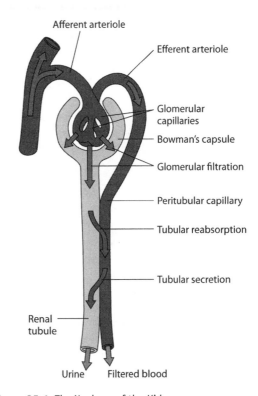

Figure 35.1 The Nephron of the Kidney.

functions of the kidney. Each nephron receives unfiltered blood from an afferent arteriole which divides into capillaries of the glomerulus. The glomerulus is contained in a structure known as Bowman's capsule. The glomerulus filters urea and other waste products from the blood. The glomerular filtrate enters Bowman's space, diffuses into the renal tubule, and then travels along the renal tubule that is lined by a single layer of specialized endothelial cells and surrounded by capillaries. As the glomerular filtrate traverses the renal tubule, salt, water, glucose, and other small molecules are reabsorbed from the filtrate into the blood, and additional waste products (e.g., ammonia, hydrogen, and potassium ions) are secreted from the blood into the urine. Urine exits the nephron via collecting ducts at the end of the renal tubule. Filtered arteriole blood exits the nephron through the efferent arteriole.

Renal function is clinically determined by measuring the glomerular filtration rate (GFR). This is accomplished by injecting a standard bolus of inulin into the blood and measuring the rate of its excretion in the urine. Inulin is a compound that is neither secreted nor reabsorbed by the kidney. Thus, inulin excretion can be used to accurately determine the volume of fluid that is being filtered by the glomeruli of the kidneys per unit of time. A useful indirect measure of the GFR can be obtained by measuring the creatinine clearance (the amount of creatinine removed from the blood by the kidneys) over a 24-hour period. Creatinine is a breakdown product of muscle metabolism and is freely filtered by the kidneys. Since a small amount of creatinine is secreted from the blood into the urine, the creatinine clearance slightly overestimates the GFR. Creatinine clearance values are also routinely corrected for body mass (muscle mass).

DIAGNOSIS OF CHRONIC KIDNEY DISEASE

Kidney disease is often diagnosed by the symptom complex of protein (albumin) in the urine, hypertension, and edema. These common symptoms of kidney disease were originally described in 1827 by the English physician, Richard Bright. Albeit, these symptoms are manifest in many forms of kidney disease and more sophisticated methods of differentiating the various types of kidney disease have now been developed (Cameron, 1972a,1972b,1972c).

Kidney disease can be categorized as either acute or chronic. Acute diseases of the kidneys such as acute glomerulonephritis are often infectious in origin and may arise due to bacteria (beta-hemolytic streptococci, escherichia coli, pseudomonas), viruses (hepatitis B, mumps, varicella, infectious mononucleosis), as well as parasites (malaria, schistosomiasis). Glomerulonephritis usually arises *not* as a direct consequence of the infection, but rather because antigen-antibody immune complexes specifically directed against the infectious agent become entrapped in the ultrafine filtration system of the glomeruli. Such entrapped immune complexes activate complement, thereby causing inflammation and subsequent damage to the basement membrane

Table 35.1	Stages of Kidney Disease
Stage of CKD	GFR in ml per min per 1.74 m^2
0 (Normal)	GFR > 90, No Proteinuria
1 (Abnormal)	GFR > 90, Proteinuria
2 (Mild)	GFR 60–89
3 (Moderate)	GFR 30–59
4 (Severe)	GFR 15–29
5 (Kidney Failure)	GFR < 15 (End Stage Renal Disease)

CKD = Chronic Kidney Disease
GFR = Glomerular Filtration Rate

of the glomeruli; hence the name "*immune-complex*" glomerulonephritis (Cameron, 1972a, 1972b, 1972c; Robbins and Cotran, 1979). The continued presence of this process can lead to chronic glomerulonephritis.

Chronic kidney disease is pathologically classified into nephrosis and nephritis. Nephrosis implies kidney disease with proteinuria (excess loss of protein in the urine) in the absence of inflammatory disease. Nephritis implies an inflammatory disease of the kidneys evidenced by the presence of inflammatory cells of the immune system. In chronic forms of either of these conditions, there is damage to the kidneys resulting in dysfunctional filtration of blood and alterations in the volume and composition of urine excreted. Irrespective of the pathology, the diagnosis of kidney disease is largely based upon the GFR and the presence of protein or abnormal substances in the urine.

Normal values of the glomerular filtration rate (GFR), adjusted for body surface area, are similar in men and women, in the range of 90–130 ml/min/1.73m^2. The severity of chronic kidney disease is categorized into the following six stages, which depend on both the GFR and the presence of protein in the urine (proteinuria).

GLOBAL PATTERN OF CHRONIC KIDNEY DISEASE

Chronic diseases have surpassed infectious diseases as the major causes of morbidity and mortality worldwide, a phenomenon known as the *epidemiologic transition*. The transition is particularly evident in the emerging pattern of morbidity and mortality due to chronic kidney disease. According to reports from the World Health Organization, the mortality from nephritis or nephrosis climbed from 536,000 in 1990 to 739,000 in 2004 (Murray and Lopez, 1997; WHO, 2004). The estimated global dialysis population for

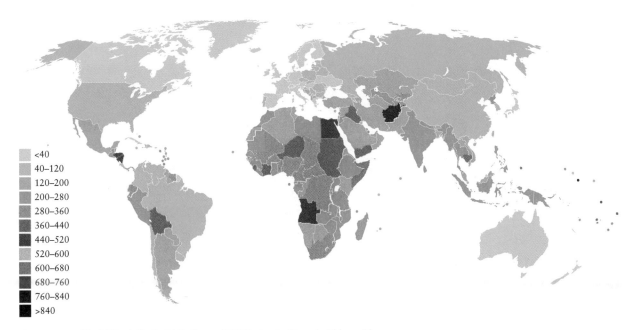

Figure 35.2 Disability Adjusted Life Years (DALY) due to Chronic Kidney Disease.

Source: Data from World Health Organization. The global burden of disease: 2004 update. Geneva, WHO, 2008. Available at www.who.int /evidence/bod.

end-stage renal disease has increased from 1.1–2 million since 2001 and is expanding at a rate of about 7% per year with an aggregate cost of more the $1 trillion (Moeller, Gioberge, and Brown, 2002).

Figure 35.2 characterizes the global burden of kidney disease by the disability-adjusted life years (DALY) that are lost annually from either death or disability caused by end-stage renal failure. Disease burdens are highest throughout Africa and certain regions of the Middle East, Southern Asia, and South America. Populations living in these regions are heavily exposed to infection by endemic parasites that are capable of compromising renal function. Principal risk factors in the developed nations of North America, Western Europe, and Australasia include type 2 diabetes, hypertension, and obesity.

Chronic Kidney Disease in Developing Countries

As shown in **Figure 35.2**, high DALYs are evident throughout Africa and in certain regions of the Middle East, Southern Asia, and South America. Interestingly, there is significant overlap of the DALYs from renal disease in these regions (particularly in Africa) with high DALYs due to malarial infection as well as infection of the urinary tract by the parasitic schistosome worm (see **Figure 35.3** and **Figure 35.4** below). Numerous reports provide evidence that chronic malaria or chronic schistosomiasis (also called *bilharzias*), parasitic conditions that affect millions of Africans, markedly heighten the risk of chronic renal failure (Cameron, 1972a,1972b,1972c;

Oyediran, 1979; Mahakur et al., 1983; Martinelli et al., 1989; Collins and Jeffery, 2007).

Some plasmodial (malarial) infections are capable of causing acute renal failure whereas others are more likely to cause chronic disease. In a hospital survey conducted in Gujarat state in western India during 1988–1992, malarial plasmodial infection by *P. vivax* or *P. falciparum* caused tubular necrosis and acute renal failure in 1.6% and 12.8% of cases, respectively (Rajapurkar, 1994); and in a similar hospital survey in northern India, acute renal failure occurred in 1.1% of cases with malarial infection. Pathogenesis is related to parasitemia-induced deformities in red blood cells such that deformed red blood cells are filtered in the kidney, causing occlusion of small blood vessels and ischemic damage to renal tubules.

Plasmodium malariae causes "*quartan malaria,*" an infectious condition that may persist for many years. The term quartan malaria refers to the 4 fever spikes that occur in infected patients at regular 3-month intervals during the year. The relationship between quartan malaria and the nephrotic syndrome (massive proteinuria, low blood albumin, generalized edema, hypertension, and hyperlipidemia) was initially recognized by Giglioli in 1930 and has since been noted by many investigators in regions where *P. malariae* is endemic (Giglioli, 1930; Cameron, 1972a,1972b,1972c; Collins and Jeffery, 2007). Persistent quartan malaria can lead to chronic glomerulonephritis and renal failure by continual

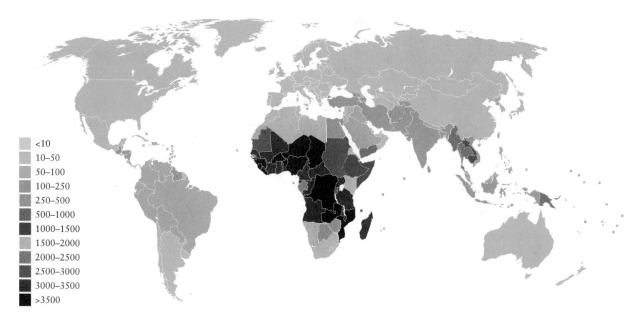

Figure 35.3 Disability Adjusted Life Years (DALY) due to Malaria, 2004.

Source: Data from World Health Organization. The global burden of disease: 2004 update. Geneva, WHO, 2008. Available at www.who.int /evidence/bod.

deposition of malarial antigen-antibody complexes in the glomeruli (Dixon, 1966).

Urinary tract schistosomiasis can also cause renal failure due to obstructive uropathy, pyelonephritis, or bladder carcinoma (occurring usually 10–20 years after the initial infection). In addition, immune complexes that contain schistosome antigens may deposit in the glomeruli, leading to glomerulonephritis and amyloidosis (Barsoum, 2003). Furthermore, leishmaniasis (also called *kala-azar*), another parasitic disease that is prevalent in Afghanistan and certain nations of the Middle East, Southern Asia, and Africa, has been found to cause renal failure and hydronephrosis (edematous

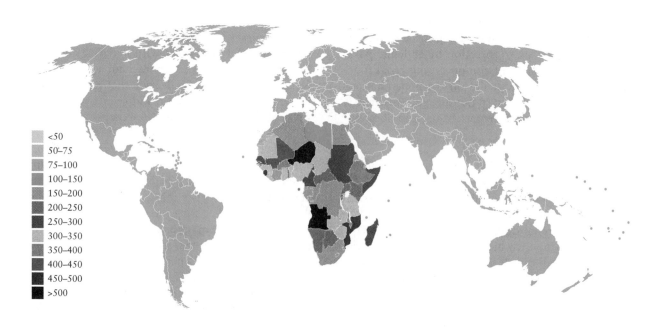

Figure 35.4 Disability Adjusted Life Years (DALY) due to Schistosmiasis, 2004.

Source: Data from World Health Organization. The global burden of disease: 2004 update. Geneva, WHO, 2008. Available at www.who.int /evidence/bod.

kidneys due to urinary obstruction) in chronically infected patients (Prasad, Sen, and Ganguly, 1992; Prakash et al., 2007). Some of these nations may have a double burden of disease due to obstructive uropathy and glomerulonephritis caused by infectious parasites as well as chronic kidney disease caused by chronic noninfectious conditions such as diabetes and hypertension (Naicker, 2003).

Chronic Kidney Disease in Developed Countries

As a consequence of the epidemiologic transition from infectious to chronic diseases and the resultant increase in longevity, the world population has experienced a dramatic change in the causes of end-stage renal disease. In nations of the developed world, the profile of risk factors for chronic kidney disease closely resembles that for cardiovascular disease. Type 2 diabetes is now the major cause, and other chronic conditions, principally hypertension, hyperlipidemia, smoking, and obesity, are contributing factors. In the United States, diabetes and hypertension are estimated to account for 44% and 27%, respectively, of the cases of chronic kidney failure (National Kidney and Urologic Diseases Information Clearinghouse, 2008).

Similar to most chronic conditions, chronic kidney disease develops slowly over a period of time and is generally a consequence of the progression of diabetes and hypertension or other underlying processes. The primary causes of kidney failure in the United States are shown in **Figure 35.5** and selected risk factors are discussed in the following section.

DIABETIC NEPHROPATHY

Diabetic nephropathy is a clinical syndrome characterized by persistent albuminuria that is confirmed on at least 2 occasions 3–6 months apart, a relentless decline in the glomerular filtration rate (GFR) and elevated arterial blood pressure. Diabetic nephropathy is the leading cause of chronic renal failure in the United States and other Western societies. It is also one of the most significant long-term complications in terms of morbidity and mortality for individual patients with diabetes. According to the United States Renal Data System National Health Interview Survey, between 1984–2002 the incidence of end-stage renal disease attributed to diabetes increased from 29.7 to 151.3 per 1 million population corresponding to a 409% increase. Diabetes is now responsible for more than 40% of all cases of end-stage renal disease in the United States (Ritz and Orth, 1999; National Kidney and Urologic Diseases Information Clearinghouse, 2008).

Many epidemiologic studies provide consistent evidence that diabetes as well as prediabetes are significant risk factors for the development of kidney disease. Investigators at the University of Wisconsin–Madison conducted a long-term prospective study of 1,460 individuals diagnosed with diabetes in order to determine the incidence of proteinuria. During 10 years of follow-up, proteinuria developed in 28% of younger individuals (< 30 years of age at baseline) compared to 33% of older individuals not taking insulin and 40% of older individuals taking insulin.

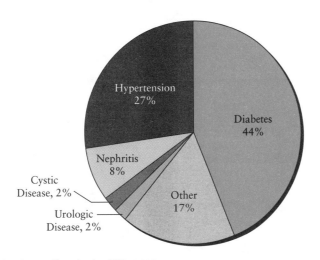

Figure 35.5 Primary Causes of Kidney Failure in the USA, 2008.

Source: Data from US National Kidney and Urologic Diseases Information Clearinghouse (2008).

The risk was highest for individuals with multiple risk factors (high glycosylated hemoglobin, hypertension, and smoking) suggesting that modification of all three of these factors should be considered in the prevention of diabetic nephropathy (Klein et al., 1995).

In the Framingham Heart Study, 2,398 subjects free of chronic kidney disease were drawn from the *Framingham offspring cohort* and given an oral glucose tolerance test during 1991–1995. After seven years of follow-up, the odds of developing chronic kidney disease was increased for incident diabetic cases (OR = 1.7) and prevalent diabetic cases (OR = 1.9) compared to subjects who were not diabetic at baseline. These estimates were adjusted for classical risk factors of cardiovascular disease (hypertension, smoking, cholesterol, and obesity). The *crude* unadjusted disease odds was also increased for individuals with prediabetic fasting glucose or impaired glucose tolerance (OR = 1.6); however, adjustment for classical risk factors of cardiovascular disease explained much of the risk associated with prediabetic status (Fox et al., 2005).

Both type 1 diabetes and type 2 diabetes predispose to diabetic nephropathy. In a New Jersey study of 717 African Americans with type 1 diabetes, the prevalence of proteinuria increased with age and duration of diabetes, e.g., proteinuria was present in 85% of subjects over 44 years of age and 72% of subjects who had undergone treatment for type 1 diabetes for 25 years or more. Hypertension and poor glycemic control were also significant predictive factors (Roy, 2004).

Epidemiological studies show that the prevalence of proteinuria increases with the duration of either type 1 or type 2 diabetes (**Figure 35.6**). Beginning at about 10 years after diagnosis, the prevalence increases exponentially for each type and is only slightly higher for type 2 diabetes. Furthermore, without aggressive therapy and tight glycemic control, progression to renal failure is expected in 60% or more of patients within 5 years of the onset of proteinuria (Hasslacher et al., 1989; Keller et al., 1996; Ritz and Orth, 1999).

Results of randomized clinical trials provide convincing evidence that the risk of developing proteinuria and end-stage renal disease in diabetic patients can be significantly reduced in diabetic patients by improving glycemic control using either insulin or oral antihyperglycemic agents (Kawazu et al., 1994; UK Prospective Diabetes Study, 1998). Nevertheless, the target level of glycosylated hemoglobin for optimal control remains under study (Ismail et al., 1999).

Chronic diabetes induces several pathological changes in the kidney including thickening of the glomerular basement membrane, proliferation of the mesangial cells (phagocytic cells), and glomerular sclerosis (scarring) due to hyaline narrowing of blood vessels and ischemia (lack of oxygen). Various molecular mechanisms have been postulated to explain these effects. Hyperglycemia causes the formation of advanced glycosylation end products (AGE) and release of cytokines, e.g., transforming growth factor beta (TGF-beta) and protein kinase-C, all of which can lead to hyperfiltration, cellular hypertrophy, and renal injury (Cooper, 1998). In particular, the excessive accumulation of advanced glycosylation end products (AGE) has been found to markedly accelerate the progression

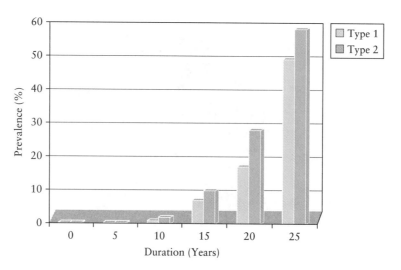

Figure 35.6 Proteinuria and Duration of Diabetes.

Source: Data from Ritz E, Orth SR (1999). Nephropathy in patients with type 2 diabetes mellitus. *N Engl J Med* 341:1127-1133; Hasslacher et al (1989). Similar risks of nephropathy in patients with type I or type II diabetes mellitus. *Nephrol Dial Transplant* 4:859–863.

of diabetic nephropathy to end-stage renal disease (Makita et al., 1991).

HYPERTENSION AND CHRONIC KIDNEY DISEASE

Many epidemiologic investigations have shown that sustained high blood pressure leads to impairment of kidney function; and reciprocally, reducing blood pressure has clearly been shown to have beneficial impact on kidney function.

In the Multiple Risk Factor Intervention Trial (MRFIT), 332,544 men aged 35–57 years of age at baseline were screened during 1973–1975 and followed for detection of end-stage renal disease or death from renal death using the National Death Index and the Social Security Administration. During an average of 16 years of follow-up, 814 subjects were either treated for or died of end-stage renal disease (ESRD). The results showed a strong graded relationship between both systolic and diastolic blood pressure and the development of ESRD (**Figure 35.7**). Compared to normotensive subjects, the relative risk of ESRD for patients with severe hypertension (systolic blood pressure > 210 mm Hg or diastolic blood pressure > 120 mm Hg) was increased by more than 20-fold (RR = 22.1). Increases in the risk due to rising blood pressure retained statistical significance after adjustment for other risk factors including age, race, diabetes, history of myocardial infarction, serum cholesterol, and cigarette smoking. The investigators concluded that increased blood pressure is a strong independent risk factor for the development of ESRD (Klag et al., 1996).

A review of cross-sectional, case-control, and prospective epidemiological studies confirmed that increasing blood pressure is an independent predictor of renal insufficiency and end-stage renal disease. As shown in **Figure 35.7**, the relationship appears to be continuous throughout the entire range of blood pressure (Klag et al., 1996; Whelton et al., 1996).

Randomized clinical trials indicate that effective regulation of blood pressure in hypertensive subjects by the administration of antihypertensive agents attenuates the progressive loss of renal function (Mogenson, 1999). Beneficial effects of blood pressure control on renal function have also been observed for patients with *both* diabetes and hypertension (Nielsen et al., 1997; Ismail et al., 1999) as well as for patients with proteinuric renal disease (Peterson et al., 1995).

The optimal target for blood pressure reduction in hypertensive patients has not been resolved and remains under study (Ruilope and Garia-Robles, 1997). In a meta-analysis of 11 randomized clinical trials involving 1,860 nondiabetic patients with hypertension, the greatest reduction in the rate of progression of renal disease was observed for patients achieving systolic blood pressures in the range of 110–129 mm Hg as opposed to lesser values (Jafar et al., 2003). Furthermore, in the *UK Prospective Diabetes Study*, even moderate lowering of blood pressure led to major reductions in the risk of both cardiovascular and renal events (UK Prospective Diabetes Study, 1998). Nevertheless, in a randomized clinical trial specifically designed to determine the optimal target for blood pressure reduction in hypertensive patients, the incidence of major cardiovascular events was 50% less in patients with a target diastolic blood pressure

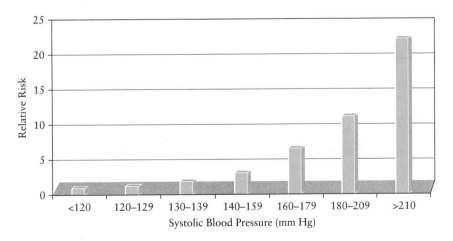

Figure 35.7 Hypertension and End Stage Renal Disease.

Source: Data from Klag MJ, Whelton PK, Randall BL, Neaton JD, Brancati FL, Ford CE, Shulman NB, Stamler (1996). Blood pressure and end-stage renal disease in men. *N Engl J Med* 334:13–18.

of 80 mm Hg compared to 90 mm Hg (Hansson et al., 1998). Thus, while there is general agreement that elevated blood pressure must be reduced to attenuate progression of renal failure and cardiovascular disease, controversy remains as to the optimal target for individual patients.

BLOOD LIPIDS, CHOLESTEROL, AND CHRONIC KIDNEY DISEASE

As enumerated in the preceding discussion, the profile of risk factors for chronic kidney disease in developed countries is similar to that for cardiovascular disease. Nevertheless, the role of high cholesterol in the development of chronic kidney disease was uncertain until investigators designed clinical-epidemiologic studies to either match out effects or adjust for confounding primarily due to diabetes and hypertension while also accounting for other factors such as age, gender, body mass, and smoking.

Early studies examined the association of blood lipids with progression of renal disease in patients with type 1 diabetes. In a small case control study conducted by investigators at Guys Hospital in London, lipid profiles were studied in 20 diabetic patients with microalbuminuria (cases) and 20 matched diabetic patients without microabluminiuria (controls). Cases with renal disease had significantly higher concentrations of LDL-cholesterol, triglycerides, and apolipoprotein B, and significantly lower concentrations of HDL-cholesterol than controls without renal disease (Jones et al., 1989).

Subsequently, investigators in Sweden conducted a prospective follow-up study of 30 patients with type 1 diabetes and nephropathy to assess the relationship between blood lipids and progression of renal disease. Results showed that high levels of serum cholesterol, triglycerides, and apolipoprotein B were correlated with a more rapid decline in glomerular filtration rate and deterioration of kidney function (Mulec et al., 1990).

In a cross-sectional study conducted in the United States, blood lipids and urinary albumin were studied in a sample of 428 women and 540 men patients with type 1 diabetes from the *Diabetes Control and Complications Trial/Epidemiology of Diabetes Interventions and Complications* (*DCCT/ EDIC*) cohort. Using multivariate analysis to adjust for duration and control of diabetes, hypertension, and body mass index, the investigators found that increased levels of triglycerides, total cholesterol, and LDL-cholesterol were significantly associated with

increasing urinary albumin and worsening of renal function (Jenkins et al., 2003).

Similar findings regarding the role of lipids in the progression of renal disease have also been reported for patients with type 2 diabetes. In a prospective study of patients with type 2 diabetes conducted in Tel Aviv, Israel, 574 patients aged 40–60 years who had normal renal function and were normotensive at baseline were followed to determine effects of plasma lipids and other factors (hemoglobin A1C, blood pressure, body mass index, and smoking) on urinary albumin excretion rate. After 7.8 years of average follow-up, total cholesterol, blood pressure, and hemoglobin A1C were found to be the main factors associated with increased albuminuria and deterioration of renal function. Notably, patients with high levels of all 3 risk factors were 43 times more likely to develop microalbuminuria than patients with normal values (Ravid et al., 1998).

Effects of cholesterol have also been observed in patients with type 2 diabetes and overt nephropathy. A *post hoc* analysis of 1,513 patients with (type 2) diabetic nephropathy enrolled in the *Reduction of Endpoints in NIDDM with the Angiotensin II Antagonist Losartan* (*RENALL*) study showed that both total cholesterol and LDL cholesterol measured at baseline were independent risk factors for endstage renal disease (Appel et al., 2003).

Specific components of the lipid profile appear to have a more prominent role in the development of renal disease than others. Investigators in Sweden demonstrated a significant association between triglyceride-rich apolipoprotein B and the rate of progression in nondiabetic patients with chronic kidney disease (Sammuelsson et al., 1998).

In the Atherosclerosis Risk in Communities Study (ARIC), 15,792 men and women aged 45–64 years at baseline were tested for total cholesterol, HDL-cholesterol, LDL-cholesterol, apolipoproteins A and B, and triglycerides and followed for a 3-year period to determine the risk of declining kidney function. The study showed that declining kidney function (assessed by increasing urinary creatinine) was significantly associated with high levels of triglycerides and low levels of HDL-cholesterol and apolipoprotein A (Muntner et al., 2000).

Investigators in France examined the role of triglycerides, LDL-cholesterol, and apolipoprotein A in the progression of nephropathy among 297 patients with type 1 diabetes. After adjustment for blood pressure and the duration and control of diabetes, the relative risk for progression to a higher stage of nephropathy was twofold higher in patients with elevated levels of triglycerides compared to subjects with normal levels. The results indicate that high triglyceride levels are an independent predictor of declining renal function in patients with type 1 diabetes (Hadjadj et al., 2004).

Findings of observational studies showing renal effects of blood lipids set the stage for randomized clinical trials of antilipemic agents (statins) to examine their therapeutic impact for patients with chronic kidney disease. In a systematic review and meta-analysis of randomized controlled trials, 27 studies with 39,704 participants were identified that reported assessment of kidney function (glomerular filtration rate and/or proteinuria) in patients who took statins compared to those who did not. Overall, statin treatment was found to significantly slow the progression of renal dysfunction, particularly among subjects with cardiovascular disease (Fried et al., 2001; Sandhu et al., 2006).

Patients with chronic kidney disease characteristically have altered lipid metabolism manifesting as elevated blood levels of triglycerides, free fatty acids, and LDL-cholesterol and reduced HDL-cholesterol. In general, high levels of cholesterol and particularly LDL-cholesterol are related to atherogenesis and the development of atheromas in blood vessels including those that nourish the kidney. Sequelae include thromboembolic events leading to ischemic tissue damage. A related condition known as hyaline arteriolar nephrosclerosis is a form of renal disease in which cholesterol-laden hyaline material narrows the renal arterioles leading to atrophy of the renal tubules, renal dysfunction, and hypertension

(Baker and Selikoff, 1952). Hypertriglyceridemia is a prominent feature of chronic kidney disease wherein damage to the kidneys is associated with the flux of excess free fatty acids and triglycerides that deposit in the renal tubules (Johnson, Stahl, and Zager, 2005).

OBESITY AND CHRONIC KIDNEY DISEASE

Obesity is an integral component in the *web of causation* of chronic kidney disease. Obesity is an independent risk factor for both diabetes and hypertension, and as discussed earlier, these two conditions account for more than 70% of chronic kidney disease. Furthermore, obesity is primarily due to excess body fat with increased numbers of lipid-laden fat cells that are capable of secreting bioactive substances that participate in the pathogenesis of kidney disease and other cardiovascular conditions.

In a study conducted in the United States during 1965–1984, the relationship between body mass and end-stage renal disease (ESRD) was assessed among 320,252 men and women enrolled in the *Kaiser Permanente* healthcare delivery system in northern California. Estimates of relative risk for overweight and obese individuals (classes I, II, and II) were based on 1,471 incident cases of ESRD diagnosed after more than 8.3 million person-years of follow-up. Compared with normal weight persons (BMI < 25), the pattern of risk shows a striking dose response curve with increasing body mass (**Figure 35.8**) (Hsu et al., 2006).

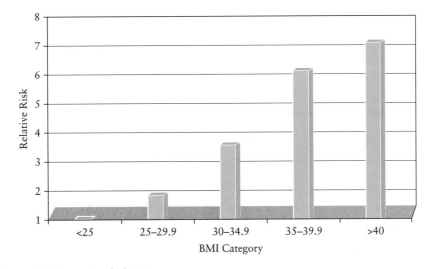

Figure 35.8 Obesity and End Stage Renal Disease.

Source: Data from Hsu C, McCulloch CE, Iribarren C, Darbinian J, Go AS (2006). Body mass index and risk for end-stage renal disease. *Ann Intern Med* 144:21–28.

A voluminous amount of evidence from the epidemiologic literature on obesity and kidney disease has been retrieved, reviewed, and analyzed. In a recent meta-analysis, data from 25 cohort studies, 3 cross-sectional studies, and 19 case-control studies published during 1980–2006 were pooled and relative risk estimates derived according to body mass index. Combined results from prospective studies reflect an increase in the relative risk of all types of kidney disease (including kidney cancer) for overweight individuals (RR = 1.41) and obese individuals (RR = 1.83). Restriction of estimates to noncancerous outcomes yielded similar results (RR = 1.53 and 1.66, respectively). The evidence also suggests that obesity has a slightly stronger effect in women than men (Wang et al., 2008).

The impact of weight loss on kidney function has been examined in randomized clinical trials. Several types of weight loss interventions have been assessed including exercise, diet, medication, and bariatric surgery. In a meta-analysis of 13 trials involving 522 patients with varying stages of obesity, weight loss intervention reduced proteinuria by 1.7 g and microalbuminuria by 14 mg. The combined results showed that each 1 kg of weight loss decreased proteinuria by 110 mg and microabuminuria by 1.1 mg. These effects were observed across different designs and methods of weight loss (Afshinnia et al., 2010).

Diseases that are linked to obesity, including chronic kidney disease, are related to excess fat and secretions of the fat cell population. The adipocyte (fat cell) is *not* simply a storage depot for fat. Far from it, adipocytes are capable of secreting a variety of hormone-like peptides (called adipokines) that have significant impact on human physiology. Indeed, the adipokine profile has been found to influence a wide variety of cellular mechanisms and functions including appetite/satiety, energy balance, immunity, inflammation, insulin sensitivity, angiogenesis, blood pressure, lipid metabolism, and endocrine homeostasis.

In particular, when the adipocyte population becomes engorged with *triacylglycerol* (the storage form of fat), macrophage infiltration is stimulated and pathogenic adipokines are secreted. For example, *tumor necrosis factor*, *interleukin 6*, and *resistin* have been linked to the development of insulin resistance and type 2 diabetes. *Angiotensinogen* released by fat cells has been implicated in the onset of hypertension and *plasminogen activating inhibitor* promotes thrombus formation. Fat cells can also release inflammatory *prostaglandins* that heighten the risk of atherogenesis and thromboembolic events.

Reciprocally, weight loss and reduction of adipose tissue induces secretion of beneficial adipokines such as *adiponectin* and *leptin* that have been found to increase insulin sensitivity and reduce blood pressure and inflammation. Clearly, modification of the adipokine profile holds significant potential for the prevention and therapy of obesity-related disease. As pointed out by Ronti and colleagues in their update of the endocrine functions of adipose tissue: "*In-depth understanding of the pathophysiology and molecular actions of adipokines may, in the coming years, lead to effective therapeutic strategies designed to protect against atherosclerosis in obese patients*" (Ronti, Lupattelli, and Mannarino, 2006).

SMOKING AND CHRONIC KIDNEY DISEASE

A number of epidemiologic investigations have demonstrated that smoking is a significant independent predictor of albuminuria (Dales et al., 1978; Mimran et al., 1994; Mulder et al., 1999). Furthermore, several studies of patients with diabetes found that smokers are at greater risk than nonsmokers for the development of diabetic nephropathy (Christiansen, 1978; Chase et al., 1991; Orth, Ritz, and Schrier, 1997).

In an important international matched-pair case control investigation of end-stage renal failure (ESRF) involving 72 patients with inflammatory or noninflammatory renal disease (cases) and 72 matched control subjects from 9 centers in Germany, Italy, and Austria, the odds ratios for ESRF showed a significant linear dose response with pack-years of smoking: OR = 3.5 for 5–15 pack-years and OR = 5.8 for > 15 pack-years compared to < 5 pack-years of smoking. Notably, the investigators also found that smokers who were treated with angiotensin-converting enzyme inhibitors (ACE inhibitors) attenuated their risk of disease progression (Orth et al., 1998). In the Multiple Risk Factor Intervention Trial (MRFIT), smoking was also identified as an independent risk factor for the development of ESRF (Whelton et al., 1995). It is also of note that diabetic individuals who quit smoking have been observed to have significantly better renal function than comparable subjects who continue to smoke (Sawicki et al., 1994).

There is strong biological plausibility for an etiologic link between smoking and renal dysfunction. Clinical-pathologic investigations have shown that smoking plays a prominent role in the genesis of atherosclerotic renal artery stenosis and ischemic nephropathy (Black et al., 1983; Oberai, Adams, and

High, 1984). Smoking may also induce inflammation and heighten vasoconstriction (endothelin) versus vasodilatation (nitric oxide) in the renal arterioles (Ritz and Orth, 1999). Clearly, smoking cessation should be a prominent component in the management of patients diagnosed with renal disease.

ALCOHOL ABUSE, GOUT AND KIDNEY DISEASE

Alcohol abuse and particularly heavy consumption of beer predisposes to hyperuricemia (excess urinary uric acid) and precipitation of monosodium uric acid crystals in synnovial joints (a condition commonly called gout) (Choi et al., 2004). Uric acid crystals frequently produce damage to the kidneys and occasionally cause the development of uric acid kidney stones (nephrolithiasis) (Robbins and Cotran, 1979).

In a cohort of the *Health Professionals Follow-up Study*, the risk of incident kidney stones was increased by twofold among men who reported a history of gout (RR = 2.12). The investigators concluded that gout is an independent risk factor for nephrolithiasis (Kramer et al., 2003). Furthermore, patients with chronic gout are predisposed to kidney failure. As pointed out nearly 50 years ago by RW Rundles, "*Nephropathy in gout may develop acutely but it is usually chronic, insidious, and slowly progressive. In gout, the formation of urate stones is often a major manifestation of the disease and the one complication most amenable to correction by allopurinol therapy*" (Rundles, 1966).

Perneger and colleagues examined the association of alcohol consumption and end stage renal disease in a population based case control study conducted in Maryland, Virginia, and West Virginia and the District of Columbia (Washington, DC). They found that persons consuming 2 or more alcoholic drinks per day were 4 times more likely to develop end stage renal disease than those with no exposure. The corresponding attributable risk estimate was 9 percent. Lesser amounts of alcohol were not found to be harmful (Perneger et al., 1999). Similar results were reported by Shankar and colleagues who studied a cohort of 3,392 adults in Wisconsin. They found that consumption of 4 or more alcoholic drinks daily increased the risk of chronic kidney disease by twofold and the combination of chronic smoking and heavy drinking increased the risk by fivefold (Shankar, Klein, and Klein, 2006).

In contrast, Menon and colleagues found no association with decline in kidney function and alcohol consumption in a prospective cohort study of 4,343 elderly men and women from four U.S. communities (Menon et al., 2010). Furthermore, some studies have observed that moderate levels of alcohol consumption (1 drink per day) have a beneficial effect on kidney function (Schaeffner et al., 2005). Clearly, additional studies are needed to clarify the dose response of kidney function and alcohol intake.

CHRONIC GLOMERULONEPHRITIS

Despite the tremendous global impact of diabetes and other chronic conditions, glomerulonephritis continues to play a significant role in the pathogenesis of chronic kidney disease throughout the world. However, recent surveys of the member nations of the World Health Organization show great disparity between developed and developing nations in the prevalence of this condition. In the highly developed nations of North America, Western Europe, Australasia, and elsewhere, glomerulonephritis is found in only 10–15% of cases; whereas in the less developed nations of Asia, Africa, and South America, glomerulonephritis is the principal pathologic condition in more than 70% of cases of chronic kidney disease (Couser, 1999; Huraib et al., 2000).

As discussed in a previous section of this chapter, glomerulonephritis usually arises due to the entrapment of antigen-antibody (immune) complexes in the basement membranes of glomeruli. The presence of such "*foreign*" immune complexes activates the complement system and inflammation ensues. Immune-mediated glomerulonephritis can arise from infections due to bacteria, viruses, or parasites. Low-grade infections that remain untreated over long periods of time have the highest propensity for pathogenesis. Malaria and schistosomiasis are prominent causative agents in developing countries, particularly in Africa (Cameron, 1972a, 1972b, 1972c). Other examples include recurring poststreptococcal disease and hepatorenal disease from chronic hepatitis. In addition, autoimmune conditions such as *systemic lupus erythematosus (SLE)* can produce renal lesions by deposition of anti-DNA:DNA complexes in the glomeruli (Robbins and Cotran, 1979). Exposure to hydrocarbons (industrial solvents and gasoline) has been examined as an environmental risk factor for glomerulonephritis although the evidence of an association is not convincing (Churchill, Fine, and Gault, 1983).

Occasionally, glomerulonephritis arises due to antibodies that are specifically directed against the glomerular basement membranes. Goodpasture's syndrome, a rare condition characterized by pulmonary hemorrhaging plus nephritis is an example of this mechanism. Less than 5% of cases of chronic glomerulonephritis are attributable to specific antibasement membrane antibodies (Robbins and Cotran, 1979).

Childhood syndromes involving renal pathology have been linked to specific genes. Alport syndrome is a rare X-linked dominant disorder that causes progressive hematuric nonimmune nephritis characterized ultrastructurally by irregular thickening, thinning, and lamellation of the glomerular basement membrane. Characteristic phenotypic features of Alport syndrome include hearing loss, ocular defects, abnormalities in platelet number and function, and esophageal, upper gastrointestinal, and genital leiomyomatosis. The genetic defect produces abnormal synthesis of collagen and other connective tissues (Flinter, Maher, and Saggar, 2003).

Autosomal dominant polycystic kidney disease accounts for approximately 10% of all cases of polycystic kidney disease (PKD). Onset typically occurs in the second or third decades of life. Enlargement of the renal cystic structures results in renin secretion and hypertension, often leading to end-stage renal disease. This condition also predisposes to the development of cerebral aneurysms, liver cysts and mitral valve prolapse. Mutations in the *PKD-1* gene on chromosome 16 account for 85% of cases, whereas mutations in the *PKD-2* gene on chromosome 4 represent the remainder. The genetic defect in PKD causes irregularities in maturation of the epithelial lining of the renal tubules (Flinter, Maher, and Saggar, 2003).

Although specific genes have not been identified for adult forms of nephropathy, studies of afflicted relatives do show characteristics of significant genetic influence. For example, there are numerous reports of familial clustering of diabetic nephropathy consistent with genetic predisposition, common environmental factors, or both (Seaquist et al., 1989; Borch-Johnson et al., 1992; Quinn et al., 1996; Bowden, 2003).

In a population-based investigation conducted in Finland, 537 families containing at least two siblings with diabetes were identified and all individuals were followed longitudinally to determine onset of diabetic nephropathy. Diabetic siblings of index cases (probands) with diabetic nephropathy were at significantly higher risk (RR = 2.3) of developing renal disease compared to siblings of control subjects without diabetic nephropathy; and furthermore, severe diabetic nephropathy in probands increased the risk in their siblings by threefold (Harjutsalo et al.,

2004). Despite the evidence supporting familial clustering of diabetic nephropathy and the heightened risk among relatives of probands, the genes involved have not been identified. Clearly, a genetic marker for nephropathy would enable early detection and treatment and facilitate screening and targeted intervention for high-risk relatives.

PREVENTION OF CHRONIC KIDNEY DISEASE

As with cardiovascular disease, chronic kidney disease develops as a consequence of a complex *web of causation* that involves multiple risk factors and causative agents. A recent review by Professor Robert Atkins of the Monash Medical Center, Victoria, Australia, provides keen insights on strategies for prevention. As he points out: "*Chronic kidney disease should not be viewed in isolation. Chronic kidney disease has a complex interrelationship with cardiovascular disease, diabetes, and hypertension. Indeed, chronic kidney disease is a major risk factor for cardiovascular disease*" (Atkins, 2005). Thus, in order to be effective, screening and prevention programs must focus not only on the detection and treatment of kidney disease, but also diabetes, hypertension, and cardiovascular diseases as well. A comprehensive profile of risk factors must be addressed including obesity, hypertension, hyperglycemia (diabetes), hyperlipidemia/hypercholesterolemia/hypertriglyceridemia, hyperuricemia (gout), smoking, alcohol abuse, lack of exercise and diet. Routine screening for microalbuminuria is essential for the early detection and treatment of kidney disease, particularly for those patients with diabetes and/or hypertension.

As a further complication, many developing nations suffer from a double burden of renal disease due to obstructive uropathy and glomerulonephritis caused by infectious parasites such as malaria and schistosomiasis or communicable bacteria and viruses, as well as that caused by chronic noninfectious conditions such as diabetes, hypertension, and obesity. In these nations, preventive and therapeutic strategies must include programs for the prevention, detection, and early effective therapy of etiologic parasitic, bacterial, and viral infections. The basic axioms of primary, secondary, and tertiary prevention involve community education and prevention of disease by lifestyle modifications, early detection of disease, and effective treatment of established disease. As pointed out by Dr. Atkins, "individual and community educational programs must be an integral part of the overall management plan" (Atkins, 2005).

TERTIARY PREVENTION OF CHRONIC KIDNEY DISEASE

Tertiary prevention is designed to restore function and inhibit disease progression after the diagnosis has been established. In regard to chronic kidney disease, a multifactorial approach is essential to prevent progression to end-stage renal disease and kidney failure. This includes effective management and control of blood pressure, blood glucose, blood lipids, and body weight, plus cessation of tobacco use through effective pharmacologic therapy plus nonpharmacologic methods such as diet, exercise, and counseling.

It is also essential for treating clinicians and healthcare workers to be aware of and correct abnormalities in other clinical parameters. For example, anemia (hemoglobin level below 11 g per deciliter) develops early in patients diagnosed with chronic kidney disease due to deficient erythropoietin production by the failing kidney. Therefore, most patients will require erythropoietin replacement to slow the progression of renal disease (Gouva et al., 2004). Nevertheless, controversy exists as to the optimal target for hemoglobin correction.

The *Correction of Hemoglobin and Outcomes in Renal Insufficiency (CHOIR)* trial used a randomized, open-label experimental study design to address the question of whether a higher target of hemoglobin correction by erythropoietin replacement in anemic patients with chronic kidney disease could provide additional clinical benefit. The study randomized 715 patients to a high hemoglobin group (target level: 13.5 g per deciliter) and 717 patients to a low hemoglobin group (target level: 11.3 g per deciliter). Surprisingly, more patients in the high hemoglobin group either died or developed congestive heart failure than in the low hemoglobin group (11.7% versus 7.5%, respectively). Furthermore, patients in the high hemoglobin group had a slightly higher rate of progression to renal replacement therapy (Singh et al., 2006). Thus, the magnitude of hemoglobin correction for optimal benefit to the patient remains in question and the specificity and mechanism of drug action should be considered and examined in more detail in future mechanistic studies.

DIALYSIS AND RENAL TRANSPLANTATION FOR END-STAGE RENAL DISEASE

End-stage renal disease (ESRD) is a devastating condition with extraordinarily high mortality and morbidity. Even in the United States where dialysis and renal transplantation are common procedures, the age adjusted case fatality rate due to ESRD is 14.3% (National Kidney and Urologic Diseases Information Clearinghouse, 2008). The high morbidity and mortality rate for ESRD patients results in reduced quality of life for the individual patient and loss of productivity. Patients also suffer from other medical conditions and complications associated with their greater risk for cardiovascular disease and other serious conditions such as hyperparathyroidism and bone disease, iron deficiency, nutritional inadequacy, inflammation, and anemia.

Hemodialysis is now being used in many developed nations of the world for the treatment of ESRD. In this procedure, blood is filtered through a semipermeable membrane to rid the body of waste, restore the proper balance of blood components, and eliminate extra fluid. While effective, hemodialysis is expensive and requires elaborate equipment and a coordinated effort by highly trained healthcare professionals as well as patients undergoing therapy.

The costs of hemodialysis for ESRD are high ($60,000–$75,000 per year for persons undergoing hemodialysis in the United States). The most recent estimates indicate that Medicare costs for ESRD have reached $20.1 billion, while non-Medicare costs have risen to $12.4 billion. The costs for the care of ESRD patients now account for 6.7% of total Medicare expenditures.

Successful renal transplantation is a life-extending procedure in patients with ESRD. In the hands of skilled transplant surgeons, transplantation has been found to extend the life of patients in renal failure by 10–15 years compared to patients sustained by hemodialysis (Wolfe et al., 1999; McDonald and Russ, 2002). Renal transplantation is an option for patients with ESRD in several developed nations (United States, United Kingdom, Spain, Italy, France, Japan, Australia, and Canada) and some developing nations (Pakistan and India). However, the primary obstacle remains the cost of the procedure (currently estimated in excess of $100,000 in the United States).

The Sindh Institute of Urology and Transplantation (SIUT) in Karachi, Pakistan, a public sector organization, performs more than 130 renal transplants per year, all from living related donors. Economic constraints, lack of public awareness, and shortage of donors limit the number of transplantation procedures. Post-transplant tuberculosis arising due to immunosuppressive drugs given to prevent transplant rejection is a special problem in developing countries. Nevertheless, the SIUT program is gaining momentum and now consists of three transplant teams of surgeons, urologists, nephrologists, pathologists, radiologists, and other support personnel.

Funding support for SIUT in a community-government partnership has increased the number of transplantations and resulted in significantly improved patient and organ survival. The SIUT program may thus serve as a model for successful renal transplantation programs in other developing nations (Rizvi et al., 2003).

In populations of developing nations, the cost of ESRD care is often prohibitive, leading to extremely high case fatality rates approaching 100% in some nations. Nevertheless, advances are being made, particularly with the use of *continuous ambulatory peritoneal dialysis* as an alternative to hemodialysis or renal transplantation for ESRD.

As opposed to hemodialysis that requires hospital-based equipment and personnel, peritoneal dialysis for ESRD can be performed by patients as home-based therapy. Peritoneal dialysis requires placement of an indwelling catheter into the peritoneal cavity for daily infusion of glucose-rich dialysate. Fluid, waste, and chemicals pass from the peritoneal capillary vessels into the peritoneum in exchange for dialysate components and the waste fluid is then drained from the peritoneum and the procedure repeated.

Peritoneal dialysis has important advantages compared to other forms of renal replacement therapy, e.g., relatively low cost, avoidance of hospital treatment, enhanced patient freedom, and improved quality of life. Complications of this procedure include infection (peritonitis) and edema (fluid overload), but these are preventable through patient education regarding infusion and drainage of diasylate and hygienic management of the catheter site. With state-of-the-art equipment, ESRD therapy by continuous ambulatory peritoneal dialysis appears to be comparable to hemodialysis if used correctly (Ronco and Amerling, 2006). Nevertheless, hemodialysis is the preferred method of treating ESRD in many societies due to the widespread misconception that it is safer and more effective than peritoneal dialysis. As pointed out by Nayak and colleagues, the future of peritoneal dialysis in the treatment of ESRD will depend upon popularization in Latin America and in Asia, especially countries such as China and India with a combined population of 2.5 billion and rapidly rising rates of diabetes, hypertension, obesity, and chronic kidney disease (Nayak et al., 2009).

● ● ● **REFERENCES**

Afshinnia, F., Wilt, T.J., Duval, S.U., Esmaeili, A., & Ibrahim, H.N. (2010). Weight loss and proteinuria: Systematic review of clinical trials and comparative cohorts. *Nephrology Dialysis Transplantation*, 25(4), 1173–1183.

Appel, G.B., Radhakrishnan, J., Avram, M.M., DeFronzo, R.A., Escobar-Jimenez, F., Campos, M.M.,...Brenner, B.M. (2003). Analysis of metabolic parameters as predictors of risk in the RENAAL study. *Diabetes Care*, 26, 1402–1407.

Atkins, R.C. (2005). The changing patterns of chronic kidney disease: The need to develop strategies for prevention relevant to different regions and countries. *Kidney International*, 68, S83–S85.

Baker, R.D., & Selikoff, E. (1952). The cholesterol of hyaline arteriolosclerosis. *Am J Pathol* 28(4), 573–581.

Barsoum, R.S. (2003). Schistosomiasis and the kidney. *Semin Nephrol*, 23(1), 34–41.

Black, H.R., Zeevi, G.R., Silten, R.M., & Smith, G.J.W. (1983). Effect of heavy cigarette smoking on renal and myocardial arterioles. *Nephron, 34*, 173–179.

Borch-Johnsen, K., Norgaard, K., Hommel, E., Mathiesen, E.R., Jensen, J.S., Deckert, T., & Parving, H.H. (1992). Is diabetic nephropathy an inherited complication? *Kidney Int, 41*, 719–722.

Bowden, D.W. (2003). Genetics of kidney disease. *Kidney International, 63*, S8–S12.

Cameron, J.S. (1972a). Bright's disease today: The pathogenesis and treatment of glomerulonephritis I. *British Medical Journal, 4*(5832), 87–90.

Cameron, J.S. (1972b). Bright's disease today: The pathogenesis and treatment of glomerulonephritis II. *British Medical Journal, 4*(5833), 160–163.

Cameron, J.S. (1972c). Bright's disease today: The pathogenesis and treatment of glomerulonephritis III. *British Medical Journal, 4*(5834), 217–220.

Chase, H.P., Garg, S.K., Marshall, G., et al. (1991). Cigarette smoking increases the risk of albuminuria among subjects with type 1 diabetes. *JAMA*, 265, 614–617.

Choi, H.K., Atkinson, K., Darlson, E.W., Willet, W., & Curhan, G. (2004). Alcohol intake and the risk of incident gout in men: A prospective study. *The Lancet, 363*(9417), 1277–1281.

Christiansen, J.S. (1978). Cigarette smoking and prevalence of microangiopathy in juvenile-onset insulin-dependent diabetes mellitus. *Diabetes Care, 1,* 146–149.

Churchill, D.N., Fine, A., & Gault, M.H. (1983). Association between hydrocarbon exposure and glomerulonephritis: An appraisal of the evidence. *Nephron, 33,* 169–172.

Collins, W.E., & Jeffery, G.M. (2007). Plasmodium malariae: Parasite and disease. *Clinical Microbiology Reviews, 20*(4), 579–592.

Cooper, M.E. (1998). Pathogenesis, prevention, and treatment of diabetic nephropathy. *Lancet, 352*(9123), 213–219.

Couser, W.G. (1999). Glomerulonephritis. *Lancet, 353*(9163), 1509–1515.

Dales, L.G., Friedman, G.D., Siegelaub, A.B., Seltzer, C.C., & Ury, H.K. (1978). Cigarette smoking habits and urine characteristics. *Nephron, 20,* 163–170.

Dixon, F.J. (1966). Comments on immunopathology. *Mil Med, 131*(Suppl.), 1233–1234.

Flinter, F., Maher, E., & Saggar, A. (2003). *The genetics of renal disease.* Oxford University Press.

Fox, C.S., Larson, M.G., Lepi, E.P., Meigs, J.B., Wilson, P.W., & Levy, D. (2005). Glycemic status and development of kidney disease: The Framingham Heart Study. *Diabetes Care, 28*(10), 2436–2440.

Fried, L.F., Orchard, T.J., Kasiske, B.L. for the Lipids and Renal Disease Progression Meta-Analysis Study Group. (2001). Effect of lipid reduction on the progression of renal disease: A meta-analysis. *Kidney International, 59,* 260–269.

Gioglioli, G. (1930). *Malarial nephritis.* London: Churchill.

Gouva, C., Nikolopoulos, P., Ioannidis, J.P., & Siamopoulos, K.C. (2004). Treating anemia early in renal failure patients slows the decline of renal

function: A randomized controlled trial. *Kidney Int, 66,* 753–760.

Hadjadj, S., Duly-Bouhanick, B., Bekherraz, A., Bridoux, F., Gallois, Y., Mauco, G.,…Marre, M. (2004). Serum triglycerides are a predictive factor for the development and the progression of renal and retinal complications in patients with type 1 diabetes. *Diabetes Metab, 30,* 43–51.

Hansson, L., Zanchetti, A., Carruthers, S.G., et al. (1998). Effects of intensive blood-pressure lowering and low-dose aspirin in patients with hypertension: Principal results of the Hypertension Optimal Treatment (HOT) randomised trial. *Lancet, 351,* 1755–1762.

Harjutsalo, V., Katoh, S., Sarti, C., Tajima, N., & Tuomilehto, J. (2004). Population-based assessment of familial clustering of diabetic nephropathy in type 2 diabetes. *Diabetes, 53*(9), 2449–2454.

Hasslacher, C., Ritz, E., Wahl, P., & Michael, C. (1989). Similar risks of nephropathy in patients with type I or type II diabetes mellitus. *Nephrol Dial Transplant, 4,* 859–863.

Hsu, C., McCulloch, C.E., Iribarren, C., Darbinian, J., & Go, A.S. (2006). Body mass index and risk for end-stage renal disease. *Ann Intern Med, 144,* 21–28.

Huraib, S., Al Khader, A., Shaheen, F., Abu Aisha, H., Souqiyyeh, M.Z., Al Mohana, F.,…Chan, N. (2000). The Spectrum of glomerulonephritis in Saudi Arabia: The results of the Saudi Registry. *Saudi J Kidney Dis Transpl, 11,* 434–441.

Ismail, N., Becker, B., Strzelczyk, P., & Ritz, E. (1999). Renal disease and hypertension in non-insulin-dependent diabetes mellitus. *Kidney Int, 55,* 1–28.

Jafar, T.H., Stark, P.C., Schmid, C.H., Landa, M., Maschio, G., deJong, P.E.,…Levey, A.S.; for the AIPRD Study Group. (2003). Progression of chronic kidney disease: The role of blood pressure control, proteinuria, and angiotensin-converting enzyme inhibition. A patient-level meta-analysis. *Ann Intern Med, 139,* 244–252.

Jenkins, A.J., Lyons, T.J., Zheng, D., Otvos, J.D., Lackland, D.T., McGee, D.,…Klein, R.L. (2003).

DCCT/EDIC Research Group: Lipoproteins in the DCCT/EDIC cohort: Associations with diabetic nephropathy. *Kidney Int, 64,* 817–828.

Johnson, A.C.M., Stahl, A., & Zager, R.A. (2005). Triglyceride accumulation in injured renal tubular cells: Alterations in both synthetic and catabolic pathways. *Kidney International, 67,* 2196–2209.

Jones, S.L., Close, C.F., Mattock, M.B., Jarrett, R.J., Keen, H., & Viverti, G.C. (1989). Plasma lipid and coagulation factor concentrations in insulin-dependent diabetic patients with microalbuminuria. *BMJ, 298,* 487–490.

Kawazu, S., Tomono, S., Shimizu, M., et al. (1994). The relationship between early diabetic nephropathy and control of plasma glucose in non-insulin-dependent diabetes mellitus: The effect of glycemic control on the development and progression of diabetic nephropathy in an 8-year follow-up study. *J Diabetes Complications, 8,* 13–17.

Keller, C.K., Bergis, K.H., Fliser, D., & Ritz, E. (1996). Renal findings in patients with short-term type 2 diabetes. *J Am Soc Nephrol, 7,* 2627–2635.

Klag, M.J., Whelton, P.K., Randall, B.L., Neaton, J.D., Brancati, F.L., Ford, C.E.,…Stamler, J. (1996). Blood pressure and end-stage renal disease in men. *N Engl J Med, 334,* 13–18.

Klein, R., Klein, B.E., Moss, S.E., & Cruickshanks, K.J. (1995). Ten-year incidence of gross proteinuria in people with diabetes. *Diabetes, 44*(8), 2436–2440.

Kramer, H.J., Choi, H.K., Atkinson, K., Stampfer, J., & Curhan, G.C. (2003). The association between gout and nephrolithiasis in men: The Health Professionals' Follow-Up Study. *Kidney International, 64,* 1022–1026.

Mahakur, A.C., Panda, S.N., Nanda, B.K., Bose, T.K., Satpathy, S.R., & Misra, Y. (1983). Malarial Acute Renal Failure. *J Assoc Phys India, 31,* 633–616.

Makita, Z., Radoff, S., Rayfield, E.J., Yang, Z., Skolnik, E., Delaney, V.,…Vlassara, H. (1991). Advanced glycosylation end products in patients with diabetic nephropathy. *N Engl J Med, 325,* 836–842.

Martinelli, R., Noblat, A.C.B., Brito, E., & Rocha, H. (1989). *Schistosoma mansoni-*induced mesangiocapillary glomerulonephritis: Influence of therapy. *Kidney International, 35,* 1227–1233.

McDonald, S.P., & Russ, G.R. (2002). Survival of recipients of cadaveric kidney transplants compared with those receiving dialysis treatment in Australia and New Zealand, 1991–2001. *Nephrol Dial Transplant, 17*(12), 2212–2219.

Menon, V., Katz, R., Mukamal, K., Kestenbaum, B., de Boer, I.H., Siscovicks, D.S., Sarnak, M.J., & Shlipak, M.G. (2010). Alcohol consumption and kidney function decline in the elderly. *Nephrol Dial Transplant, 25,* 3301–3307.

Mimran, A., Ribstein, J., DuCailar, G., & Halimi, J.M. (1994). Albuminuria in normals and essential hypertension. *J Diabetes Complications, 8,* 150–156.

Moeller, S., Gioberge, S., & Brown, G. (2002). ESRD patients in 2001: Global overview of patients, treatment modalities and development trends. *Nephrol Dial Transplant, 217,* 2071–2076.

Mogensen, C.E. (1999). Microalbuminuria, blood pressure and diabetic renal disease: Origin and development of ideas. *Diabetologia, 42,* 263–285.

Mulder, J., Pinto-Sietsma, S.J., Diercks, G.F., et al. (1999). Smoking behaviour and urinary albumin excretion (UAE) in the general population. *J Am Soc Nephrol, 10,* 175A.

Mulec, H., Johnson, S.A., & Bjorck, S. (1990). Relation between serum cholesterol and diabetic nephropathy. *Lancet, 335,* 1537–1538.

Muntner, P., Coresh, J., Smith, C., Eckfeldt, J., & Klag, M.J. (2000). Plasma lipids and risk of developing renal dysfunction: The Atherosclerosis Risk in Communities Study. *Kidney Int, 58,* 293–301.

Murray, C.J.L., & Lopez, A.D. (1997). Mortality by cause for eight regions of the world: Global burden of disease study. *Lancet, 349,* 1269–1276.

Naicker, S. (2003). End-stage renal disease in sub-Saharan and South Africa. *Kidney Int*, *63*, 119.

National Kidney and Urologic Diseases Information Clearinghouse. (2008). National Institute of Diabetes and Digestive and Kidney Diseases (NIDDK). National Institutes of Health (NIH) Publication No. 08-3925, 2008.

Nayak, K.S., Prabhu, M.V., Sinoj, K.A., Subhramanyam, S.V., & Sridhar, G. (2009). C. Ronco, C. Crepaldi, D.N. Cruz (Eds.). Peritoneal dialysis in developing countries. *Contrib Nephrol*, *163*, 270–277.

Nielsen, F.S., Rossing, P., Gall, M.A., Skott, P., Smidt, U.M., & Parving, H.H. (1997). Long-term effect of lisinopril and atenolol on kidney function in hypertensive NIDDM subjects with diabetic nephropathy. *Diabetes*, *46*, 1182–1188.

Oberai, B., Adams, C.W.M., & High, O.B. (1984). Myocardial and renal arteriolar thickening in cigarette smoking. *Atherosclerosis*, *52*, 185–190.

Orth, S.R., Ritz, E., & Schrier, R.W. (1997). The renal risks of smoking. *Kidney Int*, *51*, 1669–1677.

Orth, S.R., Stöckmann, A., Conradt, C., Ritz, E., in collaboration with Ferro, M., Kreusser, W., Picolli, G., Rambausek, M., Roccatello, D., Schäfer, K.,...Zucchelli, P. (1998). Smoking as a risk factor for end-stage renal failure in men with primary renal disease. *Kidney Int*, *54*, 926–931.

Oyediran, A.B.O.O. (1979). Renal disease due to schistosomiasis of the lower urinary tract. *Kidney International*, *16*, 15–22.

Perneger, T.V., Whelton, P.K., Puddey, I.B., & Klag, M.J. (1999). Risk of end-stage renal disease associated with alcohol consumption. *Am J Epidemiol*, *150*, 1275–1281.

Peterson, J.C., Adler, S., Burkart, J.M., et al. (1995). Blood pressure control, proteinuria, and the progression of renal disease: The Modification of Diet in Renal Disease Study. *Ann Intern Med*, *123*, 754–762.

Prakash, J., Sundar, S., Kar, B., Sharma, N., Raja, R., & Usha. (2007). Spectrum of renal disease In visceral leishmaniasis. *The Internet Journal of Tropical Medicine*, *4*(1).

Prasad, L.S., Sen, S., & Ganguly, S.K. (1992). Renal involvement in kala-azar. *Indian Journal of Medical Research*, *95*(1), 43–46.

Quinn, M., Angelico, M.C., Warram, J.H., & Krolewski, A.S. (1996). Familial factors determine the development of diabetic nephropathy in patients with IDDM. *Diabetologia*, *39*, 940–945.

Rajapurkar, M.M. (1994). Renal involvement in malaria. *J Postgrad Med*, *40*, 132–134.

Ravid, M., Brosh, D., Ravid-Safran, D., Levy, Z., & Rachmani, R. (1998). Main risk factors for nephropathy in type 2 diabetes mellitus are plasma cholesterol levels, mean blood pressure, and hyperglycemia. *Arch Intern Med*, *158*, 998–1004.

Ritz, E., & Orth, S.R. (1999). Nephropathy in patients with type 2 diabetes mellitus. *N Engl J Med*, *341*, 1127–1133.

Rizvi, S.A.H., Naqvi, S.A.A., Hussain, Z., Hashmi, A., Akhtar, F., Hussain, M.,...Jawad, F. (2003). Renal transplantation in developing countries. *Kidney International*, *63*, S96–S100.

Robbins, S.L., & Cotran, R.S. (1979). *Pathologic basis of disease*. Philadelphia: WB Saunders Company.

Ronco, C., & Amerling, R. (2006). Continuous flow peritoneal dialysis: Current state-of-the-art and obstacles to further development. *Contrib Nephrol*, *150*, 310–320.

Ronti, T., Lupattelli, G., & Mannarino, E. (2006). The endocrine function of adipose tissue: An update. *Clini Endocrinol*, *64*(4), 355–365.

Roy, M.S. (2004). Proteinuria in African Americans wih type 1 diabetes. *J Diabetes Complications*, *18*(1), 69–77.

Ruilope, L.M., & Garcia-Robles, R. (1997). How far should blood pressure be reduced in diabetic hypertensive patients? *J Hypertens Suppl*, *15*, S63–S65.

Rundles, R.W. (1966). Allopurinol in gouty nephropathy and renal dialysis. *Ann Rheum Dis, 25,* 694.

Sammuelsson, O., Attman, P., Knight-Gibson, C., Larsonn, R., Mulec, H., Weiss, L., & Alaupovic, P. (1998). Complex apolipoprotein B-containing lipoprotein particles are associated with a higher rate of progression of human chronic renal insufficiency. *J Am Soc Nephrol, 9,* 1482–1488.

Sandhu, S., Wiebe, N., Fried, L.F., & Tonelli, M. (2006). Statins for improving renal outcomes: A meta-analysis. *J Am Soc Nephrol, 17,* 2006–2016.

Sawicki, P.T., Didjurgeit, U., Muhlhauser, I., Bender, R., Heinemann, L., & Berger, M. (1994). Smoking is associated with progression of diabetic nephropathy. *Diabetes Care, 17,* 126–131.

Seaquist, E.R., Goetz, F.C., Rich, S., & Barbosa, J. (1989). Familial clustering of diabetic kidney disease: Evidence for genetic susceptibility to diabetic nephropathy. *N Engl J Med, 320,* 1161–1165.

Schaeffner, E.S., Kurth, T., de Jong, P.E., Glynn, R.J., Buring, J.E., & Gaziano, J.M. (2005). Alcohol consumption and the risk of renal dysfunction in apparently healthy men. *Arch Intern Med, 165,* 1048–1053.

Shankar, A., Klein, R., & Klein, B.E.K. (2006). The association among smoking, heavy drinking, and chronic kidney disease. *Am J Epidem, 164*(3), 263–271.

Singh, A.K., Szczech, L., Kezhen, L.T., Barnhart, H., Sapp, S., Wolfson, M., Reddan, D., for the CHOIR investigators. (2006). Correction of anemia with epoetin alfa in chronic kidney disease. *N Engl J Med, 255,* 2085–2098.

UK Prospective Diabetes Study Group. (1998). Intensive blood-glucose control with sulphonylureas or insulin compared with conventional treatment and risk of complications in patients with type 2 diabetes. *Lancet, 352,* 837–853.

Wang, Y., Chen, X., Song, Y., Caballero, B., & Cheskin, L.J. (2008). Association between obesity and kidney disease: A systematic review and meta-analysis. *Kidney Int, 73*(1), 19–33.

Whelton, P.K., Perneger, T.V., He, J., & Klag, M.J. (1996). The role of blood pressure as a risk factor for renal disease. *J Hum Hypertens, 10,* 683–689.

Whelton, P.K., Randall, B., Neaton, J., Stamler, J., Brancati, F.L., & Klag, M.J. (1995). Cigarette smoking and ESRD incidence in men screened for the MRFIT. *J Am Soc Nephrol, 6,* 408a.

Wolfe, R.A., Ashby, V.B., Milford, E.L., Ojo, A.O., Ettenger, R.E., Agodoa, L.Y.,...Port, F.K. (1999). Comparison of mortality in all patients on dialysis, patients on dialysis awaiting transplantation, and recipients of a first cadaveric transplant. *N Eng J Med, 341,* 1725–1730.

World Health Organization. (2004). *The global burden of disease: 2004 update.*

Epidemiology of Cirrhosis of the Liver

GLOBAL BURDEN OF CIRRHOSIS OF THE LIVER

Cirrhosis of the liver is responsible for nearly 800,000 deaths per year worldwide (WHO, 2009a). Annual age-adjusted mortality rates vary widely ranging from >30 male deaths per 100,000 in Mexico, Chile, and certain nations of Eastern Europe and the Russian Federation to < 5 deaths per 100,000 in some Nordic countries, Singapore, and New Zealand (La Vecchia et al., 1994; Ramstedt, 2001; Bosetti et al., 2007; Zatoński et al., 2010).

Within populations, the age-adjusted mortality rates are consistently two to threefold higher in men than women. In North America, mortality rates have declined since 1970 and have stabilized at approximately 10 per 100,000 in men and 5 per 100,000 in women. While rates have also declined in some European nations (e.g., Italy, France, and Spain), many of the populations of Eastern Europe continue to show high or increasing mortality rates from liver cirrhosis (Ramstedt, 2001; Bosetti et al., 2007; Zatoński et al., 2010).

Globally, chronic alcohol consumption and chronic liver infections by hepatitis B virus HBV) and/ or hepatitis C virus (HCV) have been the main causes of cirrhosis. More recently, the increasing prevalence of obesity and the *metabolic syndrome* has resulted

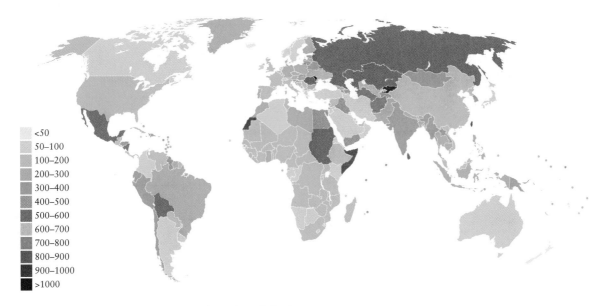

Legend:
<50
50–100
100–200
200–300
300–400
400–500
500–600
600–700
700–800
800–900
900–1000
>1000

Figure 36.1 Disability Adjusted Life Years from Liver Cirrhosis, 2004.

Source: Data from World Health Organization. The global burden of disease: 2004 update. Geneva, WHO, 2008. Available at www.who.int /evidence/bod.

in increasing incidence rates of cirrhosis secondary to nonalcoholic fatty liver disease, particularly in developed countries. Chronic liver disease and cirrhosis are important causes of morbidity and mortality throughout the world. The global pattern of disability adjusted life years (*DALY*) lost due to cirrhosis of the liver is shown in **Figure 36.1** (*DALY* = *YLL* + *YLD* where *YLL* = years of life lost due to death and *YLD* = years of life lost due to severe disability). The annual DALY rates are highest in those populations with high rates of alcoholism and chronic liver infections by HBV and/or HCV.

LIVER FUNCTION AND ANATOMY

The human liver is a vital organ that regulates a number of life-sustaining functions including the synthesis of important proteins (e.g., albumin, clotting factors and complement); metabolism and regulation of lipids, carbohydrates, and certain steroidal hormones (e.g., estrogens and androgens); synthesis and regulation of cholesterol and cholesterol byproducts (e.g., bile acids and fat soluble vitamins, A, D, E, and K); production and secretion of bile acids for digestion; the formation, storage, and release of glycogen for the regulation of blood glucose; and detoxification of chemicals and harmful substances.

The liver is located in the upper right quadrant of the abdomen. Its normal weight in adults is between 1,400–1,600 grams. The liver receives a dual blood supply consisting of the hepatic portal vein and hepatic arteries. The hepatic portal vein carries

venous blood drained from the spleen and gastrointestinal tract and the hepatic arteries supply arterial blood. Oxygen is provided from both sources; approximately half from the hepatic portal vein and half from the hepatic arteries (Robbins and Cotran, 1979). The gall bladder, which is located just beneath the liver, stores and concentrates bile produced by the liver and regulates bile secretion into the duodenum for the digestion of dietary fat (**Figure 36.2**).

The liver is organized into thousands of small lobules separated by bands of connective tissue. The parenchyma (tissue) within each lobule consists primarily of polygonal hepatocytes that carry out the multiple biosynthetic and metabolic functions of the liver. The hepatocytes are arranged in microscopic functional units called *acini* that are distributed within the lobules. Each acinus consists of hepatocytes arranged in concentric zones about hepatic arterioles and portal venules in order to facilitate selective secretion/excretion of cellular metabolites. The products of cellular synthesis and metabolism enter the blood in the sinusoids that are adjoined to the acini. Sinusoids are vascular channels that are lined by fenestrated endothelium and heavily populated by *Kupffer cells (see description below)*.

Hepatocytes are responsible for an amazing array of biochemical functions. Their cytoplasm is laden with mitochondria that are responsible for oxidative phosphorylation and energy production, and the oxidation of fatty acids. Also within the cytoplasm, the *smooth endoplasmic reticulum* is the site of synthesis of cholesterol and bile acids, conjugation of bilirubin, drugs and steroids for excretion,

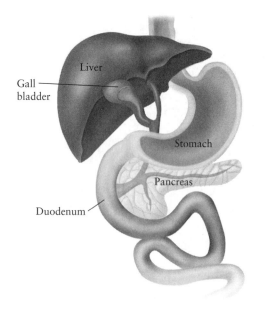

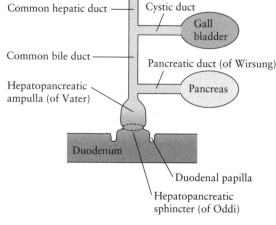

Figure 36.2 Anatomy of the Liver and Related Organs.

metabolism of drugs and steroids, and breakdown of glycogen; and the *rough endoplasmic reticulum* is the site of protein synthesis. The multiple synthetic and metabolic pathways of hepatocytes are dependent upon the presence and functional integrity of a variety of essential enzymes, e.g., the mixed function oxidase system (enzymes that oxidize toxic compounds for metabolism and excretion), cytochrome oxidase (a mitochondrial enzyme essential for respiration), and cytochrome P450 enzymes (oxidizing enzymes involved in metabolism and bioactivation of lipids, steroids, and drugs).

The liver is the detoxification center of the human body. For example, the *urea cycle* metabolizes ammonia, the principle byproduct of protein breakdown. Ammonia is highly toxic to cells, whereas urea is nontoxic and readily condensed in urine by the kidneys for excretion. One of the enzymes present in hepatocytes is alcohol dehydrogenase which catalyzes the conversion of alcohol to nontoxic metabolites for excretion. As discussed below, genetic variability in the alcohol dehydrogenase enzyme system influences the risk of developing alcoholic cirrhosis of the liver.

Kupffer cells are large phagocytic cells of the innate immune system that circulate throughout the sinusoidal network of the liver parenchyma. They were first observed by the German scientist, Karl Wilhelm von Kupffer in 1876 (Haubrich, 2004). Kupffer cells phagocytize senescent red blood cells and hepatocytes and break down hemoglobin and other cellular constituents (Robbins and Cotran, 1979).

In 1951, novel fat-storage cells lining the hepatic sinusoids were discovered by Ito (Ito, 1951). These *Ito cells* actively store lipids and retinoids and are apparently involved in liver fibrosis during the development and progression of cirrhosis (Geerts, 2001).

CIRRHOSIS OF THE LIVER: PATHOLOGY, CLINICAL SYMPTOMS, AND DIAGNOSIS

Cirrhosis of the liver is a chronic inflammatory condition that causes a sustained recursive cycle of necrosis and regeneration of hepatocytes (liver cells). The word "*cirrhosis*" derives from the Greek term *kirrhos* that means "*of yellow color*" (the orange-yellow color of the diseased liver) (Robbins and Cotran, 1979). The French physician, René Laennec, named the condition "*cirrhosis*" in his 1819 work in which he also describes the stethoscope (Roguin, 2006).

With progression of cirrhosis, there is massive relapsing inflammation and necrosis of hepatocytes admixed with fibrosis and formation of nodular scar tissue and regeneration of liver tissue. The progressive destruction of liver tissue and conversion of the normal liver architecture into fibrotic nodules causes significant derangement of many important biosynthetic and metabolic processes. Liver cirrhosis is therefore characterized by a wide range of clinical symptoms including edema, ascites, jaundice, compromised blood clotting, hyperglycemia, abnormal digestion, and buildup of toxic substances in blood and tissues. A common clinical sign of liver disease is *jaundice*, the yellowish discoloration of the skin and sclerae of the eye due to the accumulation of bilirubin (a yellow breakdown product of hemoglobin) in tissues and interstitial fluids of the body.

Advanced disease often results in obstruction of key blood vessels within the liver, e.g., the portal vein, with subsequent development of portal hypertension and ascites (fluid accumulation in the abdominal cavity) and/or bleeding esophageal varices due to shunting of blood to vessels external to the liver. Other life-threatening complications include hepatoencephalopathy and/or renal failure due to high blood concentrations of toxic substances such as ammonia and carbon tetrachloride (Robbins and Cotran, 1979; Galambos, 1985). The eventual consequences of progressive cirrhosis are liver failure and death.

PATHOGENESIS OF CIRRHOSIS OF THE LIVER

Cirrhosis of the liver has multiple etiologies, the best known of which is alcoholic cirrhosis, which is most prominent in the western world. Nevertheless, certain infectious agents now rival alcohol as the leading cause, most notably in the developing nations of Africa and Asia. Chronic liver infection by hepatitis B virus (HBV), hepatitis C virus (HBV), and hepatitis D virus (HDV) all cause a sequence of pathogenic events similar to chronic alcohol exposure, the end result of which is cirrhosis. Furthermore, the metabolic syndrome (the disease complex of diabetes, obesity, hyperlipidemia, and hypertension) has been found to heighten the development of fatty liver disease and its progression to cirrhosis, even in the absence of alcohol exposure or infectious hepatitis.

Fatty Liver

Cirrhosis is often viewed as the culmination of a series of progressive pathological changes. One of the earliest changes is the intracellular accumulation of fat by hepatocytes (*fatty change*) that results in a fatty liver (*steatosis*). The genesis of fatty change in the liver remains a topic of some controversy. In this condition, fat vacuoles laden with triglycerides appear within hepatocytes, possibly as a consequence of deranged lipid metabolism and transport in cells exposed to alcohol or other toxic substances.

In addition to chronic alcohol exposure, chronic HBV and HCV infections induce fatty liver in the majority of infected patients (Bamber et al., 1981; Hirche et al., 2007). Furthermore, a condition known as *nonalcoholic fatty liver disease* that arises in patients with the metabolic syndrome (obesity, type 2 diabetes mellitus and hyperlidemia) has recently been recognized as a distinct clinical entity with worldwide health impact (see discussion below).

Hepatitis

Hepatitis refers to inflammation of the liver, regardless of the inciting agent. The *sine qua non* of hepatitis is infiltration of the liver by inflammatory cells of the immune system, e.g., macrophages, neutrophils, and lymphocytes. Common pathological findings include areas of necrosis and liver degeneration, hyaline accumulation within hepatocytes, and micronodular and macronodular fibrosis.

Cirrhosis

Cirrhosis of the liver is a significant cause of serious illness, liver failure, and death. Pathologic hallmarks of cirrhosis include the presence of regenerating nodules of hepatocytes and the deposition of fibrotic connective tissue between these nodules. With progression of disease, these fibrotic bands continue to expand and eventually replace the entire liver architecture causing obstruction of blood flow and general disruption of liver function.

Diagnosis of Cirrhosis of the Liver

The gold standard in the diagnosis of cirrhosis is confirmation of cirrhotic liver pathology by microscopic examination of a liver biopsy. Specimens are ordinarily obtained through a percutaneous, transjugular, laparoscopic, or fine-needle approach. Clinical, laboratory, and imaging data are also useful in confirming the diagnosis of cirrhosis. For example, elevated liver enzymes (aminotransferase, alkaline phosphatase, gamma-glutamyl transferase), increased bilirubin, decreased albumin, coagulation defects, immune dysfunction, hyponatremia (low sodium), and thrombocytopenia (low platelets) are suggestive of cirrhosis. Ultrasound and other imaging techniques also aid in the diagnosis.

Major Causes of Liver Cirrhosis

Cirrhosis of the liver has multiple etiologies. As in many chronic diseases, risk factors often coexist in the same patient and synergistically increase the risk. As discussed below, cirrhosis is often the consequence of one or more of four major factors: alcoholism, hepatitis B, hepatitis C, and the metabolic syndrome. As discussed in the following sections, these factors are not mutually exclusive and when combined they synergistically increase the risk of developing liver cirrhosis.

Alcohol Abuse and Cirrhosis of the Liver: Mortality Studies

The early studies of Raymond Pearl at Johns Hopkins University found that heavy drinkers had higher mortality rates due to cirrhosis of the liver than light drinkers or abstainers (Pearl, 1926). Alcohol consumption increased substantially in many countries after World War II, which spurred scientific interest in the health effects of alcohol addiction. Postwar studies of longitudinal data revealed temporal relationships between *per capita* alcohol consumption and cirrhosis mortality rates (Jellinek and Keller, 1952; Ledermann, 1956; Seeley, 1960).

In a landmark study, Milton Terris studied relationships between *per capita* alcohol consumption and annual mortality rates due to cirrhosis of the liver in the United States, Great Britain, and Canada during 1910–1964. Long-term trends were investigated by age, gender, race, urban-rural residence, occupation, and social status. Terris noted the close parallelism between time-series curves (spanning 1910–1964) of the annual *per capita* consumption of spirits and wine (but not beer) and annual liver cirrhosis mortality in populations of the United States, the United Kingdom, and Canada (Terris, 1967).

Subsequent epidemiologic studies have consistently demonstrated that heavy drinkers and alcoholics are at elevated risk for the development of cirrhosis of the liver and have significantly higher mortality rates than the general population (Pell and D'Alonzo, 1973; Schmidt and de Lint, 1972; Bruun et al., 1975; Coates et al., 1986; Mann et al., 1993; Thun et al., 1997; Leifman and Romelsjs, 1997; Corrao, 1998; Corrao et al., 1998a). This relationship has proved to be remarkably strong and has been consistently observed across time periods and in various regions of the world (Bruun et al., 1975; Smart and Mann, 1991; Ramstedt, 2001). For example, Schmidt found a correlation of $r = 0.97$ between *per capita* consumption of alcohol and liver cirrhosis mortality rates during 1932–1977 in Ontario,

Canada. He estimated that 79% of liver cirrhosis deaths in the Ontario population were attributable to heavy alcohol intake (Schmidt, 1980).

Time series investigations reflect a lagged relationship between cirrhosis mortality and per capita alcohol consumption whereby the rate of cirrhosis mortality in a year is influenced by the alcohol consumption rates of several previous years (Ledermann, 1956; Corrao, 1998; Ramstedt, 2001). To account for this effect, Skog developed a *"distributed lag model,"* in which the effects of alcohol consumption in a year are distributed over the next several years (Skog, 1980, 1984). Using this model, he was able to explain an apparent inverse relationship between per capita alcohol consumption and cirrhosis mortality rates in Great Britain between 1931–1958 (Popham, 1970). Application of the model produced the expected positive relationship between alcohol consumption and cirrhosis mortality (Skog, 1980; Mann, Smart, and Govoni, 2003).

Results of cohort studies have added to the evidence linking alcohol abuse and mortality due to cirrhosis of the liver as well as noncirrhotic diseases and conditions. In a long-term follow-up study conducted in Denmark, 10,154 patients with cirrhosis of the liver were identified from the Danish National Registry of Patients during 1982–1989 and followed to determine time and cause of death. Relative survival was calculated as the ratio of observed survival to that expected for persons of the same age and sex in the general population. After 12 years of follow-up, 6,979 (69%) of the cirrhotic patients had died, a 12-fold increase in all-cause mortality compared to the general population. The estimated 10-year relative mortality due to alcoholic cirrhosis was 66%. Cause-specific mortality ratios were significantly increased not only for cirrhosis-related conditions, but also for ischemic heart disease, infectious disease, gastrointestinal cancer, accidents, and suicide (Sørensen et al., 2003).

Alcohol Consumption and Cirrhosis Mortality in the United States

The close temporal relationship between alcohol consumption and cirrhosis mortality is well illustrated by time-series data for the United States population collected during the 20th century (Roizen, Kerr, and Fillmore, 1999). As shown in **Figure 36.3**, US cirrhosis mortality rates for men and women were high at the beginning of the 20th century but then declined

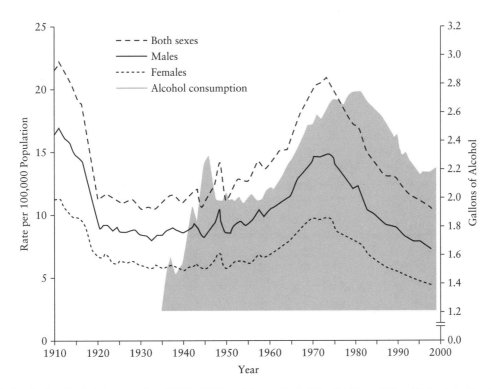

Figure 36.3 Per Capita Alcohol Consumption (1935–1997) and Age–adjusted Death Rates of Liver Cirrhosis by Gender (1910–1997) in the United States Population.

Source: Data from Mortality rate data adapted from Yoon et al. 2001; per capita alcohol consumption data from Nephew et al. 2002. Mann RE, Smart RG, Govoni R (2003). The Epidemiology of Alcoholic Liver Disease. *Alcohol Res Health* 27:209–219.

Table 36.1	Liver Function and Alcohol Intake.		
Liver Function	**No. of Cases**	**Daily Alcohol Consumption**[a]	**Years of Alcohol Abuse**
Normal	70	90	7.7
Uncomplicated Fatty Liver	118	109	7.8
Severe Steatofibrosis	48	127	10.3
Chronic Alcoholic Hepatitis	78	125	11.9
Cirrhosis	39	147	17.1

[a]Average mg per day per hour per kg body weight. Source of Data: Lelbach WK (1974). Organic pathology related to volume and patterns of alcohol use. In: Gibbins RS, Israel Y, Kalant H, eds. *Research Advances in Alcohol and Drug Problems. Vol 1.* New York: John Wiley & Sons, pp. 93–198.

Source: Data from Lelbach WK (1974). Organic pathology related to volume and patterns of alcohol use. In: Gibbins RS, Israel Y, Kalant H, eds. *Research Advances in Alcohol and Drug Problems. Vol 1.* New York: John Wiley & Sons, pp. 93–198.

precipitously with Prohibition in 1920 only to rise again when Prohibition ended in 1933. Rates peaked in 1973 and have since declined in parallel with decreasing per capita consumption levels.

International Trends of Alcohol Consumption and Cirrhosis

International studies of geographic patterns also reveal significant positive correlations between per *capita* intake of alcohol and mortality from liver cirrhosis (Schmidt and Bronetto, 1962; Schmidt and de Lint, 1972; Schmidt, 1980). Using data collected by the World Health Organization for 47 countries in 1974, Moser found a correlation of $r = 0.74$ between rates of cirrhosis mortality and per capita alcohol consumption (Moser, 1980) (**Figure 36.4**).

Important investigations have been conducted to elucidate the progression of liver disease according to the amount and duration of alcohol consumption (Hall, 1995). Lelbach studied the impact of alcohol consumption on liver function and cirrhosis development among 319 patients in an alcoholism clinic in Germany. He calculated the average amount of alcohol consumed per hour in a 24–hour day according to the severity of liver damage. As shown in **Table 36.1**, the severity of liver damage was found to be closely related to the amount and duration of alcohol intake. On average, patients with normal liver function consumed the least amount of alcohol for the shortest duration and those with cirrhosis consumed the greatest amount for the longest duration (**Table 36.1**). Patients with normal liver function had been drinking heavily for only about 8 years whereas those with cirrhosis had been drinking heavily for more than 17 years. As this research illustrates, the progression of liver damage from fatty liver to

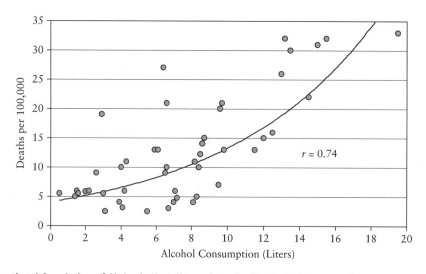

Figure 36.4 International Correlation of Cirrhosis Mortality and Per Capita Alcohol Consumption.

Source: Data from Moser J (1980). Prevention of alcohol related problems: an international review of prevention measures, policies and programmes. Published on behalf of the World Health Organization by the Alcoholism and Drug Addiction Research Foundation, Toronto, Canada. Progression of Liver Disease with Chronic Alcohol Abuse.

cirrhosis is a function of both quantity and duration of alcohol consumption (Lelbach, 1974).

While epidemiologic research has established a firm etiologic connection between heavy alcohol consumption and cirrhosis of the liver, there is considerable heterogeneity amongst studies regarding the *threshold dose* of alcohol necessary for pathogenesis as well as effects of *interactions* of alcohol with other risk factors and conditions such as viral hepatitis, smoking, and the metabolic syndrome.

Bellentani and colleagues examined relationships of daily alcohol intake, type of beverage consumed and drinking patterns with alcohol-induced liver disease in a cohort of 6,534 Italian subjects 12–65 years of age and without disease at baseline (the *Dionysos Study*). They found that the risk threshold for the development of cirrhosis or noncirrhotic liver damage was ingestion of more than 30 grams (2–3 drinks) of alcohol daily for 10 years, which corresponds to a lifetime (cumulative) alcohol intake exceeding 100 kg. The investigators concluded that the risk of developing alcohol-induced liver damage increased significantly (more than threefold) with intakes above the 30 g daily threshold; they also noted that drinking alcohol outside mealtimes or drinking multiple different alcoholic beverages increased the risk (Bellentani et al., 1997; Bellentani and Tiribelli, 2001).

To further investigate effects of low (threshold) levels of alcohol consumption, Corrao and colleagues at the University of Milano, Italy, conducted a meta-analysis of epidemiologic studies with adequate information on alcohol consumption and cirrhosis. Fifteen studies involving 3,742 cirrhotic patients were included in the analysis (2,724 from case-control studies and 1,013 from cohort studies). Though there was marked heterogeneity among studies, the results provided clear evidence that low levels of alcohol intake (25 grams per day) significantly increased the risk of developing cirrhosis of the liver (relative risk estimates ranged from 1.5–3.6 depending on the type of regression model used). Higher consumption levels (50 grams per day) were associated with relative risks ranging from 1.9–9.4. The dose response of cirrhosis risk with increasing consumption of alcohol based on a quadratic regression model is shown in **Figure 36.5**. Chronic daily intake of 25 grams of alcohol (about two alcoholic drinks) increased the risk by more than twofold in this model (Corrao et al., 1998a).

Beverage-specific Effects

Relationships between *per capita* alcohol consumption and cirrhosis mortality may vary depending on the type of alcoholic beverage consumed—beer, wine, or spirits. Indeed, the presence of beverage-specific effects could help explain why cirrhosis mortality began to decline in some populations during the 1970s *despite the continued rise in total alcohol consumption*. This pattern is exemplified by the U.S. time series data on total alcohol consumption and cirrhosis mortality shown above in **Figure 36.3**.

Researchers over the past several decades have investigated potential reasons for imperfections in temporal associations between *per capita* alcohol consumption and mortality due to liver cirrhosis (Schmidt and Bronetto, 1962; Terris, 1967; Gruenewald and Ponicki, 1995). In an analysis of time series data from the United States spanning 1949–1994, Roizen and colleagues demonstrated

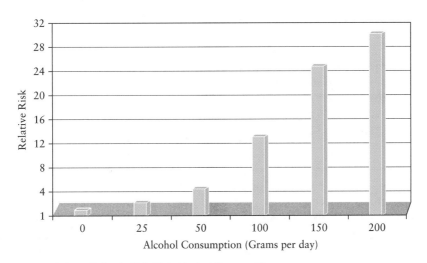

Figure 36.5 Dose Response of Liver Cirrhosis Risk With Alcohol Consumption.

Source: Data from Corrao G, Bagnardi V, Zambon A, Oorchio P (1998c). Meta-analysis of alcohol intake in relation to risk of liver cirrhosis. *Alcohol & Alcoholism* 33(4):381–392.

that the curve for total alcohol consumption lags behind the cirrhosis mortality curve whereas the curve for consumption of distilled spirits shows a better fit (Roizen et al., 1999a). They state that "*the trend-line for per capita distilled spirit consumption bears a much closer correspondence to the cirrhosis mortality trend than does per capita total alcohol consumption*" (Roizen et al., 1999b). This "*beverage-specific*" effect was initially demonstrated by Milton Terris (Terris, 1967) and suggests that per capita consumption of distilled beverages with high alcoholic content may be a better determinant of cirrhosis trends than total alcohol consumption.

Kerr and colleagues extended the analysis of distilled spirits versus total alcohol consumption as correlates of cirrhosis mortality to several other countries with similar results. Time series data were examined in Australia, Canada, New Zealand, the United Kingdom, and the United States during the years 1953–1993. In these populations, per capita consumption of distilled spirits accounted for the majority of the effects of alcohol and provided the best fit to mortality data (Kerr, Fillmore, and Marvy, 2000).

As pointed out by Mann, Smart, and Govoni in their review, *The Epidemiology of Alcoholic Liver Disease*:

"The stronger association between per capita consumption of spirits and cirrhosis mortality may be attributable to biological and sociobehavioral mechanisms." Some types of alcoholic beverages may be more toxic to the liver than others (Lelbach, 1974; Schmidt and Bronetto, 1962). In addition, consumption of certain alcoholic beverages may be associated with different drinking styles (Smart, 1996)—that is, people who tend to drink frequently and heavily, and thus are at greatest risk for developing cirrhosis, also may tend to drink spirits rather than beer or wine. Thus, drinking style may collude with biological mechanisms to significantly raise some drinkers' risk of liver disease. This interesting and important issue is the subject of ongoing investigation" (Mann, Smart, and Govoni, 2003).

Synergy of Alcohol and Tobacco in Cirrhosis of the Liver

Liu and colleagues examined the separate and joint effects of alcohol and smoking on incidence rates of liver cirrhosis and gallbladder disease in the *Million Women Study* conducted in the United Kingdom. The *Million Women Study* is an ongoing prospective study of 1,290,413 million middle-aged women (mean age = 56.1 years) in England and Scotland who were recruited through the United Kingdom National Health Service during 1996–2001. At recruitment, women provided details on the amount of alcohol they were drinking, their smoking status, and the number of cigarettes they smoked daily, as well as information on anthropometric factors, sociodemographic factors, reproductive history, use of exogenous hormones, and medical history. During a mean follow-up of 6.1 years, 2,105 women developed cirrhosis and 23,989 developed gallbladder disease yielding 5-year incidence rates of 1.3 per 1,000 persons and 15 per 1,000 persons, respectively. The risk of cirrhosis of the liver increased with increasing alcohol consumption whereas the risk of gall bladder disease appeared to decrease. Comparing women who drank ≥15 units/week with those who drank 1–2 units/week, the relative risk was 4.32 for cirrhosis and 0.59 for gallbladder disease. Increasing numbers of cigarettes smoked daily increased the risk of both conditions. Comparing current smokers of ≥20 cigarettes/day with never smokers, the relative risk was 3.76 for cirrhosis and 1.29 for gallbladder disease. Synergistic effects of alcohol and smoking were observed for the development of cirrhosis but not for gallbladder disease, e.g., the risk of developing liver cirrhosis was increased nearly 15-fold in women who drank and smoked heavily compared to women with neither exposure (**Figure 36.6**). These findings indicate that alcohol and smoking separately increase the risk of developing cirrhosis of the liver and their joint effects are particularly hazardous (Liu et al., 2009).

Chronic Viral Hepatitis and Cirrhosis of the Liver

Compounding the problem of alcoholic cirrhosis of the liver, chronic liver infections by hepatitis B virus (HBV) and/or hepatitis C virus (HCV) have emerged as major causes of liver cirrhosis in many populations. A variety of different liver viruses can infect and damage the liver including hepatitis A, B, C, D, and E.

Acute Hepatitis A and E   Hepatitis A and hepatitis E are RNA viruses that typically cause acute infection lasting only a few days. Both are transmitted by the fecal-oral route. Contaminated drinking water and food supplies have been implicated in major outbreaks. The highest rates of infection occur in regions where low standards of sanitation promote the transmission of these viruses. Hepatitis A and hepatitis E *do not* develop into chronic hepatitis or cirrhosis; however, there are case reports where acute hepatitis A/E infection has resulted in *acute* liver failure and death in immunocompromised individuals and pregnant women (Fiore, 2004; Emerson and Purcell,

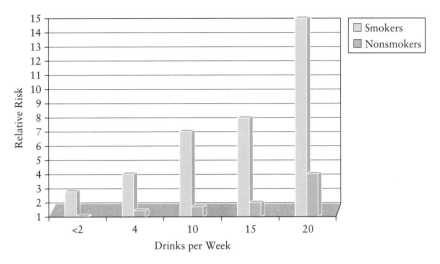

Figure 36.6 Cirrhosis of the Liver: Combined Effects of Alcohol and Tobacco in British Women.

Source: Data from Liu B, Balkwill A, Roddam A, Brown A, Beral V on behalf of the Million Women Study Collaborators (2009). Separate and joint effects of alcohol and smoking on the risks of cirrhosis and gallbladder disease in middle-aged women. *American Journal of Epidemiology* 169(2):153–160.

2003). The other hepatitis viruses (HBV, HCV, and HDV) are primarily responsible for chronic liver infections that can progress to liver cirrhosis.

Hepatitis B and Cirrhosis of the Liver   Hepatitis B virus (HBV) is a common source of viral hepatitis in humans. The virus is endemic in regions of Asia, Africa, and China and has infected approximately one-third of the world population (more than *two billion* people). The prevalence of HBV infection varies widely from 0.5% in nonendemic regions to levels exceeding 10% in endemic areas (Custer et al., 2004). It is estimated that 400 million people are chronic carriers of HBV (Williams, 2006).

Hepatitis B is a DNA virus that undergoes replication in the liver. It is similar to RNA viruses in that reverse transcriptase is used for replication. Viral transmission results from exposure to infectious blood or body fluids. In regions of the world where HBV is endemic, most HBV infections occur during infancy or early childhood. Vertical transmission from mother to baby can occur at the time of childbirth when the newborn passes through the birth canal or later, e.g., through contaminated saliva or breast milk. High rates of child to child transmission have also been documented in certain populations. (Shapiro, 1993; Locarnini, 2004).

Transmission of HBV in adults occurs through unprotected sexual contact with an infected individual or by using contaminated needles and syringes for the intravenous injection of illicit drugs. The virus can also be transmitted by transfusion with contaminated blood or blood products in countries without effective screening programs for donor blood. Nevertheless, immunocompetent adults who become infected by HBV usually clear the virus without treatment and less than 1% of individuals who become infected during adulthood will develop chronic hepatitis B. Reciprocally, approximately 95% of newborns that acquire HBV at birth are unable to clear the virus and thus become chronic carriers of HBV. Individuals with chronic HBV infection have an exceptionally high (approximately 40%) probability of eventually dying from liver cirrhosis and/or hepatocellular carcinoma (Williams, 2006).

Fung and colleagues evaluated 951 Asian men and women with chronic HBV infection to document the prevalence of severe liver fibrosis and/or cirrhosis (Fung et al., 2008). Of these patients, 319 (34%) were found to have severe fibrosis. The overall prevalence was higher in males than females (39% vs. 24%) and higher in adults with antibodies against the viral pre-core antigen (HBeAg) (58% vs. 43%). Seropositivity for HBeAg is indicative of a high viral load, prolonged immune damage and accelerated progression of liver damage. The prevalence of fibrosis/cirrhosis increased with age reaching 81% after 65 years of age (**Figure 36.7**).

Hepatitis C and Cirrhosis of the Liver   Chronic infection with hepatitis C virus (HCV) causes chronic inflammation of the liver that over time can progress to cirrhosis, hepatocellular carcinoma, or both. The global prevalence of HCV is approximately 3% (more than 200 million infected persons). The virus is endemic in many parts of the world and is primarily

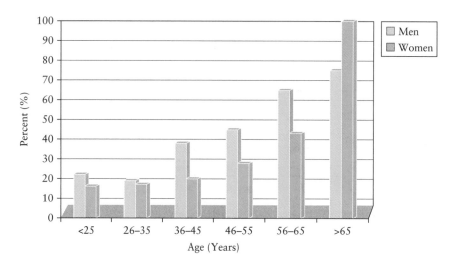

Figure 36.7 Age-Specific Prevalence of Severe Fibrosis/Cirrhosis of the Liver in Patients with Chronic HBV Infection.

Source: Data from Fung J, Lai C-L, But D, Wong D, Cheung T-K, Yuen M-F (2008). Prevalence of fibrosis and cirrhosis in chronic hepatitis B: implications for treatment and management. *American Journal of Gastroenterology* 103(6):1421–1426.

transmitted by exposure to contaminated blood or body fluids. Prevalence rates are high in many African nations and Egypt in particular. Notably, HCV can be transmitted via unsterilized injection equipment and infusion of inadequately screened blood and blood products. In Egypt, a nationwide parenteral treatment program for widespread schistosiomiasis (infection by parasitic schistosome worms) may have accidentally caused high rates of HCV infection (Frank et al., 2000). Routine donor screening in blood banks by enzyme immunoassays has achieved a sharp decline in transfusion-associated HCV transmission (Kamal, 2008).

In contrast to HBV that most often infects newborns and children, HCV is commonly first encountered in adulthood. The host response to HCV infection is highly variable. Approximately 20–40% of subjects experience clearance of the virus and spontaneous resolution of infection. Conversely, the majority of HCV infections (60–80%) become chronic and may eventually progress to cirrhosis and/or hepatocellular carcinoma. Estimates of the proportion of chronically infected persons who develop cirrhosis 20 years after initial infection vary widely: from 2–4 % in children to 20–30% in adults. Furthermore, patients who are older at the time of infection, patients with continuous exposure to alcohol, and those coinfected with HIV or HBV demonstrate accelerated progression to more advanced liver disease. Some success has been achieved in the early treatment of chronic HCV infection using interferon plus antiviral drugs (NIH Consensus Statement on Management of Hepatitis C, 2002).

Hepatitis D: Coinfection with Hepatitis B

Hepatitis D Virus (HDV) also called hepatitis *delta* is a small circular RNA virus. It appears to be a subviral satellite because it can only propagate in the presence of hepatitis B virus (HBV). Transmission of HDV can occur either via simultaneous infection with HBV (coinfection) or via infection of an individual previously infected with HBV (superinfection).

Both superinfection and coinfection with HDV result in more severe complications compared to infection with HBV alone. These complications include a greater likelihood of experiencing liver failure in acute infections and rapid progression to liver cirrhosis with an increased risk of developing liver cancer in chronic infections. In combination with hepatitis B virus, hepatitis D has a 20% mortality rate, the highest of all the acute hepatitis infections.

Synergy of Alcohol and Viral Hepatitis   Excess alcohol consumption has been found to worsen the course and outcome of viral hepatitis (Schiff and Ozden, 2003). Poynard and colleagues studied the influence of alcohol intake among 1,574 patients with hepatitis C who had not received antiviral therapy. Compared to nondrinkers, patients who drank more than 50 g of alcohol daily increased their risk of developing liver fibrosis by 34%. Furthermore, the relative risk of progression of fibrosis with heavier alcohol intake was 2.36. The effects of lower amounts of alcohol intake were not significant (Poynard, Bedossa, and Opolon, 1997).

Bellentani and colleagues analyzed hepatitis virus markers, self-reported alcohol intake, and clinical and biochemical markers of liver disease in a cohort of 6,917 Italian individuals in northern Italy (the *Dionysos Study*). As noted above in the section on alcoholic cirrhosis, daily alcohol consumption of 30 g or more independently increased the risk of cirrhosis more than threefold. Furthermore, among subjects who tested positive for HCV, 32% of heavy drinkers developed cirrhosis compared to only 10% of light drinkers (Bellentani et al., 1999).

Seef and colleagues studied 1,030 US patients enrolled in a prospective investigation of transfusion-associated HCV infection during 1968–1980. After 15 years of follow-up, 17% of patients with HCV infection developed cirrhosis compared to 2.8% of patients without hepatitis. Notably, patients with both HCV and a history of alcohol abuse were 31 times more likely to develop cirrhosis than control subjects (Seeff et al., 2001).

The deleterious impact of alcohol consumption in patients with HCV infection was dramatically demonstrated in a case control study of 285 cirrhotic patients in Italy. Only 1.4% (4 subjects) were HCV-positive and nondrinkers compared to 11.2% (32 patients) who were both HCV-positive and heavy drinkers (Corrao and Arico, 1998).

Clearly, these results provide consistent evidence that heavy alcohol use exacerbates liver disease in patients with hepatitis C and accelerates the progression of steatohepatitis to cirrhosis. Nevertheless, additional studies are needed in order to elucidate potential effects of light to moderate alcohol intake in patients with hepatitis C infection (Peters and Terrault, 2002).

Nonalcoholic Cirrhosis of the Liver

The Metabolic Syndrome   The *metabolic syndrome* (also called *Syndrome X*) is a disease complex of glucose intolerance or type 2 diabetes, hypertension, central obesity and dyslipidemia (elevated total cholesterol and triglycerides and decreased HDL cholesterol). The prevalence of this disease constellation is rising throughout the world.

The metabolic syndrome predisposes not only to atherosclerosis and catastrophic cardiovascular events (myocardial infarction and stroke), but it also promotes the development of *nonalcoholic fatty liver disease*. Nonalcoholic fatty liver disease refers to excess accumulation of fat in the liver in the absence of exposure to alcohol. It is the most prevalent of all liver diseases and is estimated to afflict 20–30% of adults in the United States and other Western countries (Angulo, 2002; Neuschwander-Teri and Caldwell, 2003). A significant fraction of individuals with nonalcoholic liver disease, perhaps

10%, develop hepatitis (inflammation of the liver). The combination of nonalcoholic fatty liver disease and hepatitis is called *nonalcoholic steatohepatitis* (*NASH*). NASH can progress to liver cirrhosis and liver failure.

Recent investigations have established that the metabolic syndrome as well as its individual components (e.g., insulin resistance, diabetes, obesity) are risk factors for the development of nonalcoholic fatty liver disease and progression to NASH, liver cirrhosis and mortality from liver failure (Angulo et al., 1999; de Ledinghen et al., 2006; Farrell and Larter, 2006; Kim and Younossi, 2008). The sequence of pathogenesis is depicted in **Figure 36.8**.

Albeit, the sequence of pathogenesis in individual patients may differ and there is the definite possibility that liver disease predisposes to insulin resistance and diabetes. There is also the issue of "*reverse causality*" in determination of the temporal sequence of pathogenesis of diabetes and liver disease. Disentangling relationships between components of the metabolic syndrome and the progression of liver disease is difficult and complex since in both conditions, ascertainment of disease onset is imprecise and often based upon clinical symptoms which may occur long after the subclinical onset of disease. While several studies have focused on this association, the question still remains; does liver disease lead to diabetes or vice versa?

German investigators examined glucose intolerance and type 2 diabetes in a group of 108 cases with liver cirrhosis and 181 control subjects without liver disease. Seventy-nine of the cirrhotic patients (73%) manifested either glucose intolerance or type 2 diabetes compared to 56% of control subjects. The crude odds ratio calculated from these data suggests that patients with either glucose intolerance or type 2 diabetes have more than a twofold increase in cirrhosis risk (crude odds ratio = 2.2). Reciprocally, the investigators did not find clinical, histological or biochemical signs of liver cirrhosis that were clearly associated with either glucose intolerance or diabetes (Müller et al., 1994).

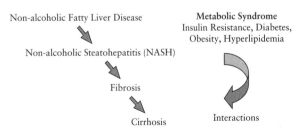

Figure 36.8 Progression of Non-alcoholic Fatty Liver Disease.

In Great Britain, Fraser and colleagues examined associations between liver enzymes, aminotransferase (ALT) and g-glutamyltransferase (GGT), and the development of diabetes in participants of the *British Women's Heart and Health Study*, a cohort of 4,286 women, ages 60–79 years at baseline, who were followed for a median of 7.3 years. Cox proportional hazards regression models were used to examine associations of liver enzymes with incident diabetes. Both ALT and GGT were associated with incident diabetes. With adjustment for age and alcohol consumption, hazard ratios increased by about 50% per standard deviation increase in logged ALT or GGT values (Fraser, Harris, and Sattar, 2009).

In the same report, Fraser and colleagues also conducted a systematic review and meta-analysis of 21 prospective, population-based studies of associations between nonalcoholic fatty liver disease and elevated liver enzymes (ALT and GGT) with the development of diabetes. Summary estimates of the relative risk (RR) of diabetes development were increased for ALT (RR = 2.02), GGT (HR = 2.94) and nonalcoholic fatty liver disease (HR = 2.52) suggesting that antecedent liver pathologies, particularly the accumulation of liver fat, are risk factors for the development of diabetes (Fraser, Harris, and Sattar, 2009).

In Bologna, Italy, Marchesini and colleagues assessed effects of the metabolic syndrome in the development of nonalcoholic steatohepatitis (NASH) among 304 patients with nonalcoholic fatty liver disease. Based on liver biopsies, 120 of these patients (cases) had nonalcoholic steatohepatitis (NASH) and

185 patients (controls) had *pure* nonalcoholic fatty liver disease. Among cases with NASH, 88% had the metabolic syndrome compared to 53% of controls with pure nonalcoholic fatty liver disease. Logistic regression analysis was used to examine the risk of developing NASH associated with the presence of the metabolic syndrome. Patients with the metabolic syndrome carried a threefold higher risk for development of NASH than those without (adjusted OR = 3.2). The metabolic syndrome was also associated with a higher risk of severe liver fibrosis (adjusted OR = 3.5). The investigators concluded that *"the metabolic syndrome puts a very large population at risk of forthcoming liver failure in the next decades"* (Marchesini et al., 2003).

In Hong Kong, China, Wong and colleagues evaluated components of the metabolic syndrome as determinants of liver cirrhosis among 1,466 patients with confirmed hepatitis B (HBV) infection. Noninvasive transient elastography (a noninvasive untrasonographic measure of liver stiffness) was use to determine the presence of liver cirrhosis in the study. The prevalence of the metabolic syndrome was higher in HBV patients with cirrhosis than those without (24% vs. 11%); after adjustment for anthropometric, biochemical and virological factors, the metabolic syndrome retained statistical significance as an independent risk factor for the development of cirrhosis in patients with chronic hepatitis B infection (OR = 1.7). Furthermore, as shown in **Figure 36.9**, the odds of developing cirrhosis shows a dose response with the number of metabolic syndrome components

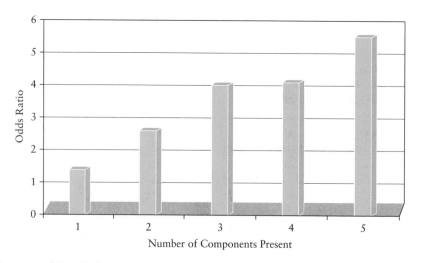

Figure 36.9 Dose Response of Liver Cirrhosis Risk and Metabolic Syndrome Components in Patients with HBV.

Source: Data from Wong G L-H, Wong V W-S, Choi P C-L, Chan A W-H, Chim A M-L, Yiu K K-L, Chan H-Y, Chan F K-L (2009). Metabolic syndrome increases the risk of liver cirrhosis in chronic hepatitis B. *Gut* 58:111-117. Metabolic Syndrome Components: Insulin Resistance or Type 2 Diabetes, Obesity, Hyperlipidemia (elevated total cholesterol and triglycerides and decreased HDL-cholesterol), Hypertension, Inflammation (elevated C-reactive protein).

present, e.g., patients manifesting all five components were over five times more likely to develop cirrhosis than those with none (Wong et al., 2009).

Stepanova and colleagues linked population data from the Third National Health and Nutrition Examination Survey (NHANES III) with nearly 18 years of mortality data from the US National Death Index to study the association of the metabolic syndrome with mortality due to liver disease. The NHANES III is a nationwide survey conducted during 1988–1994 to provide information on health and nutrition in the civilian US population. The study compared mortality in 1,556 individuals with liver disease to 13,004 individuals without disease. Underlying liver disease pathology was classified according to risk factors and viral seropositivity. There were 235 individuals with alcoholic liver disease, 66 with chronic hepatitis B, 264 with chronic hepatitis C, and 991 with nonalcoholic fatty liver disease. During more than 13 years of follow-up, a total of 3,662 individuals died in the cohort of 15,866 individuals. Mortality risks were tested by Cox regression analysis. The presence of the metabolic syndrome significantly increased mortality from liver disease for each of the underlying pathologies: Hazard ratio (HR) = 4.3 for chronic hepatitis B, HR = 3.4 for chronic hepatitis C, HR = 2.1 for alcoholic liver disease, and HR = 12.1 for nonalcoholic fatty liver disease. Furthermore, specific components of the metabolic syndrome such as diabetes, insulin resistance and obesity independently increased liver disease mortality in certain conditions, e.g., the presence of type 2 diabetes increased liver mortality in patients with chronic hepatitis B more than 30-fold (Stepanova, Zobair, and Younossi, 2010). These results provide compelling evidence that the metabolic syndrome acts independently and in concert with other risk factors to increase the mortality due to liver disease.

In summarizing the results of such studies, it is apparent that the metabolic syndrome accelerates the progression of nonalcoholic fatty liver disease and is linked to higher rates of liver failure and mortality (Marchesini and Bianchi, 2010). Conversely, the presence of nonalcoholic fatty liver disease also appears to predispose to insulin resistance and the genesis of type 2 diabetes mellitus. Various physiological mechanisms may be involved. For example, adipokines such as leptin, adiponection and resistin are secreted by metabolically active visceral adipose cells and may interact to promote liver fibrosis and/or diabetes. Increases in liver enzymes might also influence insulin resistance, e.g., elevated levels of ALT and GGT reflect increased levels of oxidative products and oxidative stress. Finally, it is likely that chronic inflammation in association with necrosis and regeneration of hepatocytes (necroinflammation) contributes significantly to the stepwise progression from fatty liver disease to steatohepatitis to fibrosis to cirrhosis to liver failure.

Gender Differences in Cirrhosis of the Liver

As discussed above, the epidemiology of cirrhosis of the liver has been linked closely to alcohol consumption. Nevertheless, several other factors (hepatitis B, hepatitis C, the metabolic syndrome and its components, particularly obesity, insulin resistance, and type 2 diabetes, and tobacco addiction) have emerged as prominent independent risk factors in the development and progression of liver disease.

An additional issue of importance is the presence of significant and long-standing gender differences in cirrhosis mortality risk and mortality rates. As shown in **Figure 36.3** earlier in this chapter, annual mortality rates from cirrhosis of the liver were more than twofold higher in US men than women throughout the 20th century. Furthermore, based on age-cause-specific mortality data published by the World Health Organization (WHO, 1997–1999), annual cirrhosis mortality rates for every age bracket are approximately two times higher in men than in women (**Figure 36.10**).

In a recent hospital-based case control study of Italian men and women, Corrao and colleagues examined the proportion of newly diagnosed cases of symptomatic liver cirrhosis attributable to three known risk factors, alcohol, hepatitis B and hepatitis C. Cases with liver cirrhosis (n = 462) were ascertained during 1989–1996 from hospitals distributed throughout Italy and controls without liver disease (n = 651) were ascertained from the same hospitals and time period. Estimates of the proportion of symptomatic liver cirrhosis attributable to alcohol intake, hepatitis B and hepatitis C infections were obtained for each individual factor and for all three factors combined. The individual population attributable risk estimates for men and women were 67.9% for alcohol, 40.1% for hepatitis C and 4.4% for hepatitis B. Taken together, these 3 risk factors explained 85.5% of liver cirrhosis in the Italian population. However, attributable risk estimates for alcohol were nearly twofold higher in men than women (85.9% vs. 46.8%) and the three factors combined explained a much higher proportion of the risk in men compared to women (98.1% vs. 67.0%). The unexplained portion of the risk in women (33%) suggests that some other factors may be involved in the genesis of liver cirrhosis in women (Corrao et al., 1998b).

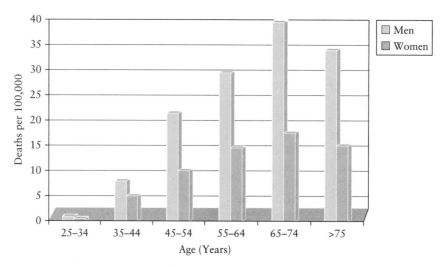

Figure 36.10 Age-Specific Mortality: Cirrhosis of the Liver.

Source: Data from World Health Organization (WHO): Annual World Health Statistics for European Nations, 1997–1999.

Gender Differences in Alcoholic Liver Disease

The twofold higher mortality due to liver cirrhosis in men compared to women undoubtedly reflects the fact that men typically drink more than women, and that the proportion of heavy drinkers and alcoholics is higher among men. However, some studies have found that at any given level of alcohol consumption, women actually have a *higher* likelihood of developing liver cirrhosis than men (Tuyns and Péquignot, 1984). As discussed in a following section of this chapter (*Genetic Predisposition to Alcoholic Liver Cirrhosis*), the heightened genetic susceptibility of women to alcoholic cirrhogenesis compared to men may be related to their lower levels of gastric alcohol dehydrogenase, the key enzyme in the metabolism of alcohol (Frezza et al., 1990).

Differences in Hepatitis B Infection

Gender differences have also been observed in the prevalence rates of cirrhogenic hepatitis viruses B and C. In most populations studied, the prevalence of chronic hepatitis B virus (HBV) infection is greater in men than women. Higher HBV infection rates in men versus women were initially reported by Blumberg and colleagues in populations of tropical climates and subsequently confirmed by investigations of blood donors, hospitalized and nonhospitalized patients, transplant and hemodialysis patients, and mental patients (London and Drew, 1977; Blumberg, 2006).

As pointed out by Baruch Blumberg (who discovered HBV in the serum of a leukemia patient in 1963), there are a number of unusual gender-related aspects of HBV infection. A significant predominance of male newborns of HBV-infected mothers has been observed in many populations where HBV is endemic. This may account for the high male to female ratios observed in China and in other areas with a high prevalence of HBV infection. The apparent "*loss of females*" in these populations can thus be ascribed, at least in part, to HBV infection (Blumberg, 2006). While the mechanism is speculative, maternal antibodies directed against HBV may cross-react with sperm to give a slight selection advantage to sperm bearing the Y chromosome.

Males infected with HBV also have a greater predilection to chronic infection than females. This finding comes from studies of HBV outbreaks in mental institutions. In one such study conducted in New York City, 49 of 317 males (15.4%) remained positive for the hepatitis B "Australia antigen" one year after an outbreak compared to only 2 of 467 females (0.43%) (Curtis et al., 1973; Goodman et al., 1971). The predominance of HBV infection and viral-induced cirrhosis among men compared to women thus contributes to the higher overall mortality rate in men due to cirrhosis of the liver.

Gender Differences in Hepatitis C Infection

Injection drug use is the single most important risk factor for acquiring hepatitis C virus (HCV). Commensurate with higher levels of drug use in men compared to women, chronic HCV infection rates are approximately twofold higher in men than women in most population-based studies. In a large national survey of 15,079 adults in the United States conducted during 1999–2002, the prevalence of HCV infection (based on HCV antibodies) was 2.1% in men compared to 1.1% in women (Armstrong et al., 2000; Armstrong et al., 2006).

Studies of special populations also reflect higher HCV infection rates in men than women. In a study of 777 patients with severe mental illness in North Carolina, HCV infection among men was nearly twice that among women. Men also had higher rates of injection needle use (23.1% vs. 12.5%), needle-sharing (17.6 vs. 7.7%) and certain other drug-related risk behaviors. In contrast, women had higher rates of sexual risk behaviors such as unprotected sex in exchange for drugs (17.8% vs. 11.2%) (Butterfield et al., 2003).

Notably, recent studies suggest that drug-related exposure to HCV may be increasing in women. In a survey of 16,000 adults in Australia, women reported higher rates of needle-sharing than men (Iversen et al., 2010). Finally, some studies suggest that women are able to clear HCV more effectively than men (Yamakawa et al., 1996) which may help explain their lower mortality rate from liver cirrhosis.

Genetic Predisposition to Alcoholic Liver Cirrhosis

Genetic factors, including those that influence alcohol metabolism, are known to influence predisposition to the development of liver cirrhosis. The primary liver enzyme that metabolizes alcohol is alcohol dehydrogenase (ADH). In humans, various forms of ADH are present that are encoded by at least seven genes. Class I ADH, which is present in the liver and the stomach, consists of three subunits encoded by three separate genes, *ADH1A, ADH1B* and *ADH1C*. Genetic expression varies according to age, gender, amount of alcohol consumed, and the alleles present at these genetic loci (Parlesak et al., 2002).

Studies in the laboratories of Charles S. Lieber at the University of Trieste, Italy, elucidated major differences in the metabolism of alcohol between men and women. In a landmark study, women were found to express lower levels of gastric ADH than men, resulting in higher blood levels of alcohol per amount consumed (Frezza et al., 1990). Alcoholic men and women were also found to metabolize alcohol more slowly than nonalcoholic subjects, and first pass metabolism was markedly decreased in alcoholic men and virtually absent in alcoholic women. The authors concluded that *"that the increased bioavailability of ethanol (alcohol) resulting from decreased gastric oxidation of ethanol may contribute to the enhanced vulnerability of women to acute and chronic complications of alcoholism"* (Frezza et al., 1990). Thus, the development of liver cirrhosis in alcoholic men and particularly in alcoholic women may in part

be related to their lower gastric ADH activity and relatively slow metabolism of alcohol compared to nonalcoholics. However, there is considerable debate regarding the issue of greater female vulnerability to alcohol and the exact mechanisms of action remain to be elucidated (Parlesak et al., 2002).

Reed and colleagues investigated genetic effects contributing to alcoholism and the development of liver cirrhosis based upon 15,924 twin pairs ascertained from the National Academy of Sciences National Research Council Twin Registry. They observed significantly higher concordance rates of alcoholism and liver cirrhosis among monozygous (identical) twins compared to dizygous (nonidentical) twins (26.7% vs. 12.2% for alcoholism and 16.9% vs. 5.3% for liver cirrhosis) and estimated that about 50% of alcohol-related end organ disease can be attributed to *additive genetic factors*. They also found that most of the genetic predisposition to liver cirrhosis was due to a *shared genetic liability for alcoholism* (Reed et al., 1996).

Human alcohol dehydrogenase (*ADH*) is under control of seven genes that are tightly clustered at position 22 on the long arm of chromosome 4 (4q22). Since the *ADH* enzymes play a major role in the pharmacokinetics of alcohol metabolism in humans, the *ADH* genes encoding these enzymes are prime candidates for genetic investigation (Edenberg, 2000).

The *Collaborative Study on the Genetics of Alcoholism* (COGA) is a large-scale study of families with and without alcoholic members ascertained from nine centers across the United States. The study was designed to identify genes that influence alcoholism and alcohol-related diseases (Edenberg, 2003). Studies of these families have elucidated polymorphisms of several ADH genes that are linked to the development of alcoholism and related conditions, e.g., liver cirrhosis (Reich et al., 1998). For example, gene variants encoding three alcohol-metabolizing enzymes, *ADH1B, ADH1C,* and *ALDH2*, have been found that heighten the risk of alcoholism (Hurley, Edenberg, and Li, 2002). Genetic variants in the promoter region of the gene encoding *ADH4* have also been found to modulate alcohol metabolism and the risk of alcoholism (Edenberg, Jerome, and Li, 1999). Genetic polymorphisms of *ADH* and their effects on alcoholism and related conditions are currently under intense study in different populations.

Zinc plays an important role in the structural integrity and efficient functioning of *ADH*. Consequently, a deficiency of zinc may compromise the metabolism of alcohol leading to sustained high blood concentrations of alcohol in those who drink. Furthermore, zinc binding to *ADH* appears to depend on the presence and spacing of specific amino acids (cysteine and histadine); thus genetic variation in zinc binding to *ADH* may also influence one's genetic susceptibility to alcohol through modification of enzyme structure and function (Auld and Bergman, 2008).

Genetic Predisposition to Viral Hepatitis and Liver Cirrhosis

A number of genetic polymorphisms have also been identified that increase susceptibility to chronic hepatitis viral infections by HBV and HCV. For example, certain alleles of the *major histocompatibility* locus, the *vitamin D receptor* locus, the *tumor necrosis factor* locus, and the *interleukin 10* locus have been found to influence the chronicity of HBV infection (Blumberg, 2006).

Investigative teams in Australia, Japan, and the United States recently conducted genome-wide studies of single nucleotide polymorphisms among patients with chronic hepatitis C infection. All three studies found that patients who carried genetic variants of the interleukin 28B interferon-lambda gene (*IL28B*) displayed altered natural and drug-induced clearance of HCV (Suppiah et al., 2009; Tanaka et al., 2009; Ge et al., 2009). These findings underscore the need for additional genetic-epidemiologic studies to clarify cirrhogenic versus protective features of genetic polymorphisms in order to guide clinical decisions regarding efficacious treatment of HCV infection based upon genotype (O'Brien, 2009).

Genetic Syndromes and Liver Cirrhosis

Primary hemochromatosis is a hereditary disease characterized by excessive absorption of iron resulting in iron overload. Excess iron in the form of hemosiderin accumulates in tissues and organs disrupting their function. The most susceptible organs are the liver, adrenal glands, heart, skin, gonads, joints and the pancreas. Patients with primary hemochromatosis can manifest a variety of pathologies including cirrhosis of the liver, polyarthritis, adrenal insufficiency, diabetes and heart failure. Affected men typically experience symptoms between the ages of 30 and 50 years. Affected women are more likely to manifest symptoms after menopause when they no longer lose iron during menstruation. The prevalence of primary hemochromatosis is highest among individuals of European descent, approximately 1 in 200. The condition is due to mutant forms of the *HFE* (high Fe) gene located on the short arm of chromosome 6. The *HFE* gene codes for a membrane protein that is essential in regulating iron absorption and transfer into cells (Feder et al., 1998).

Wilson's disease is a rare autosomal recessive genetic disorder in which copper accumulates in the liver, the brain and other tissues. This condition is rare with an annual rate of 1 to 4 cases per 100,000. Clinical signs typically occur in childhood or adolescence and include low serum *ceruloplasmin* (the transport protein for copper in the blood), the deposition of copper and formation of brownish *Kayser-Fleischer* rings in the cornea of the eye, elevated liver enzymes, polyarthritis, kidney dysfunction, and altered mental status. Wilson's disease is caused by mutant forms of the *ATP7B* gene (located on the long arm of chromosome 13) causing impairment of enzymatic incorporation of copper into ceruloplasmin and excretion of excess copper in bile. Accumulation of copper in the liver results in inflammation (hepatitis), fibrosis, cirrhosis, and ultimately liver failure. Mental disturbances (encephalopathy) may occur as a consequence of disturbances in the urea cycle and increased blood ammonia (Ala et al., 2007).

Ethnic Differences in Liver Cirrhosis

Annual estimates of the mortality rates due to liver cirrhosis differ among gender-ethnic groups of the United States. Although the absolute rates have declined dramatically during the past four decades, cirrhosis mortality remains about twofold higher for African American men than for Caucasian American men (**Figure 36.11**). Ethnic differences in mortality show a similar trend in women, although the differences are much smaller and the current rates are similar for African American and Caucasian American women (Stinson, Grant, and Dufour. 2001, Mann, Smart, and Govoni, 2003; Yoon et al., 2001, 2002).

The persisting higher mortality from liver cirrhosis in African American men compared to Caucasian American men may be a consequence of several risk factors and their interactions. Differential patterns of alcohol consumption, insulin resistance, exposure to hepatitis viruses, age, income, education, employment, genetic predisposition, familial history of alcohol/drug abuse and stress should all be considered in the complex web of causation (Jones-Webb, 1998). Differential access to alcoholism treatment services and health care may also be important (Singh and Hoyert, 2000). Notably, recent estimates suggest that Hispanic men have the highest cirrhosis mortality rates of any gender-ethnic group in the United States, approximately 12 deaths per 100,000 per year (Stinson, Grant, and Dufour, 2001; Mann, Smart, and Govoni, 2003). The observed excess cirrhosis mortality in Hispanic men is consistent with their higher prevalence of hepatitis C infection compared

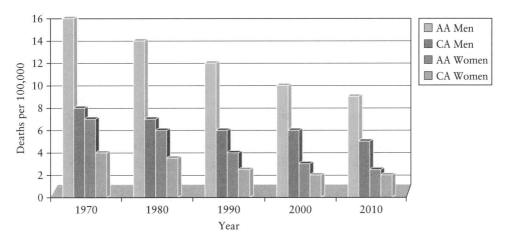

Figure 36.11 Trends in Liver Cirrhosis Mortality by Gender and Ethnicity.

Source: Data from Yoon Y–H, Yi H, Grant BF, et al. (2001). Surveillance Report #57: Liver Cirrhosis Mortality in the United States, 1970–98. Washington, DC: National Institute on Alcohol Abuse and Alcoholism. Yoon Y–H, Yi H, Grant BF, et al. (2002). Surveillance Report #60: Liver Cirrhosis Mortality in the United States, 1970–99. Washington, DC: National Institute on Alcohol Abuse and Alcoholism.

to other ethnic groups (Yen, Keeffe, and Ahmed. 2003). Ethnic differences in certain types of liver cirrhosis have also been observed within European populations (Douds et al., 2003). As pointed out by Mann and colleagues, ethnic differences have important implications for research and prevention and *"from a public health perspective, an understanding of subpopulation dynamics is critical to the development of programs for preventing alcoholic liver disease"* (Mann, Smart, and Govoni, 2003).

Coffee and Alcoholic Liver Disease

The results of several epidemiologic studies suggest that coffee consumption may protect against the development of cirrhosis of the liver, especially alcoholic cirrhosis. Klatsky and colleagues first examined the relationship between coffee and cirrhosis in a cohort of 128,934 adults ascertained through the *Kaiser Permanente Medical Care Program* in California. During 10 years of follow-up, 132 patients were hospitalized or died because of cirrhosis. The results suggested an inverse association between coffee consumption and the risk of liver cirrhosis as well as the risk of death due to cirrhosis, the effects being strongest for alcoholic cirrhosis (Klatsky and Armstrong, 1992).

More recently, Klatsky and colleagues reported findings after 22 years of follow-up of the same cohort (*n* = 125,580) during which 330 patients developed cirrhosis of the liver. As before, the study demonstrated a robust inverse dose response between coffee consumption and the risk of cirrhosis, independent

of confounders. Estimates of relative risk (RR) were RR = 0.7 for up to one cup daily, RR = 0.6 for one to three cups daily, and RR = 0.2 for four or more cups daily. No effects were noted for patients with nonalcoholic cirrhosis (Klatsky et al., 2006).

Tverdal and Skurtveit examined the relationship between coffee consumption and mortality due to liver cirrhosis in a cohort of 51,306 Norwegian adults. During 17 years of follow-up, a total of 4,207 deaths were recorded including 53 deaths from liver cirrhosis. Of the deaths due to cirrhosis, 36 were reported as alcoholic cirrhosis. The relative risk of liver cirrhosis decreased significantly with each daily increase of two cups of coffee (RR = 0.6). Furthermore, restriction of deaths to those with reported alcoholic cirrhosis gave similar results (Tverdal and Skurtveit, 2003).

Corrao and colleagues examined coffee consumption and liver cirrhosis in a case control study involving 274 cases and 458 control subjects ascertained from hospitals in Italy. They also found an inverse dose response relationship between cirrhosis risk and coffee intake. The odds ratios (OR) decreased in linear fashion for 1, 2, 3, and 4 daily cups of coffee, OR = 0.47, OR = 0.23, OR = 0.21, and OR = 0.16, respectively (Corrao et al., 2001).

An independent case control study conducted in Italy examined coffee consumption in 101 cirrhotic patients and more than 1,500 controls. Compared to individuals who had never consumed coffee, those reporting daily consumption of three or more cups reduced their risk of developing liver cirrhosis by 71% (OR = 0.29) (Gallus et al., 2002).

Investigators at the National Institutes of Health conducted an investigation of dietary caffeine consumption to evaluate effects on the progression of liver fibrosis. They examined 177 patients who underwent liver biopsy, 121 of whom had chronic hepatitis C infection. Caffeine intake was based upon completion of a detailed dietary questionnaire by each participant. In comparisons of subjects with advanced liver fibrosis (bridging fibrosis/cirrhosis) versus those with mild liver disease, individuals who consumed the equivalent of 2.25 cups of coffee daily reduced their risk of developing severe liver fibrosis by 75% (adjusted OR = 0.25). A similar effect was observed in the subset of patients with hepatitis C (OR = 0.19). The results suggest that caffeine per se has a protective effect against the progression of liver disease including those patients with chronic hepatitis C infection (Modi et al., 2010).

The combined evidence from these studies indicates that coffee protects against the development of liver cirrhosis. Consistency of results, the magnitude of the risk reductions and the presence of an inverse dose response in each of the studies support this conclusion. Mechanistically, it has been suggested that caffeine may have antioxidant effects and/or antagonist activity against adenosine receptors in the liver (Higdon and Frei, 2006).

Prevention of Cirrhosis of the Liver

Prevention of chronic cirrhosis and other forms of chronic liver disease is largely focused on the major risk factors: alcohol, viral hepatitis (particularly HBV and HCV), and components of the metabolic syndrome (insulin resistance, type 2 diabetes, obesity, hyperlipidemia, and hypertension). For greatest impact, strategies must target primary prevention of exposure, secondary prevention for early detection and treatment, and tertiary prevention to delimit disease progression.

Prevention of Alcohol-Related Cirrhosis of the Liver

Alcohol control is a complex and multifaceted health problem. Nevertheless, scientific evidence is accruing regarding the value of certain health care policies that restrict the affordability, availability and accessibility of alcohol. Policies that have proven effective in reducing public harm from alcohol consumption include raising the price of alcoholic beverages through taxation, government regulation and standardization of retail sales of alcoholic beverages, strict enforcement of laws on minimum drinking age, passage of laws lowering the legal blood alcohol levels for operation of a motor vehicle, strict enforcement of drunk driving laws and strong penalties for violators, and increased awareness, detection and treatment of alcohol abuse and alcoholism (WHO, 2010).

Many investigators have observed that the price of alcohol is inversely correlated with per capita alcohol consumption and cirrhosis mortality rates (Seeley, 1960; Bruun et al., 1975; Cook and Tauchen, 1982; Edwards et al., 1994; Ramstedt, 2001; Chaloupka, Grossman, and Saffer. 2002). The evidence strongly indicates that the most cost-effective policy to reduce alcohol-related harm is through taxation (WHO, 2009).

Numerous studies also indicate that early detection of alcohol abuse and increased membership in alcohol treatment programs such as Alcoholics Anonymous (AA) are beneficial in reducing alcohol-related harm (Romelsjš, 1987; Mann, Smart, and Anglin, 1988; Holder and Parker, 1992; Smart and Mann, 1991, 1993; Smart, 1996; Smart, Mann, and Suurvali, 1998; Smart and Mann, 2000). Reductions in cirrhosis morbidity and mortality in association with increased levels of treatment and AA membership have been observed in Canada (Mann et al., 1988), the United States (Mann et al., 1991; Holder and Parker, 1992; Smart, Mann, and Lee, 1996) and Sweden (Romelsjš, 1987; Leifman and Romelsjš, 1997). These results support the value of instituting and sustaining programs for the early detection and aggressive treatment of alcohol abuse and alcoholism.

Perhaps surprisingly, public information and school education programs have *not* proven effective in reducing alcohol-related harm in the populations studied (WHO, 2010). Notwithstanding, such programs remain important for the dissemination of accurate information and maintenance of public awareness regarding the deleterious health effects of alcohol abuse (WHO, 2010).

In consideration of these findings, the World Health Organization recently adopted an evidence-based resolution espousing *a global strategy to reduce the harmful use of alcohol* (WHO, 2010). The following statement provides a synopsis of the program:

> *"Increasing capacity of health and social welfare systems to deliver treatment and early intervention; drink-driving countermeasures; limits on the availability of alcohol; restrictions on alcohol marketing; taxation and pricing policies to discourage frequent and heavy alcohol consumption; measures to control social contexts that promote excessive drinking; and reducing the public health impact of illicit and informally produced alcohol"* (Babor, 2010).

PREVENTION OF VIRAL HEPATITIS

Hepatitis B Virus: Prevention and Control

Maurice Ralph Hilleman (1919–2005) was an American microbiologist who specialized in the development of vaccines to prevent infectious diseases. Vaccines developed in his laboratories are now routinely used to prevent measles, mumps, hepatitis A, hepatitis B, chickenpox, meningitis, pneumonia, and *Haemophilus influenzae*. Hilleman is credited with saving more lives than any other scientist of the 20th century (Offit, 2007).

National HBV vaccination programs have been in place since the early 1980s. The HBV vaccine used in these programs stimulates antibodies against the hepatitis B surface antigen (HBsAg). Vaccine efficacy is best demonstrated by *universal childhood HBV vaccination programs* which have produced significant reductions in the rates of acute and chronic hepatitis B infection and related chronic liver diseases in all populations tested (Alter, 2001; Shepard et al., 2006).

Universal Childhood Hepatitis B Vaccination

One of the first universal childhood hepatitis B vaccination programs was initiated in the population of Taiwan, which has high rates of endemic HBV. The results have been impressive. The seroprevalence of HBsAg among Taiwanese children decreased from 9.8% in 1984, the year when universal infant immunization began, to 0.7% in 1999 (Chan, Lee, and Lo, 2004). Furthermore, the incidence and mortality rates of hepatocellular carcinoma among children decreased by 49% and 75%, respectively, during the same time period (Chang et al., 1997).

In the Gambia, West Africa, the rates of HBV infection among 9-year-old children vaccinated in infancy were compared to that of unvaccinated children of the same age. Vaccinated children developed 83% fewer acute infections (8% vs. 50%) and 95% fewer chronic infections than unvaccinated children (0.6% vs. 10.0%). These results demonstrate the value of infant vaccination in protecting against acute and chronic HBV infection and suggest that immunity persists throughout the first decade of life (Viviani et al., 1999).

In Afragola, Italy, a community with very high rates of HBV infection and liver disease, the prevalence of HBsAg in males up to 12 years of age decreased from 10.5% in 1978 to 0.8% in 1993. The prevalence of individuals with antibodies to the HBV core antigen (anti-HBc) fell from 52.6 to 1.2%. Notably, the prevalence of HBsAg seropositivity among *unvaccinated* males also declined significantly, from 18% in 1978 to 5.5% in 1989. The decreased prevalence of HBsAg in the unvaccinated population suggests the phenomenon of "*herd immunity*" whereby vaccinated individuals buffer unvaccinated and susceptible individuals from exposure to HBV (Da Villa et al., 1998).

In a regional study in China, the prevalence of HBV carriers has dropped from 16% to 1.4% since the initiation of immunization in the 1990s (Cui, Wang, and Liang, 2006; Liu and Fan, 2006). In the United States, new infections with HBV declined from 260,000 in the 1980s to about 78,000 in 2001, and in Alaska where HBV is endemic, acute hepatitis B infection decreased from 215 cases per 100,000 to less than 10 cases per 100,000 as a consequence of immunization (Shepard et al., 2006).

As of May 2003, 151 of the 192 national members of the World Health Organization (WHO) had implemented universal childhood vaccination programs. There are 89 member states that have been designated as high HBV prevalence regions, and 64 of these nations now have universal infant vaccination programs. It is the goal of the WHO to soon have universal vaccination programs in all countries. The worldwide vaccination program is proceeding very well and has saved millions of people from infection, illness, and death. The following statement by Dr. Miriam Alter, Chief of Epidemiology, Hepatitis Branch, US Centers for Disease Control, exemplifies the importance of a worldwide immunization program to eliminate HBV infection:

"The primary goal of hepatitis B prevention programs is reduction of chronic hepatitis B virus (HBV) infection and HBV-related chronic liver disease. Although donor screening, risk-reduction counseling and services, and effective infection control practices can reduce or eliminate the potential risk for HBV transmission, immunization is by far the single most effective prevention measure. Worldwide, the integration of hepatitis B vaccine into existing childhood vaccination schedules has the greatest likelihood of long-term success. However, by 2000, only 116 of 215 countries had such a policy, representing 31% of the global birth cohort. In addition, efforts must be strengthened to vaccinate older adolescents and adults with high-risk behaviors or occupations in countries where most HBV transmission and the morbidity associated with acute hepatitis B occur among persons in these age groups. Although continued immunization of successive birth cohorts should achieve the eventual elimination of HBV transmission,

this will not occur for decades without success-ful vaccination of adults at increased risk for in-fection" (Alter, 2003).

Preventive measures beyond blood-banking practices include prompt identification of infected individuals, awareness of the potential for perinatal transmission, implementation of safe-injection practices, linkage of drug users to drug treatment programs, and im-plementation of community-based education and support programs to modify risk behavior. Some of these measures have been successfully implemented in the control of HIV infections, and it stands to rea-son that they would be valuable for reducing HCV transmission. Future advances in the diagnosis and management of hepatitis C require continued vigi-lance concerning the transmission of this infection, extending treatment to populations not previously evaluated in treatment trials, and the introduction of more effective therapies (Alter, 2006).

TERTIARY PREVENTION IN CIRRHOSIS OF THE LIVER

Cirrhosis of the liver is generally irreversible, and treat-ment usually focuses on preventing progression and complications. If complications cannot be controlled or when the liver ceases functioning, liver transplanta-tion is necessary. Survival from liver transplantation has improved in recent years, and the 5-year survival rate is now around 80%, depending largely on the severity of disease and other medical problems in the recipient (Kirsch, Robson, and Trey, 1995)

CONCLUSION

Cirrhosis of the liver is responsible for nearly 800,000 deaths per year worldwide. National rates vary widely as a function of the major risk factors for cir-rhosis: alcohol abuse, chronic viral hepatitis (primar-ily HBV and HCV), and components of the metabolic syndrome (insulin resistance/type 2 diabetes, visceral obesity, hyperlipidemia and hypertension). Men have a twofold higher risk than women throughout the lifespan. Other factors, e.g., smoking, genetics and ethnicity also influence the risk of cirrhosis devel-opment. Polymorphisms of genes encoding alcohol dehydrogenase, the chief enzyme in alcohol metabo-lism, have been found that modulate the risk of cir-rhosis development. Genetic factors have also been

discovered that modulate the immune response to hepatitis viral infection. Other relatively infrequent causes of liver cirrhosis include hemochromatosis (iron overload) and Wilson's disease (excess copper deposition in the liver and other tissues).

Recent declines in cirrhosis mortality rates in the United States and other developed nations are attributable to reductions in per capita consump-tion of alcohol. Nevertheless, liver cirrhosis arising from nonalcoholic fatty change has emerged as an important global health concern. Progression of this condition is related to development of the metabolic syndrome, particularly insulin resistance and obesity.

Effective prevention of alcoholic cirrhosis in-volves restriction of the affordability, availability and accessibility of alcohol plus early detection of alcohol abuse and aggressive treatment of alcohol-ism. Vaccination programs have proven extremely effective in the elimination of HBV infection. An effective vaccine against HCV has not yet been de-veloped. Primary prevention involves avoidance of exposure to HCV-contaminated blood from intra-venous drug abusers. Development of the metabolic syndrome appears largely preventable through diet and exercise for weight control maintenance of op-timal levels of blood glucose, blood pressure, and blood lipids.

REFERENCES

Adams, L.A., Lymp, J.F., St. Sauver, J., et al. (2005). The natural history of nonalcoholic fatty liver disease: A population-based cohort study. *Gastroenterology, 129*, 113–121.

Ala, A., Walker, A.P., Ashkan, K., Dooley, J.S., & Schilsky, M.L. (2007). Wilson's disease. *Lancet, 369*(9559), 397–408.

Alter, M.J. (2001). Protecting future generations through immunization against hepatitis B. *Ann Intern Med, 125*, 835–836.

Alter, M.J. (2003). Epidemiology and prevention of hepatitis B. *Semin Liver Dis, 23*(1), 39–46.

Alter, M.J. (2006). Prevention of spread of hepatitis C. *Hepatology, 36*(Suppl 1), S93–S98.

Angulo, P. (2002). Nonalcoholic fatty liver disease. *N Engl J Med, 346*, 1221–1231.

Angulo, P., Keach, J.C., Batts, K.P., et al. (1999). Independent predictors of liver fibrosis in patients with nonalcoholic steatohepatitis. *Hepatology,* *30,* 1356–1362.

Armstrong, G.L., Alter, M.J., McQuillan, G.M., & Margolis, H.S. (2000). The past incidence of hepatitis C virus infection: Implications for future burden of chronic liver disease in the United States. *Hepatology, 31,* 777–782.

Armstrong, G.L., Wasley, A., Simard, E.P., McQuillan, G.M., Kuhnert, W.L., & Alter, M.J. (2006). The prevalence of hepatitis C virus infection in the United States, 1999 through 2002. *Annals of Internal Medicine, 144*(10), 705–714.

Auld, D.S., & Bergman, T. (2008). The role of zinc for alcohol dehydrogenase structure and function. *Cell Mol Life Sci, 65,* 3961–3970.

Babor, T.F. (2010). Public health science and the global strategy on alcohol. *Bulletin of the World Health Organization, 88*(9), 641–716.

Bamber, M.A.Y., Murray, A.K., Weller, I.V.C., Morelli, A., Scheuer, P.J., Thomas, H.C., & Sherlock, S. (1981). Clinical and histological features of a group of patients with sporadic non-A, non-B hepatitis. *J Clin Pathol, 34,* 1175–1180.

Bellentani, S., Saccoccio, G., Costa, G., Tiribelli, C., Manenti, F., Sodde, M.,...Brandi, G., and the Dionysos Study Group. (1997). Drinking habits as cofactors of risk for alcohol induced liver damage. *Gut, 41,* 845–850.

Bellentani, S., Pozzato, G., Saccoccio, G., et al. (1999). Clinical course and risk factors of hepatitis C virus related liver disease in the general population: Report from the Dionysos study. *Gut, 44,* 874–880.

Bellentani, S., & Tiribelli, C. (2001). Spectrum of liver disease in the general population: Lessons from the Dionysos study. *Journal of Hepatology, 35,* 531–537.

Blumberg, B.S. (2006). The curiosities of hepatitis B virus: Prevention, sex ratio, and demography. *The Proceedings of the American Thoracic Society, 3,* 14–20.

Bosetti, C., Levi, F., Lucchini, F., Zatoniski, W.A., Negri, E., & La Vecchia, C. (2007). Worldwide mortality from cirrhosis: An update to 2002. *Journal of Hepatology, 46*(5), 827–839.

Bruun, K., Edwards, G., Lumio, M., et al. (1975). *Alcohol control policies in public health perspective.* Helsinki: Finnish Foundation for Alcohol Studies.

Butterfield, M.I., Bosworth, H.B., Meador, K.G., Stechuchak, K.M., Essock, S.M., Osher, F.C.,... Horner, R.D.; Five–Site Health and Risk Study Research Committee. (2003). Gender differences in hepatitis C infection and risks among persons with severe mental illness. *Psychiatr Serv, 54*(6), 848–853.

Chaloupka, F.J., Grossman, M., & Saffer, H. (2002). The effects of price on alcohol consumption and alcohol–related problems. *Alcohol Research & Health, 26,* 22–34.

Chan, C.Y., Lee, S.D., & Lo, K.J. (2004). Legend of hepatitis B vaccination: The Taiwan experience. *J Gastroenterol Hepatol, 19,* 121–126.

Chang, M.H., Chen, C.J., Lai, M.S., Hsu, H.M., Wu, T.C., Kong, M.S.,...Chen, D.S. for the Taiwan Childhood Hepatoma Study Group. (1997). Universal hepatitis B vaccination in Taiwan and the incidence of hepatocellular carcinoma in children. *New England Journal of Medicine, 336*(26), 1855–1859.

Coates, R.A., Halliday, M., Rankin, J., et al. (1986). Risk of fatty infiltration or cirrhosis of the liver in relation to ethanol consumption: A case–control study. *Clinical and Investigative Medicine, 9,* 26–32.

Cook, P.J., & Tauchen, G. (1982). The effect of liquor taxes on heavy drinking. *Bell Journal of Economics, 13*(2), 379–390.

Corrao, G. (1998). Liver cirrhosis mortality trends in Eastern Europe, 1970–1989. Analyses of age, period and cohort effects and of latency with alcohol consumption. *Addiction Biology, 3,* 413–422.

Corrao, G., & Arico, S. (1998). Independent and combined action of hepatitis C virus infection and alcohol consumption on the risk of symptomatic liver cirrhosis. *Hepatology, 27,* 914–919.

Corrao, G., Bagnardi, V., Zambon, A., & Oorchio, P. (1998a). Meta-analysis of alcohol intake in relation to risk of liver cirrhosis. *Alcohol & Alcoholism, 33*(4), 381–392.

Corrao, G., Zambon, A., Torchio, P., Arico, S., La Vecchia, C., & Di Orio, F. (1998b). Attributable risk for symptomatic liver cirrhosis in Italy. *Journal of Hepatology, 28,* 608–614.

Corrao, G., Zambon, A., Bagnardi, V., D'Amicis, A., Klatsky, A., Collaborative SIDECIR Group. (2001). Coffee, caffeine, and the risk of liver cirrhosis. *Ann Epidemiol, 11,* 458–465.

Cui, F.Q., Wang, X.J., & Liang, X.F. (2006). Epidemiological analysis on reported hepatitis B under 15 years in China: The report from Chinese Center for Disease Control and Prevention. *Chin J Vaccines Immunization, 12*(2006), 206–208.

Curtis, J.L., Samper, L., Rodriquez, L.A., & Garrett, M.G. (1973). Sex difference in hepatitis-associated (Australia) antigen carrier state one year after hepatitis outbreak. *Pediatrics, 52,* 441–443.

Custer, B., Sullivan, S.D., Hazlet, T.K., Iloeje, U., Veenstra, D.L., & Kowdley, K.V. (2004). Global epidemiology of hepatitis B virus. *Journal of Clinical Gastroenterology, 38*(10 Suppl 3), S158–S168.

Da Villa, G., Piccinino, F., Scolastico, C., Fusco, M., Piccinino, R., & Sepe, A. (1998). Long-term epidemiological survey of hepatitis B virus infection in a hyperendemic area (Afragola, southern Italy): Results of a pilot vaccination project. *Res Virol, 149*(5), 263–270.

de Ledinghen, V., Ratziu, V., Causse, X., et al. (2006). Diagnostic and predictive factors of significant liver fibrosis and minimal lesions in patients with persistent unexplained elevated transaminases. A prospective multicenter study. *J Hepatol, 45,* 592–599.

Douds, A.C., Cox, M.A., Iqbal, T.H., & Cooper, T.H. (2003). Ethnic differences in cirrhosis of the liver in a British city: Alcoholic cirrhosis in South Asian men. *Alcohol and Alcoholism, 38,* 148–150.

Edenberg, H.J., Jerome, R.E., & Li, M. (1999). Polymorphism of the human alcohol dehydrogenase 4 (ADH4) promoter affects gene expression. *Pharmacogenetics, 9*(1), 25–30.

Edenberg, H.J. (2000). Regulation of the mammalian alcohol dehydrogenase genes. *Progress in Nucleic Acid Research and Molecular Biology, 64,* 295–341.

Edenberg, J.H. (2003). *The collaborative study on the genetics of alcoholism: An update.* National Institute on Alcohol Abuse and Alcoholism. National Institutes of Health. Department of Health and Human Services.

Edwards, G., Anderson, P., Babor, T.F., et al. (1994). *Alcohol Policy and the Public Good.* New York: Oxford University Press.

Emerson, S.U., & Purcell, R. (2003). Hepatitis E virus. *Rev Med Virol, 13,* 145–154.

Farrell, G.C., & Larter, C.Z. (2006). Nonalcoholic fatty liver disease: From steatosis to cirrhosis. *Hepatology, 43,* S99–S112.

Feder, J.N., Penny, D.M., Irrinki, A., Lee, V.K., Lebrón, J.A., Watson, N., Schatzman, R.C. (1998). The hemochromatosis gene product complexes with the transferrin receptor and lowers its affinity for ligand binding. *Proc Natl Acad Sci USA, 95*(4), 1472–1477.

Fiore, A.E. (2004). Hepatitis A transmitted by food. *Clinical Infectious Diseases, 38,* 705–715.

Frank, C., Mohamed, M., Strickland, G., Lavanchy, D., Arthur, R., Magder, L.,…Sallam, I. (2000). The role of parenteral anti-schistosomal therapy in the spread of hepatitis C virus in Egypt. *Lancet, 355*(9207), 887–891.

Fraser, A., Harris, R., & Sattar, N. (2009). Alanine aminotransferase, gamma-glutamyltransferase, and incident diabetes: The British Women's Heart and Health Study and meta-analysis. *Diabetes Care, 32,* 741–750.

Frezza, M., Di Padova, C., Pozzato, G., Terpin, M., Baraona, E., & Lieber, C.S. (1990). High blood alcohol levels in women: The role of decreased gastric alcohol dehydrogenase activity and first–pass metabolism. *New England Journal of Medicine, 322,* 95–99.

Fung, J., Lai, C.L., But, D., Wong, D., Cheung, T.K., & Yuen, M.F. (2008). Prevalence of fibrosis and cirrhosis in chronic hepatitis B: Implications for treatment and management. *American Journal of Gastroenterology, 103*(6), 1421–1426.

Gallus, S., Tavani, A., Negri, E., & La Vecchia, C. (2002). Does coffee protect against liver cirrhosis? *Ann Epidemiol, 12,* 202–205.

Galambos, J. (1985). Epidemiology of cirrhosis in the United States of America. In P. Hall (Ed.), *Alcoholic liver disease: Pathobiology, epidemiology, and clinical aspects* (pp. 230–249). New York: John Wiley & Sons.

Ge, D., Fellay, J., Thompson, A.J., Simon, J.S., Shianna, C.V., Urban, T.J.,…Goldstein, D.B. (2009). Genetic variation in *IL28B* predicts hepatitis C treatment-induced viral clearance. *Nature, 461,* 399–401.

Geerts, A. (2001). History, heterogeneity, developmental biology, and functions of quiescent hepatic stellate cells. *Semin Liver Dis, 21*(3), 311–335.

Goodman, M., Wainwright, R.L., Weir, H.F., & Gall, J.C. Jr. (1971). A sex difference in the carrier state of Australia (hepatitis-associated) antigen. *Pediatrics, 48,* 907.

Gruenewald, P.J., & Ponicki, W.R. (1995). The relationship of alcohol sales to cirrhosis mortality. *Journal of Studies on Alcohol, 56,* 635–641.

Hall, P. (1995). Pathological spectrum of alcoholic liver disease. In P. Hall, (Ed.) *Alcoholic liver disease: Pathobiology and pathogenesis* (2nd ed., pp. 41–68). London: Edward Arnold.

Haubrich, W.S. (2004). Kupffer of Kupffer cells. *Gastroenterology, 127,* 16.

Higdon, J.V., & Frei, B. (2006). Coffee and health: A review of recent human research. *Crit Rev Food Sci Nutr, 46,* 101–123.

Hirche, T.O., Ianee, H., Hirche, A., Schneider, A., & Dietrich, C.F. (2007). Evaluation of hepatic steatosis by ultrasound in patients with chronic hepatitis C virus infection. *Liver International, 27*(6), 748–757.

Holder, H.D., & Parker, R.N. (1992). Effect of alcoholism treatment on cirrhosis mortality: A 20–year multivariate time series analysis. *British Journal of Addiction, 87,* 1263–1274.

Hurley, T.D., Edenberg, H.J., & Li, T.K. (2002). The Pharmacogenomics of alcoholism. *Pharmacogenomics: The search for individualized therapies* (pp. 417–441). Weinheim, Germany: Wiley-VCH.

Ito, T. (1951). Cytological studies on stellate cells of Kupffer and fat storing cells in the capillary wall of the human liver. *Acta Anat Nippon, 26,* 2.

Iversen, J., Wand, H., Gonnermann, A., Maher, L., on behalf of the collaboration of Australian Needle and Syringe Programs. (2010). Gender differences in hepatitis C antibody prevalence and risk behaviours amongst people who inject drugs in Australia 1998–2008. *Int J Drug Policy,* May 14. [Epub ahead of print].

Jellinek, E.M., & Keller, M. (1952). Rates of alcoholism in the United States of America, 1940–1948. *Quarterly Journal of Studies on Alcohol, 13,* 49–59.

Jones-Webb, R. (1998). Drinking patterns and problems among African–Americans: Recent findings. *Alcohol Health & Research World, 22*(4), 260–264.

Kamal, S.M. (2008). Acute hepatitis C: A systematic review. *American Journal of Gastroenterology, 103,* 1283–1297.

Kerr, W.D., Fillmore, K.M., & Marvy, P. (2000). Beverage-specific alcohol consumption and cirrhosis mortality in a group of English–speaking beer-drinking countries. *Addiction, 95,* 339–346.

Kim, C.H., & Younossi, Z.M. (2008). Nonalcoholic fatty liver disease: A manifestation of the metabolic syndrome. *Cleve Clin J Med, 75*, 721–728.

Kirsh, R., Robson, S., & Trey, C. (1995). *Diagnosis and management of liver disease.* London: Chapman and Hall.

Klatsky, A.L., & Armstrong, M.A. (1992). Alcohol, smoking, coffee, and cirrhosis. *Am J Epidemiol, 136*, 1248–1257.

Klatsky, A.L., Morton, C., Udaltsova, N., & Friedman, G.D. (2006). Coffee, cirrhosis, and transaminase enzymes. *Arch Intern Med, 166*, 1190–1195.

La Vecchia, F.L., Lucchini, F., Franceschi, S., & Negri, E. (1994). Worldwide patterns and trends in mortality from liver cirrhosis, 1955 to 1990. *Ann Epidemiol, 4*, 480–486.

Lai, M.M.C. (1994). Hepatitis delta virus. In R.G. Webster & A. Granoff (Eds.). *Encyclopedia of virology* (pp. 574–580). London: Academic Press Ltd.

Ledermann, S. (1956). *Alcool, alcoolisme, alcoolisation.* Paris: Presses Universitaires de France.

Leifman, H., & Romelsjš, A. (1997). The effects of changes in alcohol consumption on mortality and admissions with alcohol–related diagnoses in Stockholm County—A time–series analysis. *Addiction, 92*, 1523–1536.

Lelbach, W.K. (1974). Organic pathology related to volume and patterns of alcohol use. In R. Gibbins, Y. Israel, H. Kalant, (Eds.) *Research advances in alcohol and drug problems (Vol. 1)* (pp. 93–198). New York: John Wiley & Sons.

Lieber, C.S. (1989). Alcohol and nutrition: An overview. *Alcohol Health & Research World, 13*(3), 197–205.

Liu, B., Balkwill, A., Roddam, A., Brown, A., Beral, V. on behalf of the Million Women Study Collaborators. (2009). Separate and joint effects of alcohol and smoking on the risks of cirrhosis and gallbladder disease in middle-aged women. *American Journal of Epidemiology, 169*(2), 153–160.

Liu, J., & Fan, D. (2007). Hepatitis B in China. *Lancet, 369*(9573), 1582–1583.

Locarnini, S. (2004). Molecular virology of hepatitis B virus. *Seminars in liver disease, 24*(Suppl 1), 3–10.

London, W.T., & Drew, J.S. (1977). Sex differences in response to hepatitis B infection among patients receiving dialysis treatment. *Proc Natl Acad Sci, USA, 74*(6), 2561–2563.

Luo, X., Kranzler, H.R., Zuo, L., Wand, S., Schork, N.J., & Gelernter, J. (2006). Diplotype trend regression (DTR) analysis of the ADH gene cluster and ALDH2 gene: Multiple significant assocation fo alcohol dependence. *Am J Hum Genet, 78*, 973–987.

Mann, R.E., Smart, R.G., & Anglin, L. (1988). Reduction in liver cirrhosis mortality and morbidity in Canada: Demographic differences and possible explanations. *Alcoholism: Clinical and Experimental Research, 12*, 290–297.

Mann, R.E., Smart, R.G., Anglin, L., & Rush, B. (1988). Are decreases in liver cirrhosis rates a result of increased treatment for alcoholism? *British Journal of Addiction, 83*, 683–688.

Mann, R.E., Smart, R.G., Anglin, L., & Adlaf, E. (1991). Reductions in cirrhosis in the United States: Associations with per capita consumption and AA membership. *Journal of Studies on Alcohol, 52*, 361–365.

Mann, R.E., Anglin, L., Wilkins, K., et al. (1993). Mortality in a sample of convicted drinking drivers. *Addiction, 88*, 643–647.

Mann, R.E., Smart, R.G., & Govoni, R. (2003). The epidemiology of alcoholic liver disease. *Alcohol Res Health, 27*, 209–219.

Marchesini, G., & Bianchi, G. (2010). Metabolic syndrome: Relevant for all types of chronic liver diseases? *Gut, 59*, 1314–1315.

Marchesini, G., Bugianesi, E., Forlani, G., Cerelli, F., Lenzi, M., Manini, R.,…Rizzetto, M. (2003).

Nonalcoholic fatty liver, steatohepatitis, and the metabolic syndrome. *Hepatology, 37,* 917–923.

Minino, A., Arias, E., Kochanek, K.D., et al. (2002). Deaths: Final data for 2000. *National Vital Statistics Reports, 50,* 1–107.

Modi, A.A., Feld, J.J., Park, Y., Kleiner, D.E., Everhart, J.E., Liang, T.J., & Hoofnagle, J.H. (2010). Increased caffeine consumption is associated with reduced hepatic fibrosis. *Hepatology, 51,* 201–209.

Moser, J. (1980). *Prevention of alcohol related problems: An international review of prevention measures, policies and programmes.* Toronto, Canada: World Health Organization by the Alcoholism and Drug Addiction Research Foundation.

Müller, M.J., Pirlich, M., Balks, H.J., & Selberg, O. (1994). Glucose intolerance in liver cirrhosis: Role of hepatic and non-hepatic influences. *Eur J Clin Chem Clin Biochem, 32*(10), 749–758.

Offit, P.A. (2007). *Vaccinated: One man's quest to defeat the world's deadliest diseases* (p. 256). New York, NY: Smithsonian Books.

Nephew, T.M., Williams, G.D., Yi, H.Y., et al. (2002). *Surveillance report #59: Apparent per capita alcohol consumption: National, state and regional trends, 1977–99.* Washington, DC: National Institute of Alcohol Abuse and Alcoholism.

Neuschwander-Tetri, B.A., & Caldwell, S.H. (2003). Nonalcoholic steatohepatitis: Summary of an AASLD Single Topic Conference. *Hepatology, 37*(5), 1202–1219.

NIH Consensus Statement on Management of Hepatitis C. (2002). *NIH Consensus and State-of-the-science Statements, 19*(3), 1–46.

O'Brien, T.R. (2009). Interferon-alfa, interferon-λ and hepatitis. *Nature Genetics, 41,* 1048–1050.

Parlesak, A., Billinger, M.H., Bode, C., & Bode, J.C. (2002). Gastric alcohol dehydrogenase activity in man: Influence of gender, age, alcohol consumption and smoking in a Caucasian population. *Alcohol and Alcoholism (Oxford, Oxfordshire), 37*(4), 388–393.

Pearl, R. (1926). *Alcohol and longevity.* New York: Knopf.

Pell, S., & D'Alonzo, A. (1973). A five–year mortality study of alcoholics. *Journal of Occupational Medicine, 15,* 120–125.

Peters, M.G., & Terrault, N.A. (2002). Alcohol use and hepatitis C. *Hepatology, 36,* S220–S225.

Popham, R.E. (1970). Indirect methods of alcoholism prevalence estimation: A critical evaluation. In R.E. Popham (Ed.). *Alcohol and alcoholism* (pp. 678–685). Toronto: University of Toronto Press.

Poynard, T., Bedossa, P., & Opolon, P. (1997). Natural history of liver fibrosis progression in patients with chronic hepatitis C. The OBSVIRC, METAVIR CLINIVIR, and DOSVIRC groups. *Lancet, 349,* 825–832.

Ramstedt, M. (2001). Per capita alcohol consumption and liver cirrhosis mortality in 14 European countries. *Addiction, 96,* S19–S34.

Reed, T., Page, W.F., Viken, R.J., & Christian, J.C. (1996). Genetic predisposition to organ–specific endpoints of alcoholism. *Alcoholism: Clinical and Experimental Research, 20,* 1528–1533.

Rehm, J., Taylor, B., Mohapatra, S., Irving, H., Baliunas, D., Patra, J., & Roerecke, M. (2010). Alcohol as a risk factor for liver cirrhosis: A systematic review and meta-analysis. *Drug Alcohol Rev, 29*(4), 437–445.

Reich, T., Edenberg, H.J., Goate, A., Williams, J.T., Rice, J.P., Van Eerdewegh, P.,...Begleiter, H. (1998). Genome-wide search for genes affecting the risk for alcohol dependence. Am J Med Genet, 81, 207–215.

Robbins, S.L., & Cotran, R.S. (1979). *Pathologic basis of disease.* Philadelphia: W.B. Saunders Company.

Roizen, R., Fillmore, K., & Kerr, W. (1999). Overlooking Terris: A speculative reconsideration of a curious spot-blindness in the history of alcohol-control science. *Contemporary Drug Problems, 26,* 577–606.

Roizen, R., Kerr, W.C., & Fillmore, K.M. (1999). Cirrhosis mortality and per capita consumption of distilled spirits, United States, 1949–1994: Trend analysis. *British Medical Journal, 319,* 666–670.

Romelsjš, A. (1987). Decline in alcohol–related in–patient care and mortality in Stockholm County. *British Journal of Addiction, 82,* 653–663.

Roguin, A. (2006). Rene Theophile Hyacinthe Laënnec (1781–1826): the man behind the stethoscope. *Clinical Medicine & Research, 4*(3), 230–235.

Schiff, E.R., & Ozden, N. (2003). Hepatitis C and alcohol. *Alcohol Res Health, 27,* 232–239.

Schmidt, W. (1980). Cirrhosis and alcohol consumption: An epidemiologic perspective. In G. Edwards, M. Grant (Eds.). *Alcoholism: New knowledge and new responses* (pp 15–47). London, Croom Helm.

Schmidt, W., & Bronetto, J. (1962). Death from liver cirrhosis and specific alcoholic beverage consumption: An ecological study. *American Journal of Public Health, 52,* 1473–1482.

Schmidt, W., & de Lint, J. (1972). Causes of death in alcoholics. *Quarterly Journal of Studies on Alcohol, 33,* 171–185.

Seeff, L.B., Hollinger, F.B., Alter, H.J., et al. (2001). Long–term mortality and morbidity of transfusion–associated non–A, non–B, and type C hepatitis: A National Heart, Lung, and Blood Institute collaborative study. *Hepatology, 33,* 455–463.

Seeley, J.R. (1960). Death by liver cirrhosis and the price of beverage alcohol. *Canadian Medical Association Journal, 83,* 1361–1366.

Shapiro, C.N. (1993). Epidemiology of hepatitis B. *The Pediatric infectious disease journal, 12*(5), 433–437.

Shepard, C.W., Simard, E.P., Finelli, L., Fiore, A.E., & Bell, B.P. (2006). Hepatitis B virus infection: Epidemiology and vaccination. *Epidemiol Rev, 28*(1), 112–125.

Singh, G.K., & Hoyert, D.L. (2000). Social epidemiology of chronic liver disease and cirrhosis mortality in the United States,

1935–1997: Trends and differentials by ethnicity, socioeconomic status, and alcohol consumption. *Human Biology, 72,* 801–820.

Skog, O.J. (1980). Liver cirrhosis epidemiology: Some methodological problems. *British Journal of Addiction, 75,* 227–243.

Skog, O.J. (1984). The risk function for liver cirrhosis from lifetime alcohol consumption. *Journal of Studies on Alcohol, 45,* 199–208.

Smart, R.G. (1996). Behavioral and social consequences related to the consumption of different beverage types. *Journal of Studies on Alcohol, 57,* 419–424.

Smart, R.G., & Mann, R.E. (1991). Factors in recent reductions in liver cirrhosis deaths. *Journal of Studies on Alcohol, 52,* 232–240.

Smart, R.G., & Mann, R.E. (1993). Recent liver cirrhosis declines: Estimates of the impact of alcohol abuse treatment and Alcoholics Anonymous. *Addiction, 88,* 193–198.

Smart, R.G., Mann, R.E., & Lee, S.L. (1996). Does increased spending on alcoholism treatment lead to lower cirrhosis death rates? *Alcohol and Alcoholism, 31*(5), 487–491.

Smart, R.G., Mann, R.E., & Suurvali, H. (1998). Changes in liver cirrhosis death rates in different countries in relation to per capita alcohol consumption and Alcoholics Anonymous membership. *Journal of Studies on Alcohol, 59,* 245–249.

Smart, R.G., & Mann, R.E. (2000). The impact of programs for high–risk drinkers on population levels of alcohol problems. *Addiction, 95,* 37–52.

Sørensen, H.T., Thulstrup, A.M., Mellemkjar, L., Jepsen, P., Christensen, E., Olsen, J.H., & Vilstrup, H. (2003). Long-term survival and cause-specific mortality in patients with cirrhosis of the liver: A nationwide cohort. *J Clin Epidemiol,* 2003 Jan, *56*(1), 88–93.

Stepanova, M., Zobair, N.R., & Younossi, M. (2010). Components of metabolic syndrome are independent predictors of mortality in patients with chronic liver disease: A population-based study. *Gut, 59,* 1410–1415.

Stinson, F.S., Grant, B.F., & Dufour, M.C. (2001). The critical dimension of ethnicity in liver cirrhosis mortality statistics. *Alcoholism: Clinical and Experimental Research, 25,* 1181–1187.

Suppiah, V., Moldovan, M., Ahlenstiel, G., Berg, T., Weltman, M., Abate, M.L.,…George, J. (2009). IL28B is associated with response to chronic hepatitis C interferon-alpha and ribavirin therapy. *Nat Genet, 41*(10), 1100–1104.

Tanaka, Y., Nishida, N., Sugiyama, M., Kurosaki, M., Matsuura, K., Sakamoto, N.,…Mizokami, M. (2009). Genome-wide association of IL28B with response to pegylated interferon-alpha and ribavirin therapy for chronic hepatitis C. *Nat Genet, 41*(10), 1105–1109.

Terris, M. (1967). Epidemiology of cirrhosis of the liver: National and mortality data. *American Journal of Public Health, 57,* 2076–2088.

Tverdal, A., & Skurtveit, S. (2003). Coffee intake and mortality from liver cirrhosis. *Ann Epidemiol, 13,* 419–423.

Thun, M.J., Peto, R., Lopez, A.D., et al. (1997). Alcohol consumption and mortality among middle–aged and elderly U.S. adults. *New England Journal of Medicine, 337,* 1705–1714.

Tuyns, A.J., & Péquignot, G. (1984). Greater risk of ascitic cirrhosis in females in relation to alcohol consumption. *International Journal of Epidemiology, 13,* 53–57.

Viviani, S., Jack, A., Hall, A.J., Maine, N., Mendy, M., Montesano, R., & Whittle, H.C. (1999). Hepatitis B vaccination in infancy in The Gambia: Protection against carriage at 9 years of age. *Vaccine, 17*(23–24), 2946–2950.

Williams, R. (2006). Global challenges in liver disease. *Hepatology, 44*(3), 521–526.

Wong, G.L.H., Wong, V.W.S., Choi, P.C.L., Chan, A.W.H., Chim, A.M.L., Yiu, K.K.L.,…Chan, F.K.L. (2009). Metabolic syndrome increases the risk of liver cirrhosis in chronic hepatitis B. *Gut, 58,* 111–117.

World Health Organization. (2000). *The Global status report on alcohol.* Geneva, Switzerland: Department of Substance Abuse.

World Health Organization. (WHO, 2009a). Death and DALY estimates for 2004 by cause for WHO Member States (Persons, all ages). *World Health Organization,* Geneva, Switzerland.

World Health Organization. (2009b). *Evidence for the effectiveness and cost-effectiveness of interventions to reduce alcohol-related harm.* Copenhagen, Denmark: World Health Organization.

World Health Organization. (2010). *Global strategy to reduce the harmful use of alcohol* (EB126. R11). Geneva, Switzerland: World Health Organization.

Xie, X., Mann, R.E., & Smart, R.G. (2000). The direct and indirect relationships between alcohol prevention measures and alcoholic liver cirrhosis mortality. *Journal of Studies on Alcohol, 61,* 499–506.

Yamakawa, Y., Sata, M., Suzuki, H., Noguchi, S., & Tanikawa, K. (1996). Higher elimination rate of hepatitis C virus among women. *Journal of Viral Hepatitis, 3*(6), 317–321.

Yen, T., Keeffe, E.B., & Ahmed, A. (2003). The epidemiology of hepatitis C virus infection. *Journal of Clinical Gastroenterology, 36,* 47–53.

Yoon, Y.H., Yi, H., Grant, B.F., et al. (2001). *Surveillance report #57: Liver cirrhosis mortality in the United States, 1970–98.* Washington, DC: National Institute on Alcohol Abuse and Alcoholism.

Yoon, Y.H., Yi, H., Grant, B.F., et al. (2002). *Surveillance report #60: Liver cirrhosis mortality in the United States, 1970–99.* Washington, DC: National Institute on Alcohol Abuse and Alcoholism.

Zatoński, W.A., Sulkowska, U., Mańczuk, M., Rehm, J., Boffetta, P., Lowenfels, A.B., & La Vecchia, C. (2010). Liver cirrhosis mortality in Europe, with special attention to Central and Eastern Europe. *Eur Addict Res, 16,* 193–201.

Epidemiology of Osteoporosis

INTRODUCTION

Osteopororis is defined as *"a systemic skeletal disorder characterized by low bone mass and microarchitectural deterioration of bone tissue with a consequent increase in bone fragility and susceptibility to fracture"* (Consensus Development Conference, 1991). In many individuals, the *first* clinical manifestation of this disease is a low trauma bone fracture of the hip, spine, forearm, or other anatomic sites. Early detection depends upon assessment of *bone mineral density (BMD)* utilizing *dual energy X-ray absorptiometry (DXA)*.

DISCOVERY

In the early 19th century, the British surgeon, Astley Cooper, recognized the link between aging, reduction in bone density and the risk of fractures (Cooper and Cooper, 1822). Shortly thereafter, the French pathologist, Jean Lobstein, coined the term *"osteoporosis"* to describe the porous bones of patients who suffer fractures (Lobstein, 1835). More than a century later, American endocrinologist Fuller Albright found that estrogen deficiency due to menopause or oophorectomy in women induces the loss of critical bone minerals, calcium and phosphate, and leads to the development of *"postmenopausal osteoporosis"* (Albright, Bloomberg, and Smith, 1940).

PATHOGENESIS OF OSTEOPOROSIS

The underlying mechanism of osteoporosis is an imbalance between bone resorption and bone formation.

Throughout life, there is continual remodeling of bone whereby older bone is resorbed by osteoclastic cells (osteoclasts) and replaced by new bone laid down by osteoblastic cells (osteoblasts). Osteoporosis develops when excessive bone resorption and inadequate bone formation reduces bone mineral density (BMD) below a critical threshold resulting in fragile bones that are highly prone to fracture.

The delicate balance of calcium homeostasis and bone remodeling is regulated by a number of cellular and molecular factors and their interactions. Any breach in the integrity of this complex regulatory system could upset the balance of bone resorption and bone formation to provoke the pathogenesis of osteoporosis.

The major minerals in bone are calcium and phosphate. The matrix of bone is composed principally of calcium and phosphate which are combined to form a lattice network of hydroxyapatite crystals. Calcium homeostasis is regulated by the parathyroid glands which secrete parathyroid hormone and the thyroid gland which secretes calcitonin. These polypeptide hormones have opposing functions. Parathyroid hormone stimulates bone resorption by osteoclasts whereas calcitonin stimulates bone formation by osteoblasts. The balance of parathyroid hormone and calcitonin maintain the concentration of serum calcium within a narrow range (~10 mg/dl) to facilitate regular muscle contractions (heartbeat), transmission of nerve impulses, and other functions that are vital to human life. A low concentration of calcium in the blood triggers the release of parathyroid hormone which promptly acts to restore calcium homeostasis by inducing resorption of calcium from bone, retention of calcium by the kidneys, and absorption of calcium in the small intestine (Robbins and Cotran, 1979).

The active hormonal form of vitamin D, 1,25 dihydroxyvitamin D (calcitriol), is necessary for optimal intestinal absorption of calcium and phosphorus. Furthermore, vitamin D exerts a tonic inhibitory effect on parathyroid hormone synthesis. A deficiency in the active form of vitamin D can thus cause calcium deficiency in bone matrix resulting in bone weakness and fragility. The effects of vitamin D are modulated through a family of cell membrane receptors.

Estrogen is also essential for the maintenance of normal bone mineral density. Estrogen acts through estrogen receptors to stimulate bone formation by osteoblasts and inhibit bone resorption by osteoclasts. In this way, estrogen decreases the rate of bone remodeling and the amount of bone lost with each remodeling cycle.

Bone resorption involves close contact and complex molecular interactions between osteoclasts and osteoblasts. The molecular messenger, *nuclear factor kappa beta (NF-Kb)* and its receptor activators and ligands (*RANK, RANKL*) stimulate osteoclast differentiation and remodeling activity. Inflammatory prostaglandins generated by the enzymatic activity of cyclooxygenase-2 (COX-2) accelerate bone resorption. Osteoblasts produce and secrete *osteoprotegerin (OPG)*, a decoy receptor that inhibits RANKL/RANK interactions (Raisz, 2005).

DIAGNOSIS OF OSTEOPOROSIS

The World Health Organization criteria for the diagnosis of osteopenia and osteoporosis are shown in **Table 37.1**. Osteopenia is defined as BMD between 1.0–2.5 standard deviations below the mean normal adult value whereas osteoporosis is diagnosed when BMD is lower than 2.5 standard deviations below the mean. Since BMD levels follow a normal distribution, approximately 0.6% of adults have osteoporosis. Severe disease is low BMD plus one or more fragility bone fractures (WHO, 1994).

Table 37.1	Diagnostic Criteria for Osteopenia and Osteoporosis
Diagnosis	Diagnostic Criteria
Normal	BMD value within 1.0 SD of mean value
Osteopenia	BMD 1.0–2.5 SD below mean value
Osteoporosis	BMD more than 2.5 SD below mean value
Osteoporosis	Abnormal BMD plus fragility fracture

BMD = Bone Mineral Density, SD = Standard Deviation.

BONE MINERAL DENSITY (BMD) AND OSTEOPOROSIS

A team of Swedish investigators conducted a meta-analysis of prospective cohort studies published during 1985–1994 in order to determine the value of BMD in predicting bone fractures in women. Eleven separate study populations were included in the analysis. During 90,000 years of follow-up, 2,000 bone fractures were detected. Pooled results revealed that the risk of bone fracture increased by a factor of 1.5 for each standard deviation decrease in BMD. The association was stronger for hip fractures (RR = 2.6) and vertebral fractures (RR = 2.3). A review of case control studies yielded similar results. The investigators concluded that BMD can predict the fracture risk for groups of women but cannot identify specific individuals who will suffer a fracture (Marshall, Johnell, and Wedel, 1996).

INCIDENCE AND PREVALENCE OF HIP FRACTURE

In their review of the epidemiology of osteoporosis Jordan and Cooper state: "*Clinically, osteoporosis is recognized by the occurrence of low trauma fractures. Hip fracture is the most serious consequence of osteoporosis and is most closely linked to BMD compared to other types of fracture*" (Jordan and Cooper, 2002). Indeed, many epidemiologic investigations have used low/moderate trauma hip fracture as a conservative indicator of osteoporosis.

Investigators at the Mayo Clinic examined trends in the age-specific incidence and prevalence of low/moderate trauma hip fracture for the population of Rochester, Minnesota during 1928–1992. Using an indexed registry of medical records, they identified a total of 2,058 adults who suffered a hip fracture of the proximal femur due to moderate or low trauma during the 65-year time period. **Figure 37.1** shows the annual age-specific *incidence* curves by gender estimated from the most recent data, 1983–1992. The annual incidence rates rise exponentially during the last half of the lifespan peaking after age 85 years at 2,000 cases per 100,000 in men and 2,700 cases per 100,000 in women after the age of 85 years. The average rate of increase per successive year of age was about 12% in women and men; however, the overall age-adjusted annual rate in women was 66% higher than in men (136 vs. 82 per 100,000), and for each age group, the incidence rate was higher in women (Melton, Therneau, and Larson, 1998).

Figure 37.2 shows the annual age-specific *prevalence* curves by gender estimated from the 1983–1992 Rochester data. The annual prevalence rates rise

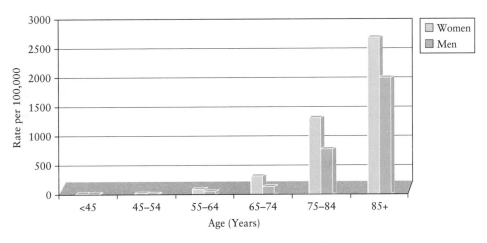

Figure 37.1 Age-Specific Incidence of Low Trauma Hip Fracture, 1983–1992, USA.

Source: Data from Melton LJ, Therneau TM, Larson DR (1998). Long-Term trends in hip fracture prevalence: the influence of hip fracture incidence and survival. *Osteoporos Int* 8:68–74.

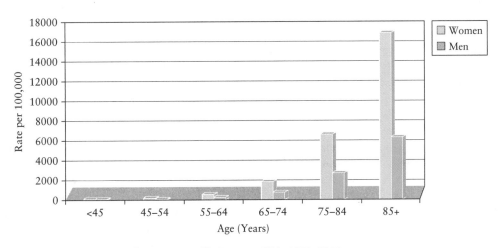

Figure 37.2 Age-Specific Prevalence of Low Trauma Hip Fracture, USA, 1983–1992.

Source: Data from Melton LJ, Therneau TM, Larson DR (1998). Long-Term trends in hip fracture prevalence: the influence of hip fracture incidence and survival. Osteoporos Int 8:68–74.

sharply after age 55 years peaking after age 85 years at about 17,000 cases per 100,000 in women and 6,000 cases per 100,000 in men. The overall age-adjusted rate in women was more than 2.3-fold higher than in men (768 vs. 333 cases per 100,000). Over the 65 year time frame of the study, the prevalence of hip fracture increased nearly fivefold in parallel with increasing longevity of the population (Melton, Therneau, and Larson, 1998).

SURVIVAL AND MORTALITY: HIP FRACTURES

Melton and colleagues also examined mortality and survival following hip fracture in the Rochester cohort. In comparison with mortality rates for the general

population there was a marked excess of deaths in both men and women during the first year following fracture. Mortality was found to be 5–10-fold higher than the general population during the first few weeks after fracture, but then gradually declined to expected levels at about 1 year post fracture. Overall, women experienced longer average survival than men following an initial hip fracture: 8.6 versus 6.1 years, respectively (Melton, Therneau, and Larson, 1998).

In a more recent analysis of the Rochester cohort, Melton and colleagues determined that the annual incidence of first hip fracture during the period 1980–2006 declined by about 1.4% per year in women while remaining unchanged in men. Among 2,434 individuals who suffered a first fracture, the cumulative risk of recurrent hip fracture after 10 years was 11% in women and 6% in men.

Interestingly, there was a significant reduction in hip fracture recurrence after 1997, corresponding to the introduction of bisphosphonate therapy for osteoporosis (Melton et al., 2009).

Results of many other studies also reflect high early mortality and disability rates among subjects who suffer hip fracture. In a study of 571 cases 50 years or older who received emergency care in metropolitan hospitals in New York City during 1997–1998, the in-hospital mortality rate was 1.6% and at 6 months postfracture, 13.5% of cases were deceased and 12.8% needed total assistance to ambulate (Hannan et al., 2005).

In Great Britain, 8,148 hip fracture cases 65 years or older who received emergency care in hospitals near Oxford during 1994–1998 were followed over 6 months postfracture. In-hospital mortality was 7.9% and 24.6% of patients died within 6 months (Goldacre, Roberts, and Yeates, 2002).

In Malmö, Sweden, all women suffering a hip fracture during 1984–1985 were followed for up to 22 years to determine mortality and the risk of a second fracture. Among 766 cases, 21% died during the first year after fracture. One-year mortality increased with age, 7%, 21%, and 33% for age groups <75, 75–84, and 85+ years, respectively, but in subsequent years after fracture, the age-adjusted relative mortality was not significantly increased compared to the general population. The 10-year risk of *second fracture* among surviving cases was estimated at 40% (von Friesendorff, Besjakov, and Akesson 2008).

GLOBAL BURDEN OF OSTEOPOROSIS

Johnnel and Kanis recently conducted a comprehensive review and analysis of hip fracture data reported by the World Health Organization with the objective of quantifying the total global burden of osteoporotic fracture. Country-specific estimates of hip fracture rates for member nations of the World Health Organization were used in the analysis. The incidence of hip fracture was estimated for men and women ages 50 years or older by 5-year age intervals based on data reported from 1990 onwards. Mean rates of hip fractures were calculated for 17 subregions of the world and subsequently collapsed into seven broad regions: Africa, America, Eastern Mediterranean, Europe, Southeast Asia, and the Western Pacific. Fracture rates at other anatomic sites (spine, forearm, humerus, and elsewhere) were extrapolated based upon age-gender-site specific data estimated from the Swedish national registry. Estimates of mortality due to osteoporotic fracture for each region were

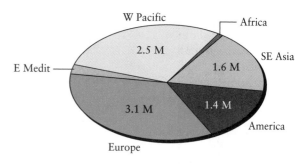

Figure 37.3 Global Distribution of Bone Fractures.

Source: Data from Johnnell O, Kanis JA (2006). An estimate of the worldwide prevalence and disability associated with osteoporotic fractures. *Osteoporos Int* 17:1726–1733.

obtained by weighting the fracture rates for each region by excess mortality rates of Swedish cases by age and gender. Disability adjusted life years (DALY = YLL+YLD) were also estimated for each region by weighting the regional age-gender-specific fracture rates by corresponding mortality and disability estimates from studies of the Swedish population (Johnnel and Kanis, 2006; Kanis et al., 2000).

Johnnel and Kanis estimated that in the year 2000, nearly 9 million osteoporotic fractures occurred in the world population. More than half of these fractures involved the hip (1.6 million), forearm (1.7 million), or spine (1.4 million). The distribution of fractures is shown by region in **Figure 37.3**. The Americas and Europe accounted for more than 50% of the worldwide burden of fractures. The total *DALY* lost from osteoporotic fractures was estimated at 5.8 million representing about 0.83% of all noncommunicable (chronic) diseases. The disease burden was greater in women (DALY = 3.7 million) than men (DALY = 2.1 million). Approximately 51% of the DALY were lost in the populations of Europe and the Americas, which comprise only about 27% of the world population. The investigators concluded that *"osteoporotic fractures are a significant cause of morbidity and mortality, particularly in the developed countries"* (Johnnel and Kanis, 2006).

RISK FACTORS FOR OSTEOPOROSIS

The pathogenesis of bone loss and osteoporosis is modulated by multiple risk factors including aging, nutritional deficiencies (vitamin D and calcium), postmenopausal estrogen deficiency in women, and various lifestyle factors including smoking, alcohol abuse, lack of exercise, low body mass, and certain environmental exposures (Cooper and Melton, 1992; Jordan and Cooper, 2002). Deficiencies in vitamin D and calcium are also prominent causes of two related bone disorders, *rickets* and *osteomalacia*. In the discussion that follows, vitamin D metabolism and regulation of calcium homeostasis are briefly reviewed and findings from randomized clinical trials of vitamin and mineral supplementation and estrogen replacement therapy are presented. Genetic factors, certain medical conditions and medications, and various other factors that modulate the risk are also covered.

Vitamin D Metabolism

The active form of vitamin D (*calcitriol*) is synthesized in humans by a cascade of reactions in the skin, liver, and kidneys (**Figure 37.4**). The initial reaction occurs in the skin where sunlight (ultraviolet light) converts the cholesterol derivative, 7-dehydrocholesterol to vitamin D3 (cholecalciferol). Cholecalciferol is subsequently transported in the blood to the liver and hydroxylated to form 25 hydroxycholecalciferol (calcidiol). Calcidiol is then transported in the blood to the proximal tubules of the kidneys where it undergoes a second hydroxylation reaction to form the active vitamin D compound 1,25 hydroxycholecalciferol (calcitriol). Calcitriol is a potent ligand of the *vitamin D receptor (VDR)*, which mediates most of the physiological actions of the vitamin. The active form of vitamin D is required for calcium and phosphorous absorption from the small intestine. In the absence of vitamin D during the early years of development, dietary calcium is not absorbed, resulting in hypocalcemia which causes severe skeletal and dental deformities, a condition known as rickets. A similar condition that is caused by vitamin D deficiency in adolescents and adults is called *osteomalacia* (Vitale, 1979).

The role of vitamin D in maintaining calcium homeostasis in the human system was elucidated in the early 20th century through the research of many investigators. McCollum and Davis initially isolated a fat soluble growth factor in butterfat and cod liver oil that was later found to prevent rickets in animals (McCollum and Davis, 1914; McCollum et al., 1922).

In 1921, Alfred Hess and L.F. Unger of Columbia University showed that by exposing rachitic children to sunlight, they were able to cure them of the disease (Hess and Unger, 1921), In 1924, the chemist Harry Steenbock and colleagues at the University of Wisconsin demonstrated that irradiation produced foodstuffs with antirachitic properties in animals, a revolutionary finding that was patented and subsequently utilized by the food industry to fortify milk, bread, cereal, and other food products with irradiated vitamin D compounds (Steenbock and Black, 1924; Steenbock, 1924). Soon thereafter, other investigators also reported that irradiation could impart antirachitic properties to inert food sources (Hume and Smith, 1924; Hess and Weinstock, 1925).

The German steroid chemist, Adolf Windhaus, eventually isolated the active form of vitamin D and was awarded the Nobel Prize "*for his studies on the constitution of the sterols and their connection with vitamins*" (Wolf, 2004). Subsequent studies by Windaus and others were instrumental in elucidating the photochemical conversion of *provitamin D* (*7-dehydrocholesterol* and *ergosterol*) to *vitamin D3* (*cholecalciferol*) (Windaus and Hess, 1926; Rosenheim and Webster, 1926; Windaus, 1931). Three decades later, investigators in the United States and England independently identified the biologically active form of vitamin D (*1,25-dihydroxycholecalciferol* or *calcitriol*) which is synthesized sequentially from cholecalciferol in the liver and kidneys (Holick et al., 1971; Holick, Schnoes, and DeLuca, 1971; Lawson et al., 1971).

Dietary sources of vitamin D include fatty fish, liver, egg yolk, and certain dairy products such as butter, cream, and cheese. Plant sources of vitamin D are limited and include certain herbs and mushrooms. In most developed countries, food staples are fortified with vitamin D to prevent deficiency. In supplements and fortified foods, vitamin D is available in two forms, vitamin D_2 (ergocalciferol) and vitamin D_3 (cholecalciferol), that differ chemically only in their side-chain structure. Vitamin D_2 is manufactured by the UV irradiation of ergosterol from yeast, and vitamin D_3 is manufactured by the irradiation of 7-dehydrocholesterol from lanolin (Holick, 2007).

Vitamin D Deficiency: Rickets and Osteomalacia

Severe deficiencies in vitamin D and/or dietary calcium and phosphorous become apparent early in life (usually by the age of 2 years) in the form of rickets.

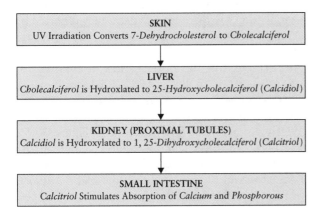

Figure 37.4 Biosynthesis of Active Vitamin D (Calcitriol).

In this condition, calcium and phosphate levels are insufficient to support normal bone development and mineralization along the growth plates of endochrondral bones. As a consequence, the bones are soft, pliable, and often deformed. A closely related condition, *osteomalacia*, refers to defective bone mineralization in adolescents and adults.

Bone formation in the human skeleton is a complex process that begins during embryogenesis and continues throughout the lifespan. Most skeletal bones involve the initial formation of an intermediate cartilaginous template, which serves as a guide for bone development. Over time, the cartilage is replaced by bone composed of calcium phosphate salts and hydroxyapatite crystals to form a dense, hard shell of endochrondral bone. The process of bone formation along cartilaginous growth plates is called *ossification*. Subsequently, the inner matrix of the newly formed bone undergoes *mineralization* by calcium and phosphorous compounds to form trabecular bone that is less dense. The inner trabecular bone matrix is heavily interlaced with small blood vessels to facilitate bone remodeling and the influx/outflux of calcium and phosphorous (Vitale, 1979).

The processes of mineralization and demineralization of bone are tightly regulated by parathyroid hormone and vitamin D, and are in a continual state of flux. Parathyroid hormone is secreted by the parathyroid glands in response to low levels of serum calcium. This hormone stimulates resorption of bone and the mobilization of calcium and phosphorous in order to maintain serum calcium within a narrow range of normality (9.5–10.5 mg/ml). Parathyroid hormone also stimulates the biosynthesis of the active form of vitamin D (calcitriol) in the renal tubules of the kidneys. Vitamin D is essential for daily maintenance of adequate stores of calcium and phosphorous in the body. Vitamin D stimulates absorption of dietary calcium and phosphorous by the small intestine while enhancing the retention of calcium by the kidneys (Vitale, 1979).

Ann Prentice of the Medical Research Council at Cambridge recently reviewed available data on vitamin D levels and calcium intake from various populations around the globe in order to characterize the prevalence of rickets and osteomalacia and nutritional deficiencies worldwide. While the fortification of milk and other food products in the mid-20th century resulted in the near eradication of rickets and osteomalacia in the United States, Europe, and other developed nations in the mid-20th century, exceptionally high prevalence rates of rickets ranging from 10% up to 70% have been found in surveys of children living in underdeveloped nations. Dr. Prentice notes that *"the prevalence of rickets, however, remains scandalously high in many parts of Asia, Africa, and the Middle East"* and she suggests *"there is an urgent need for action to address the global burden of rickets and osteomalacia"* (Prentice, 2008).

The plasma concentration of *25 hydroxycholecalciferol (25 hydroxyvitamin D)* is a useful vitamin D biomarker because it has a long half-life in the circulation and its concentration is not under tight homeostatic regulation. This biomarker therefore reflects vitamin D supply and usage over a period of time. Normal levels of 25 hydroxyvitamin D range between 20–80 ng/ml although there is debate about the lower limit (some investigators suggest a lower threshold of 30 ng/ml).

Patients with rickets or osteomalacia often have very low levels of hydroxyvitamin D. In a study of 98 patients and their families from New Delhi, India, the average level of 25 hydroxyvitamin D among patients was ~6 pg/ml with a 95% confidence interval of approximately 1–10 ng/ml. Notably, 90% of the cases with either rickets or osteomalacia were female and among 221 of their close relatives, 24% of females and 5% of males had *chemical osteomalacia* defined as hydroxyvitamin D less than 20 ng/ml. These results suggest that females are at particularly high risk (Ray et al., 2009).

In 1997, a standing committee of the US Institute of Medicine reported a consensus statement that *"persons with hydroxyvitamin D less than 20 nmols/L (8 ng/ml) probably have rickets or osteomalacia"* (Institute of Medicine, 1997). More recently, other investigators have suggested slightly higher cutpoints of 25 nmols/L (10 ng/ml) and 30 nmols/L (12 ng/ml) (Norman, 2008; Prentice, 2008).

National surveys have been conducted in Great Britain and the United States to characterize the prevalence of vitamin D deficiency at different ages. Such studies were designed to quantify the fraction of individuals with vitamin D deficiency reflected by serum levels of *25 hydroxyvitamin D (25 hydroxycholecalciferol)* less than 25 nmols/L (10 ng/ml). Surprisingly, the prevalence of low vitamin D status in Great Britain during 1992–2001 was between 5–20% in most age groups and exceeded 20% in young men and women aged 19–24 years, and in elderly women over 85 years of age (**Figure 37.5**). Furthermore, prevalence estimates ranging from 20–40% were found in certain populations likely to have little sun exposure and/or low dietary intake, particularly elderly adults living in nursing homes, certain minority groups, and individuals on special

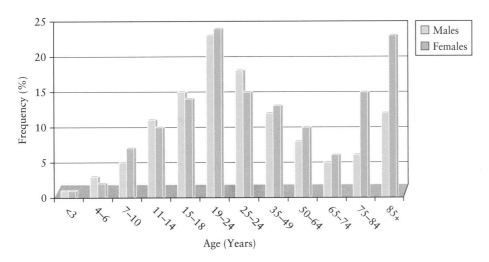

Figure 37.5 Prevalence of Low Serum Vitamin D in Great Britain, 1992–2001.

Source: Data from Gregory et al., 1995; Finch et al., 1998; Gregory et al., 2000; Ruston et al., 2003; Prentice, 2008.

diets (Gregory et al., 1995; Gregory, Lowe, and Bates, 2000; Finch, Doyle, and Lowe, 1998; Ruston, Hoare, and Gregory, 2003; Prentice, 2008). These results suggest that even in developed nations, many individuals do not have adequate levels of vitamin D and are therefore at increased risk for the development of rickets, osteomalacia, and osteoporosis (Prentice et al., 2006; Prentice, 2008).

In contrast to the vitamin D data from Great Britain, a national survey conducted in the United States during 1988–1994 yielded prevalence estimates below 5% for vitamin D deficiency irrespective of age. The relatively low prevalence of vitamin D deficiency in the United States population compared to Great Britain may partially reflect the greater sun exposure in the Southern United States population (Looker et al., 2002; Prentice, 2008).

Good nutrition is especially important for normal fetal development and good maternal health. Recent surveys suggest that vitamin D deficiency is remarkably commonplace in pregnant women of certain ethnic minority groups, even those residing in developed countries. For example, studies of pregnant women in minority groups from the Netherlands, Great Britain, New Zealand, and Australia have yielded prevalence estimates of vitamin D deficiency ranging from 50–80%. Vitamin D deficiency during pregnancy may serve as a harbinger for the subsequent development of bone disorders in mother and offspring (Prentice, 2008).

The recommended daily allowances (RDA) of vitamin D in the United States are 400 IU from birth to 1 year of age, 600 IU between the ages of 1 and 70 years, and 800 IU for individuals over 70 years of age. Intake of 600 IU is also recommended for pregnant or lactating women (Institute of Medicine, 2010). Notably, vitamin D-fortified milk is available in many developed nations and exemplifies a simple, practical, inexpensive, and effective means of preventing vitamin D deficiency, rickets, and osteomalacia (Scrimshaw, 1986). Obviously, the vitamin D status of populations in developed countries may not reflect that of some underdeveloped countries where malnutrition and nutritional deficiencies are relatively common. Albeit, there are scant data on vitamin D deficiency and related conditions in the developing world and more studies are clearly needed to accurately characterize their global impact.

Vitamin D Deficiency and Osteoporosis

Very few epidemiologic investigations have focused on vitamin D deficiency as a risk factor for osteoporosis. In Oslo, Norway, which has a high incidence of osteoporosis, investigators conducted a matched case control study to evaluate risk factors of hip fractures among the elderly. Cases admitted to Oslo hospitals for treatment of hip fracture were compared to controls matched by age and gender. Though no association was found with calcium intake, low intake of vitamin D (<100 IU) significantly increased the risk of hip fracture (OR = 3.9) (Meyer et al., 1995).

In a nested case control study of osteoporosis among Mediterranean women, Ramstam and Kanis compared the use of vitamin D supplements in 1,634 women with hip fracture aged 50 years or older to 3,532 age matched controls from 14 centers in 6 Mediterranean countries. Overall, the risk of hip fracture was reduced by 26% among those using vitamin D supplements (RR = 0.74). Observed risk reductions were greater for women 80 years and older (RR = 0.63) and those with body mass index less than 20 (RR = 0.45). The investigators concluded that vitamin D supplementation for the prevention of hip fracture might be usefully targeted to the frail and elderly (Ranstam and Kanis, 1995).

One study reflects the importance of considering endogenous levels of not only vitamin D but also estrogen. In a nested case control study of women 65 years or older, Cummings and colleagues compared serum levels of vitamin D3 (cholecalciferol) and estrogen (estradiol) at baseline in 133 women who subsequently developed hip fracture and 138 women who subsequently suffered vertebral fractures with randomly selected controls from the same cohort. Women were excluded if they took exogenous estrogen. Results revealed that women with low serum vitamin D3 levels (<23 pg/ml) were at increased risk of suffering a hip fracture (OR = 2.1) and women with low serum estrogen (<5 pg/ml) were at increased risk of suffering either a hip or vertebral fracture (OR = 2.5). Furthermore, women with undetectable free estrogen (unbound to sex hormone binding globulin) had marked increases in fracture risk (OR = 6.9 for hip fractures and OR = 7.9 for vertebral fractures). These results suggest that low serum levels of estrogen and/or vitamin D increase the fracture risk in postmenopausal women (Cummings et al., 1998).

Calcium Homeostasis

Calcium is a mineral that is essential for life. Its presence is integral to intracellular signaling, enzyme activation, transmission of nerve impulses, muscle contractions, and many other physiological processes. Blood levels of calcium must be maintained within a very narrow range (9.5–10.5 mg/ml) for these processes to remain viable. Calcium (in the form of calcium phosphate) is the primary building block of bone and is responsible for bone density and strength. Bone is the primary storage compartment of calcium and undergoes continual remodeling throughout the lifespan in order to help maintain calcium homeostasis in all tissues.

The action of vitamin D and the metabolism of calcium and phosphate are regulated by parathyroid hormone that is secreted by the parathyroid glands. Parathyroid hormone stimulates the synthesis of the active form of vitamin D (calcitriol) in the renal tubules of the kidneys plus the release of calcium and phosphate from bone. Cacitriol enhances the absorption of

dietary calcium and phosphate in the small intestine plus the retention of both minerals by the renal tubules of the kidneys. This integrated metabolic system is essential for the maintenance of calcium/phosphorous/bone homeostasis, and perturbation in any part of the system is likely to cause disease. For example, vitamin D deficiency during early bone development causes rickets since dietary calcium and phosphorous are not absorbed in the gastrointestinal tract and are thus not available to mineralize bone. Likewise, severely low levels of dietary calcium and phosphorous can produce deranged ossification and lack of bone mineralization leading to osteomalacia in adolescents and young adults, and osteoporotic fracture in the elderly (Prentice et al., 2006; Prentice, 2008).

Calcium Deficiency and Osteoporosis

Surprisingly, the results of epidemiologic investigations *do not* consistently support a beneficial effect of high calcium intake per se on bone health. For example, in a 12-year prospective study of 77,781 adult American women, Harvard investigators found *no evidence* that higher intakes of milk or calcium from food sources reduced the risk of bone fractures (Feskanich et al., 1997).

In contrast, a longitudinal study of 957 American men and women aged 50–79 years at baseline and followed for up to 14 years revealed a significant reduction in the risk of hip fractures with high calcium intake (RR = 0.60 per 198 mg per 1,000 kcal). The investigators suggest that this result *"strongly supports the hypothesis that increased dietary calcium intake protects against hip fracture"* (Holbrook, Barrett-Connor, and Wingard, 1988).

Randomized Clinical Trials
Calcium Supplementation for Prevention of Osteoporosis

A team of international investigators conducted a meta-analysis of placebo-controlled randomized clinical trials to evaluate calcium supplementation for the prevention of osteoporosis in postmenopausal women. A literature search identified 15 randomized clinical trials of 1,806 postmenopausal patients that reported bone mineral density and fracture risk with and without calcium supplementation. The combined results from these trials showed that calcium supplementation significantly reduced the rates of bone loss after two or more years of treatment. Rates of vertebral and nonvertebral fractures also decreased with calcium supplementation compared to placebo (23% and 14%, respectively) although effect measures did not reach statistical significance. The investigators concluded that calcium supplementation has a positive influence on bone mineral density (Shea et al., 2002). Notwithstanding, as discussed in the following section on vitamin D, supplementation with *calcium plus vitamin D* not only increases bone density but also appears to have significant value in the chemoprevention of osteoporotic fractures (DIPART Group, 2010).

Calcium and Vitamin D Supplementation for Prevention of Osteoporosis

Several randomized clinical trials have been conducted to assess potential chemopreventive effects of supplemental vitamin D and calcium on bone density and rates of bone fracture in postmenopausal women. Albeit, the results of these studies provide conflicting evidence regarding benefit of vitamin D supplementation to bone health.

Papadimitropoulos and colleagues conducted a meta-analysis of 25 trials that randomized postmenopausal women to standard or hydroxylated vitamin D with or without calcium supplementation versus placebo. All studies had at least one year of follow-up. The combined results showed that vitamin D supplementation reduced the incidence of vertebral fractures (RR = 0.63) and nonvertebral fractures (RR = 0.77) (Papadimitropoulos et al., 2002).

Investigators of the *US Women's Health Initiative* examined effects of calcium and vitamin D on bone density and fracture risk in a randomized placebo controlled clinical trial of postmenopausal women. They recruited 36,292 postmenopausal women, 50–79 years of age, for random assignment to receive 1,000 mg of elemental calcium (as calcium carbonate) plus 400 IU of vitamin D3 daily or placebo. Fractures were assessed over 7 years of follow-up and bone density was measured in samples of treated and untreated women in the study. Censored results on termination of the trial revealed improved bone density and a significant reduction in the hazard ratio for hip fracture (HR = 0.71) among women who received supplemental calcium plus vitamin D (Jackson et al., 2006).

Bischoff-Ferrari and colleagues conducted a meta-analysis of data extracted from randomized clinical trials of vitamin D and fracture risk in order to evaluate effects of the dose of vitamin D supplementation. Only double blind randomized clinical trials of oral vitamin D supplementation with or without supplemental calcium in older persons 60 years or older that examined hip or vertebral fractures were included. Five trials of hip fracture (9,294 participants) and 7 trials of nonvertebral fracture (9,820 participants) met the inclusion criteria. Compared to placebo, oral vitamin D at a dose of 700–800 IU daily reduced the relative risk of both hip fracture (RR = 0.74) and nonvertebral fracture (RR = 0.77), whereas no benefit was observed for lesser doses. The investigators concluded that oral vitamin D supplementation at 700–800 IU daily reduces the risk of hip and nonvertebral fractures whereas a dose of 400 IU daily is not sufficient for fracture prevention (Bischoff-Ferrari et al., 2005).

Boonen and colleagues extended the meta-analysis of Bischoff-Ferrari et al. to examine the the risk of hip fracture among individuals receiving dietary supplementation with vitamin D alone versus calcium plus vitamin D. In their analysis, the pooled relative risk estimate for vitamin D plus calcium (RR = 0.82) was 25% less than the estimate for vitamin D alone (RR = 1.10), suggesting that vitamin D reduces the risk of hip fracture only when calcium supplementation is added (Boonen at al., 2007).

Most recently, investigators of the *DIPART (vitamin D Individual Patient Analysis of Randomized Trials)* group conducted a meta-analysis of individual patient data from randomized clinical trials to evaluate independent and joint effects of oral supplementation with vitamin D and calcium. Their pooled analysis included individual patient data from 7 major randomized clinical trials of oral vitamin D supplementation with or without calcium supplementation. These trials included 68,517 participants (14.7% male) ranging in age from 47–107 years with fracture as the primary outcome. Cox regression was utilized to estimate the *hazard ratio (HR)* with adjustment for other variables. Results revealed that vitamin D in combination with calcium reduced the overall risk of fracture (HR = 0.92) and hip fracture (HR = 0.84). However, no significant effects of vitamin D alone were noted irrespective of dose. Furthermore, the analysis did not detect significant interactions with age, gender or estrogen replacement therapy. These results suggest that vitamin D supplementation alone is *ineffective* in preventing fractures, but that the *combination* of oral calcium and vitamin D reduces the risk of hip fracture and total fractures (DIPART Group, 2010).

Vitamin D and Calcium Supplementation Therapy for Bone Disease

Studies of populations residing in tropical climates where sun exposure is abundant and vitamin D levels are sufficient clearly suggest that severe dietary calcium deficiency per se can cause rachitic disease and that early detection and correction of the deficiency is beneficial. Thacher and colleagues conducted a clinical trial of 123 Nigerian children with rickets to assess the therapeutic benefit of oral supplementation with vitamin D alone, calcium alone, and combination therapy with vitamin D and calcium. After 6 months of treatment, recovery was apparent in 61% of children who received calcium, 58% of children receiving combination therapy, but only 19% of children receiving vitamin D. The investigators concluded that Nigerian children with rickets have a low intake of calcium and a better response to treatment with calcium alone or in combination with vitamin D than to vitamin D alone (Thacher et al., 1999).

In contrast, results of studies of vitamin D and calcium supplementation therapy in patients with osteoporotic fracture have not been encouraging. In a *therapeutic* trial conducted in Great Britain, elderly adults 70 years or older who had suffered an initial low-trauma fracture were randomly assigned to take 800 IU of supplemental vitamin D3 daily, 1,000 mg of supplemental calcium daily, both supplements daily, or placebo. During 24–62 months of follow-up, 698 new fractures were detected among the 5,292 participants. In comparisons of treatment groups with placebo, no significant differences were detected in the incidence of new fractures. Thus, these findings do not support oral supplementation with calcium and/or vitamin D3 as an effective therapeutic approach for the tertiary prevention of second fractures in such patients (Grant et al., 2005).

Calcium and Vitamin D: Synopsis of Findings

In summary, calcium and vitamin D are essential for bone health, and deficiencies in either agent (or both) can cause rickets and osteomalacia during the developmental years and osteoporosis later in life. The major causes of vitamin D deficiency are poor nutrition and scarce exposure to sunlight. Nutritional surveys in developing and some developed countries also reflect calcium deficiencies in a significant fraction of the population. The recent evidence from randomized clinical trials lends support to routine supplementation with *both* compounds, particularly for those at high risk. Supplemental intake of 700–800 mg of calcium *and* 400–800 IU of vitamin D is recommended as a safe, effective, and inexpensive means of preventing rickets in children, osteomalacia in adolescents and young adults, and osteoporotic fractures in the elderly (Gennari, 2001).

Estrogen and Osteoporosis

As illustrated in **Figures 37.1** and **37.2**, osteoporosis is rarely observed in premenopausal women but is a relatively common disorder in postmenopausal women. The major physiological impact of menopause is the loss of ovarian estrogens that are secreted during the menstrual cycle. Typically, serum estrogen (estradiol) is highest during the follicular phase of the menstrual cycle (~400 pg/ml) and then declines to much lower levels (~50 pg/ml) in parallel with rising progesterone levels during the luteal phase. Following menopause, estrogen (estrone) is primarily produced in fat and muscle cells by the enzymatic action of aromatase, which converts adrenal steroids to estrogen. As a consequence of the shutdown of ovarian biosynthesis, postmenopausal levels of estrogen fall dramatically to about 15% of premenopausal values (Howanitz and Howanitz, 1984).

The impact of reduced estrogen on bone remodeling in postmenopausal women is dramatic. With falling estrogen, there is a marked increase in the activity of ligands and receptors that stimulate osteoclasts (*RANK* and *RANKL*) and a marked decrease in *osteoprotegerin* (*OPG*) and other factors that stimulate osteoblasts. These changes tip the balance of bone remodeling in favor of osteoclastic bone resorption that far outpaces osteoblastic bone formation. The end result is demineralization of both the outer cortical shell and the inner trabacular matrix of bone.

Heidi Nelson of the *Oregon Health Sciences University* conducted a systematic review and evaluation of studies of *estrogen replacement therapy* (ERT) and *selective estrogen receptor modulators* (*SERMs*) to determine their value in preventing osteoporosis and bone fracture in postmenopausal women. The study was supported by the *US Agency for Healthcare Research and Quality*. Only randomized controlled trials and cohort studies were included in the analysis. Results of 22 randomized clinical trials revealed that ERT improved bone density and reduced the risk of nonvertebral fractures by 27% (RR = 0.73). In cohort studies, women who received ERT compared to those who did not showed 20–35% reductions in the adjusted relative risk of hip fracture. In studies of SERMs, both tamoxifen and raloxifene were found to increased bone density of various sites, and raloxifene reduced the risk of vertebral fractures by 41% (RR = 0.59). These results suggest that ERT and SERMs may have benefit in improving bone density and protecting against bone fractures (Nelson, 2002).

Testosterone and Osteoporosis

Though osteoporosis occurs more often in women, elderly men constitute a significant fraction (25% or more) of cases. A few studies have examined the association between testosterone deficiency (hypogonadism) and osteoporosis and the impact of testosterone replacement therapy on bone health in men.

Levels of total testosterone and free (unbound) testosterone were compared in a small case control study of 28 elderly men who suffered hip fractures and 28 healthy controls matched by age, ethnicity, and living conditions. The average serum levels of total testosterone and free testosterone were found to be significantly lower among cases than controls, and testosterone deficiency (<9 nmol/L) was present in 20 of the cases versus 9 of the controls (Crude OR = 5.3). Serum levels of hydroxvitamin D were also lower among cases. The investigators concluded that gonadal deficiency is an important risk factor for osteoporotic fracture in men and recommended that early recognition and testosterone replacement therapy be considered for prevention (Jackson, Riggs, and Spiekerman, 1992).

Investigators at Massachusett General Hospital in Boston compared bone mineral density (BMD) and other measures of body composition in 36 adult men with acquired hypogonadism and 44 untreated age-matched eugonadal controls. On average, the spinal BMD among hypogonadal men was about 10% less than controls. Cases also had about 37% higher body fat than controls. Testosterone therapy (100 mg per week) was initiated in 29 of the hypogonadal men and subjects were evaluated at 6-month intervals for 18 months. Testosterone replacement therapy produced a significant increase in lean muscle mass (7%), a significant decrease in percent body fat (14%), and a significant increase in spinal BMD (5%). Furthermore, markers of bone remodeling and resorption, serum *alkaline phosphatase* and urinary *deoxypyridinoline* excretion, decreased significantly with therapy. The investigators concluded that testosterone replacement therapy has beneficial impact on body composition and increases bone density in hypogonadal men (Katznelson et al., 1996).

Investigators at the Mayo Clinic performed a systematic review and meta-analysis of randomized placebo-controlled clinical trials to assess the effect of testosterone administration on bone health in men. Eight trials that enrolled a total of 365 patients were included in the analysis. Results revealed that intramuscular injections of testosterone improved bone mineral density (BMD) by 8% in the lumbar spine and 4% in the femoral head compared to placebo whereas transdermal injections had no significant effect. The investigators concluded that the available trials offer some evidence of the clinical efficacy of intramuscular testosterone for osteoporosis prevention and treatment in men (Tracz et al., 2006).

Low Body Mass Index and Osteoporosis

De Laet and colleagues explored the association of *body mass index (BMI)* with fracture risk using data from 12 prospective population-based cohort studies involving nearly 60,000 men and women. Results revealed an inverse relation between BMI and the risk of bone fracture. Overall, there was a risk reduction of 2% for any type of fracture per unit increase in BMI (RR = 0.98) and a risk reduction of 7% for hip fracture per unit increase in BMI (RR = 0.93). The risk of hip fracture in subjects with BMI <20 was approximately double that of subjects with BMI >25 (RR = 1.95). The protective effect of increasing BMI was similar for men and women. These effects were attenuated with adjustment for bone mineral density (BMD). The investigators concluded that *"low BMI confers a risk of substantial importance for all fractures that is largely independent of age and sex, but dependent on BMD"* (De Laet et al., 2005).

Smoking and Osteoporosis

Three meta-analyses have been published with the objective of clarifying the association between smoking and osteoporosis. Law and Hackshaw examined the association based on data from 29 cross-sectional studies and 19 cohort and case control studies involving 15,750 subjects. Results revealed that the risk of hip fracture was 41% greater in smokers than nonsmokers and that bone mineral density (BMD) declined 2% more in smokers than nonsmokers for every 10 year increase in age (Law and Hackshaw, 1997).

Ward and Klesges conducted a pooled analysis of data from 86 studies involving 40,753 subjects. Their results revealed that chronic smoking increased the lifetime risk of hip fracture by 31% in women and 40% in men. The risk of vertebral fractures was also increased by smoking (13% in women and 32% in men). Their results also suggest that about 10% of all hip fractures are attributable to smoking (Ward and Klesges, 2001).

In the most recent meta-analysis, Kanis and colleagues examined the data from 10 prospective cohort studies involving 59,232 subjects. They found that current smoking increased the overall fracture risk by 25% and the risk of hip fracture by 84% (Kanis et al., 2005a).

Several mechanisms have been postulated to explain the increased fracture risk among smokers. While definitive evidence is lacking, some studies suggest that smoking reduces bone mineral density by decreasing endogenous estrogens in women, decreasing the absorption of vitamin D and calcium, and/or increasing the adrenal secretion of glucocorticoids (Wong, Christie, and Wark, 2007).

Alcohol and Osteoporosis

Kanis and colleagues examined the association of bone fracture and alcohol consumption in a meta-analysis of data from 3 prospective cohort studies involving 5,939 men and 11,032 women. The results revealed a threshold effect of alcohol intake at 3 or more drinks per day (RR = 1.23 for any fracture and RR = 1.68 for hip fracture). Relative risk estimates by gender did not differ significantly. Lesser levels of alcohol intake had no effect on the risk. Adjustment of estimates for bone mineral density (BMD) did not change the magnitude of the estimates. These results suggest that consumption of 3 or more drinks of alcohol daily confers a significant risk increase for bone fracture that is independent of BMD (Kanis et al., 2005b).

Genetics of Osteoporosis

Osteoporosis is a polygenic disorder that is influenced by multiple genes and gene products implicated in bone resorption and bone formation. These basic processes are regulated by complex genetic, hormonal, nutritional, and environmental factors that interact to maintain homeostasis of calcium and other bone minerals and constituents. Family studies suggest that the risk of fracture in close relatives of probands (index cases) is significantly higher than nonrelatives, and twin studies have found higher concordance rates of bone fracture in monozygous twins than dizygous twins (Cooper and Melton, 1992). These findings suggest there may be major genes that modulate the risk. Candidate genes revealed by *genome wide association studies (GWAS)* and linkage analysis are integral to the control of multiple hormones (estrogen, parathyroid hormone, calcitonin, glucocorticoids), minerals (calcium and phosphorous), vitamins (vitamin D), inflammatory factors (interleukin-1, cyclooxygenase-2), and their cell membrane receptors (Rizzoli, Bonjour, and Ferrari, 2001).

Glucocorticoids and Osteoporosis

Glucocorticoid-induced osteoporosis is caused by taking anti-inflammatory steroids such as prednisone, prednisolone, dexamethasone, and cortisone. These compounds are routinely used to treat inflammatory arthritic and rheumatic conditions. Molecular studies suggest that glucocorticoids increase the expression of the receptor activator of *nuclear factor kappa beta ligand (RANKL)* and decrease expression of *osteoprotegerin (OPG)* in osteoblasts which leads to

increased differentiation and activity of osteoclasts. This mechanism and others contribute to increased bone resorption, reduced bone mineral density, and increased risk of osteoporotic fracture.

Van Staa and colleagues evaluated effects of oral corticosteroids on bone mineral density (BMD) and fracture risk by a meta-analysis of published data from 66 reports on bone density and 23 reports on fracture involving 2,891 patients who took glucocorticoids. Strong associations were found between cumulative dose and loss of BMD and between daily dose and fracture risk. The risk of fracture was found to increase within 3–6 months after the initiation of corticosteroid therapy. Risk increases were noted for any fracture (RR = 1.9), hip fracture (RR = 2.01), vertebral fracture (RR = 2.86), and forearm fracture (RR = 1.13). The risk decreased after stopping therapy. Risk estimates were not influenced by underlying disease, age, or gender. The investigators concluded that *"oral corticosteroid treatment using more than 5 mg (of prednisolone or equivalent) daily leads to a reduction in bone mineral density and a rapid increase in the risk of fracture during the treatment period"* (Van Staa, Leufkans, and Cooper, 2002).

Similar results were observed in a study of oral corticosteroid use and the risk of fractures among patients registered in the *General Practice Research Database* of the United Kingdom. The study included 244,235 patients who used oral corticosteroids and 244,235 controls. Patients taking at least 7.5 mg of prednisolone (or equivalent) daily had significantly increased risks of nonvertebral fracture (RR = 1.44), hip fracture (RR = 2.21), and vertebral fracture (RR = 2.83) compared to those taking less than 2.5 mg daily (Van Staa et al., 2000). The findings of these investigations suggest that *"the adverse skeletal effects of oral corticosteroids manifest rapidly"* and mandate that *"preventive measures against corticosteroid-induced osteoporosis should therefore be instituted as soon after the commencement of glucocorticoid therapy as possible"* (Van Staa et al., 2000). Administration of supplemental bisphosphonate plus calcium and vitamin D has been shown effective in counteracting the detrimental effects of glucocorticoids on bone health (Kwok and Tam, 2008).

Physical Activity and Osteoporosis

A team of German investigators conducted a controlled exercise trial in early postmenopausal women with low bone density. Their objective was to determine the impact of a vigorous, combined high-impact, strength, and endurance training program on bone mineral density (BMD) determined by

X-ray absorptiometry (DXA). Participants included 137 osteopenic women (BMD 1.0–2.5 standard deviations below the mean) who were 1–8 years past menopause. Women were assigned to the exercise intervention group (*n* = 86) or the control group (*n* = 51). The intervention was 14 months of exercise training with 2 joint sessions and 2 home training sessions. All women studied received 1,500 mg of calcium and 500 IU of vitamin D daily. After 14 months, BMD at the lumbar spine had *increased* by 1.3% from baseline in the exercise treatment group whereas it had *decreased* by 1.2% in the control group. Though differences at other sites were not statistically significant, BMD levels for women in the exercise group were always higher than in the control group. Muscle strength increased significantly in the treated group but declined in the controls. The investigators concluded that "*high-intensity exercise training can have a positive influence on bone density in early postmenopausal osteopenic women*" (Kemmler et al., 2003).

Several meta-analyses of exercise studies provide confirmation that physical exercise generally has a positive effect on bone mass and bone density; however, there is considerable heterogeneity from study to study in the type, duration, and intensity of exercise regimens used and the target populations treated. Kemmler and colleagues point out several general conclusions extracted from the totality of evidence: *(1) there is a strong relationship between exercise and osteogenic stimulation, (2) the exercise effects are site specific and not systemic, (3) exercises with unusual strain distributions such as aerobics or games, have a higher osteogenic stimulus than more constrained exercises such as walking or running, (4) programs that combine ground and joint reaction forces are superior to programs that apply only a single type of force, (5) physical activity of exercise seems to be more effective in the developing skeletal structure than in the elderly population, and (6) exercise effects on bone density seem to be different in pre- and postmenopausal women* (Kemmler et al., 2003).

Cadmium and Osteoporosis

Occupational or environmental exposure to cadmium is a risk factor for several skeletal and renal disorders including osteoporosis, osteomalacia, renal tubular dysfunction, hypercalciuria, and formation of renal stones. The detrimental effects of cadmium exposure were first observed during the 1950s in residents of the *Jinzu River Basin* in Japan that was heavily contaminated by cadmium discarded from zinc mining. Ingestion of cadmium-contaminated rice resulted in at least 150 cases of *itai-itai* disease, a complex of bone fractures, osteomalacia, osteoporosis, and renal dysfunction diagnosed primarily in elderly women (Hagino and Kono, 1955; Tsuchija, 1969). The cadmium content in the bones of patients with itai-itai disease was later found to be 9 times higher than normal in men and 3 times higher than normal in women (Noda and Kitagawa, 1990).

Investigators in Belgium conducted a prospective investigation designed to assess associations between cadmium exposure, bone mineral density, and the risk of fracture. Cadmium exposure was measured by urinary cadmium excretion in 506 adults (199 men and 306 women) from 10 districts of Belgium, 6 of which bordered on 3 zinc smelters. At baseline, bone density was measured at the forearm by single photon absorptiometry. Median follow-up in the study was 6.6 years. In postmenopausal women, a twofold increase in urinary cadmium was associated with a 0.01 g per cubic centimeter decrease in bone density. High urinary cadmium was associated with an increased risk of fracture in women (RR = 1.73) and height loss in men (RR = 1.60). Cadmium excretion in districts near smelters was 23% higher than in other districts corresponding to a higher rate of fracture (16.0 vs. 10.3 cases per 1,000 person years). The investigators concluded that environmental exposure to cadmium may promote skeletal demineralization, increased bone fragility, and increased risk of bone fractures (Staessen et al., 1999).

In Sweden, investigators at the Karolinska Institute examined the association of cadmium exposure and the risk of osteoporosis among samples of 520 men and 544 women, ages 16–81 years, who were environmentally or occupationally exposed to cadmium. The level of urinary cadmium was used to approximate cadmium exposure and osteoporosis was determined by measuring bone mineral density at the forearm. The results revealed a significant dose response between urinary cadmium level and osteoporosis in men over 60 years of age. The risk increased more than fivefold at the highest level of cadmium and approximately twofold for both men and women at intermediate levels (**Figure 37.6**). Results also revealed a fourfold increase in tubular proteinuria and a threefold decrease in bone mineral density among those individuals with the highest levels of urinary cadmium (Alfven et al., 2000; Alfven, Jarup, and Elinder, 2002).

Cadmium accumulates in bone and may cause damage by interfering with calcium deposition and collagen production or by stimulating inflammatory prostaglandins that heighten bone resorption (Kazantzis, 2004). As Lars Jarup of the Imperial

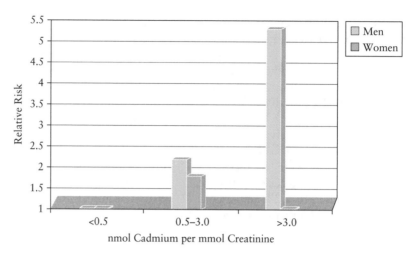

Figure 37.6 Dose Response of Osteoporosis Risk by Level of Urinary Cadmium.

Source: Data from Alfven T, Elinder CG, Carlson MD, Grubb A, Hellstrom L (2000). Low-level cadmium exposure and osteoporosis, *J Bone Mineral Res* 15(8):1579–1586.

College of Medicine in London points out in his review of cadmium overload and toxicity:

> "*As techniques are perfected for detecting smaller amounts of trace elements in various tissues of the body, investigators are finding that the threshold for toxicity of trace elements is much lower than expected. Further research on cadmium is needed to reveal the mechanisms of toxicity and true environmental and occupational exposure limits*" (Jarup, 2002).

Antecedent Disease and Osteoporosis

Multiple chronic diseases and conditions are associated with the development of osteoporosis. Endocrine disorders can lead to abnormal levels of key hormones that accelerate bone remodeling, bone loss, and increase the risk of osteoporotic bone fracture. Examples include *hypogonadal* conditions such as *Turner's syndrome* (*XO genotype*) and *Klinefelter's syndrome* (*XXY genotype*), adrenal disorders (*Cushing's syndrome*), and disorders of the thyroid (*thyrotoxicosis*) and parathyroid glands (*hyperparathyroidism*). Furthermore, there is much current interest in not only the master hormones secreted by target endocrine organs of the hypothalamic-pituitary axes (gonads, adrenals, thyroid and parathyroid glands), but also the effects of releasing factors secreted by the pituitary gland on bone remodeling (Imam et al., 2009).

Patients with arthritic and/or autoimmune conditions are at increased risk due to inherent inflammation and/or treatment with corticosteroids (prednisone). For example, patients with *systemic lupus erythematosus* (*SLE*) have been found to have nearly five times the fracture risk of the general population (Ramsey-Goldman et al., 1999).

Calcium deficiency can arise from malnutrition and/or malabsorption disorders (lactose intolerance, colitis), or by renal nephropathies that reduce calcium reabsorption in the renal tubules. Chronic kidney disease has also been found to reduce the biosynthesis of calcitriol, the active form of vitamin D. In general, any condition that directly or indirectly compromises bone metabolism can lead to loss in bone mineral density and osteoporotic fracture (Martin and Gonzalez, 2007).

PRIMARY PREVENTION OF OSTEOPOROSIS

The risk of osteoporotic fracture can be reduced by making appropriate lifestyle choices. Recommended guidelines include regular daily aerobic exercise (walking, jogging, biking, swimming), sufficient intake of dietary calcium, vitamin D and other nutrients essential for healthy bones, exposure to sunlight (at least 30 minutes daily), avoidance of smoking, restriction of alcohol consumption, and individual strategies to prevent falls. Effective chemopreventive supplements include the combination of calcium and vitamin D. Bisphosphonates are also effective in high risk subjects (USPSTF, 2011).

Screening for Osteoporosis (Secondary Prevention)

The US Preventive Services Task Force recently recommended that all women 65 years of age or older should be screened for osteoporosis by bone densitometry.

Guidelines for screening younger women incorporate the presence of risk factors and specific "*clinical decision rules*" which take into account age, BMI, smoking status, alcohol use, family history, medical history, medication history, and history of previous falls (Hippisley-Cox and Coupland, 2009; USPSTF, 2011).

Tertiary Prevention

In confirmed osteoporosis, *bisphosphonate* drugs are the first line of treatment in women. Other effective drugs that may be prescribed on an individual basis include estrogen replacement therapy (ERT) or selective estrogen receptor modulators (SERM) in women and testosterone in men. Other hormonal abnormalities should also be addressed. Lifestyle changes to modify risk are essential to complement medication. Potential side effects of all prescribed drugs must be carefully considered. For example, ERT heightens the risk of breast cancer and endometrial cancer (USPSTF, 2011; Roush, 2011).

● ● ● REFERENCES

Albright, F., Bloomberg, E., & Smith, P.H. (1940). Postmenopausal osteoporosis. *Trans Assoc Am Physicians*, *55*, 298–305.

Alfven, T., Elinder, C.G., Carlson, M.D., Grubb, A., & Hellstrom, L. (2000). Low-level cadmium exposure and osteoporosis. *J Bone Mineral Res*, *15*(8), 1579–1586.

Alfven, T.L., Jarup, L., & Elinder, C.G. (2002). Cadmium and lead in blood in relation to low bone mineral density and tubular proteinuria. *Environ Health Perspect*, *110*, 699–702.

Bischoff-Ferrari, H.A., Willett, W.C., Wong, J.B., Giovannucci, E., Dietrich, T., & Dawson-Hughes, B. (2005). Fracture prevention with vitamin D supplementation: A meta-analysis of randomized controlled trials. *JAMA*, *293*, 2257–2264.

Boonen, S., Lips, P., Bouillon, R., Bischoff-Ferrari, H.A., Vanderschueren, D., & Haentjens, P. (2007). Need for additional calcium to reduce the risk of hip fracture with vitamin D supplementation: Evidence from a comparative meta-analysis of randomized controlled trials. *J Clin Endocrinol Metab*, *92*, 1415–1423.

Consensus Development Conference. (1991). Prophylaxis and treatment of osteoporosis. *Osteoporosis Int*, *1*, 114–117.

Cooper, A., & Cooper, B.B. (1822). *A treatise on dislocations, and on fractures of the joints*. London, United Kingdom: Churchill.

Cooper, C., & Melton, L.J. (1992). Epidemiology of osteoporosis. *Trends Endocrinol Metab*, *3*, 224–229.

Cummings, S.R., Browner, W.S., Bauer, D., Stone, K., Ensrud, K., & Ettinger, B. (1998). *Endogenous hormones and the risk of hip and vertebral fractures among older women*. N Engl J Med, 339, 733–738.

DIPART Group. (2010). *Patient level pooled analysis of 68,500 patients from seven major vitamin D fracture trials in US and Europe*. BMJ, 340, b5463.

De Laet, C., Kanis, J.A., Odén, A., Johanson, H., Johnell, O., Delmas, P.,…Tenenhouse, A. (2005). Body mass index as a predictor of fracture risk: A meta-analysis. *Osteoporos Int*, *16*(11), 1330–1338.

Feskanich, D., Willett, W.C., Stampfer, M.J., & Colditz, G.A. (1997). Milk, dietary calcium and bone fractures in women: A 12-year prospective study. *Amer J Public Health*, *87*, 992–997.

Finch, S., Doyle, W., & Lowe, C. (1998). *National diet and nutrition survey: People aged 65 years and over. Vol 1: Report of the diet and nutrition survey*. London: The Stationery Office.

Gennari, C. (2001). Calcium and vitamin D nutrition and bone disease of the elderly. *Public Health Nutr*, *4*(2B), 547–559.

Goldacre, M.J., Roberts, S.E., & Yeates, D. (2002). Mortality after admission to hospital with fractured neck of femur: Database study. *BMJ*, *325*, 868–869.

Grant, A.M., Avenell, A., Campbell, M.K., McDonald, A.M., MacLennan, G.S., McPherson, G.C.,…Wallace, W.A.; RECORD Trial Group. (2005). Oral vitamin D3 and calcium for secondary prevention of low-trauma fractures in elderly people (*Randomised Evaluation of Calcium Or vitamin D, RECORD*): A randomized placebo-controlled trial. *Lancet*, *365*(9471), 1621–1628.

Gregory, J.R., Collins, D.L., Davies, P.S.W., Hughes, J.M., & Clarke, P.C. (1995). *National diet and nutrition survey: Children aged 1.5 to 4.5 years.* London: HMSO.

Gregory, J., Lowe, C., & Bates, C. (2000). *National diet and nutrition survey: young people aged 4 to 18 years.* (Vol. 1). *Report of the diet and nutrition survey.* London: The Stationery Office.

Hagino, N., & Kono, M. (1955). A study on the cause of itai-itai disease. *Proceedings of the 17th Meeting of the Japanese Society of Clinical Surgeons.*

Hannan, E.L., Magaziner, J., Wang, J.J., Eastwood, E.A., Silberzweig, S.B., Gilbert, M.,… Siu, A.L. (2005). Mortality and locomotion 6 months after hospitalization for hip fracture. *JAMA, 285*(21), 2793–2794.

Hess, A.F., & Unger, L.J. (1921). The cure of infantile rickets by artificial light and by sunlight. *Proc Soc Exp Biol Med, 18,* 298.

Hess, A.F., & Weinstock, M. (1925). A further report on imparting antirachitic properties to inert substances by ultra-violet irradiation. *J Biol Chem, 63,* 297–307.

Hippisley-Cox, J., & Coupland, C. (2009). Predicting risk of osteoporotic fracture in men and women in England and Wales: prospective derivation and validation of Qfracture scores. *BMJ, 339,* b4229.

Holbrook, T.L., Barrett-Connor, E., & Wingard, D.L. (1988). Dietary calcium and risk of hip fracture: 14-year prospective population study. *Lancet, 332*(8619), 1046–1049.

Holick, M.F., Schnoes, H.K., DeLuca, H.F., Suda, T., & Cousins, R.J. (1971). Isolation and identification of 1,25-dihydroxy-cholecalciferol. A metabolite of vitamin D active in intestine. *Biochemistry, 10*(14), 2799–2804.

Holick, M.F., Schnoes, H.K., & DeLuca, H.F. (1971). Identification of 1,25-dihydroxycholecalciferol, a form of vitamin D3 metabolically active in the intestine. *Proc Natl Acad Sci USA, 68*(4), 803–804.

Holick, M.F. (2007). Vitamin D deficiency. *N Engl J Med, 357,* 266–281.

Howanitz, J.H., & Howanitz, P.J. (1984). Evaluation of endocinre function. In J.B. Henry (Ed.), *Todd, Sanford & Davidsohn clinical diagnosis and management by laboratory methods* (17th ed., pp. 299–345). Philadelphia: WB Saunders Company.

Hume, E.M., & Smith, H.H. (1924). The effect of irradiation of the environment with ultra-violet light upon the growth and calcification of rats, fed on a diet deficient in fat-soluble vitamins: The part played by irradiated sawdust. *Biochem J, 18,* 1334–1345.

Imam, A., Iqbal, J., Blair, H.C., Davies, T.F., Huang, C.L., Zallone, A., Zaidi, M., & Sun, L. (2009). Role of the pituitary-bone axis in skeletal pathophysiology. *Curr Opin Endocrinol Diabetes Obes, 16*(6), 423–429.

Institute of Medicine. (1997). Standing Committee on the Scientific Evaluation of Dietary Reference Intakes, Food and Nutrition Board, Institute of Medicine. *Vitamin D. Dietary reference intakes for calcium, magnesium, phosphorus, vitamin D, and fluoride.* Washington, DC: National Academy Press.

Institute of Medicine. (2010). *Dietary reference intakes for vitamin D and calcium.* US National Academy of Sciences.

Jackson, J.A., Riggs, M.W., & Spiekerman, A.M. (1992). Testosterone deficiency as a risk factor for hip fractures in men: A case-control study. *Am J Med Sci, 304*(1), 4–8.

Jackson, R.D., LaCroix, A.Z., Gass, M., Wallace, R.B., Robbins, J., Lewis, C.E.,… Barad, D.; Women's Health Initiative Investigators. (2006). Calcium plus vitamin D supplementation and the risk of fractures. *N Engl J Med, 16, 354*(7), 669–683.

Jarup, L. (2002). Cadmium overload and toxicity. *Nephrol Dial Transplant, 17*(Suppl 2), 35–39.

Johnnell, O., & Kanis, J.A. (2006). An estimate of the worldwide prevalence and disability associated with osteoporotic fractures. *Osteoporos Int, 17,* 1726–1733.

Jordan, K.M., & Cooper, C. (2002). Epidemiology of osteoporosis. *Best Practice & Research Clinical Rheumatology, 16*(5), 795–806.

Kanis, J.A., Oden, A., Johnell, O., Jonsson, B., De Laet, C., & Dawson, A. (2000). The burden of osteoporotic fractures: A method for setting intervention thresholds. *Osteoporos Int, 12,* 417–427.

Kanis, J., Johnell, O., Oden, A., Johansson, H., De Laet, C., Eisman, J.A.,...Tenenhouse, A. (2005a). Smoking and fracture risk: A meta-analysis. *Osteoporos Int, 16,* 155–162.

Kanis, J.A., Johansson, H., Johnell, O., Oden, A., De Laet, C., Eisman, J.A.,...Tenenhouse, A. (2005b). Alcohol intake as a risk factor for fracture. *Osteoporos Int, 16*(7), 737–742.

Katznelson, L., Finkelstein, J.S., Schoenfeld, D.A., Rosenthal, D.I., Anderson, E.J., & Klibanski, A. (1996). Increase in bone density and lean body mass during testosterone administration in men with acquired hypogonadism. *The Journal of Clinical Endocrinology, & Metabolism, 81*(12), 4358–4365.

Kazantzis, G. (2004). Cadmium, osteoporosis and calcium metabolism. *Biometals, 17*(5), 493–498.

Kemmler, W., Engelke, K., Weineck, J., Hensen, J., & Kalender, W.A. (2003). The Erlangen Fitness Osteoporosis Prevention Study: A controlled exercise trial in early postmenopausal women with low bone density—First-year results. *Arch Phys Med Rehabil, 84,* 673–682.

Kwok, L.W., & Tam, L.S. (2008). Recent advances in the management of steroid induced osteoporosis. *Hong Kong Bull Rheum Dis, 8,* 12–18.

Law, M.R., & Hackshaw, A.K. (1997). A meta-analysis of cigarette smoking, bone mineral density and risk of hip fracture: Recognition of a major effect. *Br Med J, 315,* 841–846.

Lawson, D.E., Fraser, D.R., Kodicek, E., Morris, H.R., & Williams, D.H. (1971). Identification of 1,25-dihydroxycholecalciferol, a new kidney hormone controlling calcium metabolism. *Nature, 230*(5291), 228–230.

Lobstein, J.G.C.F.M. (1835). *Lehrbuch der pathologischen Anatomie.* Stuttgart: Bd II.

Looker, A.C., Dawson-Hughes, B., Calvo, M.S., Gunter, E.W., & Sahyoun, N.R. (2002). Serum 25-hydroxyvitamin D status of adolescents and adults in two seasonal sub-populations from NHANES III. *Bone, 30,* 771–777.

Marshall, D., Johnell, O., & Wedel, H. (1996). Meta-analysis of how well measures of bone density predict occurrence of osteoporotic fractures. *British Medical Journal, 312,* 1254–1259.

Martin, K.J., & Gonzalez, E.A. (2007). Metabolic bone disease in chronic kidney disease. *J Am Soc Nephrol, 18,* 875–885.

McCollum, E.V., & Davis, M. (1914). Observations on the isolation of the substance in butter fat which exerts a stimulating effect on growth. *J Biol Chem, 19,* 245–250.

McCollum, E.V., Simmonds, N., Becker, J.E., & Shipley, P.G. (1922). Studies on experimental rickets. XXI. An experimental demonstration of the existence of a vitamin which promotes calcium deposition. *J Biol Chem, 53,* 293–312.

Melton, L.J., Therneau, T.M., & Larson, D.R. (1998). Long-Term trends in hip fracture prevalence: The influence of hip fracture incidence and survival. *Osteoporos Int, 8,* 68–74.

Melton, L., Kearns, A., Atkinson, E., Bolander, M., Achenbach, S., Huddleston, J., Therneau, T., et al. (2009). Secular trends in hip fracture incidence and recurrence. *Osteoporosis Int, 20*(5), 687–694.

Meyer, H.E., Henriksen, C., Falch, J.A., Pedersen, J.I., & Tverdal, A. (1995). Risk factors for hip fracture in a high incidence area: A case-control study from Oslo, Norway. *Osteoporos Int, 5*(4), 239–246.

Nelson, H.D. (2002). Hormone replacement therapy and osteoporosis. *Systematic evidence review, 12,*

(p. 43). Washington, DC: Agency for Healthcare Research and Quality, US Department of Health and Human Services.

Noda, M., & Kitagawa, M. (1990). A quantitative study of iliac bone histopathology in 62 cases with itai-itai disease. *Cacif Tissue Int, 47,* 66–74.

Norman, A.W. (2008). From vitamin D to hormone D: Fundamentals of the vitamin D endocrine system essential for good health. *American Journal of Clinical Nutrition, 88*(2), 4915–4995.

Papadimitropoulos, E., Wells, G., Shea, B., Gillespie, W., Weaver, B., Zytaruk, N.,...Guyatt, G. (2002). Meta-analysis of the efficacy of vitamin D treatment in preventing osteoporosis in postmenopausal women. *Endocrine Reviews, 23*(4), 560–569.

Prentice, A., Schoenmakers, I., Laskey, M.A., De Bono, S., Ginty, F., & Goldberg, G.R. (2006). Nutrition and bone growth and development. *Proc Nutr Soc, 65,* 348–360.

Prentice, A. (2008). Vitamin D deficiency: a global perspective. *Nutr Rev, 66*(10 Suppl 2), S153–S164.

Raisz, L.G. (2005). Pathogenesis of osteoporosis: Concepts, conflicts, and prospects. *J Clin Invest, 115*(12), 3318–3325.

Ramsey-Goldman, R., Dunn, J.E., Huang, C.F., Dunlop, D., Rairie, J.E., Fitzgerald, S., & Manzi, S. (1999). Frequency of fractures in women with systemic lupus erythematosus: Comparison with United States population data. *Arthritis Rheum, 42*(5), 882–890.

Ranstam, J., & Kanis, J.A. (1995). Influence of age and body mass on the effects of vitamin D on hip fracture risk. *Osteoporos Int, 5*(6), 450–454.

Ray, D., Goswami, R., Gupta, N., Tomar, N., Singh, N., & Sreenivas, V. (2009). Predisposition to vitamin D deficiency osteomalacia and rickets in females is linked to their 25(OH)D and calcium intake rather than vitamin D receptor gene polymorphism. *Clinical Endocrinology, 71*(3), 334–340.

Rizzoli, R., Bonjour, J.P., & Ferrari, S.L. (2001). Osteoporosis, genetics and hormones. *Journal of Molecular Endocrinology, 26,* 79–94.

Robbins, S.L., & Cotran, R.S. (1979). *Pathologic basis of disease.* Philadelphia: W.B. Saunders Company.

Rosenheim, O., & Webster, T.A. (1926). Further observations on the photo-chemical formation of vitamin D. *J Soc Chem Ind, 45,* 932.

Roush, K. (2011). Prevention and treatment of osteoporosis in postmenopausal women: A review. *Am J Nurs, 111*(8), 26–35.

Ruston, D., Hoare, L., & Gregory, J. (2003). *The national diet and nutrition survey: Adults aged 19 to 64 years. (vol. 4). Nutritional status (anthropometry and blood analytes), blood pressure and physical activity.* London: The Stationery Office.

Scrimshaw, N.S. (1986). Nutrition and preventive medicine. In: J.M. Last (Ed.). *Maxcy-Rosenau public health and preventive medicine* (12th ed., pp. 1515–1542). Norwalk, Connecticut: Appleton-Century-Croft.

Shea, B., Wells, G., Cranney, A., Zytaruk, N., Robinson, V., Griffith, L.,...Guyatt, G. (2002). Meta-analysis of calcium supplementation for the prevention of postmenopausal osteoporosis. *Endocrine Reviews, 23*(4), 552–559.

Staessen, J., Roels, H., Emelianov, D., Kuznetsova, T., Thijs, L., Vangronsveld, J., & Fagard, R. (1999). Environmental exposure to cadmium, forearm bone density, and risk of fractures: Prospective population study. Public Health and Environmental Exposure to Cadmium (PheeCad) Study Group. *Lancet, 353*(9159), 1140–1144.

Steenbock, H., & Black, A. (1924). Fat-soluble vitamins: The induction of growth-promoting and calcifying properties in a ration by exposure to ultraviolet light. *Journal of Biological Chemistry, 62,* 405–422.

Steenbock, H. (1924). The induction of growth promoting and calcifying properties in a ration by exposure to light. *Science, 60,* 224–225.

Thacher, T.D., Fischer, P.R., Pettifor, J.M., Lawson, J.O., Isichei, C.O., Reading, J.C., & Chan, G.M. (1999). A comparison of calcium, vitamin D, or both for nutritional rickets in Nigerian children. *N Engl J Med, 341,* 563–568.

Tracz, M.J., Sideras, K., Boloña, E.R., Haddad, R.M., Kennedy, C.C., Uraga, M.V.,…Montoir, V.M. (2006). Testosterone use in men and its effects on bone health. A systematic review and meta-analysis of randomized placebo-controlled trials. *The Journal of Clinical Endocrinology, & Metabolism, 91*(6), 2011–2016.

Tsuchija, K. (1969). Causation of ouch-ouch disease (Itai-itai byo): An introduction review. Part 1, nature of disease. *Keio J Med, 18,* 181–194.

US Preventive Services Task Force. (2011). Screening for osteoporosis: U.S. preventive services task force recommendation statement. *Annals of Internal Medicine, 154*(5), 356–364.

Van Staa, T.P., Leufkens, H.G., Abenhaim, L., Zhang, B., & Cooper, C. (2000). Use of oral corticosteroids and risk of fractures. *J Bone Mineral Res, 15,* 993–1000.

Van Staa, T.P., Leufkens, H.G., & Cooper, C. (2002). The epidemiology of corticosteroid induced osteoporosis: A meta-analysis. *Osteoporos Int, 13,* 777–787.

Vitale, J.J. (1979). Nutritional disease. In S.L. Robbins and R.S. Cotran (Eds.) *Pathologic basis of disease* (2nd ed., pp. 483–520). Philadelphia: WB Saunders Company.

von Friesendorff, M., Besjakov, J., & Akesson, K. (2008). Long-term survival and fracture risk after hip fracture: A 22-year follow-up in women. *J Bone Mineral Res, 23*(11), 1832–1841.

Ward, K.D., & Klesges, R.C. (2001). A meta-analysis of the effects of cigarette smoking on bone mineral density. *Calcif Tissue Int, 68,* 259–270.

WHO. (1994). *Assessment of fracture risk and its application to screening for postmenopausal women.* Geneva, Switzerland: World Health Organization.

Windaus, A., & Hess, A. (1926). Sterine und antirachitisches Vitamin. Nachrichten von der Gesellschaft der Wissenschaften zu Göttingen, 175–184.

Windaus, A. (1931). The chemistry of irradiated ergosterol. *Proc R Soc (Lond), 108,* 568–575.

Wolf, G. (2004). The discovery of vitamin D: The contribution of Adolf Windaus. *Nutr, 134,* 1299–1302.

Wong, P.K.K., Christie, J.J., & Wark, J.D. (2007). The effects of smoking on bone health. *Clinical Science, 113,* 233–241.

CHAPTER

38

Epidemiology of Arthritis

INTRODUCTION

Arthritis is an inflammatory disease of one or more synovial joints of the skeletal system. Synovial joints facilitate motion (flexion, extension, rotation, abduction) and are divisible into ball and socket joints (shoulder and hip), hinge joints (elbow and knee), pivot joints (atlas and axis), condyloid joints (wrist), saddle joints (thumb), and gliding joints (fingers). Arthritis has multiple forms and several classification systems have been proposed based upon etiology, the joints involved, and other symptoms. This chapter focuses on the three major forms of arthritis: osteoarthritis (degenerative joint disease), rheumatoid arthritis (an autoimmune disorder), and gout (due to uric acid crystals). Other forms that are briefly covered include ankylosing spondylitis, juvenile arthritis, and suppurative arthritis (due to infection). The approximate distribution of incident cases of these forms of arthritis in the adult US population is shown in **Table 38.1**.

Table 38.1	Forms of Arthritis
Type	**Relative Frequency (%)**
Osteoarthritis	80%
Rheumatoid Arthritis	10%
Gouty Arthritis	5%
Ankylosing Spondylitis	2%
Juvenile Arthritis	1%
Suppurative Arthritis	1%
Other Variants	1%

Source: CDC (2011). Arthritis. Centers for Disease Prevention and Control, Atlanta, Georgia, 2011.

SYNOVIAL JOINTS

As pointed out by Robbins and Cotran in their discussion of diseases of the musculoskeletal system: *"the joints are ideally structured to serve their function as the hinges of the skeletal system."* Bones are firmly connected at the joint capsule by ligaments, tendons, and muscles. Within the joint space, three primary components, *articular cartilage, synovial membranes, and synovial fluid*, interact to provide a smooth gliding surface for joint flexion/rotation/extension and weight-bearing throughout the lifespan (Robbins and Cotran, 1979). **Figure 38.1** depicts the cellular components of a typical synovial joint.

Again quoting Robbins and Cotran: *"the articular cartilage is a unique connective tissue which serves as an elastic shock absorber and wear-resistant, weight-bearing surface."* Cartilage is devoid of nerves, lymphatics, and blood vessels, and does not normally undergo cell division. However, chondrocytes are present that sustain the continual turnover of cartilage by actively synthesizing its two essential components, collagen and proteoglycans (Robbins and Cotran, 1979).

The *synovial membranes* line the joint capsule. These membranes consist of a single layer of phagocytic cells and secretory cells. The phagocytes guard the joint capsule against infection while the secretory cells actively produce and secrete *synovial fluid* into the joint space. Synovial fluid is a remarkably viscous substance that helps facilitate flexion of all joints as well as rotation of certain complex joints. Under normal conditions, the synovial fluid is sterile and does not contain lymphoctyes or other immune cells. However, in arthritic conditions, the synovial fluid is often infiltrated by lymphocytes and other immune cells in association with chronic inflammation.

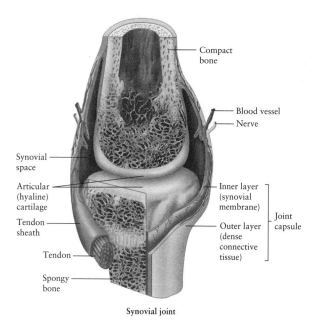

Figure 38.1 Normal Synovial Joint.

PATHOGENESIS OF ARTHRITIS

Regardless of etiology, the sine qua non of arthritis is inflammatory involvement of one or more synovial joints. At the molecular level, proinflammatory cytokines and mediators such as interleukin-1, tumor necrosis factor alpha, prostaglandins, leukotrienes, and nitric oxide interact to promote chronic inflammation and damage to the articular cartilage and other tissues of the joint capsule. Taking osteoarthritis as a prime example, the cumulative effects of mechanical stress and strain over many years eventually induce constitutive upregulation of key enzymes (cyclooxygenase, lipoxygenase, arginase, nitric oxide synthetase) and proinflammatory mediators (prostaglandins, leukotrienes, nitric oxide) conducive to chronic inflammation and arthritis in tissues of the joint capsule (Weinberg, Fermor, and Guilak, 2007).

OSTEOARTHRITIS (DEGENERATIVE JOINT DISEASE)

The most common form of arthritis is *osteoarthritis*. This form is a slowly progressive disorder that typically manifests late in life. The condition principally afflicts the weight-bearing joints and is characterized clinically by pain, inflammation, deformity, and limitation of motion. Radiographic studies of afflicted joints reveal the presence of focal erosive lesions, cartilage destruction, subchrondral sclerosis,

cyst formation, and large osteophytes (bone spurs) at the joint margins (Mankin, 1974).

Osteoarthritis is often attributed to the *"wear and tear of aging"* and is thus referred to as *degenerative joint disease*. According to one theory of pathogenesis, weight-bearing joints or joints subjected to sustained repetitive trauma undergo focal cartilaginous erosion and osteolytic changes that over time extend and produce widespread damage to the articular cartilage. Such damage heightens friction and resistance to motion in the joint thereby inducing chronic inflammation which exacerbates the progression of disease. There is also a marked increase in the rate of collagen synthesis in arthritic joints compared to nonarthritic joints. However, newly formed cartilage is more prone to injury and damage, which also favors disease progression. Some investigators therefore suggest that the pathogenesis of osteoarthritis is best defined as a failure of repair processes to keep pace with joint damage from chronic excessive mechanical stress (Brandt, Dieppe, and Radin, 2009).

DIAGNOSIS OF OSTEOARTHRITIS

The most widely using classification schemes for osteoarthritis are based on the radiological appearance of the joint. The radiological hallmarks are joint space narrowing, sclerosis, and formation of bone spurs and cysts. Severity is graded based on a 0–4 scale (Kellgren and Lawrence, 1958: Kellgren, 1962). Based solely on radiographic findings, osteoarthritis is classified as: 0–absent, 1–doubtful, 2–minimal, 3–moderate, and 4–severe. Joints of the hips, knees, spine, thumbs, and fingers are most often affected by osteoarthritis.

INCIDENCE AND PREVALENCE OF OSTEOARTHRITIS

Osteoarthritis is clearly a disease of the aging process. As shown in **Figure 38.2**, age-specific annual *incidence rates* estimated for American men and women increase exponentially from middle age and peak after 70 years of age (Oliveria et al., 1995).

Age-specific annual *prevalence rates* of osteoarthritis of the knee estimated from surveys of European men and women are shown in **Figure 38.3**. Remarkably, after 80 years of age, the annual rates exceed 32,000 per 100,000 in women and approach 20,000 per 100,000 in men. It is notable that the age-specific prevalence rates of knee osteoarthritis for women exceed corresponding rates for men by

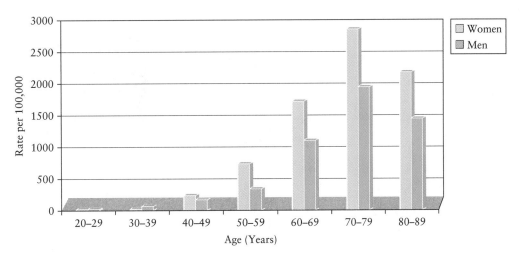

Figure 38.2 Age-Specifc Incidence of Osteoarthritis.

Source: Data from Oliveria SA, Felson DT, Reed JI, Cirillo PA, Walker AM (1995). Incidence of symptomatic hand, hip, and knee osteoarthritis among patients in a health maintenance organization. *Arthritis & Rheumatism* 38(8):1134–1141.

50–60% after about 55 years of age. In contrast to the striking gender difference in the prevalence of *knee osteoarthritis*, the corresponding prevalence rates of *hip osteoarthritis* are only slightly higher in women compared to men (Symmons, Mathers, and Pfleger, 2006a). Surveys of US adults have yielded similar findings. Based on prevalence data from the Third National Health and Nutrition Examination Survey (NHANES III), among adults over 60 years of age, 42% of women had *knee osteoarthritis* compared to 31% of men, whereas the prevalence of *hip osteoarthritis* in women barely exceeded that in men (27% vs. 26%) (Lawrence et al., 2008).

DISABILITY IN OSTEOARTHRITIS

While osteoarthritis per se is not a life-threatening disease, it is the leading cause of disability in many populations of the world, particularly those with greater longevity. Worldwide, osteoarthritis was responsible for approximately 14.3 million years of life lost due to disability (YLD) in 2000, which is approximately 3% of the total disability. The global annual rate of YLD in women (2.9 per 1,000) is about 60% higher than the rate in men (1.8 per 1,000) (Symmons, Mathers, and Pfleger, 2006a).

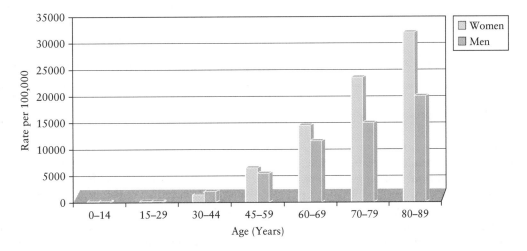

Figure 38.3 Age-Specific Prevalence of Osteoarthritis of the Knee.

Source: Data from Symmons D, Mathers C, Pfleger B (2006). Global burden of osteoarthritis in the year 2000. In Global Burden of Disease 2000. World Health Organization, Geneva, Switzerland.

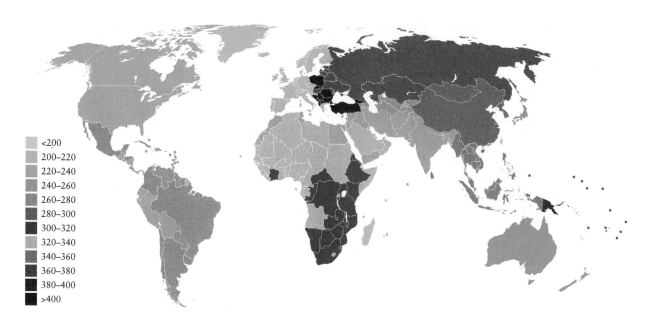

Figure 38.4 Disability Adjusted Life Years (DALY): Osteoarthritis, 2004.

Source: Data from World Health Organization. The global burden of disease: 2004 update. Geneva, WHO, 2008. Available at www.who.int /evidence/bod.

The global pattern of *disability adjusted life years (DALY)* due to osteoarthritis is shown in **Figure 38.4**. Recall that *DALY = YLL + YLD* where *YLL = years of life lost due to premature death* and *YLD = years of life lost due to disability*. The DALY for osteoarthritis primarily reflect years of life lost from disability (YLD) rather than years of life lost from premature death (YLL) since very few deaths are attributed to osteoarthritis. The highest rates are evident in populations without access to adequate treatment such as Russia, China, and sub-Saharan Africa (WHO, 2009).

TIME TRENDS IN OSTEOARTHRITIS PREVALENCE

Since the incidence and prevalence rates of osteoarthritis increase dramatically with age, the extended life expectancy of many populations around the globe will undoubtedly result in greater numbers of patients with this condition. But an even more disturbing relationship that will undoubtedly amplify the global burden of osteoarthritis is its etiologic link with obesity. Indeed, the number of afflicted adults in the United States population increased nearly 30% during 1995–2005 (27 million in 2005 vs. 21 million in 1995) concurrent with the obesity epidemic that has plagued the nation (Lawrence et al., 2008). Since

osteoarthritis is an irreversible, progressive, and often disabling condition, this trend is expected to produce a corresponding increase in the years of productive life lost to disability.

Based upon a recent analysis of the National Health Interview Survey (NHIS) for 2007–2009, 49.9 million U.S. adults currently have *self-reported physician-diagnosed arthritis* (osteoarthritis, rheumatoid arthritis, gout, lupus, or fibromyalgia) and 21.1 million have *arthritis-attributable activity limitation*. Results suggest that the number of cases is increasing by nearly 1 million per year in the U.S. population and that the prevalence is highest among obese individuals (33.8% in obese women 25.2% in obese men) (Cheng et al., 2010; CDC, 2011).

RISK FACTORS FOR OSTEOARTHRITIS

Aside from aging, the major risk factors for the development of osteoarthritis include being female (after age 55 years), being overweight or obese, and previous major trauma or sustained repetitive trauma to specific joints. Positive family history also appears to increase the risk. As discussed in the following paragraphs, there is some evidence suggesting an etiologic link between diabetes and osteoarthritis, and a possible *protective* effect of smoking; however, the current evidence supporting these associations is equivocal.

Obesity and Osteoarthritis

In an analysis of cross sectional data from the first United States National Health and Nutrition Examination Survey of 1971–1975 (NHANES I), Jennifer Anderson and David Felson examined associations of a variety of putative risk factors with osteoarthritis of the knee. A total of 5,193 adults, aged 35–74 years, 315 of whom had osteoarthritis of the knee diagnosed by radiography contributed data for analysis. After controlling for confounders, the investigators found a significant dose response in the risk of knee osteoarthritis with increasing body mass in both men and women (**Figure 38.5**). The risk increased more than fourfold among obese men (OR = 4.78) and more than sevenfold among women with gravid obesity (OR = 7.37). Results also revealed an increase in the risk associated with occupational knee bending demands (OR = 2.45) and an excess of osteoarthritis among African American women (OR = 2.12). Based on these findings, the authors suggested that obesity is a causative factor in the genesis of osteoarthritis of the knee (Anderson and Felson, 1988).

Maradee Davis and colleagues also used the NHANES I data to examine the association of obesity and osteoarthritis of the knee. They compared 75 subjects with *unilateral* osteoarthritis and 226 subjects with *bilateral* disease to 3,584 normal subjects. Radiologic studies of each subject were used to define the presence of osteoarthritis (grades 2–4). Obesity was defined as body mass index (BMI) of 30 or higher. Results revealed that obesity increased the risk of *bilateral* knee osteoarthritis (adjusted OR = 7.92) and to a lesser extent, *unilateral* knee osteoarthritis (adjusted OR = 3.45). Controlling for age, gender, serum cholesterol, serum uric acid, body fat distribution, bone density, and blood pressure did not diminish these effects, suggesting a lack of influence of these factors in modulating the osteoarthritis risk attributable to obesity (Davis, Ettinger, and Neuhaus, 1990).

In additional studies of the NHANES I database, Davis and colleagues found associations between obesity and osteoarthritis of joints of the hands and feet, and they also determined that prior knee injury was a strong independent risk factor for unilateral osteoarthritis (OR = 16.3 and OR = 10.9 for injury to the right and left knee, respectively). However, they *did not* find significant differences between men and women in the strength of the associations of obesity with osteoarthritis. As a consequence, they suggest the need to examine other factors such as reproductive history, endogenous estrogens, and anthropometric measures in order to identify factors that heighten the osteoarthritis risk in women compared to men (Davis et al., 1988, 1989, 1990).

Trauma and Osteoarthritis

Blagojevic and colleagues conducted an extensive review and meta-analysis of studies of risk factors for osteoarthritis of the knee in older adults. Of 2,233 published studies screened, 85 were selected for inclusion in the analysis based on quality and inclusion of risk estimates with confidence intervals. Data were

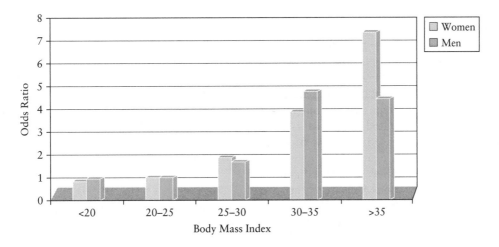

Figure 38.5 Risk of Knee Osteoarthritis With Increasing Body Mass.

Source: Data from Anderson JJ, Felson DT (1988). Factors associated with osteoarthritis of the knee in the first National Health and Nutrition Examination Survey (HANES I). Evidence for an association with overweight, race, and physical demands of work. *Amer J Epidemiol* 128(1):179–189.

abstracted from 42 cohort studies and 43 case control studies. The results revealed that previous knee trauma (pooled OR = 3.86), obesity (pooled OR = 2.63), presence of Heberden's nodes (pooled OR = 1.49), and female gender (pooled OR = 1.84) were the strongest risk factors. Some studies also found evidence of increased risk with regular strenuous exercise, history of high physical workload, certain repetitive physical activities (kneeling and squatting), and increased bone mineral density. Smoking was examined in 18 studies (8 case control studies and 10 cohort studies) and the combined data across all studies suggested a small protective effect (pooled OR = 0.84). However, the risk reduction was only evident in case control studies (OR = 0.60) and not cohort studies (OR = 0.97). The authors suggest that easily identifiable risk factors such as obesity, knee injury, and nodal hand osteoarthritis can be targeted for prevention of disabling knee osteoarthritis (Blagojevic et al., 2010).

Type 2 Diabetes Mellitus and Osteoarthritis

Wain and colleagues initially suggested a relationship between diabetes and osteoarthritis based upon a small study of 30 patients with diabetes and 30 matched controls (Waine, Nevinny, and Rosenthal, 1961). Subsequent studies have been conducted to examine the relationship, some finding significant associations and others not.

Engstrom and colleagues recently examined a Swedish cohort of 5,171 elderly adults to quantify associations between lifestyle habits, body mass, blood pressure, HDL-cholesterol, triglycerides, glucose, and C-reactive protein (CRP), and the risk of developing osteoarthritis. Baseline data were collected during 1991–1994. A total of 120 subjects developed severe hip osteoarthritis and 89 developed knee osteoarthritis during 12 years of follow-up. The presence of the *metabolic syndrome* (disease complex of type 2 diabetes, obesity, and high blood pressure) significantly increased the risk of knee osteoarthritis (RR = 2.1) but the risk was attenuated by adjustment for obesity (RR = 1.1). Elevated CRP was associated with a significant increase in the risk of knee osteoarthritis in women, but again, adjustment for other factors attenuated the effect. The investigators concluded that these associations were largely attributable to confounding (Engstrom et al., 2008).

Francis Berenbaum of the Pierre and Marie Curie University in Paris recently reviewed the observational and experimental evidence supporting an association between diabetes and the development of osteoarthritis. Based upon a *"positive signal"* from the available data, Dr. Berenbaum proposes a general paradigm whereby *advanced glycosylation end products (AGEs)* and *reactive oxygen species (ROS)* in patients with hyperglycemia incite chondrocyte and synovial reactivity leading to osteoarthritis (Berenbaum, 2010). Nevertheless, it is important to note that obesity is a major risk factor for both diabetes and osteoarthritis, and meaningful estimates of independent effects of hyperglycemia must therefore be carefully adjusted for measures of body mass. Clearly, additional studies are needed to clarify whether there is an etiologic link between hyperglycemia and the development of osteoarthritis.

Genetics of Osteoarthritis

Involvement of the distal interphalangeal joints of the fingers in osteoarthritis is often marked by the presence of distinct sclerotic nodules called *Heberden's nodes*. These nodes are more likely to develop in females with osteoarthritis than males; and furthermore, early studies of familial osteoarthritis suggested that genetic factors may predispose to their development (Stecher, 1941; Lawrence and Moore, 1952; Kellgren, Lawrence, and Bier, 1963). Additional evidence supporting a role for genetic factors in the development of osteoarthritis came from a study of twins which revealed that the concordance for nodal osteoarthritis in monozygous twins was approximately double that in dizygous twins (Lawrence, 1977).

Other studies have linked Heberden's nodes in osteoarthritis to specific haplotypes of the *human leukocyte antigen (HLA)* system (Ercilla et al., 1977; Pattrick et al., 1989), and studies of afflicted twins and siblings have revealed a number of genetic polymorphisms and point mutations associated with defective collagen biosynthesis and repair that may predispose to the development of osteoarthritis (Williams and Jimenez, 1995). In addition, as pointed out by Holderman and colleagues in their review of the genetics of osteoarthritis, *"mutations in genes coding for cartilage components other than collagen, or for control factors such as enzymes, inhibitors, and signal transduction mediators may lead to similar clinical end points"* (Holderbaum, Haqqi, and Moskowitz, 1999).

Smoking and Osteoarthritis

To determine if smoking is protective against the development of osteoarthritis, Hui and colleagues conducted a review of the literature and meta-analysis of published observational studies with relevant data. They identified 48 studies involving 537,730 subjects for analysis: 8 cohort studies, 21 cross sectional studies, and 19 case control studies.

Overall, results revealed a small protective effect of smoking (OR = 0.87). However, the effect was stronger in hospital-based case control studies (OR = 0.65) than community-based case control studies (OR = 0.90), cohort studies (OR = 0.92) or cross sectional studies (OR = 0.89). The investigators suggest that the observed protective effect of smoking in hospital-based case control studies may be due to selection bias of hospital controls with smoking-related conditions (Hui, Doherty, and Zhang, 2011).

PREVENTION OF OSTEOARTHRITIS

Major global efforts have been initiated to reduce the burden of osteoarthritis and other forms of arthritis. Programs include the *US National Arthritis Plan*, the *European League Against Rheumatism* (EULAR), and the *International League of Associations for Rheumatology* (ILAR). Furthermore, during 2000–2010, the World Health Organization launched the *Monitor Project of the Bone and Joint Decade* to better quantify the global burden of musculoskeletal disorders such as osteoarthritis and develop strategies for their prevention (Khaltaev et al., 2003). Education is key to self-management and prevention. Notably, the Internet has become a significant tool used by advocates to inform and mobilize grassroots attention to effect change in behavior and lifestyle (Leong and Euller-Ziegler, 2004). Active prevention of arthritic conditions obviously targets those risk factors that contribute to joint damage: obesity, excessive repetitive stress and strain to the joints, lack of aerobic exercise, dehydration, and poor nutrition. Maintenance of ideal weight, avoidance of repetitive joint trauma, regular aerobic exercise, generous water intake, and good nutrition with sufficient calcium, phosphorous, and vitamin D are essential components of a preventive strategy.

Tertiary Prevention of Osteoarthritis Sequela

The underlying disease process of osteoarthritis has thus far proven to be irreversible. Nevertheless, some evidence has accrued suggesting that weight reduction, regular nontraumatic aerobic exercise (e.g., swimming, bike riding), and sustained use of analgesics such as aspirin, ibuprofen, or acetaminophen may effectively arrest disease progression (Brandt and Flusser, 1991).

Clinical Trials of Glucosamine and Chondroitin

In recent years, formulations of glucosamine and chondroitin have been marketed as effective therapeutic agents for patients with osteoarthritis. Recently, a team of European investigators conducted a comprehensive review and meta-analysis of the available data from randomized clinical trials of these agents to determine their therapeutic efficacy in reducing joint pain and progression of osteoarthritis of the hip or knee. Ten large-scale randomized controlled clinical trials that compared glucosamine, chondroitin, or their combination with placebo were included in the investigation. Each trial enrolled at least 200 patients with osteoarthritis of the hip or knee, a total of 3,803 patients overall. The results revealed *no significant differences* in either pain relief or disease progression between patients receiving active treatment versus placebo. The investigators concluded that compared with placebo, glucosamine, and chondroitin, used either separately or in combination, *do not* reduce joint pain or produce beneficial changes in the joints of patients with osteoarthritis. They also suggest that prescribing these compounds to patients who have not received treatment should be discouraged (Wandel et al., 2010).

Clinical Trials of Weight Reduction

Investigators in Denmark conducted a meta-analysis of randomized clinical trials designed to assess changes in pain and function achieved by weight loss in overweight patients with knee osteoarthritis. Four trials involving 454 patients were included in the study. Results revealed significant reductions in pain (OR = 0.20) and disability (OR = 0.23) associated with an average weight reduction of 6.1 kg. The investigators concluded that disability could be significantly improved with a 5.1% reduction in weight from baseline which was achievable within a 20-week period (Christensen et al., 2007).

It is also important to note that relief of osteoarthritic symptoms may be achieved by arthroplasty or joint replacement surgery. As pointed out by Symmons and colleagues in their review of the global burden of osteoarthritis: "*total joint replacement is a highly cost effective operation for severe osteoarthritis and provides good pain relief and improvement in mobility and quality of life in the majority of patients in the United States*" (Symmons, Mathers, and Pfleger, 2006a).

RHEUMATOID ARTHRITIS

Rheumatoid arthritis is a systemic inflammatory autoimmune disease that affects multiple synovial joints in a symmetrical pattern. The disease is thus succinctly characterized as *symmetrical inflammatory polyarthritis*. The inflammatory process induces excessive proliferation of connective tissue cells that form a *"pannus"* of hyperplastic cells within the joint capsule. Eventually, these cells invade and erode the articular cartilage causing deformities and destruction of the joint and loss of function. The condition usually begins in the small joints of the hands and feet and then progresses to the larger joints. Extra-articular features are commonly found in patients with rheumatoid arthritis including rheumatoid skin nodules, vasculitis, pericarditis, pulmonary fibrosis, and peripheral amyloidosis (Robbins and Cotran, 1979; Symmons, Mathers, and Pfleger, 2006b).

Pathogenesis of Rheumatoid Arthritis

In their textbook, *Pathogenesis of Disease*, Robbins and Cotran state that "*virtually all patients with classic rheumatoid arthritis have rheumatoid factor in their sera.*" *Rheumatoid factor* is an autoantibody that binds to other immunoglobulins (IgG and IgM) to form immune complexes. According to one model of the pathogenesis of rheumatoid arthritis, these complexes attack specific antigenic targets within the joint space leading to complement activation and release of lysosomal enzymes by macrophages and other immune cells. This destructive cascade produces irreparable damage to the joint cartilage (Robbins and Cotran, 1979).

Diagnosis of Rheumatoid Arthritis

Rheumatoid arthritis is diagnosed by the presence of a sufficient number of characteristic signs and symptoms including morning stiffness, joint pain and tenderness, symmetrical soft tissue swelling of joints, subcutaneous nodules, radiographic changes in joints, and positive rheumatoid factor. *Classical rheumatoid arthritis* is defined when all criteria are positive (Ropes et al., 1958; Arnett et al., 1988).

Incidence and Prevalence of Rheumatoid Arthritis

Investigators at the Mayo Clinic estimated the age-specific incidence of rheumatoid arthritis among adults living in Rochester, Minnesota, and followed during 1955–1994. During this time period, 609 Rochester residents (445 women and 164 men) fulfilled the 1987 American College of Radiology criteria for the diagnosis of rheumatoid arthritis. As depicted in **Figure 38.6**, the age-specific incidence curves differ dramatically by gender. In women, rates begin to rise during late adolescence peaking at 116 cases per 100,000 during ages 55–64 years after which they remain high until age 85. In contrast, rates in men rise steadily after about age 30 peaking at 102 cases per 100,000 during ages 75–84 years. Across the entire lifespan, the incidence in women is approximately twice that in men (Gabriel, Crowson, and O'Fallon, 1999; Doran et al., 2002). Similar age-specific incidence patterns have been reported for men and women in Great Britain (Symmons et al., 2002; Symmons, Mathers, and Pfleger, 2006b).

Age-specific prevalence rates estimated from combined surveys of European populations are shown in **Figure 38.7**. Based on these estimates, after the age of 65 years, approximately 3% of women have rheumatoid arthritis compared to 1.5% of men (Symmons et al., 2002; Symmons, Mathers, and Pfleger, 2006b).

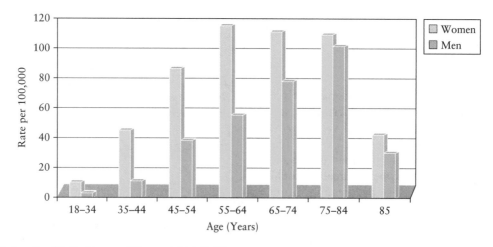

Figure 38.6 Age-Specific Incidence of Rheumatoid Arthritis.

Source: Data from Gabriel SE, Crowson CS, O'Fallon WM (1999). The epidemiology of rheumatoid arthritis in Rochester, Minnesota, 1955–1985. *Arthritis & Rheumatism* 42(3):415–420.

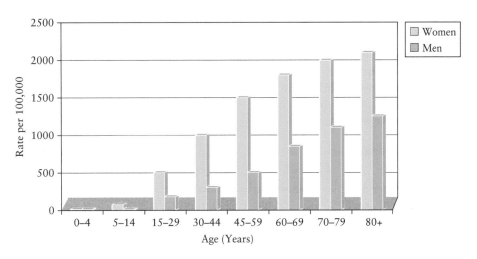

Figure 38.7 Age-Specific Prevalence of Rheumatoid Arthritis.

Source: Data from Symmons D, Mathers C, Pfleger B (2006). Global burden of rheumatoid arthritis in the year 2000. In Global Burden of Disease 2000. World Health Organization, Geneva, Switzerland.

Disability in Rheumatoid Arthritis

Rheumatoid arthritis initially causes erosion of the cartilage of synovial joints. Without treatment, there is inevitable progression of the process to contiguous bone which eventually results in destruction and deformity of the joints and severe disability. Furthermore, rheumatoid arthritis is clearly associated with several conditions that cause premature death such as end stage kidney disease and cardiovascular disease.

The excess deaths among patients with rheumatoid arthritis have been attributed to its extra-articular manifestations presumably arising from circulating autoimmune complexes and/or the cumulative inflammatory burden of the disease.

The global pattern of *DALY* due to rheumatoid arthritis is shown in **Figure 38.8**. Rates appear highest in nations of the Russian Federation, Eastern Europe, and Central and South America. However,

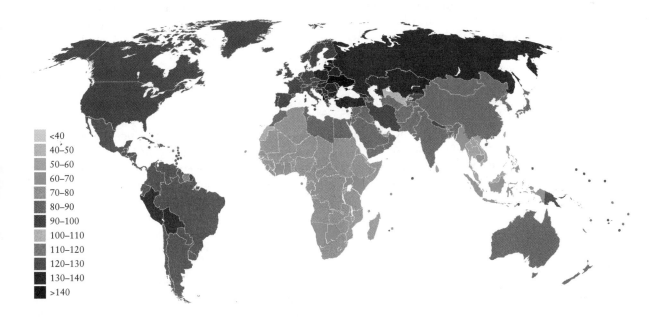

Figure 38.8 Disability Adjusted Life Years (DALY): Rheumatoid Arthritis.

Source: Data from World Health Organization. The global burden of disease: 2004 update. Geneva, WHO, 2008. Available at www.who.int /evidence/bod.

it should be recognized that the estimates for these regions (as well as most other developing nations) are based upon scanty data and further investigations and surveys are needed to improve our understanding of intra and inter-regional variability in morbidity and mortality rates from rheumatoid arthritis (Symmons, Mathers, and Pfleger, 2006b).

Time Trends in Rheumatoid Arthritis: Morbidity and Mortality

Population surveys of member nations of the World Health Organization in 1990 and 2000 suggest that both morbidity and mortality attributable to rheumatoid arthritis are increasing. During this period, YLD from rheumatoid arthritis increased from 3.2 to 4.5 million and YLL increased from 118,000 to 148,000 (Symmons, Mathers, and Pfleger, 2006b). These increases have occurred in parallel with the *epidemiologic transition* in which the global burden of chronic diseases has surpassed infectious and parasitic conditions. Notably, several debilitating and life-threatening chronic diseases frequently occur in patients with rheumatoid arthritis.

A recent study of patients treated at the Mayo Clinic in the United States reported *no improvement* in mortality from rheumatoid arthritis over the last four decades (Doran et al., 2002). A cohort study of 1,049 patients in the Netherlands also failed to reveal any improvement in survival. In fact, the mortality rate among these subjects was 40% higher than in the general population. A total of 207 patients died during up to 23 years of follow-up and excess mortality emerged at about 10 years after diagnosis. The leading causes of death were cardiovascular disease, cancer, infection, and respiratory disease. Significant baseline predictors of mortality included gender (male), early age at diagnosis, rheumatoid factor, disability, and comorbidity. The investigators advocate better disease control in all age groups and suggest that comorbid conditions be treated more aggressively to help improve survival of patients with rheumatoid arthritis (Radovits et al., 2010).

Risk Factors for Rheumatoid Arthritis

Only a few risk factors have been clearly identified in the development of rheumatoid arthritis. Multiple studies suggest that genetic factors are extremely important, and as with other autoimmune conditions, being female carries an approximate twofold increase in the risk compared to being male. The available evidence also suggests that smoking increases the risk in both men and women, whereas use of the oral contraceptive pill appears to reduce the risk in women.

Genetics of Rheumatoid Arthritis

There is substantial evidence to suggest that genetic factors contribute significantly to the etiopathogenesis of rheumatoid arthritis. Concordance rates for rheumatoid arthritis are fourfold higher in monozygous twins (12–15%) than dizygous twins (3–4%) and the rates among full siblings of probands (index cases) are higher than expected (Aho et al., 1986; Silman et al., 1993).

The association between rheumatoid arthritis and HLA-DR4 was first demonstrated more than 30 years ago (Statsny, 1978) and it was soon discovered that several genes that determine susceptibility to rheumatoid arthritis reside in the HLA region of chromosome 6 (Deighton et al., 1989). It has now been determined that specific "shared epitopes" encoded by certain class II HLA alleles may interact with pathogenic microbes such as Epstein Barr virus to incite the autoimmune reactions of rheumatoid arthritis (Gregerson, Silver, and Winchester, 1987; Weyand et al., 1992; Ollier and MacGregor, 1995). Nevertheless, other genes are likely to be involved and genome-wide association studies of afflicted relatives are now being conducted to identify them (Symmons and Harrison, 2000).

Female Hormones and Rheumatoid Arthritis

As shown in **Figures 38.6** and **38.7**, the incidence and prevalence rates of rheumatoid arthritis in women are more than double the rates in men. The excess female risk is most apparent during the premenopausal years and then dissipates slightly in old age. One interpretation of this biological phenomenon is that reproductive hormones are responsible; perhaps estrogen heightens the risk in women and androgen lessens the risk in men. Two findings appear to counter this viewpoint: (1) premenopausal women who take the oral contraceptive pill (a combination of estrogen and progestin) appear to have a *reduced* risk of later developing progressive disease, and (2) postmenopausal hormone replacement therapy has *not* been found to influence either the development or the progression of rheumatoid arthritis.

Oral Contraceptives and Rheumatoid Arthritis

Some epidemiologic studies have reported that premenopausal women who take the oral contraceptive pill have a reduced risk of later developing rheumatoid arthritis. Nevertheless, findings differ from study to study. Spector and Hochberg therefore undertook a review of the published studies and performed a meta-analysis of the data. Their analysis included data from 9 independent studies, 6 case control studies, and 3 cohort studies. The overall pooled odds ratio across studies (OR = 0.73) suggested a protective effect; however, studies of hospital cases yielded a stronger effect (OR = 0.49) than studies of population-based cases (OR = 0.95). One interpretation of these results is that the oral contraceptive pill may not have a protective effect against the development of rheumatoid arthritis but rather may prevent progression to severe disease (Spector and Hochberg, 1990).

It is of further interest that longitudinal studies of populations in Great Britain, Finland, and the United States suggest that the incidence rates of rheumatoid arthritis declined significantly during the last half of the 20th century (Linos et al., 1980; Silman, 1988; Hochberg, 1990; Kaipiainen-Seppänen et al., 1996; Abdel-Nasser et al., 1997; Doran et al., 2002; Helmick et al., 2008). For example, in a study of residents of Rochester, Minnesota, the age-adjusted incidence rates estimated for successive 10-year intervals during the 40-year period, 1955–1994 decreased by 52% in women and 30% in men (**Figure 38.9**). Interestingly, the steeper decline in women coincides with the introduction and widespread use of the oral contraceptive pill which began in about 1960 (Doran et al., 2002).

Hormone Replacement Therapy and Rheumatoid Arthritis

The Women's Health Initiative (WHI) randomized controlled trials conducted in the United States evaluated the effects of postmenopausal hormone replacement (estrogen alone and estrogen + progestin) compared with placebo on the development and progression of rheumatoid arthritis. Among 27,347 participants, 63 prevalent cases and 105 incidence cases of rheumatoid arthritis were identified during 7.1 years and 5.6 years of follow-up in the 2 trials. No statistically significant differences were detected in the risk of developing rheumatoid arthritis or the severity of rheumatoid arthritis between the postmenopausal hormone treatment groups and placebo (Walitt et al., 2008).

Female Gender and Rheumatoid Arthritis

An alternative hypothesis that has been advanced to explain the female excess of autoimmune conditions such as rheumatoid arthritis compared to men is the mosaic nature of the active X chromosome in the female genotype. According to the Lyon hypothesis, as cell lineages develop during embryogenesis, either the maternal X or the paternal X remains active and the reciprocal X is inactivated and becomes a Barr body. In theory, if the X activation/inactivation process is a random event, then 50% of cell lineages would be expected to have an active paternal X and 50% an active maternal X. However, if the X activation/inactivation process is skewed so that one X is preferentially activated in cells of the immune system, the ability of the immune system to recognize self may be compromised thus leading to autoimmune reactivity (Mignon, 2006).

Smoking and Rheumatoid Arthritis

Smoking has been examined as a risk factor for rheumatoid arthritis in a number of epidemiologic investigations. To assess the strength and consistency of the

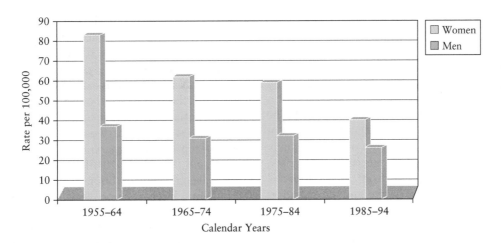

Figure 38.9 Decline in the Incidence of Rheumatoid Arthritis, USA, 1955–1994.

Source: Data from Doran MF, Pond GR, Crowson CS, O'Fallon WM, Gabriel SE (2002). Trends in incidence and mortality in rheumatoid arthritis in Rochester, Minnesota, over a forty-year period. *Arthritis & Rheumatism* 46(3):625–631.

association in men and women, a team of Japanese investigators conducted a meta-analysis of available data from published reports. Sixteen studies were included in the analysis, 11 case control studies and 5 cohort studies. The case control studies included 4,764 cases and 13,647 controls, and the cohort studies identified 9,121 cases from among 566,044 participants. The summary odds ratios for 20 or more pack years of smoking clearly indicated that smoking was a risk factor in both men (OR = 2.31) and women (OR = 1.75). Estimates were similar for case control and cohort studies. Interestingly, the presence of rheumatoid factor appeared to strengthen the effect of smoking in men but not in women. These results suggest that heavy smokers, whether male or female, have an approximate twofold increase in the risk of developing rheumatoid arthritis. The investigators speculate that smoking may increase the risk by accentuating the dysfunction of T lymphocytes (Sugiyama et al., 2010).

Prevention and Control of Rheumatoid Arthritis

Other than avoidance of smoking, there are no methods that have been clearly shown to reduce the risk of developing rheumatoid arthritis. Early diagnosis and initiation of therapy is imperative in preventing disease progression and limiting disability. Nonsteroidal anti-inflammatory drugs show benefit in reducing pain and inflammation, steroids (prednisone) offer symptomatic relief, and methotrexate, sulphasalazine, and/or injectable gold and new agents directed against inflammatory cytokines may slow disease progression. In addition to drug therapy, orthopedic surgery may be of benefit for patients with severe disabling deformities (Symmons, Mathers, and Pfleger, 2006b).

GOUT

Gout is characterized by *"transient but recurrent attacks of acute arthritis evoked by the precipitation of monosodium uric acid crystals from supersaturated body fluids"* (Robbins and Cotran, 1979). The classic form of gout predominantly affects joints of the great toe (85% of patients) but other joints may also become involved (ankles, heels, knees, wrists, fingers, and elbows). With progression, there is destruction of articular cartilage and subchondral bone leading to chronic disabling arthritis.

The Dutch scientist Antonie van Leeuwenhoek, known as *"the father of microbiology,"* first described the microscopic appearance of urate crystals in 1679 (Pillinger, Rosenthal, and Abeles, 2007).

In 1848 the English physician Alfred Baring Garrod recognized that excess uric acid in the blood was the cause of gout (Storey, 2001).

The pathognomonic microscopic lesion of gout is called a tophus, a periarticular mass of urate crystals surrounded by fibroblasts admixed with macrophages, lymphocytes, and foreign body giant cells. Uric acid crystals frequently produce damage to the kidneys and occasionally cause the development of uric acid kidney stones. Patients with gout also commonly manifest hypertension, hypertriglyceridemia, hyperlipidemia, and hyperglycemia (Robbins and Cotran, 1979).

Uric Acid Metabolism and Gout

The development of gout is preceded by chronic hyperuricemia due to overproduction and/or increased retention of uric acid. Hyperuricemia arises from retention due to dysfunction in renal uric acid excretion in about 90% of cases, and overproduction of uric acid in the remaining 10% of cases. Overproduction of uric acid can be caused by enzymatic defects in uric acid synthesis and degradation, excess intake of purines and other substrates of uric acid, and/or excess intake of alcohol or other drugs that heighten uric acid synthesis and/or interfere with renal clearance. Disorders that cause excessive cell destruction and release of nucleic acids and purines into the bloodstream can also produce hyperuricemia. Serum uric acid levels exceeding 7 mg/dl are highly conducive to the precipitation of uric acid crystals in bodily fluids and tissues, particularly in the synovial fluid (Klinenberg, 1977).

Recently, investigators at Boston University examined the gender-specific relationship between serum uric acid and the incidence of gout among 2,476 women and 1,951 men who were followed for up to 52 years as a component of the Framingham Heart Study. A total of 304 incident cases of gout were detected in the study, 104 in women and 200 in men. Notably, the risk of gout begins to increase at a threshold level of about 5 mg/dl and increases exponentially in both men and women. However, the risk estimates for women are about 50% less than men for each incremental increase in serum uric acid (**Figure 38.10**). In multivariate analyses, several comorbid conditions were also found to independently increase the risk including obesity (RR = 2.74), alcohol intake exceeding one drink daily (RR = 3.10), hypertension (RR = 1.82), and diuretic use (RR = 2.39). The risk also increased with increasing age (RR = 1.24 per 5 years). The investigators concluded that *"higher levels of serum uric acid increase*

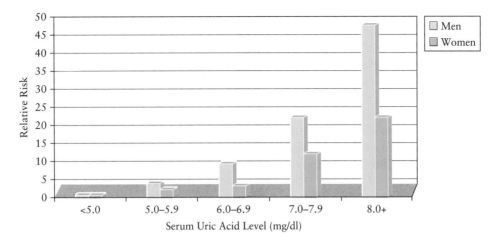

Figure 38.10 Dose Response in Risk of Gout with Increasing Serum Uric Acid in Women and Men.

Source: Data from Bhole V, de Vera M, Rahman MM, Krishnan E, Choi H (2010). Epidemiology of gout in women: Fifty-two–year followup of a prospective cohort. *Arthritis & Rheumatism* 62(4):1069–1076.

the risk of gout in a graded manner among women, but the rate of increase is lower than that among men" (Bhole et al., 2010).

Incidence and Prevalence of Gout

The incidence and prevalence of gout appear to be rising in many populations around the globe in conjunction with the *epidemiologic transition*. Factors related to the increase include increasing longevity concurrent with increasing rates of comorbid conditions such as hypertension, obesity, diabetes, the metabolic syndrome, cardiovascular disease, and kidney disease. Such conditions likely impair the renal clearance of uric acid leading to hyperuricemica (elevated serum uric acid) which is the forerunner of gout development. These conditions in combination with other factors (genetic predisposition, alcohol consumption, dietary purines, and the use of certain drugs) have produced marked increases in the rates of gout. In the United States, compilation of self-reported data derived from national surveys suggest that approximately 3.0 million adults had gout in 2008, an increase of 42% from 2.1 million cases who self-reported gout in 1995 (Lawrence et al., 2008).

Evidence that the *incidence* of gout is increasing in the US population comes from a longitudinal study of adults in Rochester, Minnesota. In this population sample, the age-gender adjusted annual incidence of acute gout increased from 4.5 to 6.2 cases per 10,000 person years during the 10-year interval from 1977–1978 to 1987–1988 and the incidence of *primary gout* (restricted to patients not taking diuretics)

increased from 2.0 to 4.6 per 10,000 during the same time period (Arromdee et al., 2002).

Evidence that the *prevalence* of gout is increasing in the US population comes from a prospective study of a managed care population of 8 million adults. During the period 1990–1999, the prevalence of gout or hyperuricemia in the cohort increased from 21 to 41 cases per 1,000 for adults 75 years or older, and from 21 to 31 cases per 1,000 for adults ages 65–74 years. Prevalence rates for younger age groups remained low and were relatively stable over the time period of study (Wallace et al., 2004).

In the United Kingdom, examination of 1.7 million adults in the *General Practitioner Research Database* yielded an annual gout *incidence* of about 14 per 10,000 person-years during 1990–1999. Interestingly, the incidence remained relatively stable over that time period reflecting a different pattern than the US data. Nevertheless, rates for adults over 65 years of age increased by about 40% during 1990–1994, and in the 65–84 year age group, there was an overall increase of 31% from 29 to 38 cases per 10,000 during the entire decade of the study. The annual prevalence of gout estimated from the 1999 data was 14 per 1,000 overall with peaks of 73 per 1,000 at 75–84 years in men and 28 per 1,000 at 85 years or older in women. In comparisons with osteoarthritis patients from the same cohort, patients with gout were more likely to have cardiovascular disease, hypertension, diabetes or chronic renal failure, or have used drugs known to impair renal clearance of uric acid such as diuretics or cyclosporine (Mikuls et al., 2005). Notably, the overall prevalence estimate from the 1999 survey was more than five times higher than the prevalence estimate from a similar national study conducted in Great Britain during the 1970s (Currie, 1979).

Age Distribution of Gout

Gout differs dramatically from rheumatoid arthritis and osteoarthritis, joint diseases that strike twice as many females as males. In contrast, approximately 90% of newly diagnosed cases of gout are males. In men, the annual prevalence rate of gout begins to increase before age 30, climbing to a peak of more than 70 cases per 1,000 in the 8th decade of life. The prevalence rates in women remain much lower than men throughout life and do not increase substantially until after menopause (**Figure 38.11**).

Disability from Gout

Chronic gouty arthritis is the most disabling phase of the disease. This phase generally appears over a span of years of increasing severity of acute attacks with spread to multiple joints. Aggressive therapy significantly reduces the risk of developing the chronic phase. Approximately 90% of patients with chronic disease eventually develop nephropathy, a life-threatening condition.

Risk Factors for Gout

Risk factors for the development of gout include male gender, renal dysfunction, excessive alcohol intake, high dietary intake of purines, exposure to certain drugs (specifically those that influence renal clearance of uric acid) and various comorbid conditions (particularly type 2 diabetes, obesity, and the metabolic syndrome). Patients with hypertension, hyperlipidemia, and/or cardiovascular disease are also at increased risk for the development of hyperuricemia and subsequently, gout. Selected risk factors are briefly discussed in the following sections (Weaver, 2008).

Gender and Gout

As shown in **Figure 38.11**, rates of gout in men of reproductive age far surpass those of women. Clinical studies have determined that during the reproductive years, the serum concentrations of uric acid in men are on average approximately 1 mg/dl higher than women. However, following menopause, serum levels of uric acid of women tend to approach those of men. The gender difference in uric acid concentration has been attributed to a beneficial effect of endogenous estrogens that promote more efficient uric acid clearance by the kidneys (Rider et al., 2004; Choi, 2008).

Kidney Dysfunction and Gout

There is a general consensus in the field of gout research that about 90% of all gout cases are due to defective renal clearance of uric acid. It is therefore important to emphasize that *any chronic condition that compromises kidney function can potentially upset the delicate balance of uric acid clearance resulting in hyperuricemia and gout*. Many of these conditions are discussed elsewhere in this text. They include type 2 diabetes and the metabolic syndrome,

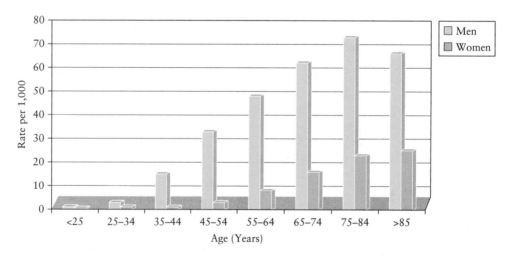

Figure 38.11 Age-Specific Prevalence of Gout.

Source: Data from Mikuls TR, Farrar JT, Bilker WB, Fernandes S, Schumacher HR Jr, Saag KG (2005). Gout epidemiology: results from the UK General Practice Research Database, 1990–1999. *Ann Rheum Dis* 64:267–272.

obesity, atherosclerosis, hypertension, dyslipidemia, and other cardiovascular conditions, and nephritis, nephrosis and other forms of kidney disease.

Of special interest is the association between gout and the disease complex known as the *metabolic syndrome*. This complex is defined by the presence of at least three of the following criteria: obesity, hypertension, hyperglycemia or type 2 diabetes, high serum triglycerides and low high-density lipoprotein cholesterol. Using data collected from 8,807 adults of the Third National Health and Nutrition Examination Survey (NHANES III) conducted during 1988–1994, a team of Harvard investigators examined the prevalence of the metabolic syndrome among 223 cases with physician-diagnosed gout and 8,584 controls without gout and quantified the magnitude of the association by estimating prevalence odds ratios. The prevalence of the metabolic syndrome was 62.8% among cases with gout and 25.4% among controls. After adjusting for age and gender, the odds of having the metabolic syndrome was strongly associated with the presence of gout (OR = 3.05). The association was elevated in women (OR = 3.97) and men (OR = 2.79). Furthermore, significant associations were noted for individual components of the metabolic syndrome: obesity (OR = 2.55), elevated triglycerides (OR = 1.90), low HDL cholesterol (OR = 1.60), hypertension (OR = 2.41), and hyperglycemia (OR = 2.14). According to the investigators,

> *"these findings indicate that the prevalence of metabolic syndrome is remarkably high among individuals with gout. Given the serious complications associated with metabolic syndrome, this frequent comorbidity should be recognized*

and taken into account in long-term treatment and overall health of individuals with gout" (Choi et al., 2007).

Drugs and Gout

Numerous drugs have been found to increase serum uric acid and therefore may potentially increase the risk of gout in certain individuals. They do so primarily by decreasing uric acid clearance by the kidney. For example, thiazide diuretics, salicylates, pyrazinamide (a drug for tuberculosis), nicotinate (a supplementary form of inositol, niacin and vitamin B3), insulin, beta blockers, and cyclosporine (an immunosuppressive drug) have all been found to increase reabsorption of uric acid by the renal tubules and with prolonged use can induce hyperuricemia and ultimately gout (Choi, Mount, and Reginato, 2005; Choi, 2008).

Obesity and Gout

Results of numerous investigations suggest that abdominal obesity increases the risk of developing gout. Choi and colleagues examined the relationship in a longitudinal cohort of 47,150 male participants with no history of gout at baseline ascertained from the *US Health Professionals Follow-up Study*. They also examined associations with hypertension and use of diuretics. During 12 years of follow-up, 730 incident cases of gout were confirmed. Results revealed a significant dose response in the risk of developing gout with increasing body mass (**Figure 38.12**). Compared to men who had maintained a stable weight (within 4 lbs) since age 21 years, the risk of developing gout increased twofold in those who had

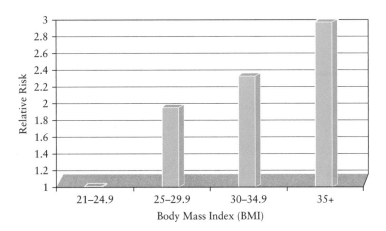

Figure 38.12 Dose Response in the Risk of Gout with Body Mass Index in Men.

Source: Data from Choi HK, Atkinson K, Karlson EW, Curhan (2005). Obesity, weight change, hypertension, diuretic use, and risk of gout in men, the Health Professionals Follow-up Study. *Arch Intern Med* 165:742–748.

gained 30 lbs or more (RR = 1.99). Reciprocally, those who had lost 10 lbs or more reduced their risk significantly (RR = 0.61). Hypertension and use of diuretics also independently increased the risk (RR = 2.33 and 1.77, respectively). The investigators concluded that "*adiposity and weight gain are strong risk factors for gout in men, while weight loss is protective*" (Choi et al., 2005).

Alcohol and Gout

Chronic alcohol consumption has been linked to the development of gout in numerous epidemiologic investigations. Yet, risk levels for specific alcoholic beverages have not been thoroughly explored. Choi and colleagues therefore used the extensive database of the *US Health Professionals Follow-up Study* to investigate levels and sources of alcohol consumption and the risk of developing gout. As already discussed, the study included 47,150 males with no history of gout at baseline who were followed over 12 years during 1986–1998. During this time, 730 incident cases of gout were detected. Results revealed a significant dose response in the risk of gout with increasing intake of alcohol (**Figure 38.13**). In comparisons of specific alcoholic beverages, beer had the strongest effect (RR = 1.49 per 12 oz serving per day) followed by spirits (RR = 1.15 per shot of per day) and wine (RR = 1.04 per 4 oz glass per day). Thus, while alcohol consumption per se is clearly a strong risk factor, there appears to be substantial variation in the risk according to the type of alcoholic beverage (Choi et al., 2004a).

Alcohol intake causes elevation of serum uric acid by at least two general biological mechanisms. First, *alcohol dehydrogenase*, the liver enzyme responsible for alcohol degradation (oxidation) in humans, triggers a cascade of reduction/oxidation (redox) reactions of adenine nucleotides resulting in the production of purines and uric acid (Faller and Fox, 1982); and second, excess hydrogen ions from *nicotinamide adenine dinucleotide* (NAD) reduction during alcohol oxidation contributes to the reduction of pyruvate and the formation of *lactate*, which in turn causes retention of uric acid in the renal proximal tubules (Lieber, 2005). It is important to note that several other factors may also be involved in the hyperuricemic impact of alcohol consumption including dehydration, ketosis, level of exercise, content of purines, or other contaminants in alcoholic beverages and various comorbidities (Yamamoto, Moriwaki, and Takahashi, 2005).

Dietary Factors and Gout

Choi and colleagues also used the *US Health Professionals Follow-up Study* to investigate associations between selected dietary factors (meat and vegetables rich in purines and dairy products) and the risk of developing gout. In this analysis, the investigators found that men in the highest quintiles of meat and seafood consumption were at increased risk compared to those in the lowest quintile (RR = 1.41 and 1.51, respectively). In contrast, the risk decreased with increasing consumption of low-fat dairy products (RR = 0.56 for the highest compared

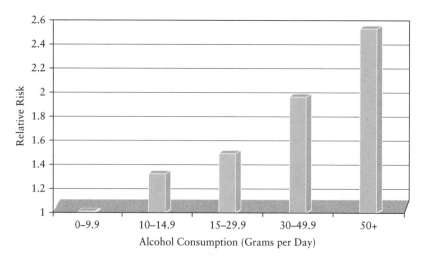

Figure 38.13 Dose Response in the Risk of Gout with Increasing Alcohol Consumption in Men.

Source: Data from Choi HK, Atkinson K, Darlson EW, Willet W, Curhan G (2004). Alcohol intake and the risk of incident gout in men: a prospective study. *The Lancet* 363(9417):1277–1281.

to the lowest quintile). Notably, the risk of gout was unchanged by consumption of purine-rich vegetables. These results suggest that high consumption of meat and seafood increase the risk of developing gout, presumably because of their high purine content, whereas high consumption of low-fat dairy products conferred a protective effect, possibly due to the uricosuric properties of casein and other milk proteins (Choi et al., 2004b).

Genetics of Gout

Genetic factors are important determinants of susceptibility to hyperuricemia and gout. Hyperuricemia and gout are particularly common in certain ethnic groups (Filipinos, Samoans, Maori, and other South Pacific Islanders) likely due to the combination of a high seafood diet rich in purines coupled with genetic factors that heighten predisposition.

In early studies of families, hyperuricemia was found to be extremely common among the close relatives of patients with gout. In 1940, Talbott investigated 136 relatives of 27 patients with gout and found hyperuricemia in 27 male and 7 female relatives (Talbott, 1940). Smyth and colleagues later studied 87 relatives of 19 probands (index cases) in 19 families and found hyperuricemia in 27 close relatives. They suggested that hyperuricemia is an autosomal dominant genetic condition (Smyth, Cotterman, and Freyberg, 1948).

Subsequently, James Neel and colleagues at the University of Michigan determined serum uric acid levels for 271 members of the 19 families first studied by Smyth, Cotterman, and Freyberg. While first degree relatives of probands had higher levels than more distant relatives, spouses, or population controls, the extended distributional pattern in these families suggested that hyperuricemia is a multifactorial genetic trait rather than under control of a single autosomal gene (Neel et al., 1965). Though there are rare monogenic syndromes that predispose to hyperuricemia and gout, there is now a firm consensus that these traits usually follow a multifactorial pattern of inheritance (Richett and Bardin, 2010).

Perhaps the most important cause of hyperuricemia is *reduced clearance of uric acid by the kidneys*. This function is controlled by a family of urate transport molecules that are expressed in the renal collecting tubules. These molecules include the fructose transporter *SLC2A9* (*GLUT9*), urate transporter 1 (*URAT1*), organic anion transporters (*OAT1, OAT2,* and *OAT3*), multidrug resistance protein (*MRP4*), sodium-coupled monocarboxyl transporters (*SMCT*), and human ATP-binding cassette (*ABCG2*). Other checkpoints in the regulation of serum uric acid include hepatic production and degradation of uric acid, monosodium crystal formation, and initiation of the acute inflammatory response. Multiple genes are thus involved in the regulation of uric acid clearance and *genome wide association studies* (*GWAS*) are being conducted to identify them. Indeed, genetic polymorphisms that compromise the function of two major regulators of renal uric acid transport have already been discovered, *SLC2A9* and *ABCG2* (Vitart et al., 2008; Choi, 2010; Merriman and Dalbeth, 2011).

Three monogenic syndromes have been well characterized in the literature. *Lesch-Nyhan syndrome* is a rare X-linked genetic disorder that affects only males. The incidence is approximately 1 in 380,000 live male births. Males with this syndrome manifest physical handicaps, mental retardation, kidney dysfunction, and gout. The syndrome is caused by a mutation in a gene on the long arm of the X chromosome that encodes the enzyme, *hypoxanthine-guanine phosphoribosyl transferase*, or *HPRT*, which catalyzes the recycling of hypoxanthine and guanine, reactions that are necessary to prevent the buildup of uric acid. Complete absence of HPRT enzyme activity leads to markedly elevated uric acid levels in the blood (hyperuricemia) that produce the symptoms that define the syndrome. Other rare genetic syndromes that predispose to gout include *familial juvenile hyperuricemic nephropathy* (*medullary cystic kidney disease)* and *phosphoribosylpyrophosphate synthetase* (*PRS*) *superactivity*. These also involve inborn errors of metabolism that result in hyperuricemia and gout (Robbins and Cotran, 1979; Bleyer and Hart, 2006).

Prevention and Therapy of Gout

Gout typically progresses through distinct clinical phases: (1) asymptomatic hyperuricemia, (2) recurrent acute attacks of gouty arthritis interspersed with asymptomatic periods, and (3) chronic gouty arthritis or tophaceous gout. Asymptomatic hyperuricemia is common and can often be reversed by nonpharmacologic methods such as reducing intake of dietary purines, limiting alcohol consumption, reducing weight if overweight or obese, maintaining blood pressure, blood lipids and blood glucose within normal limits, avoiding nephrotoxic drugs, and drinking generous amounts of water daily. The excruciatingly painful symptoms of gout can be effectively treated by administration of nonsteroidal anti-inflammatory drugs (NSAIDs), steroids, or colchicine. Pharmacologic treatment of hyperuricemia with urate-lowering drugs such as allopurinol or probenecid has led to a dramatic reduction in long-term gouty arthritis and tophaceous gout. Furthermore, hemodialysis has markedly improved survival among patients who develop gouty nephropathy (Harris, Siegel, and Alloway, 1999; Luk and Simkin, 2005).

ANKYLOSING SPONDYLITIS

Ankylosing spondylitis (also called Marie-Strümpell disease) is a highly inflammatory form of arthritis of the spine. This disorder is characterized by back pain and stiffness, and loss of spinal mobility due to compression and ultimate fusion of sacroiliac joints and vertebrae. Diagnosis is typically made based upon symptoms and radiography. The anatomic and pathological changes in the spine are indistinguishable from those of rheumatoid arthritis.

Longitudinal examination of a population cohort in Rochester, Minnesota during 1935–1973 revealed an annual age-adjusted incidence of 11.0 per 100,000 in males and 4.0 per 100,000 in females. In this study, the incidence peaked during ages 25–34 years and the male-to-female ratio was approximately 4 to 1 (Carter et al., 1979).

There are extreme geographic and ethnic differences in the prevalence of ankylosing spondylitis. Prevalence rates exceeding 60 per 1,000 have been observed in surveys of North American Indians markedly exceeding rates found in Caucasian populations in the United States and Europe (Hochberg, 1984). These ethnic differences in prevalence closely reflect population differences in the frequency of the histocompatibililty antigen, HLA-B27.

Heredity plays a strong role in predisposing to the development of ankylosing spondylitis. In family studies, approximately 25% of close relatives of probands (index cases) have been found to manifest symptomatic or asymptomatic disease (Hochberg, Bias, and Arnett, 1978). Most notably, individuals who carry the HLA-B27 antigen are at high risk for the development of ankylosing spondylititis (Schlosstein et al., 1973; Brewerton et al., 1973). The HLA-B27 is found in 90–95% of patients of European origin with ankylosing spondylitis compared to 8% in the general population. However, only about 5% of individuals in the general population who carry HLA-B27 will develop ankylosing spondylitis; therefore HLA-B27 has little value as a biomarker for the disease (Reveille, Ball, and Khan, 2001).

The exact mechanism by which HLA-B27 confers disease susceptibility has not been determined. Conceivably, this antigen triggers an autoimmune response by killer T cells that incites inflammation in the spinal synovium. Family studies suggest that HLA-B27 contributes about 40% of the overall genetic risk for ankylosing spondylitis and that other antigens of the major histocompatibility locus on chromosome 6 contribute to the remaining risk (Reveille, Ball, and Khan, 2001).

Various infectious agents have also been found in association with HLA-B27 and ankylosing spondylitis. For example, HLA-B27 and certain *Klebsiella* species have been found to cross react (Ebringer et al., 1977; Gezcy and Yap, 1982). One interpretation of such findings is that specific infectious agents or other environmental triggers may interact with HLA-B27 and/or other antigens of the major histocompatibility locus to incite autoimmune reactivity leading to ankylosing spondylitis (Reveille, 2006).

While there is no cure for ankylosing spondylitis, aerobic exercise, good posture, and certain medications have been found to be effective in preventing/relieving symptoms. Medications for pain relief include nonsteroidal anti-inflammatory drugs (NSAIDs), selective cyclcooxygenase-2 (COX-2) blockers, and opiods. Disease modifying antirheumatic drugs (*DMARDS*) such as cyclosporine, methotrexate, sulfasalazine, prednisone, and TNF-a antagonists have shown benefit in reducing immunoreactivity. Patients with ankylosing spondylitis often manifest comorbid inflammatory conditions such as ulcerative colitis, Crohn's disease, pulmonary fibrosis, vasculitis, and uveitis which must be recognized and treated (McVeigh and Cairns, 2006).

JUVENILE IDIOPATHIC ARTHRITIS

Juvenile idiopathic arthritis refers to a spectrum of arthritic conditions diagnosed in children or adolescents ages 16 years or younger. The diagnosis is made based upon a detailed history and physical examination, radiography, and laboratory tests. Overall, girls are affected approximately twice as often as boys. The incidence peaks between ages 1–3 years. As noted in the following discussion, the age of onset and the gender ratio vary by subtype (Hoffart and Sherry, 2010).

The nomenclature of childhood arthritis has undergone revision and continues to evolve with research and discovery. In past years, the terms *juvenile rheumatoid arthritis* and *juvenile chronic arthritis* were commonly used to describe slightly different forms of childhood arthritis, thereby compromising comparability of studies. In 1997, a committee of international investigators established uniform

Table 38.2	Major Subtypes of Juvenile Idiopathic Arthritis				
Subtype	**Freq**	**Joints**	**Pattern**	**F:M**	**Biomarker**
Oligoarticular	50%	4 or less	Asymmetric	2:1	ANA+
Polyarticular	30%	5 or more	Symmetric	2:1	RF×
Systemic	10%	Multiple	Asymmetric	1:1	Increased CRP

Relative frequencies are approximate. Other less common forms of juvenile idiopathic arthritis have also been defined (Enthesitis-Related Arthritis and Psoriatic Arthritis). These forms account for less than 10% of cases.

ANA = Antinuclear Antibodies, RF = Rheumatois Factor, CRP = C-Reactive Protein.

criteria for the diagnosis of childhood arthritis and recommended using "*juvenile idiopathic arthritis*" to describe all forms of childhood arthritis. The term "*idiopathic*" means that the exact cause is unknown. Three major subtypes of *juvenile idiopathic arthritis* are defined: *oligoarticular, polyarticular,* and *systemic disease* (Fink, 1995; Petty et al., 1998, 2004). Characteristics of the three major forms of *juvenile idiopathic arthritis* are shown in **Table 38.2**.

Oligoarticular juvenile idiopathic arthritis accounts for approximately 50% of cases. It is defined as arthritis that affects 4 or fewer joints during the first 6 months of disease. The female:male ratio of this subtype is approximately 2:1. Patients are typically young girls, ages 1–4 years, with involvement of the large joints of the lower extremities (knees and ankles). Approximately 70% of patients have *antinuclear antibodies (ANA)* whereas *rheumatoid factor* is absent. Inflammation of the eye (uveitis) is common in this subtype.

Polyarticular juvenile idiopathic arthritis accounts for about 30% of cases. It is defined as arthritis that affects five or more joints within the first six months of disease. The female-to-male ratio of this subtype is approximately 2:1. Children with disease are typically negative for rheumatoid factor whereas adolescents are positive. Both small and large joints may be affected and the pattern of arthritic joints is typically symmetric. Eye inflammation is less common in this subtype.

Systemic juvenile idiopathic arthritis (also called *Still's disease*) accounts for approximately 10% of cases. The early phase of systemic disease is characterized by fever, rash, lymphadenopathy, hepatosplenomegaly, and inflammation of peripherial membranes of the heart and lungs (pericarditis and pleuritis, respectively). Life-threatening coagulopathy may develop in this early phase. Notably, arthritic symptoms are often not detected until weeks or even months after the initial acute febrile episode; consequently, definitive diagnosis may be delayed. The female:male ratio of this subtype is approximately 1:1, and onset is most common in the early years of childhood. About one-third of patients progress to chronic destructive arthritis.

Enthesitis-related arthritis refers to inflammatory arthritis in association with *inflammatory tendonitis (enthesitis)*. This subtype is most common in boys, ages 8 years and older. Patients often manifest ankylosing spondylitis and inflammatory bowel disease and carry HLA-B27.

Psoriatic juvenile idiopathic arthritis is characterized by the development of psoriasis (inflammatory dermatitis) and subsequently, polyarticular arthritis. This subtype is more common in young girls with seropositivity for antinuclear antibodies (Petty et al., 1998; Petty et al., 2004; Hoffart and Sherry, 2010).

From the preceding discussion, it is obvious that juvenile idiopathic arthritis encompasses a heterogeneous group of disorders. While their pathogenesis is not fully understood, molecular studies suggest an autoimmune basis wherein cells of the immune system attack molecular targets in the joint capsule. This autoimmune reactivity appears to be largely dependent upon genetic factors that are triggered by specific environmental factors. The best documented associations are with genetic variants of the *human leukocyte antigen (HLA)* complex such as *HLA-A, HLA-DR/DQ,* and *HLA-DP*. Such genes encode molecules that facilitate the presentation of antigenic peptides to T lymphocytes of the immune system; conceivably, polymorphisms in these genes trigger an autoimmune response, particularly during periods of infection by viruses or bacteria that demonstrate mimicry with autoantigens. Other genes may also be involved, particularly those that encode inflammatory cytokines, prostaglandins, leukotrienes, and their cell membrane receptors. *Genome wide association studies (GWAS)* and studies of candidate genes to determine linkage and gene expression are in progress with the goal of identifying molecular targets for effective prevention and therapy (Førre and Smerdel, 2002; Prahalad, 2004).

Estimates of the annual incidence and prevalence of juvenile idiopathic arthritis vary widely from study to study, even in the same populations. Australian investigators Prudence Manner and Carol Bower reviewed epidemiologic studies of childhood arthritis published during 1966–2002 to identify possible reasons for the wide-ranging estimates of prevalence and incidence. Results from 34 studies were reviewed. Annual prevalence estimates ranged from 0.07–4.01 per 1,000, a 57-fold difference between extremes, and annual incidence estimates ranged from 8–226 per 100,000, a 28-fold difference between extremes. Factors contributing to the wide range of estimates included differences among studies in diagnostic criteria, case ascertainment, disease recognition (particularly inactive cases), and small sample sizes in some studies (Manner and Bower, 2002).

Investigators at the Mayo Clinic in the United States examined a longitudinal inception cohort for trends in the incidence of juvenile rheumatoid arthritis. The study utilized the diagnostic retrieval system of the *Rochester Epidemiology Project* to screen medical records of all residents of Rochester, Minnesota for diagnoses of juvenile rheumatoid arthritis during the 33 year period, 1960–1993. A total of 65 cases with juvenile rheumatoid arthritis were identified (48 females and 17 males). Among cases, 72% had oligoarticular disease, 17% had polyarticular disease, and 11% had systemic disease. As shown in **Figure 38.14**, two peaks in the onset of disease were observed, the first in early childhood (ages 2–3 years) and the second during adolescence (ages 12–15 years). Overall, the annual incidence rate was 11.7 per 100,000; however, rates estimated for successive time periods, 1960–1969, 1970–1979, and 1980–1993 showed a declining trend (15.0, 14.1, and 7.8 per 100,000, respectively). Furthermore, examination of moving averages of the yearly incidence rates revealed the presence of cyclic patterns with peaks in 1967, 1975, and 1987. The investigators suggest that the declining incidence and cyclic nature of the data may reflect effects of infectious agents or other environmental factors on the etiopathogenesis of juvenile rheumatoid arthritis (Peterson et al., 1996).

Juvenile idiopathic arthritis per se is seldom life-threatening and a significant fraction of patients, perhaps 50%, eventually enter remission with no or minimal functional loss. However, it is important to note that there is currently no cure for juvenile idiopathic arthritis. The primary goals of therapy are to eliminate active disease, normalize joint function, preserve normal growth, and prevent long-term joint damage. Recent evidence suggests that early aggressive therapy of newly diagnosed patients may effectively reduce the risk of devastating consequences such as permanent joint disability or blindness from chronic uveitis. In their comprehensive review of antirheumatic drugs used in the treatment of childhood arthritis, Hayward and Wallace suggest that "*there is a therapeutic window of opportunity in which to target interventions to optimize long-term outcomes in children with juvenile idiopathic arthritis*" (Hayward and Wallace, 2009).

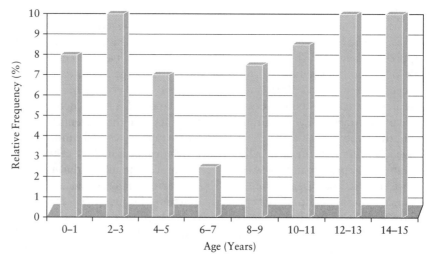

Figure 38.14 Onset of Juvenile Rheumatoid Arthritis in US Children.

Source: Data from Peterson LS, Mason T, Nelson AM, O'Fallon WM, Gabriel SE (1996). Juvenile rheumatoid arthritis in Rochester, Minnesota 1960–1993. Is the epidemiology changing? *Arthritis & Rheumatism* 39(8):1385–1390.

SUPPURATIVE (SEPTIC) ARTHRITIS

Suppurative or septic arthritis refers to the invasion of the joint space by bacteria, viruses, or other microbes. Typically, bacteria emanating from an infection localized at another anatomic site seed the joint space by dissemination through the bloodstream. The most common causes of suppurative arthritis are *staphylococci* and *streptococci* (in adults), *gonococci* (in young adults), *Hemophilus influenza* and *Pseudomonas aeruginosa* (in children), and *Escherichia coli* (in the elderly, IV drug users, and seriously ill patients). *Tuberculosis arthritis* is a common development of active pulmonary tuberculosis in children and adults living in regions of the world where *Tuberculosis mycobacteria* are endogenous (Robbins and Cotran, 1979). In developed countries where joint replacement is relatively common, subjects with artificial joints are at increased risk of developing suppurative arthritis due to *staphylococci, streptococci,* and other infectious agents. Prompt recognition and effective antimicrobial therapy for the underlying infectious agent is required for the preservation of normal joint function in patients who develop suppurative arthritis (Robbins and Cotran, 1979; Kaandorp et al., 1997; Weston et al., 1999).

• • • REFERENCES

Abdel-Nasser, A.M., Rasker, J.J., & Valkenburg, H.A. (1997). Epidemiological and clinical aspects relating to the variability of rheumatoid arthritis. *Seminars in Arthritis & Rheumatism, 27*(2), 123–140.

Aho, K., Markku, K., Tuiminen, J., & Kaprio, J. (1986). Occurrence of rheumatoid arthritis in a nationwide series of twins. *J Rheumatol, 13,* 899–902.

Anderson, J.J., & Felson, D.T. (1988). Factors associated with osteoarthritis of the knee in the first National Health and Nutrition Examination Survey (HANES I). Evidence for an association with overweight, race, and physical demands of work. *Amer J Epidemiol, 128*(1), 179–189.

Arnett, F.C., Edworthy, S.M., Bloch, D.A., McShane, D.J., Fries, J.F., & Cooper, N.S. (1988). The American Rheumatism Association 1987 revised criteria for the classification of rheumatoid arthritis. *Arthritis & Rheumatism, Arthritis Care & Research, 31*(3), 315–324.

Arromdee, E., Michet, C.J., Crowson, C.S., O'Fallon, W.M., & Gabriel, S.E. (2002). Epidemiology of gout: Is the incidence rising? *J Rheumatol, 29,* 2403–2406.

Berenbaum, F. (2010). Diabetes-induced osteoarthritis: From a new paradigm to a new phenotype. *Ann Rheum Dis,* doi:10.1136/ard.2010.146399.

Bhole, V., de Vera, M., Rahman, M.M., Krishnan, E., & Choi, H. (2010). Epidemiology of gout in women: Fifty-two–year followup of a prospective cohort. *Arthritis & Rheumatism, 62*(4), 1069–1076.

Blagojevic, M., Jinks, C., Jeffery, A., & Jordan, K.P. (2010). Risk factors for onset of osteoarthritis of the knee in older adults: A systematic review and meta-analysis. *Osteoarthritis and Cartilage, 18*(1), 24–33.

Bleyer, A.J., & Hart, T.C. (2006). Genetic factors associated with gout and hyperuricemia. *Adv Chronic Kidney Dis, 13*(2), 124–130.

Brandt, K.D., & *Flusser,* D. (1991). Osteoarthritis. In: N. Bellamy (Ed.) Prognosis in the rheumatic diseases (pp. 11–35). Lancaster, England: Kluwer Academic Publishers.

Brandt, K.D., Dieppe, P., & Radin, E. (2009). Etiopathogenesis of osteoarthritis. *Med Clin North Am, 93*(1), 1–24.

Brewerton, D.A., Hart, F.D., Nicholls, A., Caffrey, M., James, D.C.O., & Sturrock, R.D. (1973). Ankylosing spondylitis and HL-A 27. *Lancet, 1,* 904–907.

Carter, E.T., McKenna, C.H., Brian, D.D., & Kurland, L.T. (1979). Epidemiology of ankylosing spondylitis in Rochester, Minnesota: 1935–1974. *Arthritis Rheum, 22,* 365–370.

CDC. (2011). *Arthritis.* Atlanta, Georgia: Centers for Disease Prevention and Control.

Cheng, Y.J., Hootman, J.M., Murphy, L.B., Langmaid, G.A., & Helmick, C.G. (2010). Prevalence of doctor-diagnosed arthritis and arthritis-attributable activity limitation—United States, 2007–2009. *MMWR; 59*(39), 1261–1265.

Choi, H.K., Atkinson, K., Darlson, E.W., Willet, W., & Curhan, G. (2004a). Alcohol intake and the risk of incident gout in men: A prospective study. *Lancet, 363*(9417), 1277–1281.

Choi, H.K., Atkinson, K., Karlson, E.W., Willett, W., & Curhan, G. (2004b). Purine-rich foods, dairy and protein intake, and the risk of gout in men. *N Engl J Med, 350*(11), 1093–1103.

Choi, H.K., Atkinson, K., Karlson, E.W., & Curhan, G. (2005). Obesity, weight change, hypertension, diuretic use, and risk of gout in men, the Health Professionals Follow-up Study. *Arch Intern Med, 165*, 742–748.

Choi, H.K., Mount, D.B., & Reginato, A.M. (2005). Pathogenesis of gout. *Ann Intern Med, 143*(7), 499–516.

Choi, H.K., Ford, E.S., Chaovang, L., & Curhan, G. (2007). Prevalence of the metabolic syndrome in patients with gout: The Third National Health and Nutrition Examination Survey. *Arthritis Care & Research, 57*(2), 109–115.

Choi, H.K. (2008). Gout: Epidemiology, pathology and pathogenesis. In J.H. Klipper, J.H. Stone, L.J. Crofford P.H. White (Eds.) *Primer on Rheumatic Diseases*, (13th ed., pp. 250–257). Springer.

Choi, H.K. (2010). Genetics of gout. *Curr Opin Rheumatol, 22*, 144–151.

Christensen, R., Bartels, E.M., Astrup, A., & Bliddal, H. (2007). Effect of weight reduction in obese patients diagnosed with knee osteoarthritis: A systematic review and meta-analysis. *Ann Rheum Dis, 66*, 433–439.

Currie, W. (1979). Prevalence and incidence of the diagnosis of gout in Great Britain. *Ann Rheum Dis, 38*, 101–106.

Davis, M.A., Ettinger, W.H., & Neuhaus, J.M. (1990). Obesity and osteoarthritis of the knee: Evidence From the National Health and Nutrition Examination Survey (NHANES I). *Seminars in Arthritis and Rheumatism, 20*(3), 34–41.

Davis, M.A., Ettinger, W.H., Neuhaus, J.M., & Hauck, W.W. (1988). Sex differences in osteoarthritis of the knee. The role of obesity. *American Journal of Epidemiology, 127*(5), 1019–1030.

Davis, M.A., Neuhaus, J.M., Ettinger, W.H., & Muller, W.H. (1990). Body fat distribution and osteoarthritis. *American Journal of Epidemiology, 132*, 701–707.

Davis, M.A., Ettinger, W.H., Neuhaus, J.M., Cho, S.A., & Hauck, W.W. (1989). The association of knee injury and obesity with unilateral and bilateral osteoarthritis of the knee. *American Journal of Epidemiology, 130*(2), 278–288.

Deighton, C.M., Walker, D.J., Griffiths, I.D., & Roberts, D.F. (1989). The contribution of HLA to rheumatoid arthritis. *Clin Gen, 36*, 178–182.

Doran, M.F., Pond, G.R., Crowson, C.S., O'Fallon, W.M., & Gabriel, S.E. (2002). Trends in incidence and mortality in rheumatoid arthritis in Rochester, Minnesota, over a forty-year period. *Arthritis & Rheumatism, 46*(3), 625–631.

Ebringer, R., Cooke, D., Cawdell, D.R., Cowing, P., & Ebringer, S. (1977). Ankylosing spondylitis: *Klebsiella* and HLA-B27. *Rheumatol Rehabil, 16*, 190–196.

Engstrom, G., de Verdier, M.G., Rollof, J., Nilsson, P.M., & Lohmander, L.S. (2008). C-reactive protein, metabolic syndrome and incidence of severe hip and knee osteoarthritis. A population-based cohort study. *Osteoarthritis and Cartilage, 17*(2), 168–173.

Ercilla, M.C., Brancos, M.A., Breysse, Y., Alonso, J., Vives, J., & Castillo, R. (1977). HLA antigens in Forestier's disease, ankylosing spondylitis and polyarthrosis of the hands. *J Rheumatol, 4*, 89–93.

Faller, J., & Fox, I.H. (1982). Ethanol-induced hyperuricemia: Evidence for increased urate production by activation of adenine nucleotide turnover. *N Engl J Med, 307*(26), 1598–1602.

Fink, C.W. (1995). Proposal for the development of classification criteria for idiopathic arthritides of childhood. *J Rheumatol, 22*, 1566–1569.

Førre, O., & Smerdel, A. (2002). Genetic epidemiology of juvenile idiopathic arthritis. *Scand J Rheumatol, 31*(3), 123–128.

Gabriel, S.E., Crowson, C.S., & O'Fallon, W.M. (1999). The epidemiology of rheumatoid arthritis in Rochester, Minnesota, 1955–1985. *Arthritis & Rheumatism, 42*(3), 415–420.

Gezcy, A.F., & Yap, J. (1982). A survey of isolates of *Klebsiella pneumoniae* which cross-react with HLA-B27-associated cell-surface structure on the lymphocytes of patients with ankylosing spondylitis. *J Rheumatol, 9,* 96–100.

Gregerson, P.K., Silver, J., & Winchester, R.J. (1987). The shared epitope hypothesis—An approach to understanding the molecular genetics of susceptibility to rheumatoid arthritis. *Arthritis Rheum, 30,* 1205–1213.

Harris, M.D., Siegel, L.B., & Alloway, J.A. (1999). Gout and hyperuricemia. In *American family physician* (pp. 925–936).

Hayward, K., & Wallace, C.A. (2009). Recent developments in anti-rheumatic drugs in pediatrics: treatment of juvenile idiopathic arthritis. *Arthritis Res Ther, 11,* 216.

Helmick, C.G., Felson, D.T., Lawrence, R.C., Gabriel, S., Hirsch, R., Kwoh, C.K., . . . Stone, J.H., National Arthritis Data Workgroup. (2008). Estimates of the prevalence of arthritis and other rheumatic conditions in the United States. Part I. *Arthritis Rheum, 58,* 15–25.

Hochberg, M.C., Bias, W.B., & Arnett, F.C. (1978). Family studies in HLA-B27-associated arthritis. *Medicine, 57,* 463–475.

Hochberg, M.C. (1984). Epidemiology. In A. Calin (Ed.): *Spondylarthropathies.* Grune and Stratton.

Hochberg, M.C. (1990). Changes in the incidence and prevalence of rheumatoid arthritis in England and Wales, 1970–1982. *Semin Arthritis Rheum, 19,* 294–302.

Hoffart, C., & Sherry, D.D. (2010). Early identification of juvenile idiopathic arthritis. *J Musculoskel Med, 27,* 52–56.

Holderbaum, D., Haqqi, T.M., & Moskowitz, R.W. (1999). Genetics and osteoarthritis: Exposing the iceberg. *Arthritis & Rheumatism, 42*(2), 397–405.

Hui, M., Doherty, M., & Zhang, W. (2011). Does smoking protect against osteoarthritis? Meta-analysis of observational studies. *Ann Rheum Dis, 70,* 1231–1237.

Kaandorp, C.J., Dinant, H.J., van de Laar, M.A., Moens, H.J., Prins, A.P., & Dijkmans, B.A. (August 1997). Incidence and sources of native and prosthetic joint infection: A community based prospective survey. *Ann Rheum Dis, 56*(8), 470–475.

Kaipiainen-Seppänen, O., Aho, K., Isomäki, H., & Laakso, M. (1996). Incidence of rheumatoid arthritis in Finland during 1980–1990. *Ann Rheum Dis, 55,* 608–611.

Khaltaev, N., Pfleger, B., Woolf, A.D., Mathers, C., Adesson, K., Hazes, J.M., & Symmons, D. (2003). Assessing the burden of musculoskeletal conditions: A joint World Health Organization–Bone and Joint Decade project. *Arthritis Res Ther, 5*(Suppl 3), 174.

Kellgren, J.H., & Lawrence, J.S. (1958). Osteoarthritis and disk degeneration in an urban population. *Annals Rheum Dis, 17,* 388–397.

Kellgren, J.H. (1962). Diagnostic criteria for population studies. *Bulletin on the Rheumatic Diseases, 13,* 291–292.

Kellgren, J.H., Lawrence, J.S., & Bier, F. (1963). Genetic factors in generalized osteoarthrosis. *Ann Rheum Dis, 22,* 237–255.

Klinenberg, J.R. (1977). Hyperuricemia and gout. *Med Clin, NA, 61,* 299.

Lawrence, J.S., & Moore, J. (1952). Generalized osteoarthritis and Heberden's nodes. *British Medical Journal, 1,* 181–187.

Lawrence, J.S. (1977). *Rheumatism in populations.* London: W Heinemann Medical Books.

Lawrence, R.C., Felson, D.T., Helmick, C.G., Arnold, L.M., Choi, H., Deyo, R.A., . . . Wolfe, F., for the National Arthritis Data Workgroup. (2008). Estimates of the prevalence of arthritis and other rheumatic conditions in the United States. Part II. *Arthritis Rheum, 58*(1), 26–35.Leong, A.L., & Euller-Ziegler, L. (2004). Patient advocacy and arthritis: Moving forward. *Bulletin of the World Health Organization, 82*(2), 115–120.

Lieber, C.S. (2005). Hyperuricemia induced by alcohol. *Arthritis & Rheumatism*, 8(4), 786–798.

Linos, A., Worthington, J.W., O'Fallon, W.M., & Kurland, L.T. (1980). The epidemiology of rheumatoid arthritis in Rochester, Minnesota: A study of incidence, prevalence, and mortality. *American Journal of Epidemiology*, 111(1), 87–98.

Luk, A.J., & Simkin, P.A. (2005). Epidemiology of Hyperuricemia and Gout. *Am J Manag Care*, 11, S435–S442.

Mankin, H.J. (1974). The reaction of articular cartilage to injury and osteoarthritis. *New Eng J Med*, 291, 1285–1335.

Manners, P.J., & Bower, C. (2002). Worldwide prevalence of juvenile arthritis why does it vary so much? *J Rheumatol*, 29, 1520–1530.

McVeigh, C.M., & Cairns, A.P. (2006). Clinical review: Diagnosis and management of ankylosing spondylitis. *BMJ*, 33(7568), 581–585.

Merriman, T.R., & Dalbeth, N. (2011). The genetic basis of hyperuricaemia and gout. *Joint Bone Spine*, 78(1), 35–40.

Mignon, B.R. (2006). The Role of X inactivation and cellular mosaicism in women's health and sex-specific diseases. *JAMA*, 295, 1428–1433.

Mikuls, T.R., Farrar, J.T., Bilker, W.B., Fernandes, S., Schumacher, H.R. Jr., & Saag, K.G. (2005). Gout epidemiology: Results from the UK General Practice Research Database, 1990–1999. *Ann Rheum Dis*, 64, 267–272.

Neel, J.V., Rakic, M.T., Davidson, R.T., Valkenburg, H.A., & Mikkelsen, W.M. (1965). Studies on hyperuricemia II. A reconsideration of the distribution of serum uric acid values in the families of Smyth, Cotterman, and Freyberg. *American J Human Genetics*, 17(1), 14–22.

Ollier, W.E.R., & MacGregor, A. (1995). Genetic epidemiology of rheumatoid disease. *Br Med Bull*, 51, 267–285.

Oliveria, S.A., Felson, D.T., Reed, J.I., Cirillo, P.A., & Walker, A.M. (1995). Incidence of symptomatic hand, hip, and knee osteoarthritis among patients in a health maintenance organization. *Arthritis & Rheumatism*, 38(8), 1134–1141.

Pattrick, M., Manhire, A., Ward, A.M., & Doherty, M. (1989). HLA-A, B antigens and a1-antitrypsin phenotypes in nodal generalised osteoarthritis and erosive osteoarthritis. *Ann Rheum Dis*, 48, 470–475.

Peterson, L.S., Mason, T., Nelson, A.M., O'Fallon, W.M., & Gabriel, S.E. (1996). Juvenile rheumatoid arthritis in rochester, minnesota 1960–1993. Is the epidemiology changing? *Arthritis & Rheumatism*, 39(8), 1385–1390.

Petty, R.E., Southwood, T.R., Baum, J., Bhettay, E., Glass, D.N., Manners, P., et al. (1998) Revision of the proposed classification criteria for juvenile idiopathic arthritis: Durban, 1997. *J Rheumatol*, 25, 1991–1994.

Petty, R.E., Southwood, T.R., Manners, P., Baum, J., Glass, D.N., Goldenberg, J.,…Woo, P. International League of Associations for Rheumatology. (2004). International League of Associations for Rheumatology. International League of Associations for Rheumatology classification of juvenile idiopathic arthritis: second revision, Edmonton 2001. *J Rheumatol*, 31, 390–392.

Pillinger, M.H., Rosenthal, P., & Abeles, A.M. (2007). Hyperuricemia and gout: New insights into pathogenesis and treatment. *Bulletin of the NYU Hospital for Joint Diseases*, 65(3), 215–221.

Prahalad, S. (2004). Genetics of juvenile idiopathic arthritis: An update. *Curr Opin Rheumatol*, 16(5), 588–594.

Radovits, B.J., Fransen, J., Shamma, S., Eijsbouts, A.M., van Riel, P.L.C.M., & Laan, R.F.J.M. (2010). Excess mortality emerges after 10 years in an inception cohort of early rheumatoid arthritis. *Arthritis Care & Research*, 62(3), 362–370.

Reveille, J.D., Ball, E.J., & Khan, M.A. (2001). HLA-B27 and genetic predisposing factors in spondyloarthropathies. *Current Opinion in Rheumatology*, 13, 265–272.

Reveille, J.D. (2006). Major histocompatibility genes and ankylosing spondylitis. *Best Practice &*

Research Clinical Rheumatology, *20*(3), 601–609.

Richette, P., & Bardin, T. (2010). Gout. *Lancet*, *375*(9711), 318–328.

Rider, L.G., Giannini, E.H., Bruneer, H.I., et al. (2004). International consensus on preliminary definitions of improvements in adult and juvenile myositis. *Arthritis Rheum*, *50*, 2281–2290.

Robbins, S.L., & Cortran, R.S. (1979). *Pathologic basis of disease* (2nd ed.). Philadelphia: WB Saunders Company.

Ropes, M.W., Bennet, G.A., Cobb, S., Jacox, R., & Jessar, R.A. (1958). Revision of diagnostic criteria for rheumatoid arthritis. *Bulletin on the Rheumatic Diseases*, *9*, 175–176.

Schlosstein, L., Terasaki, P.I., Bluestone, R., & Pearson, C.M. (1973). High association of an HL-A antigen, W27, with ankylosing spondylitis. *The New England Journal of Medicine*, *288*, 704–706.

Silman, A.J. (1988). Has the incidence of rheumatoid arthritis declined in the United Kingdom? *Br J Rheumatol*, *27*, 77–79.

Silman, A., MacGregor, A., Thomson, W., Hooligan, S., Carty, D., & Farhan, A. (1993). Twin concordance rates for rheumatoid arthritis: Results from a nationwide study. *Br J Rheumatol*, *32*, 903–907.

Smyth, C.J., Cotterman, C.W., & Freyberg, R.H. (1948). The genetics of gout and hyperuricemia: An analysis of nineteen families. *J Clin Invest*, *27*(6), 749–759.

Spector, T.D., & Hochberg, M.C. (1990). The protective effect of the oral contraceptive pill on rheumatoid arthritis: An overview of the analytic epidemiological studies using meta-analysis. *J Clin Epidemiol*, *43*(11), 1221–1230.

Statsny, P. (1978). Association of the B cell alloantigen DRw4 with rheumatoid arthritis. *N Engl J Med*, *298*, 869–871.

Stecher, R.M. (1941). Heberden's nodes: Heredity in hypertrophic arthritis of finger joints. *Am J Med Sci*, *201*, 801–809.

Storey, G.D. (2001). Alfred Baring Garrod (1819–1907). *Rheumatology (Oxford, England)*, *40*(10), 1189–1190.

Sugiyama, D., Nishimura, K., Tamaki, K., Tsuji, G., Nakazawa, T., Morinobu, A., & Kumagai, S. (2010). Impact of smoking as a risk factor for developing rheumatoid arthritis: A meta-analysis of observational studies. *Ann Rheum Dis*, *69*, 70–81.

Symmons, D., & Harrison, B. (2000). Early inflammatory polyarthritis: Results from the norfolk arthritis register with a review of the literature. I. Risk factors for the development of inflammatory polyarthritis and rheumatoid arthritis. *Rheumatology*, *39*(8), 835–843.

Symmons, D., Turner, G., Webb, R., Aslen, P., Barret, E., Lunt, M.,…Silman, A. (2002). The prevalence of rheumatoid arthritis in the United Kingdom; new estimates for a new century. *Rheumatology*, *41*(7), 793–800.

Symmons, D., Mathers, C., & Pfleger, B. (2006a). Global burden of osteoarthritis in the year 2000. In *Global Burden of Disease 2000*. Geneva, Switzerland: World Health Organization.

Symmons, D., Mathers, C., & Pfleger, B. (2006b). Global burden of rheumatoid arthritis in the year 2000. In *Global burden of disease 2000*. Geneva, Switzerland: World Health Organization.

Talbott, J.H. (1940). Serum urate in relatives of gouty patients. *J Clin Invest*, *19*, 645.

Vitart, V., Rudan, I., Hayward, C., et al. (2008). SLC2A9 is a newly identified urate transporter influencing serum urate concentration, urate excretion and gout. *Nat Genet*, *40*(4), 437–442.

Waine, H., Nevinny, D., & Rosenthal, J. (1961). Assocation of osteoarthritis and diabetes mellitus. *Tufts Folia Med*, *8*, 13–19.

Walitt, B., Pettinger, M., Weinstein, A., Katz, J., Torner, J., Wasko, M.C., & Howard, B.V. for the Women's Health Initiative. (2008). Effects of postmenopausal hormone therapy on rheumatoid arthritis: The Women's Health Initiative randomized controlled trials. *Arthritis Rheum*, *59*(3), 302–310.

Wallace, K.L., Riedel, A.A., Joseph-Ridge, N., & Wortmann, R. (2004). Increasing Prevalence ofg and hyperuricemia over 10 years among older adults in a managed care population. *J Rheumatol, 31*, 1582–1587.

Wandel, S., Jüni, P., Tendal, B., Nüesch, E., Villiger, P.M., Welton, N.J., Reichenbach, S., & Trelle, S. (2010). Effects of glucosamine, chondroitin, or placebo in patients with osteoarthritis of hip or knee: Network meta-analysis. *BMJ, 341*, D4675.

Weaver, A. (2008). Epidemiology of gout. *Cleve Clin J Med, 75*(Suppl 5), S9–S12.

Weinberg, J.B., Fermor, B., & Guilak, F. (2007). Nitric oxide synthase and cyclooxygenase interactions in cartilage and mensiscus: Relationship to joint physiology, arthritis and tissue repair. *Subcellular Biochemistry, 42*, 31–62.

Weston, V.C., Jones, A.C., Bradbury, N., Fawthrop, F., & Doherty, M. (1999). Clinical features and outcome of septic arthritis in a single UK Health District 1982–1991. *Ann Rheum Dis, 58*(4), 214–219.

Weyand, C.M., Hicok, K.C., Conn, D.L., & Goronzy, J.J. (1992). The influence of HLA-DRB1 genes on disease severity in rheumatoid arthritis. *Annals of Internal Medicine, 117*(10), 801–806.

WHO. (2009). Death and DALY estimates for 2004 by cause for WHO Member States (Persons, all ages). *WHO Disease and Injury Estimates*. World Health Organization.

Williams, C.J., & Jimenez, S.A. (1995). Heritable diseases of cartilage caused by mutations in collagen genes. *J Rheumatol, 22*, 28–33.

Yamamoto, T., Moriwaki, Y., & Takahashi, S. (2005). Effect of ethanol on metabolism of purine bases (hypoxanthine, xanthine and uric acid). *Clinica chimica Acta, 356*(1–2), 35–57.

Epidemiology of Alzheimer's Disease

INTRODUCTION

Alzheimer's disease is the most common form of dementia accounting for more than 50% of all cases. This incurable, degenerative, terminal disease was first described by German psychiatrist and neuropathologist, Alois Alzheimer, in 1907 (Alzheimer, 1907). Onset typically occurs after age 65 years; although there are familial forms of Alzheimer's disease that develop earlier in life.

The second most common type of dementia is *vascular dementia* which accounts for most of the remaining cases. Vascular dementia refers to loss of brain function due to decreased cerebral blood flow often secondary to mini-strokes that occlude the cerebral arterioles and smaller blood vessels. Vascular dementia is discussed later in this chapter.

The pathologic hallmark of Alzheimer's disease is a significant loss of neurons in the brain. Compared with the healthy adult brain which contains more than 100 billion neurons, the Alzheimers' brain is characterized by dramatic shrinkage from cell loss and widespread debris from dead and dying neurons. Progression of disease ultimately results in complete loss of memory and absence of normal brain function. Fatality is often due to pneumonia in a bedridden, totally incapacitated patient.

Alzheimer's disease predominantly strikes adults late in life. As a consequence, incidence and prevalence rates are highest in developed nations whose populations contain greater numbers of elderly people. Age-specific incidence rates of dementia based on data from 23 published studies are shown in **Figure 39.1**. Rates are slightly higher in women than men and peak

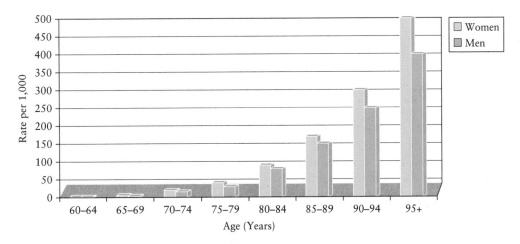

Figure 39.1 Age-Specific Incidence of Alzheimer's Disease by Gender.

Source: Data from Jorm AF, Jolley D (1998). The incidence of dementia: a meta-analysis. *Neurology* 51:728–733.

during the ninth decade of life. The rates approximately double for each successive 5-year age interval, and among women over the age of 95 years, the cumulative (5 year) risk of developing Alzheimer's disease is about 50% (Jorm and Jolley, 1998).

DIAGNOSIS AND PROGRESSION OF ALZHEIMER'S DISEASE

The specific criteria used to diagnose Alzheimer's disease and other forms of dementia are defined in the *Diagnostic and Statistical Manual of Mental Disorders, Fourth Edition (DSM-IV)*. Early symptoms of Alzheimer's disease include memory deficits, confusion, irritability, aggression, mood swings, and behavioral changes. The diagnosis is made by behavioral and cognitive tests, and brain scans that reveal characteristic morphological changes in the brain. Alzheimer's disease is characterized by the loss of neurons and synapses in the cerebral cortex and subcortical regions of the brain, particularly in the hippocampus, a key memory center located in the medial temporal lobe. The loss of neurons results in marked atrophy of the affected regions. Imaging studies using *magnetic resonance imaging* (MRI) and *positron emission tomography* (PET) have documented reductions in the size of specific regions of the brain in patients as they progressed from mild cognitive impairment to Alzheimer's disease (Förstl and Kurz, 1999; Waldemar et al., 2007).

Progression of disease brings the gradual loss of all bodily functions and, ultimately, death. Since Alzheimer's disease is incurable and progressive, patient management and care are essential. However, caregivers are often faced with overwhelming social, psychological, physical, and economic pressures.

GLOBAL INCIDENCE OF ALZHEIMER'S DISEASE

Based on a meta-analysis of age-specific incidence data from 23 studies, Jorm and Jolley found that the incidence of Alzheimer's disease doubles for each 5-year age interval after the age of 65 years (**Figure 39.1**). This corresponds to an *incidence doubling time* of 5 years, definable as the chronological number of years required for the age-specific incidence to double in magnitude (Jorm and Jolley, 1998).

Investigators at Johns Hopkins University recently conducted an updated meta-analysis of published age-specific incidence rates of Alzheimer's disease in order to characterize regional and gender differences in the incidence doubling times as well as

the rates. Their analysis was based upon age-specific incidence rates reported in 27 publications. Age-specific incidence rates of Alzheimer's disease were modeled by log-linear regression for men and women of six geographic regions (Africa, Asia, Europe, Latin America, North America, and Oceania). As expected, incidence rates varied considerably and were higher in men than women, and higher in populations of developed nations than developing nations. For example, the incidence at age 80 years was 1.37% for women, 1.06% for men, 2.06% for North American populations, 1.48% for European populations, and 0.83% for populations of other nations. Nevertheless, regression analysis revealed *no significant differences in* the *incidence doubling times* by gender or by region. Overall, the incidence of Alzheimer's disease increased by about 13% with each advancing year of age, which yields an overall incidence doubling time of 5.5 years. The homogeneity of incidence doubling times suggests that progression of Alzheimer's disease is similar across populations, whereas differences in the magnitude of the incidence rates could reflect differences in environmental and/or genetic factors that influence disease onset, or differences in clinical thresholds for case diagnosis (Ziegler-Graham et al., 2008).

GLOBAL PREVALENCE OF ALZHEIMER'S DISEASE

According to published estimates from different sources, the number of living Alzheimer's patients increased from about 24 million in 2001 to 36 million in 2010, an increase of more than 1.2 million prevalent cases per year (Ferri et al., 2005; World Health Organization, 2006; Brookmeyer et al., 2007; World Alzheimer Report, 2010). This increase primarily reflects the increasing longevity of the world population and underscores the growing health burden of dementia in the aged. Recent reports suggest that unless effective interventions are discovered and implemented, the global prevalence of Alzheimer's disease and other forms of dementia will double every 20 years and surpass 80 million by 2040 (Brookmeyer, Gray, and Kawas, 1998; Ferri et al, 2005; Brookmeyer et al., 2007).

ALZHEIMER'S DISEASE: SURVIVAL AND CASE FATALITY

Survival following the diagnosis of Alzheimer's disease is reduced by at least 50% compared to the general population. Albeit, median survival times and case fatality rates are highly variable and depend on several factors including the severity of disease at the time of diagnosis, the age and gender of the patient, the level of care, and the rate of disease progression. In general, studies of patients from different locations and in different settings reveal that younger patients survive longer than older patients, women survive longer than men, and patients with mild disability at diagnosis survive longer than those with severe disability. Selected studies of survival and related measures in patients with Alzheimer's disease are discussed in the following paragraphs.

Investigators at the University of Turku in Finland examined the survival experience of 218 patients with Alzheimer's disease and 115 patients with *vascular dementia* secondary to stroke. For the Alzheimers' patients, the 14-year survival rate was 2.4% compared to 16.6% for the general population, median survival was 5 years, and 68% of deaths were directly attributed to dementia. Advanced disability and male gender were independently found to increase the relative risk of dying by about twofold. Survival measures were similar for patients with dementia due to vascular disease (Mölsä, Marttila, and Rinne, 1986).

Investigators in the Netherlands used mortality data from the *Rotterdam Study*, a population-based prospective study of elderly adults, to estimate overall and severity-specific mortality for patients with dementia. Results revealed that dementia was associated with increased mortality in all age, sex, and disease severity groups. In comparison to healthy individuals from the Dutch population, mortality rate ratios for subjects with dementia were increased more than twofold in men (RR = 2.1) and women (RR = 2.3) (Witthaus et al., 1999).

Investigators at McGill University in Montreal, Canada, used data from the *Canadian Study of Health and Aging* to evaluate the survival experience of 821 subjects with dementia (396 with Alzheimer's disease, 252 with possible Alzheimer's disease, and 173 with vascular dementia). The investigators noted that previous studies failed to include persons with rapidly progressive disease who died before they could be enrolled, thus introducing a type of bias referred to as *"length or survivor bias."* After adjustment for length bias, the median survival was 3.1 years for patients with probable Alzheimer's disease, 3.5 years for patients with possible Alzheimer's disease, and 3.3 years for patients with vascular dementia. As in other studies, female gender and younger age of onset were significant predictors of longer survival. The investigators concluded that with appropriate adjustment, survival following onset of dementia is much shorter than previously thought (Wolfson et al., 2001).

Investigators at Johns Hopkins University in Baltimore, Maryland, studied the survival of 108 incident cases of Alzheimer's disease in the *Baltimore Longitudinal Study of Aging*. The median survival was 8.3 years for those diagnosed at age 65 years compared to 3.4 years for those diagnosed at age 90 years. Diagnoses at ages 65 and 90 years were associated with approximately 67% and 39% reductions in median life span, respectively (Brookmeyer et al., 2002).

Investigators at the University of Washington in Seattle studied the survival of 521 patients with newly recognized Alzheimer's disease. The median survival was 4.2 years in men and 5.7 years in women. Men had significantly poorer survival than women across all age groups, and survival was decreased in all age groups compared to the US population (Bowen et al., 1996; Larson et al., 2004).

Investigators at Columbia University in New York studied the survival of 323 incident cases of Alzheimer's disease. The *annual case fatality rate* was slightly higher in men than women (11.6 vs. 9.9 deaths per 100 person years) and trended upwards with age at diagnosis (7.0, 9.1, and 16.1 per 100 person years for patients diagnosed at <75, 75–84, and 85+ years, respectively). The median survival for all patients was 6.0 years, but those diagnosed before age 75 years survived twice as long as those diagnosed after age 85 years (median survival times, 9.9 vs. 4.4 years. respectively). The presence of diabetes or hypertension at the time of diagnosis also increased the risk of death (RR = 2.57 and RR = 1.99, respectively) (Helzner et al., 2008).

Investigators at the University of Pittsburg conducted a nested case control study of Alzheimer's disease in a community-based cohort of 1,670 elderly subjects in Pennsylvania. Cases and controls were ascertained during 15 years of follow-up. Based on 330 incident cases, the overall mean survival was 5.9 years; however, survival was significantly longer for patients with earlier onset (8.3 years for onset before age 75 years vs. 3.8 years for onset at 85 years or older). There was no difference in mean survival between men and women. Based on a Cox regression analysis of 273 cases and 546 controls, the adjusted hazard ratio for mortality was 1.40, indicating that patients with Alzheimer's disease had a 40% increased risk of dying compared to those without dementia (Ganguli et al., 2005).

Investigators at the University of Cambridge in England studied the survival of 438 incident cases of Alzheimer's disease or other forms of dementia ascertained from multiple centers in England and Wales. The subjects were ascertained from a population-based cohort of 13,004 individuals enrolled in 1991 and followed until 2005. The overall median survival was 4.5 years, but survival among patients diagnosed before 70 years of age was more than double that among those diagnosed after age 80 years (10.7 vs. 4.3 years, respectively). Other significant predictors of mortality included male gender and severe disability (Xie et al., 2008).

Investigators affiliated with the *Medical Research Council General Practice Research Framework* in London conducted a case control study of survival involving patients from 353 general medicine practices comprising the *Health Improvement Network* in the United Kingdom. The study compared survival in 22,529 patients with dementia to 112,645 controls without dementia. In addition, the annual incidence of dementia was estimated during 1997–2007 for the entire network population. During the 11-year time frame of study, the annual incidence of dementia remained relatively stable at about 4 cases per 1,000 person years at risk. The median survival among patients with dementia decreased from 6.7 years for patients diagnosed before age 70 years to 1.9 years for those diagnosed at 90 years or older. Most notably, in the first year after diagnosis, the mortality rate was more than three times greater in patients with dementia than in those without (adjusted RR = 3.68). In subsequent years, the mortality rates remained more than twofold higher among patients with dementia (mean adjusted RR = 2.42). Adjustment for comorbidities and other factors had little effect on the rate ratios. The investigators suggest that *"the high risk of death in the first year after diagnosis may reflect diagnoses made at times of crisis or late in the disease trajectory"* (Rait et al., 2010).

ALZHEIMER'S DISEASE: GLOBAL MORTALITY

Similar to the incidence and prevalence, mortality rates due to Alzheimer's disease vary widely among populations around the globe. Low rates reflect short longevity as in sub-Saharan Africa where the life span is less than 50 years and the annual Alzheimers' mortality rate is less than 1 death per 100,000. Intermediate mortality rates are characteristic of nations in transition such as India and China, whereas much higher rates exceeding 20 deaths per 100,000 are evident in the populations of developed countries such as the United States (Alzheimer's Association, 2010).

Due to the *"epidemiologic transition"* and the gradual aging of the world population, it has become evident that the mortality due to Alzheimer's disease has increased dramatically in most popula-

tions during the past few decades. However, mortality estimates are typically based upon the reported *underlying cause of death* on death certificates, and Alzheimer's disease and other forms of dementia are often *unlisted* as either the principle cause or a contributing cause of death, even in decedents known to have severe antecedent dementia.

As pointed out by Hoyert and Rosenberg of the US National Center for Health Statistics (NCHS):

> *"Generally, more than one cause of death is reported on the death certificate, and together these causes are referred to as "multiple causes of death." For each death certificate, one of the causes is referred to as an "underlying cause of death," defined as the disease or injury that initiated the train of events leading directly to death or the circumstances of the accident or violence that produced the fatal injury. To classify medical terms on the death certificate, NCHS uses the International Classification of Diseases. Generally, the underlying cause is the item tabulated and presented for statistical purposes in the United States and other countries"* (Hoyert and Rosenberg, 1997).

Based upon the cause of death listed on death certificates in the United States population, mortality rates attributed to Alzheimer's disease increased dramatically during 1979–1995, from about 2 per 100,000 in 1979 to 38 per 100,000 in 1995 among individuals over the age of 65 years. *However, mortality rates computed from death certificates with Alzheimer's disease listed as one of multiple causes are more than double the rates based on only the underlying cause of death.* For example, in 1995 Alzheimer's disease was listed as the underlying cause of death on 20,230 death certificates, while it appeared as one of multiple causes of death on 40,836 death certificates (Hoyert and Rosenberg, 1997, 1999).

Reporting inaccuracies for Alzheimer's disease and dementia have also been noted in studies of decedents known to have terminal stage disease. Investigators in Boston examined the death certificates of 165 decedents in a cohort of patients in nursing homes who had advanced dementia due to Alzheimer's disease or other forms of senile dementia. Despite the terminal nature of dementia among these individuals, neither Alzheimer's disease nor dementia was recorded on the death certificates of 37% of decedents. Furthermore, among 115 decedents diagnosed with terminal Alzheimer's disease, only 27% of death certificates mentioned Alzheimer's disease as a cause of death. These results raise concerns about the accuracy of the global mortality statistics on Alzheimer's disease and other forms of dementia (Wachterman, Kiely, and Mitchel, 2008).

In addition to the underreporting of certain conditions such as Alzheimer's disease and dementia, changes in coding and reporting practices can have a marked influence on disease rates. Mortality rates attributed to Alzheimer's disease in the US population during 1980–2010 are shown in **Figure 39.2**. It is important to note that prior to 1999, physicians completing death certificates often coded Alzheimer's disease as senile dementia, likely resulting in se- vere *underestimates* of cause-specific mortality. Consolidation into a single code took place in the 10th revision of the *International Classification of Diseases*, which was implemented around the turn of the century. Thus, the rates in the United States and many other populations after the year 1999 show a distinct "jump" compared to the prior rates due to the change in ICD coding rather than biological phenomena. Such spikes in disease rates are often a consequence of reporting changes, which must be taken into account in the examination of time trends (Griffiths and Rooney, 2006).

Irrespective of the ICD coding change in 1999, it is clear from the US data that the annual mortality rates due to Alzheimer's disease are trending upward. Furthermore, the US trends in reported mortality rates for Alzheimer's disease are consistent with those in several other developed countries including Canada, England, Australia, Norway, Japan, and Sweden (Newman and Bland, 1987; Martyn and Pippard, 1988; Jorm, Henderson, and Jacomb, 1989; Flaten, 1989; Imaizumi, 1992; Hallberg, 2009). In these countries

as in the United States, mortality rates attributable to Alzheimer's disease have increased dramatically.

The World Health Organization (WHO) periodi- cally reports the global number of deaths based upon compilation of the causes listed on samples of death certificates from various regions of the world. In 2002, WHO reported that Alzheimer's disease was respon- sible for 397,000 (0.7%) of nearly 58 million deaths (WHO, 2003). However, as already discussed, it is likely that mortality rates are severely underestimated from death certificates, even in developed nations.

An alternative method of calculating mortality is derived from the annual case fatality rate. Numerous studies suggest that the median survival among newly diagnosed Alzheimer's patients is approximately 5 years, which converts to an annual case fatality rate of about 13%, and since Alzheimers' patients have an approximate twofold higher mortality than nor- mal individuals of the same age, their *excess annual mortality* is approximately 6%. Thus, the number of worldwide deaths directly attributable to Alzheimer's disease in 2002 can be estimated as 6% of 24 million prevalent cases or approximately 1.44 million. Since the case fatality rate of Alzheimer's patients has remained stable, the total number of attributable deaths in 2010 is 6% of 36 million prevalent cases or approximately 2.16 million.

It is noteworthy that an alternative indirect method gives a similar value, e.g., if the 397 million deaths reported due to Alzheimer's disease on death certificates in 2002 represents only 27% of the actual deaths, then the total number of deaths attributable to Alzheimer's disease is 397 million/0.27 = 1.47 million deaths.

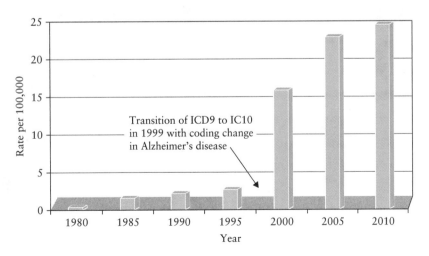

Figure 39.2 Trend of Annual Mortality for Alzheimer's Disease, USA, 1980–2010.

Source: Data from Hoyert DL, Rosenberg HM (1999). Mortality from Alzheimer's disease: an update. *Natl Vital Stat Rep* 47(20):1-8. Alzheimer's Association (2010). Alzheimer's Disease Facts and Figures. Alzheimer's Association, Washington DC, 2010.

The major factor responsible for the increasing incidence, prevalence, and mortality rates of Alzheimer's disease is undoubtedly the increasing longevity in populations throughout the world. It is also likely that greater awareness of symptoms among physicians has increased the recording of Alzheimer's disease on death certificates. Obviously, it is important to separate increases due to death certificate diagnoses because of growing awareness of the disease from true increases caused by biological changes in pathogenesis. Although death rates represent a potential measure of the public health impact of Alzheimer's disease, variations in the accuracy of diagnosis and in the completion of death certificates limit the value of mortality data in estimating the true burden of this disease.

ALZHEIMER'S DISEASE: DISABILITY ADJUSTED LIFE YEARS (DALY)

Figure 39.3 shows the global pattern of disability adjust life years (DALY) lost from Alzheimers' disease and other forms of dementia during 2004. The highest DALY are evident in the older populations of the developed world including North America, Europe, Scandinavia, Japan, and Australia. Based on estimates reported by the World Health Organization, dementia contributed 11.2% of years lived with disability in people aged 60 years and older, which is more than stroke, musculoskeletal disorders, cardiovascular disease, and all forms of cancer. The disability burden for dementia, estimated by an international and multidisciplinary expert consensus, was higher than all other health conditions, apart from spinal-cord injury and terminal cancer.

BURDEN OF ALZHEIMER'S DISEASE IN THE UNITED STATES

It is estimated that 5.4 million Americans are living with Alzheimer's disease. Of these, 5.2 million are 65 years or older and the remaining 200,000 cases have early onset disease. During 2000–2008, mortality due to Alzheimer's disease increased by about 66%, making it the 6th leading cause of death in the United States (see **Figure 39.2**). Based on review of the underlying cause of death listed on death certificates, 74,632 (17.6%) of the 2,423,712 deaths that occurred in the United States during 2007 were attributed to Alzheimer's disease (Xu et al., 2010).

PATHOLOGY OF ALZHEIMER'S DISEASE

Alzheimer's disease is characterized by the loss of neurons and synapses in the cerebral cortex and subcortical regions of the brain. The loss of neurons results in marked atrophy of the affected regions. Imaging studies using *magnetic resonance imaging* (MRI) and *positron emission tomography* (PET)

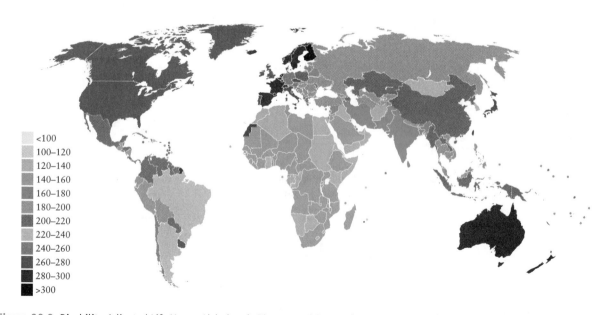

Figure 39.3 Disability Adjusted Life Years: Alzheimer's Disease and Dementia, 2004.

Source: Data from World Health Organization. The global burden of disease: 2004 update. Geneva, WHO, 2008. Available at www.who.int /evidence/bod.

have documented reductions in the size of specific regions of the brain in patients as they progressed from mild cognitive impairment to Alzheimer's disease (Waldemar et al., 2007).

Postmortem studies of the brains of Alzheimer's patients have revealed distinct features including diminished brain size, increased ventricle size, characteristic plaques and tangles in the white matter, and millions of dead or dying neurons. Using a silver staining technique, Alois Alzheimer and his contemporary rival, Oskar Fischer, first identified neuritic plaques and neurofibrillary tangles in postmortem specimens of cerebral cortex from afflicted patients (Goedert, 2009). The neurofibrillary tangles characteristic of Alzheimer's brains are laden with *beta amyloid* and deranged *tau protein* that are associated with pathogenesis and the loss of neuronal function (Tiraboschi et al., 2004).

Amyloid plaques and neurofibrillary tangles are clearly visible by microscopy in brains of those afflicted by Alzheimer's disease. Neurofibrillary tangles are aggregates of a microtubule-associated protein, *tau protein,* which has become hyperphosphorylated and accumulates inside the neurons. Amyloid plaques are made up of small peptide fragments called *beta-amyloid.* Beta-amyloid is derived from a larger transmembrane protein, *amyloid precursor protein,* that is critical for neuron growth, survival, and postinjury repair. In Alzheimer's disease, the degradation of amyloid precursor protein is disrupted and fibrils of beta-amyloid form clumps that deposit outside neurons in dense formations known as senile plaques (Turner et al., 2003).

In his initial studies, Alzheimer noted the presence of *inflammation* and *gliosis* in postmortem specimens of brain tissue from afflicted patients. The inflammatory response is typically localized around beta-amyloid plaques and is characterized by influx of proinflammatory microglia and astrocytes (Akiyama et al., 2000). Furthermore, biochemical markers of inflammation such as cyclosocygenase-2 (COX-2), complement factors, and certain chemokines and cytokines have been found in excess in brain tissues of Alzheimer's patients (Yasojima et al., 2000). The sequence of pathogenesis of Alzheimer's disease has not yet been determined, and it is unknown whether inflammation is an *effect* of the disease process or a *causative factor* in the initiation and progression of disease.

Recent studies have noted the presence of *beta-amyloid* and *tau protein* in the cerebrospinal fluid of most patients with Alzheimer's disease (Marksteiner, Hinterhuber, and Hinterhuber, 2007). Furthermore, in follow-up studies of subjects with mild cognitive impairment, these CSF biomarkers were found to accurately predict progression to Alzheimer's disease, suggesting they may have a role in the early detection of disease (De Meyer et al., 2010).

RISK FACTORS OF ALZHEIMER'S DISEASE

The primary risk factor for Alzheimer's disease is age. As initially suggested by Jorm and Jolley and confirmed by others, the incidence doubles every 5 years after 65 years of age for men and women of all populations studied (Jorm and Jolley, 1998; Ziegler-Graham et al., 2008). Nevertheless, postmortem studies of the brains of centenarians reveal that Alzheimer's disease and/or other forms of brain pathology are not always the inevitable outcome of the aging process (den Dunnen et al., 2008).

Alzheimer's Disease and Cardiovascular Risk Factors

In patients with Alzheimer's disease, cerebral infarcts due to mini-strokes often contribute to the progression of disease, and most cases display not only the characteristic pathologic findings of Alzheimer (amyloid deposition, neurofibrillary tangles, and inflammation) but also atherosclerosis, ischemia, and disruption of the blood brain barrier (Querfurth and LaFerla, 2010). *Indeed, all of the classical risk factors for ischemic heart disease and stroke have been found to increase the risk of Alzheimer's disease.* Selected studies of smoking, hypertension, hypercholesterolemia, hyperglycemia, and obesity are discussed in the following paragraphs.

The mortality rates due to cardiovascular diseases such as ischemic heart disease and stroke have declined substantially during the last few decades in populations of many developed nations. These declines have primarily been attributed to reductions in cigarette smoking, coupled with effective detection and treatment of heart disease, hypertension, diabetes and hyperlipidemia, plus regular exercise, improved nutrition, and possibly the intake of low dose aspirin. Since there is some evidence implicating cardiovascular risk factors in the development of neurodegenerative diseases, investigators have searched for corresponding trends in the development of Alzheimer's disease and other forms of dementia. Correlative secular trends are evident in two such studies conducted in the United States and Japan.

A team of investigators from multiple US centers investigated secular trends in the age-specific prevalence and incidence rates of Alzheimer's disease and dementia in elderly cohorts from communities in Minnesota, Illinois, and Indiana, and in the nationwide *US Health and Retirement Study*. Results of the study were mixed. In the cohorts from individual communities, there were no significant trends in either the incidence or the prevalence of Alzheimer's disease or dementia. However, in the *Health and Retirement* cohort, the prevalence of dementia declined from 12.2% in 1993 to 8.7% in 2002, suggesting that public health and medical interventions targeting cardiovascular conditions may also have had a favorable impact on neurological health (Rocca et al., 2011).

Investigators at Kyushu University in Fukuoka, Japan, examined secular trends in the prevalence of Alzheimer's disease and vascular dementia in a prospective cohort residing in the rural community of Hisayama. The study included four cross-sectional examinations conducted in 1985, 1992, 1998, and 2005. Results revealed a significant *increase* in the age and gender-adjusted prevalence of Alzheimer's disease and all-cause dementia. The overall prevalence of Alzheimer's disease increased from 1.1% in 1985 to 3.8% in 2005. The greatest prevalence increase, from 5% in 1985 to 15% in 2005, was observed among individuals who were 80 years and older. These results suggest that increasing rates of metabolic disorders such as obesity, hypercholesterolemia, and glucose intolerance may be associated with the rising prevalence of Alzheimer's disease in the Japanese population (Sekita et al., 2010).

Hypertension, Hypercholesterolemia, and Alzheimer's Disease

As part of a longitudinal study in Gothenburg, Sweden, a team of neuroscientists analyzed the relation between blood pressure and the development of dementia among 382 elderly adults. The cohort was followed for up to 15 years and participants were examined periodically to detect neurological changes. Participants who developed dementia at age 79 years or older had significantly higher mean systolic and diastolic blood pressures at baseline compared to those who remained disease free (178 vs. 164 mm Hg, and 101 vs. 92 mm Hg, respectively). Furthermore, dementia cases with cerebral white matter lesions (mini-infarcts) by computed tomography had significantly higher baseline blood pressure levels than control subjects. It was also noted that the blood pressures of cases declined to lower levels in the years just before diagnosis. The investigators concluded that longstanding hypertension may increase the risk of developing dementia by inducing small vessel disease and white matter lesions in the brain (Skoog et al., 1996).

The *Honolulu Heart Program* of the *Honolulu Asian Aging Study* was designed to investigate the association of midlife blood pressure and the development of Alzheimer's disease or other forms of dementia in Japanese-American men. Participants ($n = 3,703$) were enrolled and examined during 1965–1971 and subsequently reexamined in 1991. Odds ratios (OR) were estimated for baseline levels of systolic and diastolic blood pressure with stratification by the presence/absence of treatment with anti-hypertensive medications. Estimates were adjusted for age, education, apolipoprotein (APOEε4) genotype, smoking, and alcohol intake. Among untreated subjects with elevated blood pressure at baseline, the risk of developing Alzheimer's disease or dementia was significantly increased compared to normotensive subjects. Elevated diastolic levels resulted in fourfold risk increases (OR = 3.8 for 90–94 mm Hg and OR = 4.3 for 95 mm Hg or higher) and elevated systolic levels increased the risk nearly fivefold (OR = 4.8 for 160 mm Hg or higher). Notably, men who received antihypertension therapy were *not* at increased risk. These results suggest that untreated hypertension during middle age is a significant risk factor for the development of dementia later in life (Launer et al., 2000).

Investigators at the University of Kuopio in Finland examined associations of blood pressure and serum cholesterol with the development of Alzheimer's disease in a prospective population-based study in eastern Finland. Participants were enrolled in 1972 and followed for an average of 21 years. A total of 1,449 participants took part in the study. The results revealed that hypertension (systolic blood pressure exceeding 160 mm Hg) and hypercholesterolemia (serum cholesterol exceeding 240 mg per dl) diagnosed in midlife (mean age, 54 years) were independently associated with increased risks of developing Alzheimer's disease later in life (mean onset, 75 years). Compared to subjects with normal blood pressure and serum cholesterol, the odds of developing disease was increased more than twofold in subjects with hypertension (OR = 2.3) or hypercholesterolemia (RR = 2.1), and the disease odds increased more than threefold for subjects with both risk factors (OR = 3.5). These findings suggest that high blood pressure and elevated cholesterol are risk factors, not only for cardiovascular disease, but also for Alzheimer's disease and dementia (Kivipelto et al., 2001).

Several randomized placebo-controlled clinical trials have been conducted to evaluate effects of antihypertensive medications in reducing the risk of developing dementia or slowing progression of disease. The results of these investigations are mixed, with some showing benefit and others not.

In an extended study of patients enrolled in the double blind, placebo-controlled *Systolic*

Hypertension in Europe (Syst-Eur) Trial, 1,485 elderly patients continued therapy with antihypertensive agents (primarily nitrendipine) whereas 1,417 control subjects were not treated. During 3.9 years of total follow-up, the mean systolic blood pressure in the treated group was 7.0 mm Hg less than the untreated group, and the incidence rate of dementia in the treated group was 55% less than in the untreated group (3.3 cases vs. 7.4 cases per 1,000 person-years). After adjustment for age, gender, entry blood pressure, and other factors, the hazard ratio for patients treated with the long acting antihypertensive agent, nitrendipine, was 0.38 (Forette et al., 2002).

The *Perindopril Protection Against Recurrent Stroke Study (PROGRESS)* was a randomized, double-blind, placebo-controlled clinical trial designed to evaluate the development of dementia with and without active treatment to control blood pressure among patients with a prior history of stroke or transient ischemic attacks. A total of 6,105 subjects were randomized to receive either antihypertensive medications (perindopril with or without indapamide) or placebo. During a mean follow-up of 3.9 years, 193 (6.3%) of 3,051 treated subjects developed dementia compared to 217 (7.1%) of 3,054 subjects who received placebo, a risk reduction of 12%. Furthermore, cognitive decline occurred less often in the treatment group compared to the placebo group (9.1% vs. 11.0%). Patients who suffered recurrent strokes were found to benefit the most from active blood pressure therapy (Tzourio et al., 2003).

In the *Hypertensive Old People in Edinburgh (HOPE)* study, 81 elderly dementia-free individuals with hypertension were treated with antihypertensive medications (captopril or bendrofluazid) for 6 months and evaluated for cognitive changes from baseline by a battery of psychometric tests. Individuals with the greatest reductions in systolic blood pressure (at least 19 mm Hg) had significantly improved cognition compared to those with reductions of 5 mm Hg or less (Starr, Whalley, and Deary, 1996).

While these studies suggest that long-term adequate blood pressure control may reduce the risk of developing dementia and improve cognition in subjects with hypertension, other studies have failed to disclose any significant benefit of therapy. Additional well-designed clinical trials will be required to clarify the effects of medications that lower blood pressure on cognitive decline (Reitz, Brayne, and Mayeux, 2011).

Smoking and Alzheimer's Disease

Epidemiologic investigations of smoking and Alzheimer's disease have yielded mixed results with some showing increases in the risk and others showing decreases. In order to clarify the findings and eliminate possible biases, investigators at the University of California in San Francisco conducted a meta-analysis of the relationship between smoking and Alzheimer's disease with adjustment for study design, study quality, secular trends, and *tobacco affiliation of study authors*. Analysis of 14 cohort studies *without* tobacco industry affiliation yielded a significantly *increased* relative risk (RR = 1.45) whereas analysis of 3 studies *with* tobacco industry affiliation yielded a *decreased* relative risk (RR = 0.60). Limiting the analysis to only cohort studies with at least average quality (based on scientific journal impact score) yielded an even higher relative risk (RR = 1.74). Based upon analysis of those studies *without tobacco industry affiliation*, the investigators concluded that smoking is a significant risk factor for the development of Alzheimer's disease (Cataldo, Prochaska, and Glantz, 2010).

Insulin Resistance, Diabetes, and Alzheimer's Disease

Several epidemiologic investigations have examined the risk of developing Alzheimer's disease in subjects with insulin resistance and/or diabetes. In the US Framingham community-based prospective cohort, 202 elderly participants with diabetes mellitus and 2,008 subjects of similar age without diabetes were identified for study. All subjects were dementia free at baseline, and risk subgroups were defined by apolipoprotein E genotype and plasma homocysteine levels. Individuals were followed for up to 20 years to detect incident cases of Alzheimer's disease. Among subjects *without* apolipoprotein E4 or elevated plasma homocysteine, the risk of developing Alzheimer's disease was increased nearly threefold in diabetic versus nondiabetic subjects (RR = 2.98). The effect of diabetes in this group was strongest for subjects aged 75 years or older (RR = 4.77). The investigators concluded that diabetes may increase the risk in the absence of other known risk factors (Akomolafe et al., 2006).

Similar results were reported for a community-based cohort of 1,173 elderly individuals in Sweden. At baseline, all subjects were free of dementia and diabetes, but 47 subjects had "*borderline diabetes*" with plasma glucose levels in the range, 120–140 mg per dl. During 9 years of follow-up, 397 subjects developed dementia and 207 developed Alzheimer's disease. Borderline diabetes at baseline was associated with an increased risk of developing dementia (HR = 1.67) or Alzheimer's disease (HR = 1.77). In stratified analyses, the risk associated with antecedent borderline diabetes was found entirely in those individuals who were *noncarriers* of the APOEε4 allele. Furthermore, the presence of severe systolic hypertension was found to accentuate the risk in individuals with borderline diabetes (Xu et al., 2007).

Investigators at New York Upstate Medical University examined associations of Alzheimer's disease with body mass, diabetes, metabolic syndrome, and insulin resistance by meta-analyses of published prospective epidemiologic investigations. For the nine studies that focused on diabetes, the pooled estimate of risk was significantly elevated (RR = 1.54) and the test for heterogeneity was not significant (Profenno, Porsteinsson, and Faraone, 2010).

Despite these epidemiologic findings of an association between antecedent diabetes and the development of Alzheimer's disease, other studies that have incorporated neuropathologic examination of postmortem brain specimens from decedents with dementia have failed to confirm the link. For example, a team of investigators in Chicago examined the neuropathology of postmortem specimens from 233 elderly men who underwent extensive annual neurological evaluations prior to death. While antecedent diabetes was associated with an increased odds of cerebral infarction (OR = 2.47), no association was found between diabetes and pathologically confirmed Alzheimer's disease (Arvanitakis et al., 2006).

Some randomized clinical trials have shown that antidiabetic drugs are of benefit to patients with cognitive impairment. In a paired crossover study conducted at the Veteran's Administration Hospital in Seattle, Washington, 26 memory-impaired subjects and 35 normal controls were given either intranasal insulin or saline on separate occasions to assess acute effects on cognition. Insulin administration was found to facilitate recall in memory-impaired subjects who were *negative* for APOEε4, but not in subjects who were *positive* for APOEε4 or in normal control subjects (Reger et al., 2005).

Other studies also suggest that the cognitive benefit of antidiabetic therapy in patients with Alzheimer's disease may be genotype-specific for APOEε4. Investigators in North Carolina studied cognitive effects of the oral diabetic medication, *rosiglitazone*, in a randomized clinical trial of 511 patients diagnosed with mild to moderate Alzheimer's disease. Rosaglitzone belongs to a class of drugs that modulate the nuclear membrane receptor, *peroxisome proliferator-activated receptor* (PPAR)-γ. Subjects were evaluated at baseline and after 24 weeks of study. Overall, no significant differences in cognition were detected between patients receiving therapy at any dose of rosiglitazone and those receiving placebo. However, on stratification for APOEε4 genotype, patients who were *negative* for APOEε4 achieved significant benefit from treatment, whereas those who were *positive* for APOEε4 did not (Risner et al., 2006).

It is also noteworthy that a randomized clinical trial conducted in Japan found that administration of a PPAR-γ agonist, pioglitazone, improved cognitive function in patients with type 2 diabetes and mild Alzheimer's disease (Sato et al., 2009). In animal models of Alzheimer's disease, PPARγ agonists have been shown to inhibit inflammatory gene expression, alter amyloid β peptide homeostasis, and exhibit neuroprotective effects (Jiang, Heneka, and Landreth, 2008).

Obesity and Alzheimer's Disease

Epidemiologic investigations have also focused on the development of Alzheimer's disease in overweight and obese individuals. In Sweden, a representative cohort of 392 adults without dementia at baseline were followed from age 70–88 years to evaluate associations of body mass, blood pressure, smoking, and other factors with the development of Alzheimer's disease. During 18 years of follow-up, 93 participants developed dementia. Results revealed that among women, for every unit increase in body mass index, the risk of Alzheimer's disease increased by 36% (Gustafson et al., 2003).

In the United States, investigators examined associations between body mass during midlife and the subsequent development of Alzheimer's disease or vascular dementia in a large and diverse cohort (*n* = 10,136) consisting of members of the *Kaiser-Permante Health Care Delivery System*. Participants were examined at ages 40–45 years and later assessed for neurological disease an average of 36 years later. Compared to individuals with normal body mass index (BMI <25) in midlife, obese subjects (BMI >30) were at increased risk for Alzheimer's disease (HR = 3.10) and vascular dementia (HR = 5.01). Furthermore, individuals overweight during midlife (BMI = 25–30) were found to have a twofold increase in the risk of developing either condition. These findings suggest that increased body mass during midlife is a significant risk factor for the development of Alzheimer's disease or vascular dementia late in life (Whitmer et al., 2007).

As noted in the previous section, investigators at New York Upstate Medical University examined associations of Alzheimer's disease with body mass and diabetes by meta-analyses of published prospective epidemiologic investigations. Combining data from nine studies, they found that diabetes increased the risk of developing Alzheimer's disease (combined RR = 1.54). For the eight studies that examined effects of obesity, the pooled estimate of risk was also elevated (RR = 1.59), but there was significant heterogeneity among studies, possibly due to differences in the age of participants at enrollment and length of follow-up (Profenno, Porsteinsson, and Faraone, 2010).

While *midlife obesity* appears to be a risk factor for Alzheimer's disease late in life, many subjects who develop dementia have been found to *lose* a significant amount of weight shortly before diagnosis. Changes in weight were closely monitored over 20 years in a prospective cohort study of 134 men and 165 women living in southern California. During follow-up, 36 men and 24 women were diagnosed with Alzheimer's disease. Compared to individuals who remained normal, significant weight losses were evident in both men and women who later developed Alzheimer's disease (Barrett-Connor et al., 1996).

A component of the *Honolulu-Asia Aging Study* was designed to assess the relationship between weight change and the development of dementia. In this population-based investigation, 1,890 Japanese-American men were weighed on 6 separate occasions between 1965–1999 and screened for dementia during 1991–1999. The 112 cases that developed dementia during the study were compared to 1,778 controls who remained free of neurological disease. Though there were no differences in weight between cases and controls in the first 26 years of study, during the 6 year period prior to diagnosis of dementia, cases had excess average weight loss (~2 kg) compared to controls (Stewart et al., 2005). Weight loss in association with Alzheimer's disease is also associated with greater disease severity, accelerated progression of disease, and increased mortality (White, Pieper, and Schmader, 1998).

Homocysteine and Alzheimer's Disease

Homocysteine is an amino acid that differs from cysteine by the addition of a single methyl group. Blood levels of homocysteine are reduced by B vitamins such as riboflavin and folic acid and some epidemiologic studies have found that high homocysteine levels and low levels of the B vitamins increase the risk of developing cardiovascular disease. However, in a recent review and meta-analysis of 8 randomized clinical trials involving 24,210 participants, there was no evidence that homocysteine-lowering interventions at any dosage or in any combination reduces the risk of developing myocardial infarction, stroke, or other cardiovascular conditions (Martí-Carvajal et al., 2009).

Investigators at Boston University conducted a prospective cohort study of 1,062 elderly adults (667 women and 425 men) to examine the relation of plasma homocysteine and the development of dementia. The study cohort was derived from participants in the *Framingham Study*. Homocysteine and other variables (age, gender, apolipoprotein E genotype, folic acid, and other cardiovascular risk factors) were measured at baseline. Over a median follow-up of 8 years, dementia developed in 111 subjects including 83 cases of Alzheimer's disease. Results revealed significant risk increases in dementia (adjusted RR = 1.4) and Alzheimer's disease (adjusted RR = 1.8) with each 1 standard deviation increase in the log-transformed level of homocysteine. Among individuals with baseline homocysteine levels exceeding 14 micromol per liter, the risk of Alzheimer's disease nearly doubled. These results suggest that elevated plasma homocysteine may be an independent risk factor for the development of Alzheimer's disease and dementia (Seshadri et al., 2002). Nevertheless, results of randomized clinical trials of homocysteine reduction are required before recommendations can be made about the use of B vitamins for the prevention of dementia (Clarke, 2007).

Estrogen Therapy and Alzheimer's Disease

Some epidemiologic investigations have found that estrogen replacement therapy (ERT) exerts a protective effect against the development of Alzheimer's disease. Investigators from the University of Southern California explored ERT and the development of Alzheimer's disease in a nested case control study within the prospective *Leisure World Cohort Study* of 8,877 elderly women. Leisure World is a retirement community in Laguna Hills, California. Among 2,529 women who died during 1981–1992, 138 cases of Alzheimer's disease were identified. Controls were matched to the cases at a 4:1 ratio by birth date and death date. Results revealed a significant reduction in the odds of developing Alzheimer's disease among ERT users compared to nonusers (OR = 0.69) suggesting that ERT may be useful for preventing or delaying the onset of dementia (Paganini-Hill and Henderson, 1994).

Investigators from Columbia University studied effects of ERT in 1,124 elderly women who were initially free of Alzheimer's disease, Parkinson's disease, and stroke, and who were taking part in a longitudinal study of aging and health in a New York City community. Overall, 156 of the women reported taking estrogen after onset of menopause. Results revealed a significant reduction in risk among ERT users compared to nonusers (RR = 0.40), and furthermore, the onset of Alzheimer's disease was significantly delayed in women who used ERT. Notably, none of 23 women who were taking estrogen at study enrollment developed Alzheimer's disease. The investigators concluded that estrogen use in postmenopausal women may delay the onset and decrease the risk of Alzheimer's disease (Tang et al., 1996).

In the US *Baltimore Longitudinal Study of Aging*, 472 postmenopausal women were followed for up to 16 years to examine the incidence of Alzheimer's disease among those who received ERT versus those who did not. Thirty-four incident cases were detected, 9 among ERT users and 25 among nonusers (RR = 0.46) indicating that ERT may have significant chemopreventive activity against Alzheimer's disease (Kawas et al., 1997).

A team of US investigators examined gender differences in the incidence of dementia among 1,357 men and 1,889 women as well as effects of ERT in women residing in Cache County, Utah, during 1995–2000. Compared to nonusers, women who used ERT for 10 or more years had a reduced risk of developing Alzheimer's disease (26 cases among 1,066 users compared with 58 cases among 800 nonusers, adjusted HR = 0.41). Women who used ERT were also at lower risk than men (HR = 0.77) (Zandi et al., 2002).

The *Women's Health Initiative* (WHI) included two randomized double-blind, placebo-controlled clinical trials of hormone replacement therapy (HRT) to assess effects on cardiovascular outcomes such as myocardial infarction and stroke, certain cancers (breast cancer, endometrial cancer, colon cancer), and several other conditions. A component of these trials, the *Women's Health Initiative Memory Study* (WHIMS), assessed effects of HRT on the development of dementia *in women who were at least 65 years of age*. Two trials were conducted in the WHI, estrogen plus progesterone (n = 4,532 women), and estrogen therapy alone (n = 2,947 women). Women who were randomized to receive active hormones received conjugated equine estrogens, 0.625 mg each day, and medroxyprogesterone acetate, 2.5 mg each day. Those in the estrogen plus progestin arm were followed from 1995–2002, and those in the estrogen arm were followed from 1995–2004. In the estrogen plus progestin trial, 61 women developed dementia, 40 receiving estrogen plus progestin, and 21 receiving placebo, yielding a hazard ratio of 2.05. In the estrogen trial, 47 participants were diagnosed with dementia, 28 receiving estrogen, and 19 receiving placebo, yielding a hazard ratio of 1.49. When data from the 2 treatment arms

were pooled, the overall hazard ratio for HRT was 1.76. The results of these randomized clinical trials therefore suggest that HRT *increases* rather than decreases the risk of developing dementia among elderly women (Shumaker et al., 2003, 2004).

In brief, HRT was found to *increase* rather than decrease the risk of heart attack, stroke, and blood clots. Risk increases were also noted for breast cancer and endometrial cancer whereas risk reductions were noted for colon cancer and bone fractures (osteoporosis). Obviously, the risk benefit ratio from these studies *does not* favor the administration of postmenopausal estrogens.

The WHIMS results conflict with the findings of many epidemiologic studies wherein women who began taking HRT coincident with the onset of menopause had a *lower* risk of developing Alzheimer's disease or dementia. The WHIMS findings of higher rates of dementia among elderly women who received estrogen alone or estrogen plus progesterone compared to those who received placebo were therefore surprising. Albeit, it is strenuously argued by some investigators that administration of HRT to women 65 years of age or older in the WHIMS component of WHI was too late in life to offer protection. It is possible that hormone therapy initiated nearer the onset of menopause might protect against some dementias while therapy delayed for a decade or more after menopause may not. A recent review article by Elizabeth Barrett-Connor and Gail Laughlin exemplifies the state of the science in regard to the effects of hormone replacement therapy on human brain function:

"There are more than 200 published scientific papers showing that estrogen has favorable effects on brain tissue and physiology in cell culture and animal models including non-human primates. The biological plausibility for a neuroprotective estrogen effect is overwhelming. However, most studies of endogenous estrogen and cognitive decline or dementia in women fail to show protection, and some suggest harm. Failure to find any consistent association might reflect the limitations of a single time of estrogen assay or poor assay sensitivity. More than half of the observational studies of hormone therapy suggest benefit. Nearly all long-term clinical trials fail to show benefit, and the longer trials tend to show harm. Failure to adequately adjust for self-selection of healthier and wealthier women and publication bias could account for some, or all, of the protective effect attributed to estrogen in observational studies. Overall, the evidence does not convincingly support the prescription

of early or late postmenopausal estrogen therapy to preserve cognitive function or prevent dementia" (Barrett-Connor and Laughlin, 2009).

Nonsteroidal Anti-Inflammatory Drugs and Alzheimer's Disease

Since Alzheimer's disease has an inflammatory component, a number of epidemiologic investigations have examined *nonsteroidal anti-inflammatory drugs (NSAIDs)* as possible chemopreventive agents. Recently, a team of epidemiologists at Johns Hopkins University conducted a meta-analysis of these studies. Combining the data from 5 prospective studies, they found significant risk reductions with regular use of nonaspirin NSAIDs (RR = 0.71) or aspirin (RR = 0.83). The combined data from 8 case control studies showed even greater risk reductions (RR = 0.47 for nonaspirin NSAIDS and RR = 0.55 for aspirin). These findings suggest that regular use of NSAIDs, particularly nonaspirin NSAIDs such as ibuprofen, may protect against the development of Alzheimer's disease (Szekely, Town, and Zandi, 2007).

Certain other drugs may also have chemopreventive potential against the development of Alzheimer's disease. For example, a few studies have reported risk reductions among individuals taking agents with antiangiogenic effects such as lipid lowering statins, histamine H2 receptor blockers, and calcium channel blockers. It has been noted that inflammation and ischemia, two key factors in the pathogenesis of dementia and Alzheimer's disease, are powerful stimulants of *angiogenesis* in blood vessels. Some investigators therefore recommend a new focus of laboratory and clinical studies to assess the effects of angiogenesis in the pathogenesis of Alzheimer's disease (Vagnucci and Li, 2003).

GENETICS OF ALZHEIMER'S DISEASE

Most cases of Alzheimer's disease are sporadic with no evidence of genetic predisposition. Nevertheless, 5–10% of cases are familial, whereby multiple relatives of a multigenerational pedigree are affected. In such multigenerational pedigrees, certain genes have been found to influence the onset of Alzheimer's disease.

Presenilin 1

The *presenilin 1 gene (PSEN1)* located on the long arm of chromosome 14 was identified by Sherrington and colleagues (1995). Multiple missense mutations of the *PSEN1* gene cause familial Alzheimer's disease.

In such families, individuals who inherit a mutated *PSEN1* gene nearly always develop Alzheimer's disease before age 50 years. The *PSEN1* protein is an essential component of the enzymatic complex, γ-secretase, that cleaves amyloid beta peptide from amyloid precursor protein. Mutant forms of *PSEN1* disrupt the process causing deposition of beta amyloid fragments in and around neurons.

Presenilin 2

The *presenilin 2 gene (PSEN2)* located on the long arm of chromosome 1 is very similar in structure and function to *PSEN1*, and mutations in *PSEN2* also cause familial Alzheimer's disease. As with *PSEN1*, mutant forms of *PSEN2* cause early onset of disease. The gene was identified in the laboratories of Rudolph Tanzi and Gerry Schellenberg in 1995 (Levy-Lahad et al., 1995). A subsequent study showed that *PSEN1* and *PSEN2* proteins are both expressed in mammalian neuronal cells (Kovacs et al., 1996). The *PSEN2* protein is also a critical component of the enzymatic complex, γ-secretase, that cleaves amyloid beta peptide from amyloid precursor protein.

Amyloid beta Precursor Protein

Mutations in the gene that encodes *amyloid beta precursor protein (APP)* also cause familial Alzheimer's disease. Specifically, individuals who inherit mutations that modify expression of the *APP* gene located on the long arm of chromosome 21 are at increased risk. Furthermore, virtually all individuals with Down syndrome (trisomy 21) who have an extra copy of the *APP* gene develop Alzheimer's disease before age 40 years (Tanzi and Parson, 2000).

Apolipoprotein E4

Apolipoproteins are proteins that bind to lipids (such as cholesterol and fatty acids) to form macromolecules called *lipoproteins*, which in turn transport lipids through the blood and lymph. Apolipoproteins also serve as coenzymes in important catalytic reactions such as the formation of arachidonic acid from other fatty acids by *lipoprotein lipase* and transfer of fatty acids in lecithin to cholesterol to form cholesterol esters by *lecithin-cholesterol-acyl-transferase*. Furthermore, apoliproteins are ligands for tissue specific receptors in the distribution of lipids to target tissues throughout the body.

Six major classes of apolipoproteins have been identified (A, B, C, D, E, and H) plus several subclasses and hundreds of polymorphic forms. Apolipoproteins were initially identified and classified according to function by investigators at the US

National Institutes of Health (Fredrickson, Levy, and Lees, 1967).

The apolipoprotein, APOE, is encoded by a gene on the long arm of chromosome 19. Several alleles have been identified at the *APOE* locus, and individuals who carry the allele for *apolipoprotein-E4*, *APOEε4*, are at increased risk for the development of Alzheimer's disease and atherosclerosis (Pericak-Vance et al., 1991). Apolipoproteins carry cholesterol and fatty acids in the blood, and they also bind to proteins, including *amyloid beta precursor protein*, and target them for biodegradation. In individuals with *APOEε4*, there is diminished binding of amyloid precursor protein leading to accumulation of amyloid in the brain and other tissues (Jiang et al., 2008; Bertram and Tanzi, 2008).

Sortilin-Related Receptor

Normal expression of the *sortilin-related receptor 1 (SORL1) gene* is essential for the recycling of amyloid precursor protein within neurons, and mutant forms of the gene have been found to promote the accumulation of excess amyloid b peptide in neuronal tissues. The neuronal accumulation of amyloid b peptide is a central event in the pathogenesis of Alzheimer's disease. The *SORL1* gene is located on chromosome 1 and is a member of a family of transmembrane receptors that are highly expressed in the central nervous system. The protein, *sortilin*, and the family of sortilin receptors work in concert with *apolipoprotein b* to regulate the uptake, sorting, intracellular transport, and release of proteins and very low density lipoproteins.

Rogaeva and colleagues examined genetic associations between Alzheimer's disease and single nucleotide polymorphisms of genes known to regulate vacuolar protein sorting, including *SORL1*, among more than 6,000 individuals from familial and population studies. They identified two genetic variants of *SORL1* associated with an increased risk of developing Alzheimer's disease late in life, and suggested that inherited or acquired changes in *SORL1* expression or function are in the causal pathway of pathogenesis (Rogaeva et al., 2007).

These initial findings have been replicated in several subsequent studies and validated in a meta-analysis of all published data on *SORL1* and Alzheimer's disease from studies conducted in the United States, the Netherlands, Canada, Belgium, the United Kingdom, Singapore, Japan, Sweden, Germany, France, and Italy. Upon pooling the data for 12,464 cases of Alzheimer's disease and 17,929 controls and making adjustments for multiple testing, several single nucleotide polymorphisms of the *SORL1* gene were discovered in distinct linkage disequilibrium blocks in association with significant increases in the risk of developing Alzheimer's disease (Reitz et al., 2011).

Insulin-Degrading Enzyme

Insulin-degrading enzyme is a zinc-binding protease of the metalloprotease family capable of cleaving short polypeptides. This enzyme was first identified by its ability to degrade the beta chain of the polypeptide hormone, insulin. In 2001, Japanese investigators Igor Kurochkin and Sataro Goto discovered that insulin degrading enzyme can degrade amyloid β peptide, the principal component of amyloid that accumulates in the pathogenesis of Alzheimer's disease (Kurochkin and Goto, 1994). Subsequently, both *in vitro* and *in vivo* studies have consistently shown an association between the expression of insulin degrading enzyme, amyloid β degradation, and the development of Alzheimer's disease (Qiu and Folstein, 2006). For example, genetically engineered "knockout" mice lacking both alleles of the *insulin-degrading enzyme (IDE) gene* exhibit a 50% decrease in amyloid β degradation resulting in cerebral accumulation of amyloid and onset of Alzheimer's symptoms (Farris et al., 2003). Furthermore, human studies of genetically inherited forms of Alzheimer's disease show reduction in both the genetic expression and catalytic activity of insulin-degrading enzyme among affected individuals (Cook et al., 2003; Kim et al., 2007).

It has been noted that deficiencies of insulin-degrading enzyme can be caused by genetic variation or by the diversion of enzymatic biodegradation from amyloid β to insulin in the presence of hyperinsulinemia. Furthermore, medications that target diabetes, insulin resistance and hyperinsulinemia have been found to improve cognition in only those Alzheimers' patients who are *negative* for *APOEε4* (the gene that predisposes to late onset alzheimer's disease). Further studies are obviously needed to clarify the cascade of pathogenesis and identify genotype-specific molecular targets for the effective prevention and therapy of Alzheimer's disease (Qiu and Folstein, 2006). An added complexity is achieving the physiologically appropriate balance between the degradation of insulin and amyloid β in the human brain.

VASCULAR DEMENTIA

Vascular dementia (often referred to as *multi-infarct dementia*) is the second most common form of dementia in older adults. This form of dementia accounts for approximately 30% of all dementia cases.

It is caused by thrombotic and/or embolic occlusion of small cerebral blood vessels. Impedance of blood flow produces ischemia and infarction of brain tissue, eventually leading to diminished brain function and dementia.

In recent years, there is growing recognition that many cases of dementia in elderly patients involve a combination of pathogenic processes, most commonly those that characterize Alzheimer's disease and ischemic cerebrovascular disease. As noted earlier in this chapter, Alzheimer's disease and vascular dementia often coexist, especially in older patients with dementia, and there are many cardiovascular risk factors that are common to both conditions including hypertension, smoking, ischemic heart disease, hypercholesterolemia, insulin resistance, and diabetes mellitus (Hébert and Brayne, 1995).

LEWY BODY DEMENTIA

Lewy body dementia is characterized microscopically by the presence of Lewy bodies which are clumps of *alpha-synuclein* and *ubiquitin* protein in neurons, detectable in postmortem brain specimens. The synucleins are intracellular proteins that appear to regulate vesicular transport processes in neurons (Lavedan, 1998). Ubiquitin is a ubiquitous molecule that tags other proteins for degradation in the proteosomes of the cell. The 2004 Nobel Prize in Chemistry was awarded jointly to Aaron Ciechanover, Avram Hershko, and Irwin Rose for their discovery of ubiquitin-mediated protein degradation (Ciechanover, Hershko, and Rose, 2004).

Other features of Lewy body dementia include the loss of *cholinergic neurons* and declining levels of the neurotransmitter, *acetylcholine*. The presenting signs and symptoms of Lewy body dementia overlap with other neurodegenerative conditions, particularly Parkinson's disease. However, disease onset is typically acute and progression is rapid, which distinguishes this form of dementia from Alzheimer's disease and vascular dementia, which show a more gradual course (Okasaki, Lipkin, and Aronson, 1961).

Lewy bodies are named after the German neurologist, Friedrich Lewy, who described eosinophilic, intracytoplasmic inclusion bodies in the neurons of the *substantia nigra* and other regions of the brain in postmortem specimens from patients with Parkinson's disease (Lewy, 1912). Lewy body dementia is distinguished from Parkinson's disease by the rapid onset of dementia within one year of the onset of Parkinsonian symptoms (bradykinesia, rigidity, and gait disturbance) and the presence of recurrent hallucinations and delusional behavior, which rarely occur in patients with Parkinson's disease. Patients with Lewy body dementia are also hypersensitive to neuroleptic medications and may become catatonic and develop life-threatening muscle rigidity on administration of commonly used drugs such as haloperidol or thioridazine (Weintraub and Hurtig, 2007).

Lewy body dementia accounts for approximately 10% of all forms of dementia. As in other dementias, its prevalence increases with age, and peak onset occurs in the seventh decade of life. Men are afflicted slightly more often than women. While most cases of Lewy body dementia are sporadic, kindreds with familial disease have been reported, some involving genetic mutations in the *alpha-synuclein gene* (*SNCA*) on chromosome 4 (Obi et al. 2008).

MIXED FORMS OF DEMENTIA

Figure 39.4 shows the profile of dementias based upon pathology and neuroimaging data collected in the Hisayama Study of elderly men and women in Japan. During 1985–2002, 251 patients developed dementia and were evaluated by either postmortem pathology (*n* = 164) or neuroimaging (*n* = 87). As shown, the most common form of dementia in the study was Alzheimer's disease, which accounted for about 48% of all dementias. Alzheimer's disease was also found in 8% of the cases with combined pathologies. *Vascular dementia* accounted for about 30% of dementias but also contributed to another 5% of cases in combination with Alzheimer's disease. Likewise, *Lewy body dementia* constituted 5% of dementias, but was also found in about 6% of patients with either Alzheimer's disease or vascular dementia. The three principal entities, Alzheimer's disease, vascular dementia, and Lewy body dementia, alone or in combination, comprised approximately 95% of all dementias (Matsui et al., 2009). It is noteworthy that dementia involving combinations of these pathologies have been found to reflect the additive effects of each of the independent neuropathies (Schneider et al., 2007).

Though the predominant form of dementia diagnosed among living patients is Alzheimer's disease, recent results from the *Honolulu-Asia Aging Study* suggest there is often a lack of agreement between the clinical diagnosis and postmortem neuropathological findings. Investigators at Kuakini Medical Center in Honolulu compared clinical and postmortem neuropathological findings for 363 Japanese-American men diagnosed with dementia during life. The results reflect a predominance of cases clinically diagnosed with Alzheimer's disease (56%) compared to only

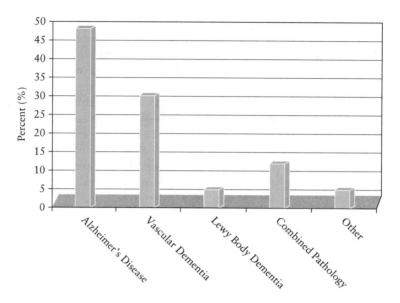

Figure 39.4 Pathologic Profile of Dementia.

Source: Data from Matsui Y, Tanizaki Y, Arima H, Yonemoto K, Doi Y, Ninomiya T, Sasaki K (2009). Incidence and survival of dementia in a general population of Japanese elderly: the Hisayama study. *J Neurol Neurosurg Psychiatry* 80:366–370.

19% based upon neuropathologic findings. Mixed pathologies accounted for 40% of cases by neuropathology compared to only 17% by clinical assessment. Among the cases with mixed neuropathologic findings, 10% manifested *Lewy bodies* and approximately 20% manifested Alzheimer's disease combined with vascular dementia. Approximately 14% of cases did not manifest any dominant neuropathologic features (**Figure 39.5**). The investigators state that "*the results suggest that clinical diagnosis of dementia made during life may fail to reflect the pathogenic complexity of this condition in very*

elderly persons." Nevertheless, they also note that there is an interval of time between the clinical diagnosis and death "*which is sufficiently long and variable that imperfect correlations with functioning during life are to be expected*" (White et al., 2005).

PREVENTION OF DEMENTIA

Dementing illnesses attributable to mixed pathologies (Alzhiemer's disease, vascular dementia, and Lewy body dementia) become progressively more common

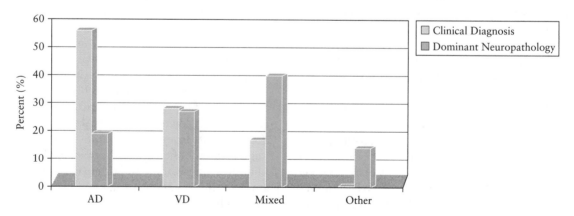

Figure 39.5 Comparison of Clinical Diagnoses and Neuropathologic Findings in Dementia.

Source: Data from White L, Small BJ, Petrovitch H, Ross GW, Masaki K, Abbott RD, Hardman J, Davis D, Nelson J, Markesbery W (2005). Recent clinical-pathologic research on the causes of dementia in late life: update from the Honolulu-Asia Aging Study. *J Geriatr Psychiatry Neurol* 18(4):224–227.

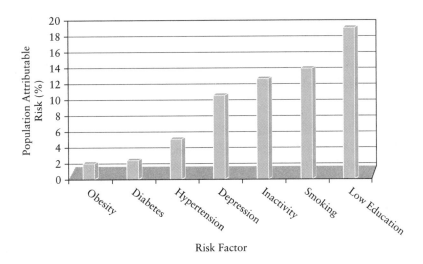

Figure 39.6 Population Attributable Risk: Alzheimer's Disease.

Source: Data from Barnes DE, Yaffe K (2011). The projected effect of risk factor reduction on Alzheimer's disease prevalence. *The Lancet Neurology* 10(9):819–828.

with advancing age, as expected on the basis of the strong associations of all three of these processes with aging. Currently available medications provide only modest clinical benefits once a patient has developed dementia. Avoidance of cardiovascular risk factors coupled with the early detection and effective treatment of hypertension, hyperlipidemia, and hyperinsulinemia therefore constitute a reasonable strategy to reduce the onset of dementia and progression of cognitive decline in old age (WHO, 2006). As pointed out by Langa, Foster, and Larson in their review of emerging concepts in the prevention and therapy of *mixed dementia*:

> *"Given the growing epidemiological and clinical evidence for the coexistence of Alzheimer's disease and vascular dementia and the potential common pathway leading from cerebral ischemia to both conditions, aggressive identification and treatment of cardiovascular risk factors in middle aged and older individuals may represent an important strategy for decreasing the incidence of dementia and for slowing the progression of cognitive decline. Clinicians should address treatment and/or lifestyle changes for the risk factors of hypertension, hyperlipidemia, diabetes, and physical inactivity for patients with early Alzheimer's disease, vascular dementia, or mixed dementia as a potential strategy for improving quality of life and delaying the progression of cognitive decline. In addition, prevention of recurrent strokes through the identification and treatment of atrial fibrillation and carotid*

> *vascular occlusive disease, as well as the appropriate use of anticoagulation for thromboembolic disease will also likely reduce the incidence or progression of vascular dementia and mixed dementia"* (Langa, Foster, and Larson, 2004).

Recently, Deborah Barnes and Kristine Yaffe comprehensively reviewed the available epidemiologic literature to estimate the global risk attributable to seven modifiable risk factors (hypertension, diabetes mellitus, obesity, smoking, depression, physical inactivity, and low education) and project effects of reducing exposure levels. For each risk factor, the relative risk (RR) was estimated by meta-analysis and the prevalence (q) was estimated by combining the data from current population surveys. The population attributable risk, $PAR = q(RR\text{-}1)/[q(RR\text{-}1) + 1]$, is the proportion of people with disease in the population that can be attributed to a given risk factor (assuming the relative risk is an accurate measure of causation). The results revealed that about half of all prevalent cases worldwide are attributable to the seven selected risk factors (**Figure 39.6**). Based upon a projection for the world population, the investigators suggest that risk reductions of 25% in all 7 factors could potentially prevent 3 million cases of Alzheimer's disease per year (Barnes and Yaffe, 2011).

● ● ● **REFERENCES**

Akiyama, H., Barger, S., Barnum, S., et al. (2002). Inflammation and Alzheimer's disease. *Neurobiol Aging*, 21(3), 383–421.

Akomolafe, A., Beiser, A., Meigs, J.B., Au, R., Green, R.C., Farrer, L.A.,...Seshadri, S. (2006). Diabetes mellitus and risk of developing Alzheimer disease: Results from the Framingham Study. *Arch Neurol, 63*(11), 1551–1555.

Alzheimer, A. (1907). Über eine eigenartige Erkrankung der Hirnrinde [About a peculiar disease of the cerebral cortex]. *Allgemeine Zeitschrift fur Psychiatrie und Psychisch-Gerichtlich Medizin, 64*(1–2), 146–148.

Alzheimer's Association. (2010). *Alzheimer's disease facts and figures*. Washington, DC: Alzheimer's Association.

Arvanitakis, Z., Schneider, J.A., Wilson, R.S., Li, Y., Arnold, S.E., Wang, Z., & Bennett, D.A. (2006). Diabetes is related to cerebral infarction but not to AD pathology in older persons. *Neurology, 67*, 1960–1965.

Barnes, D.E., & Yaffe, K. (2011). The projected effect of risk factor reduction on Alzheimer's disease prevalence. *Lancet Neurology, 10*(9), 819–828.

Barrett-Connor, E., Edelstein, S.L., Corey-Bloom, J., & Wiederholt, W.C. (1996). Weight loss precedes dementia in community-dwelling older adults. *J Am Geriatr Soc, 44*, 1147–1152.

Barrett-Connor, E., & Laughlin, G.A. (2009). Endogenous and exogenous estrogen, cognitive function, and dementia in postmenopausal women: Evidence from epidemiologic studies and clinical trials. *Semin Reprod Med, 27*(3), 275–282.

Bertram, L., & Tanzi, R.E. (2008). Thirty years of Alzheimer's disease genetics: The implications of systematic meta-analyses. *Nature Reviews Neuroscience, 9*(10), 768–778.

Bowen, J.D., Malter, A.D., Sheppard, L., Kukull, W.A., McCormick, W.C., Teri, L., & Larson, E.B. (1996). Predictors of mortality in patients diagnosed with probable Alzheimer's disease. *Neurology, 47*(2), 433–439.

Brookmeyer, R., Gray, S., & Kawas, C. (1998). Projections of Alzheimer's disease in the United States and the public health impact of delaying disease onset. *American Journal of Public Health, 88*(9), 1337–1342.

Brookmeyer, R., Corrada, M.M., Curriero, F.C., & Kawas, C. (2002). Survival following a diagnosis of Alzheimer disease. *Arch Neurol, 59*, 1764–1767.

Brookmeyer, R., Johnson, E., Ziegler-Graham, K., & Arrighi, H.M. (2007). Forecasting the global burden of Alzheimer's disease. *Alzheimer's and Dementia, 3*(3), 186–191.

Cataldo, J.K., Prochaska, J.J., & Glantz, S.A. (2010). Cigarette smoking is a risk factor for Alzheimer's disease: An analysis controlling for tobacco industry affiliation. *Journal of Alzheimer's Disease, 19*(2), 465–480.

Ciechanover, A., Hershko, A., & Rose, I. (2004). The Nobel Prize in Chemistry 2004.

Clarke, R. (2007). Homocysteine, B vitamins, and the risk of dementia. *American Journal of Clinical Nutrition, 85*(2), 329–330.

Cook, D.G., Leverenz, J.B., McMillan, P.J., Kulstad, J.J., Ericksen, S., Roth, R.A., . . . Craft, S. (2003). Reduced hippocampal insulin-degrading enzyme in late-onset alzheimer's disease is associated with the apolipoprotein E-epsilon4 allele. *Am J Pathol, 162*(1), 313–319.

De Meyer, G., Shapiro, F., Vanderstichele, H., Vanmechelen, E., Engelborghs, S., De Deyn, P.P.,...Trojanowski, J.Q., for the Alzheimer's Disease Neuroimaging Initiative. (2010). Diagnosis-independent Alzheimer disease biomarker signature in cognitively normal elderly people. *Arch Neurol, 67*(8), 949–956.

den Dunnen, W.F., Brouwer, W.H., Bijlard, E., Kamphuis, J., van Linschoten, K., Eggens-Meijer, E., & Holstege, G. (2008). No disease in the brain of a 115-year-old woman. *Neurobiol Aging, 29*(8), 1127–1132.

Farris, W., Mansourian, S., Chang, Y., Lindsley, L., Eckman, E.A., Frosch, M.P.,...Guenette, S. (2003). Insulin-degrading enzyme regulates the levels of insulin, amyloid beta-protein, and the beta-amyloid precursor protein intracellular domain in vivo. *Proc Natl Acad Sci, USA, 100*(7), 4162–4167.

Ferri, C.P., Prince, M., Brayne, C., Brodaty, H., Fratiglioni, L., Manguli, M.,…Scasufca, M, for Alzheimer's Disease International. (2005). Global prevalence of dementia: A Delphi consensus study. *Lancet, 366,* 2112–2117.

Flaten, T.P. (1989). Mortality from dementia in Norway, 1969–1983. *J Epidemiol Community Health, 43,* 285–289.

Forette, F., Seux, M.L., Staessen, J.A., Thijs, L., Babarskiene, M.R., Babeanu, S.,…Birkenhäger, W.H., Systolic Hypertension in Europe Investigators. (2002). The prevention of dementia with antihypertensive treatment: New evidence from the Systolic Hypertension in Europe (Syst-Eur) study. *Arch Intern Med, 162*(18), 2046–2052.

Förstl, H., & Kurz, A. (1999). Clinical features of Alzheimer's disease. *European Archives of Psychiatry and Clinical Neuroscience, 249*(6), 288–290.

Fredrickson, D.S., Levy, R.I., & Lees, R.S. (1967). Fat transport in lipoproteins—An integrated approach to mechanisms and disorders. *New England Journal of Medicine, 276*(1), 34–42.

Ganguli, M., Dodge, H.H., Shen, C., Pandav, R.S., & DeKosky, S.T. (2005). Alzheimer disease and mortality: A 15-year epidemiological study. *Arch Neurol, 62*(5), 779–784.

Griffiths, C., & Rooney, C. (2006). Trends in mortality from Alzheimer's disease, Parkinson's disease and dementia, England and Wales, 1979–2004. *Health Statistics Quarterly, 30,* 6–14.

Gustafson, D., Rothenberg, E., Blennow, K., Steen, B., & Skoog, I. (2003). An 18-year follow-up of overweight and risk of Alzheimer Disease. *Arch Intern Med, 163,* 1524–1528.

Hallberg, O. (2009). Is increased mortality from Alzheimer's disease in Sweden a reflection of better diagnostics? *Current Alzheimer Research, 6*(6), 471–475.

Hébert, R., & Brayne, C. (1995). Epidemiology of vascular dementia. *Neuroepidemiology, 14,* 240–257.

Helzner, E.P., Scarmeas, N., Cosentino, S., Tang, M.X., Schupf, N., & Stern, Y. (2008). Survival in Alzheimer disease, a multiethnic, population-based study of incident cases. *Neurology, 71*(19), 1489–1495.

Hoyert, D.L., & Rosenberg, H.M. (1997). Alzheimer's disease as a cause of death in the United States. *Public Health Reports, 112,* 497–505.

Hoyert, D.L., & Rosenberg, H.M. (1999). Mortality from Alzheimer's disease: An update. *Natl Vital Stat Rep, 47*(20), 1–8.

Imaizumi, Y. (1992). Mortality rate of Alzheimer's disease in Japan: Secular trends, marital status, and geographical variations. *Acta Neurol Scand, 86*(5), 501–505.

Jiang, Q., Lee, C.Y., Mandrekar, S., Wilkinson, B., Cramer, P., Zelcer, N.,…Landreth, G.E. (2008). ApoE promotes the proteolytic degradation of amyloid beta. *Neuron (United States: Cell Press), 58*(5), 681–693.

Jiang, Q., Heneka, M., & Landreth, G.E. (2008). The role of peroxisome proliferator-activated receptor-gamma (PPARγ) in Alzheimer's disease: Therapeutic implications. *CNS Drugs, 22,* 1–14.

Jorm, A.F., & Jolley, D. (1998). The incidence of dementia: A meta-analysis. *Neurology, 51,* 728–733.

Jorm, A.F., Henderson, A.S., & Jacomb, P.A. (1989). Regional differences in mortality from dementia in Australia: An analysis of death certificate data. *Acta Psychiatr Scan, 79,* 179–185.

Kawas, C., Resnick, S., Morrison, A., Brookmeyer, R., Corrada, M., Zonderman, A., . . . Metter, E. (1997). A prospective study of estrogen replacement therapy and the risk of developing Alzheimer's disease. The Baltimore Longitudinal Study of Aging. *Neurology, 48*(6), 1517–1521.

Kim, M., Hersh, L.B., Leissring, M.A., Ingelsson, M., Matsui, T., Farris, W., Lu, A.,…Tanzi, R.E. (2007). Decreased catalytic activity of the insulin-degrading enzyme in chromosome 10-linked

Alzheimer disease families. *J Biol Chem, 282*(11), 7825–7832.

Kivipelto, M., Helkala, E.L., Laakso, M.P., Hänninen, T., Hallikainen, M., Alhainen, K.,... Nissinen, A. (2001). Midlife vascular risk factors and Alzheimer's disease in later life: Longitudinal, population based study. *BMJ, 322*(7300), 1447–1451.

Kovacs, D.M., Fausett, H.J., Page, K.J., Kim, T.W., Moir, R.D., Merriam, D.E.,...Wasco, W. (1996), Alzheimer-associated presenilins 1 and 2: neuronal expression in brain and localization to intracellular membranes in mammalian cells. *Nature Medicine, 2*, 224–229.

Kurochkin, I.V., & Goto, S. (1994). Alzheimer's beta-amyloid peptide specifically interacts with and is degraded by insulin degrading enzyme. *FEBS Lett, 345*(1), 33–37.

Langa, K.M., Foster, N.L., & Larson, E.B. (2004). Mixed dementia: Emerging concepts and therapeutic implications. *JAMA, 292*(23), 2901–2908.

Larson, E.B., Shadlen, M.F., Wang, L., McCormick, W.C., Bowen, J.D., Teri, L., & Kukull, W.A. (2004). Survival after initial diagnosis of Alzheimer disease. *Ann Intern Med, 140*, 501–509.

Launer, L.J., Ross, G.W., Petrovitch, H., Masaki, K., Foley, D., White, L.R., & Havlik, R.J. (2000). Midlife blood pressure and dementia: The Honolulu-Asia aging study. *Neurobiol Aging, 21*, 49–55.

Lavedan, C. (1998). The synuclein family. *Genome Res, 8*(9), 871–80.

Levy-Lahad, E., Wasco, W., Poorkaj, P., Romano, D.M., Oshima, J.M., Pettingell, W.H.,...Tanzi, R.E. (1995). Candidate gene for the chromosome 1 familial Alzheimer's disease locus. *Science, 269*, 973–977.

Lewy, F.H. (1912). Paralysis agitans. In M. Lewandowsky (Ed.) *Handbuch der neurologie* (pp. 920–933). Springer Verlag.

Marksteiner, J., Hinterhuber, H., & Hinterhuber, C. (2007). Cerebrospinal fluid biomarkers for diagnosis of Alzheimer's disease: Beta-amyloid(1-42), tau, phospho-tau-181 and total protein. *Drugs Today, 43*(6), 423–431.

Martí-Carvajal, A.J., Solà, I., Lathyris, D., & Salanti, G. (2009). Homocysteine lowering interventions for preventing cardiovascular events. *Cochrane Database Syst Rev, 4*:CD006612.

Martyn, C.N., & Pippard, E.C. (1988). Usefulness of mortality data in determining the geography and time trends of dementia. *J Epidemiol Community Health, 42*, 134–137.

Matsui, Y., Tanizaki, Y., Arima, H., Yonemoto, K., Doi, Y., Ninomiya, T., & Sasaki, K. (2009). Incidence and survival of dementia in a general population of Japanese elderly: The Hisayama study. *J Neurol Neurosurg Psychiatry, 80*, 366–370.

Mölsä, P.K., Marttila, R.J., & Rinne, U.K. (1986). Survival and cause of death in Alzheimer's disease and multi-infarct dementia. *Acta Neurol Scand, 74*(2), 103–107.

Newman, S.C., & Bland, R.C. (1987). Canadian trends in mortality from mental disorders, 1965–1983. *Acta Psychiatr Scan, 76*, 1–7.

Obi, T., Nishioka, K., Ross, O.A., Terada, T., Yamazaki, K., Sugiura, A.,...Hattori, N. (2008). Clinicopathologic study of a SNCA gene duplication patient with Parkinson disease and dementia. *Neurology, 70*(3), 238–241.

Okasaki, H., Lipkin, L.E., & Aronson, S.M. (1961). Diffuse intracytoplasmic inclusions (Lewy type) associated with progressive dementia and quadriparesis in flexion. *Journal Neuropathology and Experimental Neurology, 20*, 237–244.

Paganini-Hill, A., & Henderson, V.W. (1994). Estrogen deficiency and risk of Alzheimer's Disease in Women. *Am J Epidemiol, 140*, 256–261.

Pericak-Vance, M.A., Bebout, J.L., Gaskell, P.C. Jr., Yamaoka, L.H., Hung, W.Y., Alberts, M.J.,... Roses, A.D. (1991). Linkage studies in familial Alzheimer disease: Evidence for chromosome 19 linkage. *Am J Hum Gene, 48*(6), 1034–1050.

Profenno, L.A., Porsteinsson, A.P., & Faraone, S.V. (2010). Meta-analysis of Alzheimer's disease risk with obesity, diabetes, and related disorders. *Biol Psychiatry, 67*(6), 505–512.

Qiu, W.Q., & Folstein, M.F. (2006). Insulin, insulin-degrading enzyme and amyloid-beta peptide in Alzheimer's disease: Review and hypothesis. *Neurobiol Aging, 27*(2), 190–198.

Querfurth, H.W., & LaFerla, F.M. (2010). Alzheimer's disease. *N Engl J Med, 362*, 329–344.

Rait, G., Walters, K., Bottomley, C., Petersen, I., Iliffe, S., & Nazareth, I. (2010). Survival of people with clinical diagnosis of dementia in primary care: Cohort study. *BMJ, 341*, c3584.

Reger, M.A., Watson, G.S., Frey, W.H. II, Baker, L.D., Cholerton, B., Keeling, M.L.,...Craft, S. (2005). Effects of intranasal insulin on cognition in memory-impaired older adults: Modulation by APOE genotype. *Neurobiol Aging, 27*(3), 451–458.

Reitz, C., Brayne, C., & Mayeux, R. (2011). Epidemiology of Alzheimer disease. *Nat Rev Neurol, 7*(3), 137–152.

Reitz, C., Cheng, R., Rogaeva, E., Lee, J.H., Tokuhiro, S., Zou, F.,...Mayeux, R., Genetic and Environmental Risk in Alzheimer Disease 1 Consortium. (2011). Meta-analysis of the association between variants in SORL1 and Alzheimer disease. *Arch Neurol, 68*(1), 99–106.

Risner, M.E., Saunders, A.M., Altman, J.F., Ormandy, G.C., Craft, S., Foley, I.M.,... Roses, A.D., Rosiglitazone in Alzheimer's Disease Study Group. (2006). Efficacy of rosiglitazone in a genetically defined population with mild-to-moderate Alzheimer's disease. *Pharmacogenomics J, 6*(4), 246–254.

Rocca, W.A., Petersen, R.C., Knopman, D.S., Hebert, L.E., Evans, D.A., Hall, K.S.,...White, L.R. (2011). Trends in the incidence and prevalence of Alzheimer's disease, dementia, and cognitive impairment in the United States. *Alzheimers Dement, 7*(1), 80–93.

Rogaeva, E., Men, Y., Lee, J.H., Gu, Y., Kawarai, T., Zou, F.,...St. George-Hyslop, P. (2007).

The neuronal sortilin-related receptor SORL1 is genetically associated with Alzheimer disease. *Nature Genet, 39*, 168–177.

Sato, T., Hanyu, H., Hirao, K., Kanetaka, H., Sakura, H., & Iwamoto, T. (2009). Efficacy of PPAR-γ agonist pioglitazone in mild Alzheimer disease. *Neurobiol Aging*, doi, 10.1016.

Schneider, J.A., Arvanitakis, Z., Bang, W., & Bennett, D.A. (2007). Mixed brain pathologies account for most dementia cases in community-dwelling older persons. *Neurology, 69*(24), 2197–2204.

Sekita, A., Ninomiya, T., Tanizaki, Y., Doi, Y., Hata, J., Yonemoto, K.,...Kiyohara, Y. (2010). Trends in prevalence of Alzheimer's disease and vascular dementia in a Japanese community: The Hisayama Study. *Acta Psychiatrica Scandinavica, 122*(4), 319–325.

Seshadri, S., Beiser, A., Selhub, J., Jacques, P.F., Rosenberg, I.H., D'Agostino, R.B.,...Wolf, P.A. (2002). Plasma homocysteine as a risk factor for dementia and Alzheimer's disease. *N Engl J Med, 346*(7), 476–483.

Sherrington, R., Rogaev, E.I., Liang, Y., Rogaeva, E.A., Levesque, G., Ikeda, M.,... St. George, P.H. (1995). Cloning of a gene bearing missense mutations in early-onset familial Alzheimer's disease. *Nature, 375*, 754–760.

Shumaker, S.A., Legault, C., Rapp, S.R., Thal, L., Wallace, R.B., Ockene, J.K., . . . Wactawski-Wende, J., for the WHIMS Investigators. (2003). Estrogen plus progestin and the incidence of dementia and mild cognitive impairment in postmenopausal women: The Women's Health Initiative Memory Study: A randomized controlled trial. *JAMA, 289*, 2651–2662.

Shumaker, S.A., Legault, C., Kuller, L., Rapp, S.R., Thal, L., Lane, D.S.,...Coker, L.H., for the Women's Health Initiative Memory Study. (2004). Conjugated equine estrogens and encidence of probable dementia and mild cognitive impairment in postmenopausal women. Women's Health Initiative Memory Study. *JAMA, 291*(24), 2947–2958.

Skoog, I., Lernfelt, B., Landahl, S., Palmertz, B., Andreasson, L.A., Nilsson, L.,...Svanborg, A. (1996). 15-year longitudinal study of blood pressure and dementia. *Lancet*, *347*, 1141–1145.

Starr, J.M., Whalley, L.J., & Deary, I.J. (1996). The effects of antihypertensive treatment on cognitive function: Results from the HOPE study. *J Am Geriatr Soc*, *44*(4), 411–415.

Stewart, R., Masaki, K., Xue, Q.L., Peila, R., Petrovitch, H., & White, L.R. (2005). A 32-year prospective study of change in body weight and incident dementia: The Honolulu-Asia Aging Study. *Arch Neurol*, *62*, 55–60.

Szekely, C.A., Town, T., & Zandi, P.P. (2007). NSAIDs for the chemoprevention of Alzheimer's disease. *Subcell Biochem*, *42*, 229–248.

Tang, M.X., Jacobs, D., Stern, Y., Marder, K., Schofield, P., Gurland, B.,...Mayeux, R. (1996). Effect of oestrogen during menopause on risk and age at onset of Alzheimer's disease. *Lancet*, *348*(9025), 429–432.

Tanzi, R., & Parson, A. (2000). *Decoding darkness: The search for the genetics causes of Alzheimer's disease*. Perseus Press.

Tiraboschi, P., Hansen, L.A., Thal, L.J., & Corey-Bloom, J. (2004). The importance of neuritic plaques and tangles to the development and evolution of AD. *Neurology*, *62*(11), 1984–1989.

Turner, P.R., O'Connor, K., Tate, W.P., & Abraham, W.C. (2003). Roles of amyloid precursor protein and its fragments in regulating neural activity, plasticity and memory. *Prog Neurobiol*, *70*(1), 1–32.

Tzourio, C., Anderson, C., Chapman, N., Woodward, M., Neal, B., MacMahon, S., Chalmers, J., PROGRESS Collaborative Group. (2003). Effects of blood pressure lowering with perindopril and indapamide therapy on dementia and cognitive decline in patients with cerebrovascular disease. *Arch Intern Med*, *163*(9), 1069–1075.

Vagnucci, Jr. A.H., & Li, W.W. (2003). Alzheimer's disease and angiogenesis. *Lancet*, *361*, 605–608.

Wachterman, M., Kiely, D.K., & Mitchel, S.L. (2008). Reporting dementia on the death certificates of nursing home residents dying with dnd-stage dementia. *JAMA*, *300*(22), 2608–2610.

Waldemar, G., Dubois, B., Emre, M., Georges, J., McKeith, I.G., Rossor, M.,...Winblad, B. (2007). Recommendations for the diagnosis and management of Alzheimer's disease and other disorders associated with dementia: EFNS guideline. *Eur J Neurol*, *14*(1), e1–e26.

Weintraub, D., & Hurtig, H.I. (2007). Presentation and management of psychosis in Parkinson's disease and dementia with Lewy bodies. *American Journal of Psychiatry*, *164*(10), 1491–1498.

White, H., Pieper, C., & Schmader, K. (1998). The association of weight change in Alzheimer's disease with severity of disease and mortality: A longitudinal analysis. *J Am Geriatr Soc*, *46*, 1223–1227.

White, L., Small, B.J., Petrovitch, H., Ross, G.W., Masaki, K., Abbott, R.D.,...Markesbery, W. (2005). Recent clinical-pathologic research on the causes of dementia in late life: Update from the Honolulu-Asia Aging Study. *J Geriatr Psychiatry Neurol*, *18*(4), 224–227.

Whitmer, R.A., Gunderson, E.P., Quesenberry, C.P. Jr., Zhou, J., & Yaffe, K. (2007). Body mass index in midlife and risk of Alzheimer disease and vascular dementia. *Curr Alzheimer Res*, *4*, 103–109.

Witthaus, E., Ott, A., Barendregt, J.J., Breteler, M., & Bonneux, L. (1999). Burden of mortality and morbidity from dementia. *Alzheimer Disease & Associated Disorders*, *13*(3), 176–181.

Wolfson, C., Wolfson, D.B., Asgharian, M., M'Lan, C.E., Ostbye, T., Rockwood, K., & Hogan, D.B. (2001). Clinical progression of dementia study group. A reevaluation of the duration of survival after the onset of dementia. *N Engl J Med*, *344*(15), 1111–1116.

World Alzheimer Report. (2010). *The global economic impact of dementia*. London, UK: Alzheimer's Disease International.

World Health Organization. (2003). *The global burden of disease*. Geneva: Switzerland: World Health Organization.

World Health Organization. (2006). *Neurological disorders: Public health challenges* (pp. 42–55). Geneva, Switzerland: World Health Organization.

Xie, J., Brayne, C., Matthews, F.E., Medical Research Council Cognitive Function and Aging Study collaborators. (2008). Survival times in people with dementia: Analysis from population based cohort study with 14 year follow-up. *BMJ*, *336*(7638), 258–262.

Xu, W., Qiu, C., Winblad, B., & Fratiglioni, L. (2007). The effect of borderline diabetes on the risk of dementia and Alzheimer's disease. *Diabetes*, *56*, 211–216.

Xu, J., Kochaniek, K.D., Murphy, S.L., & Tejada-Vera, B. (2010). Deaths: Final data for 2007. *National Vital Statistics Reports*, *58*(9). Hyattsville, MD: National Center for Health Statistics.

Yasojima, K., Schwab, C., McGeer, E.G., & McGeer, P.L. (2000). Human neurons generate C-reactive protein and amylid P: Upregulation in Alzheimer's disease. *Brain Res*, *887*(1), 80–89.

Zandi, P.P., Carlson, M.C., Plassman, B.L., Welsh-Bohmer, K.A., Mayer, L.S., Steffens, D.C., & Breitner, J.S. for the Cache County Memory Study Investigators. (2002). Hormone replacement therapy and incidence of Alzheimer disease in older women. *JAMA*, *288*(17), 2123–2129.

Ziegler-Graham, K., Brookmeyer, R., Johnson, E., & Arrighi, H.M. (2008). Worldwide variation in the doubling time of Alzheimer's disease incidence rates. *Alzheimer's and Dementia*, *4*(5), 316–323.

Epidemiology of Parkinson's Disease

INTRODUCTION

Parkinson's disease is a degenerative disorder of the central nervous system involving the massive death and destruction of *dopamine* synthesizing neurons of the *substantia nigra* in the midbrain. Early symptoms of Parkinson's disease are tremor and shaking of the extremities, "cogwheel" rigidity of the joints, slowness of movement (bradykinesia), difficulty in walking, and loss of balance. These primary motor symptoms of Parkinson's disease are collectively called *"parkinsonism."* As the disease progresses, cognitive and behavioral symptoms often arise and dementia may occur.

The *substantia nigra* is a bilateral structure located in the midbrain that plays an important role in regulating a variety of neurological functions including mood, memory, cognition, addiction, learning, reward, and movement. *Substantia nigra* is Latin for *black substance*, so named because it contains high levels of brownish-black *neuromelanin* in dopaminergic neurons. Parkinson's disease is caused by the death of dopaminergic neurons due to their accumulation of the nuclear protein, *alpha-synuclein*, within intracellular inclusions called *Lewy bodies* in the *substantia nigra pars compacta*.

Cells of the *substantia nigra* produce and supply the neurotransmitter, dopamine, to the *basal ganglia* of the human brain. The basal ganglia consist of clusters of tightly interconnected nerve cells within the core of the forebrain. The primary structures are the caudate nucleus, the putamen, the globus pallidus, and the thalamus (**Figure 40.1**). The putamen and caudate nucleus together are often referred to as the *corpus striatum*. These neural structures within

the basal ganglia receive and process nerve impulses from the cerebral cortex which are then relayed back to the cortex through the thalamus to trigger precise, rapid, coordinated voluntary movements, and thought processes.

The cell bodies of neurons in the substantia nigra synthesize the neurotransmitter, *dopamine*, which travels in a network of axons (the *pars compacta*) to cell bodies in the basal ganglia. In Parkinson's disease, destruction of the substantia nigra results in depletion of dopamine in the basal ganglia. Without dopamine, the processing and transmission of signals by the neuronal circuits of the basal ganglia are disrupted and parkinsonian symptoms appear.

HISTORY OF PARKINSON'S DISEASE

The disease is named after the English physician, James Parkinson, who initially described its characteristic signs and symptoms among six patients with the *"shaking palsy"* in 1817. In his *Essay on the Shaking Palsy*, Parkinson accurately described the characteristic resting tremor, abnormal posture and gait, slowness of movement, paralysis, diminished muscle strength, and progression of disease over time (Parkinson, 1817).

In 1912, the German neurologist, Friedrich Lewy, described microscopic particles in the brains of patients who had died from Parkinson's disease (Lewy, 1912). Such eosinophilic inclusion bodies are called *Lewy bodies*. A few years later, the Russian neuropathologist, Konstantin Tretiakoff reported that the *substantia nigra* was the specific area of

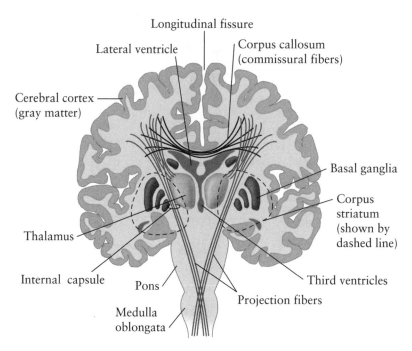

Figure 40.1 The Human Basal Ganglia.

the brain affected in patients with Parkinson's disease (Tretiakoff, 1919). Nearly four decades later, the Swedish investigator, Arvid Carlsson, correctly concluded from many years of laboratory investigations that Parkinson's disease arises due to depletion of the neurotransmitter, dopamine, from the *basal ganglia* of the brain (Carlsson, 1959). Carlsson was later awarded the 2000 Nobel Prize in Physiology or Medicine for his work on dopamine (Carlsson, Greengard, and Kandel, 2000).

A critical step in understanding the development of Parkinson's disease was made through genetic studies of familial disease. Identification of missense mutations in the gene encoding *alpha-synuclein* in patients from these families provided the first clue that this protein could be involved in the molecular chain of pathogenesis (Polymeropoulos et al., 1997; Polymeropoulos, 1998; Krüger et al., 1998).

Subsequently, Micheal Goedert, Maria Grazia Spillantini, and colleagues at the University of Cambridge identified the protein, *alpha-synuclein*, as the major component of Lewy bodies in Parkinson's disease (Spillanitini et al., 1997, 1998). Due to the inordinate accumulation of this protein in dead and dying neurons of the substantia nigra, Parkinson's disease has become known as a form of "*synucleinopathology*" (Goedert, 2001).

PATHOLOGY OF PARKINSON'S DISEASE

The classic pathologic feature of Parkinson's disease is the accumulation of the protein, *alpha-synuclein*, within intracellular inclusions of dopaminergic neurons in the *para compacta* of the *substantia nigra* of the *basal ganglia* of the midbrain. These inclusions are called *Lewy bodies* named after the German neurologist, Friedrich Lewy, who discovered them nearly a century ago in postmortem specimens of brain tissues from patients with Parkinson's disease (Lewy, 1912). These inclusions within neurons in the substantia nigra of the midbrain are also responsible for the development of a type of dementia called *Lewy body dementia*. Lewy body dementia is distinguishable from Parkinson's disease by the acute nature of dementia onset, in contrast to patients with Parkinson's disease who may develop dementia many years after their diagnosis (Weintraub and Hurtig, 2007; Holt et al., 2010; Schulz-Schaeffer, 2010).

In addition to *alpha-synuclein*, the Lewy bodies of Parkinson's disease also contain *ubiquitin*, a small ubiquitous protein that normally attaches to other intracellular proteins and targets them for degradation within proteasomes. Proteasomes are intracellular micromachines that degrade proteins into elemental amino acids in a process called proteolysis. Misfolded proteins such as alpha-synuclein also accumulate in the dopaminergic projections (axons) that supply dopamine to the basal ganglia. These events produce the death and destruction of dopaminergic neurons of the substantia nigra and generalized depletion of dopamine in the basal ganglia of the brain (see **Figure 40.1**). The loss of this essential neurotransmitter leads to the well-known motor function impairments (resting tremor, rigidity, and bradykinesia) that characterize Parkinson's disease.

The pigment *neuromelanin* is a form of melanin that is found principally in the dopaminergic neurons of the midbrain. Its origin and function in these cells has been a longstanding mystery. Recent biochemical studies suggest that neuromelanin forms from the oxidation of cytosolic dopamine and subsequently serves to protect dopaminergic neurons by binding to ionic iron, quinones, and other free radicals (Sulzer et al., 2000).

Numerous pathologic investigations have demonstrated that the degeneration of dopaminergic neurons in Parkinson's disease is associated with robust *microglia activation*. In this phenomenon, microglia undergo a remarkable transition from quiet nursing cells to a reactive state, in which they undergo hypertrophy, proliferation (gliosis), and altered gene expression. Reactive microglia are capable of secreting neurotrophic factors that promote neuronal survival, but they can also secrete *proinflammatory* and *neurotoxin factors*. Notably, the chief regulatory enzyme of the inflammatory prostaglandin cascade, cyclooxygenase-2 (*COX-2*), is overexpressed in the reactive microglia of patients with Parkinson's disease, but not in normal subjects. Thus, *inflammogenesis* may significantly contribute to the dopaminergic cell loss of Parkinson's disease (Knott, Stern, and Wilkin, 2000; Hald, Van Beek, and Lotharious, 2007; Ardestani, 2010).

INCIDENCE AND PREVALENCE OF PARKINSON'S DISEASE

Parkinson's disease is the second most common neurodegenerative disease after Alzheimer's disease. In the US population, this condition is diagnosed in about 1% of adults over the age of 60 years and 4% over the age of 80 years (Lonnecke and Breteler, 2006). However, reported estimates of prevalence and incidence show wide disparities among populations, most likely due to differences in methodology and inadequate case finding. Nevertheless, genetic, environmental, and behavioral factors may also contribute to the variability in rates as discussed in this section.

Nebraska became the first and only state in the United States to create a Parkinson's disease registry. Since 1997, the registry has provided information about the incidence and prevalence of the disease in the general population of Nebraska. Based upon analysis of physician-reported cases during 1997–2006, the population of Nebraska has relatively high incidence and prevalence rates of Parkinson's disease compared to other populations. For the entire population of the state, the annual crude prevalence was estimated at 329 cases per 100,000. It is possible that the high rates of Parkinson's disease in Nebraska are due to heavy use of and exposure to pesticides in what is largely a farming area. Well designed epidemiologic studies are needed to elucidate and confirm such effects (Strickland and Bertoni, 2003; Safranak, Theis, and Krause, 2007).

Clusters of Parkinson's disease have been discovered in certain ethnic groups. For example, in a population-based screening of individuals over the age of 60 years in an Amish community, 15 prevalent cases were found among 213 individuals, yielding an extraordinarily high annual crude prevalence rate of 5,703 cases per 100,000. Farming and carpentry were the usual occupations among male participants and homemaking among female participants. All subjects used well water throughout their lives and, according to Amish custom, none used electricity. Homes were thus lighted and heated by propane gas. Notably, only two individuals with Parkinson's disease were first-degree relatives, suggesting that environmental exposures rather than genetic factors contributed to the excess prevalence of Parkinson's disease in this community (Racette et al., 2009).

High prevalence rates have also been observed in other cultures. In 1988, a door to door survey was conducted to screen for neurological diseases among 14,010 members of the Parsi colony, an Islamic religious sect living in Bombay, India. A total of 46 individuals were found to have Parkinson's disease, yielding an extremely high crude prevalence of 328.3 per 100,000. Genetic factors were postulated to play a role due to the high frequency of consanguineous marriages in the Parsis community (Bharucha et al., 1988).

Investigators at the University of Rochester in New York utilized prevalence estimates from 15 different countries to project the number of individuals with Parkinson's disease in nations with the largest populations in Europe and worldwide. Prevalence estimates for 2005 were derived for individuals at least 50 years of age in 5 European nations (Germany, France, United Kingdom, Italy, and Spain) and the world's 10 most populous nations (China, India, United States, Indonesia, Brazil, Pakistan,

Bangladesh, Russia, Nigeria, and Japan). Estimates were derived from age-specific prevalence data reported in 62 published articles plus census data for each country. By the most conservative estimate, 4.1 million individuals over the age of 50 years were living with Parkinson's disease in these nations during 2005 (Dorsey et al., 2007).

Muangpaisan and colleagues systematically reviewed estimates of the prevalence and incidence of Parkinson's disease from 21 publications for populations in the nations of Asia. Surveys of populations in China (6), Japan (5), India (3), Taiwan (2), Singapore (2), Israel (1), Korea (1), and Saudi Arabia (1) were included in the investigation. Age-standardized prevalence rates ranged from 51 to 177 per 100,000 in door to door surveys and from 36–68 per 100,000 in record-based surveys. Standardized incidence rates also varied widely ranging from 1.5 per 100,000 in a door to door survey of 29 provinces in China to 8.7 per 100,000 in Taiwan. On average, the rates for Asian populations are about 50% lower than rates observed in large studies of non-Asian populations conducted throughout Europe, North America, South America, and Australia. For example, prevalence estimates in 30 studies of non-Asian populations ranged from 101–439 per 100,000 in door to door surveys and from 61–141 per 100,000 in record based surveys, and incidence rates ranged from 15–28 per 100,000 in door to door surveys and from 6.1–17.4 per 100,000 in record based surveys. Since prevalence is a multiplicative function of incidence and duration of disease (prevalence = incidence × duration), the relatively low prevalence rates in non-Asian populations could reflect relatively poor survival due to lack of access to health care and treatment. However, varying methodologies and differences in diagnostic criteria and case-finding strategies undoubtedly contribute to the wide variation in reported estimates of prevalence and incidence of Parkinsons' disease worldwide (Muangpaisan, Hori, and Brayne, 2009).

Driver and colleagues estimated the age-specific incidence and lifetime risk of Parkinson's disease in the Physician's Health Study, a prospective national cohort of 21,970 US male physicians aged 40–84 years at baseline and followed over 23 years. They identified 563 cases in the cohort yielding a crude annual incidence rate of 121 cases per 100,000 person years. The cumulative risk of disease for ages 45–100 years was estimated at 6.7% and the annual incidence for men over the age of 65 years was 224 per 100,000. The incidence among chronic smokers was about 30% less than among nonsmokers (Driver et al., 2009).

Estimates of the incidence of Parkinson's disease vary widely, even within countries. The incidence of Parkinson's disease in the US Physician's Health Study (224 per 100,000 for men over 65 years of age) is more than twofold higher than estimates derived from other US population samples: 119 per 100,000 in Manhattan, 113 per 100,000 in Minnesota, and 100 per 100,000 in Los Angeles. Comparative estimates for European populations are higher than the US estimates: 261 per 100,000 in Rotterdam, 360 per 100,000 in Central Spain, and 461 per 100,000 in Italy. A number of factors may contribute to this wide variation including differences in the age and longevity of the populations studied, methods of case finding, criteria for the diagnosis of Parkinson's disease, and the prevalence of smoking (Driver et al., 2009).

The characteristic pattern of the age-specific incidence of Parkinson's disease is depicted for men and women in **Figure 40.2**. Data are from the prospective cohort in Olmsted County, Minnesota (Bower et al.,

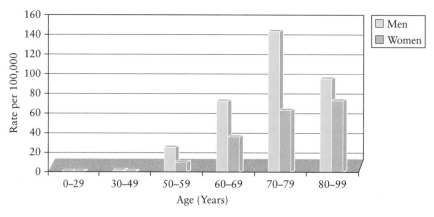

Figure 40.2 Annual Age-Specific Incidence of Parkinson's Disease.

Source: Data from Bower JH, Maraganore DM, McDonnell SK, Rocca WA (1999). Incidence and distribution of parkinsonism in Olmsted County, Minnesota, 1976–1990. *Neurology* 52(6):1214-20.

1999). As shown, Parkinson's disease is rarely diagnosed before the age of 50 years but then increases exponentially with age. Rates are higher in men than women for all age brackets but appear to equilibrate after the age of 80 years. The peak onset in men occurs about a decade earlier than in women.

A study in Northern California compared the incidence of Parkinson's disease by age, gender, and ethnicity in members of the *Kaiser Permanente Medical Care Program*. Among 588 cases diagnosed during 1994–1995, only 24 (4%) were diagnosed before the age of 50 years. Annual incidence rates peaked during ages 80–89 years for both men (191 per 100,000) and women (71 per 100,000). Hispanics had the highest overall rates and African Americans the lowest, although sample sizes were small in all ethnic groups except for non-Hispanic Caucasians. Additional studies are therefore needed to confirm the presence of ethnic differences (Van Den Eeden et al., 2003).

As longevity increases worldwide, the burden of chronic diseases of old age, including Parkinson's disease, will undoubtedly rise. Without intervention, the prevalence of Parkinson's disease is expected to approach 9 million by the year 2030, more than double the number of cases in 2005. Population-based registries are needed in order to assess the burden of neurodegenerative diseases and guide the health, social, and economic policies of the future (Dorsey et al., 2007).

SURVIVAL, DEMENTIA, AND MORTALITY IN PARKINSON'S DISEASE

Compared to the general population, patients who develop Parkinson's disease have increased mortality and shortened survival. Furthermore, most studies suggest that dementia often occurs as a consequence of disease progression, affecting nearly two-thirds of patients with long-term survival.

Investigators of the *Rochester Epidemiology Project* in Minnesota examined the survival of incident cases of Parkinson's disease in the *Olmsted County Cohort* during 1976–1995. Cases (*n* = 196) were matched by age and gender to disease-free controls (*n* = 185) from the same population and all individuals were followed to determine the time of death. A total of 110 cases and 79 controls died during follow-up. The mortality rate was 1.6 times higher in cases than controls, and median survival was 10.3 years for the cases and 13.4 years for controls. These results demonstrate that patients with Parkinson's disease have a significantly higher risk of dying compared to matched controls from the general population (Elbaz et al., 2003).

In the United Kingdom, measures of survival for a community-based cohort of patients with Parkinson's disease were compared with the age and gender matched population of England and Wales. The study compared the ages at death, life expectancies, and standardized mortality ratios (SMR) for patients with and without dementia. A total of 166 patients participated in the study, of which 91 died after only 4 years of follow-up. The SMR was threefold higher in demented patients (SMR = 3.10) than nondemented patients (SMR = 1.15), and among patients diagnosed between ages 55–74 years of age, the life expectancy for demented patients was markedly shortened (7.5 years) compared to nondemented patients (12.4 years). These results suggest that dementia severely compromises the survival of patients with Parkinson's disease whereas those who do not develop dementia experience near normal survival (Hobson, Meara and Ishihara-Paul, 2010).

Similar results were observed in a study of 90 incident cases of Parkinson's disease conducted at the University of Leeds in the United Kingdom. Compared to disease-free controls, patients with Parkinson's disease had 1.64 times higher mortality and shorter median survival (9.1 years compared to more than 13 years). Furthermore, mortality was increased nearly twofold in patients with dementia versus those without (Hughes et al., 2004).

Dementia is a common feature of patients with Parkinson's disease. For example, in a meta-analysis of 24 studies, the average prevalence among 1,767 patients was 25% (Aarsland, Zaccai, and Brayne, 2005). Furthermore, prospective studies of nondemented patients with Parkinson's disease have consistently shown that their risk of developing dementia cumulates at a rate of approximately 10% per year. Investigators in Norway found an annual incidence of 95 per 1,000 person years among 171 patients (Aarsland et al., 2001) and investigators in Wales found a similar rate of 107 per 1,000 person years among 86 patients (Hobson and Meara, 2004). These estimates reflect a sixfold risk increase compared to matched subjects without Parkinson's disease and yield a cumulative rate of 65% for 10 years of survival. This estimate is consistent with a study in Denmark in which 71 (66%) of 108 patients with Alzheimer's disease developed dementia during 8 years of follow-up (Aarsland et al., 2003) and an extended study in Norway in which 140 (60%) of 233 patients developed dementia during 12 years of follow-up (Buter et al., 2008).

Investigators at the University of North Carolina conducted a meta-analysis of dementia and polymorphisms of *apoplipoprotein E* (*APOE*) in patients with Parkinson's disease. Their analysis revealed an elevated risk of dementia among patients with *APOE ε4* (OR = 1.6); however, there was significant heterogeneity among study results and additional studies are needed to confirm the association (Huang et al., 2006).

A team of investigators examined the survival of 288 male patients with newly diagnosed Parkinson's disease compared to 51,012 disease-free men in the *US Health Professionals Follow-up Study*. The study specifically examined effects of duration of disease and smoking. During 15 years of follow-up, 92 cases (32%) died compared to 8,485 controls (17%). After adjustment for age, men with Parkinson's disease had 60% higher mortality than controls. The relative risk of death increased with duration of disease: RR = 1.1 for 1–5 years, RR = 2.3 for 6–10 years, and RR = 3.5 after 10 years. Smoking increased mortality by twofold among controls but conferred no additional risk of death among patients with Parkinson's disease (Chen et al., 2006).

Based upon the median survival from a number of prospective studies (~10 years), the annual risk of death for a patient with newly diagnosed Alzheimer's disease is approximately 6.7% which is 1.6 times greater than the general population (excess risk = 2.5%). Assuming there are 4.1 million prevalent cases worldwide, a crude estimate of the excess number of global deaths attributable to Alzheimer's disease is 0.025 × 4.1 million = 102,500. This estimate is likely to be conservative as a consequence of under-reporting and substandard patient care in less developed countries.

DISABILITY ADJUSTED LIFE YEARS: PARKINSON'S DISEASE

Once diagnosed, Parkinson's disease invariably progresses over time. Without treatment, motor symptoms (tremor, unsteady gait, bradykinesia, and cogwheel rigidity) worsen quickly and may lead to ambulation and disability within a few years. Medications such as levodopa can effectively delay progression for a time; however, such drugs have been found to produce a more rapid decline in cognitive function in some patients. Inevitably, patients develop autonomic disturbances, sleeplessness, mood alterations, cognitive decline, and dementia, all of which greatly increase disability and mortality (Poewe, 2006).

The 2004 pattern of *disability adjusted life years* (*DALY*) due to Parkinson's disease as shown in **Figure 40.3** (WHO, 2009). Since the incidence peaks among the elderly, DALY values tend to be higher in developed countries whose populations have the greatest longevity. Nevertheless, populations with the highest DALY are those in war torn areas of the Middle East, such as Iraq and Afghanistan. Such populations have been subjected to unusually high levels of certain environmental neurotoxins including pesticides, fuel vapors, combustion products from oil well fires

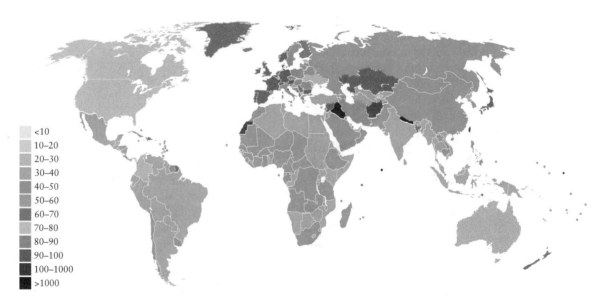

	<10
	10–20
	20–30
	30–40
	40–50
	50–60
	60–70
	70–80
	80–90
	90–100
	100–1000
	>1000

Figure 40.3 Disability Adjusted Life Years, Parkinson's Disease, 2004.

Source: Data from World Health Organization. The global burden of disease: 2004 update. Geneva, WHO, 2008. Available at www.who.int/evidence/bod.

and open pit fires, nerve gases, and depleted uranium (Golomb, 2008; Friedl, Grate, and Proctor, 2009).

Another outlier with high DALY lost from Parkinson's disease is the small nation of Nepal that borders northeastern India in the Himalayan mountain range. Risk factors in the Napelese population include lack of oxygen, nutritional deficiencies in iodine, zinc, and other minerals, and outbreaks of Japanese encephalitis due to a mosquito-born virus, all of which might contribute to the development of parkinsonism (De Pedro-Cuesta, 1987; Pradhan et al., 1999; Kanda et al., 2000; Ramakrishnan, 2002; Brewer et al., 2010).

Notably, some patients from populations of the Middle East are characterized by very early onset (the average age at diagnosis was 36 years in one series of 60 patients) and novel genetic polymorphisms in the *leucine rich repeat kinase 2* (*LRRK2*) gene, which is discussed in a following section of this chapter on the genetics of Parkinson's disease). These results suggest that genetic factors may play a more dominant role in the pathogenesis of Parkinson's disease in certain populations due to the relatively high frequency of consanguineous marriages (Shojaee et al., 2009; Elahi, 2009).

RISK FACTORS FOR PARKINSON'S DISEASE

The pathogenesis of Parkinson's disease is complex and involves both genetic and environmental factors. Though many risk factors and protective factors have been proposed, conclusive evidence is lacking for most. The two consistently observed relationships are an increased risk in those exposed to pesticides and a reduced risk in smokers. In recent years, the roles of some individual genes and molecular pathways have been elucidated, which has advanced our understanding of this disease (Lonneke and Breteler, 2006). Selected studies are discussed in the following paragraphs.

Genetics of Parkinson's Disease

In a community-based study, investigators at Columbia University in New York assessed the risk of Parkinson's disease among 1,458 first-degree relatives of 233 index cases (probands). Compared to relatives of disease-free controls, relatives of the cases were 2.3 times more likely to develop Parkinson's disease. The risk estimates were highest among Caucasian male relatives but similar for siblings and parents of the probands. The results support the existence of genetic factors that influence susceptibility to pathogenesis (Marder et al., 1996).

Tanner and colleagues assessed the role of genetics in the development of Parkinson's disease by comparing the concordance and discordance of disease in monozygous and dizygous twins. The study examined 19,842 male twins enrolled from the National Academy of Sciences World War II Veteran Twins Registry. Across all ages, the pairwise concordance rates were *not* significantly higher for monozygous versus dizygous twins (15.5% and 11.1%, respectively). However, within 16 twin pairs with diagnosis before 50 years of age, the concordance among monozygous twins was 100% compared to 17% for dizygous twins (RR = 6.0). The investigators concluded that genetic factors may be important for early onset disease but *do not* play a major role when Parkinson's disease is diagnosed after the age of 50 years (Tanner et al., 1999).

Autosomal Dominant Genes and Parkinson's Disease

Alpha-synuclein   The gene that encodes *alpha-synuclein* (*SNCA*) is located on the long arm of human chromosome 4. Carriers of mutant forms of *SNCA* are at high risk for developing Parkinson's disease. A mutant *SNCA* allele was first identified in a large Italian kindred in which heterozygous gene carriers manifested early-onset Parkinson's disease in an *autosomal dominant* inheritance pattern (Polymeropoulos et al., 1997; Polymeropolous, 1998). Mutated *SNCA* alleles have since been discovered in several multigenerational families in which Parkinson's disease is inherited as an autosomal dominant syndrome. Mutations in SNCA disrupt the normal processing of alpha-synuclein within dopaminergic cells, leading to the formation of Lewy bodies and cell death (Hardy et al., 2006).

LRRK2 and Dardarin   Funayama and colleagues performed a genome-wide linkage analysis of a Japanese kindred with an *autosomal dominant* inheritance pattern of parkinsonism among relatives. Patients in the kindred manifested the classic clinical symptoms of Parkinson's disease but Lewy bodies were *absent* in postmortem specimens of the substantia nigra. Findings revealed genetic linkage of disease susceptibility to a mutant gene on the long arm of chromosome 12 that encodes the leucine rich repeat protein kinase, *LRRK2* (Funayama et al., 2002).

Subsequent genetic studies have identified scores of families in which carriers of missense mutations of *LRRK2* developed late onset Parkinson's disease. However, postmortem studies of brainstem specimens from these patients have revealed marked heterogeneity in the presence and composition of inclusion bodies within degenerating neurons of the substantia nigra. To date, more than 20 mutant alleles of *LRRK2* have been identified; however, the penetrance of these alleles is highly variable and there is marked heterogeneity in the deposition of misfolded proteins and degeneration of dopaminergic neurons among gene carriers (Zimprich et al., 2004).

The *LRRK2* gene encodes the complex protein, *dardarin*, which is a leucine-rich protein kinase that phosphorylates other proteins and regulates protein catabolism and metabolism within neurons. A team of investigators cloned the *LRRK2* gene from afflicted members of Spanish families with heritable parkinsonism. Since these families were of *Basque* descent, they named the *LRRK2* protein, *dardarin*, after the Basque word *dardar* which means tremor (Paisán-Ruíz et al., 2004).

Autosomal Recessive Genes and Parkinson's Disease

Japanese investigators identified gene deletions in the long arm of chromosome 6 in a *rare* form of early-onset parkinsonism, showing an autosomal recessive inheritance pattern. Postmortem studies of afflicted patients revealed depletion of dopaminergic neurons in the substantia nigra but *without* Lewy bodies (Kitada et al., 1998). The deleted gene, *Parkin*, encodes *E3 ligase* that regulates ubiquitylation of proteins for degradation in proteasomes of neurons. Either deletions or missense mutations of the *Parkin* gene can lead to the accumulation of misfolded proteins within dopaminergic neurons and development of parkinsonism (Lim, Dawson, and Dawson, 2006; Hardy et al., 2006).

Other rare mutations have also been noted in association with parkinsonism. Mutations in the *PTEN-induced kinase gene* (*PINK-1*) located on the short arm of chromosome 1 have been identified in families with early onset Parkinson's disease. The *PINK-1* gene encodes a protein kinase that is essential for normal mitochondrial function in neurons (Rogaeva et al., 2004).

Molecular studies of these genes and the search for others that influence the pathogenesis of Parkinson's disease are continuing at a rapid pace. The molecular genetics of this condition as well as other forms of neurodegenerative disease can be expected to elucidate molecular targets for effective therapy and/or chemoprevention.

MPTP and Parkinson's Disease

Interest in environmental exposures, particularly pesticides, metals, and industrial solvents rose substantially following the discovery that exposure to high levels of *1-methyl-4-phenyl-1,2,3,6-tetrahydro-pyridine* (*MPTP*) causes acute onset of parkinsonian symptoms. This discovery was made by J. William Langston and colleagues who studied several young intravenous drug users in California who developed irreversible parkinsonian symptoms after injecting narcotics contaminated with MPTP (Langston et al., 1983; Langston and Palfreman, 1996).

Subsequent investigations determined that MPTP crosses the blood-brain barrier where it is activated by monoamine oxidase (Langston et al., 1984; Langston, 1985). The active metabolite of MPTP causes parkinsonian symptoms by inducing pathologic changes in dopaminergic neurons confined to the substantia nigra. Notably, the active metabolite of MPTP (MPP+) bears a close structural similarity to the herbicide, paraquat, which suggests that exposure to herbicides and/or pesticides might also elevate the risk. As noted in a review of the epidemiology of Parkinson's disease, "*the established neurotoxin properties of some widely used pesticides (e.g., organophosphorous insecticides) and the chemical similarity of paraquat MPP+ are logical reasons to focus on these exposures*" (Checkoway and Nelson, 1999).

While MPTP *per se* is not neurotoxic, it readily crosses the blood-brain barrier where it is converted to MPP+ by the enzyme *monoamine oxidase B* (*MOA-B*) of glial cells. The neurotoxic cation MPP+ has been found to kill dopamine-producing neurons in the pars compacta of the substantia nigra by interfering with the electron transport chain of mitochondria (Richardson et al., 2005).

Paraquat is the trade name for *N, N'-dimethyl-4,4'-bipyridinium dichloride*, one of the most widely used herbicides in the world. When ingested, pure paraquat is highly toxic to mammals, including humans, potentially leading to acute respiratory distress and death. There are no specific antidotes for paraquat and in third world countries it is a major suicide agent. A related compound, *rotenone*, is a poisonous extract of certain plant species, primarily *Derris* and *Lonchocarpus*, that is widely used as an insecticide. Similar to the ionic metabolite of MPTP, both paraquat and rotenone exert toxic effects on the dopeminergic neurons of the midbrain by interfering with the electron transport chain in mitochondria or the production of free radicals (Richardson et al., 2005).

Herbicides, Pesticides, and Parkinson's Disease

Findings linking MPTP exposure to parkinsonism in humans stimulated epidemiologic studies of Parkinson's disease and exposure to pesticides and herbicides, since many of these compounds are similar in structure to MPTP. In an early ecological study conducted in the rural population of Quebec, Canada, more than 5,000 cases were identified during 1980–1984 and prevalence rates calculated and compared among 9 hydrographic regions. The study revealed that the rates of Parkinson's disease varied unevenly throughout the province and regions with the highest rates were characterized by intensive market gardening and the highest levels of pesticide use (Barbeau et al., 1987).

In Hong Kong, Suzanne Ho and colleagues conducted a case control study of Parkinson's disease comparing the use of pesticides and herbicides among 34 cases and 105 controls. They found a significant increase in the odds ratio associated with previous use of pesticides and/or herbicides (OR = 3.6), although the participants were unable to provide details on the specific types of chemicals used (Ho, Wee, and Lee, 1989).

Priyadarshi and colleagues performed a meta-analysis of 19 studies of Parkinson's disease and pesticide exposure published between 1989–1999. Findings revealed a significant increase in the overall risk (OR = 1.94) and combined estimates from studies in the US (OR = 2.15), Canada (OR = 1.94), Europe (OR = 1.76), and Asia (OR-2.53) were similar. Nevertheless, there was significant heterogeneity among studies possibly due to differences in case definition and the methods used to define exposure (Priyadarshi et al., 2000).

Results of subsequent studies in the past few years continue to support an association of exposure to pesticides/herbicides and the development of Parkinson's disease. In France, a case control study compared pesticide exposure in 81 cases and 252 population-based controls. The study revealed a positive association between occupational pesticide exposure and the odds of developing Parkinson's disease (OR = 2.2) (Baldi et al., 2003).

Investigators at the American Cancer Society examined pesticide exposure and the risk of developing Parkinson's disease among participants of the *Cancer Prevention Study II Nutrition Cohort*, a longitudinal investigation of US men and women initiated in 1992. A total of 143,325 individuals who were disease-free at baseline were followed for up to 10 years to detect the development of incident cases of Parkinson's disease. Exposure to pesticides was reported by 7,864 participants including farmers and ranchers. Regardless of occupation, individuals exposed to pesticides had a 70% higher incidence of Parkinson's disease than those not exposed (RR = 1.7). The investigators suggest the need

for future studies to identify specific chemicals that increase the risk (Ascherio et al., 2006).

Investigators at Duke University conducted a family-based study of 319 cases and 296 disease-free relatives to assess the relationship between Parkinson's disease and pesticide exposure. Cases reported pesticide exposure more often than controls (OR = 1.61) and cumulative exposure to pesticides showed a dose-response pattern with the risk (Hancock et al., 2008).

Caroline Tanner, William Langston, and colleagues affiliated with the *Parkinson's Institute* in Sunnyvale, California, have conducted two separate investigations to elaborate associations between the risk of developing Parkinson's disease and exposure to pesticides and herbicides. In a multicenter case control study, lifelong occupational and job histories were utilized to determine pesticide and herbicide exposures among 519 cases and 511 controls. The results revealed an increased disease risk with overall pesticide use (OR = 1.90) and especially with pesticides such as rotenone that have found to be mechanistically associated with experimental parkinsonism (OR = 2.20). The highest risk (OR = 2.59) was noted for dichlorophenoxyacetic acid (2, 4-D), a neurotoxin known to uncouple oxidative phosphorylation in mitochondria that is one of the most widely used herbicides worldwide (Tanner et al., 2009).

In a subsequent nested case control study, the lifetime exposure histories to herbicides and pesticides were compared in 110 incident cases and 358 controls frequency-matched by age, gender, and location. All individuals were ascertained from the *US Agricultural Health Study*, a prospective cohort of more than 89,000 agricultural workers. Findings revealed an increased disease risk with exposure to pesticides such as rotenone that inhibit mitochondrial function (OR = 2.0) and with agents such as paraquat that cause oxidative stress (OR = 2.5) (Tanner et al., 2011).

Overall, the results of multiple epidemiologic investigations provide consistent evidence that pesticide/herbicide exposure is linked to the development of Parkinson's disease. Furthermore, specific compounds found to increase the risk are known to form reactive oxygen species and cause mitochondrial dysfunction, the same mechanisms linked to the destruction of dopaminergic neurons in the midbrain in experimental animal models of Parkinson's disease.

Environmental Risk Factors and Parkinson's Disease

In 1837, John Couper described parkinsonian symptoms in five men who worked in a chemical plant grinding the black oxide of manganese ore. The manganese ore grinders exhibited gait disturbance, loss of balance, paralysis of facial muscles, impaired ability to hear and speak, and drooling, but the cardinal sign of Parkinson's disease, resting tremor, was notably absent. Couper's essay is regarded as the first report of severe neurotoxicity in humans resulting from manganese exposure (Couper, 1837).

More than a century later, Rodier conducted a survey of nervous system abnormalities among 3,849 workers employed in 3 manganese mines in Morocco. His findings revealed 151 workers with parkinsonian-like symptoms, 132 of whom held jobs drilling blast holes that entailed the most intense manganese exposures. The peak prevalence of *manganism* with intense exposure was 43.5% among workers aged 30–44 years (Rodier, 1955; Checkoway, 2010).

Many subsequent investigations have examined the effects of manganese exposure in both humans and nonhuman primates. The available evidence from behavioral, neuroimaging, neurochemical, and neuropathological studies suggests that manganese accumulation in the brain produces an *atypical form of parkinsonism,* which is *not* associated with degeneration of the dopaminergic neurons in the subtantia nigra as in classical Parkinson's disease. Rather, manganese poisoning may inihibit the release of dopamine at the synapses of dopaminergic neurons with neurons in the basal ganglia (Guilarte, 2010).

A number of case control epidemiologic investigations have been conducted in search of other environmental exposures that influence the risk of developing Parkinson's disease. Most such studies suffer from lack of detailed information about the type, frequency, intensity, and duration of exposure.

The *Geoparkinson Study* is a large international case control study of Parkinson's disease designed to assess associations of genetic and environmental risk factors with the development of Parkinson's disease. Standardized personal interviews were conducted to collect information on lifetime exposure to solvents, pesticides, iron, copper, and manganese for 767 cases and 1,989 controls. Participants were ascertained at centers in Scotland, Italy, Sweden, Romania, and Malta. Levels of exposure for each subject were estimated by a job exposure matrix and subjective modeling. Logistic regression analysis revealed a dose-response in risk with increasing exposure to pesticides: OR = 1.13 for low exposure and OR = 1.41 for high exposure; increased risk with a history of repeated traumatic loss of consciousness (OR = 2.53); and decreased risk with chronic tobacco use (OR = 0.50). Results for other environmental factors including exposure to solvents, iron, manganese, or copper were null. The findings of this large international study suggest that pesticide exposure and head trauma have causative roles in the genesis of Parkinson's disease, but to not support links with other environmental risk factors (Dick et al., 2007).

Smoking and Parkinson's Disease

As pointed out by Checkoway and Nelson in their review of the epidemiology of Parkinson's disease:

> *"Apart from the increasing incidence of Parkinson's disease with age, the most consistently reported epidemiologic finding has been an inverse association with cigarette smoking. Decreased risks, by about 50% among smokers compared to nonsmokers have been reported from many case control studies, some of which demonstrated strong inverse dose-response relations. Cohort studies in which smoking data were obtained before cases' diagnoses substantiate the negative association with smoking"* (Checkoway and Nelson, 1999).

Recently, 305,468 participants of the *National Institutes of Health American Association of Retired Persons (AARP) Diet and Health Cohort* were studied to evaluate the relative importance of smoking duration in reducing the risk. A total of 1,662 participants developed Parkinson's disease during the study. Compared to never smokers, disease odds were reduced among past smokers (OR = 0.78) and current smokers (OR = 0.56) and the risk declined as the duration of smoking increased (Chen et al., 2010).

A team of US investigators from multiple institutions conducted a pooled meta-analysis of available published studies to clarify associations of age of smoking onset, time since quitting, and other measures of smoking and tobacco use with the risk of developing Parkinson's disease. Eight case control studies (2,328 cases and 4,113 controls) and three cohort studies (488 cases and 4,880 controls) were included in the analysis. The pooled data confirmed a dose-dependent reduction in the risk of developing Parkinson's disease with duration of cigarette smoking as well as other forms of tobacco use. These effects were not influenced by gender or education. The investigators state that *"although the numerous adverse health effects of cigarette smoking may eventually limit the clinical implications of the epidemiologic findings on smoking and Parkinson's disease, research to reveal the underlying chemicals and mechanisms are warranted"* (Ritz et al., 2007).

Coffee and Parkinson's Disease

Several studies have also observed an inverse association between coffee consumption and the risk of developing Parkinson's disease. Investigators at Harvard University conducted a systematic review and meta-analysis to summarize the evidence for both coffee consumption and cigarette smoking. Results for smoking were based on 44 case control studies and 4 cohort studies, and results for coffee consumption were based on 8 case control and 5 cohort studies. Compared with never smokers, the relative risk of developing Parkinson's disease was 0.80 for past smokers and 0.39 for current smokers, and the risk declined by about 20% for each additional 10 pack-years of smoking. Compared with noncoffee drinkers, the relative risk of developing Parkinson's disease was 0.69 for coffee drinkers, and the risk declined by about 10% for each additional cup of coffee per day. Results therefore provide strong evidence that smoking and drinking coffee both lower the risk of developing Parkinson's disease (Hernán et al., 2002).

Nonsteroidal Anti-Inflammatory Drugs and Parkinson's Disease

In addition to the loss of dopminergic neurons in the substantia nigra of the midbrain, inflammation and microgliosis have also been noted in the pathogenesis of Parkinson's disease. These findings have stimulated interest in potential chemopreventive effects of nonsteroidal anti-inflammatory drugs (NSAIDs).

Two major prospective studies have focused on NSAIDs and Parkinson's disease: the *Health Professionals Follow-up Study* in men and the *Nurses Health Study* in women. Prospective cohorts of 44,057 men and 98,845 women free of Parkinson's disease, stroke, and cancer at baseline participated in the study. In both cohorts, questionnaires were mailed every two years to ascertain updated information on health status and medical diagnoses. During follow-up (1986–2000 for men and 1980–1998 for women), 415 incident cases were detected (236 in men and 236 in women). Participants who reported regular use of aspirin or nonaspirin NSAIDs (primarily ibuprofen) were found to have a significant reduction in their risk of developing Parkinson's disease (RR = 0.55). Risk reductions were similar for men and women. These results suggest that NSAIDs have neuroprotective effects against the development of Parkinson's disease and are consistent with other epidemiologic findings showing that these compounds

also reduce the risk of developing Alzheimer's disease (Chen et al., 2003).

TERTIARY PREVENTION IN PARKINSON'S DISEASE

Parkinson's disease invariably progresses with time. Without treatment, motor symptoms often advance rapidly and patients may lose independent ambulation and become bedridden in just a few years. Medications such as levodopa, dopamine agonists, monoamine oxidase (MAO) inhibitors, anticholinergics, and amantadine have been instrumental in delaying the progression of motor symptoms by more than a decade (WHO, 2006). Although levodopa continues to be the gold standard of treatment for the cardinal motor features of Parkinson's disease, its chronic use is associated with potentially disabling motor complications and psychosis. Atypical (second generation) antipsychotic medications are routinely administered to patients who develop psychosis; however, additional studies are needed to assess the effects of specific drugs on morbidity, mortality, and disease progression (Weintraub and Hurtig, 2007; Holt et al., 2010).

Future prospects to improve outcomes and the quality of life in patients with Parkinson's disease include gene therapy to restore the chemical balance of neurotransmitters within the circuitry of the basal ganglia. In animal models of parkinsonism, gene transfer of glutamic acid decarboxylase to modulate *gamma-aminobutyric acid (GABA)* in the subthalamic nucleus has been found to improve basal ganglia function, and most recently, a randomized clinical trial of this procedure in human patients produced significant improvement in motor function among patients who received gene therapy compared to those who received placebo at 6 months of follow-up (Lewitt et al., 2011).

• • • REFERENCES

Aarsland, D., Andersen, K., Larsen, J.P., Lolk, A., Nielsen, H., & Kragh-Sorensen, P. (2001). Risk of dementia in Parkinson's disease: A community-based, prospective study. *Neurology, 56*(6), 730–736.

Aarsland, D., Andersen, K., Larsen, J.P., Lolk, A., & Kragh-Sorensen, P. (2003). Prevalence and characteristics of dementia in Parkinson disease: An 8-year prospective study. *Arch Neurol, 60*(3), 387–392.

Aarsland, D., Zaccai, J., & Brayne, C. (2005). A systematic review of prevalence studies of dementia in Parkinson's disease. *Mov Disord*, *20*(10), 1255–1263.

Ardestani, M.S. (2010). Parkinson's disease, the inflammatory pathway and anti-inflammatory drugs: An overview. *J Med Sci*, *10*(3), 49–58.

Ascherio, A., Chen, H., Weisskopf, M.G., O'Reilly, E., McCuloough, M.L., Calle, E.E.,...Thun, M.J. (2006). Pesticide exposure and risk for Parkinson's disease. *Annals of Neurology*, *60*(2), 197–203.

Baldi, I., Cantagrel, A., Lebailly, P., Tison, F., Dubroca, B., Chrysostome, V., Dartigues, J.F., & Brochard, P. (2003). Association between Parkinson's disease and exposure to pesticides in southwestern France. *Neuroepidemiology*, *22*, 305–310.

Barbeau, A., Roy, M., Bernier, G., Campanella, G., & Paris, S. (1987). Ecogenetics of Parkinson's disease: Prevalence and environmental aspects in rural areas. *Can J Neurol Sci*, *14*(1), 36–41.

Bharucha, N.E., Bharucha, E.P., Bharucha, A.E., Bhise, A.V., & Schoenberg, B.S. (1988). Prevalence of Parkinson's disease in the Parsi community of Bombay, India. *Arch Neurol*, *45*(12), 1321–1323.

Bower, J.H., Maraganore, D.M., McDonnell, S.K., & Rocca, W.A. (1999). Incidence and distribution of parkinsonism in Olmsted County, Minnesota, 1976–1990. *Neurology*, *52*(6), 1214–1220.

Brewer, G.J., Kanzer, S.H., Zimmerman, E.A., Molho, E.S., Celmins, D.F.,...Dick, R. (2010). Subclinical zinc deficiency in Alzheimer's disease and Parkinson's disease. *Am J Alzheimers Dis Other Demen*, *25*(7), 572–575.

Buter, T.C., van den Hout, A., Matthews, F.E., Larsen, J.P., Brayne, C., & Aarsland, D. (2008). Dementia and survival in Parkinson disease: A 12-year population study. *Neurology*, *70*(13), 1017–1022.

Carlsson, A. (1959). The occurrence, distribution and physiological role of catecholamines in the nervous system. Pharmacol Rev, *11*(2, Part 2), 490–493.

Carlsson, A., Greengard, P., & Kandel, E.R. (2000). The Nobel Prize in Physiology or Medicine, 2000.

Checkoway, H., & Nelson, L.M. (1999). Epidemiologic approaches to the study of Parkinson's disease etiology. *Epidemiology*, *10*, 327–336.

Checkoway, H. (2010). Documenting neurotoxicity from occupational manganese exposure. *Occup Environ Med*, *67*, 362–363

Chen, H., Shang, S.M., Hernán, M.A., Schwarzschild, M.A., Willett, W.C., Colditz, G.A.,...Ascherio, A. (2003). Nonsteroidal anti-inflammatory drugs and the risk of Parkinson disease. *Arch Neurol*, *60*, 1059–1064.

Chen, H., Shumin, M., Zhang, S.M., Schwarzschild, M.A., Hernán, M.A., & Ascherio, A. (2006). Survival of Parkinson's disease patients in a large prospective cohort of male health professionals. *Movement Disorders*, *21*(7), 1002–1007.

Chen, H., Huang, X., Guo, X., Mailman, R.B., Park, Y., Kamel, F.,...Blair, A. (2010). Smoking duration, intensity, and risk of Parkinson disease. *Neurology*, *74*(11), 878–884.

Couper, J. (1837). On the effects of black oxide of manganese when inhaled into the lungs. *Brit Ann Med Pharm*, *1*, 41–42.

De Pedro-Cuesta, J. (1987). Studies on the prevalence of paralysis agitans by tracer methodology. *Acta Neurol Scand*, *75*(Suppl 112), 1–106.

Dick, F.D., De Palma, G., Ahmadi, A., Scott, N.W., Prescott, G.J., Bennett, J.,...Felice, A. (2007). Environmental risk factors for Parkinson's disease and parkinsonism: The Geoparkinson study. *Occup Environ Med*, *64*, 666–672.

Dorsey, E.R., Constantinescu, R., Thompson, J.P., Biglan, K.M., Holloway, R.G., Kieburtz, K.,...Tanner, C.M. (2007). Projected number of people with Parkinson disease in the most populous nations, 2005 through 2030. *Neurology*, *68*(5), 384–386.

Driver, J.A., Logroscino, G., Gaziano, J.M., & Kurth, T. (2009). Incidence and remaining lifetime risk of Parkinson disease in advanced age. *Neurology, 72*(5), 432–438.

Elahi, E. (2009). A study of Parkinsons's disease in Iranian patients. *Genetics in the 3rd Millennium, 7*(3), 1749–1752.

Elbaz, A., Bower, J.H., Peterson, B.J., Maraganore, D.M., McDonnell, S.K., Ahlskog, J.E.,...Rocca, W.A. (2003). Survival study of Parkinson disease in Olmsted county, Minnesota. *Arch Neurol, 60*, 91–96.

Friedl, K.E., Grate, S., & Proctor, S.P. (2009). Neurotoxicological interactions with physical and psychological stressors. In: RTO-TR-HFM-057, Defense Technical Information Center (DTIC), 2009, Chapter 9, 1–22.

Funayama, M., Hasegawa, K., Kowa, H., Saito, M., Tsuji, S., & Obata, F. (2002). A new locus for Parkinson's disease (PARK8) maps to chromosome 12p11.2-q13.1. Ann Neurol, 51, 296–301.

Goedert, M. (2001). Alpha-synuclein and neurodegenerative diseases. *Nat Rev Neurosci, 2*(7), 492–501.

Golomb, B.A. (2008). Acetylcholinesterase inhibitors and Gulf War illnesses. *Proc Natl Acad Sci USA, 105*, 4295–4300.

Guilarte, T.R. (2010). Manganese and Parkinson's disease: A critical review and new findings. *Environ Health Perspect, 118*(8), doi:10.1289/ehp.0901748.

Hald, A., Van Beek, J., & Lotharious. (2007). Inflammation in Parkinson's disease. *Subcellular Biochemistry, 42*, 249–279.

Hancock, D.B., Martin, E.R., Mayhew, G.M., Stajich, J.M., Jewett, R., Stacy, M.A.,...Scott, W.K. (2008). Pesticide exposure and risk of Parkinson's disease: A family-based case-control study. *BMC Neurology, 8*, 6, doi:10.1186/1471-2377-8-6.

Hardy, J., Cai, H., Cookson, M.R., Gwinn-Hardy, K., & Singleton, A. (2006). Genetics of Parkinson's disease and parkinsonism. *Annals of Neurology, 60*(4), 389–398.

Hernán, M.A., Takkouche, B., Caamano-Isorna, F., & Gestal-Otero, J.J. (2002). A meta-analysis of coffee drinking, cigarette smoking, and the risk of Parkinson's disease. *Ann Neurol, 52*, 276–284.

Ho, S.C., Woo, J., & Lee, C.M. (1989). Epidemiologic study of Parkinson's disease in Hong Kong. *Neurology, 39*, 1314–1318.

Hobson, P., & Meara, J. (2004). Risk and incidence of dementia in a cohort of older subjects with Parkinson's disease in the United Kingdom. *Mov Disord, 19*(9), 1043–1049.

Hobson, P., Meara, J., & Ishihara-Paul, L. (2010). The estimated life expectancy in a community cohort of Parkinson's disease patients with and without dementia, compared with the UK population. *J Neurol Neurosurg Psychiatry, 81*, 1093–1098.

Holt, R.J., Sklar, A.R., Darkow, T., Goldberg, G.A., Johnson, J.C., & Harley, C.R. (2010). Prevalence of Parkinson's disease-induced psychosis in a large US managed care population. *J Neuropsychiatry Clin Neurosci, 22*, 105–110.

Huang, X., Chen, P., Kaufer, D.I., Trouster, A.I., & Poole, C. (2006). Apolipoprotein E and dementia in Parkinson Disease: A meta-analysis. *Arch Neurol, 63*, 189–193.

Hughes, T.A., Ross, H.F., Mindham, R.H., & Spokes, E.G. (2004). Mortality in Parkinson's disease and its association with dementia and depression. *Acta Neurol Scand, 110*(2), 118–123.

Kanda, A., Ebihara, S., Arai, H., Takeda, A., & Sasaki, H. (2000). Parkinson's disease and impaired chemosensitivity to hypoxia. *Lancet, 356*(9247), 2100.

Kitada, T., Asakawa, S., Hattori, N., Matsumine, H., Yamamura, Y., Minoshima, S.,...Shimizu, N. (1998). Mutations in the parkin gene cause autosomal recessive juvenile parkinsonism. Nature, 392, 605–608.

Knott, C., Stern, G., & Wilkin, G.P. (2000). Inflammatory regulators in Parkinson's disease: iNOS, lipocortin-1, and cyclooxygeneases-1 and 2. *Mol Cell Neurosci, 16*, 724–739.

Krüger, R., Kuhn, W., Müller, T., Woitalla, D., Graeber, M., Kösel, S.,...Riess, O. (1998). Ala30Pro mutation in the gene encoding alpha-synuclein in Parkinson's disease. *Nat Genet, 18,* 106–108.

Langston, J.W., Ballard, P., Tetrud, J.W., & Irwin, I. (1983). Chronic parkinsonism in humans due to a product of meperidine-analog synthesis. *Science, 219,* 979–980.

Langston, J.W., Forno, L.S., Rebert, C.S., & Irwin, I. (1984). Selective nigral toxicity after systemic administration of 1-methyl-4-pheny1-1,2,5,6-tetrahydropyridine (MPTP) in the squirrel monkey. *Brain Res, 292,* 390–394.

Langston, J.W. (1985). MPTP and Parkinson's disease. *Trends in Neurosci, 8,* 79–83.

Langston, J.W., & Palfreman, J. (1996). *The Case of the frozen addicts: How the solution of an extraordinary medical mystery spawned a revolution in the understanding and treatment of Parkinson's disease.* New York: Pantheon.

Lewitt, P.A., Rezai, A.R., Leehey, M.A., Ojemann, S.G., Flaherty, A.W., Eskandar, E.N.,...Feigin, A. (2011). AAV2-*GAD* gene therapy for advanced Parkinson's disease: A double-blind, sham-surgery controlled, randomised trial. *Lancet Neurology, 10*(4), 309–319.

Lewy, F.H. (1912). Paralysis agitans. In "Handbuch der Neurologie" (Edited by: M. Lewandowsky). Berlin: Springer Verlag, pp. 920–933.

Lim, K.L., Dawson, V.L., & Dawson, T.M. (2006). Parkin-mediated lysine 63-linked polyubiquitination: A link to protein inclusions formation in Parkinson's and other conformational diseases? Neurobiol Aging, 27, 524–529.

Lonneke, M.L. de Lau & Breteler, M.M.B. (2006). Epidemiology of Parkinson's disease. *Lancet Neurology, 5*(6), 525–535.

Marder, K., Tank, M.X., Mejia, H., Alfaro, B., Cote, L., Louis, E.,...Mayeux, R. (1996). Parkinson's disease among first-degree relatives: A community-based study. *Neurology, 47*(1), 155–160.

Muangpaisan, W., Hori, H., & Brayne, C. (2009). Systematic review of the prevalence and incidence of Parkinson's disease in Asia. *J Epidemiol, 19*(6), 281–293.

Paisán-Ruíz, C., Jain, S., Evans, E.W., Gilks, W.P., Simón, J., van der Brug, M.,...Singleton, A.B. (2004). Cloning of the gene containing mutations that cause PARK8-linked Parkinson's disease. *Neuron, 44*(4), 595–600.

Parkinson, J. (1817). *An essay on the shaking palsy.* London: Sherwood, Neely and Jones.

Poewe, W. (2006). The natural history of Parkinson's disease. *J Neurol, 253*(Suppl 7), VII/2–VII/6.

Polymeropoulos, M.H., Lavedan, C., Leroy, E., Ide, S.E., Dehejia, A., Dutra, A.,...Nussbaum, R.L. (1997). Mutation in the alpha-synuclein gene identified in families with Parkinson's disease. *Science, 276,* 2045–2047.

Polymeropoulos, M.H. (1998). Autosomal dominant Parkinson's disease and alpha-synuclein. *Ann Neurol, 44*(3 Suppl 1), S63–S64.

Pradhan, S., Pandey, N., Shashank, S., Gupta, R.K., & Mathur, A. (1999). Parkinsonism due to predominant involvement of substantia nigra in Japanese encephalitis. *Neurology, 53,* 1781–1786.

Priyadarshi, A., Khuder, S.A., Schaub, E.A., & Shrivastava, S. (2000). A meta-analysis of Parkinson's disease and exposure to pesticides. *Neurotoxicology, 21*(4), 435–440.

Racette, B.A., Good, L.M., Kissel, A.B., Criswell, S.R., & Perlmutter, J.S. (2009). A population-based study of parkinsonism in an Amish community. *Neuroepidemiology, 33*(3), 225–230.

Ramakrishnan, U. (2002). Prevalence of micronutrient malnutrition worldwide. *Nutrition Reviews, 60*(5), S46–SA2.

Richardson, J.R., Quan, Y., Sherer, T.B., Greenamyre, J.T., & Miller, G.W. (2005). Paraquat neurotoxicity is distinct from that of MPTP and rotenone. *Toxicol Sci, 88*(1), 193–201.

Ritz, B., Ascherio, A., Checkoway, H., Marder, K.S., Nelson, L.M., Rocca, W.A.,...Gorell, J. (2007). Pooled analysis of tobacco use and risk of Parkinson disease. *Arch Neurol, 64*, 990–997.

Rodier, J. (1955). Manganese poisoning in Moroccan miners. *Br J Ind Med, 12*, 21–35.

Rogaeva, E., Johnson, J., Lang, A.E., Gulick, C., Gwinn-Hardy, K., Kawarai, T.,...Singleton, A.B. (2004). Analysis of the PINK1 gene in a large cohort of cases with Parkinson disease. *Arch Neurol, 61*(12), 1898–1904.

Safranak, T.J., Theis, M., & Krause, J. (2007). The Nebraska Parkinson's Disease Registry. Nebraska Department of Health and Human Services.

Schulz-Schaeffer, W.J. (2010). The synaptic pathology of alpha-synuclein aggregation in dementia with Lewy bodies, Parkinson's disease and Parkinson's disease dementia. *Acta Neuropathol, 120*(2), 131–143.

Shojaee, S., Fazlali, Z., Ghazavi, F., Banihosseini, S.S., Kazemi, M.H., Parsa, K.,...Elahi, E. (2009). Identification of four novel potentially Parkinson's disease associated *LRRK2* variations among Iranian patients. *Neuroscience, 467*(2), 53–57.

Spillantini, M.G., Schmidt, M.L., Lee, V.M., Trojanowski, J.Q., Jakes, R., & Goedert, M. (1997). Alpha-synuclein in Lewy bodies. *Nature, 388*(6645), 839–840.

Spillantini, M.G., Crowther, R.A., Jakes, R., Hasegawa, M., & Goedert, M. (1998). Alpha-synuclein in filamentous inclusions of Lewy bodies from Parkinson's disease and dementia with lewy bodies. *Proc Natl Acad Sci USA, 95*(11), 6469–6473.

Strickland, D., & Bertoni, J.M. (2003). Parkinson's prevalence estimated by a state registry. *Movement Disorders, 19*(3), 318–323.

Sulzer, D., Bogulavsky, J., Larsen, K.E., Behr, G., Karatekin, E., Kleinman, M.H.,...Zecca, L. (2000). Neuromelanin biosynthesis is driven by xxcess cytosolic catecholamines not zccumulated by synaptic vesicles. *Proceedings of the National Academy of Science USA, 97*(22), 11869–11874.

Tanner, C.M., Ottman, R., Goldman, S.M., Ellenberg, J., Chan, P., Mayeux, R., & Langston, J.W. (1999). Parkinson disease in twins: An etiologic study. *JAMA, 281*(4), 341–346.

Tanner, C.M., Ross, G.W., Jewell, S.A., Hauser, R.A., Jankovic, J., Factor, S.A.,...Langston, J.W. (2009). Occupation and risk of parkinsonism: A multicenter case-control study. *Arch Neurol, 66*(9), 1106–1113.

Tanner, C.M., Kamel, F., Ross, G.W., Hoppin, J.A., Goldman, S.M., Korell, M.,...Langston, J.W. (2011). Rotenone, Paraquat and Parkinson's disease. *Environ Health Perspect*, doi:10.1289/ehp.1002839.

Tretiakoff, K. (1919). Contribution a l'Etude de L'Anatomie pathologique du Locus Niger de Soemmering avec quelques déductions relatives à la pathogénie des troubles du tonus musculaire et De La Maladie de Parkinson. Doctoral Disseration, University of Paris, 1919.

Van Den Eeden, S.K., Tanner, C.M., Bernstein, A.L., Fross, R.D., Leimpeter, A., Bloch, D.A., & Nelson, L.M. (2003). Incidence of Parkinson's disease: Variation by age, gender, and race/ethnicity. *Am J Epidemiol, 157*(11), 1015–1022.

Weintraub, D., & Hurtig, H.I. (2007). Presentation and management of psychosis in Parkinson's disease and dementia with Lewy bodies. *American Journal of Psychiatry, 164*(10), 1491–1498.

World Health Organization. (2006). *Neurological disorders: Public health challenges* (pp. 140–150). Geneva, Switzerland, World Health Organization.

World Health Organization. (2009). Age-standardized DALYs per 100,000 by cause and member state, 2004. Health statistics and health information systems. *Global burden of disease.* World Health Organization.

Zimprich, A., Biskup, S., Leitner, P., Lichtner, P., Farrer, M., Lincoln, S.,...Gasser, T. (2004). Mutations in LRRK2 cause autosomal-dominant parkinsonism with pleomorphic pathology. *Neuron, 44*(4), 601–607.

Epidemiology of Schizophrenia

INTRODUCTION

Schizophrenia is a mental condition characterized by hallucinations, delusions, suicidal ideation, paranoia, and other disturbances of thought processes and cognition. The signs and symptoms of schizophrenia are highly variable and often categorized as positive, negative, and cognitive.

A century ago, the noted Swiss psychiatrist, Eugen Bleuler, coined the term "*schizophrenia*" from the Greek roots for schizo (split) and phrene (mind). However, the term was not meant to imply split personality but rather the fragmented thinking process of patients with the disorder. Bleuler was also the first to categorize schizophrenia according to its positive and negative symptoms (Bleuler, 1911, 1931).

Positive symptoms refer to abnormal and sometimes bizarre psychotic thoughts and behaviors including auditory and visual hallucinations and "*delusions of grandeur*" and "*delusions of persecution.*" Afflicted persons often exhibit unusual, dysfunctional and/or disorganized thought processes, and agitated repetitive body movements. Patients with severe "*end stage*" disease develop catatonia, a mental state of immobilization and failure to respond.

Negative symptoms include a flat affect of expression and speech, lack of pleasure in ordinary life, inability to carry out planned activities, and failure to speak and communicate with others. Cognitive symptoms refer to memory deficits, failure to focus, and inability to use information in a logical fashion.

The onset of schizophrenia differs by gender, peaking during late adolescence and young adulthood in males, and 10–20 years later in females (**Figure 41.1**). Following the peak times of onset, the rates gradually decline with age, although the

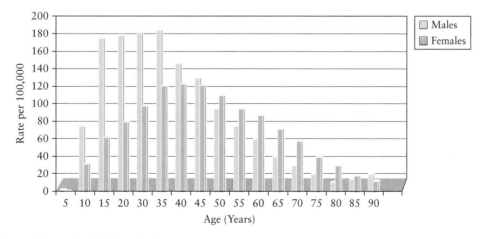

Figure 41.1 Age at Diagnosis of Schizophrenia.

Source: Data from Center for Chronic Disease Prevention and Control, Health Canada, Hospital Morbidity File, Canadian Institute for Health Information, 1999/2000.

condition may develop at any time during the lifespan. The onset is highly variable and may be either acute or preceded by a long prodromal phase. For example, negative symptoms may precede the development of the more overt positive signs by several years (Hafner, Maurer, and Loffler, 1999; Beiser et al., 1993).

INCIDENCE OF SCHIZOPHRENIA

In past years, there was a longstanding dogmatic opinion that the prevalence and the incidence of schizophrenia varied little from population to population (Eaton, 1985, 1991; Jablensky, 2000). However, recent studies based upon rigorously compiled data using standardized techniques of diagnosis and case reporting have revealed wide variability in both the incidence and prevalence amongst populations (McGrath, 2005, 2006).

McGrath and colleagues systematically reviewed and compared published incidence rates of schizophrenia for the period 1965–2001. Their review included 1,458 rate estimates derived from 100 core population studies, 24 migrant studies, 23 cohort studies, and 14 studies of special populations from 33 different countries. Results revealed an asymmetric distribution of annual incidence rates with a median value of 15.2 per 100,000. Omitting the upper and lower 10% of all estimates, the rates still varied five-fold from 7.7–43.0 per 100,000. On average, rates were higher in males than females (RR = 1.40) and tended to be higher in urban areas than rural areas. Rates were also higher in migrants than native born persons (RR = 4.6). These findings indicate the presence of considerable variation in the incidence rates of schizophrenia around the world due to the influence of cultural, urban, and geographic factors (McGrath et al., 2004).

PREVALENCE OF SCHIZOPHRENIA

McGrath and colleagues also systematically reviewed published estimates of the prevalence of schizophrenia. They identified 188 studies that provided 1,721 prevalence estimates, 132 from population-based core studies, 15 from migrant studies, and 41 from studies of special populations. The median point prevalence was 460 per 100,000 with a range from 310 to 1,000 for the 10th and 90th percentiles. In contrast to the incidence which is higher in males, there was no difference in prevalence between males and females. However, migrants had 1.8-times higher

prevalence values than native-born individuals, and populations of developed countries had higher values than those of less-developed countries (median estimates: 330 vs. 260 per 100,000, respectively). Furthermore, the prevalence rates were higher for populations living at higher altitudes (McGrath et al, 2008).

MORTALITY FROM SCHIZOPHRENIA

The systematic literature review by McGrath and colleagues identified 37 studies that estimated the standardized mortality rate (SMR) for patients with schizophrenia. A total of 561 SMR estimates were derived from these studies for analysis. The median MSR for all-cause mortality was 2.6 with a range of 1.2 to 5.8 for the 10th and 90th percentiles. Mortality from suicide was elevated nearly 13-fold (SMR = 12.9). The results also revealed a secular trend of standardized mortality rates during the period 1970–1990, increasing from 1.8 to 3.2 (McGrath et al., 2008).

Disability Adjusted Life Years (DALY) Lost: Schizophrenia

The *disabililty adjusted life years (DALY)* lost due to schizophrenia tend to be highest in Oceania, the Middle East, and Southeast Asia, while the nations of Australia, Japan, United States, and Western Europe have lower values (**Figure 41.2**). Marked differences are apparent in some populations despite their relative geographical proximity. For example, the DALY for schizophrenia in Indonesia is nearly twice that of Australia (the nations with the highest and lowest respective DALY).

Overall, the divergent pattern of lower DALY in more developed nations may reflect significant advances that have been made in the treatment of schizophrenia in recent decades; in fact, many patients treated judiciously with antipsychotic medications for acute schizophrenic episodes have been found to recover and lead relatively normal lives with little disability or increased mortality (Bleuler, 1972; Harding and Zahniser, 1994). Nevertheless, in a recent international study of 1,633 cases of schizophrenia from 18 participating centers, patients from developing nations such as India, Nigeria, and Columbia were found to have a 40% higher recovery rate than patients from developed nations in Europe, the United States, and Japan (Sartorius, Jablensky, and Shapiro, 1977; Sartorius et al., 1986; Leff et al., 1992). This surprising result is discussed in greater detail in the next section of this chapter.

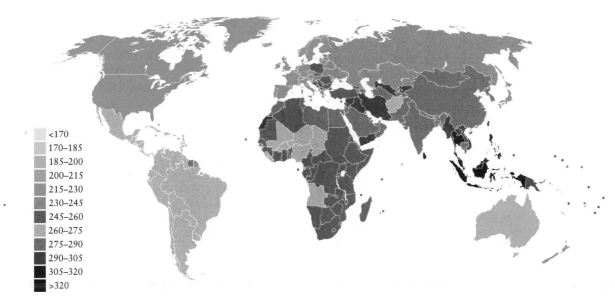

Figure 41.2 Disability Adjusted Life Years: Schizophrenia, 2004.

Source: Data from World Health Organization. The global burden of disease: 2004 update. Geneva, WHO, 2008. Available at www.who.int /evidence/bod.

COURSE OF SCHIZOPHRENIA

The course of schizophrenia is highly variable from patient to patient. In a classic investigation, Manfred Bleuler (the son of Eugen Bleuler) followed 100 male and 108 female patients in *Burghölzli Psychiatric Hospital* in Zurich, Switzerland during 1942–1965. Patients ranged in age from 17–67 years at the time the study began and were followed up to 23 years. Bleuler differentiated patients according to onset (acute vs. chronic) and progression or regression of disease. Among 194 evaluable patients, 76 (39%) manifested a simple course of unrelenting disease progression and 118 (61%) manifested an undulating course characterized by periods of remission interspersed with episodic disease. At the end of follow-up, 45 patients (23%) had progressed to severe end stage disease (catatonia), 105 (54%) were stable with mild to moderate disease, and 44 (23%) had recovered (Bleuler, 1972).

Many other studies have been conducted to examine the course of schizophrenia in patients ascertained from populations throughout the world. Most of these have found even higher rates of recovery than observed in the classic investigation by Bleuler, thus dispelling the myth that schizophrenia is an incurable mental illness. Selected studies are summarized in the following paragraphs.

In the *Iowa 500 Study* in the United States, 186 patients were followed for an average of 35 years and 46% either improved or recovered (Clancy et al., 1974). In the *Bonn Hospital Study* in Germany,

502 patients were followed for an average of 22.4 years. Findings revealed that 22% of patients had complete remission of symptoms and 43% had remission with mild cognitive disturbances (Huber, Gross, and Schüttler, 1978). In the *Lausanne Study* in Switzerland, findings were reported for 289 patients followed up to 64 years. Results indicated that 27% of patients recovered, 22% reached an end stage of mild disease, 24% reached an end stage of moderately severe disease, and 18% suffered severe end stage disease (Ciompi and Müller, 1976). At the *Chestnut Lodge Psychiatric Hospital* in the United States, 446 patients received long-term residential psychotherapy for an average of 15 years. At the end of study, 36% of patients had recovered and 64% were either chronically ill or marginally functional (McGlashan, 1984). In the *Japanese Long-Term Study*, 105 patients ascertained at Gumma University Hospital were followed up to 27 years. Of these, 31% recovered, 46% improved, and 23% regressed (Ogawa et al., 1987). The *Vermont Longitudinal Research Project* followed 269 patients for an average of 32 years. The study involved an innovative rehabilitation program with community and social support of all patients. Results revealed that 45% of patients recovered and 68% were assessed as having good social and psychological function at last contact (Harding et al., 1987). A comparative cohort of 269 patients from Maine received standard psychiatric care and were followed an average of 36 years. Results revealed that 49% of patients improved and demonstrated good social

and psychological function at followup (DeSisto et al., 1995). The *Cologne Long Term Study* in Germany followed 148 patients for an average of 25 years. Results revealed complete recovery among 7% of patients and better than expected outcomes for 58% of patients (Marneros et al., 1989).

The World Health Organization *International Study of Schizophrenia (ISOS)* was designed to examine disease outcomes in 18 culturally diverse cohorts of schizophrenia patients. The study included 14 cohorts of incident cases and 4 cohorts of prevalent cases, a total of 1,633 patients with schizophrenia or related psychotic diseases. Patients were evaluated for disease status after 15 and 25 years of followup. Results revealed a recovery rate of 56% among patients in the incident cohorts and 60% among patients in the prevalence cohorts. A notable finding was that the recovery rate was higher among patients in centers of developing nations than developed nations (56% vs. 39%) (Sartorius, Jablensky, and Shapiro, 1977; Sartorius et al., 1986; Leff et al., 1992). This surprising result was reconfirmed in a reanalysis of the ISOS data, suggesting the presence of factors in developing nations that favor recovery from schizophrenia (Hopper and Wanderling, 2000).

Findings of the *International Study of Schizophrenia (ISOS)* have prompted other investigations of mortality and morbidity associated with schizophrenia in developing nations. Cohen and colleagues at Harvard University conducted a literature review and tabulation of data from 23 longitudinal studies of schizophrenia in 11 low and middle-income countries. Clinical outcomes including suicide, patterns of disease course, disability and social outcomes such as marital status and occupation, and access to treatment were reviewed. Results revealed wide variation in clinical outcomes, standard of care, patterns of disease course, disability, social dysfunction, and suicide rates with relatively high levels of "poor outcomes" reported in some developing countries (Brazil, China, and Nigeria) but not in others (India and Indonesia). The investigators suggest the need for continuing studies "*to better understand how neuropsychiatric processes and social worlds interact to shape the lives of persons with schizophrenia in low- and middle-income countries*" (Cohen et al., 2008).

SUICIDE IN SCHIZOPHRENIA

Suicide is the leading cause of premature death among patients with schizophrenia. However, there is some controversy concerning the magnitude of suicide risk that apparently arose from early reports of *proportionate mortality* (the fraction of deceased patients who committed suicide), which is not the same as the *case fatality rate from suicide* or the *cumulative incidence of suicide* among all patients. Based on his studies in Switzerland, Bleuler reported that 12.8% of *deceased patients* died from suicide (Bleuler, 1972). Tsuang later reported a similar estimate of 10.1% among decedents in the United States (Tsuang, 1978).

It is important to note that these early estimates reflect *proportionate mortality* due to suicide among only deceased patients rather than the case fatality or cumulative incidence of suicide among all patients. Estimates of proportionate mortality and case fatality due to suicide would yield similar results only when either all patients are observed until death or if suicides occur at a constant rate over time relative to other causes of death.

Investigators at the Mayo Clinic in Rochester, Minnesota, conducted a meta-analysis of cohort studies of patients with schizophrenia to accurately quantify their lifetime (cumulative) suicide risk. Studies included 32 studies of prevalent cases (n = 25,578 patients) and 29 studies of incident cases (n = 22,958 patients). The lifetime prevalence of suicide was estimated at 5.6% and the cumulative lifetime incidence of suicide was estimated at 4.9%. The approximate pattern of the cumulative suicide risk among schizophrenics is depicted in **Figure 41.3**. The cumulative risk of suicide rises linearly in the early years after diagnosis of schizophrenia, but then plateaus at approximately 5% after about 20 years. These results demonstrate that unless all subjects are followed until death, the proportionate mortality estimated from only decedents would markedly exceed the case fatality, since nearly all suicides are committed within a few years of diagnosis and the majority of schizophrenic patients exhibit long-term survival with 95% ultimately dying from other causes. As pointed out, this pattern "*highlights the significant effect of suicide concentrated early in the course of illness*" and "*implies that suicide-prevention interventions are best directed at persons early in the course of their schizophrenic illness*" (Palmer, Pankratz, and Bostwick., 2005).

Numerous investigations have been conducted to identify and treat those schizophrenic patients who have suicidal ideation and are at high risk of committing suicide. In the *Chestnut Lodge Study* of 322 patients diagnosed with schizophrenia or related disorders, 40% of patients reported suicidal ideation, 23% reported suicide attempts, and 6.5% died from suicide. The suicide rate among patients with paranoid schizophrenia was higher (12%) than

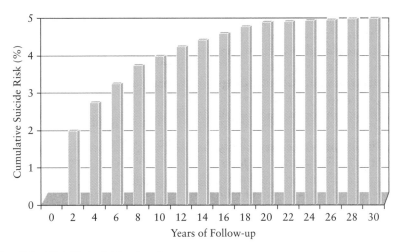

Figure 41.3 Cumulative Risk of Suicide in Schizophrenia.

Source: Data from Palmer BA, Pankratz VS, Bostwick JM (2005). The lifetime risk of suicide in schizophrenia: a reexamination. *Arch Gen Psychiatry* 62:247–253.

among other patients. The investigators concluded that "*suicide may emerge from a nondelusional but acutely painful awareness of the illness process, negative expectations of the future, depleted self-esteem, and hopelessness*" (Fenton et al., 1997).

Investigators at Oxford conducted a meta-analysis of studies of suicide among patients with schizophrenia to elucidate the risk factors and formulate preventive measures. Systematic review of the literature identified 29 studies for analysis including 5 cohort studies and 24 case control studies. Findings revealed an increased risk of suicide among patients with fear of mental disintegration (OR = 12.1), previous suicide attempts (OR = 4.09), recent loss (OR = 4.03), poor adherence to treatment (OR = 3.75), drug misuse (OR = 3.21), depression (OR = 3.03), and agitation or motor restlessness (OR = 2.61). Hallucinations and delusions were associated with reductions in risk (OR~0.50). Based on these results, the investigators suggested that

> "*prevention of suicide is thus likely to result from active treatment of affective symptoms and syndromes, improving adherence to treatment, use of medication that may have special anti-suicidal effects, and maintaining special vigilance in patients with risk factors, especially when faced with significant loss events*" (Hawton et al., 2005).

In 1997, Mark Williams published his "*Cry of Pain*" model of psychological conditions under which suicide is more likely together with possible intervention strategies. According to this model, suicidal risk is elevated by untoward environmental stressors; intractable feelings of hopelessness, defeat, and entrapment; negative perceptions of oneself, others, and circumstances; a perceived absence of rescue factors; and access to methods of suicide (Williams, 1997). Various approaches involving cognitive-behavioral psychotherapy are currently being explored for the treatment of depression and suicidal ideation (Johnson, Gooding, and Tarrier, 2008; Rasmussen et al., 2010).

MODELS OF PATHOGENESIS: SCHIZOPHRENIA

A longstanding hypothesis proposes that schizophrenia is caused by excess *dopamine* production and release by the mesolimbic neurons of the *substantia nigra* in the midbrain. This hypothesis links the hallucinatory and delusional symptoms of schizophrenia to hyperactivity of dopaminergic circuits in the forebrain. The dopamine hypothesis of schizophrenia is supported by pharmacologic evidence that phenothiazines and other drugs that reduce dopaminergic activity show therapeutic efficacy in patients with schizophrenia, whereas drugs such as amphetamines and cocaine that promote dopaminergic activity induce psychotic symptoms. Furthermore, the administration of levodopa to patients with Parkinson's disease induces paranoid ideation and auditory hallucinatory symptoms that are indistinguishable from those observed in some patients with schizophrenia. Indeed, the antidopaminergic impact of neuroleptic drugs is the cornerstone of the dopamine hypothesis of schizophrenia (Meltzer and Stahl, 1976).

A corollary of the dopamine hypothesis of schizophrenia suggests there are increased levels of *dopamine receptors* in neurons of the basal ganglia. There are two major types of dopamine receptors, *D1* and *D2*, and several subtypes. Antipsychotic drugs directed against *D2* have shown some therapeutic efficacy in the treatment of schizophrenia (Girault and Greengard, 2004).

A second hypothesis that has gained credibility in recent years postulates an imbalance of dopamine and a second neurotransmitter, glutamate, that works through activation of its cell membrane receptor, *N-methy-D-aspartate* (*NMDA*). This hypothesis is based upon the effects of phencyclidine (PCP), a general anesthetic that was abandoned for clinical use because a significant fraction of patients who received it experienced disturbing thoughts and feelings on emergence from anesthesia. Specifically, PCP was found to induce the full spectrum of psychotic symptoms (disorganized thinking, hallucinations and delusions, flat affect, and social withdrawal) that characterize patients with schizophrenia.

Molecular studies have since revealed that PCP inhibits the activity of glutamate by blocking the NMDA receptor. Glutamate normally serves as the *"brake"* for dopaminergic activity in the brain, and blockade of the NMDA receptor results in hyperactivity of dopaminergic pathways. Thus, both the dopaminergic and the glutamate neurotransmitter systems appear to be involved in the pathogenesis of schizophrenia. Specifically, if NMDA receptors are either deficient or fail to function properly, the regulation of dopamine by glutamate is interrupted leading to schizophrenic symptoms (Jentsch and Roth, 1999; Goff and Coyle, 2001; Mechri et al., 2001).

RISK FACTORS OF SCHIZOPHRENIA

Genetics of Schizophrenia

Genetic factors undoubtedly play an important role in the development of schizophrenia. Studies of schizophrenia in twins reveal that the risk approaches 50% in monozygous twins which is about threefold higher than in dizygous twins, and familial studies reflect 6- to 13-fold increases in the risk among first-degree relatives of cases (probands) compared to relatives of disease-free controls (**Table 41.1**). Nevertheless, spouses of patients have a twofold increase in risk, and adopted children of affected mothers have roughly the same risk as dizygotic

Table 41.1	Genetic Risk of Schizophrenia
Genetic Risk Category	**Risk (%)**
General Population	1%
Spouse of Patient	2%
Parent of Patient	6%
Sibling of Patient	9%
Offspring of Patient	13%
Adopted Child of Patient	17%
Dizygotic Twin	17%
Monozygotic Twin	48%

Source: Data from Tsuang M (2000). Schizophrenia: genes and environment. *Biol Psychiatry* 47(3):210–220.

twins, indicating the importance of shared environmental factors (Tsuang, 2000).

Investigators at the University of North Carolina conducted a meta-analysis of 12 twin studies in order to estimate the *heritability of additive genetic effects* that influence the liability to schizophrenia. Results revealed a heritability estimate of 81%, although there was also evidence of significant common or shared environmental influences. The investigators concluded that *"schizophrenia is a complex trait that results from genetic and environmental etiological influences"* (Sullivan, Kendler, and Neale, 2003).

Intensive research is now focused on finding genes that influence predisposition to the development of schizophrenia. To date, several genes have been discovered that show significant linkage with schizophrenia.

Catechol-O-methyltransferase is one of several enzymes that methylates and inactivates catecholamine neurotransmitters such as dopamine, epinephrine, and norepinephrine. In humans, catechol-O-methyltransferase is encoded by the *COMT* gene on the long arm of chromosome 22. Some studies have suggested that dysfunctional genetic variants of *COMT* predispose to the development of schizophrenia, particularly on exposure to *cannabis* during adolescence (Caspi et al., 2005).

The *Neuregulin 1 gene* (*NRG1*) on the short arm of chromosome 8 encodes a glycoprotein that modulates neuronal migration and formation of synapses during fetal development. Neuregulin is also involved in regulating myelination of neurons and signaling between glia and neurons. Dysfunctional genetic variants of *NRG1* have been found in association with the development of schizophrenia (Harrison and Law, 2005).

Other candidate schizophrenia liability genes include *dysbindin, disrupted-in-schizophrenia 1 (DISC1), regulator of G-protein signaling 4 (RGS4),* and *metabotropic glutamate receptor-3 (GRM3),* all of which likely encode proteins that influence NMDA-receptor-mediated glutamate transmission and/or signaling by dopamine and gamma-amino-butyric acid (GABA). These genes and the proteins they encode could serve as specific molecular targets for therapy (Harrison and Weinberger, 2005; Straub and Weinberger, 2006).

Male Gender and Schizophrenia

In 1919, Emil Kraepelin, one of the founders of modern psychiatry, asserted that *"the male sex appears in general to suffer somewhat more frequently from dementia praecox than the female"* (Kraepelin, 1919). Nevertheless, the general view that there is no gender difference in the lifetime risk of developing schizophrenia persisted throughout most of the 20th century.

André Aleman and colleagues at the University of Amsterdam re-examined the issue of male gender as a risk factor based on a meta-analysis of gender-specific estimates of the incidence of schizophrenia derived from 49 studies published during 1980–2002. Results revealed a 42% increase in the incidence in males compared to females (RR = 1.42). Furthermore, the increased risk in males persisted for individuals diagnosed after the age of 65 years (RR = 1.32) (Aleman, Kahn, and Selten, 2003).

Apart from the 40% excess of schizophrenia in males compared to females, other distinct gender differences have been noted in the onset, symptoms, and outcomes of the disorder. Female patients are characterized by later onset of symptoms, depression and mood changes, a better ability to adjust to their environment, higher familial risk, and response to lower dosages of antipsychotic medications. In contrast, male patients are more likely to manifest a flat affect, lack of communication, and social isolation (Cannon and Clarke, 2005).

Season of Birth and Schizophrenia

Multiple studies of patients with schizophrenia conducted in different climates and in different populations consistently reveal a slightly higher frequency of patients that are born during the winter months (Davies et al., 2003; Carrion-Baralt et al., 2006).

Torrey and colleagues at the National Institute of Mental Health Neuroscience Center in Washington DC reviewed 86 studies including 437,710 cases, 411,874 from in the Northern Hemisphere countries, and 25,836 from countries in the Southern Hemisphere countries. Despite methodological differences amongst studies, the results were remarkably consistent in showing a 5–8% excess of cases born during the winter and spring months and a similar deficit of cases born during the summer and fall months. This effect was not influenced by gender, social class, race, pregnancy or birth complications, clinical subtypes, or neurological measures. Although unproven, it is hypothesized that heightened seasonal exposure of the developing fetal brain to environmental toxins, infectious agents, and/or nutritional/energy deficiencies during the second trimester, when early differentiation and maturation of neurons and neuronal circuits are occurring, may elevate the risk of subsequently developing schizophrenia (Torrey et al., 1997).

Obstetric Complications and Schizophrenia

Many studies have focused on obstetric complications during labor and delivery as risk factors for the subsequent development of schizophrenia. Rosanoff and colleagues first suggested there may be a link between cerebral birth trauma during delivery and the development of schizophrenia based upon a study of 142 twin pairs that were either concordant or discordant for the disorder (Rosanoff et al., 1934). More than 20 years later, Pasamanick and colleagues published their classic study of mental disorders diagnosed among individuals with a history of obstetric complications in Baltimore. Based upon the results, they suggested a *"continuum of reproductive causality"* whereby brain damage incurred during pregnancy and birth complications can lead to a gradient of subsequent injury and mental disorders including fetal and neonatal death, cerebral palsy, epilepsy, mental deficiency, and behavioral disorders (Pasamanick, Rogers, and Lilienfield, 1956). In 1967, Stabenau and Pollin published an analysis of the birth histories of 100 pairs of monozygotic twins discordant for schizophrenia and reported that significantly more of the schizophrenic twins had been the lighter of the two at birth and had experienced birth complications, particularly asphyxia (Stabenau and Pollin, 1967).

Subsequent studies have also revealed associations between serious pregnancy or obstetric complications and the development of schizophrenia. In a meta-analysis of data from 16 published case control studies and two cohort studies, a past history of obstetric complications increased the odds of developing schizophrenia by twofold. Subgroup analyses revealed significant risk increases for a number of obstetric complications including premature rupture of membranes, prematurity, resuscitation at time of delivery, low birth weight (<2,500 grams), preeclampsia, and forceps delivery (Geddes and Lawrie, 1995; Geddes et al., 1999).

In a later meta-analysis of eight prospective cohort studies, multiple obstetric complications were found to significantly increase the risk of developing schizophrenia. Of these, the strongest risk factor was gestational diabetes (RR = 7.76) followed by placenta abruption (RR = 4.02), very low birth weight (RR = 3.89), and emergency Cesarean section (RR = 3.24). Significant risk increases were also noted for uterine atony, rhesus incompatibility, asphyxia, bleeding in pregnancy, and preeclampsia. The investigators categorized obstetric risk into three groups: (1) complications of pregnancy (bleeding, preeclampsia, diabetes, and rhesus incompatibility), (2) abnormal fetal growth and development (low birth weight, congenital malformations, and small head circumference), and (3) complications of delivery (asphyxia, uterine atony, and emergency Cesarean section) (Cannon, Jones, and Murray, 2002).

Maternal Infection and Schizophrenia

Infection during fetal development has been linked to the subsequent occurrence of schizophrenia in a number of epidemiologic investigations. Various infectious agents with predilection for evolving neural tissues have been implicated. Selected studies are discussed below.

Influenza and Schizophrenia

Mednick and colleagues at the University of Southern California were the first to find a link between *prenatal* infection and schizophrenia. The investigation involved long-term follow-up of a birth cohort of individuals from Helsinki, Finland, whose birth dates coincided with the 1957 A2 influenza epidemic. Results revealed that potential fetal exposure to influenza during the second trimester of pregnancy (the period of rapid neuron formation) significantly elevated the risk of subsequently being diagnosed with schizophrenia (Mednick, 1970; Mednick et al., 1988).

Since this initial investigation, many others have examined maternal influenza as a risk factor for schizophrenia in offspring. Recently, investigators in Denmark conducted a nested case control study of schizophrenia and obstetric complications in which they compared 1,039 incident cases to 24,826 individually matched controls. Participants were ascertained from the *Danish National Longitudinal Registry System*. Though several obstetric risk factors were identified, maternal influenza was by far the strongest, increasing the risk more than eightfold (RR = 8.2). Risk estimates ranged from 1.5–2.9 for other obstetrical factors such as lack of prenatal care, prematurity, preeclampsia, hemorrhaging during delivery, manual extraction, and maternal sepsis. These results suggest that fetal neurodevelopment may be significantly compromised by maternal influenza as well as other obstetric complications, and such effects may persist and manifest later in life in the form of schizophrenia (Byrne et al., 2007).

Rubella and Schizophrenia

The *Rubella Birth Defects Evaluation Project* was established at New York University Medical Center in 1964 to examine the clinical manifestations of congenital rubella and formulate appropriate management techniques. The project identified a birth cohort of 214 individuals whose mothers tested positive for rubella, and these individuals were followed over time to assess psychiatric outcomes. Psychiatric evaluations were conducted after 20 years to determine the incidence of nonaffective psychosis in comparison to an unexposed birth cohort of 766 individuals from Saratoga County and Albany, New York. Results revealed more than a fivefold increase in the incidence of nonaffective psychosis in rubella-exposed subjects compared to nonexposed subjects (16% vs. 3%, RR = 5.2). Since the rubella virus is known to cross the placenta, infect the fetal brain, disrupt organogenesis, and cause encephalitis, these findings suggest that rubella infection during fetal development causes schizophrenia-like neurodevelopmental disorders (Brown et al., 2000).

Toxoplasmosis gondii and Schizophrenia

There is consistent evidence that individuals with antibodies to the feline protozoan parasite, *Toxoplasmosis gondii*, have a higher prevalence of schizophrenia than those without. Since 1953, a total of 19 studies of *Toxoplasmosis gondii* antibodies in persons with schizophrenia and other severe psychiatric disorders versus controls have been published. Among these, 18 reported a higher percentage of antibodies in the affected persons and in 11 studies the difference was statistically significant (Torrey and Yolken, 2003). In the two largest studies, Kozar and colleagues reported antibodies in 495 (52%) of psychiatric inpatients compared with 170 (25%) of 681 controls (Kozar, 1953), and Roch and Varela detected antibodies in 836 (86%) of 973 patients with schizophrenia versus 30% in the general population (Roch and Varela, 1966).

Two case control studies have examined childhood exposure to cats as a risk factor for the development of schizophrenia. In one study, 84 (51%) of 165 cases versus 65 (38%) of 165 matched controls had owned a house cat in childhood (OR = 1.59). In the other study, 136 (52%) of 262 cases versus 219 (42%) of 522 matched controls owned a cat between birth and age 13 (OR = 1.53) (Torrey and Yolken, 1995; Torrey, Rawlings, and Yolken, 2000).

In humans, *Toxoplasma* is an important cause of abortions and stillbirths after primary infection in pregnant women. The organism is capable of crossing the placenta and infecting the fetus and is known to cause a variety of congenital abnormalities and neurological symptoms including hydrocephaly, microcephaly, intracranial calcifications, deafness, seizures, cerebral palsy, damage to the retina, and mental retardation (Torrey and Yolken, 2003).

Notably, a recent study in the laboratories of Glenn McConkey at the University of Leeds found that *Toxoplasmosis gondii* produces and secretes two key enzymes needed for the biosynthesis of dopamine, *phenylalananine hydroxylase* and *tyrosine hydroxylase*. Conceivably, active infection with this parasite may contribute to the pathogenesis of schizophrenia and other forms of psychosis through overstimulation of dopaminergic circuitry in the brain (Gaskell et al., 2009). As a consequence of these investigations, clinical trials are now being conducted to assess effects of antimicrobial agents specific for *Toxoplasma* in patients with schizophrenia.

These reports and many others suggest that a variety of infectious agents may elevate the risk of developing schizophrenia in the offspring of mothers who became infected during pregnancy. Infectious agents that cross the placenta and infect the fetal brain at a critical time in development may affect the differentiation and maturation of neurons, synapses, receptors, and other components of the central nervous system. Multiple factors could elicit such neurological changes including the direct impact of live viruses or bacteria, the influx of immune cells and release of inflammatory cytokines, temperature changes associated with fever and febrile illness, and antibodies that cross react with neurological tissues (Boksa, 2008).

Cannabis and Schizophrenia

The association between cannabis (also known as marijuana or hashish) and schizophrenia was recognized long ago (Warnock, 1903; Moreau, 1973). Though the exact mechanisms of action remain to be clarified, the results of several recent prospective studies provide compelling evidence of a cause and effect relationship between cannabis exposure and the development of this disorder (Hall and Degenhardt, 2000).

In a large longitudinal study, 45,570 Swedish male conscripts (persons enlisted in the military by compulsion) were followed over a 15-year period to determine the association of self-reported use of cannabis and the development of schizophrenia. A total of 246 cases were identified in the *Swedish National Register of Psychiatric Care* during follow-up. Results reflect a pronounced dose response of the exposure-specific incidence with cannabis use, increasing more than sixfold among heavy users compared to nonusers (**Figure 41.4**). These effects

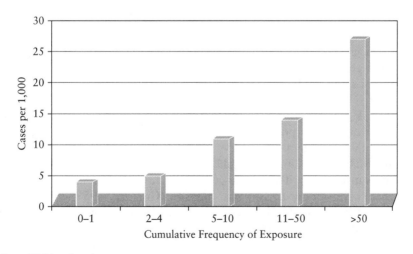

Figure 41.4 Cannabis and Schizophrenia.

Source: Andréasson S, Allebeck P, Engström A, Rydberg U (1987). Cannabis and schizophrenia: a longitudinal study of Swedish conscripts. *Lancet* 330(8574):1483–1486.

persisted with adjustment for potential social and psychological confounders indicating *"that cannabis is an independent risk factor for schizophrenia"* (Andréasson et al., 1987).

The association of cannabis and schizophrenia was also examined in the *Dunedin Multidisciplinary Health and Development Birth Cohort* of 1,037 individuals born in Dunedin, New Zealand during 1972–1973. Information on adolescent drug use was obtained by self report at ages 15 and 18 years of age, and psychiatric status was assessed at 26 years of age. The analysis focused on a subset of 759 subjects with complete data on adult psychiatric outcomes, adolescent use of illicit substances (including cannabis), and childhood psychotic syndromes. The findings revealed that individuals who began regular cannabis use before age 15 years were nearly seven times more likely to be diagnosed with symptoms of schizophrenia (OR = 6.91). This effect persisted with adjustment for the presence of psychotic symptoms during childhood. Based on results, the investigators advised that *"cannabis use among psychologically vulnerable adolescents should be strongly discouraged by parents, teachers, and health practitioners"* (Arseneault et al., 2002).

In the *Netherlands Mental Health Survey and Incidence Study*, a population sample of 4,045 individuals was followed during 1997–1999 to assess effects of cannabis exposure on the development of psychotic disorders. Baseline cannabis use was found to be a risk factor for the development of psychotic symptoms in a dose response pattern. Compared to nonuse, any level of cannabis use increased the risk more than threefold (OR = 3.25) and daily use increased the risk nearly sevenfold (OR = 6.81) (van Os et al., 2002).

In a retrospective cohort study, investigators in Denmark identified 535 patients treated for cannabis-induced psychosis through the Danish Psychiatric Central Register and followed their course for at least 3 years to determine their risk of developing schizophrenia. Among these individuals, 44.5% developed schizophrenia-spectrum disorders. In a separate analysis, individuals in the cannabis-exposed cohort developed disease earlier than who had no history of exposure (24.6 years vs. 30.7 years in males and 28.9 years vs. 33.1 years in females). The investigators concluded that cannabis-induced psychosis is a strong prognostic factor for the development of schizophrenia-spectrum disorders (Arendt et al., 2005).

Henquet and colleagues examined the association of cannabis use and psychosis in a meta-analysis of published prospective studies. Seven studies were included in their analysis, all of which focused on either schizophrenia *per se* or psychotic outcomes related to schizophrenia. Prior history of cannabis use increased the risk of psychosis by about twofold (Pooled OR = 2.1). There was no evidence of heterogeneity among studies (Henquet et al., 2005).

An international team of investigators conducted a meta-analysis to clarify the timing of onset of psychotic disorders among individuals exposed to cannabis compared to those with no exposure. Data were extracted from 83 studies for analysis. The combined data revealed that the mean onset of psychosis occurred 2.7 years earlier in individuals who used cannabis (Large et al., 2011).

The totality of epidemiologic evidence therefore suggests that regular cannabis use precipitates the development of schizophrenia in some individuals. As pointed out in a recent review of human studies of cannabis and schizophrenia:

> *"Converging lines of evidence suggest that cannabinoids can produce a full range of transient schizophrenia-like positive, negative, and cognitive symptoms in some healthy individuals. Also clear is that in individuals with an established psychotic disorder, cannabinoids can exacerbate symptoms, trigger relapse, and have negative consequences on the course of the illness. The mechanisms by which cannabinoids produce transient psychotic symptoms, while unclear may involve dopamine, GABA, and glutamate neurotransmission. However, only a very small proportion of the general population exposed to cannabinoids develop a psychotic illness. It is likely that cannabis exposure is a "component cause" that interacts with other factors to "cause" schizophrenia or a psychotic disorder, but is neither necessary nor sufficient to do so alone"* (D'Souza, Sewell, and Ranganathan, 2009).

Parental Age and Schizophrenia

Advanced *paternal age* was first proposed as a risk factor for schizophrenia in a report by Gregory in 1959. In the study, fathers of 1,000 patients newly admitted to Canadian hospitals were, on average, 2–3 years older than fathers in the general population (Gregory, 1959). Results of most subsequent studies lend support to this association (Granville-Grossman, 1966; Hare and Moran, 1979; Kinnell, 1983; Brown et al., 2002; Dalman and Allebeck, 2002; Byrne et al., 2003).

In Israel, Malaspina and colleagues studied the association of paternal age and schizophrenia in a population birth cohort of 87,907 individuals born in Jerusalem from 1964–1976. Cases were identified in the cohort by linking records to the *Israel Psychiatric Registry*. During the follow-up period which ended in 1998, a total of 658 cases were diagnosed with either schizophrenia or nonaffective psychosis. Compared with offspring of fathers younger than 25 years of age, the relative risk of schizophrenia increased monotonically with each successive 5-year paternal age group, reaching 2.02 and 2.96 in offspring of fathers aged 45–49 years and 50 years or older, respectively. In contrast, *maternal age* had no effect on the risk (Malaspina et al., 2001).

In Sweden, Sipos and colleagues conducted a population-based cohort study of 712,014 individuals born in Sweden between 1973–1980 to investigate the association of paternal age at conception and the risk of developing schizophrenia in the offspring. A total of 639 cases of schizophrenia and 1,311 cases of nonaffective psychosis were identified in the cohort by linking records to the *Swedish Inpatient Discharge Register* during 1989–2001. After adjustment for obstetric complications, socioeconomic factors, family history, and other factors, the overall hazard ratio for each 10 year increase in paternal age was 1.46. The association was present only in patients *without* a family history of schizophrenia, suggesting that accumulation of *de novo* mutations in sperm may elevate the risk (Sipos et al., 2004).

Autoimmune Diseases and Schizophrenia

Various autoimmune disorders have been linked to schizophrenia, some that apparently increase the risk and others that either have no effect or may even decrease the risk. The evidence appears strongest for a positive association with celiac disease and a negative association with rheumatoid arthritis (Ganguli, Brar, and Rabin, 1994).

Celiac disease is a rare autoimmune disorder caused by immunoreactivity of cells lining the small intestine to gliadin, a prolamin (gluten protein) found in wheat and other grains such as barley and rye. Symptoms include malabsorption of gluten-containing products, inflammatory bowel disease, chronic diarrhea, and failure to thrive in infants. The condition occurs primarily in genetically susceptible individuals that inherit specific alleles of the *human leukocyte antigen (HLA)* locus on chromosome 6. Nearly half a century ago, celiac disease was proposed as a risk factor for schizophrenia based primarily on case reports and ecological data showing a correlation between national changes in wheat intake and hospital admissions of schizophrenic patients (Dohan, 1966, 1980).

An international team of investigators recently examined the association of celiac disease and schizophrenia in a case control study of 7,997 incident cases admitted to Danish psychiatric facilities during 1981–1998 and nearly 20,000 disease-free controls from the general population matched by year of birth and gender. Only celiac disease diagnosed before the onset of schizophrenia was considered in the study. The rate of celiac disease was found to be threefold higher amongst cases than controls (1.5 vs. 0.5 per 1,000, adjusted RR = 3.2). These results suggest that patients with celiac disease who develop schizophrenia may respond to removal of gluten from the diet (Eaton et al., 2004). Though the mechanism of action is not fully understood, studies of celiac disease in humans show the presence of circulating gluten antibodies and T-cells activated by gluten breakdown products with neurotoxic and psychoactive effects (Hadjivassiliou et al., 2010).

In a subsequent investigation, William Eaton and colleagues in Denmark used the *Danish National Medical Register System* to examine the association of schizophrenia with any form of antecedent autoimmune disease. The dataset included 7,704 cases of schizophrenia diagnosed during 1981 to 1998 and a matched sample of controls from the general population. Data were also ascertained for the parents of cases and controls. Only autoimmune diseases occurring before the diagnosis of schizophrenia were considered in the analysis. Findings revealed a 45% increase in the risk of schizophrenia among individuals with a medical or familial history of *any form of autoimmune disease*. Risk increases were noted for celiac disease, thyrotoxicosis (Grave's disease), hemolytic anemia (antibodies against red blood cells), and several other forms of autoimmunity. These results suggest that some autoimmune conditions have risk factors in common with schizophrenia (Eaton et al., 2006).

In contrast to the positive associations observed between schizophrenia and several autoimmune disorders, many studies have consistently shown that individuals with schizophrenia are *less* likely to develop *rheumatoid arthritis*. For example, Eaton and colleagues reviewed data from 14 epidemiologic investigations and concluded that "*there is sufficient evidence for the negative association between the two disorders to justify further research*" (Eaton, Hayward, and Ram, 1992). In a subsequent meta-analysis of 15 epidemiologic studies, the risk of developing rheumatoid arthritis in schizophrenic patients was well below that in patients with other psychiatric conditions (OR = 0.29) (Oken and Schulzer, 1999).

Rheumatoid arthritis is a chronic systemic inflammatory condition of the synovial joints and other tissues that eventually leads to the massive destruction of synovial membranes and cartilage. This disorder is associated with the sustained presence of *rheumatoid factor*, an autoantibody that binds to synovial membranes, collagen, and articular cartilage thus promoting persistent inflammation, complement activation, and other destructive and lytic processes. Conceivably, one or more infectious agents are capable of inducing the production of rheumatoid factor in susceptible individuals which in turn incites a recursive autoimmune reaction directed primarily against synovial membranes and articular cartilage (Robbins and Cotran, 1979).

Allelic combinations of the *human leukocyte antigen* (*HLA*) loci on chromosome 6 have been examined in autoimmune and psychiatric conditions. These genetic loci are components of the *major histocompatibility complex* (*MHC*) of genes on chromosome 6 which encode antigens and other components of the immune system. Since there are six major HLA loci (A, B, C, DP, DQ, and DR) as well as a large number of other genes within the MHC, thousands of genotypic combinations are possible.

Notably, certain HLA alleles have been found in association with the development of several of the autoimmune conditions that apparently influence schizophrenia risk, e.g., celiac disease with *HLA-DQ2 and DQ8*; thyroiditis with *HLA DR3*; and rheumatoid arthritis with *HLA DR4* (Thorsby and Benedicte, 2005). Furthermore, preliminary results of linkage studies suggest there are genes that influence susceptibility to schizophrenia located on the short arm of chromosome 6 (Mayilyan and Weinberger, 2008). It is therefore plausible that certain HLA genotypic configurations may either predispose to both autoimmunity and schizophrenia, or reciprocally, have divergent impact on the etiopathogenesis of these disorders. Identification of such genes, the antigens they encode and the cellular functions influenced may elucidate molecular targets for effective molecular intervention.

TERTIARY PREVENTION IN SCHIZOPHRENIA

Guidelines for the treatment of patients with schizophrenia have been comprehensively reviewed by several authorities in the field (Royal Australian and New Zealand College of Psychiatrists, 2005). There is general agreement that the judicious use of antipsychotic agents plays a significant role in the treatment of schizophrenia and other psychotic disturbances. However, as noted by Manfred Bleuler, among his patients who maintained long-standing remission or a stable recovery, not a single one had received chronic neuroleptic medication. Instead, the patients were given medication during acute phases and never for longer than a few weeks after recovery from their acute episode (Bleuler, 1972). More recently, in their assessment of the long-term follow-up literature on schizophrenic patients, Harding and Zahniser found that 25–50% of patients in recovery were completely off medications and functioning well without further symptoms (Harding and Zahniser, 1994).

Coexistent substance abuse is common in patients with schizophrenia and is potentially responsible for a myriad of collateral health problems including deterioration of psychiatric symptoms. Substance abuse should therefore be candidly addressed with the aim of tapering and ultimately eliminating exposure. An integrated motivational approach to care is advocated with family and community support and intensive case management by a psychiatrist during acute episodes of psychosis and periods of vulnerability (Ziedonis et al., 2005).

● ● ● REFERENCES

Aleman, A., Kahn, R.S., & Selten, J.P. (2003). Sex differences in the risk of schizophrenia: Evidence from meta-analysis. *Archives of General Psychiatry, 60*(6), 565–571.

Andréasson, S., Allebeck, P., Engström, A., & Rydberg, U. (1987). Cannabis and schizophrenia: A longitudinal study of Swedish conscripts. *Lancet, ii,* 1483–1485.

Arendt, M., Rosenberg, R., Foldager, L., Perto, G., & Munk-Jorgensen, P. (2005). Cannabis-induced psychosis and subsequent schizophrenia-spectrum disorders: Follow-up study of 535 incident cases. *Br J Psychiatry, 187,* 510–515.

Arseneault, L., Cannon, M., Poulton, R., Murray, R., Caspi, A., & Moffitt, T.E. (2002). Cannabis use in adolescence and risk for adult psychosis: Longitudinal prospective study. *BMJ (Clinical Research Edition), 325*(7374), 1212–1213.

Beiser, M., Erickson, D., Fleming, J.A., & Iacono, W.G. (1993). Establishing the onset of psychotic illness. *The American Journal of Psychiatry, 150*(9), 1349–1354.

Bleuler, E. (1911). *Dementia praecox or The group of schizophrenias.* (Engl. Trans. 1961) New York International Universities Press.

Bleuler, M. (1931). Schizophrenia: Review of work of Professor Eugen Bleuler. *Archives of Neurology and Psychiatry, 26,* 610–627.

Bleuler, M. (1972). *The schizophrenic disorders: Long-term patient and family studies.* London: Yale University Press.

Boksa, P. (2008). Maternal infection during pregnancy and schizophrenia. *J Psychiatry Neurosci, 33*(3), 183–185.

Brown, A.S., Cohen, P., Greenwald, S., & Susser, E. (2000). Nonaffective psychosis after prenatal exposure to rubella. *The American Journal of Psychiatry, 157*(3), 438–443.

Brown, A.S., Schaefer, C.A., Wyatt, R.J., Begg, M.D., Goetz, R., Bresnahan, M.A.,...Susser, E.S. (2002). Paternal age and risk of schizophrenia in adult offspring. *The American Journal of Psychiatry, 159*(9), 1528–1533.

Byrne, M., Agerbo, E., Ewald, H., Eaton, W.W., & Mortensen, P.B. (2003). Parental age and risk of schizophrenia: A case-control study. *Archives of General Psychiatry, 60*(7), 673–678.

Byrne, M., Agerbo, E., Bennedsen, B., Eaton, W.W., & Mortensen, P.B. (2007). Obstetric conditions and risk of first admission with schizophrenia: A Danish national register based study. *Schizophr Res, 97*(1–3), 51–59.

Cannon, M., & Clarke, M.C. (2005). Schizophrenia: Epidemiology and risk factors. *Psychiatry, 4*(10), 7–10.

Cannon, M., Jones, P.B., & Murray, R.M. (2002). Obstetric complications and schizophrenia: Historical and meta-analytic review. *The American Journal of Psychiatry, 159*(7), 1080–1092.

Carrion-Baralt, J.R., Smith, C.J., Rossy-Fullana, E., Lewis-Fernandez, R., Davis, K.L., & Silverman, J.M. (2006). Seasonality effects on schizophrenic births in multiplex families in a tropical island. *Psychiatry Research, 142*(1), 93–97.

Caspi, A., Moffitt, T.E., Cannon, M., McClay, J., Murray, R., Harrington, H.,...Craig, I.W. (2005). Moderation of the effect of adolescent-onset cannabis use on adult psychosis by a functional polymorphism in the catechol-O-methyltransferase gene: Longitudinal evidence of a gene x environment interaction. *Biological Psychiatry, 57*(10), 1117–1127.

Center for Chronic Disease Prevention and Control, Health Canada, Hospital Morbidity File, Canadian Institute for Health Information, 1999/2000.

Ciompi, L., & Müller, C. (1976). *Lebensweg und alter der schizophrenen, eine katamnestische langzeitstudie bis ins senium.* Berlin: Springer.

Clancy, J., Tsuang, M.T., Norton, B., & Winokur, G. (1974). The Iowa 500: A comprehensive study of mania, depression and schizophrenia. *J Iowa Med Soc, 64*(9), 394–396.

Cohen, A., Patel, V., Thara, R., & Gureje, O. (2008). Questioning an axiom: Better prognosis for schizophrenia in the developing world? *Schizophr Bull, 34*(2), 229–244.

Dalman, C., & Allebeck, P. (2002). Paternal age and schizophrenia: Further support for an association. *The American Journal of Psychiatry, 159*(9), 1591–1592.

Davies, G., Welham, J., Chant, D., Torrey, E.F., & McGrath, J. (2003). A systematic review and meta-analysis of Northern Hemisphere season of birth studies in schizophrenia. *Schizophrenia Bulletin, 29*(3), 587–593.

DeSisto, M.J., Harding, C.M., McCormick, R.V., Ashikaga, T., & Brooks, G.W. (1995). The Maine and Vermont three-decade studies of serious mental illness. Matched comparison of cross-sectional outcome. *The British Journal of Psychiatry, 167,* 331–338.

Dohan, F. (1966). Cereals and schizophrenia-data and hypothesis. *Acta Psychiatrica Scand, 42,* 125–152.

Dohan, F.C. (1980). Hypothesis: Genes and neuroactive peptides from food as cause of schizophrenia. *Advances in Biochemical Psychopharmacology, 22,* 535–548.

D'Souza, D.C., Sewell, R.A., & Ranganathan, M. (2009). Cannabis and psychosis/schizophrenia: Human studies. *Eur Arch Psychiatry Clin Neurosci*, 259(7), 413–431.

Eaton, W.W., Mortensen, P.B., Agerbo, E., Byrne, M., Mors, O., & Ewald, H. (2004). Coeliac disease and schizophrenia: Population based case control study with linkage of Danish national registers. *BMJ* (*Clinical Research Edition*), 328(7437), 438–439.

Eaton, W.W. (1985). Epidemiology of schizophrenia. *Epidemiologic Reviews*, 7, 105–126.

Eaton, W.W. (1991). Update on the epidemiology of schizophrenia. *Epidemiologic Reviews*, 13, 320–328.

Eaton, W.W., Hayward, C., & Ram, R. (1992). Schizophrenia and rheumatoid arthritis: A review. *Schizophr Res*, 6(3), 181–192.

Eaton, W.W., Byrne, M., Ewald, H., Mors, O., Chen, C.Y., Agerbo, E., & Mortensen, P.B. (2006). Association of schizophrenia and autoimmune diseases: Linkage of Danish national registers. *Am J Psychiatry*, 163(3), 521–528.

Fenton, W.S., McGlashan, T.H., Victor, B.J., & Blyler, C.R. (1997). Symptoms, subtype, and suicidality in patients with schizophrenia spectrum disorders. *Am J Psychiatry*, 154, 199–204.

Ganguli, R., Brar, J.S., & Rabin, B.S. (1994). Immune abnormalities in schizophrenia: Evidence for the autoimmune hypothesis. *Harvard Review of Psychiatry*, 2(2), 70–83.

Gaskell, E.A., Smith, J.E., Pinney, J.W., Westhead, D.R., & McConkey, G.A. (2009) A unique dual activity amino acid hydroxylase in *Toxoplasma gondii*. *PLoS ONE*, 4(3), e4801.

Geddes, J.R., & Lawrie, S.M. (1995). Obstetric complications and schizophrenia: A meta-analysis. *Br J Psychiatry*, 167, 786–793.

Geddes, J.R., Verdoux, H., Takei, N., Lawrie, S.M., Bovet, P., Eagles, J.M.,...Murray, R.M. (1999). Schizophrenia and complications of pregnancy and labor: An individual patient data meta-analysis. *Schizophrenia Bulletin*, 25(3), 413–423.

Girault, J-A., Greengard, P. (2004). The neurobiology of dopamine signaling. *Arch Neurol* 61, 641–644.

Goff, D.C., & Coyle, R.J. (2001). The emerging role of glutamate in the pathophysiology and treatment of schizophrenia. *Am J Psychiatry*, 158, 1367–1368.

Granville-Grossman, K.L. (1966). Parental age and schizophrenia. *Br J Psychiatry*, 112(490), 899–905.

Gregory, I. (1959). Factors influencing first admission rates to Canadian mental hospitals: III; An analysis by education, marital status, country of birth, religion, and rural-urban residence, 1950–1952. *Canadian Journal of Psychiatry*, 4, 133–151.

Hadjivassiliou, M., Sanders, D.S., Grünewald, R.A., Woodroofe, N., Boscolo, S., & DAeschlimann, D. (2010). Gluten sensitivity: From gut to brain. *Lancet Neurol*, 9, 318–330.

Hafner, H., Maurer, K., & Loffler, W. (1999). Onset and prodromal phase as determinants of the course. In W.F. Gattaz, & H. Hafner, (eds.) *Search for the causes of schizophrenia: Vol IV, Balance of the century* (pp. 35–58). Darmstadt: Steinkopf Springer.

Hall, W., & Degenhardt, L. (2000). Cannabis use and psychosis: A review of clinical and epidemiological evidence. *The Australian and New Zealand Journal of Psychiatry*, 34(1), 26–34.

Harding, C.M., Brooks, G.W., Ashikaga, T., Strauss, J.S., & Breier, A. (1987). The Vermont longitudinal study of persons with severe mental illness, I: methodology, study sample, and overall status 32 years later. *Am J Psychiatry*, 144, 718–726.

Harding, C.M., & Zahniser, H. (1994). Empirical correction of seven myths about schizophrenia with implications for treatment. *Acta Psychiatr Scand Suppl*, 384, 140–146.

Hare, E.H., & Moran, P.A. (1979). Raised parental age in psychiatric patients: Evidence for the constitutional hypothesis. *Br J Psychiatry*, 134, 169–177.

Harrison, P.J., & Law, A.J. (2005). Neuregulin 1 and schizophrenia: Genetics, gene expression, and neurobiology. *Biological Psychiatry, 60*(2), 132–140.

Harrison, P.J., & Weinberger, D.R. (2005). Schizophrenia genes, gene expression, and neuropathology: On the matter of their convergence. *Molecular Psychiatry, 10*, 40–68.

Hawton, K., Sutton, L., Haw, C., Sinclair, J., & Deeks, J.J. (2005). Schizophrenia and suicide: Systematic review of risk factors. The British *Journal of Psychiatry, 187*, 9–20.

Henquet, C., Murray, R., Linszen, D., & van Os, J. (2005). The environment and schizophrenia: The role of cannabis use. *Schizophrenia Bulletin, 31*(3), 608–612.

Hopper, K., & Wanderling, J. (2000). Revisiting the developed versus developing country distinction in course and outcome in schizophrenia: Results from ISOS, the WHO-collaborative follow-up project. *Schizophrenia Bulletin, 26*(4), 835–846.

Huber, G., Gross, G., & Schüttler, R. (1978). *Schizophrenie: Eine verlaufsund sozialpsychiatrische langzeitstudie.* Berlin: Springer.

Jablensky, A. (2000). Epidemiology of schizophrenia: The global burden of disease and disability. *Eur Arch Psychiatry Clin Neurosci, 250*, 274–285.

Jentsch, J.D., & Roth, R.H. (1999). The neuropsychopharmacology of phencyclidine: From NMDA receptor hypofunction to the dopmaine hypothesis of schizophrenia. *Neuropsychopharmacology, 20*, 201–225.

Johnson, J., Gooding, P., & Tarrier, N. (2008). Suicide risk in schizophrenia: Explanatory models and clinical implications, the schematic appraisal model of suicide (SAMS). *Psychology and Psychotherapy: Theory, Research and Practice, 81*, 55–77.

Kinnell, H.G. (1983). Parental age in schizophrenia. *Br J Psychiatry, 142*, 204.

Kozar, Z. (1953). Badania nad toksoplazmoza wśród umyslowo chorych. *Bull Inst Mar Trop Med Gdańsk, 5*, 134–145.

Kraepelin, E. (1919). *Dementia Praecox and Paraphrenia.* (R.M. Barclay, Trans.). New York, NY: Krieger.

Large, M., Sharma, S., Compton Slade, T., & Nielssen, O. (2011). Cannabis use and earlier onset of psychosis: A systematic meta-analysis. *Arch Gen Psychiatry*, doi:10.1001/archgenpsychiatry.2011.5.

Leff, J., Sartorius, N., Jablensky, A., Korten, A., & Ernberg, G. (1992). The international pilot study of schizophrenia: Five-year follow-up findings. *Psychological Medicine, 22*(1), 131–145.

Malaspina, D., Harlap, S., Fennig, S., Heiman, D., Nahon, D., Feldman, D., & Susser, E.S. (2001). Advancing paternal age and the risk of schizophrenia. *Archives of General Psychiatry, 58*(4), 361–367.

Marneros, A., Deister, A., Rohde, A., Steinmeyer, E.M., & Jünemann, H. (1989). Long-term outcome of schizoaffective and schizophrenic disorders: A comparative study. *European Archives of Psychiatry and Clinical Neuroscience, 238*(3), 118–125.

Mayilyan, K.R., & Weinberger, D.R. (2008). Involvment of the HLA diversity in schizoprhenia, supporting data and perspectives. *ASHI Quarterly*, Third Quarter, 74–77.

McGlashan, T.H. (1984). The Chestnut Lodge Follow-up Study II. Long-term outcome of schizophrenia and the affective disorders. *Arch Gen Psychiatry, 41*(6), 586–601.

McGrath, J., Saha, S., Welham, J., El Saadi, O., MacCauley, C., & Chant, D. (2004). A systematic review of the incidence of schizophrenia: The distribution of rates and the influence of sex, urbanicity, migrant status and methodology. *BMC Medicine, 2*, 13. DOI: 10.1186/1741-7015-2-13.

McGrath, J.J. (2005). Myths and plain truths about schizophrenia epidemiology, the NAPE lecture 2004. *Acta Psychiatr Scand, 111*(1), 4–11.

McGrath, J.J. (2006). Variations in the incidence of schizophrenia: Data versus dogma. *Schizophr Bull, 32*, 195–197.

McGrath, J., Saha, S., Chant, D., & Welham, J. (2008). Schizophrenia: A concise overview of incidence, prevalence, and mortality. *Epidemiol Rev*, 30(1), 67–76.

Mechri, A., Saoud, M., Khiari, G., d'Amato, T., Dalery, J., & Gaha, L. (2001). Glutaminergic hypothesis of schizophrenia: Clinical research studies with ketamine. *Encephale*, 27(1), 53–59.

Mednick, S.A. (1970). Breakdown in individuals at high risk for schizophrenia: Possible predispositional perinatal factors. *Ment Hyg*, 54, 51–63.

Mednick, S.A., Machon, R.A., Huttunen, M.O., & Bonett, D. (1988). Adult schizophrenia following prenatal exposure to an influenza epidemic. *Arch Gen Psychiatry*, 45(2), 189–192.

Meltzer, H.Y., & Stahl, S.M. (1976). The dopamine hypothesis of schizophrenia: A review. *Schizophr Bull*, 2, 19–76.

Moreau, J. (1973). *Hashish and mental illness*. New York: Raven.

Ogawa, K., Miya, M., Watarai, A., Nakazawa, M., Yuasa, S., & Utena, H. (1987). A long-term follow-up study of schizophrenia in Japan with special reference to the course of social adjustment. *The British Journal of Psychiatry*, 151, 758–765.

Oken, R.J. & Schulzer, M. (1999). Schizophrenia and rheumatoid arthritis: The negative association revisited. *Schizophrenia Bulletin*, 25, 625–638.

Palmer, B.A., Pankratz, V.S., & Bostwick, J.M. (2005). The lifetime risk of suicide in schizophrenia: A reexamination. Arch Gen Psychiatry, 62, 247–253.

Pasamanick, B., Rogers, M.E., & Lilienfield, A.M. (1956). Pregnancy experience and the development of behavior disorder in children. *Am J Psychiatry*, 112, 613–618.

Rasmussen, S., Fraser, L., Gotz, M., MacHale, S., Mackie, R., Masterton, G.,...O'Connor, R.C. (2010). Elaborating the Cry of Pain model of suicidality: Testing a psychological model in a sample of first-time and repeat self-harm patients. *British Journal of Clinical Psychology*, 49, 15–30.

Robbins, S.L., & Cotran, R.S. (1979). *Pathologic basis of disease*. Philadelphia: W.B. Saunders Company.

Roch, E., & Varela, G. (1966). Diversos aspectos de la investigación sobre toxoplasmosis en México. Resultados obtenidos en 29 883 reacciones de Sabin y Feldman efectuadas de 1953 a 1965. *Rev Invest Salud Públ (Méx)*, 26, 31–49.

Rosanoff, A.J., Handy, L.M., Plesset, I.R., & Brush, S. (1934). The etiology of so-called schizophrenic psychoses: With special reference to their occurrence in twins. *Am J Psychiatry*, 91, 247–286.

Royal Australian and New Zealand College of Psychiatrists Clinical Practice Guidelines Team for the Treatment of Schizophrenia and Related Disorders. (2005). Royal Australian and New Zealand College of Psychiatrists clinical practice guidelines for the treatment of schizophrenia and related disorders. *Aust N Z J Psychiatry*, 39(1–2), 1–30.

Sartorius, N., Jablensky, A., & Shapiro, R. (1977). Two-year follow-up of the patients included in the WHO International Pilot Study of Schizophrenia. *Psychol Med*, 7(3), 529–541.

Sartorius, N., Jablensky, A., Korten, A., Ernberg, G., Anker, M., Cooper, J.E., & Day, R. (1986). Early manifestations and first-contact incidence of schizophrenia in different cultures. A preliminary report on the initial evaluation phase of the WHO Collaborative Study on determinants of outcome of severe mental disorders. *Psychological Medicine*, 16(4), 909–928.

Sipos, A., Rasmussen, F., Harrison, G., Tynelius, P., Lewis, G., Leon, D.A., & Gunnell, D. (2004). Paternal age and schizophrenia: A population based cohort study. *BMJ (Clinical research Edition)*, 329(7474), 1070.

Stabenau, J.R., & Pollin, W. (1967). Early characteristics of monozygotic twins discordant for schizophrenia. *Arch Gen Psychiatry*, 17, 723–734.

Straub, R.E., & Weinberger, D.R. (2006). Schizophrenia genes: From famine to feast. *Biol Psychiatry*, *60*, 81–83.

Sullivan, P.F., Kendler, K.S., & Neale, M.C. (2003). Schizophrenia as a complex trait: Evidence from a meta-analysis of twin studies. *Arch Gen Psychiatry*, *60*(12), 1187–1192.

Thorsby, E.M., & Benedicte, A.L. (2005). HLA associated genetic predisposition to autoimmune diseases: Genes involved and possible mechanisms. *Transplant Immunology*, *14*(3–4), 175–182.

Torrey, E.F., Miller, J., Rawlings, R., & Yolken, R.H. (1997). Seasonality of births in schizophrenia and bipolar disorder: A review of the literature. *Schizophrenia Research*, *28*(1), 1–38.

Torrey, E.F., & Yolken, R.H. (1995). Could schizophrenia be a viral zoonosis transmitted from house cats? *Schizophrenia Bulletin*, *21*(2), 167–171.

Torrey, E.F., Rawlings, R., & Yolken, R.H. (2000). The antecedents of psychoses: A case-control study of selected risk factors. *Schizophr Res*, *46*, 17–23.

Torrey, E.F., & Yolken, R.H. (2003). Toxoplasma gondii and schizophrenia. *Emerging Infectious Diseases*, *9*(11), 1375–1380.

Tsuang, M.T. (1978). Suicide in schizophrenics, manics, depressives, and surgical controls: A comparison with general population suicide mortality. *Arch Gen Psychiatry*, *35*, 153–155.

Tsuang, M. (2000). Schizophrenia: Genes and environment. *Biol Psychiatry*, *47*(3), 210–220.

van Os, J., Bak, M., Hanssen, M., Bijl, R.V., de Graaf, R., & Verdoux, H. (2002). Cannabis use and psychosis: A longitudinal population-based study. *American Journal of Epidemiology*, *156*(4), 319–327.

Warnock, J. (1903). Insanity from hasheesh. *J Ment Sci*, *49*, 96–110.

Williams, J.M.G. (1997). *Cry of pain.* Harmondsworth Penguin.

Ziedonis, D.M., Smelson, D., Rosenthal, R.N., Batki, S.L., Green, A.I., Henry, R.J.,…Weiss, R.D. (2005). Improving the care of individuals with schizophrenia and substance use disorders: Consensus recommendations. *J Psychiatr Pract*, *11*(5), 315–339.

42

Epidemiology of Epilepsy

INTRODUCTION

An epileptic seizure is caused by a crescendo of action potentials in one or more circuits of the brain. Symptoms can range from total sustained muscle contraction (tonus) to violent rhythmic jerking and shaking of all muscle groups (clonus), depending upon which neuronal circuits are misfiring.

The Greek term "*epilepsy*," meaning "*seizure*," was coined to describe neurologic symptoms of violent spasmodic jerking and shaking admixed with intermittent paralysis in afflicted patients. According to a consensus statement, epilepsy refers to the abnormal and excessive discharge of a set of neurons in the brain resulting in transitory abnormal neurological phenomena that may include alterations of consciousness, motor sensory, autonomic, and/or psychic events (Commission on Epilepsy and Prognosis, ILAE, 1993).

DIAGNOSIS OF EPILEPSY

Epilepsy is diagnosed by confirmation of 2 or more unprovoked seizures separated by at least 24 hours in an individual. Abnormal findings may also be present in electroencephalogram (EEG) studies and imaging studies of the brain. Since other neurological events can mimic seizures, particularly in children, a careful history must be taken in order to document the exact nature of the "seizure" and arrive at a correct diagnosis. Stimuli that may incite seizure-like symptoms include illness, infection, physical or emotional trauma, medications, and use of illicit drugs.

True seizures are characterized by inappropriate rhythmic limb movements and/or muscle contractions (clonus) often interrupted by sustained muscle contraction (tonus). Seizures invariably involve altered consciousness and unresponsiveness to verbal commands during the episode. Immediately following a seizure, persisting focal findings (delay in restoration of normal speech, sight, hearing, cognition, and motor function) can often be used to pinpoint the area of the brain affected.

Electroencephalogram (EEG) studies are recommended in the evaluation of individuals with suspected seizures or epilepsy. Tracings should be obtained in the awake and sleep states in close proximity to an event. Characteristic epileptiform patterns of brain waves can help confirm the diagnosis and elucidate the affected regions of the brain.

Neuroimaging studies are also recommended for individuals who have suffered a seizure. Such studies may reveal structural abnormalities such as tumors, congenital malformations, vascular anomalies, infections, and traumatic injuries. Magnetic resonance imaging (MRI) is preferred over other imaging procedures in studies of the brain.

TYPES OF SEIZURES

As pointed out by Sander and Shorvon in their comprehensive review of the epidemiology of the epilepsies, "*Many different conditions, with different causes and outcomes, may express themselves solely by the occurrence of recurrent epileptic seizures. Epilepsy is a collection of syndromes and conditions rather than a single disease...*" (Sander and Shorvon, 1996). Hence, it is important to consider the different types of seizures in discussion of the epidemiology of epilepsy.

Table 42.1	Major Types of Epileptic Seizures
Type of Seizure	**Neurologic Characteristics**
Partial Seizure	*Focal area of neuron discharge*
Simple	No loss of consciousness
Complex	Loss of consciousness
Secondary Generalization	Evolvement to generalized seizure
Generalized Seizure	*Widespread neschuron diarge*
Petit Mal	Unresponsiveness
Myclonic	Sporadic muscle contractions
Clonic	Abnormal bilateral repetitive contractions
Tonic	Sustained muscle contraction
Atonic	Loss of muscle tone
Grand Mal	Clonic-Tonic symptoms
Status Epilepticus	*Unrelenting seizure activity*

Source: Classification scheme is derived from the following references: Commission on Classification and Terminology of the International League Against Epilepsy (1989). Proposal for revised classification of epilepsies and epileptic syndromes. *Epilepsia* 30:389–399. Commission on Epilepsy and Prognosis, International League Against Epilepsy (1993). Guidelines for epidemiologic studies on epilepsy. *Epilepsia* 34:592–596.

Types of seizure are categorized according to the location of dysfunctional neuronal circuits in the brain and the extent of consciousness with corresponding impact on motor and cognitive function. There are more than 40 different types of seizures and only the main types will be discussed in this chapter. The major seizure types are summarized in **Table 42.1** and briefly outlined in the following paragraphs.

A partial or focal seizure refers to a specific localized cerebral area in which the neurons are excessively firing. A simple seizure is one in which there is no loss of consciousness, and a complex seizure is one in which there is impaired awareness or loss of consciousness. Thus, a simple partial seizure refers to localized brain dysfunction without loss of consciousness, whereas a complex partial seizure refers to localized brain dysfunction and unconsciousness.

Simple seizures are subclassified according to the profile of symptoms: motor impairment involving muscle contraction and rigidity; cognitive impairment affecting vision, hearing, smell, taste, or touch; and memory or emotional disturbances.

Complex partial seizures are characterized by impaired awareness of surroundings or loss of consciousness. Other characteristics include automatisms such as lip smacking, chewing, fidgeting, and other inappropriate involuntary repetitive movements. A partial seizure will occasionally evolve into a generalized seizure wherein the patient loses consciousness and manifests other signs and symptoms of widespread neuronal discharge.

A generalized seizure is one involving both cerebral hemispheres with widespread cerebral dysfunction and corresponding impact on many motor and cognitive functions. All generalized seizures involve the loss of consciousness. These are subdivided into six types: *absence (petit mal), myoclonic, clonic, tonic, atonic,* and *tonic-clonic (grand mal) seizures.*

Absence (petit mal) seizures cause a brief loss of consciousness for a few seconds without other symptoms. Such seizures typically interrupt normal childhood activity and may reoccur several times throughout the day.

Myoclonic seizures consist of sporadic "jerking" muscle contractions of very short duration whereas *clonic* seizures involve inappropriate repetitive rhythmic movements simultaneously occurring on both sides of the body.

Tonic seizures are characterized by sustained contraction of muscles whereas *atonic* seizures involve the loss of muscle tone, particularly in the arms and legs that often results in a fall.

The most dramatic of the generalized seizures is the *grand mal* seizure, in which the patient first loses consciousness and manifests generalized contraction of all muscles (the tonic phase) for 30–60 seconds followed by violent uncontrolled spasmodic muscle contractions (the clonic phase) for 30–60 seconds, after which the patient enters into a deep coma (the posticteral phase) that may last up to 30 minutes. Grand mal seizures can be fatal and are characterized by incontinence, tongue biting, convulsions, and accidental injury.

A catastrophic event in a patient with epilepsy is the occurrence of *status epilepticus.* This life-threatening condition is defined as the presence of intense unrelenting seizure activity lasting longer than 30 minutes. Status epilepticus occurs in about 1 in 5 patients who have been diagnosed with epilepsy.

Accurate classification according to seizure type involves extensive testing by an electroencephalogram (EEG) which records tracings of brain waves from different regions of the brain. Such tests are often unavailable in epidemiologic investigations of epilepsy that are conducted in the field.

TYPES OF EPILEPSY

Although epilepsy is defined as the occurrence of two or more unprovoked seizures in an individual, the different types of epilepsy are classified not only by the type of seizure, but also according to a number of other features including the age at diagnosis, known underlying causes (trauma, stroke, tumor, infection), genetic factors, the part of the brain involved, the severity and frequency of seizure activity, EEG findings, response to antiepileptic drugs, and prognosis. A consensus statement from the *International League Against Epilepsy (ILAE)* categorizes epilepsy according to two dichotomies: localization-related versus generalized disease, and idiopathic versus symptomatic or cryptogenic disease (Commission on Epilepsy and Prognosis, ILAE, 1993). Major epilepsy syndromes classified by this system are summarized in **Table 42.2.**

It is important to realize that in the nomenclature of epilepsy research, *idiopathic* disease refers to epilepsy with a *genetic* basis, *symptomatic* disease has a known underlying cause (developmental delay, trauma, tumor, infection), and *cryptogenic* disease has a known structural anomaly in the brain but the cause has not been definitively elucidated. Another term that has been used for *symptomatic* disease is *remote symptomatic epilepsy.*

Localization-related (focal) epilepsy is characterized by partial seizures due to excessive firing of a focal group of neurons. This type may be idiopathic, symptomatic, or cryptogenic.

Generalized epilepsy is characterized by generalized seizures due to excessive firing of neurons distributed throughout the brain. This type may also be idiopathic, symptomatic, or cryptogenic.

As discussed in the following section, several *idiopathic* (genetic) focal epilepsy syndromes have been described, including *benign epilepsy with centrotemporal spikes (Rolandic epilepsy)*, benign occipital epilepsies of childhood (*Panayiotopolous syndrome and Gestault syndrome*), and *nocturnal frontal lobe epilepsy*. These syndromes have specific EEG characteristics, respond well to antiepileptic medication, and usually remit with age. In contrast, *symptomatic* focal epilepsies are often more malignant, with higher rates of medical intractability, and lower remission rates (Panayiotopolous et al., 2008; Taylor et al., 2008). According to the *International Classification of Epilepsies and Epileptic Syndromes* proposed by the *International League Against Epilepsy (ILAE)* in 1989, *cryptogenic* epilepsies are presumed to be *symptomatic* but with unknown etiology (Commission on Classification and Terminology of the International League Against Epilepsy, 1989).

It is also important to realize that epileptic phenotypes are extraordinarily heterogeneous, and despite extensive clinical investigation, a large fraction of patients are unclassifiable according to etiology. Investigators at the Mayo Clinic recently examined the incidence and classification of new onset epilepsy in a population-based group of children in Olmstead County Minnesota. All children with newly diagnosed epilepsy from 1980 to 2004 were classified by mode of onset, etiology and syndrome using criteria of the

Table 42.2	**Major Epilepsy Syndromes**	
Type of Epilepsy	**Localization-Related**	**Generalized**
Idiopathic (Genetic)	• Benign Rolandic	• Childhood Absence
	• Benign Occipital	• Juvenile Absence
	• Nocturnal FL	• Dravet syndrome
		• Juvenile Myoclonic
		• Tonic-Clonic
Symptomatic or Cryptogenic	• Temporal Lobe	• West syndrome
	• Frontal Lobe	• Lennox-Gastaut
	• Parietal Lobe	
	• Occipital Lobe	

Source: Classification scheme is derived from the following references: Commission on Classification and Terminology of the International League Against Epilepsy (1989). Proposal for revised classification of epilepsies and epileptic syndromes. *Epilepsia* 30:389–399. Commission on Epilepsy and Prognosis, International League Against Epilepsy (1993). Guidelines for epidemiologic studies on epilepsy. *Epilepsia* 34:592–596.

International League Against Epilepsy (ILAE). The adjusted annual incidence rate of new onset epilepsy in children was 44.5 cases per 100,000. Rates were highest in the first year of life and diminished with age. The mode of onset was focal in 68%, generalized (bilateral) in 23%, spasmodic in 3%, and unknown in 5% of cases. Approximately half of children had unknown etiology, and among the remaining cases, 78 (22%) were idiopathic (genetic) and 101 (28%) were structural or metabolic. The investigators concluded that *"Nearly half of childhood epilepsy is of 'unknown' etiology"* (Wirrell et al., 2011).

EPILEPSY SYNDROMES

The epilepsy syndromes listed in **Table 42.2** plus other selected epilepsy syndromes are briefly defined in the following paragraphs. A number of epilepsy syndromes have been identified that are caused by heritable deleterious genes and/or chromosomal aberrations. Relevant genetic findings are discussed for selected idiopathic (genetic) syndromes.

Idiopathic (Genetic) Localization-Related (Focal) Syndromes

- *Benign Rolandic epilepsy* of childhood (benign centrotemporal lobe epilepsy) occurs in children under 13 years of age, with peak onset in late childhood prior to puberty. Apart from their seizure disorder, children with this type of epilepsy are otherwise normal. This syndrome features simple partial seizures that involve facial muscles and frequently cause drooling. Although most episodes are brief, seizures sometimes spread and generalize. Seizures are typically nocturnal and confined to sleep. The EEG may demonstrate spike discharges in the centrotemporal region (Rolandic sulcus) of the brain. Seizures may require anticonvulsant treatment, but sometimes are infrequent enough to allow physicians to defer treatment. Seizures usually cease at puberty. Genetic studies of families with affected children suggest an autosomal dominant inheritance pattern with high gene penetrance (Bali et al., 2007) and linkage with the gene encoding the α7 subunit of the acetylcholine receptor (*CHRNA7*) on the long arm of chromsome 15 (Neubauer et al., 1998). It is noteworthy that this same gene has also been linked to the development of *juvenile myoclonic epilepsy*, as discussed later (Elmslie et al., 1997).

- *Benign occipital epilepsies of childhood* are broadly classified into 2 forms, one with early onset typically before the age of 5 years (*Panayiotopoulos syndrome*) and the other with later onset between 5–10 years of age (*Gastaut syndrome*). *Panayiotopoulos syndrome* is characterized by prolonged autonomic seizures of occipital origin, often lasting more than 30 minutes, thus constituting autonomic *status epilepticus* (Panayiotopoulos, 2007). In contrast, Gastaut syndrome is characterized by frequent brief seizures with visual hallucinations, ictal blindness, and illusions (Gastaut, 1982). Though some family studies of EEG patterns have suggested an autosomal dominant inheritance pattern (Kuzniecky and Rosenblatt, 1987), a lack of concordance among monozygous twins implies that somatic mutations and epigenetic or environmental factors are also likely to play a role in the benign occipital epilepsies of childhood (Taylor et al., 2008).

- *Nocturnal frontal lobe epilepsy* is an inherited epileptic disorder that causes seizures during sleep. Onset is usually in childhood. These seizures arise in the frontal lobes and consist of complex motor movements, such as hand clenching, arm raising/lowering, and knee bending. Vocalizations such as shouting, moaning, or crying are also common. Mutations in genes encoding subunits of nicotinic acetylcholine receptors on chromosomes 15 and 20 are responsible for this syndrome. The inheritance pattern is autosomal dominant with high penetrance of the deleterious genes (Steinlein et al., 1995; Berkovic and Scheffer, 1997; Phillips et al., 1998).

- *Primary reading epilepsy* is a rare form of reflex epilepsy classified as idiopathic and localization-related. Nearly all seizures in this syndrome are precipitated by reading (usually reading aloud). Reading in susceptible individuals triggers characteristic myoclonic seizures. Inheritance of this syndrome appears to be polygenic (Berkovic and Scheffer, 1997).

Idiopathic (Genetic) Generalized Syndromes

- *Childhood absence epilepsy* affects children under 13 years of age. Peak onset is at 5–6 years of age. Children with this form of epilepsy have recurrent absence seizures, brief episodes of unresponsive staring, sometimes with minor motor features such as eye blinking or subtle chewing. The EEG finding is generalized 3 Hz spike and wave discharges. Occasionally, patients develop generalized tonic-clonic (grand mal) seizures. This condition carries a good prognosis because children do not usually show cognitive decline or neurological deficits, and the seizures in the majority of patients cease spontaneously with growth and maturation. Though childhood absence epilepsy displays a complex pattern of polygenic inheritance, recent familial and genetic studies have elucidated major genes that may heighten susceptibility. A study of 50 Austrian families with affected children detected significant disequilibrium in polymorphisms of the genes encoding the γ-aminobutyric acid (GABA) type-A receptor subunits α5 (GABRA5) and β3 (GABRB3) located on the long arm of chromosome 15 (Feucht et al., 1999); and a gene-sequencing study conducted in China detected 12 missense mutations in the T-type calcium channel gene on the short arm of chromosome 16 among 118 patients with this syndrome compared to none among 230 normal controls (Chen et al., 2003).

- *Juvenile absence epilepsy* is similar to the childhood form but seizures begin during the teenage years. Patients with this syndrome occasionally manifest generalized tonic-clonic (grand mal) seizures and progression to juvenile myoclonic epilepsy is relatively common. Though the inheritance pattern of juvenile absence epilepsy is complex, genetic studies suggest that defective glutamate receptor genes on chromosome 21 may contribute to the genesis of this syndrome (Sander et al., 1997a).

- *Dravet syndrome* (severe myoclonic epilepsy of infancy) is a rare neurodevelopmental disorder (1 in 40,000 births) characterized by severe epilepsy that does not respond well to treatment. This syndrome was first described by the French psychiatrist, Charlotte Dravet, in 1978. Dravet studied at the Centre Saint Paul at the University of Marseille, under the supervision of Henri Gastaut, who first described the Lennox-Gastaut syndrome. Seizures in Darvet syndrome are often prolonged and may progress to status epilepticus, a medical emergency. Mutations in the voltage-gated sodium channel SCN1A gene are the main genetic cause of Dravet syndrome. A recent large series of 333 patients were screened using direct gene sequencing and gene amplification techniques. Point mutations in the SCN1A gene were detected in 228 (68%) of cases, 161 of which had not previously been reported. Missense mutations were the most common mutation type. Furthermore, additional genetic deletions and rearrangements were identified in 14 of the 105 patients without SCN1A point mutations. Based on their results, the investigators state: "*These findings widely expand the SCN1A mutation spectrum identified and highlight the importance of screening the coding regions with both direct sequencing and a quantitative method*" (Depieene et al., 2009).

- *Juvenile myoclonic epilepsy* is most often diagnosed during the teenage years. Patients have normal cognition and are otherwise neurologically intact. The most common seizures are myoclonic jerks, although generalized tonic-clonic (grand mal) seizures and absence seizures may also occur. Myoclonic jerks usually cluster in the early morning after awakening. The EEG reveals generalized 4–6 Hz spike wave discharges or multiple spike discharges. Interestingly, patients are often diagnosed when they have their first generalized tonic-clonic seizure when they experience sleep deprivation (e.g., during the freshman year in college after staying up late to study for exams). Alcohol withdrawal can also be a precipitating factor in breakthrough seizures. Though seizure risk is lifelong, the majority of patients are able to successively manage their condition with anticonvulsant medication and avoidance of seizure precipitants. Genetic studies of juvenile myoclonic epilepsy have generally revealed complex polygenic inheritance. However, a recent study of 34 pedigrees, each with one or more affected relatives, revealed linkage of susceptibility to the gene encoding the α7 subunit of the nicotinic acetylcholine receptor (CHRNA7) on the long arm of chromosome 15. Based on these results, the investigators suggest they may have discovered a major susceptibility locus for juvenile myoclonic epilepsy (Elmslie et al., 1997).

- *Unverricht-Lundborg disease* is the most common form of an uncommon group of genetic epilepsy disorders called *progressive myoclonic epilepsies*. This genetic disorder is caused by a mutation in the *cystatin B gene* that encodes a protein that inhibits proteases that leak out of lysosomes in the cell (Turk and Bode, 1991; Joensuu, Lehesjoki, and Kopra, 2008). The disease is named after the German physician, Heinrich Unverricht, who first described it in 1891, and the Swedish physician, Herman Bernhard Lundborg, who provided greater detail in 1903. The syndrome occurs in children between the ages of 6–16 years, most from the Baltic and Mediterranean regions of Europe. The disease is characterized by recurrent myoclonic and tonic-clonic seizures that become progressively more frequent and severe over time. The condition is usually progressive. Depression is prevalent among patients and their life expectancy is less than 25 years (Kalviainen et al., 2008).

- *Tonic-clonic (grand mal) seizures on awakening* is an uncommon epileptic syndrome characterized by recurrent generalized tonic-clonic (*grand mal*) seizures when the patient awakens from sleep. About 70% of cases are diagnosed during adolescence; however, onset is highly variable ranging from early childhood into the fourth decade of life. An important feature of this syndrome is that patients with any of the other syndromes of idiopathic generalized epilepsy, which are characterized by minor seizures, may experience generalized tonic-clonic (grand mal) seizures, usually of the awakening type. Such seizures are severe and potentially dangerous since they may progress to *status epilepticus*. The genetic basis of tonic-clonic seizures on awakening is complex. Associations with the nicotinic acetylcholine receptor and GABA receptor subunit genes on chromosome 15, certain genes of the major histocompatibility locus on chromosome 6, and putative susceptibility loci on chromosomes 2, 3, and 14 have been reported (Schmitz et al., 1997; Elmslie et al., 1997; Sander et al., 1997b; Janz, 2000).

Symptomatic or Cryptogenic Localization-related Syndromes

Symptomatic localization-related epilepsies are divided by the location of the epileptic lesion in the brain, since the symptoms of the seizures predominantly reflect the region of the brain disrupted rather than the cause of the lesion. Tumors, vascular and cavernous malformations, head trauma, infection, and cerebral infarcts can all cause epileptic foci in different regions of the brain.

- *Epilepsies of the frontal lobe, temporal lobe, parietal lobe, and occipital lobe* arise from lesions in the corresponding regions of the brain that cause seizures. Symptomatic causes include brain stroke, tumors, head trauma, infection, and congenital malformations.

- *Rasmussen's encephalitis* is a rare progressive, inflammatory brain lesion. This condition is most often diagnosed in children under the age of 10 years, but it can also occur in adolescents and adults. Initial symptoms are simple-partial or complex-partial seizures that may progress to *epilepsia partialis continua* (*simple partial status epilepticus*). Neuroimaging shows inflammatory encephalitis on one side of the brain that may spread if not treated. Dementia and hemiparesis are also commonly found in patients with this syndrome. Though the cause of encephalitis remains unknown, pathogenesis apparently involves an autoimmune attack against certain types of membrane receptors of the neurotransmitter, glutamate (Takahashi et al., 2005).

- *Mesial temporal lobe epilepsy* is the most common cryptogenic form of epilepsy. In most cases, the epileptogenic region corresponds to sclerosis (scarring) found in the midline (mesial) temporal structures (the hippocampus, amygdala, and parahippocampal gyrus). It is hypothesized that brain damage from traumatic injury, infection, a brain tumor, lack of oxygen, and/or seizure activity causes sustained inflammation leading to the formation of the scar tissue. However, a recent study detected *human herpes virus 6B* (*HHV-6B*) in brain specimens from 15 of 24 patients with mesial temporal sclerosis, in contrast to 0 of 14 specimens from patients with other syndromes. These results suggest that HHV-6B infection may contribute to the pathogenesis of mesial temporal lobe epilepsy (Fotheringham et al., 2007). Seizures begin in late childhood and adolescence and are poorly controlled by anticonvulsant medications. Most patients have complex partial seizures that are occasionally preceded by an aura. Seizures may progress to secondary generalized tonic-clonic (grand mal) seizures.

Generalized Symptomatic or Cryptogenic Syndromes

- *West syndrome* is a form of childhood epilepsy diagnosed by the triad of developmental delay, infantile seizures (spasms), and an arrhythmic EEG pattern. Onset occurs before the age of 2 years with a peak between 8 and 9 months. Approximately 1 in 3,500 infants are afflicted.

Causation may be symptomatic, cryptogenic, or idiopathic (genetic). A common cause is *tuberous sclerosis*, a genetic disorder that causes tumors to form in many different organs, primarily in the brain, eyes, heart, kidney, skin, and lungs. Several types of brain lesions can occur in individuals with tuberous sclerosis and up to 90% of children with this condition develop epilepsy. Briefly, the condition is caused by mutations in either of two genes, *TSC1* or *TSC2*, that encode proteins (*hamartin* and *tuberin*) that are essential for normal cell proliferation and differentiation. Other causes of West syndrome include congenital disorders (Down syndrome), infection, and traumatic brain injury; albeit, the etiology is unknown in 40–50% of cases. The prognosis for children with West syndrome varies with the underlying cause. Unfortunately, most surviving patients have persisting cognitive impairment and continuing seizures and usually progress to *Lennox-Gastaut syndrome* (Cowan and Hudson, 1991).

- *Lennox-Gastaut syndrome* consists of the triad of developmental delay or childhood dementia, mixed generalized seizures, and a characteristic EEG pattern of 2 Hz slow spike waves. Onset occurs between 2 and 18 years of age. Approximately 26 of 1,000 children are afflicted by the age of 10 years. As in West syndrome, causation may be symptomatic, cryptogenic, or idiopathic (genetic). Indeed, surviving patients with West syndrome often progress to Lennox-Gastaut syndrome. Most patients have astatic seizures (drop attacks), tonic seizures, tonic-clonic seizures, atypical absence seizures, and sometimes, complex partial seizures. Anticonvulsants are usually only partially successful in treatment (Trevathan, Murphy, and Yeargin-Allsopp, 1997).

- *Ohtahara syndrome* is a rare, severe epilepsy syndrome that usually begins in the first few days or weeks of life. Characteristic seizures are in the form of stiffening spasms with an EEG pattern of high voltage spikes followed by suppressed activity. Most infants with the disorder show significant underdevelopment of part or all of the cerebral hemispheres. The prognosis is poor with about half of the infants dying in the first year of life. Nearly all surviving infants are severely intellectually disabled and many have cerebral palsy. There is no effective treatment. A number of children have underlying structural brain abnormalities (Clarke et al., 1987).

Table 42.3	Special Syndromes
Type	**Description**
Febrile (Fever) Seizure	Seizure and convulsions associated with infection and fever
Isolated Seizure	Solitary unprovoked partial seizure without recurrence
Circumstantial Seizure	Seizure activity provoked by environmental or physiologic stimulus

Other Epileptic Categories

Two additional categories have been defined to accommodate other forms of epilepsy and seizure activity. *Undetermined epilepsy* is characterized by seizures that cannot be accurately categorized as either partial or generalized. Undetermined epilepsy syndromes include neonatal seizures, severe myoclonic seizures, and the *Landau-Kleffner syndrome*, a rare, childhood neurological disorder characterized by the sudden or gradual development of aphasia (the inability to understand or express language).

Special syndromes are not definable as epilepsy *per se* but rather are entities characterized by seizures. These include febrile (fever) seizures, unprovoked solitary seizures, and circumstantial or situation-related seizures that are triggered by specific environmental or physiological stimuli (**Table 42.3**).

FEBRILE (FEVER) SEIZURES AND EPILEPSY

Febrile (fever) seizures are convulsions induced by fever in infants or small children. During a febrile seizure, the child often loses consciousness and shakes, moving limbs on both sides of the body; or less commonly, the child becomes rigid or manifests muscle contractions in only one portion of the body such as the arm, leg, or the right or left side only. Febrile seizures ordinarily last for 1–2 minutes, although there is extreme variability in duration, from a few seconds up to 15 minutes or more. The majority of children who exhibit febrile seizures have body temperatures exceeding 102°F. Most such seizures occur during the early hours of elevated body temperature.

Acute febrile miniseizures are relatively common during the first years of life affecting about 5% of children before the age of 5 years. The incidence of febrile seizures is highest during the first months of life and then progressively declines until about age 10 years when the risk becomes negligible.

It is important to realize that children with febrile seizures are not considered to have epilepsy, since epilepsy is defined as two or more *unprovoked* seizures. In fact, the vast majority of febrile seizures are of short duration and harmless. During a febrile seizure, there is a slight chance of accidental injury; however, there is no evidence to suggest that *short* febrile seizures cause brain damage.

Approximately 1 in 25 children will have at least 1 febrile seizure, and 1 in 3 of those with a 1st febrile seizure will have additional febrile seizures. Febrile seizures most commonly occur between the ages of 6 months and 5 years. Factors that increase the risk of having recurrent febrile seizures are early onset of the first febrile seizure, frequent infection and fever, and familial history of febrile seizures among family members.

Investigators in Greece examined the recurrence of febrile seizures among 260 children with a first episode between 3 months and 6 years of age. The median follow-up was 4.3 years with evaluations every 4–6 months and at the time of each recurrence. The strongest risk factors for recurrence were early onset, familial history of febrile seizures, and low temperature prior to the initial seizure (Pavlidou et al., 2008).

Investigators in the United States examined the recurrence of febrile seizures among 428 children who were assessed every 3 months for at least 2 years after their first episode. Recurrent febrile seizures occurred in 126 (31.8%) of these children; 73 (17.1%) had only 1 recurrence, 38 (8.9%) had 2 recurrences, and 25 (5.8%) had 3 or more recurrences. Early age at onset, history of febrile seizures in a first-degree relative (parent or sibling), low fever preceding the first seizure, and brief interval between fever and seizure onset were strong independent predictors of recurrent febrile seizures. The investigators suggest that these four factors can be used to define groups of patients with high versus low probability of developing recurrent febrile seizures (Berg et al., 1997).

Febrile seizures were once considered to be an early warning sign of impending epilepsy. However, most children (over 90%) affected by febrile seizures recover completely over time without developing epilepsy. Furthermore, risk factors that predict subsequent febrile seizures (early onset, recurrent fever, and familial history) have *not* consistently been found to predict the development of epilepsy; and reciprocally, most risk factors associated with epilepsy have *not* been found to increase the risk of recurrent febrile seizures. Nevertheless, some studies suggest that certain types of recurrent febrile seizures *do* increase the risk of subsequently developing epilepsy and the association remains under intense investigation (Berg, 1992).

A study conducted in Singapore examined neurological outcomes among 476 children initially hospitalized for febrile seizures during infancy. During more

than 7 years of follow-up, 10 of these children (2.1%) had one or more unprovoked seizures and 5 children (1.1%) became epileptic. The incidence of epilepsy among children with a febrile seizure lasting 30 minutes or more was increased nearly 9-fold compared to children with shorter seizures (12.1% vs. 1.4%); and the incidence of epilepsy was increased nearly 6-fold among children with a familial history of epilepsy compared to those with no familial history (9.1% vs. 1.6%). Gender, ethnicity, age at onset, and number of recurrent febrile seizures did not influence the risk (Lee, 1989).

Investigators at Rotterdam in the Netherlands reexamined the risk factors for febrile seizures and associations with epilepsy in a pooled analysis of individual data from five follow-up studies that incorporated standardized definitions of febrile seizures, complex seizures and risk factors. Among 2,496 children with fever seizures, 32% had 1, 15% had 2, and 7% had 3 or more recurrent febrile seizures after a first episode. The hazard of recurrent febrile seizures was greatest between the ages of 12 and 24 months, and the risk of having additional febrile seizures more than doubled with each successive recurrence. Recurrence risk was also increased by a history of *either febrile or unprovoked seizures* in a first-degree relative (parent or sibling) and low temperature preceding the first febrile seizure. Notably, early onset of febrile seizure (less than 12 months), familial history of unprovoked seizures, and an initial partial fever seizure (affecting only one part of the body) were found to significantly increase the risk of subsequently developing complex seizures and epilepsy (Offringa et al., 1994).

In a landmark study, investigators in Denmark evaluated the association between febrile seizures and epilepsy in a long-term population-based cohort of 1.54 million persons born during 1978–2002, including 49,587 children with febrile seizures, 16,481 individuals with epilepsy, and 2,149 individuals who developed epilepsy after febrile seizures. At 23 years of follow-up, the cumulative incidence of epilepsy among individuals who had childhood febrile seizures was 6.9%, more than 5 times higher than individuals with no history of febrile seizures (adjusted RR = 5.4). The risk remained high during the entire follow-up period but was particularly high shortly after the first febrile seizure (**Figure 42.1**). Familial history of epilepsy, history of cerebral palsy, and low APGAR score at birth were also found to independently elevate the risk of epilepsy development. The investigators suggest that febrile seizures may be the first sign of epilepsy, or share common risk factors with epilepsy, or may cause brain damage (edema of the hippocampus) predisposing to epilepsy in certain individuals (Vestergaard et al., 2007).

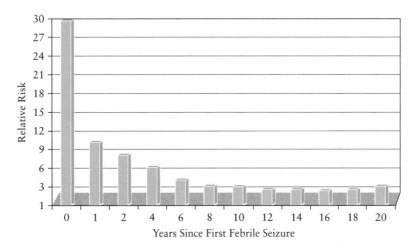

Figure 42.1 Epilepsy Risk and Febrile Seizures.

Source: Data from Vestergaard M, Pedersen CB, Sidenius P, Olsen J, Christensen J (2007). The long-term risk of epilepsy after febrile seizures in susceptible subgroups. *Am J Epidemiol* 165(8):911–918.

ISOLATED SEIZURES

Occasionally, an individual may experience a single solitary seizure or a cluster of seizures in a short span of time during or following an illness or injury without any further episodes. Such "isolated seizures" can be provoked by any number of factors such as head trauma, infection, stress, etc. Often no identifiable cause can be found. Such events clearly *do not* meet the criteria for the diagnosis of epilepsy: 2 or more unprovoked seizures separated by at least 24 hours in time.

CIRCUMSTANTIAL (SITUATION-RELATED) SEIZURES

Circumstantial seizures are stimulated by identifiable environmental or physiological causes such as stress, trauma, hormones, alcohol, drugs, sleep deprivation, infection, vascular disease, cancer, endocrine disorders, and a variety of other conditions. This "wastebasket" category includes *nonepileptic* patients with solitary seizures for which the cause can be inferred from patient-related circumstances and situations.

STATUS EPILEPTICUS

One seizure type that deserves special mention is *status epilepticus*, a catastrophic life-threatening continuous seizure lasting longer than 30 minutes. Status epilepticus can occur as an amplification of one of the aforementioned epileptic syndromes or it can occur spontaneously without warning due to a variety of other causes. Indeed, epilepsy is only *one* cause of status epilepticus found in only about one-third of patients. Other predominant causes include infectious diseases (particularly in children), strokes, hemorrhage, brain tumors, metabolic diseases, drug overdose, alcohol abuse, and head trauma. Status epilepticus can be focal, generalized, or complex, involving both focal and generalized seizure activity. The condition is surprisingly common, particularly among infants and young children and older adults (**Figure 42.2**). Case fatality rates of status epilepticus range from 10% in children to nearly 50% in the elderly (DeLorenzo et al., 1995).

Status epilepticus has been found to have a strong genetic basis. Corey and colleagues examined the role of genetic factors in status epilepticus using the population-based *Virginia Twin Registry*. Their study included 70 individuals with at least 1 episode of status epilepticus and 318 individuals with verified seizures among 332 twin pairs. Status epilepticus occurred in 21 (13.2%) of 158 individuals with febrile seizures and 49 (22.0%) of 223 individuals with afebrile seizures. The age at first occurrence of status epilepticus ranged from 2 months to 59 years. The overall concordance rate of status epilepticus was 31% among monozygous twins and 0 among dizygous twins. Furthermore, among monozygous twin pairs with epilepsy, 67% were also concordant for status epilepticus. The investigators concluded that genetic factors contribute significantly to the genesis of status epilepticus (Corey et al., 1998; Corey, Pellock, and DeLorenzo, 2004).

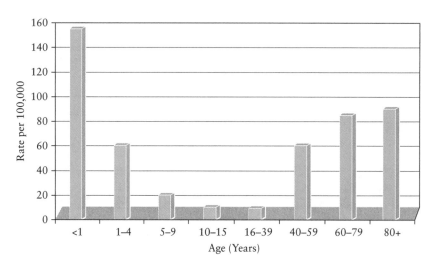

Figure 42.2 Age-Specific Incidence of Status Epilepticus.

Source: Data from DeLorenzo RJ, Pelloch JM, Towne AR, Boggs JG (1995). Epidemiology of status epilepticus. *J Clin Neurophysiol* 12:316–325.

The twin studies of status epilepticus therefore reflect a definite genetic predisposition to this life-threatening condition. Nevertheless, causation is obviously multifactorial involving a combination of genetic and environmental factors. As already discussed in this chapter, certain monogenic epileptic syndromes involving mutations in key genes have been identified (*GABRA5, GABRB3, SCN1A, CHRNA7*). However, these syndromes are relatively rare and as pointed out in a recent review, *"mutations in a single gene can produce different epilepsy phenotypes in different individuals as a result of modifying genetic or environmental factors"* (Schauwecker, 2009). Epigenetic effects might also contribute to the phenotypic heterogeneity of status epilepticus. Obviously, further studies are needed to elucidate major genes that contribute to the genesis of status epilepticus.

GLOBAL BURDEN OF EPILEPSY

The World Health Organization reports that about 50 million people worldwide have epilepsy, 40 million of whom reside in developing nations with little or no access to treatment. Indeed, 15–20 million people with this condition receive no medication (Scott, Lhatoo, and Sander, 2001; World Health Organization, 2001).

Incidence of Epilepsy and Unprovoked Seizure

The worldwide distribution of epilepsy reflects marked variability. Socioeconomically deprived people are clearly at higher risk. The annual incidence rates are highest in resource-poor countries, particularly those in sub-Saharan Africa and Latin America, ranging from 100–200 per 100,000 (Singhal et al., 1998; Scott, Lhatoo, and Sander, 2001). Rates are much lower in industrialized countries such as the United States, the United Kingdom, Australia, and Western Europe ranging from 23–54 per 100,000 (Jallon, 2002). Relatively low annual incidence rates have also been reported for population samples from China (29–35 per 100,000) and India (38–60 per 100,000). However, studies of these populations are sparse, and additional prospective population-based studies are needed for confirmation (Li et al., 1985; Mani et al., 1998; Sawhney et al., 1999; Wang et al., 2003; Ray et al., 2002; Mac et al., 2007).

Kotsopoulos and colleagues reviewed reported estimates of the incidence of epilepsy and unprovoked seizures published during 1966–1999 and conducted a meta-analysis of these data. Forty studies of population samples from around the globe were included in their analysis. The median annual age-adjusted incidence rate was 47 per 100,000 for epilepsy and 56 per 100,000 for unprovoked seizures. Males had slightly higher rates of epilepsy than females (51 vs. 46 per 100,000) and developing countries had higher rates than developed countries (69 vs. 43 per 100,000). In developing countries, rates tended to be higher in children than the elderly, perhaps due to shortened life expectancies and fewer survivors of stroke, tumors, and neurodegenerative conditions that heighten susceptibility to seizure. As discussed later in this chapter, such populations are more prone

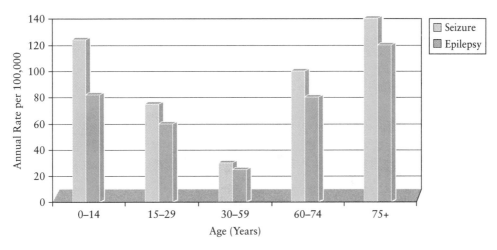

Figure 42.3 Age-Specific Incidence of Epilepsy and Unprovoked Seizure.

Source: Data from Kotsopoulos IAW, Van Merode T, Kessels FGH, De Krom MCTFM, Knottnerus JA (2002). Systematic review and meta-analysis of incidence studies of epilepsy and unprovoked seizures. *Epilepsia* 43(11):1402–1409. Hauser WA, Annegers JF, Kurland LT (1993). Incidence of epilepsy and unprovoked seizures in Rochester, Minnesota: 1935–1984. *Epilepsia* 34:453–468.

to endemic infectious and parasitic conditions (cryptocercosis, onchocerciasis) that increase the risk of childhood seizure. Childhood rates in some developed countries declined over the time span covered, perhaps due to improving prenatal and antenatal care; in contrast, rates in the elderly increased, likely due to better survival of stroke and other conditions that predispose to seizures (Kotsopoulos et al., 2002). The composite distribution of age-specific incidence is a U-shaped curve with high rates in children and the elderly (**Figure 42.3**).

Prevalence of Epilepsy

Epilepsy is often a lifelong disorder that persists in an individual for many decades. Annual prevalence rates are therefore much higher than the incidence rates, varying widely worldwide from 1–20 per 1,000 with a median rate of about 7 per 1,000. High annual prevalence rates have been reported for impoverished nations in sub-Saharan Africa and Latin America (15–20 per 1,000) whereas much lower values have been reported for industrialized nations. Rates in the United States, the United Kingdom, Australia, and European nations range from 1–10 per 1,000 with a median of 5 per 1,000. A recent review of reported prevalence rates for population samples from Asian nations found a range of 1.5 per 1,000 in Japan to 10 per 1,000 in Pakistan with a median of 6 per 1,000 (Li et al., 1985; Singhal, 1998; Sridharan and Murthy, 1999; Scott, Lhatoo, and Sander, 2001; Wang et al., 2003; Huang et al., 2002; Fong et al., 2003; Bharucha, 2003; Mannan, 2004; Mac et al., 2007).

Disability Adjusted Life Years (DALY) Lost From Epilepsy

The *disability adjusted life years (DALY)* that are lost due to epilepsy reflect a public health burden of tremendous dimensions. Rates are highest in impoverished nations where there is little access to treatment (**Figure 42.4**).

EPILEPSY MORTALITY

Individuals with epilepsy die from four major causes: *status epilepticus* (often due to lack of anticonvulsant medications), *suicide* associated with depression, *trauma* associated with seizures, and *sudden unexpected death in epilepsy*. Those at highest risk for epilepsy-related deaths usually have underlying neurological impairment or poorly controlled seizures whereas those with mild to moderate epilepsy are at much lower risk for epilepsy-related death.

Epilepsy Mortality in Developing Countries

The case fatality and mortality rates reported for epileptic patients appear to be highest in developing nations and rural areas where there is little access to treatment. For example, in a study of epileptic patients conducted in rural Ethiopia, most patients were treated with local herbs, holy water, and amulets, whereas less than 2% received antiepileptic drugs. Injuries from burns or trauma suffered during seizures were found in 14% of patients. During the 2-year study period, 8 of the 9 reported deaths among

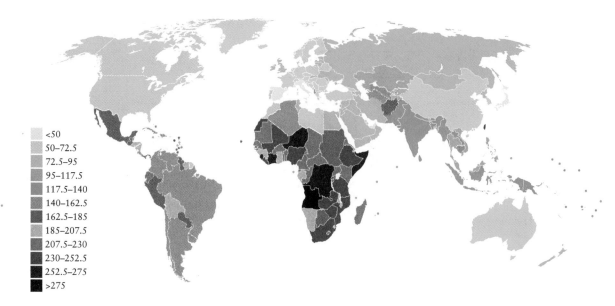

Figure 42.4 Disability Adjusted Life Years Due to Epilepsy, 2004.

Source: Data from: World Health Organization. The global burden of disease: 2004 update. Geneva, WHO, 2008. Available at www.who.int /evidence/bod.

patients were due to status epilepticus and 1 due to burns suffered when the patient fell into a domestic fire during a seizure (Tekle-Haimanot et al., 1990).

In a study conducted in a rural area of Cameroon in Central Africa, 37 (29%) of 128 patients with epilepsy died compared to 6 (5%) of 128 matched controls during 10 years of follow-up (RR = 6.2). The most frequent causes of death among epileptic patients were status epilepticus, sudden unexpected death in epilepsy, and drowning (Kamgno, Pion, and Boussinesq, 2003).

A recent study of patients living in a mountainous region of Laos revealed a *case fatality rate* of 91 deaths per 1,000 person-years. *None* of these patients had access to standard therapy with antiepileptic medications (Tran et al., 2006).

An international team of investigators traced the mortality experience of 103 *untreated* epileptic patients from a rural area of Bolivia over a 10-year period. Ten deaths were recorded yielding an overall mortality rate of 10 deaths per 1,000 person-years. The standardized mortality rate was elevated among patients with *remote symptomatic epilepsy* (SMR = 3.0) but not among patients with idiopathic disease (Nicoletti et al., 2009).

Investigators in Shanghai examined the mortality experience of 2,455 *prevalent* cases of epilepsy ascertained from 8 rural counties of 6 provinces in China with a population of 3,185,000 people. Patients were older than 2 years with a history of at least 2 convulsion seizures in the previous 12 months. Most were

started on monotherapy with phenobarbital as part of a community-based intervention study (which is described in last section of this chapter on epileptic therapy). Standard mortality ratios (SMR) were computed by age using the 2004 Chinese population as the reference group. During the year of study, 35 deaths were recorded, 471 patients withdrew, and 91 patients were lost to follow-up. The SMR for all ages was 3.9, but estimates were much higher in the younger age groups (**Figure 42.5**). The principal causes of death among young patients were suicide or drowning, whereas older patients died primarily from myocardial infarction, stroke, cancer, or pneumonia (Ding et al., 2006).

Epilepsy Treatment Gap

The *epilepsy treatment gap*, defined as the proportion of people with active epilepsy who require treatment but do not receive it, has been proposed as a useful parameter to compare access to and quality of care for epilepsy patients across populations. Prior anecdotal and descriptive estimates suggest that the treatment gap is much higher in low-income than high-income countries.

Wang and colleagues carried out a door-to-door survey to determine the prevalence of epilepsy and the proportion of patients receiving treatment amongst 55,000 people living in rural areas of China. The lifetime prevalence was 7.0 per 1,000 and 41% of all patients had *not* received any appropriate treatment. The prevalence of active epilepsy was 4.6 per 1,000

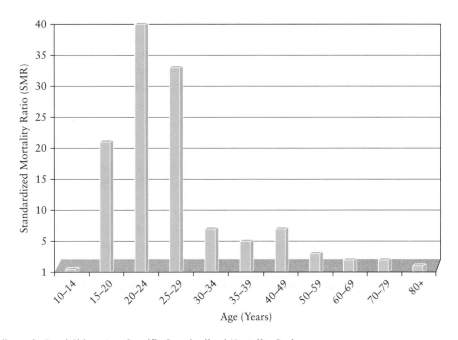

Figure 42.5 Epilepsy in Rural China: Age-Specific Standardized Mortality Ratios.

Source: Data from Ding D, Wang W, Wu J, Ma G, Dai Z, Yang B, Wang T, Yuan C, Hong Z, de Boer HM, Prilipko L, Sander JW (2006). Premature mortality in people with epilepsy in rural China: a prospective study. *Lancet Neurol* 5:823–827.

and 63% of individuals with active epilepsy had not received antiepileptic therapy in the week before the survey (Wang et al., 2003).

Meyer and colleagues at the World Health Organization recently examined the treatment gap for patients with active epilepsy in 54 populations from 28 countries based upon a comprehensive review of relevant published data. Their review encompassed studies spanning nearly 30 years, from 1978–2006, and included samples of patients from Africa, Asia, Europe, Australia, and North and South America. Results revealed a wide range of treatment gaps from 6% in Singapore to 100% in Bolivia. Treatment gaps of less than 10% were observed for patient populations in Taiwan, Norway, Singapore, the United Kingdom, Ireland, the United States, and selected populations in Argentina, Brazil, and France. In sharp contrast, treatment gaps greater than 95% were found in rural China, Ethiopia, the Gambia, the Lao People's Republic, Nigeria, Pakistan, Panama, Togo, Uganda, the United Republic of Tanzania, and Zambia. Wide variability was also noted within some countries. For example, treatment gaps in India ranged from 22% for patients in urban areas to 90% for patients living in rural villages. The results of this systematic review of the literature clearly reflect dramatic global disparities in the care and treatment of epilepsy patients. Treatment gaps for active epilepsy exceeded 75% in most low-income countries

and 50% in most middle-income countries, whereas high-income countries had treatment gaps of less than 10%. The investigators concluded their report with the following statement: "*Increased commitment by the global health community is needed to reduce the treatment gap and thereby reduce the potentially devastating social consequences and poor health outcomes resulting from untreated epilepsy*" (Meyer et al., 2010).

Epilepsy Mortality in Developed Countries

The case fatality and mortality rates due to epilepsy are markedly lower in developed nations than developing nations. For example, long-term studies in the United States, the United Kingdom, Australia, several European nations, some South American nations, and urban populations in China and India have found case fatality rates ranging from 1–10 deaths per 1,000 person-years (Mac et al., 2007). As one might expect, survival is significantly better among patients who achieve early long-term remission from epileptic symptoms without reliance on medications. Recent studies are discussed below suggesting that more than half of patients who receive early treatment successfully achieve long-term remission without seizure activity.

Sillanpää and Shinnar examined the mortality experience of a Finnish cohort of 245 cases with childhood epilepsy (160 incident cases and 95 prevalent cases) followed for more than 40 years. Follow-up examinations were conducted every fifth year and detailed information was collected including the age and cause of death. A total of 60 patients died during follow-up yielding an overall case fatality rate of 24%. The overall death rate was 6.9 deaths per 1,000 person-years (5.3 deaths per 1,000 person years for incident cases only). Subjects with *remote symptomatic epilepsy* secondary to neurological impairment (cognitive impairment, developmental delay, cerebral palsy, or autism) or neurological insult (head trauma, stroke, or meningitis) were compared to those with idiopathic or cryptogenic epilepsy (of indeterminate origin). Mortality among subjects with *remote symptomatic epilepsy* was more than threefold higher than among subjects with idiopathic or cryptogenic epilepsy (11.1 vs. 3.2 deaths per 1,000 person-years, RR = 3.5). Among the 60 deaths observed in the cohort, 33 (55%) were attributed to epilepsy *per se* and 26 (43%) were attributed to the underlying neurologic condition. Among the epilepsy-related deaths, 18 were due to *sudden unexplained death in epilepsy*, 9 were due to seizure or *status epilepticus*, and 6 were due to drowning. Notably, only 4 deaths occurred among 103 patients who achieved 5-year remission and were not receiving medication at last follow-up (1.5 deaths per 1,000 person years), compared to 5 deaths among 35 patients in 5-year remission and receiving medication at last follow-up (11.2 deaths per 1,000 person years), and 51 deaths among 107 subjects who did not achieve 5-year remission (15.9 deaths per 1,000 person years). Early deaths (during childhood) were primarily due to underlying neurologic conditions whereas later deaths (during adulthood) were mostly due to epilepsy-related events (Sillanpää and Shinnar, 2010).

A team of Swedish investigators conducted a comprehensive review of epilepsy mortality data reported in the literature for developed countries. In population-based cohorts of incident disease with 7–29 years of follow-up, standardized mortality ratios ranged from 1.6–3.0, and survivorship following the diagnosis of epilepsy was 91%, 85%, and 83% at 5, 10, and 15 years, respectively. Mortality in patients from Iceland, France, Sweden, and the United Kingdom did not differ significantly from the general population, whereas mortality among US patients was increased. Notably, all studies reported increased standardized mortality ratios for patients with *remote symptomatic epilepsy* ranging from 2.2–6.5. The highest mortality ratios occurred among patients diagnosed with epilepsy or other neurological disorders at birth. Excess mortality was also high among elderly patients, primarily due to underlying disor-

ders such as stroke, cancer, other neurodegenerative conditions, and pneumonia. The most common seizure-related cause of death among epileptic children and adolescents was sudden unexpected death (Forsgren et al., 2005).

SUICIDE AND EPILEPSY

Suicide is a major cause of death among patients with epilepsy and its impact is often underestimated. Pompili and colleagues recently examined this phenomenon in a meta-analysis of 29 published studies. Their analysis included 50,814 patients, 187 of whom committed suicide. Overall, the annual suicide rate among patients with epilepsy was estimated at 32.5 per 1,000, which was 8.5 times higher than in the general population (matched by age group, country, and year). However, rates varied widely and perhaps surprisingly, some cohorts of epileptic patients actually had lower suicide rates than their comparison populations. Suicide risk appears to be increased by intractable epilepsy, depression, and surgical intervention, particularly temporal lobectomy, whereas low rates are associated with early therapy and freedom from seizure activity, particularly without medication. The investigators state that "*despite intensive efforts, effective prediction and prevention strategies remain elusive*" and they encourage further studies to address "*the role played by mood disorders, treatment-resistant epilepsy, and surgical treatment in the precipitation of suicide*" (Pompili et al., 2005).

EPILEPSY RISK FACTORS

From the preceding discussion, it is obvious that the term "*epilepsy*" encompasses a vast collection of syndromes and conditions, each having its own defining features and characteristics. Likewise, multiple risk factors have been implicated in the etiopathogenesis of the epilepsies. Indeed, the risk of developing epilepsy varies widely according to age, gender, genetic predisposition, physiology, medical history, behavior, and external environment.

By definition, *idiopathic epileptic syndromes* have a significant genetic basis whereas *circumstantial (situation-related) epilepsy* is associated with environmental exposures and/or physiological processes or disturbances. Risk factors for circumstantial epilepsy include age (epilepsy is most commonly diagnosed in children and elderly adults), male gender, head trauma, stroke, cardiovascular disease, encephalitis (infection of the brain), brain tumors and other cancers, certain metabolic conditions, alcohol and other drugs, and prolonged febrile seizures in childhood. Frankly, any exposure that causes brain damage or interrupts normal brain function should be regarded as a potential risk factor for the development of epileptic seizures.

The risk factors for early onset disease during childhood and late onset disease in the elderly are dramatically different. Young patients develop epilepsy as a consequence of genetic predisposition, trauma, infection, and febrile seizures, whereas elderly patients develop epilepsy secondary to cerebrovascular disease (stroke), metabolic conditions (type 2 diabetes), cancer, other neurodegenerative conditions (Alzheimer's disease), and alcohol abuse and/ or withdrawal. It is also noteworthy that about 30% of first acute seizures among the elderly are *status epilepticus* requiring emergency care. It is emphasized that about 50% of epilepsy cases in children and 30–50% of elderly patients are not classifiable with respect to known causes or risk factors (Hauser and Kurland, 1975; Hauser, Annegers, and Kurland, 1993; Forsgren et al., 1996; Sirven, 1998; Wirrell et al., 2011). Selected studies of the risk factors for epilepsy are discussed in the following paragraphs.

Fetal Alcohol Syndrome and Epilepsy

Investigators at Queens University in Ontario, Canada, examined the association between *fetal alcohol spectrum disorder* and the subsequent development of epilepsy. The investigation identified 425 exposed subjects, 86 with fetal alcohol syndrome, and 339 with alcohol-related neurodevelopmental disorder. Among all 425 subjects, 25 (5.9%) developed confirmed epilepsy, approximately 10 times the prevalence in the general population. Exposure during the first trimester was the predominant pattern of fetal alcohol exposure among the epileptic patients. The investigators suggest the need for future studies to clarify the pathogenic mechanisms that link prenatal alcohol exposure to a reduced seizure threshold (Bell et al., 2010).

Alcohol Abuse and Epilepsy

Samokhvalov and colleagues conducted a systematic review and meta-analysis of published epidemiologic data to characterize the association between alcohol consumption and the risk of developing epilepsy. Their analysis is based upon 18 published studies that quantified the association between alcohol consumption and epilepsy risk. Results reveal a significant dose response in the risk of epilepsy with increasing alcohol consumption (**Figure 42.6**). The data suggest that a threshold level of about 4 alcoholic drinks per day (48 g of pure alcohol) is sufficient to significantly elevate the risk (Samokhvalov et al., 2010).

Various hypotheses have been advanced to explain the link between alcohol abuse and epilepsy risk. These include alcohol toxicity to neurons, hypoxia due to alcohol-related cerebrovascular disease, brain damage due to traumatic injury, and a "*kindling theory.*" The kindling theory suggests that repeated withdrawal from alcohol including natural withdrawal during sleep over many years gradually reduces the epileptogenic threshold (Ballenger and Post, 1978).

Stroke and Epilepsy

Stroke is a major risk factor for the development of epileptic seizures. In an international prospective multicenter study, Bladin and colleagues followed 1,897 consecutive patients with acute stroke to determine

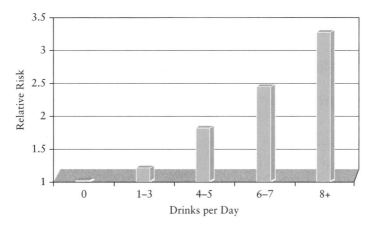

Figure 42.6 Epilepsy Risk and Alcohol Consumption.

Source: Data from Samokhvalov AV, Irving H, Mohapatra S, Rehm J (2010). Alcohol consumption, unprovoked seizures, and epilepsy: a systematic review and meta-analysis. *Epilepsia* 51(7):1177–1184.

the incidence of seizures overall and by type of stroke. They found that 8.6% of 1,632 patients with ischemic stroke had seizures, compared to 10.6% of 265 patients with hemorrhagic stroke. Among patients who suffered an ischemic stroke, 4.8% had seizures within 2 weeks (3.4% within 24 hours); and among patients who suffered hemorrhagic strokes, 7.9% had seizures within 2 weeks (6.0% within 24 hours). Epilepsy was diagnosed in 47 (2.5%) of stroke patients (Bladin et al., 2000). Similar results have been observed in several other studies (Olsen, Hagenhaven, and Thage, 1987; Kilpatrick et al., 1990; So et al., 1996; Reith et al., 1997).

Longer-term studies suggest that the risk of developing epileptic seizures persists for several years following stroke (Awada, Omojola, and Obeid, 1999). In a British prospective study of 675 patients with a first stroke (545 of whom had cerebral infarction), the 5-year actuarial risk of seizure was 11.5% (Burn et al., 1997). In a US study of stroke patients in Olmstead County, Minnesota, the cumulative risk of seizure development was 7.4% at 5 years and 8.9% at 10 years (So et al., 1996). Such population-based studies have found 20–40-fold increases in seizure risk relative to the general population. *Status epilepticus* can also occur following a stroke, involving 31% of stroke patients with seizures in 1 large study. Status epilepticus was the initial seizure type in more than half of these patients (Rumbach et al., 2000).

Type 1 Diabetes Mellitus and Epilepsy

Idiopathic generalized epilepsies, which account for about 30% of all patients with epilepsy, have no apparent cause other than genetic predisposition. Due to a long-term clinical impression that epilepsy and type 1 diabetes are possibly related, investigators in the United Kingdom reviewed the medical histories of 518 patients with confirmed idiopathic generalized epilepsy to quantify their prevalence of type 1 diabetes compared to the general population. Seven cases of type 1 diabetes were identified among the patient cohort which was 4.4 times the number expected. In 6 of the 7 patients, the onset of type 1 diabetes preceded the development of epilepsy. These results suggest there may be an etiologic link between the two conditions, possibly due to precipitation of seizures by hypoglycemic episodes; however, additional studies are needed for confirmation (McCorry et al., 2006).

Type 2 Diabetes and Epilepsy

Patients with type 2 diabetes have been found to be at increased risk for the development of acute epileptic seizures in a number of studies. Investigators in Stockholm, Sweden, conducted a nested case control study of 933 patients 15 years or older with newly diagnosed unprovoked seizures and 6,039 controls matched to the cases by gender, year of diagnosis, and catchment area. Results revealed significant increases in the odds of seizure associated with prior hospitalization for diabetes (OR = 1.9), myocardial infarction (OR = 1.7), cerebral infarction (OR = 9.4), intracerebral hemorrhage (OR = 7.2), subarachnoid hemorrhage (OR = 7.2), and transient ischemic attack (OR = 3.2) (Adelöw et al., 2011).

In patients with type 2 diabetes, the onset of epileptic seizure is often associated with nonketotic hyperglycemia. Several types of epileptic seizures have been reported in patients with nonketotic hyperglycemia, and early recognition and swift correction of the condition by administration of insulin and rehydration are essential to prevent serious morbidity and mortality (Singh, Gupta, and Strobus, 1973; Brick, Gutrecht, and Ringel, 1989; Scherer, 2005).

Glucose Homeostasis and Epilepsy

Acute seizures including status epilepticus have been reported for diabetic patients at both ends of the spectrum of inadequate glucose control: those with *nonketogenic hyperglycemia* and those with *hypoglycemia*. Numerous reports have appeared in the literature describing epileptic seizures in diabetic children and adults associated with hypoglycemia (Malouf and Brust, 1985; Lahat, Barr, and Bistritzer, 1995) and with hyperglycemia (Singh, Gupta, and Strobus, 1973; Askenasy, Streifler, and Carasso, 1977; Sirven, 1998).

Body Mass and Epilepsy

Investigators in the United Kingdom conducted a retrospective cohort study using the data from *The Health Improvement Network* (*THIN*) to examine incidence rates of seizures by different levels of body mass index (BMI). Individuals with BMI of 30 or more were classified as obese. The annual incidence of seizures among obese subjects (34.8 cases per 100,000) was similar to the rate among subjects with normal weight (35.8 cases per 100,000). However, underweight subjects with BMI less than 18.5 and gravidly obese subjects with BMI greater than 40 had elevated seizure rates (RR = 1.6 and 1.8, respectively). These findings suggest that individuals at the extremes of body mass are susceptible to seizure development (Gao, Juhaeri, and Dai, 2008).

Parasitic Infection and Epilepsy

Cysticercosis is a systemic infection caused by the pork tapeworm *Taenia solium*. Humans acquire the parasite by ingesting its eggs in food or water contaminated by feces of infected individuals. Neurocysticercosis is caused by infection of the central nervous system and/or brain by the larval stage of *Taenia solium*. This condition is a major cause of neurologic disease in developing countries of Latin America, South America, Africa, and Asia. Neurocysticercosis is the underlying cause of many seizures in these populations, and is primarily responsible for the higher incidence of epilepsy in developing versus industrialized nations.

Human *toxocariasis* is another parasitic zoonotic infection found primarily in populations of developing nations. Infection is caused by *Toxocara canis*, a common roundworm found in dogs and cats. Humans ingest eggs of the parasite in contaminated food and fomites. The larvae of *Toxocara canis* can migrate into the central nervous system and cause neurologic symptoms including epilepsy.

Nicoletti and colleagues have conducted extensive studies of zoonotic infections and epilepsy throughout the world. In rural Bolivia, they compared serologies of 113 cases with confirmed epilepsy (59 with partial seizures and 54 with generalized seizures) to 233 controls matched by age, gender, and location. Cases and controls were assessed serologically for antibodies against both *T. canis and T. solium*. Results revealed significant increases in the odds of epilepsy among individuals seropositive for *T. solium* (OR = 1.85) and *T. canis* (OR = 2.85). Stronger associations were found for epileptic individuals with late onset partial seizures diagnosed after age 15 years (OR = 3.66 for *T. solium* and OR = 18.2 for *T. canis*). Findings suggest that both neurocysticercosis and toxoceriasis contribute to the high rates of epilepsy in developing countries (Nicoletti et al., 2002).

Additional studies of epileptic patients from the same region of Bolivia using both neuroradiologic and serologic testing confirmed the presence of neurocysticercosis in 27% of cases. The investigators note that cysticercosis and other zoonotic conditions are preventable and treatable. The results therefore suggest that elimination of these parasitic infections could markedly reduce the morbidity and mortality due to epilepsy in endemic areas (Nicoletti et al., 2005).

Onchocerciasis, also known as *river blindness*, is a parasitic infection caused by *Onchocerca volvulus*, a small nematode (roundworm) that is transmitted to humans through the bite of a blackfly of the genus *Simulium*. The larval nematodes spread to many tissues of the body including the retina of the eye and in some cases the brain. The worms carry a symbiotic bacteria, *Wolbachia pipientis*, and when the worms die, *Wobachia* symbionts are released triggering a host immune response that causes intense itching and necrosis of infected tissues. The vast majority of these infections occur in populations living along the riverbanks of sub-Saharan Africa where the blackfly lives, hence the term "*river blindness.*" An estimated 18 million people suffer from onchocerciasis and approximately 270,000 are blind. Onchocerciasis can be effectively treated with two doses of an antiparasitic drug called ivermectin taken 6 months apart every 3 years (World Health Organization, 2010).

Due to the high prevalence of onchocerciasis in regions with high rates of epilepsy and the predilection of this parasite for neural tissues, a number of epidemiologic investigations have been conducted in search of a cause and effect relationship; albeit, the results of these studies have been inconsistent.

A team of investigators conducted a matched case control study 187 cases and 374 controls in three northwestern towns of the Central African Republic. Each case was matched to two controls by gender, age, residence, treatment with ivermectin (an antiparasitic drug), date of last use, and the number of doses. Onchocerciasis infection was assessed by the presence of microfilaria in a skin biopsy. Active infections were detected in 39.6% of cases and 35.8% of controls. The mean dermal parasitic load was 26 microfiliaria per mg of skin in cases and 24 microfiliaria per mg of skin in controls, and the odds of epilepsy due to infection was only marginally elevated (OR = 1.21) (Druet-Cabanac et al., 1991).

Investigators in Cameroon compared 72 patients with epilepsy to 72 controls matched by age, gender, and location. Cases were ascertained from 14 villages in central Cameroon where onchocerciasis is endemic. On average, the microfiliaral load per skin snip was twice as high among cases compared to controls (288 vs. 141), supporting the existence of a link between onchocerciasis infection and the development of epilepsy. The investigators speculate that null results observed in some populations may be due to ivermectin control measures implemented in the past two decades (Boussinesq et al., 2002).

More recently, Druet-Cabanac and colleagues conducted a meta-analysis of available data from epidemiologic studies of onchocerciasis and epilepsy. Nine African studies were included in the analysis. The combined estimate of relative risk barely missed statistical significance (RR = 1.21, p < 0.06), and the investigators suggest that additional research is needed to confirm a causal relationship and clarify the neurological pathogenicity of onchocerciasis (Druet-Cabanac et al., 2004).

Estrogen and Estrogen Replacement Therapy

Catamenial epilepsy is when partial seizures cluster around certain phases of a woman's menstrual cycle. Three major types of catamenial epilepsy have been defined: perimenstrual, periovulatory, and periluteal. In each type, seizure activity is increased by about two-fold during the corresponding time of the menstrual cycle. The perimenstrual type is associated with drastic decreases in serum levels of both estrogen and progesterone, the periovulatory type coincides with a spike in serum estrogren just prior to ovulation, and the periluteal type is associated with abnormally low levels of progesterone throughout the luteal phase of the menstrual cycle. All three types are characterized by heightened serum levels of estrogen relative to progesterone, and most treatment regimens for catamenial epilepsy involve the adminstration of progestins (Herzog, 2008).

Hormone replacement therapy has traditionally been used in menopausal women with epilepsy to alleviate their menopausal symptoms such as hot flashes and vaginal dryness. However, recent studies suggest that hormone therapy may actually increase seizure activity.

Investigators at Cornell University in New York City conducted a small randomized double-blind placebo-controlled clinical trial to evaluate the effects of estrogen and medroxyprogesterone in postmenopausal women with epilepsy. Investigators randomized 21 eligible epileptic patients, ages 42–62 years, to receive either estrogen plus progesterone or placebo. Five of seven women receiving high dose hormone therapy and 4 of 8 women receiving low dose hormone therapy had worsening seizure frequency compared to 1 of 6 women receiving placebo. The investigators concluded there was a dose-related increase in seizure frequency in postmenopausal women who received hormone replacement therapy (Harden et al., 2006).

EPILEPSY: TREATMENT AND PROGNOSIS

The cornerstone of epileptic treatment is administration of anticonvulsant and antipsychotic medications antecedent to seizures or during times of high stress. In the United States, there are more than 20 medications that are approved for the treatment of epilepsy. Recent studies suggest that with early diagnosis and accurate differentiation between generalized and partial seizures coupled with administration of targeted anticonvulsant medications as needed to inhibit seizures and minimize side effects, the majority of patients with idiopathic or cryptogenic disease are able to achieve sustained freedom from seizure activity.

In patients with symptomatic epilepsy (with known etiology), effective treatment involves not only the management of seizure activity but also intervention to address the underlying pathology.

Investigators at the Mayo Clinic compared long-term outcomes in children with newly diagnosed epilepsy identified in Olmstead County, Minnesota, during 1980–2004. Among 359 cases, 215 (60%) had nonidiopathic focal epilepsy and of these, 206 were followed to determine recurrent seizure activity over time. Cases were classified as having symptomatic epilepsy if their disease had a known structural or metabolic etiology and cryptogenic if not. Ninety-five cases were classified as cryptogenic and 111 as symptomatic. Median follow-up exceeded 11 years in both groups. Long-term outcome was significantly better among cases with cryptogenic epilepsy than those with symptomatic epilepsy. At last follow-up, only 7% of patients with cryptogenic epilepsy were experiencing intractable seizures compared to 40% of patients with symptomatic epilepsy, and of those achieving freedom from seizure activity, 68% of the cryptogenic group were off antiepileptic medications compared to 46% of the symptomatic group. Furthermore, approximately one-third of children with cryptogenic epilepsy experienced no further seizures after the initiation of treatment. The investigators concluded that more than half of nonidiopathic epilepsy is cryptogenic (without an identifiable cause) and children with this epileptic subtype have an excellent long-term prognosis (Wirrell et al., 2010),

Early epilepsy diagnosis and intervention has also proven successful in rural communities. Investigators at the Beijing Neurosurgical Institute conducted a community-based intervention study to evaluate the efficacy of monotherapy with phenobarbital in patients diagnosed with convulsive epilepsy in primary healthcare clinics in eight rural counties of China. Local physicians who completed a specialized training course carried out the screening, treatment, and follow-up. The study enrolled 2,455 patients. In 68% of patients who completed 12 months of treatment, seizure frequency was decreased by at least 50%, and a third of patients became seizure-free. Furthermore, 72% of patients who completed 24 months' treatment had at least 50% reduction in seizure frequency and a quarter of patients remained seizure-free. The study confirms the value of intervention and monotherapy in treating patients with convulsive epilepsy in rural populations (Wang et al., 2006).

• • • REFERENCES

Adelöw, C., Andersson, T., Ahlbom, A., & Tomson, T. (2011). Prior hospitalization for stroke, diabetes, myocardial infarction, and subsequent risk of unprovoked seizures. *Epilepsia, 52*(2), 301–307.

Askenasy, J.J., Streifler, M., & Carasso, R. (1977). Moderate nonketotic hyperglycemia—a cause of focal epilepsy: Report of two cases and review of literature. *Eur Neurol, 16*, 51–61.

Awada, A.M., Omojola, M.F., & Obeid, T. (1999). Late epileptic seizures after cerebral infarction. *Acta Neurol Scand, 99*, 265–268.

Bali, B., Kull, L.L., Strug, L.J., Clarke, T., Murphy, P.L., Akman, C.I.,...Pal, D.K. (2007). Autosomal dominant inheritance of centrotemporal sharp waves in rolandic epilepsy families. *Epilepsia, 48*(12), 2266–2272.

Ballenger, J.C., & Post, R.M. (1978). Kindling as a model for alcohol withdrawal syndromes. *Br J Psychiatry, 133*, 1–14.

Bell, S.H., Stade, B., Reynolds, J.N., Rasmussen, C., Anderew, G., Hwang, P.A., & Carlen, P.L. (2010). The remarkably high prevalence of epilepsy and seizure history in fetal alcohol spectrum disorders. *Alcohol Clin Exp Res, 34*(6), 1084–1089.

Berg, A.T. (1992). Febrile seizures and epilepsy: The contributions of epidemiology. *Paediatr Perinat Epidemiol, 6*(2), 145–152.

Berg, A.T., Shinnar, S., Darefsky, A.S., Holford, T.R., Shapiro, E.D., Salomon, M.E.,...Hauser, A.W. (1997). Predictors of recurrent febrile seizures: A prospective cohort study. *Arch Pediatr Adolesc Med, 151*(4), 371–378.

Berkovic, S.F., & Scheffer, I.E. (1997). Epilepsies with single gene inheritance. *Brain Dev, 19*, 13–18.

Bharucha, N.E. (2003). Epidemiology of epilepsy in India. *Epilepsia, 44*, 9–11.

Bladin, C.F., Alexandrov, A.V., Bellavance, A., Bornsetin, N., Chambers, B., Coté, R.,...Norris, J.W. for the Seizures After Stroke Study. (2000). Seizures after stroke: A prospective multicenter study. *Arch Neurol, 57*, 1617–1622.

Boussinesq, M., Pion, S.D.S., & Demanqa-Nqanque, & Kamqno, J. (2002). Relationship between onchocerciasis and epilepsy: A matched case-control study in the Mbam Valley, Republic of Cameroon. *Transactions of the Royal Society of Tropical Medicine and Hygiene, 96*(5), 537–541.

Brick, J., Gutrecht, J., & Ringel, R. (1989). Reflex epilepsy and non-ketotic hyperglycemia in the elderly: A specific neuroendocrine syndrome. *Neurology, 39*, 394–349.

Burn, J., Dennis, M., Bamford, J., Sandercock, P., Wade, D., & Warlow, C. (1997). Epileptic seizures after a first stroke: The Oxfordshire Community Stroke Project. *BMJ, 315*, 1582–1587.

Chen, Y., Lu, J., Pan, H., Zhang, Y., Wu, H., Xu, K.,...Wu, X. (2003). Association between genetic variation of *CACNA1H* and childhood absence epilepsy. *Ann Neurol, 54*, 239–243.

Clarke, M., Gill, J., Noronha, M., & McKinlay, I. (1987). Early infantile epileptic encephalopathy with suppression burst: Ohtahara syndrome. *Dev Med Child Neurol, 29*, 520–528.

Commission on Classification and Terminology of the International League Against Epilepsy. (1989). Proposal for revised classification of epilepsies and epileptic syndromes. *Epilepsia, 30*, 389–399.

Commission on Epilepsy and Prognosis, International League Against Epilepsy. (1993). Guidelines for epidemiologic studies on epilepsy. *Epilepsia, 34*, 592–596.

Corey, L.A., Pellock, J.M., Boggs, J.G., Miller, L.L., & DeLorenzo, R.J. (1998). Evidence for a genetic predisposition for status epilepticus. *Neurology, 50*(2), 558–560.

Corey, L.A., Pellock, J.M., & DeLorenzo, R.J. (2004). Status epilepticus in a population-based Virginia twin sample. *Epilepsia, 45*(2), 159–165.

Cowan, L.D., & Hudson, L.S. (1991). The epidemiology and natural history of infantile spasms. *J Child Neurol, 6*, 355–364.

DeLorenzo, R.J., Pelloch, M., Towne, A.R., & Boggs, J.G. (1995). Epidemiology of status epilepticus. *J Clin Neurophysiol, 12*, 316–325.

Depieene, C., Trouillard, O., Saint-Martin, C., Gourfinkel-An, I., Bouteiller, D., Carpentier,

W.,...LeGuern, E. (2009). Spectrum of *SCN1A* gene mutations associated with Dravet syndrome: Analysis of 333 patients. *J Med Genet, 46,* 183–191.

Ding, D., Wang, W., Wu, J., Ma, G., Dai, Z., Yang, B.,...Sander, J.W. (2006). Premature mortality in people with epilepsy in rural China: A prospective study. *Lancet Neurol, 5,* 823–827.

Druet-Cabanac, M., Preux, P.M., Bouteille, B., Bernet-Bernady, P., Dunand, J., Hopkins, A.,...Dumas, M. (1991). Onchocerciasis and epilepsy: A matched case-control study in the Central African Republic. *Am J Epidemiol, 149,* 565–570.

Druet-Cabanac, M., Boussinesq, M., Dongmo, L., Farnarier, G., Bouteille, B., & Preux, P.M. (2004). Review of epidemiological studies searching for a relationship between onchocerciasis and epilepsy. *Neuroepidemiology, 23*(3), 144–149.

Elmslie, F.V., Rees, M., Williamson, M.P., Kerr, M., Kjeldsen, M.J., Pang, K.A.,...Gardiner, R.M. (1997). Genetic Mapping of a major susceptibility locus for juvenile myoclonic epilepsy on chromosome 15q. *Hum Mol Genet, 6*(8), 1329–1334.

Feucht, M., Fuchs, K., Pichlbauer, E., Hornik, K., Scharfetter, J., Goessler, R.,...Aschauer, H. (1999). Possible association between childhood absence epilepsy and the gene encoding GABRB3. *Biological Psychiatry, 46*(7), 997–1002.

Fong, G.C.Y., Mak, W., Cheng, T.S., et al. (2003). A prevalence study of epilepsy in Hong Kong. *Hong Kong Med J, 9,* 252–257.

Forsgren, L., Bucht, G., Eriksson, S., & Bergmark, L. (1996). Incidence and clinical characterization of unprovoked seizures in adults: A prospective population-based study. *Epilepsia, 37,* 224–229.

Forsgren, L., Hauser, W.A., Olafsson, E., Sander, J.W., Sillanpää, M., & Tomson, T. (2005). Mortality of epilepsy in developed countries: A review. *Epilepsia, 46*(Suppl 11), 18–27.

Fotheringham, J., Donati, D., Akhyani, N., Fogdell-Hahn, A., Vortmeyer, A., Heiss, J.D.,...Jacobson, S. (2007). Association of human herpesvirus-6B with mesial temporal lobe epilepsy. *PLoS Med, 4*(5), e180.

Gao, S., Juhaeri, J., & Dai, W.S. (2008). The incidence rate of seizures in relation to BMI in UK adults. *Obesity, 16*(9), 2126–2132.

Gastaut, H. (1982). A new type of epilepsy: Benign partial epilepsy of childhood with occipital spike-waves. *Clin Electroencephalogr, 13,* 13–22.

Harden, C.L., Herzog, A.G., Nikolov, B.G., Koppel, B.S., Christos, P.J., Fowler, K.,...Hauser, W.A. (2006). Hormone replacement therapy in women with epilepsy: A randomized, double-blind, placebo-controlled study. *Epilepsia, 47*(9), 1447–1451.

Hauser, W.A., & Kurland, L.T. (1975). The epidemiology of epilepsy in Rochester, Minnesota, 1935 through 1967. Epilepsia, *16,* 1–66.

Hauser, W.A., Annegers, J.F., & Kurland, L.T. (1993). Incidence of epilepsy and unprovoked seizures in Rochester, Minnesota: 1935–1984. *Epilepsia, 34,* 453–468.

Herzog, A.G. (2008). Catamenial epilepsy: Definition, prevalence, pathophysiology and treatment. *Seizure, 17*(2), 151–159.

Huang, M., Hong, Z., Zeng, J., et al. (2002). The prevalence of epilepsy in rural Jinshan in Shanghai. *Zhonghua Liu Xing Bing Xue Za Zhi, 23,* 345–346.

Jallon, P. (2002). Epilepsy and epileptic disorders, an epidemiological marker? Contribution of descriptive epidemiology. *Epileptic Disord, 4,* 1–13.

Janz, E. (2000). Epilepsy with grand mal on awakening and sleep-waking cycle. *Clinical Neurophysiology, 111*(Supplement 2), S103–S110.

Joensuu, T., Lehesjoki, A.E., & Kopra, O. (2008). Molecular background of EPM1-Unverricht-Lundborg disease. *Epilepsia, 49,* 557–563.

Kalviainen, R., Khyuppenen, J., Koskenkorva, P., Eriksson, K., Vanninen, R., & Mervaala, E.

(2008). Clinical picture of EPM1-Unverricht-Lundborg disease. *Epilepsia*, 49, 549–556.

Kamgno, J., Pion, S.D.S., & Boussinesq, M. (2003). Demographic impact of epilepsy in Africa: Result of a 10 year cohort study in a rural area of Cameroon. *Epilepsia*, 44, 956–963.

Kilpatrick, C.J., Davis, S.M., Tress, B.M., Rossiter, S.C., Hopper, J.L., & Vandendriesen, M.L. (1990). Epileptic seizures in acute stroke. *Arch Neurol*, 47(2), 157–160.

Kotsopoulos, I.A.W., Van Merode, T., Kessels, F.G.H., De Krom, M.C.T.F.M., & Knottnerus, J.A. (2002). Systematic review and meta-analysis of incidence studies of epilepsy and unprovoked seizures. *Epilepsia*, 43(11), 1402–1409.

Kuzniecky, R., & Rosenblatt, B. (1987). Benign occipital epilepsy: A family study. *Epilepsia*, 28(4), 346–350.

Lahat, E., Barr, J., & Bistritzer, T. (1995). Focal epileptic episodes associated with hypoglycemia in children with diabetes. *Clin Neurol Neurosurg*, 97(4), 314–316.

Lee, W.L. (1989). Long-term outcome of children with febrile seizures. *Ann Acad Med Singapore*, 18(1), 32–34.

Li, S.C., Schoenberg, B.S., Wang, C.C., et al. (1985). Epidemiology of epilepsy in urban areas of the People's Republic of China. *Epilepsia*, 26, 391–394.

Mac, T.L., Tran, D.S., Quet, F., Odermatt, P., Preux, P.M., & Tan, C.T. (2007). Epidemiology, aetiology, and clinical management of epilepsy in Asia: A systematic review. *The Lancet Neurology*, 6, 533–543.

Malouf, R., & Brust, J.C.M. (1985). Hypoglycemia: Causes, neurologic manifestations, and outcomes. *Ann Neurol*, 17, 421–430.

Mani, K.S., Rangan, G., Srinivas, H.V., et al. (1998). The Yelandur study: A community-based approach to epilepsy in rural South India: Epidemiological aspects. *Seizure*, 7, 281–288.

Mannan, M.A. (2004). Epilepsy in Bangladesh. *Neurol Asia*, 9, 18.

McCorry, D., Nicolson, A., Smith, D., Marson, A., Feltbower, R.G., & Chadwick, D.W. (2006). An association between type 1 diabetes and idiopathic generalized epilepsy. *Ann Neurol*, 59(1), 204–206.

Meyer, A.C., Dua, T., Ma, J., Saxena, S., & Birbeck, G. (2010). Global disparities in the epilepsy treatment gap: A systematic review. *Bulletin of the World Health Organization*, 88, 260–266.

Neubauer, B.A., Fiedler, B., Himmelein, B., Kämpfer, F., Lässker, U., Schwabe, G.,… Stephani, U. (1998). Centrotemporal spikes in families with rolandic epilepsy: Linkage to chromosome 15q14. *Neurology*, 51(6), 1608–1612.

Nicoletti, A., Bartoloni, A., Reggio, A., Bartalesi, F., Roselli, M., Sofia, V.,…Hall, A.J. (2002). Epilepsy, cysticercosis, and toxocariasis: A population-based case-control study in rural Bolivia. *Neurology*, 58, 1256–1261.

Nicoletti, A., Bartoloni, A., Sofia, V., Bartalesi, F., Rosdao Chavez, J., Osinaga, R.,…Hall, A.J. (2005). Epilepsy and neurocysticercosis in rural Bolivia: A population-based survey. *Epilepsia*, 46(7), 1127–1132.

Nicoletti, A., Sofia, V., Vitale, G., Bonelli, S.I., Bejarano, V., Bartalesi, F.,…Bartoloni, A. (2009). Natural history and mortality of chronic epilepsy in an untreated population of rural Bolivia: A follow-up after 10 years. *Epilepsia*, 50(10), 2199–2206.

Offringa, M., Bossuyt, P.M., Lubsen, J., Ellenberg, J.H., Nelson, K.B., Knudsen, F.U.,…Larsen, S. (1994). Risk factors for seizure recurrence in children with febrile seizures: A pooled analysis of individual patient data from five studies. *J Pediatr*, 124(4), 574–584.

Olsen, T.S., Hagenhaven, H., & Thage, O. (1987). Epilepsy after stroke. *Neurology*, 37, 1209–1212.

Panayiotopoulos, C.P. (2007). The birth and evolution of the concept of Panayiotopoulos syndrome. *Epilepsia*, 48, 1041–1034.

Panayiotopoulos, C.P., Michael, M., Sanders, S., Valeta, T., & Koutroumanidis, M. (2008). Benign childhood focal epilepsies: Assessment of established and newly recognized syndromes. *Brain, 131*(Pt 9), 2264–2286.

Pavlidou, E., Tzitiridou, M., Kontopoulos, E., & Panteliadis, C.P. (2008). Which factors determine febrile seizure recurrence? A prospective study. *Brain Dev, 30*(1), 7–13.

Phillips, H.A., Scheffer, L.E., Crossland, K.M., Bhatia, K.P., Fish, D.R., Marsden, C.D.,... Mulley, J.C. (1998). Autosomal dominant nocturnal frontal-lobe epilepsy: Genetic heterogeneity and evidence for a second Locus at 15q24. *The American Journal of Human Genetics, 63*(4), 1108–1116.

Pompili, M., Girardi, P., Ruberto, A., & Tatarelli, R. (2005). Suicide in the epilepsies: A meta-analytic investigation of 29 cohorts. *Epilepsy Behav, 7*(2), 305–310.

Ray, B.K., Bhattacharya, S., Kundu, T.N., et al. (2002). Epidemiology of epilepsy-Indian perspective. *J Indian Med Assoc, 100*, 322–326.

Reith, J., Jorgensen, H.S., Nakayama, H., Raaschou, H.O., & Olsen, T.S. (1997). Seizures in acute stroke: Predictors and prognostic significance. The Copenhagen Stroke Study. *Stroke, 28*, 1585–1589.

Rumbach, L., Sablot, D., Berger, E., Tatu, L., Vuiller, F., & Moulin, T. (2000). Status epilepticus in stroke: Report on a hospital-based cohort. *Neurology, 54*, 350–354.

Samokhvalov, A.V., Irving, H., Mohapatra, S., & Rehm, J. (2010). Alcohol consumption, unprovoked seizures, and epilepsy: A systematic review and meta-analysis. *Epilepsia, 51*(7), 1177–1184.

Sander, J.W., & Shovron, S.D. (1996). Epidemiology of the epilepsies. *J Neurol Neurosurg Psychiatry, 61*(5), 433–443.

Sander, T., Hildmann, T., Kretz, R., Fürst, R., Sailer, U., Bauer, G.,...Janz, D. (1997a). Allelic association of juvenile absence epilepsy with a GluR5 kainate receptor gene (*GRIK1*) polymorphism. *Amer J Med Gen, 74*(4), 416–421.

Sander, T., Bockenkamp, B., Hildmann, T., Blasczyk, R., Kretz, R., Wienker, T.F.,...Ziegler, A. (1997b). Refined mapping of the epilepsy susceptibility locus EJM 1 on chromosome 6. *Neurology, 49*, 842–847.

Sawhney, I.M., Singh, A., Kaur, P., et al. (1999). A case control study and one year follow-up of registered epilepsy cases in a resettlement colony of North India, a developing tropical country. *J Neurol Sci, 165*, 31–35.

Schauwecker, P.E. (2009). The genetics of status epilepticus. *Epilepsia, 50*(Suppl 12), 22–24.

Scherer, C. (2005). Seizures and non-ketotic hyperglycemia. *Presse Med, 34*(15), 1084–1086.

Schmitz, B., Gardiner, R.M., Janz, D., & Beck-Mannagetta, G. (1997). Linkage analysis between idiopathic generalized epilepsies and the GABA a receptor α5, β3 and γ3 subunit gene cluster on chromosome 15. *Acta Neurol Scand, 96*, 1–7.

Scott, R.A., Lhatoo, S.D., & Sander, J.W. (2001). The treatment of epilepsy in developing countries: Where do we go from here? *Bull World Health Organ, 79*, 344–351.

Sillanpää, M., & Shinnar, S. (2010). Long-term mortality in childhood-onset epilepsy. *N Engl J Med, 363*, 2522–2529.

Singh, B.M., Gupta, D.R., & Strobus, R.J. (1973). Nonketotic hyperglycemia and Epilepsia, partialis continua. *Arch Neurol, 29*, 1887–1900.

Singhal, B.S. (1998). Neurology in developing countries: A population perspective. *Arch Neurol, 55*, 1019–1021.

Sirven, J.I. (1998). Epilepsy in older adults: Causes, consequences and treatment. *J American Geriatrics Society, 46*, 1291–1301.

So, E.L., Annegers, J.F., Hauser, W.A., O'Brien, P.C., & Whisnant, J.P. (1996). Population-based study of seizure disorders after cerebral infarction. *Neurology, 42*, 350–355.

Sridharan, R., & Murthy, B.M. (1999). Prevalence and pattern of epilepsy in India. *Epilepsia, 40*, 631–636.

Steinlein, O.K., Mulley, J.C., Propping, P., Wallace, R.H., Phillips, H.A., Sutherland, G.R.,…Berkovic, S.F. (1995). A missense mutation in the neuronal nicotinic acetylcholine receptor α4 subunit is associated with autosomal dominant nocturnal frontal lobe epilepsy. *Nat Genet, 11*, 201–203.

Takahashi, Y., Mori, H., Mishina, M., Watanabe, M., Kondo, N., Shimomur, J.,…Fujiwar, T. (2005). Autoantibodies and cell-mediated autoimmunity to NMDA-type GluRepsilon2 in patients with Rasmussen's encephalitis and chronic progressive Epilepsia, partialis continua. *Epilepsia, 46*(Suppl 5), 152–158.

Taylor, I., Berkovic, S.F., Kivity, S., & Scheffer, I.E. (2008). Benign occipital epilepsies of childhood: Clinical features and genetics. *Brain, 131*(9), 2287–2294.

Tekle-Haimanot, R., Forsgren, L., Abebe, M., Gebre-Mariam, A., Heijbel, J., Holmgren, G., & Ekstedt, J. (1990). Clinical and electroencephalographic characteristics of epilepsy in rural Ethiopia: A community-based study. *Epilepsy Research, 7*(3), 230–239.

Tran, D.S., Odermatt, P., Le, T.O., Huc, P., Druet-Cabanac, M., Barennes, H.,…Preux, P.M. (2006). Prevalence of epilepsy in a rural district of central Lao PDR. *Neuroepidemiology, 26*, 199–206.

Trevathan, E., Murphy, C.C., & Yeargin-Allsopp, M. (1997). Prevalence and descriptive epidemiology of Lennox-Gastaut syndrome among Atlanta children. *Epilepsia, 38*(2), 1283–1288.

Turk, V., & Bode, W. (1991). The cystatins: protein inhibitors of cysteine proteinases. *FEBS Lett, 285*(2), 213–219.

Vestergaard, M., Pedersen, C.B., Sidenius, P., Olsen, J., & Christensen, J. (2007). The long-term risk of epilepsy after febrile seizures in susceptible subgroups. *Am J Epidemiol, 165*(8), 911–918.

Wang, W.Z., Wu, J.Z., Wang, D.S., Dai, X.Y., Yang, B., Wang, T.P.,…Sander, J.W. (2003). The prevalence and treatment gap in epilepsy in China: An ILAE/IBE/WHO study. *Neurology, 60*, 1544–1545.

Wang, W.Z., Wu, J.Z., Ma, G.Y., Dai, X.Y., Yang, B., Wang, T.P.,…Sander, J.W. (2006). Efficacy assessment of phenobarbital in epilepsy: A large community-based intervention trial in rural China. *Lancet Neurol, 5*, 6–52.

Wirrell, E.C., Grossardt, B.R., Wong-Kisiel, L.C., & Nickels, K.C. (2011). Incidence and classification of new-onset epilepsy and epilepsy syndromes in children in Olmsted County, Minnesota from 1980 to 2004: A population-based study. *Epilepsy Res*, Apr 7 [Epub ahead of print].

Wirrell, E.C., Grossardt, B.R., So, E.L., & Nickels, K.C. (2010). A population-based study of long-term outcomes of cryptogenic focal epilepsy in childhood: Cryptogenic epilepsy is probably not symptomatic epilepsy. *Epilepsia, 52*(4), 738–745.

World Health Organization. (2001). *Epilepsy: Epidemiology, aetiology and prognosis.* WHO Factsheet, 2001, 165. World Health Organization.

World Health Organization. (2010). *Water-related diseases: Onchocerciasis.* World Health Organization.

43

Epidemiology of Multiple Sclerosis

Zachary M. Harris & Randall E. Harris

INTRODUCTION

Multiple sclerosis is an autoimmune inflammatory disease in which the myelin sheaths surrounding the axons of neurons (nerve cells) are damaged or destroyed, leading to demyelination and scarring as well as a broad spectrum of signs and symptoms. The name *multiple sclerosis* refers to scars (scleroses), particularly in the white matter of the brain and spinal cord. Disease onset usually occurs in young adults between the ages of 20–40 years. Multiple sclerosis is diagnosed roughly twice as often in women compared to men (Weinshenker, 1994).

Multiple sclerosis compromises the communication of neurons in the central nervous system. Neurons communicate with one another by transmitting electrical impulses (action potentials) down their long filamentous tentacles (axons) to the synapses (junctions between neurons). Axons are wrapped in myelin that provide essential insulation to facilitate the rapid directed electrical transmission of nerve impulses (**Figure 43.1**). Myelin is a lipoprotein that

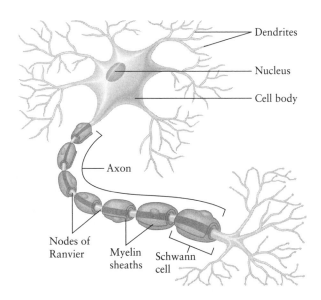

Figure 43.1 Nerve Axion and Myelin Sheath.

is synthesized by *glia*, cells that support and nurture neurons. In multiple sclerosis, the body's own immune system attacks and damages myelin and/or glial cells. When myelin is lost, the axons can no longer effectively conduct nerve impulses.

DISCOVERY OF MULTIPLE SCLEROSIS

The French neurologist, Jean-Martin Charcot, first recognized multiple sclerosis as a distinct disease in 1868. Charcot named the condition *sclerose en plaques* and characterized its diagnosis by the neurologic triad of nystagmus (oscillating eye movements), intention tremor, and scanning (staccato) speech (Charcot, 1868). Earlier in 1838, Robert Carswell and Jean Cruveilhier had published detailed descriptions and drawings of pathologic lesions in brain and spinal cord specimens from patients who had died from the disease (Compston, 1988).

Sydney Allison spearheaded the use of population-based studies of multiple sclerosis and other neurologic conditions in the early 20th century. His early studies of the populations in Wales and Northern Ireland characterized salient clinical and epidemiologic features of the disease including its onset during early adult life, an excess in females, occasional familial clustering, and the progressive, often episodic, nature of disability and decline in most patients resulting in shortened life expectancy (Allison, 1931; Allison and Millar, 1954).

DIAGNOSIS OF MULTIPLE SCLEROSIS

Since almost any neurological symptom can appear in patients with multiple sclerosis, other conditions must be ruled out in reaching the diagnosis. Despite sophisticated diagnostic tools and techniques, the diagnosis of multiple sclerosis remains one of exclusion, meaning that other likely diseases must be eliminated before a conclusive diagnosis of multiple sclerosis can be made.

An international panel of experts has recently developed a system to clarify the diagnosis of multiple sclerosis that makes use of neurological imaging (magnetic resonance imaging [MRI]), analysis of cerebral spinal fluid for IgG antibodies, and testing for visual evoked action potentials. According to this system, confirmation of multiple sclerosis is based upon the number of attacks of neurological symptoms characteristic of multiple sclerosis combined with the number and location of lesions identified (McDonald et al., 2001; Polman et al., 2005).

COURSE OF MULTIPLE SCLEROSIS

Multiple sclerosis is a complex debilitating condition with high morbidity and mortality. Often, the disease follows a biphasic course where a relapsing-remitting stage is followed by a more severe progressive stage. Relapsing-remitting multiple sclerosis is characterized by transient episodes of dysfunction caused by inflammation of the nervous system with rapid recovery. Onset of these attacks can include paresthesia (numbness), diplopia (double vision), scotoma (visual anomalies), sensory and motor disorders of limbs, and cerebellar incoordination (lack of balance). After a variable amount of time (months to years), the relapsing-remitting stage of multiple sclerosis may advance to an episodic downhill course of progressively worse symptoms culminated by blindness due to retrobulbar neuritis, ataxia, incontinence, paraplegia, major system failure, and death. This so-called secondary progressive type is untreatable and the main cause of permanent disability in the multiple sclerosis patient population. Patients presenting with relapsing-remitting multiple sclerosis may never advance to the progressive stage of the disease. On the other hand, many patients who have no previous history of transient neurologic attacks present with progressive multiple sclerosis and are said to have primary progressive multiple sclerosis. Intellectual deterioration is not a common feature of relapsing-remitting multiple sclerosis, although cognitive impairment can be seen in progressive multiple sclerosis. There is no cure for multiple sclerosis and despite intensive efforts, the average life expectancy is reduced by about 10 years compared to the general population.

GLOBAL BURDEN OF MULTIPLE SCLEROSIS

The World Health Organization recently launched a major collaborative initiative to determine the global epidemiology of multiple sclerosis and characterize the resources needed to diagnose, inform, treat, rehabilitate, and provide services to people who develop the disease. As a part of this effort, 112 countries representing 87.8% of the world population were surveyed during 2005–2007 in order to gather epidemiologic data on the incidence, prevalence, morbidity, and mortality of multiple sclerosis. The survey detected more than 1.3 million people with multiple sclerosis, 630,000 in Europe, 520,000 in the Americas, 66,000 in the Eastern Mediterranean, 56,000 in the Western Pacific, 31,500 in Southeast Asia, and 11,000 in

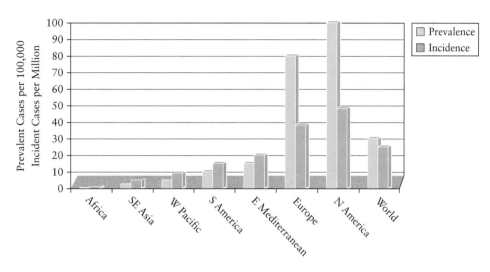

Figure 43.2 Prevalence and Incidence of Multiple Sclerosis by Region, 2008.

Source: Data from World Health Organization (2008). Atlas Multiple Sclerosis Resources in the World, 2008. Geneva, Switzerland.

Africa. It is noted that these figures underestimate the total worldwide burden of multiple sclerosis since no data were available for some countries with huge populations such as the Russian Federation (World Health Organization, 2008).

GLOBAL PREVALENCE AND INCIDENCE OF MULTIPLE SCLEROSIS

Globally, the annual prevalence of multiple sclerosis was found to be extraordinarily variable, ranging from less than 1 case per 100,000 in Africa to 176 cases per 100,000 in Hungary. The median prevalence was 30 per 100,000. Rates exceeded 100 cases per

100,000 in North America (United States, Canada) and several European countries (Hungary, Germany, Czech Republic, Norway, Denmark, Poland), whereas far lower rates (less than 10 cases per 100,000) were reported by most countries in Africa, Southeast Asia, the Western Pacific, and South America (**Figure 43.2**). By income category, prevalence rates were substantially higher in high income countries than low income countries (**Figure 43.3**).

Annual incidence rates are also shown in **Figure 43.2** and **Figure 43.3**. These rates are markedly lower than the prevalence rates and are given as *cases per million*. The median annual incidence among all reporting countries was 25 cases per million with a range from less than 1 in Africa to 290 cases per

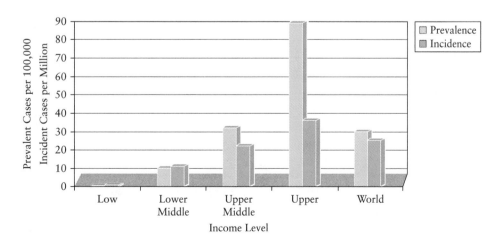

Figure 43.3 Prevalence and Incidence of Multiple Sclerosis by Income, 2008.

Source: Data from World Health Organization (2008). Atlas Multiple Sclerosis Resources in the World, 2008. Geneva, Switzerland.

million in the small Eastern Mediterranean nation of Croatia. The global pattern of incidence is similar to the prevalence; high rates are found in high income developed countries and low rates in low income developing countries.

It is likely that these prevalence and incidence patterns largely reflect the enhanced diagnostic and reporting capabilities of developed nations with higher standards of living and more extensive healthcare systems. Nevertheless, the WHO survey results confirm that multiple sclerosis is a "global disease" that occurs in all populations. Accurate quantification of the burden of multiple sclerosis in less developed countries is expected to improve as diagnostic facilities such as MRI become more widely available and accessible (World Health Organization, 2008).

DEMOGRAPHY OF MULTIPLE SCLEROSIS

Despite the wide international variability in the prevalence and incidence rates, certain epidemiologic features of multiple sclerosis have been found to be relatively invariant. In the recent WHO survey of multiple sclerosis, 60–70% of cases were diagnosed prior to age 40 years and the mean age of onset was around 29 years for all regions and income groups in both men and women. Furthermore, there was a consistent 2 to 1 female to male ratio of both the incidence and prevalence of multiple sclerosis, irrespective of income level. The pattern of age-specific incidence depicted in **Figure 43.4** reflects the excess female risk at all ages (World Health Organization, 2008).

CASE FATALITY AND LIFE EXPECTANCY

Several studies have reported that patients with multiple sclerosis have reduced life expectancy and higher mortality than individuals from the general population. However, there is considerable variability among studies and a wide range of reported median survival times.

Sadovnick and colleagues examined the case fatality rate and life expectancy of patients with multiple sclerosis in a large cohort of patients followed in Vancouver, Canada. The case fatality among patients with severe disability was four times higher than controls without disease. In contrast, excluding deaths by suicide, case fatality among patients with mild to moderate disability was 1.6 times higher than controls matched by age and gender. Life tables constructed for the patient cohort indicated that the overall life expectancy of multiple sclerosis is approximately 7 years less than the general population (Sadovnick et al., 1992).

Grytten and colleagues examined survival and cause of death among 878 patients diagnosed with multiple sclerosis and living in Hordaland County, Norway. Survival and mortality data for the patient cohort were compared with the general Norway population matched by age, gender, and calendar year. During more than 50 years of follow-up, 198 patients died. The median survival from onset was 41 years for patients with multiple sclerosis versus 49 years in the general population, and the overall mortality among patients was 2.7 times higher than expected. Median survival was greater in women than men (43 years vs. 36 years) and greater for younger patients with onset less than 30 years of age

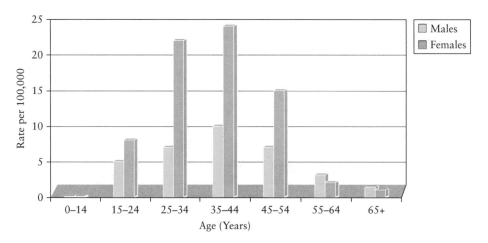

Figure 43.4 Annual Age-Specific Incidence of Multiple Sclerosis.

Source: Data from World Health Organization (2008). Atlas Multiple Sclerosis Resources in the World, 2008. Geneva, Switzerland.

versus older patients with onset after 50 years of age (45 years vs. 23 years). Nevertheless, the standard mortality ratio (SMR) was highest among patients with early onset (SMR = 5.4 for onset before age 20 years) and declined with later onset (SMR = 1.2 for onset after age 60 years). Patients with primary progressive disease had 1.6 times higher overall mortality than those with relapsing-remitting disease. Among the 198 decedents, 144 (73%) had multiple sclerosis listed on their death certificates and 113 (57%) had multiple sclerosis listed as the primary cause of death. Other notable causes of death included cardiovascular disease (16%), infectious disease (9%), cancer (6%), and accident or suicide (3%) (Grytten et al., 2008).

Similar findings were reported for a cohort of 386 patients with multiple sclerosis living in Oslo, Norway. Patients were diagnosed between 1940–1980 and followed until 2006. A total of 263 patients (68%) died during follow-up. Median survival from the time of onset was 35 years, which was approximately 11 years less than expected in the general population. The crude annual mortality rate was 21.6 per 1,000 person-years and the all-cause standard mortality ratio was 2.5. The most frequent underlying cause of death recorded on death certificates was multiple sclerosis (50%). Other leading causes of death were cardiovascular disease (14%), cancer (10%), infection (10%), and accident or suicide (5%). The investigators also noted that excess mortality first appeared during the second decade after disease onset in this patient cohort (Smestad, Sandvik, and Celius, 2009).

SUICIDE IN MULTIPLE SCLEROSIS

Several studies have found that the risk of suicide is elevated in patients with multiple sclerosis. In a nationwide investigation in Denmark, 53 of 5,525 patients committed suicide within the period 1953–1985. These data yielded a cumulative lifetime risk of 1.95% and a standard mortality ratio of 1.83. The suicide risk was 50% higher among males than females and was highest within the first 5 years after diagnosis (Stenager et al., 1992). Similar results have been reported for other cohorts of patients with multiple sclerosis (Fredrikson et al., 2003; Bronnum-Hansen et al, 2005).

GLOBAL MORTALITY: MULTIPLE SCLEROSIS

According to the underlying cause of death listed on death certificates, only a small fraction of patients with multiple sclerosis die every year, perhaps 2–3%

on average. Thus, the annual mortality rate due to multiple sclerosis in the world population is relatively low (~3 deaths per million). According to data reported by member nations of the World Health Organization, multiple sclerosis accounted for less than 20,000 deaths in 2004. Nevertheless, as the disease progresses, disability also increases as does the *disability adjusted life years* (the sum of years lost due to premature death and years lost due to disability).

Disability Adjusted Life Years: Multiple Sclerosis

The global distribution of *disability adjusted life years* (*DALY*) lost due to multiple sclerosis is depicted for WHO member nations in **Figure 43.5**. As with the patterns of prevalence and incidence (**Figure 43.2** and **Figure 43.3**), the DALY are higher in developed nations with more advanced diagnostic, treatment, and reporting capabilities.

AUTOIMMUNITY AND MULTIPLE SCLEROSIS

Multiple sclerosis is generally characterized as a cell-mediated autoimmune disease of the central nervous system. This concept is supported by its higher frequency in females compared to males (which is similar to many other autoimmune disorders such as *systemic lupus erythematosis* and *rheumatoid arthritis*); its association with other autoimmune conditions in individual patients and amongst relatives of index cases; the presence of autoantibodies to myelin and glial cell antigens in the serum and cerebral spinal fluid of patients; and transient amelioration of disease activity during periods of immunosuppression such as pregnancy. As in other autoimmune conditions, specific haplotypes of the human leukocyte antigen (HLA) have been identified that predispose to multiple sclerosis. Furthermore, *experimental autoimmune encephalomyelitis* is an animal model that is analogous to human multiple sclerosis (Weiner, 1998; Marrie, 2004).

Female predominance is characteristic of all autoimmune conditions including multiple sclerosis. Autoimmunity reflects a reaction of the immune system against "*self.*" In patients with multiple sclerosis, IgG antibodies targeting myelin and glial cells can be detected in sera and cerebral spinal fluid as well as in specimens of lesions. These antibodies stimulate killer T cells to attack glial cells in the brain and spinal cord resulting in demyelination and axonal dissection of neurons.

The genesis of autoimmunity and its predominance in females remains enigmatic. One hypothesis

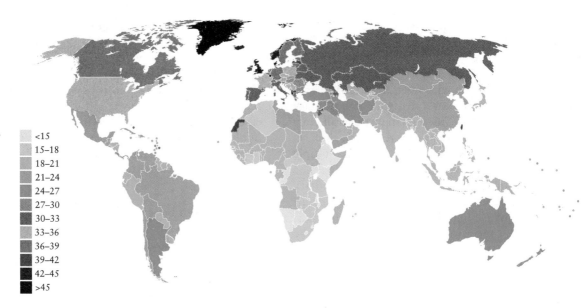

Figure 43.5 Global Disability Adjusted Years: Multiple Sclerosis, 2004.

Source: Data from World Health Organization. The global burden of disease: 2004 update. Geneva, WHO, 2008. Available at www.who.int /evidence/bod.

postulates incompatibility of X chromosomes. Since either the paternal or the maternal X chromosome is inactivated in cell lineages early during embryogenesis, the genotype of the human female is actually a *mosaic* of active and inactivated paternal and maternal X chromosomes. This phenomenon was described by Mary Lyon in 1961 and is called the "*Lyon hypothesis*" (Lyon, 1961). Inactivated X chromosomes are called "*Barr bodies*" named after Murray Barr who first described them (Barr and Bertram, 1949). Conceivably, incompatibility of the paternal and maternal X chromosomes might lead to immunoreactivity, particularly if neuronal tissues contain the active X chromosome from one parent and immune cells contain the other. In the context of other stimuli such as a viral infection, this could occasionally lead to failure of the immune system to recognize "self," thereby leading to an autoimmune reaction. Various permutations of this hypothesis have appeared in the literature (Willer, Sadovnick, and Ebers, 2002).

PATHOGENIC MECHANISMS IN MULTIPLE SCLEROSIS

Disruption of the Blood-Brain Barrier

Disruption of the blood-brain barrier has been found to precede the development of multiple sclerosis (Kermode et al., 1990). The blood-brain barrier

consists of tight junctions between the endothelial cells that line the capillaries and other blood vessels of the brain and spinal cord. Under normal conditions, these tight junctions prevent entrance of T cells into neurological tissues; however, many viruses and certain other infectious agents may compromise the blood-brain barrier and allow T cells to pass through (**Figure 43.6**). Upon clearance of the infection, the T cells are trapped inside the brain and may stimulate immunoreactivity and inflammation. Notably, dysregulation of the blood-brain barrier and transendothelial migration of activated leukocytes and their release of inflammatory cytokines and chemokines are among the earliest cerebrovascular abnormalities seen in multiple sclerosis brains (Minagar and Alexander, 2003).

Inflammation

Inflammation is a chief pathologic hallmark of relapsing-remitting multiple sclerosis. According to one model, T cells gain entrance into the brain through the blood-brain barrier and become immunoreactive, thereby stimulating a cascade of destructive inflammatory processes including axon transection, myelin degradation, and glial cell death.

Localized foci of demyelination are present in white and gray matter in the brains of multiple sclerosis patients. Imaging these lesions using MRI with gadolinium enhancement provides the most conclusive evidence for a diagnosis of relapsing-remitting multiple sclerosis. Lesions can be pathologically

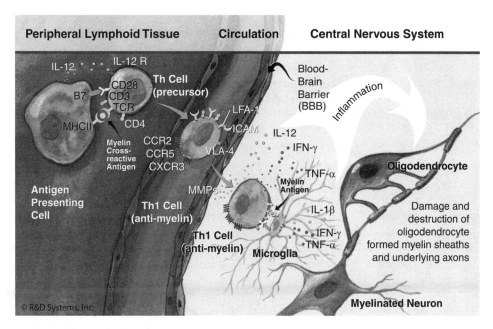

Figure 43.6 Lymphocyte Penetration of Blood-Brain Barrier.
Source: Courtesy of R&D systems, Inc. Minneapolis, MN, USA.

characterized as immunologically active or chronic by various degrees of microgliosis, astrocytosis, myelin vacuolation or loss, and axonal transection. Demyelinated lesions will undergo a reparative process whereby oligodendrocytes replace lost myelin with a thinner but still functional sheath. These repaired lesions are called shadow lesions and are of intense interest because they exhibit a natural mechanism whereby the brain replaces lost myelin.

Remyelination Failure

The principal cell responsible for myelin formation and repair is the oligodendrocyte, a glial cell that synthesizes and maintains myelin for up to 40 nerve axons in the central nervous system (Weinshenker, 1994; Weiner, 1998; Compston and Coles, 2002). Failure of remyelination by oligodendroctyes is thought to be largely responsible for sustained neurological symptoms in patients with progressive multiple sclerosis. Inability of oligodendrocytes to migrate into demyelinated areas and for oligodendrocyte progenitors to mature are possible reasons why lesions enter a chronically demyelinated phase. *Hyaluronan (hyaluronic acid)* is a large glycosaminoglycan that polymerizes to form a polygel scaffold that is essential for cell migration, adhesion, differentiation, maturation, and proliferation in many tissues including the brain. Recent studies have identified deposits of hyaluronan in lesions from multiple sclerosis patients, and this material has been found to inhibit the maturation of oligodendrocyte precursor cells

in vitro. Degradation products of hyaluronan may thus contribute to remyelination failure by blocking the maturation of oligodendrocytes (Back et al., 2005). Most recently, this inhibitory process has been found to depend upon upregulation of specific toll-like receptors that activate the innate immune system (Sloane et al., 2010).

Axonal Injury

Irresponsiveness of progressive multiple sclerosis to immunomodulatory therapies suggests a completely different pathogenenic mechanism of this disease stage. Focused research efforts are being made at investigating the role of Wallerian degeneration and axonal transection in chronic multiple sclerosis disability. Axonal destruction appears early in the disease course in both lesions and normal white and gray matter areas and accumulates with disease progression. It is thought that axonal transection is at first clinically silent because the central nervous system compensates for neuroaxonal loss. However, once a threshold of axonal loss is reached, the neurodegenerative component of the disease becomes a major determinent of clinical disability (Trapp et al., 1999)

Chronic Cerebrospinal Venous Insufficiency

A recent theory advanced to explain the pathogenesis and progression of multiple sclerosis involves a vascular condition known as *chronic cerebrospinal venous insufficiency*, which is characterized by abnormal cerebral venous strictures of unknown origin and loss of venous outflow from the brain. Surgical repair of such lesions has been shown effective for some patients with multiple sclerosis in preliminary trials, but confirmation of benefit awaits the results of further testing (Zamboni et al., 2009).

Genetics of Multiple Sclerosis

Multiple sclerosis is a complex autoimmune disease involving the interaction of both genetic and environmental factors. Genetic susceptibility is indicated by studies of twins and relatives of index cases (probands). Monozygous twins have higher disease concordance (~20%) than dizygous twins (~5%), and full siblings of probands have approximately twice the risk of half-siblings (Sadovnick et al., 1993; Dyment, Ebers, and Sadovnick, 2004). Nevertheless, the high *lack of concordance* among monozygous twins (~80%) indicates that environmental factors undoubtedly play a significant role in the genesis of multiple sclerosis.

Genetic variation at the major histocompatability complex (MHC) on chromosome 6 has been found to influence the risk of developing multiple sclerosis (**Figure 43.7**). Several genetic polymorphisms of the *human leukocyte antigen (HLA)* system appear to either increase or decrease the risk. In addition, recent studies have identified polymorphisms of genes encoding *T-cell receptors* (which bind to HLA

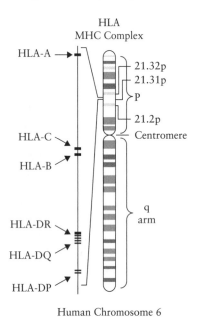

Figure 43.7 The Major Histocompatibility Complex (MHC) and Human Leukocyte Antigen (HLA) System on Chromosome 6.

Source: Courtesy of Philip Deitiker.

antigens) and the *cytotoxic T-cell leukocyte antigen* (which downregulates the T-cell antigenic response) that increase susceptibility. Genetic investigations are currently in progress in several laboratories to identify specific genotypes that confer susceptibility or resistance to the genesis of multiple sclerosis (Dyment, Ebers, and Sadovnick, 2004).

Ethnic Differences in Multiple Sclerosis

In 1988, George Lowis reviewed the international literature to identify the main demographic and sociocultural features of multiple sclerosis in different ethnic groups. He noted that the highest rates were found in regions largely inhabited by Caucasians and the lowest in those areas with primarily non-Caucasian populations, and also that racially different groups living in the same geographic area had divergent rates, with higher rates predominating in Caucasians and lower rates in non-Caucasians. Within racial groups, Lowis also noted that the prevalence increased with increasing latitude and suggested that while racial (genetic) factors may contribute to the distribution of multiple sclerosis, environmental agents predominantly influence the risk, irrespective of race (Lowis et al., 1988).

More recently, Mario Pugliatti, Stefano Sotgiu, and Giulio Rosati reviewed the extensive body of literature on multiple sclerosis and attempted to refine its geographic distribution using prevalence data from surveys conducted in different regions and at different times. Their review focused on prevalence estimates for ethnically distinct populations of several broad geographic areas (Europe, North and South America, Asia, Africa, the Middle East, and Australasia). Based upon findings of wide divergence in prevalence rates for populations in close geographic proximity, they suggest that genetic factors have a significant influence on susceptibility and resistance. For example, repeated surveys of populations living on the Italian peninsula have yielded rates in the range of 40–70 per 100,000, in striking contrast to the small island of Sardinia located 200 km to the west of the Italian mainland. Prevalence rates of multiple sclerosis in Sardinians were among the highest in the world, ranging from 144–152 per 100,000. The genetically isolated population of this small island also has one of the highest rates of type 1 diabetes, another autoimmune condition. Summarizing their results, the investigators state

"The rarity of multiple sclerosis in Samis, Turkmen, Uzbeks, Kazakhs, Kirgizis, native Siberians, North and South Amerindians, Canadian Hutterites, Chinese, Japanese, African blacks,

and New Zealand Maoris, and its high risk in Sardinians, Parsis and Palestinians, as well as in South African English-speaking whites as compared to Afrikaners, point to differential racial susceptibility as an important determinant of the worldwide uneven geographic distribution of the disease"

and suggest that the geography of multiple sclerosis can be viewed as *"a discontinuous distribution of genetic alleles of susceptibility, conferring risks that are subsequently modified and influenced by environment"* (Rosati, 2001; Pugliatti, Sotgiu, and Rosati, 2002).

Environmental Risk Factors for Multiple Sclerosis

Many different environmental factors have been proposed as risk factors for multiple sclerosis. These include sun exposure, infection, vaccinations, climate, stress, occupation, drug use, and diet (Marrie, 2004; Ascherio and Munger, 2007a, 2007b). Selected epidemiologic studies of environmental factors are discussed next.

Geographic Variation in Multiple Sclerosis

Ecological studies of multiple sclerosis rates suggest there is a north-to-south gradient in the northern hemisphere and a south-to-north gradient in the southern hemisphere; that is, multiple sclerosis appears to be less common in people living near the equator. The early epidemiologic studies of Charles Limberg, Lenoard Kurland, and E.D. Acheson were instrumental in showing the distinct latitudinal gradient in the rates of multiple sclerosis in the northern and southern hemispheres (Limberg, 1950; Kurland 1952; Acheson et al., 1960) and many subsequent investigations have confirmed its existence (Leibowitz, Sharon, and Alter, 1967; Kuroiwa, Shibasaki, and Ikeda, 1983; van der Mei et al., 2001; Marrie, 2004; Ascherio and Munger, 2007b), Cold climate, deficient sunlight, and low vitamin D have been investigated as possible causes of the latitude gradient in the rates. Notwithstanding, it has been pointed out that there are notable exceptions to this pattern that cannot be explained by a prevalence-latitude relationship (Pugliatti, Sotgiu, and Rosati, 2002; Rosati, 2001).

Sunlight, Vitamin D, and Multiple Sclerosis

Investigations of a potential link between multiple sclerosis, sun exposure, and vitamin D are complicated by a number of issues including difficulties in accurately measuring exposure and the complexities of vitamin D metabolism in humans. Under normal physiologic conditions, ultraviolet light converts *7-dehydroxcholesterol* in the skin to *previtamin D3* which is rapidly converted to *vitamin D3 (cholecalciferol)*. Cholecalciferol and a related form of vitamin D, *ergocalciferol*, can also be obtained from dietary sources.

Vitamin D3 is carried to the liver complexed with *vitamin D3 binding protein*, where it is converted to *25-hydroxy vitamin D (calcidiol)*, which is the major circulating form of vitamin D. Subsequently, in the kidney, the enzyme *1-alpha-hydroxylase* converts calcidiol to *1,25-dihydroxy vitamin D (calcitriol)* the biologically active form of the molecule (Holick, 2005).

Evidence from both *in vitro* investigations and animal studies suggests that vitamin D influences the risk of developing multiple sclerosis. In molecular studies, calcitriol has been found to dampen the innate immune response by inducing secretion of anti-inflammatory cytokines by T cells (Von Essen et al., 2010). Furthermore, in animal studies, the administration of biologically active vitamin D has been shown to prevent the onset of *experimental autoimmune encephalitis* (an experimental mouse model of multiple sclerosis) as well as its progression (Lemire and Archer, 1991; Cantorna, Hayes, and DeLuca, 1996; Cantorna, 2008).

A team of investigators at Harvard University recently examined the association of dietary vitamin D in two large prospective cohorts of women, the Nurses Health Study (92,253 women followed from 1980–2000) and the Nurses Health Study II (95,310 women followed from 1991 to 2001). Diet was assessed at baseline and updated every 4 years thereafter. During follow-up, 173 incident cases of multiple sclerosis were detected. Pooled results from the two cohorts revealed that women in the highest quintile of total vitamin D intake had a significantly reduced risk of developing multiple sclerosis compared to women with low intake (RR = 0.67). When the sources of vitamin D were stratified, supplementary vitamin D intake (at least 400 international units daily) was inversely associated with the risk (OR = 0.59) but not dietary vitamin D (Munger et al., 2004).

Munger and colleagues also evaluated the potential protective effect of vitamin D by examining levels of 25-hydroxyvitamin D (calcidiol) in serum samples of 247 cases with multiple sclerosis and matched controls. Sera were obtained from the US Department of Defense Serum Repository of more than 7 million military personnel. Multiple sclerosis cases were identified from Army and Navy physical disability databases for 1992–2004 and each case was matched to two disease-free controls by age, gender, ethnicity, and dates of blood collection.

Results revealed an inverse dose response in the risk of developing multiple sclerosis with increasing levels of 25-hydroxy vitamin D, but only for Caucasians. The disease odds were reduced by 62% among individuals in the highest quintile (above 99.1 nmol/L) compared to those in the lowest quintile (OR = 0.38). No significant associations were found between serum levels of vitamin D and multiple sclerosis for members of other ethnic groups, although these individuals had lower 25-hydroxyvitamin D levels than Caucasians. The investigators suggest their results support *"a protective role for vitamin D in multiple sclerosis"* (Munger et al., 2006; Ascherio, Munger, and Simon, 2010).

Investigators at the University of California in Los Angeles investigated sun exposure and multiple sclerosis in 79 disease-discordant monozygous twin pairs. The analysis compared sun exposure in the affected twin with that of the unaffected twin in a pair-matched case control design. Results revealed that for each unit increase in a sun exposure index, the odds of developing multiple sclerosis *decreased* by 25%. Findings suggest a protective effect of sun exposure that is independent of genetic susceptibility (Islam et al., 2007).

In a recent case control study conducted at multiple sites in Australia, Robyn Lucas and colleagues compared sun exposure and serum levels of vitamin D in 216 cases with multiple sclerosis to 395 controls without disease matched by age, gender, and location. Results revealed that the odds of developing a first demyelinating event *decreased* by 30% per 1,000 kilojoule increase in exposure to ultraviolet light, and independently decreased by 7% per 10 nmol/L increase in the serum level of 25-hydroxy-vitamin D. The investigators concluded that sun exposure and vitamin D levels may independently influence the risk of developing multiple sclerosis but advocated further evaluation in clinical trials. Postulated mechanisms for these effects include immunosuppression by sun exposure and downregulation of innate immunity by vitamin D (Lucas et al., 2011).

Investigators at the University of California, San Francisco, examined the association between serum levels of 25-hydroxyvitamin D3 and the rate of relapse among 110 pediatric patients with multiple sclerosis. They found that for every 10 ng/ml increase in the level of 25-hydroxyvitamin D3, the rate of subsequent relapse decreased by 34% (Mowry et al., 2010). Similar results were reported by investigators at the University of Melbourne for a prospective cohort of 145 adult patients with relapsing-remitting multiple sclerosis. They found that for each 10 nmol/L increase in 25-hydroxyvitamin D3, the risk of relapse decreased by 12% (Simpson et al., 2010).

The totality of observational evidence therefore suggests that vitamin D may have both chemopreventive and therapeutic value in reducing the burden of multiple sclerosis. Multicenter double-blind placebo-controlled randomized clinical trials of vitamin D supplementation are currently in progress to elucidate such effects in patients with multiple sclerosis.

Infection and Multiple Sclerosis

Scores of microbial infectious agents have been proposed as potential triggers in the pathogenesis of multiple sclerosis; however, no specific microbe has been clearly substantiated as causative. Findings supporting a viral etiology include pathological evidence of infection in the brain and cerebrospinal fluid of most patients, the association of several viruses with *human demyelinating encephalitis* (a condition with similarities to multiple sclerosis), and induction of demyelination in animals by viral infection. Many childhood infections have been studied including measles, mumps, rubella, varicella, human herpes virus type 6, retroviruses, and *Chlamydia pneumoniae*. Albeit, results for specific microbes either reflect no association whatsoever or are inconsistent from study to study. One possible exception is Epstein-Barr virus (EBV), which infects up to 90% of the population by adulthood. Several serological studies have detected significantly higher frequencies of EBV antibodies in the sera and cerebral spinal fluid of multiple sclerosis patients compared to controls, and some studies have found an increased risk among individuals with a history of infectious mononucleosis (which is caused by EBV infection). Nevertheless, some investigators have reported null results and additional well-designed studies are needed to confirm or refute this association (Marrie, 2004; Ascherio and Munger, 2007a).

John Kurtzke and colleagues conducted a series of epidemiologic investigations of multiple sclerosis in the population living in the Faroe Islands which are located between Scotland and Iceland in the North Atlantic Ocean. His studies suggest that multiple sclerosis was introduced into the native population by British troops who occupied the islands during 1940–1945. Kurtzke described the temporal pattern of disease in the Faroe Island population over half a century as *"four successive epidemics beginning in 1943"* and suggested that multiple sclerosis is the rare outcome of infection by a transmissible agent, perhaps a retrovirus (Kurtzke, 1993).

There is also some evidence that parasitic infection by *Borrelia burgdorferi*, the etiologic agent of Lyme disease, occasionally manifests symptoms characteristic of multiple sclerosis. Several studies have found that patients diagnosed with multiple sclerosis have positive serologic reactions to Borrelia antigen, and characteristic spirochytes of the organism have been found in postmortem studies of brain tissues of afflicted patients. Results suggest there may be an association between Lyme borreliosis and multiple sclerosis (Marshall, 1988).

The age at the time of infection has also been examined as a risk factor for development of multiple sclerosis. A recent review of 19 studies found reasonable consistency among studies in showing that infection by any one of a number of agents (measles, mumps, varicella, rubella) at a relatively late age during childhood (after 6 years of age) was associated with a greater odds of developing multiple sclerosis. As pointed out by Ruth Ann Marrie in her review of the environmental epidemiology of multiple sclerosis: *"It is possible that any one of several agents could produce the same result under the appropriate circumstances (a genetically susceptible host at a critical time of exposure)"* (Marrie, 2004).

Studies of Multiple Sclerosis in Migrants

Perhaps surprisingly, there is general agreement of results from studies of multiple sclerosis rates in migrants. People migrating from a high risk area to a low risk area experience a decrease in disease rates, whereas people migrating from a low risk area to a high risk area retain their low rates. These findings suggest that the risk of disease is established early in life and prior to the time of migration (Gale and Martyn, 1995).

Vaccination and Multiple Sclerosis

A series of case reports in France raised particular concern about demyelinating events developing after hepatitis B vaccination. In a nested case control study of 192 women with multiple sclerosis and 645 matched controls, Aschero and colleagues found no effect of hepatitis B vaccination at any time before disease onset (OR = 0.9) (Ascherio et al., 2001). Similarly, other case control studies found no evidence of an association; furthermore, results of both case control and cohort studies have consistently reported no association between the development of multiple sclerosis and other childhood vaccinations (measles, mumps, rubella) (Marrie, 2004; Ascherio and Munger, 2007b).

Organic Solvents and Multiple Sclerosis

Several studies have assessed the association between exposure to organic solvents and multiple sclerosis. A meta-analysis of case control studies found a 70%

increase in overall risk (pooled OR = 1.7) (Landtblom et al., 1996). However, a subsequent review of 14 epidemiologic studies revealed inconsistencies and methodological issues with risk estimates ranging from 0.4–4.9 (Marrie, 2004). Though a link between multiple sclerosis and exposure to organic solvents cannot be excluded, additional studies are needed for definitive proof of an association.

Tobacco and Multiple Sclerosis

Many epidemiologic investigations have examined tobacco use as a risk factor for multiple sclerosis. Handel and colleagues recently reviewed the literature on smoking and multiple sclerosis and performed a meta-analysis of risk estimates from eligible studies. They included data from 14 studies of 3,052 cases and 457,619 controls in their analysis. Results revealed an approximate 50% increase in the risk for smokers compared to nonsmokers (RR = 1.52). The risk of secondary disease was also elevated by continuation of the smoking habit among patients (RR = 1.88). The investigators concluded that smoking significantly heightens the risk of developing multiple sclerosis and suggested the need for further research to clarify interactions with other risk factors (Handel et al., 2011).

PREVENTION AND THERAPY OF MULTIPLE SCLEROSIS

Though there is no known cure for multiple sclerosis, intensive research is focused on finding effective drugs and other modalities to prevent attacks, return function after attacks, and prevent disability and decline from progressive disease. Corticosteroids are typically used to manage acute attacks and certain immunomodulatory drugs (interferon-b, glatiramer acetate) have proven effective in some patients. A variety of monoclonal antibodies that target specific molecules in the immunopathogenesis of multiple sclerosis are currently being investigated in randomized clinical trials (WHO, 2006: Pozzilli and Prosperini, 2010). Therapies aimed at enhancing natural mechanisms of remyelination in the brain hold promise for the treatment of progressive multiple sclerosis and as such are of intense interest in current neurological research. There is also much interest in the use of supplementary or vitamin D analogs for the prevention and management of multiple sclerosis. Randomized clinical trials are currently in progress to evaluate the potential benefit of vitamin D therapy for patients with relapsing-remitting multiple sclerosis (Cantorna, 2008).

• • • **REFERENCES**

Acheson, E.D., Bachrach, C.A., & Wright, F.M. (1960). Some comments on the relationship of the distribution of multiple sclerosis to latitude, solar radiation, and other variables. *Acta Psychiatrica Scandinavica, 35*(S147), 132–147.

Allison, R.S. (1931). Disseminated sclerosis in North Wales: An inquiry into its incidence, frequency, distribution and other etiological factors. *Brain, 53*, 391–430.

Allison, R.S., & Millar, J.H.D. (1954). Prevalence of disseminated sclerosis in Northern Ireland. *Ulster Med J, 23*(Suppl 2), 1–27.

Ascherio, A., Zhang, S.M., Hernan, M.A., Olek, M.J., Coplan, P.M., Brodovicz, K., & Walker, A.M. (2001). Hepatitis B vaccination and the risk of multiple sclerosis. *N Engl J Med, 344*, 327–332.

Ascherio, A., & Munger, K.L. (2007a). Environmental risk factors for multiple sclerosis. Part I: The role of infection. *Ann Neurol, 61*(4), 288–299.

Ascherio, A., & Munger, K.L. (2007b). Environmental risk factors for multiple sclerosis. Part II: Noninfectious factors. *Ann Neurol, 61*(6), 504–513.

Ascherio, A., Munger, K.L., & Simon, K.C. (2010). Vitamin D and multiple sclerosis. *Lancet Neurol, 9*(6), 599–612.

Back, S.A., Tuohy, T.M., Chen, H., Wallingford, N., Craig, A., Struve, J.,...Sherman, L.S. (2005). Hyaluronan accumulates in demyelinated lesions and inhibits oligodendrocyte progenitor maturation. *Nat Med, 11*(9), 966–972.

Barr, M.L., & Bertram, E.G. (1949). A morphological distinction between neurones of the male and female, and the behaviour of the nucleolar satellite during accelerated nucleoprotein synthesis. *Nature, 63*(4148), 676–677.

Bronnum-Hansen, H., Stenager, E., Nylev, S.E., & Koch-Henriksen, N. (2005). Suicide among Danes with multiple sclerosis. *J Neurol Neurosurg Psychiatr, 76*, 1457–1159.

Cantorna, M.T., Hayes, C.E., & DeLuca, H.F. (1996). 1,25-Dihydroxyvitamin D_3 reversibly blocks the progression of relapsing encephalomyelitis, a model of multiple sclerosis. *Proc Natl Acad Sci USA, 93*, 7861–7864.

Cantorna, M.T. (2008). Vitamin D and multiple sclerosis: An update. *Nutr Rev, 66*(10 Suppl 2), S135–S138.

Charcot, J. (1868). Histologie de la sclerose en plaques. *Gazette des hopitaux, Paris, 41*, 554–555.

Compston, A. (1988). The 150th anniversary of the first depiction of the lesions of multiple sclerosis. *J Neurol Neurosurg Psychiatr, 51*(10), 1249–1252.

Compston, A., & Coles, A. (2002). Multiple sclerosis. *Lancet, 359*(9313), 1221–1231.

Dyment, D.A., Ebers, G.C., & Sadovnick, A.D. (2004). Genetics of multiple sclerosis. *Lancet, 3*, 104–110.

Fredrikson, S., Cheng, Q., Jiang, G.X., & Wasserman, D. (2003). Elevated suicide risk among patients with multiple sclerosis in Sweden. *Neuroepidemiology, 22*, 146–152.

Gale, C.R., & Martyn, C.N. (1995). Migrant studies in multiple sclerosis. *Prog Neurobiol, 47*, 425–448.

Grytten, T.N., Lie, S.A., Aarseth, J.H., Nyland, H., & Myhr, K.M. (2008). Survival and cause of death in multiple sclerosis: Results from a 50-year follow-up in Western Norway. *Mult Scler, 14*(9), 1191–1198.

Handel, A.E., Williamson, A.J., Disanto, G., Dobson, R., Giovannoni, G., & Ramagopalan, S.V. (2011) Smoking and multiple sclerosis: An updated meta-analysis. *PLoS ONE, 6*(1), e16149. doi:10.1371.

Holick, M.F. (2005). Photobiology of vitamin D. In D. Feldman, J. Pike, & F. Glorieux, (Eds.). *Vitamin D* (2nd ed., pp. 37–46). New York: Elsevier Academic Press.

Islam, T., Gauderman, W.J., Cozen, W., & Mack, T.M. (2007). Childhood sun exposure influences risk of multiple sclerosis in monozygotic twins. *Neurology, 69*, 381–388.

Kermode, A.G., Thompson, A.J., Tofts, P., MacManus, D.G., Kendall, B.E., Kingsley,

D.P.E.,…McDonald, W.I. (1990). Breakdown of the blood-brain barrier precedes symptoms and other MRI signs of new lesions in multiple sclerosis. *Brain*, *113*, 1477–1489.

Kurland, L.T. (1952). Epidemiologic characteristics of multiple sclerosis. *Am J Med*, *21*, 561–571.

Kuroiwa, Y., Shibasaki, H., & Ikeda, M. (1983). Prevalence of multiple sclerosis and its north-to-south gradient in Japan. *Neuroepidemiology*, *2*, 62–69.

Kurtzke, J.F. (1993). Epidemiologic evidence for multiple sclerosis as an infection. *Clin Microbiol Rev*, *6*(4), 382–427.

Landtblom, A.M., Flodin, U., Soderfeldt, B., Wolfson, C., & Axelson, O. (1996). Organic solvents and multiple sclerosis: A synthesis of the current evidence. *Epidemiology*, *7*, 429–433.

Leibowitz, U., Sharon, D., & Alter, M. (1967). Geographical considerations in multiple sclerosis. *Brain*, *90*, 871–886.

Lemire, J.M., & Archer, D.C. (1991). 1,25-Dihydroxyvitamin D_3 prevents the in vivo induction of murine experimental autoimmune encephalomyelitis. *J Clin Invest*, *87*, 1103–1107.

Limberg, C.C. (1950). The geographic distribution of multiple sclerosis and its estimated prevalence in the United States. In *Multiple sclerosis and the demyelinating diseases. Proceedings of the Association for Research in Nervous and Mental Disease* (December 10–11, 1948), (vol. 28, pp. 15–24). Baltimore: Williams and Wilkins.

Lowis, G.W. (1988). Ethnic factors in multiple sclerosis: A review and critique of the epidemiological literature. *Int J Epidemiol*, *17*(1), 14–20.

Lucas, R.M., Ponsonby, A.L., Dear, K., Valery, P.C., Pender, M.P., Taylor, B.V.,…McMichael, A.J. (2011). Sun exposure and vitamin D are independent risk factors for CNS demyelination. *Neurology*, *76*(6), 540.

Lyon, M.F. (1961). Gene action in the X-chromosome of the mouse (*Mus musculus L.*) *Nature*, *190*(4773), 372–373.

Marrie, R.A. (2004). Environmental risk factors in multiple sclerosis aetiology. *The Lancet Neurology*, *3*(12), 709–718.

Marshal, V. (1988). Multiple Sclerosis is a chronic central nervous system infection by a spirochetal agent. *Medical Hypothesis 25*, 89–92.

McDonald, W.I., Compston, A., Edan, G., Goodkin, D., Hartung, H.P., Lublin, F.D.,…Wolinsky, J.S. (2001). Recommended diagnostic criteria for multiple sclerosis: Guidelines from the International Panel on the Diagnosis of Multiple Sclerosis. *Ann Neurol*, *50*(1), 121–127.

Minagar, A., & Alexander, J.S. (2003). Blood-brain barrier disruption in multiple sclerosis. *Multiple Sclerosis*, *9*, 540–549.

Mowry, E.M., Krupp, L.B., Milazzo, M., Chabas, D., Strober, J.B., Belman, A.L.,…Waubant, E. (2010). Vitamin D status is associated with relapse rate in pediatric-onset multiple sclerosis. *Ann Neurol*, *67*(5), 618–624.

Munger, K.L., Zhang, S.M., O'Reilly, E., Hernán, M.A., Olek, M.J., Willett, W.C., & Ascherio, A. (2004). Vitamin D intake and incidence of multiple sclerosis. *Neurology*, *62*(1), 60–65.

Munger, K.L., Levin, L.I., Hollis, B.W., Howard, N.S., & Ascherio, A. (2006). Serum 25-hydroxyvitamin D levels and risk of multiple sclerosis. *JAMA*, *296*(23), 2832–2838.

Polman, C.H., Reingold, S.C., Edan, G., Filippi, M., Hartung, H.P., Kappos, L.,…Wolinsky, J.S. (2005). Diagnostic criteria for multiple sclerosis: 2005 revisions to the "McDonald Criteria". *Ann Neurol*, *58*(6), 840–646.

Pozzilli, C., & Prosperini, L. (2010). Recent advances in the management of multiple sclerosis. *European Neurological Journal*, *2*(1), 41–48.

Pugliatti, M., Sotgiu, S., & Rosati, G. (2002). The worldwide prevalence of multiple sclerosis. *Clin Neurol Neurosurg*, *104*, 182–191.

Rosati, G. (2001). The prevalence of multiple sclerosis in the world: an update. *Neurol Sci*, *22*(2), 117–139.

Sadovnick, A.D., Ebers, G.C., Wilson, R.W., & Paty, D.W. (1992). Life expectancy in patients attending multiple sclerosis clinics. *Neurology*, *42*(5), 991–994.

Sadovnick, A.D., Armstrong, H., Rice, G.P.A., Bulman, D., Hashimoto, L., Paty, D.W.,…Ebers, G.C. (1993). A population-based study of multiple sclerosis in twins: Update. *Ann Neurol,* *33,* 281–285.

Simpson, S. Jr., Taylor, B., Blizzard, L., Ponsonby, A.L., Pittas, F., Tremlett, H.,...van der Mei, I. (2010). Higher 25-hydroxyvitamin D is associated with lower relapse risk in multiple sclerosis. *Ann Neurol, 68*(2), 193–203.

Sloane, J.A., Batt, C., Ma, Y., Harris, Z.M., Trapp, B., & Vartanian, T. (2010). Hyaluronan blocks oliogdendrocyte progenitor maturation and remyelination through TLR2. *CProc Nat Acad Sci USA, 107*(25), 11555–11560.

Smestad, C., Sandvik, L., & Celius, E.G. (2009). Excess mortality and cause of death in a cohort of Norwegian multiple sclerosis patients. *Mult Scler, 15*(11), 1263–1270.

Stenager, E.N., Stenager, E., Koch-Henriksen, N., Brønnum-Hansen, H., Hyllested, K., Jensen, K., & Bille-Brahe, U. (1992). Suicide and multiple sclerosis: An epidemiological investigation. *J Neurol Neurosurg Psychiatry, 55*(7), 542–545.

Trapp, B.D., Ransohoff, R.M., Fisher, E., & Rudick, R.A. (1999). Neurodegeneration in multiple sclerosis: Relationship to neurological disability. *Neuroscientist, 5*(1), 48–57.

van der Mei, I.A.F., Ponsonby, A.L., Blizzard, L., & Dwyer, T. (2001). Regional variation in multiple sclerosis prevalence in Australia and its association with ambient ultraviolet radiation. *Neuroepidemiology, 20,* 168–174.

Von Essen, M.R., Kongsbak, M., Schjerling, P., Olgaard, K., Ødum, N., & Geisler, C. (2010). Vitamin D controls T cell antigen receptor signaling and activation of human T cells. *Nature Immunology, 22,* 344–349.

Weiner, H.L. (1998). A 21 point unifying hypothesis on the etiology and treatment of multiple sclerosis. *Can J Neurol Sci, 25,* 93–101.

Weinshenker, B.G. (1994). Natural history of multiple sclerosis. *Ann Neurol, 36*(Suppl), S6–S11.

Willer, C.J., Sadovnick, A.D., & Ebers, G.C. (2002). Microchimerisms in autoimmunity and transplantation: Potential relevance to multiple sclerosis. *J Neuroimmunol, 126,* 126–133.

World Health Organization. (2006). *Neurological disorders: Public health challenges* (pp. 85–94). Geneva, Switzerland, World Health Organization.

World Health Organization. (2008). Atlas Multiple Sclerosis Resources in the World, 2008. Geneva, Switzerland.

Zamboni, P., Galeotti, R., Menegatti, E., Tacconi, G., Dall'Ara, G., Bartolomei, I., & Salvi, F. (2009). Chronic cerebrospinal venous insufficiency in patients with multiple sclerosis. *J Neurol Neurosurg Psychiatry, 80,* 392–399.

44

Epidemiology of Suicide

INTRODUCTION

Suicide is now the 13th leading cause of death in the world population. Each year, more than 1 million individuals die by their own hand (WHO, 2002). Suicide is often committed out of perceived despair and hopelessness due to an underlying chronic mental disorder such as depression, bipolar disorder, schizophrenia, epilepsy, multiple sclerosis, alcoholism, and drug abuse. Indeed, the presence of a mental disorder is the predominant risk factor for suicide, and it is generally acknowledged that more than 90% of those who committed suicide had a psychiatric diagnosis at the time of death (Bertolote and Fleischmann, 2002a). Undesirable circumstances (financial crises, interpersonal conflicts, terminal disease, chronic pain, debilitation, and other untoward situations) also play a significant role. The most common methods of committing suicide are by firearms, poisons, knives, drowning, hanging, suffocation, and jumping from heights.

Suicide rates are based upon death certificates and likely reflect underreporting in certain populations. As pointed out by Bertolote and Fleischmann in their review of global suicide,

> "The official figures on suicide made available to WHO by its Member States are based on death certificates signed by legally authorized personnel, usually doctors and, to a lesser extent, police officers. Generally speaking, these professionals do not misrepresent the information. However, suicide may be hidden and underreported for several reasons, e.g. as a result of prevailing social or religious attitudes. In some places, it is believed that suicide is underreported by a percentage between 20% and 100%. This underlines the importance of bringing about corrections and improvement on a worldwide basis" (Bartolote and Fleischmann, 2002a).

The global distribution of suicide shows considerable variability amongst nations ranging from 1–32 suicides per 100,000 per year (**Figure 44.1**). Exceedingly high rates (over 20 suicides per 100,000) are found in certain nations of the Russian Federation (Lithuania, Slovenia, Ukraine, Latvia, Slovenia), in Eastern Europe (Kazakhstan, Belarus, Hungary), and in sub-Saharan Africa (Guyana, Somalia). In recent years, all of these nations have been ravaged by famine, war, and poverty, conditions that are inescapably associated with depression, hopelessness, and despair. Suicide rates tend to be lower in populations with a higher standard of living, although there are notable exceptions. For example, rates are high in Japan (24 per 100,000) and certain Scandinavian countries (18 per 100,000 in Finland and 16 per 100,000 in Sweden) and low in Islamic countries of the Middle East.

GENDER AND SUICIDE

In nearly all nations, the suicide rate in males far exceeds the rate in females. In the impoverished country of Lithuania, which has the highest rate in the world (32 suicides per 100,000), the male rate is nearly 7 times higher than the female rate (59 per 100,000 versus 9 per 100,000). Male to female ratios of suicide rates are in the range of 3 to 4 for most other countries (**Table 44.1**). One notable exception is in China, where females have the highest suicide rate in the world (15 per 100,000), which is even higher than males (13 per 100,000). Japanese women also have a high suicide rate (14 per 100,000).

Bertolote and Fleischmann compared the age-specific distributions of suicide rates for males and females based upon rates reported by 62 WHO member nations in 1998 (**Figure 44.2**). These average rates highlight the predominance of suicide in males compared to females throughout the lifespan.

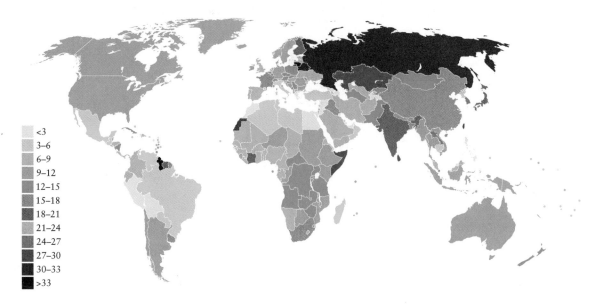

Figure 44.1 Global Distribution of Suicide, 2004.

Source: Data from: World Health Organization. The global burden of disease: 2004 update. Geneva, WHO, 2008. Available at www.who.int/evidence/bod.

Rates increase dramatically during adolescence and early adulthood, and in many populations suicide is one of the leading causes of death among individuals aged 15–24 years. Suicide rates then continue to rise throughout the lifespan, most significantly at approximately 50 years of age in men and 60 years of age in women (Bertolote and Fleischmann, 2002b).

Hawton and van Heeringen recently reviewed 144 studies of suicide in order to identify and evaluate signficant risk factors in different populations and formulate preventive strategies. While differences were noted by age, gender, and population, they found general agreement regarding the significance of several major suicide risk factors.

The major risk factors for suicide among the young include suicidal thoughts, psychiatric disorders (such as depression, impulsive aggressive behavior, bipolar disorders, and anxiety disorders), and drug and/or alcohol abuse. Other important contributory factors include previous suicide attempts and/or episodes of self-harm; family disruption and discord; familial history of suicide; violence and/or drug abuse; recent loss of a parent, sibling, or close friend; physical and sexual abuse; homelessness; and homosexual

Table 44.1	Crude Suicide Rates by Gender		
Country	**Males**	**Females**	**Ratio**
Lithuania	58.5	8.8	6.6
Hungary	37.1	8.8	4.2
Japan	36.8	13.7*	2.6
Finland	27.3	9.5	2.9
Sweden	26.0	6.3	4.1
Canada	17.9	5.4	3.3
UK	17.7	5.4	3.3
USA	17.7	4.5	3.9
India	12.2	9.1	1.3
China	13.3	14.8*	0.9
Brazil	7.3	1.9	3.8

Source: Data from World Health Organization, (2002). Mortality and burden of disease estimates for WHO member states in 2002. World Health Organization. 2002.

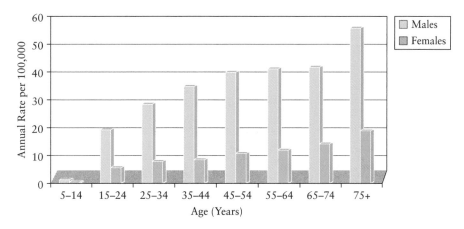

Figure 44.2 Age-Specific Rates of Suicide in Males and Females, 1998.

Source: Data from Bertolote JM, Fleischmann A (2002). Suicide and psychiatric diagnosis: a worldwide perspective. *World Psychiatry* 1(3):181–185.

and/or bisexual orientation. The risk is also increased if there is access to firearms.

Major risk factors for suicide among the elderly include a previous suicide attempt, presence of chronic depression or other psychiatric disorder, chronic debilitating disease, unemployment, lack of independence, social isolation (some studies have shown this is especially so in older males who are recently widowed), and access to means, such as the availability of firearms in the home (Hawton and van Heeringen, 2009).

TIME TRENDS IN SUICIDE RATES

Bertolote and Fleischmann also examined the gender-specific time trends in global suicide rates between 1950–1995. In their analysis, suicide rates reported by WHO member nations were averaged by gender and year, and plotted. During this 45-year time span, the suicide rate increased by 49% in males and 33% in females. The investigators cautioned, however, that the 1950 data are based on only 11 countries whereas the later estimates are the average rates for 62 countries that reported on suicide (Bertolote and Fleischman, 2002b).

Investigators associated with the Karolinska Institute in Sweden investigated gender differences and time trends in global suicide rates among adolescents, ages 15–19 years, using data reported by the World Health Organization. Data were available from 90 countries representing most regions of the world. Across all countries, suicide accounted for 9.1% of all reported deaths. The mean annual suicide rate in males was 2.5 times higher than females (10.5 per 100,000 versus 4.1 per 100,000) and the male rate was higher than the female rate in 85 of the 90 countries. Exceptions were noted in China, Cuba,

Ecuador, El Salvador, and Sri Lanka, where females had a slightly higher rate than males. Time trends and patterns were also examined for 26 countries that reported suicide data during 1965–1999. Eighteen of these were European countries of Western Europe, Central Europe, and Scandinavia and eight were non-European countries (United States, Canada, Australia, New Zealand, Japan, Singapore, and Mauritius). The data revealed twofold higher suicide rates among young males of non-European nations and a disturbing rising trend in suicide among young males of both sets of countries (**Figure 44.3**). Female rates were also higher in the non-European countries but remained relatively stable over time. The investigators conclude that "*suicide among young people is a major health problem in many societies, and preventive measures are strongly recommended*" (Wasserman, Cheng, and Jian, 2005).

Figure 44.4 depicts the age-specific rates of suicide in the United States for three time periods spanning 1930–2007. As noted by several investigators, there has been a dramatic shift in the pattern of age-specific rates in recent decades (Stockard and O'Brien, 2003; Wasserman, Cheng, and Jian, 2005; O'Brien and Stockard, 2006). In 1930, the suicide rate increased monotonically with age and the highest levels occurred among the elderly. In contrast, the patterns of 1965–2007 reflect increases in the rates of suicide during adolescence and young adulthood and declines in the rates among the elderly. In 2007, the highest suicide rates in the United States occurred during middle age. The rise in suicide rates among middle-aged US adults is likely due to a combination of factors including circumstantial depression because of retirement, unemployment, declining health, and/or the heavy use of prescription drugs.

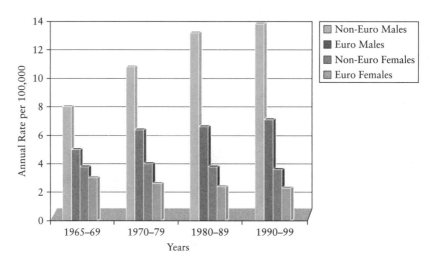

Figure 44.3 Time Trends in Global Suicide Rates, Ages 15–19 Years.

Source: Data from Wasserman D, Cheng Q, Jian G-X (2005). Global suicide rates among young people aged 15-19. *World Psychiatry* 4(2):114–120.

SUICIDE AND MENTAL DISORDERS

In order to discuss the implications of psychiatric diagnosis for suicide prevention, Bertolote and Fleischmann reviewed the psychiatric literature on mental disorders and suicide published during 1959–2001. Their review included 31 papers with information on the presence/absence of mental disorders among 15,629 cases of suicide. Of these, 7,424 cases (47.5%) had been admitted at least once to a psychiatric hospital or ward whereas 8,205 cases (52.5%) had not. All diagnoses of mental disorders were coded according to either the *International Classification of Diseases* (ICD) or the *Diagnostic and Statistical Manual of Mental Disorders* (DSM).

The investigators noted that more than 90% of the cases included for study were from developed nations of North America, Europe, Australia, and New Zealand. As expected, 99.9% of previously hospitalized cases had an established psychiatric disorder; but surprisingly, the vast majority (96.8%) of the cases who had never been hospitalized were also found to have an antecedent mental disorder. The frequency of mental disorders among suicide cases with and without a history of being a psychiatric inpatient are compared in **Figures 44.5A** and **44.5B**.

The predominant psychiatric disorder in both sets of suicide cases was mood disorder. This condition includes depression, bipolarity, and mania. Schizophrenia, substance abuse, (particularly alcohol

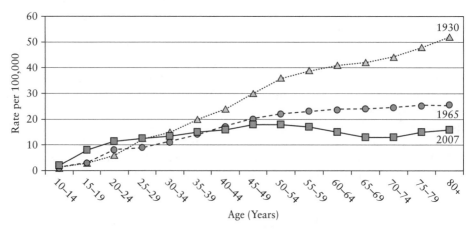

Figure 44.4 Age Distributions of Suicide Rates in the United States, 1930–2007.

Source: Data from Stockard J, O'Brien RM (2003). Cohort variations and changes in age-specific suicide rates over time: explaining variation in youth suicide. *Social Forces* 81(2):605–642. Centers for Disease Control (2007). Atlanta, Georgia, USA.

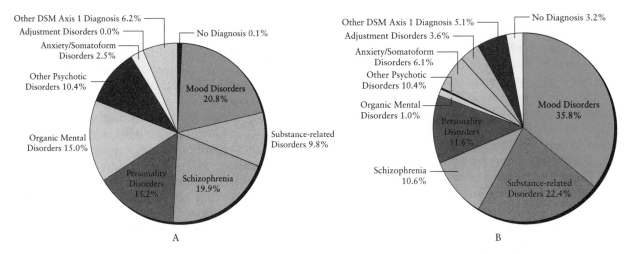

Figure 44.5 (A) Mental Disorders and Suicide: Psychiatric Inpatients; (B) Mental Disorders and Suicide: General Population.

Source: Data from Bertolote JM, Fleischmann A (2002). Suicide and psychiatric diagnosis: a worldwide perspective. *World Psychiatry* 1(3):181–185.

abuse), and personality disorders was also present in 10% or more of cases in both groups. Organic conditions (epilepsy, Parkinson's disease, multiple sclerosis, strokes, tumors) were prominent among previously hospitalized cases (15%) but not cases from the general population (1%). It is important to note that these conditions are not mutually exclusive and may combine to accentuate the risk of suicide. For example, schizophrenia in combination with psychotic disorders was present in more than 30% of suicide victims that had been previously hospitalized for a psychiatric condition. Based upon these results, the investigators recommend a multifaceted approach to suicide prevention including appropriate therapy for mental disorders, control of the availability of toxic substances and medicines, restricted access to firearms and other weapons, preventive public health measures (detoxification of domestic gas and car emissions, erection of barriers to deter jumping from high places), and responsible media reporting about suicide (Bertolote and Fleischmann, 2002b).

Similar results were reported by Arsenault-Lapierre and colleagues based upon their review of 3,275 suicides from 27 studies in which psychological autopsy studies of cases were performed. In a psychological autopsy, interviews are conducted with key informants and official medical records are examined to extract information regarding demography, psychiatric disorders, comorbidity, and other relevant data. Among all suicide cases, 87.3% had been diagnosed with a mental disorder prior to suicide. However, in comparisons of males and females, major gender differences became apparent. Male suicide cases had higher odds of substance abuse (OR = 3.58), personality disorders

(OR = 2.01), and childhood disorders (OR = 4.95), whereas female cases had higher odds of affective disorders (OR = 1.52) and depression (OR = 1.89). Results suggest that most suicides are committed by those with a history of psychiatric illness, but that suicidal males and females have differential psychiatric profiles (Arsenault-Lapierre, Kim, and Turecki, 2004).

GEOGRAPHIC PATTERNS OF SUICIDE

Suicide in China

Investigators from Harvard University and the Beijing *Suicide Research and Prevention Center* examined suicide rates in China by gender, age, and region (urban or rural) based upon mortality data provided by the Chinese Ministry of Health for 1995–1999. Suicide was found to be the 5th leading cause of death in China, accounting for 3.6% of all deaths and claiming 287,000 victims per year. The mean annual suicide rate was 23 per 100,000. The suicide rate was 25% higher in females than males, mainly because of the large number of suicides in young women living in rural communities. Gender-specific suicide rates in rural communities were threefold higher than in urban communities, and in rural areas, ingestion of lethal pesticides that are readily accessible in the homes of most residents is the preferred method of committing suicide (Phillips, Li, and Zhang, 2002).

Investigators in Beijing conducted a case control study of 152 individuals who attempted suicide and 152 matched controls to evaluate the role of mental illness and other potential risk factors. Three independent risk factors were identified for suicidal behavior: severe acute stress (OR = 67.5), presence of mental illness (OR = 13.9), and depression due to negative life events in the previous year (OR = 5.3). In contrast to findings in other populations, the relative frequency of mental illness among Chinese suicide cases was relatively low (38%). The investigators concluded that mental illness is an important risk factor of attempted suicide, but not an essential precondition (Li, Yang, and Zhang, 2001).

The Chinese government policy that restricts the number of children and favors male versus female progeny has also been suggested as a risk factor for suicide in Chinese women. David Reardon provides an interesting discussion of the high suicide rate among Chinese women and the potential role of strictly enforced birth quotas in China. Chinese women face the prospect of being pressured into having abortions, particularly in rural areas. Reardon states that *"the preference for boys in rural areas has led to infanticide and selective abortion of female fetuses which may cause impacted grief and sense of devaluation of women's self worth"* (Reardon, 2002). Notably, induced abortion has been found to significantly increase the risk of suicide (Morgan et al., 1997) and suicidal ideation after abortion is likely related to unresolved grief and depression rather than preexisting psychiatric illness (Burke and Reardon, 2002; Law and Liu, 2008).

USA Suicide Belt

Suicide is the 11th leading cause of death in the United States, responsible for 34,598 deaths in 2007. As in other populations, rates are 3–4 times higher in males than females, and the *"web of causation"* usually involves some combination of the following conditions and risk factors: psychiatric illness (particularly depression), substance abuse (particularly alcohol abuse), debilitating/terminal illness (cancer, HIV disease), familial history of mental disorder, substance abuse, violence, physical and/or sexual abuse, and other undesirable circumstances (financial and/or interpersonal crises). Firearms are readily accessible in the United States and the instrument of destruction in 55% of all suicides (Moscicki, 2001).

It has long been recognized that the western intermountain region of the United States (Montana, Idaho, Wyoming, Colorado, Utah, Nevada, Arizona, and New Mexico) has a higher suicide rate than the rest of the country in what has been labeled the *suicide belt* (**Figure 44.6**). Factors contributing to the high rates in these populations include widespread poverty and depression, abuse of alcohol and other drugs, easy access to firearms and other weapons, and circumstances that can quickly fuel financial crises and interpersonal conflicts. For example, individuals who experience a major losing spree at the

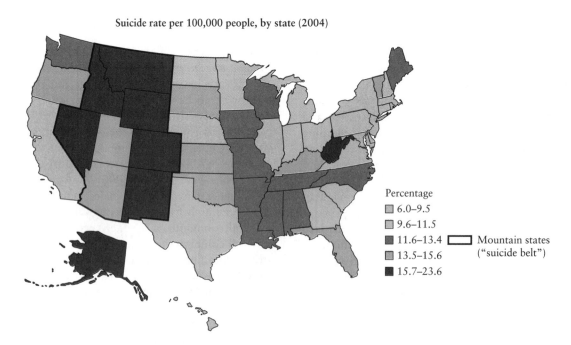

Suicide rate per 100,000 people, by state (2004)

Percentage
- 6.0–9.5
- 9.6–11.5
- 11.6–13.4   ☐ Mountain states
- 13.5–15.6   ("suicide belt")
- 15.7–23.6

Figure 44.6 Suicide Belt of the United States.

Source: National Institute of Mental Health, National Suicide Rate Map, http://mentalhealth.gov/statistics/4NAT_MAP.shtml. Accessed November 7th, 2011.

gambling tables and amass insurmountable debt have been known to commit suicide on site.

Individuals at the University of California examined the relative mortality from suicide among out-of-state visitors to three standardized metropolitan statistical areas with longstanding legalized gambling: Atlantic City in Atlantic County, New Jersey; Las Vegas in Clark County, Nevada; and Reno in Washoe County, Nevada. The relative mortality from suicide among "*out-of-state visitors*" to these three counties was compared to the average relative mortality from suicide among "*out-of-state visitors*" to all other counties in the United States. The relative mortality rates due to suicide for visitors to Las Vegas, Reno, and Atlantic City were 4.3%, 2.3%, and 1.9%, respectively, compared to 1.0% for other US counties. The corresponding proportionate mortality ratios adjusted for age, gender, race, and geographic location were 160, 149, and 152 for the 3 gambling counties. These results suggest that gamblers are more suicide-prone than other interstate travelers of the same gender, age, race, and geographic region. The investigators suggest three explanations of results: gambling prompts some individuals to commit suicide; gambling settings attract suicidal people; or both processes are at work (Phillips, Welty, and Smith, 1997).

Ethnicity and Suicide

Bertolote and Fleischmann examined rates of suicide according to the predominant religious denomination of countries. Results revealed a remarkable difference between countries of Islamic faith and countries of other prevailing religions. In Muslim (Islamic) countries where suicide is strictly forbidden, the suicide rates are very near zero (**Figure 44.7**). These data suggest

that religious preference is a major determinant of suicidal ideation (Bertolote and Fleischmann, 2002b).

SUICIDE ATTEMPTS AND COMPLETED SUICIDE

The strongest known predictor of suicide is a suicide attempt. The suicide risk among individuals who have attempted suicide is hundreds of times higher than the general population. Approximately 10–15% of individuals who attempt suicide will eventually commit suicide. The risk is highest shortly after an attempt and gradually declines over time (Schmidtke et al., 2001).

Parasuicide refers to suicide attempts or gestures where there is no actual intention of completing the act. Parasuicide is difficult to distinguish from an actual attempt to commit suicide and should be considered a major risk factor for a future completed suicide.

Investigators in Helsinki, Finland, conducted a long-term study of morbidity and mortality among 100 patients who attempted suicide by self-poisoning. Patients were followed for up to 37 years to determine their cause-specific mortality and the relative frequency of completed suicide. Two of the patients were lost to follow-up. Among the 98 remaining subjects, 13 (13.2%) committed suicide (7 women and 6 men), 8 by drug overdose, 4 by hanging, and 1 by jumping. Eight of the 13 suicides were committed 15 or more years after the first attempt, and suicides continued to accumulate in the cohort over nearly 40 years of follow-up. These results clearly show that a first suicide attempt is an indicator of high risk for completed suicide throughout the adult lifetime (Suominen et al., 2004).

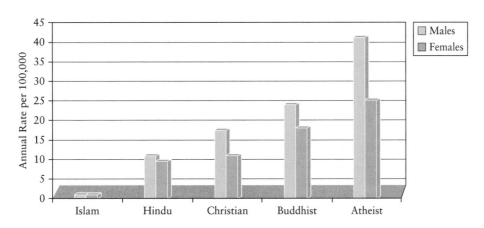

Figure 44.7 Suicide Rates by Religion.

Source: Data from Bertolote JM, Fleischmann A (2002). A global perspective in the epidemiology of suicide. *Suicidologi* 7(2):6–8.

GENETICS OF SUICIDE

Several lines of evidence suggest that suicidal behavior has a significant genetic component. For example, suicidal behavior has been shown to cluster in families, and twin studies have demonstrated that monozygous twins have greater concordance for suicidal behavior than dizygous twins. Recently, molecular studies have found associations of suicidal risk with polymorphisms of the gene encoding *tryptophan hydroxylase* (Roy, Rytander, and Sarchiapone, 1997). Notably, tryptophan hydroxylase is the rate-limiting enzyme in the biosynthetic pathway of *serotonin* (5 hydroxytryptamine or 5-HT). Serotonin functions as neurotransmitter in the brain and central nervous system and is well known for its "*mood elevating*" effects. Several molecular studies have also noted associations of suicidal behavior with polymorphisms of genes encoding serotonin transporters and serotonin receptors. Results of these early molecular studies therefore suggest that genetic variation in the serotonin regulating genes may be associated with depression, suicidal ideation, and completed suicide (Du et al., 2001). However, it has been pointed out that the genetics of suicidal behavior is undoubtedly complex, and likely involves post-transcriptional, post-translational, and/or epigenetic phenomena as well as genetic mutations and polymorphisms (Arango et al., 2003).

ANTIDEPRESSANT DRUGS AND SUICIDE

Though little objective evidence exists on the impact of antidepressant drugs on suicide ideation, there is a long-standing concern that antidepressants might actually induce suicidality early in treatment. Debate on this question intensified in 1990 with a report of 6 adult patients who became suicidal after treatment with fluoxetine (Prozac), a *selective serotonin reuptake inhibitor* (*SSRI*) (Teicher, Glod, and Cole, 1990). This report prompted a meta-analysis of data from randomized clinical trials of fluoxetine to assess possible adverse effects, but the results *did not* reveal increased suicidality among patients who received the drug (Beasley et al., 1991).

Subsequently, three separate meta-analyses of data from a large number of placebo controlled randomized clinical trials of antidepressant drugs *did not* find significant differences between those assigned to drug versus placebo in rates of attempted or completed suicide (Khan, Warner, and Brown, 2000; Storosum et al., 2001; Hammad et al., 2003). It is important to note that these findings are based upon trials of adults and may not be relevant to children and adolescent patients.

Published reports of the emergence of self-destructive behavior in children and adolescents treated with fluoxetine and other antidepressants motivated a renewed concern about potential drug-induced suicide ideation in pediatric patients (King et al., 1991; Olfson et al., 2003). In 2006, investigators from the US Food and Drug Administration reported the results of their meta-analysis of 23 placebo-controlled randomized clinical trials of antidepressants used in the treatment of pediatric patients with major depressive or anxiety disorders. Evaluable data were available for 4,582 patients enrolled in these studies. *While there were no completed suicides in any of the trials*, the findings suggested an increase in the risk of suicidality across all antidepressant drugs tested (RR = 1.95). The risk increase with *selective serotonin reuptake inhibitors* was slightly less than other classes of antidepressants but remained significant (RR = 1.66). The investigators concluded that "*the use of antidepressant drugs in pediatric patients is associated with a modestly increased risk of suicidality.*" However, they also pointed out that other pertinent data seem inconsistent with these findings (Hammad, Laughren, and Racoosin, 2006).

For example, the rate of suicide in adolescent males, ages 15–19 years, declined by 31% in the United States during 1992–2002, concurrent with increased prescriptions for antidepressants in this age group (Stockard and O'Brien, 2003; CDC, 2007). Furthermore, suicide autopsy studies have failed to find evidence of antidepressant drug use in adolescent victims (Leon et al., 2004). Nevertheless, as a precautionary measure, the FDA has modified antidepressant drug labeling to include a "*black box*" warning regarding risk of suicide ideation. The warning states that "*antidepressant medicines may increase suicidal thoughts or actions in some children, teenagers, and young adults when the medicine is first started*" (US FDA, 2007).

Recently, a team of investigators from The Ohio State University conducted an independent meta-analysis to assess the suicidal effects of antidepressants used for the treatment of pediatric depression and obsessive compulsive and anxiety disorders. Their analysis included data from 27 trials enrolling a total of 5,310 patients. There were no completed suicides in these trials and medication produced significant symptom relief for all types of disorders. Nevertheless, consistent with the findings of the FDA meta-analysis, there was a small overall increase in the risk of treatment-emergent suicidal ideation and/or suicide attempt (Bridge et al., 2007).

CLASSIFICATION OF SUICIDE

Various types of suicide have been defined in the literature. One of the most famous classifications of suicide types was published in 1897 by the famous French sociologist, Emile Durkeim. He categorized suicide into four types (egoistic, altruistic, anomic, and fatalistic) according to integration and regulation in social groups rather than by individual characteristics (Durkheim, 1897). Durkheim's social theory of suicidal behavior suffers from the "ecological fallacy" whereby the diseases contracted by individuals do not necessarily reflect the populations that they live in. Despite its limitations, Durkheim's work on suicide has influenced proponents of control theory and is often mentioned as a classic sociological study (Pope, 1976).

In modern epidemiology, diseases (including suicide) are most accurately described and classified by the special characteristics of afflicted individuals rather than the general characteristics of groups or populations. As discussed already, suicidal behavior usually involves a complex web of causative factors, and conceivably, combinations of these factors could be used to derive a workable classification scheme. However, there is no consensus among experts in the field of suicide research regarding standardized nomenclature for the classification of suicide. Most recently, David Lester has proposed an interesting classification scheme that parallels the classification of murder and manslaughter. According to his scheme, there are five basic types of "*self-inflicted*" murder: first-degree suicide (the act was premeditated with intent to kill), second-degree suicide (the act was not premeditated with intent to kill), third-degree suicide (an act of self-harm that was not intended to kill but did), voluntary suicide (the act was provocated by severe psychiatric stress, e.g., intended rape), and involuntary suicide (the act was due to negligence or recklessness, e.g., alcohol or drug overdose). It is suggested that the majority of cases of suicide can be classified according to this scheme (Lester, 2009). Albeit, this classification would have to be extended to encompass some special forms of suicidal behavior, all of which directly involve *other individuals as either accessories or victims*.

Assisted Suicide and Euthanasia

Assisted suicide is when an individual solicits the help of another person to commit suicide. There is considerable debate regarding legal, religious, and moral issues surrounding assisted suicide versus one's personal "*right to die.*" Medically assisted suicide (*euthanasia*) is currently a controversial ethical issue involving people who are terminally ill, in extreme pain, or have (perceived or construed) minimal quality of life due to injury or illness. While euthanasia is illegal in most jurisdictions, the practice is legal with certain restrictions in Belgium, Switzerland, the Netherlands, and the state of Oregon. Recently, the *Social, Health, and Family Affairs Committee* of the *Council of Europe*, representing 45 nations, issued a report which called upon European nations to consider decriminalizing euthanisia (Marty, 2003). Three statements from the report are of primary interest.

1. Nobody has the right to impose on the terminally-ill and the dying the obligation to live out their life in unbearable suffering and anguish where they themselves have persistently expressed the wish to end it.

2. There is no implied obligation on any health worker to take part in an act of euthanasia, nor can such an act be interpreted as the expression of lesser consideration for human life.

3. Governments of Council of Europe member states are asked to collect and analyze empirical evidence about end-of-life decisions; to promote public discussion of such evidence; to promote comparative analysis of such evidence in the framework of the Council of Europe; and, in the light of such evidence and public discussion, to consider whether enabling legislation authorizing euthanasia should be envisaged.

In Switzerland where euthanasia was legalized in 1941, the number of assisted suicides has risen dramatically in the past two decades (**Figure 44.8**). Furthermore, in recent years, increasing numbers of individuals from other countries have entered Switzerland to undergo euthaniasia, a practice called *tourist suicide*. For example, in 1995, 45% of more than 400 assisted suicides involved individuals from outside the country (Bosshard, 2010).

Investigators at the University of Zurich analyzed all cases of assisted suicide in Switzerland facilitated by two "right to die" organizations during 2001–2004. Their objective was to quantify the predominant reasons for euthanasia and characterize its epidemiologic features. Among 421 assisted suicides, 65% were women, 61% were from outside Switzerland, and 75% were suffering from fatal diseases such as multiple sclerosis or amyotrophic lateral sclerosis. Among the 25% of cases who did not have a fatal illness, chronic pain, and debilitation, depression and "*weariness of life*" were common reasons given for undergoing euthanasia (Fischer et al., 2008).

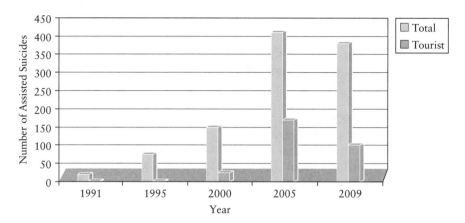

Figure 44.8 Euthanasia in Switzerland, 1991–2009.

Source: Data from Bosshard G (2010). Assisted suicide and euthanasia (EAS) in Europe with special regard to Switzerland. Briefing Report to End of Life Assistance (Scotlland) Bill Committee. May, 2010.

Murder-Suicide

Murder-suicide is an act of murder followed by suicide of the perpetrator. *Familicide* is a type of murder-suicide in which a spouse and one or more children are murdered, or in which parents and/or other relatives are murdered followed by suicide of the perpetrator. Spree killings are another form of murder-suicide that ends in suicide by the perpetrators, such as in several school shootings that have occurred in the United States and elsewhere.

Peter Marzuk and colleagues reviewed the epidemiology, patterns, and major determinants of murder-suicide with the objective of identifying individuals who either commit this type of violence or are at greatest risk to become a victim. Data and relevant information were obtained from articles, books, and monographs published during 1966–1992. In the United States, the annual incidence of murder-suicide episodes was about 2 per million person-years accounting for 1,000–1,500 deaths per year. Incidence rates were relatively constant in those populations reporting data and no significant time trends were noted. The investigators found that "*the principal perpetrators are young males with intense sexual jealousy, depressed mothers, or despairing elderly men with ailing spouses. The principal victims are female sexual partners or consanguineous relatives, usually young children*" (Marzuk, Tardiff, and Hirsch, 1992).

Rare Forms of Suicide

Other rare types of suicide have been described. Fortunately, such episodes are extraordinarily rare and as a consequence, there is little epidemiologic data pertaining to any of them.

A *copycat suicide* is defined as emulation of another suicide based on accounts or depictions of the original suicide in the media or elsewhere.

A *cult suicide* is a term used to describe mass suicide by the members of groups that have been considered cults. In some cases all or nearly all members have committed suicide at the same time and place as ordered by the cult leader.

Mass suicide is when a number of people kill themselves for the same ideological reason. Suicide missions, kamikaze and suicide terrorist attacks are military or paramilitary forms of mass suicide. An *honor suicide* is when a person commits suicide to escape the shame of an immoral or cowardly action.

An *Internet suicide* is a suicide conducted in full view of the public via the Internet, or pursuant to a suicide pact made between individuals who meet on the Internet. The majority of Internet suicides have been reported in Japan.

Suicide by cop is when a suicidal individual deliberately threatens a law enforcement officer or other armed individual with the goal of provoking a lethal response.

A *suicide pact* describes suicide in two or more individuals who agree to die together. Such pacts usually involve married or romantic partners, particularly elderly couples.

It is stressed that these forms of suicide are extraordinarily rare with a very low lifetime risk, perhaps less than 1 per million. Despite this, such episodes are often sensationalized by exhaustive media coverage which may in fact influence suicidal and violent behavior in others. One of the earliest known associations between the media and suicide arose from Goethe's novel *Die Leiden des Jungen Werther*

(*The Sorrows of Young Werther*) published in 1774, in which the hero shoots himself after an ill-fated love affair. Shortly after its publication, there were many reports of young men who committed suicide by the same method. Hence the term "*Werther effect*" has persisted in the literature to describe imitation (or copycat) suicides. Obviously, sensationalized reporting of such cases in the media is to be discouraged (Schmidtke and Schaller, 1998).

PREVENTION OF SUICIDE

Prevention of suicide is a major public health challenge in all countries of the world. In 1993, six broad guidelines were proposed by the World Health Organization to prevent suicidal behavior: timely diagnosis and effective treatment of those with depression and other mental disorders, restricting possession of firearms and other weapons, detoxification of domestic gas, detoxification of car emissions, control of availability of poisons and toxic substances, and "*toning down*" sensationalized reports of suicide in the press (WHO, 1993).

Shortly thereafter, Gunnell and Frankel reviewed the literature on the efficacy of various methods of suicide prevention. Though evidence of efficacy was found lacking for single interventions, the investigators advocated further testing of a multifaceted approach that includes restricting access to firearms and weapons of self-destruction, educating general practitioners on how to recognize and treat depression and other psychiatric disorders, limiting over-the-counter and prescription drugs that are most often taken in fatal overdoses, implementing population-based registries of parasuicide and suicide, and modifying car exhaust design to prevent exposure to carbon monoxide. The investigators also noted that patients recently discharged from psychiatric hospitals and those with a history of parasuicide are at particularly high risk; hence, such patients should be carefully monitored and managed appropriately with antidepressant medications. The following statement from this report is particularly poignant:

> "*Inevitably, many of those who commit suicide are suffering from longstanding mental or physical distress and for them life has become unbearable. For others suicide occurs as a result of a crisis, either as a consequence of relationship breakdown or financial difficulties, in the context of a vulnerable personality type. Suicide offers an escape from an intolerable, although probably transient period of emotional turmoil.*

> *If appropriate help and protection can be offered during this period, suicide can be prevented"* (Gunnell and Frankel, 1994).

● ● ● **REFERENCES**

Arango, V., Huang, Y.Y., Underwood, M.D., & Mann, J.J. (2003). Genetics of the serotonergic system in suicidal behavior. *Journal of Psychiatric Research, 37,* 375–386.

Arsenault-Lapierre, G., Kim, C., & Turecki, G. (2004). Psychiatric diagnoses in 3275 suicides: A meta-analysis. *BMC Psychiatry, 4,* 37.

Beasley, C.M. Jr., Dornseif, B.E., Bosomworth, J.C., Sayler, M.E., Rampey, A.H. Jr., Heiligenstein, J.H.,...Masica, D.N. (1991). Fluoxetine and suicide: A meta-analysis of controlled trials of treatment for depression. *BMJ, 303,* 685–692.

Bertolote, J.M., & Fleischmann, A. (2002a). Suicide and psychiatric diagnosis: A worldwide perspective. *World Psychiatry, 1*(3), 181–185.

Bertolote, J.M., & Fleischmann, A. (2002b). A global perspective in the epidemiology of suicide. *Suicidologi, 7*(2), 6–8.

Bosshard, G. (2010). Assisted suicide and euthanasia (EAS) in Europe with special regard to Switzerland. Briefing Report to End of Life Assistance (Scotland) Bill Committee. May, 2010.

Bridge, J.A., Iyengar, S., Salary, C.B., Barbe, R.P., Birmaher, B., Pincus, H.A.,...Brent, D.A. (2007). Clinical response and risk for reported suicidal ideation and suicide attempts in pediatric antidepressant treatment: A meta-analysis of randomized controlled trials. *JAMA, 297*(15), 1683–1696.

Burke, T., & Reardon, D.C. (2002). *Forbidden grief: The unspoken pain of abortion.* Springfield, IL: Acorn Books.

Centers for Disease Control. (2007). Atlanta, Georgia, USA.

Du, L., Faludi, G., Palkovits, M., Bakish, D., & Hrdina, P.D. (2001). Serotonergic genes and suicidality. *Crisis, 22*(2), 54–60.

Durkheim, E. (1897). *Le Suicide*. Paris, France.

Fischer, S., Huber, C.A., Imhof, L., Imhof, R.M., Furter, M., Ziegler, S.J., & Bosshard, G. (2008). Suicide assisted by two Swiss right-to-die organisations. *J Med Ethics, 34*, 810–814.

Gunnell, D., & Frankel, S. (1994). Prevention of suicide: Aspirations and evidence. *BMJ, 308*(6938), 1227–1233.

Hammad, T., Mosholder, A., Boehm, G., Racoosin, J.A., & Laughren, T. (2003). Incidence of suicide in randomized controlled trials of patients with major depressive disorder [abstract]. *Pharmacoepidemiol Drug Safety, 12*, S156.

Hammad, T.A., Laughren, T., & Racoosin, J. (2006). Suicidality in pediatric patients treated with antidepressant drugs. *Arch Gen Psychiatry, 63*, 332–339.

Hawton, K., & van Heeringen, K. (2009). Suicide. *The Lancet, 373*(9672), 1372–1381.

Khan, A., Warner, H.A., & Brown, W.A. (2000). Symptom reduction and suicide risk in patients treated with placebo in antidepressant clinical trials. *Arch Gen Psychiatry, 57*, 311–317.

King, R.A., Riddle, M.A., Chappell, P.B., Hardin, M.T., Anderson, G.M., & Lombroso, P. (1991). Emergence of self-destructive phenomena in children and adolescents during fluoxetine treatment. *J Am Acad Child Adolesc Psychiatry, 30*, 179–186.

Law, S., & Liu, P. (2008). Suicide in China: Unique demographic patterns and relationship to depressive disorder. *Curr Psychiatry Rep, 10*(1), 80–86.

Leon, A.C., Marzuk, P.M., Tardiff, K., & Teres, J.J. (2004). Paroxetine, other antidepressants, and youth suicide in New York City: 1993 through 1998. *J Clin Psychiatry, 65*, 915–918.

Lester, D. (2009). A proposal for a nomenclature for suicide. *Psychological Reports, 105*, 685–686.

Li, X.Y., Yang, R.S., & Zhang, C. (2001). A case-control study of the risk factors in attempted suicide. *Chin J Epidemiol, 22*, 281–283.

Olfson, M., Shaffer, D., Marcus, S.C., & Greenberg, T. (2003). Relationship between antidepressant medication treatment and suicide in adolescents. *Arch Gen Psychiatry, 60*, 978–982.

Marty, D. (2003). *Euthanasia*. Report: Social, Health and Family Affairs Committee, Doc 9898, Sep 10, 2003.

Marzuk, P.M., Tardiff, K., & Hirsch, C.S. (1992). The epidemiology of murder-suicide. *JAMA, 267*, 3179–3183.

Morgan, C.M., Evan, M., Peter, J.R., & Currie, C. (1997). Mental health may deteriorate as a direct effect of induced abortion. *BMJ, 314*, 902.

Moscicki, E.K. (2001). Epidemiology of completed and attempted suicide: Toward a framework for prevention. *Clinical Neuroscience Research, 1*, 310–323.

O'Brien, R.M., & Stockard, J. (2006). A common explanation for the changing age distributions of suicide and homicide in the United States, 1930 to 2000. *Social Forces, 84*(3), 1539–1557.

Phillips, D.P., Welty, W.R., & Smith, M.M. (1997). Elevated suicide levels associated with legalized gambling. *Suicide and Life Threatening Behavior*, Dec 27(4), 373–378.

Phillips, M.R., Li, X., & Zhang, Y. (2002). Suicide rates in China, 1995–1999. *Lancet, 359*, 835–840.

Pope, W. (1976). *Durkheim's suicide: A classic analyzed*. Chicago: University of Chicago Press.

Reardon, D.C. (2002). Suicide rates in China. *Lancet, 359*, 2274.

Roy, A., Rytander, G., & Sarchiapone, M. (1997). Genetics of suicide: Family studies and molecular genetics. *Annals of the New York Academy of Sciences, 836*, 135–157.

Schmidtke, A., & Schaller, S. (1998). What do we do about media effects on imitation of suicidal behaviour. In: D. De Leo, A. Schmidtke, S. Schaller (Eds.). *Suicide prevention: A holistic approach* (pp. 121–137). Dordrecht: Kluwer Academic Publishers.

Schmidtke, A., Bille-Brahe, U., De Leo, D., Kerkhof, A., & Wasserman, D. (2001). *Suicidal behaviour in Europe: Results from the WHO/EURO multicentre study on suicidal behaviour*. Bern: Hogrefe & Huber.

Stockard, J., & O'Brien, R.M. (2003). Cohort variations and changes in age-specific suicide rates over time: Explaining variation in youth suicide. *Social Forces*, *81*(2), 605–642.

Storosum, J.G., van Zweiten, B.J., van den Brink, W., Gersons, B.P.R., & Broekmans, A.W. (2001). Suicide risk in placebo-controlled studies of major depression. *Am J Psychiatry*, *158*, 1271–1275.

Suominen, K., Isometsa, E., Suoka, J., Haukka, J., Achte, K., & Lonnquiest, J. (2004). Completed suicide after a suicide attempt: A 37 year follw-up study. *Am J Psychiatry*, *161*, 563–564.

Teicher, M.H., Glod, C., & Cole, J.O. (1990). Emergence of intense suicidal preoccupation during fluoxetine treatment. *Am J Psychiatry*, *147*, 207–210.

US FDA. (2007). *Antidepressant use in children, adolescents, and adults. Revisions to medication guide, antidepressant medicines, depression and other serious mental illnesses, and suicidal thoughts or actions*. United States Food and Drug Administration.

Wasserman, D., Cheng, Q., & Jian, G.X. (2005). Global suicide rates among young people aged 15–19. *World Psychiatry*, *4*(2), 114–120.

World Health Organization. (1993). *Guidelines for the primary prevention of mental, neurological and psychosocial disorders: Suicide*. Geneva, Switzerland: Division of Mental Health, World Health Organization.

World Health Organization. (2002). *Mortality and burden of disease estimates for WHO member states in 2002*. World Health Organization.

World Health Organization. (2009). *Mortality and burden of disease estimates for WHO member states in 2004*. Geneva, Switzerland, World Health Organization.

45

Epidemiology of Tuberculosis

INTRODUCTION

Tuberculosis is a common infectious disease caused by *Mycobacterium tuberculosis*. The infection typically attacks the lungs but can also spread to other organs including the meninges, lymph nodes, skeletal system, and genitourinary tract. Tuberculosis is a communicable disease that is disseminated by coughing and sneezing. Most infections in humans are asymptomatic and become latent, but about 10% of latent infections eventually progress to active disease. Without treatment, active tuberculosis has a case fatality rate exceeding 50% (Jasmer, Nahid, and Hopewell, 2002).

Classic symptoms of active tuberculosis are chronic cough with blood-tinged sputum, fever, night sweats, and profound weight loss. Historically, tuberculosis was called "consumption" since patients were virtually consumed from within by the disease. The definitive diagnosis of tuberculosis relies on chest X-rays, a tuberculin skin test (Mantoux test), blood serology, and microscopic examination of cultures of biological specimens (Konstantinos, 2010).

HISTORICAL RECORD OF TUBERCULOSIS

Tuberculosis has ravaged the human population for thousands of years. The causative microbe, *Mycobacterium tuberculosis*, has been detected in mummies (3000 BC), prehistoric human remains (7000 BC), and the remains of bison (15000 BC) (Zink et al., 2003; Hershkovitz et al., 2008; Rothschild et al., 2001). Hippocrates identified *phthisis* (the Greek term for tuberculosis) as the most widespread disease of his time (460 BC). Afflicted

patients had intractable fever and hemoptysis (pulmonary hemorrhage), which was almost always fatal (Herzog, 1998).

Discovery of Mycobacterium Tuberculosis

The bacillus causing tuberculosis, *Mycobacterium tuberculosis*, was identified and described in 1882 by the famed German microbiologist, Robert Koch. It has been estimated that during the 18th and 19th centuries, tuberculosis was responsible for the deaths of more than *1 billion people*. In the year that Koch made his discovery, 7 million people died from tuberculosis (Waddington, 2004). Koch also synthesized a vaccine from killed bacteria that he called "*tuberculin*." Although ineffective as a treatment, tuberculin testing became routine in detecting bovine tuberculosis leading to the elimination of the disease in livestock (Waddington, 2004). Robert Koch's discovery of the *tubercle bacillus*, and his subsequent development of measures to prevent the spread of tuberculosis have had a profound impact on human history and undoubtedly spared many lives. The Nobel Prize in physiology or medicine was awarded to Dr. Koch in 1905 "*for his investigations and discoveries in relation to tuberculosis*" (Koch, 1905).

Tuberculosis in the 19th and 20th Centuries

Tuberculosis was one of the leading causes of death in the United States, Europe, and many other countries throughout the 19th century and the early 20th century. Those infected with tuberculosis were isolated from society and placed in sanatoriums to prevent dissemination of the disease. Therapies for the "*white plague*" were of little benefit until the development of an effective vaccine in France and the subsequent discovery of streptomycin in the United States.

The antituberculosis *Bacille Calmette-Guérin vaccine* was conceived and developed between 1905 and 1921 at the Pasteur Institutes in France by Albert Camette and Camille Guérin. Their vaccine was eventually proven to be of value in preventing tuberculosis in humans, but was not widely used until after World War II (Comstock, 1994; Bonah, 2005).

Selman Waksman was an American biochemist and microbiologist whose research promoted the discovery of streptomycin and several other antibiotics. In 1952, Waksman was awarded the Nobel Prize in Physiology or Medicine in recognition of "*his discovery of streptomycin, the first antibiotic active against tuberculosis*" (Waksman, 1952).

Due to the effective use of antibiotics for patients with latent and active disease during the last half of the 20th century, the death rates from tuberculosis plummeted in the United States and other developed countries. Nevertheless, with the emergence of multidrug resistant strains of *Mycobacterium tuberculosis (MDR-TB)* and coinfections with HIV, there has been a resurgence of tuberculosis that has become a global public health emergency in many regions of the world (WHO, 2007).

GLOBAL BURDEN OF TUBERCULOSIS IN THE 21ST CENTURY

Based upon recent global surveys of member nations and territories, the World Health Organization reports that approximately *one-third of the world population* is infected with *Mycobacterium tuberculosis*. As shown in **Figure 45.1**, most of the more than *2 billion* individuals who are seropositive for *Mycobacterium tuberculosis* (~80%) are found in 22 developing countries, most of which are located in Asia and sub-Saharan Africa (World Health Organization, 2007, 2009, 2010).

The prevalence of seropositive individuals varies by location and also by age. In developing countries such as the United States, Canada, European, and Australasian nations, the rates remain low (less than 1%) throughout the lifespan. In contrast, rates in endemic areas, such as sub-Saharan Africa, India, China, and Russia rise dramatically with age approaching nearly 100% in some populations. **Figure 45.2** shows the prevalence of seropositive individuals by age based upon tuberculin testing among 1,061 individuals in Cape Town, South Africa. All individuals surveyed were HIV negative. Note that by age 35, the prevalence of seropositive individuals is nearly 90% (Wood et al., 2010).

INCIDENCE AND PREVALENCE OF ACTIVE TUBERCULOSIS

During 2007, the World Health Organization conducted its most recent global survey to determine the incidence, prevalence, and mortality of tuberculosis among its 196 member nations and territories. The survey captured nearly all (99.7%) of the world population (WHO, 2007). The following statistics quoted from the 2009 WHO Report capture the

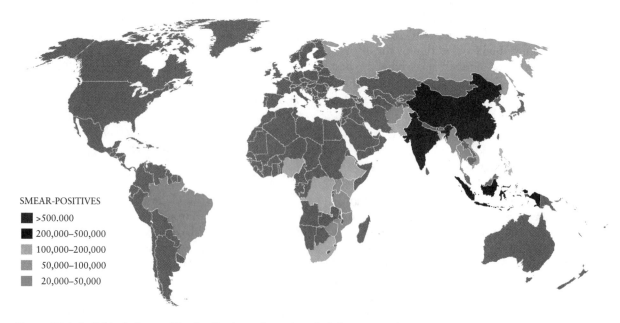

SMEAR-POSITIVES

- ■ >500.000
- ■ 200,000–500,000
- 100,000–200,000
- 50,000–100,000
- 20,000–50,000

Figure 45.1 Individuals Seropositive for *Mycobacterium tuberculosis* in 22 countries.

Source: Data from World Health Organization (2007). Tuberculosis. World Health Organization, Geneva, Switzerland.

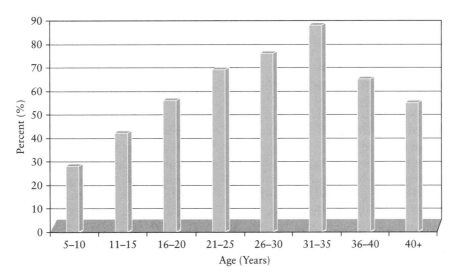

Figure 45.2 Age-Specific Prevalence of Tuberculin Seropositivity in South Africa.

Source: Data from Wood R, Liang H, Wu H, Middelkoop K, Oni T, Rangaka MX, Wilkinson RJ, Bekker L-G, Lawn SD (2010). Changing prevalence of TB infection with increasing age in high TB burden townships in South Africa. *Int J Tuberc Lung Dis* 13(4):406–412.

essence of the global burden of tuberculosis (TB) and related conditions.

> *"Globally, there were an estimated 9.27 million incident cases of TB in 2007. This is an increase from 9.24 million cases in 2006, 8.3 million cases in 2000, and 6.6 million cases in 1990. Most of the estimated numbers of cases in 2007 were in Asia (55%) and Africa (31%), with small proportions of cases in the Eastern Mediterranean Region (6%), the European Region (5%), and the Region of the Americas (3%). The five countries that rank first to fifth in terms of total numbers of cases in 2007 are India (2.0 million), China (1.3 million), Indonesia (0.53 million), Nigeria (0.46 million), and South Africa (0.46 million). Of the 9.27 million incident TB cases in 2007, an estimated 1.37 million (15%) were HIV-positive; 79% of these HIV-positive cases were in the African Region and 11% were in the South-East Asia Region."*

> *"There were an estimated 13.7 million prevalent cases of TB in 2007 (206 per 100 000 population), a decrease from 13.9 million cases (210 per 100 000 population) in 2006."*

> *"An estimated 1.3 million deaths occurred among HIV negative incident cases of TB (20 per 100 000 population) in 2007. There were an additional 456,000 deaths among incident TB cases who were HIV-positive; these deaths are classified as HIV deaths in the International Statistical Classification of Diseases (ICD-10). The 456,000 deaths among HIV-positive incident TB cases equate to 33% of HIV-positive*

incident cases of TB and 23% of the estimated 2 million HIV deaths in 2007."

The 9.3 million incident (new) cases of tuberculosis observed in 2007 converts to an annual global incidence rate of 139 per 100,000, slightly less than the incidence observed in 2004 (142 per 100,000). However, the annual incidence rates varied by tenfold amongst nations, from less than 25 per 100,000 in developed nations of North America, Europe, and Australasia to more than 300 per 100,000 in many of the impoverished nations of sub-Saharan Africa. Swaziland in Central Africa had the highest incidence (1,200 per 100,000) and Canada one of the lowest (2 per 100,000).

Relatively high national incidence rates were observed in India (168 per 100,000) and China (98 per 100,000), yielding 2 million and 1.3 million new cases, respectively. Rates were also high in Indonesia (530,000 new cases), Nigeria (460,000 new cases), and South Africa (460,000 new cases). The highest incidence in South America was observed in Brazil (48 per 100,000). Portugal and Spain had the highest incidence rates among Western European nations (30 cases per 100,000). Rates were comparatively low in the United Kingdom (15 per 100,000) and the United States (4 per 100,000).

TUBERCULOSIS: MORTALITY

Approximately 1.8 million people died from tuberculosis in 2007; of these, 456,000 (~25%) were co-infected with the Human Immunodeficiency Virus

(HIV), and the remainder were HIV-negative. More than 80% of deaths from tuberculosis occurred in Southeast Asia and sub-Saharan Africa where coinfection with HIV is common. As discussed in the following section on HIV-tuberculosis coinfection, case fatality rates are markedly elevated in coinfected patients who do not have access to both *highly active antiretroviral therapy (HAART)* and combination antibiotic therapy for tuberculosis.

The WHO investigators estimated that about 110,000 deaths were caused by multi*drug resistant tuberculosis (MDR-TB)* or *extensively drug resistant tuberculosis (XDR-TB)*. In high burden regions of the world, these strains have been found in 10–20% of patients with active tuberculosis, compared to less than 5% of patients in other areas. Resistant strains of *Tuberculosis mycobacterium* require special regimens of antibiotics taken for long periods of time. Such antibiotics are expensive and not readily available in most societies, and as a consequence, the case fatality rates are inordinately high (50% or more) among individuals infected with MDR-TB or XDR-TB (WHO, 2009).

Annual mortality rates ranged from less than 10 per 100,000 in North America, Europe and Australasia to greater than 70 per 100,000 in sub-Saharan Africa. Rates were intermediate in Southeast Asia (31 per 100,000), Eastern Mediterranean countries (18 per 100,000) and the islands of the West Pacific (13 per 100,000). The global pattern of mortality due to tuberculosis is similar to the pattern of disability adjusted life years shown in **Figure 45.3**.

DISABILITY ADJUSTED LIFE YEARS (DALY): TUBERCULOSIS

The pattern of *disability adjusted life years (DALY)* lost due to premature death and disability from tuberculosis reflects high rates in sub-Saharan Africa, Southeast Asia, the Russian Federation, and some countries in South America (Figure 45.3). Childhood deaths from tuberculosis contribute heavily to the DALY. Of the 2 million total deaths from tuberculosis in 2007, nearly one-fourth (470,000) occurred in children under the age of 15 years. Furthermore, without adequate treatment, tuberculosis is a progressive disease that causes significant disability. The pattern of DALY due to tuberculosis therefore reflects early childhood death and progressive disability among afflicted adults in the impoverished populations of Africa, Asia, and other regions with high incidence and prevalence rates.

TUBERCULOSIS IN THE UNITED STATES

Every year, the United States Centers for Disease Control (CDC) reports results from the *National Tuberculosis Surveillance System* for the previous

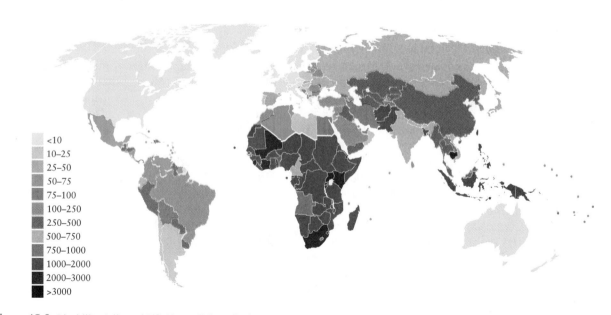

Figure 45.3 Disability Adjusted Life Years: Tuberculosis, 2004.

Source: Data from World Health Organization. The global burden of disease: 2004 update. Geneva, WHO, 2008. Available at www.who.int/evidence/bod.

year (CDC, 2010a). In 2009, a total of 11,540 new cases of active tuberculosis were reported in the United States. The overall incidence rate was 3.8 cases per 100,000, a decrease of 77% from the rate of 7.6 per 100,000 reported in 1993. The rate in foreign-born persons was 18.6 per 100,000, nearly 11 times higher than in US-born persons (1.7 per 100,000). The rate of tuberculosis in foreign-born persons has decreased 45% from the rate of 33.8 per 100,000 reported in 1993 (**Figure 45.4**).

There are marked ethnic differences in the rates of active tuberculosis in the United States. The rates among Hispanics and African Americans (7 per 100,000) were approximately 8 times higher than among non-Hispanic Caucasians (0.9 per 100,000), and rates among Asians were nearly 26 times higher (23.3 per 100,000). In 2009, 4 countries accounted for 50.1% of the tuberculosis cases in foreign-born persons: Mexico (1,574), the Philippines (799), India (523), and Vietnam (514). In 2009, among persons with tuberculosis and a known human immunodeficiency virus (HIV) test result, 10.2% (690 of 6,743) were coinfected with HIV (CDC, 2010a).

TRANSMISSION OF TUBERCULOSIS

When people suffering from active pulmonary tuberculosis cough, sneeze, speak, or spit, they expel infectious aerosolized droplets 0.5–5 µm in diameter. A single sneeze can release up to 40,000 droplets, each of which may transmit the disease since the infectious dose of tuberculosis is very low and inhaling fewer than 10 bacteria may cause an infection.

People with prolonged, frequent, or intense contact with patients who have active tuberculosis are at particularly high risk of becoming infected. A person with active untreated tuberculosis can infect 10–15 other people per year. Others at risk include people in areas where tuberculosis is common, people who inject drugs using unsanitary needles, residents and employees of high-risk congregate settings, medically underserved and low-income populations, high-risk racial or ethnic minority populations, children exposed to adults in high-risk categories, patients immunocompromised by conditions such as HIV/AIDS, people who take immunosuppressant drugs, and healthcare workers serving these high-risk clients (Cole and Cook, 1998).

In endemic areas, community acquisition of latent tuberculosis infection is common. In a recent study of school children in South Africa where *Mycobacterium tuberculosis* and HIV are endemic, the annual rate of new infection based upon tuberculin skin testing was 4.1% resulting in a prevalence of 52% among adolescents by 17 years of age (Middlekoop et al., 2008).

Mycobacterium tuberculosis can only be transmitted by patients with active disease. The probability of transmission from one person to another depends upon the number of infectious droplets expelled by a carrier, the effectiveness of ventilation, the duration of exposure, and the virulence of the *Mycobacterium tuberculosis* strain. The chain of transmission can be broken by isolating patients with active disease and starting effective therapy. After 2 weeks of treatment, patients with nonresistant active tuberculosis generally cease to be contagious. In newly infected

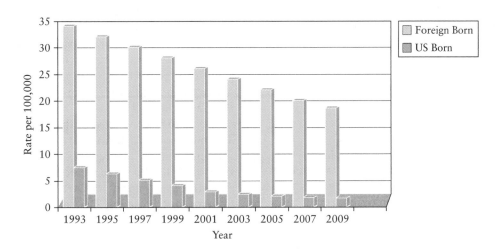

Figure 45.4 Rates of Tuberculosis in the USA, 1993–2009.

Source: Data from Centers for Disease Control (2010a). Reported Tuberculosis in the United States, 2009. Atlanta, GA: US Department of Health and Human Services, CDC, October 2010.

individuals, there is a 21–28 day incubation period before the bacterium can be transmitted to others. Tuberculosis is also a "food-borne" infectious disease and can be transmitted by ingestion of contaminated meat and milk. *Mycobacterium bovis*, once a common cause of tuberculosis, was virtually eliminated from human populations of developing countries after the introduction of pasteurized milk (Robbins and Cotran, 1979; Tweddle and Livingstone, 1994; Thoen, Lobue, and de Kantor, 2006).

PATHOGENESIS OF TUBERCULOSIS

Infection begins when mycobacteria reach the pulmonary alveoli where they invade and replicate within the endosomes of alveolar macrophages. Within macrophages, mycobacteria are shielded from oxidative and enzymatic damage by their highly resistant lipid cell walls. Macrophages, lymphocytes, and fibroblasts aggregate around infected cells to form a granuloma which is characteristic of *latent* tuberculosis infection. Tuberculosis is thus classified as a *granulomatous* inflammatory condition. In many patients with tuberculosis, the infection waxes and wanes. Over time, the cores of tuberculous granulomas become necrotic with the texture of soft white cheese, a pathologic feature known as *caseous necrosis*. Tissue destruction and necrosis are balanced by healing and fibrosis. With successful therapy, granulomatous lesions are totally replaced by scar tissue. However, upon eruption from granulomas, live mycobacteria can disseminate through the bloodstream to other tissues and organs causing the formation of secondary lesions in peripheral lymph nodes, kidneys, brain, and bone. Disseminated tuberculosis (miliary tuberculosis) is most common in infants and the elderly. Without early treatment, the case fatality rate of this condition approaches 100% (Robbins and Cotran, 1979; Kim et al., 2003).

RISK FACTORS FOR TUBERCULOSIS

Risk factors for tuberculosis are divisible into those that influence transmission of the mycobacterium, and those modulate the course of latent versus active infection. Individual studies of mycobacterial transmission and resistance to infection in humans are complicated by a variety of issues including the ethics and morality of conducting such investigations and the absence of a validated measure of exposure. Epidemiologic studies are therefore limited to ecological studies of the prevalence of coinfection by *Mycobacterium tuberculosis* and HIV, and individual studies of other noninfectious factors that heighten or lessen the risk of developing active disease among those who have latent tuberculosis.

HIV and Tuberculosis

Among the 9.27 million incident cases of tuberculosis in 2007, an estimated 1.37 million (14.8%) were HIV-positive. Of these, 79% were found in sub-Saharan Africa and 11% in Southeast Asia. The heaviest burden of this coepidemic of tuberculosis and HIV infections is in sub-Saharan Africa. In South Africa and Swaziland, approximately 1% of the population develops tuberculosis annually and these two nations account for more than 40% of all cases of HIV-associated tuberculosis. In 2007, more than 465,000 deaths were attributed to HIV-tuberculosis coinfections. Most of these deaths (~ 70%) occurred in 5 countries: 131,000 in India, 112,000 in China, 43,000 in Russia, 16,000 in South Africa, and 15,000 in Bangladesh (WHO, 2009, 2010).

In patients with HIV infection, the risk of developing active tuberculosis is contingent upon prophylaxis and therapy. In Barcelona, Spain, Guelar and colleagues conducted a prospective study of 839 HIV-infected patients to examine effects of immune status (tuberculin positivity) and prophylaxis with isoniazid among patients with a positive tuberculin test. During 52 months of follow-up, active tuberculosis developed in 23 (3.1%) of 733 patients with a negative tuberculin test (2.4 cases per 100 patient-years). Among tuberculin positive patients, active tuberculosis developed in 7 of 26 patients who did not receive isoniazid prophylaxis (16.2 cases per 100 patient-years), 4 of 61 patients who completed 9 months of prophylaxis (8.9 cases per 100 patient years), and none of 19 patients who continued prophylaxis until the end of study. These results suggest that sustained prophylaxis with isoniazid provides significant protection against the development of active tuberculosis in patients with HIV infection (Guelar et al., 1993).

In a study conducted at the University of Cape Town in South Africa, investigators compared the incidence rate of tuberculosis in 264 patients with HIV disease who were treated with *highly active antiretrovirus therapy* (*HAART*) to the rate in 760 patients not receiving HAART. Results revealed that HAART reduced the incidence of tuberculosis by 81% in patients with HIV disease (2.4 vs. 9.7 cases per 100 patient-years); furthermore, the protective effect of HAART was greatest in symptomatic patients and those with advanced immune suppression (Badri, Wilson, and Wood, 2002).

The results of these and other trials indicate that with appropriate therapy and management, tuberculosis can be averted in HIV-infected patients. However, due to the high cost and intensive nature of patient management, most patients in developing countries simply do not have access to such therapy and therefore develop coinfections with HIV and tuberculosis. For example, the WHO survey of 2007 suggests that in regions with a high prevalence of HIV-positive individuals such as South Africa and Swaziland, the incidence of active tuberculosis is increased more than twenty-fold in HIV-positive individuals compared to HIV-negative individuals (WHO, 2009). In coinfected patients, immunosuppression due to HIV often results in extra-pulmonary and disseminated tuberculosis; reciprocally, the presence of tuberculosis has been noted to increase the viral load of HIV. The case fatality rate among coinfected individuals is extraordinarily high.

Gandhi and colleagues recently examined the prevalence of MDR-TB and XDR-TB and the consequences of coinfection with HIV in a rural area of South Africa. During 2005 and 2006, sputum samples were collected from 1,539 patients. Of these, 221 (14.3%) had MDR-TB and 53 (3.4%) had XDR-TB. More than half (55%) of patients with XDR-TB had never been previously treated for tuberculosis. Most notably, all XDR-TB cases tested positive for HIV. Among cases with XDR-TB, the median survival was only 16 days and nearly all (52 of 53) died within a few weeks. Results therefore suggest that XDR-TB is readily transmitted to HIV-infected patients in the South African population and coinfected patients have little chance of survival (Gandhi et al., 2006).

Childhood Tuberculosis

Accurate estimates of the burden of tuberculosis in children are unavailable for many populations. This is because cases with active pulmonary disease are detected by virtue of "positive smears" of sputum samples, and most children with active disease (up to 95%) simply do not produce enough sputum for testing. As a consequence, tuberculosis rates based upon "smear positive" cases probably only represent about 5–10% of the actual cases (Rekha and Swaminathan, 2007; Lighter and Rigaud, 2009).

Infection rates in children can be monitored by periodic tuberculin skin tests; however, without such testing, primary infection in children is predominantly asymptomatic and goes unrecognized in the vast majority (~90%) of cases. Recent studies conducted in endemic areas have noted twofold higher seroconversion rates among young children with sustained exposure to female caregivers with HIV and tuberculosis coinfection compared to children without such exposure (Kenyon et al., 2002). However, the seroconversion rate is also high in children from endemic regions due to community acquisition of mycobacterial infection (see **Figure 45.2**).

Young children who become infected with *Mycobacterium tuberculosis* are at high risk for the development of active disease. As shown in **Figure 45.5**, the risk is highest during the first year of life when the immune system is most immature and then declines dramatically in subsequent years as immunocompetence rises. Meningitis and military tuberculosis, conditions with high case fatality rates, are common in those infants with primary infection. Furthermore, infected children frequently manifest

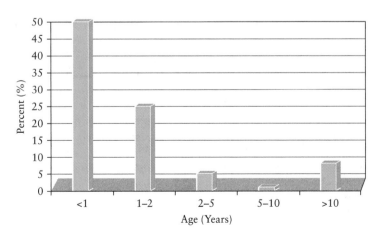

Figure 45.5 Risk of Developing Active Tuberculosis in Infected Children.

Source: Data from Marais BJ, Gie RP, Schaaf HS, Hesseling AC, Obihara CC, Atarke JJ, Enarson DA (2004). The natural history of childhood intra-thoracic tuberculosis: a critical review of literature from the pre-chemotherapy era. *Int J Tuberc Lung Dis* 9(4):392–402.

progression to these life-threatening conditions without significant prior symptoms (Marais et al., 2004).

Pregnancy and Tuberculosis

The greatest burden of tuberculosis in women occurs during the childbearing years. Eighty percent of all mortality due to tuberculosis in women occurs in this age group (WHO, 2009).

A number of studies have noted that HIV infection and tuberculosis during pregnancy are a particularly deadly combination and are independent risk factors for maternal mortality (Tripathy and Tripathy, 2003; Mofenson and Laughon, 2007). In communities where tuberculosis and HIV infection are endemic, pregnant women are at high risk of acquiring both infections. In Durban, South Africa, a dramatic increase in the case load of tuberculosis in pregnant women was observed from 1996–1998; notably, there was a tenfold increase in the rate of tuberculosis among the women who were HIV-positive and 72% of these cases were attributed to HIV infection. Furthermore, more than 10% of these young mothers died (Pillay et al., 2001).

In a study conducted in Zambia, tuberculosis accounted for 25% of all nonobstetric maternal deaths and AIDS was present in 92% of cases with tuberculosis (Ahmed et al., 1990).

In a study of maternal mortality in South Africa, there was a 3.2-fold increase in the relative risk of death in mothers with TB-HIV coinfection compared with HIV-uninfected mothers with tuberculosis infection, and 54% of maternal deaths caused by tuberculosis were attributable to coinfection with HIV. Furthermore, in tertiary care hospitals in South Africa, TB-HIV coinfection accounted for 14–15% of all maternal mortality (Khan et al., 2001).

A team of investigators conducted a cross-sectional survey to identify HIV status and cases of active tuberculosis among pregnant women in six clinics in Sowet, South Africa. During 2008–2009, 3,963 pregnant women were enrolled and screened for tuberculosis, of whom 1,454 (36.7%) were HIV-seropositive. Active pulmonary tuberculosis was diagnosed in 10 HIV-seropositive women (6.9 per 1,000) and 5 HIV-seronegative women (2.0 per 1,000). Results suggest a threefold higher burden of active tuberculosis in pregnant women who are HIV-seropositive (Gounder et al., 2011).

The deadly combination of tuberculosis and HIV infection has also been noted among pregnant women in developed countries. In New York City, Margono and colleagues reviewed the medical records of 18 pregnant women diagnosed with tuberculosis between 1985–1992 at 2 metropolitan hospitals. Eleven of the women were tested for HIV and 7 (64%) were positive. The investigators concluded that cases of active tuberculosis associated with HIV infection are increasing among pregnant women and recommended early tuberculin skin testing in HIV-positive women of reproductive age and the initiation of appropriate preventive strategies to reduce morbidity and mortality from tuberculosis (Margono et al., 1994).

Lynne Mofenson and Barbara Laughon of the United States National Institute of Child Health and Human Development point to five lines of evidence to support tuberculin testing among pregnant women who are HIV positive to facilitate targeted prophylaxis in those found to have latent tuberculosis:

> *"(1) TB-HIV coinfection is frequent in many resource-limited settings, (2) HIV infection is the strongest risk factor for progression of latent TB to active TB disease, (3) tests are available to identify TB infection, (4) there is an intervention available that is effective in preventing progression from infection to disease, (5) and the development of TB disease in HIV-infected pregnant and postpartum women is associated with significant maternal and infant mortality"* (Mofenson and Laughon, 2007).

Consensus guidelines have been issued regarding tuberculin testing and treatment of tuberculosis during pregnancy. The following statement is quoted from the Centers for Disease Control (CDC, 2010b).

> *"Untreated tuberculosis represents a greater hazard to a pregnant woman and her fetus than does its treatment. Treatment of pregnant women should be initiated whenever the probability of TB is moderate to high. Infants born to women with untreated TB may be of lower birth weight than those born to women without TB and, rarely, the infant may be born with TB. Although the drugs used in the initial treatment regimen cross the placenta, they do not appear to have harmful effects on the fetus. Tuberculin skin testing is considered both valid and safe throughout pregnancy. The special TB blood test is safe to use during pregnancy, but has not been evaluated for diagnosing M. tuberculosis infection in pregnant women. Other tests are needed to show if a person has TB disease."*

Noninfectious Risk Factors

A number of noninfectious risk factors have been elucidated that heighten the risk of developing active tuberculosis among patients with latent disease.

These include chronic smoking, pulmonary silicosis, chronic obstructive pulmonary diseases (emphysema, chronic bronchitis, asthma), immunosuppressive exposures other than HIV (chemotherapy for malignancy, immunosuppressive drugs), metabolic diseases (diabetes, autoimmune conditions), and other physiologic stressors (pregnancy, poor nutrition).

Silicosis and Active Tuberculosis

In 1948, J.H. Lee reported findings of a study of 100 miners who developed pulmonary silicosis. Of these 100 patients, 65 were proven to also have active tuberculosis by positive sputum, postmortem examination, or other bacteriological tests (Lee, 1948). Silica particles increase the risk of developing active tuberculosis by irritating the respiratory system and interfering with macrophage function (Robbins and Cotran, 1979).

Diabetes and Active Tuberculosis

Several studies have suggested that type 2 diabetes increases the risk of developing active tuberculosis . To clarify and quantify the association, Jeon and Murray conducted a meta-analysis of data from 13 observational studies containing 1,786,212 participants and 17,698 cases of active tuberculosis. In a random effects model, diabetes was found to increase the risk more than threefold (RR = 3.11). However, case control studies were heterogeneous with odds ratios ranging from 1.16–7.83. Nevertheless, the results clearly show that diabetes increases the risk of developing active tuberculosis, and the investigators suggest that *"active case finding and treatment of latent TB and efforts to diagnose, detect, and treat DM may have a beneficial impact on TB control"* (Jeon and Murray, 2008). Mechanistically, diabetes has been found to modulate chemotaxis, phagocytosis, activation, and antigen presentation by phagocytes in response to *Mycobacterium tuberculosis*. (Moutschen, Scheen, and Lefebvre, 1992; Dooley and Chaisson, 2009).

Smoking and Tuberculosis

An international team of investigators recently studied the association between tobacco smoking and active tuberculosis in a sizeable cohort of the general population of Taiwan. The study included 17,699 participants who completed a standardized health interview survey and were followed during 2001–2004. Smoking status and other variables were measured by in-person interviews at baseline and incident cases of active tuberculosis were identified from the *Taiwan National Health Insurance* database. During 3.3 years of follow-up, 57 new cases of active tuberculosis were detected. Overall, current smoking was associated with an increase in the risk (OR = 1.94).

These results are similar to findings of several case control studies and suggest that tobacco smoking increases the risk of developing active tuberculosis (Lin et al., 2009).

Bates and colleagues conducted a meta-analysis of the epidemiologic studies that provided relative risk estimates quantifying the association between tuberculosis infections and tobacco smoking. They included data from 24 studies in their analysis. Findings revealed that smoking increases the risk of developing active tuberculosis by up to 60% (RR = 1.6). The combined evidence from these studies therefore indicates that smoking is a risk factor for the development of active tuberculosis among individuals with latent disease (Bates et al., 2007).

Dietary Risk Factors

Certain other risk factors and conditions have been implicated in the genesis of active tuberculosis. As one might expect, pulmonary diseases such as emphysema, chronic bronchitis and asthma, and exposure to immunosuppressive drugs during chemotherapy or organ transplant procedures have all been found to heighten the risk. Some studies have found vitamin deficiencies to be associated with risk. For example, in a review and meta-analysis of seven studies vitamin D and active tuberculosis yielded an overall risk reduction of 32% for individuals with high versus low serum levels (Nnoaham and Clarke, 2008). In addition, conditions reflecting poor nutrition or malnutrition are 2–3 times more common among patients with active tuberculosis than patients with latent disease (Schaible and Kaufmann, 2007).

Genetic Susceptibility to Tuberculosis

Studies of monozygous and dizygous twins have found some evidence that genetic factors may modulate susceptibility or resistance to the development of tuberculosis. One recent genetic study of 516 cases and 514 healthy controls in the Hong Kong Chinese population revealed that specific polymorphisms of the interleukin 12 gene may influence the risk (Tso et al., 2004). Nevertheless, these preliminary findings await independent confirmation in other laboratories.

MULTIDRUG RESISTANT TUBERCULOSIS (MDR-TB) AND EXTENSIVELY DRUG-RESISTANT TUBERCULOSIS (XDR-TB)

By definition, *multidrug resistant tuberculosis (MDR-TB)* does not respond to first line drugs (isoniazid and rifampicin) and *extensively drug-resistant tuberculosis (XDR-TB)* is also resistant to three or more of the six classes of second-line drugs (and often does not respond to any drug). Drug resistant tuberculosis is rapidly disseminating throughout the world. In a recent survey of 109 member nations conducted by the World Health Organization, cases of MDR-TB were found in all participating countries and cases of XDR-TB were found in 55 (50%) of the countries sampled (Donald and van Helden, 2009).

A team of investigators recently examined characteristics of MDR-TB and XDR-TB in Shanghai, one of the largest cities in Asia (population ~23 million). In the study, MDR-TB cases were identified by testing for resistance to first-line drugs (isoniazid and rifampicin) in all culture positive cases of tuberculosis, and XDR-TB cases were identified by testing for resistance to second line drugs in the MDR-TB cases. During 2004–2007, 4,379 culture-positive cases of tuberculosis were diagnosed. Of these, 247 (5.6%) were infected with MDR-TB and 11 (6.3%) of 175 MDR-TB cases tested were found to carry XDR-TB. Among patients with MDR-TB, 57% responded to treatment with second-line drugs. It is notable that more than half of the patients infected by resistant strains of tuberculosis were newly diagnosed without any history of treatment for tuberculosis. Thus, community acquisition of resistant tuberculosis strains is a serious public health problem in Shanghai (Zhao et al., 2009).

ANTIBIOTIC RESISTANCE IN MYCOBACTERIUM TUBERCULOSIS

The development of antibiotic resistance by *Mycobacterium tuberculosis* has been extensive studied and reviewed. Dartmouth microbiologist Jay Dalton provides a succinct but thorough treatise in which he states:

> "Tuberculosis has become a threat again in the modern era of antimicrobial warfare, because its unique characteristics give it enormous potential for developing resistance to even the strongest antibiotics. Tuberculosis combines one of the slowest division rates among bacteria with a hardy cell wall defense system. Both of these factors stretch treatment into a multiple month process, creating a massive window for human error in the form of incorrect or missed dosages. Similarly, this slow pace of infection increases the possibility of evolution-based antimicrobial resistance by giving tuberculosis bacteria time to mutate. For these reasons, multi-drug resistant tuberculosis is one of the biggest health threats*

of this generation and the discovery of new treatment methods will be essential in the ongoing fight against this disease" (Dalton, 2009).

Dalton points out that the cell wall of *Mycobacterium tuberculosis* is a major determinant of its virulence due to a high content of mycolic acid and other lipids that form a protective shield against cationic proteins, lysozymes, and oxygen radicals of phagocytosis. This waxy hydrophobic cell wall resists sustained exposure to acids, detergents, oxidants, and antibiotics, thereby facilitating survival of the bacterium for long periods of time. Indeed, even a *short* treatment course for active tuberculosis involves a minimum of 6 months of combined antibiotic therapy: 2 months of isoniazid, rifampin, and pyrazinamide followed by 4 months of isoniazid, rifamate, and rimactane. The long period of treatment required for success is due to the slow reproductive rate and resistant cell wall of the bacterium and it is within this time period that mutations may accumulate and confer bacterial resistance (Dalton, 2009).

PREVENTION OF TUBERCULOSIS

Tuberculosis, malaria, and HIV/AIDS are the three major infectious diseases of poverty. Together they account for nearly 5 million deaths per year.

The control and prevention of tuberculosis involves primary, secondary, and tertiary prevention. While no vaccine is available that provides reliable protection for adults, vaccination using the *Bacille Calmette-Guérin vaccine (BCG)* offers significant protection in children and is widely used worldwide. Approximately 85% of infants in 172 countries were immunized in 1993 (WHO, 1995).

One country that *does not* widely administer BCG is the United States where tuberculosis remains relatively uncommon. Vaccination is only recommended for infants or children with negative skin test results who are continually exposed to untreated or ineffectively treated patients or will be continually exposed to multidrug-resistant tuberculosis (MDR-TB); and for healthcare workers considered on an individual basis in settings in which a high percentage of MDR-TB patients have been found, transmission of MDR-TB is likely, and TB control precautions have been implemented and were not successful (CDC, 2010b).

Mantoux tuberculin skin tests are widely used for routine screening of children and high risk individuals. Early detection and effective treatment of active cases are essential for prevention and control.

Most recently, the World Health Organization has implemented a *STOP TB Strategy* for its member nations, with the objective of dramatically reducing the global burden of tuberculosis. The WHO strategy has six principal components:

1. Pursue high-quality *DOTS* (*Directly Observed Treatment Short-course*) expansion and enhancement.
2. Address TB/HIV, MDR-TB, XDR-TB, and other special challenges.
3. Contribute to health system strengthening.
4. Engage all care providers.
5. Empower people with TB, and communities, through partnership.
6. Enable and promote research.

The program builds on the success of DOTS while also explicitly addressing the key challenges facing tuberculosis prevention and control. Its goal is to dramatically reduce the global burden of tuberculosis by 2015 by ensuring that all patients with tuberculosis, including those coinfected with HIV and those with MDR-TB and XDR-TB, benefit from universal access to high-quality diagnosis and patient-centered treatment. The *STOP TB Strategy* also supports the development of new and effective tools to prevent, detect and treat tuberculosis (WHO, 2008).

● ● ● REFERENCES

Ahmed, Y., Mwaba, P., Chintu, C., Grange, J.M., Ustianowski, A., & Zumla, A. (1990). A study of maternal mortality at the University Teaching Hospital, Lusaka, Zambia: The emergence of tuberculosis as a major nonobstetric cause of maternal death. *Int J Tuberc Lung Dis, 3,* 675–680.

Badri, M., Wilson, D., & Wood, R. (2002). Effect of highly active antiretroviral therapy on incidence of tuberculosis in South Africa: A cohort study. *Lancet, 359*(9323), 2059–2064.

Bates, M.N., Khalakdina, A., Pai, M., Chang, L., Lessa, F., & Smith, K.R. (2007). Risk of tuberculosis from exposure to tobacco smoke: A systematic review and meta-analysis. *Arch Intern Med, 167*(4), 335–342.

Bonah, C. (2005). The 'experimental stable' of the BCG vaccine: Safety, efficacy, proof, and standards, 1921–1933. *Stud Hist Philos Biol Biomed Sci, 36*(4), 696–721.

Centers for Disease Control. (2010a). *Reported tuberculosis in the United States, 2009*. Atlanta, GA: US Department of Health and Human Services, CDC.

Centers for Disease Control. (2010b). Ethnographic Guides: Promoting Cultural Sensitivity—A Practical Guide for Tuberculosis Programs. Atlanta, GA: US Department of Health and Human Services, CDC, January, 2010.

Cole, E., & Cook, C. (1998). Characterization of infectious aerosols in health care facilities: An aid to effective engineering controls and preventive strategies. *Am J Infect Control, 26*(4), 453–464.

Comstock, G. (1994). The International Tuberculosis Campaign: A pioneering venture in mass vaccination and research. *Clin Infect Dis, 19*(3), 528–540.

Dalton, J. (2009). Antibiotic resistance of tuberculosis. *DUJS Online*, 22 Feb 2009.

Donald, P.R., & van Helden, P.D. (2009). The global burden of tuberculosis—Combating drug resistance in difficult times. *N Engl J Med, 360*(23), 2393–2395.

Dooley, K.E., & Chaisson, R.E. (2009). Tuberculosis and diabetes mellitus: Convergence of two epidemics. *Lancet Infect Dis, 9*(12), 737–746.

Gandhi, N.R., Moll, A., Sturm, A.W., Pawinski, R., Govender, T., Lalloo, U.,…Friedland, G. (2006). Extensively drug-resistant tuberculosis as a cause of death in patients co-infected with tuberculosis and HIV in a rural area of South Africa. *The Lancet, 368*(9547), 1575–1580.

Gounder, C.R., Wada, N.I., Kensler, C., Violari, A., McIntyre, J., Chaisson, R.E., & Martinson, N.A. (2011). Active tuberculosis case-finding among pregnant women presenting to antenatal clinics in Soweto (2011). *South Africa Journal of Acquired Immune Deficiency Syndromes*, doi:10.1097.

Guelar, A., Gatell, J.M., Verdejo, J., Podzamczer, D., Lozano, L., Aznar, E., Miró, J.M.,…González, J. (1993). A prospective study of the risk of tuberculosis among HIV-infected patients. *AIDS, 7*(10), 1345–1349.

Hershkovitz, I., Donoghue, H.D., Minnikin, D.E., Besra, G.S., Lee, O.Y.C., Gernaey, A.M.,… Spigelman, M. (2008). Detection and molecular characterization of 9000-year-old *Mycobacterium tuberculosis* from a neolithic settlement in the Eastern Mediterranean. *PLoS ONE, 3*(10), e3426.

Herzog, B.H. (1998). History of tuberculosis. *Respiration, 65,* 5–15.

Jasmer, R.M., Nahid, P., & Hopewell, P.C. (2002). Clinical practice. Latent tuberculosis infection. *N Engl J Med, 347*(23), 1860–1866.

Jeon, C.Y., & Murray, M.B. (2008). Diabetes mellitus increases the risk of active tuberculosis: A systematic review of 13 observational studies. *PLoS Med, 5*(7), e152.

Kenyon, T.A., Creek, T., Laserson, K., Makhoa, M., Chimidza, N., Mwasekaga, M.,…Binkin, N. (2002). Risk factors for transmission of Mycobacterium tuberculosis from HIV-infected tuberculosis patients, Botswana. *International Journal of Tuberculosis and Lung Disease, 6*(10), 843–850.

Khan, M., Pillay, T., Moodley, J.M., & Connolly, C.A. (2001). Maternal mortality associated with tuberculosis-HIV-1 co-infection in Durban, South Africa. *AIDS, 15,* 1857–1863.

Kim, J., Park, Y., Kim, Y., Kang, S., Shin, J., Park, I., & Choi, B. (2003). Miliary tuberculosis and acute respiratory distress syndrome. *Int J Tuberc Lung Dis, 7*(4), 359–364.

Koch, R. (1905). The Nobel Prize in Physiology or Medicine, 1905.

Konstantinos, A. (2010). Testing for tuberculosis. *Australian Prescriber, 33*(1), 12–18.

Lee, J.H. (1948). Tuberculosis and silicosis. *Can Med Assoc J, 58*(4), 349–353.

Lighter, J., & Rigaud, M. (2009). Diagnosing childhood tuberculosis: Traditional and innovative modalities. *Curr Probl Pediatr Adolesc Health Care, 39,* 61–88.

Lin, H.H., Ezzati, M., Chang, H.Y., & Murray, M. (2009). Association between tobacco smoking and active tuberculosis in Taiwan: Prospective cohort study. *Am J Respir Crit Care Med, 180*(5), 475–480.

Marais, B.J., Gie, R.P., Schaaf, H.S., Hesseling, A.C., Obihara, C.C., Atarke, J.J., & Enarson, D.A. (2004). The natural history of childhood intra-thoracic tuberculosis: A critical review of literature from the pre-chemotherapy era. *Int J Tuberc Lung Dis, 9*(4), 392–402.

Margono, F., Mroueh, J., Garely, A., White, D., Duerr, A., & Minkoff, H.L. (1994). Resurgence of active tuberculosis among pregnant women. *Obstet Gynecol, 83*(6), 911–914.

Middlekoop, K., Bekker, L.G., Myer, L., Dawson, R., & Wood, R. (2008). Rates of tuberculosis transmission to children and adolescents in a community with a high prevalence of HIV Infection among adults. *Clin Infect Dis, 47*(3), 349–355.

Mofenson, L.M., & Laughon, B.E. (2007). Human immunodeficiency virus, *Mycobacterium tuberculosis*, and pregnancy: A deadly combination. *Clin Infect Dis, 45*(2), 250–253.

Moutschen, M.P., Scheen, A.J., & Lefebvre, P.J. (1992). Impaired immune responses in diabetes mellitus: Analysis of the factors and mechanisms involved. Relevance to the increased susceptibility of diabetic patients to specific infections. *Diabetes Metab, 18,* 187–201.

Nnoaham, K.E., & Clarke, A. (2008). Low serum vitamin D levels and tuberculosis: A systematic review and meta-analysis. *International journal of epidemiology, 37*(1), 113–119.

Pillay, T., Khan, M., Moodley, J., Adhikari, M., Padayatchi, N., Naicker, V.,…Coovadia, H.M. (2001). The increasing burden of tuberculosis in pregnant women, newborns and infants under 6 months of age in Durban, KwaZulu-Natal. *S Afr Med J, 91*(11), 983–987.

Rekha, B., & Swaminathan, S. (2007). Childhood tuberculosis—Global epidemiology and the impact of HIV. *Paediatric Respiratory Reviews, 8*(2), 99–106.

Robbins, S.L., & Cotran, R.S. (1979). *Pathologic basis of disease* (2nd ed.). Philadelphia: WB Saunders Co.

Rothschild, B., Martin, L., Lev, G., Bercovier, H., Bar-Gal, G., Greenblatt, C.,...Brittain, D. (2001). *Mycobacterium tuberculosis* complex DNA from an extinct bison dated 17,000 years before the present. *Clin Infect Dis, 33*(3), 305–311.

Schaible, U.E., & Kaufmann, S.H. (2007). Malnutrition and infection: Complex mechanisms and global impacts. *PLoS medicine, 4*(5), e115.

Thoen, C., Lobue, P., & de Kantor, I. (2006). The importance of *Mycobacterium bovis* as a zoonosis. *Vet Microbiol, 112*(2–4), 339–345.

Tripathy, S.N., & Tripathy, S.N. (2003). Tuberculosis and pregnancy. *Int J Gynaecol Obstet, 80*, 247–253.

Tso, H.W., Lau, Y.L., Tam, C.M., Wong, H.S., & Chiang, K.S. (2004). Associations between *IL12B* polymorphisms and tuberculosis in the Hong Kong Chinese population. *J Infect Dis, 190*(5), 913–919.

Tweddle, N., & Livingstone, P. (1994). Bovine tuberculosis control and eradication programs in Australia and New Zealand. *Vet Microbiol, 40*(1–2), 23–39.

Waddington, K. (2004). To stamp out so terrible a malady: Bovine tuberculosis and tuberculin testing in Britain, 1890–1939. *Med Hist, 48*(1), 29–48.

Waksman, S.A. (1952). The Nobel Prize in Physiology or Medicine 1952.

Wood, R., Liang, H., Wu, H., Middelkoop, K., Oni, T., Rangaka, M.X.,...Lawn, S.D. (2010). Changing prevalence of TB infection with increasing age in high TB burden townships in South Africa. *Int J Tuberc Lung Dis, 13*(4), 406–412.

World Health Organization. (1995). *WHO statement on BCG revaccination for the prevention of tuberculosis*. Geneva: World Health Organization.

World Health Organization. (2007). *Tuberculosis*. Geneva, Switzerland: World Health Organization.

World Health Organization. (2008). *Implementing the STOP TB strategy*. Geneva, Switzerland: World Health Organization.

World Health Organization. (2009). *Epidemiology. Global tuberculosis control: epidemiology, strategy, financing* (pp. 6–33). Geneva, Switzerland: World Health Organization.

World Health Organization. (2010). *WHO tuberculosis factsheet*. Geneva, Switzerland: World Health Organization.

Zhao, M., Li, X., Xu, P., Shen, X., Gui, X., Gui, X.,...Gao, Q. (2009). Transmission of MDR and XDR tuberculosis in Shanghai, China. *PLoS ONE, 4*(2), e4370. doi:10.1371.

Zink, A., Sola, C., Reischl, U., Grabner, W., Rastogi, N., Wolf, H., & Nerlich, A. (2003). Characterization of *Mycobacterium tuberculosis* complex DNAs from Egyptian mummies by spoligotyping. *J Clin Microbiol, 41*(1), 359–367.

46

Epidemiology of Malaria

INTRODUCTION

Malaria is a zoonotic infectious disease transmitted to humans by *Anopheles* species of mosquitoes. The disease is caused by a plasmodium (microscopic worm) that is carried in mosquito saliva. Humans become infected when an infected mosquito inserts its long hollow needle-like proboscis through the skin and sucks up blood.

Four species of malaria infect and cause disease in humans. Severe life-threatening malaria is most commonly caused by *Plasmodium falciparum*. Other species, *Plasmodium vivax*, *Plasmodium ovale*, and *Plasmodium malariae* generally cause infections with milder symptoms that are rarely fatal. Parasitic *Plasmodium* species also infect birds, reptiles, monkeys, chimpanzees, and rodents.

Malaria is caused by the proliferation of malarial parasites within red blood cells (erythrocytes), typically producing fever and headache and in severe cases progressing to anemia, coma, and death.

Malaria is most common in tropical and subtropical regions of the world near the equator, including much of sub-Saharan Africa, Asia, and Central America. Significant rainfall and warm temperatures enable mosquitoes that serve as vectors of malarial transmission to breed continuously.

HISTORY OF MALARIA

In 2700 BC, the symptoms of malaria were accurately described in ancient Chinese medical writings in the *Nei Ching*, the *Chinese Canon of Medicine*. During the second century BC, the *Qinghao* plant (*Artemisia annua*) was described in the Chinese medical treatise,

52 Remedies. Derivatives of this extract, known collectively as *artemisinins*, are very potent and effective antimalarial drugs that are still used today, especially in combination with other drugs (Wright et al., 2010).

Following their arrival in the New World, Spanish Jesuit missionaries learned from indigenous Indian tribes of a medicinal tree bark used for the treatment of fevers. The Countess of Chinchón, the wife of the Viceroy of Peru, was cured of fever by an extract of this bark and the tree was subsequently named *Cinchona* after the countess. The active compound in Cinchona bark is the antimalarial, quinine. Along with artemisinins, quinine is one of the most effective antimalarial drugs available today (Greenwood, 1992).

In 1880, Charles Louis Alphonse Laveran, a French army surgeon stationed in Constantine, Algeria, was the first to detect parasites in the blood of a patient suffering from malaria. Laveran was awarded the 1907 Nobel Prize (Laveran, 1907).

In 1897, Ronald Ross, a British officer in the Indian Medical Service, demonstrated that malaria parasites are transmitted to and from humans by mosquitoes. In further work, Ross showed that bird malaria is transmitted by mosquitoes and that the life cycle of the parasite involves a sporogonic cycle (the time interval during which the parasite developed in the mosquito). Ross also described in great detail the use of bed nets to protect against malarial transmission by mosquitoes. Ross was awarded the Nobel Prize in 1902 (Ross, 1902).

Camillo Golgi, an Italian neurophysiologist, established that malarial fever coincided with the rupture and release of merozoites into the blood stream. For their discoveries in the field of neurology,

Golgi and his colleague, Santiago Ramón y Cajal, were awarded the Nobel Prize in 1906 (Golgi and Cajal, 1906).

Chloroquine was discovered by Hans Andersag in 1934 at Bayer laboratories in Germany. Chloroquine was established as an effective and safe antimalarial drug after World War II and is still being used today. Nevertheless, many malarial strains have now developed chloroquine resistance (Jensen and Melhorn, 2009).

Fred Soper, an American epidemiologist and public health administrator, was called the "*General Patton*" of mosquito eradication. During 1927–1962, Soper directed successful campaigns in several regions of the world to eliminate malaria and yellow fever by draining swamps and spraying insecticides to eradicate the mosquito population by reducing their breeding sites. One of his early successes was the total eradication of the *Anopheles gambiae* mosquito population and elimination of malaria from certain regions of Brazil. Soper spearheaded the *Global Malaria Eradication Program* that helped eliminate the disease from the developed world and from many parts of the developing world. He was a strong advocate of the *judicious* use of the insecticide, dichloro-diphenyl-trichloroethane (DDT), to selectively eliminate species of *Anopheles* mosquitoes, the vectors of malaria transmission. Fred Soper, the *mosquito killer*, directed massive campaigns to eliminate malaria by the eradication of plasmodium-infected mosquitoes and his efforts undoubtedly spared the lives of millions of people (Gladwell, 2001).

The insecticidal property of DDT was discovered in 1939 by Paul Müller in Switzerland. This compound was widely and successfully used for malaria elimination and control in many countries at the end of World War II. For example, targeted spraying with DDT had virtually eliminated malaria from the United States population by 1951. Müller was awarded the Nobel Prize in 1948 (Müller, 1948).

In 1955, members of the World Health Organization submitted an ambitious proposal at the World Health Assembly for the eradication of malaria worldwide. This global program involved house spraying with insecticides (DDT), antimalarial drug treatment, and surveillance. Though the initial efforts of this program were successful in some populations, it was eventually abandoned due to lack of funding and various other reasons. Strong opposition to the use of DDT was voiced in the book *Silent Spring* by Rachel Carson who emphasized its persistence in the environment and potential for causing long-term damage to the ecosystem (Gladwell, 2001).

LIFE CYCLE OF PLASMODIA

Female mosquitoes of the *Anopheles* genus are primary hosts and the vectors of transmission. Humans and other vertebrates are considered secondary (intermediate) hosts. The life cycle of plasmodia is extraordinarily complex and involves both sexual and asexual replication (**Figure 46.1**).

Young pregnant *Anopheles* female mosquitoes ingest the malaria parasite by feeding on the blood of an infected human carrier. Infected mosquitoes carry *Plasmodium sporozoites* in their salivary glands. Sporozoites differentiate into male or female gametes that undergo *sexual recombination* in the gut of the mosquito. Sexual fusion of gametes produces an *ookinete* that penetrates the gut lining and produces an *oocyst* in the gut wall. When the oocyst ruptures, it releases new sporozoites that migrate through the mosquito's body to the salivary glands, where they can infect a new human host. The sporozoites are injected into the skin and blood with the mosquito's saliva when the mosquito ingests a human blood meal.

Upon entering the human bloodstream, sporozoites migrate to the liver where they infect liver cells (hepatocytes). Within the cytoplasm of hepatocytes, sporozoites undergo transformation into merozoites that multiply asexually for 1–4 weeks. Infected hepatocytes eventually rupture releasing thousands of merozoites into the blood stream where they infect erythrocytes (red blood cells). Within erythrocytes, merozoites continue to multiply *asexually*, periodically rupturing their host cells and invading other erythrocytes. Various forms of merozoites have been detected in red blood cells (ring forms, trophozoites, and schizonts). Clinically, waves of fever are associated with repeating cycles of erythrocytic infection, rupture, and release of merozoites in the same individual.

PATHOGENESIS OF MALARIA

The clinical symptoms of malaria are caused by the asexual erythrocytic (blood stage) parasites. When merozoites invade erythrocytes, they digest hemoglobin, the oxygen-carrying molecule of the body. A toxic breakdown product of hemoglobin (hemozoin pigment) and other toxic factors accumulate and are released into the bloodstream along with newly invasive merozoites when the infected cells lyse (rupture). The hemozoin and other toxic factors stimulate macrophages and other immune cells to produce cytokines and other soluble factors which

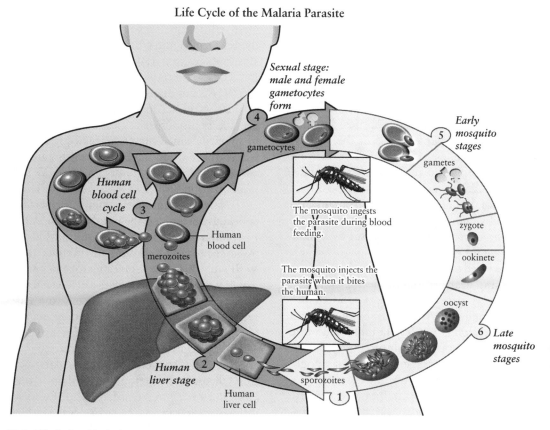

Figure 46.1 Life Cycle of Malaria.

incite fever, rigors, and potentially fatal immunoreactive pathophysiology.

Plasmodial parasites spend most of their human life cycle within hepatocytes and erythroctyes and are therefore protected from attack by the immune system. One exception is in the spleen where infected erythrocytes are immobilized, identified, and destroyed. However, *Plasmodium falciparum* has developed a mechanism to avoid passage through the spleen whereby infected erythrocytes, particularly those with mature trophozoites, adhere to the vascular endothelium of venular blood vessel walls and do not freely circulate in the blood. The sequestration of infected erythrocytes in the small blood vessels of the brain is the pathogenic mechanism of *cerebral malaria.*

Two malarial species, *Plasmodium vivax* and *Plasmodium ovale,* can remain dormant for long periods of time in hepatocytes. The dormant liver stage parasites are called *hypnozoites.* Reactivation and relapse are particularly characteristic of subspecies of *Plasmodium vivax,* which are endemic in India and the equatorial regions of Central and South America (Chin, 1973; Cogswell, 1992).

Plasmodium malariae is the most persistent of the malarial species and can coexist in the human system as a chronic infectious disease over a period of many years. Infections in untreated or inadequately treated individuals are often asymptomatic and can induce the formation of antigen-antibody complexes that deposit in the glomeruli of the kidneys. Chronic *Plasmodium malariae* infections are commonly detected in individuals living in the equatorial regions of South America and Africa and are a primary cause of the nephrotic syndrome and kidney failure (Chin, 1973).

Malarial infection, particularly due to *Plasmodium falciparum,* can quickly turn fatal. Life-threatening complications include cerebral malarial infection, hyperparasitemia when more than 5% of erythrocytes are infected by malarial parasites, severe anemia due to hemolysis (massive destruction of red blood cells), splenic rupture, acute respiratory distress syndrome, abnormalities in blood coagulation, low blood pressure due to cardiovascular collapse, acute kidney failure, metabolic acidosis (excessive acidity in the blood and tissues), and/or hypoglycemia (Chen, Schlichtherle, and Wahlgren, 2000).

GLOBAL BURDEN OF MALARIA

Incidence and Mortality

In 2006, the World Health Organization conducted a survey of 109 of its member nations and territories to characterize the global incidence, prevalence, and mortality of malaria. Only those countries classified as "malaria-endemic" participated in the survey. Estimates of the number of cases of malaria were obtained by adjusting the reported cases for coverage of the population and the parasite-positivity rate. Estimates of the number of deaths from malaria were obtained by multiplying the estimated number of *Plasmodium falciparum* malaria cases by a fixed case-fatality rate for each country.

Results revealed that malaria causes 250 million cases of fever and nearly 1 million deaths annually. Most cases (98%) were diagnosed in sub-Saharan Africa (86%), Southeast Asia (9%), or the Eastern Mediterranean region (3%). It is notable that more than half of all cases occurred in just five African countries (Nigeria, Democratic Republic of Congo, Ethiopia, United Republic of Tanzania, and Kenya). Of the 250 million cases, 230 million (92%) were due to *Plasmodium falciparum*, and in Africa, 98% of cases were due to this strain of malaria.

The vast majority of malarial deaths (91%) occurred in sub-Saharan Africa and 85% occurred in children under the age of 5 years of age. Pregnant women, individuals with HIV/AIDS, and elderly individuals (over 65 years of age) were especially vulnerable accounting for 8%, 5%, and 2% of malarial deaths, respectively. Southeast Asia and the Eastern Mediterranean region each contributed about 4% of malarial deaths.

These data reflect little change since 1992 when the WHO conducted a similar survey of malaria in these same nations. Furthermore, these figures are likely underestimates of the global burden of malaria, since many cases occur in rural areas where there is no access to health care, and as a consequence, they are undocumented (World Health Organization, 2008).

Using different methodology, Robert Snow and colleagues estimated the number of incident cases of *Plasmodia falciparum* malaria during 2002 to be 515 million, more than double the number reported by WHO in 2006. These investigators also suggest that a higher fraction of new cases (30%) occur outside of Africa (**Figure 46.2**). Their estimates were based upon reported clinical attack rates of only the most virulent malarial strain, *Plasmodia falciparum*. Estimates were derived from 83 studies conducted in 22 countries of 5 WHO regions. Using these data, a classification scheme was developed according to the *median annual attack rates (cases per 1,000)* observed in different geographic areas: 39 areas were classified as hypoendemic (43 per 1,000), 25 as mesoendemic (171 per 1,000), and 8 were holo/hyperendemic (873 per 1,000). The number of new cases for each WHO region was estimated by weighting attack rates by the corresponding populations of the geographic areas within that region (Snow et al., 2005).

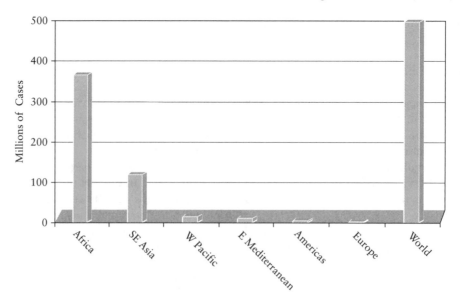

Figure 46.2 New Cases of *Plasmodium falciparum Malaria*, 2002.

Source: Data from Snow RW, Guerra CA, Noor AM, Myint HY, Hay SI (2005). The global distribution of clinical episodes of Plasmodium falciparum malaria. *Nature* 434:214–217.

Snow and colleagues chose not to estimate mortality from *Plasmodium falciparum* using their methodology *"because of the paucity of prospective epidemiological descriptions of cause-specific mortality outside Africa"* (Snow et al., 2005). Nevertheless, they point out that the risk of death after a clinical attack of *Plasmodium falciparum* may be tenfold higher in sub-Saharan Africa than nations outside of Africa, likely because of lack of access to prompt treatment.

Case Fatality: Plasmodium Falciparum Malaria

Malaria represents a medical emergency and may rapidly progress to severe complications and death without prompt and appropriate treatment. Severe malaria is almost exclusively caused by *Plasmodium falciparum*. Major complications of severe malaria include cerebral malaria, pulmonary edema, acute renal failure, severe anemia, and/or bleeding. Acidosis and hypoglycemia are the most common metabolic complications. Any of these complications can develop rapidly and progress to death within hours or days. In many patients, several of these complications exist together or evolve in rapid succession within a few hours.

Malaria can be particularly devastating in infants and young children. Among 1,357 Gambian children hospitalized with malaria, 179 (13.2%) died within 6 months of admission. Case fatality rates were high in patients with cerebral malaria plus severe anemia (17%), cerebral anemia (16%), severe anemia (8%), or hypoglycemia (33%). Among those with cerebral malaria, 11% suffered major residual neurological deficits such as hemiplegia, cortical blindness, aphasia, and/or ataxia. Onset of severe anemia tended to occur before the age of 3 years whereas onset of cerebral malaria

was more typical during ages 3–5 years (**Figure 46.3**) (Brewster, Kwiatkowski, and White, 1990).

Murphy and Breman conducted an extensive review and analysis of published case fatality rates for children of sub-Saharan Africa who were less than 5 years of age when diagnosed with malaria. Their review included 3,275 cases of cerebral malaria and 3,723 cases of malarial anemia diagnosed and treated in multiple centers in sub-Saharan Africa. Results revealed that cerebral malaria has an overall case fatality rate of 19% and malarial anemia has a case fatality rate of 13%. The case fatality rate was also high among children presenting with respiratory distress, hypoglycemia, or overlapping symptoms due to malaria (18%). Furthermore, low birth weight babies born to infected mothers had a case fatality rate of 38%. Based on these case fatality rates, the investigators suggest that the annual death toll from early childhood malaria in sub-Saharan Africa could be as high as 2.26 million (Murphy and Breman, 2001).

Both fetal and maternal mortality are elevated among pregnant women who develop malarial infections. In a review of published data on maternal mortality due to anemia, severe malarial anemia was found to elevate maternal mortality more than threefold (Brabin, Hakimi, and Pelletier, 2001).

Disability Adjusted Life Years: Malaria

The *disability adjusted life years* (*DALY*) lost from malaria reflects the high burden of deaths in early childhood plus disability due to chronic infection, particularly neurological deficits due to cerebral malaria. As shown in **Figure 46.4**, the highest DALY are evident in sub-Saharan Africa, similar to other infectious diseases of poverty such as tuberculosis and HIV/AIDS.

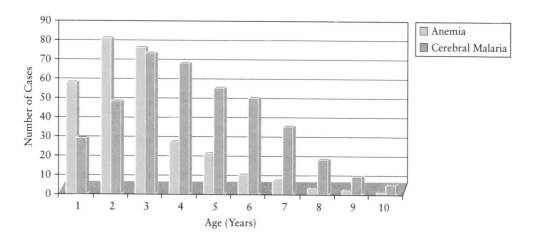

Figure 46.3 Age Distribution of Malaria in Gambian Children.

Source: Data from Brewster DR, Kwiatkowski D, White NJ (1990). Neurological sequelae of cerebral malaria in children. *Lancet* 336(8722):1039–1043.

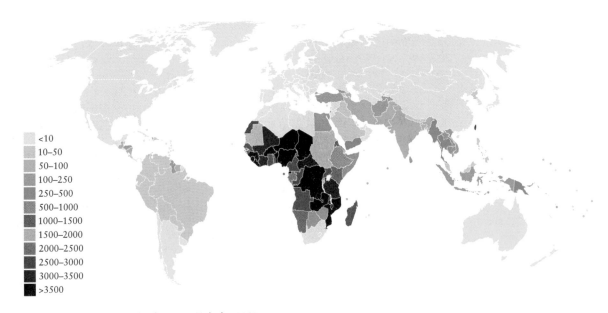

Figure 46.4 Disability Adjusted Life Years: Malaria, 2007.

Source: Data from World Health Organization. The global burden of disease: 2004 update. Geneva, WHO, 2008. Available at www.who.int/evidence/bod.

GENETIC RESISTANCE TO MALARIA

The devastation wreaked upon the human population by malaria has taken some unexpected twists and turns. Due to the predilection of plasmodium species for infants and children who often died of malaria before reaching reproductive age, *malarial resistance genes* have been fixed at high frequencies in populations residing in endemic areas.

Sickle Cell Anemia and Malaria

Sickle cell anemia is an autosomal recessive genetic disorder characterized by red blood cells that assume an abnormal, rigid, sickle shape. The condition was discovered in 1910 by Chicago physician James Herrick in the blood of a young boy with anemia from the West Indies (Herrick, 1910). A later report demonstrated that the sickling was associated with low erythrocyte oxygen content (Hahn and Gillespie, 1927). Epidemiologic studies soon revealed that the trait was relatively common in populations with endemic malaria because it protects red blood cells from infection by *Plasmodium falciparum*. The sickle cell trait is caused by a single base pair change in the gene for hemoglobin on chromosome 11 (Pauling et al., 1949; Ashley-Koch, Yang, and Olney, 1998). Individuals homozygous for the mutated gene have a morphologically altered form of hemoglobin (hemoglobin S) that forms "tactoid" crystals in red blood cells causing them to transform into a "sickle" shape. Hemoglobin S is not particularly efficient at carrying oxygen to tissues; hence individuals who are homozygous for the sickle cell gene usually become anemic. However, the sickled cells are not favorable hosts for the *Plasmodium falciparum* merozoites, and consequently, individuals with sickle cell anemia who live in regions endemic for malaria are protected from *falciparum* infection during childhood and survive to reproduce and pass the gene to subsequent generations. Recent studies have confirmed that the sickle cell gene is most common in populations of sub-Saharan Africa, the Middle East, and India, coincident with the historically high rates of malaria in these regions (Piel et al., 2010).

Glucose-6-Phosphate Dehydrogenase Deficiency and Malaria

Glucose-6-phosphate dehyrogenase (G6PD) is an X-linked enzyme that protects red blood cells from oxidative stress. Infants with deficiencies in G6PD can develop neonatal jaundice and hemolytic anemia following certain environmental stimuli. Populations endemic for malaria have high rates of G6PD deficiencies that may afford protection against certain types of plasmodium infections. Louicharoen and colleagues investigated the effects of a common G6PD deficiency variant in Southeast Asia, the *G6PD-Mahidol* variant, in patients with *Plasmodiuim vivax* or *Plasmodium falciparum* malaria. They examined parasite density in blood samples from 400 individuals with *Plasmodium falciparum* infection and 227 individuals with *Plasmodiuim vivax* infection.

They found that the density of *vivax* parasites was reduced by 30% in heterozygous females and by 61% in homozygous females for the Mahidol G6PD mutation. The G6PD-variant had no effect on parasite density among patients with *falciparum* infection. Their results suggest that *Plasmodium vivax* has been a driving force behind the strong selective advantage conferred by this mutation (Louicharoen et al., 2009).

CONTROL OF MALARIA

The complex life cycle of the malarial plasmodia presents several opportunities for intervention including mosquito eradication, prevention of mosquito strikes, plasmodium eradication, and treatment of malarial infections. Recently, the World Health Organization launched a global program designed to reduce the burden of malaria worldwide (WHO, 2010). The program advocates combinations of four basic components.

Vector Control

Vector control remains the most generally effective measure to prevent malaria transmission and therefore the cornerstone of the four basic technical elements of the WHO Global Malaria Control Strategy. Elements of vector control include distribution of insecticide treated bed nets, targeted spraying of insecticides and larvicides, and drainage of mosquito breeding sites to reduce populations of *Anopheles* mosquitoes. Malaria transmission can be reduced substantially by preventing mosquito bites by distribution of inexpensive mosquito nets and insect repellents, or by mosquito-control measures such as spraying insecticides inside houses and draining standing water where mosquitoes lay their eggs.

The malaria life cycle involves plasmodial infection of not only humans, but also mosquitoes. Obviously, curbing infection in the susceptible mosquito population could have a major impact in preventing spread into humans and other species. As pointed out by George Dimopoulos and colleagues of the Johns Hopkins Malaria Research Institute:

"Recent efforts in the areas of vector biology and vector-borne diseases have focused on blocking infection of the insect as a means of disease control. A better understanding of the interactions between the parasite and the mosquito vector is crucial to achieving this goal. For instance, boosting the anti-Plasmodium immune response by temporally expressing Rel2 [the gene that regulates interleukin 2 of the innate immune system]

or a specific effector molecule in transgenic mosquitoes could create mosquito populations refractory to parasite infection. The introduction into and stable transmission of inhibitory bacteria in natural mosquito populations might also be a means of controlling Plasmodium transmission that does not require genetic modification or release of mosquitoes. Exploiting the anti-Plasmodium immune response of the mosquito is yet another potential mechanism for combating Plasmodium infections worldwide" (Cirimotich et al., 2010).

Early Diagnosis and Treatment

Early diagnosis of malaria and its effective and timely treatment reduces morbidity and prevents death from malaria. Advanced diagnostic tools (microscopy and rapid diagnostic tests) and effective drug therapies (artemisinin-based combination treatments) administered by highly trained healthcare personnel facilitate effective case management with a high probability of cure.

Identification of High Risk Groups

Some population groups are at considerably higher risk of contracting severe malaria than others. High-risk groups include pregnant women, patients with HIV/AIDS, nonimmune travelers, and in high transmission areas, children less than 5 years of age. Such individuals warrant special measures for prevention and treatment of malaria, and to mitigate their risk, consideration should be given to their specific circumstances and the tools and strategies available.

Coinfection with HIV has been found to increase the severity and case fatality of malaria in a number of studies. A team of international investigators recently assessed the impact of coinfection by HIV-1 and malaria in 41 countries of sub-Saharan Africa. Overall, the data suggest that the HIV-1 epidemic had increased the incidence of malaria by 1.3% and malarial deaths by 4.9%. However, in the countries of southern Africa that have high rates of HIV-1 infections in rural areas (Botswana, Zimbabwa, Swaziland, South Africa, and Namibia), the incidence of clinical malaria increased by 28% and the mortality from malaria increased by 114% (Korenromp et al., 2005).

Mounting evidence has also revealed pathologic interactions between HIV and malaria in coinfected patients. A transient (one-log) elevation in the HIV viral load had been observed during febrile malaria episodes; and reciprocally, the severity and symptoms of malaria are enhanced in HIV-infected patients (Abu-Raddad, Patnaik, and Kublin, 2006).

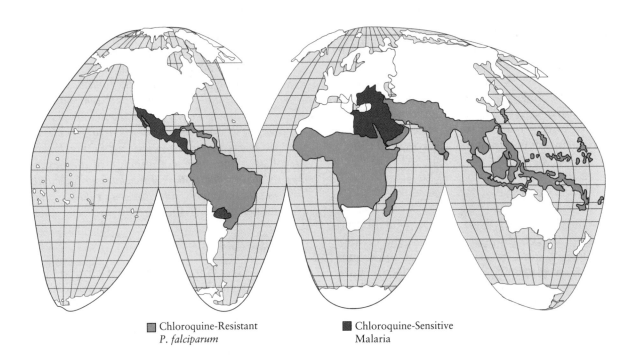

□ Chloroquine-Resistant
  P. falciparum

■ Chloroquine-Sensitive
  Malaria

Figure 46.5 Global Malarial Resistance to Chloroquine, 2005.

Source: Data from World Health Organization (2004). World Malaria Report. Geneva, Switzerland, 2004.

Surveillance, Monitoring, and Evaluation

Monitoring and evaluation are essential components of the WHO Global Malaria Program. Monitoring measures the implementation of the range of strategic activities, while evaluation measures the extent to which objectives are being reached.

Chloroquine Resistance of Malaria

A disturbing feature in the fight against malaria is the development of large-scale resistance by *Plasmodia falciparum* to several antimalarial drugs, most notably chloroquine (**Figure 46.5**). Nevertheless, a variety of antimalarial medications are available and most recently, the treatment of *Plasmodium falciparum* infections in endemic countries has been transformed by the use of combinations of drugs containing an *artemisinin* derivative. Severe malaria is treated with intravenous or intramuscular quinine, or increasingly, the artemisinin derivative *artesunate* which appears to be superior to quinine in both children and adults.

• • • REFERENCES

Abu-Raddad, L., Patnaik, P., & Kublin, J. (2006). Dual infection with HIV and malaria fuels the spread of both diseases in sub-Saharan Africa. Science, *314*(5805), 1603–1606.

Ashley-Koch, A., Yang, Q., & Olney, R.S. (1998). Hemoglobin S allele and sickle cell disease. *American Journal of Epidemiology, 151*(9), 839–845.

Brabin, B.J., Hakimi, M., & Pelletier, D. (2001). An analysis of anemia and pregnancy-related maternal mortality. *J Nutr, 131*(2S–2), 604S–614S.

Brewster, D.R., Kwiatkowski, D., & White, N.J. (1990). Neurological sequelae of cerebral malaria in children. *Lancet, 336*(8722), 1039–1043.

Chen, Q., Schlichtherle, M., & Wahlgren, M. (2000). Molecular aspects of severe malaria. *Clin Microbiol Rev, 13*(3), 439–450.

Chin, W. (1973). Malaria. In J.M. Last (Ed.) *Maxey-Rosenau public health and preventive medicine* (12th ed., pp. 361–370). Norwalk, Connecticut: Appleton-crofts.

Cirimotich, C.M., Dong, Y., Garver, L.S., Sim, S., & Dimopoulos, G. (2010). Mosquito immune defenses against Plasmodium infection. *Dev Comp Immunol, 34*(4), 387–395.

Cogswell, F.B. (1992). The hypnozoite and relapse in primate malaria. *Clin Microbiol Rev*, 5(1), 26–35.

Gladwell, M. (2001). The mosquito killer. Annals of Public Health. *The New Yorker*, July 2, 2001.

Golgi, C., & Cajal, S.R. (1906). The Nobel Prize in Physiology or Medicine, 1906.

Greenwood, D. (1992). The quinine connection. *J Antimicrob Chemother*, 30(4), 417–427.

Hahn, V.E., & Gillespie, E.B. (1927). Report of a case greatly improved by splenectomy. Experimental study of sickle cell formation. *Arch Intern Med*, 39(2), 233–254.

Herrick, J.B. (1910). Peculiar elongated and sickled shaped corpuscles in a case of severe anemia. *AMA Arch Intern Med*, 6, 517.

Jensen, M., & Mehlhorn, H. (2009). Seventy-five years of Resochin in the fight against malaria. *Parasitology Research*, 105(3), 609–627.

Korenromp, E.L., Williams, B.G., de Vlas, S.J., Gouws, E., Gilks, C.F., & Ghys, P.D. (2005). Malaria attributable to the HIV-1 epidemic, Sub-Saharan Africa. *Emerg Infect Dis*, [serial on the Internet].

Laveran, C.L. (1907). The Nobel Prize in Physiology or Medicine, 1907.

Louicharoen, C., Patin, E., Paul, R., Nuchprayoon, I., Witoonpanich, B., Peerapittayamongkol, C.,...Sakuntabhai, A. (2009). Positively selected *G6PD*-Mahidol mutation reduces *Plasmodium vivax* density in Southeast Asians. *Science*, 326(5959), 1546–1549.

Müller, P.H. (1948). The Nobel Prize in Physiology or Medicine 1948. Nobelprize.org.

Murphy, S.C., & Breman, J.G. (2001). Gaps in the childhood malaria burden in Africa: Cerebral malaria, neurological sequelae, anemia, respiratory distress, hypoglycemia, and complications of pregnancy. In J.G. Breman, A. Egan, & G.T. Keusch (Eds.). The intolerable burden of malaria: A new look at the numbers. Supplement to Volume 64(1) of the *American Journal of Tropical Medicine and Hygiene*.

Pauling, L., Itano, H.A., Singer, S.J., & Wells, I.C. (1949). Sickle cell anemia, a molecular disease. *Science*, 110, 543–548.

Piel, F.B., Patil, A.P., Howes, R.E., Nyangiri, O.A., Gething, P.W., Williams, T.N.,...Hay, S.I. (2010). Global distribution of the sickle cell gene and geographical confirmation of the malaria hypothesis. *Nature Communications, 1*(8), 104–108.

Ross, R. (1902). The Nobel Prize in Physiology or Medicine, 1902.

Snow, R.W., Guerra, C.A., Noor, A.M., Myint, H.Y., & Hay, S.I. (2005). The global distribution of clinical episodes of *Plasmodium falciparum* malaria. *Nature, 434*, 214–217.

World Health Organization. (2004). World Malaria Report. Geneva, Switzerland, 2010.

World Health Organization. (2008). World Malaria Report. Geneva, Switzerland, 2008.

World Health Organization. (2010). World Malaria Report. Geneva, Switzerland, 2010.

Wright, C.W., Linley, P.A., Brun, R., Wittlin, S., & Hsu, E. (2010). Ancient Chinese methods are remarkably effective for the preparation of artemisinin-rich extracts of qing hao with potent anti-malarial activity. *Molecules, 15*(2), 804–812.

Epidemiology of HIV/AIDS

INTRODUCTION

The *acquired immunodeficiency syndrome* (*AIDS*) is a disease of the immune system caused by infection with the *human immunodeficiency virus* (*HIV*). The condition is therefore called HIV/AIDS. The infection progressively reduces the integrity of the immune system and renders afflicted individuals susceptible to opportunistic infections and certain types of cancer.

HIV can be transmitted from person to person in blood, semen, or vaginal fluid. Viral entry into the adult human system typically occurs when bodily fluids containing live virus come into contact with mucous membranes of the vagina, anus, or oral cavity. AIDS is therefore classified as a sexually transmitted disease (STD). HIV can also be transmitted by contaminated hypodermic needles, and from an infected mother to her baby during pregnancy, childbirth, or in breastmilk.

HIV/AIDS is a modern day pandemic, causing death and disability throughout the world. The most recent global survey conducted by the World Health Organization in 2009 found that 33.3 million individuals worldwide are living with HIV/AIDS. In that year, 2.6 million new HIV infections were detected and 1.8 million people died from HIV/AIDS. Most of the deaths from HIV/AIDS (76%) occur in sub-Saharan Africa. In this region, 22.5 million people are living with HIV/AIDS.

HISTORY OF HIV/AIDS

AIDS Outbreaks, United States

The initial report of the condition now known as HIV/AIDS described five homosexual young men in Los Angeles who had developed multiple opportunistic infections including a rare type of pneumonia caused by *Pneumocystis carinii* (MMWR, 1981a). This was quickly followed by reports of homosexual men living in New York, San Francisco, and Los Angeles who had developed various opportunistic infections plus a rare tumor characteristic of immunodeficiency, Kaposi sarcoma (MMWR, 1981b, 1982a). The combination of opportunistic infections and Kaposi sarcoma was subsequently reported in Haitians, drug addicts, hemophiliacs and other transfusion recipients, infants, female sex contacts of afflicted men, prisoners, and Africans (MMWR, 1982b, 1982c, 1982d, 1982e; Masur et al., 1981, 1982; MMWR, 1983a, 1983b). Many other complications were typical of these patients including candidiasis, cytomegalovirus infection, mycobacterial infection, herpes infection, toxoplasmosis, fungal infection, varicella, and non-Hodgkin's lymphoma.

Discovery of HIV

Early theories of causation that were advanced to explain these outbreaks included exposure to multiple viruses and agents such as cytomegalovirus, Epstein Barr virus (Sonnabend, Witkin, and Purtilo, 1983), sperm cell antibodies (Mavligit et al., 1984), and amyl nitrite (Goedert, Neuland, and Wallen, 1982). The prominence of homosexual men and intravenous drug addicts with opportunistic infections among the early cases of AIDS suggested an etiologic agent that was blood-borne and sexually transmitted and caused severe immunosuppression.

The search for a novel virus responsible for AIDS was highly competitive and widely publicized. The causal RNA retrovirus, later named the *human immunodeficiency virus* (*HIV*) was first isolated in France in 1983 by Françoise Barré-Sinoussi and colleagues in the laboratory of Luc Montaignier (Barré-Sinoussi et al., 1983). The same virus was also isolated from several AIDS patients by Robert Gallo and colleagues at the National Institutes of Health and by Jay Levy and colleagues in San Francisco (Gallo et al., 1984; Levy et al., 1984). Shortly thereafter, Montaignier's group isolated a closely related virus in West African patients; hence the original virus was designated *HIV-1* and the West African virus *HIV-2*. Based upon their discovery of HIV-1 and HIV-2, the French group suggested that *"these viruses existed long before the current AIDS epidemics. Their biological properties are conserved in spite of limited sequence homology; this may help the determination of the structure-function relationships of the different viral elements"* (Guyader et al., 1987).

HIV LIFE CYCLE

The life cycle of HIV can be succinctly described in six steps.

1. Binding and Fusion: HIV begins its life cycle when it binds to a CD4 receptor and one of two coreceptors on the surface of a CD4+ T-lymphocyte. The virus then fuses with the host cell. After fusion, the virus releases RNA, its genetic material, into the host cell.

2. Reverse Transcription: An HIV enzyme called *reverse transcriptase* converts the single-stranded HIV RNA to double-stranded HIV DNA.

3. Integration: The newly formed HIV DNA enters the host cell's nucleus, where an HIV enzyme called integrase integrates the HIV DNA within the host cell's DNA. The integrated HIV DNA is called *provirus*. The provirus may remain inactive for several years, producing few or no new copies of HIV.

4. Transcription: When the host cell receives a signal to become active, the provirus uses a host enzyme called RNA polymerase to create copies of the HIV genomic material, as well as shorter strands of messenger RNA (mRNA). The mRNA is used as a blueprint to make long chains of HIV proteins.

5. Assembly: An HIV enzyme called *protease* cuts the long chains of HIV proteins into smaller individual proteins. As the smaller HIV proteins come together with copies of HIV's RNA genetic material, a new virus particle is assembled.

6. Budding: The newly assembled virus *"buds"* from the host cell. During budding, the new virus incorporates part of the cell's outer envelope. This envelope, which acts as a covering, is studded with protein/sugar combinations called HIV glycoproteins. These HIV glycoproteins are necessary for the virus to bind CD4 and coreceptors. The new copies of HIV can now move on to infect other cells (**Figure 47.1**).

The RNA genome of HIV contains nine genes that regulate its cell cycle. Three genes, *gag*, *pol*, and *env* encode structural proteins to make new virus

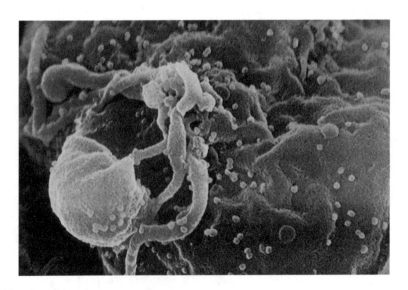

Figure 47.1 HIV Budding From T Lymphocyte.

Source: Courtesy of C. Goldsmith, P. Feorino, E. L. Palmer, W. R. McManus/CDC.

particles. The six remaining genes (*tat, rev, nef, vif, vpr,* and *vpu*) are regulatory genes that control specific processes such as binding to CD4 cells, entry into the host cell, integration into the host cell DNA, activation and transcription of viral genes, regulation of viral replication, and the budding process (Hope and Trono, 2000).

HIV/AIDS IN THE UNITED STATES

Parameters describing the HIV/AIDS epidemic in the United States (incidence and prevalent cases and deaths) during 1985–2005 are plotted in **Figure 47.2**. In 1993, the definition of AIDS was modified to include those patients with a CD4-lymphocyte count below 200 cells per cubic millimeter or below 14% of the lymphocytic population. The epidemic peaked during 1993–1995 and has since declined.

The mode of transmission of HIV has changed dramatically over the course of the epidemic in the United States. The largest proportionate increase occurred in cases attributable to heterosexual transmission, from 5% in 1983 to 31% in 2005. Most heterosexual cases (90%) were women, suggesting a marked preeminence of male to female transmission. In contrast, the relative frequency of cases identified as men who have sex with men has decreased from

71% to around 50%. The proportion of cases identified as acquiring HIV by intravenous drug abuse has stabilized at approximately 15% (CDC, 2007; Osmond, 2003; Fenton, 2007).

The race and ethnicity of new cases of HIV/AIDS has also changed dramatically over time (**Figure 47.3**). The relative frequency of Caucasian cases dropped from 60% in 1981 to 28% in 2005 whereas the frequency of African American cases rose from 25% to 50% over the same time period. Hispanics also account for a high fraction of cases (~20%). Currently, men who have sex with men and African American men and women bear a disproportionate burden of death and disability from HIV/AIDS (CDC, 2007; Osmond, 2003; Fenton, 2007).

HIV/AIDS IN AFRICA

According to the 2009 survey results on HIV/AIDS from the World Health Organization, approximately 22.5 million people living in sub-Saharan African have HIV/AIDS. This constitutes about 72% of all HIV/AIDS cases worldwide. In that year, 1.8 million new cases were detected and 1.4 million HIV/AIDS patients died. The adult prevalence (5%) in sub-Saharan Africa is fivefold higher than any other region in the world and AIDS continues to be the

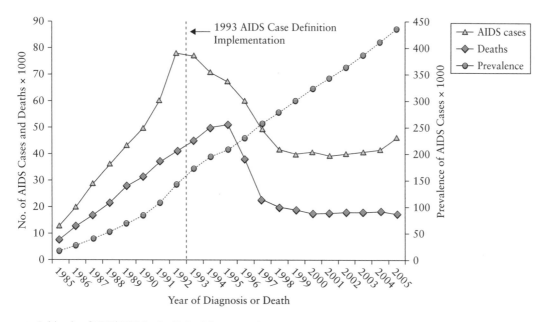

Figure 47.2 Epidemic of HIV/AIDS in the United States, 1985–2005.

Source: Reproduced from Centers for Disease Control (2007). Epidemiology of HIV Infection (through 2005). Slide 2: Diagnoses of HIV Infection among Adults and Adolescents, by Sex, 2006—2009—40 States and 5 U.S. Dependent Areas. Atlanta, Georgia. http://www.cdc.gov/hiv/topics/surveillance/resources/slides/general/index.htm. Accessed November 8th, 2011.

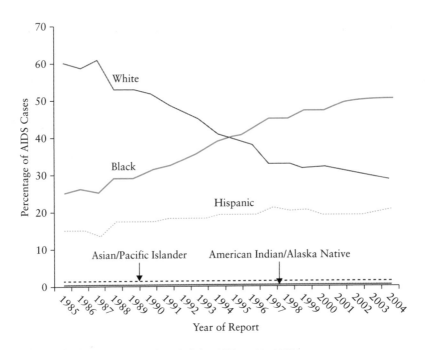

Figure 47.3 Relative Frequency of HIV/AIDS Cases by Ethnicity, USA, 1985–2005.

Source: Reproduced from Centers for Disease Control (2007). Epidemiology of HIV Infection (through 2005). Slide 22: AIDS Diagnoses among Adults and Adolescents, by Race/Ethnicity and Year of Diagnosis, 1985–2009—United States and Dependent Areas. Atlanta, Georgia. http://www.cdc.gov/hiv/topics/surveillance/resources/slides/general/index.htm. Accessed November 8th, 2011.

leading cause of mortality in this region (**Figure 47.4**). Unlike other regions, most people living with HIV in sub-Saharan Africa are women (61%).

The *disability adjusted life years* (*DALY*) attributable to HIV/AIDS is shown in **Figure 47.5**. The pattern reflects extraordinarily high values for most of the 47 countries in sub-Saharan Africa. Life expectancy has fallen dramatically in the worst-affected

countries; for example, during the period 1980–2005, it is estimated that life expectancy fell from 65 to 35 years in Botswana (Kallings, 2008).

Notably, the global pattern of DALY due to HIV/AIDS shows substantial overlap with the DALY due to other common infectious diseases such as tuberculosis, hepatitis B, hepatitis C, and malaria. Indeed, the clustering of such infectious agents in poverty

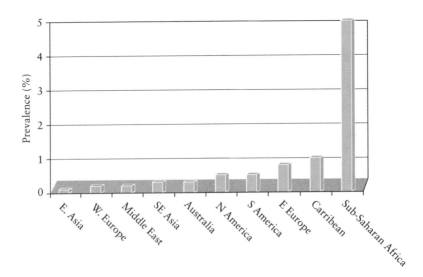

Figure 47.4 Global Prevalence of HIV/AIDS, 2009.

Source: Data from WHO (2010). World Health Statistics 2010. World Health Organization Statistical Information System (WHOSIS), Geneva, Switzerland.

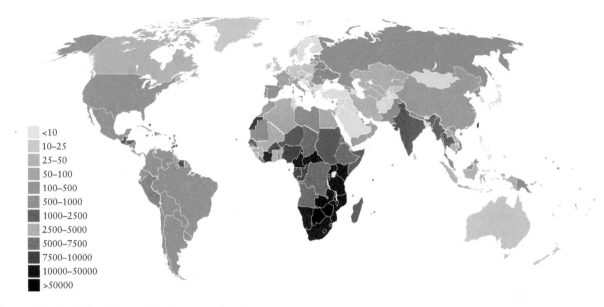

Figure 47.5 Disability Adjusted Life Years, HIV/AIDS, 2004.

Source: Data from World Health Organization. The global burden of disease: 2004 update. Geneva, WHO, 2008. Available at www.who.int/evidence/bod.

stricken regions of the world has led to dramatic increases in coinfections that contribute significantly to the global toll of death and disability.

ORIGIN OF HIV

It is likely that HIV/AIDS existed in sub-Saharan Africa long before its recognition in the United States. In West Africa, viruses similar to HIV-1 and HIV-2 have been found in chimpanzees and monkeys. It is hypothesized that such viruses entered the human population by direct exposure to contaminated blood and tissues during the slaughter of primates for meat (Hahn et al., 2000).

COINFECTIONS INVOLVING HIV

The geographic pattern of HIV/AIDS overlaps with several other infectious conditions. The *disability adjusted life years (DALY)* lost due to HIV/AIDS shown in **Figure 47.5** is largely a consequence of death and disability due to coinfection of HIV patients with human herpes virus 8, hepatitis B, hepatitis C, tuberculosis, and malaria.

HIV and Human Herpes Virus 8 (HHV-8)

Kaposi sarcoma has already been discussed. This tumor occasionally develops in individuals who are severely immunocompromised such as those

with HIV infection. Kaposi sarcoma became widely known as one of the defining conditions of the *acquired immunodeficiency syndrome (AIDS)* during the 1980s. Although associated with HIV disease, Kaposi sarcoma is actually caused by another virus, *human herpes virus 8 (HHV-8)*.

In 1994, Yuan Chang, Patrick Moore, and Ethel Cesarman at Columbia University in New York isolated a novel herpes virus from the tumor cells of a Kaposi sarcoma. They later sequenced the virus and identified it as the eighth human herpes virus; hence it was given the name, HHV-8. This virus has since been found in all Kaposi sarcomas tested and is considered the cause of the disease (Chang et al., 1994; Moore and Chang, 1995; Cesarman et al., 1995).

Kaposi sarcoma arises from the endothelial cells that line lymphatic vessels. The tumor is characterized by the formation of vascular channels engorged with red blood cells giving it a dark red papular appearance. Kaposi sarcoma is typically found on the skin, but metastatic spread to other sites is common, especially the mouth, the gastrointestinal tract, and the respiratory tract. Kaposi sarcoma is associated with significant morbidity and mortality worldwide (Parkin et al., 2005).

Herpes viruses can be transmitted by intimate sexual contact and by transplantation of contaminated organs. *In sub-Saharan Africa where high rates of HHV-8 prevail, Kaposi sarcoma is the most common of all cancers.* As with other herpes viral infections, HHV-8 may persist in a dormant state for many years, only to be reactivated by conditions of severe immunosuppression such as HIV disease. Active HHV-8 infection specifically initiates and promotes malignant transformation of the lymphatic endothelium in the genesis of Kaposi sarcoma (Chang et al., 1994; Moore and Chang, 1995; Cesarman et al., 1995).

Before the epidemic of AIDS, Kaposi sarcoma was rare in Western countries, comprising only 0.3% of all cancers in men and 0.1% in women in the United States and Europe. Following onset of the HIV epidemic, rates of Kaposi sarcoma increased dramatically among men in developed nations. In the United States, the annual incidence rates peaked in 1989 at 9.6 per 100,000. Since that time, rates have declined to pre-AIDS levels, presumably in response to effective combined chemotherapy for HIV disease by *highly active antiretroviral therapy (HAART)* (Stebbing, Portsmouth, and Bassard, 2003).

In many parts of Africa, post-AIDS rates of Kaposi sarcoma have continued to increase in populations with high endemic rates and little access to effective therapy, such as Uganda, Malawi, Zimbabwe, and Swaziland . Indeed, *Kaposi sarcoma is now the most common cancer in men and the second most common cancer in women in many nations of sub-Saharan Africa* (Parkin et al., 2005).

HIV and Hepatitis B Virus

Coinfection with human immunodeficiency virus (HIV) and hepatitis B virus (HBV) is common due to shared modes of transmission. In areas of low HBV endemicity, such as North America, Australia, and Europe, HBV and HIV infection are usually acquired in adolescence or adulthood through sexual contact or intravenous drug injection. In areas of low HBV endemicity, the prevalence of chronic coinfection is around 5–7% among HIV-infected individuals (Alter, 2006). In countries with intermediate and high HBV endemicity, the main routes of transmission of HBV are perinatal or in early childhood; in these countries, HBV and HIV coinfection rates are 10–20% (Lee, Ko, and Lee, 2008; Nyirenda, Beadsworth, and Stephany, 2008; Diop-Ndiaye and Toure-Kane, 2008).

The rate of progression and complications from viral hepatitis are accelerated in patients with HIV coinfection (Puoti, Torti, and Ripamonti, 2003; Thio, Seaberg, and Skolasky, 2002). After acquiring HBV infection, HIV infected individuals are 6 times more likely to develop chronic hepatitis B than HIV negative individuals (Bodsworth, Cooper, and Donovan, 1991; Hadler, Judson, and

O'Maeely, 1991; Gatanaga et al., 2000). This risk of progressive HBV disease and liver cirrhosis and failure is higher with lower CD4 lymphocyte counts (Biggar, Goedert, and Hoofnagle, 1987; Laukamm-Josten, Muller, and Bienzle, 1988). There is also evidence that HIV infected individuals with low CD4 counts are at a greater risk of developing hepatocelllular carcinoma (Clifford, Rickenbach, and Polesel, 2008).

HIV and Hepatitis C Virus

Approximately one-third of HIV-infected patients in Europe and the United States are coinfected with hepatitis C virus (HCV). Such patients have been found to be at high risk for the development and progression of liver disease, particularly those receiving *highly active antiretroviral therapy (HAART)*. Treatment with HAART has been found to reduce morbidity and mortality from HIV; however, the adverse effects of HAART include liver toxicity, which may hasten the progression of liver cirrhosis in patients coinfected with HCV. Notably, the introduction of *pegylated interferon* in combination with ribavirin has improved the treatment options for patients with HIV and HCV coinfection (Rockstroh and Spengler, 2004).

HIV and Tuberculosis

Recent data reported by the World Health Organization suggests that rates of coinfection with HIV and the *Mycobacterium tuberculosis* are increasing in many populations. Briefly, 1.37 million individuals have HIV/AIDS and tuberculosis, most of whom (~80%) are in sub-Saharan Africa. In 2007, more than 465,000 deaths were attributed to HIV-tuberculosis infections, with 70% occurring in 5 countries (India, China, Russia, South Africa, and Bangladesh) (WHO, 2010a, 2010b).

In patients with HIV/AIDS who are tuberculin-positive, the risk of developing active tuberculosis is high and prophylaxis with isoniazid is warranted (Guelear et al., 1993). Furthermore, HAART has been found to reduce the incidence of tuberculosis in patients with HIV/AIDS (Badri, Wilson, and Wood, 2002). Results suggest that appropriate therapy can reduce the onset of active tuberculosis in patients with HIV/AIDS. However, without therapy, immunosuppression due to HIV often results in disseminated forms of multidrug resistant tuberculosis (MDR-TB) or extensively resistant tuberculosis (XDR-TB) and rapid demise of coinfected patients (Gandhi et al., 2006).

HIV and Malaria

Coinfection with HIV has been found to increase the severity and case fatality of malaria, particularly in sub-Saharan African where the most virulent malarial strain, *Plasmodium falciparum*, is endemic. In nations with high rates of HIV-1 infections, the incidence of clinical malaria has increased nearly 30% and malaria-related mortality has increased more than 100% (Korenromp et al., 2005). Synergistic increases have been noted in the HIV viral load and the severity of malarial symptoms in coinfected patients (Abu-Raddad, Patnaik, and Kublin, 2006).

PREVENTION AND CONTROL OF HIV/AIDS

The successful prevention and control of HIV/AIDS depends upon interrupting transmission of the virus. The main features of prevention are avoiding sexual contact with any HIV-infected individual, avoiding use of injectable drugs, avoiding contact with contaminated bodily fluids, and practicing universal precautions (for healthcare workers). All blood products and blood donors should be carefully screened to avoid contamination. Accurate information about HIV/AIDS prevention and control should be disseminated to the general public, preferably before sexual activity begins.

The majority of HIV infections are acquired through unprotected sexual activity between partners, one of whom has HIV. The primary mode of HIV infection worldwide is through sexual contact between members of the opposite sex. The male latex condom, if used correctly without oil-based lubricants, is the single most effective available technology to reduce the sexual transmission of HIV and other sexually transmitted infections. Studies on couples where one partner is infected show that with consistent condom use, HIV infection rates for the uninfected partner are below 1% per year (Cayley, 2004).

Antiretroviral treatment of infected patients has been found to significantly reduce the sexual transmission of HIV by reducing the level of virus in bodily fluids. In a recent multicenter study conducted in Botswana, Brazil, India, Kenya, Malawi, South Africa, Thailand, Zimbabwe, and the United States, 1,763 couples discordant for HIV-positivity were randomly assigned to either a treatment group where the HIV-positive partner received antiretroviral drugs immediately or a control group where no drug was given. Out of 28 HIV infections that developed among study participants who were HIV-negative at baseline, 27 developed among members of the untreated couples. The early preventive treatment therefore led to a 96% reduction in HIV transmission to HIV-negative partners, strong evidence of the value of early intervention with antiretroviral therapy in such couples (Warren, 2011).

Healthcare workers should follow universal precautions to reduce their risk of exposure to contaminated blood. These precautions include wearing gloves, masks, protective eyewear or shields, and gowns or aprons that prevent exposure of the skin or mucous membranes to blood-borne pathogens. Frequent and thorough washing of the skin immediately after being contaminated with blood or other bodily fluids reduces the chance of infection. Sharp objects like needles, scalpels, and glass, are carefully disposed of to prevent needle stick injuries with contaminated items (Kerr et al., 2007).

Injection of illicit drugs using contaminated needles and syringes is a major mode of HIV transmission among intravenous drug abusers. Harm reduction strategies such as needle-exchange programs have been used with some success in reducing rates of HIV infection associated with intravenous drug abuse (Wodak and Cooney, 2006).

To avoid mother-to-child transmission, HIV-infected mothers are encouraged to avoid breastfeeding their infant and instead use replacement feeding that is acceptable, feasible, affordable, sustainable, and safe. However, if replacement feeding is unavailable, exclusive breastfeeding is recommended during the first months of life and discontinued as soon as possible (WHO, 2006).

One way to change risky behavior is health education. Several studies have shown the positive impact of culturally adapted educational programs advocating cautious sexual behavior. In 2010, a United Nations AIDS Inter-Agency Task Team encouraged more research on the actual implementation of sex-education programs (such as teacher training, access to related services through schools and the community, or parental attitudes to HIV and AIDS education), and more longitudinal studies on the deeper complexities of the relationship between education and HIV prevention and control (Lakhanpal and Ram, 2008; Rindermann and Meisenberg, 2009).

● ● ● REFERENCES

Abu-Raddad, L., Patnaik, P., & Kublin, J. (2006). Dual infection with HIV and malaria fuels the spread of both diseases in sub-Saharan Africa. *Science, 314*(5805), 1603–1606.

Alter, M.J. (2006). Epidemiology of viral hepatitis and HIV co infection. *J Hepatol, 44*(1 Suppl), S6–S9.

Badri, M., Wilson, D., & Wood, R. (2002). Effect of highly active antiretroviral therapy on incidence of tuberculosis in South Africa: A cohort study. *Lancet, 359*(9323), 2059–2064.

Barré-Sinoussi, F., Chermann, J.C., Rey, F., Nugeyre, M.T., Chamaret, S., Gruest, J.,… Montagnier, L. (1983). Isolation of a T-lymphotropic retrovirus from a patient at risk for acquired immune deficiency syndrome (AIDS). *Science, 220,* 868–871.

Biggar, R.J., Goedert, J.J., & Hoofnagle, J. (1987). Accelerated loss of antibody to hepatitis B surface antigen among immnodeficient homosexual men infected with HIV. *N Engl J Med, 316,* 360.

Bodsworth, N.J., Cooper, D.A., & Donovan, B. (1991). The influence of human immunodeficiency virus virus type 1 infection on the development of the hepatitis B carrier state. *J Infect Dis, 163,* 1138–1140.

Cayley, W.E. Jr. (2004). Effectiveness of condoms in reducing heterosexual transmission of HIV. *Am Fam Physician, 70*(7), 1268–1269.

CDC. (2007). *AIDS surveillance—general epidemiology (through 2005).* Atlanta, Georgia: Centers for Disease Control and Prevention, US Department of Health and Human Services.

Cesarman, E., Chang, Y., Moore, P.S., Said, J.W., & Knowles, D.M. (1995). Kaposi's sarcoma-associated herpesvirus-like DNA sequences in AIDS-related body-cavity-based lymphomas. *N Engl J Med, 332*(18), 1186–1191.

Chang, Y., Cesarman, E., Pessin, M.S., Lee, F., Culpepper, J., Knowles, D.M., & Moore, P.S. (1994). Identification of herpesvirus-like DNA sequences in AIDS-associated Kaposi's sarcoma. *Science, 266,* 1865–1869.

Clifford, G.M., Rickenbach, M., & Polesel, J. (2008). Influence of HIV-related immunodeficiency on the risk of hepatocellular carcinoma. *AIDS, 22,* 2135–2141.

Diop-Ndiaye, H., & Toure-Kane, C. (2008). Hepatitis B, C seroprevalence and delta virus in HIV-1 Senegalese patients at HAART initiation (retrospective study). *J Med Virol, 80,* 1332–1336.

Fenton, K.A. (2007). Changing epidemiology of HIV/AIDS in the United States: Implications for enhancing and promoting HIV testing strategies. *Clin Infect Dis, 45*(Suppl 4), S213–S220.

Gallo, R.C., Salahuddin, S.Z., Popovic, M., Shearer, G.M., Kaplan, M., Haynes, B.F.,… Safai, B. (1984). Frequent detection and isolation of cytopathic retroviruses (HTLV-III) from patients with AIDS and at risk for AIDS. *Science, 224*(4648), 500–503.

Gandhi, N.R., Moll, A., Sturm, A.W., Pawinski, R., Govender, T., Lalloo, U.,…Friedland, G. (2006). Extensively drug-resistant tuberculosis as a cause of death in patients co-infected with tuberculosis and HIV in a rural area of South Africa. *The Lancet, 368*(9547), 1575–1580.

Gatanaga, H., Yasuoka, A., Kikuchi, Y., Tachikawa, N., & Oka, S. (2000). Influence of prior HIV-1 infection on the development of chronic hepatitis B infection. *Eur J Clin Microbiol Infect Dis, 19,* 237–239.

Goedert, J.J., Neuland, C.Y., & Wallen, W.C. (1982). Amyl nitrite may alter T lymphocytes in homosexual men. *Lancet, 1,* 412–416.

Guelar, A., Gatell, J.M., Verdejo, J., Podzamczer, D., Lozano, L., Aznar, E.,… González, J. (1993). A prospective study of the risk of tuberculosis among HIV-infected patients. *AIDS, 7*(10), 1345–1349.

Guyader, M., Emerman, M., Sonigo, P., Clavel, F., Montagnier, L., & Alizon, M. (1987). Genome organization and transactivation of the human immunodeficiency virus type 2. *Nature, 326*(6114), 662–669.

Hadler, S.C., Judson, F.N., & O'Maeely, P.M. (1991). Outcome of hepatitis B virus infection in homosexual men and its relation to prior human immunodeficiency virus infection. *J Infect Dis, 163,* 454–459.

Hahn, B.H., Shaw, G.M., De Cock, K.M., & Sharp, P.M. (2000). AIDS as a zoonosis: Scientific and public health implications. *Science, 287,* 607–614.

Hope, T.J., & Trono, D. (2000). Structure, expression and regulation of the HIV genome.

HIV InSite. University of California, San Francisco.

Kallings, L.O. (2008). The first postmodern pandemic: 25 years of HIV/AIDS. *J Intern Med*, 263(3), 218–243.

Kerr, T., Kimber, J., Debeck, K., & Wood, E. (2007). The role of safer injection facilities in the response to HIV/AIDS among injection drug users. *Current HIV/AIDS Reports*, 4(4), 158–164.

Korenromp, E.L., Williams, B.G., de Vlas, S.J., Gouws, E., Gilks, C.F., & Ghys, P.D. (2005). Malaria attributable to the HIV-1 epidemic, Sub-Saharan Africa. *Emerg Infect Dis*, [serial on the Internet].

Lakhanpal, M., & Ram, R. (2008). Educational attainment and HIV/AIDS prevalence: A cross-country study. *Economics of Education Review*, 27, 14–21.

Laukamm-Josten, U., Muller, O., & Bienzle, U. (1988). Decline of naturally acquired antibodies to hepatitis B surface antigen in HIV-1 infected homosexual men. *AIDS*, 2, 400–401.

Lee, H.C., Ko, N.Y., & Lee, N.Y. (2008). Seroprevalence of viral hepatitis and sexually transmitted disease among adults with recently diagnosed HIV infection in southern Taiwan, 2000-5: Upsurge in hepatitis C virus infections among injection drug users. *J Formos Med Assoc*, 107, 404–411.

Levy, J.A., Hoffman, A.D., Kramer, S.M., Landis, J.A., Shimabukuro, J.M., & Oshiro, L.S. (1984). Isolation of lymphocytopathic retroviruses from San Francisco patients with AIDS. *Science*, 225(4664), 840–842.

Masur, H., Michelis, M.A., Greene, J.B., Onorato, I., Stouwe, R.A., Holzman, R.S.,...Cunningham-Rundles, S. (1981). An outbreak of community-acquired *Pneumocystis carinii* pneumonia: Initial manifestation of cellular immune dysfunction. *N Engl J Med*, 305(24), 1431–1438.

Masur, H., Michelis, M.A., Wormser, G.P., Lewin, S., Gold, J., Tapper, M.L.,...Cunningham-Rundles, S. (1982). Opportunistic infection in previously healthy women. Initial manifestations of a community-acquired cellular immunodeficiency. *Ann Intern Med*, 97(4), 533–539.

Mavligit, G.M., Talpaz, M., Hsia, F.T., Wong, W., Lichtiger, B., Mansell, P.W., & Mumford, D.M. (1984). Chronic immune stimulation by sperm alloantigens: support for the hypothesis that spermatozoa induce immune dysregulation in homosexual males. *JAMA*, 251, 237–241.

MMWR. (1981a). Pneumocystis pneumonia—Los Angeles. *Morb Mortal Wkly Rep*, 30, 250–252.

MMWR. (1981b). Kaposi's sarcoma and Pneumocystis pneumonia among homosexual men—New York City and California. *Morb Mortal Wkly Rep*, 30, 305–308.

MMWR. (1982a). A cluster of Kaposi's sarcoma and *Pneumocystis carinii* pneumonia among homosexual male residents of Los Angeles and Orange Counties, California. *Morb Mortal Wkly Rep*, 31, 305–307.

MMRW. (1982b). Opportunistic infections and Kaposi's sarcoma among Haitians in the United States. *Morb Mortal Wkly Rep*, 31, 353–354.

MMWR. (1982c). Pneumocystis carinii pneumonia among persons with hemophilia A. *Morb Mortal Wkly Rep*, 31, 365–367.

MMWR. (1982d). Possible transfusion-associated acquired immune deficiency syndrome (AIDS)—California. *Morb Mortal Wkly Rep*, 31, 652–654.

MMWR. (1982e). Unexplained immunodeficiency and opportunistic infections in infants—New York, New Jersey, California. *Morb Mortal Wkly Rep*, 31, 665–667.

MMWR. (1983a). Immunodeficiency among female sexual partners of males with acquired immune deficiency syndrome (AIDS)—New York. *Morb Mortal Wkly Rep*, 31, 697–698.

MMWR. (1983b). Acquired immune deficiency syndrome (AIDS) in prison inmates—New York, New Jersey. *Morb Mortal Wkly Rep*, 31, 700–701.

Moore, P.S., Gao, S.J., Dominguez, G., Cesarman, E., Lungu, O., Knowles, D.M.,...Chang, Y. (1996). Primary characterization of a herpesvirus agent associated with Kaposi's sarcoma. *The Journal of Virology*, *70*(1), 549–558.

Moore, P.S., and Chang, Y. (1995). Detection of herpesvirus-like DNA sequences in Kaposi's sarcoma in patients with and without HIV infection. *N Engl J Med*, *332*(18), 1181–1185.

Nyirenda, M., Beadsworth, M.B., & Stephany, P. (2008). Prevalence of infection with hepatitis B and C virus and co infection with HIV in medical inpatients in Malawi. *J Infect*, *57*, 72–77.

Osmond, D.H. (2003). Epidemiology of HIV/AIDS in the United States. *HIV InSite*. University of California, San Francisco.

Parkin, D.M., Bray, F., Ferlay, J., & Pisani, P. (2005). Global Cancer Statistics, 2002. *CA Cancer J Clin*, *55*, 74–108.

Puoti, M., Torti, C., & Ripamonti, D. (2003). Severe hepatotoxicity during combination antiretroviral therapy treatment: Incidence, liver histology, and outcome. *J Acquir Immune Defic Syndr*, *32*, 259–267.

Rindermann, H., & Meisenberg, G. (2009). Relevance of education and intelligence at the national level for health: The case of HIV and AIDS. *Intelligence*, *37*, 383–395.

Rockstroh, J.K., & Spengler, U. (2004). HIV and hepatitis C virus co-infection. *Lancet Infect Dis*, *4*(7), 437–444.

Sonnabend, J., Witkin, S.S., & Purtilo, D.T. (1983). Acquired immunodeficiency syndrome, opportunistic infections, and malignancies in male homosexuals. A hypothesis of etiologic factors in pathogenesis. *JAMA*, *249*(17), 2370–2374.

Stebbing, J., Portsmouth, & Bassard, B. (2003). How does HAART lead to the resolution of Kaposi's sarcoma? *J Antimicrob Chemother*, *51*(5), 1095–1098.

Thio, C.L., Seaberg, E.C., & Skolasky, R.L. (2002). HIV-1, hepatitis B virus, and risk of liver-related mortality in the Multi-Center AIDS Cohort Study (MACS). *Lancet*, *360*, 1921–1926.

Warren, M. (2011). Earlier initiation of HIV treatment led to a 96 percent reduction in HIV transmission to the uninfected partner. AIDS Vaccine Advocacy Coalition (AVAC).

WHO. (2006). *HIV and Infant Feeding Technical Consultation, Consensus statement*. Geneva, Switzerland: World Health Organization.

WHO. (2010a). *Report on the global AIDS epidemic*. Geneva, Switzerland: World Health Organization.

WHO. (2010b). *WHO tuberculosis factsheet*. Geneva, Switzerland: World Health Organization.

Wodak, A., & Cooney, A. (2006). Do needle syringe programs reduce HIV infection among injecting drug users: A comprehensive review of the international evidence. *Substance Use & Misuse*, *41*(6–7), 777–813.

Index